ENCYCLOPEDIA OF AMERICAN HISTORICAL DOCUMENTS

VOLUME I

ENCYCLOPEDIA OF AMERICAN HISTORICAL DOCUMENTS

VOLUME I

Edited by Susan Rosenfeld

Facts On File, Inc.

Encyclopedia of American Historical Documents

Facts On File, Inc.
132 West 31st Street
New York NY 10001

Library of Congress Cataloging-in-Publication Data

Encyclopedia of American Historical Documents / edited by Susan Rosenfeld
p. cm.
Includes bibliographical references and index.
ISBN 0-8160-4995-5 (set)—ISBN 0-8160-5993-4 (vol. 1)—
ISBN 0-8160-5994-2 (vol. 2)—ISBN 0-8160-5995-0 (vol. 3)
1. United States—History—Sources—Encyclopedias. I. Rosenfeld, Susan C.
E173.E54 2004
973'.03—dc21   2003051610

Facts On File books are available at special discounts when purchased in bulk
quantities for businesses, associations, institutions, or sales promotions. Please call
our Special Sales Department in New York at (212) 967-8800 or (800) 322-8755.

You can find Facts On File on the World Wide Web at http://www.factsonfile.com

Text adaptation by Theresa Montoya and Cathy Rincon
Cover design by Cathy Rincon

Printed in the United States of America

VB FOF 10 9 8 7 6 5 4 3 2 1

This book is printed on acid-free paper.

Contents

Volume III

Era 7: THE EMERGENCE OF MODERN AMERICA (ca. 1901–1929)   1165

Progressivism   1166

Preface

★ ————————————————————————————————————

Encyclopedia of American Historical Documents is a valuable ready reference for anyone interested in American history. Its documents were culled from a number of sources, most notably *Landmark Documents in American History*. *Landmark Documents* contains more than 1,600 documents, almost all in their entirety, that correspond to the 10 eras of the National American History Standards (www.sscnet.ucla.edu/nchs/standards). It is an unparalleled resource that also contains biographies, images, and a time line. However, it is available only to subscribing Internet users. The *Encyclopedia* contains between approximately 50 and 65 documents per era, a number of them excerpts only, especially those that fall under Eras 9 and 10 (1945–present).

The introduction provides a brief overview of the project and sets out the way in which documents were selected and some caveats for using them. Each era begins with an overview of the entire period. While these are based on the overviews provided by the American History Standards, they are mostly original works by this editor, and they cover the topics represented in the documents.

Each document also has an introduction. These describe when and why the document was created and explain its significance for its own time, for American history in general, and, if applicable, its relevance today. In addition, the introductions also discuss related documents not included in the encyclopedia. Many introductions are taken in whole or in part from *Landmark Documents*. Often, however, I supply additional information.

The selection of documents is completely my own. However, I would like to thank my editor, Owen Lancer; Sabrina Schram, who located a number of documents for Eras 1 and 2; and the reference librarians at Wayne State University, Detroit, Michigan, and in Annapolis, Maryland, who assisted me. I would also like to thank my husband, Fred Stielow, for his support throughout this project.

—Susan Rosenfeld
Annapolis, Maryland

Introduction

Encyclopedia of American Historical Documents contains records of major significance from the period of European exploration of the Americas (15th century) to the present, including documents that address terrorism in the wake of the September 11, 2001, attacks. Organization and themes are drawn from the standards for each of the 10 eras of the National American History Standards for grades 9–12 (www.sscnet.ucla.edu/nchs/standards). For each era, the documents are presented by topic (usually a combination of several "standards") in roughly chronological order. These five themes run through each of the 10 eras:

1. Diversity of people in America
2. Development, establishment, and maintenance of American democracy
3. The American environment
4. Development of American economy and technology
5. Intellectual life and popular culture

Often, documents relate to more than one of the major themes; in these cases, these documents were placed under the topic for which they had the greatest impact or relevance.

A selection of suggested representative readings by topic is included after the overview of each era. Most selections are more general books suitable for high school students, rather than scholarly monographs or works that focus on a narrow topic or geographical area. With the exception of a few classics, such as *The Education of Henry Adams* (Era 6), the list consists of recent works. The sources from which documentary selections are derived were omitted from these lists.

Not every "landmark" document could be included in this compilation. Fortunately, many of the documents are available in standard reference works or on the Internet (although some may be accessible only to database subscribers).

The documents were selected using several criteria:

1. *Only one document on a particular topic.* Other relevant documents are noted in the introduction and in a "See also" list following the document.
2. *Documents with resonance for the 21st century.* These were given preference over documents with only contemporary importance. For example, the

Nuclear Non-Proliferation Treaty, which is still in effect and still controversial, was selected over the Nuclear Test Ban Treaty of 1963.

3. *Documents that represent turning points in U.S. history and culture.* These include such items as landmark Supreme Court decisions, international treaties, and texts related to scientific and cultural matters, such as Darwin's *On the Origin of Species* or the announcement of the eradication of polio.

4. *Documents that have multiple significance for U.S. history and culture.* For example, both the Kennedy-Nixon debates, which had political significance and which demonstrated the increasing influence of television on American culture, and the comments on the Equal Rights Amendment by Congresswoman Shirley Chisholm, the first African-American woman to be nominated for president by a major political party, were included.

5. *Controversial items.* These are important for evaluating controversial issues, as examples such as the Three-fifths Compromise of 1787 and Truman's 1947 Loyalty Program, included in the text, underscore the complexities of historical situations in their times.

Copyright restrictions limit reproduction, particularly in the most recent years, but also for certain edited or translated earlier documents. Lyrics to popular music of the Vietnam era, for example, such as Bob Dylan's "The Times They Are A-Changing," an antiwar anthem, and "The Ballad of the Green Beret," which applauded the American military, helped define American culture in the Vietnam era, but they could not be included because of their copyright. Another problem related to the reproduction of documents, such as those about the European and African legacies of the United States, is lack of easily available and uncopyrighted translations.

Still another difficulty concerns racial descriptions of blacks and Indians in exploration narratives and even in government documents. In the early part of American history, descriptions of Native Americans and many of those regarding people of African heritage come almost exclusively from literate people of European descent, and they are often unflattering at best. The descriptions included provide a more comprehensive and accurate portrayal of daily life, as well as demonstrate how these groups were perceived; others show how the Native Americans perceived Europeans and European Americans.

Those caveats aside, *Encyclopedia of American Historical Documents* provides a comprehensive picture of American history from the voyages of Eric the Red and Columbus through the passage of the Homeland Security Bill.

ERAS 1 TO 3

ERA 1
Three Worlds Meet
(BEGINNINGS TO CA. 1620)

Era 1 brings together the influences of Europe, people native to the New World, and people native to Africa. It provides an introduction into how our diverse American society was created. In this section, five long-range changes set in motion principally by the Columbian voyages are addressed:

1. Redistribution of the world's population, including millions of Europeans, most voluntarily, but with some criminals given a choice between execution and immigration—the New World or the next world. At least 10–12 million Africans also come to the New World enslaved. Most are sent to South America and the Caribbean.
2. England, France, Portugal, Spain, and Holland establish trading outposts and colonial communities in Africa and South Asia as well as the New World.
3. Large amounts of gold, silver, and New World commodities such as tobacco fostered commercial expansion and capitalist enterprise.
4. As the new colonies emerge far from the monarchies that spawn them, ideas of representative government are able to take hold.
5. New World plantations require a large work force that can withstand the climate and harsh conditions. African

slavery provides it. Slaves become a vital component for Europeans in South America, the Caribbean, and eventually the southern United States.

The first set of documents here goes back to the earliest known European contact with North America and includes a number of exploration narratives. These not only describe the hardships suffered by early explorers but provide their comments about the native peoples they encountered and the environment they observed. In the next set, treaties, charters, and other legal and religious documents that influenced the peopling of the New World are represented, including two of the major influences on the Protestant Reformation. The third set provides a glimpse into the lives of the sorts of people who came to America in the 16th and 17th centuries: a 16th-century English family and a 17th-century victim of the African slave trade. It also includes an introduction to an argument for the English to explore the New World and a treatise lamenting the effect of the tobacco trade on British commerce. The fourth covers the experiences of the earliest colonists in what is now the northeastern United States, and the last covers the beginnings of representative government in New England and Virginia.

European Exploration

Saga of Eric the Red, ca. 1387

This excerpt from a version of the *Saga of Eric the Red* found in the *Flateyar-bok* (Songbook) (ca. 1387 C.E.) recounts the discovery of North America by Leif Ericsson. About 1000 C.E., Leif, son of Eric the Red, went in search of a new land to the west that had been spotted earlier by the sailor Biarni Heriulfsson. Leif encountered three islands, Helluland (thought to be modern-day Labrador), Markland (modern Newfoundland), and Vinland, where he and his crew spent the winter before returning to Greenland. The exact location of Vinland (called Wineland in this translation) is in dispute. In 1963 the remains of a Norse settlement were found at L'Anse-aux-Meadows in northern Newfoundland, but despite the proven authenticity of the artifacts, scholars continue to suggest sites for Vinland ranging from New England to Virginia.

There was now much talk about voyages of discovery. Leif, the son of Eric the Red, of Brattahlid, visited Biarni Heriulfsson and bought a ship of him, and collected a crew, until they formed altogether a company of thirty-five men. Leif invited his father, Eric, to become the leader of the expedition, but Eric declined, saying that he was then stricken in years, and adding that he was less able to endure the exposure of sea life than he had been. Leif replied that he would nevertheless be the one who would be most apt to bring good luck and Eric yielded to Leif's solicitation, and rode from home when they were ready to sail. When he was but a short distance from the ship, the horse which Eric was riding stumbled, and he was thrown from his back and wounded his foot, whereupon he exclaimed, "It is not designed for me to discover more lands than the one in which we are now living, nor can we now continue longer together." Eric returned home to Brattahlid, and Leif pursued his way to the ship with his companions, thirty-five men. One of the company was a German, named Tyrker. They put the ship in order; and, when they were ready, they sailed out to sea, and found first that land which Biarni and his shipmates found last. They sailed up to the land, and cast anchor, and launched a boat, and went ashore, and saw no grass there. Great ice mountains lay inland back from the sea, and it was as a [tableland of] flat rock all the way from the sea to the ice mountains; and the country seemed to them to be entirely devoid of good qualities. Then said, Leif "It has not come to pass with us in regard to this land as with Biarni, that we

have not gone upon it. To this country I will now give a name, and call it Helluland." They returned to the ship, put out to sea, and found a second land. They sailed again to the land, and came to anchor, and launched the boat, and went ashore. This was a level wooded land; and there were broad stretches of white sand where they went, and the land was level by the sea. Then said Leif, "This land shall have a name after its nature; and we will call it Markland." They returned to the ship forthwith, and sailed away upon the main with north-east winds, and were out two "doegr" before they sighted land. They sailed toward this land, and came to an island which lay to the northward off the land. There they went ashore and looked about them, the weather being fine, and they observed that there was dew upon the grass, and it so happened that they touched the dew with their hands, and touched their hands to their mouths, and it seemed to them that they had never before tasted anything so sweet as this. They went aboard their ship again and sailed into a certain sound, which lay between the island and a cape, which jutted out from the land on the north, and they stood in westering past the cape. At ebb-tide, there were broad reaches of shallow water there, and they ran their ship aground there, and it was a long distance from the ship to the ocean; yet were they so anxious to go ashore that they could not wait until the tide should rise under their ship, but hastened to the land, where a certain river flows out from a lake. As soon as the tide rose beneath their ship, however, they took the boat and rowed to the ship, which they conveyed up the river, and so into the lake, where they cast anchor and carried their hammocks ashore from the ship, and built themselves booths there. They afterward determined to establish themselves there for the winter, and they accordingly built a large house. There was no lack of salmon there either in the river or in the lake, and larger salmon than they had ever seen before. The country thereabouts seemed to be possessed of such good qualities that cattle would need no fodder there during the winters. There was no frost there in the winters, and the grass withered but little. The days and nights there were of more nearly equal length than in Greenland or Iceland. On the shortest day of winter, the sun was up between "eykarstad" and "dagmalastad." When they had completed their house, Leif said to his companions, "I propose now to divide our company into two groups, and to set about an exploration of the country. One-half of our party shall remain at home at the house, while the other half shall investigate the land;

and they must not go beyond a point from which they can return home the same evening, and are not to separate [from each other]. Thus they did for a time. Leif, himself, by turns joined the exploring party, or remained behind at the house. Leif was a large a powerful man, and of a most imposing bearing—a man of sagacity, and a very just man in all things.

It was discovered one evening that one of their company was missing; and this proved to be Tyrker, the German. Leif was sorely troubled by this, for Tyrker had lived with Leif and his father for a long time, and had been very devoted to Leif when he was a child. Leif severely reprimanded his companions, and prepared to go in search of him, taking twelve men with him. They had proceeded but a short distance from the house, when they were met by Tyrker, whom they received most cordially. Leif observed at once that his foster-father was in lively spirits. Tyrker had a prominent forehead, restless eyes, small features, was diminutive in stature, and rather a sorry-looking individual withal, but was, nevertheless, a most capable handicraftsman. Leif addressed him, and asked, "Wherefore art thou so belated, foster-father mine, and astray from the others?" In the beginning Tyrker spoke for some time in German, rolling his eyes and grinning, and they could not understand him; but after a time he addressed them in the Northern tongue: "I did not go much further [than you], and yet I have something of novelty to relate. I have found vines and grapes." "Is this indeed true, foster-father?" said Leif. "Of a certainty it is true," quoth he, "for I was born where there is no lack of either grapes or vines." They slept the night through, and on the morrow Leif said to his shipmates, "We will now divide our labors, and each day will either gather grapes or cut vines and fell trees, so as to obtain a cargo of these for my ship." They acted upon this advice, and it is said that their after-boat was filled with grapes. A cargo sufficient for the ship was cut, and when the spring came they made their ship ready, and sailed away; and from its products Leif gave the land a name, and called it Wineland. They sailed out to sea, and had fair winds until they sighted Greenland and the fells below the glaciers.

Source:

Arthur M. Reeves. *The Finding of Wineland the Good: The Icelandic Discovery of America.* London, 1890.

Christopher Columbus, Journal, 1492

The journal Columbus kept during his first voyage to the Americas in 1492 no longer exists in its original form. The available text was abridged and edited by the Spanish priest Bartolomé de Las Casas, an early missionary in the New World

and a noted champion of native peoples, particularly in his historical works on the Indies. The revisions by de Las Casas account for the variant use of first and third person in reference to Columbus throughout the manuscript. In the section below, Columbus recounts his departure from the city of Granada in May and the discovery of land the following October, and he describes the indigenous people he mistakenly named *Indians*. Columbus assumed the people were simple because they were naked and did not have metal weapons. He also assumed that they would be readily converted to Christianity "as they appear to have no religion." Columbus may have been attempting to construct an idea of the natives as future Christians in order to please his sponsors, King Ferdinand and Queen Isabella, the "Catholic Monarchs" who instituted the Spanish Inquisition in 1478 to create a homogenous Christian population in Spain. Columbus would undertake three more journeys across the Atlantic in his lifetime, exploring Trinidad, Venezuela, the Orinoco River Delta, Cape Honduras, Nicaragua, Costa Rica, Veragua, and Panama, but never reaching the spice-rich Orient he set out to find. He died in Spain in 1506, still believing he had reached "the Indies."

IN THE NAME OF OUR LORD JESUS CHRIST
Whereas, Most Christian, High, Excellent, and Powerful Princes, King and Queen of Spain and of the Islands of the Sea, our Sovereigns, this present year 1492, after your Highnesses had terminated the war with the Moors reigning in Europe, the same having been brought to an end in the great city of Granada, where on the second day of January, this present year, I saw the royal banners of your Highnesses planted by force of arms upon the towers of the Alhambra, which is the fortress of that city, and saw the Moorish king come out at the gate of the city and kiss the hands of your Highnesses, and of the Prince my Sovereign; and in the present month, in consequence of the information which I had given your Highnesses respecting the countries of India and of a Prince, called Great Can, which in our language signifies King of Kings, how, at many times he, and his predecessors had sent to Rome soliciting instructors who might teach him our holy faith, and the holy Father had never granted his request, whereby great numbers of people were lost, believing in idolatry and doctrines of perdition. Your Highnesses, as Catholic Christians, and princes who love and promote the holy Christian faith, and are enemies of the doctrine of Mahomet, and of all idolatry and heresy, determined to send me, Christopher Columbus, to the above-mentioned countries of India, to see the said princes, people, and territories, and to learn their disposition and the proper method of converting them to our holy faith; and furthermore directed that I should not proceed by land to the East, as is customary, but by a Westerly route, in which direction we have hitherto no

certain evidence that any one has gone. So after having expelled the Jews from your dominions, your Highnesses, in the same month of January, ordered me to proceed with a sufficient armament to the said regions of India, and for that purpose granted me great favors, and ennobled me that thenceforth I might call myself Don, and be High Admiral of the Sea, and perpetual Viceroy and Governor in all the islands and continents which I might discover and acquire, or which may hereafter be discovered and acquired in the ocean; and that this dignity should be inherited by my eldest son, and thus descend from degree to degree forever. Hereupon I left the city of Granada, on Saturday, the twelfth day of May, 1492, and proceeded to Palos, a seaport, where I armed three vessels, very fit for such an enterprise, and having provided myself with abundance of stores and seamen, I set sail from the port, on Friday, the third of August, half an hour before sunrise, and steered for the Canary Islands of your Highnesses which are in the said ocean, thence to take my departure and proceed till I arrived at the Indies, and perform the embassy of your Highnesses to the Princes there, and discharge the orders given me. For this purpose I determined to keep an account of the voyage, and to write down punctually every thing we performed or saw from day to day, as will hereafter appear. Moreover, Sovereign Princes, besides describing every night the occurrences of the day, and every day those of the preceding night, I intend to draw up a nautical chart, which shall contain the several parts of the ocean and land in their proper situations; and also to compose a book to represent the whole by picture with latitudes and longitudes, on all which accounts it behooves me to abstain from my sleep, and make many trials in navigation, which things will demand much labor.

Friday, 3 August 1492. Set sail from the bar of Saltes at 8 o'clock, and proceeded with a strong breeze till sunset, sixty miles or fifteen leagues south, afterwards southwest and south by west, which is the direction of the Canaries.

Source:

Internet Medieval Sourcebook. Available on-line URL: www.fordham.edu/halsall/sbook.html. Accessed October 2003.

Giovanni da Verrazano, "Report to Francis I," 1524

In 1524, under the patronage of King Francis I of France, Giovanni da Verrazano sailed from the island of Madeira near Portugal to the eastern coast of North America. Verrazano landed at Cape Fear in present-day North Carolina and sailed up the coast. Along the way, he stopped at New York Harbor, Block Island, and Narragansett Bay, and he reached Newfoundland before sailing home. In this excerpt from his report to Francis I, Verrazano sails into New York Harbor and sights a "very big river," known today as the Hudson River. He does not land, however, due to a sudden wind that forces his ships back out to sea. He continues northward and sights Block Island off the coast of Rhode Island, which he names *Aloysia* in honor of the king's mother. Verrazano then sails on to Newport, Rhode Island, where he encounters the Wampanoag Indians, whom he describes as an exceptionally beautiful and noble people. Verrazano's voyage established France's claim to lands in the New World.

. . . At the end of a hundred leagues we found a very agreeable situation located within two small prominent hills, in the midst of which flowed to the sea a very big river, which was deep within the mouth: and from the sea to the hills of that (place) with the rising of the tides, which we found eight feet any laden ship might have passed. On account of being anchored off the coast in good shelter, we did not wish to adventure in without knowledge of the entrances. We were with the small boat, entering the said river to the land, which we found much populated. The people, almost like the others, clothed with the feathers of birds of various colors, came toward us joyfully, uttering very great exclamations of admiration, showing us where we could land with the boat more safely. We entered said river, within the land, about half a league, where we saw it made a very beautiful lake with a circuit of about three leagues: Through which they (the Indians) went, going from one and another part to the number of XXX of their little barges, with innumerable people, who passed from one shore and the other in order to see us. In an instant, as is wont to happen in navigation, a gale of unfavorable wind blowing in from the sea, we were forced to return to the ship, leaving the said land with much regret because of its commodiousness and beauty, thinking it was not without some properties of value, all of its hills showing indications of minerals.

Called Angouleme from the principality which thou attainedst in lesser fortune, and the bay which that land makes Santa Margarita from the name of thy sister who vanquishes the other matrons of modesty and talent.

The anchor raised, sailing toward the coast, as thus the land turned, having traveled LXXX leagues always in sight of it, we discovered an island triangular in form, distant ten leagues from the continent, in size like the island of Rhodes, full of hills, covered with trees, much populated (judging) by the continuous fires along all the surrounding shore which we saw they made. We baptized it in the name of your most illustrious mother, Aloysia; not anchoring there on account of the unfavorableness of the weather.

We came to another land, distant from the island XV leagues, where we found a very beautiful port, and before we entered it, we saw about XX barges of the people who came with various cries of wonder round about the ship. Not approaching nearer than fifty paces, they halted. looking at the edifice (i.e. the ship), our figures and clothes: then all together they uttered loud shout, signifying that they were glad. Having reassured them somewhat, imitating their gestures, they came so near that we threw them some little bells and mirrors and many trinkets. having taken which, regarding them with laughter. They entered the ship confidently. There were among them two Kings, of as good stature and form as it would be possible to tell: the first of about XXXX years, the other a young man of XXIII years, the clothing of whom was thus: the older had on his nude body a skin of a stag, artificially adorned like a damask with various embroideries: the head bare, the hair turned back with various bands, at the neck a broad chain ornamented with many stones of diverse colors. The young man was almost in the same style. This is the most beautiful people and the most civilized in customs that we have found in his navigation. They excel us in size: the are of bronze color, some inclining more to whiteness, others to tany color: the face sharply cut, the hair long and black, upon which they bestow the greatest study in adorning it; the eyes black and alert, the bearing kind and gentle, imitating much the ancient (manner). Of the other paris of the body I will not speak to Your Majesty, having all the proportions which belong to very well built man. Their women are of the same beauty and charm; very graceful; of comely mien and agreeable aspect; of habits and behavior as much according to womanly custom as pertains to human nature: they go nude with only one skin of the stag embroidered like the men and some wear on the arms very rich skins of the lynx; the head bare, with various arrangements of braids, composed of their own hair, which hang on one side and the other of the breast. Some use other hair arrangements like the women of Egypt and of Syria use, and these are they who are advanced in age and are joined in wedlock. They have in the ears various pendant trinkets as the orientals are accustomed to have, the men like the women, among which we saw many plates wrought from copper, by whom it is prized more than gold; which, on account of its color, they do not esteem; wherefore among all it is held by them more worthless; on the other hand rating blue and red above any other. That which they were given by us which they most valued were little bells, blue crystals and other trinkets to place in the ears and on the neck. They did not prize cloth of silk and of gold nor even of other kind nor did they care to have them: likewise with metals like steel and iron; for many times showing them our arms they did not conceive admiration for them nor ask for them, only examining the workmanship. They did the same with the mirrors: suddenly looking at them, they refused them laughing. They are very liberal, so much so that all which they have they give away. We formed a great friendship with them, and one day, before we had entered with the ship in the port, remaining on account of the unfavorable weather conditions, anchored a league at sea, they came tn great numbers in their little barges to the ship, having painted and decked the face with various colors, showing to us it was evidence of good feeling, bringing to us their food, signaling to us where for the safety of the ship we ought anchor in the port, continually accompanying us until we cast anchor there.

Source:

A translation by E. H. Hall, 1910. Newsday. com "Giovanni da Verrazano's Report to Francis I, July 8, 1524: The History of the *Dauphine* and Its Voyage." Available on-line. URL: www.newsday.com/extras/lihistory/vault/hs215a1v.htm. Accessed October 2003.

The Journey of
Álvar Núñez Cabeza de Vaca, 1542
Translated by Fanny Bandelier (1905)

The document below details the experiences of a conquistador who left Spain in 1527 and was one of a handful of survivors of his expedition. He returned 10 years later. In between he was shipwrecked several times, came close to starving to death or dying of thirst on numerous occasions, was enslaved by Indians, and was also recognized as a great healer. His adventures took him from present-day Florida into Texas and present-day Mexico. When back again among "Christians," he related stories of jeweled cities that he had heard from the Indians, which became the "Seven Cities of Cibola" legend that spurred other conquistadores, notably Francisco Vásquez de Coronado, whose men found the Grand Canyon.

The following excerpts, from a very long narrative, are a sample of Cabeza de Vaca's hardships, observations on Indian life, explanations of how he communicated with Indians where no interpreter was available, and descriptions of the terrain. Because he wandered over such a great distance and encountered so many different native cultures, the excerpts here are representative of the narrative, not of the diversity of people and environment he wrote about.

On the 27th day of the month of June, 1527, the Governor Panfilo de Narvaez departed from the port of San Lucar de Barrameda, with authority and orders from Your Majesty to conquer and govern the provinces that extend from the river of the Palms to the Cape of the Florida, these provinces being on the main land. The fleet he took along consisted of five vessels, in which went about 600 men. . . . We arrived at the Island of Santo Domingo, where we remained nearly forty-five days, supplying ourselves with necessary things, especially horses. Here more than 140 men of our army forsook us, who wished to remain, on account of the proposals and promises made them by the people of the country. From there we started and arrived at Santiago (a port in the Island of Cuba) where, in the few days that we remained the Governor supplied himself again with people, arms and horses. . . .

✿   ✿   ✿

Sixty people and twenty horses perished on [two] ships [that were lost in a hurricane while in Cuba]. . . . In this condition we were until the 5th day of the month of November, when the Governor, with his four vessels, arrived. The people on board of the ships and those he found [thirty members of de Vaca's crew who were on the land] were so terrified by what had happened that they were afraid to set to sea again in winter and begged the Governor to remain there for that season, and he, seeing their good will and that of the inhabitants, wintered at that place . . . until the 20th day of February . . . . At that time the Governor . . . took along . . . 400 men and eighty horses, on four vessels and one brigantine.

✿   ✿   ✿

[After battling more storms] we crossed to the coast of Florida, sighting land on Tuesday, the 12th day of the month of April. We coasted the way of Florida, and on Holy Thursday cast anchor at the mouth of a bay, at the head of which we saw certain houses and habitations of Indians.

On . . . Good Friday the Governor disembarked, with as many men as his little boats would hold, and as we arrived at the huts or houses of the Indians we had seen, we found them abandoned and deserted. . . . One of those houses was so large that it could hold more than 300 people. . . . The next day the Governor hoisted flags in behalf of Your Majesty and took possession of the country in Your Royal name, exhibited his credentials, and was acknowledged as Governor according to Your Majesty's commands. . . . He then ordered the remainder of the men to disembark, also the forty-two horses left (the others having perished on account of the great storms and the long time they had been on sea), and these few that remained were so thin and weak that they could be of little use for the time. The next day the Indians of that village came, and, although they spoke to us, as we had no interpreters we did not understand them; but they made many gestures and threats, and it seemed as if they beckoned to us to leave the country. Afterward, without offering any molestation, they went away.

After another day the Governor resolved to penetrate inland to explore the country and see what it contained. We went with him . . . with forty men, among them six horsemen, who seemed likely to be of but little use. We took the direction of the north, and at the hour of vespers reached a very large bay, which appeared to sweep far inland. After remaining there that night and the next day, we returned to the place where the vessels and the men were. The Governor ordered the brigantine to coast towards Florida in search of the port which Miruelo, the pilot, had said he knew, but he had missed it. . . .

✿   ✿   ✿

After the brigantine left we again penetrated inland. . . . After a march of four leagues, captured four Indians, to whom we showed maize in order to find out if they knew it, for until then we had seen no trace of it. They told us that they would take us to a place where there was maize and they led us to their village, at the end of the bay nearby, and there they showed us some that was not yet fit to be gathered. There we found many boxes for merchandise from Castilla. In every one of them was a corpse covered with painted deer hides. The commissary thought this to be some idolatrous practice, so he burnt the boxes with the corpses. We also found pieces of linen and cloth, and feather head dresses that seemed to be from New Spain, and samples of gold.

We inquired of the Indians (by signs) whence they had obtained these things and they gave us to understand that, very far from there, was a province called Apalachen in which there was much gold. They also signified to us that in that province we would find everything we held in esteem. . . .

✿   ✿   ✿

On Saturday, the 1st of May, [the governor] ordered that they should give to each one of those who had to go with him, two pounds of ship-biscuit and one-half pound of bacon, and thus we set out upon our journey inland. The number of people we took along was three hundred. . . . We marched for fifteen days, living on the supplies we had taken with us, without finding anything else to eat but palmettos like those of Andalusia. In all this time we did not meet a soul, nor did we see a house or village, and finally reached a river, which we crossed with much trouble, by swimming and on rafts. It took us a day to ford the river on account of the swiftness of its current. When we got across, there came towards us some two hundred Indians, more or less; the Governor went to meet them, and after he talked to them by signs they acted in such a manner that we were obliged to set upon them and seize five or six, who took us to their houses, about half a league from there, where we found a large quantity of corn ready for harvest. We gave infinite thanks to our Lord for having helped us in such great need, for, as we were not used to such exposures, we felt greatly exhausted, and were much weakened by hunger.

❉   ❉   ❉

. . . We left the next day, always in quest of . . . Apalachen . . . , taking as guides those whom we had captured, and marched until the 17th of June without finding an Indian who would dare to wait for us. Finally there came to us a chief, whom an Indian carried on his shoulders. He wore a painted deerskin, and many people followed him, and he was preceded by many players on flutes made of reeds. He came the place where the Governor was and stayed an hour. We gave him to understand by signs that our aim was to reach Apalachen, but from his gestures it seemed to us that he was an enemy of the Apalachen people and that he would go and help us against them. We gave him beads and little bells and other trinkets, while he presented the Governor with the hide he wore. Then he turned back and we followed him.

❉   ❉   ❉

We travelled until the day after St. John's Day, when we came in sight of Apalachen, without having been noticed by the Indians of the land. . . . We had also suffered greatly from hunger, for, although we found corn occasionally, most of the time we marched seven or eight leagues without any. And many there were among us who besides suffering great fatigue and hunger, had their backs covered with wounds from the weight of the armor and other things they had to carry. . . . But to find ourselves at last where we wished to be and where we had been assured so much food and gold would be had, made us forget a great deal of our hardships and weariness.

Once in sight of Apalachen, the Governor commanded me to enter the village with nine horsemen and fifty foot. So the inspector and I undertook this. Upon penetrating into the village we found only women and boys. . . . While we were walking about, [the men] came and began to fight, shooting arrows at us. They killed the inspector's horse, but finally fled and left us. We found there plenty of ripe maize ready to be gathered and much dry corn already housed. We also found many deer skins and among them mantles made of thread and of poor quality, with which the women cover parts of their bodies. They had many vessels for grinding maize. The village contained forty small and low houses, reared in sheltered places, out of fear of the great storms that continuously occur in the country. . . .

The country between our landing place and the village and country of Apalachen is mostly level; the soil is sand and earth. All throughout it there are very large trees and open forests containing nut trees, laurels and others of the kind called resinous, cedar, juniper, wateroak, pines, oak

and low palmetto. . . . Everywhere there are many lagoons, large and small, some very difficult to cross, partly because they are so deep, partly because they are covered with fallen trees. . . . There is much maize in this province and the houses are scattered all over the country. . . . The animals we saw there were three kinds of deer, rabbits and hares, bears and lions and other wild beasts, among them one that carries its young in a pouch on its belly as long as the young are small, until they are able to look for their sustenance, and even then, when they are out after food and people come, the mother does not move until her little ones are in the pouch again. The country is very cold; it has good pasture for cattle; there are birds of many kinds in large numbers: geese, ducks, wild ducks, muscovy ducks, Ibis, small white herons (Egrets), herons and partridges. We saw many falcons, marsh-hawks, sparrow-hawks, pigeon-hawks and many other birds. Two hours after we arrived at Apalachen the Indians that had fled came back peaceably, begging us to give back to them their women and children, which we did. The Governor, however, kept with him one of their caciques [chiefs], at which they became so angry as to attack us the following day. They did it so swiftly and with so much audacity as to set fire to the lodges we occupied, but when we sallied forth they fled to the lagoons nearby, on account of which and of the big corn patches, we could not do them any harm beyond killing one Indian. The day after, Indians from a village on the other side came and attacked us in the same manner, escaping in the same way, with the loss of a single man. We remained at this village for twenty-five days. . . .

❉   ❉   ❉

. . . In a fight some of our people were wounded, in spite of their good armor. There were men that day who swore they had seen two oak trees, each as thick as the calf of a leg, shot through and through by arrows, which is not surprising if we consider the force and dexterity with which they shoot. I myself saw an arrow that had penetrated the base of a poplar tree for half a foot in length. All the many Indians from Florida we saw were archers, and, being very tall and naked, at a distance they appear giants. . . . Those people are wonderfully built, very gaunt and of great strength and agility. Their bows are as thick as an arm, from eleven to twelve spans long, shooting an arrow at 200 paces with unerring aim.

❉   ❉   ❉

[They had more difficulties with Indians, and neither food nor water.] With death as our only prospect . . . and considering these and many other inconveniences and that we had tried many expedients, we finally resorted to a very difficult one, which was to build some craft in which to leave the land. It seemed impossible, as none of us knew how to construct ships. We had no tools, no iron, no smithery, no oakum, no pitch, no tackling; finally, nothing of what was indispensable. Neither was there anybody to instruct us in shipbuilding, and, above all, there was nothing to eat, while the work was going on, for those who would have to perform the task. Considering all this, we agreed to think it over. Our parley ceased for that day, and everyone went off, leaving it to God, Our Lord, to put him on the right road according to His pleasure.

The next day God provided that one of the men should come, saying that he would make wooden flues, and bellows of deerskin, and as we were in such a state that anything appearing like relief seemed acceptable, we told him to go to work, and agreed to make of our stirrups, spurs, cross-bows and other iron implements the nails, saws and hatchets and other tools we so greatly needed for our purpose.

❖ ❖ ❖

The work on these was done by the only carpenter we had, and progressed so rapidly that, beginning on the fourth day of August, on the twentieth day of the month of September, five barges of twenty-two elbow lengths each were ready, caulked with palmetto oakum and tarred with pitch, which a Greek called Don Teodoro made from certain pines. Of the husk of palmettos, and of the tails and manes of the horses we made ropes and tackles, of our shirts sails, and of the junipers that grew there we made the oars, which we thought were necessary, and such was the stress in which our sins had placed us that only with very great trouble could we find stones for ballast and anchors of the barges, for we had not seen a stone in the whole country. We flayed the legs of the horses and tanned the skin to make leather pouches for carrying water.

❖ ❖ ❖

In all these parts we saw no mountains nor heard of any, and before embarking we had lost over forty men through sickness and hunger, besides those killed by Indians. On the twenty-second day of the month of September we had eaten up all the horses but one. We embarked in the following order: In the barge of the Governor there were forty-nine men, and as many in the one entrusted to the purser and the commissary. The third barge he placed in charge of Captain Alonso del Castillo and of Andres Dorantes, with forty-eight men; in another he placed two captains, named Tellez and Penalosa, with forty-seven men. The last one he gave to the inspector and to me, with forty-nine men, and, after clothing and supplies were put on board, the sides of the barges only rose half a foot above the water. Besides, we were so crowded as to be unable to stir. So great is the power of need that it brought us to venture out into such a troublesome sea in this manner, and

without any one among us having the least knowledge of the art of navigation.

❖ ❖ ❖

At the end of these thirty days, and when we were in extreme need of water and hugging the coast. . . . It was Our Lord's pleasure, who many a time shows His favor in the hour of greatest distress, that at sunset we turned a point of land and found there shelter and much improvement. . . . The Indians . . . were tall and well built, and carried neither bows nor arrows. We followed them to their lodges . . . in front of the lodges we saw many jars with water, and great quantities of cooked fish. The Chief of that land offered all to the Governor and led him to his abode. The dwellings were of matting and seemed to be permanent. When we entered the home of the chief he gave us plenty of fish, while we gave him of our maize, which they ate in our presence, asking for more. So we gave more to them, and the Governor presented him with some trinkets. While with the cacique at his lodge, half an hour after sunset, the Indians suddenly fell upon us and upon our sick people on the beach. . . . They also attacked the house of the cacique, where the Governor was, wounding him in the face with a stone. . . . Those of us who were there, seeing the Governor hurt, placed him aboard the barge and provided that most of the men should follow him to the boats. Some fifty of us remained on land to face the Indians, who attacked thrice that night, and so furiously as to drive us back every time further than a stone's throw. . . . Not one of us escaped unhurt.

❖ ❖ ❖

The Governor had with him the healthiest and strongest men, in no way could we follow or keep up with him. . . . As I could not follow him, I went after the other barge. . . . We travelled together for four days, our daily ration being half a handful of raw maize. . . . A storm overtook us, in which the other barge was lost. God's great mercy preserved us from being drowned in that weather.

It being winter and the cold very great, and as we had been suffering so many days from hunger and from the injuries we received from the waves, that the next day people began to break down, so that when the sun set all those aboard of my barge had fallen in a heap and were so near dying that few remained conscious, and not five men kept on their feet.

❖ ❖ ❖

Close to shore a wave took us and hurled the barge a horse's length out of water. With the violent shock nearly all the people who lay in the boat like dead came to themselves, and, seeing we were close to land, began to crawl out on all fours. As they took to some rocks, we built a fire and toasted some of our maize. We found rain water, and with the warmth of the fire people revived and began to cheer up. The day we arrived there was the sixth of the month of November.

⁕   ⁕   ⁕

Then we embarked. Two crossbow shots from shore a wave swept over us, we all got wet, and being naked and the cold very great, the oars dropped out of our hands. The next wave overturned the barge. The inspector and two others clung to her to save themselves, but the contrary happened; they got underneath the barge and were drowned.

The shore being very rough, the sea took the others and thrust them, half dead, on the beach of the same island again, less the three that had perished underneath the barge.

The rest of us, as naked as we had been born, had lost everything, and while it was not worth much, to us it meant a great deal. It was in November, bitterly cold, and we in such a state that every bone could easily be counted, and we looked like death itself. Of myself I can say that since the month of May I had not tasted anything but toasted maize, and even sometimes had been obliged to eat it raw. Although the horses were killed during the time the barges were built, I never could eat of them, and not ten times did I taste fish. This I say in order to explain and that any one might guess how we were off. On top of all this, a north wind arose, so that we were nearer death than life. It pleased Our Lord that . . . we found wood with which we built big fires and then with many tears begged Our Lord for mercy and forgiveness of our sins. Every one of us pitied not only himself, but all the others whom he saw in the same condition.

To this island we gave the name of the Island of Ill-Fate. The people on it are tall and well formed; they have no other weapons than bows and arrows. . . . The men have one of their nipples perforated from side to side and sometimes both; through this hole is thrust a reed as long as two and a half hands and as thick as two fingers; they also have the under lip perforated and a piece of cane in it as thin as the half of a finger. The women do the hard work. People stay on this island from October till the end of February, feeding on . . . roots . . . taken from under the water in November and December. They have channels made of reeds and get fish only during that time. . . . At the end of February they remove to other parts in search of food, because the roots begin to sprout and are not good any more.

Of all the people in the world, they are those who most love their children and treat them best, and should the child of one of them happen to die, parents and relatives bewail it, and the whole settlement, the lament last-

ing a full year, day after day. Before sunrise the parents begin to weep, after them the tribe, and the same they do at noon and at dawn. At the end of the year of mourning they celebrate the anniversary and wash and cleanse themselves of all their paint. They mourn all their dead in this manner, old people excepted, to whom they do not pay any attention, saying that these have had their time and are no longer of any use, but only take space, and food from the children.

Their custom as to bury the dead, except those who are medicine men among them, whom they burn, and while the fire is burning, all dance and make a big festival, grinding the bones to powder. At the end of the year. . . they scarify themselves and give to the relatives the pulverized bones to drink in water. Every man has a recognized wife, but the medicine men enjoy greater privileges, since they may have two or three, and among these wives there is great friendship and harmony.

⁕   ⁕   ⁕

On the island I have spoken of they wanted to make medicine men of us without any examination or asking for our diplomas, because they cure diseases by breathing on the sick, and with that breath and their hands they drive the ailment away. So they summoned us to do the same in order to be at least of some use. We laughed, taking it for a jest, and said that we did not understand how to cure.

⁕   ⁕   ⁕

Their manner of curing is as follows: When one is ill they call in a medicine man, and after they are well again not only do they give him all they have, but even things they strive to obtain from their relatives. All the medicine man does is to make a few cuts where the pain is located and then suck the skin around the incisions. They cauterize with fire, thinking it very effective, and I found it to be so by my own experience. Then they breathe on the spot where the pain is and believe that with this the disease goes away.

The way we treated the sick was to make over them the sign of the cross while breathing on them, recite a Pater noster and Ave Maria, and pray to God, Our Lord, as best we could to give them good health and inspire them to do us some favors. Thanks to His will and the mercy He had upon us, all those for whom we prayed, as soon as we crossed them, told the others that they were cured and felt well again.

⁕   ⁕   ⁕

All the people of this country go naked; only the women cover part of their bodies with a kind of wool that grows on trees. The girls go about in deer skins. They are very liberal towards each other with what they have. There is no ruler among them. All who are of the same descendancy cluster together. There are two distinct languages spoken on the island. . . .

Trading along with my wares I penetrated inland as far as I cared to go and along the coast as much as forty or fifty leagues. My stock consisted mainly of pieces of seashells and cockles, and shells with which they cut a fruit which is like a bean, used by them for healing and in their dances and feasts. This is of greatest value among them, besides shell-beads and other objects. These things I carried inland, and in exchange brought back hides and red ochre with which they rub and dye their faces and hair; flint for arrow points, glue and hard canes where-with to make them, and tassels made of the hair of deer, which they dye red. This trade suited me well because it gave me liberty to go wherever I pleased; I was not bound to do anything and no longer a slave. Wherever I went they treated me well, and gave me to eat for the sake of my wares. My principal object in doing it, however, was to find out in what manner I might get further away. I became well known among them; they rejoiced greatly when seeing me and. . . those who did not know me would desire and endeavor to meet me for the sake of my fame [as a healer].

❊   ❊   ❊

Nearly six years I spent thus in the country, alone among them and naked, as they all were themselves. The reason for remaining so long was that I wished to take with me a Christian called Lope de Oviedo, who still lingered on the island. . . . In the end I got him to come.

[de Vaca finds other Christians and learns the fate of others on his expedition.] The purser, with the friars, had stranded with their barge among the rivers, and, while they were proceeding along the coast, the barge of the Governor and his men came. . . . The Governor did not land that night, but remained on his barge with a pilot and a page who was sick. They had neither water nor anything to eat aboard, and at midnight a northerner set in with such violence that it carried the barge out into the sea, without anybody noticing it. They had for an anchor only a stone, and never more did they hear of him.

❊   ❊   ❊

At last the Christians escaped through flight, and remained with the other Indians, whose slaves they agreed to become. But, although serving them, they were so ill-treated, that no slaves, nor men in any condition of life, were ever so abused. Not content with cuffing and beating them and pulling out their beards for mere pastime, they killed three out of the six only because they went from one lodge to another. . . .

It is a custom of theirs to kill even their own children for the sake of dreams, and the girls when newly born they throw away to be eaten by dogs. The reason why they do it is (as they say) that all the others of that country are their enemies with whom they are always at war, and should they marry their daughters they might multiply so much as to be able to overcome them and reduce them to slavery. Hence they prefer to kill the girls rather than see them give birth to children who would become their foes.

We asked them why they did not wed the girls among themselves. They replied it was bad to marry them to their own kin, and much better to do away with their daughters than to leave them to relatives or to enemies. This custom they have in common with their neighbors, the Iguaces, and no other tribe of that country has it. When they want to get married they buy their wives from their enemies. The price paid for a woman is a bow, the best to be had, with two arrows, and if he has no bow he gives a net as much as a fathom in width and one in length. They kill their own children and buy those of strangers. Marriage only lasts as long as they please. For a mere nothing they break up wedlock.

❊   ❊   ❊

The men do not carry burdens or loads, the women and old men have to do it, for those are the people they least esteem. They have not as much love for their children as those spoken of before. Some among them are given to unnatural vices. The women are compelled to do very hard work. . . . They spend most of the night in stirring the fire to dry those roots which they eat, and at daybreak they begin to dig and carry firewood and water to their houses and attend to other necessary matters. Most of these Indians are great thieves, for, although very liberal towards each other, as soon as one turns his heads his own son or the father grabs what he can. They are great liars and drunkards and take something in order to become intoxicated. They are so accustomed to running that, without resting or getting tired, they run from morning till night in pursuit of a deer, and kill a great many. . . . Their huts are of matting placed over four arches. They carry them on their back and move every two or three days in quest of food; they plant nothing that would be of any use.

They are a very merry people, and even when famished do not cease to dance and celebrate their feasts and ceremonials. Their best times are when "tunas" (prickly pears) are ripe, because then they have plenty to eat and spend the time in dancing and eating day and night.

❊   ❊   ❊

When I had been with the Christians for six months, waiting to execute our plans, the Indians went for "tunas". . . and as we were about to flee the Indians began fighting among themselves over a woman and cuffed and struck and hurt each other, and in great rage each one took his lodge and went his own way. So we Christians had to part, and in no manner could we get together again until the year following. During that time I fared very badly, as well from lack of food as from the abuse the Indians gave me. So badly was I treated that I had to flee three times from my masters, and they all went in my pursuit ready to kill me. But God, Our Lord, in His infinite goodness, protected and saved my life.

❖   ❖   ❖

From the Island of Ill-Fate on, all the Indians whom we met as far as to here have the custom of not cohabiting with their wives when these are pregnant, and until the child is two years old.

Children are nursed to the age of twelve years, when they are old enough to gather their own food. We asked them why they brought their children up in that way and they replied, it was owing to the great scarcity of food all over that country, since it was common (as we saw) to be without it two or three days, and even four, and for that reason they nursed the little ones so long to preserve them from perishing through hunger. And even if they should survive, they would be very delicate and weak. When one falls sick he is left to die in the field unless he be somebody's child. Other invalids, if unable to travel, are abandoned; but a son or brother is taken along.

There is also a custom for husbands to leave their wives if they do not agree, and to remarry whom they please; this applies to the young men, but after they have had children they stay with their women and do not leave them.

❖   ❖   ❖

They all are warriors and so astute in guarding themselves from an enemy as if trained in continuous wars. . . . When in places where their enemies can offend them, they set their lodges on the edge of the roughest and densest timber and dig a trench close to it in which they sleep. The men at arms are hidden by brushwood and have their loopholes, and are so well covered and concealed that even at close range they cannot be seen. . . . To the densest part of the forest they open a very narrow trail and there arrange a sleeping place for their women and children. . . . In case there are no forests wherein they can hide thus and prepare their ambushes, they settle on the plain wherever it appears most appropriate, surrounding the place with trenches protected by brushwood. In these they open loopholes through which they can reach the enemy with arrows, and those parapets they build for the night. . . .

In this whole country they make themselves drunk by a certain smoke for which they give all they have. . . .

❖   ❖   ❖

During the time I was among them I saw something very repulsive, namely, a man married to another. Such are impotent and womanish beings, who dress like women and perform the office of women, but use the bow and carry big loads. Among these Indians we saw many of them; they are more robust than the other men, taller, and can bear heavy burdens.

❖   ❖   ❖

Alonso del Castillo and Estevanico, the negro [one of the survivors who was reunited with de Vaca], left with the women as guides, and the woman who was a captive took them to a river that flows between mountains, where there was a village, in which her father lived, and these were the first abodes we saw that were like unto real houses. . . .

So we went on our way and traversed the whole country to the South Sea, and our resolution was not shaken by the fear of great starvation, which the Indians said we should suffer (and indeed suffered). . . . All along the river, and in the course of these seventeen days we received plenty of cowhides. . . . Our food consisted (for each day) of a handful of deer-tallow, which for that purpose we always sought to keep. . . .

Among the houses there were several made of earth, and others of cane matting; and from here we travelled more than a hundred leagues, always meeting permanent houses and a great stock of maize and beans, and they gave us many deer (-hides) and blankets of cotton better than those of New Spain. They also gave us plenty of beads made out of the coral found in the South Sea; many good turquoises, which they get from the north; they finally gave us all they had; and Dorantes they presented with five emeralds, shaped as arrow-points, which arrows they use in their feasts and dances. As they appeared to be of very good quality, I asked whence they got them from, and they said it was from some very high mountains toward the north, where they traded for them with feather-bushes and parrot-plumes, and they said also that there were villages with many people and very big houses.

Among those people we found the women better treated than in any other part of the Indies as far as we have seen. They wear skirts of cotton that reach as far as the knee, and over them half-sleeves of scraped deerskin, with strips that hang down to the ground, and which they clean with certain roots, that clean very well and thus keep them tidy. The shirts are open in front and tied with strings; they wear shoes.

All those people came to us that we might touch and cross them; and they were so obtrusive as to make it difficult to endure since all, sick and healthy, wanted to be crossed. . . . All those people believed that we came from Heaven. What they do not understand or is new to them they are wont to say it comes from above.

✿   ✿   ✿

We travelled over a great part of the country, and found it all deserted, as the people had fled to the mountains, leaving houses and fields out of fear of the Christians. . . . They brought us blankets, which they had been concealing from the Christians, and gave them to us, and told us how the Christians had penetrated into the country before, and had destroyed and burnt the villages, taking with them half of the men and all the women and children, and how those who could escaped by flight. Seeing them in this plight, afraid to stay anywhere, and that they neither would nor could cultivate the soil, preferring to die rather than suffer such cruelties, while they showed the greatest pleasure at being with us. . . . It clearly shows how, in order to bring those people to Christianity and obedience unto Your Imperial Majesty, they should be well treated, and not otherwise.

✿   ✿   ✿

I took with me the negro and eleven Indians and, following the trail, went in search of the Christians. . . . I came upon four Christians on horseback. . . . I spoke first, and told them to lead me to their captain, and we went together to Diego de Alcaraza, their commander.

✿   ✿   ✿

We had many and bitter quarrels with the Christians, for they wanted to make slaves of our Indians, and we grew so angry at it that at our departure we forgot to take along many bows, pouches and arrows, also the five emeralds, and so they were left and lost to us. We gave the Christians a great many cow-skin robes, and other objects, and had much trouble in persuading the Indians to return home and plant their crops in peace. They insisted upon accompanying us until, according to their custom, we should be in the custody of other Indians, because otherwise they were afraid to die; besides, as long as we were with them, they had no fear of the Christians and of their lances. At all this the Christians were greatly vexed, and told their own interpreter to say to the Indians how we were of their own race, but had gone astray for a long while, and were people of no luck and little heart, whereas they were the lords of the land, whom they should obey and serve. The Indians gave all that talk of theirs little attention. . . . In short, they recalled all our deeds, and praised them highly, contrasting them with the conduct of the others.

✿   ✿   ✿

We went on with the idea of insuring the liberty of the Indians, and, when we believed it to be assured, the opposite took place. The Spaniards had planned to fall upon those Indians we had sent back in fancied security and in peace, and that plan they carried out.

✿   ✿   ✿

After baptizing the children we left for the village of San Miguel, where, on our arrival, Indians came and told how many people were coming down from the mountains, settling on the plain, building churches and erecting crosses; in short, complying with what we had sent them word to do. Day after day we were getting news of how all was being done and completed.

✿   ✿   ✿

[After] San Miguel [we went to] the town of Compostela, where the Governor, Nuño de Guzman, resided. . . . The Governor received us very well, giving us of what he had, for us to dress in; but for many days I could bear no clothing, nor could we sleep, except on the bare floor. Ten or twelve days later we left for Mexico. On the whole trip we were well treated by the Christians; many came to see us on the road, praising God for having freed us from so many dangers. We reached Mexico . . . and were very well received by the Viceroy and the Marquis of the Valley, who presented us with clothing, offering all they had. On the day of Saint James there was a festival, with bull-fight and tournament.

✿   ✿   ✿

When winter was past, Andres Dorantes and I left Mexico . . . . We arrived [at the port of Lisbon] on the ninth of August, vespers of Saint Laurentius day, of the year 1537.

And, in testimony of, that what I have stated in the foregoing narrative is true, I hereunto sign my name: Cabeza de Vaca

Source:
Public Broadcasting Service/PBS. Archives of the West. "The Journey of Alvar Nuñez Cabeza De Vaca (1542)." Available on-line. URL: www.pbs.org/weta/thewest/resources/archives/one/cabeza.htm. Downloaded June 2003.

Arthur M. Barlowe, "Exploration of Virginia," 1584

In March of 1584, Sir Walter Raleigh received a patent from Queen Elizabeth I granting him permission to establish colonies in North America. The following month he commissioned an exploratory voyage, headed by Captains Philip Amadas and Arthur M. Barlowe, to search out possible locations for a new colony. Amadas and Barlowe set out from England on April 27, 1584, and reached Roanoke Island, off the coast of present-day North Carolina, which would eventually be the site of Jamestown, the first permanent English settlement in North America. It is thought that, in an effort to attract settlers to the New World, the beauty of the land and the friendliness of the native inhabitants was somewhat exaggerated. Certain phrases in the account, such as, "The soil is the most plentiful, sweet, fruitful and wholesome of all the world," tend to support this theory. Following some introductory paragraphs about the journey, the excerpt below opens with a description of the island.

Barlowe's account, first published in Holingshed's *Chronicles* in 1587, was subsequently also published in Richard Hakluyt's *The Principall Navigations Voiages Traffiques & Discoveries of the English Nation.* First published in 1589, Hakluyt's *Voyages* was and continues to be a major source of firsthand accounts of the earliest English explorations and attempts at colonization.

This Island had many goodly woodes full of Deere, Conies, Hares, and Fowle, even in the middest of Summer in incredible abundance. The woodes are not such as you finde in Bohemia, Muscovia, or Hercynia, barren and fruitless, but the highest and reddest Cedars of the world, farre bettering the Ceders of the Âcores, of the Indies, or Lybanus, Pynes, Cypres, Sassaphras, the Lentisk, or the tree that beareth the Masticke, the tree that beareth the rine of blacke Sinamon, of which Master Winter brought from the streights of Magellan, and many other of excellent smell and qualitie. We remained by the side of this Island two whole dayes before we saw any people of the Countrey: the third day we espied one small boate rowing towardes us having in it three persons: this boat came to the Island side, foure harquebuz-shot from our shippes, and there two of the people remaining, the third came along the shoreside towards us, and wee being then all within boord, he walked up and downe upon the point of the land next unto us: then the Master and the Pilot of the Admirall, Simon Fernandino, and the Captaine Philip Amadas, my selfe, and others rowed to the land, whose comming this fellow attended, never making any shewe of feare or doubt. And after he had spoken of many things not understood by us, we brought him with his owne good liking, aboord the ships, and gave him a shirt, a hat & some other things, and made him taste of our wine, and our meat, which he liked very wel: and after having viewed both barks, he departed, and went to his owne boat againe, which hee had left in a little Cove or Creeke adjoyning: as soone as hee was two bow shoot into the water, he fell to fishing, and in lesse then halfe an houre, he had laden his boate as deepe, as it could swimme, with which hee came againe to the point of the lande, and there he devided his fish into two parts, pointing one part to the ship, and the other to the pinnesse: which, after he had (as much as he might) requited the former benefites received, departed out of our sight.

The next day there came unto us divers boates, and in one of them the Kings brother, accompanied with fortie or fiftie men, very handsome and goodly people, and in their behaviour as mannerly and civill as any of Europe. His name was Granganimeo, and the King is called Wingina, the country Wingandacoa, and now by her Majestie Virginia. The maner of his comming was in this sort: hee left his boates altogether as the first man did a little from the shippes by the shore, and came along to the place over against the ships, followed with fortie men. When he came to the place, his servants spread a long matte upon the ground, on which he sate downe, and at the other ende of the matte foure others of his companie did the like, the rest of his men stood round about him, somewhat a farre off: when we came to the shore to him with our weapons, hee never mooved from his place, nor any of the other foure, nor never mistrusted any harme to be offred from us, but sitting still he beckoned us to come and sit by him, which we performed: and being set hee made all signes of joy and welcome, striking on his head and his breast and afterwardes on ours, to shewe wee were all one, smiling and making shewe the best he could of all love, and familiaritie. After hee had made a long speech unto us, wee presented him with divers things, which hee received very joyfully, and thankefully. None of the company durst speake one worde all the time: onely the foure which were at the other ende, spake one in the others eare very softly.

The King is greatly obeyed, and his brothers and children reverenced: the King himselfe in person was at our being there, sore wounded in a fight which hee had with the King of the next countrey, called Wingina, and was shot in two places through the body, and once cleane through the thigh, but yet he recovered: by reason whereof and for that hee lay at the chiefe towne of the country, being six dayes journey off, we saw him not at all.

After we had presented this his brother with such things as we thought he liked, wee likewise gave somewhat to the other that sat with him on the matte: but presently he arose and tooke all from them and put it into his owne basket, making signes and tokens, that all things ought to bee delivered unto him, and the rest were but his servants, and followers. A day or two after this we fell to trading with them, exchanging some things that we had, for Chamoys, Buffe, and Deere skinnes: when we shewed him all our packet of merchandize, of all things that he sawe, a bright tinne dish most pleased him, which hee presently tooke up and clapt it before his breast, and after made a hole in the brimme thereof and hung it about his necke, making signes that it would defende him against his enemies arrowes: for those people maintaine a deadly and terrible warre, with the people and King adjoyning. We exchanged our tinne dish for twentie skinnes, woorth twentie Crownes, or twentie Nobles: and a copper kettle for fiftie skins woorth fifty Crownes. They offered us good exchange for our hatchets, and axes, and for knives, and would have given any thing for swordes: but wee would not depart with any. After two or three dayes the Kings brother came aboord the shippes, and dranke wine, and eat of our meat and of our bread, and liked exceedingly thereof: and after a few dayes overpassed, he brought his wife with him to the ships, his daughter and two or three children: his wife was very well favoured, of meane stature and very bashfull: shee had on her backe a long cloake of leather, with the furre side next to her body, and before her a piece of the same: about her forehead shee had a bande of white Corall, and so had her husband many times: in her eares shee had bracelets of pearles hanging downe to her middle, (whereof wee delivered your worship a little bracelet) and those were of the bignes of good pease. The rest of her women of the better sort had pendants of copper hanging in either eare, and some of the children of the Kings brother and other noble men, have five or sixe in either eare: he himselfe had upon his head a broad plate of golde, or copper for being unpolished we knew not what mettal it should be, neither would he by any meanes suffer us to take it off his head, but feeling it, would bow very easily. His apparell was as his wives, onely the women weare their haire long on both sids, and the men but on one. They are of colour yellowish, and their haire black for the most part, and yet we saw children that had very fine aburne, and chestnut coloured haire.

After that these women had bene there, there came downe from all parts great store of people, bringing with them leather, corall, divers kindes of dies very excellent, and exchanged with us: but when Granganimeo the kings brother was present, none durst trade but himselfe: except such as weare red pieces of copper on their heads like himselfe: for that is the difference betweene the noble men, and the governours of the countreys, and you have understood since by these men, which we brought home, that no people in the worlde cary more respect to their King, Nobilitie, and Governours, then these doe. The Kings brothers wife, when she came to us (as she did many times) was followed with forty or fifty women alwayes: and when she came into the shippe, she left them all on land, saving her two daughters, her nurse and one or two more. The Kings brother always kept this order, as many boates as he would come withall to the shippes, so many fires would hee make on the shore a farre off, to the end we might understand with what strength and company he approached. Their boates are made of one tree, either of Pine or of Pitch trees: a wood not commonly knowen to our people, nor found growing in England. They have no edge-tooles to make them withall: if they have any they are very fewe, and those it seemes they had twentie yeres since, which, as those two men declared, was out of a

wrake which happened upon their coast of some Christian ship, being beaten that way by some storme and outragious weather, whereof none of the people were saved, but only the ship, or some part of her being cast upon the sand, out of whose sides they drew the nayles and the spikes, and with those they made their best instruments. The manner of making their boates is thus: they burne downe some great tree, or take such as are winde fallen, and putting gumme and rosen upon one side thereof, they set fire into it, and when it hath burnt it hollow, they cut out the coale with their shels, and ever where they would burne it deeper or wider they lay on gummes, which burne away the timber, and by thie meanes they fashion very fine boates, and such as will transport twentie men. Their oares are like scoopes, and many times they set with long pooles, as the depth serveth.

The Kings brother had great liking of our armour, a sword, and divers other things which we had: and offered to lay a great boxe of pearle in gage for them: but we refused it for this time, because we would not make them knowe, that we esteemed thereof, untill we had understoode in what places of the countrey the pearle grew: which now your Worshippe doeth very well understand. He was very just of his promise: for many times we delivered him merchandize upon his word, but ever he came within the day and performed his promise. He sent us every day a brase or two of fat Bucks, Conies, Hares, Fish the best of the world. He sent us divers kindes of fruites, Melons, Walnuts, Cucumbers, Gourdes, Pease, and divers rootes, and fruites very excellent good, and of their Countrey corne, which is very white, faire and well tasted, and groweth three times in five moneths: in May they sow, in July they reape, in June they sow, in August they reape: in July they sow, in September they reape: onely they cast the corne into the ground breaking a little of the soft turfe with a wodden mattock, or pickeaxe: our selves prooved the soile, and put some of our Pease in the ground, and in tenne dayes they were of fourteene ynches high: they have also Beanes very faire of divers colours and wonderfull plentie: some growing naturally, and some in their gardens, and so have they both wheat and oates.

The soile is the most plentifull, sweete, fruitfull and wholsome of all the worlde: there are above foureteene severall sweete smelling timber trees, and the most part of their underwoods are Bayes and such like: they have those Okes that we have, but farre greater and better. After they had bene divers times aboord our shippes, my selfe, with seven more went twentie mile into the River, that runneth towards the Citie of Skicoak, which River they call Occam: and the evening following, wee came to an island, which they call Raonoak, distant from the harbour by which we entred, seven leagues: and at the North end thereof was a village of nine houses, built of Cedar, and fortified round about with sharpe trees, to keepe out their enemies, and the entrance into it made like a turne pike very artificially; when wee came towardes it, standing neere unto the waters side, the wife of Granganimo the Kings brother came running out to meete us very cheerefully and friendly, her husband was not then in the village; some of her people shee commanded to drawe our boate on shore for the beating of the billoe: others she appointed to cary us on their backes to the dry ground, and others to bring our oares into the house for feare of stealing. When we were come into the utter roome, having five roomes in her house, she caused us to sit downe by a great fire, and after tooke off our clothes and washed them, and dryed them againe: some of the women plucked off our stockings and washed them, some washed our feete in warme water, and shee her selfe tooke great paines to see all things ordered in the best maner shee could, making great haste to dresse some meate for us to eate.

After we had thus dryed our selves, she brought us into the inner roome, where shee set on the boord standing along the house, some wheate like furmentie, sodden Venison, and roasted, fish sodden, boyled, and roasted, Melons rawe, and sodden rootes of divers kindes, and divers fruites: their drinke is commonly water, but while the grape lasteth, they drinke wine, and for want of caskes to keepe it, all the yere after they drink water, but it is sodden with Ginger in it, and blacke Sinamon, and sometimes Sassaphras, and divers other wholesome, and medicinable hearbes and trees. We were entertained with all love and kindnesse, and with as much bountie (after their maner) as they could possibly devise. We found the people most gentle, loving, and faithfull, voide of all guile and treason, and such as live after the maner of the golden age. The people onely care howe to defend themselves from the cold in their short winter, and to feed themselves with such meat as the soile affoordeth: there meate is very well sodden and they make broth very sweet and savorie: their vessels are earthen pots, very large, white and sweete, their dishes are wodden platters of sweet timber: within the place where they feede was their lodging, and within that their Idoll, which they worship, of whome they speake incredible things. While we were at meate, there came in at the gates two or three men with their bowes and arrowes from hunting, whom when wee espied, we beganne to looke one towardes another, and offered to reach our weapons: but as soone as shee espied our mistrust, shee was very much mooved, and caused some of her men to runne out, and take away their bowes and arrowes and breake them, and withall beate the poore fellowes out of the gate againe. When we departed in the evening and would not tary all night, she was very sory, and gave us into our boate our supper halfe dressed, pottes and all, and brought us to our boateside, in which wee lay all night, remooving the same

a prettie distance from the shoare: shee perceiving our jealousie, was much greived, and sent divers men and thirtie women, to sit all night on the banke side by us, and sent us into our boates five mattes to cover us from the raine, using very many wordes to intreate us to rest in their houses: but because wee were few men, and if wee had miscaried, the voyage had bene in very great danger, wee durst not adventure any thing, though there was no cause of doubt: for a more kinde and loving people there can not be found in the worlde, as farre as we have hitherto had triall. Beyond this Island there is the maine lande, and over against this Island falleth into this spacious water, the great river called Occam by the inhabitants on which standeth a towne called Pomeiock, & six dayes journey from the same is situate their greatest citie called Skicoak, which this people affirme to be very great: but the Savages were never at it, only they speake of it by the report of their fathers and other men, whom they have heard affirme it to bee above one houres journey about.

Into this river falleth another great river, called Cipo, in which there is found great store of Muskles in which there are pearles: likewise there descendeth into this Occam, another river, called Nomopana, on the one side whereof standeth a great towne called Chawanook, and the Lord of that towne and countrey is called Pooneno: this Poomeno is not subject to the king of Wingandacoa, but is a free Lord: beyond this country is there another king, whom they cal Menatonon, and these three Kings are in league with each other. Towards the Southwest, foure dayes journey is situate a towne called Sequotan, which is the Southernmost towne of Wingandacoa, neere unto which, six and twentie yeres past there was a ship cast away, whereof some of the people were saved, and those were white people, whome the countrey people preserved.

And after ten dayes remaining in an out Island unhabited, called Wocokon, they with the help of some of the dwellers of Sequotan, fastened two boates of the countrey together & made mastes unto them, and sailes of their shirtes, and having taken into them such victuals as the countrey yeelded, they departed after they had remained in this out Island 3 weekes: but shortly after it seemed they were cast away, for the boates were found upon the coast, cast a land in another Island adjoyning: other then these, there was never any people apparelled, or white of colour, either seene or heard of amongst these people, and these aforesaid were seen onely of the inhabitants of Secotan, which appeared to be very true, for they wondred marvelously when we were amongst them at the whitenes of our skins, ever coveting to touch our breasts, and to view the same. Besides they had our ships in marvelous admiration, & all things els were so strange unto them, as it appeared that none of them had ever seene the like. When we discharged any piece, were it but an hargubuz, they would tremble thereat for very feare, and for the strangenesse of the same: for the weapons which themselves use are bowes and arrowes: the arrowes are but of small canes, headed with a sharpe shell or tooth of a fish sufficient ynough to kill a naked man. Their swordes be of wood hardened: likewise they use wooden breastplates for their defence. They have besides a kinde of club, in the end whereof they fasten the sharpe hornes of a stagge, or other beast. When they goe to warres they cary about with them their idol, of whom they aske counsel, as the Romans were woont of the Oracle of Apollo. They sing songs as they march towardes the battell in stead of drummes and trumpets: their warres are very cruell and bloody, by reason whereof, and of their civill dissentions which have happened of late yeeres amongst them, the people are marvelously wasted, and in some places the countrey left desolate.

Adjoyning to this countrey aforesaid called Secotan begginneth a countrey called Pomovik, belonging to another king whom they call Piamacum, and this king is in league with the next king adjoyning towards the setting of the Sunne, and the countrey Newsiok, situate upon a goodly river called Neus: these kings have mortall warre with Wingina king of Wingandacoa: but about two yeeres past there was a peace madde betweene the King Piemacum, and the Lord of Secotan, as these men which we have brought with us to England, have given us to understand: but there remaineth a mortall malice in the Secotanes, for many injuries and slaughters done upon them by this Piemacum. They invited divers men, and thirtie women of the best of his countrey to their towne to a feast: and when they were altogether merry, & praying before their Idol, (which is nothing els but a meer illusion of the devil) the captaine or Lord of the town came suddenly upon them, and slewe them every one, reserving the women and children: and these two have often times since perswaded us to surprize Piemacum his towne, having promised and assured us, that there will be found in it great store of commodities. But whether their perswasion be to the ende they may be revenged of their enemies, or for the love of they beare to us, we leave that to the tryall hereafter.

Beyond the Island called Roanoak, are maine Islands very plentifull of fruits and other naturall increases, together with many townes, and villages, along the side of the continent, some bounding upon the Islands, and some stretching up further into the land.

When we first had sight of this countrey, some thought the first land we saw to bee the continent: but after we entred into the Haven, we saw before us another mighty long Sea: for there lyeth along the coast a tracte of Islands, two hundreth miles in length, adjoyning to the Ocean sea, and betweene the Islands, two or three entrances: when you are entred betweene them (these Islands being very narrow for the most part, as in most places six miles broad, in some places lesse, in fewe more) then there appeareth another great Sea, containing in bredth in some places, forty, and in some fifty, in some twenty miles over, before you come unto the continent: and in this inclosed Sea there are above an hundreth Islands of divers bignesses, whereof one is sixteene miles long, at which we were finding it a most pleasant and fertile ground, replenished with goodly Cedars, and divers other sweete woods, full of Corrants, of flaxe, and many other notable commodities, which we at that time had no leasure to view. Besides this Island there are many, as I have sayd, some of two or three, or foure, or five miles, some more, some lesse, most beautifull and pleasant to behold, replenished with Deere, Conies, Hares and divers beasts, and about them the goodliest and best fish in the world, and in greatest abundance.

Thus Sir, we have acquainted you with the particulars of our discovery, made this present voyage, as farre foorth as the shortnesse of the time we there continued would affoord us take view of: and so contenting our selves with this service at this time, which wee hope hereafter to inlarge, as occasion and assistance shalbe given, we resolved to leave the countrey, and to apply our selves to returne for England, which we did accordingly, and arrived safely in the West of England about the middest of September.

And whereas wee have above certified you of the countrey taken in possession by us, to her Majesties use, and so to yours by her Majesties grant, wee thought good for the better assurance thereof to record some of the particular Gentleman, & men of accompt, who then were present as witnesses of the same, that thereby all occasion of cavill to the title of the countrey, in her Majesties behalfe may be prevented, which otherwise, such as like not the action may use and pretend, whose names are:

Captaines:
Master Philip Amadas,
Master Arthur Barlow,

Of the Companie:
William Greenevile,
John Wood,
James Browewich,
Henry Greene,
Benjamin Wood,
Simon Ferdinando,
Nicholas Petman,
John Hewes,

We brought home also two of the Savages being lustie men whose names were Wanchese and Manteo.

See also CHARTER TO SIR WALTER RALEIGH, 1584.

Source:
Richard Hakluyt. *The Principal Navigations Voyages Traffiques and Discoveries of the English Nation.* Edited by Richard Hakluyt and Edmund Goldsmid. Edinburgh: E. & G. Goldsmid, 1885–1890.

Richard Hakluyt, "Discourse Concerning Westerne Planting," 1584

The purpose of this unpublished state paper, written by Richard Hakluyt in 1584 was to stir interest in colonization of the Western Hemisphere. Hakluyt was an ordained minister in the Church of England and served as chaplain to the English ambassador in Paris in the 1580s. It was there that his interest in the explorations of the European powers was fueled. He later published a collection of eyewitness accounts and other records of English and foreign explorers in an enlarged, reconstructed edition called *The Principal Navigations, Voyages and Discoveries of the English Nation (1598–1600),* one of the most important collections of exploration documents in existence. Only Chapter XX has been reproduced in this volume.

Chapter XX

A brefe collection of certaine reasons to induce her Majestie and the state to take in hande the westerne voyadge and the plantinge there.

1. The soyle yeldeth, and may be made to yelde, all the severall comodities of Europe, and of all kingdomes, domynions, and territories that England tradeth withe, that by trade of marchandize cometh into this realme.

2. The passage thither and home is neither to longe nor to shorte, but easie, and to be made twise in the yere.

3. The passage cutteth not nere the trade of any prince, nor nere any of their contries or territories, and is a safe passage, and not easie to be annoyed by prince or potentate whatsoever.

4. The passage is to be perfourmed at all times of the yere, and in that respecte passeth our trades in the Levant Seas within the Straites of Juberalter, and the trades in the seas within the Kinge of Denmarkes Straite, and the trades to the portes of Norwey and of Russia, &c.; for as in the south weste Straite there is no passage in somer by lacke of windes, so within the other places there is no passage in winter by yse and extreme colde.

5. And where England nowe for certen hundreth yeres last passed, by the peculiar comoditie of wolles, and of later yeres by clothinge of the same, hath raised it selfe from meaner state to greater wealthe and moche higher honour, mighte, and power then before, to the equallinge of the princes of the same to the greatest potentates of this parte of the worlde; it cometh nowe so to passe, that by the greate endevour of the increase of the trade of wolles in Spaine and in the West Indies, nowe daily more and more multiplienge, that the wolles of England, and the clothe made of the same, will become base, and every day more base then other; which, prudently weyed, yt behoveth this realme, yf it meane not to returne to former olde meanes and basenes, but to stande in present and late former honour, glorye, and force, and not negligently and sleepingly to slyde into beggery, to foresee and to plante at Norumbega or some like place, were it not for any thing els but for the hope of the vent of our woll indraped, the principall and in effecte the onely enrichinge contynueinge naturall comoditie of this realme. And effectually pursueinge that course, wee shall not onely finde on that tracte of lande, and especially in that firme northwarde (to whome warme clothe shalbe righte wellcome), an ample vente, but also shall, from the north side of that firme, finde oute knowen and unknowen ilandes and domynions replenished with people that may fully vent the aboundaunce of that our comoditie, that els will in fewe yeres waxe of none or of small value by forreine aboundaunce, &c.; so as by this enterprice wee shall shonne the ymmynent mischefe hanginge over our heades, that els muste nedes fall upon the realme, without breache of peace or sworde drawen againste this realme by any forreine state; and not offer our auncient riches to scornefull neighboures at home, nor sell the same in effecte for nothinge, as wee shall shortly, if presently it be not provaided for. The increase of the wolles of Spaine and America is of highe pollicie, with greate desire of our overthrowe, endevoured; and the goodnes of the forren wolles our people will not enter into the consideration of, nor will not beleve aughte, they be so sotted with opinion of their owne; and, yf it be not foresene and some such place of vent provided, farewell the goodd state of all degrees in this realme.

6. This enterprise may staye the Spanishe Kinge from flowinge over all the face of that waste firme of America, yf wee seate and plante there in time, in tyme I say, and wee by plantinge shall lett him from makinge more shorte and more safe returnes oute of the noble portes of the purposed places of our plantinge, then by any possibilitie he can from the parte of the firme that nowe his navies by ordinary courses come from, in this that there is no comparison betwene the portes of the coastes that the Kinge of Spaine dothe nowe possesse and use, and the portes of the coastes that our nation is to possesse by plantinge at Norumbega, and on that tracte faste by, more to the northe and northeaste, and in that there is from thence a moche shorter course, and a course of more temperature, and a course that possesseth more contynuaunce of ordinary windes, then the present course of the Spanishe Indian

navies nowe dothe. And England possessinge the purposed place of plantinge, her Majestie may, by the benefete of the seate, havinge wonne goodd and royall havens, have plentie of excellent trees for mastes, of goodly timber to builde shippes and to make greate navies, of pitche, tarr, hempe, and all thinges incident for a navie royall, and that for no price, and withoute money or request. Howe easie a matter may yt be to this realme, swarminge at this day with valiant youthes, rustinge and hurtfull by lacke of employment, and havinge goodd makers of cable and of all sortes of cordage, and the best and moste connynge shipwrights of the worlde, to be lordes of all those sees, and to spoile Phillipps Indian navye, and to deprive him of yerely passage of his treasure into Europe, and consequently to abate the pride of Spaine and of the supporter of the greate Antechriste of Rome, and to pull him downe in equallitie to his neighbour princes, and consequently to cutt of the common mischefes that come to all Europe by the peculiar aboundaunce of his Indian treasure, and thiss withoute difficultie.

7. This voyadge, albeit it may be accomplished by barke or smallest pynnesse for advise or for a necessitie, yet for the distaunce, for burden and gaine in trade, the marchant will not for profitts sake use it but by shippes of greate burden; so as this realme shall have by that meane shippes of greate burden and of greate strengthe for the defence of this realme, and for the defence of that newe seate, as nede shall require, and withall greate increase of perfecte seamen, which greate princes in time of warres wante, and which kinde of men are neither nourished in fewe daies nor in fewe yeres.

8. This newe navie of mightie newe stronge shippes, so in trade to that Norumbega and to the coastes there, shall never be subjecte to arreste of any prince or potentate, as the navie of this realme from time to time hath bene in the portes of thempire, in the portes of the Base Contries, in Spaine, Fraunce, Portingale, &c., in the tymes of Charles the Emperour, Fraunces the Frenche kinge, and others; but shall be alwayes free from that bitter mischeefe, withoute grefe or hazarde to the marchaunte or to the state, and so alwaies readie at the comaundement of the prince with mariners, artillory, armor, and munition, ready to offende and defende as shalbe required.

9. The greate masse of wealthe of the realme imbarqued in the marchantes shippes, caried oute in this newe course, shall not lightly, in so farr distant a course from the coaste of Europe, be driven by windes and tempestes into portes of any forren princes, as the Spanishe shippes of late yeres have bene into our portes of the Weste Contries, &c.; and so our marchantes in respecte of private state, and of the realme in respecte of a generall safetie from venture of losse, are by this voyadge oute of one greate mischefe.

10. No forren commoditie that comes into England comes withoute payment of custome once, twise, or thrise, before it come into the realme, and so all forren comodities become derer to the subjectes of this realme; and by this course to Norumbega forren princes customes are avoided; and the forren comodities cheapely purchased, they become cheape to the subjectes of England, to the common benefite of the people, and to the savinge of greate treasure in the realme; whereas nowe the realme becomethe poore by the purchasinge of forreine comodities in so greate a masse at so excessive prices.

11. At the firste traficque with the people of those partes, the subjectes of this realme for many yeres shall chaunge many cheape comodities of these partes for thinges of highe valor there not estemed; and this to the greate inrichinge of the realme, if common use faile not.

12. By the greate plentie of those regions the marchantes and their factors shall lye there cheape, buye and repaire their shippes cheape, and shall returne at pleasure withoute staye or restrainte of forreine prince; whereas upon staies and restraintes the marchaunte raiseth his chardge in sale over of his ware; and, buyenge his wares cheape, he may mainteine trade with smalle stocke, and withoute takinge upp money upon interest; and so he shalbe riche and not subjecte to many hazardes, but shalbe able to afforde the comodities for cheape prices to all subjectes of the realme.

13. By makinge of shippes and by preparinge of thinges for the same, by makinge of cables and cordage, by plantinge of vines and olive trees, and by makinge of wyne and oyle, by husbandrie, and by thousandes of thinges there to be done, infinite nombers of the Englishe nation may be set on worke, to the unburdenynge of the realme with many that nowe lyve chardgeable to the state at home.

14. If the sea coste serve for makinge of salte, and the inland for wine, oiles, oranges, lymons, figges, &c., and for makinge of yron, all which with moche more is hoped, withoute sworde drawen, wee shall cutt the combe of the Frenche, of the Spanishe, of the Portingale, and of enemies, and of doubtfull frendes, to the abatinge of their wealthe and force, and to the greater savinge of the wealthe of the realme.

15. The substaunces servinge, wee may oute of those partes receave the masse of wrought wares that now wee receave out of Fraunce, Flaunders, Germanye, &c.; and so wee may daunte the pride of some enemies of this realme, or at the leaste in parte purchase those wares, that nowe wee buye derely of the Frenche and Flemynge, better cheape; and in the ende, for the parte that this realme was wonte to receave, dryve them oute of trade to idlenes for the settinge of our people on worke.

16. Wee shall by plantinge there inlarge the glory of the gospell, and from England plante sincere relligion, and provide a safe and a sure place to receave people from all partes of the worlde that are forced to flee for the truthe of Gods worde.

17. If frontier warres there chaunce to aryse, and if thereupon wee shall fortifie, yt will occasion the trayninge upp of our youthe in the discipline of warr, and make a nomber fitt for the service of the warres and for the defence of our people there and at home.

18. The Spaniardes governe in the Indies with all pride and tyranie; and like as when people of contrarie nature at the sea enter into gallies, where men are tied as slaves, all yell and crye with one voice, *Liberta, liberta,* as desirous of libertie and freedome, so no doubte whensoever the Queene of England, a prince of such clemencie, shall seate upon that firme of America, and shalbe reported throughe oute all that tracte to use the naturall people there with all humanitie, curtesie, and freedome, they will yelde themselves to her governement, and revolte cleane from the Spaniarde, and specially when they shall understande that she hathe a noble navie, and that she aboundeth with a people moste valiaunte for theyr defence. And her Majestie havinge Sir Fraunces Drake and other subjectes already in credite with the Symerons, a people or great multitude alreadye revolted from the Spanishe governemente, she may with them and a fewe hundrethes of this nation, trayned upp in the late warres of Fraunce and Flaunders, bringe greate things to passe, and that with greate ease; and this broughte so aboute, her Majestie and her subjectes may bothe enjoye the treasure of the mynes of golde and silver, and the whole trade and all the gaine of the trade of marchandize, that nowe passeth thither by the Spaniardes onely hande, of all the comodities of Europe; which trade of marchandize onely were of it selfe suffycient (withoute the benefite of the riche myne) to inriche the subjectes, and by customes to fill her Majesties coffers to the full. And if it be highe pollicie to mayneteyne the poore people of this realme in worke, I dare affirme that if the poore people of England were five times so many as they be, yet all mighte be sett on worke in and by workinge lynnen, and suche other thinges of marchandize as the trade into the Indies dothe require.

19. The present shorte trades causeth the maryner to be cast of, and ofte to be idle, and so by povertie to fall to piracie. But this course to Norumbega beinge longer, and a contynuaunce of themployment of the maryner, dothe kepe the maryner from ydlenes and from necessitie; and so it cutteth of the principal actions of piracie, and the rather because no riche praye for them to take cometh directly in their course or any thing nere their course.

20. Many men of excellent wittes and of divers singuler giftes, overthrowen by suertishippe, by sea, or by some folly of youthe, that are not able to live in England, may there be raised againe, and doe their contrie goodd service; and many nedefull uses there may (to greate purpose) require the savinge of greate nombers, that for trifles may otherwise be devoured by the gallowes.

21. Many souldiers and servitours, in the ende of the warres, that mighte be hurtfull to this realme, may there be unladen, to the common profite and quiet of this realme, and to our forreine benefite there, as they may be employed.

22. The frye of the wandringe beggars of England, that growe upp ydly, and hurtfull and burdenous to this realme, may there be unladen, better bredd upp, and may people waste contries to the home and forreine benefite, and to their owne more happy state.

23. If Englande crie oute and affirme, that there is so many in all trades that one cannot live for another, as in all places they doe, this Norumbega (if it be thoughte so goodd) offreth the remedie.

Thomas Hariot, *Briefe and True Report of the New Found Land of Virginia,* 1588

This document, written by Thomas Hariot and illustrated by John White in 1588, revealed the true findings of the colonizing expedition led by Sir Walter Raleigh that had landed on Roanoke Island, off the Virginia coast. The text emphasized geographical and environmental items of interest, including native plants that could be used for food. It also describes the indigenous people. However, the report became more famous for John White's visual record, which consisted of 23 watercolor paintings from a collection of at least 63. These included representations of the life and habits of the Native Americans as well as the "flora and fauna" of the land, and they were even known to have influenced geographers in their study of the coastline of the Chesapeake Bay. White's paintings were engraved for the *True Report of Virginia* by Theodore de Bry, and the document was published in a second edition in 1590. The excerpts here include the first and last parts. Consult the source for the entire document.

Rafe Lane One of Her Maiesties
Equieres and Governour of the Colony in Virginia above mentioned for the time there resident. To the gentle Reader, wisheth all happiness in the Lord.

Lbeit (Gentle Reader) the credite of the reports in this treatise contained, can little be furthered by the testimony of one as my selfe, through affection judged partiall, though without desert: Neverthelesse forsomuch as I haue beene requested by some my particular friends, who conceiue more rightly of me, to deliver freely my knowledge of the same; not onely for the satisfying of them, but also for the true enformation of anie other whosoeuer, that comes not with a prejudicate minde to the reading thereof: Thus much upon my credit I am to affirme: that things universally are so truely set downe in this treatise by the author thereof, an Actor in the Colony & a man no lesse for his honestly then learning commendable: as that I dare boldely auouch it may very well passe with the credit of trutheuen amongst the most true relations of this age. Which as for mine own part I am readie any way with my word to acknowledge, so also (of the certaintie thereof assured by mine owne experience) with this my publike assertion, I doe affirmed the same. Farewell in the Lorde.

To the Adventurers, Fauourers, and Welwillers of the Enterprise for the Inhabiting and Planting in Virginia.

Since the first undertaking by Sir Walter Raleigh to deale in the action of discovering of that Countrey which is now called and known by the name of *Virginia;* many voyages having bin thither made at sundrie times of his great charge; as first in the yeere 1584, and afterwards in the yeeres 1585, 1586, and now oflare this last yeare of 1587: There have bin diners and variable reporters with some slaunderous and shamefull speeches bruited abroad by many that returned from thence. Especially of that discouery which was made by the Colony transported by Sir Richard Greinuile in the yeare 1585, being of all the others the most principal and as yet of most effect, the time of their abode in the countrey beeing a whole yeare, when as in the other voyage before they staied but fixe weekes; and the others after were onelie for supply and transportation, nothing more being discovered then had been before, Which reports haue not done a litle wrong to many that otherwise would haue also fauoured & adventured in the action, to the honour and benefite of our nation, besides the particular profite and credite which would redound to them selues the dealers therein; as I hope by the sequele of events to the shame of those that haue auouched the contrary shalbe manifest; if you the adventures, fauourers, and welwillers do but either encrease in number, or in opinion continue, or having bin doubtfull renewe your good liking and furtherance to deale therein according to the worthinesse thereof alreadye found and as you shall understand hereafter to be requisite. Touching which worthiness through cause of the diuersitie of relations and reportes, manye of your opinions coulde not bee firme, nor the mindes of some that are well disposed, bee setled in any certaintie.

I haue therefor thought it good beeing one that have beene in the discouerie and in dealing with the naturall inhabitantes specially imploied; and having therefore seene and knowne more then the ordinarie: to imparte so much unto you of the fruites of our labours, as that you may knowe howe iniuriously the enterprise is slaundered. And that in publike manner at this present chiefelie for two respectes.

First that some of you which are yet ignorant or doubtfull of the state thereof, may see that there is sufficient cause why the cheese enterpriser with the fauour of her Maiestie, notwithstanding suche reporters; hath not onelie since continued the action by sending into the countrey againe, and replanting this last yeere a new Colony; but is also readie, according as the times and meanes will affoorde, to follow and prosecute the same.

Secondly, that you seeing and knowing the continuance of the action by the view hereof you may generally know & learne what the countrey is; & thervpon consider how your dealing therein if it proceede, may returne you profit and gaine; bee it either by inhabiting & planting or otherwise in furthering thereof. And least that the substance of my relation should be doubtful unto you, as of others by reason of their diuersitie: I will first open the cause in a few wordes wherefore they are so different; referring my selfe to your favourable constructions, and to be adjudged of as by good consideration you shall finde cause. Of your companie that returned some for their misdemenour and ill dealing in the countrey, have beene there worthily punished; who by reason of their badde natures, have maliciously not onelie spoken ill of their Gouernours; but for their sakes slaundered the countrie it selfe. The like also have those done which where of their confort.

Some beeing ignorant of the state thereof, notwithstanding since their returne amongst their friendes and acquaintance and also others, especially if they were in companie where they might not be gainesaide; woulde seeme to knowe so much as no men more; and make no men so great trauailers as themselves. They stood so much as it maie seeme vppon their credite and reputation that having been at twelve moneth in the countrey, it woulde have beene a great disgrace unto them as they thought, if they coulde not have saide much whether it were true or false. Of which some have spoken of more then ever they saw or otherwise knew to bee there; othersome have not bin ashamed to make absolute deniall of that which although not by them, yet by others is most certainely and there plentifully knowne. And othersome make difficulties of those things they have no skill of.

The cause of their ignorance was, in that they were of that many that were never out of the Iland where wee were seated, or not farre, or at the leastwise in few places els, during the time of our aboade in the countrey; or of that many that after golde and siluer was not so soone found, as it was by them looked for, had little or no care of any other thing but to pamper their bellies; or of that many which had little understanding, less discretion, and more tongue then was needfull or requisite.

Some also were of a nice bringing up, only in cities or townes, or such as never (as I may say) had seene the world before. Because there were not to bee found any English cities, nor such faire houses, nor at their owne wish any of their olde accustomed daintie food, nor any soft beds of downe or fethers; the countrey was to them miserable, & their reports thereof according.

Because my purpose was but in briefe to open the cause of the varietie of such speeches; the particularities of them, and of many enuious, malicious, and slaunderous reports and devises els, by our owne countrey men besides; as trifles that are not worthy of wise men to bee thought upon, I meane not to trouble you with all: but will passe to the commodities, the substance of that which I have to make relation of unto you.

The treatise whereof for your more readie view & easier understanding I will divide into three special parts. In the first I will make declaration of such commodities there alreadie found or to be raised, which will not onely serve the ordinary turnes of you which are and shall bee the planters and inhabitants, but such an overplus sufficiently to bee yelded, or by men of skill to bee provided, as by way of trafficke and exchaunge with our owne nation of England, will enrich your selves the providers; those that shal deal with you; the enterprisers in general; and greatly profit our owne countrey men, to supply the with most things which heretofore they have bene faine to provide, either of strangers or of our enemies: which commodities for distinction sake, I call *Merchantable.*

In the second, I will set downe all the commodities which wee know the countrey by our experience doeth yeld of it selfe for victuall, and sustenance of mans life; such as is usually fed vpo by the inhabitants of the countrey, as also by us during the time we were there.

In the last part I will make mention generally of such other commodities besides, as I am able to remember, and as I shall thinke behoofull for those that shall inhabite, and plant there to knowe of; which specially concerne building, as also some other necessary uses: with a briefe description of the nature and maners of the people of the countrey.

The first part of merchantable commodities

Silke of grasse or grasse Silke: There is a kind of grasse in the countrey vppon the blades whereof there groweth very good silke in forme of a thin glittering skin to bee stript of. It groweth two foote and a halfe high or better: the blades are about two foot in length, and half inch broad. The like groweth in Persia, which is in the selfe same climate as *Virginia,* of which very many of the silke workes that come from thence into Europe are made. Hereof if it be planted and ordered as in Persia, it cannot in reason be otherwise,

but that there will rise in shorte time great profite to the dealers therein; seeing there is so great vse and vent thereof as well in our countrey as els where. And by the meanes of sowing & planting it in good ground, it will be farre greater, better, and more plentiful then it is. Although notwithstanding there is great store thereof in many places of the countrey growing naturally and wilde. Which also by proof here in England, in making a piece of silke Grogran, we found to be excellent good.

Worme Silke: In manie of our journeys we found silke wormes fayre and great; as bigge as our ordinary walnuttes. Although it hath not beene our happe to have found such plentie as elsewhere to be in the countrey we have heard of; yet seeing that the countrey doth naturally breede and nourish them, there is no doubt but if art be added in planting of mulbery trees and others fitte for them in commodious places, for their feeding and nourishing; and some of the carefully gathered and husbanded in that sort as by men of skill is knowne to be necessarie: there will rise as great profite in time to the *Virginians,* as thereof doth now the Persians, Turkes, Italians and Spaniards.

Flaxe and Hempe: The trueth is that of Hempe and Flaxe there is no great store in any one place together, by reason it is not planted but as the soile doth yeeld it of itselfe; and howsoever the lease, and stemme or stalke doe differ from ours; the stuffe by the iudgemet of men of skill is altogether as good as ours. And if not, as further proofe should finde otherwise; we have that experience of the soile, as that there cannot bee shewed anie reason to the contrary, but that it will grow there excellent well; and by planting will be yeelded plentifully: seeing there is so much ground whereof of some may well be applyed to such purposes. What benefite heereof may growe in cordage and linnens who can not easily vnderstand?

Allum: There is a veine of earth along the sea coast for the space of fourtie or fiftie miles, whereof by the judgement of some of that have made triall heere in England, is made good *Allum,* of that kinde which is called *Roche Allum.* The richness of such a commoditie is so well knowne that I neede not saye any thing thereof. The same earth doth also yeelde *White Copresse, Nitrum,* and *Alumen plumeum,* but nothing so plentifully as the common *Allum;* which be also of price and profitable.

Wapeih, a kinde of earth so called by the naturall inhabitants; very like to *terra Sigillata:* and having beene refined, it hath beene found by some of our Phisitions and Chirurgeons to bee of the same kinde of vertue and more effectuall. The inhabitants use it very much for the cure of sores and woundes: there is in diuers places great plentie, and in some places of a blewe sort.

Pitch, Tarre, Rozen, and *Turpentine:* There are those kindes of trees which yeelde them abundantly and great store. In the very same Iland where wee were seated, being fifteene miles of length, and fiue or six miles in breadth, there are fewe trees but of the same kind; the whole Iland being full.

Sassafras, called by the inhabitantes *Winauk,* a kinde of wood of most pleasant and sweete smel; and of most rare vertues in phisick for the cure of many diseases. It is foud be experience to bee farre better and of more vses then the wood which is called *Guaiacum,* or *Lignum vite.* For the description, the manner of vsing the manifolde vertues thereof, I referre you to the booke of *Monardus,* translated and entituled in English, *The ioyfulnesses from the West Indies.*

Cedar, a very sweet wood & fine timber; wherof if nests of chests be there made, or timber therof fitted for sweet & fine bedsteads, tables, deskes, lutes, virginalles & many things else, (of which there hath beene proofe made already,) to make vp fraite with other principal commodities will yeeld profite.

Wine: There are two kinds of grapes that the soile doth yeeld naturally: the one is small and sowre of the ordinarie bignesse as ours in England: the other farre greater & of himselfe lushious sweet. When they are planted and husbanded as they ought, a principall commoditie of wines by them may be raised.

Oyle: There are two fortes of *Walnuttes* both holding oyle, but the one farre more plentifull then the other. When there are milles & other deuises for the purpose, a commodity of them may be raised because there are infinite store. There are also three seuerall kindes of *Berries* in the forme of Oke akornes, which also by the experience and vse of the inhabitantes, wee finde to yeelde very good and sweete oyle. Furthermore the *Beares* of the countrey are commonly very fatte, and in some places there are many: their fatnesse because it is so liquid, may well be termed oyle, and hath many special vses.

Furres: All along the Sea coast there are great store of *Otters,* which beeyng taken by weares and other engines made for the purpose, will yeelde good profite. Wee hope also of *Marterne furres,* and make no doubt by the relation of the people but that in some places of the countrey there are store: although there were but two skinnes that came to out handes. *Luzarnes* also we haue understanding of, although for the time we saw none.

Deare Skinnes dressed after the manner of *Chamoes* or undressed are to be had of the naturall inhabitants thousands yeerely by way of trafficke for trifles: and no more wast or spoyle of Deare then is and hath beene ordinarily in time before.

Ciuet cattes: In our trauailes, there was founde one to haue beene killed by a saluage or inhabitant: and in another place the smell where one or more had lately beene before: whereby we gather besides then by the relation of the people that there are some in the countrey: good profite will rise by them.

Iron: In two places of the countrey specially, one about fourescore and the other six score miles from the Fort or place where wee dwelt: wee founde neere the waterside the ground to be rockie, which by the triall of a minerall man, was founde to holde yron richly. It is founde in manie places of the countrey else. I knowe nothing to the contrarie, but that it maie bee allowed for a good marchantable commoditie, considering there the small charge for the labour and feeding of men: the infinite store of wood: the want of wood and deerenesse thereof in England: & the necessity of ballasting of shippes.

Copper: A hundred and fiftie miles into the maine in two townes wee founde with the inhabitaunts diuerse small plates of copper, that had beene made as wee understood, by the inhabitantes that dwell farther into the countrey: where as they say are mountaines and Riuers that yeelde also whyte graynes of Mettall, which is to bee deemed *Siluer.* For confirmation whereof at the time of our first arriuall in the Countrey, I sawe with some others with mee, two small peeces of siluer grosly beaten about the weight of a Testrone, hangyng in the eares of a *Wiroans* or *chiefe Lorde* that dwelt about fourescore myles from us: of whom thorowe enquiry, by the number of dayes and the way, I learned that it had come to his handes from the fame place or neere, where I after understood the copper was made and the white graynes of mettall founde. The aforesaide copper wee also founde by triall to holde siluer.

Pearle: Sometimes in feeding on muscles we founde some pearle; but it was our hap to meete with ragges, or of a pide colour; not hauing yet discouered those places where we hearde of better and more plentie. One of our companie; a man of skill is such matters, had gathered together from among the sauage people aboute fiue thousande: of which number he chose so many as made a fayre chaine, which for their likenesse and vniformitie in roundnesse, orientnesse, and pidenesse of many excellent colours, with equalitie in greatnesse, were verie fayre and rare; and had therefore beene presented to her Maiestie, had wee not by casualtie and through extremity of a storme, lost them with many things els in comming away from the countrey.

Sweete Gummes of diuers kindes and many other Apothecary drugges of which wee will make speciall mention, when we shall receiue it from such men of skill in that kynd, that in taking reasonable paines shall discouer them more particularly then wee haue done; and than now I can make relation of, for want of the examples I had prouided and gathered, and are nowe lost, with other thinges by causualtie before mentioned.

Dyes of diuers kindes: There is *Shoemake* well knowen, and vsed in England for blacke; the seede of an hearbe called *Wasewowr;* little small rootes called *Chappacor;* and the barke of the tree called by the inhabitaunts *Tangomockomindge:* which Dies are for diuers sortes of red: their goodnesse for our English clothes remayne yet to be proued. The inhabitants use them onely for the dying of hayre; and colouring of their faces, and Mantles made of Deare skinnes; and also for the dying of Rushes to make artificiall workers withall in their Mattes and Baskettes; hauing no other thing besides that they account of, apt to use them for. If they will not proue merchantable there is no doubt but the Planters there shall finde apte uses for them, as also for other colours which wee knowe to be there.

Oade; a thing of so great vent and use amongst English Diers, which cannot bee yeelded sufficiently in our owne countrey for spare of ground; may bee planted in *Virginia,* there being ground enough. The grouth therof need not to be doubted, when as in the Ilandes of the Asores it groweth plentifully, which is in the same climate. So likewise of *Madder.*

We carried thither *Suger canes* to plant which beeing not so well preserued as was requisit, & besides the time of the yere being past for their setting when we arriued, wee could not make that proofe of them as wee desired. Nothwithstanding, seeing that they grow in the same climate, in the South part of Spaine and in Barbary, our hope in reason may yet cotinue. So likewise for *Orenges,* and *Lemmons:* there may be planted also *Quinses.* Wherby may grow in reasonable time if the actio be diligently prosecuted, no small commodities in *Sugers, Suckets,* and *Marmalades.*

Many other commodities by planting may there also bee raised, which I leave to your discret and gentle considerations: and many also bee there which yet we have not discovered. Two more commodities of great value one of certaintie, and the other in hope, not to be planted, but there to be raised & in short time to be provided and prepared, I might have specified. So likewise of those commodities already set downe I might have said more; as of the particular places where they are founde and best to be planted and prepared: by what meanes and in what reasonable space of time they might be raised to profit and in what proportion; but because others then welwillers might bee therewithall acquainted, not to the good of the action, I have wittingly omitted them: knowing that to those that are well disposed I have uttered, according to my promise and purpose, for this part sufficient.

The Second part of suche commodities as *Virginia is knowne to yeelde for victuall and sustenance* of mans life, vsually fed vpon by the *naturall inhabitants: as also by us during the time of our aboad. And first of such as are sowed and busbanded.*

Pagatowr, a kinde of graine so called by the inhabitants; the fame in the West Indies is called *Mayze*: English men call it *Guinney wheate* or *Turkie wheate,* according to the names of the countreys from whence the like hath beene brought. The graine is about the bignesse of our ordinary English peaze and not much different in forme and shape: but of divers colours: some white, some red, some yellow, and some blew. All of them yeelde a very white and sweete flowre: beeing used according to his kinde it maketh a very good bread. Wee made of the same in the country some mault, whereof was brued as good ale as was to bee desired. So likewise by the help of hops therof may bee made as good Beere. It is a graine of marueilous great increase; of a thousand, fifteene hundred and some two thousand sold. There are three sortes, of which two are ripe in an eleven and twelve weekes at the most sometimes in ten, after the time they are set, and are then of height in stalke about six or seuen foote. The other sort is ripe in fourteene, and is about ten foote high; of she stalkes some beare foure heads, some three, some one, and two: every head containing five, sixe, or seven hundred graines within a fewe more or lesse. Of these graines besides bread, the inhabitants make victuall eyther by parching them; or seething them whole vntill they be broken; or boyling the floure with water into a pappe.

Okindgier, called by us *Beanes,* because in greatnesse & partly in shape they are like to the Beanes in England; saving that they are flatter, of more divers colours, and some pide. The lease also of the stemme is much different. In taste they are altogether as good as our English peaze.

Wickonzowr, called by us *Peaze,* in respect of the beanes for distinctio sake, because they are much lesse; although in forme they little differ; but in goodnesse of tast much, & are far better then our English peaze. Both the beanes and peaze are ripe in tenne weekes after they are set. They make them victuall either by boyling them all to pieces into a broth; or boiling them whole vntill they bee soft and beginne to breake as is used in England, eyther by themselves or mixtly together: Sometime they mingle of the wheate with them. Sometime also beeing whole sodden, they bruse or pound them in a morter, & thereof make loaues or lumps of dowishe bread, which they use to eat for varietie.

Macocqwer, according to their seuerall formes called by us, *Pompions, Mellions,* and *Gourdes,* because they are of the like formes as those kindes in England. In *Virginia* such of seuerall formes are of one taste and very good, and do also spring from one feed. There are of two sorts; one is ripe in the space of a moneth, and the other in two moneths.

There is an hearbe which in Dutch is called *Melden.* Some of those that I describe it vnto, take it to be a kinde of Orage; it groweth about foure or fiue foote high: of the seede thereof they make a thicke broth, and pottage of a very good taste: of the stalke by burning into ashes they make a kinde of salt earth, wherewithall many use sometimes to season their brothes; other salte they knowe not. Wee our selues vsed the leaues also forpothearbes.

There is also another great hearbe in forme of a Marigolde, about sixe foote in height; the head with the floure is a spanne in breadth. Some take it to bee *Planta Solis:* of the feedes heereof they make both a kinde of bread and broth.

All the aforesaide commodities for victuall are set or sowed, sometimes in groundes a part and seuerally by theselues; but for the most part together in one ground mixtly: the manner thereof with the dressing and preparing of the ground because I will note vnto you the fertilitie of the soile; I thinke good briefly to describe.

The ground they never fatten with mucke, dounge or any other thing; neither plow nor digge it as we in England, but onely prepare it in sort as followeth. A fewe daies before they sowe or set, the men with wooden instruments, made almost in forme of mattockes or hoes with long handles; the women with short peckers or parers, because they vse them sitting, of a foote long and a bout fiue inches in breadth: doe onely breake the vpper part of the ground to raise vp the weedes, grasse, & old stubbes of corne stalkes with their rootes. The which after a day or twoes drying in the Sunne, being scrapte vp into many small heapes, to save them labour for carrying them away; they burne into ashes. (And whereas some may thinke that they vse the ashes for to better the grounde; I say that then they woulde eyther disperse the ashes abroade; which wee obserued they doe not, except the heapes bee too great: or els would take speciall care to set their corne where the ashes lie, which also wee finde they are carelesse of.) And this is all the husbanding of their ground that they use.

Then their setting or sowing is after this maner. First for their corne, beginning in one corner of the plot, with a pecker they make a hole, wherein they put soure graines with that care they touch not one another, (about an inch asunder) and couer them with the moulde againe: and so through out the whole plot, making such holes and vsing them after such maner: but with this regard that they bee made in rankes, every ranke differing from other halfe a fadome or a yarde, and the hole also in euery ranke, as much. By this meanes there is a yarde spare ground betwene euery hole: where according to discretion here and there, they set as many Beanes and Peaze: in divers places also among the feedes of *Macocqwer Melden* and *Plant a solis.*

The ground being thus set according to the rate by vs experimented, an English Acre conteining fourtie pearches in length, and foure in breadth, doeth there yeeld in croppe or ofcome of corne, beanes, and peaze, at the leaft two hundred London Bushelles: besides the *Macocqwer; Melden,* and *Planta solis:* When as in England fourtie bushelles of our wheate yeelded out of such an acre is thought to be much. I thought also good to note this vnto you, you which shall inhabite and plant there, maie know how specially that countrey corne is there to be preferred before ours: Besides the manifold waies in applying it to victuall, the increase is so much that small labour and paines is needful in respect that must be vsed for ours. For this I can assure you that according to the rate we have made proofe of, one man may prepare and husbandso much grounde (hauing once borne corne before) with lesse then foure and twentie houres labour, as shall yeelde him victuall in a large proportion for a twelue moneth, if hee haue nothing else, but that which the same ground will yeelde, and of the kinde onelie which I haue before spoken of: the saide ground being also but of fiue and twentie yards square, And if neede require, but that there is ground enough, there might be raised out of one and the selffame ground two haruestes or ofcomes; for they sowe or set and may at anie time when they thinke good from the middest of March vntill the ende of Iune: so that they also set when they haue eaten of their first croppe. In some places of the country notwithstanding they haue two haruests, as we haue heard, out of one and the same ground.

For English corne nevertheles whether to use of not to vse it, you that inhabite maie do as you shall haue father cause to thinke best. Of the grouth you need not to doubt: for barlie, oates and peaze, we haue seene proof of, not beeing purposely sowen but fallen casually in the worstfort of ground, and yet to be as faire as any we haue ever seene here in England. But of wheat because it was musty and had taken salt water wee could make no triall: and of rye we had none. Thus much haue I digressed and I hope not vnnecessarily: nowe will I returne againe to my course and intreate of that which yet remaineth apperteining to this Chapter.

There is an herbe which sowed a part by it selfe & is called by the inhabitants *vppowoc:* In the West Indies it hath diuers names, according to the seuerall places & countries where it groweth and is vsed: The Spaniardes generally call it *Tobacco.* The leaues there of being dried and brought into powder: they vse to take the fume or smoke thereof by sucking it through pipes made of claie into their stomacke and heade; from whence it purgeth superfluous fleame & other grosse humors, openeth all the pores & passages of the body: by which meanes the vse thereof, not only preserveth the body from obstruction;

but also if any be, so that they have not beene of too long continuance, in short time breaketh them: wherby their bodies are notably preserued in health, & know not many greevous disease wherewithall wee in England are oftentimes afflicted.

This *Uppowoc* is of so precious estimation amongest the, that they thinke their gods are maruelously delighted therewith: Whereupon sometime they make hallowed fires & cast some of the pouder therein for a sacrifice: being in a storme vppon the waters, to pacifie their gods, they cast some up into the aire and into the water: so a weare for fish being newly set vp, they cast some therein and into the aire: also an escape of danger, they cast some into the aire likewise: but all done with strange gestures, stamping, somtime dauncing, clapping of hands, holding vp of hands, & staring vp the heaues, vttering therewithal and chaterring strange words & noises.

We our selues during the time we were there vsed to suck it after their manner, as also since our returne, & have found manie rare and wonderful experiments of the vertues thereof; of which the relation woulde require a volume by it selfe: the vse of it by manie of late, men & women of great calling as else, and some learned Phisitions also, is sufficient witnes.

And there are all the commodities for sustenance of life that I know and can remember they vse to husband: all else that followe are founde growing naturally or wilde.

Of Rootes

Openauk are a kind of roots of round forme, some of the bignes of walnuts, some far greater, which are found in moist & marish grounds growing many together one by another in ropes, or as thogh they were fastened with a string. Being boiled or fodden they are very good meate.

Okeepenauk are also of roud shape, found in dry grouds: some are of the bignes of a mans head. They are to be eaten as they are taken out of the ground, for by reason of their drinesse they will neither roste nor seeth. Their tast is not so good as of the former rootes, notwithstanding for want of bread & somtimes for varietie the inhabitats vse to eate them with fish or flesh, and in my iudgement they doe as well as the houshold bread made of rie heere in England.

Kaishucpenauk a white kind of roots about the bignes of hen egs & nere of that forme: their tast was not so good to our seeming as of the other, and therfore their place and manner of growing not so much cared for by vs: the inhabitants nowithstanding used to boile & eate many.

Tsinaw a kind of roote much like vnto y which in England is called the *China root* brought from the East Indies. And we know not anie thing to the contrary but that it maie be of the same kind. These roots grow manie together in great clusters and doe bring foorth a brier stalke, but the leafe is shape far vnlike; which beeing supported by the trees it groweth neerest vnto, wil reach or climbe to the top of the highest. From these roots while they be new or fresh beeing chopt into small pieces & stamp, is strained with water a iuice that maketh bread, & also being boiled a very good spoonermeate in maner of a gelly, and is much better in tast if it bee tempered with oyle. This *Tsinaw* is not of that sort which by some was caused to be brought into England for the *China roote*, for it was discouered since, and is in vse as is aforesaid: but that which was brought hither is not yet knowne neither by vs nor by the inhabitants to serue for any vse of purpose; although the rootes in shape are very like.

Coscushaw, some of our company tooke to bee that kinde of roote which the Spaniards in the West Indies call *Cassauy*, whereupon also many called it by that name: it groweth in very muddie pooles and moist groundes. Being dressed according to the countrey maner, it maketh a good bread, and also a good sponemeate, and is vsed very much by the inhabitants: The iuice of this root is poison, and therefore heede must be taken before any thing be made therewithall: Either the rootes must bee first sliced and dried in the Sunne, or by the fire, and then being pounded into floure wil make good bread: or els while they are greene they are to bee pared, cut into pieces and stampt; loues of the same to be laid neere or ouer the fire vntill it be soure, and then being well pounded againe, bread, or spone meate very god in taste, and holsome may be made thereof.

Habascon is a roote hoat taste almost of the forme and bignesse of a Parseneepe, of it selfe it is no victuall, but onely a helpe beeing boiled together with other meates.

There are also *Leekes* differing little from ours in England that grow in many places of the coutrey, of which, when we came in places where they were, wee gathered and eate many, but the naturall inhabitants neuer.

Of Fruites

Chestnuts, there are in divers places great store: Some they vse to eate rawe, some they stampe and boile to make spoonemeate, and with some being fodde they make such a manner of dowe bread as they vse of their beanes before mentioned.

Walnuts. There are two kindes of Walnuts, and of the infinit store: In many places where very great woods for many miles together the third part of trees are walnut-trees. The one kind is of the same taste and forme or litle differing from ours of England, but that they are harder and thicker shelled: the other is greater and hath a verie ragged and harde shell: but the kernell great, verie oylie and sweete. Besides their eating of them after our ordinarie maner, they breake them with stones and pound them in morters with water to make a milk which they vse to put into some sorts of their spoonmeate; also among their fodde wheat, peaze, beanes and pompions which maketh them haue a farre more pleasant taste.

Medlars a kind of verie good fruit, so called by vs chieflie for these respectes: first in that they are not good until they be rotten: then in that they open at the head as our medlars, and are about the same bignesse: otherwise in taste and colour they are farre different: for they are as red as cheries an very sweet: but whereas the cherie is sharpe sweet, they are lushious sweet.

Metaque funnauk, a kinde of pleasaunt fruite almost of the shape & bignes of English peares, but that they are of a perfect red colour as well within as without. They grow on a plant whose leaues are verie thicke and full of prickles as sharpe as needles. Some that haue bin in the Indies, where they haue seen that kind of red die of great price which is called *Cochinile* to grow, doe describe his plant right like vnto this of *Meraquefunnauk* but whether it be the true *cochinile* or a bastard or wilde kind, it cannot yet be certified seeing that also as I heard, *Cochinile* is not of the fruite but founde on the leaues of the plant; which leaues for such matter we haue not so specially obserued.

Grapes there are of two forts which I mentioned in the marchantable commodities.

Straberies there are as good & as great as those which we haue in our English gardens.

Mulberies, Applecrabs, Hurts or *Hurtleberies,* such as wee haue in England.

Sacquenummener a kinde of berries almost like vnto capres but somewhat greater which grow together in clusters vpon a plant or herb that is found in shalow waters: being boiled eight or nine hours according to their kind are very good meate and holesome, otherwise is they be eaten they will make a man for the time franticke or extremely sicke.

There is a king of *read* which beareth of feed almost like vnto ourrie or wheat, & being boiled is good meate.

In our trauailes in some places wee founde *wilde peaze* like vnto ours in England but that they were lesse, which are also good meate.

Of a kinde of fruite or berrie in forme of Acornes

There is a kind of berrie or acorne, of which there are fiue forts that grow on seueral kinds of trees; the one is called *Sagatemener,* the second *Osamener,* the third *Pummuckoner.* These kind of a corns they vse to drie vpon hurdles made of reeds with fire vnderneath almost alter the maner as we dry malt in Englad. When they are to be vsed they first water them vntil they be soft & then being fod they make a good victual, either to eate so simply, or els being also pounded, to make loaues or lumpes of bread. These be also the three kinds of which, I said before, the inhabitants vsed to make sweet oyle.

An other sort is called *Sapummener* which being boiled or parched doth eate and taste like vnto chestnuts. They sometime also make bread of this sort.

The fifth sort is called *Mangummenauk,* and is the acorne of their kind of oake, the which beeing dried after the manner of the first sortes, and afterward watered they boile them, & their seruants or sometime the chiefe the selues, either for variety or for want of bread, doe eate them with their fish or flesh.

Of Beastes

Deare, in some places there are great store: neere vnto the fea coast they are of the ordinarie bignes as ours in England, & some lesse: but further vp into the countrey where there is better feed they are greater: they differ from ours onely in this, their tailes are longer and the snags of their hornes looke backward.

Conies, Those that we haue seen & al that we can heare of are of a grey colour like vnto hares: in some places there are such plentie that all the people of some townes make them mantles of the furre of flue of the skinnes of those they vsually take.

Saquenuckot & *Maquowoc;* two kindes of small beastes greater then conies which are very good meat. We neuer tooke any of them our selues, but sometime eate of such as the inhabitants had taken & brought vnto vs.

Squirels which are of a grey colour, we haue take & eate.

Beares which are all of black colour. The beares of this countrey are good meat; the inhabitants in time of winter do vse to take & eate manie, so also somtime did wee. They are taken commonlie in this sort. In some Ilands or places where they are, being hunted for, as soone as they haue spiall of a man they presently run awaie, & then being chased they clime and get vp the next tree they can, from whence with arrowes they are shot downe starke dead, or with those wounds that they may after easily be killed; we sometime shotte them downe with our caleeuers.

I haue the names of eight & twenty seuerall sortes of beasts which I haue heard of to be here and there dispersed in the coutrie, especially in the maine: of which there are only twelue kinds that we haue yet discouered, & of those that be good meat we know only them before mentioned. The inhabitants somtime kil the *Lyon* & eat him: & we sometime as they came to our hands of their *Wolves* or *wolvish Dogges,* which I haue not set downe for good meat, least that some would vnderstand my iudgement therin to be more simple than needeth, although I could alleage the difference in taste of those kindes from ours, which by some of our company haue beene experimented in both.

Of Foule

Tvrkie cockes and *Turkie hennes: Stockdoues: Partridgess Cranes: Hernes:* & in winter great store of *Swannes* & *Geese.* Of all sortes of foule I have the names in the countrie language offourescore and fixe of which number besides those that be named, we haue taken, eaten, & haue the pictures as they were there drawne with the names of the inhabitaunts of seuerall strange sortes of water foule eight, and seueteene kinds of land foul, although wee haue seen and eaten of many more, which for want of leasure there for the purpose coulde not bee pictured: and after wee are better furnished and stored vpon further discovery, with their strange beastes, fishe, trees, plants, and hearbes, they shall bee also published.

There are also *Parats, Faulcons, & Marlin haukes,* which although with vs they bee not vsed for meate, yet for other causes I thought good to mention.

Of Fishe

For foure monethes of the yeere, February, March, Aprill and May, there are plentie of *Sturgeons:* And also in the same monethes of *Herrings,* some of the ordinary bignesse as ours in England, but the most part farre greater, of eighteene, twentie inches, and some two foote in length and better; both these kindes of fishe in those monethes are most plentifull, and in best season, which wee founde to bee most delicate and plesaunt meate.

There are also *Troutes: Porpoises: Rayes: Oldwines: Mullets: Plaice:* and very many other sortes of excellent good fish, which we haue taken & eaten, whose names I know not but in the countrey language; wee haue of twelue sorts more the pictures as they were drawn in the countrey with their names.

The inhabitants vse to take the two maner of wayes, the one is by a kind of wear made of reedes which in that countrey are very strong. The other way which is more strange, is with poles made sharpe at one ende, by shooting them into the fish after the maner as Irishmen cast dartes; either as they are rowing in their boates or els as they are wading in the shallowes for the purpose.

There are also in many places plentie of these kindes which follow.

Seacrabbes, such as we haue in England.

Oysters, some very great, and some small; some rounde and some of a long shape: They are founde both in salt water and brackish, and those that we had out of salt-water are far better than the other as in our owne countrey,

Also *Muscles: Scalopes: Periwinkles:* and *Creuifes.*

Seekanauk, a kinde of crustie shell fishe which is good meate, about a foote in breadth, hauing a crustie tayle, many legges like a crab; and her eyes in her backe. They are founde in shallowes of salt waters; and sometime on the shoare.

There are many *Tortoyses* both of lande and sea kinde, their backes & bellies are shelled very thicke: their head, feete, and taile, which are in appearance, feeme ougly as though they were members of a serpent or venemous; but notwithstanding they are very good meate, as also their egges. Some haue bene founde of a yard in bredth and better.

And thus haue I made relation of all sortes of victuall that we fed vpon for the time we were in *Virginia,* as also the inhabitants themselues, as farre foorth as I knowe and can remember or that are specially worthy to bee remembred.

The third and last part of such other *thinges* as is *behoofull for those which shall* plant and inhabit to know of; with a description of the nature and manners of the *people of the countrey.*

Of Commodities for Building and other necessary vses

Those other things which I am more to maker rehearsall of, are such as concerne building, and other mechanicall necessarie vses; as diuers fortes of trees for house & ship timber, and other vses els; Also lime, stone, and brick, least that being not mentioned some might have bene doubted of, or by some that are malicious reported the contrary.

Okes, these are as faire, straight, tall, and as good timber as any can be, and also great store, and in some places very great.

Walnut trees, as I haue saide before very many, some haue bene seen excellent faire timber of foure & five fadome, & above fourescore foot streight without bough.

Firre trees fit or masts of ships, some very tall & great.

Rakiock a kind of trees so called that are sweet wood of which the inhabitants that were neere vnto vs doe commonly make their boats or Canoes of the forms of trowes; only with the helpe of fire, hatchets of stones, and shels; we haue known some so great being made in that sort of one tree that they haue carried well xx. men at once, besides much baggage: the timber being great, tal, streight, soft, light, & yet tough enough I thinke (besides other vses) to be fit also for masts of ships.

Cedar a sweet wood good for feelings, Chefts, Boxes, Bedsteedes, Lutes, Virginals, and many things els, as I haue also said before. Some of our company which haue wandered in some places where I haue not bene, haue made certaine affirmation of *Cyprus* which for such and other excellent vses, is also a wood of price and no small estimation.

Maple, and also *Wich-hazle,* wherof the inhabitants vse to make their bowes.

Holly a necessary thing for the making of birdlime.

Willowes good for the making of weares and weeles to take fish after the English manner, although the inhabitants vse only reedes, which because they are so strong as also flexible, do serue for that turne very well and sufficiently.

Beech and *Ashe,* good for caske, hoopes: and if neede require, plow worke, as also for many things els.

Elme.

Sassafras trees.

Ascopo a kinde of tree very like vnto Lawrell, the barke is hoat in taft and spicie, it is very like to that tree which Monardus describeth to bee *Cassia Lignea* of the West Indies.

There are many other strange trees whose names I knowe not but in the *Virginia* language, of which I am not nowe able, neither is it so conuenient for the present to trouble you with particular relation: seeing that for timber and other necessary vses I haue named sufficient: And of many of the rest but that they may be applied to good vse, I know no cause to doubt.

Now for Stone, Bricke and Lime, thus it is. Neere vnto the Sea coast where wee dwelt, there are no kinde of stones to bee found (except a fewe small pebbles about foure miles off) but such as haue bene brought from far-farther out of the maine. Informe of our voiages wee haue beene diuers hard raggie stones, great pebbles, and a kinde of grey stone like vnto marble, of which the inhabitants make their hatchets to cleeue wood. Vpon inquirie wee heard that a little further vp into the Countrey were of all fortes verie many, although of Quarries they are ignorant, neither haue they vse of any store whereupon they should haue occasion to seeke any. For if euerie housholde baue one or two to cracke Nuttes, grinde shelles, whet copper, and sometimes other stones for hatches, they haue enough: neither vse they any digging, but onely for graues about three foote deepe: and therefore no maruaile that they know neither Quarries, nor lime stones, which both may bee in places neerer than they wot of.

In the meane time vntil there bee discouerie of sufficient store in some place or other conuenient, the want of you which are and shalbe the planters therein may be as well supplied by Bricke: for the making whereof in diuers places of the countrey there is clay both excellent good, and plentie; and also by lime made of Oister shels, and of others burnt, after the maners as they vse in the Iles of Tenet and Shepy, and also in diuers other places of England: Which kinde of lime is well knowne to bee as good as any other. And of Oister shels there is plentie enough: for besides diuers other particular places where are abundance, there is one shallowe sounde along the coast, where for the space of many miles together in length, and two or three miles in breadth, the grounde is nothing els beeing but halfe a foote or a foote vnder water for the most part.

This much can I say further more of stones, that about 120 miles from our fort neere the water in the side of a hill was founde by a Gentleman of our company, a great veine of hard ragge stones, which I thought good to remember vnto you.

Of the Nature and Manners of the People

It resteth I speake a word or two of the naturall inhabitants, their natures and manners, leauing large discourse thereof vntill time more conuenient hereafter: nowe onely so farre foorth, as that you may know, how that they in respect of troubling our inhabiting and planting, are not to be feared; but that they shall haue cause both to feare and loue vs, that shall inhabite with them.

They are a people clothed with loose mantles made of Deere skins, & aprons of the fame rounde about their middles; all els naked; of such a difference of statures only as wee in England; hauing no edge tooles or weapons of yron or steele to offend vs withall, neither know they how to make any: those weapons y they haue, are onlie bowes made of Witch hazle, & arrowes of reeds; flat edged truncheons also of wood about a yard long, neither haue they any thing to defed theselues but targets made of bards; and some armours made of stickers wickered together with thread.

Their townes are but small, & neere the sea coast but few, some containing but 10. or 12. houses: some 20. The greatest that we haue seene haue bene but of 30. Houses: if they be walled it is only done with barks of trees made fast to stakes, or els with poles onely fixed vpright and close one by another. Their houses are made of small poles made fast at the tops in rounde forme after the maner as is vsed in many arbories in our gardens of England, in most towns couered with barkes, and in some with artificiall mattes made of long rushes; from the tops of the houses downe to the ground. The length of them is commonly double to the breadth, in some places they are but 12. and 16. yardes long, and in other some wee haue seene of foure and twentie.

In some places of the countrey one onely towne belongeth to the government of a *Wiroans* or chiefe Lorde; in other some two or three, in some fixe, eight, & more; the greatest *Wiroans* that yet we had dealing with had but eighteene townes in his gouernment, and able to make not above seuen or eight hundred fighting men at the most: The language of every gouernment is different from any other, and the farther they are distant the greater is the difference.

Their maner of warres amongst themselues is either by sudden surprising one another most commonly about the dawning of the day, or moone light; or els by ambushes, or some suttle devises: Set battels are very rare, except it fall out where there are many trees, where eyther part may haue some hope of defence, after the deliuerie of euery arrow, in leaping behind some or other.

If there fall out any warres between vs & them, what their fight is likely to bee, we hauing aduantages against them so many maner of waies, as by our discipline, our strange weapons and deuises els; especially by ordinance great and small, it may be easily imagined; by the experience we haue had in some places, the turning vp of their heeles against vs in running away was their best defence.

In respect of vs they are a people pocre and for want of skill and iudgement in the knowledge and vse of our things, doe esteeme our trifles before thinges of greater value: Notwithstanding in their proper manner considering the want of such meanes as we haue, they seeme very ingenious; For although they haue no such tooles, nor any such craftes, sciences and artes as wee; yet in those thinges they doe, they shewe excellencie of wit. Any by howe much they vpon due consideration shall finde our manner of knowledges and craftes to exceede theirs in perfection, and speed for doing or execution, by so much the more is it probable that they shoulde desire our friendships & loue, and haue the greater respect of pleasing and obeying vs. Whereby may bee hoped if meanes of good gouernment bee vsed, that they may in short time be brought to ciuilitie, and the imbracing of true religion.

Some religion they haue alreadie, which although it be farre from the truth, yet beyng as it is, there is hope it may bee the easier and sooner reformed.

The beleeue that there are many Gods which they call *Montoac,* but of different and degrees; one onely chiefe and great God, which hath bene from all eternitie. Who as they affirme when hee purposed to make the worlde, made first other goddes of a principall order to bee as meanes and instruments to be vsed in the creation and gouernment to follow; and after the Sunne, Moone, and Starres, as pettie goddes and the instruments of the other order more principall. First they say were made waters, out of which by the gods was made all diuersitie of creatures that are visible or invisible.

For mankind they say a woman was made first, which by the woorking of one of the goddes, conceiued and brought foorth children: And in such sort they say they had their beginning.

But how manie yeeres or ages haue passed since, they say they can make no relation, hauing no letters nor other such meanes as we to keepe recordes of the particularities of times past, but onelie tradition from father to sonne.

The thinke that all the goods are of humane shape, & therefore they represent them by images in the formes of men, which they call *Kewasowok* one alone is called *Kewas;* Them they place in houses appropriate or temples which they call *Machicomuck;* Where they woorship, praie, sing, and make manie times offering unto them. In some *Machicomuck* we haue seene but on *kewas,* in some two, and in other some three; The common sort thinke them to be also gods.

They beleeue also the immorralitie of the soule, that after this life as soone as the soule is departed from the bodie according to the workes it hath done, it is eyther carried to heauen the habitacle of gods, there to enjoy perpetuall blisse and happinesse, or els to a great pitte or hole, which they thinke to bee in the furthest partes of their part of the worlde towarde the sunne set, there to burne continually: the place they call *Popogusso.*

For the confirmation of this opinion, they tolde mee two stories of two men that had been lately dead and reuiued againe, the one happened but few yeres before our comming into the countrey of a wicked man which hauing beene dead and buried, the next day the earth of the graue beeing seene to moue, was taken vp againe; Who made declaration where his soule had beene, that is to saie very neere entering into *Popogusso,* had not one of the gods saued him & gaue him leaue to returne againe, and teach his friends what they should doe to avoid that terrible place of torment.

The other happened in the same yeere wee were there, but in a towne that was threescore miles from vs, and it was tolde mee for straunge newes that one beeing dead, buried and taken vp againe as the first, shewed that although his bodie had lien dead in the graue, yet his soule as aliue, and had trauailed farre in a long broade waie, on both sides whereof grewe most delicate and pleasaunt trees, bearing more rare and excellent fruites then euer hee had seene before or was able to expresse, and at length came to most braue and faire houses, neere which hee met his father, that had beene dead before, who gaue him great charge to goe backe againe and shew his friends what good they were to doe to enjoy the pleasures of that place, which when he had done he should after come againe.

What subtilty soeuer be in the *Wiroances* and Priestes, this opinion worketh so much in manie of the common and simple sort of the people that it maketh them haue great respect to their Gouernours, and also great care what they do, to avoid torment after death, and to enjoy blisse; although notwithstanding there is punishment ordained for malefactours, as stealers, whoremoongers, and other sortes of wicked doers; some punished with death, some with forfeitures, some with beating, according to the greatnes of the factes.

And this is the summe of their religio, which I learned by hauing special familiaritie with some of their priestes. Wherein they were not so sure grounded, nor gaue such credite to their traditions and stories but through conuersing with vs they were brought into great doubts of their owne, and no small admiration of ours, with earnest desire in many, to learne more than we had meanes for want of perfect vtterance in their language to expresse.

Most thinges they sawe with vs, as Mathematicall instruments, sea compasses, the vertue of the loadstone in drawing yron, a perspectiue glasse whereby was shewed manie strange sightes, burning glasses, wildefire woorkes, gunnes, bookes, writing and reading, spring clocks that seeme to goe of themselues, and manie other thinges that wee had, were so straunge vnto them, and so farre exceeded their capacities to comprehend the reason and meanes how they should be made and done, that they thought they were rather the works of gods then of men, or at the leastwise they had bin giuen and taught vs of the gods. Which made manie of them to haue such opinion of vs, as that if they knew not the trueth of god and religion already, it was rather to be had from vs, whom God so specially loued then from a people that were so simple as they found themselues to be in comparison of vs. Whereupon greater credite was giuen vnto that we spake of concerning such matters.

Manie times and in euery towne where I came, according as I was able, I made declaration of the contentes of the Bible; that therein was set foorth the true and onelie God, and his mightie woorkes, that therein was contayned the true doctrine of saluation through Christ, with manie particularities of Miracles and chiefe poyntes of religion, as I was able then to vtter, and thought fitte for the time. And although I told them the booke materially & of it self was not of anie such vertue, as I thought they did concieue, but onely the doctrine therein contained; yet would many be glad to touch it; to embrace it, to kisse it, to hold it to their brests and heades, and stroke oner all their bodie with it; to shewe their hungrie desire of that knowledge which was spoken of.

The *Wiroans* with whom we dwelt called *Wingina*, and many of his people would be glad many times to be with vs at our praiers, and many times call vpon vs both in his owne towne, as also in others wither he sometimes accompanied vs, to pray and sing Psalmes; hoping thereby to bee partaker of the same effectes which wee by that meanes also expected.

Twise this *Wiroans* was so grieuously sicke that he was like to die, and as hee laie languishing, doubting of anie helpe by his owne priestes, and thinking he was in such daunger for offending vs and thereby our god, sent for some of vs to praie and bee a meanes to our God that it would please him either that he might liue or after death dwell with him in blisse; so likewise were the requestes of manie others in the like case.

On a time also when their corne began to wither by reason of a drouth which happened extraordinarily, fearing that it had come to passe by reason that in some thing they had displeased vs, many woulde come to vs & desire vs to praise to our God of England, that he would preserue their corne, promising that when it was ripe we also should be partakers of the fruite.

There could at no time happen any strange sicknesse, losses, hurtes, or any other crosse vnto them, but that they would impute to vs the cause or means therof for offending or not pleasing vs. One other rare and strange accident, leauing others, will I mention before I ende, which mooued the whole countrey that either knew or hearde of vs, to haue vs in wonderfull admiration.

There was no towne where we had any subtile deuise practised against vs, we leauing it vnpunished or not reuenged (because wee fought by all meanes possible to win them by gentleness) but that within a few dayes after our departure from euerie such towne, the people began to die very fast, and many in short space; in some townes about twentie, in some fourtie, in some sixtie, & in one six score, which in trueth was very manie in respect of their numbers. This happened in no place that wee coulde learne but where wee had bene, where they vsed some practise against vs, and after such time; The disease also so strange, that they neither knew what it was, not how to cure it; the likely by report of the oldest men in the countrey neuer happened before, time out of minde. A thing specially obserued by vs as also by the naturall inhabitants themselues.

Insomuch that when some of the inhabitantes which were our friends & especially the *Wiroans Wingina* had obserued such effects in foure or fiue towns to follow their wicked practises, they were perswaded that it was the worke of our God through our meanes, and that wee by him might kil and slaie whom wee would without weapons and not come neere them.

And thereupon when it had happened that they had vnderstanding that any of their enemies had abused vs in our iourneyes, hearing that wee had wrought no reuenge with our weapons, & fearing upon some cause the matter should so rest: did come and intreate vs that we woulde bee a meanes to our God that they as others that had dealt with vs might in like fort die; alleaging howe much it would be for our credite and profire, as also theirs; and hoping furthermore that we would do so much at their requests in respect of the friendship we protesse them.

Whose entreaties although wee shewed that they were vngodlie, affirming that our God would not subject him selfe to anie such praiers and requestes of men: that in deede all thinges haue beene and were to be done according to his good pleasure as he had ordained: and that we to shew our selues his true servants ought rather to make petition for the contrarie, that they with them might liue together with vs, bee made partakers of his truth & serue him in righteousnes; but notwitstanding in such fort, that wee referre that as all other thinges, to bee done according to his diuine will & pleasure, and as by his wisedome he had ordained to be best.

Yet because the effect sell out so sodainly and shortly after according to their desires, they thought neuertheless it came to passe by our meanes, and that we in vsing such speeches vnto them did but dissemble the matter, and therefore came vnto vs to giue vs thankes in their manner that although wee satisfied them not in promise, yet in deedes and effect we had fulfilled their desires.

This maruelous accident in all the countrie wrought so strange opinions of vs, that some people could not tel whether to think vs gods or men, and the rather because that all the space of their sicknesse, there was no man of ours knowne to die, or that was specially sicke: they noted also that we had no women amongst vs, neither that we did care for any of theirs.

Some therefore were of opinion that wee were not borne of women, and therefore not mortall, but that wee were men of an old generation many yeeres past then risen againe to immortalitie.

Some woulde likewise seeme to prohesie that there were more of our generation yet to come, to kill theirs and take their places, as some thought the purpose was by that which was already done.

Those that were immediately to come after vs they imagined to be in the aire, yet inuisible & without bodies, & that they by our intreaty & for the loue of vs did make the people to die in that fort as they did by shooting inuisible bullets into them.

To confirme this opinion their phisitions to excuse their ignorance in curing the difease, would not be ashamed to say, but earnestly make the simple people beleue, that the strings of blood that they sucked out of the sicke bodies, were the strings wherewithall the inuisible bullets were tied and cast.

Some also thought that we shot them selues our of our pieces from the place where we dwelt, and killed the people in any such towne that had offended vs as we lifted, how farre distant from vs soeuer it were.

And other some said that it was the special woorke of God for our sakes, as wee our selues haue cause in some forte to thinke no lesse, whatsoeuer some doe or maie imagine to the contrarie, specially some Astrologers knowing of the Eclipse of the Sunne which wee saw the same yeere before in our voyage thy ther ward, which vnto them appeared very terrible. And also of a Comet which beganne to appeare but a few daies before the beginning of the said sicknesse. But to conclude them from being the speciall causes of so special an accident, there are farther reasons then I thinke fit at this present to bee alleadged.

There their opinions I haue set downe the more at large that it may appeare vnto you that there is good hope they may be brought through discreet dealing and gouernement to the imbracing of the trueth, and consequently to honour, obey, feare and love vs.

And although some of our companie towardes the ende of the yeare, shewed themselues too fierce, in slaying some of the people, in some towns, vpon causes that on our part, might easily enough haue been borne withall: yet not withstanding because it was on their partiustly deserued, the alteration of their opinions generally & for the most part concerning vs is the lesse to bee doubted. And whatsoeuer els they maybe, by carefulnesse of our selues neede nothing at all to be feared.

The best neuerthelesse in this as in all actions besides is to be endeuoured and hoped, & of the worst that may happen notice to bee taken with consideration, and as much as may be eschewed.

The Conclusion

Now I haue as I hope made relation not of so fewe and smal things but that the countrey of men that are indifferent & wel disposed maie be sufficiently liked: If there were no more knowen then I haue mentioned, which doubtlesse and in great reason is nothing to that which remaineth to bee discoured, neither the soile, nor commodities. As we haue reason so to gather by the differece we found in our trauails; for although all which I have before spoke of, have bin discovered & experimented not far fro the sea coast where was our abode & most of our trauailing: yet somtimes as we made our iourneies farther into the maine and countrey; we found the foyle to bee fatter; the trees greater and to growe thinner; the grounde more firme and deeper mould; more and larger champions; finer grasse and as good as euer we saw any in England; in some places rockie and farre more high and hillie ground; more plentie of their fruites; more abundance of beastes; the more inhabited with people, and of greater pollicie & larger dominions, with greater townes and houses.

Why may wee not then looke for in good hope from the inner parts of more and greater plentie, as well of other things, as of those which wee haue alreadie discouered? Vnto the Spaniardes happened the like in discovering the maine of the West Indies. The maine also of this countrey of *Virginia*, extending some wayes so many hundreds of leagues, as otherwise then by the relation of the inhabitants wee haue most certaine knowledge of, where yet no Christian Prince hath any possession or dealing, cannot but yeeld many kinds of excellent commodities, which we in our discouerie haue not yet seene.

What hope there is els to be gathered of the nature of the climate, being answerable to the Iland of *Japan*, the land of *China, Persia, Iury*, the Ilandes of *Cyprus* and *Candy*, the South parts of *Greece, Italy,* and *Spaine,* and of many other notable and famous countreis, because I meane not to be tedious, I leaue to your own consideration.

Whereby also the excellent temperature of the ayre there at all seasons, much warmer then in England, and neuer so violently hot, as sometimes is vnder & between the Tropikes, or nere them; cannot bee vnknowne vnto you without farther relation.

For the holsomnesse thereof I neede to say but thus much: that for all the want of prouision, as first of English victuall; excepting for twentie daies, wee liued only by drinking water and by the victual of the countrey, of which some sorts were very straunge vnto us, and might haue bene thought to haue altered our temperatures in such sort as to haue brought vs into some greeuous and dangerous diseases: secondly the want of English meanes, for the taking of beastes, fish, and foule, which by the helpe only of the inhabitants and their meanes, coulde not bee so suddenly and easily prouided for vs, nor in so great numbers & quantities, nor of the choise as otherwise might haue bene to out better satisfaction and contentment. Some want also wee had of clothes. Furthermore, in all our trauailes which were most speciall and often in the time of winter, our lodging was in the open aire vpon the grounde. And yet I say for all this, there were but foure of our whole, company (being one hundred and eight) that died all the yeere and that but at the latter ende thereof and vpon none of the aforesaide causes. For all foure specially three were feeble, weake, and sickly persons before euer they came thither, and those that knewe them much marueyled that they liued so long beeing in that case, or had aduentured to trauaile. Seeing therefore the ayre there is so temperate and holsome, the soyle to fertile and yeelding such commodities as I haue before mentioned, the voyage also thither to and fro beeing sufficiently experimented, to bee perfourmed thrise a yeere with ease and at any season thereof: And the dealing of *Sir Water Raleigh* so liberall in large giuing and graunting lande there, as is alreadie knowen, with many helpes and furtherances els: (The least that hee hath graunted hath beene fiue hundred acres to a man onely for the aduenture of his person): I hope there remaine no cause wherby the action should be misliked.

If that those which shall thither trauaile to inhabite and plant bee but reasonably prouided for the first yere as those are which were transported the last, and beeing there doe vse but that diligence and care as is requisite, and as they may with ease: There is no doubt but for the time following they may haue victuals that is excellent good and plentie enough; some more English fortes of cattaile also hereafter, as some haue bene before, and are there yet remaining, may and shall bee God willing thither transported: So likewise our kinde of fruites, rootes, and hearbes may bee there planted and sowed, as some haue

been alreadie, and prove wel. And in short time also they may raise of those sortes of commodities which I haue spoken of as shall both enrich themselves, as also others that shall deale with them.

And this is all the fruites of our labours, that I haue thought necessary to aduertise you of at this present: what els concerneth the nature and manners of the inhabitants of *Virginia:* The number with the particularities of the voyages thither made; and of the actions of such that haue bene by *Sir Water Raleigh* Therein and there imployed, many worthy to bee remembered: as of the first discouerers of the Countrey: of our Generall for the time *Sir Richard Greinsuile;* and after his departure, of our Gouernour there Master *Rase Lane;* with diuers other directed and imployed vnder theyr gouernement: Of the Captaynes and Masters of the voyages made since for transportation; of the Gouernour and assistants of those alredie transported, as of many persons, accidents, and thinges els, I haue ready in a discourse by itself in manner of a Chronicle according to the course of times, and when time shall bee thought convenient shall be also published.

Thus referring my relation to your fauourable constructions, expecting good successe of the action, from him which is to be acknowledged the authour and gouernour not only of this but of all things els, I take my leaue of you, this moneth of *February. 1588.*

FINIS.

See also ARTHUR M. BARLOWE, "EXPLORATION OF VIRGINIA," 1584.

Source:

Thomas Hariot. "Briefe and True Report of the New Found Land of Virginia." Virginia State Archives. Facts On File. American History Online. URL: www.factsonfile.com.

Bartholomew Gosnold to His Father (Letters from Jamestown), 1602

Letter from an explorer who became an early inhabitant of the Jamestown colony and member of the colony's governing council. Bartholomew Gosnold writes on his return to England that he reached "the latitude of 41 degrees," which indicates that he was in the New York/New England area. Gosnold was a noted navigator who explored much of the New England coast and was the first European to sight Martha's Vineyard.

My duty remembered, &c. Sir, I was in good hope that my occasions would have allowed me so much liberty, as to have come unto you before this time; otherwise I would have written more at large concerning the country from whence we lately came, than I did: but not well remembering what I have already written (though I am assured that there is nothing set down disagreeing with the truth,) I thought it fittest not to go about to add anything in writing, but rather to leave the report of the rest till I come myself; which now I hope shall be shortly, and so soon as with conveniency I may. In the mean time, notwithstanding whereas you seem not to be satisfied by that which I have already written, concerning some especial matters; I have here briefly (and as well as I can) added these few lines for your further satisfaction: and first, as touching that place where we were most resident, it is the latitude of 41 degrees, and one third part; which albeit it be so much to the southward, yet it is more cold than those parts of Europe, which are situated under the same parallel: but one thing is worth the noting, that notwithstanding the place is not so much subject to cold as England is, yet did we find the spring to be later there, than it is with us here, by almost a month: this whether it happened accidentally this last spring to be so, or whether it be so of course, I am not very certain; the latter seems most likely, whereof also there may be given some sufficient reason, which now I omit; as for the acorns we saw gathered on heaps, they were of the last year, but doubtless their summer continues longer than ours.

We cannot gather, by anything we could observe in the people, or by any trial we had thereof ourselves, but that it is as healthful a climate as any can be. The inhabitants there, as I wrote before, being of tall stature, comely proportion, strong, active, and some of good years, and as it should seem very healthful, are sufficient proof of the healthfulness of the place. First, for ourselves (thanks be to God) we had not a man sick two days together in all our voyage; whereas others that went out with us, or about that time on other voyages (especially such as went upon reprisal,) were most of them infected with sickness, whereof they lost some of their men, and brought home a many sick, returning notwithstanding long before us. But Verrazano, and others (as I take it, you may read in the Book of Discoveries,) do more particularly entreat of the age of the people in that coast. The sassafras which we brought we had upon the islands; where though we had little disturbance, and reasonable plenty; yet for that the greatest part of our people were employed about the fitting of our house, and such like affairs, and a few (and those but easy laborers) undertook this work, the rather because we were informed before our going forth, that a ton was sufficient to cloy England, and further, for that we had resolved upon our return, and taken view of our victual, we judged it then needful to use expedition; which afterward we had more certain proof of; for when we came to an anchor before Portsmouth, which was some four days after we made the land, we had not one cake of bread, nor any drink, but a little vinegar left: for these and other reasons, we returned no otherwise laden than you have heard. And thus much I hope shall suffice till I can myself come to give you further notice, which though it be not so soon as I could have wished, yet I hope it shall be in convenient time.

In the mean time, craving your pardon, for which the urgent occasions of my stay will plead, I humbly take my leave.

7th September, 1602
Your dutiful son,
Barth. Gosnold.

Source:

J. Franklin Jameson. *Narratives of Early Virginia.* New York: Charles Scribner's Sons, 1907.

The Legal and Religious Basis for
European Settlement in the New World

Ferdinand and Isabella, The Edict of the Expulsion from Spain, 1492

This edict, issued at Granada, Spain, on March 30, 1492, describes the ghettoization and expulsion of Jews from Spain. Jews who did not leave were subject to the Inquisition, in which heretics (non-Catholics) were tortured and burned to death. Muslims, who previously had been driven from all of Iberia but Granada, were also expelled or subjected to the Inquisition. Jewish and Muslim cultures had thrived together before Spain was united under Ferdinand and Isabella in 1469. Jews called Maranos openly converted while secretly practicing Jewish rituals and chose to remain after 1492. Some of these families immigrated to South America during the 17th century but the Inquisition followed them. Others eventually settled in the relatively more tolerant northeastern colonies of New York and Rhode Island. Many Maranos moved from South America into what is now Mexico and the southwestern United States. In recent years, a number of American descendants of Maranos, who practiced both Catholicism and certain Jewish rituals, have returned to Judaism.

Whereas, having been informed that in these our kingdoms, there were some bad Christians who judaised and apostatized from our holy Catholic faith, the chief cause of which was the communication of Jews with Christians; . . . in the year 1480, We ordered the . . . Jews in all the cities, towns, and places in our kingdoms and dominions, to separate into Jewries and places apart, where they should live and reside, hoping by their separation alone to remedy the evil. Furthermore, We have . . . . given orders that inquisition should be made in our . . . . kingdoms, . . . and . . . many guilty persons have been discovered . . . And as we are informed by the inquisitors, and many other religious, ecclesiastical, and secular persons, that great injury . . . does result . . . from the participation, society, and communication they . . . hold with Jews, who it appears always endeavor in every way they can to subvert our holy Catholic faith, and to make faithful Christians withdraw and separate themselves from them, and attract and pervert them to their injurious opinions and belief, instructing them in the ceremonies and observances of their religion, holding meetings where they read and teach them what they are to believe and observe according to their religion;

seeking to circumcise them and their children; giving them books from which they may read their prayers; and explaining to them the fasts they are to observe; assembling with them to read and to teach them the histories of their law, notifying to them the festivals previous to their occurring, and instructing them what they are to do and observe thereon; giving and carrying to them from their houses unleavened bread, and meat slaughtered with ceremonies; instructing them what they are to refrain from, . . . in food as in other matters, for the due observance of their religion, and persuading them all they can to profess and keep the law of Moses:

❊   ❊   ❊

. . . We knew the certain remedy for all these injuries and inconveniences was to separate the . . . Jews from all communication with Christians, and banish them from all our kingdoms, yet We were desirous to content ourselves by ordering them to quit all the cities, towns, and places of Andalusia, where it appears, they had done the greatest mischief, considering that would suffice, and that those of other cities, towns and places would cease to do and commit the same.

But We are informed that neither that, nor the execution of some of the Jews, who have been guilty of . . . crimes and offenses against Our holy Catholic faith, has been sufficient for a complete remedy to obviate and arrest so great an opprobrium and offense to the Catholic faith and religion.

And as it . . . appears, that the . . . Jews, wherever they live and congregate, daily increase in continuing their wicked and injurious purposes; . . . We command this our edict to be issued, whereby We command all Jews and Jewesses, of whatever age they may be, that live, reside, and dwell in our said kingdoms and dominions, . . . that by the end of the month of July next, of the present year 1492, they depart from all Our said kingdoms and dominions, with their sons, daughters, man-servants, maid-servants, and Jewish attendants, both great and small, of whatever age they may be; and they shall not presume to return to, nor reside therein, or in any part of them, either as residents, travelers, or in any other manner whatever, under pain that if they do not perform and execute the same . . . they incur the penalty of death, and confiscation of all their property to our treasury . . .

And We command and forbid any person or persons of Our . . . kingdoms, of whatsoever rank, station, or condition they may be . . . to receive, shelter, protect, or defend any Jew or Jewess, after . . . the end of July, . . . henceforward for ever and ever, under pain of losing all their property, vassals, castles, and other possessions; and furthermore forfeit to Our treasury any sums they have, or receive from Us.

And that the . . . Jews and Jewesses may be the better able to dispose of themselves, their property, and estates, We hereby take and receive them under Our security, protection, and royal safeguard; and insure to them and their properties, that . . . until . . . the end of the . . . month of July, they may travel in safety, and may enter, sell, barter, and alienate all their moveable and immovable property, and freely dispose thereof at their pleasure. And that during the said time, no harm, injury, or wrong whatever shall be done to their persons or properties . . .

We likewise grant permission and authority to the said Jews and Jewesses, to export their wealth and property, by sea or land, from our said kingdoms and dominions, provided they do not take away gold, silver, money, or other articles prohibited by the laws of our kingdoms, but in merchandise and goods that are not prohibited.

And We command all the justices of our kingdoms, that they cause the whole of the above herein contained to be observed and fulfilled, and that they do not act contrary hereto; and that they afford all necessary favor, under pain of being deprived of office, and the confiscation of all their property to our exchequer.

Source:
"The Edict of the Expulsion from Spain." *Gates to Jewish Heritage.* Available on-line. URL: www.jewishgates.com/file.asp?File_ID=7.

Papal Bull Inter Caetera of 1493

Treaty concluded by Pope Alexander VI on May 4, 1493, that drew an imaginary line 100 leagues west of the Cape Verde Islands in order to decide the future of Columbus's discoveries in terms of territorial claims. There was much dispute involving the lands discovered by Columbus between Spain and Portugal. King John II of Portugal believed these discoveries were made in the region south and west of Guinea, thus presenting a problem concerning Portuguese control over Guinea. The Papal Bull Inter Caetera made the final decision that Portugal would have claim to all rights and possessions that it already held east of the imaginary line drawn by Alexander VI, while Spain would have the right to trade, colonize, and explore anywhere west of this line. An amendment of the bull was created in September 1493, giving Spain the right to the "eastern regions and to India." Nine months later, in the Treaty of Tordesillas, Spain agreed to move the line west of the Cape Verde Islands, giving Portugal a claim to what is now Brazil.

Alexander, bishop, servant of the servants of God, to the illustrious sovereigns, our very dear son in Christ, Ferdinand, king, and our very dear daughter in Christ, Isabella, queen of Castile, Leon, Aragon, Sicily, and Granada, health and apostolic benediction. Among other works well pleasing to the Divine Majesty and cherished of our heart, this assuredly ranks highest, that in our times especially the Catholic faith and the Christian religion be exalted and be everywhere increased and spread, that the health of souls be cared for and that barbarous nations be overthrown and brought to the faith itself. Wherefore inasmuch as by the favor of divine clemency, we, though of insufficient merits, have been called to this Holy See of Peter, recognizing that as true Catholic kings and princes, such as we have known you always to be, and as your illustrious deeds already known to almost the whole world declare, you not only eagerly desire but with every effort, zeal, and diligence, without regard to hardships, expenses, dangers, with the shedding even of your blood, are laboring to that end; recognizing also that you have long since dedicated to this purpose your whole soul and all your endeavors—as witnessed in these times with so much glory to the Divine Name in your recovery of the kingdom of Granada from the yoke of the Saracens—we therefore are rightly led, and hold it as our duty, to grant you even of our own accord and in your favor those things whereby with effort each day more hearty you may be enabled for the honor of God himself and the spread of the Christian rule to carry forward your holy and praiseworthy purpose so pleasing to immortal God. We have indeed learned that you, who for a long time had intended to seek out and discover certain islands and mainlands remote and unknown and not hitherto discovered by others, to the end that you might bring to the worship of our Redeemer and the profession of the Catholic faith their residents and inhabitants, having been up to the present time greatly engaged in the siege and recovery of the kingdom itself of Granada were unable to accomplish this holy and praiseworthy purpose; but the said kingdom having at length been regained, as was pleasing to the Lord, you, with the wish to fulfill your desire, chose our beloved son, Christopher Columbus, a man assuredly worthy and of the highest recommendations and fitted for so great an undertaking, whom you furnished with ships and men equipped for like designs, not without the greatest hardships, dangers, and expenses, to make diligent quest for these remote and unknown mainlands and islands through the sea, where hitherto no one had sailed; and they at length, with divine aid and with the utmost diligence sailing in the ocean sea, discovered certain very remote islands and even mainlands that hitherto had not been discovered by others; wherein dwell very many peoples living in peace, and, as reported, going unclothed, and not eating flesh. Moreover, as your aforesaid envoys are of opinion, these very peoples living in the said islands and countries believe in one God, the Creator in heaven, and seem sufficiently disposed to embrace the Catholic faith and be trained in good morals. And it is hoped that, were they instructed, the name of the Savior, our Lord Jesus Christ, would easily be introduced into the said countries and islands. Also, on one of the chief of these aforesaid islands the said Christopher has already caused to be put together and built a fortress fairly equipped, wherein he has stationed as garrison certain Christians, companions of his, who are to make search for other remote and unknown islands and mainlands. In the islands and countries already discovered are found gold, spices, and very many other precious things of divers kinds and qualities. Wherefore, as becomes Catholic kings and princes, after earnest consideration of all matters, especially of the rise and spread of the Catholic faith, as was the fashion of your ancestors, kings of renowned memory, you have purposed with the favor of divine clemency to bring under your sway the said mainlands and islands with their residents and inhabitants and to bring them to the Catholic faith. Hence, heartily commending in the Lord this your holy and praiseworthy purpose, and desirous that it be duly accomplished, and that the name of our Savior be carried into those regions, we exhort you very earnestly in the Lord and by your reception of holy baptism, whereby you are bound to our apostolic commands, and by the bowels of the mercy of our Lord Jesus Christ, enjoin strictly, that inasmuch as with eager zeal for the true faith you design to equip and dispatch this expedition, you purpose also, as is your duty, to lead the peoples dwelling in those islands and countries to embrace the Christian religion; nor at any time let dangers or hardships deter you therefrom, with the stout hope and trust in your hearts that Almighty God will further your undertakings. And, in order that you may enter upon so great an undertaking with greater readiness and heartiness endowed with the benefit of our apostolic favor, we, of our own accord, not at your instance nor the request of anyone else in your regard, but of our own sole largess and certain knowledge and out of the fullness of our apostolic power, by the authority of Almighty God conferred upon us in blessed Peter and of the vicarship of Jesus Christ, which we hold on earth, do by tenor of these presents, should any of said islands have been found by your envoys and captains, give, grant, and assign to you and your heirs and successors, kings of Castile and Leon, forever, together with all their dominions, cities, camps, places, and villages, and all rights, jurisdictions, and appurtenances, all islands and mainlands found and to be found, discovered and to be discovered towards the west and south, by drawing and establishing a line from the Arctic pole, namely the north, to the Antarctic pole, namely the south, no matter whether the said mainlands and islands are found and to be found in the direction of India or towards any other quarter, the said line to be distant one hundred leagues towards the west and south from any of the islands commonly known as the Azores and Cape Verde. With this proviso however that none of the islands and mainlands, found and to be found, discovered and to be discovered, beyond that said line towards the west and south, be in the actual possession of any Christian king or prince up to the birthday of our Lord Jesus Christ just past from which the present year one thousand four hundred and ninety-three begins. And we make, appoint, and depute you and your said heirs and successors lords of them with full and free power, authority, and jurisdiction of every kind; with this proviso however, that by this our gift, grant, and assignment no right acquired by any Christian prince, who may be in actual possession of said islands and mainlands prior to the said birthday of our Lord Jesus Christ, is hereby to be understood to be withdrawn or taken away. Moreover we command you in virtue of holy obedience that, employing all due diligence in the premises, as you also promise—nor do we doubt your compliance therein in accordance with your loyalty and royal greatness of spirit—you should appoint to the aforesaid mainlands and islands worthy, God-fearing, learned, skilled, and experienced men, in order to instruct the aforesaid inhabitants and residents in the Catholic faith and train them in good morals. Furthermore, under penalty of excommunication *late sententie* to be incurred *ipso facto,* should anyone thus contravene, we strictly forbid all persons of whatsoever rank, even imperial and royal, or of whatsoever estate, degree, order, or condition, to dare, without your special permit or that of your aforesaid heirs and successors, to go for the purpose of trade or any other reason to the islands or mainlands, found and to be found, discovered and to be discovered, towards the west and south, by drawing and establishing a line from the Arctic pole to the Antarctic pole, no matter whether the mainlands and islands, found and to be found, lie in the direction of India or toward any other quarter whatsoever, the said line to be distant one hundred leagues towards the west and south, as is aforesaid, from any of the islands commonly known as the Azores and Cape Verde; apostolic constitutions and ordinances and other decrees whatsoever to the contrary notwithstanding. We trust in Him from whom empires and governments and all good things proceed, that, should you, with the Lord's guidance, pursue this holy and praiseworthy undertaking, in a short while your hardships and endeavors will attain the most felicitous result, to the happiness and glory of all Christendom. But inasmuch as it would be difficult to have these present letters sent to all places where desirable, we wish, and with similar accord and knowledge do decree, that to copies of them, signed by the hand of a public notary commissioned therefor, and sealed with the seal of any ecclesiastical officer or ecclesiastical court, the same respect is to be shown in court and outside as well as anywhere else as would be given to these presents should they thus be exhibited or shown. Let no one, therefore, infringe, or with rash boldness contravene, this our recommendations, exhortation, requisition, gift, grant, assignment, constitution, deputation, decree, mandate, prohibition, and will. Should anyone presume to attempt this, be it known to him that he will incur the wrath of Almighty God and of the blessed apostles Peter and Paul. Given at Rome, at St. Peter's, in the year of the incarnation of our Lord one thousand four hundred and ninety-three, the fourth of May, and the first year of our pontificate.

Gratis by order of our most holy lord, the pope. June. For the referendary, A. de Mucciarellis. For J. Bufolinus, A. Santoseverino. L. Podocatharus.

Source:

Francis Garvin Davenport, ed. *European Treaties Bearing on the History of the United States and Its Dependencies to 1648,* Washington, D.C., 1917. pp. 71–78.

Henry VII, King of England, "Letters Patent to John Cabot," 1496

Patent secured by Italian explorer John Cabot (Giovanni Caboto) from King Henry VII of England on March 5, 1496, to look for a western route to the Spice Islands by plotting a course north of Columbus's. John Cabot and his sons, Lewis, Sebastian, and Santius, were granted the right to sail to and conquer—under the English flag—any new lands they could find. Setting sail from Bristol on May 2, 1497, Cabot made a landfall on the North American mainland along the Labrador coast and paved the way for the founding of the English colonies in America. He returned to Bristol on August 6, 1497.

Sebastian, and Santius for the discouerie of new and unknowen lands.

Henry, by the grace of God, king of England and France, and lord of Ireland, to all to whom these presents shall come, Greeting.

Be it knowen that we haue giuen and granted, and by these presents do giue and grant for vs and our heires, to our welbeloued Iohn Cabot citizen of Venice, to Lewis, Sebastian, and Santius, sonnes of the sayd Iohn, and to the heires of them, and euery of them, and their deputies, full and free authority, leaue, and power to saile to all parts, countreys, and seas of the East, of the West, and of the North, vnder our banners and ensignes, with fiue ships of what burthen or quantity soeuer they be, and as many mariners or men as they will haue with them in the sayd ships, vpon their owne proper costs and charges, to seeke out, dicouer, and finde whatsoeuer isles, countreys, regions or prouinces of the heathen and infidels whatsoeuer they be, and in what part of the world soeuer they be, which before this time haue bene vnknowen to all Christians: we haue granted to them, and also to euery of them, the heires of them, and euery of them, and their deputies, and haue giuen them license to set vp our banners and ensignes in euery village, towne, castle, isle, or maine land of them newly found. And that the aforesayd Iohn and his sonnes, or their heires and assignes may subdue, occupy and possesse all such townes, cities, castles and isles of them found, which they can subdue, occupy and possesse, as our vassals, and lieutenants, getting vnto vs the rule, title, and jurisdiction of the same villages, townes, castles, & firme Land so found. Yet so that the aforesayd Iohn, and his sonnes and heires, and their deputies, be holden and bounden of all the fruits, profits, gaines, and commodities growing of such nauigation, for euery their voyage, as often as they shall arriue at our port of Bristoll (at which port they shall be bound and holden onely to arriue) all manner of necessary costs and charges by them made, being deducted, to pay vnto vs in wares or money the fift part of the capitall gaine so gotten. We giuing and granting vnto them and to their heires and deputies, that they shall be free from all paying of customes of all and singular such merchandize as they shall be free from all paying of customes of all and singular they shall bring with them from those places so newlie found.

And moreouer, we haue given and granted to them, their heires and deputies, that all the firme lands, isles, villages, townes, castles and places whatsoeuer they be that they shall chance to finde, may not of any other of our subjects be frequented or visited without the licence of the foresayd Iohn and his sonnes, and their deputies, vnder payne of forfeiture as well of their ships as of all and singular goods of all them that shall presume to saile to those places so found. Willing, and most straightly commanding all and singular our subjects as well on land as on sea, appointed officers, to giue good assistance to the aforesaid Iohn, and his sonnes and deputies, and that as well in arming and furnishing their ships or vessels, as is prouision of quietnesse, and in buying of victuals for their money, and all other things by them to be prouided necessary for the sayd nauigation, they do giue them all their helpe and fauour. In witnesse whereof we have caused to be made these our lettres patents. Witnesse our selfe at Westminister, the fift day of March, in the eleuenth yeere of our reigne.—

Source:
Henry Steele Commager, ed. *Documents of American History.* New York: F.S. Crofts & Co., 1934.

Charter to Sir Walter Raleigh, 1584

Patent received by Sir Walter Raleigh from Queen Elizabeth I on March 25, 1584, for the right to establish a colony in the New World. Six months after his half brother Sir Humphrey Gilbert was killed during his second attempt at establishing a colony in America, Raleigh received this charter (almost identical to Gilbert's) from the queen; he responded by sending out several expeditions and by establishing the ill-fated colony on Roanoke Island in present-day North Carolina. He was later charged with treason, imprisoned in the Tower of London, and ultimately executed after falling out of favor following Elizabeth's death in 1603.

Charter in Favor of Sir Walter Ralegh, Knight,
For the Discovery and Planting of New Lands in America

Elizabeth by the grace of God of England, France and Ireland Queene, defender of the faith, &c. To all people to whom these presents shal come, greeting. Know ye that of our especial grace, certaine science, & meere motion, we haue giuen and graunted, and by these presents for vs, our heires and successors doe giue and graunt to our trusty and welbeloued seruant Walter Ralegh Esquire, and to his heires and assignes for euer, free liberty & licence from time to time, and at all times for euer hereafter, to discouer, search, finde out, and view such remote, heathen and barbarous lands, countreis, and territories, not actually possessed of any Christian prince, nor inhabited by Christian people, as to him, his heires and assignes, and to euery or any of them shall seeme good, and the same to haue, holde, occupy & enjoy to him, his heires and assignes for euer, with all prerogatiues, commodities, iurisdictions, royalties, priuiledges, franchises and preeminences, thereto or thereabouts both by sea and land, whatsoeuer we by our letters patents may grant, and as we or any of our noble progenitors haue heretofore granted to any person or persons, bodies politique or corporate: and the saide Walter Ralegh, his heires and assignes, and all such as from time to time, by license of us, our heires and successors, shal goe or trauaile thither to inhabite or remaine, there to build and fortifie, at the discretion of the said Walter Ralegh, his heires &

assignes, the statutes or act of Parliament made against fugitiues, or against such as shall depart, remaine or continue out of our Realme of England without license, or any statute, act, law, or any ordinance whatsoeuer to the contrary in any wife notwithstanding.

And we do likewise by these presents, or our especial grace, meere motion, and certaine knowledge, for us, our heires and successors, giue and graunt full authoritie, libertie and power to the said Walter Ralegh, his heires and assignes, and euery of them, that he and they, and euery or any of them shall and may at all and euery time and times hereafter, haue, take, and leade in the sayde voyage, and trauaile thitherward, or to inhabite there with him or them, and euery or any of them, such and so many of our subjects as shall willingly accompany him or them, and euery or any of them: and to whom also we doe by these presents, giue full libertie and authoritie in that behalfe, and also to haue, take and employ, and use sufficient shipping and furniture for the transportations, and Nauigations in that behalfe, so that none of the same persons or any of them be such as hereafter shall be restrained by us, our heires or successors.

And further that the said Walter Ralegh his heires and assignes, and euery of them, shall haue, holde, occupie and enjoy to him, his heires and assignes, and euery of them for euer, all the soyle of all such landes, territories, and Countreis, so to be discouered and possessed as aforesaid, and of all such Cities, Castles, Townes, Villages, and places in the same, with the right, royalties, franchises, and iurisdictions, as well marine as other within the sayd landes, or Countreis, or the seas thereunto adioyning, to be had, or used, with full power to dispose thereof, and of euery part in fee simple or otherwise, according to the order of the lawes of England, as neere as the same conueniently may be, at his, and their will and pleasure, to any persons then being, or that shall remaine within the allegiance of us, our heires and successors: reseruing alwayes to us, our heires and successors, for all seruices, dueties, and demaunds, the fift part of all the oare of golde and siluer, that from time to time, and at all times after such discouerie, subduing and possessing, shall be there gotten and obtained: All which lands, Countreis, and territories shall for euer be holden of the said Walter Ralegh, his heires and assignes, of us, our heires and successors, by homage, and by the sayd payment of the said fift part, reserued onely for all seruices. And moreouer, we do by these presents, for us, our heires and successors, giue and grant licence to the said Walter Ralegh, his heires, and assignes, and euery of them, that he, and they, and euery or any of them, shall and may from time to time, and at all times for euer hereafter, for his and their defence, encounter and expulse, repell and resist aswell by sea as by lande, and by all other wayes whatsoeuer, all and euery such person and persons whatsoeuer, as without especiall liking and licence of the sayd Walter Ralegh, and of his heires and assignes, shall attempt to inhabite within the sayde Countreys, or any of them, or within the space of two hundreth leagues neere to the place or places within such Countreys as aforesayde (if they shall not bee before planted or inhabited within the limits as aforesayd with the subiects of any Christian Prince being in amitie with us) where the sayd Walter Ralegh, his heires, or assignes, or any of them, or his, or their, or any of their associats or company, shall within six yeeres (next ensuing) make their dwellings or abidings, or that shall enterprise or attempt at any time hereafter unlawfully to annoy, eyther by Sea or Lande the sayde Walter Ralegh, his heires or assignes, or any of them, or his or their, or any of his or their companies: giuing and graunting by these presents further power and authoritie to the sayd Walter Ralegh, his heires and assignes, and euery of them from time to time, and at all times for euer hereafter, to take and surprise by all maner of meanes whatsoeuer, all and euery those person or persons, with their Shippes, Vessels, and other goods and furniture, which without the licence of the sayde Walter Ralegh, or his heires, or assignes, as aforesayd, shalbe found traffiquing into any Harbour, or Harbours, Creeke, or Creekes, within the limits aforesayd, (the subiects of our Realmes and Dominions, and all other persons in amitie with us, trading to the New-found lands for fishing as heretofore they haue commonly vsed, or being driuen by force of a tempest, or shipwracke onely excepted:) and those persons, and euery of them, with their shippes, vessels, goods, and furniture to deteine and possesse as of good and lawfull prize, according to the discretion of him the sayd Walter Ralegh, his heires, and assignes, and euery, or any of them. And for uniting in more perfect league and amitie, of such Countryes, landes, and territories so to be possessed and inhabited as aforesayd with our Realmes of England and Ireland, and the better incouragement of men to these enterprises: we doe by these presents, graunt and declare that all such Countries, so hereafter to be possessed and inhabited as is aforesayd, from thencefoorth shall be of the allegiance of us, our heires and successours. And wee doe graunt to the sayd Walter Ralegh, his heires, and assignes, and to all, and euery of them, and to all, and euery other person and persons, being of our allegiance, whose names shall be noted or entred in some of our Courts of recorde within our Realme of England, that with the assent of the sayd Walter Ralegh, his heires or assignes, shall in his iourneis for discouerie, or in the iourneis for conquest hereafter trauaile to such lands, countreis and territories, as aforesayd, and to their, and to euery of their heires, that they, and euery or any of them, being eyther borne within our sayde Realmes of England or Irelande, or in any other place within our allegiance, and which hereafter shall be

inhabiting within any the Lands, Countryes, and Territories, with such licence (as aforesayd) shall and may haue all the priuiledges of free Denizens, and persons natiue of England, and within our allegiance in such like ample maner and forme, as if they were borne and personally resident within our said Realme of England, any law, custome, or usage to the contrary notwithstanding.

And forasmuch as upon the finding out, discouering, or inhabiting of such remote lands, countries, and territories as aforesaid, it shalbe necessary for the safety of all men, that shall aduenture themselues in those iourneyes or voyages, to determine to liue together in Christian peace, and ciuill quietnesse eche with other, whereby euery one may with more pleasure and profit enioy that whereunto they shall atteine with great paine and perill, wee for us, our heires and successors, are likewise pleased and contented, and by these presents doe giue & grant to the said Walter Ralegh, his heires and assignes for euer, that he and they, and euery or any of them, shall and may from time to time for euer hereafter, within the said mentioned remote lands and countries, in the way by the seas thither, and from thence, haue full and meere power and authoritie to correct, punish, pardon, gouerne, and rule by their and euery or any of their good discretions and policies, as well in causes capitall, or criminall, as ciuil, both marine and other, all such our subiects, as shal from time to time aduenture themselues in the said iourneis or voyages, or that shall at any time hereafter inhabite any such lands, countreis, or territories as aforesayd, or that shall abide within 200. leagues of any of the sayde place or places, where the sayde Walter Ralegh, his heires or assignes, or any of them, or any of his or their associats or companies, shall inhabite within 6. yeeres next ensuing the date hereof, according to such statutes, lawes and ordinances as shall be by him the sayd Walter Ralegh, his heires and assignes, and euery or any of them deuised, or established, for the better gouernment of the said people as aforesaid. So always as the said statutes, lawes, and ordinances may be, as nere as conueniently may bee, agreeable to the forme of the lawes, statutes, gouernment, or pollicie of England, and also so as they be not against the true Christian faith, nowe professed in the Church of England, nor in any wife to withdrawe any of the subiects or people of those lands or places from the alleagance of us, our heires and successours, as their immediate Soueraigne under God.

And further, we doe by these presents for us, our heires and successors, giue and grant ful power and authoritie to our trustie and welbeloued Counsailour Sir William Cecill knight, Lorde Burghley, or high Treasourer of England, and to the Lorde Treasourer of England for us, our heires and successors, for the time being, and to the priuie Counsaile of us, our heires and successors, or any foure or more of them for the time being, that he, they, or any foure or more of them, shall and may from time to time, and at all times hereafter, under his or their handes or Seales by vertue of these presents, authorise and license the sayd Walter Ralegh, his heires and assignes, and euery or any of them by him, & by themselues, or by their, or any of their sufficient Atturnies, Deputies, Officers, Ministers, Factors, and seruants, to imbarke & transport out of our Realme of England and Ireland, and the Dominions thereof, all or any of his or their goods, and all or any the goods of his and their associats and companies, and euery or any of them, with such other necessaries and commodities of any our Realmes, as to the sayde Lorde Treasurer, or foure or more of the priuie Counsaile, of us our heires and successors for the time being (as aforesaid) shalbe from time to time by his or their wisedomes, or discretions thought meete and conuenient, for the better reliefe and supportation of him the sayde Walter Ralegh, his heires, and assignes, and euery or any of them, and of his or their or any of their associats and companies, any act, statute, law, or any thing to the contrary in any wife notwithstanding.

Prouided alwayes, and our wil and pleasure is, and we do hereby declare to all Christian kings, princes, and states, that if the sayde Walter Ralegh, his heires or assignes, or any of them, or any other by their licence or appointment, shall at any time or times hereafter robbe or spoile by sea or by land, or doe any act of vniust or vnlawfull hostilitie, to any of the subiects of us, our heires or successors, or to any of the subiects of any the kings, princes, rulers, Gouernours, or estates, being then in perfect league and amitie with us, our heires and successors, and that upon such iniurie, or upon iust complaint of any such Prince, Ruler, Gouernour or estate, or their subiects, wee, our heires and successors, shall make open Proclamation within any the portes of our Realme of England, that the saide Walter Ralegh, his heires and assignes, and adherents or any to whom these our Letters patents may extende, shall within the termes to bee limited, by such Proclamation, make full restitution, and satisfaction of all such iniuries, done: so as both we and the said Princes, or other so complaining, may hold us and themselues fully contended: And that if the said Walter Ralegh, his heires an assignes, shall not make or cause to be made satisfaction accordingly within such time so to be limited, that then it shal be lawful to us, our heires and successors, to put the sayde Walter Ralegh, his heires and assignes, and adherents, and all the inhabitants of the saide places to be discouered (as is aforesaid) or any of them out of our allegeance and protection, and that from and after such time of putting out of protection of the sayde Walter Ralegh, his heires, assignes and adherents, and others so to be put out, and the said places within their habitation, pos-

session and rule, shall be out of our allegeance and protection, and free for all Princes and others to pursue with hostilitie, as being not our subiects, nor by us any way to be auouched, maintained, or defended, not to be holden as any of ours, nor to our protection, or dominion, or allegeance any way belonging: for that expresse mention of the cleere yeerely value of the certaintie of the premisses, or any part thereof, or of any other gift, or grant by us, or any our progenitors, or predecessors to the said Walter Ralegh, before this time made in these presents bee not expressed, or any other grant, ordinance, prouision, proclamation, or restraint to the contrary thereof, before this time, giuen, ordained, or prouided, or any other thing, cause, or matter whatsoeuer, in any wife notwithstanding. In witnesse whereof, wee haue caused these our letters to be made Patents. Witnesse our selues, at Westminster the fiue and twentie day of March, in the fixe and twentith yeere of our Raigns.

Source:
University of North Carolina at Chapel Hill Libraries. Documenting the American South. URL: hhtp.docsouth.unc.edu/ nc/barlowe/barlowe.html. Accessed October 2003.

First Charter of Virginia, April 10, 1606

Charter provided to incorporate two companies, the London Company and the Plymouth Company, by King James I on April 10, 1606. These two companies were given the rights to produce a colony on any land then known as Virginia or any other territories belonging to England in the New World. The London Company was the first to settle in America, founding the colony of Jamestown in Virginia on May 14, 1607. The First Charter of Virginia gave these settlers the right to claim all lands, as well as 100 miles into the mainland, as English territory. Each new colony was ordained to have a council containing 13 men, while a separate council of 13 men would also be provided by King James in England for management and support. The charter declared all children born in these new colonies citizens of England.

James, by the Grace of God, King of *England, Scotland, France,* and *Ireland,* Defender of the Faith, etc. Whereas our loving and well-disposed Subjects, Sir *Thomas Gates,* and Sir *George Somers,* Knights, *Richard Hackluit,* Clerk, Prebendary of *Westminster,* and *Edward-Maria Wingfield, Thomas Hanham,* and *Ralegh Gilbert,* Esqrs. *William Parker,* and *George Popham,* Gentlemen, and divers others of our loving Subjects, have been humble Suitors unto us, that We would vouchsafe unto them our Licence, to make Habitation, Plantation, and to deduce a colony of sundry of our People into that part of *America* commonly called Virginia, and other parts and Territories in *America,* either appertaining unto us, or which are not now actually possessed by any *Christian* Prince or People, situate, lying, and being all along the Sea Coasts, between four and thirty Degrees of *Northerly* Latitude from the Equinoctial Line, and five and forty Degrees of the same Latitude, and in the main Land between the same four and thirty and five and forty Degrees, and the Islands thereunto adjacent, or within one hundred Miles of the Coast thereof;

And to that End, and for the more speedy Accomplishment of their said intended Plantation and Habitation there, are desirous to divide themselves into two several Colonies and Companies; the one consisting of certain Knights, Gentlemen, Merchants, and other Adventurers, of our City of *London* and elsewhere, which are, and from time to time shall be, joined unto them, which do desire to begin their Plantation and Habitation in some fit and convenient Place, between four and thirty and one and forty Degrees of the said Latitude, alongst the Coasts of *Virginia,* and the Coasts *America* aforesaid: And the other consisting of sundry Knights, Gentlemen, Merchants, and other Adventurers, of our Cities of *Bristol* and *Exeter,* and of our Town of *Plimouth,* and of other Places, which do join themselves unto that Colony, which do desire to begin their Plantation and Habitation in some fit and convenient Place, between eight and thirty Degrees and five and forty Degrees of the said Latitude, all alongst the said Coasts of *Virginia* and *America,* as that Coast lyeth:

We, greatly commending, and graciously accepting of, their Desires for the Furtherance of so noble a Work, which may, by the Providence of Almighty God, hereafter tend to the Glory of his Divine Majesty, in propagating of *Christian* Religion to such People, as yet live in Darkness and miserable Ignorance of the true Knowledge and Worship of God, and may in time bring the Infidels and Savages, living in those parts, to human Civility, and to a settled and quiet Government: Do, by these our Letters Patents, graciously accept of, and agree to, their humble and well-intended Desires;

And do therefore, for Us, our Heirs, and Successors, grant and agree, that the said Sir *Thomas Gates,* Sir *George Somers, Richard Hackluit,* and *Edward-Maria Wingfield,* Adventurers of and for our City of *London,* and all such others, as are, or shall be, joined unto them of that Colony, shall be called the *first Colony;* And they shall and may begin their said first Plantation and Habitation, at any Place upon the said Coast of *Virginia* or *America,* where they shall think fit and convenient, between the said four and thirty and one and forty Degrees of the said Latitude; And that they shall have all the Lands, Woods, Soil, Grounds, Havens, Ports, Rivers, Mines, Minerals,

Marshes, Waters, Fishings, Commodities, and Hereditaments, whatsoever, from the said first Seat of their Plantation and Habitation by the Space of fifty Miles of *English* Statute Measure, all along the said Coast of *Virginia* and *America,* towards the *West* and *Southwest,* as the Coast lyeth, with all the Islands within one hundred Miles directly over against the same Sea Coast; And also all the Lands, Soil, Grounds, Havens, Ports, Rivers, Mines, Minerals, Woods, Waters, Marshes, Fishings, Commodities, and Hereditaments, whatsoever, from the said Place of their first Plantation and Habitation for the space of fifty like *English* Miles, all alongst the said Coasts of *Virginia* and *America,* towards the *East* and *Northeast,* or towards the *North,* as the Coast lyeth, together with all the Islands within one hundred Miles, directly over against the said Sea Coast; And also all the Lands, Woods, Soil, Grounds, Havens, Ports, Rivers, Mines, Minerals, Marshes, Waters, Fishings, Commodities, and Hereditaments, whatsoever, from the same fifty Miles every way on the Sea Coast, directly into the main Land by the Space of one hundred like *English* Miles; And shall and may inhabit and remain there; and shall and may also build and fortify within any the same, for their better Safeguard and Defense, according to their best Discretion, and the Discretion of the Council of that Colony; And that no other of our Subjects shall be permitted, or suffered, to plant or inhabit behind, or on the Backside of them, towards the main Land, without the Express License or Consent of the Council of that Colony, thereunto in Writing first had and obtained.

And we do likewise, for Us, our Heirs, and Successors, by these Presents, Grant and agree, that the said *Thomas Hanham,* and *Ralegh Gilbert, William Parker,* and George Popham, and all others of the Town of *Plimouth* in the County of *Devon,* or elsewhere, which are, or shall be, joined unto them of that Colony, shall be called the *second Colony;* And that they shall and may begin their said Plantation and Seat of their first Abode and Habitation, at any Place upon the said Coast of *Virginia* and *America,* where they shall think fit and convenient, between eight and thirty Degrees of the said Latitude, and five and forty Degrees of the same Latitude; And that they shall have all the Lands, Soils, Grounds, Havens, Ports, Rivers, Mines, Minerals, Woods, Marshes, Waters, Fishings, Commodities, and Hereditaments, whatsoever, from the first Seat of their Plantation and Habitation by the Space of fifty like *English* Miles, as is aforesaid, all alongst the said Coasts of *Virginia* and *America,* towards the *West* and *Southwest,* or towards the *South,* as the Coast lyeth, and all the Islands within one hundred Miles, directly over against the said Sea Coast; And also all the Lands, Soils, Grounds, Havens, Ports, Rivers, Mines, Minerals, Woods, Marshes, Waters, Fishings, Commodities, and Hereditaments, whatsoever, from the said Place of their first Plantation and Habitation for the Space of fifty like Miles, all alongst the said Coast of *Virginia* and *America,* towards the *East* and *Northeast,* or towards the *North,* as the Coast lyeth, and all the Islands also within one hundred Miles directly over against the same Sea Coast; And also all the Lands, Soils, Grounds, Havens, Ports, Rivers, Woods, Mines, Minerals, Marshes, Waters, Fishings, Commodities, and Hereditaments, whatsoever, from the same fifty Miles every way on the Sea Coast, directly into the main Land, by the Space of one hundred like *English* Miles; And shall and may inhabit and remain there; and shall and may also build and fortify within any the same for their better Safeguard, according to their best Discretion, and the Discretion of the Council of that Colony; And that none of our Subjects shall be permitted, or suffered, to plant or inhabit behind, or on the back of them, towards the main Land, without express Licence of the Council of that Colony, in Writing thereunto first had and obtained.

Provided always, and our Will and Pleases herein is, that the Plantation and Habitation of such of the said Colonies, as shall last plant themselves, as aforesaid, shall not be made within one hundred like *English* Miles of the other of them, that first began to make their Plantation, as aforesaid.

And we do also ordain, establish, and agree, for Us, our Heirs, and Successors, that each of the said Colonies shall have a Council, which shall govern and order all Matters and Causes, which shall arise, grow, or happen, to or within the same several Colonies, according to such Laws, Ordinances, and Instructions, as shall be, in that behalf, given and signed with Our Hand or Sign Manual, and pass under the Privy Seal of our realm of *England;* Each of which Councils shall consists of thirteen Persons, to be ordained, made, and removed, from time to time, according as shall be directed and comprised in the same instructions; And shall have a several Seal, for all Matters that shall pass or concern the same several Councils; Each of which Seals, shall have the King's Arms engraven on the one Side thereof, and his Portraiture on the other; And that the Seal for the Council of the said first Colony shall have engraven round about, on the one Side, these Words; *Sigillum Regis Magnae Britanniae, Franciae, & Hiberniae;* on the other Side this Inscription round about; *Pro Concilio primae Coloniae Virginiae.* And the Seal for the Council of the said second Colony shall also have engraven, round about the one Side thereof, the aforesaid Words; *Sigillum Regis Magnae Britanniae, Franciae, & Hiberniae;* and on the other Side; *Pro Concilio secundae Coloniae Virginiae:*

And that also there shall be a Council, established here in *England,* which shall, in like Manner, consist of thirteen Persons, to be, for that Purpose, appointed by Us, our Heirs and Successors, which shall be called our *Council of Virginia;* And shall, from time to time, have the superior Managing and Direction, only of and for all Matters that shall or may concern the Government as well as of the said several Colonies, as of and for any other Part or Place, within the aforesaid Precincts of four and thirty and five and forty Degrees above mentioned; Which Council shall, in like manner, have a Seal, for Matters concerning the Council or Colonies, with the like Arms and Portraiture, as aforesaid, with this inscription, engraven round about on the one Side; *Sigillum Regis Magnae Britanniae, Franciae, & Hiberniae;* and round about on the other Side, *Pro Concilio suo Virginiae.*

And moreover, we do Grant and agree, for Us, our Heirs and Successors; that the said several Councils of and for the said several Colonies, shall and lawfully may, by Virtue hereof, from time to time, without any Interruption of Us, our Heirs or Successors, give and take Order, to dig, mine, and search for all Manner of Mines of Gold, Silver, and Copper, as well within any part of their said several Colonies, as for the said main Lands on the Backside of the same Colonies; And to Have and enjoy the Gold, Silver, and Copper, to be gotten thereof, to the Use and Behoof of the same Colonies, and the Plantations thereof; Yielding therefore to Us, our Heirs and Successors, the fifth Part only of all the same Gold and Silver, and the fifteenth Part of all the same Copper, so to be gotten or had, as is aforesaid, without any other Manner of Profit or Account, to be given or yielded to Us, our Heirs, or Successors, for or in Respect of the same:

And that they shall, or lawfully may, establish and cause to be made a Coin, to pass current there between the people of those several Colonies, for the more Ease of Traffick and Bargaining between and amongst them and the Natives there, of such Metal, and in such Manner and Form, as the said several Councils there shall limit and appoint.

And we do likewise, for Us, our Heirs, and Successors, by these Presents, give full Power and Authority to the said Sir *Thomas Gates,* Sir *George Somers, Richard Hackluit, Edward-Maria Wingfield, Thomas Hanham, Ralegh Gilbert, William Parker,* and *George Popham,* and to every of them, and to the said several Companies, Plantations, and Colonies, that they, and every of them, shall and may, at all and every time and times hereafter, have, take, and lead in the said Voyage, and for and towards the said several Plantations, and Colonies, and to travel thitherward, and to abide and inhabit there, in every the said Colonies and Plantations, such and so many of our Subjects, as shall willingly accompany them or any of them, in the said Voyages and Plantations; With sufficient Shipping, and Furniture of Armour, Weapons, Ordinance, Powder, Victual, and all other things, necessary for the said Plantations, and for their Use and Defence there: Provided always, that none of the said Persons be such, as shall hereafter be specially restrained by Us, our Heirs, or Successors.

Moreover, we do, by these Presents, for Us, our Heirs, and Successors Give and grant License unto the said Sir *Thomas Gates,* Sir *George Somers, Richard Hackluit, Edward-Maria Wingfield, Thomas Hanham, Ralegh Gilbert, William Parker,* and *George Popham,* and to every of the said Colonies, that they, and every of them, shall and may, from time to time, and at all times forever hereafter, for their several Defences, encounter, expulse, repel, and resist, as well by Sea as by Land, by all Ways and Means whatsoever, all and every such Person and Persons, as without the special License of the said several Colonies and Plantations, shall attempt to inhabit within the said several Precincts and Limits of the said several Colonies and Plantations, or any of them, or that shall enterprise or attempt, at any time hereafter, the Hurt, Detriment, or Annoyance, of the said several Colonies or Plantations:

Giving and granting, by these Presents, unto the said Sir *Thomas Gates,* Sir *George Somers, Richard Hackluit, Edward-Maria Wingfield,* and their Associates of the said first Colony, and unto the said *Thomas Hankam, Ralegh Gilbert, William Parker,* and *George Popham,* and their Associates of the said second Colony, and to every of them, from time to time, and at all times for ever hereafter, Power and Authority to take and surprise, by all Ways and Means whatsoever, all and every Person and Persons, with their Ships, Vessels, Goods and other Furniture, which shall be found trafficking, into any Harbour of Harbours, Creek or Creeks, or Place, within the Limits or Precincts of the said several Colonies and Plantations, not being of the same Colony, until such time, as they, being of any Realms, or Dominions under our Obedience, shall pay, or agree to pay, to the Hands of the Treasurer of that Colony, within whose Limits and Precincts they shall so traffick, two and a half upon every Hundred, of any thing, so by them trafficked, bought, or sold; And being Strangers, and not Subjects under our Obeysance, until they shall pay five upon every Hundred, of such Wares and Merchandise, as they shall traffick, buy, or sell, within the Precincts of the said several Colonies, wherein they shall so traffick, buy, or sell, as aforesaid; Which Sums of Money, or Benefit, as aforesaid, for and during the Space of one and twenty Years, next ensuing the Date hereof, shall be wholly employed to the Use, Benefit, and Behoof of the said several Plantations, where such Traffick shall be made; And after the said one and twenty Years ended, the same shall be taken to the Use of Us, our Heirs, and Successors, by such Officers and Ministers as by Us, our Heirs, and Successors, shall be thereunto assigned or appointed.

And we do further, by these Presents, for Us, our Heirs, and Successors, Give and grant unto the said Sir *Thomas Gates,* Sir *George Somers, Richard Hackluit,* and

Edward- Maria Wingfield, and to their Associates of the said first Colony and Plantation, and to the said *Thomas Hanham, Ralegh Gilbert, William Parker,* and *George Popham,* and their Associates of the said second Colony and Plantation, that they, and every of them, by their Deputies, Ministers, and Factors, may transport the Goods, Chattels, Armour, Munition, and Furniture, needful to be used by them, for their said Apparel, Food, Defence, or otherwise in Respect of the said Plantations, out of our Realms of *England* and *Ireland,* and all other or Dominions, from time to time, for and during the Time of seven Years, next ensuing the Date hereof, for the better Relief of the said several Colonies and Plantations, without any Customs, Subsidy, or other Duty, unto Us, our Heirs, or Successors, to be yielded or payed for the same.

Also we do, for Us, our Heirs, and Successors, Declare, by these Presents, that all and every the Persons being our Subjects, which shall dwell and inhabit within every or any of the said several Colonies and Plantations, and every of their children, which shall happen to be born within any of the Limits and Precincts of the said several Colonies and Plantations, shall have and enjoy all Liberties, Franchises, and Immunities, within any of our other Dominions, to all Intents and Purposes, as if they had been abiding and born, within this our Realm of *England,* or any other of our said Dominions.

Moreover, our gracious Will and Pleasure is, and we do, by these Presents, for Us, our Heirs, and Successors, declare and set forth, that if any Person or Persons, which shall be of any of the said Colonies and Plantations, or any other which shall traffick to the said Colonies and Plantations, or any of them, shall, at any time or times hereafter, transport any Wares, Merchandises, or Commodities, out of any of our Dominions, with a Pretence to land, sell, or otherwise dispose of the same, within any the Limits and Precincts of any of the said Colonies and Plantations, and yet nevertheless, being at Sea, or after he hath landed the same within any of the said Colonies and Plantations, shall carry the same into any other Foreign Country, with a Purpose there to sell or dispose of the same, without the Licence of Us, our Heirs, and Successors, in that Behalf first had and obtained; That then, all the Goods and Chattels of such Person or Persons, so offending and transporting, together with the said Ship or Vessel, wherein such Transportation was made, shall be forfeited to Us, our Heirs, and Successors.

Provided always, and our Will and Pleasure is, and we do hereby declare to all Christian Kings, Princes, and States, that if any Person or Persons which shall hereafter be of any of the said several Colonies and Plantations, or any other, by his, their, or any of their Licence and Appointment, shall, at any Time or Times hereafter, rob or spoil, by Sea or Land, or do any Act of unjust and unlawful Hostility to any the Subjects of Us, our Heirs, or Successors, or any the Subjects of any King, Prince, Ruler, Governor, or State, being then in League or Amitie with Us, our Heirs, or Successors, and that upon such Injury, or upon just Complaint of such Prince, Ruler, Governor, or State, or their Subjects, We, our Heirs, or Successors, shall make open Proclamation, within any of the Ports of our Realm of *England,* commodious for that purpose, That the said Person or Persons, having committed any such Robbery, or Spoil, shall within the term to be limited by such Proclamations, make full Restitution or Satisfaction of all such Injuries done, so as the said Princes, or others so complaining, may hold themselves fully satisfied and contented; And, that if the said Person or Persons, having committed such Robbery or Spoil, shall not make, or cause to be made Satisfaction accordingly, within such Time so to be limited, That then it shall be lawful to Us, our Heirs, and Successors, to put the said Person or Persons, having committed such Robbery or Spoil, and their Procurers, Abettors, and Comforters, out of our Allegiance and Protection; And that it shall be lawful and free, for all Princes, and others to pursue with hostility the said offenders, and every of them, and their and every of their Procurers, Aiders, abettors, and comforters, in that behalf.

And finally, we do for Us, our Heirs, and Successors, Grant and agree, to and with the said Sir *Thomas Gates,* Sir *George Somers, Richard Hackluit, Edward-Maria Wingfield,* and all others of the said first colony, that We, our Heirs, and Successors, upon Petition in that Behalf to be made, shall, by Letters Patent under the Great Seal of *England,* Give and Grant, unto such Persons, their Heirs and Assigns, as the Council of that Colony, or the most part of them, shall, for that Purpose, nominate and assign all the Lands, Tenements, and Hereditaments, which shall be within the Precincts limited for that Colony, as is aforesaid, To be holden of Us, our Heirs, and Successors, as of our Manor at *East-Greenwich,* in the County of *Kent,* in free and common Soccage only, and not in Capite:

And do in like Manner, Grant and Agree, for Us, our Heirs, and Successors, to and with the said *Thomas Hanham, Ralegh Gilbert, William Parker,* and *George Popham,* and all others of the said second Colony, That We, our Heirs, and Successors, upon Petition in that Behalf to be made, shall, by Letters-Patent, under the Great Seal of *England,* Give and Grant, unto such Persons, their Heirs, and Assigns, as the Council of that Colony, or the most Part of them, shall for that Purpose nominate and assign, all the Lands, Tenements, and Hereditaments, which shall be within the Precincts limited for that Colony, as is aforesaid. To be holden of Us, our Heirs, and Successors, as of our Manor of *East-Greenwich,* in the County of *Kent,* in free and common Soccage only, and not in Capite:

All which Lands, Tenements, and Hereditaments, so to be passed by the said several Letters- Patent, shall be sufficient Assurance from the said Patentees, so distributed and divided amongst the Undertakers for the Plantation of the said several Colonies, and such as shall make their Plantations in either of the said several Colonies, in such Manner and Form, and for such Estates, as shall be ordered and set down by the Council of the said Colony, or the most part of them, respectively, within which the same Lands, Tenements, and Hereditaments shall lye or be; Although express Mention of the true yearly Value or Certainty of the Premises, or any of them, or of any other Gifts or Grants, by Us or any of our Progenitors or Predecessors, to the aforesaid Sir *Thomas Gates,* Knt. Sir *George Somers,* Knt. *Richard Hackluit, Edward-Maria Wingfield, Thomas Hanham, Ralegh Gilbert, William Parker,* and *George Popham,* or any of them, heretofore made, in these Presents, is not made; Or any Statute, Act, Ordinance, or Provision, Proclamation, or Restraint, to the contrary hereof had, made, ordained, or any other Thing, Cause, or Matter whatsoever, in any wise notwithstanding. In Witness whereof, we have caused these our Letters to be made Patents; Witness Ourself at *Westminster,* the tenth Day of *April,* in the fourth Year of our Reign of *England, France,* and *Ireland,* and of *Scotland* the nine and thirtieth.

Lukin *Per breve de privato Sigillo.*

Source:

Documents Illustrative of American History, 1606–1863, with introductions and references by Howard W. Preston. New York: G. P. Putnam's Sons, 1886.

Virginia Company of London, Instructions for the Virginia Colony, 1606

In the early 17th century, after the failure of colonization efforts by Humphrey Gilbert and Sir Walter Raleigh, England turned away from granting liberal land patents to individuals. Joint-stock companies, the forerunners of modern corporations, were now employed to settle and turn a profit in England's new lands. One of the first of these was the Virginia Company of London, chartered by King James I in 1606. The Instructions below, written by earlier colonists (Richard Hakluyt, the younger, is thought to be one of the authors), were meant to serve as a guide for the new colonists. They were also meant to ensure that the colonists pursued the company's two main objectives: trade and profit. Colonists were instructed to look for a northwest passage to the spice-rich East and to obtain gold, silver, and other precious metals, such as copper, from either the native inhabitants or through their own explorations.

As we doubt not but you will have especial care to observe the ordinances set down by the King's Majesty and delivered unto you under the Privy Seal; so for your better directions upon your first landing we have thought good to recommend unto your care these instructions and articles following.

When it shall please God to send you on the coast of Virginia, you shall do your best endeavour to find out a safe port in the entrance of some navigable river, making choice of such a one as runneth farthest into the land, and if you happen to discover divers portable rivers, and amongst them any one that hath two main branches, if the difference be not great, make choice of that which bendeth most toward the North-West for that way you shall soonest find the other sea.

When you have made choice of the river on which you mean to settle, be not hasty in landing your victuals and munitions; but first let Captain Newport discover how far that river may be found navigable, that you make election of the strongest, most wholesome and fertile place; for if you make many removes, besides the loss of time, you shall greatly spoil your victuals and your caske, and with great pain transport it in small boats.

But if you choose your place so far up as a bark of fifty tuns will float, then you may lay all your provisions ashore with ease, and the better receive the trade of all the countries about you in the land; and such a place you may perchance find a hundred miles from the river's mouth, and the further up the better. For if you sit down near the entrance, except it be in some island that is strong by nature, an enemy that may approach you on even ground, may easily pull you out; and if he be driven to seek you a hundred miles [in] the land in boats, you shall from both sides of the river where it is narrowest, so beat them with your muskets as they shall never be able to prevail against you.

And to the end that you be not surprised as the French were in Florida by Melindus, and the Spaniard in the same place by the French, you shall do well to make this double provision. First, erect a little stoure at the mouth of the river that may lodge some ten men; with whom you shall leave a light boat, that when any fleet shall be in sight, they may come with speed to give you warning. Secondly, you must in no case suffer any of the native people of the country to inhabit between you and the sea coast; for you cannot carry yourselves so towards them, but they will grow discontented with your habitation, and be ready to guide and assist any nation that shall come to

invade you; and if you neglect this, you neglect your safety.

When you have discovered as far up the river as you mean to plant yourselves, and landed your victuals and munitions; to the end that every man may know his charge, you shall do well to divide your six score men into three parts; whereof one party of them you may appoint to fortifie and build, of which your first work must be your storehouse for victuals; the other you may imploy in preparing your ground and sowing your corn and roots; the other ten of these forty you must leave as centinel at the haven1s mouth. The other forty you may imploy for two months in discovery of the river above you, and on the country about you; which charge Captain Newport and Captain Gosnold may undertake of these forty discoverers. When they do espie any high lands or hills, Captain Gosnold may take twenty of the company to cross over the lands, and carrying a half dozen pickaxes to try if they can find any minerals. The other twenty may go on by river, and pitch up boughs upon the bank's side, by which the other boats shall follow them by the same turnings. You may also take with them a wherry, such as is used here in the Thames; by which you may send back to the President for supply of munition or any other want, that you may not be driven to return for every small defect.

You must observe if you can, whether the river on which you plant doth spring out of mountains or out of lakes. If it be out of any lake, the passage to the other sea will be more easy, and [it] is like enough, that out of the same lake you shall find some spring which run[s] the contrary way towards the East India Sea; for the great and famous rivers of Volga, Tan[a]is and Dwina have three heads near joynd; and yet the one falleth into the Caspian Sea, the other into the Euxine Sea, and the third into the Paelonian Sea. In all your passages you must have great care not to offend the naturals [natives], if you can eschew it; and imploy some few of your company to trade with them for corn and all other . . . victuals if you have any; and this you must do before that they perceive you mean to plant among them; for not being sure how your own seed corn will prosper the first year, to avoid the danger of famine, use and endeavour to store yourselves of the country corn.

Your discoverers that pass over land with hired guides, must look well to them that they slip not from them: and for more assurance, let them take a compass with them, and write down how far they go upon every point of the compass; for that country having no way nor path, if that your guides run from you in the great woods or desert, you shall hardly ever find a passage back.

And how weary soever your soldiers be, let them never trust the country people with the carriage of their weapons; for if they run from you with your shott, which they only fear, they will easily kill them all with their arrows. And whensoever any of yours shoots before them, be sure they may be chosen out of your best marksmen; for if they see your learners miss what they aim at, they will think the weapon not so terrible, and thereby will be bould to assault you.

Above all things, do not advertize the killing of any of your men, that the country people may know it; if they perceive that they are but common men, and that with the loss of many of theirs they diminish any part of yours, they will make many adventures upon you. If the country be populous, you shall do well also, not to let them see or know of your sick men, if you have any; which may also encourage them to many enterprizes.

You must take especial care that you choose a seat for habitation that shall not be over burthened with woods near your town; for all the men you have, shall not he able to cleanse twenty acres a year; besides that it may serve for a covert for your enemies round about.

Neither must you plant in a low or moist place, because it will prove unhealthfull. You shall judge of the good air by the people; for some part of that coast where the lands are low, have their people blear eyed, and with swollen bellies and legs; but if the naturals he strong and clean made, it is a true sign of a wholesome soil.

You must take order to draw up the pinnace that is left with you, under the fort: and take her sails and anchors ashore, all but a small kedge to ride by; least some ill-dispositioned persons slip away with her.

You must take care that your marriners that go for wages, do not mar your trade; for those that mind not to inhabite, for a little gain will debase the estimation of exchange, and hinder the trade for ever after; and therefore you shall not admit or suffer any person whatsoever, other than such as shall be appointed by the President and Counsel there, to buy any merchandizes or other things whatsoever.

It were necessary that all your carpenters and other such like workmen about building do first build your storehouse and those other rooms of publick and necessary use before any house be set up for any private person: and though the workman may belong to any private persons yet let them all work together first for the company and then for private men.

And seeing order is at the same price with confusion, it shall be adviseably done to set your houses even and by a line, that your street may have a good breadth, and be carried square about your market place and every street's end opening into it; that from thence, with a few field pieces, you may command every street throughout; which market place you may also fortify if you think it needfull.

You shall do well to send a perfect relation by Captaine Newport of all that is done, what height you are seated, how far into the land, what commodities you find, what soil, woods and their several kinds, and so of all other things else to advertise particularly; and to suffer no man to return but by pasport from the President and Counsel, nor to write any letter of anything that may discourage others.

Lastly and chiefly the way to prosper and achieve good success is to make yourselves all of one mind for the good of your country and your own, and to serve and fear God the Giver of all Goodness, for every plantation which our Heavenly Father hath not planted shall be rooted out.

Source:
University of Kansas. Available on-line. URL: www.ku.edu/carrie/docs/texts/virginia_instructions.html. Accessed October 2003.

Second Charter of Virginia, 1609

Second charter instituted by King James I on May 23, 1609, concerning the Virginia Company, now settled in Jamestown. Affairs of the Virginia Company were very badly managed in the first three years of its existence. This charter made fundamental changes in the first charter by once again splitting up the London and Plymouth Companies. In addition, the many royal councils of the first charter were replaced by one company council. Most importantly, control of the colony was put in the hands of the treasurer and his council, to be known as the "Treasurer and Company of Adventurers and Planters of the City of London for the first Colony in Virginia."

King James I endowed a third charter on March 12, 1612, giving the Virginia Company jurisdiction of the island of Bermuda and any other islands situated in the ocean bordering the coast of Virginia. This third charter also provided the company with a more democratic government, giving them a higher degree of independence. This included the council meeting once a week for better order and government, as well as allowing a group of at least five members of the council, always including the treasurer or his deputy, to be considered a sufficient court for handling all matters within the colony. Bermuda was subsequently sold, and this charter was made null when Virginia became a royal colony in 1624.

James, by the Grace of God, King of *England, Scotland, France,* and *Ireland,* Defender of the Faith, &c. To all, to whom these Presents shall come, Greeting. Whereas, at the humble Suit and Request of sundry our loving and well-disposed Subjects, intending to deduce a Colony, and to make Habitation and Plantation of sundry our People in that Part of *America* commonly called Virginia, and other Parts and Territories in *America,* either appertaining unto Us, or which are not actually possessed of any *Christian* Prince of People, within certain Bounds and Regions, We have formerly, by our Letters patents, bearing Date the tenth Day of *April,* in the fourth Year of our Reign of *England, France,* and *Ireland,* and of *Scotland* the nine and thirtieth, Granted to Sir *Thomas Gates,* Sir *George Somers,* and others, for the more speedy Accomplishment of the said Plantation and Habitation, that they should divide themselves into two Colonies (the one consisting of divers Knights, Gentlemen, Merchants, and others, or our City of *London,* called the First Colony; And the other consisting of divers Knights, Gentlemen, and others, of our Cities of *Bristol, Exeter,* and Town of *Plimouth,* and other Places, called the Second Colony). And have yielded and granted many and sundry Privileges and Liberties to each Colony, for their quiet settling and good Government therein, as by the said Letters-patents more at large appeareth.

Now, forasmuch as divers and sundry of our loving Subjects, as well Adventurers, as Planters, of the said first Colony, which have already engaged themselves in furthering the Business of the said Colony and Plantation, and do further intend, by the Assistance of Almighty God, to prosecute the same to a happy End, have of late been humble Suitors unto Us, that (in Respect of their great Charges and the Adventure of many of their Lives, which they have hazarded in the said Discovery and Plantation of the said Country) We would be pleased to grant them a further Enlargement and Explanation of the said Grant, Privileges, and Liberties, and that such Counsellors, and other Officers, may be appointed amongst them, to manage and direct their affairs, as are willing and ready to adventure with them, as also whose Dwellings are not so far remote from the City of *London* , but they may, at convenient Times, be ready at Hand, to give their Advice and Assistance, upon all Occasions requisite.

We greatly affecting the effectual Prosecution and happy success of the said Plantation, and commending their good desires therein, for their further Encouragement in accomplishing so excellent a Work, much pleasing to God, and profitable to our Kingdom, do of our especial Grace, and certain Knowledge, and mere Motion, for Us, our Heirs, and Successors, Give, Grant, and Confirm, to our trusty and well-beloved Subjects, Robert, Earl of Salisbury, (and others) . . . and to such and so many as they do, or shall hereafter admit to be joined with them, in the form hereafter in these presents expressed, whether they go in their Persons to be Planters there in the said Plantation, or whether they go not, but adventure their monies, goods, or Chattles, that they shall be one Body or Commonalty per-

petual, and shall have perpetual Succession and one common Seal to serve for the said Body or Commonalty, and that they and their Successors shall be known, called, and incorporated by the Name of *The Treasurer and Company of Adventures and Planters of the City of London, for the first Colony in Virginia.* And that they and their Successors shall be from henceforth forever enabled to take, acquire, and purchase by the Name aforesaid (Licence for the same from Us, our Heirs, and Successors, first had and obtained) any Manner of Lands, Tenements, and Hereditaments, Goods and Chattles, within our Realm of England, and Dominion of Wales. And that they, and their Successors, shall likewise be enabled by the Name aforesaid, to plead and be impleaded, before any of our Judges or Justices in any of our Courts, and in any Actions or Suits whatsoever. And we do also of our special Grace, certain Knowledge, and mere Motion, give, grant and confirm, unto the said Treasurer and Company, and their Successors, under the Reservations, Limitations, and Declarations hereafter expressed, all those Lands, Countries, and Territories, situate, lying, and being in that Part of *American,* called *Virginia,* from the Point of Land, called Cape or *Point Comfort,* all along the Sea Coast to the Northward, two hundred miles, and from the said Point of *Cape Comfort,* all along the Sea Coast to the Southward, two hundred Miles, and all that Space and Circuit of Land, lying from the Sea Coast of the Precinct aforesaid, up into the Land throughout from Sea to Sea, West and Northwest; And also all the Islands lying within one hundred Miles along the Coast of both Seas of the Precinct aforesaid.

And forasmuch as the good and prosperous Success of the said Plantation, cannot but chiefly depend next under the Blessing of God, and the Support of our Royal Authority, upon the provident and good Direction of the whole Enterprise, by a careful and understanding Council, and that it is not convenient, that all the Adventures shall be so often drawn to meet and assemble, as shall be requisite for them to have Meetings and Conference about the Affairs thereof; Therefore we do ordain, establish and confirm, that there shall be perpetually one Council here resident, according to the Tenour of our former Letters-Patents; Which Council shall have a Seal for the better Government and Administration of the said Plantation, besides the legal Seal of the Company or Corporation, as in our former Letters-Patents is also expressed.

And the said Thomas Smith, We do ordain to be Treasurer of the said Company; which Treasurer shall have Authority to give Order for the Warning of the Council, and summoning the Company to their Courts and Meetings. And the said Council and Treasurer, or any of them shall be from henceforth nominated, chosen, continued, displaced, changed, altered and supplied, as Death, or other several Occasions shall require, out of the Company of the said Adventurers, by the Voice of the greater part of the said Company and Adventurers, in their Assembly for that Purpose: Provided always, That every Counsellor so newly elected, shall be presented to the Lord Chancellor of *England,* or to the Lord High Treasurer of *England,* or to the Lord Chamberlain of the Household of Us, our Heirs and Successors for the Time being, to take his Oath of a Counsellor to Us, our Heirs and Successors, for the said Company of Adventurers and Colony in *Virginia.*

And further, of our special Grace, certain Knowledge, and mere Motion, for Us, our Heirs and Successors, we do, by these Presents, Give and Grant full Power and Authority to our said Council here resident, as well at this present time, as hereafter from time to time, to nominate, make, constitute, ordain and confirm, by such Name or Names, Stile or Stiles, as to them shall seem good, And likewise to revoke, discharge, change, and alter, as well all and singular Governors, Officers, and Ministers, which already have been made, as also which hereafter shall be by them thought fit and needful to be made or used for the Government of the said Colony and Plantation: And also to make, ordain, and establish all Manner of Orders, Laws, Directions, Instructions, Forms and Ceremonies of Government and Magistracy, fit and necessary for and concerning the Government of the said Colony and Plantation; And the same, at all Times hereafter, to abrogate, revoke, or change, not only within the Precincts of the said Colony, but also upon the Seas, in going and coming to and from the said Colony, as they in their good Discretion, shall think to be fittest for the Good of the Adventurers and inhabitants there.

And we do further by these presents Ordain and establish, that the said Treasurer and Council here resident, and their successors or any four of them being assembled (the Treasurer being one) shall from time to time have full Power and Authority to admit and receive any other Person into their Company, Corporation, and Freedom; And further in a General Assembly of Adventurers, with the consent of the greater part upon good Cause, to disfranchise and put out any Person or Persons out of the said Freedom or Company.

And forasmuch as it shall be necessary for all such our loving Subject as shall inhabit within the said Precincts of *Virginia* aforesaid, to determine to live together in the Fear and true Worship of Almighty God, Christian Peace and Civil Quietness each with other, whereby every one may with more Safety, Pleasure and Profit enjoy that whereunto they shall attain with great Pain and Peril; We for Us, our Heires, and Successors are likewise pleased and contented, and by these Presents do Give and Grant unto the said Treasurer and Company, and their Successors, and to such

Governors, Officers, and Ministers, as shall be by our said Council constituted and appointed according to the Natures and Limits of their Offices and Places respectively, that they shall and may from Time to Time, for every hereafter, within the said Precincts of *Virginia,* or in the way by Sea thither and from thence, have full and absolute Power and Authority to correct, punish, pardon, govern, and rule all such the Subjects of Us, our Heires, and Successors as shall from Time to Time adventure themselves in any Voyage thither, or that shall at any Time hereafter, inhabit in the Precincts and Territories of the said Colony as aforesaid, according to such Orders, Ordinances, Constitutions, Directions, and Instructions, as by our said Council as aforesaid, shall be established; And in Defect thereof in case of Necessity, according to the good Discretion of the said Governor and Officers respectively, as well in Cases capital and criminal, as civil, both Marine and other; So always as the said Statutes, Ordinances and Proceedings as near as conveniently may be, be agreeable to the Laws, Statutes, Government, and Policy of this our Realm of *England.* And we do further of our special Grace, certain Knowledge, and mere Motion, grant, declare, and ordain, that such principal Governor, as from Time to Time shall duly and lawfully be authorized and appointed in Manner and Form in these Presents heretofore expressed, shall have full Power and Authority, to use and exercise Martial Law in Cases of Rebellion or Mutiny, in as large and ample Manner as our Lieutenants in our Counties within this our Realm of *England* have or ought to have, by Force of their Commissions of Lieutenancy.

And lastly, because the principal Effect which we can desire or expect of this Action, is the Conversion and Reduction of the People in those Parts unto the true Worship of God and Christian Religion, in which Respect we should be loath that any Person should be permitted to pass that we suspected to affect the Superstitions of the Church of *Rome,* we do hereby declare, that it is our Will and Pleasure that none be permitted to pass in any Voyage from Time to Time to be made into the said Country, but such as first shall have taken the Oath of Supremacy; For which Purpose, we do by these Presents give full Power and Authority to the Treasurer for the Time being, and any three of the Council, to tender and exhibit the said Oath, to all such Persons as shall at any Time be sent and employed in the said Voyage. Although express Mention of true yearly Value or Certainty of the Premises, or any of them, or of any other Gifts or Grants by Us, or any of our Progenitors or Predecessors to the aforesaid Treasurer and Company heretofore made in these Presents, is not made; Or any Act, Statute, Ordinance, Provision, Proclamation, or Restraint, to the contrary hereof had, made, ordained, or provided, or any other Thing, Cause, or Matter whatsoever in any wise notwithstanding. In Witness whereof, We have caused these our Letters to be made Patent. Witness ourself at *Westminster*, the 23d Day of *May*, in the seventh Year of our Reign of *England, France*, and *Ireland*, and of Scotland the °°°°

Per Ipsum Regem. Lukin.

See also VIRGINIA COMPANY OF LONDON, INSTRUCTIONS FOR THE VIRGINIA COLONY, 1606.

Source:

Documents Illustrative of American History, 1606–1863, with introductions and references by Howard W. Preston. New York: G. P. Putnam's Sons, 1886.

Leyden Agreement of 1618

An affirmation of loyalty to King James I of England and religious orthodoxy attached to an application for a Virginia land patent. Issued in 1618, the Leyden Agreement was written by religious leaders of the Leyden (Netherlands) congregation of separatists. The group received a patent to settle in the colonies from the Virginia Company.

Seven Artikes which ye Church of Leyden sent to ye Counsell of England to bee considered of in respeckt of their judgements occationed about theer going to Virginia Anno 1618

1. To ye confession of fayth published in ye name of ye Church of England & to every artikell theerof wee do with ye reformed churches wheer wee live & also els where assent wholy.

2. As wee do acknolidg ye docktryne of fayth theer tawght so do wee ye fruites and effeckts of ye same docktryne to ye begetting of saving fayth in thousands in ye land (conformistes and reformistes as ye are called) wth whom also as wth our bretheren we do desyer to keepe speritu-all communion in peace and will pracktis in our parts all lawfull thinges.

3. The Kings Majesty wee acknoledge for Supreame Governer in his Dominion in all causes and over all parsons, and ye none maye decklyne or apeale from his authority or judgement in any cause whatsoever, byt y in all thinges obedience is dewe unto him, ether active, if ye thing commanded be not agaynst God's woord, or passive yf itt bee, except pardon can bee obtayned.

4. Wee judg itt lawfull for his Majesty to apoynt bishops; civill overseers, or officers in awthoryty onder hime, in ye severall provinces, dioses, congregations or parrishes to oversee ye Churches and governe them civilly according to ye Lawes of ye Land, untto whom ye ar in all thinges to

give an account & by them to bee ordered according to Godlynes.

5. The authoryty of ye present bishops in ye Land wee do acknowlidg so far forth as ye same is indeed derived from his Majesty untto them and as ye proseed in his name, whom we will also theerein honor in all things and hime in them.

6. Wee beleeve yt no sinod, classes, convocation or assembly of Ecclesiasticall officers hath any power or awthoryty att all but as ye same by ye Majestraet geven unto them.

7. And lastly, wee desyer to geve untto all Superiors dew honnor to preserve ye untiy of ye speritt wth all ye feare God, to have peace wth all men what in us lyeth & wheerin wee err to bee instructed by any.

Subscribed by John Robinson and Willyam Bruster.

Source:

Henry Steele Commager, ed. *Documents of American History*. New York: F.S. Crofts & Co., 1934.

James I,
Charter of New England, 1620

This charter, granted in 1620 by England's King James I, named several English lords and noblemen to a body known as the Council of New England. This council was incorporated to establish a colony in the area roughly equivalent to modern-day New England. The council was invested with many powers, including the right to trade, grant lands, raise armies, make laws, and appoint officials. In effect, the charter was setting up a feudal system of government that granted fiefdoms to the various council members. This plan was complicated by infighting among the council members over territorial borders and the difficulties associated with ruling a mini-empire without a compelling physical presence, since the lords chose to remain in England. The separatist Pilgrims in Plymouth and the middle-class merchant Puritans who founded the Massachusetts Bay Colony eventually established their own rights to the land they settled. In 1629 New England Council member Robert, earl of Warwick, surrendered part of the 1620 patent to William Bradford, head of the Plymouth Colony. The Massachusetts Bay Company, wishing to avoid the entanglements of the original charter, bypassed the Council of New England altogether and took its own charter from the crown in 1629.

JAMES, by the Grace of God, King of England, Scotland, France and Ireland, Defender of the Faith, &c. to all whom these Presents shall come, Greeting, Whereas, upon the humble Petition of divers of our well disposed

Subjects, that intended to make several Plantations in the Parts of America, between the Degrees of thirty-ffoure and ffourty-five; We according to our princely Inclination, favouring much their worthy Disposition, in Hope thereby to advance the in Largement of Christian Religion, to the Glory of God Almighty, as also by that Meanes to streatch out the Bounds of our Dominions, and to replenish those Deserts with People governed by Lawes and Magistrates, for the peaceable Commerce of all, that in time to come shall have occasion to traffique into those Territoryes, granted unto Sir Thomas Gates, Sir George Somers, Knights, Thomas Hanson, and Raleigh Gilbert, Esquires, and of their Associates, for the more speedy Accomplishment thereof, by our Letters-Pattent, bearing Date the Tenth Day of Aprill, in the Fourth Year of our Reign of England, France and Ireland, and of Scotland the ffourtieth, free Liberty to divide themselves into two several Collonyes; the one called the first Collonye, to be undertaken and advanced by certain Knights, Gentlemen, and Merchants, in and about our Cyty of London; the other called the Second Collonye, to be undertaken and advanced by certaine Knights, Gentlemen, and Merchants, and their associates, in and about our Citties of Bristol, Exon, and our Towne of Plymouth, and other Places, as in and by our said Letters-Pattents, amongst other Things more att large it doth and may appears. And whereas, since that Time, upon the humble Petition of the said Adventurers and Planters of the said first Collonye, We have been graciously pleased to make them one distinct and entire Body by themselves, giving unto them their distinct Lymitts and Bounds, and have upon their like humble Request, granted unto them divers Liberties, Priveliges, Enlargements, and Immunityes, as in and by our severall Letters-Patents it doth and may more at large appears. Now forasmuch as We have been in like Manner humbly petitioned unto by our trusty and well beloved Servant, Sir fferdinando Gorges, Knight, Captain of our ffort and Island by Plymouth, and by certain the principal Knights and Gentlemen Adventurers of the said Second Collonye, and by divers other Persons of Quality, who now intend to be their Associates, divers of which have been at great and extraordinary Charge, and sustained many Losses in seeking and discovering a Place fitt and convenient to lay the Foundation of a hopeful Plantation, and have divers Years past by God's Assistance, and their own endeavours, taken actual Possession of the Continent hereafter mentioned, in our Name and to our Use, as Sovereign Lord thereof, and have settled already some of our People in Places agreeable to their Desires in those Parts, and in Confidence of prosperous Success therein, by the Continuance of God's Devine Blessing, and our Royall Permission, have resolved in a more plentifull and effectual Manner to prosecute the same, and to that Purpose and Intent have desired of Us, for their better Encouragement and Satisfaction herein, and that they may avoide all Confusion, Questions, or Differences between themselves, and those of the said first Collonye, We would likewise be graciously pleased to make certaine Adventurers, intending to erect and. establish fishery, Trade, and Plantacion, within the Territoryes, Precincts, and Lymitts of the said second Colony, and their Successors, one several distinct and entire Body, and to grant unto them, such Estate, Liberties, Priveliges, Enlargements, and Immunityes there, as in these our Letters-Pattents hereafter particularly expressed and declared. And for asmuch as We have been certainly given to understand by divers of our good Subjects, that have for these many Years past frequented those Coasts and Territoryes, between the Degrees of Fourty and Fourty-Eight, that there is noe other the Subjects of any Christian King or State, by any Authority from their Soveraignes, Lords, or Princes, actually in Possession of any of the said Lands or Precincts, whereby any Right, Claim, Interest, or Title, may, might, or ought by that Meanes accrue, belong, or appertaine unto them, or any of them. And also for that We have been further given certainly to knowe, that within these late Yeares there hath by God's Visitation reigned a wonderfull Plague, together with many horrible Slaugthers, and Murthers, committed amoungst the Sauages and brutish People there, heertofore inhabiting, in a Manner to the utter Destruction, Deuastacion, and Depopulacion of that whole Territorye, so that there is not left for many Leagues together in a Manner, any that doe claime or challenge any Kind of Interests therein, nor any other Superiour Lord or Souveraigne to make Claime "hereunto, whereby We in our Judgment are persuaded and satisfied that the appointed Time is come in which Almighty God in his great Goodness and Bountie towards Us and our People, hath thought fitt and determined, that those large and goodly Territoryes, deserted as it were by their naturall Inhabitants, should be possessed and enjoyed by such of our Subjects and People as heertofore have and hereafter shall by his Mercie and Favour, and by his Powerfull Arme, be directed and conducted thither. In Contemplacion and serious Consideracion whereof, Wee have thougt it fitt according to our Kingly Duty, soe much as in Us lyeth, to second and followe God's sacred Will, rendering reverend Thanks to his Divine Majestie for his gracious favour in laying open and revealing the same unto us, before any other Christian Prince or State, by which Meanes without Offence, and as We trust to his Glory, Wee may with Boldness go on to the settling of soe hopefull a Work, which tendeth to the reducing and Conversion of such Sauages as remaine wandering in Desolacion and Distress, to Civil Societie and Christian Religion, to the Inlargement of our own Dominions, and the Aduancement of the Fortunes of such of our good Subjects as shall willingly intresse themselves in the said Imployment, to whom We cannot but give singular Commendations for their soe worthy Intention and Enterprize; Wee therefore, of our especiall Grace, mere Motion, and certaine Knowledge, by the Aduice of the Lords and others of our Priuy Councell have for Us, our Heyrs and Successors, graunted, ordained, and established, and in and by these Presents, Do for Us, our Heirs and Successors, grant, ordaine and establish, that all that Circuit, Continent, Precincts, and Limitts in America, lying and being in Breadth from Fourty Degrees of Northerly Latitude, from the Equnoctiall Line, to Fourty-eight Degrees of the said Northerly Latitude, and in length by all the Breadth aforesaid throughout the Maine Land, from Sea to Sea, with all the Seas, Rivers, Islands, Creekes, Inletts, Ports, and Havens, within the Degrees, Precincts and Limitts of the said Latitude and Longitude, shall be the Limitts; and Bounds, and Precints of the second Collony: And to the End that the said Territoryes may forever hereafter be more particularly and certainly known and distinguished, our Will and Pleasure is, that the sa.ne shall from henceforth be nominated, termed, and called by the Name of New-England, in America; and by that Name of New-England in America, the said Circuit, Precinct, Limitt, Continent, Islands, and Places in America, aforesaid, We do by these Presents, for Us, our Heyrs and Successors, name, call, erect, found and establish, and by that Name to have Continuance for ever.

And for the better Plantacion, ruling, and governing of the aforesaid New-England, in America, We will, ordaine, constitute, assigne, limits and appoint, and for Us, our Heyrs and Successors, Wee, by the Advice of the Lords and others of the said priuie Councill, do by these Presents ordaine, constitute, limett, and appoint, that from henceforth, there shall be for ever hereafter, in our Towne of Plymouth, in the County of Devon, one Body politicque and corporate, which shall have perpetuall Succession, which shall consist of the Number of fourtie Persons, and no more, which shall be, and shall be called and knowne by the Name the Councill established at Plymouth, in the County of Devon for the planting, ruling, ordering, and governing of New-England, in America; and for that Purpose Wee have, at and by the Nomination and Request of the said Petitioners, granted, ordained, established, and confirmed; and by these Presents, for Us, our Heyres and Successors, doe grant, ordaine, establish, and confirme, our right trusty and right well beloved Cosins and Councillors Lodovick, Duke of Lenox, Lord Steward of our Houshold, George Lord Marquess Buckingham, our High Admiral of England, James Marquess Hamilton, William Earle of Pembrocke, Lord Chamberlaine of our Houshold, Thomas Earl of Arundel, and our right trusty and right well beloved Cosin, William Earl of Hathe, and right trusty and right well beloved Cosin and Councellor, Henry Earle of Southampton, and our right trusty and right well beloved Cousins, William Earle of Salisbury, and Robert Earle of Warwick, and our right trusty and right well beloved John Viscount Haddington, and our right trusty and well beloved Councellor Edward Lord Zouch, Lord Warden of our Cincque Ports, and our trusty and well beloved Edmond Lord Sheffield, Edward Lord Gorges, and our well beloved Sir Edward Seymour, Knight and Barronett, Sir Robert Manselle, Sir Edward Zouch, our Knight Marshall, Sir Dudley Diggs, Sir Thomas Roe, Sir fferdinando Gorges, Sir Francis Popham, Sir John Brook, Sir Thomas Gates, Sir Richard Hawkins, Sir Richard Edgcombe, Sir Allen Apsley, Sir Warwick Hale, Sir Richard Catchmay, Sir John Bourchier, Sir Nathaniel Rich, Sir Edward Giles, Sir Giles Mompesson, and Sir Thomas Wroth, Knights; and our well beloved Matthew Sutcliffe, Dean of Exeter, Robert Heath, Esq; Recorder of our Cittie of London, Henry Bourchier, John Drake, Rawleigh Gilbert, George Chudley, Thomas Hamon, and John Argall, Esquires, to be and in and by these Presents; We do appoint them to be the first modern and present Councill established at Plymouth, in the County of Devon, for the planting, ruling, ordering, and governing of New-England, in America; and that they, and the Suruiuours of them, and such as the Suruluours and Suruinor of them shall, from tyme to tyme elect, and chuse, to make up the aforesaid Number of fourtie Persons, when, and as often as any of them, or any of their Successors shall happen to decease, or to be removed from being of the said Councill, shall be in, and by these Presents, incorporated to have a perpetual Succession for ever, in Deed, Fact, and Name, and shall be one Bodye corporate and politicque; and that those, and such said Persons, and their Successors, and such as shall be elected and chosen to succeed them as aforesaid, shall be, and by these Presents are, and be incorporated, named, and called by the Name of the Councill established at Plymouth, in the County of Devon, for the planting, ruling, and governing of New-England, in America; and them the said Duke of Lenox, Marquess Buckingham, Marquess Hamilton, Earle of Pembroke, Earle of Arundell, Earle of hathe, Earle of Southampton, Earle of Salisbury, Earle of Warwick, Viscount Haddington, Lord Zouch, Lord Sheffield, Lord Gorges, Sir Edward Seymour, Sir Robert Mansell, Sir Edward Zouch, Sir Dudley Diggs, Sir Thomas Roe, Sir fferdinando Gorges, Sir ffrancis Popham, Sir John Brooks, Sir Thomas Gates, Sir Richard Hawkins, Sir Richard Edgcombe, Sir Allen Apsley, Sir Warwick Heale, Sir Richard Catchmay, Sir John Bourchier, Sir Nathaniell Rich, Sir Edward Giles, Sir Giles Mompesson, Sir Thomas Wroth, Knights; Matthew Suttcliffe, Robert Heath, Henry Bourchier, John Drake, Rawleigh Gilbert, George Chudley, Thomas Haymon, and John Argall, Esqrs. and their successors, one Body corporate and politick, in Deed and Name, by the Name of the Councell established att Plymouth, in the County of Devon for the planting, ruling, and governing of New-England, in America. Wee do by these Presents, for Us, our Heyres and Successors, really and fully incorporate, erect, ordaine. name, constitute, and establish, and that by the same Name of the said Councill, they and their Successors for ever hereafter be incorporated, named, and called, and shall by the same Name have perpetual Succession. And further, Wee do hereby for Us, our Heires and Successors, grant unto the said Councill established aft Plymouth, that they and their Successors, by the same Name, be and shall be, and shall continue Persons able and capable in the Law, from time to time, and shall by that Name, of Councill aforesaid, have full Power and Authority, and lawful Capacity and Habilily, as well to purchase, take, hold, receive, enjoy, and to have, and their Successors for ever, any Manors, Lands, Tenements, Rents, Royalties, Privileges, Immunities, Reversions, Annuities, Hereditaments, Goods, and Chattles whatsoever, of or from Us, our Heirs, and Successors, and of or from any other Person or Persons whatsoever, as well in and within this our Realme, of England, as in and within any other Place or Places whatsoever or wheresoever; and the same Manors, Lands, Tenements, and Hereditaments, Goods or Chattles, or any of them, by the same Name to alien and sell, or to do, execute, ordaine and performe all other Matters and Things whatsoever to the said Incorporation and Plantation concerning and-belonging.

And further, our Will and Pleasure is, that the said Councill, for the time being, and their Successors, shall have full Power and lawful authority, by the Name aforesaid, to sue, and be sued; implead, and to be impleaded; answer, and to be answered, unto all Manner of Courts and Places that now are, or hereafter shall be, within this our Realme and elsewhere, as well temporal as spiritual, in all Manner of Suits and Matters whatsoever, and of what Nature or Kinde soever such Suite or Action be or shall be. And our Will and Pleasure is, that the said flourty Persons, or the greater Number of them, shall and may, from time to time, and at any time hereafter, at their owne Will and Pleasure, according to the Laws, Ordinances, and Orders of or by them, or by the greater Part of them, hereafter in Manner and forme in these Presents mentioned, to be agreed upon, to elect and choose amongst themselves one of the said dourty Persons for the Time being, to be President of the said Councill, which President soe elected and chosen, Wee will, shall continue and be President of the said Councill for so long a Time as by the Orders of the said Councill, from time to time to be made, as hereafter is mentioned, shall be thought fitt, and no longer; unto which President, or in his Absence, to any such Person as by the Order of the said Councill shall be thereunto

appointed, Wee do give Authority to give Order for the warning of the said Council, and summoning the Company to their Meetings. And our Will and Pleasure is, that from time to time, when and so often as any of the Councill shall happen to decease, or to be removed from being of the said Councell, that then, and so often, the Survivors of them the said Councill, and no other, or the greater Number of them, who then shall be from time to time left and remaininge, and who shall, or the greater Number of which that shall be assembled at a public Court or Meeting to be held for the said Company, shall elect and choose one or more other Person or Persons to be of the said Councill, and which from time to time shall be of the said Councill, so that the Number of Bounty Persons of the said Councill may from time to time be supplied: Provided always that as well the Persons herein named to be of the said Councill, as every other Councellor hereafter to be elected, shall be prevented Lord Chancellor of England, or to the Lord High Treasurer of England, or to the Lord Chamberlaine of the Household of Us, our Heires and Successors for the Time being, to take his and their Oath and Oathes of a Councellor and Councellors to Us, our Heirs and Successors, for the said Company and Collonye in New-England.

And further, Wee will and grant by these Presents, for Us, our Heires and Successors, unto the said Councill and their Successors, that they and their Successors shall have and enjoy for ever a Common Seale, to be engraver according to their Discretions; and that it shall be lawfull for them to appoint whatever Seale or Seales, they shall think most meete and necessary, either for their Use, as they are one united Body incorporate here, or for the publick of their Gouvernour and Ministers of New-England aforesaid, whereby the Incorporation may or shall scale any Manner of Instrument touching the same Corporation, and the Manors, Lands, Tenements, Rents, Reversions, Annuities, Hereditaments, Goods, Chattles, Affaires, and any other Things belonging unto, or in any wise appertaininge, touching, or concerning the said Councill and their Successors, or concerning the said Corporation and plantation in and by these our Letters-Patents as aforesaid founded, erected, and established.

And Wee do further by these Presents, for Us, our Heires and Successors, grant unto the said Councill and their Successors, that it shall and may be lawfull to and for the said Councill, and their Successors for the Time being, in their discretions, from time to time to admits such and so many Person and Persons to be made free and enabled to trade traffick unto, within, and in New-England aforesaid, and unto every Part and Parcell thereof, or to have, possess, or enjoy, any Lands or Hereditaments in New-England aforesaid, as they shall think fitt, according to the Laws, Orders, Constitutions, and Ordinances, by the said

Councill and their Successors from time to time to be made and established by Virtue of, and according to the true Intent of these Presents, and under such Conditions, Reservations, and agreements as the said Councill shall set downe, order and direct, and not otherwise. And further, of our especiall Grace, certaine Knowlege, and mere Motion, for Us, our Heires and Successors, Wee do by these Presents give and grant full Power and Authority to the said Councill and their Successors, that the said Councill for the Time being, or the greater Part of them, shall and may, from time to time, nominate, make, constitute, ordaine, and confirms by such Name or Names, Style or Styles, as to them shall seeme Good; and likewise to revoke, discharge, change, and alter, as well all and singular, Governors, Officers, and Ministers, which hereafter shall be by them thought fill and needful to be made or used, as well to attend the Business of the said Company here, as for the Government of the said Collony and Plantation, and also to make, ordaine, and establish all Manner of Orders, Laws, Directions, Instructions, Forms, and Ceremonies of Government and Magistracy fitt and necessary for and concerning the Government of the said Collony and Plantation, so always as the same be not contrary to the Laws and Statutes of this our Realme of England, and the same att all Times hereafter to abrogate, revoke, or change, not only within the Precincts of the said Collony, but also upon the Seas in going and coming to and from the said Collony, as they in their good Discretions shall thinke to be fittest for the good of the Adenturers and Inhabitants there.

And Wee do further of our especiall Grace, certaine Knowledge, and mere Motion, grant, declare, and ordain, that such principall Governor, as from time to time shall be authorized and appointed in Manner and Forme in these Presents heretofore expressed, shall haue full Power and Authority to use and exercise marshall Laws in Cases of Rebellion, Insurrection and Mutiny in as large and ample Manner as our Lieutenants in our Counties within our Realme of England have or ought to have by Force of their Commission of Lieutenancy. And for as much as it shall be necessary for all our lovinge Subjects as shall inhabit within the said Precincts of New-England aforesaid, to determine to live together in the Feare and true Worship of Allmighty God, Christian Peace, and civil Quietness, each with other, whereby every one may with more Safety, Pleasure, and Profist, enjoye that whereunto they shall attaine with great Pain and Perill, Wee, for Us, our Heires and Successors, are likewise pleased and contented, and by these Presents do give and grant unto the said Council and their Successors, and to such Governors, Officers, and Ministers, as shall be by the said Councill constituted and appointed according to the Natures and Limitts of their Offices and Places respectively, that they shall and may,

from time to time for ever heerafter, within the said Precincts of New-England, or in the Way by the Seas thither, and from thence have full and absolute Power and Authority to correct, punish, pardon, governe, and rule all such the Subjects of Us, our Heires and Successors, as shall from time to time adventure themselves in any Voyage thither, or that shall aft any Time heerafter inhabit in the Precincts or Territories of the said Collony as aforesaid, according to such Laws, Orders, Ordinances, Directions, and Instructions as by the said Councill aforesaid shall be established; and in Defect thereof, in Cases of Necessity, according to the good Discretions of the said Governors and Officers respectively, as well in Cases capital and criminal, as civill, both marine and others, so allways as the said Statutes, Ordinances, and Proceedings, as near as conveniently may be, agreeable to the Laws, Statutes, Government and Policie of this our Realme of England. And furthermore, if any Person or Persons,-Adventurers or Planters of the said Collony, or any other, aft any Time or Times heerafter, shall transport any Moneys, Goods, or Merchandizes, out of any of our Kingdoms, with a Pretence or Purpose to land, sell, or otherwise dispose of the same within the Limitts and Bounds of the said Collony, and yet nevertheless being att Sea, or after he hath landed within any Part of the said Collony shall carry the same into any other fforaigne Country with a Purpose there to sell and dispose thereof, that then all the Goods and Chattles of the said Person or Persons so offending and transported, together with the Ship or Vessell wherein such Transportation was made, shall be forfeited to Us, our Heires and Successors.

And Wee do further of our especial Grace, certaine Knowledge, and meere Motion for Us, our Heirs and Successors for and in Respect of the Considerations aforesaid, and for divers other good Causes and Considerations, us thereunto especially moving, and by the Advice of the Lords and Others of our said Privy Councill have absolutely giuen, granted, and confirmed, and do by these Presents absolutely give, grant, and confirm unto the said Councill, called the Counceil established att Plymouth in the County of Devon for the planting, ruling, and governing of New-England in America, and unto their Successors for ever, all the aforesaid Lands and Grounds, Continent, Precinct, Place, Places and Territoryes, viz, the aforesaid Part of America, lying, and being in Breadth from ffourty Degrees of Northerly Latitude from the Equinoctiall Line, to ffourty-eight Degrees of the said Northerly Latitude inclusively, and in Length of, and within all the Breadth aforesaid, throughout the Maine Land from Sea to Sea, together also, with the Firme Lands, Soyles, Grounds Havens, Ports, Rivers, Waters, Fishings, Mines, and Mineralls, as well Royall Mines of Gold and Silver, as other Mine and Mineralls, precious Stones, Quarries, and all, and singular other

Comodities, Jurisdictions, Royalties, Priveliges, Franchises, and Preheminences, both within the same Tract of Land upon the Maine, and also within the said Islands and Seas adjoining: Provided always, that the said Islands, or any of the Premises herein before mentioned, and by these Presents intended and meant to be granted, be not actually possessed or inhabited by any other Christian Prince or Estate, nor he within the Bounds, Limitts, or Territoryes, of that Southern Collony Heretofore by us granted to be planted by diverse of our loving Subjects in the South Parts, to have and to hold, possess and enjoy, all, and singular, the aforesaid Continent, Lands, Territoryes, Islands, Hereditaments and Precincts, Sea Waters, Fishings, with all, and all Manner their Commodities, Royalties, Liberties, Preheminences and Profitts, that shall arise from thence, with all and singular. their Appertenances, and every Part and Parcell thereof, and of them, to and unto the said Councell and their Successors and Assignes for ever, to the sole only and proper Use, Benefit and Behooffe of them the said Council and their Successors and Assignes for ever, to be holden of Us, our Heires, and Successors, as of our Manor of East-Greenwich, in our County of Kent, in free and common Soccage and not in in Capite, nor by Knight's Service; yielding and paying therefore to Us, our Heires, our Successors, the fifth Part, of the Ores of Gold and Silver, which from time to time, and aft all times hereafter, shall happen to be found, gotten, had, and obtained, in or within any the said Lands, Limitts, Territoryes, and Precincts, or in or within any Part or Parcell thereof, for, or in Respect of all, and all Manner of Dutys, Demands, and Services whatsoever, to be done, made, or paid to Us, our Heires, and Successors.

And Wee do further of our especiall Grace, certaine Knowledge and meere Motion, for Us, and our Heires, and Successors, give and grant to the said Councell, and their Successors for ever by these Presents, that it shall be lawfull and free for them and their Assignes, att all and every time and times hereafter, out of our Realmes or Dominions whatsoever, to take, load, carry, and transport in, and into their Voyages, and for, and towards the said Plantation in New-England, all such and so many of our loveing Subjects, or any other Strangers that will become our loving Subjects, and live under our Allegiance, as shall willingly accompany them in the said Voyages and Plantation, with Shipping, Armour, Weapons, Ordinances, Munition, Shott, Victuals, and all Manner of Cloathing, Implements, Furniture, Beasts, Cattle, Horses, Mares, and all other Things necessary for the said Plantation, and for their Use and Defence, and for Trade with the People there, and in passing and returning to and fro, without paving or yielding, any Custom or Subsidie either inwards or outwards, to Us, our Heires, or Successors, for the same, for the Space of seven Years, from the Day of the Date of these Presents, provided, that none of the said

Persons be such as shall be hereafter by special Name restrained by Us, our Heire, or Successors.

And for their further Encouragement, of our especial Grace and Favor, Wee do by these Presents for Us, our Heires, and Successors, yield and grant, to and with the said Councill and their Successors, and every of them, their Factors and Assignes, that they and every of them, shall be free and quits from all Subsidies and Customes in NewEngland for the Space of seven Years, and from all Taxes and Impositions for the Space of twenty and one Yeares, upon all Goods and Merchandizes aft any time or times hereafter, either upon Importation thither, or Exportation from thence into our Realme of England, or into any our Dominions by the said Councill and their Successors their Deputies, Factors, and Assignes, or any of them, except only the five Pounds per Cent. due for Custome upon all such Goods and Merchandizes, as shall be brot and imported into our Realme of England, or any other of our Dominions, according to the ancient Trade of Marchants; which five Pounds per Cent. only being paid, it shall be thenceforth lawful and free for the said Adventurers, the same Goods and Merchandize to export and carry out of our said Dominions into fforraigne Parts, without any Custom, Tax, or other Duty to be paid to Us, our Heires, or Successors, or to any other Officers or Ministers of Us, our Heires, or Successors; provided, that the said Goods and Merchandizes be shipped out within thirteene Months after theire first Landing within any Part of those Dominions.

And further our Will and Pleasure is, and Wee do by these Presents charge, comand, warrant, and authorize the said Councill, and their Successors, or the major Part of them, which shall be present and assembled for that Purpose, shall from time to time under their comon Seale, distribute, convey, assigne, and sett over, such particular Portions of Lands, Tenements, and Hereditaments, as are by these Presents, formerly granted unto each our loveing Subjects, naturally borne or Denisons, or others, as well Adventurers as Planters, as by the said Company upon a Comission of Survey and. Distribution, executed and returned for that Purpose, shall be named, appointed, and allowed, wherein our Will and Pleasure is, that Respect be had as well to the Proportion of the Adventurers, as to the special Service, Hazard, Exploit, or Meritt of any Person so to be recompensed, advanced, or rewarded, and wee do also, for Us, our Heires, and Successors, grant to the said Councell and their Successors and to all and every such Governours, other Officers, or Ministers, as by the said Councill shall be appointed to have Power and Authority of Government and Command in and over the said Collony and Plantation, that they and every of them, shall, and lawfully may, from time to time, and aft all Times hereafter for ever, for their severall Defence and Safety, encounter, expulse, repel, and resist by Force of Arms, as well by Sea as by Land, and all Ways and Meanes whatsoever, all such Person and Persons, as without the speciall Licence of the said Councell and their Successors, or the greater Part of them, shall attempt to inhabitt within the said severall Precincts and Limitts of the said Collony and Plantation. And also all, and every such Person or Persons whatsoever, as shall enterprise or attempt att any time hereafter Destruction, Invasion, Detriment, or Annovance to the said Collony and Plantation; and that it shall be lawfull for the said Councill, and their Successors, and every of them, from Time to Time, and att all Times heereafter, and they shall have full Power and Authority, to take and surprize by all Ways and Means whatsoever, all and every such Person and Persons whatsoever, with their Ships, Goods, and other Furniture, trafficking in any Harbour, Creeke, or Place, within the Limitts and Precintes of the said Collony and Plantations, and not being allowed by the said Councill to be adventurers or Planters of the said Collony. And of our further Royall Favor, Wee have granted, and for Us, our Heires, and Successors, Wee do grant unto the said Councill and their Successors, that the said Territoryes, Lands, Rivers, and Places aforesaid, or any of them, shall not be visited, frequented, or traded unto, by any other of our Subjects, or the Subjects of Us, our Heires, or Successors, either from any the Ports and Havens belonging or appertayning, or which shall belong or appertayne unto Us, our Heires, or Successors, or to any forraigne State, Prince, or Pottentate whatsoever: And therefore, Wee do hereby for Us, our Heires, and Successors, charge, command, prohibit and forbid all the Subjects of Us, our Heires, and Successors, of what Degree and Quality soever, they be, that none of them, directly, or indirectly, presume to vissitt, frequent, trade, or adventure to traffick into, or from the said Territoryes, Lands, Rivers, and Places aforesaid, or any of them other than the said Councill and their Successors, Factors, Deputys, and Assignes, unless it be with the License and Consent of the said Councill and Company first had and obtained in Writing, under the comon Seal, upon Pain of our Indignation and Imprisonment of their Bodys during the Pleasure of Us, our Heires or Successors, and the Forfeiture and Loss both of theire Ships and Goods, wheresoever they shall be found either within any of our Kingdomes or Dominions, or any other Place or Places out of our Dominions.

And for the better effecting of our said Pleasure heerein Wee do heereby for Us, our Heires and Successors, give and grant full Power and Authority unto the said Councill, and their Successors for the time being, that they by themselves, their Factors, Deputyes, or Assignes, shall and may from time to time, and at all times heereafter, attach, arrest, take, and seize all and all Manner of Ship and Ships, Goods, Wares, and Merchandizes whatsoever, which

shall be bro't from or carried to the Places before mentioned, or any of them, contrary to our Will and Pleasure, before in these Presents expressed. The Moyety or one halfe of all which Forfeitures Wee do hereby for Us, our Heires and Successors, give and grant unto the said Councill, and their Successors to their own proper Use without Accompt, and the other Moyety, or halfe Part thereof, Wee will shall be and remaine to the Use of Us, our Heires and Successors. And we likewise have condiscended and granted, and by these Presents, for Us, our Heires and Successors, do condiscend, and grant to and with the said Councill and their Successors, that Wee, our Heires or Successors, shall not or will not give and grant any Lybertye, License, or Authority to any Person or Persons whatsoever, to saile, trade, or trafficke unto the aforesaid parts of New-England, without the good Will and Likinge of the said Councill, or the greater Part of them for the Time Hinge, let any their Courts to be assembled. And Wee do for us, our Heires and Successors, give and grant unto the said Councill, and their Successors, that whensoever, or so often as any Custome or Subsidie shall growe due or payable unto Us, our Heires or Successors, according to the Limitation and Appointment aforesaid by Reason of any Goods, Wares, Merchandizes, to be shipped out, or any Returne to be made of any Goods, Wares, or Merchandizes, unto or from New-England, or any the Lands Territoryes aforesaid, that then so often, and in such Case the ffarmers, Customers, and Officers of our Customes of England and Ireland, and every of them, for the Time being, upon Request made unto them by the said Councill, their Successors, Factors, or Assignes, and upon convenient Security to be given in that Behalfe, shall give and allowe unto the said Councill and their Successors, and to all Person and Persons free of the said Company as aforesaid, six Months Time for the Payment of the one halfe of all such Custome and Subsidie, as shall be due, and payable unto Us, our Heires and Successors for the same, for which these our Letterspattent, or the Duplicate, or the Enrolrnent thereof, shall be Onto our said Officers a sufficient Warrant and Discharge. Nevertheless, our Will and Pleasure is, that if any of the said Goods, Wares, and Merchandizes, which be, or shall be, aft any Time heereafter, ended and exported out of any of our Realmes aforesaid, and shall be shipped with a Purpose not to be carried to New-England aforesaid, that then such Payment, Duty, Custome, Imposition, or Forfieture, shall be paid and belong to Us, our Heires and Successors, for the said Goods, Wares, and Merchandices, so fraudulently sought to be transported, as if this our Grant had not been made nor granted: And Wee do for Us, our Heires and Successors, give and grant unto the said Councill and theire Successors for ever, by these Presents, that the said President of the said Company, or his Deputy for the Time being, or any two others of the said Councill, for the said Collony in New-England, for the Time beinge, shall and may, and aft all Times heereafter, and from time to time, have full Power and Authority, to minister and give the Oath and Oaths of Allegiance and Supremacy, or either of them, to all and every Person and Persons, which shall aft any Time and Times heereafter, goe or pass to the said Collony in New-England. And further, that it shall be like-wise-be lawful for the said President, or his Deputy for the Time being, or any two others of the said Councill for the said Collony of New-England for the Time being, from time to time, and aft all Times heerafter, to minister such a formal Oath, as by their Discretion shall be reasonably devised, as well unto any Person and Persons imployed or to be imployed in, for, or touching the said Plantation, for their honest, faithfull, and just Discharge of their Service, in all such Matters as shall be committed unto them for the Good and Benefist of the said Company, Collony, and Plantation, as also unto such other Person or Persons, as the said President or his Deputy, with two others of the said Councill, shall thinke meete for the Examination or clearing of the Truth in any Cause whatsoever, concerning the said Plantation, or any Business from thence proceeding, or hereunto belonging.

And to the End that now lewd or ill-disposed Persons, Saylors, Soldiers, Artificers, Labourers, Husbandmen, or others, which shall receive Wages, Apparel, or other Entertainment from the said Councill, or contract and agree with the said Councill to goe, and to serve, and to be imployed, in the said Plantation, in the Collony in New England, do afterwards withdraw, hide, and conceale themselves, or refuse to go thither, after they have been so entertained and agreed withall; and that no Persons which shall be sent and imployed in the said Plantation, of the said Collony in New-England, upon the Charge of the said Councill, doe misbehave themselves by mutinous Seditions, or other notorious Misdemeanors, or which shall be imployed, or sent abroad by the Governour of New England or his Deputy, with any Shipp or Pinnace, for Provision for the said Collony, or for some Discovery, or other Business or Affaires concerninge the same, doe from thence either treacherously come back againe, or returne into the Realme of Englande by Stealth, or without Licence of the Governour of the said Collony in New-England for the Time being, or be sent hither as Misdoers or Offendors; and that none of those Persons after theire Returne from thence, being questioned by the said Councill heere, for such their Misdemeanors and Offences, do, by insolent and contemptuous Carriage in the Presence of the said Councill shew little Respect and Reverence, either to the Place or Authority in which we have placed and appointed them and others, for the clearing of their Lewdness and Misdemeanors committed in New-England, divulge vile and scandalous Reports of the Country of New-England, or of the Government or Estate of the said Plantation and Collony, to bring the said Voyages and Plantation into Disgrace and Contempt, by Meanes whereof, not only the Adventurers and Planters already engaged in the said Plantation may be exceedingly abused and hindered, and a great number of our loveing and well-disposed Subjects, otherways well affected and inclined to joine and adventure in so noble a Christian and worthy Action may be discouraged from the same, but also the Enterprize itself may be overthrowne, which cannot miscarry without some Dishonour to Us and our Kingdome: Wee, therefore, for preventing so great and enormous Abuses and Misdemeanors, Do, by these Presents for Us, our Heires, and Successors, give and grant unto the said President or his Deputy, or such other Person or Persons, as by the Orders of the said Councill shall be appointed by Warrant under his or their Hand or Hands, to send for, or cause to-be apprehended, all and every such Person and Persons, who shall be noted, or accused, or found at any time or times hereafter to offend or misbehave themselves in any the Affaires before mentioned and expressed; and upon the Examination of any such Offender or Offenders, and just Proofe made by Oathe taken before the said Councill, of any such notorious Misdemeanours by them comitted as aforesaid, and also upon any insolent, contemptuous, or irreverent Carriage or Misbehaviour, to or against the said Councill, to be shewed or used by any such Person or Persons so called, convened, and appearing before them as aforesaid, that in all such Cases, our said Councill, or any two or more of them for the Time being, shall and may have full Power and Authority, either heere to bind them over with good Sureties for their good Behaviour, and further therein to proceed, to all Intents and Purposes as it is used in other like Cases within our Realme of England, or else at their Discretions to remand and send back the said offenders, or any of them, to the said Colony of New-England, there to be proceeded against and punished as the Governour's Deputy or Councill there for the Time being, shall think meete, or otherwise according to such Laws and Ordinances as are, and shall be, in Use there, for the well ordering and good Government of the said Colony.

And our Will and Pleasure is, and Wee do hereby declare to all Christian Kings, Princes, and States, that if any Person or Persons which shall hereafter be of the said Collony or Plantation, or any other by License or Appointment of the said Councill, or their Successors, or otherwise, shall at any time or times heereafter, rob or spoil, by Sea or by Land, or do any Hurt, Violence, or unlawfull Hostillity to any of the Subjects of Us, our Heires, or Successors, or any of the Subjects of any King, Prince, Ruler, or Governour, or State, being then in League and Amity with Us, our Heires and Successors, and that upon such

Injury, or upon just Complaint of such Prince, Ruler, Governour, or State, or their Subjects, Wee, our Heires, or Successors shall make open Proclamation within any of the Ports of our Realme of England commodious for that Purpose, that the Person or Persons having committed any such Robbery or Spoile, shall within the Term limited by such a Proclamation, make full Restitution or Satisfaction of all such Injuries done, so as the said Princes or other, so complaining, may hold themselves fully satisfied and contented. And if that the said Person or Persons having committed such Robery or Spoile, shall not make or cause to be made Satisfaction accordingly within such Terme so to be limited, that then it shall be lawful for Us, our Heires, and Successors, to put the said Person or Persons our of our Allegiance and Protection; and that it shall be lawful and free for all Princes to prosecute with Hostillity the said Offenders and every of them, their, and every of their Procurers, Aidors, Abettors, and Comforters in that Behalfe. Also, Wee do for Us, our Heires, and Successors, declare by these Presents, that all and every the Persons, beinge our Subjects, which shall goe and inhabitt within the said Collony and Plantation, and every of their Children and Posterity, which shall happen to be born within the Limitts thereof, shall have and enjoy all Liberties, and ffranchizes, and Immunities of free Denizens and naturall Subjects within any of our other Dominions, to all Intents and Purposes, as if they had been abidinge and born within this our Kingdome of England, or any other our Dominions.

And lastly, because the principall Effect which we can desire or expect of this Action, is the Conversion and Reduction of the People in those Parts unto the true Worship of God and Christian Religion, in which Respect, Wee would be loath that any Person should be permitted to pass that Wee suspected to affect the Superstition of the Chh of Rome, Wee do hereby declare that it is our Will and Pleasure that none be permitted to pass, in any Voyage from time to time to be made into the said Country, but such as shall first have taken the Oathe of Supremacy; for which Purpose, Wee do by these Presents give full Power and Authority to the President of the said Councill, to tender and exhibit the said Oath to all such Persons as shall at any time be sent and imployed in the said Voyage. And Wee also for us, our Heires and Successors, do covenant and grant to and with the Councill, and their Successors, by these Presents, that if the Councill for the time being, and their Successors, or any of them, shall at any time or times heereafter, upon any Doubt which they shall conceive concerning the Strength or Validity in Law of this our present Grant, or be desirous to have the same renewed and confirmed by Us, our Heires and Successors, with Amendment of such Imperfections and Defects as shall appear fitt and necessary to the said Councill, or their Successors, to be reformed and amended on the Behalfe of Us, our Heires and Successors, and for the furthering of the Plantation and Government, or the Increase, continuing, and flourishing thereof, that then, upon the humble Petition of the said Councill for the time being, and their Successors, to us, our Heires and Successors, Wee, our Heires and Successors, shall and will forthwith make and pass under the Great Seall of England, to the said Councill and theire Successors, such further and better Assurance, of all and singular the Lands, Grounds, Royalties, Privileges, and Premisses aforesaid granted, or intended to be granted, according to our true Intent and Meaneing in these our Letters-patents, signified, declared, or mentioned, as by the learned Councill of Us, our Heires, and Successors, and of the said Company and theire Successors shall, in that Behalfe, be reasonably devised or advised. And further our Will and Pleasure is, that in all Questions and Doubts, that shall arise upon any Difficulty of Instruction or Interpretation of any Thing contained in these our Letters-pattents, the same shall be taken and Interpreted in most ample and beneficial Manner, for the said Council and theire Successors, and every Member thereof. And Wee do further for Us, our Heires and Successors, charge and comand all and singular Admirals, Vice-Admirals, Generals, Commanders, Captaines, Justices of Peace, Majors, Sheriffs, Bailiffs Constables, Customers, Comptrollers, Waiters, Searchers, and all the Officers of Us, our Heires and Successors, whatsoever to be from time to time, and att all times heereafter, in all Things aiding, helping, and assisting unto the said Councill, and their Successors, and unto every of them, upon Request and Requests by them to be made, in all Matters and Things, for the furtherance and Accomplishment of all or any the Matters and Things by Us, in and by these our Letters-pattents, given, granted, and provided, or by Us meant or intended to be given, granted, and provided, as they our said Officers, and the Officers of Us, our Heires and Successors, do tender our Pleasure, and will avoid the contrary att their Perills. And Wee also do by these Presents, ratifye and confirm unto the said Councill and their Successors, all Priveliges, Franchises, Liberties, Immunities granted in our said former Letters-patents, and not in these our Letters-patents revoked, altered, changed or abridged, altho' Expressed, Mentioned, &c.

In Witness, &c.
Witnes our selfe at Westminster,
the Third Day of November, in the Eighteenth Yeare of
our Reign over England, &c.
Par Breve de Privato Sigillo, &c.

Source:
Francis Newton Thorpe, ed. *The Federal and State Constitutions Colonial Charters, and Other Organic Laws of the States,*

Territories, and Colonies Now or Heretofore Forming the United States of America. Washington, D.C.: Government Printing Office, 1909.

Mayflower Compact, 1620

Agreement signed by 41 male Pilgrims before disembarking from the *Mayflower* in Provincetown Harbor on November 11, 1620; it stated that they would submit to the will of the majority in whatever regulations of government were agreed upon. The compact committed them to "frame such just and equal laws . . . as shall be thought most meet and convenient for the general good of the colony. . . ." It also bound them to constitute offices for the general good of the proposed colony and to hold in check dissenters who had threatened to strike out for themselves when Pilgrim leaders decided to land at Plymouth instead of Virginia. The compact was patterned after their church covenant, which placed religious authority in the congregation. The Mayflower Compact was intended to preserve order until a patent could be obtained, and it remained in force until 1691. With it, a form of democratic government had been established by Europeans in New England.

In the name of God, amen. We, whose names are underwritten, the loyal subjects of our dread sovereign lord King James, by the grace of God, of Great Britain, France, and Ireland, King, Defender of the Faith, etc. Having undertaken for the glory of God, and advancement of the Christian faith, and honor of our King and Country, a voyage to plant the first colony in the northern parts of Virginia, do by these presents, solemnly and mutually in the presence of God and of one another, covenant and combine ourselves together into a civil body politic, for our better ordering and preservation, and furtherance of the ends aforesaid; and by virtue hereof do enact, constitute, and frame, such just and equal laws, ordinances, acts, constitutions, and offices, from time to time, as shall be thought most meet and convenient for the general good of the colony; unto which we promise all due submission and obedience. In witness whereof we have hereunto subscribed our names at Cape Cod the eleventh of November, in the reign of our sovereign lord King James of England, France, and Ireland, the eighteenth, and of Scotland, the fifty-fourth. Anno Domini, 1620.

Mr. John Carver Mr. William Bradford Mr. Edward Winslow Mr. William Brewster Isaac Allerton Miles Standish John Alden John Turner Francis Eaton James Chilton John Craxton John Billington Joses Fletcher John Goodman Mr. Samuel Fuller Mr. Christopher Martin Mr. William Mullins Mr. William White Mr. Richard Warren John Howland Mr. Stephen Hopkins Digery Priest Thomas Williams Gilbert Winslow Edmund Margesson Peter Brown Richard Bitteridge George Soule Edward Tilly John Tilly Francis Cooke Thomas Rogers Thomas Tinker John Ridgate Edward Fuller Richard Clark Richard Gardiner Mr. John Allerton Thomas English Edward Doten Edward Liester

Source:

John Scott, ed. *Living Documents in American History.* New York: Washington Square Press, 1964–68.

Early Settlements and Government in the English Colonies

Ralph Lane, Account of the First Roanoke Colony, 1585–1586

An account of the first English colony in North America by its overseer, Ralph Lane. Established under the authority of Sir Walter Raleigh in August 1585 on Roanoke Island in present-day North Carolina, the colony lasted only 10 months. When Sir Richard Grenville, the leader of the expedition, was delayed in his return with desperately needed supplies, the settlers abandoned the colony and returned to England with Sir Francis Drake in June 1586. Grenville finally arrived a few weeks after the colonists had left. Unwilling to completely surrender the colony, Grenville left 15 men at the deserted fort and sailed for England. When a new colony arrived in 1587, they found only the skeleton of one man. The disappearance of Grenville's men foreshadowed the fate of the famous "Lost

Colony" of Roanoke, the second English attempt at colonization in the New World. The account below is divided into two sections: In the first part, Lane describes the colonists' efforts to survive in the new land, find riches, and coexist with the native peoples. The second part offers an explanation as to why the colonists chose to leave with Drake, who had just returned from plundering the Spanish colony of St. Augustine. Excerpts of these sections are included here.

───────────── ❧ ─────────────

The First Part Declaring the Peculiarities of the Countrey of Virginia:

First therefore touching the particularities of the Country, you shall understand that our discovery of the same hath been extended from the Island of Roanoak, (the same having been the place of our settlement or inhabitation) into the South, into the North, into the Northwest, and into the West.

The uttermost place to the Southward of any discovery was Secotan, being by estimation fourscore miles distant from Roanoak. The passage from thence was through a broad sound within the main, the same being without sight of land, and yet full of flats and shoals: we had but one boat with four oars to pass through the same, which boat could not carry above fifteen men with their furniture, baggage, and victual for seven days at the most: and as for our pinnesse, besides that she drew too deep water for that shallow sound, she would not stir for an oar: for these and other reasons (winter also being at hand) we thought good wholly to leave the discovery of those parts until our stronger supply.

To the Northward our furthest discovery was to the Chesepians, distant from Roanoke about 130. miles, the passage to it was very shallow and most dangerous, by reason of the breadth of the sound, and the little succor that upon any flaw was there to be had.

But the territory and soil of the Chesepians (being distant fifteen miles from the shore) was for pleasantness of seat, for temperature of Climate, for fertility of soil, and for the commodity of the Sea, besides multitude of Bears (being an excellent good victual) with great woods of Sassafras, and Walnut trees, is not to be excelled by any other whatsoever.

There be sundry Kings, whom they call Weroances, and Countries of great fertility adjoining to the same, as the Mandoages, Tripanicks, and Opossians, which all came to visit the Colony of the English, which I had for a time appointed to be resident there.

To the Northwest the farthest place of our discovery was to Chawanook distant from Roanoak about 130. miles. Our passage thither lies through a broad sound, but all fresh water, and the channel of a great depth, navigable for good shipping, but out of the channel full of shoals.

❀   ❀   ❀

Between Muscamunge and Chawanook upon the left hand as we pass thither, is a goodly high land, and there is a Town which we called The blind Town, but the Savages called it Ohanoak, and hath a very goodly corn field belonging unto it: it is subject to Chawanook.

Chawanook it self is the greatest Province & Seigniory lying upon that River, and the very Town it self is able to put 700. fighting men into the field, besides the force of the Province it self.

The King of the said Province is called Menatonon, a man impotent in his limbs, but otherwise for a Savage, a very grave and wise man, and of a very singular good discourse in matters concerning the state, not only of his own Country, and the disposition of his own men, but also of his neighbors round about him as well far as near, and of the commodities that each Country yielded. When I had him prisoner with me, for two days that we were together, he gave me more under-standing and light of the Country than I had received by all the searches and Savages that before I or any of my company had had conference with: it was in March last past 1586. Amongst other things he told me, that going three days journey in a Canoe, up his River of Chawanook, and then descending to the land, you are within four days journey to pass over land Northeast to a certain Kings country, whose Province lies upon the Sea, but his place of greatest strength is an Island situated, as he desribed unto me, in a Bay, the water round about the Island very deep.

❀   ❀   ❀

He showed me that the said King was with him at Chawanook two years before, & brought him certain Pearls, but the same of the worst sort, yet was he fain to buy them of him for copper at a dear rate, as he thought. He gave me a rope of the same pearls, but they were black, and naught, yet many of them were very great, and a few amongst a number very sparkling and round, all which I lost with other things of mine, coming aboard Sir Francis Drake his Fleet: yet he told me that the said King had great store of Pearls that were white, great, and round, and that his black Pearls his men did take out of shallow water, but the white Pearls his men fished for in very deep water.

It seemed to me by his speech, that the said King had traffic with white men that had clothes as we have, for these white Pearls, and that was the reason that he would not depart with other then with black Pearls, to those of the same country.

The king of Chawanook promised to give me guides to go over land into that kings country whensoever I would: but he advised me to take good store of men with me, and good store of victual, for he said, that king would be loath to suffer any strangers to enter into his Country, and especially to meddle with the fishing for any Pearls there, and that he was able to make a great many of men into the field, which he said would fight very well.

✤   ✤   ✤

For Pemisapan, who had changed his name of Wingina upon the death of his brother Granganimo, had given both the Choanists, and Mangoaks word of my purpose touching them, I having been enforced to make him privy to the same, to be served by him of a guide to the Mangoaks, and yet he did never rest to solicit continually my going upon them, certifying me of a general assembly even at that time made by Menatonon at Chawanook of all his Weroances, and allies to the number of three thousand bows, preparing to come upon us at Roanoke, and that the Mangoaks also were joined in the same confederacy, who were able of themselves to bring as many more to the enterprise: And true it was that at that time the assembly was held at Chawanook about us, as I found at my coming thither, which being unlooked for did so dismay them, as it made us have the better hand at them. But this confederacy against us of the Choanists and Mangoaks was altogether and wholly procured by Pemisapan him-selfe, as Menatonon confessed unto me, who sent them continual word, that our purpose was fully bent to destroy them: on the other side he told me, that they had the like meaning towards us.

He in like sort having sent word to the Mangoaks of mine intention to pass up into their River, and to kill them (as he said) both they and the Moratoks, with whom before we were entered into a league, and they had ever dealt kindly with us, abandoned their Towns along the River, and retired themselves with their women, and their Corn within the main: insomuch as having passed three days voyage up the River, we could not meet a man, nor find a grain of Corn in any their Towns: whereupon considering with my self that we had but two days victual left, and that we were then 160. miles from home, besides casualty of contrary winds or storms, and suspecting treason of our own Savages in the discovery of our voyage intended, though we had no intention to be hurtful to any them, otherwise then for our copper to have had corn of them: I at night upon the Corps of guard, before the putting forth of Sentinels, advertised the whole company of the case we stood in for victual, and of mine opinion that we were betrayed by our own Savages, and of purpose drawn forth by them upon vain hope to be in the end starved, seeing all the Country fled before us, and therefore while we had those two days victual left, I thought it good for us to make our return homeward, and that it were necessary for us to get the other side of the Sound of Weopomeiok in time, where we might be relieved upon

the weirs of Chypanum, and the womens Town, although the people were fled.

✤   ✤   ✤

And that which made me most desirous to have some doings with the Mangoaks either in friendship or otherwise to have had one or two of them prisoners, was, for that it is a thing most notorious to all the country, that there is a Province to the which the said Mangoaks have recourse and traffic up that River of Moratoc, which has a marvelous and most strange Mineral. This Mine is so notorious amongst them, as not only to the Savages dwelling up the said river, and also to the Savages of Chawanook, and all them to the Westward, but also to all them of the main: the Countries name is of fame, and is called Chaunis Temoatan.

The Mineral they say is Wassador, which is copper, but they call by the name of Wassador every metal whatsoever: they say it is of the color of our copper, but our copper is better then theirs: and the reason is for that it is redder and harder, whereas that of Chaunis Temoatan is very soft, and pale: they say that they take the said metal out of a river that falls very swift from high rocks and hills, and they take it in shallow water: the manner is this. They take a great bowl by their description as great as one of our targets, and wrap a skin over the hollow part thereof, leaving one part open to receive in the mineral: that done, they watch the coming down of the current, and the change of the color of the water, and then suddenly chop down the said bowl with the skin, and receive unto the same as much oar as will come in, which is ever as much as their bowl will hold, which presently they cast into a fire, and forthwith it melted, and does yield in five parts, at the first melting, two parts of metal for three parts of oar. Of this metal the Mangoaks have so great store, by report of all the Savages adjoining, that they beautify their houses with great plates of the same: and this to be true, I received by report of all the country, and particularly by young Skiko, the King of Chawanooks son my prisoner, who also himself had been prisoner with the Mangoaks, and set down all the particularities to me before mentioned: but he had not been at Chawnis Temoatan himself: for he said, it was twenty days journey overland from the Mangoaks, to the said Mineral Country, and that they passed through certain other territories between them and the Mangoaks, before they came to the said Country.

Upon report of the premises, which I was very inquisitive in all places where I came to take very particular information of, by all the Savages that dwelt towards those parts, and especially of Menatonon himself, who in every thing did very particularly inform me, and promised me guides of his own men, who should pass over with me, even to the said Country of Chaunis Temoatan (for overland from Chawanook to the Mangoaks is but one day's journey from Sun rising to Sun setting, whereas by water it is seven days with the soonest:) These things, I say, made me very desirous by all means possible to recover the Mangoaks, and to get some of that their copper for an assay, and therefore I willingly yielded to their resolution: But it fell out very contrary to all expectation, and likelihood: for after two days travel, and our whole victual spent, lying on shore all night, we could never see man, only fires we might perceive made alongst the shore where we were to pass, and up into the Country, until the very last day. In the evening whereof, about three of the clock we heard certain Savages call as we thought, Manteo, who was also at that time with me in the boat, whereof we all being very glad, hoping of some friendly conference with them, and making him to answer them, they presently began a song, as we thought, in token of our welcome to them: but Manteo presently betooke him to his piece, and told me that they meant to fight with us: which word was not so soon spoken by him, and the light horseman ready to put to shore, but there lighted a volley of their arrows amongst them in the boat, but did no hurt (God be thanked) to any man. Immediately, the other boat lying ready with their shot to scour the place for our hand weapons to land upon, which was presently done, although the land was very high and steep, the Savages forthwith quitted the shore, and betooke themselves to flight: we landed, and having fair and easily followed for a small time after them, who had wooded themselves we know not where: the Sun drawing then towards the setting, and being then assured that the next day if wee would pursue them, though we might happen to meet with them, yet we should be assured to meet with none of their victual, which we then had good cause to think of: therefore choosing for the company a convenient ground in safety to lodge in for the night, making a strong Corps of guard, and putting out good Sentinels, I determined the next morning before the rising of the Sun to be going back again, if possibly we might recover the mouth of the river, into the broad sound, which at my first motion I found my whole company ready to assent unto: for they were now come to their Dogges porridge, that they had bespoken for themselves if that befell them which did, and I before did mistrust we should hardly escape. The end was, we came the next day by night to the Rivers mouth within four or five miles of the same, having rowed in one day down the current, as much as in four days we had done against the same: we lodged upon an Island, where we had nothing in the world to eat but pottage of Sassafras leaves, the like whereof for a meat was never used before as I think. The broad sound we had to pass the next day all fresh and fasting: that day the wind blew so strongly, and the billow so great, that there was no possibility of passage without sinking of our boats. This was upon Easter eve,

which was fasted very truely. Upon Easter day in the morning the wind coming very calm, we entered the sound, and by four of the clock we were at Chipanum, whence all the Savages that we had left there were fled, but their weirs did yield us some fish, as God was pleased not utterly to suffer us to be lost: for some of our company of the light horsemen were far spent. The next morning we arrived at our home Roanoke . . . .

I have set down this Voyage somewhat particularly, to the end it may appear unto you (as true it is) that there wanted no great good will from the most to the least amongst us, to have perfected this discovery of a good Mine, by the goodness of God, or a passage to the South-sea, or some way to it, and nothing else can bring this Country in request to be inhabited by our nation. And with the discovery of either of the two above showed, it will be the most sweet and healthy climate, and therewithall the most fertile soil (being manured) in the world: and then will Sassafras, and many other roots and gums there found make good marchandise and lading for shipping, which otherwise of themselves will not be worth the fetching.

❊   ❊   ❊

Thus Sir, I have though simply, yet truly set down unto you, what my labor with the rest of the gentlemen, and poor men of our company (not without both pain and peril, which the Lord in his mercy many ways delivered us from) could yield unto you, which might have been performed in some more perfection, if the Lord had been pleased that only that which you had provided for us had at the first been left with us, or that he had not in his eternal providence now at the last set some other course in these things. . . .

The Second Part Touching the Conspiracie of Pemisapan, the Discovery of the Same, and at the Last, of Our Request to Depart with Sir Francis Drake for England:

Ensenore a Savage father to Pemisapan being the only friend to our nation that we had amongst them, and about the King, died the 20 of April 1586. He alone had before opposed himself in their consultations against all matters proposed against us, which both the King and all the rest of them after Grangemoes death, were very willing to have preferred. And he was not only by the mere providence of God during his life, a means to save us from hurt, as poisonings and such like, but also to do us very great good, and singularly in this.

The King was advised and of himself disposed, as a ready means to have assuredly brought us to ruin in the month of March 1586 himself also with all his Savages to have run away from us, and to have left his ground in the Island unsowed: which if he had done, there had been no possibility in common reason, (but by the immediate hand of God) that we could have been preserved from starving out of hand. For at that time we had no weirs for fish, neither could our men skill of the making of them, neither had we one grain of Corn for seed to put into the ground.

In mine absence on my voyage that I had made against the Chaonists, and Mangoaks, they had raised a rumor among themselves, that I and my company were part slain, and part starved by the Chaonists, and Mangoaks. One part of this tale was too true, that I and mine were like to be starved, but the other false.

Nevertheless until my return it took such effect in Pemisapans breast, and in those against us, that they grew not only into contempt of us, but also (contrary to their former reverend opinion in show, of the Almighty God of heaven, and Jesus Christ whom we serve and worship, whom before they would acknowledge and confess the only God) now they began to blaspheme, and flatly to say, that our Lord God was not God, since he suffered us to sustain much hunger, and also to be killed of the Renapoaks, for so they call by that general name all the inhabitants of the whole main, of what province soever. Insomuch as old Ensenore, neither any of his fellows, could for his sake have no more credit for us: and it came so far that the king was resolved to have presently gone away as is aforesaid.

❖   ❖   ❖

Within certain days after my return from the said journey, Menatonon sent a messenger to visit his son the prisoner with me, and sent me certain pearls for a present, or rather, as Pemisapan told me, for the ransom of his son, and therefore I refused them: but the greatest cause of his sending then, was to signify unto me, that he had commanded Okisko King of Weopomiok, to yield himself servant, and vassal to the great Weroanza of England, and after her to Sir Walter Raleigh: to perform which commandment received from Menatonon, the said Okisko jointly with this Menatonons messenger sent four and twenty of his principal men to Roanoak to Pemisapan, to signify that they were ready to perform the same, and so had sent those his men to let me know that from that t ime forward, he, and his successors were to acknowledge her Majesty their only Sovereign, and next unto her, as is aforesaid

All which being done, and acknowledged by them all, in the presence of Pemisapan his father, and all his Savages in counsel then with him, it did for the time thoroughly (as it seemed) change him in disposition toward us: Insomuch as forthwith Ensenore won this resolution of him, that out of hand he should go about, and withal, to cause his men to set up weirs forthwith for us: both which he at that present went in hand withall, and did so labor the expedition

of it, that in the end of April he had sowed a good quantity of ground, so much as had been sufficient, to have fed our whole company (God blessing the growth) and that by the belly, for a whole year: besides that he gave us a certain plot of ground for our selves to sow. All which put us in marvelous comfort, if we could pass from April until the beginning of July, (which was to have been the beginning of their harvest,) that then a new supply out of England or else our own store would well enough maintain us: All our fear was of the two months betwixt, in which mean space if the Savages should not help us with Cassavi, and China, and that our weirs should fail us, (as often they did,) we might very well starve, notwithstanding the growing corn, like the starving horse in the stable, with the growing grass, as the proverb is: which we very hardly had escaped but only by the hand of God, as it pleased him to try us. For within few days after, as before is said, Ensenore our friend died, who was no sooner dead, but certain of our great enemies about Pemisapan, as Osacan a Werowance, Tanaquiny and Wanchese most principally, were in hand again to put their old practices in use against us, which were readily embraced, and all their former devices against us renewed, and new brought in question. But that of starving us, by their forbearing to sow, was broken by Ensenore in his life, by having made the King all at one instant to sow his ground, not only in the Island, but also at Dasamonquepeio in the main, within two leagues over against us. Nevertheless there wanted no store of mischievous practices among them. . . . Pemisapan with his troop above named should have executed me, and some of our Weroances (as they called all our principal officers,) the main forces of the rest should have come over into the Island, where they meant to have dispatched the rest of the company. . . .

❖   ❖   ❖

Now to the end that we might be the fewer in number together, and so be the more easily dealt withal (for in deed ten of us with our arms prepared, were a terror to a hundred of the best sort of them,) they agreed and did immediately put it in practice, that they should not for any copper sell us any victuals whatsoever: besides that in the night they should send to have our weirs robbed, and also to cause them to be broken, and once being broken never to be repaired again by them. By this means the King stood assured, that I must be enforced for lack of sustenance there, to disband my company into sundry places to live upon shell fish, for so the Savages themselves do . . . while their grounds be in sowing, and their corn growing: which failed not his expectation. For the famine grew so extreme among us, or weirs failing us of fish, that I was enforced to send Captain Stafford with 20. with him to Croatoan my Lord Admirals Island to serve two turns in one, that is to say, to feed himself and his company, and also to keep watch if any shipping came upon the coast to warn us of the same. I sent M. Pridiox with the pinnesse to Hatorask, and ten with him, with the Provost Marshal to live there, and also to wait for shipping: also I sent every week 16. or 20. of the rest of the company to the main over against us, to live of Casada and oysters.

✿   ✿   ✿

My purpose was to have relied my self with Menatonon, and the Chaonists, who in truth as they are more valiant people and in greater number then the rest, so are they more faithful in their promises, and since my late being there had given many tokens of earnest desire they had to join in perfect league with us, and therefore were greatly offended with Pemisapan and Weopomeiok for making him believe such tales of us.

✿   ✿   ✿

The day of their assembly aforesaid at Roanoke was appointed the 10. of June: all which the premises were discovered by Skyco, the King Menatonon his son my prisoner, who having once attempted to run away, I laid him in the shackles, threatening to cut off his head, whom I remitted at Pemisapans request: whereupon he being persuaded that he was our enemy to the death, he did not only feed him with himself, but also made him acquainted with all his practices. On the other side, the young man finding himself as well used at my hand, as I had means to show, and that all my company made much of him, he flatly discovered all unto me, which also afterwards was revealed unto me by one of Pemisapans own men, that night before he was slain.

These mischiefs being all instantly upon me and my company to be put in execution, it stood me in hand to study how to prevent them, and also to save all others, which were at that time as aforesaid so far from me: whereupon I sent to Pemisapan to put suspicion out of his head, that I meant presently to go to Croatoan, for that I had heard of the arrival of our fleet, (though I in truth had neither heard nor hoped for so good adventure,) and that I meant to come by him, to borrow of his men to fish for my company, & to hunt for me at Croatoan, as also to buy some four days provision to serve for my voyage.

✿   ✿   ✿

The alarm given, they took themselves to their bows, and we to our arms: some three or four of them at the first were slain with our shot: the rest fled into the woods. The next morning with the light horsemen & one Canoe taking 25 with the Colonel of the Chesepians, and the Sergeant major, I went to Dasamonquepeio: and being landed, sent Pemisapan word by one of his own Savages that met me at the shore, that I was going to Croatoan, and meant to take him in the way to complain unto him of Osocon, who the night past was conveying away my prisoner, whom I had there present tied in an handlock. Hereupon the king did abide my coming to him, and finding my self amidst seven or eight of his principal Weroances and followers, (not regarding any of the common sort) I gave the watch-word agreed upon, (which was, Christ our victory) and immediately those his chief men and himself had by the mercy of God for our deliverance, that which they had purposed for us. The king himself being shot thorow by the Colonel with a pistol, lying on the ground for dead, & I looking as watchfully for the saving of Manteos friends, as others were busy that none of the rest should escape, suddenly he started up, and ran away as though he had not been touched, insomuch as he overran all the company, being by the way shot through the buttocks by mine Irish boy with my petronell. In the end an Irish man serving me, one Nugent, and the deputy provost, undertook him; and following him in the woods, overtook him: and I in some doubt least we had lost both the king & my man by our own negligence to have been intercepted by the Savages, we met him returning out of the woods with Pemisapans head in his hand.

This fell out the first of June 1586, and the eight of the same advertisement to me from captain Stafford, lying at my lord Admirals Island, that he had discovered a great fleet of three and twenty sails: but whether they were friends or foes, he could not yet discern. He advised me to stand upon as good guard as I could.

✿   ✿   ✿

He brought me a letter from the General Sir Francis Drake, with a most bountiful and honorable offer for the supply of our necessities to the performance of the action we were entered into; and that not only of victuals, munition, and clothing, but also of barks, pinnesses, and boats; they also by him to be victualled, manned, and furnished to my contentment.

✿   ✿   ✿

Hereupon calling such Captains and gentlemen of my company as then were at hand, who were all as privy as my self to the Generals offer: their whole request was to me, that considering the case that we stood in, the weakness of our company, the small number of the same, the carrying away of our first appointed bark, with those two especial Masters, with our principal provisions in the same, by the very hand of God as it seemed, stretched out to take us from thence; considering also, that his second offer, though most honorable of his part, yet of ours not to be taken, insomuch as there was no possibility for her with any safety to be brought into the harbor: seeing furthermore, our hope for supply with Sir Richard Greenvill, so undoubtedly promised us before Easter, not yet come, neither then likely to come this year, considering the doings in England for Flanders, and also for America, that therefore I would resolve my self with my company to go into England in that fleet, and accordingly to make request to the General in all our names, that he would be pleased to give us present passage with him. Which request of ours by my self delivered unto him, he most readily assented unto: and so he sending immediately his pinnesses unto our Island for the fetching away of a few that there were left with our baggage, the weather was so boisterous, & the pinnesses so often on ground, that the most of all we had, with all our Cards, Books and writings were by the Sailors cast overboard, the greater number of the fleet being much aggrieved with their long and dangerous abode in that miserable road.

From whence the General in the name of the Almighty, weighing his anchors (having bestowed us among his fleet) for the relief of whom he had in that storm sustained more peril of wreck then in all his former most honorable actions against the Spaniards, with praises unto God for all, set sail the nineteenth of June 1586, and arrived in Portsmouth the seven and twentieth of July the same year.

Source:

Richard Hakluyt. *The Principal Navigations Voyages Traffiques and Discoveries of the English Nation.* Edited by Richard Hakluyt and Edmund Goldsmid. Edinburgh: E. & G. Goldsmid, 1885–1890.

The "Lost Colony" of Roanoke, 1587

In 1587 Sir Walter Raleigh sent a new colony to Virginia to replace the failed colony of 1586. Unlike the first group, this settlement included women and children and was more community-oriented than the previous military-style outpost. The colonists had invested in the venture and were promised land and a voice in their own government in return. John White, a veteran of the first colony, was appointed governor, and 12 men were designated "assistants" in the new "City of Raleigh." Unfortunately, the second colony did not fare much better than the first. They had planned to land further north, in the Chesapeake Bay area, where the land would be easier to farm, but the ship's captain refused to take them that far, so the colonists were forced to establish a colony on the ruins of the first settlement. Then intermittent hostilities with the Indians escalated when the English mistook the friendly Croatoans for an unfriendly tribe and attacked them in retaliation for the murder of colonist George Howe. These factors, combined with a shortage of food and a three-year delay in receiving new supplies, all contributed to the colony's fate.

Before the year was out, John White left his daughter, Eleanor, and newborn granddaughter, Virginia Dare, the first English child born in the New World, and returned to England for supplies. The outbreak of war with Spain, however, kept him in England for three more years, and it was not until March of 1590 that he was able to sail to the Roanoke colony. White, who was primarily a passenger on this voyage, had little control over a captain and crew that took a greater interest in piracy than the relief expedition. White and the crew reached Hatorask, near Roanoke Island, in August and spotted smoke on the island but found the settlement deserted when they arrived. Before his departure three years earlier, White and the settlers had agreed that if it were necessary for them to move to another location, they would carve the name of the new place on a tree at the old site. If they were in any danger, they were to inscribe a cross over the name. When White arrived he found the letters *croatoan* carved on a tree outside the main fort. There was no cross, so White assumed they had safely removed to a nearby island where the friendly Croatoan Indians lived. However, before he could seek the colonists there, a storm blew in and forced the expedition to return to England. White could not put together another voyage to search for the colony, and Sir Walter Raleigh, whose patent of discovery had expired in 1590, was also unable to charter a successful relief effort, despite several attempts to do so. When the Jamestown colonists arrived in 1607, they resumed the search for the missing colony. Investigations into Indian accounts of Europeans living in the area proved fruitless, and no survivors were ever found. Today, more than 400 years later, the fate of the "Lost Colony" remains a mystery.

The excerpt below recounts the arrival of the second group of colonists, their interactions with the Indians, the birth of Virginia Dare, and the colonists' decision to send White back to England for supplies.

The fourth Voyage made to Virginia with three ships, in the yere 1587. Wherein was transported the second Colonie

In the yeere of our Lord 1587. Sir Walter Ralegh intending to persevere in the planting of his Countrey of Virginia, prepared a newe Colonie of one hundred and fiftie men to be sent thither, under the charge of John White, whom hee appointed Governour, and also appointed unto him twelve Assistants, unto whom hee gave a Charter, and incorporated them by the name of Governour and Assistants of the Citie of Ralegh in Virginia.

July

The two and twentieth of July wee arrived safe at Hatorask, where our ship and pinnesse ankered: the Governour went aboard the pinnesse, accompanied with fortie of his best men, intending to passe up to Roanoak foorthwith, hoping there to finde those fifteene Englishmen, which Sir Richard Grinvile had left there the yeere before, with whom hee meant to have conference, concerning the state of the Countrey, and Savages, meaning after he had done so, to returne againe to the fleete, all passe along the coast, to the Bay of Chesepiok, where we intended to make our seate and forte, according to the charge given us among other directions in writing under the hande of Sir Walter Ralegh: but assoone as we were put with our pinnesse from the ship, a Gentleman by the meanes of Ferdinando, who was appointed to returne for England, called to the sailers in the pinnesse, charging them not to bring any of the planters backe againe, but to leave them in the Island, except the Governour, & two or three such as he approved, saying that the Summer was farre spent, wherefore hee would land all the planters in no other place. Unto this were all the saylers, both in the pinnesse, and shippe, perswaded by the Master, wherefore it booted not the Governour to contend with them, but passed to Roanoak, and the same night at sunne-set went aland on the Island, in the place where our fifteene men were left, but we found none of them, nor any signe that they had bene there, saving onely wee found the bones of one of those fifteene, which the Savages had slaine long before.

The three and twentieth of July the Governour with divers of his company, walked to the North ende of the Island, where Master Ralfe Lane had his forte, with sundry necessary and decent dwelling houses, made by his men about it the yeere before, where wee hoped to find some signes, or certaine knowledge of our fifteene men. When we came thither, we found the fort rased downe, but all the houses standing unhurt, saving that the neather roomes of them, and also of the forte, were overgrowen with Melons of divers sortes, and Deer within them, feeding on those Melons: so wee returned to our company, without hope of ever seeing any of the fifteene men living.

The eight and twentieth, George Howe, one of our twelve Assistants was slaine by divers Savages, which were come over to Roanoak, either of purpose to espie our company, and what number we were, or else to hunt Deere, whereof were many in the Island. These Savages being secretly hidden among high reedes, where oftentimes they find the Deere asleep, and so kill them, espied our man wading in the water alone, almost naked, without any weapon, save only a smal forked sticke, catching Crabs therewithal, and also being strayed two miles from his company, and shot at him in the water, where they gave him sixteen wounds with their arrowes: and after they had slaine him with their wooden swords, they beat his head in pieces, and fled over the water to the maine.

On the thirtieth of July Master Stafford and twenty of our men passed by water to the Island of Croatan, with Manteo, who had his mother, and many of his kinred

dwelling in that island, of whom wee hoped to understand some newes of our fifteene men, but especially to learne the disposition of the people of the countrey towards us, and to renew our old friendship with them. At our first landing they seemed as though they would fight with us: but perceiving us begin to march with our shot towardes them, they turned their backes, and fled. Then Manteo their countrey man called to them in their owne language, whom, assoone as they heard, they returned, and threwe away their bowes and arrows, and some of them came unto us, embracing us and entertaining us friendly, desiring us not to gather or spill any of their corne, for that they had but little. We answered them, that neither their corne, nor any other nor any other thing of theirs should be diminished by any of us, and that our comming was onely to renew the old love, that was betweene us and them at the first, and to live with them as brethren and friends: which answere seemed to please them well, wherefore they requested us to walke up to their Towne, who there feasted us after their maner, and desired us earnestly, that there might bee some token or badge given them of us, whereby we might know them to be our friends, when we met them any where out of the Towne or Island. They told us further, that for want of some such badge, divers of them were hurt the yeere before, being found out of the Island by Master Lane his company, where of they shewed us one, which at that very instant lay lame, and had lien of that hurt ever since: but they sayd, they knew our men mistooke them, and hurt them in stead of Winginos men, wherefore they held us excused.

August

The next day we had conference further with them, concerning the people of Secotan, Aquascogoc, & Pomeiok, willing them of Croatan to certifie the people of those townes, that if they would accept our friendship, we would willingly receive them againe, and that all unfriendly dealings past on both parts, should be utterly forgiven and forgotten. To this the chiefe men of Croatan answered, that they would gladly doe the best they could, and within seven dayes, bring the Wiroances and chiefe Governours of those townes with them, to our Governour at Roanoak, or their answere. We also understood of the men of Croatoan, that our man Master Howe was slaine by the remnant of Winginos men dwelling then at Dasamonguepeuk, with whom Wanchese kept companie: and also we understood by them of Croatoan, how that the 15 Englishmen left at Roanoak the yeere before, by Sir Richard Grinvile, were suddenly set upon, by 30 of the men of Secota, Aquascogoc, and Dasamonguepek, in manner following. They conveyed themselves secretly behind the trees, neere the houses where our men carelesly lived: and having perceived that of those fifteene they could see but eleven only, two of those Savages appeared to the 11 Englishmen, calling to them by friendly signes, that but two of their chiefest men should come unarmed to speake with those two Savages, who seemed also to bee unarmed. Wherefore two of the chiefest of our Englishmen went gladly to them: but whilest one of those Savages traiterously imbraced one of our men, the other with his sworde of wood, which he had secretly hidden under his mantell, strooke him on the head and slew him, and presently the other eight and twenty Savages shewed them selves: the other Englishman perceiving this, fled to his company, whom the Savages pursued with their bowes, and arrowes, so fast, that the Englishmen were forced to take the house, wherein all their victuall, and weapons were: but the Savages, foorthwith set the same on fire: by meanes wherof our men were forced to take up such weapons as came first to hand, and without order to runne foorth among the Savages, with whom they skirmished above an howre. In this skirmish another of our men was shotte into the mouth with an arrow, where hee died: and also one of the Savages was shot into the side by one of our men, with a wild fire arrow, whereof he died presently. The place where they fought was of great advantage to the Savages, by meanes of the thicke trees, behinde which the Savages through their nimblenes, defended themselves, and so offended our men with their arrowes, that our men being some of them hurt, retyred fighting to the water side, where their boat lay, with which they fled towards Hatorask. By that time they had rowed but a quarter of a mile, they espied their foure fellows coming from a creeke thereby, where they had bene to fetch Oysters: these foure they received into their boate, leaving Roanoak, and landed on a little Island on the right hand of our entrance into the harbour of Hatorask, where they remayned a while, but afterward departed, whither as yet we know not.

Having nowe sufficiently dispatched our businesse at Croatoan, the same day we departed friendly, taking our leave, and came aboord the fleete at Hatorask.

The eight of August, the Governour having long expected the comming of the Wiroanses of Pomeiok, Aquascogoc, Secota, and Dasamonguepeuk, seeing that the seven dayes were past, within which they promised to come in, or to send their answeres by the men of Croatoan, and no tidings of them heard, being certainly also informed by those men of Croatoan, that the remnant of Wingina his men, which were left alive, who dwelt at Dasamonquepeuk, were they which had slaine George Howe, and were also at the driving of our eleven Englishmen from Roanoak, hee thought to deferre revenge thereof no longer. Wherefore the same night about midnight, he passed over the water, accompanied with Captaine Stafford, and 24 men, wherof Manteo was one, whom we tooke with us to be our guide to the place where those Savages dwelt, where he behaved himselfe toward us as a most faithfull Englishman.

The next day, being the 9 of August, in the morning so early that it was yet darke, we landed neere the dwelling place of our enemies, & very secretly conveyed our selves through the woods, to that side, where we had their houses betweene us and the water: and having espied their fire, and some sitting about it, we presently set on them: the miserable soules herewith amazed, fled into a place of thicke reedes, growing fast by, where our men perceiving them, shot one of them through the bodie with a bullet, and therewith we entred the reedes, among which we hoped to acquite their evill doing towards us, but we were deceived, for those Savages were our friends, and were come from Croatoan to gather the corne & fruit of that place, because they understood our enemies were fled immediately after they had slaine George Howe, and for haste had left all their corne, Tobacco, and Pompions standing in such sort, that al had bene devoured by the birds, and Deere, if it had not bene gathered in time: but they had like to have payd deerely for it: for it was so darke, that they being naked, and their men and women appareled all so like others, wee knew not but that they were al men: and if that one of them which was a Wiroances wife had not had a child at her backe, shee had bene slaine in stead of a man, and as hap was, another Savage knew master Stafford, and ran to him, calling him by his name, whereby hee was saved. Finding our selves thus disappointed of our purpose, we gathered al the corne, Pease, Pompions, and Tabacco that we found ripe, leaving the rest unspoiled, and tooke Menatoan, his wife, with the yong child and the other Savages with us over the water to Roanoake. Although the mistaking of these Savages somewhat grieved Manteo, yet he imputed their harme to their owne folly, saying to them, that if their Wiroances had kept their promise in comming to the Governour at the day appointed, they had not knowen that mischance.

The 13 of August our Savage Manteo, by the commandement of Sir Walter Ralegh, was christened in Roanoak, and called Lord thereof, and as Dasamonguepek, in reward of his faithfull service.

The 18 Elenor, daughter of the Governour, and wife to Ananias Dare one of the Assistants, was delivered of a daughter in Roanoak, and the same was christened there the Sonday following, and because this child was the first Christian borne in Virginia, shee was named Virginia. By this time our ships had unladen the goods and victuals of the planters, and began to take in wood, and fresh water, and to new calke and trimme them for England: the planters also prepared their letters and tokens to send backe into England.

The next day the 22 of August, the whole company both of the Assistants and planters came to the Governour, and with one voice requested him to returne himselfe into England, for the better and sooner obtaining of supplies, and other necessaries for them: but he refused it, and alleaged many sufficient causes, why he would not: the one was, that he could not so suddenly returne backe againe without his great discredite, leaving the action, and so many whome hee partly had procured through his perswasions, to leave their native countrey, and undertake that voyage, and that some enemies to him and the action at his returne into England would not spare to slander falsly both him and the action, by saying, hee went to Virginia, but politikely, and to no other end but to leade so many into a countrey, in which hee never meant to stay himselfe, and there to leave them behind him. Also he alleaged, that seeing they intended to remove 50 miles further up into the maine presently, he being then absent, his stuffe and goods might be both spoiled, & most of them pilfered away in the cariage, so that at his returne he should be either forced to provide himselfe of all such things againe, or else at his comming againe to Virginia find himselfe utterly unfurnished, whereof already he had found some proofe, being but once from them three dayes. Wherefore he concluded that he would not goe himselfe.

The next day, not onely the Assistants but divers others, as well women as men, began to renew their requests to the Governour againe, to take upon him to returne into England for the supply, and dispatch of all such things as there were to be done, promising to make him their bond under all their handes and seales for the safe preserving of all his goods for him at his returne to Virginia, so that if any part thereof were spoyled or lost, they would see it restored to him, or his Assignes, whensoever the same should be missed and demanded: which bond, with a testimony under their hands and seales, they forthwith made, and delivered into his hands. The copie of the testimony I thought good to set downe.

May it please you, her Majesties subjects of England, we your friends and countrey-men, the planters in Virginia, doe by these presents let you and every of you to understand, that for the present and speedy supply of certaine our knowen and apparent lackes and needes, most requisite and necessary for the good and happy planting of us, or any other in this land of Virginia, wee all of one minde & consent, have most earnestly intreated, and uncessantly requested John White, Governour of the planters in Virginia, to passe into England, for the better and more assured help, and setting forward of the foresayd supplies: and knowing assuredly that he both can best, and wil labour and take paines in that behalfe for us all, and he not once, but often refusing it, for our sakes, and for the honour and maintenance of the action, hath at last, though much against his will, through our importunacie, yielded to leave his governement, and all his goods among us, and

himselfe in all our behalfes to passe into England, of whose knowledge and fidelitie in handling this matter, as all others, we doe assure ourselves by these presents, and will you to give all credite thereunto, the 25 of August 1587.

The Governour being at the last through their extreame intreating constrayned to returne into England, having then but halfe a dayes respite to prepare himselfe for the same, departed from Roanoak the seven and twentieth of August in the morning, and the same day about midnight, came aboord the Flieboat, who already had weyed anker, and rode without the barre, the Admirall riding by them, who but the same morning was newly come thither againe. The same day both the ships weyed anker, and set saile for England.

Source:

Richard Hakluyt. *The Principal Navigations Voyages Traffiques and Discoveries of the English Nation.* Edited by Richard Hakluyt and Edmund Goldsmid. Edinburgh: E. & G. Goldsmid, 1885–1890.

Constitution of the Iroquois, Late 16th Century

During the latter half of the 16th century, the Iroquois, led by Dekanawidah, a Huron prophet from the north, and Hiawatha, a Mohawk medicine man, formed a confederacy known as the League of Five Nations. This union joined the Mohawk, Onondaga, Seneca, Oneida, and Cayuga tribes into one nation. Later, in 1715, the Tuscarora, who had moved north to avoid warfare with white settlers, were adopted into the confederacy. The name *Iroquois* is derived from the French pronunciation of the Algonquian word *ireohkwa*, which means "real adders" or "snakes." The Iroquois people refer to themselves collectively as the Haudenosaunee, meaning "people of the longhouse." The Haudenosaunee originally lived communally in long, rectangular wooden houses. They thought of their confederacy as one big longhouse that stretched across the territory of the combined nations. The Constitution of the Iroquois Nations, or Gayanashagowa, the Great Binding Law, was most likely solidified in the culture's oral tradition between 1450 and 1500, but a written form did not appear until the early 20th century. The league is the earliest example of a structured democracy in North America and predates democratic governments in many European nations. It has been suggested that the U.S. Constitution is somewhat indebted to the Iroquois Constitution. There are certain resemblances, including the division of both governments into three parties (or branches) in order to maintain a system of checks and balances. However, unlike the U.S. Constitution, the Iroquois Constitution dictates a much broader range of social and cultural laws, including the society's matrilineal nature and instructions for adoption and funeral ceremonies.

The Constitution of the Iroquois Nations: The Great Binding Law, Gayanashagowa

1. I am Dekanawidah and with the Five Nations' Confederate Lords I plant the Tree of Great Peace. I plant it in your territory, Adodarhoh, and the Onondaga Nation, in the territory of you who are Firekeepers.

I name the tree the Tree of the Great Long Leaves. Under the shade of this Tree of the Great Peace we spread the soft white feathery down of the globe thistle as seats for you, Adodarhoh, and your cousin Lords.

We place you upon those seats, spread soft with the feathery down of the globe thistle, there beneath the shade of the spreading branches of the Tree of Peace. There shall you sit and watch the Council Fire of the Confederacy of the Five Nations, and all the affairs of the Five Nations shall be transacted at this place before you, Adodarhoh, and your cousin Lords, by the Confederate Lords of the Five Nations.

2. Roots have spread out from the Tree of the Great Peace, one to the north, one to the east, one to the south and one to the west. The name of these roots is the Great White Roots and their nature is Peace and Strength.

If any man or any nation outside the Five Nations shall obey the laws of the Great Peace and make known their disposition to the Lords of the Confederacy, they may trace the Roots to the Tree and if their minds are clean and they are obedient and promise to obey the wishes of the Confederate Council, they shall be welcomed to take shelter beneath the Tree of the Long Leaves.

We place at the top of the Tree of the Long Leaves an Eagle who is able to see afar. If he sees in the distance any evil approaching or any danger threatening he will at once warn the people of the Confederacy.

3. To you Adodarhoh, the Onondaga cousin Lords, I and the other Confederate Lords have entrusted the caretaking and the watching of the Five Nations Council Fire.

When there is any business to be transacted and the Confederate Council is not in session, a messenger shall be dispatched either to Adodarhoh, Hononwirehtonh or Skanawatih, Fire Keepers, or to their War Chiefs with a full statement of the case desired to be considered. Then shall Adodarhoh call his cousin (associate) Lords together and consider whether or not the case is of sufficient importance to demand the attention of the Confederate Council. If so, Adodarhoh shall dispatch messengers to summon all the Confederate Lords to assemble beneath the Tree of the Long Leaves.

When the Lords are assembled the Council Fire shall be kindled, but not with chestnut wood, and Adodarhoh shall formally open the Council.

Then shall Adodarhoh and his cousin Lords, the Fire Keepers, announce the subject for discussion.

The Smoke of the Confederate Council Fire shall ever ascend and pierce the sky so that other nations who may be allies may see the Council Fire of the Great Peace.

Adodarhoh and his cousin Lords are entrusted with the Keeping of the Council Fire.

4. You, Adodarhoh, and your thirteen cousin Lords, shall faithfully keep the space about the Council Fire clean and you shall allow neither dust nor dirt to accumulate. I lay a Long Wing before you as a broom. As a weapon against a crawling creature I lay a staff with you so that you may thrust it away from the Council Fire. If you fail to cast it out then call the rest of the United Lords to your aid.

5. The Council of the Mohawk shall be divided into three parties as follows: Tekarihoken, Ayonhwhathah and Shadekariwade are the first party; Sharenhowaneh, Deyoenhegwenh and Oghrenghrehgowah are the second party, and Dehennakrineh, Aghstawenserenthah and Shoskoharowaneh are the third party.

The third party is to listen only to the discussion of the first and second parties and if an error is made or the proceeding is irregular they are to call attention to it, and when the case is right and properly decided by the two parties they shall confirm the decision of the two parties and refer the case to the Seneca Lords for their decision. When the Seneca Lords have decided in accord with the Mohawk Lords, the case or question shall be referred to the Cayuga and Oneida Lords on the opposite side of the house.

6. I, Dekanawidah, appoint the Mohawk Lords the heads and the leaders of the Five Nations Confederacy. The Mohawk Lords are the foundation of the Great Peace and it shall, therefore, be against the Great Binding Law to pass measures in the Confederate Council after the Mohawk Lords have protested against them.

No council of the Confederate Lords shall be legal unless all the Mohawk Lords are present.

7. Whenever the Confederate Lords shall assemble for the purpose of holding a council, the Onondaga Lords shall open it by expressing their gratitude to their cousin Lords and greeting them, and they shall make an address and offer thanks to the earth where men dwell, to the streams of water, the pools, the springs and the lakes, to the maize and the fruits, to the medicinal herbs and trees, to the forest trees for their usefulness, to the animals that serve as food and give their pelts for clothing, to the great winds and the lesser winds, to the Thunderers, to the Sun, the mighty warrior, to the moon, to the messengers of the Creator who reveal his wishes and to the Great Creator who dwells in the heavens above, who gives all the things useful to men, and who is the source and the ruler of health and life.

Then shall the Onondaga Lords declare the council open.

The council shall not sit after darkness has set in.

8. The Firekeepers shall formally open and close all councils of the Confederate Lords, and they shall pass upon all matters deliberated upon by the two sides and render their decision.

Every Onondaga Lord (or his deputy) must be present at every Confederate Council and must agree with the majority without unwarrantable dissent, so that a unanimous decision may be rendered. If Adodarhoh or any of his cousin Lords are absent from a Confederate Council, any other Firekeeper may open and close the Council, but the Firekeepers present may not give any decisions, unless the matter is of small importance.

9. All the business of the Five Nations Confederate Council shall be conducted by the two combined bodies of Confederate Lords. First the question shall be passed upon by the Mohawk and Seneca Lords, then it shall be discussed and passed by the Oneida and Cayuga Lords. Their decisions shall then be referred to the Onondaga Lords (Firekeepers) for final judgement.

The same process shall obtain when a question is brought before the council by an individual or a War Chief.

10. In all cases the procedure must be as follows: when the Mohawk and Seneca Lords have unanimously agreed upon a question, they shall report their decision to the Cayuga and Oneida Lords who shall deliberate upon the question and report a unanimous decision to the Mohawk Lords. The Mohawk Lords will then report the standing of the case to the Firekeepers, who shall render a decision as they see fit in case of a disagreement by the two bodies, or confirm the decisions of the two bodies if they are identical. The Firekeepers shall then report their decision to the Mohawk Lords who shall announce it to the open council.

11. If through any misunderstanding or obstinacy on the part of the Firekeepers, they render a decision at variance with that of the Two Sides, the Two Sides shall reconsider the matter and if their decisions are jointly the same as before they shall report to the Firekeepers who are then compelled to confirm their joint decision.

12. When a case comes before the Onondaga Lords (Firekeepers) for discussion and decision, Adodarho shall introduce the matter to his comrade Lords who shall then discuss it in their two bodies. Every Onondaga Lord except Hononwiretonh shall deliberate and he shall listen only. When a unanimous decision shall have been reached by the two bodies of Firekeepers, Adodarho shall notify Hononwiretonh of the fact when he shall confirm it. He shall refuse to confirm a decision if it is not unanimously agreed upon by both sides of the Firekeepers.

13. No Lord shall ask a question of the body of Confederate Lords when they are discussing a case, question or proposition. He may only deliberate in a low tone with the separate body of which he is a member.

14. When the Council of the Five Nation Lords shall convene they shall appoint a speaker for the day. He shall be a Lord of either the Mohawk, Onondaga or Seneca Nation.

The next day the Council shall appoint another speaker, but the first speaker may be reappointed if there is no objection, but a speaker's term shall not be regarded more than for the day.

15. No individual or foreign nation interested in a case, question or proposition shall have any voice in the Confederate Council except to answer a question put to him or them by the speaker for the Lords.

16. If the conditions which shall arise at any future time call for an addition to or change of this law, the case shall be carefully considered and if a new beam seems necessary or beneficial, the proposed change shall be voted upon and if adopted it shall be called, "Added to the Rafters."

Rights, Duties and Qualifications of Lords

17. A bunch of a certain number of shell (wampum) strings each two spans in length shall be given to each of the female families in which the Lordship titles are vested. The right of bestowing the title shall be hereditary in the family of the females legally possessing the bunch of shell strings and the strings shall be the token that the females of the family have the proprietary right to the Lordship title for all time to come, subject to certain restrictions hereinafter mentioned.

18. If any Confederate Lord neglects or refuses to attend the Confederate Council, the other Lords of the Nation of which he is a member shall require their War Chief to request the female sponsors of the Lord so guilty of defection to demand his attendance of the Council. If he refuses, the women holding the title shall immediately select another candidate for the title.

No Lord shall be asked more than once to attend the Confederate Council.

19. If at any time it shall be manifest that a Confederate Lord has not in mind the welfare of the people or disobeys the rules of this Great Law, the men or women of the Confederacy, or both jointly, shall come to the Council and upbraid the erring Lord through his War Chief. If the complaint of the people through the War Chief is not heeded the first time it shall be uttered again and then if no attention is given a third complaint and warning shall be given. If the Lord is contumacious the matter shall go to the council of War Chiefs.

The War Chiefs shall then divest the erring Lord of his title by order of the women in whom the titleship is vested. When the Lord is deposed the women shall notify the

Confederate Lords through their War Chief, and the Confederate Lords shall sanction the act. The women will then select another of their sons as a candidate and the Lords shall elect him. Then shall the chosen one be installed by the Installation Ceremony.

When a Lord is to be deposed, his War Chief shall address him as follows:

"So you, ———, disregard and set at naught the warnings of your women relatives. So you fling the warnings over your shoulder to cast them behind you.

"Behold the brightness of the Sun and in the brightness of the Sun's light I depose you of your title and remove the sacred emblem of your Lordship title. I remove from your brow the deer's antlers, which was the emblem of your position and token of your nobility. I now depose you and return the antlers to the women whose heritage they are."

The War Chief shall now address the women of the deposed Lord and say:

"Mothers, as I have now deposed your Lord, I now return to you the emblem and the title of Lordship, therefore repossess them."

Again addressing himself to the deposed Lord he shall say:

"As I have now deposed and discharged you so you are now no longer Lord. You shall now go your way alone, the rest of the people of the Confederacy will not go with you, for we know not the kind of mind that possesses you. As the Creator has nothing to do with wrong so he will not come to rescue you from the precipice of destruction in which you have cast yourself. You shall never be restored to the position which you once occupied."

Then shall the War Chief address himself to the Lords of the Nation to which the deposed Lord belongs and say:

"Know you, my Lords, that I have taken the deer's antlers from the brow of ———, the emblem of his position and token of his greatness."

The Lords of the Confederacy shall then have no other alternative than to sanction the discharge of the offending Lord.

20. If a Lord of the Confederacy of the Five Nations should commit murder the other Lords of the Nation shall assemble at the place where the corpse lies and prepare to depose the criminal Lord. If it is impossible to meet at the scene of the crime the Lords shall discuss the matter at the next Council of their Nation and request their War Chief to depose the Lord guilty of crime, to "bury" his women relatives and to transfer the Lordship title to a sister family.

The War Chief shall address the Lord guilty of murder and say:

"So you, ——— (giving his name) did kill ——— (naming the slain man), with your own hands! You have

comitted a grave sin in the eyes of the Creator. Behold the bright light of the Sun, and in the brightness of the Sun's light I depose you of your title and remove the horns, the sacred emblems of your Lordship title. I remove from your brow the deer's antlers, which was the emblem of your position and token of your nobility. I now depose you and expel you and you shall depart at once from the territory of the Five Nations Confederacy and nevermore return again. We, the Five Nations Confederacy, moreover, bury your women relatives because the ancient Lordship title was never intended to have any union with bloodshed. Henceforth it shall not be their heritage. By the evil deed that you have done they have forfeited it forever."

The War Chief shall then hand the title to a sister family and he shall address it and say:

"Our mothers, ———, listen attentively while I address you on a solemn and important subject. I hereby transfer to you an ancient Lordship title for a great calamity has befallen it in the hands of the family of a former Lord. We trust that you, our mothers, will always guard it, and that you will warn your Lord always to be dutiful and to advise his people to ever live in love, peace and harmony that a great calamity may never happen again."

21. Certain physical defects in a Confederate Lord make him ineligible to sit in the Confederate Council. Such defects are infancy, idiocy, blindness, deafness, dumbness and impotency. When a Confederate Lord is restricted by any of these condition, a deputy shall be appointed by his sponsors to act for him, but in case of extreme necessity the restricted Lord may exercise his rights.

22. If a Confederate Lord desires to resign his title he shall notify the Lords of the Nation of which he is a member of his intention. If his coactive Lords refuse to accept his resignation he may not resign his title.

A Lord in proposing to resign may recommend any proper candidate which recommendation shall be received by the Lords, but unless confirmed and nominated by the women who hold the title the candidate so named shall not be considered.

23. Any Lord of the Five Nations Confederacy may construct shell strings (or wampum belts) of any size or length as pledges or records of matters of national or international importance.

When it is necessary to dispatch a shell string by a War Chief or other messenger as the token of a summons, the messenger shall recite the contents of the string to the party to whom it is sent. That party shall repeat the message and return the shell string and if there has been a sumons he shall make ready for the journey.

Any of the people of the Five Nations may use shells (or wampum) as the record of a pledge, contract or an agreement entered into and the same shall be binding as soon as shell strings shall have been exchanged by both parties.

24. The Lords of the Confederacy of the Five Nations shall be mentors of the people for all time. The thickness of their skin shall be seven spans—which is to say that they shall be proof against anger, offensive actions and criticism. Their hearts shall be full of peace and good will and their minds filled with a yearning for the welfare of the people of the Confederacy. With endless patience they shall carry out their duty and their firmness shall be tempered with a tenderness for their people. Neither anger nor fury shall find lodgement in their minds and all their words and actions shall be marked by calm deliberation.

25. If a Lord of the Confederacy should seek to establish any authority independent of the jurisdiction of the Confederacy of the Great Peace, which is the Five Nations, he shall be warned three times in open council, first by the women relatives, second by the men relatives and finally by the Lords of the Confederacy of the Nation to which he belongs. If the offending Lord is still obdurate he shall be dismissed by the War Chief of his nation for refusing to conform to the laws of the Great Peace. His nation shall then install the candidate nominated by the female name holders of his family.

26. It shall be the duty of all of the Five Nations Confederate Lords, from time to time as occasion demands, to act as mentors and spiritual guides of their people and remind them of their Creator's will and words. They shall say:

"Hearken, that peace may continue unto future days!

"Always listen to the words of the Great Creator, for he has spoken.

"United people, let not evil find lodging in your minds.

"For the Great Creator has spoken and the cause of Peace shall not become old.

"The cause of peace shall not die if you remember the Great Creator."

Every Confederate Lord shall speak words such as these to promote peace.

27. All Lords of the Five Nations Confederacy must be honest in all things. They must not idle or gossip, but be men possessing those honorable qualities that make true royaneh. It shall be a serious wrong for anyone to lead a Lord into trivial affairs, for the people must ever hold their Lords high in estimation out of respect to their honorable positions.

28. When a candidate Lord is to be installed he shall furnish four strings of shells (or wampum) one span in length bound together at one end. Such will constitute the evidence of his pledge to the Confederate Lords that he will live according to the constitution of the Great Peace and exercise justice in all affairs.

When the pledge is furnished the Speaker of the Council must hold the shell strings in his hand and address the opposite side of the Council Fire and he shall commence his address saying: "Now behold him. He has now become a Confederate Lord. See how splendid he looks." An address may then follow. At the end of it he shall send the bunch of shell strings to the oposite side and they shall be received as evidence of the pledge. Then shall the opposite side say:

"We now do crown you with the sacred emblem of the deer's antlers, the emblem of your Lordship. You shall now become a mentor of the people of the Five Nations. The thickness of your skin shall be seven spanss—which is to say that you shall be proof against anger, offensive actions and criticism. Your heart shall be filled with peace and good will and your mind filled with a yearning for the welfare of the people of the Confederacy. With endless patience you shall carry out your duty and your firmness shall be tempered with tenderness for your people. Neither anger nor fury shall find lodgement in your mind and all your words and actions shall be marked with calm deliberation. In all of your deliberations in the Confederate Council, in your efforts at law making, in all your official acts, self interest shall be cast into oblivion. Cast not over your shoulder behind you the warnings of the nephews and nieces should they chide you for any error or wrong you may do, but return to the way of the Great Law which is just and right. Look and listen for the welfare of the whole people and have always in view not only the present but also the coming generations, even those whose faces are yet beneath the surface of the ground—the unborn of the future Nation."

29. When a Lordship title is to be conferred, the candidate Lord shall furnish the cooked venison, the corn bread and the corn soup, together with other necessary things and the labor for the Conferring of Titles Festival.

30. The Lords of the Confederacy may confer the Lordship title upon a candidate whenever the Great Law is recited, if there be a candidate, for the Great Law speaks all the rules.

31. If a Lord of the Confederacy should become seriously ill and be thought near death, the women who are heirs of his title shall go to his house and lift his crown of deer antlers, the emblem of his Lordship, and place them at one side. If the Creator spares him and he rises from his bed of sickness he may rise with the antlers on his brow. The following words shall be used to temporarily remove the antlers: "Now our comrade Lord (or our relative Lord) the time has come when we must approach you in your illness. We remove for a time the deer's antlers from your brow, we remove the emblem of your Lordship title. The Great Law has decreed that no Lord should end his life with the antlers on his brow. We therefore lay them aside

in the room. If the Creator spares you and you recover from your illness you shall rise from your bed with the antlers on your brow as before and you shall resume your duties as Lord of the Confederacy and you may labor again for the Confederate people."

32. If a Lord of the Confederacy should die while the Council of the Five Nations is in session the Council shall adjourn for ten days. No Confederate Council shall sit within ten days of the death of a Lord of the Confederacy. If the Three Brothers (the Mohawk, the Onondaga and the Seneca) should lose one of their Lords by death, the Younger Brothers (the Oneida and the Cayuga) shall come to the surviving Lords of the Three Brothers on the tenth day and console them. If the Younger Brothers lose one of their Lords then the Three Brothers shall come to them and console them. And the consolation shall be the reading of the contents of the thirteen shell (wampum) strings of Ayonhwhathah. At the termination of this rite a successor shall be appointed, to be appointed by the women heirs of the Lordship title. If the women are not yet ready to place their nominee before the Lords the Speaker shall say, "Come let us go out." All shall leave the Council or the place of gathering. The installation shall then wait until such a time as the women are ready. The Speaker shall lead the way from the house by saying, "Let us depart to the edge of the woods and lie in waiting on our bellies." When the women title holders shall have chosen one of their sons the Confederate Lords will assemble in two places, the Younger Brothers in one place and the Three Older Brothers in another. The Lords who are to console the mourning Lords shall choose one of their number to sing the Pacification Hymn as they journey to the sorrowing Lords. The singer shall lead the way and the Lords and the people shall follow. When they reach the sorrowing Lords they shall hail the candidate Lord and perform the rite of Conferring the Lordship Title.

33. When a Confederate Lord dies, the surviving relatives shall immediately dispatch a messenger, a member of another clan, to the Lords in another locality. When the runner comes within hailing distance of the locality he shall utter a sad wail, thus: "Kwa-ah, Kwa-ah, Kwa-ah!" The sound shall be repeated three times and then again and again at intervals as many times as the distance may require. When the runner arrives at the settlement the people shall assemble and one must ask him the nature of his sad message. He shall then say, "Let us consider." Then he shall tell them of the death of the Lord. He shall deliver to them a string of shells (wampum) and say: "Here is the testimony, you have heard the message." He may then return home. It now becomes the duty of the Lords of the locality to send runners to other localities and each locality shall send other messengers until all Lords are notified. Runners shall travel day and night.

34. If a Lord dies and there is no candidate qualified for the office in the family of the women title holders, the Lords of the Nation shall give the title into the hands of a sister family in the clan until such a time as the original family produces a candidate, when the title shall be restored to the rightful owners. No Lordship title may be carried into the grave. The Lords of the Confederacy may dispossess a dead Lord of his title even at the grave.

Election of Pine Tree Chiefs

35. Should any man of the Nation assist with special ability or show great interest in the affairs of the Nation, if he proves himself wise, honest and worthy of confidence, the Confederate Lords may elect him to a seat with them and he may sit in the Confederate Council. He shall be proclaimed a 'Pine Tree sprung up for the Nation' and shall be installed as such at the next assembly for the installation of Lords. Should he ever do anything contrary to the rules of the Great Peace, he may not be deposed from office—no one shall cut him down—but thereafter everyone shall be deaf to his voice and his advice. Should he resign his seat and title no one shall prevent him. A Pine Tree chief has no authority to name a successor nor is his title hereditary.

Names, Duties and Rights of War Chiefs

36. The title names of the Chief Confederate Lords' War Chiefs shall be: Ayonwaehs, War Chief under Lord Takarihoken (Mohawk) Kahonwahdironh, War Chief under Lord Odatshedeh (Oneida) Ayendes, War Chief under Lord Adodarhoh (Onondaga) Wenenhs, War Chief under Lord Dekaenyonh (Cayuga) Shoneradowaneh, War Chief under Lord Skanyadariyo (Seneca). The women heirs of each head Lord's title shall be the heirs of the War Chief's title of their respective Lord. The War Chiefs shall be selected from the eligible sons of the female families holding the head Lordship titles.

37. There shall be one War Chief for each Nation and their duties shall be to carry messages for their Lords and to take up the arms of war in case of emergency. They shall not participate in the proceedings of the Confederate Council but shall watch its progress and in case of an erroneous action by a Lord they shall receive the complaints of the people and convey the warnings of the women to him. The people who wish to convey messages to the Lords in the Confederate Council shall do so through the War Chief of their Nation. It shall ever be his duty to lay the cases, questions and propositions of the people before the Confederate Council.

38. When a War Chief dies another shall be installed by the same rite as that by which a Lord is installed.

39. If a War Chief acts contrary to instructions or against the provisions of the Laws of the Great Peace, doing so in the capacity of his office, he shall be deposed

by his women relatives and by his men relatives. Either the women or the men alone or jointly may act in such a case. The women title holders shall then choose another candidate.

40. When the Lords of the Confederacy take occasion to dispatch a messenger in behalf of the Confederate Council, they shall wrap up any matter they may send and instruct the messenger to remember his errand, to turn not aside but to proceed faithfully to his destination and deliver his message according to every instruction.

41. If a message borne by a runner is the warning of an invasion he shall whoop, "Kwa-ah, Kwa-ah," twice and repeat at short intervals; then again at a longer interval. If a human being is found dead, the finder shall not touch the body but return home immediately shouting at short intervals, "Koo-weh!"

Clans and Consanguinity
42. Among the Five Nations and their posterity there shall be the following original clans: Great Name Bearer, Ancient Name Bearer, Great Bear, Ancient Bear, Turtle, Painted Turtle, Standing Rock, Large Plover, Deer, Pigeon Hawk, Eel, Ball, Opposite-Side-of-the-Hand, and Wild Potatoes. These clans distributed through their respective Nations, shall be the sole owners and holders of the soil of the country and in them is it vested as a birthright.

43. People of the Five Nations members of a certain clan shall recognize every other member of that clan, irrespective of the Nation, as relatives. Men and women, therefore, members of the same clan are forbidden to marry.

44. The lineal descent of the people of the Five Nations shall run in the female line. Women shall be considered the progenitors of the Nation. They shall own the land and the soil. Men and women shall follow the status of the mother.

45. The women heirs of the Confederated Lordship titles shall be called Royaneh (Noble) for all time to come.

46. The women of the Forty Eight (now fifty) Royaneh families shall be the heirs of the Authorized Names for all time to come. When an infant of the Five Nations is given an Authorized Name at the Midwinter Festival or at the Ripe Corn Festival, one in the cousinhood of which the infant is a member shall be appointed a speaker. He shall then announce to the opposite cousinhood the names of the father and the mother of the child together with the clan of the mother. Then the speaker shall announce the child's name twice. The uncle of the child shall then take the child in his arms and walking up and down the room shall sing: "My head is firm, I am of the Confederacy." As he sings the opposite cousinhood shall respond by chanting, "Hyenh, Hyenh, Hyenh, Hyenh," until the song is ended.

47. If the female heirs of a Confederate Lord's title become extinct, the title right shall be given by the Lords of the Confederacy to the sister family whom they shall elect and that family shall hold the name and transmit it to their (female) heirs, but they shall not appoint any of their sons as a candidate for a title until all the eligible men of the former family shall have died or otherwise have become ineligible.

48. If all the heirs of a Lordship title become extinct, and all the families in the clan, then the title shall be given by the Lords of the Confederacy to the family in a sister clan whom they shall elect.

49. If any of the Royaneh women, heirs of a titleship, shall wilfully withhold a Lordship or other title and refuse to bestow it, or if such heirs abandon, forsake or despise their heritage, then shall such women be deemed buried and their family extinct. The titleship shall then revert to a sister family or clan upon application and complaint. The Lords of the Confederacy shall elect the family or clan which shall in future hold the title.

50. The Royaneh women of the Confederacy heirs of the Lordship titles shall elect two women of their family as cooks for the Lord when the people shall assemble at his house for business or other purposes. It is not good nor honorable for a Confederate Lord to allow his people whom he has called to go hungry.

51. When a Lord holds a conference in his home, his wife, if she wishes, may prepare the food for the Union Lords who assemble with him. This is an honorable right which she may exercise and an expression of her esteem.

52. The Royaneh women, heirs of the Lordship titles, shall, should it be necessary, correct and admonish the holders of their titles. Those only who attend the Council may do this and those who do not shall not object to what has been said nor strive to undo the action.

53. When the Royaneh women, holders of a Lordship title, select one of their sons as a candidate, they shall select one who is trustworthy, of good character, of honest disposition, one who manages his own affairs, supports his own family, if any, and who has proven a faithful man to his Nation.

54. When a Lordship title becomes vacant through death or other cause, the Royaneh women of the clan in which the title is hereditary shall hold a council and shall choose one from among their sons to fill the office made vacant. Such a candidate shall not be the father of any Confederate Lord. If the choice is unanimous the name is referred to the men relatives of the clan. If they should disapprove it shall be their duty to select a candidate from among their own number. If then the men and women are unable to decide which of the two candidates shall be named, then the matter shall be referred to the Confederate Lords in the Clan. They shall decide which candidate

shall be named. If the men and the women agree to a candidate his name shall be referred to the sister clans for confirmation. If the sister clans confirm the choice, they shall refer their action to their Confederate Lords who shall ratify the choice and present it to their cousin Lords, and if the cousin Lords confirm the name then the candidate shall be installed by the proper ceremony for the conferring of Lordship titles.

Official Symbolism

55. A large bunch of shell strings, in the making of which the Five Nations Confederate Lords have equally contributed, shall symbolize the completeness of the union and certify the pledge of the nations represented by the Confederate Lords of the Mohawk, the Oneida, the Onondaga, the Cayuga and the Senecca, that all are united and formed into one body or union called the Union of the Great Law, which they have established. A bunch of shell strings is to be the symbol of the council fire of the Five Nations Confederacy. And the Lord whom the council of Firekeepers shall appoint to speak for them in opening the council shall hold the strands of shells in his hands when speaking. When he finishes speaking he shall deposit the strings on an elevated place (or pole) so that all the assembled Lords and the people may see it and know that the council is open and in progress. When the council adjourns the Lord who has been appointed by his comrade Lords to close it shall take the strands of shells in his hands and address the assembled Lords. Thus will the council adjourn until such time and place as appointed by the council. Then shall the shell strings be placed in a place for safekeeping. Every five years the Five Nations Confederate Lords and the people shall assemble together and shall ask one another if their minds are still in the same spirit of unity for the Great Binding Law and if any of the Five Nations shall not pledge continuance and steadfastness to the pledge of unity then the Great Binding Law shall dissolve.

56. Five strings of shell tied together as one shall represent the Five Nations. Each string shall represent one territory and the whole a completely united territory known as the Five Nations Confederate territory.

57. Five arrows shall be bound together very strong and each arrow shall represent one nation. As the five arrows are strongly bound this shall symbolize the complete union of the nations. Thus are the Five Nations united completely and enfolded together, united into one head, one body and one mind. Therefore they shall labor, legislate and council together for the interest of future generations. The Lords of the Confederacy shall eat together from one bowl the feast of cooked beaver's tail. While they are eating they are to use no sharp utensils for

if they should they might accidentally cut one another and bloodshed would follow. All measures must be taken to prevent the spilling of blood in any way.

58. There are now the Five Nations Confederate Lords standing with joined hands in a circle. This signifies and provides that should any one of the Confederate Lords leave the council and this Confederacy his crown of deer's horns, the emblem of his Lordship title, together with his birthright, shall lodge on the arms of the Union Lords whose hands are so joined. He forfeits his title and the crown falls from his brow but it shall remain in the Confederacy. A further meaning of this is that if any time any one of the Confederate Lords choose to submit to the law of a foreign people he is no longer in but out of the Confederacy, and persons of this class shall be called "They have alienated themselves." Likewise such persons who submit to laws of foreign nations shall forfeit all birthrights and claims on the Five Nations Confederacy and territory. You, the Five Nations Confederate Lords, be firm so that if a tree falls on your joined arms it shall not separate or weaken your hold. So shall the strength of the union be preserved.

59. A bunch of wampum shells on strings, three spans of the hand in length, the upper half of the bunch being white and the lower half black, and formed from equal contributions of the men of the Five Nations, shall be a token that the men have combined themselves into one head, one body and one thought, and it shall also symbolize their ratification of the peace pact of the Confederacy, whereby the Lords of the Five Nations have established the Great Peace.

The white portion of the shell strings represent the women and the black portion the men. The black portion, furthermore, is a token of power and authority vested in the men of the Five Nations.

This string of wampum vests the people with the right to correct their erring Lords. In case a part or all the Lords pursue a course not vouched for by the people and heed not the third warning of their women relatives, then the matter shall be taken to the General Council of the women of the Five Nations. If the Lords notified and warned three times fail to heed, then the case falls into the hands of the men of the Five Nations. The War Chiefs shall then, by right of such power and authority, enter the open concil to warn the Lord or Lords to return from the wrong course. If the Lords heed the warning they shall say, "we will reply tomorrow." If then an answer is returned in favor of justice and in accord with this Great Law, then the Lords shall individualy pledge themselves again by again furnishing the necessary shells for the pledge. Then shall the War Chief or Chiefs exhort the Lords urging them to be just and true.

Should it happen that the Lords refuse to heed the third warning, then two courses are open: either the men may decide in their council to depose the Lord or Lords or to club them to death with war clubs. Should they in their council decide to take the first course the War Chief shall address the Lord or Lords, saying: "Since you the Lords of the Five Nations have refused to return to the procedure of the Constitution, we now declare your seats vacant, we take off your horns, the token of your Lordship, and others shall be chosen and installed in your seats, therefore vacate your seats."

Should the men in their council adopt the second course, the War Chief shall order his men to enter the council, to take positions beside the Lords, sitting between them wherever possible. When this is accomplished the War Chief holding in his outstretched hand a bunch of black wampum strings shall say to the erring Lords: "So now, Lords of the Five United Nations, harken to these last words from your men. You have not heeded the warnings of the women relatives, you have not heeded the warnings of the General Council of women and you have not heeded the warnings of the men of the nations, all urging you to return to the right course of action. Since you are determined to resist and to withhold justice from your people there is only one course for us to adopt." At this point the War Chief shall let drop the bunch of black wampum and the men shall spring to their feet and club the erring Lords to death. Any erring Lord may submit before the War Chief lets fall the black wampum. Then his execution is withheld.

The black wampum here used symbolizes that the power to execute is buried but that it may be raised up again by the men. It is buried but when occasion arises they may pull it up and derive their power and authority to act as here described.

60. A broad dark belt of wampum of thirty-eight rows, having a white heart in the center, on either side of which are two white squares all connected with the heart by white rows of beads shall be the emblem of the unity of the Five Nations.

The first of the squares on the left represents the Mohawk nation and its territory; the second square on the left and the one near the heart, represents the Oneida nation and its territory; the white heart in the middle represents the Onondaga nation and its territory, and it also means that the heart of the Five Nations is single in its loyalty to the Great Peace, that the Great Peace is lodged in the heart (meaning the Onondaga Lords), and that the Council Fire is to burn there for the Five Nations, and further, it means that the authority is given to advance the cause of peace whereby hostile nations out of the Confederacy shall cease warfare; the white square to the right of

the heart represents the Cayuga nation and its territory and the fourth and last white square represents the Seneca nation and its territory.

White shall here symbolize that no evil or jealous thoughts shall creep into the minds of the Lords while in Council under the Great Peace. White, the emblem of peace, love, charity and equity surrounds and guards the Five Nations.

61. Should a great calamity threaten the generations rising and living of the Five United Nations, then he who is able to climb to the top of the Tree of the Great Long Leaves may do so. When, then, he reaches the top of the tree he shall look about in all directions, and, should he see that evil things indeed are approaching, then he shall call to the people of the Five United Nations assembled beneath the Tree of the Great Long Leaves and say: "A calamity threatens your happiness." Then shall the Lords convene in council and discuss the impending evil. When all the truths relating to the trouble shall be fully known and found to be truths, then shall the people seek out a Tree of Ka-hon-ka-ah-go-nah, and when they shall find it they shall assemble their heads together and lodge for a time between its roots. Then, their labors being finished, they may hope for happiness for many days after.

62. When the Confederate Council of the Five Nations declares for a reading of the belts of shell calling to mind these laws, they shall provide for the reader a specially made mat woven of the fibers of wild hemp. The mat shall not be used again, for such formality is called the honoring of the importance of the law.

63. Should two sons of opposite sides of the council fire agree in a desire to hear the reciting of the laws of the Great Peace and so refresh their memories in the way ordained by the founder of the Confederacy, they shall notify Adodarho. He then shall consult with five of his coactive Lords and they in turn shall consult with their eight brethern. Then should they decide to accede to the request of the two sons from opposite sides of the Council Fire, Adodarho shall send messengers to notify the Chief Lords of each of the Five Nations. Then they shall despatch their War Chiefs to notify their brother and cousin Lords of the meeting and its time and place. When all have come and have assembled, Adodarhoh, in conjunction with his cousin Lords, shall appoint one Lord who shall repeat the laws of the Great Peace. Then shall they announce who they have chosen to repeat the laws of the Great Peace to the two sons. Then shall the chosen one repeat the laws of the Great Peace.

64. At the ceremony of the installation of Lords if there is only one expert speaker and singer of the law and the Pacification Hymn to stand at the council fire, then when this speaker and singer has finished addressing one

side of the fire he shall go to the opposite side and reply to his own speech and song. He shall thus act for both sides of the fire until the entire ceremony has been completed. Such a speaker and singer shall be termed the "Two Faced" because he speaks and sings for both sides of the fire.

65. I, Dekanawida, and the Union Lords, now uproot the tallest pine tree and into the cavity thereby made we cast all weapons of war. Into the depths of the earth, down into the deep underearth currents of water flowing to unknown regions we cast all the weapons of strife. We bury them from sight and we plant again the tree. Thus shall the Great Peace be established and hostilities shall no longer be known between the Five Nations but peace to the United People.

Laws of Adoption

66. The father of a child of great comliness, learning, ability or specially loved because of some circumstance may, at the will of the child's clan, select a name from his own (the father's) clan and bestow it by ceremony, such as is provided. This naming shall be only temporary and shall be called, "A name hung about the neck."

67. Should any person, a member of the Five Nations Confederacy, specially esteem a man or woman of another clan or of a foreign nation, he may choose a name and bestow it upon that person so esteemed. The naming shall be in accord with the ceremony of bestowing names. Such a name is only a temporary one and shall be called "A name hung about the neck." A short string of shells shall be delivered with the name as a record and a pledge.

68. Should any member of the Five Nations, a family or person belonging to a foreign nation submit a proposal for adoption into a clan of one of the Five Nations, he or they shall furnish a string of shells, a span in length, as a pledge to the clan into which he or they wish to be adopted. The Lords of the nation shall then consider the proposal and submit a decision.

69. Any member of the Five Nations who through esteem or other feeling wishes to adopt an individual, a family or number of families may offer adoption to him or them and if accepted the matter shall be brought to the attention of the Lords for confirmation and the Lords must confirm adoption.

70. When the adoption of anyone shall have been confirmed by the Lords of the Nation, the Lords shall address the people of their nation and say: "Now you of our nation, be informed that such a person, such a family or such families have ceased forever to bear their birth nation's name and have buried it in the depths of the earth. Henceforth let no one of our nation ever mention the original name or nation of their birth. To do so will be to hasten the end of our peace.

Laws of Emigration

71. When any person or family belonging to the Five Nations desires to abandon their birth nation and the territory of the Five Nations, they shall inform the Lords of their nation and the Confederate Council of the Five Nations shall take cognizance of it.

72. When any person or any of the people of the Five Nations emigrate and reside in a region distant from the territory of the Five Nations Confederacy, the Lords of the Five Nations at will may send a messenger carrying a broad belt of black shells and when the messenger arrives he shall call the people together or address them personally displaying the belt of shells and they shall know that this is an order for them to return to their original homes and to their council fires.

Rights of Foreign Nations

73. The soil of the earth from one end of the land to the other is the property of the people who inhabit it. By birthright the Ongwehonweh (Original beings) are the owners of the soil which they own and occupy and none other may hold it. The same law has been held from the oldest times. The Great Creator has made us of the one blood and of the same soil he made us and as only different tongues constitute different nations he established different hunting grounds and territories and made boundary lines between them.

74. When any alien nation or individual is admitted into the Five Nations the admission shall be understood only to be a temporary one. Should the person or nation create loss, do wrong or cause suffering of any kind to endanger the peace of the Confederacy, the Confederate Lords shall order one of their war chiefs to reprimand him or them and if a similar offence is again committed the offending party or parties shall be expelled from the territory of the Five United Nations.

75. When a member of an alien nation comes to the territory of the Five Nations and seeks refuge and permanent residence, the Lords of the Nation to which he comes shall extend hospitality and make him a member of the nation. Then shall he be accorded equal rights and privileges in all matters except as after mentioned.

76. No body of alien people who have been adopted temporarily shall have a vote in the council of the Lords of the Confederacy, for only they who have been invested with Lordship titles may vote in the Council. Aliens have nothing by blood to make claim to a vote and should they have it, not knowing all the traditions of the Confederacy, might go against its Great Peace. In this manner the Great Peace would be endangered and perhaps be destroyed.

77. When the Lords of the Confederacy decide to admit a foreign nation and an adoption is made, the Lords

shall inform the adopted nation that its admission is only temporary. They shall also say to the nation that it must never try to control, to interfere with or to injure the Five Nations nor disregard the Great Peace or any of its rules or customs. That in no way should they cause disturbance or injury. Then should the adopted nation disregard these injunctions, their adoption shall be annuled and they shall be expelled. The expulsion shall be in the following manner: The council shall appoint one of their War Chiefs to convey the message of annulment and he shall say, "You (naming the nation) listen to me while I speak. I am here to inform you again of the will of the Five Nations' Council. It was clearly made known to you at a former time. Now the Lords of the Five Nations have decided to expel you and cast you out. We disown you now and annul your adoption. Therefore you must look for a path in which to go and lead away all your people. It was you, not we, who committed wrong and caused this sentence of annulment. So then go your way and depart from the territory of the Five Nations and from the Confederacy."

78. Whenever a foreign nation enters the Confederacy or accepts the Great Peace, the Five Nations and the foreign nation shall enter into an agreement and compact by which the foreign nation shall endeavor to pursuade other nations to accept the Great Peace.

Rights and Powers of War

79. Skanawatih shall be vested with a double office, duty and with double authority. One-half of his being shall hold the Lordship title and the other half shall hold the title of War Chief. In the event of war he shall notify the five War Chiefs of the Confederacy and command them to prepare for war and have their men ready at the appointed time and place for engagement with the enemy of the Great Peace.

80. When the Confederate Council of the Five Nations has for its object the establishment of the Great Peace among the people of an outside nation and that nation refuses to accept the Great Peace, then by such refusal they bring a declaration of war upon themselves from the Five Nations. Then shall the Five Nations seek to establish the Great Peace by a conquest of the rebellious nation.

81. When the men of the Five Nations, now called forth to become warriors, are ready for battle with an obstinate opposing nation that has refused to accept the Great Peace, then one of the five War Chiefs shall be chosen by the warriors of the Five Nations to lead the army into battle. It shall be the duty of the War Chief so chosen to come before his warriors and address them. His aim shall be to impress upon them the necessity of good behavior and strict obedience to all the commands of the War Chiefs. He shall deliver an oration exhorting them with great zeal to be brave and courageous and never to be guilty of cowardice. At the conclusion of his oration he shall march forward and commence the War Song and he shall sing:

> Now I am greatly surprised
> And, therefore I shall use it—
> The power of my War Song.
> I am of the Five Nations
> And I shall make supplication
> To the Almighty Creator.
> He has furnished this army.
> My warriors shall be mighty
> In the strength of the Creator.
> Between him and my song they are
> For it was he who gave the song
> This war song that I sing!

82. When the warriors of the Five Nations are on an expedition against an enemy, the War Chief shall sing the War Song as he approaches the country of the enemy and not cease until his scouts have reported that the army is near the enemies' lines when the War Chief shall approach with great caution and prepare for the attack.

83. When peace shall have been established by the termination of the war against a foreign nation, then the War Chief shall cause all the weapons of war to be taken from the nation. Then shall the Great Peace be established and that nation shall observe all the rules of the Great Peace for all time to come.

84. Whenever a foreign nation is conquered or has by their own will accepted the Great Peace their own system of internal government may continue, but they must cease all warfare against other nations.

85. Whenever a war against a foreign nation is pushed until that nation is about exterminated because of its refusal to accept the Great Peace and if that nation shall by its obstinacy become exterminated, all their rights, property and territory shall become the property of the Five Nations.

86. Whenever a foreign nation is conquered and the survivors are brought into the territory of the Five Nations' Confederacy and placed under the Great Peace the two shall be known as the Conqueror and the Conquered. A symbolic relationship shall be devised and be placed in some symbolic position. The conquered nation shall have no voice in the councils of the Confederacy in the body of the Lords.

87. When the War of the Five Nations on a foreign rebellious nation is ended, peace shall be restored to that nation by a withdrawal of all their weapons of war by the

War Chief of the Five Nations. When all the terms of peace shall have been agreed upon a state of friendship shall be established.

88. When the proposition to establish the Great Peace is made to a foreign nation it shall be done in mutual council. The foreign nation is to be persuaded by reason and urged to come into the Great Peace. If the Five Nations fail to obtain the consent of the nation at the first council a second council shall be held and upon a second failure a third council shall be held and this third council shall end the peaceful methods of persuasion. At the third council the War Chief of the Five nations shall address the Chief of the foreign nation and request him three times to accept the Great Peace. If refusal steadfastly follows the War Chief shall let the bunch of white lake shells drop from his outstretched hand to the ground and shall bound quickly forward and club the offending chief to death. War shall thereby be declared and the War Chief shall have his warriors at his back to meet any emergency. War must continue until the contest is won by the Five Nations.

89. When the Lords of the Five Nations propose to meet in conference with a foreign nation with proposals for an acceptance of the Great Peace, a large band of warriors shall conceal themselves in a secure place safe from the espionage of the foreign nation but as near at hand as possible. Two warriors shall accompany the Union Lord who carries the proposals and these warriors shall be especially cunning. Should the Lord be attacked, these warriors shall hasten back to the army of warriors with the news of the calamity which fell through the treachery of the foreign nation.

90. When the Five Nations Council declares war any Lord of the Confederacy may enlist with the warriors by temporarily renouncing his sacred Lordship title which he holds through the election of his women relatives. The title then reverts to them and they may bestow it upon another temporarily until the war is over when the Lord, if living, may resume his title and seat in the Council.

91. A certain wampum belt of black beads shall be the emblem of the authority of the Five War Chiefs to take up the weapons of war and with their men to resist invasion. This shall be called a war in defense of the territory.

Treason or Secession of a Nation

92. If a nation, part of a nation, or more than one nation within the Five Nations should in any way endeavor to destroy the Great Peace by neglect or violating its laws and resolve to dissolve the Confederacy, such a nation or such nations shall be deemed guilty of treason and called enemies of the Confederacy and the Great Peace. It shall then be the duty of the Lords of the Confederacy who remain faithful to resolve to warn the offending people. They shall be warned once and if a second warning is necessary they

shall be driven from the territory of the Confederacy by the War Chiefs and his men.

Rights of the People of the Five Nations

93. Whenever a specially important matter or a great emergency is presented before the Confederate Council and the nature of the matter affects the entire body of the Five Nations, threatening their utter ruin, then the Lords of the Confederacy must submit the matter to the decision of their people and the decision of the people shall affect the decision of the Confederate Council. This decision shall be a confirmation of the voice of the people.

94. The men of every clan of the Five Nations shall have a Council Fire ever burning in readiness for a council of the clan. When it seems necessary for a council to be held to discuss the welfare of the clans, then the men may gather about the fire. This council shall have the same rights as the council of the women.

95. The women of every clan of the Five Nations shall have a Council Fire ever burning in readiness for a council of the clan. When in their opinion it seems necessary for the interest of the people they shall hold a council and their decisions and recommendations shall be introduced before the Council of the Lords by the War Chief for its consideration.

96. All the Clan council fires of a nation or of the Five Nations may unite into one general council fire, or delegates from all the council fires may be appointed to unite in a general council for discussing the interests of the people. The people shall have the right to make appointments and to delegate their power to others of their number. When their council shall have come to a conclusion on any matter, their decision shall be reported to the Council of the Nation or to the Confederate Council (as the case may require) by the War Chief or the War Chiefs.

97. Before the real people united their nations, each nation had its council fires. Before the Great Peace their councils were held. The five Council Fires shall continue to burn as before and they are not quenched. The Lords of each nation in future shall settle their nation's affairs at this council fire governed always by the laws and rules of the council of the Confederacy and by the Great Peace.

98. If either a nephew or a niece see an irregularity in the performance of the functions of the Great Peace and its laws, in the Confederate Council or in the conferring of Lordship titles in an improper way, through their War Chief they may demand that such actions become subject to correction and that the matter conform to the ways prescribed by the laws of the Great Peace.

Religious Ceremonies Protected

99. The rites and festivals of each nation shall remain undisturbed and shall continue as before because they

were given by the people of old times as useful and necessary for the good of men.

100. It shall be the duty of the Lords of each brotherhood to confer at the approach of the time of the Midwinter Thanksgiving and to notify their people of the approaching festival. They shall hold a council over the matter and arrange its details and begin the Thanksgiving five days after the moon of Dis-ko-nah is new. The people shall assemble at the appointed place and the nephews shall notify the people of the time and place. From the beginning to the end the Lords shall preside over the Thanksgiving and address the people from time to time.

101. It shall be the duty of the appointed managers of the Thanksgiving festivals to do all that is needed for carrying out the duties of the occasions. The recognized festivals of Thanksgiving shall be the Midwinter Thanksgiving, the Maple or Sugar-making Thanksgiving, the Raspberry Thanksgiving, the Strawberry Thanksgiving, the Corn-planting Thanksgiving, the Corn Hoeing Thanksgiving, the Little Festival of Green Corn, the Great Festival of Ripe Corn and the complete Thanksgiving for the Harvest. Each nation's festivals shall be held in their Long Houses.

102. When the Thansgiving for the Green Corn comes the special managers, both the men and women, shall give it careful attention and do their duties properly.

103. When the Ripe Corn Thanksgiving is celebrated the Lords of the Nation must give it the same attention as they give to the Midwinter Thanksgiving.

104. Whenever any man proves himself by his good life and his knowledge of good things, naturally fitted as a teacher of good things, he shall be recognized by the Lords as a teacher of peace and religion and the people shall hear him.

The Installation Song

105. The song used in installing the new Lord of the Confederacy shall be sung by Adodarhoh and it shall be:

"Haii, haii Agwah wi-yoh
A-kon-he-watha
Ska-we-ye-se-go-wah
Yon-gwa-wih
Ya-kon-he-wa-tha
Haii, haii It is good indeed
(That) a broom,—
A great wing,
It is given me
For a sweeping instrument."

106. Whenever a person properly entitled desires to learn the Pacification Song he is privileged to do so but he must prepare a feast at which his teachers may sit with him and sing. The feast is provided that no misfortune may befall them for singing the song on an occasion when no chief is installed.

Protection of the House

107. A certain sign shall be known to all the people of the Five Nations which shall denote that the owner or occupant of a house is absent. A stick or pole in a slanting or leaning position shall indicate this and be the sign. Every person not entitled to enter the house by right of living within it upon seeing such a sign shall not approach the house either by day or by night but shall keep as far away as his business will permit.

Funeral Addresses

108. At the funeral of a Lord of the Confederacy, say:

"Now we become reconciled as you start away. You were once a Lord of the Five Nations' Confederacy and the United People trusted you. Now we release you for it is true that it is no longer possible for us to walk about together on the earth. Now, therefore, we lay it (the body) here. Here we lay it away. Now then we say to you, 'Persevere onward to the place where the Creator dwells in peace. Let not the things of the earth hinder you. Let nothing that transpired while yet you lived hinder you. In hunting you once took delight; in the game of Lacrosse you once took delight and in the feasts and pleasant occasions your mind was amused, but now do not allow thoughts of these things to give you trouble. Let not your relatives hinder you and also let not your friends and associates trouble your mind. Regard none of these things.'

"Now then, in turn, you here present who were related to this man and you who were his friends and associates, behold the path that is yours also! Soon we ourselves will be left in that place. For this reason hold yourselves in restraint as you go from place to place. In your actions and in your conversation do no idle thing. Speak not idle talk neither gossip. Be careful of this and speak not and do not give way to evil behavior. One year is the time that you must abstain from unseemly levity but if you can not do this for ceremony, ten days is the time to regard these things for respect."

109. At the funeral of a War Chief, say: "Now we become reconciled as you start away. You were once a War Chief of the Five Nations' Confederacy and the United People trusted you as their guard from the enemy." (The remainder is the same as the address at the funeral of a Lord.)

110. At the funeral of a Warrior, say: "Now we become reconciled as you start away. Once you were a devoted provider and protector of your family and you were ever ready to take part in battles for the Five Nations' Confederacy. The United People trusted you." (The remainder is the same as the address at the funeral of a Lord.)

111. At the funeral of a young man, say: "Now we become reconciled as you start away. In the beginning of your career you are taken away and the flower of your life is withered away." (The remainder is the same as the address at the funeral of a Lord.)

112. At the funeral of a chief woman, say: "Now we become reconciled as you start away. You were once a chief woman in the Five Nations' Confederacy. You once were a mother of the nations. Now we release you for it is true that it is no longer possible for us to walk about together on the earth. Now, therefore, we lay it (the body) here. Here we lay it away. Now then we say to you, 'Persevere onward to the place where the Creator dwells in peace. Let not the things of the earth hinder you. Let nothing that transpired while you lived hinder you. Looking after your family was a sacred duty and you were faithful. You were one of the many joint heirs of the Lordship titles. Feastings were yours and you had pleasant occasions . . ." (The remainder is the same as the address at the funeral of a Lord.)

113. At the funeral of a woman of the people, say: "Now we become reconciled as you start away. You were once a woman in the flower of life and the bloom is now withered away. You once held a sacred position as a mother of the nation. (Etc.) Looking after your family was a sacred duty and you were faithful. Feastings . . . (etc.)" (The remainder is the same as the address at the funeral of a Lord.)

114. At the funeral of an infant or young woman, say: "Now we become reconciled as you start away. You were a tender bud and gladdened our hearts for only a few days. Now the bloom has withered away . . . (etc.). Let none of the things that transpired on earth hinder you. Let nothing that happened while you lived hinder you." (The remainder is the same as the address at the funeral of a Lord.)

115. When an infant dies within three days, mourning shall continue only five days. Then shall you gather the little boys and girls at the house of mourning and at the funeral feast a speaker shall address the children and bid them be happy once more, though by a death, gloom has been cast over them. Then shall the black clouds roll away and the sky shall show blue once more. Then shall the children be again in sunshine.

116. When a dead person is brought to the burial place, the speaker on the opposite side of the Council Fire shall bid the bereaved family cheer their minds once again and rekindle their hearth fires in peace, to put their house in order and once again be in brightness for darkness has covered them. He shall say that the black clouds shall roll away and that the bright blue sky is visible once more. Therefore shall they be in peace in the sunshine again.

117. Three strings of shell one span in length shall be employed in addressing the assemblage at the burial of the dead. The speaker shall say: "Hearken you who are here, this body is to be covered. Assemble in this place again ten days hence for it is the decree of the Creator that mourning shall cease when ten days have expired. Then shall a feast be made." Then at the expiration of ten days the speaker shall say:

"Continue to listen you who are here. The ten days of mourning have expired and your minds must now be freed of sorrow as before the loss of a relative. The relatives have decided to make a little compensation to those who have assisted at the funeral. It is a mere expression of thanks. This is to the one who did the cooking while the body was lying in the house. Let her come forward and receive this gift and be dismissed from the task." In substance this shall be repeated for every one who assisted in any way until all have been remembered.

Source:

University of Oklahoma Law Center. "The Iroquois Constitution." Available on-line. URL: www.law.uo.edu/hist/iroquois. html. Accessed June 2003.

John Smith, *The Generall Historie of Virginia, New England, and the Summer Isles, 1607–1614*

This excerpt from Captain John Smith's *Generall Historie of Virginia, New England and the Summer Isles*, written in 1624, recounts the hardships endured by the settlers at Jamestown, his capture in 1607 by Powhatan Indians, and his ultimate rescue by Pocahontas, the king's 12-year-old daughter. Although it is one of the most famous stories to emerge from colonial America, the veracity of the tale has been questioned by historians. Smith (1580–1631), a soldier, adventurer, and explorer, had been known to exaggerate his exploits, and his earliest accounts of his captivity in Virginia do not mention Pocahontas. By 1614 Smith's independent and sometimes difficult nature had alienated the Virginia Company, as well as other potential sponsors for his adventures. He spent the remainder of his life writing about his past. In 1616 Pocahontas became a minor celebrity when she toured England with her husband, John Rolfe, for the Virginia Company. Her portrait was painted, and she visited with King James I and Queen Anne. Before her arrival, Smith wrote a letter of introduction to Queen Anne that praised Pocahontas for rescuing him and for bringing food to the colonists during the winter of 1607. This was the first time Smith had mentioned Pocahontas in connection with his captivity, and while the letter may have been meant to create a favorable impression of the Indian princess on the Queen, it also reintroduced Smith back into the royal spotlight. Eight years later, in 1624, he published the more detailed and embellished account below.

⸺⸺⸺⸺⸺⸺⸺⸺ ❧ *⸺⸺⸺⸺⸺⸺⸺⸺*

I.

It might well be thought, a country so fair (as Virginia is) and a people so tractable, would long ere this have been quietly possessed, to the satisfaction of the adventurers, and the eternizing of the memory of those that effected it. But because all the world do see a failure; this following treatise shall give satisfaction to all indifferent readers, how the business has been carried: where no doubt they will easily understand and answer to their question, how it came to pass there was no better speed and success in those proceedings.

Captain Bartholomew Gosnold, one of the first movers of this plantation, having many years solicited many of his friends, but found small assistance; at last prevailed with some gentlemen, as Captain John Smith, Master Edward-maria Wingfield, Master Robert Hunt, and divers others, who depended a year upon his projects, but nothing could be effected, till by their great charge and industry, it came to be apprehended by certain of the nobility, gentry, and merchants, so that his Majesty by his letters patents, gave commission for establishing councils, to direct here; and to govern, and to execute there. To effect this, was spent another year, and by that, three ships were provided, one of 100 tons, another of 40 and a pinnace of 20. The transportation of the company was committed to Captain Christopher Newport, a mariner well practiced for the western parts of America. But their orders for government were put in a box, not to be opened, nor the governors known until they arrived in Virginia.

On the 19 of December, 1606, we set sail from Blackwall, but by unprosperous winds, were kept six weeks in the sight of England; all which time, Master Hunt our preacher, was so weak and sick, that few expected his recovery. Yet although he were but twenty miles from his habitation (the time we were in the Downes) and notwithstanding the stormy weather, nor the scandalous imputations (of some few, little better than atheists, of the greatest rank among us) suggested against him, all this could never force from him so much as a seeming desire to leave the business, but preferred the service of God, in so good a voyage, before any affection to contest with his godless foes whose disastrous designs (could they have prevailed) had even then overthrown the business, so many discontents did then arise, had he not with the water of patience, and his godly exhortations (but chiefly by his true devoted examples) quenched those flames of envy, and dissension. . . .

II.

The first land they made they called Cape Henry; where thirty of them recreating themselves on shore, were assaulted by five savages, who hurt two of the English very dangerously.

That night was the box opened, and the orders read, in which Bartholomew Gosnol, John Smith, Edward Wingfield, Christopher Newport, John Ratliff, John Martin, and George Kendall, were named to be the council, and to choose a president among them for a year, who with the council should govern. Matters of moment were to be examined by a jury, but determined by the major part of the council, in which the president had two voices.

Until the 13 of May they sought a place to plant in; then the council was sworn, Master Wingfield was chosen president, and an oration made, why Captain Smith was not admitted of the council as the rest.

Now falls every man to work, the council contrive the fort, the rest cut down trees to make place to pitch their tents; some provide clapboard to relade the ships, some make gardens, some nets, etc. The savages often visited us kindly. The president's overweening jealousy would admit no exercise at arms, or fortification but the boughs of trees cast together in the form of a half moon by the extraordinary pains and diligence of Captain Kendall.

Newport, Smith, and twenty others, were sent to discover the head of the river: by divers small habitations they passed, in six days they arrived at a town called Powhatan, consisting of some twelve houses, pleasantly seated on a hill; before it three fertile isles, about it many of their cornfields, the place is very pleasant, and strong by nature, of this place the Prince is called Powhatan, and his people Powhatans. To this place the river is navigable: but higher within a mile, by reason of the rocks and isles, there is not passage for a small boat, this they call the falls. The people in all parts kindly entreated them, till being returned within twenty miles of Jamestown, they gave just cause of jealousy: but had God not blessed the discoverers otherwise than those at the fort, there had then been an end of that plantation; for at the fort, where they arrived the next day, they found 17 men hurt, and a boy slain by the savages, and had it not chanced a cross bar shot from the ships struck down a bough from a tree among them, that caused them to retire, our men had all been slain, being securely all at work, and their arms in dry fats.

Hereupon the president was contented the fort should be pallisaded, the ordnance mounted, his men armed and exercised: for many were the assaults, and ambuscades of the savages, and our men by their disorderly straggling were often hurt, when the savages by the nimbleness of their heels well escaped.

What toil we had, with so small a power to guard our workmen by day, watch all night, resist our enemies, and effect our business, to relade the ships, cut down trees, and prepare the ground to plant our corn, etc., I refer to the reader's consideration.

Six weeks being spent in this manner, Captain Newport (who was hired only for our transportation) was to return with the ships.

Now Captain Smith, who all this time from their departure from the Canaries was restrained as a prisoner upon the scandalous suggestions of some of the chiefs (envying his repute) who fained he intended to usurp the government, murder the council, and make himself king, that his confederates were dispersed in all the three ships, and that divers of his confederates that revealed it, would affirm it; for this he was committed as a prisoner.

Thirteen weeks he remained thus suspected, and by that time the ships should return they pretended out of their commiserations, to refer him to the council in England to receive a check, rather than by particulating his designs make him so odious to the world, as to touch his life, or utterly overthrow his reputation. But he so much scorned their charity, and publicly defied the uttermost of their cruelty; he wisely prevented their policies, though he could not suppress their envy; yet so well he demeaned himself in this business, as all the company did see his innocency, and his adversaries' malice, and those suborned to accuse him, accused his accusers of subornation; many untruths were alleged against him; but being so apparently disproved, begat a general hatred in the hearts of the company against such unjust commanders, that the president was adjudged to give him 2001; so that all he had was seized upon, in part of satisfaction, which Smith presently returned to the store for the general use of the colony. Many were the mischiefs that daily sprung from their ignorant (yet ambitious) spirits; but the good doctrine and exhortation of our preacher Master Hunt reconciled them, and caused Captain Smith to be admitted of the council.

The next day all received the communion, the day following the savages voluntarily desired peace, and Captain Newport returned for England with news; leaving in Virginia 100 the 15 of June 1607. Being thus left to our fortunes, it fortuned that within ten days scarce ten among us could either go, or well stand, such extreme weakness and sickness oppressed us. And thereat none need marvel, if they consider the cause and reason, which was this.

While the ships stayed, our allowance was somewhat bettered, by a daily proportion of biscuit, which the sailors would pilfer to sell, give, or exchange with us, for money, sassafras, furs, or love. But when they departed, there remained neither tavern, beer house, nor place of relief, but the common kettle. Had we been as free from all sins as gluttony, and drunkenness, we might have been canonized for Saints; but our president would never have been admitted, for ingrossing to his private, oatmeal, sack, oil, aquavitse, beef, eggs, or what not, but the kettle; that indeed he allowed equally to be distributed, and that was

half a pint of wheat, and as much barley boiled with water for a man a day, and this having fried some 26 weeks in the ship's hold, contained as many worms as grains; so that we might truly call it rather so much bran than corn, our drink was water, our lodgings castles in the air.

With this lodging and diet, our extreme toil in bearing and planting pallisades, so strained and bruised us, and our continual labor in the extremity of the heat had so weakened us, as were cause sufficient to have made us as miserable in our native country, or any other place in the world.

From May, to September, those that escaped, lived upon sturgeon, and sea-crabs, fifty in this time we buried, the rest seeing the president's projects to escape these miseries in our pinnace by flight (who all this time had neither felt want nor sickness) so moved our dead spirits, as we deposed him; and established Ratcliff in his place, (Gosnol being dead) Kendall deposed. Smith newly recovered, Martin and Ratcliff was by his care preserved and relieved, and the most of the soldiers recovered with the skillful diligence of Master Thomas Wotton our surgeon general.

But now was all our provision spent, the sturgeon gone, all helps abandoned, each hour expecting the fury of the savages; when God the patron of all good endeavors, in that desperate extremity so changed the hearts of the savages, that they brought such plenty of their fruits, and provision, as no man wanted. . . .

III.

But our comedies never endured long without a tragedy; some idle exceptions being muttered against Captain Smith, for not discovering the head of Chickahamania river, and taxed by the council, to be too slow in so worthy an attempt. The next voyage he proceeded so far that with much labor by cutting of trees insunder he made his passage; but when his barge could pass no farther, he left her in a broad bay out of danger of shot, commanding none should go ashore till his return: himself with two English and two savages went up higher in a canoe; but he was not long absent, but his men went ashore, whose want of government gave both occasion and opportunity to the savages to surprise one George Cassen, whom they slew, and much failed not to have cut off the boat and all the rest.

Smith little dreaming of that accident, being got to the marshes at the river's head, twenty miles in the desert, had his two men slain (as is supposed) sleeping by the canoe, while himself by fowling sought them victual: who finding he was beset with 200 savages, two of them he slew, still defending himself with the aid of a savage his guide whom he bound to his arm with his garters, and used him as a buckler, yet he was shot in his thigh a little, and had many arrows that stuck in his clothes but no great hurt, till at last they took him prisoner.

When this news came to Jamestown, much was their sorrow for his loss, few expecting what ensued.

Six or seven weeks those Barbarians kept him prisoner, many strange triumphs and conjurations they made of him, yet he so demeaned himself among them, as he not only diverted them from surprising the fort, but procured his own liberty, and got himself and his company such estimation among them, that those savages admired him more than their own Quiyouckosucks. . . .

At last they brought him to Meronocomoco, where was Powhatan their emperor. Here more than two hundred of those grim courtiers stood wondering at him, as he had been a monster; till Powhatan and his train had put themselves in their greatest braveries. Before a fire upon a seat like a bedstead, he sat covered with a great robe, made of Rarowcun (raccoon?) skins, and all the tails hanging by. On either hand did sit a young wench of 16 or 18 years, and along on each side the house, two rows of men, and behind them as many women, with all their heads and shoulders painted red: many of their heads bedecked with the white down of birds; but every one with something: and a great chain of white beads about their necks.

At his entrance before the king, all the people gave a great shout. The queen of Appamatuck was appointed to bring him water to wash his hands, and another brought him a bunch of feathers, instead of a towel to dry them: having feasted him after their best barbarous manner they could, a long consultation was held, but the conclusion was, two great stones were brought before Powhatan: then as many as could laid hands on him, dragged him to them, and thereon laid his head, and being ready with their clubs, to beat out his brains, Pocahontas the king's dearest daughter, when no entreaty could prevail, got his head in her arms, and laid her own upon his to save him from death: whereat the Emperor was contented he should live to make him hatchets, and her bells, beads, and copper; for they thought him as well of all occupations as themselves. For the king himself will make his own robes, shoes, bowes, arrows, pots; plant, hunt, or do anything so well as the rest.

Two days after, Powhatan having disguised himself in the most fearful manner he could, caused Captain Smith to be brought forth to a great house in the woods, and thereupon a mat by the fire to be left alone. Not long after from behind a mat that divided the house, was made the most doleful noise he ever heard; then Powhatan more like a devil than a man, with some two hundred more as black as himself, came unto him and told him now they were friends, and presently he should go to Jamestown, to send

him two great guns, and a grindstone, for which he would give him the country of Capahowosick, and forever esteem him as his son Nantaquoud.

IV.

So to Jamestown with 12 guides Powhatan sent him. That night they quartered in the woods, he still expecting (as he had done all this long time of his imprisonment) every hour to be put to one death or other: for all their feasting. But almighty God (by his divine providence) had mollified the hearts of those stern barbarians with compassion. The next morning betimes they came to the fort, where Smith having used the savages with what kindness he could, he showed Rawhunt, Powhatan's trusty servant, two demi-culverins and a millstone to carry Powhatan: they found them somewhat too heavy; but when they did see him discharge them, being loaded with stones, among the boughs of a great tree loaded with icicles the ice and branches came so tumbling down, that the poor savages ran away half dead with fear. But at last we regained some conference with them, and gave them such toys; and sent to Powhatan, his women, and children such presents, as gave them in general full content.

Now in Jamestown they were all in combustion, the strongest preparing once more to run away with the pinnace; which with the hazard of his life, with Sakre falcon and musket shot, Smith forced now the third time to stay or sink.

Some no better than they should be, had plotted with the president, the next day to have put him to death by the Levitical law, for the lives of Robinson and Emry; pretending the fault was his that had led them to their ends: but he quickly took such order with such lawyers, that he laid them by the heels till he sent some of them prisoners for England.

Now every once in four or five days, Pocahontas with her attendants, brought him so much provision, that saved many of their lives, that else for all this had starved with hunger.

Thus from numb death our good God sent relief,
The sweet assuager of all other grief.

His relation of the plenty he had seen, especially at Werawocomoco, and of the state and bounty of Powhatan, (which till that time was unknown) so revived their dead spirits (especially the love of Pocahontas) as all men's fear was abandoned.

Thus you may see what difficulties still crossed any good endeavor; and the good success of the business being thus often brought to the very period of destruction; yet you see by what strange means God has still delivered it.

As for the insufficiency of them admitted in commission, that error could not be prevented by the electors;

there being no other choice, and all strangers to each other's education, qualities, or disposition. And if any deem it a shame to our Nation to have any mention made of those enormities, let him peruse the Histories of the Spaniard's Discoveries and Plantations, where they may see how many mutinies, disorders, and dissensions have accompanied them, and crossed their attempts: which being known to be particular men's offenses; does take away the general scorn and contempt, which malice, presumption, coveteousness, or ignorance might produce; to the scandal and reproach of those, whose actions and valiant resolutions deserve a more worthy respect.

V.

Now whether it had been better for Captain Smith, to have concluded with any of those several projects, to have abandoned the country, with some ten or twelve of them, who were called the better sort, and have left Master Hunt our preacher, Master Anthony Gosnol, a most honest, worthy, and industrious gentleman, Master Thomas Wotton, and some 27 others of his countrymen to the fury of the savages, famine, and all manner of mischiefs, and inconveniences, (for they were but forty in all to keep possession of this large country;) or starve himself with them for company, for want of lodging: or but adventuring abroad to make them provision, or by his opposition to preserve the action, and save all their lives; I leave to the censure of all honest men to consider. . . .

Source:

John Smith. *The General Historie of Virginia, New England, and the Summer Isles.* London: Printed by I. D. and I. H. for Michael Sparkes, 1624.

John Rolfe to the Governor of Virginia, (Letters from Jamestown), 1613

John Rolfe, an early inhabitant of the Jamestown colony and member of the colony's governing council, is requesting permission to marry Pocahontas, daughter of the powerful Indian chief Powhatan and the purported savior of Captain John Smith. Pocahontas and Rolfe were married in 1613, and their union secured a peace between the Indians and the colonists that lasted until 1622, five years after her death.

Letter of John Rolfe to Sir Thomas Dale

The coppie of the Gentle-mans letters to Sir Thomas Dale, that after married Powhatans daughter, containing the reasons moving him thereunto.

Honourable Sir, and most worthy Governor:

When your leasure shall best serve you to peruse these lines, I trust in God, the beginning will not strike you into a greater admiration, then the end will give you good content. It is a matter of no small moment, concerning my own particular, which here I impart unto you, and which toucheth mee so neerely, as the tendernesse of my salvation. Howbeit I freely subject my selfe to your grave and mature judgement, deliberation, approbation, and determination; assuring my selfe of your zealous admonitions, and godly comforts, either perswading me to desist, or incouraging me to persist therin, with a religious and godly care, for which (from the very instant, that this began to roote it selfe within the secret bosome of my brest) my daily and earnest praiers have bin, still are, and ever shall be produced forth with as sincere a godly zeale as I possibly may to be directed, aided and governed in all my thoughts, words, and deedes, to the glory of God, and for my eternal consolation. To persevere wherein I never had more neede, nor (till now) could ever imagine to have bin moved with the like occasion.

But (my case standing as it doth) what better worldly refuge can I here seeke, then to shelter my selfe under the safety of your favourable protection? And did not my ease proceede from an unspotted conscience, I should not dare to offer to your view and approved judgement, these passions of my troubled soule, so full of feare and trembling in hypocrisie and dissimulation. But knowing my owne innocency and godly fervor, in the whole prosecution hereof, I doubt not of your benigne acceptance, and clement construction. As for malicious depravers, and turbulent spirits, to whom nothing is tastful but what pleaseth their unsavory paalat, I passe not for them being well assured in my perswasion (by the often trial and proving of my selfe, in my holiest meditations and praiers) that I am called hereunto by the spirit of God; and it shall be sufficient for me to be protected by your selfe in all vertuous and pious indevours. And for my more happie proceeding herein, my daily oblations shall ever be addressed to bring to passe so good effects, that your selfe, and all the world may truely say: This is the worke of God, and it is marvelous in our eies.

But to avoid tedious preambles, and to come neerer the matter: first suffer me with your patence, to sweepe and make cleane the way wherein I walke, from all suspicions and doubts, which may be covered therein, and faithfully to reveale unto you, what should move me hereunto.

Let therefore this my well advised protestation, which here I make betweene God and my own conscience, be a sufficient witnesse, at the dreadfull day of judgement (when the secret of all mens harts shall be opened) to condemne me herein, if my chiefest intent and purpose be not, to strive with all my power of body and minde, in the undertaking of so mightie a matter, no way led (so farre forth as mans weakenesse may permit) with the unbridled desire of carnall affection: but for the good of this plantation, for the honour of our countrie, for the glory of God, for my owne salvation, and for the converting to the true knowledge of God and Jesus Christ, an unbeleeving creature, namely Pokahuntas. To whom my hartie and best thoughts are, and have a long time bin so intagled, and inthralled in so intricate a laborinth, that I was even awearied to unwinde my selfe thereout. But almighty God, who never faileth his, that truly invocate his holy name hath opened the gate, and led me by the hand that I might plainely see and discerne the safe paths wherein to treade.

To you therefore (most noble Sir) the patron and Father of us in this countery doe I utter the effects of this setled and long continued affection (which hath made a mightie warre in my mediations) and here I doe truely relate, to what issue this dangerous combate is come unto, wherein I have not onely examined, but throughly tried and pared my thoughts even to the quick, before I could Snde and fit wholesome and apt applications to cure so daungerous an ulcer. I never failed to offer my daily and faithfull praiers to God, for his sacred and holy assistance. I forgot not to set before mine eies the frailty of mankinde, his prones to evill, his indulgencie of wicked thoughts, with many other imperfections wherein man is daily insnared, and oftentimes overthrowne, and them compared to my present estate. Nor was I ignorant of the heavie displeasure which almightie God conceived against the sonnes of Levie and Israel for marrying strange wives, nor of the inconveniences which may thereby arise, with other the like good motions which made me looke about warily and with good circumspection, into the grounds and principall agitations, which thus should provoke me to be in love with one whose education hath bin rude, her manners barbarous, her generation accursed, and so discrepant in all nurtriture frome my selfe, that oftentimes with feare and trembling, I have ended my private controversie with this: surely these are wicked instigations, hatched by him who seeketh and delighteth in mans destruction; and so with fervent praiers to be ever preserved from such diabolical assaults (as I tooke those to be) I have taken some rest. Thus-when I had thought I had obtained my peace and quitnesse, beholde another, but more gracious tentation hath made breaches into my holiest and strongest meditations; with which I have bin put to a new traill, in a straighter manner then the former: for besides the many passions and sufferings which I have daily, hourely, yea and in my sleepe indured, even awaking mee to astonishment, taxing mee with remisnesse, and carlesnesse, refusing and neglecting to performe the duetie of a good Christian, pulling me by the eare, and crying: why dost not thou indevour to make her a Christian? And these have happened to my greater wonder, ven when she hath bin furthest seper-

ated from me, which in common reason (were it not an undoubted worke of God) might breede forgetfulnesse of a farre more worthie creature. Besides, I say the holy spirit of God often demaunded of me, why I was created?

If not for transitory pleasures and worldly vanities, but to labour in the Lords vineyard, there to sow and plant, to nourish and increase the fruites thereof, daily adding witt the good husband in the Gospell, somewhat to the tallent, that in the end the fruites may be reaped, to the comfort of the laborer in this life, and his salvation in the world to come? And if this be, as undoubtedly this is, the service Jesus Christ requireth of his best servant: wo unto him that hath these instruments of pietie put into his hands and wilfillly despiseth to worke with them. Likewise, adding hereunto her great apparance of love to me, her desire to be taught and instructed in the knowledge of God, her capablenesse of understanding, her aptnesse and willingnesse to receive anie good impression, and also the spirituall, besides her owne incitements stirring me up hereunto.

What should I doe? Shall I be of so untoward a disposition, as to refuse to leade the blind into the right way? Shall I be so unnaturall, as not to give bread to the hungrie? or uncharitable, as not to cover the naked? Shall I despise to actuatethese pious dueties of a Christian? Shall the base feare of displeasing the world, overpower and with holde mee from revealing unto man these spirituall workes of the Lord, which in my meditations and praiers, I have daily made knowne unto him? God forbid. I assuredly trust hee hath thus delt with me for my eternall felicitie, and for his glorie: and I hope so to be guided by his heavenly graice, that in the end by my faithfilll paines, and christianlike labour, I shall attaine to that blessed promise, Pronounced by that holy Prophet Daniell unto the righteous that bring many unto the knowledge of God. Namely, that they shall shine like the starres forever and ever. A sweeter comfort cannot be to a true Christian, nor a greater incouragement for him to labour all the daies of his life, in the performance thereof, nor a greater gaine of consolation, to be desired at the hower of death, and in the day of judgement.

Againe by my reading, and conference with honest and religious persons, have I received no small encouragement, besides serena mea conscientia, the cleerenesse of my conscience, clean from the filth of impurity, quoe est instar muri ahenei, which is unto me, as a brasen wall. If I should set down at large, the perhioations and godly motions, which have striven within mee, I should but make a tedious and unnecessary volume. But I doubt not these shall be sufficient both to certifie you of my tru intents, in discharging of my dutie to God, and to your selfe, to whose gracious providence I humbly submit my selfe, for his glory, your honour, our Countreys good, the benefit of this Plantation, and for the converting of one unregenerate, to regeneration; which I beseech God to graunt, for his deere Sonne Christ Jesus his sake. Now if the vulgar sort, who square all mens actions by the base rule of their owne filthinesse, shall taxe or taunt me in this my godly labour: let them know, it is not any hungry appetite, to gorge my selfe with incontinency; sure (if I would, and were so sensually inclined) I might satisfie such desire, though not without a seared conscience, yet with Christians more pleasing to the eie, and lesse fearefull in the offence unlawfully committed. Nor am I in so desperate an estate, that I regard not what becommeth of mee; nor am I out of hope but one day to see my Country, nor so void of friends, nor mean in birth, but there to obtain a mach to my great content: nor have I ignorantly passed over my hopes there, or regardlessly seek to loose the love of my- friends, by taking this course: I know them all, and have not rashly overslipped any.

But shal it please God thus to dispose of me (which I earnestly desire to fulfill my ends before sette down) I will heartely accept of it as a godly taxe appointed me, and I will never cease, (God assisting me) untill I have accomplished, and brought to perfection so holy a worke, in which I will daily pray God to blesse me, to mine, and her eternall happines. And thus desiring no longer to live, to enjoy the blessings of God, then this my resolution doth tend to such godly ends, as are by me before declared: not doubting of your favourable acceptance, I take my leave, beseeching Almighty God to raine downe upon you, such plenitude of his heavenly graces, as your heart can wish and desire, and so I rest,

At your command
most willing to be
disposed off,
John Rolfe

Source:
J. Franklin Jameson. *Narratives of Early Virginia*. New York: Charles Scribner's Sons, 1907.

Edward Winslow's Letter, 1621

This letter, dated December 12, 1621, was written by Edward Winslow, one of the early governors of the Plymouth Colony. It appears in *Mourt's Relation*, a journal of the Pilgrims' first year in New England. Published in England in 1622, the journal is thought to be the work of Winslow and another prominent Plymouth governor, William Bradford. In the letter below, Winslow discusses the character of the Indians, the climate, the landscape, and the food available in this new land. He also recounts the arrival of new men to the colony, discusses the goods the Pilgrims have sent back to England, and offers advice to new settlers on what they should bring. Most inter-

esting perhaps is his description of the autumn feast the Pilgrims shared with the Indians, which became the basis for the modern American holiday of Thanksgiving. Winslow ends his account of the feast by saying, "And although it be not always so plentiful as it was at this time with us, yet by the goodness of God we are so far from want, that we often wish you partakers of our plenty."

Although I received no letter from you by this ship, yet forasmuch as I know you expect the performance of my promise, which was, to write unto you truly and faithfully of all things, I have therefore at this time sent unto you accordingly, referring you for further satisfaction to our more large relations.

You shall understand that in this little time a few of us have been here, we have built seven dwelling-houses and four for the use of the plantation, and have made preparation for divers others. We set last spring some twenty acres of Indian corn, and sowed some six acres of barley and peas; and according to the manner of the Indians, we manured our ground with herrings, or rather shads, which we have in great abundance, and take with great ease at our doors. Our corn did prove well; and, God be praised, we had a good increase of Indian corn, and our barley indifferent good, but our peas not worth the gathering, for we feared they were too late sown. They came up very well, and blossomed; but the sun parched them in the blossom.

Our harvest being gotten in, our governor sent four men on fowling, that so we might, after a special manner, rejoice together after we had gathered the fruit of our labors. They four in one day killed as much fowl as, with a little help beside, served the company almost a week. At which time, among other recreations, we exercised our arms, many of the Indians coming among us, and among the rest their greatest king, Massasoit, with some ninety men, whom for three days we entertained and feasted; and they went out and killed five deer, which they brought to the plantation, and bestowed on our governor, and upon the captain and others. And although it be not always so plentiful as it was at this time with us, yet by the goodness of God we are so far from want, that we often wish you partakers of our plenty.

We have found the Indians very faithful in their covenant of peace with us, very loving, and ready to pleasure us. We often go to them, and they come to us. Some of us have been fifty miles by land in the country with them, the occasions and relations whereof you shall understand by our general and more full declaration of such things as are worth the noting. Yea, it has pleased God so to possess the Indians with a fear of us and love unto us, that not only the greatest king among them, called Massasoit, but also all the princes and peoples round about us, have either made suit unto us, or been glad of any occasion to make peace with us; so that seven of them at once have sent their messengers to us to that end. Yea, an isle at sea, which we never saw, hath also, together with the former, yielded willingly to be under the protection and subject to our sovereign lord King James. So that there is now great peace amongst the Indians themselves, which was not formerly, neither would have been but for us; and we, for our parts, walk as peaceably and safely in the wood as in the highways in England. We entertain them familiarly in our houses, and they as friendly bestowing their venison on us. They are a people without any religion or knowledge of any God, yet very trusty, quick of apprehension, ripe-witted, just.

For the temper of the air here, it agrees well with that in England; and if there be any difference at all, this is somewhat hotter in summer. Some think it to be colder in winter; but I cannot out of experience so say. The air is very clear, and not foggy, as has been reported. I never in my life remember a more seasonable year than we have here enjoyed; and if we have once but kine, horses, and sheep, I make no question but men might live as contented here as in any part of the world. For fish and fowl, we have great abundance. Fresh cod in the summer is but coarse meat with us. Our bay is full of lobsters all the summer, and affords a variety of other fish. In September we can take a hogshead of eels in a night, with small labor, and can dig them out of their beds all the winter. We have muscles and othus at our doors. Oysters we have none near, but we can have them brought by the Indians when we will. All the spring-time the earth sends forth naturally very good salad herbs. Here are grapes, white and red, and very sweet and strong also; strawberries, gooseberries, raspberries, etc.; plums of three sorts, white, black, and red, being almost as good as a damson; abundance of roses, white, red and damask; single, but very sweet indeed. The country wants only industrious men to employ; for it would grieve your hearts if, as I, you had seen so many miles together by goodly rivers uninhabited; and withal, to consider those parts of the world wherein you live to be even greatly burdened with abundance of people. These things I thought good to let you understand, being the truth of things as near as I could experimentally take knowledge of, and that you might on our behalf give God thanks, who hath dealt so favorably with us.

Our supply of men from you came the 9th of November, 1621, putting in at Cape Cod, some eight or ten leagues from us. The Indians that dwell thereabout were they who were owners of the corn which we found in caves, for which we have given them full content, and are in great league with them. They sent us word there was a ship near unto them, but thought it to be a Frenchman; and indeed for ourselves we expected not a friend so soon. But when we perceived that she made for our bay, the governor commanded a great piece to be shot off, to call home such as were abroad at work. Whereupon every man, yea boy, that could handle a gun, were ready, with full resolution that, if she were an enemy, we would stand in our just defense, not fearing them. But God provided better for us than we supposed. These came all in health, not any being sick by the way, otherwise than by sea-sickness, and so continue at this time, by the blessing of God. . . .

When it pleased God we are settled and fitted for the fishing business and other trading, I doubt not but by the blessing of God the gain will give content to all. In the meantime, that we have gotten we have sent by this ship; and though it be not much, yet it will witness for us that we have not been idle, considering the smallness of our number all this summer. We hope the merchants will accept of it, and be encouraged to furnish us with things needful for further employment, which will also encourage us to put forth ourselves to the uttermost.

Now because I expect your coming unto us, with other of our friends, whose company we much desire, I thought good to advertise you of a few things needful. Be careful to have a very good bread-room to put your biscuits in. Let your cask for beer and water be iron-bound, for the first tire, if not more. Let not your meat be dry-salted; none can better do it than the sailors. Let your meal be so hard trod in your cask that you shall need an adz or hatchet to work it out with. Trust not too much on us for corn at this time, for by reason of this last company that came, depending wholly upon us, we shall have little enough till harvest. Be careful to come by some of your meal to spend by the way; it will much refresh you. Build your cabins as open as you can, and bring good store of clothes and bedding with you. Bring every man a musket or fowling-piece. Let your piece be long in the barrel, and fear not the weight of it, for most of our shooting is from stands. Bring juice of lemons, and take it fasting; it is of good use. For hot waters, aniseed water is the best; but use it sparingly. If you bring anything for comfort in the country, butter or salad oil, or both, is very good. Our Indian corn, even the coarsest, makes as pleasant meat as rice; therefore spare that, unless to spend by the way. Bring paper and linseed oil for your windows, with cotton yarn for your lamps. Let your shot be most for big fowls, and bring store of powder and shot. I forbear further to write for the present, hoping to see you by the next return. So I take my leave, commending you to the Lord for a safe conduct unto us, resting in him,

Your loving friend,
E. W.

Source:

Edward Winslow and William Bradford. *Mourt's Relation: A Journal of the Pilgrims at Plymouth*, 1622.

Thomas Dale, "Lawes Divine, Morall and Martiall," 1612

Laws written by Thomas Dale in 1612 to bring order to colonial Virginia. Jamestown, the first English settlement in America, was established in 1607 by the Virginia Company of London. By the winter of 1609, many colonists, discouraged by bad times and starvation, tried to flee. However, they returned once they met ships bringing supplies and new colonists. Thomas Dale found the settlement in rebellion, with a large disinclination to work. As deputy governor, he issued a criminal code that placed the colonists under martial law; he is remembered for its merciless austerity, including recommending that a food thief be tied to a tree until he starved.

For the Colony in Virginea Brittania. Lawes Divine, Morall and Martiall, etc.

Alget qui non Ardet.

Res nostrae subinde non sunt, quales quis optaret, sed quales esse possunt.

Printed at London for Walter Burre. 1612.

To the Right Honorable, the Lords of the Councell of Virginia.

Noblest of men, though tis the fashion now Noblest to mix with basest, for their gaine; Yet doth it fare farre otherwise with you, That scorne to turn to Chaos so againe, And follow your supreme distinction still, Till of most noble, you become divine And imitate your maker in his will, To have his truth in blackest nations shine. What had you beene, had not your Ancestors Begunne to you, that make their nobles good? And where white Christians turn in maners Mores You wash Mores white with sacred Christian bloud This wonder the, that others nothing make Forth then (great Lords) for your Lords Saviors sake.

By him, all whose duty is tributary to your Lordships, and unto so excellent a cause.

William Strachey.

To the constant, mighty, and worthie friends, the Committies, Assistants unto his Majesties Councell for the Colonie in Virginea-Brittania.

When I went forth upon this voyage, (Right worthy Gentlemen) true it is, I held it a service of dutie, (during the time of my unprofitable service, and purpose of stay in the Colonie, for which way else might I adde unto the least hight of so Heroicke and pious a building) to propose unto myself to be (though an unable) Remembrancer of all accidents, occurrences, and undertakings thereunto, adventitiall: In most of which since the time our right famous sole Governour then, now Lieutenant Generall Sir Thomas

Gates Knight, after the ensealing of his Commission hasted to our fleete in the West, there staying for him, I have both in the Bermudas, and since in Virginia beene a a sufferer and an eie witnesse, and the full storie of both in due time shall consecrate unto your viewes, as unto whom by right it appertaineth, being vowed patrones of a worke, and enterprise so great, then which no object nor action (the best of bests) in these time, may carry with it in the like fame, honour, or goodnesse.

Howbet since many impediments, as yet must detaine such my observations in the shadow of darknesse, (untill I shall be able to deliver them perfect unto your judgements why I shall provoke and challenge) I do in the meane time present a transcript of the Toparchia or State of those duties, by which their Colonie stands regulated and commaunded, that such may receive due checke, who malitiously and desperately heretofore have censured of it, and by examining of which they may be right sorie so to have defaulked from us as if we lived there lawlesse, without obedience to our Countrey, or observance of Religion to God.

Nor let it afflict the patience of such full and well instructed judgments, unto whom many of these constitutions and Lawes Divine or Marshall may seeme auncient and common, since these grounds are the same constant, Asterismes, and starres, which must guide all that travell in these perplexed wayes, and paths of publique affairs; and whosoever shall wander from them, shall but decline a hazardous and by-course to bring their purposes to good effect.

Nor let another kind quarrell or traduce the Printing of them to be delivered in particular to officers and private Souldiers for their better instruction, especially unto a Company for the grievous, unsettled and unfurnished, since we know well how short our memories are oftentimes, and unwilling to give storage to the better things, and such things as limit and bound mankind in their necessariest duties.

For which it transcends not the reach of his understanding, who is conversant, if but as for a festivall exercise, (every privy Moone) in reading of a booke, that records and edicts for manners or civil duties, have usually beene fixed upon ingraven Tables, for the Commons daily to overlooke: a custome more especially cherished by those not many yeeres since in Magnuza who have restored (as I may say) after so great a floud and rage of abused goodnesse, all Lawes, literature and Vertue againe, which had well nigh perished, had not the force of piety and sacred reason remaining in the bosomes of some few, opposed itselfe against the fury of so great a calamity, of whom it is an undenyable truth, that the meanes and way whereby they reduced the generall defection, was by printing thereby so houlding uppe those involved principles; and

Instructions wherein (as in a mirror), the blind and wandering judgement might survaye, what those knowledges were, which taught both how to governe, and how to obey, (the end indeed of sociable mankinds Creation) since without order and governement, (the onely hendges, whereupon, not onely the safety, but the being of all states doe turne and depend) what society may possible subsist, or commutative goodnesse be practised. And thus lawes being published, every common eye may take survey of their duties, and carrying away the tenour of the same, meditate, and bethinke how safe, quiet, and comely it is to be honest, just, and civill.

And indeed all the sacred powers of knowledge and wisedome are strengthened by these two waies, either by a kind of divine nature, which his happy creation hath blessed him with, the vertue whereof comprehendeth, foreseeth and understandeth the truth and cleerenesse of all things: or by instruction and tradition from others, which must improve his wants, and by experience render him perfect, awaking him in all seasons a vigilant observer of civill cautions and ordinances, an excellent reason inforcing no lesse unto the knowledge of him that will shine a starre in the firmament, where good men move, and that is, that no man doth more ill then hee that is ignorant.

For the avoiding of which, and to take away the plea of *I did not know* in him that shall exorbitate or goe aside with any delinquencie which may be dangerous in example or execution, albeit true it is how hee is indeede the good and honest man that will be good, and to that needeth fewe other precepts. It hath appeared most necessary unto our present Ethnarches Deputy Governor Sir Thomas Dale knight Marshall, not onely to exemplifie the old Lawes of the Colony, by Sir Thomas Gates published and put in execution by our Lord Generall Laware during his time one whole yeere of being there, but by vertue of his office, to prescribe and draw new, with their due penaltyes, according unto which wee might live in the Colony justly one with another, and performe the generall service for which we first came thither, and with so great charges and expences, are now setled and maintained there.

For my paines, and gathering of them, as I know they will be right welcom to such young souldiers in the Colony who are desirous to learne and performe their duties, so I assure me, that by you I shall bee encouraged to go on in the discharge of greater offices by examining and favouring my good intention in this, and in what else my poore knowledge or faithfulnesse may enable me to be a servant in so beloved and sacred a businesse. And even so committing to your still most abstract, grave and unsatisfied carefulnesse, both it and myselfe, I wish returne of seven fold into such his well inspired bosome, who hath lent his

helping hand unto this new Sion. From my lodging in the blacke Friers.

At your best pleasures, either to returne unto the Colony, or to pray for the successe of it heere.

William Strachey.

Articles, Lawes, and Orders, Divine, Politique, and Martiall for the Colony in Virginea: first established by Sir Thomas Gates Knight, Lieutenant Generall, the 24th of May 1610. exemplified and approved by the Right Honourable Sir Thomas West Knight, Lord Lawair, Lord Governour and Captaine Generall the 12th of June 1610. Againe exemplified and enlarged by Sir Thomas Dale Knight, Marshall, and Deputie Governour, the 22nd of June. 1611.

Whereas his Majestie like himselfe a most zealous Prince hath in his owne Realmes a principall care of true Religion, and reverence to God, and hath alwaies strictly commaunded his Generals and Governours, with all his forces wheresoever, to let their waies be like his ends, for the glorie of God.

And forasmuch as no good service can be performed, or warre well managed, where militarie discipline is not observed, and militarie discipline cannot be kept, where the rules or chiefe parts thereof, be not certainely set downe, and generally knowne, I have (with the advise and counsell of Sir *Thomas Gates* Knight, Lieutenant Generall) adhered unto the lawes divine, and orders politique, and martiall of his Lordship (the same exemplified) an addition of such others, as I have found either the necessitie of the present State of the Colonie to require, or the infancie, and weaknesse of the body thereof, as yet able to digest, and doe now publish them to all persons in the Colonie, that they may as well take knowledge of the Lawes themselves, as of the penaltie and punishment, which without partialitie shall be inflicted upon the breakers of the same.

1. First since we owe our highest and supreme duty, our greatest, and all our allegeance to him, from whom all power and authoritie is derived, and flowes as from the first, and onely fountaine, and being especiall souldiers emprest in this sacred cause, we must alone expect our successe from him, who is onely the blesser of all good attempts, the King of kings, the commaunder of commaunders, and Lord of Hostes, I do strictly commaund and charge all Captaines and Officers, of what qualitie or nature soever, whether commanders in the field, or in towne, or townes, forts or fortresses, to have care that the Almightie God bee duly and daily served, and that they call upon their people to heare Sermons, as that also they diligently frequent Morning and Evening praier themselves by their owne exemplar and daily life, and dutie herein,

encouraging others thereunto, and that such, who shall often and wilfully absent themselves, be duly punished according to the martiall law in that case provided.

2. That no man speake impiously or maliciously, against the holy and blessed Trinitie, or any of the three persons, that is to say, against God the Father, God the Son, and God the holy Ghost, or against the knowne Articles of the Christian faith, upon paine of death.

3. That no man blaspheme Gods holy name upon paine of death, or use unlawful oathes, taking the name of God in vaine, curse, or banne, upon paine of severe punishment for the first offence so committed, and for the second, to have bodkin thrust through his tongue, and if he continue the blaspheming of Gods holy name, for the third time so offending, he shall be brought to a martiall court, and there receive censure of death for his offence.

4. No man shall use any traiterous words against his Majesties Person, or royall authority upon paine of death.

5. No man shall speake any word, or do any act, which may tend to the derision, or despight of Gods holy word upon paine of death: Nor shall any man unworthily demeane himselfe unto any Preacher, or Minister of the same, but generally hold them in all reverent regard, and dutiful intreatie, otherwise he the offender shall openly be whipt three times, and ask publike forgivenesse in the assembly of the congregation three several Saboth daies.

6. Everie man and woman duly twice a day upon the first towling of the Bell shall upon the working daies repaire unto the Church, to hear divine Service upon pain of losing his or her dayes allowance for the first omission, for the second to be whipt, and for the third to be condemned to the Gallies for six Moneths. Likewise no man or woman shall dare to violate or breake the Sabboth by any gaming, publique, or private abroad, or at home, but duly sanctifie and observe the same, both himselfe and his familie, by preparing themselves at home with private prayer, that they may be the better fitted for the publique, according to the commandements of God, and the orders or our Church, as also every man and woman shall repaire in the morning to the divine service, and Sermons preached upon the Saboth day, and in the afternoon to divine service, and Catechising, upon paine for the first fault to lose their provision, and allowance for the whole weeke following, for the second to lose the said allowance, and also to be whipt, and for the third to suffer death.

7. All Preachers or Ministers within this our Colonie, or Colonies, shall in the Forts, where they are resident, after divine Service, duly preach every Sabbath day in the forenoone, and Catechise in the afternoone, and weekely say the divine service, twice every day, and preach every Wednesday, likewise every Minister where he is resident, within the same Fort, or Fortresse, Townes or Towne, shall chuse unto him, foure of the most religious and better dis-

posed as well to informe of the abuses and neglects of the people in their duties, and service to God, as also to the due reparation, and keeping of the Church handsome, and fitted with all reverent observances thereunto belonging: likewise every Minister shall keepe a faithful and true Record, or Church Booke, of all Christnings, Marriages, and deaths of such our people, as shall happen within their Fort, or Fortresses, Townes or Towne at any time, upon the burthen of a neglectfull conscience, and upon paine of losing their Entertainement.

8. He that upon pretended malice, shall murther or take away the life of any man, shall bee punished with death.

9. No man shal commit the horrible, and detestable sins of Sodomie upon pain of death; and he or she that can be lawfully convict of Adultery shall be punished with death. No man shall ravish or force any woman, maid or Indian, or other, upon pain of death, and know the that he or shee, that shall commit fornication, and evident proofe made thereof, for their first fault shall be whipt, for their second they shall be whipt, and for their third they shall be whipt three times a weeke for one month, and ask publique forgivenesse in the Assembly of the Congregation.

10. No man shall bee found guilty of Sacriledge, which is a Trespasse as well committed in violating and abusing any sacred ministry, duty or office of the Church, irreverently, or prophanely, as by beeing a Church robber, to filch, steale or carry away any thing out of the Church appertaining thereunto, or unto any holy, and consecrated place, to the divine Service of God, which no man should doe upon paine of death: likewise he that shall rob the store of any commodities therein, of what quality soever, whether provisions of victuals, or of Arms, Trucking stuffe, Apparrell, Linnen, or Wollen, Hose or Shooes, Hats or Caps, Instruments or Tooles of Steele, Iron, etc. or shall rob from his fellow souldier, or neighbour, any thing that is his, victuals, apparell, household stuffe, toole, or what necessary else soever, by water or land, out of boate, house, or knapsack, shall bee punished with death.

11. Hee that shall take an oath untruly, or beare false witnesse in any cause, or against any man whatsoever, shall be punished with death.

12. No manner of person whatsoever, shall dare to detract, slaunder, calumniate, or utter unseemely, and unfitting speeches, either against his Majesties Honourable Councell for this Colony, resident in England, or against the Committees, Assistants unto the said Councell, or against the zealous indeavors, and intentions of the whole body of Adventurers for this pious and Christian Plantation, or against any publique booke, or bookes, which by their mature advise, and grave wisdomes, shall be thought fit, to be set foorth and publisht, for the advance-

ment of the good of this Colony, and the felicity thereof, upon paine for the first time so offending, to bee whipt three severall times, and upon his knees to acknowledge his offence and to aske forgivenesse upon the Saboth day in the assembly of the congregation, and for the second time so offending to be condemned to the Galley for three yeares, and for the third time so offending to be punished with death.

13. No matter of Person whatsoever, contrarie to the word of God (which tyes every particular and private man, for conscience sake to obedience, and duty of the Magistrate, and such as shall be placed in authoritie over them), shall detract, slaunder, calumniate, murmur, mutenie, resist, disobey, or neglect the commaundments, either of the Lord Governour, and Captaine Generall, the Lieutenant Generall, the Martiall, the Councell, or any authorised Captaine, Commaunder or publike Officer, upon paine for the first time so offending to be whipt three severall times, and upon his knees to acknowledge his offence, with asking forgivenesse upon the Saboth day in the assembly of the congregation, and for the second time so offending to be condemned to the Gally for three yeares: and for the third time so offending to be punished with death.

14. No man shall give any disgracefull words, or commit any act to the disgrace of any person in this Colonie, or any part thereof, upon paine of being tied head and feete together, upon the guard everie night for the space of one moneth, besides to bee publikely disgraced himselfe, and be made uncapable ever after to possesse any place, or execute any office in this imployment.

15. No man of what condition soever shall barter, trucke, or trade with the Indians, except he be thereunto appointed by lawful authority, upon paine of death.

16. No man shall rifle or dispoile, by force or violence, take away any thing from any Indian comming to trade, or otherwise, upon paine of death.

17. No Cape Marchant, or Provant Master, or Munition Master, or Truck Master, or keeper of any store, shall at any time imbezell, sell, or give away any thing under his Charge to any Favorite, of his, more then unto any other, whome necessity shall require in that case to have extraordinary allowance of Provisions, nor shall they give a false accompt unto the Lord Governour, and Captaine Generall, unto the Lieuetenant Generall, unto the Marshall, or any deputed Governor, at any time having the commaund of the Colony, with intent to defraud the said Colony, upon paine of death.

18. No man shall imbezel or take away the goods of any man that dyeth, or is imployed from the town or Fort where he dwelleth in any other occasioned remote service, for the time, upon pain of whipping three severall times, and restitution of the said goods againe, and in danger of

incurring the penalty of the tenth Article, if so it may come under the construction of theft. And if any man die and make a will, his goods shall be accordingly disposed; if hee die intestate, his goods shall bee put into the store, and being valued by two sufficient praisers, his next of kinne (according to the common Lawes of England), shall from the Company, Committies, or adventurers, receive due satisfaction in monyes, according as they were praised, by which meanes the Colonie shall be the better furnished; and the goods more carefully preserved, for the right heire, and the right heire receive content for the same in *England.*

19. There shall be no Capttain, Master, Marriner, saylor, or any else of what quality or condition soever, belonging to any Ship or Ships, at this time remaining, or which shall hereafter arrive within this our River, bargaine, buy, truck or trade with any one member in this Colony, man, woman, or child, for any toole or instrument of iron, steel or what else, whether appertaining to Smith Carpenter, Joyner, Shipwright, or any manuall occupation, or handicraft man whatsoever, resident within our Colonie, nor shall they buy or bargaine, for any apparell, linnen, or wollen, houshold-stuffe, bedde, bedding, sheete towels, napkins, brasse, pewter, or such like, eyther for ready money, or provisions, nor shall they exchange their provisions, of what quality soever, whether Butter, Cheese, Bisket, meal, Oatmele, Aquavite, oyle, Bacon, any kind of Spice, or such like, for any such aforesaid instruments, or tooles, Apparell, or household-stuffe, at any time, or so long as they shall here remain, from the date of these presents upon paine of losse of their wages in *England,* confiscation and forfeiture of such their monies and provisions, and upon peril beside of such corporall punishment as shall be inflicted upon them by verdict and censure of a martiall Court: Nor shall any officer, souldier, or Trades man, or any else of what sort soever, members of this Colony, dare to sell any such Toole, or instruments, necessary and usefull, for the businesse of the Colonie, or trucke, sell, exchange, or give away his apparell, or household stuffe of what sort soever, unto any such Seaman, either for mony, or any such foresaid provisions, upon paine of 3 times severall whipping, for the one offender, and the other upon perill of incurring censure, whether of disgrace, or addition of such punishment, as shall bee thought fit by a Court martiall.

20. Whereas sometimes heeretofore the covetous and wide affections of some greedy and ill disposed Seamen, Saylers, and Marriners, laying hold upon the advantage of the present necessity, under which the Colony sometimes suffered, have sold unto our people, provisions of Meale, Oatmeale, Bisket, Butter, Cheese etc., at unreasonable rates, and prises unconscionable: for avoiding the like to bee now put in practise, there shall no Captain, Master,

Marriner, or Saylor, or what Officer else belonging to any ship, or shippes, now within our river, or heereafter which shall arrive, shall dare to bargaine, exchange, barter, truck, trade, or sell, upon paine of death, unto any one Landman member of this present Colony, any provisions of what kind soever, above the determined valuations, and prises, set downe and proclaimed, and sent therefore unto each of your severall ships, to bee fixed upon your Maine mast, to the intent that want of due notice, and ignorance in this case, be no excuse, or plea, for any one offender herein.

21. Sithence we are not to bee a little carefull, and our young Cattell, and Breeders may be cherished, that by the preservation, and increase of them, the Colony heere may receive in due time assured and great benefite, and the adventurers at home may be eased of so great a burthen, by sending unto us yeerely supplies of this kinde, which now heere for a while, carefully attended, may turne their supplies unto us into provisions of other qualities, when or these wee shall be able to subsist our selves, and which wee may in short time, be powerful enough to doe, if we wil according to our owne knowledge of what is good for our selves, forbeare to work into our own wants, againe, by over hasty destroying, and devouring the stocks, and authors of so profitable succeeding a Commodity, as increase of Cattel, Kine, Hogges, Goates, Poultrie etc. must of necessity bee granted, in every common mans judgement, to render unto us: Now know thee therefore, these promises carefully considered, that it is our will and pleasure, that every one, of what quality or condition soever hee bee, in his present Colony, to take due notice of this our Edict, whereby wee do strictly charge and command, that no man shall dare to kill, or destroy any Bull, Cow, Calfe, Mare, Horse, Colt, Goate, Swine, Cocke, Henne, Chicken, Dogge, Turkie, or any tame Cattel, or Poultry, of what condition soever; whether his owne, or appertaining to another man, without leave from the Generall, upon paine of death in the Principall, and in the accessary, burning in the Hand, and losse of his eares, and unto the concealer of the same foure and twenty houres whipping, with addition of further punishment, as shall be thought fitte by the censure, and verdict of a Martiall Court.

22. There shall no man or woman, Launderer or Launderesse, dare to wash any uncleane Linnen, drive bucks, or throw out the water or suds of fowle cloathes, in the open streete, within the Pallizadoes, or within forty foote of the same, nor rench, and make cleane, any kettle, pot, or pan, or such like vessell within twenty foote of the olde well, or new Pumpe: nor shall any one aforesaid, within lesse then a quarter of one mile from the Pallizadoes, dare to doe the necessities of nature, since by these unmanly, slothfull, and loathsome immodesties, the whole Fort may bee choaked, and poisoned with ill aires, and so

corrupt (as in all reason cannot but much infect the same) and this shall they take notice of, and avoide, upon paine of whipping and further punishment, as shall be thought meete, by the censure of a martiall Court.

23. No man shall imbezell, lose, or willingly breake, or fraudulently make away, either Spade, Shovell, Hatchet, Axe, Mattocke, or other toole or instrument uppon paine of whipping.

24. Any man that hath any edge toole, either of his owne, or which hath heeretofore beene belonging to the store, see that he bring it instantly to the storehouse, where he shall receive it againe by a particular note, both of the toole, and of his name taken, that such a toole unto him appertaineth, at whose hands, upon any necessary occasion, the said toole may be required, and this shall he do, upon paine of severe punishment.

25. Every man shall have an especial and due care, to keepe his house sweete and cleane, as also so much of the streete, as lieth before his door, and especially he shall so provide, and set his bedstead whereon he lieth, that it may stand three foote at least from the ground, as he will answere the contrarie at a martiall Court.

26. Every tradesman in their severall occupation, trade and function, shall duly and daily attend his worke upon his said trade or occupation, upon perill for his first fault, and negligence therein, to have his entertainment checkt for one moneth, for his second fault three moneth, for his third one yeare, and if he continue still unfaithfull and negligent therein, to be condemned to the Gally for three yeare.

27. All overseers of workemen, shall be carefull in seeing that performed, which is given them in charge, upon paine of such punishment as shall be inflicted upon him by a martiall Court.

28. No souldier or tradesman, but shall be readie, both in the morning, and in the afternoone, upon the beating of the Drum, to goe out unto his worke, nor shall hee return home, or from his worke, before the Drum beate againe, and the officer appointed for that businesse, bring him of, upon perill for the first fault to lie upon the Guard head and heeles together all night, for the second time so faulting to be whipt, and for the third time so offending to be condemned to the Gallies for a yeare.

29. No man or woman, (upon paine of death) shall runne away from the Colonie, to Powhathan, or any savage Weroance else whatsoever.

30. He that shall conspire any thing against the person of the Lord Governour, and Captaine Generall, against the Lieutenant Generall, or against the Marshall, or against any publike service commaunded by them, for the dignitie, and advancement of the good of the Colony, shall be punished with death: and he that shall have knowledge of any such pretended act of disloyalty or treason, and shall not

reveale the same unto his Captaine, or unto the Governour of that fort or towne wherein he is, within the space of one houre, shall for the concealing of the same after that time, be not onely held an accessary, but alike culpable as the principall traitor or conspirer, and for the same likewise he shall suffer death.

31. What man or woman soever, shall rob any garden, publike or private, being set to weed the same, or wilfully pluck up therein any roote, herbe, or flower, to spoile and wast or steale the same, or robbe any vineyard, or gather up the grapes, or steale any eares of the corne growing, whether in the ground belonging to the same fort or towne where he dwelleth, or in any other, shall be punished with death.

32. Whosoever Seaman, or Landman of what qualitie, or in what place of commaund soever, shall be imployed upon any discovery, trade, or fishing voiage into any of the rivers within the precincts of our Colonie, shall for the safety of those men who are committed to his commaund, stand upon good and carefull guard, for the prevention of any treachery in the Indian, and if they touch upon any shore, they shal be no lesse circumspect, and warie, with good and carefull guard day and night, putting forth good Centinell, and observing the orders and discipline of watch and ward, and when they have finished the discovery, trade, or fishing, they shall make hast with all speed, with such Barke or Barkes, Pinisse, Gallie, Ship. etc. as they shall have the commaund of, for the same purpose, to *James towne* againe, not presuming to goe beyond their commission, or to carry any such Barke or Barkes, Gally, Pinnice, Ship, etc. for England or any other countrey in the actuall possession of any Christian Prince, upon perill to be held an enemie to this plantation, and traitor there-unto, and accordingly to lie liable unto such censure of punishment (if they arrive in England) as shall be thought fit by the Right Honourable Lords, his Majesties Councell for this Colonie, and if it shall so happen, that he or they shall be prevented, and brought backe hither againe into the Colonie, their trecherous flight to be punished with death.

33. There is not one man nor woman in this Colonie now present, or hereafter to arrive, but shall give up an account of his and their faith, and religion, and repaire unto the Minister, that by his conference with them, hee may understand, and gather, whether heretofore they have beene sufficiently instructed, and catechised in the principles and grounds of Religion, whose weaknesse and ignorance herein, the Minister finding, and advising them in all love and charitie, to repaire often unto him, to receive therein a greater measure of knowledge, if they shal refuse so to repaire unto him, and he the Minister give notice thereof unto the Governour, or that chiefe officer of that towne or fort, wherein he or she, the parties so offending

shall remaine, the Governour shall cause the offender for his first time of refusall to be whipt, for the second time to be whipt twice, and to acknowledge his fault upon the Saboth day, in the assembly of the congregation, and for the third time to be whipt every day until he hath made the same acknowledgement, and asked forgivenesse for the same, and shall repaire unto the Minister, to be further instructed as aforesaid: and upon the Saboth when the Minister shall catechise, and of him demaund any question concerning his faith and knowledge, he shall not refuse to make answere upon the same perill.

34. What man or woman soever, Laundrer or Laundresse appointed to wash the foule linnen of any one labourer or souldier, or any one else as it is their duties so to doe, performing little, or no other service for their allowance out of the store, and daily provisions, and supply of other necessaries, unto the Colonie, and shall from the said labourer or souldier, or any one else, of what qualitie whatsoever, either take any thing for washing, or withhold or steale from him any such linnen committed to her charge to wash, or change the same willingly and wittingly, with purpose to give him worse, old and torne linnen for his good, and proofe shall be made thereof, she shall be whipped for the same, and lie in prison till she make restitution of such linnen, withheld or changed.

35. No Captaine, Master, or Mariner, of what condition soever, shall depart or carry out of our river, any Ship, Barke, Barge, Gally, Pinnace etc. Roaders belonging to the Colonie, either now therein, or hither arriving, without leave and commission from the Generall or chiefe Commaunder of the Colonie upon paine of death.

36. No man or woman whatsoever, members of this Colonie, shall sell or give unto any Captaine, Marriner, Master, or Sailer, etc. any commoditie of this countrey, of what quality soever, to be transported out of the Colonie, for his or their owne private uses, upon paine of death.

37. If any souldier indebted, shall refuse to pay his debts unto his creditor, his creditor shall informe his Captaine, if the Captaine cannot agree the same, the creditor shall informe the Marshals civill and principall officer, who shall preferre for the creditor a bill of complaint at the Marshals Court, where the creditor shal have Justice.

All such Bakers as are appointed to bake bread, or what else, either for the store to be given out in generall, or for any one in particular, shall not steale nor imbezell, loose, or defraud any man of his due and proper weight and measure, nor use any dishonest and deceiptfull tricke to make the bread weigh heavier, or make it courser upon purpose to keepe backe any part or measure of the flower or meale committed unto him, nor aske, take, or detaine any one loafe more or lesse for his hire or paines for so baking, since whilest he who delivered unto him such meale or flower, being to attend the businesse of the

Colonie, such baker or bakers are imposed upon no other service or duties, but onely so to bake for such as do worke, and this shall hee take notice of, upon paine for the first time offending herein of losing his eares, and for the second time to be condemned a yeare to the Gallies, and for the third time offending, to be condemned to the Gallies for three yeares.

All such cookes as are appointed to seeth, bake or dresse any manner of way, flesh, fish, or what else, of what kind soever, either for the generall company, or for any private man, shall not make lesse, or cut away any part or parcel of such flesh, fish, etc. Nor detaine or demaund any part or parcell, as allowance or hire for his so dressing the same, since as aforesaid of the baker, hee or they such Cooke or Cookes, exempted from other publike works abroad, are to attend such seething and dressing of such publike flesh, fish, or other provisions of what kinde soever, as their service and duties expected from them by the Colony, and this shall they take notice of, upon paine for the first time offending herein, of losing his eares, and for the second time to be condemned a yeare to the Gallies: and for the third time offending to be condemned to the Gallies for three yeares.

All fishermen, dressers of Sturgeon or such like appointed to fish, or to secure the said Sturgeon for the use of the Colonie, shall give a just and true account of all such fish as they shall take by day or night, of what kinde soever, the same to bring into the Governour: As also of all such kegges of Sturgeon or Caviare as they shall prepare and cure upon perill for the first time offending heerein, of loosing his eares, and for the second time to be condemned a yeare to the Gallies, and for the third time offending, to be condemned to the Gallies for three yeares.

Every Minister or Preacher shall every Sabboth day before Catechising, read all these lawes and ordinances, publikely in the assembly of the congregation upon paine of his entertainment check for that weeke.

The Summarie of the Marshall Lawes
Thee are now further to understand, that all these prohibited, and forefended trespasses and misdemenors, with the injoyned observance of all these thus repeated, Civill and Politique Lawes, provided, and declared against what Crimes soever, whether against the divine Majesty of God, or our soveraigne, and Liege Lord, King *James*, the detestable crime of Sodomie, Incest, Blasphemie, Treason against the person of the principall Generals, and Commaunders of this Colonie, and their designs, against detracting, murmuring, calumniating, or slaundering of the Right Honourable the Councell resident in England, and the Committies there, the general Councell, and chiefe Commaunders heere, as also against intemperate

raylings, and base unmanly speeches, uttered in the disgrace one of another by the worser sort, by the most impudent, ignorant, and prophane, such as have neither touch of humanitie, nor of conscience amongst ourselves, against Adultery, Fornication, Rape, Murther, Theft, false witnessing in any cause, and other the rest of the Civil, and Politique Lawes and Orders, necessarily appertaining, and properly belonging to the Government of the State and Condition of the present Colony, as it now subsisteth: I say thee are to know, that all these thus joyned, with their due punishments, and perils heere declared, and published, are no lesse subject to the Martiall law, then unto the Civil Magistrate, and where the Alarum, Tumult, and practise of arms, are not exercised, and where these now following Lawes, appertaining only to Martiall discipline, are diligently to be observed, and shall be severely executed.

1. No man shall willingly absent himself, when hee is summoned to take the oath of Supremacy, upon paine of death.

2. Every Souldier comming into this Colonie, shall willingly take his oath to serve the King and the Colonie, and to bee faithfull, and obedient to such Officers, and Commaunders, as shall be appointed over him, during the time of his aboard therein, according to the Tenor of the oath in that case provided, upon paine of being committed to the Gallies.

3. If any Souldier, or what maner of man else soever, of what quality or condition soever he be, shal tacitely compact, with any Sea-man, Captain, Master, or Marriner, to convay himselfe a Board any shippe, with intent to depart from, and abandon the Colony, without a lawful Passe from the Generall, or chiefe commander of the Colonie, at that time, and shall happen to bee prevented, and taken therwith, before the shippe shall depart out of our Bay, that Captaine, Maister or mariner, that shall so receive him, shall lose his wages, and be condemned to the Gallies for three yeeres, and he the sworne servant of the Colony, Souldier, or what else, shall bee put to death with the Armes which he carrieth.

4. When any select, and appointed Forces, for the execution and performance of any intended service, shall bee drawne into the field, and shall dislodge from one place unto another, that Souldier that shall quit, or forsake his Colors, shall be punished with death.

5. That Souldier that shall march upon any service, shall keepe his Ranke and marching, the Drum beating, and the Ensigne displayed, shall not dare to absent himselfe, or stray and straggle from his ranke, without leave granted from the cheefe Officer, upon paine of death.

6. All Captaines shall command all Gentlemen, and Common Souldiers in their Companies, to obey their Sergeants, and Corporals, in their offices, without resisting, or injuring the said Officers, upon paine, if the injurie

be by words, he the offender shal aske his Officer pardon in the place of Arms, in the mead of the troopes. If by Act, he the offender shall passe the pikes.

7. That Souldier that in quarrel with an other shall call upon any of his companions, or Countrimen to assist, and abette him, shall bee put to death with such Armes as he carrieth.

8. Hee that shall begin a mutiny, shall bee put to death with such Armes as he carrieth.

9. Where a quarrell shall happen betweene two or more, no man shall betake him unto any other Arms then his sword, except he be a Captaine or Officer, upon paine of being put to death with such Armes as he shall so take.

10. If a Captaine or Officer of a Companie shall come where two or more are fighting with their drawne swords, so soone as hee shall cry Hold, and charge them to forbeare, those that have their swords in their hands so drawne, shall not dare to strike or thrust once after upon paine of passing the Pikes.

11. That Souldier that having a quarrell with an other, shall gather other of his acquaintance, and Associates, to make parties, to bandie, brave second, and assist him therin, he and those braves, seconds, and assistants shall passe the Pikes.

12. He that shall way-lay any man by advantage taken, thereby cowardly to wound, or murther him shall passe the Pikes.

13. If any discontentment shall happen betweene Officers, or Souldiers, so as the one shall give words of offence, unto the other, to moove quarrell, the Officer or Souldier shall give notice thereof, to his Corporall, or superior officer, and the Corporall, or superior officer, shall commit the offender, and if it happen between Commanders, the officer offended shall give notice to the Generall, or Marshal, that he may be committed, who for the first offence shall suffer three daies imprisonment, and make the officer wronged, satisfaction before his squadron to repair him, and satisfie him, without base submission, which may unworthy him to carry Armes. And the officer, or Souldier so offended, having satisfaction offered, shall with all willingnes receive it, for which both producing it to his Officer, and accepting of satisfaction, hee shall bee reputed an officer, or souldier well governed in himselfe, and so much the fitter to be advanced in Commaund over others, and if any shall upbraid him, for not having sought a savage headlong revenge against his fellow, the officer or souldier so upbraiding, shall bee punished and make satisfaction as the first offender, and if any shal so offend the second time he shall suffer ten nights lying head and heeles together, with Irons upon the guard, and have his entertainement checkt for one month, and make satisfaction to the officer or souldier, as before remembred, and for the third offence, hee shall bee committed to the Gal-

lies three yeeres. And if upon the first offence given by any officer or souldier, upon any other, in words as aforesaid, and the other returne injurious words againe, they shall both be taken as like offenders, and suffer like punishment, saving that he who gave the first offence, shall offer first repaire unto the offended, which he the offended shall accept, and then shal hee proceed to returne the like satisfaction unto the other, and if any shall bee obstinate in this point of repaire, and satisfaction, hee shall suffer sharped and severe punishment, until hee shall consent unto it, the words or manner of satisfaction, to be given unto the Party, or parties offended, shall be appointed by the chiefe officer of the Company, under whom the officer, or souldier shall happen to bee, with the knowledge of the provost Marshall, provided, that if the Officer or souldier shall desire it, hee may appeale unto the chiefe officer of the Garrison, or unto the Marshall, if hee shall be present to Judge of the equity of the satisfaction. And if any Lanceprizado, Corporall, or other officer, shall happen to bee present, or shall take knowledge of any such offence offered of one partie, or Quarrell sought and accepted of more parties, he shall presently cause the partie, or parties so offending to bee committed to prison, the due execution may follow, as is formerly provided. And if any Lanceprizado, Corporall, or superior officer shall neglect his or their duty, or duties heerein appointed, by not bringing the offender, and their offences, to the knowledge of the superior office, that satisfaction as aforesaid, upon the fault committed, may orderly follow, the officer so offending, shal for his first omission, negligence, and contempt, suffer ten daies Imprisonment, for the second twenty, and for the third losse of his place, and to bee put to the duty of a Centinell: And if any officer or Souldier shall be present when two or more shall draw weapons, with intent to fight, or shall fight, they shall presently doe their best to part them, and if he be an officer he shall commit them, or put them under safe guard to bee committed, and if hee bee a private souldier, hee shall give notice to the provost, marshall, or unto the first officer that he shall meet with, of the parties offending, who shall presently take order, that they may be apprehended, and committed to the Provost Martialcy, and if any officer or souldier, shall happen to see any officer or souldier so fighting, and shall not doe his best to part them, without favouring one part or other, hee shall bee punished at the discretion of the officer in chiefe, and the punishment shall extend to the taking away of life, if the cause shal so require, and if any officer, or souldier shall know of any purpose in any to fight, and shall not stay them, or discover them to such officers, as are competent to stay them, but that they goe to fight, and doe accordingly fight, that officer, or souldier shall bee taken, and shall bee punished cleerely and in the same sort, as the offence deserveth punishment betweene them fighting.

14. That officer, or Souldier that shall challenge another to fight, and hee that shall carry any Challenge, knowing it to be a Challenge, and he that accepteth any such Challenge with a purpose and returne of answere, to meete the saide Challenger to fight with him, in this case they shall all three be held alike culpable, and lie subject to the Censure of a Martiall Court.

15. That officer who shal command the guard and let such Challengers and Challenged, passe the ports, upon his knowledge to fight, shall be casseird, and if the officer be under the degree of a Captaine, hee shall bee put to doe the duty of a Centinell.

16. No officer shall strike any souldier, for any thing, not concerning the order, and duty of service, and the publique worke of the Colony, and if any officer shall so doe, hee shall bee punished as a private man in that case, and bee held unworthy to command, so perverting the power of his place and authority.

17. No man shall be Captaine of the watch at any time, under the degree of an Ensigne.

18. He that shall take the name of God in vain or shall play at Cards or dice, upon the Court of guard, for the first time so offending, he shall bee committed to prison, there to lie in Irons for three daies, for the second time so offending, hee shall be whipt, and for the third time so offending hee shall bee condemned to the Gallies for one yeere.

19. Hee that shall absent himselfe from the Court of Guard, uppon his watch above one houre without leave of his Corporall or superior officer, shall for his first time so offending, at the relieving of the watch bee committed to prison, and there to lye in Irons for 3 dayes, for the second time he shall be committed to prison and there lye in irons for one weeke, and have his entertainement checkt for one weeke, and for the third time, hee shall be committed to the Gallies for six moneths.

20. He that shall swagger, and give injurious words upon the court of guard, for the first offence, hee shall aske forgivenesse upon his knees, of the officers, and rest of the Guard, before the Captain of the watch at that time: for his second time so offending, he shall bee committed to the Gallies for one yeere.

21. He that draweth his sword upon the Court of Guard, shall suffer death by the Armes which he weareth.

22. He that should draw his sword in a towne of Garrison, or in a Campe shall lose his right hand.

23. That souldier that shall goe out of the Fort, Towne or Campe, other then by the ordinary guards, issues, waies, or ports, shall suffer death by the Armes which he carrieth.

24. He that shall abuse and injurie the Serjeant Major, the provost Marshall, either by word, or deede, if hee be a Captaine, hee shall be casseird, if a Souldier he shall passe the pikes.

25. When the Officer or Souldier shall have committed any Crime, or have made breach of the publique Lawes, his Captaine shall commit him unto the serjeant Major, who having taken his examination, shall send him to the Provost Marshall, committed unto prison, that he may bee brought to be censured by a court Marshall.

26. No Souldier shall withstand or hinder the Provost Marshall, or his men in the execution of his office, upon paine of death.

27. All Captaines, Lieutenants, Serjeants, and Corporals, shall be diligent at convenient times, to traine and exercise their Companies, and shall have a care of their Armes, as they tender their entertainment, and upon pain of casseiring, and other corporall punishment, as shall be inflicted by vertue of a Marshall court.

28. No man shall goe twelve score from the quarter, his colours, towne or fort, without leave of his Captaine, upon paine for the first time of whipping, for the second offence to be committed to the Gallies for one yeare, and for the third offence to suffer death.

29. No man shall sell, give, imbezell, or play away his Armes, or any part thereof, upon paine of death.

30. No common Souldier shall sell, or make away any of his apparell, which is delivered unto him by the Colonie, or out of the store, upon paine of whipping.

31. No man shall depart from his guard without leave of his officer, upon paine of punishment: and who so shall be set Centinell, shall not depart from it, until he be relieved, nor sleepe thereof upon paine of death.

32. No man shall offer any violence, or contemptuously resist or disobey his Commaunder, or doe any act, or speake any words which may tend to the breeding of any disorder or mutinie in the towne or field, or disobey any principall Officers directions upon paine of death.

33. He that shall not appeare upon the guard, or not repaire unto his colours, when the Drum upon any occasion shall beate either upon an Alarum, or to attend the businesse which shall be then commaunded, shall for his first offence lie in Irons upon the court of guard all one night, and for his second be whipt, and for the third be condemned to the Gallies for one yeare.

34. That Souldier who fighting with an enemie, shall lose his Armes, or runne away cowardly, or yeeld himselfe but upon apparant and great constraints or without having performed, first the part of a good souldier, and an honest man, shall suffer death with the armes which he carrieth.

35. That Souldier that shall let go any caution delivered upon a treatie, or any prisoner or warre by his negligence, shall be punished with death.

36. No Souldier shall let goe any prisoner of war, which he hath taken without consent of his Captaine, who shall advertise the chiefe Commaunder, upon paine of being committed to the Gallies for one yeare.

37. That Souldier which upon an assault, or taking of any towne, that shall not follow his colours, and the victory, but shall fall to pillage for his private profit, after the place taken, shall suffer death with the armes which he weareth.

38. No Souldier may speake or have any private conference with any of the salvages, without leave of his Captaine, nor his Captaine without leave of his chiefe Officer, upon paine of death.

39. When the Marshall or Governour of a towne, shall demaund a Souldier that hath made breach of these lawes, that Captaine or any other that shall conceale him, or assist him to flie away, shall bee punished with the punishment which the fact of the said fugitive deserved.

40. That Captaine shall *ipso facto,* find any Souldier breaking these fore declared lawes and ordinances, of whatsoever company he shall be, he shall commit him to the Provost Marshall to be punished according as the offence committed commeth under the construction of the Martiall law in that case provided.

41. No Souldier shall unprofitably waste his pouder, shot, or match, by shooting it idly away, or at birds, beasts, or fowle, but shall give an account unto his Corporall of the same, who shall certifie his Captain upon peril for his first fault so committed, to be committed to prison, there to lie in Irons head and heeles togither eight and forty hours, for the second to be condemned six moneths to the Gallies, and for the third offence to be condemned two yeares to the Gallies.

42. All Captaines, Officers, and common Souldiers, or others of what condition soever, members of the Colonie, shall doe their endeavours to detect, apprehend, and bring to punishment all offenders, and shall assist the officer of that place for that purpose, as they will answere the contrary at our Marshall court.

43. All other faults, disorders, and offences that are not mentioned in these Lawes, Articles, and Orders shall be and are supplied in the instructions which I have set downe, and now shall be delivered unto every Captain, and other Officer, so farre forth as the infancie, and as yet weake condition of this our present Colony will suffer, and which shall be punished according to the generall custome, and therefore I commaund all men to looke to their charges, and him that hath no charge to looke to his owne carriage, and to keepe himselfe within the bounds of dutie, for the discipline shall be strictly kept, and the offenders against the lawes thereof severely punished.

44. Whosoever shall give offence to the Indians in that nature, which truly examined, shall found to have beene cause of breach of their league, and friendship, which with so great travaile, desire, and circumspection, we have or shall at any time obtaine from them without commission so to doe, from him that hath authorities for the same, shall be punished with death.

45. Whosoever shall willfully, or negligently set fire on any Indian dwelling house, or *Quioquisock* house or temple, or upon any storehouse, or garner of graine, or provision of what quality soever, or disvaledge, ransacke, or ill intreat the people of the countrey, where any warre, or where through any march shall be made except it be proclaimed, or without commandement of the chiefe officers shall be punished with death.

46. Whosoever shall not do his endeavour and best to regaine and recover his colours, if by hap it fall into the Indians hands shall lie subject to the censure of a Marshall court.

47. Whosoever shall faine himself sick, upon the point of fight, or when any worke is to be done or slip away from the service of either, shall be punished by death.

48. Whosoever shall raise any question, brabble or braule in the watch, or Amboscado, or in Scout, or Sentinel in any other effect, or make any noise or rumor where silence, secrecie, and covert is to be required, shall be punished with death.

49. Whosoever shall not retreat when the drum or trumpet soundeth the same, whether it be upon any sallies, made out of any town or fortres, or in skirmish, or in any incounter, shall be punished with death.

50. It now resteth, that all Captaines and supreme officers, whether governor in towne, fort or fortes, or Captaine of companies shall be advised to do their indevors joyntly, and to agree in one accord, that the true and never failing Justice, may be executed with all integrity of all these foredeclared lawes, according to the dignitie, power, and censure of the Martiall court, that by the exemplar lives, and honourable practises of all that is good and vertuous, all things may be governed in good order, as no doubt, our Right Honorable Lord Generall doth assure himselfe, that all good and upright men that have the feare of God, and his service, and their owne honour in regard, will demean themselves no lesse, then according to the dignity of their place, and charge of their command, the united powers of his Lordships knowledge, being so full of approved noblenesse, and the well knowne, and long time exercised grounds of Piety, as without question he cannot but desire rather a little number of good men, obedient and tractable, submitting to good order and discipline, then a great armie, composed of vitious prophane, quarrellous, disobedient, and ignoble persons, wherefore in his Lordships behalfe, I must intreat all Governors, Captains, Officers, and Soldiers, and neverthelesse do injoyne, ordaine and command them to carry themselves in their severall duties and charges, according to the intention of his Lordship, declared by these present Ordinances.

51. Every Captaine shall cause to be read all these lawes which concerne martiall discipline, every weeke

upon his guard day, unto his company upon paine of censure of a Martiall court.

A Praier duly said Morning and Evening upon the Court of Guard, either by the Captaine of the watch himselfe, or by some one of his principall officers.

Merciful Father, and Lord of heaven and earth, we come before thy presence to worship thee in calling upon thy name, and giving thankes unto thee, and though our duties and our verie necessities call us heereunto: Yet we confesse our hearts to be so dull and untoward, that unlesse thou be mercifull to us to teach us how to pray, we shall not please thee, nor profit our selves in these duties.

Wee therefore most humbly beseech thee to raise up our hearts with thy good spirit, and so to dispose us to praier, that with true fervencie of heart, feeling of our wants, humblenesse of minde, and faith in thy gracious promises, we may present our suites acceptably unto thee by our Lord and Saviour Jesus Christ.

And thou our Father of al mercies, that hast called us unto thee, heare us and pitie thy poore servants, we have indeed sinned wonderously against thee through our blindnesse of mind, prophanesse of spirit, hardnesse of heart, selfe love, worldlinesse, carnall lusts, hypocrisie, pride vanitie, unthankfulnesse, infidelitie, and other native corruptions, which being bred in us, and with us, have defiled us even from the wombe, and unto this day, and have broken out as plague sores into innumerable transgressions of all thy holy lawes, (the good waies whereof we have wilfully declined,) and have many times displeased thee, and our own consciences in chusing those things which thou hast most justly and severely forbidden us. And besides all this wee have outstood the gracious time and meanes of our version, or at least not stooped and humbled our selves before thee, as wee ought, although we have wanted none of those helpes, which thou vouchsafest unto thy wandering children to fetch them home withall, for we have had together with thy glorious workers, thy word calling upon us without with thy spirit within, and have been solicited by promises, by threatnings, by blessings, by chastisings, and by examples, on all hands: And yet our corrupted spirits cannot become wise before thee, to humble themselves, and to take heede as we ought, and wish to do.

Wherefore O Lord God, we do acknowledge thy patience to have beene infinite and incomparable, in that thou hast been able to hold thy hands from revenging thy self upon us thus long, and yet pleasest to hold open the dore of grace, that we might come it unto thee and be saved.

And now O blessed Lord God, we are desirous to come unto thee, how wretched soever in our selves, yea our very wretchednesse sends us unto thee: unto thee with whom the fatherlesse, and he that hath no helper findeth mercy, we come to thee in thy Sons name not daring to come in our owne: In his name that came for us, we come to thee, in his mediation whom thou hast sent: In him O Father, in whom thou hast professed thy selfe to be well pleased, we come unto thee, and doe most humbly beseech thee to pittie us, and to save us for thy mercies sake in him.

O Lord our God our sins have not outbidden that bloud of thy holy Son which speaks for our pardon, nor can they be so infinite, as thou art in thy mercies, and our hearts (O God thou seest them,) our hearts are desirous to have peace with thee, and war with our lusts, and wish that they could melt before thee, and be dissolved into godly mourning for all that filth that hath gone through them, and defiled them. And our desires are now to serve and please thee, and our purposes to endevour it more faithfully, we pray thee therefore for the Lord Jesus sake seale up in our consciences thy gracious pardon of all our sinnes past, and give us to feele the consolation of this grace shed abroad in our hearts for our eternall comfort and salvation: and that we may know this perswasion to be of thy spirit, and not of carnall presumption, (blessed God) let those graces of thy spirit, which doe accompanie salvation, be powred out more plentifully upon us, encrease in us all godly knowledge, faith, patience, temperance, meekenesse, wisedome, godlinesse, love to thy Saints and service, zeale of thy glory, judgement to discerne the difference of good and ill, and things present which are temporary, and things to come which are eternall.

Make us yet at the last wise-hearted to lay up our treasure in heaven, and to set our affections more upon things that are above, where Christ sits at thy right hand: And let all the vaine and transitory inticements of this poore life, appeare unto us as they are, that our hearts may no more be intangled and bewitched with the love of them.

O Lord O God, our God, thou hast dearely bought us for thine owne selfe, give us so honest hearts as may be glad to yeeld the possession of thine owne. And be thou so gracious, as yet to take them up, though we have desperately held thee out of them in times past, and dwell in us, and raigne in us by thy spirit, that we may be sure to raigne with thee in thy glorious kingdome, according to thy promise through him that hath purchased that inheritance for all that trust in him.

And seeing thou doest so promise these graces to us, as that thou requirest our industrie and diligence in the use of such meanes as serve thereto (good Lord) let us not so crosse our praiers for grace, as not to seeke that by diligence, which we make shew to seeke by prayer, least our owne waies condemne us of hypocrisie. Stirre us up therefore (O Lord) to the frequent use of prayer, to reading, hearing, and meditating of thy holy word, teach us to profit by the conversation of thy people, and to be profitable in our owne, make us wise to apprehend all opportunities of doing or receiving spirituall good, strengthen us with grace to observe our hearts and waies, to containe them in good order, or to reduce them quickly, let us never thinke any company so good as thine, nor any time so well spent, as that which is in thy service, and beautifying of thine Image in our selves or others.

Particularly we pray thee open our eies to see our naturall infirmities, and to discover the advantages which Satan gets thereby. And give us care to strive most, where we are most assaulted and endamaged.

And thou O God, that hast promised to blesse thine owne ordinances, blesse all things unto us, that we may grow in grace and in knowledge, and so may shine as light in this darke world, giving good example to all men, and may in our time lie downe in peace of a good conscience, embaulmed with a good report, and may leave thy blessings entailed unto ours after us for an inheritance.

These O Father, are our speciall suits, wherein wee beseech thee to set forth the wonderful riches of thy grace towards us, as for this life, and the things thereof, we crave them of thee so farre as may be for our good, and thy glory, beseeching thee to provide for us as unto this day in mercy. And when thou wilt humble or exalt us, governe us so long, and so farre in all conditions and changes, as we may cleave fast unto thee our God unchangeably, esteeming thee our portion and sufficient inheritance for evermore. Now what graces we crave for our selves, which are here before thy presence, we humbly begge for all those that belong unto us, and that by dutie or promise wee owe our praiers unto, beseeching thee to be as gracious unto them, as unto our own souls, and specially to such of them, as in respect of any present affliction or temptation may be in speciall needs of some more speedie helpe or comfort from thy mighty hand.

Yea our Lord God we humbly desire to blesse with our praiers the whole Church more specially our nation, and therein the kings Majestie our Soveraigne, his Queene and royall seede, with all that be in authoritie under him, beseeching thee to follow him and them with those blessings of thy protection and direction, which may preserve them safe from the malice of the world, and of Satan, and may yeeld them in their great places faithfull to thee for the good of thy people, and their owne eternall happinesse and honour.

We beseech thee to furnish the Churches with faithfull and fruitfull ministers, and to blesse their lives and labours for those mercifull uses, to which thou hast ordained them, sanctifie thy people O God, and let them not deceive themselves with a formalitie of religion in steed of the power thereof, give them grace to profit both by those favours, and by those chasticements which thou hast sent successively or mixedly amongst them. And Lord

represse that rage of sinne, and prophanesse in all Christian states which breeds so much Apostacy and defection, threatning the taking away of this light from them: Confound thou O God all the counsel and practises of Satan and his ministers, which are or shall be taken up against thee, and the kingdome of thy deare sonne. And call in the Jewes together with the fulnesse of the gentiles, that thy name may be glorious in al the world, the dayes of iniquity may come to an end, and we with all thine elect people may come to see thy face in glorie, and be filled with the light thereof for evermore.

And now O Lord of mercie, O Father of the spirits of all flesh, looke in mercie upon the Gentiles, who yet know thee not, O gracious God be mercifull to us, and bless us, and not us alone, but let thy waies be knowne upon earth, and thy saving health amongst all nations: we praise thee, and we blesse thee: But let the people praise thee O God, yea let all the people praise thee, and let these ends of the world remember themselves and turne to thee the God of their salvation. And seeing thou hast honoured us to choose us out to beare thy name unto the Gentiles: we therefore beseech thee to bless us, and this our plantation, which we and our nation have begun in thy feare, and for they glory. We know O Lord, we have the divel and all the gates of hel against us, but if thou O Lord be on our side, we care not who be against us. O therfore vouchsafe to be our God and let us be a part and portion of thy people, confirme thy covenant of grace and mercy with us, which thou hast made to thy Church in Christ Jesus. And seeing Lord the highest end of our plantation here, is to set up the standard, and display the banner of Jesus Christ, even here where satans throne is Lord, let our labor be blessed in laboring the conversion of the heathen. And because thou usest not to work such mighty works by unholy means, Lord sanctifie our spirits, and give us holy harts, that so we may be thy instruments in this most glorious work: lord inspire our souls with thy grace, kindle in us zeale of thy glory: fill our harts with thy feare, and our tongues with thy praise, furnish us all from the highest to the lowest with all gifts and graces needful not onely for our salvation, but for the discharge of our duties in our severall places, adorne us with the garments of Justice, mercy, love, pitie, faithfulnesse, humility, and all vertues, and teach us to abhor al vice, that our lights may so shine before these heathen, that they may see our good works, and so be brought to glorifie thee our heavenly Father.

And seeing Lord we professe our selves thy servants, and are about thy worke, Lord blesse us, arme us against difficulties, strength us against all base thoughts and temptations, that may make us looke backe againe. And seeing by thy motion and work in our harts, we have left our warme nests at home, and put our lives into our hands principally to honour thy name, and advance the kingdome of thy son, Lord gives us leave to commit our lives into thy hands: let thy Angels be about us, and let us be as Angels of God sent to this people, And so blesse us Lord, and so prosper all our proceedings, that the heathen may never say unto us, where is now your God: Their Idols are not so good as silver and gold, but lead and copper, and the works of their own hands. But thou *Jehovah* art our God, and we are the works of thy hands: O then let *Dagon* fall before thy Arke, let Satan be confounded at thy presence, and let the heathen see it and be ashamed, that they may seeke thy face, for their God is not as our God, themselves being Judges. Arise therfore O Lord, and let thine enemies be scattered, and let them that hate thee flie before thee: As the smoke vanisheth, so let Satan and his delusions come to nought and as wax melteth before the fire, so let wickednes, superstition, ignorance and idolatry perish at the presence of thee our God. And wheras we have by undertaking this plantation undergone the reproofs of the base world, insomuch as many of our owne brethren laugh us to scorne, O Lord we pray thee fortifie us against this temptation: let *Sanballat,* and *Tobias,* Papists and players, and such other *Amonits* and *Horonits* the scum and dregs of the earth, let them mocke such as helpe to build up the wals of Jerusalem, and they that be filthy, let them be filthy still, and let such swine still wallow in their mire, but let not the rod of the wicked fal upon the lot of the righteous, let not them put forth their hands to such vanity, but let them that feare thee, rejoyce and be glad in thee, and let them know, that it is thou O Lord, that raignest in England, and unto the ends of the world. And seeing this work must needs expose us to many miseries, and dangers of soule and bodie, by land and sea, O Lord we earnestly beseech thee to receive us into thy favour and protection, defend us from the delusion of the divel, the malice of the heathen, the invasions of our enemies, and mutinies and dissentions of our own people, knit our hearts altogether in faith and feare of thee, and love one to another, give us patience, wisedome and constancy to goe on through all difficulties and temptations, til this blessed work be accomplished, for the honour of thy name, and glory of the Gospel of Jesus Christ: That when the heathen do know thee to be their God, and Jesus Christ to be their salvation, they may say, blessed be the King and Prince of England, and blessed be the English nation, and blessed for ever be the most high God, possessor of heaven and earth, that sent them amongst us: And heere O Lord we do upon the knees of our harts offer thee the sacrifice of praise and thanksgiving, for that thou hast moved our harts to undertake the performance of this blessed work, with the hazard of our person, and the hearts of so many hundreds of our nation to assist it with meanes and provision, and with their holy praiers, Lord looke mercifully upon them all, and for

that portion of their substance which they willingly offer for thy honour and service in this action, recompence it to them and theirs, and reward it seven fold into their bosomes with better blessings: Lord blesse England our sweet native countrey, save it from Popery, this land from heathenisme, and both from Atheisme. And Lord heare their praiers for us, and us for them, and Christ Jesus our glorious Mediator for us all. Amen.

Source:

David H. Flaherty, ed., compiled by William Strachey. *For the Colony in Virginea Britannia, Lawes Divine, Morall and Martiall, etc.* Charlottesville: University of Virginia Press, 1969.

John Pory, Secretary of the Jamestown Council, to Sir Dudley Carleton, English Envoy to The Hague, (Letters from Jamestown), 1619

The letter from an early inhabitant of the Jamestown colony and member of the colony's governing council was written two months after the council's inaugural meeting on August 4, 1619. This meeting was the first European legislative assembly in North America. In the excerpt here, Pory's high praise for the colony's assets may have been an attempt to impress the English official and gain further financial backing.

Letter of John Pory, Secretary of Virginia, to Sir Dudley Carleton

As touching the quality of this country, three thinges there bee which in fewe yeares may bring this Colony to perfection; the English plough, Vineyards, and Cattle. For the first, there be many grounds here cleared by the Indians to our handes, which being much worne out, will beare no more of their corne, which requireth an extrordinary deale of sappe and substance to nourish it; but of our graine of all sortes it will bear great abundance. . . .

Vines here are in suche abundance, as where soever a man treads, they are ready to embrace his foote. I have tasted here of a great black grape as big as a Damascin, that hath a true Muscatell-taste; the vine whereof now spending itselfe to the to pps of high trees, if it were reduced into a vineyard, and there domesticated, would yield incomparable fruite. The like or a better taste have I founde in a lesser sorte of black grapes. White grapes also of great excellency I have hearde to be in the country; but they are very rare, nor did I ever see or taste of them. For cattle, they do mightily increase here, both kine, hogges and goates, and are much greater in stature, then the race of them first brought out of England. No lesse are our horses and mares likely to multiply, which proove of a delicate shape, and of as good spirite and metall.

All our riches for the present doe consiste in Tobacco, wherein one man by his owne labour hath in one yeare raised to himselfe to the value of 200l sterling; and another by the meanes of six servants hath cleared at one crop a thousand pound English. These be true, yet indeed rare examples, yet possible to be done by others. Our principall wealth (I should have said) consisteth in servants: But they are chardgeable to be furnished with armes, apparell and bedding and for their transportation an d casual, both at sea, and for their first yeare commonly at lande also: But if they escape, they prove very hardy, and sound able men.

. . . But to leave the Populace, and to come higher; the Governour here, who at his first coming, besides a great deale of worth in his person, brought onely his sword with him, was at his late being in London, together with his lady, out of his meer gett ings here, able to disburse very near three thousand pounde to furnishe huimselfe for his voiage. And once within seven yeares, I am persuaded (absit invidia verbo) that the Governours place here may be as profittable as the lord Deputies of Irland."

Source:

J. Franklin Jameson. *Narratives of Early Virginia.* New York: Charles Scribner's Sons, 1907.

Ordinance of Virginia, 1621

This document, written by the Virginia Company and dated July 24, 1621, authorized the convening of the first Assembly of Virginia. The first document for this purpose was lost, and this ordinance is believed to be an almost exact reproduction. The Assembly of Virginia took place on July 30, 1619, and marks the first representative legislature in America. It formed two supreme councils: The Council of State was named to assist the governor in daily business, while the General Assembly was formed to create laws for the colony as a combined body, consisting of the aforementioned council and two burgesses from every town in Virginia.

An Ordinance and Constitution of the Treasurer, Council, and Company in England for a Council of State and General Assembly. Dated July 21, 1621.

To all People, to whom these Presents shall come, be seen, or heard, the Treasurer, Council, and Company of Adventurers and Planters for the city of London for the first Colony of Virginia, send Greeting. Know ye, that we, the said Treasurer, Council, and Company, taking into our

careful Consideration the present State of the said Colony of Virginia, and intending, by the Divine Assistance, to settle a Form of Government there, as may be the greatest Benefit and Comfort of the People, and whereby all Injustice, Grievances, and Oppression may be prevented and kept off as much as possible from the said Colony, have thought fit to make our Entrance by ordering and establishing such Supreme Councils, as may not only be assisting to the Governor for the Time being, in the Administration of Justice, and the executing of other Duties to this Office belonging; but also by their vigilant Care and Prudence, may provide, as well for a Remedy of all Inconveniences, growing from time to time, as also for the advancing of Increase, Strength, Stability and Prosperity of the said Colony:

We therefore, the said Treasurer, Council, and Company, by Authority directed to us from his Majesty under the Great Seal, upon mature Deliberation, Do hereby order and declare, that, from henceforward, there shall be Two Supreme Councils in Virginia, for the better government of the Colony aforesaid.

One of which Councils to be called the Council of State (and whose office shall chiefly be assisting, with their Care, Advice, and Circumspection, to the said Governor) shall be chosen, nominated, placed, and displaced, from time to time, by us, the said Treasurer, Council, and Company, and our Successors:

Which Council of State shall consist for the present, only of these persons, as are here inserted, viz., Sir Francis Wyat, Governor of Virginia, Captain Francis West, Sir George Yeardley, Knight, Sir William Neuce, Knight, Marshal of Virginia, Mr. George Sandys, Treasurer, Mr. George Thorpe, Deputy of the College, Captain Thomas Neuce, Deputy for the Company, Mr. Pawlet, Mr. Leech, Captain Nathaniel Powell, Mr. Christopher Davidson, Secretary, Dr. Pots, Physician to the Company, Mr. Roger Smith, Mr. John Berkeley, Mr. John Rolfe, Mr. Ralph Hamer, Mr. John Pountis, Mr. Michael Lapworth, Mr. Harwood, Mr. Samuel Macock: Which said Counsellors and Council we earnestly pray and desire, and in his Majesty's Name strictly charge and command, that all Factions, Partialities, and sinister respect laid aside, they bend their Care and Endeavours to assist the said Governor; first and principally, in the Advancement of the Honour and Service of God, and the Enlargement of his Kingdom amongst the Heathen People; and next, in erecting of the said Colony in due obedience to his Majesty, and all lawful Authority from his Majesty's Directions; and lastly, in maintaining the said People in Justice and Christian Conversation amongst themselves, and in Strength and Ability to withstand their Enemies. And this Council, to be always, or for the most Part, residing about or near the Governor.

The other, more generally to be called by the Governor, once Yearly, and no oftener, but for very extraordinary and important Occasions, shall consist, for the present, of the said Council of State and of two Burgesses out of every Town, Hundred, or other particular Plantation, to be respectively chosen by the Inhabitants: Which Council shall be called the General Assembly, wherein (as also in the said Council of State) all Matters shall be decided, determined, and ordered, by the greater Part of the Voices then present; reserving to the Governor always a Negative Voice. And this General Assembly shall have free Power to treat, consult and conclude, as well of all emergent Occasions concerning the Public Weal of the said Colony and every Part thereof, as also to make, ordain, and enact such general Laws and Orders, for the Behoof of the said Colony, and the good Government thereof, as shall from time to time appear necessary or requisite:

Whereas in all other Things, we require the said General Assembly, as also the said Council of State, to imitate and follow the Policy of the Form of Government, Laws, Customs, and Manner of Trial and other Administration of Justice, used in the Realm of England, as near as may be, even as ourselves, by his Majesty's Letters-patent, are required:

Provided, that no Law or Ordinance, made in the said General Assembly, shall be or continue in Force or Validity, unless the same shall be solemnly ratified and confirmed, in a General Quarter Court of the said Company here in England, and so ratified, be returned to them under our Seal: It being our Intent to afford the like Measure also unto the said Colony that after the Government of the said Colony shall once have been well framed and settled accordingly, which is to be done by Us, as by Authority derived from his Majesty, and the same shall have been so by Us declared, no Orders of Court afterwards shall bind the said Colony, unless they be ratified in like Manner in the General Assemblies.

In Witness whereof we have hereunto set our Common Seal, the 24th of July, 1621, and in the Year of the Reign of our Sovereign Lord, James, King of England, etc., the . . . and of Scotland the . . .

Source:

Documents Illustrative of American History, 1606–1863, with introductions and references by Howard W. Preston. New York: G. P. Putnam's Sons, 1886.

SUGGESTED READING

European Exploration; The Legal and Religious Basis for European Settlement in the New World

Kenneth R. Andrews, *Trade, Plunder, and Settlement: Maritime Enterprise and the Genesis of the British Empire, 1480–1630.* New York: Cambridge University Press, 1984.

Ralph Davis, *The Rise of the Atlantic Economies.* Ithaca, N.Y.: Cornell University Press, 1973.

L. McAlister, *Spain and Portugal in the New World, 1492–1700.* Minneapolis, Minn.: University of Minnesota Press, 1984.

Samuel E. Morison, *The European Discovery of America: The Voyages.* New York: Oxford University Press, 1971.

Early Settlements and Government in the English Colonies

Samuel Eliot Morrison, ed. *William Bradford, Of Plymouth Plantation.* New York: Knopf, 2001.

Ivor Noel Hume, *The Virginia Adventure: Roanoke to James Towne, an Archaeological and Historical Odyssey.* Charlottesville, Va.: University Press of Virginia, 1997.

David J. Weber, *The Spanish Frontier in North America.* New Haven, Conn.: Yale University Press, 1992.

ERA 2
Colonization and Settlement
(CA. 1620–1762)

★ ───

The earliest attempts at New World colonization occurred in the 16th century and included the settlement of St. Augustine, in what is now Florida. However, this chapter concentrates on the English colonies that came to fruition in the 17th and early 18th centuries and eventually became the earliest states. Most important to the English government in this period were its Caribbean colonies, which produced sugar and molasses and fulfilled the mercantile ideal—colonies producing goods for the enrichment of the mother country. The continental North American colonies were not founded solely for commercial reasons. The several proprietary colonies founded after 1630—Maryland, New Jersey, Pennsylvania and Delaware, and the Carolinas—belonged to individuals who received charters from the king. Maryland and Pennsylvania, founded by a Catholic and a Quaker proprietor, respectively, proposed religious toleration, as did Rhode Island. Maryland and the Carolinas envisioned benevolent baronial societies. Massachusetts and Connecticut sought to establish Puritan theocracies, while Georgia, also a proprietary colony, provided a haven for British convicts. American-style representative government derives from the 17th century charters, even those governed by proprietors. The various charters compose the first part of Era 2.

During the 17th century, the colonial cities were what we would now call frontier towns. Frontier conditions persisted throughout this entire era in all but a few cities and communities between the East Coast and the Appalachian Mountains. Life was often difficult. The second section explores colonial life from various points of view, including that of an indentured servant and of an English captive discussing her Native American captors. Other aspects of colonial life are represented by Jonathan Edwards's famous sermon "Sinners in the Hands of an Angry God," illustrating the religious ideas prevalent among many New Englanders and New Yorkers, and testimonies from the Salem witchcraft trials.

Legal matters and rebellions dominate the next section, including laws that governed daily life. England suffered two major rebellions during the 17th century, with parallel events also occurring in the New World, including the 1647 rebellion of Protestants that Margaret Brent helped quell in Maryland and Jacob Leisler's rebellion in New York in 1689 that followed England's "Glorious Revolution." Well before England began taxing its North American colonies, their citizens had developed their own political institutions to the point where they chafed at too much control from overseas. This section ends with two documents that express this nascent desire for independence.

The Establishment of Colonies and Settlements

Peter Schagen, Letter to the States General on the Purchase of Manhattan, 1626

Report explaining Peter Minuit's purchase of Manhattan Island in 1626. Dutch settlers purchased the island from the resident Manhattan tribal leaders (who didn't actually own the land) in exchange for trinkets of little value. Two years earlier, Dutch settlers had begun laying the foundations for a town at the southern tip of the island, calling the settlement New Amsterdam. The decision to purchase this island hinged on the fact that it could be easily defended and was centrally located among other Dutch settlements. The colony was run by the Dutch West India Company, a joint stock company. In 1640 it gave up its trade monopoly and allowed other Dutch merchants to invest in the town. By 1645 Dutch settlers had completely eradicated the Manhattan tribe.

High and Mighty Lords:

Yesterday, arrived here the Ship the Arms of Amsterdam, which sailed from New Netherland, out of the River Mauritius, on the 23rd September. They report that our people are in good heart and live in peace there; the Women also have borne some children there. They have purchased the Island Manhattes from the Indians for the value of 60 guilders; 'tis 11,000 morgens in size. They had all their grain sowed by the middle of May, and reaped by the middle of August. They send thence samples of summer grain; such as wheat, rye, barley, oats, buckwheat, canary seed, beans and flax.

The cargo of the aforesaid ship is:—7246 Beaver skins. 178 1/2 Otter skins. 675 Otter skins. 48 Minck skins. 36 Wild cat skins. 33 Mincks. 34 Rat skins.

Considerable Oak timber and Hickory. Herewith, High and Mighty Lords, be commended to the mercy of the Almighty.

In Amsterdam, the 5th November, Ad 1626. Received 7th November, 1626.

Your High Mightinesses' obedient,
(Signed) P. Schagen.

Source:

E. B. O'Callaghan. *Documents Relative to the Colonial History of the State of New York*. Vol. 1. Albany, N.Y.: Weed, Parsons, 1853–87.

Charter of the Colony of New Plymouth, 1629

This charter, also known as the Warwick Patent, granted legal rights to the land between Narragansett Bay, in present-day Rhode Island, and Cohasset, on the Massachusetts coast, to Governor William Bradford and other founders of the Plymouth Colony. A 1620 patent granted by England's King James I had appropriated the entire territory of New England for several noblemen who were incorporated into the Council for New England. The charter below, signed by council member Robert, Earl of Warwick, transfers part of the original land grant to Bradford. William Bradford helped organize the Pilgrims' journey on the *Mayflower* and drafted the Mayflower Compact after their arrival in 1620. He was elected governor of the colony 30 times. His written accounts of life in the colony, *Mourt's Relation* (with Edward Winslow) and *A History of Plymouth Plantation*, offer invaluable insights into the lives of the Pilgrims. In 1640 he relinquished his proprietary control over the colony to the freemen, or voters, of Plymouth.

To all to whom these presents shall come greetinge: Whereas our late sovereigns lord king James for the advancement of a collonie and plantacon in the cuntry called or knowne by the name of New Englande in America, by his highnes letters patients under the greate scale of Englande bearingedate att Westminster the third day of November in the eighteenth yeare of his highnes raigne of England, &c. did give graunte and confirms unto the right honoble Lodowicke late lord duke of Lenox, George late marques of Buckingham, James marques Hamilton, Thomas earle of Arundell, Robert earle of Warwicke and Ferdinando Gorges, Knight, and divers others whose names are expressed in the said letters pattents and their successors that they should be one bodie pollitique and corporate perpeturely consistinge of forty persons, and that they should have perpetual succession and one common scale to serve for the said body and that they and their successors should be incorporated called and knowne by the name of the Councill established at Plymouth in the county of Devon for the planting, rulinge orderinge and governinge of New Englande in America, and alsoe of his speciall grace certaine knowledge and more motion did give graunte and confirms unto the said presidents and councill and their successors forever under the reservations limitations and declaracons in the said letters pattents expressed, all that part and portion of the said country called New-England in America scituate, and lyinge and being in breadth from ffourty degrees northerly latitude from the equinoctiall line to ffourty eight degrees of the said northerly latitude inclusively, and in length of and in all the breadth aforesaide throughout the maine land from sea to sea, together alsoe with all the firms landes soyles grounds creeks inletts havens portes seas rivers islands waters fishinges mynes and mineralls as well royall mines of gold and silver as other mines and mineralls pretious stones quarries and all and singular the commodities juris-diccons royalties privileges ffranchises and preheminences both within the said tracte of lands upon the maine, as also within the said islands and seas adioyninge: To have hold possesse and enjoy all and singuler the foresaid continents landes territories islands hereditaments and prcints sea waters fishinges with all and all manner their commodities royalties privileges preheminences and proffitts that shall arise from thence, with all and singuler their appurtenaces and every parte and parcell thereof unto the said councell and their successors and assignee forever: To be holden of his Matie, his heirs and successors as of his mannor of East Greenwiche in the county of Kent in free and common soccage and not *in capite* nor by Knights service yeeldinge and payinge therefore to the said late king's Matie, his heires and successors the fifte parte of the oare of gold and silver which from tyme to tyme and aft all tymes from the date of the said letters pattents sholbe there gotten had and obtained for and in respect of all and all manner of duties demands and services whatsoever to be done made and paid unto his said late Matie, his heirs and successors as in and by the said letters patients amongst sundry other privileges and matters therein contained more fully and at large it doth and may appease. Now knowe ye that the said councell by virtue and authority of his said late Man letters patients and for and in consideracon that William Bradford and his associatts have for these nine yeares lived in New Englande aforesaid and have there inhabited and planted a towne called by the name of New Plimouth att their own proper costs and charges: And now seeinge that by the spe-ciall providence of God, and their extraordinary care and industry they have increased their plantacon to neere three hundred people, and are uppon all occasions able to relieve any new planters or others his Mats subjects whoe may fall uppon that coaste; have given granted bargained sould enfeofed allotted assigned and sett over and by these presents doe cleerly and absolutely give graunt bargaine sell alien enfeoffe allots assigne and confirme unto the said William Bradford, his heires associatts and assignee all that part of New-Englande in America aforesaid and tracte and tractes of lande that lye within or betweene a certaine riv-olet or rundlett there commonly called Coa hassett alias Cona hassett towards the north, and the river commonly

called Naragansets river towards the south; and the great westerne ocean towards the east, and betweene and within a straight line directly extendinge upp into the maine land towards the west from the mouth of the said river called Naragansetts river to the utmost limitts and bounds of a cuntry or place in New Englande called Pokenacutt alias Sowamsett westward, and another like straight line extendinge itself directly from the mouth of the said river called Coahassett alias-Cone hassett towards the west so farr upp into the maine lande westwardes as the utmost limitts of the said place or cuntry commonly called Poken-cutt alias Sowamsett doe extend, together with one half of the said river called Naragansetts and the said rivolett or rundlett called Coahassett alias Conahassett and all lands rivers waters havens creeks ports fishings fowlings and all hereditaments proffitts comodities and emoluments what-soever situate lyinge and beinge or ariseinge within or betweene the said limitts and bounds or any of them. And for as much as they have noe conveniente place-either of tradinge or ffishinge within their own precints whereby (after soe longe travell and great paines,) so hopefull a plantacon may subsiste, as alsoe that they may bee incour-aged the better to proceed in soe pious a worke which may especially tend to the propagation of religion and the great increase of trade to his Mats realmes, and advancemente of the publique plantacon, the said councell have further given graunted bargained sold enfeoffed allotted assigned and sett over and by these presentes doe cleerely and abso-lutely give graunte bargaine sell alien enfeoffe allots assigne and confirme unto the said William Bradford his heires associate and assignee all that tracte of lande or parte of New England in America aforesaid wch lyeth within or betweene and extendeth itself from the utmost limitts of Cobbiseconte alias Comasee-Conte which adjoineth to the river of Kenebeke alias Kenebekike towards the westerne ocean and a place called the falls att Mequamkike in America aforesaid, and the space of fif-teene Englishe miles on each side of the said river com-monly called Kenebek river, and all the said river called Kenebek that lies within the said limitts and bounds east-ward westward northward or southward laste above men-tioned, and all lands grounds soyles rivers waters fishings hereditamts and proffitts whatsoever situate lyinge and beinge arisinge happeninge or accrueinge, or which shall arise happen or accrue in or within the said limitts and boundes or either of them together with free ingresse egresse and regresse with shipps boates shallopps and other vessels from the sea commonly called the westerne ocean to the said river called Kennebek and from the said river to the said westerne ocean, together with all prerog-atives rights royalties jurisdiccons, preveledges ffranchises liberties and guerenities, and alsoe marine liberty with the escheats and casualties thereof the Admiralty Jurisdiccon excepted with all the interest right title claime and demande whatsoever which the said councell and their successors now have or ought to have and claime or may have and acquire hereafter in or to any the said porcons or tractes of land hereby menconed to be graunted, or any the premisses in as free large ample and beneficiall manner to all intents, construccons and purposes whatsoever as the said councell by virtue of his Mats said letters pattents may or can graunte; to have and to horde the said tracte and tractes of lande and all and singular the premisses above menconed to be graunted with their and every of their appurtenances to the said William Bradford his heires associatts and assignee forever, to the only proper and absolute use and behoofe of the said William Bradford his heires associate and assignee forever; Yeeldinge and payinge unto our said soveraigne Lord the Kinge, his heires and successors forever one-fifte parte of the oare of the mines of gold and silver and one other fifte parte thereof to the presidents and councell, which shall be had possessed and obtained within the precints aforesaid for all services and demands whatsoever. And the said councell doe further graunt and agree to and with the said William Bradford his heires associatts and assignee and every of them, his and their Factors agents tenants and servants and all such as hee or they shall send and employ aboute his said particular plantacon, shall and may from tyme to tyme Freely and lawfully goe and returne trade and traffique as well with the Englishe as any of the natines within the precints aforesaid, with liberty of fishinge uppon any parte of the sea coaste and sea shoares of any the seas or islands adjacente and not beinge inhabited or otherwise disposed of by order of the said presidents and councell: also to importe exporte and transports their goods and merchandise aft their wills and pleasures paying only such duty to the Kings Matie, his heires and successors as the said Presidente and councell doe or ought to pay without any other taxes impositions burdens and restraints upon them to be imposed. And further the said councell doe graunt and agree to and with the said William Bradford his heires associatts and assignee, that the persons transported by him or any of them shall not be taken away, ymployed or commanded either by the Governor for the tyme beinge of New Englande or by any other authority there, from the business and employments of the said William Bradford and his associatts his heires and assignee; necessary [to the] defence of the cuntry preservacon of the peace suppressinge of tumults within the lands, trialls in matters of justice by appeale uppon spetiall occasion only excepted. Alsoe it shall be lawfull and free for the said William Bradford his associatts his heires and assignee aft all tymes hereafter to incorporate by some usual or ffit name and title, him or themselves or the people there inhabitinge under him or them with liberty to them and their successors from tyme to tyme to frame, and make orders ordi-

nances and constitucons as well for the better governmt of their affaires here and the receavinge or admittinge any to his or their society as alsoe for the better governmt of his or their people and affaires in New Englande or of his and their people att sea in goeinge thither, or returninge from thence, and the same to putt in execucon or cause to be putt in execucon by such officers and ministers as he and they shall authorize and depute: Provided that the said lawes and orders be not repugnante to the lawes of Englande, or the frame of governments by the said presidents councell hereafter to be established. And further it shall be lawfull and free for the said William Bradford, his heires associate and assignee to transports cattle of all kinds, alsoe powder shot ordnance and municon from tyme to tyme as shal be necessary for their strength and safety hereafter for their several defence; to encounter expulse repell and resiste by force of armes as well by sea as by lande, by all waies and meanes whatsoever. And by virtue of the authority to Us derived by his said late Mats letters pattents to take apprehend seize and make prize of all such persons their shipps and goods as shall attempte to inhabite or trade with the savage people of that cuntry within the severall precincts and limitts of his and their severall plantacon, or shall enterprise or attempt aft any tyme destruccon invasion detriment or annoyance to his and their said plantacon; the one moiety of which goods soe siezed and taken it shal be lawfull for the said William Bradford his heires associate and assignee to take to their own use and behoofe; the other moiety thereof to be delivered by the said William Bradford his heires associats and assignee to such officer and officers as shalbe appointed to receave the same for his Mats use. And the said councell do hereby covenante and declare that it is their intense and meaninge for the good of this plantacon that the said William Bradford his associate his or their heires or assignee shall have and enjoy whatsoever privilege or privileges of what kinde soever, as are expressed or intended to be graunted in and by his said late Mats letters pattents, and that in as large and angle manner as the said councell thereby now may or hereafter can graunte, coyninge of money excepted. And the said councell for them and their successors doe covenante and graunte to the said William Bradford, his heires associates and assignee by these presents, that they the said councell shall at any time hereafter uppon request aft the only proper costs and charges of the said William Bradford, his heires associate and assignee doe make suffer execute and willingly consent unto any further act or actes, conveyance or conveyances, assurance or assurances whatsoever, for the good and perfect investing assureinge and conveyinge and sure makinge of all the aforesaid tracte and tractes of landes royalties mines mineralls woods fishinges and all and singular their appurtenances, unto the said William Bradford his heires associate and assignee as by him or them or his or their heires or assignee, or his or their councell learned in the law shalbe devised, advised and required. And lastly know yee that wee the said counsell have made constituted deputed authorized and appointed Captaine Miles Standish, or in his absence Edward Winslowe, John Howlande and John Alden, or any of them to be our true and lawful attorney and attornies jointly and severally in our name and steed to enter into the said tracte and tractes of lande and other the premises with their appurtenances, or into some parte thereof in the name of the whole for us and in our names to take possession and seisin thereof, and after such possession and seisin thereof or of some parte thereof in the name of the whole had and taken; then for us and in our names to deliver the full and peacable possession and seisin of all and singular the said menconed tobe graunted premisses unto the said William Bradford his heires assoctatts and assignee or to his or their certaine attorney or atturnies in that behalf ratifyinge alloweinge and confirminge all whatsoever our said atturney doe in or about the premisses. In witness whereof, the aid councell established aft Plimouth in the county of Devon for the plantinge rulinge orderinge and governinge of New England in America have hereunto putt their scale the thirteenth day of January in fifte yeare of the raigne of our Soveraigne Lord Charles by the grace of God, Kinge of Englande Scotland Fraunce and Ireland defender of the ffaithe &c. Anno Domi 1629.

(SEAL) R. Warwicke.

See also JAMES I, CHARTER OF NEW ENGLAND, 1620.

Source:

Francis Newton Thorpe, ed. *The Federal and State Constitutions, Colonial Charters, and Other Organic Laws of the States, Territories, and Colonies Now or Heretofore Forming the United States of America*. Washington, D.C.: Government Printing Office, 1909.

Massachusetts Bay Colony Charter, 1629

Royal charter of 1629 that confirmed to a group of influential Puritans, merchants, and others the power to trade and colonize in New England between the Charles and Merrimack Rivers. It gave to the approximately 1,000 immigrants local powers of self-government and general court jurisdiction to admit new members as a means of limiting the voting in the colony to those of their own religious beliefs;—consequently, within a few years the enterprise was transformed from a trading company into a theocracy almost devoid of outside control. Dissent resulted in the voluntary exile of founders of Connecticut and the forced exile of founders of Rhode Island towns. On January 1, 1680, New Hampshire was formally

separated from the Massachusetts Bay Colony and became an independent royal colony with four major towns: Portsmouth, Hampton, Dover, and Exeter. Its charter appointed a council and commissioned John Cutt as president of the council. The new government was endowed with the power to preside over civil and criminal matters and to make intercessions on behalf of the English Crown. However, John Cutt died within a year of his appointment, and the province entered a 20-year period of social and political instability. Between 1689 and 1696, New Hampshire lost approximately one-tenth of its population to Indian attacks. Many residents advocated reannexation with Massachusetts, but London officials decided on a compromise: New Hampshire would remain an independent state, but it would share a governor with Massachusetts. This arrangement remained in effect until 1740, when New Hampshire was granted its own royal governor as a result of boundary disputes with Massachusetts.

CHARLES, by the Grace of God, Kinge of England, Scotland, France, and Ireland, Defendor of the Fayth, etc., To all to whome theis Presentes shall come, Greeting. Whereas our most deare and royall father Kinge James, of blessed memory, by his Highness letters patentes beareing date of Westminster the third day of November, in the eighteenth yeare of his raigne, Hath given and graunted unto the Councell established at Plymouth in the County of Devon, for the planting, ruling, ordering, and governing of Newe England in America, and to their successors and assignes for ever: All that parte of America lyeing and being in bredth from forty degrees of northerly latitude from the equinoctiall lyne, to forty eight degrees of the saide northerly latitude inclusively, and in length of and within all the breadth aforesaid throughout the maine landes from sea to sea, together, also, with all the firme landes, soyles, groundes, havens, portes, rivers, waters, fishing, mynes, and myneralls, aswell royall mynes of gould and silver, as other mynes and myneralls, precious stones, quarries, and all and singuler other commodities, jurisdictions, royalties, priviledges, franchises, and prehemynences, both within the said tract of lande upon the mayne, and also within the islandes and seas adjoining: Provided alwayes, That the saide islandes or any the premises by the said letters patentes intended and meant to be graunted were not then actuallie possessed or inhabited by any other Christian Prince or State, nor within the boundes, lymittes, or territories of the Southerne Colony then before graunted by our said deare father, to be planted by divers of his loveing subjectes in the south partes. To have and to houlde, possesse, and enjoy all and singuler the aforesaid continent, landes, territories, islands, hereditamentes, and precinctes, seas, waters, fishinges, with all and all manner their commodities, royalties, liberties, prehemynences, and profittes that should from thenceforth arise from thence, with all and singuler their appurtenances, and every parte and parcell thereof, unto the saide Councell and their successors and assignes for ever, To the sole and proper use, benefitt, and behoofe of them the saide Councell and their successors and assignes for ever: To be houlden of our saide most deare and royall father, his heires, and successors, as of this manner of Eastgreenewich, in the County of Kent, in free and common Soccage, and not in Capite nor by Knightes Service. Yeildinge and paying therefore to the saide late Kinge, his heires, and successors the fifte parte of the oare of gould and silver which should, from tyme to tyme, and at all tymes then after, happen to be found, gotten, had, and obteyned in, att, or within any of the saide landes, lymyttes, territories, and precinctes, or in or within any parte or parcell thereof, for or in respect of all and all manner of duties, demaunds, and services whatsoever to be don, made, or paide to our saide dear father, the late Kinge, his heires, and successors, As in and by the saide letters patentes (amongest sundrie other clauses, powers, priviledges, and grauntes therein conteyned) more at large appeareth. And whereas the saide Councell, established at Plymouth, in the County of Devon, for the plantinge, ruling, ordering, and governing of Newe England in America, have, by their deede, indented under their common seale, bearing date the nyneteenth day of March last past, in the third yeare of our raigne, given, graunted, bargained, spulde, enfeoffed, aliened, and confirmed to Sir Henry Rosewell, Sir John Young, knightes, Thomas Southcott, John Humphrey, John Endecott, and Symon Whetcombe, their heires and associates for ever, All that parte of Newe England in America aforesaid which lyes an extendes betweene a greate river there commonlie called Monomack, alias Merriemack, and a certen other river there called Charles river, being in the bottome of a certayne bay there commonlie called Massachusettes, alias Mattachusettes, alias Massatusettes bay, and also all and singuler those landes an hereditamentes whatsoever lyeing within the space of three English myles on the south parte of the saide Charles river, or of any or everie parte thereof: And also all and singuler the landes and hereditamentes whatsoever, lyeing and being within the space of three English myles to the southwarde of the southermost parte of the saide bay, called Massachusettes, alias Mattachusetes, alias Massatusetes, bay: And also all those landes and hereditamentes whatsoever which lye and be within the space of three English myles to the northward of the saide river called Monomack, alias Merrymack, or to the northward of any and every parte thereof: And all landes and hereditamentes whatsoever, lyeing within the lymyttes aforesaide, north and south, in latitude and bredth, and in length and longitude, of and within all the bredth aforesaide, throughout the mayne landes there, from the Atlantick and westerne sea and ocean on the east

parte, to the south sea on the west parte, and all landes and groundes, place and places, soyles, woodes and wood groundes, havens, portes, rivers, waters, fishinges, and hereditamentes whatsoever, lyeing within the said boundes and lymyttes, and everie parte and parcell thereof: And also all islandes lyeing in America aforesaide, in the saide seas, or either of them, on the westerne or easterne coastes or partes of the saide tractes of lande by the saide indenture mentioned to be given, graunted, bargained, sould, enfeoffed, aliened, and confirmed, or any of them: And also all mynes and myneralls, as well royall mynes of gould and silver, as other mynes and myneralls whatsoever in the saide landes and premises, or any parte thereof: And all jurisdictions, rightes, royalties, liberties, freedomes, ymmunities, priviledges, franchises, preheminences, and commodities whatsoever, which they, the saide Councell, established at Plymouth, in the County of Devon, for the planting, ruling, ordering, and governing of Newe England in America, then had or might use, exercise, or enjoy in and within the saide landes and premises by the saide indenture mentioned to be given, graunted, bargained, sould, enfeoffed, and confirmed, or in or within any parte or parcell thereof. To have and to hould the saide parte of Newe England in America which lyes and extendes and is abutted as aforesaide, and every parte and parcell thereof: And all the saide islandes, rivers, portes, havens, waters, fishinges, mynes and minerals, jurisdictions, franchises, royalties, liberties, priviledges, commodities, hereditamentes, and premisses whatsoever, with the appurtenances, unto the saide Sir Henry Rosewell, Sir John Younge, Thomas Southcott, John Humfrey, John Endecott, and Simon Whetcombe, their heires and assignes, and their associattes, to the onlie proper and absolute use and behoofe of the said Sir Henry Rosewell, Sir John Younge, Thomas Southcott, John Humfrey, John Endecott, and Symon Whettcombe, their heires and assignes, and their associattes, for evermore. To be houlden of us, our heires and successors, as of our mannor of Eastgreenewich, in the County of Kent, in free and common Socage, and not in Capite, nor by knightes service, yeilding and payeing therefore unto us, our heires and successors, the fifte parte of the oare of goulde and silver which shall, from tyme to tyme, and all tymes hereafter, happen to be founde, gotten, had, and obteyned in any of the saide landes within the saide lymyttes, or in or within any parte thereof, for and in satisfaction of all manner duties, demaunds, and services whatsoever, to be donn, made, or paid to us, our heires or successors, as in and by the said recited indenture more at large maie appeare. Nowe knowe yee, that wee, at the humble suite and petition of the saide Sir Henry Rosewell, Sir John Younge, Thomas Southcott, John Humfrey, John Endecott, and Simon Whetcombe, and of others whome they have associated unto them, have, for divers good causes and considerations us moveing, graunted and confirmed, And by theis presentes of our especiall grace, certen knowledge, and meere motion, doe graunt and confirme unto the saide Sir Henry Rosewell, Sir John Younge, Thomas Southcott, John Humfrey, John Endecott, and Simon Whetcombe, and to their associates hereafter named, (videlicet,) Sir Richard Saltonstall, knight, Isaack Johnson, Samuel Aldersey, John Ven, Mathew Cradock, George Harwood, Increase Nowell, Richard Perry, Richard Bellingham, Nathaniell Wright, Samuell Vassall, Theophilus Eaton, Thomas Goffe, Thomas Adams, John Browne, Samuell Browne, Thomas Hutchins, William Vassall, William Pinchion, and George Foxcrofte, their heires and assignes, All the saide parte of Newe England in America, lyeing and extending betweene the boundes and lymittes in the said recited indenture expressed, and all landes and groundes, place and places, soyles, woodes and wood groundes, havens, portes, rivers, waters, mynes, mineralls, jurisdictions, rightes, royalties, liberties, freedomes, immunities, priviledges, franchises, preheminences, hereditamentes, and commodities whatsoever to them the saide Sir Henry Rosewell Sir John Younge, Thomas Southcott, John Humfrey, John Endecott, and Simon Whetcombe, their heires and assignes, and to their associattes, by the saide recited indenture given, graunted, bargayned, solde, enfeoffed, aliened, and confirmed, or mentioned or intended thereby to be given, graunted, bargayned, sold, enfeoffed, aliened, and confirmed. To have and to hould the saide parte of Newe England in America, and other the premisses hereby mentioned to be graunted and confirmed, and every parte and parcell thereof, with the appurtenances, to the saide Sir Henry Rosewell, Sir John Younge, Sir Richard Saltonstall, Thomas Southcott, John Humfrey, John Endecott, Simon Whetcombe, Isaack Johnson, Samuell Aldersey, John Ven, Mathewe Cradock, George Harwood, Increase Nowell, Richard Pery, Richard Bellingham, Nathaniell Wright, Samuell Vassall, Theophilus Eaton, Thomas Goffe, Thomas Adams, John Browne, Samuell Browne, Thomas Hutchins, William Vassall, William Pinchion, and George Foxcrofte, their heires and assignes for ever, to their onlie proper and absolute use and behoofe for evermore. To be holden of us, our heires and successors, as of our mannor of Eastgreenewich aforesaid, in free and common Socage, and not in Capite nor by knightes service, and also yeilding and paying therefore to us, our heires and successors, the fifte parte onlie of all oare of gould and silver, which, from tyme to tyme, and att all tymes hereafter shalbe there gotten, had, or obteyned, for all services, exactions, and demaunds whatsoever, according to the tenure and reservation in the said recited indenture expressed. And further knowe yee, That, of our more especiall grace, certen knowledg, and meere motion, Wee have given and graunted, And by theis presentes doe for us, our heires and successors, give and graunt unto the said Sir

Henry Rosewell, Sir John Younge, Sir Richard Saltonstall, Thomas Southcott, John Humfrey, John Endecott, Symon Whetcombe, Isaack Johnson, Samuell Aldersey, John Ven, Mathewe Cradock, George Harwood, Increase Nowell, Richard Pery, Richard Bellingham, Nathaniel Wright, Samuell Vassall, Theophilus Eaton, Thomas Goffe, Thomas Adams, John Browne, Samuell Browne, Thomas Hutchins, William Vassall, William Pinchion, and George Foxcrofte, their heires and assignes, All that parte of Newe England in America which lyes and extendes betweene a great river there commonlie called Monomack river, alias Merrimack river, and a certain other river there called Charles river, being in the bottome of a certen bay there commonlie called Massachusettes, alias Mattachusettes, alias Massatusettes bay: And also all and singuler those landes and hereditamentes whatsoever, lyeing within the space of three Englishe myles on the south parte of the saide river called Charles river, or of any or every parte thereof; And also all and singuler the landes and hereditamentes whatsoever lyeing and being within the space of three Englishe myles to the southward of the southermost parte of the said baye called Massachusettes, alias Mattachusettes, alias Massatusetes bay: And also all those landes and hereditamentes whatsoever which lye and be within the space of three English myles to the northward of the saide river called Monomack, alias Merrymack, or to the norward of any and every parte thereof, and all landes hereditamentes whatsoever, lyeing within the lymittes aforesaide, north and south, in latitude and bredth, and in length and longitude, and of within all the bredth aforesaide, throughout the mayne landes there from the Atlantick and westerne sea and ocean on the east parte, to the south sea on the west parte: And all landes and groundes, place and places, soyles, woodes and wood groundes, havens, portes, rivers, waters, and hereditamentes whatsoever, lyeing within the said boundes and lymyttes, and every parte and parcell thereof, and also all islandes in America aforesaide, in the saide seas, or either of them, on the westerne or easterne coastes, or partes of the saide tractes of landes hereby mentioned to be given and graunted, or any of them, and all mynes and myneralls, aswell royall mynes of gould and silver as other mynes and myneralls whatsoever, in the said landes and premises, or any parte thereof, and free libertie of fishing in or within any the rivers or waters within the boundes and lymyttes aforesaid, and the seas thereunto adjoining: And all fishes, royal fishes, whales, balan, sturgions, and other fishes, or what kinde or nature soever that shall at any tyme hereafter be taken in or within the saide seas or waters, or any of them, by the said Sir Henry Rosewell, Sir John Younge, Sir Richard Saltonstall, Thomas Southcott, John Humfrey, John Endecott, Simon Whetcombe, Isaack Johnson, Samuell Aldersey, John Ven, Mathewe Cradock, George Harwood, Increase Noell, Richard Pery, Richard Bellingham, Nathaniell Wright, Samuell Vassall, Theophilus Eaton, Thomas Goffe, Thomas Adams, John Browne, Samuell Browne, Thomas Hutchins, William Vassall, William Pinchion, and George Foxcrofte, their heires and assignes, or by any other person or persons whatsoever there inhabiting, by them, or any of them, to be appointed to fishe therein. Provided, always, that yf the said landes, islandes, or any other the premises herein before mentioned, and by theis presentes intended and meant to be graunted, were, at the tyme of the graunting of the saide former letters patentes, dated the third day of November, in the eighteenth yeare of our said deare fathers raigne aforesaide, actuallie possessed or inhabited by any other Christian Prince or State, or were within the boundes, lymyttes, or territories of that Southerne Colony then before graunted by our said late father to be planted by divers of his loveing subjectes in the south partes of America, That then this present graunt shall not extend to any such partes or parcells thereof, soe formerly inhabited or lyeing within the boundes of the southerne plantation as aforesaide, but as to those partes or parcells soe possessed or inhabited by such Christian Prince or State, or being within the bounders aforesaid, shalbe utterly voyd, theis presentes or any thinge therein conteyned to the contrarie notwithstanding. To have and to hould, possesse and enjoy the saide partes of Newe England in America, which lye, extend, and are abutted as aforesaid, and every parte and parcell thereof: And all the islandes, rivers, portes, havens, waters, fishinges, fishes, mynes, myneralls, jurisdictions, franchises, royalties, liberties, privileges, commodities, and premises whatsoever, with the appurtenances, unto the said Sir Henry Rosewell, Sir John Younge, Sir Richard Saltonstall, Thomas Southcott, John Humfrey, John Endecott, Simon Whetcombe, Isaack Johnson, Samuell Aldersey, John Ven, Mathewe Cradock, George Harwood, Increase Nowell, Richard Perry, Richard Bellingham, Nathaniell Wright, Samuell Vassall, Theophilus Eaton, Thomas Goffe, Thomas Adams, John Browne, Samuell Browne, Thomas Hutchins, William Vassall, William Pinchion, and George Foxcroft, their heires and assignes forever, to the onlie proper and absolute use and behoufe of the said Sir Henry Rosewell, Sir John Younge, Sir Richard Saltonstall, Thomas Southcott, John Humfrey, John Endecott, Simon Whetcombe, Isaac Johnson, Samuell Aldersey, John Ven, Mathewe Cradocke, George Harwood, Increase Nowell, Richard Pery, Richard Bellingham, Nathaniell Wright, Samuell Vassall, Theophilus Eaton, Thomas Goffe, Thomas Adams, John Browne, Samuell Browne, Thomas Hutchins, William Vassall, William Pinchion, and George Foxcroft, their heires and assignes forevermore. To be holden of us, our heires and successors, as of our mannor of Eastgreenewich, in our Countie of Kent, within our realme of England, in free and common soccage, and not in Capite nor by knightes service, and also yeilding and

paying therefore to us, our heires and successors, the fifte parte onlie of all oare of gould and silver which, from tyme to tyme, and at all tymes hereafter, shalbe there gotten, had, or obteyned for all services, exactions, and demaundes whatsoever. Provided alwaies, and our expresse will and meaninge is, That onlie one fifte parte of the gould and silver oare abovementioned in the whole, and noe more, be reserved or payeable unto us, our heires and successors, by collour or vertue of theis presentes. The double reservations or recitalls aforesaid, or any things herein conteyned, notwithstanding. And forasmuch as the good and prosperous successe of the plantation of the saide partes of Newe England aforesaid intended by the said Sir Henry Rosewell, Sir John Younge, Sir Richard Saltonstall, Thomas Southcott, John Humfrey, John Endecott, Simon Whetcombe, Isaack Johnson, Samuell Aldersey, John Ven, Mathewe Cradock, George Harwood, Increase Noell, Richard Pery, Richard Bellingham, Nathaniell Wright, Samuell Vassall, Theophilus Eaton, Thomas Goffe, Thomas Adams, John Browne, Samuell Browne, Thomas Hutchins, William Vassall, William Pinchion, and George Foxcrofte, to be speedily sett upon, cannot but chiefly depend next under the blessing of Almightie God and the support of our royall authoritie, upon the good government of the same, To the ende that the affaires and busyssinesses which, from tyme to tyme, shall happen and arise concerning the saide landes and the plantation of the same, maie be the better mannaged and ordered. Wee have further hereby, of our especiall grace, certen knowledge, and meere motion, given, graunted, and confirmed, And for us, our heires and successors, doe give, graunt, and confirme unto our saide trustie and welbeloved subjectes, Sir Henry Rosewell, Sir John Younge, Sir Richard Saltonstall, Thomas Southcott, John Humfrey, John Endicott, Simon Whetcombe, Isaack Johnson, Samuell Aldersey, John Ven, Mathewe Cradock, George Harwood, Increase Nowell, Richard Pery, Richard Bellingham, Nathaniell Wright, Samuel Vassall, Theophilus Eaton, Thomas Goffe, Thomas Adams, John Browne, Samuell Browne, Thomas Hutchins, William Vassall, William Pinchion, and George Foxcrofte: And for us, our heires and successors, wee will and ordeyne, That the saide Sir Henry Rosewell, Sir John Yong, Sir Richard Saltonstall, Thomas Southcott, John Humfrey, John Endicott, Symon Whetcombe, Isaack Johnson, Samuell Aldersey, John Ven, Mathewe Cradock, George Harwood, Increase Noell, Richard Pery, Richard Bellingham, Nathaniell Wright, Samuell Vassall, Theophilus Eaton, Thomas Goffe, Thomas Adams, John Browne, Samuell Browne, Thomas Hutchins, William Vassal, William Pinchion, and George Foxcrofte, and all such others as shall hereafter be admitted and made free of the Company and Society hereafter mentioned, shall, from tyme to tyme, and at the tymes for ever hereafter, be, by vertue of theis presentes, one body corporate and politique in fact and name, by the name of the Governor and Company of the Mattachusettes Bay in New England: And them by the name of the Governor and Company of the Mattachusettes Bay in Newe England, one bodie politique and corporate in deede, fact, and name, Wee doe for us, our heires and successors, make, ordeyne, constitute, and confirme by theis presentes, and that by that name they shall have perpetuall succession: And that by the same name they and their successors shall, and maie be capeable and enabled, aswell to implead and to be impleaded, and to prosecute, demaund, and aunswere, and be aunsweared unto, in all and singuler suites, causes, quarrells, and actions of what kinde or nature soever. And also to have, take, possesse, acquire, and purchase any landes, tenementes, or hereditamentes, or any goodes or chattells, And the same to lease, graunt, demise, alien, bargaine, sell, and dispose of as other our liege people of this our realme of England, or any other corporation or body politique of the same maie lawfullie doe: and, further, that the said Governor and Companye and their successors maie have for ever one common seale, to be used in all causes and occasions of the said Company, and the same seale maie alter, chaunge, breake, and newe make, from tyme to tyme, at their pleasures. And our will and pleasure is, And wee doe hereby for us, our heires and successors, ordeyne and graunte, That, from henceforth for ever, there shalbe one Governor, one Deputy Governor, and eighteene Assistantes of the same Company, to be from tyme to tyme constituted, elected, and chosen out of the freemen of the saide Company, for the tyme being, in such manner and forme as hereafter in theis presents is expressed. Which said officers shall applie themselves to take care for the best disposeing and ordering of the generall buysines and affaires of, for, and concerning the saide landes and premises hereby mentioned to be graunted, and the plantacion thereof, and the government of the people there. And for the better execution of our royall pleasure and graunte in this behalf, wee doe, by theis presentes, for us, our heires and successors, nominate, ordeyne, make, and constitute our wellbeloved the saide Mathewe Cradocke to be the first and present Governor of the said Company, and the saide Thomas Goffe to be Deputy Governor of the saide Company, and the saide Sir Richard Saltonstall, Issack Johnson, Samuell Aldersey, John Ven, John Humfrey, John Endecott, Simon Whetcombe, Increase Noell, Richard Pery, Nathaniell Wright, Samuell Vassall, Theophilus Eaton, Thomas Adams, Thomas Hutchins, John Browne, George Foxcrofte, William Vassal, and William Pinchion to be the present Assistantes of the saide Company, to continue in the saide severall offices respectivelie for such tyme and in such manner as in and by theis presentes is hereafter declared and appointed. And, further, wee will, and by theis presentes for us, our heires and successors, doe ordeyne and graunt, That the

Governor of the saide Company, for the tyme being, or in his absence, by occasion of sicknes or otherwise, the Deputie Governor, for the tyme being, shall have authoritie, from tyme to tyme, upon all occasions, to give order for the assembling of the saide Company, and calling them together to consult and advise of the business and affaires of the saide Company. And that the said Governor, Deputie Governor, and Assistantes of the saide Company, for the tyme being, shall or maie once every moneth, or oftener at their pleasures, assemble, and houlde, and keepe a Courte or Assemblie of themselves, for the better ordering and directing of their affaires. And that any seaven or more persons of the Assistantes, togither with the Governor or Deputie Governor, soe assembled, shalbe saide, taken, held, and reputed to be, and shalbe, a full and sufficient Courte or Assemblie of the saide Company for the handling, ordering, and dispatching of all such buysinesses and occurrentes as shall, from tyme to tyme, happen touching or concerning the said Company or plantation, and that there shall or maie be held and kept by the Governor or Deputie Governor of the said Company, and seaven or more of the said Assistantes, for the tyme being, upon every last Wednesday in Hillary, Easter, Trinity, and Michas termes respectivelie for ever, one greate, generall, and solempe Assemblie, which foure Generall Assemblies shalbe stiled and called the Foure Greate and Generall Courtes of the saide Company: In all and every or any of which saide Great and Generall Courtes soe assembled, wee doe, for us, our heires and successors, give and graunte to the said Governor and Company, and their successors, That the Governor, or, in his absence, the Deputie Governor, of the saide Company for the tyme being, and such of the Assistantes and freemen of the saide Company as shalbe present, or the greater nomber of them soe assembled, whereof the Governor or Deputie Governor and six of the Assistantes, at the least to be seaven shall have full power and authoritie to choose, nominate, and appointe such and soe many others as they shall thinke fitt, and that shall be willing to accept the same, to be free of the said Company and Body, and them into the same to admitt, and to elect and constitute such officers as they shall thinke fitt and requisite for the ordering, mannaging, and dispatching of the affaires of the saide Governor and Company and their successors, And to make lawes and ordinances for the good and welfare of the saide Company, and for the government and ordering of the saide landes and plantation, and the people inhabiting and to inhabite the same, as to them from tyme to tyme shalbe thought meete. Soe as such lawes and ordinances be not contrarie or repugnant to the lawes and statutes of this our realme of England. And our will and pleasure is, And wee doe hereby for us, our heires and successors, establish and ordeyne, That yearely once in the yeare for ever hereafter, namely, the last Wednesday in Easter tearme yearely, the

Governor, Deputy Governor, and Assistantes of the said Company, and all other officers of the saide Company, shalbe, in the Generall Court or Assembly to be held for that day to tyme, newly chosen for the yeare ensueing by such greater parte of the said Company for the tyme being, then and there present, as is aforesaid. And yf it shall happen the present Governor, Deputy Governor, and Assistantes by theis presentes appointed, or such as shall hereafter be newly chosen into their roomes, or any of them, or any other of the officers to be appointed for the said Company, to dye or to be removed from his or their severall offices or places before the saide generall day of election, (whome wee doe hereby declare for any misdemeanor or defect to be removeable by the Governor, Deputie Governor, Assistantes, and Company, or such greater parte of them in any of the publique Courtes to be assembled as is aforesaid,) That then, and in every such case, it shall and maie be lawfull to and for the Governor, Deputie Governor, Assistantes, and Company aforesaide, or such greater parte of them soe to be assembled as is aforesaid, in any of their assemblies, to proceade to a newe election of one or more others of their Company in the roome or place, roomes or places, of such officer or officers soe dyeing or removed, according to their discretions. And ymmediatly upon and after such election and elections made of such Governor, Deputie Governor, Assistant or Assistantes, or any other officer of the saide Company in manner and forme aforesaid, the authoritie, office, and power before given to the former Governor, Deputie Governor, or other officer and officers soe removed, in whose steede and place newe shalbe shoe chosen, shall, as to him, and them, and everie of them, cease and determine. Provided, also, and our will and pleasure is, That aswell such as are by theis presentes appointed to be the present Governor, Deputie Governor, and Assistantes of the said Company as those that shall succeed them, and all other officers to be appointed and chosen as aforesaid, shall, before they undertake the execution of their saide offices and places, respectivelie take their corporall oathes for the due and faithful performance of their duties in their severall offices and places, before such person or persons as are by theis presentes hereunder appointed to take and receive the same; That is to saie, the saide Mathewe Cradock, whoe is hereby nominated and appointed the present Governor of the saide Company, shall take the saide oathes before one or more of the Masters of our Courte of Chauncery for the tyme being, unto which Master or Masters of the Chauncery Wee doe, by theis presentes, give full power and authoritie to take and administer the said oathe to the said Governor accordinglie. And after the saide Governor shalbe soe sworne, then the said Deputy Governor and Assistants, before by theis presentes nominated and appointed, shall take the said severall oathes to their offices and places respectivelie

belonging before the said Mathew Cradock, the present Governor, soe formerlie sworne as aforesaid. And every such person as shalbe, as the tyme of the annuall election, or otherwise upon death or removeall, be appointed to be the newe Governor of the said Company, shall take the oathes to that place belonging before the Deputy Governor or two of the Assistantes of the said Company, at the least, for the tyme being. And the newe elected Deputie Governor and Assistantes, and all other officers to be hereafter chosen as aforesaide, from tyme to tyme, to take the oathes to their places respectivelie belonging before the Governor of the said Company for the tyme being. Unto which said Governor, Deputie Governor, and Assistantes, Wee doe by theis presents give full power and authoritie to give and administer the said oathes respectively, according to our true meaning hearein before declared, without any commission or further warrant to be had and obteyned of us, our heires or successors in that behalf. And wee doe further, of our especiall grace, certen knowledge, and meere motion, for us, our heires and successors, give and graunte to the said Governor and Company, and their successors for ever, by theis presentes, That it shalbe lawfull and free for them and their assignes, at all and every tyme and tymes hereafter, out of any our realms or domynions whatsoever, to take leade, carry, and transport for and into their voyages, and for and towardes the said plantation in Newe England, all such and soe many of our loving subjectes, or any other strangers that will become our loving subjectes, and live under allegiance, as shall willinglie accompany them in the same voyages and plantation, and also shipping, armour, weapons, ordinance, munition, powder, shott, corne, victualls, and all manner of clothing, implements, furniture, beastes, cattle, horses, mares, marchandizes, and all other thinges necessarie for the saide plantation, and for their use and defence, and for trade with the people there, and in passing and returning to and fro, any lawe, or statute to the contrarie hereof in any wise notwithstanding, and without payeing or yielding any custome, or subsedie either inward or outward to us, our heires or successors, for the same, by the space of seaven yeares, from the day of the date theis presentes. Provided, that none of the saide persons be such as shalbe, hereafter by especiall name restrayned by us, our heires or successors. And for their further encouragement, Of our especiall grace and favor, wee doe by theis presentes for us, our heires and successors, yeild and graunt to the saide Governor and Company, and their successors, and every of them, their factors and assignes, That they and every of them shalbe free and quitt from all taxes, subsidies, and customes in Newe England for the like space of seaven yeares, and from all taxes and impositions for the space of twenty and one yeares upon all goodes and merchandises at any tyme or tymes hereafter, either upon importation thither, or exportation from thence into our realme of England, or into any other our domynions, by the said Governor and Company, and their successors, their deputies, factors, and assignes, or any of them, except onlie the five poundes per centum due for custome upon all such goodes and merchandizes, as after the saide seaven yeares shalbe expired shalbe brought or imported into our realme of England, or any other of our dominions, according to the auncient trade of merchantes, which five poundes per centum onlie being paide, it shall be thenceforth lawfull and free for the said adventures the same goodes and merchandizes to export and carry out of our said domynions into forraine partes, without any custome, tax, or other dutie to be paid to us, our heires or successors, or to any other officers or ministers of us, our heires and successors. Provided, that the said goodes and merchandizes be shipped our within thirteene monethes after their first landing within any parte of the saide domynions. And wee doe for us, our heires and successors, give and graunte unto the saide Governor and Company and their successors, That whensoever, or soe often any custome or subsedie shall growe due or payeable unto us, our heires or successors, according to the lymittation and appointment aforesaide, by reason of any goodes, wares, or merchandizes to be shipped out, or any retorne to be made of any goodes, wares, or merchandizes, unto or from the said partes of New England hereby mentioned to be graunted as aforesaide, or any the landes or territories aforesaide, That then and soe often and in such case the farmors, customers, and officers of our customes of England and Ireland, and everie of them for the tyme being, upon request made to them by the saide Governor and Company, or their successor, factors, or assignes, and upon convenient security to be given in that behalf, shall give and allowe unto the said Governor and Company, and their successors, and to all and everie person and persons free of that company as aforesaide, six monethes tyme for the payement of the one halfe of all such custome and subsidy as shalbe due and payeable unto us, our heires and successors, for the same, For which theis our letters patentes, or the duplicate or the inrollment thereof, shalbe unto our saide officers a sufficient warrant and discharge. Nevertheless, our will and pleasure is, That yf any of the saide goodes, wares, and merchandize which be or shalbe at any tyme hereafter landed or exported out of any of our realms aforesaide, and shalbe shipped with a purpose not to be carried to the partes of Newe England aforesaide, but to some other place, That then such payment, dutie, custome, imposition, or forfeyture shalbe paid or belonge to us, our heires and successors, for the said goodes, wares, and merchandize soe fraudulently sought to be transported, as yf this our graunte had not benn made nor graunted. And wee doe further will, And by theis presentes for us, our heires and successors, firmely enjoin and commaunde as well the Treasorer, Chauncellor, and Barons of

the Exchequer of us, our heires and successors, as also all and singuler the customers, farmors, and collectors of the customes, subsidies, and impostes and other the officers and ministers of us, our heires and successors, whatsoever, for the tyme being, That they and every of them, upon the shewing forth unto them of theis letters patentes, or the duplicate or exemplification of the same, without any other writt or warrant whatsoever from us, our heires or successors, to be obteyned or sued forth, doe and shall make full, whole, entire, and due allowance and cleare discharge unto the saide Governor and Company, and their successors, of all customes, subsidies, impositions, taxes, and duties whatsoever that shall or maie be claymed by us, our heires and successors, of or from the said Governor and Company and their successors, for or by reason of the said goodes, chattels, wares, merchandizes, and premises to be exported out of our saide domynions, or any of them, into any parte of the saide landes or premises hereby mentioned to be given, graunted, and confirmed, or for or by reason of any of the saide goodes, chattells, wares, or merchandizes to be imported from the said landes and premises hereby mentioned to be given, graunted, and confirmed, into any of our saide dominions or any parte thereof, as aforesaide, excepting onlie the saide five poundes per centum hereby reserved and payeable after the expiration of the saide terme of seaven yeares, as aforesaid, and not before. And theis our letters patentes, or the inrollment, duplicate, or exemplification of the same shalbe for ever hereafter from time to tyme, as well to the Treasorer, Chauncellor, and Barons of the Exchequer of us, our heires and successors, as to all and singuler the customers, farmors, and collectors of the customes, subsidies, and impostes of us, our heires and successors, and all searchers and other the officers and ministers whatsoever of us, our heires and successors for the time being, a sufficient warrant and discharge in this behalf. And further, our will and pleasure is, And wee doe hereby, for us, our heires and successors, ordeyne, declare, and graunte to the saide Governor and Company, and their successors, That all and every the subjectes of us, our heires or successors, which shall goe to and inhabite within the saide landes and premisses hereby mentioned to be graunted, and every of their children which shall happen to be borne there, or on the seas in goeing thither or retorning from thence, shall have and enjoy all liberties and immunities of free and naturall subjectes within any of the domynions of us, our heires or successors, to all intentes, constructions, and purposes whatsoever, as yf they and everie of them were borne within the realme of England. And that the Governor and Deputie Governor of the said Company for the tyme being, or either of them, and any two or more of such of the saide Assistances as shalbe thereunto appointed by the saide Governor and Company, at any of their courtes of assemblies to be held as aforesaide, shall and maie att all tymes, and from tyme to tyme hereafter, have full power and authoritie to minister and give the oathe and oathes of supremacie and allegiance, or either of them, to all and everie person and persons which shall at any tyme of tymes hereafter goe or passe to the landes and premises hereby mentioned to be graunted to inhabite in the same. And wee doe, of our further grace, certen knowledg and meere motion, give and graunt to the saide Governor and Company, and their successors, That it shall and maie be lawfull to and for the Governor of Deputie Governor and such of the Assistantes and Freemen of the said Company for the tyme being as shalbe assembled in any of their Generall Courtes aforesaide, or in any other Courtes to be specially summoned and assembled for that purpose, or the greater parte of them, (whereof the Governor or Deputie Governor and six of the Assistantes, to be alwaies seaven,) from tyme to tyme to make, ordeine, and establishe all manner of wholesome and reasonable orders, lawes, and statutes, and ordinances, directions, and instructions not contrarie to the lawes of this our realme of England, aswell for setling of the formes and ceremonies of government and magistracy fitt and necessary for the said plantation and the inhabitantes there, and for nameing and stiling of all sortes of officers, both superior and inferior, which they shall finde needefull for that governement and plantation, and the distinguishing and setting forth of the severall duties, powers, and lymyttes of every such office and place, and the formes of such oathes warrantable by the lawes and statutes of this our realme of England as shalbe respectivelie ministred unto them, for the execution of the said severall offices and places, as also for the disposing and ordering of the elections of such of the said officers as shalbe annuall, and of such others as shalbe to succeede in case of death or removeall, and ministring the said oathes to the newe elected officers, and for impositions of lawfull fynes, mulctes, imprisonment, or other lawfull correction, according to the course of other corporations in this our realme of England, and for the directing, ruling, and disposeing of all other matters and thinges whereby our said people, inhabitantes there, maie be soe religiously, peaceablie, and civilly governed, as their good life and orderlie conversation maie wynn and incite the natives of country to the knowledg and obedience of the onlie true God and Savior of mankinde, and the Christian fayth, which, in our royall intention and the adventurers free profession, is the principall ende of this plantation. Willing, commaunding, and requiring, and by theis presentes for us, our heires and successors, ordeyning and appointing, That all such orders, lawes, statutes, and ordinances, instructions, and directions, as shalbe soe made by the Governor or Deputie Governor of the said Company, and such of the Assistantes and Freemen as aforesaide, and published in writing under their common seale, shalbe carefullie and dulie observed, kept, performed, and putt in execution, according to the true intent and meaning of the same. And theis our letters patentes, or the duplicate or exemplification thereof, shalbe to all and everie such officers, superior and inferior, from tyme to tyme, for the putting of the same orders, lawes, statutes, and ordinances, instructions, and directions in due execution against us, our heires and successors, insufficient warrant and discharge. And wee doe further, for us, our heires and successors, give and graunt to the said Governor and Company, and their successors, by theis presentes, That all and everie such cheife commaunders, captaines, governors, and other officers and ministers, as by the said orders, lawes, statutes, ordinances, instructions, or directions of the said Governor and Company for the tyme being, shalbe from tyme to tyme hereafter ymploied either in the government of the saide inhabitantes and plantation, or in the waye by sea thither or from thence, according to the natures and lymyttes of their offices and places respectively, shall from tyme to tyme hereafter for ever within the precinctes and partes of Newe England hereby mentioned to be graunted and confirmed, or in the waie by sea thither, or from thence, have full and absolute power and authoritie to correct, punishe, pardon, governe, and rule all such the subjectes of us, our heires and successors, as shall from tyme to tyme adventure themselves in any voyadge thither or from thence, or that shall at any tyme hereafter inhabite within the precinctes and partes of Newe England aforesaid, according to the orders, lawes, ordinances, instructions, and directions aforesaid, not being repugnant to the lawes and statutes of our realme of England, as aforesaid. And wee doe further, for us, our heires and successors, give and graunte to the said Governor and Company and their successors, by theis presentes, That it shall and maie be lawfull to and for the cheife commaunders, governors, and officers of the said company for the time being, who shalbe resident in the said parte of Newe England in America, by theis presentes graunted, and others there inhabiting, by their appointment and direction from tyme to tyme, and at all tymes hereafter, for their speciall defence and safety, to incounter, expulse, repell, and resist by force of armes, aswell by sea as by lande, and by all fitting waies and meanes whatsoever, all such person and persons as shall at any tyme hereafter attempt or enterprise the destruction, invasion, detriment, or annoyance to the said plantation or inhabitantes: And to take and surprise, by all waies and meanes whatsoever, all and every such person and persons, with their shippes armour, munition, and other goodes, as shall in hostile manner invade or attempt the defeating of the said plantation, or the hurt of the said Company and inhabitantes. Nevertheles, our will pleasure is, And wee doe hereby declare to all Christian Kinges, Princes, and States, That yf any person or persons which shall hereafter be of the said Company or plantation, or any other, by lycense or appointment of the said Governor and Company for the tyme being, shall at any tyme of tymes here-after, robb or spoyle by sea or by land, or doe any hurt, vio-lence, or unlawfull hostility to any of the subjectes of us, our heires or successor, or any of the subjectes of any Prince or State being then in league and amytie with us, our heires and successors, and that upon such injury don, and upon just complaint of such Prince or State, or their subjectes, wee, our heires or successors, shall make open proclamation within any of the partes within our realme of England commodious for that purpose, That the person or persons haveing committed any such roberie or spoyle, shall within the terme lymytted by such a proclamation make full restitution or satisfaction of all such injuries don, soe as the said Princes or others soe complayning maie hould themselves fullie satisfied and contented. And that yf the said person or persons having committed such roberry or spoile shall not make or cause to be made satis-faction accordinglie within such time soe to be lymytted, That then it shalbe lawfull for us, our heires and succes-sors, to putt the said person or persons out of our alle-giance and protection: And that it shalbe lawfull and free for all Princes to prosecute with hostilitie the said offendors and every of them, their and every of their pro-curers, ayders, abettors, and comforters in that behalf. Provided also, and our expresse will and pleasure is, And wee doe by theis presentes, for us, our heires and succes-sors, ordeyne and appoint, That theis presentes shall not in any manner enure, or be taken to abridge, barr, or hinder any of our loving subjects whatsoever to use and exercise the trade of fishing upon that coast of New England in America by theis presentes mentioned to be graunted: But that they and every or any of them shall have full and free power and liberty to continue and use their said trade of fishing upon the said coast in any the seas thereunto adjoyning, or any armes of the seas or saltwater rivers where they have byn wont to fishe, and to build and sett up upon the landes by theis presentes graunted such wharfes, stages, and workehouses as shalbe necessarie for the salt-ing, drying, keeping, and packing up of their fish, to be taken or gotten upon that coast: And to cutt downe and take such trees and other materialls there groweing, or being, or shalbe needefull for that purpose, and for all other necessarie easementes, helpes, and advantage con-cerning their said trade of fishing there, in such manner and forme as they have byn heretofore at any tyme accus-tomed to doe, without making any wilfull waste or spoyle, Any thing in theis presentes conteyned to the contrarie notwithstanding and wee doe further, for us, our heires and successors, ordeyne and graunte to the said Governor and Company, and their successors, by theis presentes, That theis our letters patentes shalbe firme, good, effectu-all, and availeable in all thinges, and to all intentes and constructions of lawe, according to our true meaning herein before declared, and shalbe construed, reputed,

and adjudged in all cases most favourablie on the behalf and for the benefitt and behoofe of the saide Governor and Company and their successors. Although expresse mention of the true yearely value or certenty of the premises, or of any of them, or of any other guiftes or grauntes by us or any of our progenitors or predecessors to the foresaid Governor or Company before this time made, in theis pre-sentes is not made, Or any statute, acte, ordinance, provi-sion, proclamation, or restrainte to the contrarie thereof heretofore had, made, published, ordeyned, or provided, or any other matter, cause, or thinge whatsoever to the contratrie thereof in any wise notwithstanding. In Witnes whereof, wee have caused theis our letters to be made patentes. Witnes ourself at Westminster, the fourth day of March, in the fourth yeare of our raigne.

Per Breve de Privato
Sigillo.
Wolseley.

Source:

Edmund S. Morgan, ed. *The Founding of Massachusetts*. Indi-anapolis, Ind.: Bobbs-Merrill, 1964. pp. 303–323.

Charter of Freedoms and Exemptions to Patroons, 1629

Charter establishing the patroon system of land tenure, set up by the Dutch West India Company on June 7, 1629. This sys-tem was used for colonization of New Netherland, in what are now the states of New York, New Jersey, Delaware, and Con-necticut. It gave any member of the charter the right to a large tract of land if he brought at his own expense at least 50 per-sons over the age of 15 years to begin a colony. The system did not take off as well as expected because Netherlanders refused to leave their country to settle in America unless they were promised freedom. Five land grants were given, but only the one granted to Killian Van Rensselaer was prosperous.

(Translation from the original Dutch)

Freedoms and Exemptions for the patroons, masters or private persons who will plant any colonies in, and send cattle to New Netherland, drawn up for the benefit of the General West India Company in New Netherland and for the profit of the patroons, masters and private persons.

I. Such participants of the said Company as may be inclined to plant any colonies in New Netherland shall be permitted to send, in the ships of this Company going thither, three or four persons to inspect the situation of the country, provided that they, with the officers and ship's company, swear to the Articles, so far as they relate to them, pay for board and passage, going and coming, six stivers a day (such as desire to mess in the cabin to pay 12 stivers) and agree to give assistance like others, in cases offensive and defensive. And if any ships be taken from the enemy, they shall receive pro rata their portions with the ship's company, each according to his quality, that is to say the colonists messing outside the cabin shall be rated with the sailors and those messing in the cabin with those of the Company's servants messing at table who receive the lowest wages.

II. However, in this matter, those persons shall have the preference who shall first have declared their intentions and applied to the Company.

III. All such shall be acknowledged patrons of New Netherland as shall agree to plant there a colony of 50 souls, upwards of 15 years old, within the space of four years after they have given notice to any Chamber of the Company here or to the commander or council there, one fourth part within one year and the remainder within three years after the sending of the first, making together four years, to the full number of 50 persons, to be shipped hence, or pain, in case of wilful neglect, of being deprived of the privileges obtained. But they are warned that the Company reserves to itself the island of the *Manhattes*.

IV. From the very hour they make known the situation of the places where they propose to settle colonies, they shall have the preference over all others to the free ownership of such lands as they shall have chosen: but in case the location should afterwards not please them or they should find themselves deceived in the selection of the land, they may, after memorializing the commander and council there, choose another place.

V. The patroons, by their agents, may, at the place where they wish to settle their colonies, [fix] their limits [so that the colony shall] extend four leagues along the coast or one side of a navigable river, to two leagues along both sides of a river, and as far inland as the situation of the occupants will permit; with the understanding that the Company retains for itself the ownership of the lands lying and remaining between the limits of the colonies, to dispose thereof when and at such time as it shall think proper, but no one else shall be allowed to come within seven or eight leagues of them without their consent unless the situation of the land thereabout be such that the commander and council for good reasons shall order otherwise; always observing that the first occupants are not to be prejudiced in the right they have obtained, except in so far as the service of the Company should require it, either for the building of fortifications or something of that sort, and that (outside of this) the [patroon of the] first settled colony shall retain the command of each bay, river or island, under the supreme jurisdiction of their High Mightinesses the States General and the Company; but the later colonies on the same river or island may appoint one or more councilors to assist him, that in consultation they may look after the interests of the colonies on the river or island.

VI. They shall forever own and possess and hold from the Company as a perpetual fief of inheritance, all the land lying within the aforesaid limits, together with the fruits, plants, minerals, rivers and springs thereof, and the high, middle and low jurisdiction, rights of fishing, fowling and grinding, to the exclusion of all others, said fief to be renewed in case of demise by doing homage to the Company and paying 20 guilders per colony within a year and six weeks, either to the Chambers here or to the commander there, each to the Chamber whence the colony was originally sent out; however no fishing or fowling shall be carried on by any one but the patroons and such as they shall permit. And in case any one should in time prosper so much as to found one or more cities, he shall have authority to appoint officers and magistrates there and to use such titles in his colony as he sees fit according to the quality of the persons.

VII. There shall likewise be granted to all patroons who shall desire the same, *Venia Testandi,* or liberty to dispose of the aforesaid fiefs by will.

VIII. The patroons may also to their profit use all lands, rivers and woods lying contiguous to them, until such time as they are taken possession of by this Company, other patroons, or private persons.

IX. Those who shall send over these colonies, shall furnish them with proper instructions in order that they may be ruled and governed conformably to the rule of government, both as to administration and justice, made, or to be made by the Assembly of the Nineteen, which [instructions] they must first lay before the directors of the respective Chambers.

X. The patroons and colonist shall be privileged to send all their people and effects thither, in ships belonging to the Company, provided they take the oath and pay the Company for bringing over the people according to the first article, and for freight of the goods five per cent cash of the cost of the goods here; without including herein, however, cattle and agricultural implements, which the Company is to carry over free, if there is room in its ships, provided that the patroons, at their own expense, fit up places for the cattle and furnish everything necessary for their support.

XI. In case it should not suit the Company to send any ships, or there should be no room in the ships sailing thither, then the said patroons, after having communicated their intentions and obtained consent from the Company in writing, may send their own ships or yachts thither, provided that, going and coming, they depart not from their ordinary course, give security to the Company for the same and take on board an assistant at the expense of the patroons as to his board and of the Company as to his monthly wages, on pain, if doing contrary hereto, of forfeiting all right and title they have obtained to the colony.

XII. Inasmuch as it is the intention of the Company to people the island of the *Manhattes* first, this island shall provisionally also be the staple port for all products and wares that are found on the North River and lands thereabouts, before they are allowed to be sent elsewhere, excepting such as are, from their nature, unnecessary there and such as can not without great loss to their owners be brought there; in this case the owners thereof must give timely notice in writing of the difficulty attending the same to the Company here, or the commander and council there, that such measures may be taken as the situation of affairs shall be found to require.

XIII. All the patroons of colonies in New Netherland and colonists living on the island of the *Manhattes* shall be at liberty to sail and traffic along the entire coast from *Florida* to *Terra Neuf,* provided that they do first return with all such goods as they shall get in trade to the island of the *Manhattes* and pay five per cent duty to the Company, in order that if possible, after proper inventory of the goods in the ship, the same may thence be sent hither. And if it should so happen that they could not return, whether from contrary currents or otherwise, the said goods may be brought nowhere but to this country, in order that they may be unladen and inventoried with the knowledge of the directors at the place where they may arrive and the aforesaid duty of five per cent paid to the Company here, on pain, if they do otherwise, of forfeiture of their goods obtained, or the true value thereof.

XIV. In case the ships of the patroons, in going or coming or in sailing along the coast from *Florida to Terra Neuf* and no further, within [the limits of] our charter should conquer any prizes from the enemy, they must bring them, or cause them to be brought, to the Chamber of the place from which they sailed in order that their honors may have the benefit thereof; the Company shall keep the one third part thereof and the remaining two thirds shall belong to them in consideration of the expense and risk at which they have been, all according to the orders of the Company.

XV. It shall also be permitted the aforesaid patroons, all along the coast of New Netherland and places circumjacent, to trade their goods, products of that country, for all sorts of merchandise that may be had there, except beavers, otters, minks and all sorts of peltry, which trade alone the Company reserves to itself. But permission for even this trade is granted at places where the Company has no agent, on the condition that such traders must bring all the peltry they may be able to secure to the island of the *Manhattes,* if it is in any way practicable, and there deliver them to the director, to be by him sent hither with the ships and goods; or, if they should come here without having done so, then to unload them with due notice to the Company and proper inventory, that they may pay to the

Company one guilder for each merchantable beaver and otter skin; the cost, insurance and all other expenses to remain at the charge of the patroons or owners.

XVI. All raw materials which the colonists of the patroons shall have obtained there, such as pitch, tar, potash, timber, grain, fish, salt, limestone and the like, shall be conveyed in the Company's ships at the rate of 18 guilders per last, four thousand weight to be accounted a last, and the Company's ship's crew shall be obliged to wheel and bring the salt on board, whereof 10 lasts make a hundred. And, in case of lack of ships or of room in the ships, they may send it over in their own ships at their own cost and enjoy in this country such freedoms and benefits as have been granted to the Company; but in either case they must pay, over and above the duty of five per cent, 18 guilders for each hundred of salt that is carried over in the Company's ships.

XVII. For all goods not mentioned in the foregoing article and which are not carried by the last there shall be paid for freight one daelder for each hundred pounds weight; and for wines, brandies, verjuice and vinegar, there shall be paid 18 guilders per cask.

XVIII. The Company promises the colonists of the patroons not to lay any duties, tolls, excise, imposts or any other contributions upon them for the space of 10 years; and after the expiration of the said 10 years, at the highest, such dues [only] as the goods pay here at present.

XIX. They will not take from the service of the patroons any of their colonists, either man or woman, son or daughter, manservant or maidservant; and, though any of these should desire it they will not receive them, much less permit them to leave their patroons and enter into the service of another, except on written consent obtained previously from their patroons and this for and during so many years as they are bound to their patroons; after the expiration whereof, the patroons shall be at liberty to bring hither such colonists as will not continue in their service and then only to set them free. And if any colonist runs away to another patroon, or, contrary to his contract, leaves his service, we promise to do everything in our power to deliver the same into the hands of his patroon or *commis* that he may be prosecuted there according to the customs of this country, as occasion may require.

XX. From all judgments given by the courts of the patroons above 50 guilders, there shall be appeal to the Company's commander and council in New Netherland.

XXI. And as to private persons who on their own account, or others who in the service of their masters here in this country shall go thither and settle as freemen in smaller numbers than the patroons, they may with the approbation of the director and council there, choose and take possession of as much land as they can properly cultivate and hold the same in full ownership either for themselves or for their masters.

XXII. They shall also have rights of hunting, as well by water as by land, in common with others in public woods and rivers and exclusively within the limits of their colonies, according to the orders of the director and council.

XXIII. Whosoever, whether colonists of the patroons for their patroons, or free men for themselves, or other private persons for their masters, shall find any shores, bays or other places suitable for fisheries or the making of salt pans may take possession thereof and work them as their own absolute property to the exclusion of all others. The patroons of colonists are granted permission also to send ships along the coast of New Netherland on the cod fishery, and with the catch to go directly to Italy or other neutral countries, provided they pay to the Company in such cases a duty of six guilders per last; and if they come to this country with their lading, they shall be free, but they shall not, under pretext of this consent or [leave] from the Company, carry any other goods to Italy on pain of peremptory punishment, it remaining at the option of the Company to put a supercargo on board each ship as in the eleventh article.

XXIV. In case any of the colonists, by his industry and diligence should discover any minerals, precious stones, crystals, marbles or the like, or any pearl fishery, the same shall be and remain the property of the patroon or patroons of such colony, provided the discoverer be given such premium as the patroon shall beforehand stipulate with his colonist by contract. And the patroons shall be exempt from the payment of any duty to the Company for the term of eight years, and for freight merely shall pay two per cent; and after the aforesaid eight years, for duty and freight, one eighth part of what the same may be worth in this country.

XXV. The Company will take all the colonists, free men as well as those that are in service, under its protection and help to defend them against all domestic and foreign attacks and violence, with the forces it has there, as much as lies in its power.

XXVI. Whosoever shall settle any colonies out of the limits of *Manhattes* Island must satisfy the Indians of that place for the land and may enlarge the limits of their colonies if they settle a proportionate number of colonists thereon.

XXVII. The patroons and colonists shall in particular endeavor as quickly as possible to find some means whereby they may support a minister and a schoolmaster, that thus the service of God and zeal for religion may not grow cool and be neglected among them, and they shall for the first, procure a comforter of the sick there.

XXVIII. The colonies that shall be established on the respective rivers or islands (that is to say, each river or island for itself), may appoint an agent, who shall give the commander and council information about that district and further matters before the council relating to his colony; of which agents one shall be changed every two years; and all colonies must, at least once in every 12 months, send an exact report of their colony and of the lands thereabout to the commander and council there.

XXIX. The colonists shall not be permitted to make any woolen, linen or cotton cloth, nor to weave any other stuffs there, on pain of being banished and peremptorily punished as oath breakers.

XXX. The Company will endeavor to supply the colonists with as many blacks as it possibly can, on the conditions hereafter to be made, without however being bound to do so to a greater extent or for a longer time than it shall see fit.

XXXI. The Company promises to finish the fort on the island of the *Manhattes,* and to put it in a posture of defense without delay. And to have these Freedoms and Exemptions approved and confirmed by their High Mightinesses the Lords States General.

Finis. At Amstelredam.

Source:
New York State Library. Albany, Van Rensselaer Bowier Manuscripts . . . Albany, N.Y.: University of the State of New York, 1908.

Cambridge Agreement of 1629

Decision signed into agreement by 12 Puritan members of the Massachusetts Bay Company, under the leadership of John Winthrop, at a meeting in Cambridge, England, on August 26, 1629; they agreed to emigrate from England to America with their families, provided the company's charter and government were also transferred abroad. Transfer of the charter meant that a business company would be changed into a plantation; by ratifying the agreement, the company repositioned its emphasis from commerce to religion. The purpose of the action was to guard against interference in the enterprise by non-Puritans in England. The agreement was authorized, and the Puritans set up a self-governing colony in New England soon afterward.

Upon due consideration of the state of the plantacion now in hand for new England, wherein wee (whose names are hereunto subscribed) have engaged ourselves: and having weighed the greatness of the worke in regard of the consequence, Gods glory and the churches good: As also in regard of the difficultyes and discouragements which in all probabilityes must be forcast upon the prosecucion of this businesse: Considering withall that this whole adventure growes upon the joynt confidence we have in each others fidelity and resolucion herein, so as no man of us would have adventured it without assurance of the rest: Now for the better encourragement of ourselves and others that shall joyne with us in this action, and to the end that every man may without scruple dispose of his estate and afayres as may best fitt his preparacion for this voyage, It is fully and faithfully agreed amongst us, and every of us doth hereby freely and sincerely promise and bynd himselfe in the word of a Christian and in the presence of God who is the searcher of all hearts, that we will so really endevour the prosecution of this worke, as by Gods assistaunce we will be ready in our persons, and with such of our severall familyes as are to go with us and such provisions as we are able conveniently to furnish ourselves withall, to embarke for the said plantacion by the first of march next, at such port or ports of this land as shall be agreed upon by the Company, to the end to passe the Seas (under Gods protection) to inhabite and continue in New England. Provided alwayes that before the last of September next the whole governement together with the Patent for the said plantacion bee first by an order of Court legally transferred and established to remayne with us and others which shall inhabite upon the said plantacion. And provided also that if any shall be hindered by such just and inevitable Lett or other cause to be allowed by 3 parts of foure of these whose names are hereunto subscribed, then such persons for such tymes and during such letts to be dischardged of this bond. And we do further promise every one for himselfe that shall fayle to be ready through his owne default by the day appointed, to pay for every dayes default the summe of 3 *li.* to the use of the rest of the Company who shall be ready by the same day and tyme.

This was done by order of Court the 29th of August, 1629.

> Rich: Saltonstall
> Tho: Dudley William Vassall Nicho: West
> Isaack Johnson John Humfrey
> Tho: Sharp Increase Nowell
> John Winthrop
> Will: Pinchon Kellam Browne
> William Colbron

Source:
Edmund S. Morgan, ed. *The Founding of Massachusetts.* Indianapolis, Ind.: Bobbs-Merrill, 1964. pp. 183–184.

Charter of Maryland, 1632

Proprietary rights to what is now the state of Maryland; granted in 1632 to George Calvert, the first lord Baltimore, who had petitioned King Charles I for the proprietary colony of Maryland on June 20, 1632. He then sent colonists, about half of whom were fellow Roman Catholics (Cecilius, like his father, George, had converted to the Catholic faith). The charter gave Cecilius as proprietor the right to collect taxes, appoint administrators, award land grants, and establish churches according to English laws. It also empowered him "to publish any Laws whatsoever . . . of and with the Advise, Assent and Approbation of the Free-men," which permitted the establishment of representative government in the province. The Maryland charter started the only Roman Catholic colony in British America.

Charles by the Grace of God, King of *England, Scotland, France,* and *Ireland,* Defendor of the Faith, &c. To all to whom these presents shall come greeting.

Whereas Our right Trusty and Wellbeloved Subject *Cecilius Calvert,* Baron of *Baltemore* in our Kingdom of *Ireland,* Sonne and heire of Sir *George Caluert* Knight, late Baron of *Baltemore* in the same Kingdome of *Ireland,* pursuing his Fathers intentions, being excited with a laudable and pious zeale for the propagation of the Christian Faith, and the enlargement of our Empire and Dominion, hath humbly besought leave of Vs, by his industry and charge, to transport an ample Colony of the *English* Nation unto a certaine Countrey hereafter described, in the parts of *American,* not yet cultivated and planted, though in some parts thereof inhabited by certaine barbarous people, having no knowledge of Almighty God, and hath humbly besought our Royall Majestie to give, grant, and confirme all the said Countrey, with certaine Priviledges and Iurisdictions, requisite for the good government, and state of his Colony, and Countrey aforesaid, to him and his heires for ever.

Know Yee therefore, that Wee favouring the Pious, and Noble purpose of the said Barons of *Baltermore,* of our speciall grace, certaine knowledge, and meere motion, have given, granted, and confirmed, and by this our present Charter, for Vs, Our Heires, and Successors, doe give, grant and confirme unto the said *Cecilius,* now Baron of *Baltemore,* his heires and Affignes, all that part of a *Peninsula,* lying in the parts of *America,* betweene the Ocean on the East, and the Bay of *Chesopeack* on the West, and divided from the other part thereof, by a right line drawne from the Promontory or Cape of Land called *Watkins Point* (situate in the foresaid Bay, neere the river of *Wighco)* on the West, unto the maine Ocean on the East; and betweene that bound on the South, unto that part of *Delaware* Bay on the North, which lieth under the fortieth degree of Northerly Latitude from the Equinoctiall, where *New-England* ends; And all that tract of land betweene the bounds aforesaid; that is to say, passing from the foresaid Bay, called *Delaware* Bay, in a right line by the degree aforesaid, unto the true Meridian of the first fountaine of the River of *Pattowmeck,* and from thence trending toward the South unto the farther banke of the fore-said River, and following the West and South side thereof unto a certaine place called *Cinquack,* situate neere the mouth of the said River, where it falls into the Bay of Chesopeack, and from thence by a straight line unto the foresaid Promontory, and place called *Watkins Point,* (So that all that tract of land divided by the line aforesaid, drawne betweene the maine Ocean, and *Watkins Point* unto the Promontory called *Cape Charles,* and all its apurtenances, doe remaine intirely excepted to us, our heires, and Successors for ever).

Wee doe also grant and confirme unto the said now Lord *Baltemore,* his heires and Assignes, all Ilands, and Iletts within the limitts aforesaid, and all and singular the Ilands and Iletts, which are, or shall be in the Ocean, within 10. Leagues from the Easterne shoare of the said Countrey, towards the East, with all and singular Ports, Harbors, Bayes, Rivers, and Inletts, belonging unto the Countrey, or Ilands aforesaid: And all the Soile, lands, Fields, Woods, Mountaines, Fennes, Lakes, Rivers, Bayes, and Inletts, situate, or being within the bounds, and limits aforesaid, with the fishing of all forts of fish, *whales, Sturgeons,* and all other royal fishes in the Sea, Bays, Inletts, or Rivers, within the premises: and the fish therein taken: and moreover all Veines, Mines, and Quarries, aswell discovered, as not discovered, of Gold, Siluer, Gemmes, and pretious stones, and all other whatsoever, be it of Stones, Mettalls, or of any other thing, or matter whatsoever, found, or to bee found within the Countrey, Iles, and limits aforesaid. And Furthermore the Patronages and Aduowsons of all Churches, which (as Christian Religion shall encrease within the Countrey, Iles, Iletts, and limits aforesaid) shall happen hereafter to bee erected: together with licence and power, to build and found Churches, Chappells, and Oratories, in convenient and fit places within the premises, and to cause them to be dedicated, and consecrated according to the Ecclesiasticall Lawes of our Kingdome of *England: Together with* all and singular the like, and as ample rights, Iurisdictions, Priviledges, Prerogatives, Royalties, Liberties Immunities, Royall rights, and franchises of what kind soever temporall, as well by Sea, as by land, within the Countrey, Iles, Iletts, and limits aforesaid; To have, exercise, use and enjoy the same, as amply as any Bishop of *Durham,* within the Bishoprick, or County *Palatine* of *Durham,* in our Kingdome of *England,* hath at any time heretofore had, held, used, or enjoyed, or of right ought, or might have had, held, used, or enjoyed.

And Him the said now Lord *Baltemore,* his Heires and Assignes, Wee doe by these Presents for Vs, Our Heires and Successors, make, create, and constitute and true and absolute Lords, and Proprietaries of the Countrey aforesaid, and of all other the Premises, (except before excepted) saving alwayes, the faith and allegeance, and Soveraigne dominion due unto Vs, Our Heires and Successors.

To Have, hold, possesse, and enjoy the sayd Countrey, Iles, Iletts, and other the Premises, unto the said now Lord *Baltemore,* his heires and assignes, to the sole and proper use and behoofe of him the said now Lord *Baltemore,* his heires and assignes for ever.

To Bee holden of Vs, Our Heires, and Successors, Kings of *England* as of Our Castle of *Windsor,* in Our County of *Berkshire,* in free and common soccage, by fealty onely, for all seruices, and not in Capite, or by Knights seruice: Yeelding and paying therefore to Vs, our Heires and Successors, two *Indian* Arrowes of those parts, to be delivered at Our said Castle of *windsor,* every yeere on the Tuesday in *Easter* weeke; and also the fifth part of all Gold and Siluer Oare within the limits aforesaid, which shall from time to time happen to be found.

Now That the said Countrey thus by Vs granted, and described, may be eminent above all other parts of the said territory, and dignified with larger titles: Know yee that wee of our further grace, certaine knowledge, and meere motion, have thought fit to erect the same Countrey and Ilands into a Province, as out of the fullnesse of Our royall Power, and Prerogative, Wee doe, for Vs, Our Heires, and Successors, erect, and incorporate them into a Province, and doe call it *Mary land,* and so from henceforth will have it called.

And Forasmvch as Wee have hereby made, and ordained the aforesaid now Lord *Baltemore,* the true Lord, and Proprietary of all the Province aforesaid: Know yee therefore moreover, that Wee, reposing especiall trust and confidence in the fidelitic, wisedome, Iustice, and Provident circumspection of the said now Lord *Baltemore,* for Vs, Our Heires and Successors, doe grant free, full, and absolute power, by vertue of these Presents, to him and his heires, for the good and happy government of the said Province, to ordaine, make, enact, and under his and their seales to publish any Lawes whatsoever, appertaining either unto the publike State of the said Province, or unto the private utility of particular Persons, according unto their best directions, of and with the aduise assent and approbation of the Free-men of the said Province, or the greater part of them, or of their delegates or deputies, whom for the enacting of the said lawes, when, and as often as neede shall require, We will that the said now Lord *Baltemore,* and his heires, shall assemble in such sort of the forme, as to him or them shall seeme best: And the same lawes duly to execute upon all people, within the said Province, and limits thereof, for the time being, or that shall be constituted under the government, and power of him or them, either sayling towards *Mary-land,* or returning from thence toward *England,* or any other of Ours, or forraine Dominions, by imposition of Penalties, Imprisonment, or any other punishment; yea, if it shall be needfull, and that the quality of the offence require it, by taking away member or life, either by him the said now Lord *Baltemore,* and his heires, or by his or their Deputies, Lievtenants, Judges, Justices, Magistrates, Officers, and Ministers to be ordained or appointed, according to the Tenor, and true intention of these Presents: And likewise to appoint and establish any Judges and Justices, Magistrates and Officers whatsoever, at sea and Land, for what causes soever, and with what power soever, and in such forme, as to the said now Lord *Baltemore,* or his heires, shall seeme most conuenient: Also to remit, release, pardon, and abolish, whether before Judgement, or after, all crimes or offences whatsoever, against the said Lawes: and to doe all and every other thing or things, which unto the complete establishment of Justice, unto Courts, Praetories, and Tribunals, formes of Judicature and maners of proceeding, do belong: although in these Presents, expresse mention be not made thereof, and by judges by them delegated, to award Processe, hold Pleas, and determine in all the said Courts and Tribunalls, all actions, suits, and causes whatsoever, as well criminal as civill, personall, reall, mixt, and praetoriall; which laws, so as aforsaid to be published, Our pleasure is, and so Wee enioyne, require, and command, shall be most absolute and available in Law, and that all the Leige people, and subjects of Vs, Our Heires and Successors, do obserue and keepe the same inuiolably, in those parts, so farre as they concerne them, under the paines therein expressed, or to be expressed: Provided nevertheless, that the said Lawes be consonant to reason, and be not repugnant or contrary, but as neere as conueniently may be agreeable to the Lawes, Statutes, Customes, and Rights of this our Kingdome of *England.*

And forasmvch, as in the Government of so great a Province, suddaine accidents doe often happen, whereunto it will be necessary to apply a remedy, before the Free-holders of the said Province, their Delegates, or Deputies, can be assembled to the making of Lawes, neither will it be conuenient, that instantly upon every such emergent occasion, so great a multitude should be called together: Therefore fore the better government of the said Province, Wee will and ordaine, and by these Presents for Vs, Our Heires, and Successors, doe grant unto the said now Lord *Baltemore,* and his heires, that the said now Lord *Baltemore* and his heires, by themselues, or by their Magistrates and Officers in that behalfe duely to be ordained as aforesaid, may make and constitute, fit and wholesome Ordinances, from time to time, within the said Province, to be kept and obserued, as well for the preservation of the Peace, as for the better government of the people there inhabiting, and publikely so notifie the same to all persons, whom the same doth, or any way may concerne; which Ordinances, Our pleasure is, shall be obserued inviolably within the said Province, under the paines therein to bee expressed. So as the said Ordinances

be consonant to reason, and be not repugnant nor contrary, but so farre as conueniently may be, agreeable with the Lawes and Statutes of Our Kingdome of *England,* and so as the said Ordinances be not expended, in any sort to bind, charge, or take away the right or interest of any person, or persons, of, or in their Life, Member, Free-hold, Goods, or Chattells.

Fvrthermore, that this new Colony may the more happily encrease by the multitude of people resorting thither, and may likewise be the more strongly defended from the incursions of Saluages, or other enemies, Pyrates and Robbers: Therefore Wee, for Vs, Our Heires and Successors, doe give and grant by those Presents, Power, licence, and liberty unto all the liege people, and subjects, both present, and future, of Vs, Our Heires, and Successors (excepting those who shall be specially forbidden) to transport themselues and families unto the said Province, with conuenient shipping, and fitting provisions, and there to settle themselues, dwell and inhabite, and to build, and fortifie Castles, Forts, and other places of strength for the publike, and their owne private defence, at the appointment of the said now Lord *Baltemore,* and his heires, the Statute of fugitives, or any other whatsoever, to the contrary of the premises, in any wise notwithstanding.

And wee will also, and of Our more speciall grace, for Vs, Our Heires, and Successors, wee doe straightly enioyne, constitute, ordaine, and command, that the said Province shall be of Our Allegiance, and that all and singular the Subjects, and Liege people of Vs, Our Heires, and Successors, transported, or to be transported into the said Province, and the children of them, and of such as shall descend from them, there already borne, or hereafter to be borne, bee, and shall be Denizens, and Lieges of Vs, Our Heires, and Successors, of Our Kingdome of *England,* and *Ireland,* and be in all things held, treated, reputed, and esteemed as the liege faithfull people of Vs, Our Heires, and Successor, borne within Our Kingdome of *England,* and likewise any Lands, Tenements, Revenues, Seruices, and other hereditaments whatsoever, within Our Kingdome of *England,* and other Our Dominions, may inherite, or otherwise purchase, receive, take, have, hold, buy, and possesse, and them may occupy, and enjoy, give, fell, aliene, and bequeath, as likewise, all Liberties, Franchises, and Priviledges, of this Our Kingdome of *England,* freely, quietly, and peaceably, have and possesse, occupy and enjoy, as Our liege people, borne, or to be borne, within Our said Kingdome of *England,* without the let, molestation, vexation, trouble, or grievance of Vs, Our Heires and Successors: any Statute, Act, Ordinance, or Provision to the contrary hereof notwithstanding.

And fvrthermore, That Our Subjects may be the rather encouraged to undertake this expedition, with ready and cheerefull minds; Know Yee, that We of Our speciall grace, certaine knowledge, and meere motion, doe give and grant, by vertue of these presents, aswel unto the said now Lord *Baltemore* and his Heires, as to all other that shall from time to time repaire unto that province, with a purpose to inhabite there, or to trade with the Natives of the said Province, full licence to Lade and Fraight in any Ports whatsoever, of Vs, Our Heires and Successors, and into the said Province of *Maryland,* by them, their servants, or assignes, to transport, all and singular, their Goods, Wares, and Merchandize; as likewise all sorts of graine whatsoever, and any other things whatsoever, necessary for food or clothing (not prohibited by the Lawes and Statutes of our Kingdomes and Dominions to bee carried out of the said kingdomes) without any lett, or molestation of Vs, Our Heires, or Successors, or of any of the officers of Vs, Our Heires, or Successors; (saving alwayes, to Vs, Our Heires, and Successors, the Impositions, Customes, and other duties and payments for the said Wares and Merchandise) any Statute, Act, Ordinance or other thing whatsoever to the contrary notwithstanding.

And because in so remote a Country, and situate amongst so many barbarous nations, the incursions aswell of the salvages themselves, as of other enemies, pyrates and robbers, may probably be feared: Therefore We have given, and for Vs, Our Heires, and Successors, doe give power by these presents, unto the now Lord *Baltemore,* his heires and assignes, by themselves, or their Captaines, or other their officers, to Leauy, Muster and Traine, all sorts of men, of what condition, or wheresoever borne, in the said Province of *Mary-Land* for the time being, and to make warre, and to pursue the Enemies and Robbers aforesaid, aswell by sea as by land, yea, even without the limits of the said Province, and (by Gods assistance) to vanquish and take them, and being taken, to put them to death by the Law of warre, or to save them at their pleasure, and to doe all and every other thing which unto the charge and office of a Captaine Generall of an Army belongeth, or hath accustomed to belong, as fully and freely, as any Captaine Generall of an army hath ever had the same.

Also, Our Will and Pleasure is, and by this Our Charter, We doe give unto the said now Lord *Baltemore,* his heires, and assignes, full power, liberty, and authority, in case of Rebellion, Tumult, or Sedition, if any should happen (which God forbid) either upon the land within the Province aforesaid, or upon the maine sea, in making a voyage thither, or returning from thence, by themselves, or their captains, deputies or other offices, to be authorized under their seales for that purpose (to whom we also for Vs, Our Heires and Successors, doe give and grant by these presents, full power and authority) to exercise Martiall Law against mutinous and seditious persons of those parts, such as shall refuse to submit themselves to his, or their government, or shall refuse to serve in the warres, or shall flie to the Enemy, or forsake their Ensignes, or by

loyterers, or stragglers, or otherwise howsoever offending against the Law, Custome, and Discipline military, as freely, and in as ample manner and forme, as any Captaine generall of an army by vertue of his office might, or hath accustomed to use the same.

Fvrthermore, That the way to honors and dignities, may not seeme to be altogether precluded and shut up, to men well borne, and such as shall prepare themselves unto this present Plantation, and shall desire to deserve well of Vs, and Our Kingdomes, both in peace and war, in so farre distant and remote a Countrey: Therefore We, for Vs, Our Heires and Suceessors, doe give free, and absolute power, unto the said now Lord *Baltemore,* his heires and assignes, to conferre favours, rewards, and honours, upon such inhabitants within the Province aforesaid, as shall deserve the same; and to invest them, with what titles and dignities soever, as he shall thinke fit, (so as they be not such as are now used in *England*) As likewise to erect and incorporate, Townes into Boroughes, and Boroughs into Cities, with convenient priuiledges and immunities, according to the merit of the inhabitants, and the fitnesse of the places, and to doe all and every other thing or things, touching the premises, which to him, or them, shall seeme meete and requisite; albeit they be such as of their owne nature might otherwise require a more speciall commandement and warrant, then in there Presents is expressed.

Wee will also, and by these Presents, for Vs, Our Heires and Successors, We doe give and grant licence, by this Our Charter, unto the said now Lord *Baltemore,* his heires and assignes, and to all the inhabitants and dwellers in the Province aforesaid, both present and to come, to import, or unlade, by themselves, or their servants factors, or assignes, all Merchandizes and goods whatsoever, that shall arise of the fruits and commodities of the said Province, either by land or sea, into any of the ports of Vs, Our Heires and Successors, in Our kingdomes of *England,* or *Ireland,* or otherwise to dispose of the said goods, in the said Ports, and if need be, within one yeere next after the unlading of the same, to lade the said merchandizes and goods againe, into the same or other ships, and to export the same into any other Countreys, either of our Dominion or forreigne, (being in Amity with Vs, Our Heires and Successors) Provided always, that they pay such Customes, Impositions, Subsidies and Duties for the same, to Vs, Our Heires and Successors, as the rest of Our Subjects of Our Kingdome of *England,* for the time being, shall be bound to pay: beyond which, We will not that the inhabitants of the foresaid Province of *Mary-land,* shall be any way charged.

And fvrthermore, of Our more ample and special Grace, certaine knowledge, and meere motion, We doe, for Vs, Our Heires and Successor, grant unto the said now Lord *Baltemore,* his heires and assignes, full and absolute power and authority, to make, erect, and constitute, within the Province of *Mary-land,* and the Iles and Iletts aforesaid, such, and so many Seaports, Harbours, Creekes, and other places, for discharge and unlading of goods and merchadises, out of Ships, Boates, and other vessels, and lading them, and in such and so many places, and with such Rights, Jurisdictions, Liberties and Priviledges unto the said ports belonging, as to him or them shall seeme most expedient. And that all and singular the Ships, Boats, and other Vessells, which shall come for merchandize and trade unto the said Province, or out of the same shall depart; shall be laden and unladen only at such Ports as shall be so erected and constituted by the said now Lord *Baltemore,* his heires or assignes, any Vse, Custome or other thing to the contrary notwithstanding; saving alwayes unto Vs, Our heires and Successors, and to all the Subjects (of Our Kingdome of *England* and *Ireland* of Vs, Our Heires and Successors, free liberty of fishing for Sea-fish, aswell in the Sea, Bayes, Inletts, and navigable Rivers as in the Harbours, Bayes and Creekes of the Province aforesaid, and the Priviledges of salting and drying their fish on the shore of the said Province, and for the same cause, to cut and take underwood, or twiggs there growing, and to build Cottages and Shedds necessary in this behalfe, as they heretofore have, or might reasonably have used; which Liberties and Priviledges, nevertheless, the Subjects aforesaid, of Vs, Our Heires and Successors, shall enjoy without any notable dammage, or injury, to be done to the said now Lord *Baltemore,* his heires, or assignes, or to the dwellers and inhabitants of the said Province, in the Ports, Creekes and shores aforesaid, and especially in the woods and Copses growing within the said Province: And if any shall doe any such dammage, or injury, he shall incurre the heavy displeasure of Vs, Our Heires and Successors, the punishment of the Lawes; and shall moreover make satisfaction.

Wee doe furthermore, will, appoint, and ordaine, and by these Presents, for Vs, Our Heires and Successors, We doe grant unto the said now Lord *Baltemore,* his heires and assignes, that he the said Lord *Baltemore,* his heires and assignes, may from time to time for ever, have and enjoy, the Customes and Subsidies, in the Ports, Harbours, and other Creekes and places aforesaid, within the Province aforesaid; payable, or due for merchandizes and wares, thereto be laded or unladed, the said Customes and Subsidies to be reasonably assessed (upon any occasion) by themselves and the people there, as aforesaid; to whom we give power by these Presents for Vs, Our Heires and Successors upon just cause, and in a due proportion, to assesse and impose the same.

And Fvrther, of Our speciall grace, and of Our certaine knowledge, and meere motion, Wee have given granted, and confirmed, and by these Presents for Vs, Our Heires and Successors, doe give, grant, and confirme unto the said now Lord *Baltemore,* his heires and assignes, full

and absolute licence, power, and authoritie, that hee the said now Lord *Baltemore,* his heires and assignes, from time to time hereafter for ever, at his, or their will, and pleasure, may assigne, aliene, grant, demise, or enfeoffe of the Premises so many, and such parts and parcells, to him or them that shall be willing to purchase the same, as they shall thinke fit, To Have and to hold to them the sayd person, or persons, willing to take or purchase the same, their heires and assignes in fee simple, or fee taile, or for terme of life, or lives, or yeeres, to bee held of the said now Lord *Baltemore,* his heires, and assignes, by such seruices, customes, and rents, as shall seeme fit to the said now Lord *Baltemore,* his heires and assignes; and not immediately of Vs, Our Heires or Successors: and to the same person or persons, and to all and every of them. Wee doe give and grant by these Presents for Vs, Our Heires and Successors, licence, authoritie, and power, that such person or persons may take the premises, or any parcell thereof, of the foresaid now Lord *Baltemore,* his heires or assignes, and the same hold to themselues, their heires, or assignes, (in what estate of inheritance soever, in fee simple, or in fee taile, or otherwise, as to them, and the now Lord *Baltemore,* his heires and assignes, shall seems expedient) of the said now Lord *Baltemore,* his heires and assignes; the statute made in the Parliament of *Edward,* Sonne of King *Henry,* late King of *England,* Our Predecessor, commonly called the Statute *Qhia emptores terrarum,* lately published in Our Kingdome of *England,* or any other Statute, Acte, Ordinance, Vse, Law, or Custome, or any other thing, cause, or matter thereupon heretofore had, done, published, ordained, or provided to the contrary, in any wise notwithstanding; And by these Presents, Wee give, and grant licence unto the said now Lord *Baltemore,* and his heires, to erect any parcells of land within the Province aforesaid, into Mannors, and in every of the said Mannors, to have, and to hold a *Court Baron,* with all things whatsoever, which to a *Court Baron,* doe belong, and to have and hold viewe of *Franck-pledge,* (for the conseruation of the peace, and the better government of those Parts,) by themselues or their stewards, or by the Lords for the time being of other Mannors, to bee deputed, when they shall bee erected: and in the same, to use all things belonging to *View of Franck-Pledge.*

And Fvrther, Our pleasure is, and by these Presents, for Vs, Our Heires, and Successors, wee doe covenant and grant to and with the said now Lord *Baltemore,* his heires and assignes; That Wee, Our Heires and Successors, shall at no time hereafter, set, or make, or cause to be set, any Imposition, Custome, or other Taxation, Rate, or Contribution whatsoever, in or upon the dwellers and inhabitants of the foresaid Province, for their Lands, Tenements, goods or Chattells within the said Province, or in or upon any goods or merchandizes, within the said Province, or to be laden, or unladen within any the Ports or harbours of the said Province: And Our pleasure is, and for Vs, Our Heires, and Successors, Wee charge and command, that this Our Declaration shall be henceforward from time to time received, and allowed in all Our Courts, and before all the Judges of Vs, Our Heires and Successors, for a sufficient and lawfull discharge payment, and acquittance; Commanding all and singular, our Officers and Ministers of Vs, our Heires and Successors, and enjoyning them upon paine of Our high displeasure, that they doe not presume at any time to attempt any thing to the contrary of the premises, or that they doe in any sort withstand the same, but that they be at all times ayding and assisting, as is fitting, unto the said now Lord *Baltemore*, and his heires, and to the Inhabitants, and Merchants of *Maryland* aforesaid, their seruants, ministers, factors and assignes, in the full use and fruition of the benefit of this Our Charter.

And Fvrther, Our pleasure is, and by these Presents for Vs, our Heires and Successors, Wee doe grant unto the said now Lord *Baltemore,* his heires and assignes, and to the Tenants, and Inhabitants of the said Province of *Mary-land,* both present, and to come, and to every of them, that the said Province, Tenants, and Inhabitants of the said *Colony* or Countrey, shall not from henceforth bee held or reputed as a member, or a part of the land of *Virginia,* or of any other Colony whatsoever, now transported, or hereafter to be transported, nor shall be depending on, or subject to their government in any thing, from whom Wee doe separate that, and them, and Our pleasure is, by these Presents that they bee separated, and that they be subject immediately to Our Crowne of *England,* as depending thereof for ever.

And if Perchance hereafter it should happen, that any doubts or questions should arise, concerning the true sence and understanding of any word, clause, or sentece contained in this Our present Charter, Wee will, ordaine, and command, that at all times, and in all things, such Interpretation bee made thereof, and allowed in any of Our Courts whatsoever, as shall be judged most aduantagious, and favourable unto the the said now Lord *Baltemore,* his heires and assignes. Provided alwayes, that no Interpretation bee admitted thereof, by which Gods Holy and Truely Christian Religion, or the allegeance due unto Vs, Our Heires and Successors, may in any thing suffer any prejudice, or diminution.

Although expresse mention bee not made in these Presents, of the true yeerely value, or certainty of the premises, or of any part thereof, or of other gifts and grants, made by Vs, Our Heires, and Predecessors, unto the said now Lord *Baltemore,* or any Statute, Acte, Ordinance, Provision, Proclamation, or restraint heretofore had, made, published, ordained, or provided, or any other thing, cause, or matter whatsoever to the contrary thereof in any wife notwithstanding.

In Witnesse whereof, Wee have caused these Our Letters to bee made Patents, Witnesse Our selfe at *Westmin-*

ster, the Twentieth day of *June,* In the Eighth yeere of Our Reigne.

Source:

The Charter of Maryland, June 20, 1632. Archives of Maryland Online. Vol. 549, pp. 9–31. Available on-line. URL: www.mdarchives.state.md.us. Accessed December 2003.

Charter of Connecticut, 1662

Legal charter for Connecticut secured by Governor John Winthrop by petition to King Charles II of England and granted on April 23, 1662. It superseded the Fundamental Orders of Connecticut while retaining and incorporating essential characteristics of the orders into the new charter. In 1687, in an attempt by England's King James II to annul the charter, England requested its surrender to Sir Edmund Andros, governor of the Dominion of New England. However, during an oration by Governor Robert Treat of Connecticut against its surrender, the lights were extinguished, and the charter was whisked away by Joseph Wadsworth and placed in a hollow tree, later known as the Charter Oak. The charter remained the basic law of Connecticut until 1818.

CHARLES the Second, by the Grace of God, King of England, Scotland, France, and Ireland, Defender of the Faith, &c. To all to whom these Presents shall come, Greeting.

Whereas by the several Navigations, Discoveries, and Successful Plantations of divers of Our loving Subjects of this Our Realm of England, several lands, Islands, Places, Colonies, and Plantations have been obtained and settled in that Part of the Continent of America called New-England, and thereby the Trade and Commerce there, hath been of late Years much increased: And whereas We have been informed by the hirable Petition of our Trusty and Well beloved John Winthrop, John Mason, Samuel Wyllys, Henry Clarke, Matthew Allyn, John Tapping, Nathan Gold, Richard Treat, Richard Lord, Henry Wolcott, John Talcott, Daniel Clarke, John Ogden, Thomas Wells, Obadias Brewen, John Clerke, Anthony Hawkins, John Deming, and Matthew Camfeild, being Persons principally interested in Our Colony or Plantation of Connecticut, in New England, that the same Colony, or the greatest part thereof, was Purchased and obtained for great and valuable Considerations, and some other Part thereof gained by Conquest, and with touch difficulty, and at the only Endeavors, Cadence, and Charges of theirs and their Associates, arced those under whom they Claim, Subdued, and Improved, and thereby become a considerable Enlargement and Addition of Our Dominions and Interest there. Now Know Ye, That in consideration thereof, and in Regard the said Colony is remote from other the English Plantations in the places aforesaid, and to the End the Affairs and Business which shall from Time to Time happen or arise concerning the same, may be duly Ordered and Managed, we have thought fit, and at the humble Petition of the Persons aforesaid, and are graciously Pleased to create and make them a Body Politicly and Corporate, with the Powers and Privileges herein after mentioned; and accordingly Our Will and Pleasure is, and of our especial Grace, certain Knowledge, and meer Motion, We have ordained, constituted and declared, and by these presents, for Us, Our Heirs and Successors, Do ordain, constitute and declare, that they the said John Winthrop, John Mason, Samuel Wyllys, Henry Clarke, Matthew Allyn, John Tapping, Nathan Gold, Richard Treat, Richard lord, Henry Wolcott, John Talcott, Daniel Clarke, John Ogden, Thomas Wells, Obadiah Bowed, John Clerke, Anthony Hawkins, John Deming, and Matthew Camfeild, and all such others as now are, or hereafter shall be admitted and made free of the Company and Society of Our Colony of Connecticut, in America, shall from Time to Time, and for ever hereafter, be One Body Corporate and politique, in Fact and Name, by the Name of, Governor and Company of the English colony of Connecticut in New-England, in America;

And that by the same Name they and their Successors shall and may have perpetual Succession, and shall and may be Persons able and capable in the Law, to plead and be impleaded, to answer and to be answered unto, to defend and be defended in all and singular Suits, Causes, Quarrels, Matters, Actions, and Things, of what Kind or Nature soever; and also to have, take, possess, acquire, and purchase Lands, Tenements, or Hereditaments, or any Goods or Chattels, and the same to lease, grant, demise, alien, bargain, sell, and dispose of, as other Our liege People of this Our Realm of England, or any other Corporation or Body Politique within the same may lawfully do. And further, That the said Governor and Company, and their Successors shall and may forever hereafter have a common Seal, to serve and use for all Causes, Matters, Things, and affairs whatsoever, of them and their Successors, and the same Seal, to alter, change, break and make new from Time to Time, at their Wills and Pleasures, as they shall think fit. And further, We will and ordain, and by these Presents, forms, our Heirs and Successors, do declare and appoint, that for the better ordering and managing of the Affairs and Business of the said Company and their Successors, there shall be One Governor, One Deputy-Governor, and Twelve Assistants, to be from time to Time constituted, elected and chosen out of the Freemen of the said Company for the Time being, in such Manner and Form as hereafter in these Presents is expressed, which said Officers shall apply themselves to take Care for the best disposing and ordering of the gen-

eral Business and all airs of and concerning the Land and Hereditaments herein after mentioned to- be granted, and the Plantation thereof, and the Government of the People thereof: And for the better Execution of Our Royal Pleasure herein, We do for Us, Our Heirs, and Successors, assign, name, constitute and appoint the aforesaid John Winthrop to be the first and present Governor of the said Company, and the said John Mason, to be the Deputy-Governor, and the said Samuel Wyllys, Matthew Allyn, Nathan Gold, Henry Clerke, Richard Treat, John Ogden, John Tapping, John Talcott, Thomas Wells, Henry Wolcott, Richard Lord, and Daniel Clerke, to be the Twelve present assistants of the said Company, to continue in the said several Offices respectively, until the second Thursday which shall be in the Month of October now next coming. And further we Will, and by these Presents for Us, Our Heirs, and Successors, Do ordain and grant, That the Governor of the said Company for the Time being, or in his Absence by occasion of Sickness, or otherwise by his Leave or Permission, the Deputy-Governor for the Time being, shall and may from Time to Time upon all Occasions, give Order for the assembling of the said Company, and calling them together to consult and advise of the Business and Affairs of the said Company, and that for ever hereafter, twice in every Year, That is to say, On every Second Thursday in October, and on every Second Thursday in May, or oftener in case it shall be requisite; the Assistants, and Freemen of the said Company, or such of them (not exceeding Two Persons from each Place, Town, or City) who shall be from Time to Time hereunto elected or deputed by the major Part of the Freemen of the respective Towns, Cities, and Places for which they shall be elected or deputed, shall have a General Meeting or Assembly, then and there to consult and advise in and about the Affairs and Business of the said Company: and that the Governor, or in his Absence the Deputy-Governor of the said Company for the Time being, and such of the Assistants and Freemen of the said Company as shall be so elected or deputed, and be present at such Meeting or Assembly, or the greatest Number of them, whereof the Governor of Deputy-Governor, and Six of the Assistants at least, to be Seven, shall be called the General Assembly, and shall have full Popover and authority to alter-and change their Days and Times of Meeting, or General-Assemblies, for electing the Governor, Deputy-Governor, and Assistants, other Officers or any other Courts, Assemblies or Meetings, and to choose, nominate and appoint such and so many other Persons as they shall; and shall be willing to accept the same, to be Free of the said Company and Body Politique, and them into the same to admit; And to elect and constitute such Officers as they shall think fit and requisite for the ordering, managing and disposing of the Affairs of the said Governor and Company, and their Successors:

And we do hereby for Us, Our Heirs and Successors, establish and ordain, That once in the Year for ever hereafter, Namely, the said Second Thursday in May, the Governor, Deputy-Governor, and Assistants of the said Company, and other Officers of the said Company, or such of them as the said General Assembly shall thinly fit, shall be in the said General Court and Assembly to be held from that Day or Time, newly chosen for the Year ensuing, by such greater Part of the said Company for the Time being, then and there present; and if the Governor, Deputy-Governor, and Assistants by these Presents appointed, or such as hereafter be newly chosen into their Rooms, or any of them, or any other the Officers to be appointed for the said Company shall die, or be removed from his or their several Offices or Places before the said general Day of Election, whom We do hereby declare for any Misdemeanor or Default, to be removable by the Governor, Assistants, and Company, or such greater Part of them in any of the said public Courts to be assembled, as is aforesaid, that then and in every such Case, it shall and may be lawful to and for the Governor, Deputy-Governor, and Assistants, and Company aforesaid, or such greater Part of them so to be assembled, as is aforesaid, in any of their Assemblies, to proceed to a new Election of one or more of their Company, in the Room or Place, Rooms or Places of such Governor, Deputy-Governor, Assistant, or other Officer or Officers so dying or removed, according to their Discretions, and immediately upon and after such Election or Elections made of such Governor, Deputy-Governor, Assistant or Assistants, or any other Officer of the said Company, in Manner and Form aforesaid, the Authority, Office and Power before given to the former Governor, Deputy-Governor, or other Officer and Officers so removed, in whose Stead and Place new shall be chosen, shall as to him and them, and every of them respectively, cease and determine.

Provided also, And Our Will and Pleasure is, That as well such as are by these Presents appointed to be the present Governor, Deputy-Governor, and Assistants of the said Company, as those that shall succeed them, and all other Officers to be appointed and chosen, as aforesaid, shall before they undertake the Execution of their said Offices and Places respectively, take their several and respective corporal Oaths for the due and faithful Performance of their Duties, in their several Offices and Places, before such Person or Persons as are by these Presents hereafter appointed to take and receive the same; That is to say, The said John Winthrop, who is herein before nominated and appointed the present Governor of the said Company, shall take the said Oath before One or more of the Masters of Our Court of Chancery for the Time being, unto which Master of Chancery, We do by these Presents give full Power and Authority to administer the Oath to the said John Winthrop accordingly: And the said John Mason,

who is herein before nominated and appointed the present Deputy-Governor of the said Company, shall take Math before the said John Winthrop, or any Two of the Assistants of the said Company, unto whom We do by these Presents give full Power and Authority to administer the said Oath to the said John Mason accordingly: And the said Saqnnel Wyllys, Henry Clerice, Matthew Allyn, John Tapping, Nathan Cold, Richard Treat, Richard Lord, Henry Wolcott, John Talcott, Daniel Clerke, John Ogden, and Thomas Wells, who are herein before nominated and appointed the present Assistants of the said Company, shall take the Oath before the said John Winthrop, and John Mason, or One of them, to whom We do hereby give full Power and Authority to administer the same accordingly.

And Our further Will and Pleasure is, that all and every Governor, or Deputy-Governor to be elected and chosen by Virtue of these Presents, shall take the said Oath before Two or more of the Assistants of the said Company for the Time being, unto whom We do by these Presents give full Power and Authority to give and administer the said Oath accordingly; and the said Assistants, and every of them, and all and every other Officer or Officers to be here after chosen from Time to Time, to take the said Oath before the Governor, or Deputy-Governor for the Time being, unto which Governor, or Deputy-Governor, We do by these Presents give full Power and Authority to administer the same accordingly. And further, Of Our more ample Grace, certain Knowledge, and meer Motion, We have given and granted, and by these presents for Us, Our Heirs and Successors, do give and grant unto the said Governor and Company of the English Colony of Connecticut, in New England, in America, and to every Inhabitant there, and to every Person and Persons trading thither, and to every such Person and Persons as are or shall be Free of the said Colony, full Power and Authority from Time to Time, and at all Times hereafter, to take Ship, Transport and carry away for and towards the Plantation and Defence of the said Colony, such of Our loving Subjects and Strangers, as shall or will willingly accompany them in, and to their said Colony and Plantation, except such Person and Persons as are or shall be therein restrained by Us, Our Heirs and Successors; and also to ship and transport all, and all Manner of Goods, Chattels, Merchandises, and other Things whatsoever that are or shall be useful or necessary for the Inhabitants of the said Colony, and may lawfully be transported thither; Nevertheless, not to be discharged of Payment to Us, our Heirs and Successors, of the Duties, Customs and Subsidies which are or ought to be paid or payable for the same.

And further, Our Will and Pleasure is, and We do for Us, Our Heirs and Successors, ordain, declare, and grant unto the said Governor and Company, and their Successors, That all, and every the Subjects of Us, Our Heirs, or

Successors, which shall go to inhabit within the said Colony, and every of their Children, which shall happen to be born there, or on the Seas in going thither, or returning from thence, shall have and enjoy all Liberties and Immunities of free Did natural Subjects within any the Dominions of Us, Our Heirs or Successors, to all Intents, Constructions and Purposes whatsoever, as if the they and every of them were born within the realm of England; And We do authorize and impower the Governor or in his Absence the Deputy governor for the Time being, to appoint Two or more of the said Assistants at any of their Courts or Assemblies to be held as aforesaid, to have Power and Authority to administer the Oath of Supremacy and Obedience to all and every Person or Persons which shall at any Time or Times hereafter go or pass into the said Colony of Connecticut, unto which said Assistants so to be appointed as aforesaid We do by these Presents give full Power and Authority to administer the said Oath accordingly. And We do further of Our especial Grace, certain Knowledge: and meer Motion, give, and grant unto the said Governor and Company of the English Colony of Connecticut, in New-England, in America, and their Successors, That it shall and may be lawful to and for the Governor, or Deputy-Governor, and such of the Assistants of the said Company for the Time being as shall be assembled in any of the General Courts aforesaid, or in any Courts to be especially summoned or assembled for that Purpose, or the greater part of them, whereof the Governor, or Deputy-Governor, and Six of the Assistants to be always Seven, to erect and make such Judicatories, for the hearing, and determining of all Actions, Causes, Matters, and Things happening within the said Colony, or Plantation, and which shall be in Dispute, and Depending there, as they shall think Fit, and Convenient, and also from Time to Time to Make, Ordain, and Establish all manner of wholesome, and reasonable Laws Statutes, Ordinances, Directions, and Instructions, not Contrary to the Laws of this Realm of England, as well for settling the Forms, and Ceremonies of Government, and Magistracy, fit and necessary for the said Plantation, and the Inhabitants there, as for Naming, and Stiling all Sorts of Officers, both Superior and Inferior, which they shall find Needful for the Government, and Plantation of the said Colony, and the distinguishing and setting forth of the several Duties, Powers, and Limits of every such Office and Place, and the Forms of such Oaths not being contrary to the Laws and Statutes of this Our Realm of England, to be administered for the Execution of the said several Offices and Places as also for the disposing and ordering of the Election of such of the said Officers as are to be annually chosen, and of such others as shall succeed in case of Death or Removal, and administring the said Oath to the newly-elected Officers, and granting necessary Commissions, and for Imposition of lawful Fines, Mulcts. Imprisonment or other Punish-

ment upon Offenders and Delinquents according to the Curse of other Corporations within this our Kingdom of England, and the same Laws, Fines, Mulcts and Executions, to alter, change, revoke, annul, release, or pardon under their Common Seal, as by the said General Assembly, or the major Part of them shall be thought fit, and for the directing, ruling and disposing of all other Matters and things, whereby Our said People Inhabitants there, may be so religiously, peaceably and civilly governed, as their good Life and orderly Conversation may win and invite the Natives of the Country to the Knowledge and Obedience of the only true GOD, and He Saviour of Mankind, and the Christian Faith, which in Our Royal Intentions, and the adventurers free Possession, is the only and principal End of this Plantation; willing, commanding and requiring, and by these Presents for Us, Our Heirs and Successors, ordaining and appointing, that all such Laws, Statutes and Ordinances, Instructions, Impositions and Directions as shall be so made by the Governor, Deputy-Governor, and Assistants as aforesaid, and published in Writing under their Common Seal, shall carefully and duly be observed, kept, performed, and put in Execution, according to the true Intent and Meaning of The same, and these Our Letters Patents, or the Duplicate, or Exemplification thereof, shall be to all and every such Officers, Superiors and Inferiors from Time to Time, for the putting of the same Orders, Laws, Statutes, Ordinances, Instructions, and Directions in due Execution, against Us, Our Heirs and Successors, a sufficient Warrant and Discharge.

And We do further for Us, Our Heirs and Successors, give and grant unto the said Governor and Company, and their Successors, by these Presents, That it shall and may be lawful to, and for the Chief Commanders, Governors and Officers of the said Company for the Time being, who shall be resident in the Parts of New-England hereafter mentioned, and others inhabiting there, by their Leave, Admittance Appointment, or Direction, from Time to Time, and at All Times hereafter, for their special Defence and Safety, to Assemble, Martial-Array, and put in warlike Posture the Inhabitants of the said Colony, and to Commissionate, Impower, and Authorize such Person or Persons as they shall think fit, to lead and conduct the said Inhabitants, and to encounter, expulse, repel and resist by Force of Arms, as well by Sea as by Land, and also to kill, slay, and destroy by all fitting Ways Enterprises, and Means whatsoever, all and every such Person or Persons as shall at any Time hereafter attempt or enterprise the Destruction, Invasion, Detriment, or Annoyance of the said Inhabitants or Plantation, and to use and exercise the Law Martial in such Cases only as Occasion shall require; and to take or surprize by all Ways and Means whatsoever, all and every such Person and Persons, with their Ships' Armour, Ammunition and other Goods of such as shall in such hostile Manner invade or attempt the defeating of the said Plantation, or the hurt of the said Company and Inhabitants, and upon just Causes to invade and destroy the Natives, or other Enemies of the said Colony. Nevertheless; Our Will and Pleasure is, and We do hereby declare unto all Christian Icings, Princes, and States, that if any Persons which shall hereafter lie of the said Company or Plantation, or any other by Appointment of the said Governor and Company for the Time being, shall at anv Time or Times hereafter rob or spoil by Sea or by Land, and do any Hurt, Violence, or unlawful Hostility to any of the Subjects of Us, Our Heirs or Successors, or any of the Subjects of any Prince or State, being then in League with Us, Our Heirs or Successors, upon Complaint of such Injury done to any such Prince or State, or their Subjects, We, Our Heirs and Successors will make open Proclamation within any Parts of Our Realm of England fit for that Purpose, thin the Person or Persons committing any such Robbery or Spoil, shall within the Time limited by such Proclamation, make full Restitution or Satisfaction of all such Injuries Lone or committed, so as the Said Prince, or others so complaining may be fully satisfied and contented; and if the said Person or Persons who shall commit any such Robbery or Spoil shall not make Satisfaction accordingly, within such Time so to be limited, that then it shall and may be lawful for Us, Our Heirs and Successors, to put such Person or Persons out of (whir Allegiance and Protection; and that it shall and may be lawful and free for all Princes or others to prosecute with Hostility such Offenders, and every of them, their, and every of their Procurers, Aiders, Abettors and Counsellors in that Behalf.

Provided also, and Our express Will and Pleasure is, and We do by these Presents for Us, Our Heirs and Successors, Ordain and Appoint, that these Presents shall not in any Manner hinder any of Our loving Subjects whatsoever to use and exercise the Trade of Fishing upon the Coast of New-England, in America, but they and every or any of them shall have full and free Power and Liberty, to continue, and use the said Trade of Fishing upon the said Coast, in any of the Seas thereunto adjoining, or any Arms of the Seas, or Salt Water Rivers where they have been accustomed to fish, and to build and set up on the. waste Land belonging to the said Colony of Connecticut, such Wharves, Stages, and Work-Houses as shall be necessary for the salting, drying, and keeping of their Fish to be taken, or gotten upon that Coast, any Thing in these Presents contained to the contrary notwithstanding. And Know Ye further, That We, of Our abundant Grace, certain Knowledge, and mere Motion, have given, granted, and confirmed, and by these Presents for Us, our Heirs and Successors, do give, grant and confirm unto the said Governor and Company, and their Successors, all that Part of Our Dominions in New-England in America, bounded on the East by Narraganset-River, commonly called Narraganset-Bay, where the said River falleth into the Sea; and on the North by the Line of the If Massachusetts-Plantation; and on the South by the Sea; and in Longitude as the Line of the Massachusetts-Colony, running from East to West, That is to say, From the said Narraganset-Bay on the East, to the South Sea on the West Part, with the Islands thereunto adjoining, together with all firm Lands, Soils, Grounds, Havens, Ports, Rivers, Waters, Dishings, Mines, Minerals, precious Stones, Quarries, and all and singular other Commodities, Jurisdictions, Royalties, Privileges, Franchises, Preheminences, and Hereditaments whatsoever, within the said Tract, Bounds, Lands, and Islands aforesaid, or to them or any of them belonging. To have and to hold the same unto the said Governor and Company, their Successors and Assigns for ever, upon Trust, and for the Use and Benefit of Themselves and their Associates, Freemen of the said Colony, their Heirs and Assigns, to be holden of Its, Our Heirs and Successors, as of Our Manor of East-Greenwich, in free and common Soccage, and not in Capite, nor by Knights Service, yielding and paying therefore to Us, Our Heirs and Successors, only the Fifth Part of all the Ore of Gold add Silver which from Time to Time, and at all Times hereafter, shall be there gotten, had, or obtained, in Lieu of all Services, Duties, and Demands whatsoever, to be to Us, our Heirs, or Successors therefore, or thereout rendered, made, or paid. And lastly, We do for Us, our Heirs and Successors, grant to the said Governor and Company, and their Successors, by these Presents, That these Our Letters Patents, shall be firm, good and effectual in the Law, to all Intents, Constructions, and Purposes whatsoever according to Our true Intent and Meaning herein before declared, as shall be construed, reputed and adjudged most favourable on the Behalf, and for the best Benefit, and Behoof of the said Governor and Company, and their Successors, although express Mention of the true Yearly Value or Certainty of the Premises, or of any of them, or of any other Gifts or Grants by Us, or by any of Our Progenitors, or Predecessors, heretofore made to the said Governor and Company of the English Colony of Connecticut, in New-England, in America, aforesaid, in these Presents is not made, or any Statute, Act, Ordinance, Provision, Proclamation, or Restriction heretofore had, made, enacted, ordained, or provided, or any other Matter, Cause, or Thing whatsoever, to the contrary thereof, in any wise notwithstanding. In Witness whereof, We have caused these Our Letters to be made Patents. Witness Ourself at Westminster, the Three and Twentieth Day of April, in the Fourteenth Year of our Reign.

By Writ of Privy Seal,
Howard

Source:
Francis Newton Thorpe, ed. *The Federal and State Constitutions, Colonial Charters, and Other Organic Laws of the States, Territories, and Colonies Now or Heretofore Forming the United States of America.* Washington, D.C.: Government Printing Office, 1909.

Charter of Carolina, 1663

A proprietary charter granting land to eight English noblemen by King Charles II in 1663 in return for their support during his bid to regain the throne from the Puritan rule of Oliver Cromwell. The area covered by the charter was enormous. The southern boundary lay near modern-day Cape Canaveral, Florida, and ran north to Albemarle Sound in North Carolina. The colony was bordered on the west by the as yet undiscovered "South Seas," which the English thought were located just beyond the Appalachian Mountains. The "Lords Proprietors" held absolute power in the colony. They designated the type of government to be installed and appointed all colonial officials. The lords of Carolina, however, ruled in absentia, and their distance from the everyday workings of the colony created tension between the settlers and the colonial governors. The Culpepper Rebellion erupted in 1677 when a group of Albemarle settlers deposed their governor and established their own council. Indian wars and piracy on the coastal towns further eroded adherence to English laws, which did not provide adequate protection from these dangers. By 1729 the heirs of the Lords Proprietors had sold their interests in the colony back to the Crown, and Carolina became a royal colony.

CHARLES the Second, by the grace of God, king of England, Scotland, France, and Ireland, Defender of the Faith, &c., To all to whom these present shall come: Greeting:

1st

Whereas our right trusty, and right well beloved cousins and counsellors, Edward Earl of Clarendon, our high chancellor of England, and George Duke of Albemarle, master of our horse and captain general of all our forces, our right trusty and well beloved William Lord Craven, John Lord Berkley, our right trusty and well beloved counsellor, Anthony Lord Ashley, chancellor of our exchequer, Sir George Carteret, knight and baronet, vice chamberlain of our household, and our trusty and well beloved Sir William Berkley, knight, and Sir John Colleton, knight and baronet, being excited with a laudable and pious zeal for the propagation of the Christian faith, and the enlargement of our empire and dominions, have humbly besought leave of us, by their industry and charge, to transport and make an ample colony of our subjects, natives of our kingdom of England, and elsewhere within our dominions, unto a certain country hereafter described, in the parts of America not yet cultivated or planted, and only inhabited by some barbarous people, who have no knowledge of Almighty God.

2d

And whereas the said Edward Earl of Clarendon, George Duke of Albemarle, William Lord Craven, John Lord Berkley, Anthony Lord Ashley, Sir George Carteret, Sir William Berkley, and Sir John Colleton have humbly besought us to give, grant and confirm unto them and their heirs, the said country, with priviledges and jurisdictions requisite for the good government and safety thereof: Know ye, therefore, that we, favouring the pious and noble purpose of the said Edward Earl of Clarendon, George Duke of Albemarle, William Lord Craven, John Lord Berkley, Anthony Lord Ashley, Sir George Carteret, Sir William Berkley, and Sir John Colleton, of our special grace, certain knowledge and meer motion, have given, granted atoll confirmed, and by this our present charter, for us, our heirs and successors, do give, grant and confirm unto the said Edward Earl of Clarendon, George Duke of Albemarle, William Lord Craven, Atolls Lord Berkley, Anthony Lord Ashley, Sir George Carteret, Sir William Berkley, and Sir John Colleton, their heirs and assigns, all that territory or tract of ground, scituate, lying and being within our dominions of America, extending from the north end of the island called Lucke island, which lieth in the southern Virginia seas, and within six and thirty degrees of the northern latitude, and to the west as far as the south seas, and so southerly as far as the river St. Matthias, which bordereth upon the coast of Florida, and within one and thirty degrees of northern latitude, and so west in a direct line as far as the south seas aforesaid; together with all and singular ports, harbours, bays, rivers, isles and islets belonging to the country aforesaid; and also all the soil, lands, fields, woods, mountlills, fields, lakes, rivers, bays and islets, scituate or being within the bounds or limits aforesaid, with the fishing of all sorts of fish, whales, sturgeons and all other royal fishes in the sea, bays, islets and rivers within the premises, and the fish therein taken; and moreover all veins, mines, quarries, as well discovered as not discovered, of gold, silver, gems, precious stones, and all other whatsoever, be it of stones, metals, or any other thing whatsoever, found or to be found within the countries, isles and limits aforesaid.

3d

And furthermore, the patronage and advowsons of all the churches and chappels, which as Christian religion shall increase within the country, isles, islets and limits aforesaid, shall happen hereafter to be erected, together with license and power to build and found churches, chappels and oratories, in convenient and fit places, within the said bounds and limits, and to cause them to be dedicated and consecrated according to the ecclesiastical laws of our kingdom of England, together with all and singular the like, and as ample rights, jurisdictions, priviledges, prerogatives, royalties, liberties, immunities and franchises of what kind soever, within the countries, isles, islets and limits aforesaid.

4th

To have, use, exercise and enjoy, and in as ample manner as any bishop of Durham in our kingdom of England, ever heretofore have held, used or enjoyed, or of right ought or could have, use, or enjoy. And them, the said Edward Earl of Clarendon, George Duke of Albemarle, William Lord Craven, John Lord Berkley, Anthony Lord Ashley, Sir George Carteret, Sir William Berkley, and Sir John Colleton, their heirs and assigns, we do by these presents, for us, our heirs and successors, make, create and constitute the true and absolute Lords Proprietors of the country aforesaid, and of all other the premises; saving always the faith, allegiance and sovereign dominion due to us, our heirs and successors, for the same, and saving also the right, title and interest of all and every our subjects of the English nation, which are now planted within the limits and bounds aforesaid (if any be). To have, hold, possess and enjoy the said country, isles, islets, and all and singular other the premises, to them the said Edward Earl of Clarendon, George Duke of Albemarle, William Lord Craven, John Lord Berkley, Anthony Lord Ashley, Sir George Carteret, Sir William Berkley, Sir John Colleton, their heirs and assigns forever, to be holden of us, our heirs and successors, as of our manner of East Greenwich in our county of Kent, in free and common soccage, and not in capite, or by knight service; yielding and paying yearly to us, our heirs and successors, for the same, the yearly rent of twenty marks of lawful money of England, at the feast of All Saints, yearly forever, the first payment thereof to begin and to be made on the feast of All Saints, which shall be in the year of our Lord one thousand six hundred and sixty-five, and also the fourth part of all gold or silver ore, which, within the limits aforesaid, shall from time to time happen to be found.

5th

And that the country, thus by us granted and described, may be dignified by us with as large titles and priviledges as any other part of our dominions and territories in that region, Know ye, that we of our further grace, certain knowledge, and meer motion, have thought fit to erect the same tract of ground, county, and island, into a province, and out of the fulness of our royal power and prerogative, we do, for us, our heirs and successors, erect, incorporate and ordain the same into a province, and call it the Province of Carolina, and so from henceforth will have it called; and forasmuch as we have hereby made and ordained the aforesaid Edward Earl of Clarendon, George Duke of Albemarle, William Lord Craven, John Lord Berkley, Anthony Lord Ashley, Sir George Carteret, Sir William Berkley, and Sir John Colleton, their heirs and assigns, the true lords and proprietors of all the province aforesaid; Know ye, therefore moreover that we, reposing especial trust and confidence in their fidelity, wisdom, justice and provident circumspection, for us, our heirs and successors, do grant full and absolute power, by virtue of these presents, to them the said Edward Earl of Clarendon, George Duke of Albemarle, William Lord Craven, John Lord Berkley, Anthony Lord Ashley, Sir George Carteret, Sir William Berkley, and Sir John Colleton, and their heirs, for the good and happy government of the said province, to ordain, make, enact, and under their seals to publish any laws whatsoever, either appertaining to the publick state of the said province, or to the private utility of particular persons, according to their best discretion, of and with the advice, assent and approbation of the freemen of the said province, or of the greater part of them, or of their delegates or deputies, whom for enacting of the said laws, when and as often as need shall require, we will that the said Edward Earl of Clarendon, George Duke of Albemarle, William Lord Craven, John Lord Berkley, Anthony Lord Ashley, Sir George Carteret, Sir William Berkley, and Sir John Colleton, and their heirs, shall from time to time assemble in such manner and form as to them shall seem best, and the same laws duly to execute upon all people within the said province and limits thereof, for the time being, or which shall be constituted under the power and government of them or any of them, either sailing towards the said province of Carolina, or returning from thence towards England, or any other of our, or foreign dominions, by imposition of penalties, imprisonment or any other punishment; yea, if it shall be needful!, and the quality of the offence requires it, by taking away member and life, either by them, the said Edward Earl of Clarendon, George Duke of Albemarle, William Lord Craven, John Lord Berkley, Anthony Lord Ashley, Sir George Carteret, Sir William Berkley, and Sir John Colleton, and their heirs, or by them or their deputies, lieutenants, judges, justices, magistrates, officers and members to be ordained or appointed according to the tenor and true intention of these presents; and likewise to appoint and establish any judges or justices, magistrates or officers whatsoever, within the said province, at sea or land, in such manner and form as unto the said Edward Earl of Clarendon, George Duke of Albemarle, William Lord Craven, John Lord Berkley, Anthony Lord Ashley, Sir George Carteret, Sir William Berkley, and Sir John Colleton and their heirs shall seem most convenient; also, to remit, release, pardon and abolish (whether before judgment or after) all crimes and offences whatsoever, against the said laws, and to do all and every other thing and things, which unto the compleat establishment of Justice unto courts, sessions, and forms of judicature and manners of proceedings therein do belong, although in these presents express mention be not made thereof; and by judges and by him or them delegated, to award process, hold pleas, and determine in all the said courts, and places of judicature, all actions, suits and causes whatsoever, as well criminal or civil, real, mixt, personal, or of any other kind or nature whatsoever; which laws, so as aforesaid to be published, our pleasure is, and we do require, enjoin and command, shall be absolute, firm and available in law, and that all the liege people of us, our heirs and successors, within the said province of Carolina, do observe and keep the same inviolably in those parts, so far as they concern them, under the pains and penalties therein expressed, or to be expressed: *Provided nevertheless*, that the said lavrs be consonant to reason, and as near as may be conveniently, agreeable to the laws and customs of this our kingdom of England.

6th

And because such assemblies of freeholders cannot be so conveniently called, as there may be occasion to require the same, we do, therefore, by these presents, give and grant unto the said Edward Earl of Clarendon, George Duke of Albemarle, William Lord Craven, John Lord Berkley, Anthony Lord Ashley, Sir George Carteret, Sir William Berkley, and Sir John Colleton, their heirs and assigns, by themselves or their magistrates, in that behalf lawfully authorized full power and authority from time to time to make and ordain fit and wholesome orders and ordinances, within the province aforesaid to be kept and observed as well for the keeping of the peace, as for the better government of the people there abiding, and to publish the same to all to whom it may concern; which ordinances, we do by these presents straightly charge and command to be inviolably observed within the said province, under the penalties therein expressed, so as such ordinances be reasonable, and not repugnant or contrary, but as near as may be, agreeable to the laws and statutes of this our kingdom of England, and so as the same ordinances do not extend to the binding, charging, or taking away of the right or interest of any person or persons, in their freehold, goods or chattels whatsoever.

7th

And to the end the said province may be more happily increased, by the multitude of people resorting thither, and may likewise be the more strongly defended from the incursions of salvages and other enemies, pirates and robbers, therefore we, for us, our heirs and successors, do give

and grant by these presents, power, license and liberty unto all the liege people of us, our heirs and successors in our kingdom of England or elsewhere, within any other our dominions, islands, colonies or plantations, (excepting those who shall be especially forbidden,) to transport themselves and families unto the said province, with convenient shipping and fitting provisions, and there to settle themselves, dwell and inhabit, any law, statute, act, ordinance, or other thing to the contrary in any wise notwithstanding. And we will also, and of our more special grace, for us, our heirs and successors, do straightly enjoin, ordain, constitute and command, that the said province of Carolina, shall be of our allegiance, and that all and singular the subjects and liege people of us, our heirs and successors, transported or to be transported into the said province, and the children of them and of such as shall descend from them, there born or hereafter to be born, be and shall be denizens and lieges of us, our heirs and successors of this our kingdom of England, and be in all things held, treated, and reputed as the liege faithful people of us, our heirs and successors, born within this our said kingdom, or any other of our dominions, and may inherit or otherwise purchase and receive, take, hold, buy and possess any lands, tenements or hereditaments within the same places, and them may occupy, possess and enjoy, give, sell, aliene and bequeathe; as likewise all liberties. franchises and priviledges of this our kingdom of England, and of other our dominions aforesaid, and may freely and quietly have, possess and enjoy, as our liege people born within the same, without the least molestation, vexation, trouble or grievance of us, our heirs and successors, any statute, act, ordinance, or provision to the contrary notwithstanding.

8th

And furthermore, that our subjects of this our said kingdom of England, and other our dominions, may be the rather encouraged to undertake this expedition with ready and cheerful minds, know ye, that we of our special grace, certain knowledge and meer motion, do give and grant by virtue of these presents, as well to the said Edward Earl of Clarendon, George Duke of Albemarle, William Lord Craven, John Lord Berkley, Anthony Lord Ashley, Sir George Carteret, Sir William Berkley, and Sir John Colleton, and their heirs, as unto all others as shall from time to time repair unto the said province, with a purpose to inhabit there, or to trade with the natives of the said province, full liberty and license to lade and freight in any port whatsoever, of us, our heirs and successors, and into the said province of Carolina, by them, their servants or assigns, to transport all and singular their goods, wares and merchandises, as likewise all sorts of grain whatsoever, and any other things whatsoever, necessary for the food and clothing, not prohibited by the laws and statutes of our kingdoms and dominions, to be carried out of the same, without any let or molestation of us, our heirs and successors, or of any other of our officers, or ministers whatsoever, saving also to us, our heirs and successors, the customs and other duties and payments, due for the said wares and merchandises, according to the several rates of the places from whence the same shall be transported. We will also, and by these presents, for us, our heirs and successors, do give and grant license by this our charter, unto the said Edward Earl of Clarendon, George Duke of Albemarle, William Lord Craven, John Lord Berkley, Anthony Lord Ashley, Sir George Carteret, Sir William Berkley, and Sir John Colleton, their heirs and assigns, and to all the inhabitants and dwellers in the province aforesaid, both present and to come, full power and absolute authority to import or unlace by themselves or their servants, factors or assigns, all merchandises and goods whatsoever, that shall arise of the fruits and commodities of the said province, either by land or by sea, into any of the ports of us, our heirs and successors, in our kingdom of England, Scotland or Ireland, or otherwise to dispose of the said goods, in the said ports; and if need be, within one year next after the unfading, to lade the said merchandises and goods again into the same or other ships, and to export the same into any other countries either of our dominions, or foreign being in amity with us, our heirs and successors, so as they pay such customs, subsidies, and other duties for the same, to us, our heirs and successors, as the rest of our subjects of this our kingdom, for the time being, shall be bound to pay, beyond which we will not, that the inhabitants of the said province of Carolina, shall be any ways charged.

9th

Provided nevertheless, and our will and pleasure is, and we have further for the consideration aforesaid, of our more especial grace, certain knowledge, and meer motion, given and granted, and by these presents, for us, our heirs and successors, do give and grant unto the said Edward Earl of Clarendon, George Duke of Albemarle, William Lord Craven, John Lord Berkley, Anthony Lord Ashley, Sir George Carteret, Sir William Berkley and Sir John Colleton, their heirs and assigns, full and free license, liberty and authority, at any time or times, from and after the feast of St. Michael the archangel, which shall be in the year of our Lord Christ, one thousand six hundred sixty and seven, as well to import, and bring into any of our dominions from the said province of Carolina, or any part thereof, the several goods and commodities, hereinafter mentioned, that is to say, silks, wines, currants, raisins, capers, wax, almonds, oyl and olives, without paying or answering to us, our heirs or successors, any custom, import, or other duty, for and in respect thereof, for and during the term and space of seven years, to commence and be accompted, from and after the first importation of four tons of any the said goods, in any one bottom, ship or vessel from the said

province, into any of our dominions, as also to export and carry out of any of our dominions, into the said province of Carolina, custom free, all sorts of tools which shall be usefull or necessary for the planters there, in the accommodation and improvement of the premises, any thing before, in these presents contained, or any law, act, statute, prohibition or other matter, or anything heretofore had, made, enacted or provided, or hereafter to be had, made, enacted or provided, to the contrary, in any wise notwithstanding.

10th

And furthermore, of our own ample and especial grace, certain knowledge, and meer motion, we do for us, our heirs and successors, grant unto the said Edward Earl of Clarendon, George Duke of Albemarle, William Lord Craven, John Lord Berkley, Anthony Lord Ashley, Sir George Carteret, Sir William Berkley and Sir John Colleton, their heirs and assigns, full and absolute power and authority to make erect and constitute, within the said province of Carolina, and the isles and islets aforesaid, such and so many seaports, harbours, creeks and other places, for discharge and unlading of goods and merchandises, out of ships, boats and other vessels, and for lading of them, in such and so many places, and with such jurisdiction, priviledges and franchises unto the said ports belonging, as to them shall seem most expedient, and that all and singular the ships, boats and other vessels, which shall come for merch an rises and trade into the said province, or shall depart out of the same, shall be laden and unladen at such ports only, as shall be erected and constituted by the said Edward Earl of Clarendon, George Duke of Albemarle, William Lord Craven, Jolm Lord Berkley, Anthony Lord Ashley, Sir George Carteret, Sir William Berkley, and Sir John Colleton, their heirs and assigns, and not elsewhere, any use, custom or any other thing to the contrary, in any wise notwithstanding.

11th

And we do furthermore will, appoint and ordain, and by these presents for us, our heirs and successors, do grant unto the said Edward Earl of Clarendon, George Duke of Albemarle, William Lord Craven, John Lord Berkley, Anthony Lord Ashley, Sir George Carteret, Sir William Berkley and Sir John Colleton, their heirs and assigns, that they the said Edward Earl of Clarendon, George Duke of Albemarle, William Lord Craven, John Lord Berkley, Anthony Lord Ashley, Sir George Carteret, Sir William Berkley and Sir John Colleton, their heirs and assigns, may from time to time forever, have and enjoy, the customs and subsidies in the ports, harbors, creeks and other places within the province aforesaid, payable for goods, merchandise and wares, there laded or to be laded, or unjaded, the said customs to be reasonably assessed, upon any occasion, by themselves, and by and with the consent of the free people there, or the greater part of them as aforesaid; to whom we give power bv these presents, for us, our heirs and successors, upon just cause and in a due proportion, to assess and impose the same.

12th

And further, of our special grace, certain knowledge, and meer motion, we have given, granted and confirmed, and by these presents, for us, our heirs and successors, do give, grant and confirm unto the said Edward Earl of Clarendon, George Duke of Albemarle, William Lord Craven, John Lord Berkley, Anthony Lord Ashley, Sir George Carteret, Sir William Berkley, and Sir John Colleton, their heirs and assigns, full and absolute license, power and authority, that the said Edward Earl of Clarendon, George Duke of Albemarle, William Lord Craven, John Lord Berkley, Anthony Lord Ashley, Sir George Carteret, Sir William Berkley, Sir John Colleton, their heirs and assigns, from time to time, hereafter, forever, at his and their will and pleasure, may assign, alien, grant, demise or enfeof the premises, or any part or parcels thereof, to him or them that shall be willing to purchase the same, and to such person or persons as they shall think fit, to have and to hold, to them the said person or persons, their heirs or assigns, in fee simple or fee tayle, or for term for life, or lives, or years, to be held of them, the said Edward Earl of Clarendon, George Duke of Albemarle, William Lord Craven, John Lord Berkley, Anthony Lord Ashley, Sir George Carteret, Sir William Berkley and Sir John Colleton, their heirs and assigns, by such rents, services and customs, as shall seem meet to the said Edward Earl of Clarendon, George Duke of Albemarle, William Lord Craven, John Lord Berkley, Anthony Lord Ashley, Sir George Carteret, Sir William Berkley, and Sir John Colleton, their heirs and assigns, and not immediately of us, our heirs and successors, and to the same person and persons, and to all and every of them, we do give and grant by these presents, for us, our heirs and successors, license, authority and power, that such person or persons, may have or take the premises, or any parcel thereof, of the said Edward Earl of Clarendon, George Duke of Albemarle, William Lord Craven, John Lord Berkley, Anthony Lord Ashley, Sir George Carteret, Sir William Berkley, and Sir John Colleton, their heirs and assigns, and the same to hold, to themselves, their heirs or assigns, in what estate of inheritance whatsoever, in fee simple, or fee tayle, or otherwise, as to them and the said Edward Earl of Clarendon, George Duke of Albemarle, William Lord Craven, John Lord Berkley, Anthony Lord Ashley, Sir George Carteret, Sir William Berkley, and Sir John Colleton, their heirs and assigns, shall seem expedient; the statute made in the parliament of Edward, son of King Henry, heretofore king of England, our predecessor, commonly called the statute of *"quia emptores terrarum;"* or any other statute, act, ordi-

nance, use, law, custom or any other matter, cause or thing heretofore published, or provided to the contrary, in any wise notwithstanding.

13th

And because many persons born, or inhabiting in the said province, for their deserts and services, may expect and be capable of marks of honor and favor, which, in respect of the great distance, cannot be conveniently conferred by us; our will and pleasure therefore is, and we do by these presents, give and grant unto the said Edward Earl of Clarendon, George Duke of Albemarle, William Lord Craven, John Lord Berkley, Anthony Lord Ashley, Sir George Carteret, Sir William Berkley, and Sir John Colleton, their heirs and assigns, full power and authority, to give and confer, unto and upon, such of the inhabitants of the said province, as they shall think do or shall merit the same, such marks of favour and titles of honour as they shall think fit so as these titles of honour be not the same as ale enjoyed by, or conferred upon any the subjects of this our kingdom of England.

14th

And further also, we do by these presents, for us, our heirs and successors, give and grant license to them, the said Edward Earl of Clarendon, George Duke of Albemarle, William Lord Craven, John Lord Berkley, Anthony Lord Ashley, Sir George Carteret, Sir William Berkley, and Sir John Colleton, their heirs and assigns, full power, liberty and license to erect, raise and build within the said province and places aforesaid, or any part or parts thereof, such and so many forts, fortresses, castles, cities, boroughs, towns, villages and other fortifications whatsoever, and the same or any of them to fortify and furnish with ordinance, powder, shot, armory, and all other weapons, ammunition, habilements of war, both offensive and defensive, as shall be thought fit and convenient for the safety and welfare of the said province and places, or any part thereof, and the same, or any of them from time to time, as occasion shall require, to dismantle, disfurnish, demolish and pull down, and also to place, constitute and appoint in and over all or any of the castles, forts, fortifications, cities, towns and places aforesaid, governors, deputy governors, magistrates, sheriffs and other officers, civil and military, as to them shall seem meet, and to the said cities, boroughs, towns, villages, or any other place or places within the said province, to grant "letters or charters of incorporation," with all liberties, franchises and priviledges, requisite and usefull, or to or within any corporations, within this our kingdom of England, granted or belonging; and in the same cities, boroughs, towns and other places, to constitute, erect and appoint such and so many markets, marts and fairs, as shall in that behalf be thought fit and necessary; and further also to erect and make in the province aforesaid, or any part thereof, so many mannors as to them shall seem meet and convenient, and in every of the said mannors to have and to hold a court baron, with all things whatsoever which to a court baron do belong, and to have and to hold views of "frank pledge" and "court leet," for the conservation of the peace and better government of those parts within such limits, jurisdictions, and precincts, as by the said Edward Earl of Clarendon, George Duke of Albemarle, William Lord Craven, John Lord Berkley, Anthony Lord Ashley, Sir George Carteret, Sir William Berkley and Sir John Colleton, or their heirs, shall be appointed for that purpose, with all things whatsoever, which to a court leet, or view of frank pledge do belong, the said court to be holden by stewards, to be deputed and authorized by the said Edward Earl of Clarendon, George Duke of Albemarle, William Lord Craven, John Lord Berkley, Anthony Lord Ashley, Sir George Carteret, Sir William Berkley, and Sir John Colleton, or their heirs, or by the lords of other manners and leets, for the time being, when the same shall be erected.

15th

And because that in so remote a country, and scituate among so many barbarous nations, and the invasions as well of salvages as of other enemies, pirates and robbers, may probably be feared; therefore we have given, and for us, our heirs and successors, do give power, by these presents, unto the said Edward Earl of Clarendon, George Duke of Albemarle, William Lord Craven, John Lord Berkley, Anthony Lord Ashley, Sir George Carteret, Sir William Berkley, and Sir John Colleton, their heirs and assigns, by themselves, or their captains, or other their officers, to levy, muster and train all sorts of men, of what condition or wheresoever born, in the said province for the time being, and to make war and pursue the enemies aforesaid, as well by sea as by land, yea, even without the limits of the said province, and by God's assistance to vanquish and take them, and being taken to put them to death by the law of war, or to save them at their pleasure; and to do all and every other thing, which unto the charge of a captain general of an army belongeth, or hath accustomed to belong, as fully and freely as any captain general of an army hath or ever had the same.

16th

Also our will and pleasure is, and by this our charter we give unto the said Edward Earl of Clarendon, George Luke of Albemarle, William Lord Craven, John Lord Berkley, Anthony Lord Ashley, Sir George Carteret, Sir William Berkley, and Sir John Colleton, their heirs and assigns, full power, liberty and authority, in case of rebellion, tumult or sedition, (if any should happen,) which God forbid, either upon the land within the province aforesaid,

or upon the main sea, in making a voyage thither, or returning from thence, by him or themselves, their captains, deputies and officers, to be authorized under his or their seals for that purpose, to whom also, for us, our heirs and successors, we do give and grant by these presents, full power and authority, to exercise martial law against mutinous and seditious persons of those parts, such as shall refuse to submit themselves to their government, or shall refuse to serve in the wars, or shall fly to the enemy, or forsake their colours or ensigns, or be loyterers or straglers, or otherwise howsoever offending against law, custom or discipline military, as freely and in as ample manner and form as any captain general of an army by vertue of his office, might or hath accustomed to use the same.

17th

And our further pleasure is, and by these presents, for us, our heirs and successors, we do grant unto the said Edward Earl of Clarendon, George Duke of Albemarle, William Lord Craven, John Lord Berkley, Anthony Lord Ashley, Sir George Carteret, Sir William Berkley, and Sir John Colleton, their heirs and assigns, and to all the tenants and inhabitants of the said province of Carolina, both present and to come, and to every of them, that the said province and the tenants and inhabitants thereof, shall not from henceforth be held or reputed a member or part of any colony whatsoever in America, or elsewhere, now transported or made, or hereafter to be transported or made; nor shall be depending on, or subject to their government in anything, but be absolutely seperated and divided from the same; and our pleasure is, by these presents, that they be seperated, and that they be subject immediately to our crown of England, as depending thereof forever; and that the inhabitants of the said Province, nor any of them, shall at any time hereafter be compelled or compellable, or be any ways subject or liable to appear or answer to any matter, suit, cause or plaint whatsoever, out of the Province aforesaid, in any other of our islands, colonies, or dominions in America or elsewhere, other than in our realm of England, and dominion of Wales.

18th

And because it may happen that some of the people and inhabitants of the said province, cannot in their private opinions, conform to the publick exercise of religion, according to the liturgy, form and ceremonies of the church of England, or take and subscribe the oaths and articles, made and established in that behalf, and for that the same, by reason of the remote distances of these places, will, we hope be no breach of the unity and uniformity established in this nation; our will and pleasure therefore is, and we do by these presents, for us, our heirs and successors, give and grant unto the said Edward Earl of Clarendon, George Duke of Albemarle, William Lord Craven, John Lord Berkley, Anthony Lord Ashley, Sir George Carteret, Sir William Berkley, and Sir John Colleton, their heirs and assigns, full and free license, liberty and authority, by such legal ways and means as they shall think fit, to give and grant unto such person or persons, inhabiting and being within the said province, or any part thereof, who really in their judgments, and for conscience sake, cannot or shall not conform to the said liturgy and ceremonies, and take and subscribe the oaths and articles aforesaid, or any of them, such indulgencies and dispensations in that behalf, for and during such time and times, and with such limitations and restrictions as they, the said Edward Earl of Clarendon, George Duke of Albemarle, William Lord Craven, John Lord Berkley, Anthony Lord Ashley, Sir George Carteret, Sir William Berkley, and Sir John Colleton, their heirs or assigns, shall in their discretion think fit and reasonable; and with this express proviso, and limitation also, that such person and persons, to whom such indulgencies and dispensations shall be granted as aforesaid, do and shall from time to time declare and continue, all fidelity, loyalty and obedience to us, our heirs and successors, and be subject and obedient to all other the laws, ordinances, and constitutions of the said province, in all matters whatsoever, as well ecclesiastical as civil, and do not in any wise disturb the peace and safety thereof, or scandalize or reproach the said liturgy, forms and ceremonies, or anything relating thereunto, or any person or persons whatsoever, for or in respect of his or their use or exercise thereof, or his or their obedience and conformity, thereunto.

19th

And in case it shall happen, that any doubts or questions should arise, concerning the true sense and understanding of any word, clause or sentence contained in this our present charter, we will, ordain and command, that at all times, and in all things, such interpretation be made thereof, and allowed in all and every of our courts whatsoever, as lawfully may be adjudged most advantageous and favourable to the said Edward Earl of Clarendon, George Duke of Albemarle, William Lord Craven, John Lord Berkley, Anthony Lord Ashley, Sir George Carteret, Sir William Berkley, and Sir John Colleton, their heirs and assigns, although express mention be not made in these presents, of the true yearly value and certainty of the premises, or any part thereof, or of any other gifts and grants made by us, our ancestors, or predecessors, to them the said Edward Earl of Clarendon, George Duke of Albemarle, William Lord Craven John Lord Berkley, Anthony Lord Ashley, Sir George Carteret, Sir William Berkley, and Sir John Colleton, or any other person or persons

whatsoever, or any statute, act, ordinance, provision, proclamation or restraint, heretofore had, made, published, ordained or provided, or any other thing, cause or matter, whatsoever, to the contrary thereof, in any wise notwithstanding.

In Witness, &c.

Witness the King, at Westminster, the four and twentieth day of March, in the fifteenth year of our reign, (1663.)

PER IPSUM REGEM.

Source:

Francis Newton Thorpe, ed. *The Federal and State Constitutions, Colonial Charters, and Other Organic Laws of the States, Territories, and Colonies Now or Heretofore Forming the United States of America.* Washington, D.C.: Government Printing Office, 1909.

Charter of Rhode Island and the Providence Plantations, 1663

Royal charter granted on July 8, 1663, by England's King Charles II to the confederation of Rhode Island and the Providence plantations. Secured by John Clarke, acting as Rhode Island's colonial agent, the charter replaced an earlier grant made in 1644. The 1663 charter established Rhode Island's western border, long disputed with Connecticut, at the Pawcatuck River; guaranteed religious freedom; and provided for an elected governor, deputy governor, assistants, and general assembly, with suffrage to be determined by the colony. The charter was kept throughout the colonial period and continued as Rhode Island's state constitution until 1842.

CHARLES THE SECOND, by the grace of God, King of England, Scotland, France and Ireland, Defender of the Faith, &c., to all to whome these presents shall come, greeting: Whereas wee have been informed, by the humble petition of our trustie and well beloved subject, John Clarke, on the behalf of Benjamine Arnold, William Brenton, William Codington, Nicholas Easton, William Boulston, John Porter, John Smith, Samuell Gorton, John Weeks, Roger Williams, Thomas Olnie, Gregorie Dexter, John Cogeshall, Joseph Clarke, Randall Holden, John Greene, John Roome, Samuell Wildbore, William Ffield, James Barker, Richard Tew, Thomas Harris, and William Dyre, and the rest of the purchasers and ffree inhabitants of our island, called Rhode-Island, and the rest of the colonie of Providence Plantations, in the Narragansett Bay, in New-England, in America, that they, pursueing, with peaceable and loyall minces, their sober, serious and religious intentions, of goalie edifieing themselves, and one another, in the holie Christian ffaith and worshipp as they were perswaded; together with the gaineing over and conversione of the poore ignorant Indian natives, in those partes of America, to the sincere professione and obedienc of the same ffaith and worship, did, not onlie by the consent and good encouragement of our royall progenitors, transport themselves out of this kingdome of England into America, but alsoe, since their arrivall there, after their first settlement amongst other our subjects in those parts, Nor the avoideing of discorde, and those manic evills which were likely to ensue upon some of those oure subjects not beinge able to beare, in these remote parties, theire different apprehensiones in religious concernements, and in pursueance of the afforesayd ends, did once againe leave theire desireable stationies and habitationes, and with excessive labour and travell, hazard and charge, did transplant themselves into the middest of the Indian natives, who, as wee are informed, are the most potent princes and people of all that country; where, by the good Providence of God, from whome the Plantationes have taken their name, upon theire labour and industrie, they have not onlie byn preserved to admiration, but have increased and prospered, and are seized and possessed, by purchase and consent of the said natives, to their ffull content, of such lands, islands, rivers, harbours and roades, as are verie convenient, both for plantationes and alsoe for buildings of shipps, suplye of pypestaves, and other merchandise; and which lyes verie commodious, in manic respects, for commerce, and to accommodate oure southern plantationes, and may much advance the trade of this oure realme, and greatlie enlarge the territories thereof; they haveinge, by neare neighbourhoode to and friendlie societie with the greate bodie of the Narragansett Indians, given them encouragement, of theire owne accorde, to subject themselves, theire people and lances, unto us; whereby, as is hoped, there may, in due tyme, by the blessing of God upon theire endeavours, bee layd a sure ffoundation of happinesse to all America:

And whereas, in theire humble addresse, they have ffreely declared, that it is much on their hearts (if they may be permitted), to hold forth a livlie experiment, that a most flourishing civill state may stand and best bee maintained, and that among our English subjects. with a full libertie in religious concernements; and that true pietye rightly grounded upon gospell principles, will give the best and greatest security to sovereignetye, and will lay in the hearts of men the strongest obligations to true loyaltye: Now know bee, that wee beinge willing to encourage the hopefull undertakeinge of oure sayd lovall and loveinge subjects, and to secure them in the free exercise and enjoyvment of all theire civill and religious rights, appertaining to them, as our loveing subjects; and to preserve

unto them that libertye, in the true Christian ffaith and worshipp of God, which they have sought with soe much travaill, and with peaceable myndes, and lovall subjectione to our royall progenitors and ourselves, to enjoye; and because some of the people and inhabitants of the same colonie cannot, in theire private opinions, conforms to the publique exercise of religion, according to the litturgy, formes and ceremonyes of the Church of England, or take or subscribe the oaths and articles made and established in that behalfe; and for that the same, by reason of the remote distances of those places, will (as wee hope) bee noe breach of the unitie and unifformitie established in this nation: Have therefore thought ffit, and doe hereby publish, graunt, ordeyne and declare, That our royall will and pleasure is, that noe person within the sayd colonye, at any tyme hereafter, shall bee any wise molested, punished, disquieted, or called in question, for any differences in opinione in matters of religion, and doe not actually disturb the civill peace of our sayd colony; but that all and everye person and persons may, from tyme to tyme, and at all tymes hereafter, freelye and fullye have and enjoye his and theire owne judgments and consciences, in matters of religious concernments, throughout the tract of lance hereafter mentioned; they behaving themselves peaceablie and quietlie, and not useing this libertie to lycentiousnesse and profanenesse, nor to the civill injurye or outward disturbeance of others; any lawe, statute, or clause, therein contayned, or to bee contayned, usage or custome of this realme, to the contrary hereof, in any wise, notwithstanding. And that they may bee in the better capacity to defend themselves, in theire just rights and libertyes against all the enemies of the Christian ffaith, and others, in all respects, wee have further thought fit, and at the humble petition of the persons aforesayd are gratiously pleased to declare, That they shall have and enjoye the benefist of our late act of indempnity and ffree pardon, as the rest of our subjects in other our dominions and territoryes have; and to create and make them a bodye politique or corporate, with the powers and priviledges hereinafter mentioned.

And accordingely our will and pleasure is, and of our especiall grace, certaine knowledge, and meere motion, wee have ordeyned, constituted and declared, and by these presents, for us, our heires and successors, doe ordeyne, constitute and declare, That they, the sayd William Brenton, William Codington, Nicholas Easton, Benedict Arnold, William Boulston, John Porter, Samuell Gorton, John Smith, John Weekes, Roger Williams, Thomas Olneye, Gregorie Dexter, John Cogeshall, Joseph Clarke, Randall Holden, John Greene, John Roome, William Dyre, Samuell Wildbore, Richard Tew, William Ffeild, Thomas Harris, James Barker, Rainsborrow,- Williams, and John Nicksonj and all such others as now are, or hereafter shall bee admitted and made ffree of the company and societie of our collonie of Providence Plantations, in the Narragansett Bay, in New England, shall bee, from tyme to tyme, and forever hereafter, a bodie corporate and politique, in fact and name, by the name of The Governor and Company of the English Colony of Rhode-Island and Providence Plantations, in New-England, in America; and that, by the same name, they and their successors shall and may have perpetuall succession, and shall and may bee persons able and capable, in the lawe, to sue and bee sued, to pleade and be impleaded, to answeare and bee answeared unto, to defend and to be defended, in all and singular suites, causes, quarrels, matters, actions and thinges, of what kind or nature soever; and alsoe to have, take, possessej acquire and purchase lands, tenements or hereditaments, or any goods or chattels, and the same to lease, graunt, demise, aliene, bargaine, sell and dispose of, at their owne will and pleasure, as other our liege people of this our realme of England, or anie corporation or bodie politique within the same, may be lawefully doe: And further, that they the sayd Governor and Company, and theire successors, shall and may, forever hereafter, have a common scale, to serve and use for all matters, causes, thinges and affaires, whatsoever, of them and their successors; and the same scale to alter, change, breake, and make new, from tyme to tyme, at their will and pleasure, as they shall thinke bitt.

And farther, wee will and ordeyne, and by these presents, for us, oure heires and successours, doe declare and apoynt that, for the better ordering and managing of the adaires and business of the sayd Company, and theire successours, there shall bee one Governour, one Deputie-Governour and ten Assistants, to bee from tyme to tyme, constituted, elected and chosen, out of the freemen of the sayd Company, for the tyme beinge, in such manner and fforme as is hereafter in these presents expressed; which sayd officers shall aplye themselves to take care for the best disposeinge and orderings of the generall businesse and adaires of, and concerneinge the lances and hereditaments hereinafter mentioned, to be graunted, and the plantation thereof and the government of the people there. And for the better execution of oure royall pleasure herein, wee doe, for us, oure heires and successours, assign, name, constitute and apoynt the aforesayd Benedict Arnold to bee the first and present Governor of the sayd Company, and the sayd William Brenton, to bee the Deputy-Governor, and the sayd William Boulston, John Porter, Roger Williams, Thomas Olnie, John Smith, John Greene, John Cogeshall, James Barker, William Ffeild, and Joseph Clarke, to bee the tenn present Assistants of the sayd Companye, to continue in the sayd severall offices, respectively, untill the first Wednesday which shall bee in the month of May now next comeing. And farther, wee will, and by these presents, for us, our heires and suc-

cessessours, doe ordeyne and graunt, that the Governor of the sayd Company, for the tyme being, or, in his absence, by occasion of sicknesse, or otherwise, by his leave and permission, the Deputy-Governor, For the tyme being, shall and may, ffrom tyme to tyme, upon all occasions, give order For the assemblinge of the sayd Company and callinge them together, to consult and advise of the businesse and affaires of the sayd Company.

And that forever hereafter, twice in every year, that is to say, on every first Wednesday in the month of May, and on every last Wednesday in October, or oftener, in case it shall bee requisite, the Assistants, and such of the ffreemen of the Company, not exceedings six persons For Newport, doure persons ffor each of the respective townes of Providence, Portsmouth and Warwicke, and two persons for each other place, towne or city, whoe shall bee, from tyme to tyme, thereunto elected or deputed by the majour parte of the ffreemen of the respective townes or places For which they shall bee so elected or deputed, shall have a generall meetings or Assembly then and there to consult, advise and determine, in and about the affaires and businesse of the said Company and Plantations. And farther, wee doe, of our especiall grace, certayne knowledge, and meere motion, give and graunt unto the sayd Governour and Company of the English Colonie of Rhode-lsland and Providence Plantations, in New-England, in America, and theire successours, that the Governour, or, in his absence, or, by his permission, the Deputy-Governour of the sayd Company, for the tyme beinge, the Assistants, and such of the Freemen of the sayd Company as shall bee soe as aforesayd elected or deputed, or soe many of them as shall bee present aft such meetinge or assemblye, as aBoresayde, shall bee called the Generall Assemblye; and that they, or the greatest parte of them present, whereof the Governour or Deputy-Governour, and six of the Assistants, at least to bee seven, shall have, and have hereby given and graunted unto them, ffull power authority, From tyme tyme, and at all tymes hereafter, to apoynt, alter and change, such dayes, tymes and places of meetinge and Generall Assemblye, as theye shall thinke ffitt; and to choose, nominate, and apoynt, such and soe manye other persons as they shall thinke ffitt, and shall be willing to accept the same, to bee Free of the sayd Company and body politique, and them into the same to admits; and to elect and constitute such offices and officers, and to graunt such needfull commissions, as they shall thinke Ott and requisite, ffor the ordering, managing and dispatching of the affaires of the sayd Governour and Company, and their successors; and from tyme to tyme, to make, ordeyne, constitute or repeal, such lawes statutes, orders and ordinances, fformes and ceremonies of government and magistracye as to them shall seeme meete for the good nad wellfare of the sayd Company, and ffor the government and ordering of the lances and hereditaments, hereinafter mentioned to be graunted, and of the people that doe, or aft any tyme hereafter shall, inhabitt or bee within the same; soe as such lawes, ordinances and constitutiones, soe made, bee not contrary and repugnant unto, butt, as neare as may bee, agreeable to the lawes of this our realme of England, considering the nature and constitutions of the place and people there; and alsoe to apoynt, order and direct, erect and settle, such places and courts of jurisdiction, ffor the heareinge and determillinge of all actions, cases, matters and things, happening within the sayd collonie and plantations, and which shall be in dispute, and depending there, as they shall thinke ffit; and alsoe to distinguish and sett forth the severall names and titles, duties, powers and limitts, of each court, office and officer, superior and inferior; and alsoe to contrive and apoynt such formes of oaths and attestations, not repugnant, but, as neare as may bee, agreeable, as aforesayd, to the lawes and statutes of this oure realme, as are conveniente and requisite, with respect to the due administration of justice, and due execution and discharge of all offices and places of trust by the persons that shall bee therein concerned; and alsoe to regulate and order the wave and manner of all elections to offices and places of trust, and to prescribe, limits and distinguish the numbers and bounces of all places, townes or cityes, within the limitts and bounds herein after mentioned, and not herein particularlie named, who have, and shall have, the power of electing and sending of ffreemen to the sayd Generall Assembly; and alsoe to order, direct and authorize the imposing of lawfull and reasonable Dynes, mulcts, imprisonments, and executing other punishments pecuniary and corporal, upon offenders and delinquents, according to the course of other corporations within this oure kingdom of England; and agayne to alter, revoke, annull or pardon, under their common scale or otherwyse, such Dynes, mulcts, imprisonments, sentences, judgments and condemnations, as shall bee thought Bitt; and to direct, rule, order and dispose of, all other matters and things, and particularly that which relates to the makinge of purchases of the native Indians, as to them shall seeme meete; wherebv oure sayd people and inhabitants, in the sayd Plantationes, may be soe religiously, peaceably and civilly governed, as that, by theire good life and orderlie conversations, they may win and invite the native Indians of the countrie to the knowledge and obedience of the onlie true God, and Saviour of mankinde; willing, commanding and requireing, and by these presents, for us, oure heires and successours, ordeyneing and apoynting, that all such lawes, statutes, orders and ordinances, instructions, impositions and directiones, as shall bee soe made by the Governour, deputye-Governour, Assistants and Freemen. Or such number of them as aforesayd, and published in writinge, under their

common scale, shall bee carefully and duely observed, kept, performed and putt in execution, according to the true intent and meaning of the same.

And these our letters patent, or the duplicate or exemplification on thereof, shall bee to all and everie such officer, superiour or inferiour, From tyme to tyme, for the putting of the same orders, lawes, statutes, ordinances, instructions and directions, in due execution, against us, oure heires and successours, a sufficient warrant and discharge. And further, our will and pleasure is, and wee doe hereby, for Vs, oure heires and successours, establish and ordeyne, that yearelie, once in the yeare, forever hereafter, namely, the aforesayd Wednesday in May, and at the towne of Newport, or elsewhere, if urgent occasion doe require, the Governour, Deputy-Governour and Assistants of the sayd Company, and other officers of the sayd Company, or such of them as the Generall Assemblye shall thinke Bitt, shall bee, in the sayd Generall Court or Assembly to bee held from that daye or tyme, newely chosen for the year ensuring, by such greater part of the sayd Company, for the tyme beinge, as shall bee then and there present; and if itt shall happen that the present Governour, Deputy-Governour and Assistants, bv these presents apoynted, or any such as shall hereafter be newly chosen into their roomes, or any of them, or any other the officers of the sayd Company, shall die or bee removed From his or their severall offices or places, before the sayd generall day of election, (whom wee doe hereby declare, for any misdemeanour or default, to be removeable by the Governour, Assistants and Company, or such greater parte of them, in any of the sayd publique courts, to bee assembled as aforesayd), that then, and in every such case, it shall and may bee lawfull to and ffor the sayd Governour, Deputy-Governour, Assistants and Company aforesayde, or such greater parte of them, soe to bee assembled as is aforesayde, in any theire assemblyes, to proceede to a new election of one or more of their Company, in the roome or place, roomes or places, of such officer or officers, soe dyeinge or removed, according to theire discretiones; and immediately upon and after such elections or elections made of such Governour, Deputy-Governour or Assistants, or any other officer of the sayd Company, in manner and forme aforesayde, the authoritie, office and power, before given to the fformer Governour, Deputy-Governour, and other officer and officers, soe removed, in whose steade and place new shall be chosen, shall, as to him and them, and every of them, respectively, cease and determine:

Provided, allwayes, and our will and pleasure is, that as well such as are by these presents apoynted to bee the present Governour, Deputy-Governour and Assistants, of the sayd Company, as those that shall succeede them, and all other officers to bee apoynted and chosen as aforesayde, shall, before the undertakeinge the execution of the sayd offices and places respectively, give theire solemn engagement, by oath, or otherwyse, for the due and fayth-full perfonnance of theire duties in their severall offices and places, before such person or persons as are by these presents hereafter apoynted to take and receive the same, that is to say: the sayd Benedict Arnold, whoa is hereinbe-fore nominated and apoynted the present Governour of the sayd Company, shall give the aforesayd engagement before William Brenton, or any two of the sayd Assistants of the sayd Company; unto whome, wee doe by these pre-senter give Bull power and authority to require and receive the same; and the sayd William Brenton, whoe is hereby before nominated and apoynted the present Deputy-Governour of the sayd Company, shall give the aforesaved engagement before the sayd Benedict Arnold, or any two of the Assistants of the sayd Company; unto whome wee doe by these presents give ffull power and authority to require and receive the same; and the sayd William Boul-ston, John Porter, Roger Williams, Thomas Olneye, John Smith, John Greene, John Cogeshall, James Barker, William Ffeild, and Joseph Clarke, whoe are hereinbefore nominated apoynted the present Assistants of the sayd Company, shall give the sayd engagement to theire offices and places respectively belongeing, before the sayd Bene-dict Arnold and William Brenton, or one of them; to whome, respectively wee doe hereby give dull power and authority to require, administer or receive the same: and further, our will and pleasure is. that all and every other future Governour or Deputy-Governour, to bee elected and chosen by vertue of these presents, shall give the sayd engagement before two or more of the sayd Assistants of the sayd Company ffor the tyme beinge; unto whome wee doe by these presents give full power and authority to require, administer or receive the same; and the sayd Assistants, and every of them, and all and every other offi-cer or officers to bee hereafter elected and chosen by vertue of these presents, from tyme to tyme, shall give the like engagements, to their offices and places respectively belonging bofere the Governour or Deputy-Governour for the tyme being; unto which sayd Governour, or Deputy-Governour, wee doe by these presents give full power and authority to require, administer or receive the same accordingly.

And wee doe likewise, for vs, oure heires and succes-sours, give and graunt vnto the sayd Governour and Com-pany and theire successours by these presents, that, for the more peaceable and orderly Government of the sayd Plantations, it shall and may bee lawfull ffor the Gov-ernour, Deputy-Governor, Assistants, and all other offi-cers and ministers of the sayd Company, in the administration of justice, and exercise of government, in the sayd Plantations, to vse, exercise, and putt in execu-tion, such methods, rules, orders and directions, not being contrary or repugnant to the laws and statutes of this oure realme, as have byn heretofore given, vsed and accus-tomed, in such cases respectively, to be putt in practice, untill att the next or some other Generall Assembly, spe-cial provision shall be made and ordeyned in the cases aforesayd. And wee doe further, for vs, oure heroes and successours, give and graunt vnto the sayd Governour and Company, and theire successours, by these presents, that itt shall and may bee lawfull to and for the sayd Gov-ernour, or in his absence, the Deputy-Governour, and majour parte of the sayd Assistants, for the tyme being, aft any tyme when the sayd Generall Assembly is not sitting, to nominate, apoynt and constitute, such and soe many commanders, governours, and military officers, as to them shall seeme requisite, for the leading, conductinge and travneing vpp the inhabitants of the sayd Plantations in martiall afiaires, and for the defence and safeguard of the sayd Plantations; and that itt shall and may bee lawfull to and for all and every such commander, governour and mil-itary officer, that shall bee soe as aforesayd, or by the Gov-ernour. or, in his absence, the Deputy-Governour, and six of the sayd Assistants, and majour parte of the Freemen of the sayd Company present att any Generall Assemblies, nominated, apoynted and constituted according to the tenor of his and theire respective commissions and direc-tions, to assemble, exercise in arms, martiall array, and putt in warlyke posture, the inhabitants of the sayd col-lonie, For theire speciall defence and safety; and to lead and conduct the sayd inhabitants, and to encounter, expulse, expell and resist, by force of armes, as well by sea as by lance; and alsoe to kill, slay and destroy, by all fitting wayes, enterprises and meaner, whatsoever, all and every such person or persons as shall, aft any tyme hereafter, attempt or enterprize the destruction, invasion, detriment or annoyance of the sayd inhabitants or Plantations; and to vse and exercise the lawe martiall in such cases only as occasion shall necessarily require; and to take or surprise, by all wayes and meanes whatsoever, all and every such person and persons, with theire shipp or shipps, armor, ammunition or other goods of such persons, as shall, in hostile manner, invade or attempt the defeating of the sayd Plantations, or the hurt of the sand Company and inhabitants; and vpon just causes, to invade and destroy the native Indians, or other enemyes of the sayd Collony. Nevertheless, our will and pleasure is, and wee doe hereby declare to the rest of oure Collonies in New Eng-land, that itt shall not bee lawefull ffor this our sayd Col-lony of Rhode-Island and Providence Plantations, in America, in New-England, to invade the natives inhabit-ing within the bounces and limitts of theire sayd Collonies without the knowledge and consent of the sand other Col-lonies. And itt is hereby declared, that itt shall not bee lawfull to or ffor the rest of the Collonies to invade or molest the native Indians, or any other inhabittants, inhabiting within the bounds and lymitts hereafter mentioned (they having subjected themselves vnto vs, and being by vs taken into our speciall protection), without the knowledge and consent of the Governour and Company of our Collony of Rhode-Island and Providence Plantations.

Alsoe our will and pleasure is, and wee doe hereby declare unto all Christian Kings, Princes and States, that if any person, which shall hereafter bee of the sayd Company or Plantations, or any other, by apoyntment of the sayd Governour and Company for the tyme beinge, shall at any tyme or tymes hereafter, rob or spoyle, by sea or land, or do any hurt, unlawfull hostillity to any of the subjects of vs, oure heires or successours, or any of the subjects of any Prince or State, beinge then in league with vs, oure heires, or successours, vpon complaint of such injury done to any such Prince or State, or theire subjects, wee, our hearer and successours, will make open proclamation within any parts of oure realme of England, ffitt ffor that purpose, that the person or persons committing any such robbery or spoyle shall, within the tyme lymitted by such proclamation, make full restitution or satisfaction of all such injuries, done or committed, soe as the sayd Prince, or others soe complaineinge, may bee fully satisfyed and contented; and if the sayd person or persons whoe shall commits any such robbery or spoyle shall not make satvsfaction, accordingly, within such tyme, soe to bee lymitted, that then wee, oure heires and successours, will putt such person or persons out of oure allegiance and protection; and that then itt shall and may bee lawefull and Tree ffor all Princes or others to prosecute, with hostillity, such offenders, and every of them, theire and every of theire procurers, adders, abettors and counsellors, in that behalfa; Provided alsoe, and oure expresse will and pleasure is, and wee doe, by these presents, For vs, our heirs and successours, ordeyne and apoynt, that these presents shall not, in any manner, hinder any of oure lovinge subjects, whatsoever, ffrom vseing and exercising the trade of ffishing vpon the coast of New-England, in America; butt that they, and every or any of them, shall have ffull and ffree power and liberty to continue and vse the trade of ffishing vpon the sayd coast, in an of the seas thereunto adjoyninge, or-any armes of the seas, or salt water, rivers and creeks, where they have been accustomed to ffish; and to build and to sett upon the waste land, belonginge to the sayd Collony and Plantations, such wharfes, stages and worke-houses as shall be necessary for the salting, drying and keepeing of theire dish, to be taken or gotten upon that coast. And ffurther, for the encouragement of the inhabitants of our sayd Collony of Providence Plantations to sett vpon the businesse of takeing whales, itt shall bee lawfull For them, or any of them, having struck whale,

dubertus, or other greate ffish, itt or them, to pursue unto any parte of that coaste, and into any bay, river, cove, creeke or shoare, belonging thereto, and itt or them, vpon sayd coaste, or in the sand bay, river, cove, creeke or shoare, belonging thereto, to kill and order for the best advantage, without molestation, they makeing noe wilfull waste or spoyle, any thinge in these presents conteyned, or any other matter or thing, to the contrary notwithstanding. And further alsoe, wee are gratiously pleased, and doe hereby declare, that if any of the inhabitants of oure sayd Collony doe sett upon the plantings of vineyards (the soyle and clymate both seemeing naturally to coneurr to the production of wynes), or bee industrious in the discovery of ffishing banks, in or about the sayd Collony, wee will, ffrom tyme to tyme, give and allow all due and fitting encouragement therein, as to others in cases of tyke nature. And further, of oure more ample grace, certayne knowledge, and meere motion, wee have given and graunted,. and by these presents, ffor vs, oure heires and successours, doe Five and graunt unto the sayd Governour and Company of the English Collony of Rhode-Island and Providence Plantations, in the Narragansett Bay, in New-England in America, and to every inhabitant there, and to every person and persons trading thither, and to every such person or persons as are or shall bee Tree of the sayd Collony, full power and authority, from tyme to tyme, and aft all tymes hereafter, to take, shipp, transport and carry away, out of any of our realmes and dominions for and towards the plantation and defence of the sayd Collony, such and soe many of oure loveing subjects and strangers as shalt or will willingly accompany them in and to their sayd Collony and Plantation; except such person or persons as are or shall be therein restrained by vs, oure heires and successours, or any law or statute of this realme: and also to shipp and transport all and all manner of goods, chattels, merchandises, and other things whatsoever, that are or shall bee vsefull or necessary ffor the sayd Plantations, and defence thereof, and vsually transported, and nott prohibited by any lawe or statute of this our realme; yielding and paying vnto vs. our heires and successours, such the rluties, custtomes and subsidies, as are or ought to bee payd or payable for the same.

And ffurther, our will and pleasure is, and wee doe, For us, our heires and successours, ordeyn, declare and graunt, vnto the sayd Governour and Company, and their successours, that all and every the subjects of vs, our heires and successours, which are already planted and settled within our sayd Collony of Providence Plantations, or which shall hereafter Roe to inhabit within the sayd Collony' and all and every of theire children, which have byn borne there, or which shall happen hereafter to bee borne there, or on the sea, goeing thither, or retourneing from thence, shall have and enjoye all libertyes and immunityes of fires and naturall subjects within any the dominions of vs, our heires or successours, to all intents, constructions and purposes, whatsoever, as if they, and every of them, were borne within the realme of England. And ffurther, know ye, that wee, of our more abundant grace, certain knowledge and meere motion, have given, graunted and confirmed, and, by these presents, for vs, our heires and successours, doe give, graunt and confirms, vnto the sayd Governour and Company, and theire successours, all that parte of Our dominiones in New-England, in America, conteyneing the Nahantick and Nanhyganset Bay, and countryes and partes adjacent, bounded on the west, or westerly, to the middle or channel of a river there, commonly called and known by the name of Pawcatuck, alias Pawcawtuck river, and soe along the sayd river, as the greater or middle streame thereof reacheth or lyes vpp into the north countrye, northward, vnto the head thereoof, and from thence, by a streight lyne drawn due north, vntill itt meets with the south lyne of the Massachusetts Collonie; and on the north, or northerly, by the aforesayd south or southerly lyne of the Massachusettes Collony or Plantation, and extending towards the east, or eastwardly, three English miles to the east and north-east of the most eastern and north-eastern parts of the aforesayd Narragansett Bay, as the sayd bay lyeth or extendeth itself from the ocean on the south, or southwardly, vnto the mouth of the river which runneth towards the towne of Providence, and from thence along the eastwardly side or banke of the sayd river (higher called by the name of Seacunck river), vp to the ffalls called Patuckett ffalls, being the most westwardly lyne of Plymouth Collony, and soe from the sayd Balls, in a streight lyne, due north, untill itt meete with the aforesayd line of the Massachusetts Collony; and bounded on the south by the ocean: and, in particular, the lands belonging to the townes of Providence, Pawtuxet, Warwicke; Misquammacok, alias Pawcatuck, and the rest vpon the maine land in the tract aforesayd, together with Rhode-Island, Blocke-Island, and all the rest of the islands and banks in the Narragansett Bay, and bordering vpon the coast of the tract aforesayd (Ffisher's Island only excepted), together with all firme lands, soyles, grounds, havens. ports rivers, waters, ffishings, mines royall, and all other mynes, mineralls, precious stones, quarries, woods, wood-grounds, rocks' slates, and all and singular other commodities, jurisdictions, royalties, priviledges, franchises, preheminences and hereditaments, whatsoever, within the sayd tract, bounds, lances, and islands, aforesayd, or to them or any of them belonging, or in any wise apperteining: to have and to hold the same, Into the sayd Governour and Company, and their successours, forever, vpon trust, for the vse and benefit of themselves and their associates, ffreemen of the sayd Collony, their heires and assignas, to be holden of vs, our heires and successours, as of the Mannor of East-Greenwich, in our county of Kent, in free and comon soccage, and not in capite, nor by knight service; Wilding and paying therefor, to vs, our heires and successours, only the Fifth part of all the oare of Fold and silver which, from tyme to tyme, and att all tymes hereafter, shall bee there gotten, had or obtained, in lieu and satisfaction of all services, duties, Dynes, forfeitures, made or to be made, claimes and demands, whatsoever, to bee to vs, our heires or successours, therefor or thereout rendered, made or paid; any graunt, or clause in a late graunt, to the Governour and Company of Connecticutt Colony, in America, to the contrary thereof in any wise notwithstanding; the aforesavd Pawcatuck river haven byn yielded, after much debate, for the fixed and certain bounces betweene these our sayd Colonies, by the agents thereof; whoe have alsoe agreed, that the sayd Pawcatuck river shall bee alsoe called alias Norrogansett or Narrogansett river; and to prevent future disputes, that otherwise might arise thereby, forever hereafter shall bee construed, deemed and taken to bee the Narragansett river in our late Irrupt to Connecticutt (colony mentioned as the easterly bounds of that Colony. And further, our will and pleasure is, that in all matters of publique controversy which may fall out betweene our Colony of Providence Plantations, and the rest of our Colonies in New-England, lit shall and may bee lawfull to and for the Governour and Company of the sayd Colony of Providence Plantations to make their appeales therein to vs, our heirs and successours. for redresse in such cases, within this our realme of England: and that itt shall bee lawfull to and for the inhabitants of the sayd Colony of Providence Plantations, without let or molestation, to passe and repasse with freedome, into and thorough the rest of the English Collonies, vpon their lawfull and civill occasions, and to converse, and hold commerce and trade, wit: such of the inhabitants of our other English Collonies as shall bee willing to admits them thereunto, they behaveing themselves peaceably among them; any act, clause or sentence, in any of the sayd Collonies provided, or that shall bee provided, to the contrary in anywise notwithstanding. And lastly, wee doe, for vs, our heires and successours, ordeyne and graunt vnto the sayd Governor and Company, and their successours, and by these presents, that these our letters patent shall be firme, good, effectuall and available in all things in the lawe, to all intents, constructions and purposes whatsoever, according to our true intent and meaning hereinbefore declared; and shall bee construed, reputed and adjudged in all cases most favorably on the behalfe, and for the benefit and behoofe, of the sayd Governor and Company, and their successours; although empress mention of the true yearly value or certainty of the premises, or any of them, or of any other gifts or graunts by vs, or by any of our progenitors or predecessors, heretofore made to the sayd Governor and Company of the English Colony of Rhode-Island and Providence Plantations, in the Narragansett Bay, New-England, in America, in these presents is not made, or any statute, act, ordinance, provision. proclamation or restriction, heretofore had, made, enacted ordeyned or provided, or any other matter, cause or thing whatsoever, to the contrary thereof in anywise notwithstanding; In witnes whereof, wee have caused these our letters to bee made patent. Witnes our Selfe att Westminster, the eighth day of July, in the Fifteenth yeare of our reigne.

By the King:
Howard.

Source:

Francis Newton Thorpe, ed. *The Federal and State Constitutions, Colonial Charters, and Other Organic Laws of the States, Territories, and Colonies Now or Heretofore Forming the United States of America.* Washington, D.C.: Government Printing Office, 1909.

Pennsylvania Charter, 1681

In 1681 King Charles II of England repaid a $16,000 debt to the late Admiral William Penn by granting his son, William Penn, Jr., a proprietary charter to 45,000 square miles of land in the New World. The new territory was named Pennsylvania in honor of Penn's father. In addition to land, the charter gave Penn the power to set up courts, conduct trade, establish cities, impose taxes, and to sell parcels of the land to private investors while retaining the title for himself. Pennsylvania remained a proprietary colony under the control of the Penn family until the American Revolution in 1776. Although Penn was aware of the land's significant commercial value, he had requested the charter primarily to establish a safe haven for the Society of Friends, or Quakers, a pacifist religious group that was heavily persecuted in England. Penn himself, who had become a Quaker during his early twenties, was expelled from Oxford for "religious non-conformity" and later charged with preaching to "an unlawful, seditious and riotous assembly." Penn's dedication to religious freedom and a liberal government shaped the character of his colony. His *First Frame of Government*, written in 1682, provided for civil liberties, elected representatives, and a local governor who acted under the authority of the ruling proprietor. Penn is also famous for signing treaties with the Delaware Indians (Lenni Lenape) that resulted in a 50-year peace between Native Americans and the colonists.

CHARLES the Second, by the Grace of God, King of England, Scotland, France, and Ireland, Defender of the Faith, &c. To all whom these presents shall come, Greeting.

WHEREAS Our Trustie and wellbeloved Subject WILLIAM PENN, Esquire, Sonne and heire of Sir WILLIAM PENN deceased, out of a commendable Desire to enlarge our English Empire, and promote such usefull comodities as may bee of Benefit to us and Our Dominions, as also to reduce the savage Natives by gentle and just mamlers to the Love of Civil Societie and Christian Religion, hath humbley besought Leave of Us to transport an ample Colonie unto a certaine Countrey hereinafter described; In the Partes of America not yet cultivated and planted; And hath likewise humbley besought Our Royall Majestie to Give, Grant, and Confirme all the said Countrey, with certaine Privileges and Jurisdictions, requisite for the good Government and Safetie of the said Countrey and Colonie, to him and his Heires forever: KNOW YE THEREFORE, That Wee, favouring the Petition and good Purpose of the said William Penn, and haveing Regard to the Memorie and Meritts of his late Father in divers Services, and perticulerlv to his Conduct, Courage, and Discretion under our Dearest Brother JAMES Duke of York, in that Signall Battell and Victorie fought and obteyned against the Dutch Fleete, command by the Heer Van Opdam, in the yeare One thousand six hundred and sixty-five: In consideration thereof, of Our Speciale grace, certaine Knowledge, and meere Motion have Given and Granted, and by this Our present Charter, for Us, Our Heires and Successors, Doe give and Grant unto the said William Penn, his Heires and Assignes, all that Tract or Parte of Land in America, with all the Islands therein conteyned, as the same is bounded on the East by Delaware River, from twelve miles distance Northwards of New Castle Towne unto the three and fortieth degree of Northerne Latitude, if the said River doeth extende so farre Northwards; But if the said River shall not extend soe farre Northward, then by the said River soe farr as it cloth extend; and from the head of the said River, the Easterne Bounds are to bee determined by a Meridian Line, to bee drawne from the head of the said River, unto the said three and fortieth Degree. The said Lands to extend westwards five degrees in longitude, to bee computed from the said Easterne Bounds; and the said Lands to bee bounded on the North by the beginning of the three and fortieth degree of Northern Latitude, and on the South by a Circle drawne at twelve miles distance from New Castle Northward and Westward unto the beginning of the fortieth degree of Northern Latitude, and then by a streight Line Westward to the Limitt of Longitude above-mentioned. WEE do also give and grant unto the said Willaim Penn, his heires and assignee, the free and undisturbed use and continuance in, and passage into and out of all and singuler Ports, Harbours, Bays, Waters, Rivers, Isles, and Inletts, belonging unto, or leading to and from the Countrey or Islands aforesaid, And all the Soyle, lands, fields, woods, underwoods, mountaines, hills, fenns, Isles, Lakes, Rivers, waters, Rivuletts, Bays, and Inletts, scituate or being within, or belonging unto the Limitts and Bounds aforesaid, togeather with the fishing of all sortes of fish, whales, Sturgeons, and all Royall and other Fishes, in the Sea, Bayes, Inletts, waters, or Rivers within the premisses, and the Fish therein taken; And also all Veines, Mines, and Quarries as well discovered as not discovered, of Gold, Silver, Gemms, and Pretious Stones, and all other whatsoever, be it Stones, Mettals, or of any other thing or matter whatsoever, found or to bee found within the Countrey, Isles, or Limitts aforesaid; AND him, the said William Penn, his heires and assignee, Wee doe by this Our Royall Charter, for Ifs, Our heires and Successors, make, create, and constitute the true and absolute Proprietarie of the Countrey aforesaid, and of all other the premisses, Saving always to Us, Our heires and Successors, the Faith and Allegiance of the said William Penn, his heires and assignee, and of all other Proprietaries, Tenants, and Inhabitants that are or shall be within the Territories and Precincts aforesaid; and Saving also, unto Us, Our heires and Successors, the Sovereignty of the aforesaid Countrey; To HAVE, hold, possess, and enjoy the said Tract of Land, Countrey, Isles, Inletts, and other the premisses unto the said William Penn, his heires and assignee, to the only Proper use and behoofe of the said William Penn, his heires and assignee for ever, to bee holden of Us, Our heires and Successors, Kings of England, as of Our Castle of Windsor in Our County of Berks, in free and comon Socage, by fealty only for all Services, and not in Capite or by Knights Service: Yielding and paying therefore to Ifs, Our heires and Successors, Two Beaver Skins, to bee delivered at Our said Castle of Windsor on the First Day of January in every Year; and also the Fifth Part of all Gold and Silver Oare, which shall from Time to Time happen to bee found within the Limitts aforesaid, cleare of all Charges. And of Our further Grace, certaine Knowledge, and meer motion, We have thought fitt to erect and We doe hereby erect the aforesaid Countrey and Islands into a Province and Seigniorie, and doe call itt PENSILVANIA, and soe from henceforth we will have itt called.

AND forasmuch as Wee have hereby made and ordained the aforesaid William Penn, his heires and assignee, the true and absolute Proprietaries of all the Lands and Dominions aforesaid, KNOW YE THEREFORE, That We reposing speciall trust and Confidence in the fidelitie, wisedom, Justice, and provident circumspection of the said William Penn for us, our heires and Successors, Doe grant free, full, and absolute power by vertue of these presents to him and his heires, and to his and their Deputies, and Lieutenants, for the good and happy government of the said countrey, to ordeyne, make, and enact and under his and their Seales to publish any Lawes whatsoever, for the raising of money for the publick use of the said Province, or for any other End, apperteyning either

unto the publick state, peace, or safety of the said Countrey, or unto the private utility of perticular persons, according unto their best discretions, by and with the advice, assent, and approbation of the Freemen of the said Countrey, or the greater parse of them, or of their Delegates or Deputies, whom for the Enacting of the said Lawes, when, and as often as need shall require, Wee will that the said William Penn and his heires, shall assemble in such sort and forme, as to him and them shall seeme best, and the same Lawes duly to execute, unto and upon all People within the said Countrey and the Limitts thereof.

AND wee doe likewise give and grant unto the said William Penn, and his heires, and to his and their Deputies and Lieutenants, full power and authoritie to appoint and establish any Judges and Justices, Magistrates and Officers whatsoever, for what Causes soever for the probates of wills, and for the granting of Administrations within the precincts aforesaid and with what Power soever, and in such forme as to the said William Penn or his heires shall seeme most convenient: Also to remits, release, pardon, and abolish whether before Judgement or after all Crimes and Of I ences whatsoever comitted within the said Countrey against the said Lawes, Treason and wilful and malitious Murder onely excepted, and in those Cases to grant Reprieves, until Our pleasure may bee known therein and to doe all and every other thing and things, which unto the compleate Establishment of Justice, unto Courts and Tribunalls, formes of Judicature, and manner of Proceedings doe belong, altho in these presents expresse mention bee not made thereof, And by Judges by them delegated, to award Processe, hold Pleas, and determine in all the said Courts and Tribunalls all Actions, Suits, and Causes whatsoever, as well Criminall as Civill, Personall, reall and mixt; which Lawes soe as aforesaid to bee published, Our Pleasure is, and soe Wee enjoyne, require, and command, shall bee most absolute and avaylable in law; and that all the Liege People and subjects of Us, Our heires and Successors, doe observe and keepe the same inviolabl in those parses, soe farr as they concerne them under the paine therein expressed, or to bee expressed. PROVIDED nevertheles, That the said Lawes bee consonant to reason, and bee not repugnant or contrarie, but as neare as conveniently may bee agreeable to the Lawes and Statutes, and rights of this Our Kingdome of England; And Saving and reserving to Us, Our heires and Successors, the receiving, heareing, and determining of the appeale and appeales of all or any Person or Persons, of, in, or belonging to the Territories aforesaid, or touching any Judgement to bee there made or given.

AND forasmuch as in the Government of soe great a Countrey, sudden Accidents doe often happen, whereunto itt will bee necessarie to apply remedie before the Freeholders of the said Province, or their Delegates or

Deputies, can bee assembled to the making of Lawes; neither will itt bee convenient that instantly upon every such emergent occasion, soe grease a multitude should be called together: Therefore for the better Government of the said Countrey Wee will, and ordaine, and by these presents, for us, our Heires and successors, Doe Grant unto the said William Penn and his heires, by themselves or by their Magistrates and Officers, in that behalfe duely to bee ordeyned as aforesaid, to make and constitute fitt and wholesome Ordinances, from time to time, within the said Countrey to bee kept and observed, as well for the preservation of the peace, as for the better government of the People there inhabiting; and publickly to notifie the same to all persons, whome the same doeth or anyway may concerne. Which ordinances, Our Will and Pleasure is shall bee observed inviolably within the said Province, under Paines therein to be expressed, soe as the said Ordinances bee consonant to reason, and bee not repugnant nor contrary, but soe farre as conveniently may bee agreeable with the Lawes of our Kingdome of England, and soe as the said Ordinances be not extended in any Sort to bind, charge, or take away the right or Interest of any person or persons, for or in their Life, members, Freehold, goods, or Chattles. And our further will and pleasure is, that the Lawes for regulateing and governing of Propertie within the said Province, as well for the descent and enjoyment of lands as likewise for the enjoyment and succession of goods and Chattles, and likewise as to Felonies, shall bee and continue the same, as they shall bee for the time being by the generall course of the Law in our Kingdome of England, untill the said Lawes shall bee altered by the said William Penn, his heires or assignee, and by the Freemen of the said Province, their Delegates or Deputies, or the greater Part of them.

AND to the End the said William Penn, or his heires, or other the Planters, Owners, or Inhabitants of the said Province, may not att any time hereafter by misconstruction of the powers aforesaid through inadvertencie or designe depart from that Faith and due allegiance, which by the lawes of this our Kingdom of England they and all our subjects, in our Dominions and Territories, always owe unto us, Our heires and Successors, by colour of any Extent or largnesse of powers hereby given, or pretended to bee given, or by force or colour of any lawes hereafter to bee made in the said Province, by vertue of any such Powers; Our further will and Pleasure is, that a transcript or Duplicate of all Lawes, which shall bee soe as aforesaid made and published within the said Province, shall within five yeares after the makeing thereof, be transmitted and delivered to the Privy Councell, for the time being, of us, our heires and successors: And if any of the said Lawes, within the space of six moneths after that they shall be soe transmitted and delivered, bee declared by us, Our heires or Successors, in Our or their Privy Councell, inconsistent

with the Sovereigntey or lawful Prerogative of us, our heires or Successors, or contrary to the Faith and Allegiance due by the legall government of this Realme, from the said William Penn, or his heires, or of the Planters and Inhabitants of the said Province, and that thereupon any of the said Lawes shall bee adjudged and declared to bee void by us, our heires or Successors, under our or their Privy Seale, that then and from thenceforth, such Lawes, concerning which such Judgement and declaration shall bee made, shall become voyd: Otherwise the said Lawes soe transmitted, shall remains, and stand in full force, according to the true intent and meaneing thereof.

FURTHERMORE, that this new Colony may the more happily increase, by the multitude of People resorting thither; Therefore wee for us, our heirs and Successors, doe Rive and grant by these presents power, Licence, and Libertie unto ail the Liege People and Subjects, both present and future, of us, our heires, and Successors, excepting those who shall bee Specially forbidden to transport themselves and Families unto the said Countrey, with such convenient Shipping as by the lawes of this our Kingdome of England they ought to use, with fitting provisions, paying only the customes therefore due, and there to settle themselves, dwell and inhabitt, and plant, for the publick and their owne private advantage.

AND FURTHERMORE, that our Subjects may bee the rather encouraged to undertake this expedicion with ready and cheerful minces, KNOW YE, That wee, of Our especial! grace, certaine knowledge, and meere motion, Doe Give and Grant by vertue of these presents, as well unto the said William Penn, and his heires, as to all others, who shall from time to time repair unto the said Countrey, with a purpose to inhabitt there, or trade with the Natives of the said Countrey, full Licence to lade and freight in any ports whatsoever, of us, our heires and Successors, according to the lawes made or to be made within our Kingdome of England, and into the said Countrey, by them, theire Servants or assignee, to transport all and singular theire wares, goods, and Merchandizes, as likewise all sorts of graine whatsoever, and all other things whatsoever, necessary for food or cloathing, not prohibited by the Lawes and Statutes of our Kingdomes and Dominiones to be carried out of the said Kingdomes, without any Lett or molestation of us, our heires and Successors, or of any of the Officers of us, our heires and Successors; saveing always to us, our heires and Successors, the legall impositions, customer, and other Duties and payments, for the said Wares and Merchandize, by any Law or Statute due or to be due to us, our heires and Successors.

AND Wee doe further, for us, our heires and Successors, Give and grant unto the said William, Penn, his heires and assignee, free and absolute power, to Divide the said Countrey and Islands into Townes, Hundreds and Counties, and to erect and incorporate Townes into Borroughs, and Borroughs into Citties, and to make and constitute faires and Marketts therein, with all other convenient priviledges and immunities, according to the merits of the inhabitants, and the Tithes of the places, and to doe all and every other thing and things touching the premisses, which to him OI them shall seeme meet and requisite, albeit they be such as of their owne nature might otherwise require a more especiall comandment and Warrant then in these presents is expressed.

WE Will alsoe, and by these presents, for us, our heires and Successors, Wee doe Give and grant Licence by this our Charter, unto the said William Penn, his heires and assignee, and to all the inhabitants and dwellers in the Province aforesaid, both present and to come, to import or unlace, by themselves or theire Servants, ffactors or assignee, all merchandises and goods whatsoever, that shall arise of the fruites and comodities of the said Province, either by Land or Sea, into any of the ports of us, our heires and successors, in our Kingdome of England, and not into any other Countrey whatsoever: And wee give him full power to dispose of the said goods in the said ports; and if need bee, within one yeare next after the unladeing of the same, to lade the said Merchandizes and Goods again into the same or other sllipps, and to export the same into any other Countreys, either of our Dominions or fforeigne, according to Lawe: Provided alwayes, that they pay such customer and impositions, subsidies and duties for the same, to Us, our heires and Successors, as the rest of our Subjects of our Kingdom of England, for the time being, shall be bound to pay, and doe observe the Acts of Navigation, and other Lawes in that behalfe made.

AND FURTHERMORE Of OUR most ample and esspeciall grace, certaine knowledge, and meere motion, Wee doe, for us, our heires and Suceessors, Grant unto the said William Penn, his heires and assignee, full and absolute power and authoritie to make, erect, and constitute within the said Province and the Isles and Islets aforesaid, such and soe many Sea-ports, harbours, Creeks, Havens, Keyes, and other places, for discharge and unladeing of goods and Merchandizes, out of the shipps, Boates, and other Vessells, and ladeing them in such and soe many Places, and with such rights, Jurisdictions, liberties and priviledges unto the said ports belonging, as to him or them shall seeme most expedient; and that all and singuler the shipps, boater, and other Vessells, which shall come for merchandise and trade unto the said Province, or out of the same shall depart, shall be laden or unladen onely at such Ports as shall be erected and constituted by the said William Penn, his heires and assignee, any use, custome, or other thing to the contrary notwithstanding. Provided, that the said William, Penn and his heires, and the Lieutenants and Governors for the time being, shall admits and receive in and about all such Ports, Havens, Creeks, and Keyes, all Officers and their Deputies, who shall from time

to time be appointed for that Purpose by the Farmers or Commissioners of our Customes for the time being.

AND Wee doe further appoint and ordaine, and by these presents, for us, our heires and Successors, Wee doe grant unto the said William Penn, his heires and assignee, That he, the said William Penn, his heires and assignee, may from time to time for ever, have and enjoy the Customes and Subsidies, in the Fortes, Harbours, and other Creeks and Places aforesaid, within the Province aforesaid, payable or due for merchandises and wares there to be laded and unladed, the said Customes and Subsidies to be reasonably assessed upon any occasion, by themselves and the People there as aforesaid to be assembled, to whom wee give power by these presents, for us, our heires and Successors, upon just cause and in dudue p'portion; to assesse and impose the same; Saveing unto us, our heires and Successors, such impositions and Customes, as by Act of Parliament are and shall be appointed.

AND it is Our further Will and plasure, that the said William Penn, his heires and assignee, shall from time to time constitute and appoint an Attorney or Agent, to Reside in or neare our City of London, who shall make knowne the place where he shall dwell or may be found, unto the Clerks of our Privy Counsell for the time being, or one of them, and shall be ready to appeare in any of our Courts aft Westminster, to Answer for any Misdemeanors that shall be committed, or by any wilfull default or neglect permitted by the said William Penn, his heires or assignee, against our Lawes of Trade or Navigation; and after it shall be ascertained in any of our said Courts, what damages Wee or our heires or Successors shall have sustained by such default or neglect, the said William Penn, his heires and assignee shall pay the same within one yeare after such taxation, and demand thereof from such Attorney: or in case there shall be noe such Attorney by the space of a yeare, or such Attorney shall not make payment of such damages within the space of one yeare, and answer such other forfeitures and penalties within the said time, as by the Acts of Parliament in England are or shall be provided according to the true intent and meaneing of these presents; then it shall be lawfull for us, our heires and Successors, to seize and Resume the government of the said Province or Countrey, and the same to retaine untill payment shall be made thereof: But notwithstanding any such Seizure or resumption of the government, nothing concerning the propriety or ownership of any Lands tenements, or other hereditaments, or goods or chattels of any the Adventurers, Planters, or owners, other then the respective Offenders there, shall be any way be affected or molested thereby.

PROVIDED alwayes, and our will and pleasure is, that neither the said William Penn, nor his heires, or any other the inhabitants of the said Province, shall at any time hereafter have or maintain any Correspondence with any other king, prince, or State, or with any of theire subjects who shall then be in Warr against us our heires or Successors; Nor shall the said William Penn, or his heires, or any other the Inhabitants of the said Province, make Warre or doe any act of Hostility against any other king, princes or State, or any of there Subjects, who shall then be in league or amity with us, our heires or successors.

AND, because in soe remote a Countrey, and scituate neare many Barbarous Nations, the incursions as well of the Savages themselves, as of other enemies, pirates and robbers, may probably be feared; Therefore Wee have given, and for us, our heires and Successors, Doe give power by these presents unto the said William Penn, his heires and assignee, by themselves or theire Captained or other their Officers, to levy, muster and traine all sorts of men, of what condition soever, or wheresoever borne, in the said Province of Pensilvania, for the time being, and to make Warre, and to pursue the enemies and Robbers aforesaid, as well by Sea as by Land, even without the Limitts of the said Province, and by God's assistance to vanquish and take them, and being taken to put them to death by the Law of Warre, or to save them, aft theire pleasure, and to doe all arid every other Thing which to the Charge and Office of a Captaine-Generall of an Army belongeth or hath accustomed to belong, as fully and Freely as any Captaine-Generall of an Army hath ever had the same.

AND FURTHERMORE, of Our especiall grace and of our certaine knowledge and meere motion, wee have given and granted, and by these presents, for us, our heires and Successors, do Give and Grant unto the said William Penn, his Heirs and Assigns, full and absolute power, licence and authoritie, that he, the said William Penn, his heires and assignee, from time to time hereafter forever, att his or theire own Will and pleasure may assigne, alien, Grant, demise, or enfeoffe of the Premises soe many and such parses or parcells to him or them that shall be willing to purchase the samej as they shall thinke fitt, To have and to hold to them the said person and persons willing to take or purchase, theire heires and assignee, in ffee-simple or ffee-taile, or for the terme of life, or lives or yeares, to be held of the said William Penn, his heires and assignee, as of the said Seigniory of Windsor, by such services, customer and rents, as shall seeme ffitt to the said William Penn, his heires and assignee, and not imediately of us, our heires and successors. AND to the same person or persons, and to all 'end every of them, wee doe give and grant by these presents, for us, our heires and successors, licence, authoritie and power, that such person or persons may take the premises, or any parcell thereof, of the aforesaid William Penn, his heires or assignee and the same hold to themselves, their heires and assignee, in what estate of inheritance soever, in ffee-simple or in ffee-taile,

or otherwise, as to him, the said William Penn, his heires and assignee, shall seem expedient: The Statute made in the parliament of EDWARD, sonne of King HENRY, late King of England, our predecessor, commonly called The Statute QUIA EMPTORES TERRARUM, lately published in our Kingdome of England in any wise notwithstanding.

AND by these presents wee give and Grant Licence unto the said William Penn, and his heires, likewise to all and every such person and persons to whom the said William Penn or his heires shall att any time hereafter grant any estate or inheritance as aforesaid, to erect any parcells of Land within the Province aforesaid into Mannors by and with the Licence to be first had and obteyned for that purpose, under the hand and Seale of the said William Penn or his heires; and in every of the said Mannors to have and to hold a Court Baron, with all thinges whatsoever which to a Court-Baron do belong, and to have and to hold View of drank-pledge for the conservation of the peace and the better government of those parses, by themselves or their Stewards, or by the Lords for the time being of other Mannors to be deputed when they shall be erected, and in the same to use all things belonging to the View of frank-pledge. AND Wee doe further grant licence and authoritie, that every such person and persons who shall erect any such Mannor or Mannors, as aforesaid, shall or may grant all or any parse of his said Lands to any person or persons, in ffee-simple, or any other estate of inheritance to be held of the said Mannors respectively, soe as noe further tenures shall be created, but that upon all further and other alienations thereafter to be made, the said lands see aliened shall be held of the same Lord and his heires, of whom the alienor did then before hold, and by the like rents and Services which were before due and accustomed.

AND FARTHER our pleasure is, and by these presents, for us, our heires and Successors, Wee doe covenant and grant to and with the said William Penn, and his heires and assignee, That Wee, our heires and Successors, shall at no time hereafter sett or make, or cause to be sets, any impossition, custome or other taxation, rate or contribution whatsoever, in and upon the dwellers and inhabitants of the aforesaid Province, for their Lands, tenements, goods or chattells within the said Province, or in and upon any goods or merchandise within the said Province, or to be laden or unladen within the ports or harbours of the said Province, unless the same be with the consent of the Proprietary, or chiefe governor, or assembly, or by act of Parliament in England.

AND Our Pleasure is, and for us, our heires and Successors, Wee charge and comand, that this our Declaration shall from henceforward be received and allowed from time to time in all our courts, and before all the Judges of us, our heires and Successors, for a sufficient and lawfull discharge, payment and acquittance; commanding all and singular the officers and ministers of us, our heires and Successors, and enjoyneing them upon pain of our high displeasure, that they doe not presume aft any time to attempt any thing to the contrary of the premisses, or that doe in any sort withstand the same, but that they be aft all times aiding and assisting, as is fitting unto the said William Penn, and his heires, and to the inhabitants and merchants of the Province aforesaid, their Servants, Ministers, doctors and Assignes, in the full use and fruition of the benefit of this our Charter.

AND Our further pleasure is and wee doe hereby, for us, our heires and Successors, charge and require, that if any of the inhabitants of the said Province, to the number of Twenty, shall at any time hereafter be desirous, and shall by any writeing, or by any person deputed for them, signify such their desire to the Bishop of London for the time being that any preacher or preachers, to be approved of by the said Bishop, may be sent unto them for their instruction, that then such preacher or preachers shall and may be and reside within the said Province, without any deniall or molestation whatsoever.

AND if perchance hereafter it should happen any doubts or questions should arise, concerning the true Sense and meaning of any word, clause, or Sentence conteyned in this our present Charter, Wee will ordaine, and comand, that att all times and in all things, such interpretation be made thereof, and allowed in any of our Courts whatsoever, as shall be adjudged most advantatacous and favourabla unto the said William Penn, his heires and assignes: Provided always that no interpretation be admitted thereof by which the allegiance due unto us, our heires and Successors may suffer any prejudice or diminution; Although express mention be not made in these presents of the true yearly value, or certainty of the premisses, or of any parse thereof, or of other gifts and grants made by us our progenitors or predecessors unto the said William Penn Any Statute, Act, ordinance, provision, proclamation, or restraint heretofore had, made, published, ordained or provided, or any other thing, cause, or matter whatsoever, to the contrary thereof in any wise notwithstanding.

IN WITNESS, &C.

Given under our Privy Seale at our Palace of Westminster the Eight and Twentieth day of February in the Three and Thirtyeth Yeare of Our Reigne.

Source:

Francis Newton Thorpe, ed. *The Federal and State Constitutions, Colonial Charters, and Other Organic Laws of the States, Territories, and Colonies Now or Heretofore Forming the United States of America.* Washington, D.C.: Government Printing Office, 1909.

Charter for the Colony of Georgia, 1732

Charter granted to James Oglethorpe by King George II on June 9, 1732, to settle the colony of Georgia. A penal reform advocate, Oglethorpe had originally planned for Georgia to be a debtors' colony, but parliamentary opposition forced him to abandon the plan. Instead, he received a 21-year charter with orders to protect Carolina and produce silk and wine. Oglethorpe arrived at Yamacraw Bluff on the Savannah River with 114 settlers on February 12, 1733.

George the second, by the grace of God, of Great Britain, France and Ireland king, defender of the faith, and so forth. To all to whom these presents shall come, greeting.

Whereas we are credibly informed, that many of our poor subjects are, through misfortunes and want of employment, reduced to great necessity, insomuch as by their labor they are not able to provide a maintenance for themselves and families; and if they had means to defray their charges of passage, and other expences, incident to new settlements, they would be glad to settle in any of our provinces in America where by cultivating the lands, at present waste and desolate, they might not only gain a comfortable subsistence for themselves and families, but also strengthen our colonies and increase the trade, navigation and wealth of these our realms. And whereas our provinces in North America, have been frequently ravaged by Indian enemies; more especially that of South-Carolina, which in the late war, by the neighboring savages, was laid waste with fire and sword, and great numbers of English inhabitants, miserably massacred, and our loving subjects who now inhabit them, by reason of the smallness of their numbers, will in case of a new war, be exposed to the late calamities; inasmuch as their whole southern frontier continueth unsettled, and lieth open to the said savages—And whereas we think it highly becoming our crown and royal dignity, to protect all our loving subjects, be they ever so distant from us; to extent our fatherly compassion even to the meanest and most unfortunate of our people, and to relieve the wants of our above mentioned poor subjects; and that it will be highly conducive for accomplishing those ends, that a regular colony of the said poor people be settled and established in the southern territories of Carolina. And whereas we have been well assured, that if we will be most graciously pleased to erect and settle a corporation, for the receiving, managing and disposing of the contributions of our loving subjects; divers persons would be induced to contribute to the uses and purposes aforesaid—Know ye therefore, that we have, for the considerations aforesaid, and for the better and more orderly carrying on of the said good purposes; of our special grace, certain knowledge and mere motion, willed, ordained, constituted and appointed, and by these presents, for us, our heirs and successors, do will, ordain, constitute, declare and grant, that our right trusty and well beloved John, lord-viscount Purcival, of our kingdom of Ireland, our trusty and well beloved Edward Digby, George Carpenter, James Oglethorpe, George Heathcote, Thomas Tower, Robert Moore, Robert Hucks, Roger Holland, William Sloper, Francis Eyles, John Laroche, James Vernon, William Beletha, esquires, A. M. John Burton, B. D. Richard Bundy, A. M. Arthur Bedford, A. M. Samuel Smith, A. M. Adam Anderson and Thomas Corane, gentlemen; and such other persons as shall be elected in the manner herein after mentioned, and their successors to be elected in the manner herein after directed; be, and shall be one body politic and corporate, in deed and in name, by the name of the Trustees for establishing the colony of Georgia in America; and them and their successors by the same name, we do, by these presents, for us, our heirs and successors, really and fully make, ordain, constitute and declare, to be one body politic and corporate in deed and in name forever; and that by the same name, they and their successors, shall and may have perpetual succession; and that they and their successors by that name shall and may forever hereafter, by persons able and capable in the law, to purchase, have, take, receive and enjoy, to them and their successors, any manors, messuages, lands, tenements, rents, advowsons, liberties, privileges, jurisdictions, franchises, and other hereditaments whatsoever, lying and being in Great Britain, or any part thereof, of whatsoever nature, kind or quality, or value they be, in fee and in perpetuity, not exceeding the yearly value of one thousand pounds, beyond reprises; also estates for lives, and for years, and all other manner of goods, chattels and things whatsoever they be; for the better settling and supporting, and maintaining the said colony, and other uses aforesaid; and to give, grant, let and demise the said manors, messuages, lands, tenements, hereditaments, goods, chattels and things whatsoever aforesaid, by lease or leases, for term of years, in possession at the time of granting thereof, and not in reversion, not exceeding the term of thirty-one years, from the time of granting thereof; on which in case no fine be taken, shall be reserved the full value, and in case a fine be taken, shall be reserved at least a moiety of the full value that the same shall reasonably and *bona fide* be worth at the time of such demise; and that they and their successors, by the name aforesaid, shall and may forever hereafter, be persons able, capable in the law, to purchase, have, take, receive, and enjoy, to them and their successors, any lands, territories, possessions, tenements, jurisdictions, franchises and hereditaments whatsoever lying and being in America, of what quantity, quality or value whatsoever they be, for the better settling and supporting and maintaining the said colony; and that by the name aforesaid they shall and may be able to sue and be

sued, plead and be impleaded, answer and be answered unto, defend and be defended, in all courts and places whatsoever, and before whatsoever judges, justices, and other officers, of us, our heirs and successors, in all and singular actions, plaints, pleas, matters, suits and demands, of what kind, nature or quality soever they be; and to act and to do, all matters and things in as ample manner and form as any other our liege subjects of this realm of Great Britain, and that they and their successors forever hereafter, shall and may have a common seal, to serve for the causes and business of them and their successors; and that it shall and may be lawful for them and their successors, to change, break, alter and make new the said seal, from time to time, and at their pleasure, and as they shall think best.

And we do further grant, for us, our heirs and successors, that the said corporation, and the common council of the said corporation, hereinafter by us appointed, may from time to time, and at all times, meet about their affairs when and where they please, and transact and carry on the business of the said corporation. And for the better execution of the purposes aforesaid, we do, by these presents, for us, our heirs and successors, give & grant to the said corporation, and their successors, that they and their successors forever, may upon the third Thursday in the month of March, yearly, meet at some convenient place to be appointed by the said corporation, or major part of them who shall be present at any meeting of the said corporation, to be had for the appointing of the said place; and that they, or two thirds of such of them, that shall be present at such yearly meeting, and at no other meeting of the said corporation, between the hours of ten in the morning and four in the afternoon of the same day, choose and elect such person or persons to be members of the said corporation, as they shall think beneficial to the good designs of the said corporation. And our further will and pleasure is, that if it shall happen that any person hereinafter by us appointed, as the common council of the said corporation, or any persons to be elected or admitted members of the said common council in the manner hereafter directed, shall die, or shall by writing under his and their hands respectively resign his or their office or offices of common council man or common council men; the said corporation, or the major part of such of them as shall be present, shall and may at such meeting, on the said third Thursday in March yearly, in manner as aforesaid, next after such death or resignation, and at no other meeting of the said corporation, into the room or place of such person or persons so dead or so resigning, elect and choose one or more such person or persons, being members of the said corporation, as to them shall seem meet; and our will is, that all and every the person or persons which shall from time to time hereafter be elected common council men of the said corporation as aforesaid, do and shall, before he or they act as common men of the said corporation, take an oath for the faithful and due execution of their office; which oath the president of the said corporation for the time being, is hereby authorized and required to administer to such person or persons elected as aforesaid. And our will and pleasure is, that the first president of the said corporation is and shall be our trusty and well-beloved, the said Lord John Viscount Percival; and that the said president shall, within thirty days after the passing this charter, cause a summons to be issued to the several members of the said corporation herein particularly named, to meet at such time and place as he shall appoint, to consult about and transact the business of said corporation. And our will and pleasure is, and we, by these presents, for us, our heirs, and successors, grant, ordain, and direct, that the common council of this corporation shall consist of fifteen in number; and we do, by these presents, nominate, constitute, and appoint our right trusty and well-beloved John Lord Viscount Percival, our trusty and beloved Edward Digby, George Carpenter, James Oglethorpe, George Heathcote, Thomas Laroche, James Vernon, William Beletha, esqrs., and Stephen Hales, Master of Arts, to be the common council of the said corporation, to continue in the said office during their good behavior. And whereas it is our royal intention, that the members of the said corporation should be increased by election, as soon as conveniently may be, to a greater number than is hereby nominated; Our further will and pleasure is, and we do hereby, for us, our heirs and successors, ordain and direct, that from the time of such increase of the members of the said corporation, the number of the said common council shall be increased to twenty-four; and that the same assembly at which such additional members of the said corporation shall be chosen, there shall likewise be elected in the manner hereinbefore directed for the election of common council men, nine persons to be the said common council men, and to make up the number thereof twenty-four. And our further will and pleasure is, that our trusty and well beloved Edward Digby, esquire, shall be the first chairman of the common council of the said corporation; and that the said lord-viscount Purcival shall be, and continue, president of the said corporation, and that the said Edward Digby shall be and continue chairman of the common council of the said corporation, respectively, until the meeting which shall be had next and immediately after the first meeting of the said corporation, or of the common council of the said corporation respectively, and no longer; at which said second meeting, and every other subsequent and future meeting of the said corporation or of the common council of the said corporation respectively, in order to preserve an indifferent rotation of the several offices, of president of the corporation, and of chairman of the common council of the said corporation we do direct and ordain that all and every the person and persons, members of the said common council for the time being, and no

other, being present at such meetings, shall severally and respectively in their turns, preside at the meetings which shall from time to time be held of the said corporation, or of the common council of the said corporation respectively; and in case any doubt or question shall at any time arise touching or concerning the turn or right of any member of the said common council to preside at any meeting of the said corporation, or at the common council of the said corporation, the same shall respectively be determined by the major part of the said corporation, or of the common council of the said corporation respectively, who shall be present at such meeting. Provided always, that no member of the said common council having served in the offices of president of the said corporation, or of chairman of the common council of the said corporation, shall be capable of being, or of serving as president or chairman at any meeting of the said corporation, or common council of the said corporation next and immediately ensuing that in which he so served as president of the said corporation or chairman of the said common council of the said corporation respectively; unless it shall so happen that at any such meeting of the said corporation, there shall not be any other member of the said common council present.

And our will and pleasure is, that at all and every of the meetings of the said corporation, or of the common council of the said corporation, the president or chairman for the time being, shall have a voice and shall vote, and shall act as a member of the said corporation or of the common council of the said corporation, at such meeting; and in case of any equality of votes, the said president or chairman for the time being, shall have and exercise a casting vote. And our further will and pleasure is, that no president of the said corporation, or chairman of the common council of the said corporation, or member of the said common council or corporation, by us by these presents appointed, or hereafter from time to time to be elected and appointed in manner aforesaid, shall have, take, or receive, directly or indirectly, any salary, fee, perquisite, benefit or profit whatsoever, for or by reason of his or their serving the said corporation, or common council of the said corporation, or president, chairman or common councilman, or as being a member of the said corporation. And our will and pleasure is, that the said herein before appointed president, chairman or common council-men, before he and they act respectively as such, shall severally take an oath for the faithful and due execution of their trust, to be administered to the president by the Chief Baron of our Court of Exchequer, for the time being, and by the president of the said corporation to the rest of the common council, who are hereby authorised severally and respectively, to administer the same. And our will and pleasure is, that all and every person and persons, shall have in his or their own name or names, or in the name or names of any person or persons in trust for him or them, or for his or their benefit, any place, office or employment of profit, under the said corporation, shall be incapable of being elected a member of the said corporation; and if any member of the said corporation during such time as he shall continue a member thereof, shall in his own name or in the name of any person or persons, in trust for him or for his benefit, have, hold or exercise, accept, possess or enjoy, any office, place or employment of profit, under the said corporation, or under the common council of the said corporation—such member shall from the time of his having, holding, exercising, accepting possessing and enjoying such office, place and employment of profit, cease to be a member of the said corporation. And we do for us, our heirs and successors, grant unto the said corporation, that they and their successors or the major part of such of them as shall be present at any meeting of the said corporation, convened and assembled for that purpose by a convenient notice thereof, shall have power from time to time, and at all times hereafter, to authorize and appoint such persons as they shall think fit to take subscriptions, and to gather and collect such moneys as shall be by any person or, persons contributed for the purposes aforesaid; and shall and may revoke and make void such authorities and appointments, as often as they shall see cause so to do.

And we do hereby for us, our heirs and successors, ordain and direct, that the said corporation shall every year lay an account in writing before the chancellor, or speaker, or commissioners, for the custody of the great seal of Great-Britain, of us, our heirs and successors; the Chief Justice of the Court of King's Bench, the Master of Rolls the Chief Justice of the Court of Common Pleas, and the chief Baron of the Exchequer of us, our heirs and successors for the time being, or any two of them; of all moneys and effects by them received or expended, for the carrying on of the good purposes aforesaid. And we do hereby, for us, our heirs and successors, give and grant unto the said corporation, and their successors, full power and authority to constitute, ordain and make, such and so many by-laws, constitutions, orders and ordinances, as to them, or the greater part of them, at their general meeting for that purpose, shall seem necessary and convenient for the well ordaining and governing of the said corporation; and the said by-laws, constitutions, orders and ordinances, or any of them, to alter and annul, as they or the major part of them then present shall see requisite: and in and by such by-laws, rules, orders and ordinances, to sell, impose and inflict, reasonable pains and penalties upon any offender or offenders, who shall transgress, break or violate the said by-laws, constitutions, orders and ordinances, so made as aforesaid, and to mitigate the same as they or the major part of them then present shall find cause, which said pains and penalties, shall and may be levied, sued for, taken, retained and recovered, by the said corporation and their successors, by their officers and servants, from time to time, to be appointed for

that purpose, by action of debt, or by any other lawful ways or means, to the use and behoof of the said corporation and their successors, all and singular: which by-laws, constitutions, orders and ordinances, so as aforesaid to be made, we will shall be duly observed and kept, under the pains and penalties therein to be contained, so always, as the said by-laws, constitutions, orders, and ordinances, pains and penalties, from time to time to be made and imposed, be reasonable and not contrary or repugnant to the laws or statutes of this our realm; and that such by-laws, constitutions and ordinances, pains and penalties, from time to time to be made and imposed; and any repeal or alteration thereof, or any of them, may be likewise agreed to be established and confirmed by the said general meeting of the said corporation, to be held and kept next after the same shall be respectively made. And whereas the said corporation intend to settle a colony, and to make an habitation and plantation in that part of our province of South-Carolina, in America, herein after described. Know ye, therefore that we greatly desiring the happy success of the said corporation, for their further encouragement in accomplishing so excellent a work have of our aforesaid grace, certain knowledge and mere motion, given and granted by these presents, for us, our heirs and successors, do give and grant to the said corporation and their successors under the reservation, limitation and declaration, hereafter expressed, seven undivided parts, the whole in eight equal parts to be divided, of all those lands, countrys and territories, situate, lying and being in that part of South-Carolina, in America, which lies from the most northern part of a stream or river there, commonly called the Savannah, all along the sea coast to the southward, unto the most southern stream of a certain other great water or river called the Alatamaha, and westerly from the heads of the said rivers respectively, in direct lines to the south seas; and all that share, circuit and precinct of land, within the said boundaries, with the islands on the sea, lying opposite to the eastern coast of the said lands, within twenty leagues of the same, which are not inhabited already, or settled by any authority derived from the crown of Great-Britain: together with all the soils, grounds, havens, ports, gulfs and bays, mines, as well royal mines of gold and silver, as other minerals, precious stones, quarries, woods, rivers, waters, fishings, as well royal fishings of whale and sturgeon as other fishings, pearls, commodities, jurisdictions, royalties, franchises, privileges and pre-eminences within the said frontiers and precincts thereof and thereunto, in any sort belonging or appertaining, and which we by our letters patent may or can grant, and in as ample manner and sort as we may or any of our royal progenitors have hitherto granted to any company, body politic or corporate, or to any adventurer or adventurers, undertaker or undertakers, of any discoveries, plantations or traffic, of, in, or unto any foreign parts whatsoever; and in as large and ample manner, as if the same were herein particularly mentioned and expressed: to have, hold, possess and enjoy, the said seven undivided parts, the whole into eight equal parts, to be divided as aforesaid, of all and singular the lands, countries and territories, with all and singular other the premises herein before by these presents granted or mentioned, or intended to be granted to them, the said corporation, and their successors forever, for the better support of the said colony, to be holden of us, our heirs and successors, as of our honour of Hamptoncourt, in our county of Middlesex in free and common soccage, and not in capite, yielding, and paying therefor to us, our heirs and successors yearly forever, the sum of four shillings for every hundred acres of the said lands, which the said corporation shall grant, demise, plant or settle; the said payment not to commence or to be made, until ten years after such grant, demise, planting or settling; and to be answered and paid to us, our heirs and successors, in such manner and in such species of money or notes, as shall be current in payment, by proclamation from time to time, in our said province of South-Carolina. All which lands, countries, territories and premises, hereby granted or mentioned, and intended to be granted, we do by these presents, make, erect and create one independent and separate province, by the name of Georgia, by which name we will, the same henceforth be called. And that all and every person and persons, who shall at any time hereafter inhabit or reside within our said province, shall be, and are hereby declared to be free, and shall not be subject to or be bound to obey any laws, orders, statutes or constitutions, which have been heretofore made, ordered or enacted by for, or as, the laws, orders, statutes or constitutions of our said province of South-Carolina, (save and except only the commander in chief of the militia, of our said province of Georgia, to our governor for the time being of South-Carolina, in manner hereafter declared;) but shall be subject to, and bound to obey, such laws, orders, statutes and constitutions as shall from time to time be made, ordered and enacted, for the better government of the said province of Georgia, in the manner hereinafter declared.

And we do hereby, for our heirs and successors, ordain, will and establish, that for and during the term of twenty-one years, to commence from the date of these our letters patent, the said corporation assembled for that purpose, shall and may form and prepare, laws, statutes and ordinances, fit and necessary for and concerning the government of the said colony, and not repugnant to the laws and statutes of England; and the same shall and may present under their common seal to us, our heirs and successors, in our or their privy council for our or their approbation or disallowance: and the said laws, statutes and ordinances, being approved of by us, our heirs and successors, in our or their privy council, shall from thence forth be in full force and virtue within our said province of Georgia. And forasmuch as the good and prosperous suc-

cess of the said colony cannot but chiefly depend, next under the blessing of God, and the support of our royal authority, upon the provident and good direction of the whole enterprise, and that it will be too great a burthen upon all the members of the said corporation to be convened so often as may be requisite, to hold meetings for the settling, supporting, ordering, and maintaining the said colony; therefore we do will, ordain and establish, that the said common council for the time being, of the said corporation, being assembled for that purpose, or the major part of them, shall from time to time, and at all times hereafter, have full power and authority to dispose of, extend and apply all the monies and effects belonging to the said corporation, in such manner and ways and by such expenses as they shall think best to conduce to the carrying on and effecting the good purposes herein mentioned and intended; and also shall have full power in the name and on account of the said corporation, and with and under their common seal, to enter under any covenants or contracts, for carrying on and effecting the purposes aforesaid. And our further will and pleasure is, that the said common council form the time being, or the major part of such common council, which shall be present and assembled for that purpose, from time to time, and at all times hereafter, shall and may nominate, constitute and appoint a treasurer or treasurers, secretary or secretaries, and such other officers, ministers and servants of the said corporation as to them or the major part of them as shall be present, shall seem proper or requisite for the good management of their affairs; and at their will and pleasure to displace, remove and put out such treasurer or treasurers, secretary or secretaries, and all such other officers, ministers and servants, as often as they shall think fit so to do; and others in the room, office, place or station of him or them so displaced, remove or put out, to nominate, constitute and appoint; and shall and may determine and appoint, such reasonable salaries, perquisites and other rewards, for their labor, or service of such officers, servants and persons as to the said common council shall seem meet; and all such officers servants and persons shall, before the acting of their respective offices, take an oath to be to them administered by the chairman for the time being of the said common council of the said corporation, who is hereby authorized to administer the same, for the faithful and due execution of their respective offices and places.

And our will and pleasure is, that all and every person and persons, who shall from time to time be chosen or appointed treasurer or treasurers, secretary or secretaries of the said corporation, in manner herein after directed, shall during such times as they shall serve in the said offices respectively, be incapable of being a member of the said corporation. And we do further of our special grace, certain knowledge and mere motion, for us, our heirs and successors, grant, by these presents, to the said corporation and their successors, that it shall be lawful for them and their officers or agents, at all times hereafter, to transport and convey out of our realm of Great-Britain, or any other of our dominions, into the said province of Georgia, to be there settled all such so many of our loving subjects, or any foreigners that are willing to become our subjects, and live under our allegiance, in the said colony, as shall be willing to go to, inhabit, or reside there, with sufficient shipping, armour, weapons, powder, shot, ordnance, munition, victuals, merchandise and wares, as are esteemed by the wild people; clothing, implements, furniture, cattle, horses, mares, and all other things necessary for the said colony, and for the use and defence and trade with the people there, and in passing and returning to and from the same. Also we do, for ourselves and successors, declare, by these presents, that all and every the persons which shall happen to be born within the said province, and every of their children and posterity, shall have and enjoy all liberties, franchises and immunities of free denizens and natural born subjects, within any of our dominions, to all intents and purposes, as if abiding and born within this our kingdom of Great-Britain, or any other of our dominions— And for the greater ease and encouragement of our loving subjects and such others as shall come to inhabit in our said colony, we do by these presents, for us, our heirs and successors, grant, establish and ordain, that forever hereafter, there shall be a liberty of conscience allowed in the worship of God, to all persons inhabiting, or which shall inhabit or be resident within our said province, and that all such persons, except papists, shall have a free exercise of their religion, so they be contented with the quiet and peaceable enjoyment of the same, not giving offence or scandal to the government. And our further will and pleasure is, and we do hereby for us, our heirs and successors, declare and grant, that it shall and may be lawful for the said common council, or the major part of them assembled for that purpose, in the name of the corporation, and under the common seal, to distribute, convey, assign and set over such particular portions of lands, tenements and hereditaments by these presents granted to the said corporation, unto such our loving subjects, natural born, denizens or others that shall be willing to become our subjects, and live under our allegiance in the said colony, upon such terms, and for such estates, and upon such rents, reservations and conditions as the same may be lawfully granted, and as to the said common council, or the major part of them so present, shall seem fit and proper. Provided always that no grants shall be made of any part of the said lands unto any person, being a member of the said corporation, or to any other person in trust, for the benefit of any member of the said corporation; and that no person having any estate or interest, in law or equity, in any part of the said lands, shall be capable of being a member of the said corporation, during the continuance of such estate or

interest. Provided also, that no greater quantity of lands be granted, either entirely or in parcels, to or for the use, or in trust for any one person, than five hundred acres; and that all grants made contrary to the true intent and meaning hereof, shall be absolutely null and void.

And we do hereby grant and ordain, that such person or persons, for the time being as shall be thereunto appointed by the said corporation, shall and may at all times, and from time to time hereafter, have full power and authority to administer and give the oaths, appointed by an act of parliament, made in the first year of the reign of our late royal father, to be taken instead of the oaths of allegiance and supremacy; and also the oath of abjuration, to all and every person and persons which shall at any time be inhabiting or residing within our said colony; and in like cases to administer the solemn affirmation to any of the persons commonly called quakers, in such manners as by the laws of our realm of Great-Britain, the same may be administered. And we do, of our further grace, certain knowledge and mere motion, grant, establish and ordain, for us, our heirs and successors, that the said corporation and their successors, shall have full power and authority, for and during the term of twenty-one years, to commence from the date of these our letters patent, to erect and constitute judicatories and courts of record, or other courts, to be held in the name of us, our heirs and successors for the hearing and determining of all manner of crimes, offences, pleas, processes, plaints, actions, matters, causes and things whatsoever, arising or happening, within the said province of Georgia, or between persons of Georgia; whether the same be criminal or civil, and whether the said crimes be capital or not capital, and whether the said pleas be real, personal or mixed: and for awarding and making out executions thereupon; to which courts and judicatories, we do hereby, for us, our heirs and successors, give and grant full power and authority, from time to time, to administer oaths for the discovery of truth in any matter in controversy, or depending before them, or the solemn affirmation, to any of the persons commonly called quakers, in such manner, as by the laws of our realm of Great-Britain, the same may be administered.

And our further will and pleasure is, that the said corporation and their successors, do from time to time, and at all times hereafter, register or cause to be registered, all such leases, grants, plantings, conveyances, settlements, and improvements whatsoever, as shall at any time hereafter be made by, or in the name of the said corporation, or any lands, tenements or hereditaments within the said province; and shall yearly send and transmit, or cause to be sent or transmitted, authentic accounts of such leases, grants, conveyances, settlements and improvements respectively, unto the auditor of the plantations for the time being, or his deputy, and also to our surveyor for the time being of our said province of South-Carolina; to whom we do hereby grant full power and authority from time to time, as often as need shall require, to inspect and survey, such of the said lands and premises, as shall be demised, granted and settled as aforesaid: which said survey and inspection, we do hereby declare, to be intended to ascertain the quitrents which shall from time to time become due to us, our heirs and successors, according to the reservation herein before mentioned, and for no other purposes whatsoever; hereby for us, our heirs and successors, strictly enjoining and commanding, that neither our or their surveyor, or any person whatsoever, under the pretext and colour of making the said survey or inspection, shall take, demand or receive, any gratuity, fee or reward, of or from, any person or persons, inhabiting in the said colony, or from the said corporation or common council thereof, on the pain of forfeiture of the said office or offices, and incurring our highest displeasure. Provided always, and our further will and pleasure is, that all leases, grants and conveyances to be made by or in the name of the said corporation, of any lands within the said province, or a memorial containing the substance and effect thereof, shall be registered with the auditor of the said plantations, of us, our heirs and successors, within the space of one year, to be computed from the date thereof, otherwise the same shall be void.

And our further will and pleasure is, that the rents, issues and all other profits, which shall at any time hereafter come to the said corporation, or the major part of them which shall be present at any meeting for that purpose assembled, shall think will most improve and enlarge the said colony, and best answer the good purposes herein before mentioned, and for defraying all other charges about the same. And our will and pleasure is, that the said corporation and their successors, shall from time to time give in to one of the principal secretaries of state, and to the commissioners of trade and plantations, accounts of the progresses of the said colony. And our will and pleasure is that no act done at any meeting of the said common council of the said corporation, shall be effectual and valid, unless eight members at least of the said common council, including the member who shall serve as chairman at the said meeting, be present, and the major part of them consenting thereunto. And our will and pleasure is, that the common council of the said corporation for the time being, or the major part of them who shall be present, being assembled for that purpose, shall from time to time, for, and during, and unto the full end and expiration of twenty-one years, to commence from the date of these our letters patent, have full power and authority to nominate, make, constitute and commission, ordain and appoint, by such name or names, style or styles, as to them shall seem meet and fitting, all and singular such governors, judges, magistrates, ministers and officers, civil and military, both by sea and land, within the said districts, as shall by them be

thought fit and needful to be made or used for the said government of the said colony; save always, and except such offices only as shall by us, our heirs and successors, be from time to time constituted and appointed, for the managing collecting and receiving such revenues, as shall from time to time arise within the said province of Georgia, and become due to us, our heirs and successors.

Provided always, and it is our will and pleasure, that every governor of the said province of Georgia, to be appointed by the common council of the said corporation, before he shall enter upon or execute the said office of governor, shall be approved by us, our heirs or successors, and shall take such oaths, and shall qualify himself in such manner, in all respects, as any governor or commander in chief of any of our colonies or plantations in America, are by law required to do; and shall give good and sufficient security for observing the several acts of parliament relating to trade and navigation, and to observe and obey all instructions that shall be sent to him by us, our heirs and successors, or any acting under our or their authority, pursuant to the said acts, or any of them. And we do by these presents for us, our heirs and successors, will, grant and ordain, that the said corporation and their successors, shall have full power for and during and until the full end and term of twenty-one years, to commence from the date of these our letters patent, by any commander or other officer or officers, by them for that purpose from time to time appointed, to train and instruct, exercise and govern a militia, for the special defence and safety of our said colony, to assemble in martial array, the inhabitants of the said colony, and to lead and conduct them, and with them to encounter, expulse, repel, resist and pursue by force of arms, as well by sea as by land, within or without the limits of our said colony; and also to kill, slay and destroy, and conquer by all fitting ways, enterprizes and means whatsoever, all and every such person or persons as shall at any time hereafter, in any hostile manner, attempt or enterprize the destruction, invasion, detriment or annoyance of our said colony; and to use and exercise the martial law in time of actual war and invasion or rebellion, in such cases, where by law the same may be used or exercised; and also from time to time to erect forts, and fortify any place or places within our said colony, and the same to furnish with all necessary ammunition, provisions and stores of war, for offence and defence, and to commit from time to time the custody or government of the same, to such person or persons as to them shall seem meet: and the said forts and fortifications to demolish at their pleasure; and to take and surprize, by all ways and means, all and every such person or persons, with their ships, arms, ammunition and other goods, as shall in an hostile manner, invade or attempt the invading, conquering or annoying of our said colony. And our will and pleasure is, and we do hereby, for us, our heirs and successors, declares and grant, that the governor and commander in chief of the province of South-Carolina, of us, our heirs and successors, for the time being, shall at all times hereafter have the chief command of the militia of our said province, hereby erected and established; and that such militia shall observe and obey all orders and directions, that shall from time to time be given or sent to them by the said governor or commander in chief; any thing in these presents before contained to the contrary hereof, in any wise notwithstanding. And, of our more special grace, certain knowledge and mere motion, we have given and granted, and by these presents, for us, our heirs and successors, do give and grant, unto the said corporation and their successors, full power and authority to import and export their goods, at and from any port or ports that shall be appointed by us, our heirs and successors, within the said province of Georgia, for that purpose, without being obliged to touch at any other port in South-Carolina. And we do, by these presents, for us, our heirs and successors, will and declare, that from and after the termination of the said term or twenty-one years, such form of government and method of making laws, statutes and ordinances, for the better governing and ordering the said province of Georgia, and the inhabitants thereof, shall be established and observed within the same, as we, our heirs and successors, shall hereafter ordain and appoint, and shall be agreeably to law; and that from and after the determination of the said term of twenty-one years, the governor of

our said province of Georgia, and all officers civil and military, within the same, shall from time to time be nominated and constituted, and appointed by us, our heirs and successors. And lastly, we do hereby, for us, our heirs and successors, grant unto the said corporation and their successors, that these our letters patent, or the enrolments or exemplification thereof, shall be in and by all things good, firm, valid, sufficient and effectual in the law, according to the true intent and meaning thereof, and shall be taken, construed and adjudged, in all courts and elsewhere in the most favorable and beneficial sense, and for the best advantage of the said corporation and their successors any omission, imperfection, defect, matter or cause, or thing whatsoever to the contrary, in any wise notwithstanding. In witness, whereof we have caused these our letters to be made patent: witness ourself at Westminster, the ninth day of June in the fifth year of our reign.

By writ of privy-seal.
Cooks.

Source:

Francis Newton Thorpe, ed. *The Federal and State Constitutions, Colonial Charters, and Other Organic Laws of the States, Territories, and Colonies Now or Heretofore Forming the United States of America.* Vol. 2. Washington, D.C.: Government Printing Office, 1909, pp. 765–777.

Settlers and Native Americans in the Colonies

Richard Frethorne, Letter from an Indentured Servant in Virginia, 1623

An indenture was a form of a contract. The two copies were written on one piece of paper and then cut from each other with an "indent" that could be matched up. Individuals too poor to pay for their passage but desiring to find a better life in the New World could "indenture" themselves to a ship master, who in turn sold the indenture to a planter. The servant worked usually for seven years, or if still a child, until his or her majority. The earliest blacks brought to America were thought to be indentured servants, rather than slaves. Convicts also were given the choice of "the new world or the next

world." Those choosing the colonies over death also were indentured. When the indenture was up, the men became freemen and had the same privileges as others of their station.

Loving and Kind Father and Mother:

My most humble duty remembered to you, hoping in god of your good health, as I myself am at the making hereof. This is to let you understand that I your child am in a most heavy case by reason of the country, [which] is such that it causeth much sickness, [such] as the scurvy and the bloody flux and diverse other diseases, which maketh the body very poor and weak. And when we are sick there is nothing to comfort us; for since I came out of the ship I never ate anything but peas, and loblollie (that is, water gruel). As for deer or venison I never saw any since I came into this land. There is indeed some fowl, but we are not allowed to go and get it, but must work hard both early and late for a mess of water gruel and a mouthful of bread and beef. A mouthful of bread for a penny loaf must serve for four men which is most pitiful. [You would be grieved] if you did know as much as I [do], when people cry out day and night—Oh! That they were in England without their limbs—and would not care to lose any limb to be in England again, yea, though they beg from door to door. For we live in fear of the enemy every hour, yet we have had a combat with them . . . and we took two alive and made slaves of them. But it was by policy, for we are in great danger; for our plantation is very weak by reason of the death and sickness of our company. For we came but twenty for the merchants, and they are half dead just; and we look every hour when two more should go. Yet there came some four other men yet to live with us, of which there is but one alive; and our Lieutenant is dead, and [also] his father and his brother. And there was some five or six of the last year's twenty, of which there is but three left, so that we are fain to get other men to plant with us; and yet we are but 32 to fight against 3000 if they should come. And the nighest help that we have is ten mile of us, and when the rogues overcame this place [the] last [time] they slew 80 persons. How then shall we do, for we lie even in their teeth? They may easily take us, but [for the fact] that God is merciful and can save with few as well as with many, as he showed to Gilead. And like Gilead's soldiers, if they lapped water, we drink water which is but weak.

And I have nothing to comfort me, nor is there nothing to be gotten here but sickness and death, except [in the event] that one had money to lay out in some things for profit. But I have nothing at all—no, not a shirt to my back but two rags (2), nor clothes but one poor suit, nor but one pair of shoes, but one pair of stockings, but one cap, [and] but two bands [collars]. My cloak is stolen by one of my fellows, and to his dying hour [he] would not tell me what he did with it; but some of my fellows saw him have butter and beef out of a ship, which my cloak, I doubt [not], paid for. So that I have not a penny, nor a penny worth, to help me too either spice or sugar or strong waters, without the which one cannot live here. For as strong beer in England doth fatten and strengthen them, so water here doth wash and weaken these here [and] only keeps [their] life and soul together. But I am not half [of] a quarter so strong as I was in England, and all is for want of victuals; for I do protest unto you that I have eaten more in [one] day at home than I have allowed me here for a week. You have given more than my day's allowance to a beggar at the door; and if Mr. Jackson had not relieved me, I should be in a poor case. But he like a father and she like a loving mother doth still help me.

For when we go to Jamestown (that is 10 miles of us) there lie all the ships that come to land, and there they must deliver their goods. And when we went up to town [we would go], as it may be, on Monday at noon, and come there by night, [and] then load the next day by noon, and go home in the afternoon, and unload, and then away again in the night, and [we would] be up about midnight. Then if it rained or blowed never so hard, we must lie in the boat on the water and have nothing but a little bread. For when we go into the boat we [would] have a loaf allowed to two men, and it is all [we would get] if we stayed there two days, which is hard; and [we] must lie all that while in the boat. But that Goodman Jackson pitied me and made me a cabin to lie in always when I [would] come up, and he would give me some poor jacks [fish] [to take] home with me, which comforted me more than peas or water gruel. Oh, they be very godly folks, and love me very well, and will do anything for me. And he much marvelled that you would send me a servant to the Company; he saith I had been better knocked on the head. And indeed so I find it now, to my great grief and misery; and [I] saith that if you love me you will redeem me suddenly, for which I do entreat and beg. And if you cannot get the merchants to redeem me for some little money, then for God's sake get a gathering or entreat some good folks to lay out some little sum of money in meal and cheese and butter and beef. Any eating meat will yield great profit. Oil and vinegar is very good; but, father, there is great loss in leaking. But for God's sake send beef and cheese and butter, or the more of one sort and none of another. But if you send cheese, it must be very old cheese; and at the cheesemonger's you may buy very food cheese for twopence farthing or halfpenny, that will be liked very well. But if you send cheese, you must have a care how you pack it in barrels; and you must put cooper's chips between every cheese, or else the heat of the hold will rot them. And look whatsoever you send me—be in never so much—look, what[ever] I make of it, I will deal truly with you. I will send it over and beg the profit to redeem me; and if I die before it come, I have entreated Goodman Jackson to send you the worth of it, who hath promised he will. If you send, you must direct your letters to Goodman Jackson, at Jamestown, a gunsmith. (You must set down his freight, because there be more of his name there.) Good father, do not forget me, but have mercy and pity my miserable case. I know if you did but see me, you would weep to see me; for I have but one suit. (But [though] it is a strange one, it is very well guarded.) Wherefore, for God's sake, pity me. I pray you to remember my love to all my friends and kindred. I hope all my brothers and sisters are in good health, and as for my part I have set down my resolution that certainly will be; that is, that the answer of this letter will be life or death to me. Therefore, good father, send as soon as you can; and if you send me any thing let this be the mark.

Richard Frethorne,
Martin's Hundred.

Source:
Susan Kingsbury, ed., *The Records of the Virginia Company of London*. Washington, D.C.: Government Printing Office, 1935, pp. 4: 58–62.

Virginia Statutes Regulating Slavery, ca. 1660–1669

Dutch traders first sold African slaves to Virginia settlers in the early 17th century. Although the number of slaves was relatively small in the first half of the century, the institution of slavery was firmly established by statutes passed in Virginia in the 1660s. These laws regulated every aspect of slavery, including how to deal with runaway slaves, the servitude of children, baptism, taxation, and punishment. They also reflected the processes by which the law developed as relations between slaves and the English settlers produced new conditions that required clarification. The laws also made clear that anyone at least half Negro was to be considered apart (and presumably inferior to) the English, regardless of their status, slave or free, and whether they had an English father. The act regarding the casual killing of slaves also made clear that at least in law slaves were considered property first.

Act XXII. English Running Away with Negroes, ca. 1660
English running away with negroes.

Bee itt enacted That case in any English servant shall run away in company with any negroes who are incapable of makeing satisfaction by addition of time, *Bee itt enacted* that the English so running away in company with them shall serve for the time of the said negroes absence as they are to do for their owne by a former act.

Act XXII. Negro Womens Children to Serve According to the Condition of the Mother, 1662
Negro womens children to serve according to the condition of the mother.

Whereas some doubts have arrisen whether children got by any Englishman upon a negro woman should be slave or ffree, *Be it therefore enacted and declared by this present grand assembly*, that all children borne in this country shalbe held bond or free only according to the condition of the mother, *And* that if any christian shall committ ffornication with a negro man or woman, hee or shee soe offending shall pay double the ffines imposed by the former act.

Act III. An Act Declaring that Baptisme of Slaves Doth Not Exempt Them from Bondage, 1667
An act declaring that baptisme of slaves doth not exempt them from bondage.

Whereas some doubts have risen whether children that are slaves by birth, and by the charity and piety of their owners made pertakers of the blessed sacrament of baptisme, should by vertue of their baptisme be made ffree; *It is enacted and declared by this grand assembly, and the authority thereof,* that the conferring of baptisme doth not alter the condition of the person as to his bondage or ffreedome; that diverse masters, ffreed from this doubt, may more carefully endeavour the propagation of christianity by permitting children, though slaves, or those of greater growth if capable to be admitted to that sacrament.

Act. VII Negro Women Not Exempted from Tax, 1668
Negro women not exempted from tax.

Whereas some doubts, have arisen whether negro women set free were still to be accompted tithable according to a former act, *It is declared by this grand assembly* that negro women, though permitted to enjoy their freedom yet ought not in all respects to be admitted to a full fruition of the exemptions and impunities of the English, and are still liable to payment of taxes.

Act I. An Act about the Casuall Killing of Slaves, 1669
An act about the casuall killing of slaves

Whereas the only law in force for the punishment of refractory servants resisting their master, mistris or overseer cannot be inflicted upon negroes, nor the obstinacy of many of them by other then violent meanes supprest, *Be it enacted and declared by this grand assembly,* if any slave resist his master (or other by his masters order correcting him) and by the extremity of the correction should chance to die, that his death shall not be accompted ffelony, but the master (or that other person appointed by the master to punish him) be acquit from molestation, since it cannot be presumed that prepensed malice (which alone makes murther ffelony) should induce any man to destroy his own estate.

Source:
Samuel Shepherd. *Statutes at Large of Virginia*. Vol. 2. New York: AMS Press, 1970. pp. 26, 170, 260, 267, 270.

Connecticut Blue Laws, 1673–1677, 1702

Colonial legislation regulating community standards of morality in Sabbath observance, dress, and habits. They came to be called *blue laws*. At the time, *blue* had a negative connotation, referring to inflexible moral standards. The English Parliament had enacted similar laws in the 14th century regulating sumptuous clothing, and later laws prohibited smoking, unnecessary work on the Sabbath, and barred certain businesses and sporting events from operating on Sundays. These laws were largely transplanted to the colonies intact and go back to the earliest years of the colonial period. Perhaps the most extreme measures were taken in New England, where, in 1651, the Massachusetts General Court declared its "complete disapproval of men and women of mean condition who wear the clothing of gentlemen" and prohibited personal adornments of gold, silk, and fur for those with estates of less than 200 pounds. The term *blue laws*, came into popular use with the publication of Reverend Samuel Peters's *General History of Connecticut* (1781), in which he ridiculed the Puritans with an imaginary code restricting mothers from kissing their children on Sundays.

Act Concerning the Dowry of Widows, 1673
That there may be some Provision made for the certain maintenance of Widows after the decease of their Husbands;

It is Ordered by the Authority of this Court; That every Married Woman (living with her Husband in this Colony, or otherwise absent from him with his consent, or through his meer default, or inevitable providence, or in cafe of Divorce, where she is the innocent party) that shall nor before Marriage be Estated by way of joynture in some Houses Lands, Tenements or other Hereditaments for term of her life, shall immediately after the death of her Husband have right and interest by way of dower in and to one third part of the real estate of her said husband that he stood of at the time of his decease in Houses and Lands, to be to her only during her natural life: And that every such Widow so endowed as aforesaid, shall maintain all such Houses, Fences and Inclosures as shall be assigned her for her Dowry, and shall leave the fame in good and sufficient reparation; the remainder of the Estate to be disposed according to the Will of the deceased, or in defect thereof according to the distribution the Court shall make thereof.

Act for Regulating and Orderly Celebrating of Marriage, 1673
For the preventing all unlawful Marriages;

It is Ordered by the Authority of this Court; That after the publication hereof, no persons shall be joyned in Mar-

riage before the intentions of the parties proceedings therein hath been published sufficiently at some publick Lecture or Town meeting in the Towns where the parties or either of them do ordinarily reside, or be set up in Writing fairly written upon some post of their Meeting House Door in publick view, there to stand so as it may be read eight dayes before such Marriage.

And whereas the power of disposal of Children in Marriage doth reside in the hands of Parents, and to prevent irregular proceeding herein;

It is Ordered by this Court; That whatsoever person from henceforth shall directly or indirectly endeavour to draw away the Affections of any Maid in this Colony, upon pretence of Marriage, before he hath obtained liberty and allowance from her Parents, Governours or Guardians, he shall forfeit for the first offence, *five pounds,* for the second offence towards the fame party *ten pounds,* and for the third offence, upon information or complaint by such Parents or Governours to any Magistrate, giving Bond to prosecute the party, he shall be committed to Prison, and upon hearing and conviction, by the next County Court, he shall be adjudged to continue in Prison until the Court of Assistants shall see cause to release him.

And as the Ordinance of Marriage is honourable amongst all, so it is meet it should be accordingly solemnized;

It is therefore Ordered by the Authority of this Court; That no person whatsoever in this Jurisdiction, shall joyn any persons together in Marriage, but the Magistrates, or such other as the General Court or Court of Assistants shall Authorize in such places where no Magistrate is near, nor shall any Magistrate or other person as aforesaid, joyn, and persons together in Marriage before the parties to be Married have been published according to Law.

Act Relating to Bills of Divorce, 1677
It is ordered by this Court that noe bill of divorce shall be granted to any man or woman lawfully marryed but in case of adultery, fraudulent contract, or willfull desertion for three years with totall neglect of duty, or seven years' providentiall absence being not heard of after due enquiry made and certifyed, such party shall be counted as legally dead to the other party; in all which cases a bill of divorce may be granted by the Court of Assistants to the agreived party who may then lawfully marry or be marryed to any other.

Act for Regulating and Orderly Celebrating of Marriage (1702)
An Act to Prevent Incestuous Marriages
Although this Court doth not take in hand to determine what is the whole breadth of the Divine Commandment, respecting unlawful Marriages, yet for preventing that

abominable Dishonesty and Confusion which might otherwise happen.

Be it Enacted by the Governour, Council and Representatives in General Court Assembled, and by the Authority of the same, That no man shall marry any woman within the degrees hereafter named in this Act, *That is to say,* No man shall marry his Grandfathers Wife, Wives Grandmother, Fathers Sister, Mothers Sister, Fathers Brothers Wife, Mothers Brothers Wife, Wives Fathers Sister, Wives Mothers Sister, Fathers Wife, Wives Mother; Daughter, Wives Daughter, Sons Wife, Sister, Brothers Wife, Wives Sister, Sons Daughter, Daughters Daughter, Sons Sons Wife, Daughters Sons Wife, Wives Sons Daughter, Wives Daughters Daughter, Brothers Daughter, Sisters Daughter, Brothers Sons Wife, Sisters Sons Wife, Wives Brothers Daughter, Wives Sisters Daughter; and if any man shall hereafter marry, or have carnal copulation with any woman, who is within the degrees before recited in this Act, every such Marriage shall be, and is hereby declared to be null and void; and all Children that shall hereafter be born of such Incestuous Marriage or Copulation, shall be for ever disabled to Inherit by Descent, or by being generally named in any Deed or Will, by Father or Mother.

And be it further Enacted by the Authority aforesaid, That every man and woman, who shall marry, or carnally know each other, being within any of the degrees before recited in this Act, and shall be convicted thereof before His Majesties Court of Assistants within this Colony, such man and woman so convicted, shall be set upon the Gallows by the space of an hour, with a Rope about their Neck, and the other end cast over the Gallows, and in the way from thence to the Common Goal, shall be severely Whipt, not exceeding forty stripes each. Also every person so offending, shall for ever after wear a Capital I of two inches long, and proportionable bigness, cut out in cloth of a contrary colour to their Cloaths, and sewed upon their upper Garments, on the outside of their arm, or on their Back in open view; and if any person or persons having been convicted and sentenced for such offence, shall at any time be found without their Letter so worn, during their aboad in this Colony, they shall by Warrant from any one Assistant or Justice of the Peace, be forthwith apprehended, and ordered to be publickly Whipt, not exceeding fifteen stripes, and so from time to time *Toties Quoties.*

And be it further Enacted by the Authority aforesaid, That if any man or woman, that shall hereafter marry contrary to the intent of this Act, and whose Marriage shall be by this Act declared null and void, shall be so hardy as to converse together as man and wife, or shall continue to dwell in the same House at any time after the publication of this Act, and be thereof convicted, or if any man and woman, who shall hereafter be divorced, or their Marriage

declared to be null and void, according to the Law of this Colony, shall Cohabit or Converse together as man and wife, and be thereof convicted, all and every such persons shall suffer the pains and penalties mentioned in an Act made, and passed by this Court, Intituled, *An act against Adultery, which in and by the said Act, are set and imposed upon such as shall be taken in Adultery.* And it shall be in the power of the Court of Assistants to assign unto any woman so separated, such reasonable part of the Estate of her late Husband, as in their discretion the circumstances of the Estate may admit, not exceeding one third part thereof.

And for preventing of all unlawful Marriages.

It is further Enacted by the Authority aforesaid, That after the Publication hereof, no person shall be joyned in Marriage, before the Intentions of the parties proceeding therein, hath been published sufficiently at some publick Lecture or Town Meeting in the Towns where the parties or either of them do ordinarily reside, or be set up in Writing fairly written upon some post of their Meeting-House door in publick views there to stand, so as it may be read eight days before such Marriage.

And whereas the power of disposal of children in Marriage doth reside in the hands of Parents, and that irregular proceedings therein may be prevented.

It is further Enacted by the Authority aforesaid, That whatsoever person shall after the publication hereof, directly or indirectly endeavour to draw away the affections of any Maid in this Colony, upon pretence of Marriage, before he hath obtained liberty and allowance from the Parents, Governours or Guardians; he shall forfeit for the first offence, *Five Pounds,* for the second offence towards the same party, *Ten Pounds,* and for the third offence, upon information or complaint by such Parents or Governours to any Assistant or Justice of the Peace, giving Bond to prosecute the party, he shall be Committed to the Prison, and upon hearing and conviction before the next County Court, he shall be adjudged to continue in Prison, until the Court of Assistants shall see cause to release him.

And as the Ordinance of Marriage is honourable amongst all, so it is meet it should be accordingly solemnized,

Be it therefore further Enacted by the Authority aforesaid, That no person whatsoever in this Colony, shall joyn any persons together in Marriage, other than a Magistrate, Justice of the Peace, and that within his own County, or Ordained Minister, and that only in the Town where he is Settled in the work of the Ministry; Nor shall any Magistrate, Justice of Peace, or Ordained Minister, presume to joyn any persons together in Marriage, before the parties to be Married have been published according to Law; Or before such Magistrate, Justice or Minister is Certified of the consent of the Parents or Guardians (if any be) of such parties: On pain of forfeiting the Sum of *Twenty Pounds,* one moiety whereof shall be to him or them that shall complain of, and prosecute the same to effect, and the other moiety to the Treasury of the County wherein the offence shall be committed.

And if any person or persons shall presume to deface, or to pull down any Publishment set up in writing, before the expiration of eight days after the time of its being set up, every such person or persons shall be fined the Sum of *Ten Shillings,* to the use of the poor of the Town where the offence is committed, he or they being thereof legally convicted, before any one Assistant or Justice of the Peace; or be Set in the Stocks one whole hour.

And it is further Enacted by the Authority aforesaid, That if any man shall wear Womens Apparel, or if any woman shall wear mens Apparel, and be thereof duly convicted; they shall be corporally punished, or fined at the discretion of the County Court, not exceeding *Five Pounds,* to the use of the County where the offence is committed, towards the defraying of the County Charges.

Source:
State Archives, Connecticut State Library, Hartford, Connecticut.

Resolutions of Germantown Mennonites Against Slavery, 1688

Statements condemning slavery issued in 1688 by the Mennonite leaders of Germantown, Pennsylvania. This document, the earliest known example of written opposition to the institution in the colonies, made clear the Mennonites' unequivocal opposition: "to bring men hither, to rob and sell them against their will, we stand against."

———————————— c∞ɔ ————————————

This is to the monthly meeting held at Richard Worrell's:

These are the reasons why we are against the traffic of men-body, as followeth: Is there any that would be done or handled at this manner? viz., to be sold or made a slave for all the time of his life? How fearful and faint-hearted are many at sea, when they see a strange vessel, being afraid it should be a Turk, and they should be taken, and sold for slaves into Turkey. Now, what is *this* better done, than Turks do? Yea, rather it is worse for them, which say they are Christians; for we hear that the most part of such negers are brought hither against their will and consent, and that many of them are stolen. Now, though they are black, we cannot conceive there is more liberty to have them slaves, as it is to have other white ones. There is a saying, that we should do to all men like as we will be done ourselves; making no difference of what generation, descent, or colour they are. And those

who steal or rob men, and those who buy or purchase them, are they not all alike? Here is liberty of conscience, which is right and reasonable; here ought to be likewise liberty of the body, except of evil-doers, which is another case. But to bring men hither, or to rob and sell them against their will, we stand against. In Europe there are many oppressed for conscience-sake; and here there are those oppressed which are of a black colour. And we who know that men must not commit adultery—some do commit adultery *in* others, separating wives from their husbands, and giving them to others: and some sell the children of these poor creatures to other men. Ah! do consider well this thing, you who do it, if you would be done at this manner—and if it is done according to Christianity! You surpass Holland and Germany in this thing. This makes an ill report in all those countries of Europe, where they hear of [it], that the Quakers do here handel men as they handel there the cattle. And for that reason some have no mind or inclination to come hither. And who shall maintain this your cause, or plead for it? Truly, we cannot do so, except you shall inform us better hereof, viz.: that Christians have liberty to practice these things. Pray, what thing in the world can be done worse towards us, than if men should rob or steal us away, and sell us for slaves to strange countries; separating husbands from their wives and children. Being now this is not done in the manner we would be done at; therefore, we contradict, and are against this traffic of men-body. And we who profess that it is not lawful to steal, must, likewise, avoid to purchase such things as are stolen, but rather help to stop this robbing and stealing, if possible. And such men ought to be delivered out of the hands of the robbers, and set free as in Europe. Then is Pennsylvania to have a good report, instead, it hath now a bad one, for this sake, in other countries; Especially whereas the Europeans are desirous to know in what manner *the Quakers* do rule in *their* province; and most of them do look upon us with an envious eye. But if this is done well, what shall we say is done evil?

If once these slaves (which they say are so wicked and stubborn men,) should join themselves—fight for their freedom, and handel their masters and mistresses, as they did handel them before; will these masters and misstresses take the sword at hand and war against these poor slaves, like, as we are able to believe, some will not refuse to do? Or, have these poor negers not as much right to fight for their freedom, as you have to keep them slaves?

Now consider well this thing, if it is good or bad. And in case you find it to be good to handel these blacks in that manner, we desire and require you hereby lovingly, that you may inform us herein, which at this time never was done, viz., that Christians have such a liberty to do so. To the end we shall be satisfied on this point, and satisfy likewise our good friends and acquaintances in our native country, to whom it is a terror, or fearful thing, that men should be handelled so in Pennsylvania.

This is from our meeting at Germantown, held ye 18th of the 2d month, 1688, to be delivered to the monthly meeting at Richard Worrell's.

Garret Henderich, Derick op de Graeff,
Francis Daniel Pastorius, Abram op de Graeff.

Source:
Henry Steele Commager, ed. *Documents of American History.* New York: F.S. Crofts & Co., 1934.

"The Narrative of the Captivity and Restoration of Mary Rowlandson," 1692

This is an example of "captivity narratives," written by European Americans who were taken prisoner during Indian uprisings. Its full title is *The sovereignty and goodness of GOD, together with the faithfulness of his promises displayed, being a narrative of the captivity and restoration of Mrs. Mary Rowlandson, commended by her, to all that desires to know the Lord's doings to, and dealings with her. Especially to her dear children and relations. The second Addition [sic] Corrected and amended. Written by her own hand for her private use, and now made public at the earnest desire of some friends, and for the benefit of the afflicted. Deut. 32.39. See now that I, even I am he, and there is no god with me, I kill and I make alive, I wound and I heal, neither is there any can deliver out of my hand.*

Although there were many instances of cooperation between local Native Americans and colonists, there were also numerous massacres on both sides. The colonial captivity narratives tended to emphasize the goodness of God in restoring these settlers to their compatriots. However, a significant number of captives, especially children, chose to remain with the Indians.

Mary Rowlandson was taken prisoner in 1775 during the bloodiest war between New Englanders and Indians, known to the English as King Philip's War, after their name for the Native American leader Metacomet, son of Massasoit, who assisted the Pilgrims. In 1671 Metacomet's nation, the Wampanoag, surrendered their weapons and agreed to abide by English law. However, skirmishes between the settlers and Indians continued. By fall the Narragansett and Nipmuck had joined the Wampanoag and the fight spread to the Connecticut River Valley in Massachusetts. Using weapons they had repaired and hidden, the Indians, in 1676, attacked Plymouth and Providence, Rhode Island, killing or capturing some 10 per-

cent of Massachusetts men, ruining more than 1,000 homes, and slaughtering Plymouth's cattle. The settlers retaliated with the help of converted "praying Indians." They prevailed after Metacomet was murdered. Many of the Indian prisoners were then sent as slaves to the Caribbean.

The portions excerpted here describe the battle in which Mary was captured, her experience while a slave of the Indians, and her return.

On the tenth of February 1675, came the Indians with great numbers upon Lancaster: their first coming was about sunrising; hearing the noise of some guns, we looked out; several houses were burning, and the smoke ascending to heaven. There were five persons taken in one house; the father, and the mother and a sucking child, they knocked on the head; the other two they took and carried away alive. There were two others, who being out of their garrison upon some occasion were set upon; one was knocked on the head, the other escaped; another there was who running along was shot and wounded, and fell down; he begged of them his life, promising them money (as they told me) but they would not hearken to him but knocked him in head, and stripped him naked, and split open his bowels. Another, seeing many of the Indians about his barn, ventured and went out, but was quickly shot down. There were three others belonging to the same garrison who were killed; the Indians getting up upon the roof of the barn, had advantage to shoot down upon them over their fortification. Thus these murderous wretches went on, burning, and destroying before them.

At length they came and beset our own house, and quickly it was the dolefulest day that ever mine eyes saw. The house stood upon the edge of a hill; some of the Indians got behind the hill, others into the barn, and others behind anything that could shelter them; from all which places they shot against the house, so that the bullets seemed to fly like hail; and quickly they wounded one man among us, then another, and then a third. About two hours (according to my observation, in that amazing time) they had been about the house before they prevailed to fire it (which they did with flax and hemp, which they brought out of the barn, and there being no defense about the house, only two flankers at two opposite corners and one of them not finished); they fired it once and one ventured out and quenched it, but they quickly fired it again, and that took. Now is the dreadful hour come, that I have often heard of (in time of war, as it was the case of others), but now mine eyes see it. Some in our house were fighting for their lives, others wallowing in their blood, the house on fire over our heads, and the bloody heathen ready to knock us on the head, if we stirred out. Now might we hear mothers and children crying out for themselves, and one another, "Lord, what shall we do?" Then I took my children (and one of my sisters', hers) to go forth and leave the house: but as soon as we came to the door and appeared, the Indians shot so thick that the bullets rattled against the house, as if one had taken an handful of stones and threw them, so that we were fain to give back. . . .

But out we must go, the fire increasing, and coming along behind us, roaring, and the Indians gaping before us with their guns, spears, and hatchets to devour us. No sooner were we out of the house, but my brother-in-law (being before wounded, in defending the house, in or near the throat) fell down dead, whereat the Indians scornfully shouted, and hallowed, and were presently upon him, stripping off his clothes, the bullets flying thick, one went through my side, and the same (as would seem) through the bowels and hand of my dear child in my arms. One of my elder sisters' children, named William, had then his leg broken, which the Indians perceiving, they knocked him on [his] head. Thus were we butchered by those merciless heathen, standing amazed, with the blood running down to our heels. My eldest sister being yet in the house, and seeing those woeful sights, the infidels hauling mothers one way, and children another, and some wallowing in their blood: and her elder son telling her that her son William was dead, and myself was wounded, she said, "And Lord, let me die with them," which was no sooner said, but she was struck with a bullet, and fell down dead over the threshold. I hope she is reaping the fruit of her good labors, being faithful to the service of God in her place. . . . the Indians laid hold of us, pulling me one way, and the children another, and said, "Come go along with us"; I told them they would kill me: they answered, if I were willing to go along with them, they would not hurt me . . .

The First Remove
Now away we must go with those barbarous creatures, with our bodies wounded and bleeding, and our hearts no less than our bodies. About a mile we went that night, up upon a hill within sight of the town, where they intended to lodge. There was hard by a vacant house (deserted by the English before, for fear of the Indians). I asked them whether I might not lodge in the house that night, to which they answered, "What, will you love English men still?" This was the dolefulest night that ever my eyes saw. Oh the roaring, and singing and dancing, and yelling of those black creatures in the night, which made the place a lively resemblance of hell. And as miserable was the waste that was there made of horses, cattle, sheep, swine, calves, lambs, roasting pigs, and fowl (which they had plundered in the town), some roasting, some lying and burning, and some boiling to feed our merciless

enemies; who were joyful enough, though we were disconsolate. . . .

The Second Remove
. . . One of the Indians carried my poor wounded babe upon a horse; it went moaning all along, "I shall die, I shall die." I went on foot after it, with sorrow that cannot be expressed. At length I took it off the horse, and carried it in my arms till my strength failed, and I fell down with it. Then they set me upon a horse with my wounded child in my lap, and there being no furniture upon the horse's back, as we were going down a steep hill we both fell over the horse's head, at which they, like inhumane creatures, laughed, and rejoiced to see it, though I thought we should there have ended our days, as overcome with so many difficulties. But the Lord renewed my strength still, and carried me along, that I might see more of His power; yea, so much that I could never have thought of, had I not experienced it.

After this it quickly began to snow, and when night came on, they stopped, and now down I must sit in the snow, by a little fire, and a few boughs behind me, with my sick child in my lap; and calling much for water, being now (through the wound) fallen into a violent fever. . . .

The Third Remove
. . . This day there came to me one Robert Pepper (a man belonging to Roxbury) who was taken in Captain Beers's fight, and had been now a considerable time with the Indians; and up with them almost as far as Albany, to see King Philip. . . . He told me he himself was wounded in the leg at Captain Beer's fight; and was not able some time to go, but as they carried him, and as he took oaken leaves and laid to his wound, and through the blessing of God he was able to travel again. Then I took oaken leaves and laid to my side, and with the blessing of God it cured me also. . . .

Nine days I sat upon my knees, with my babe in my lap, till my flesh was raw again; my child being even ready to depart this sorrowful world, they bade me carry it out to another wigwam (I suppose because they would not be troubled with such spectacles) whither I went with a very heavy heart, and down I sat with the picture of death in my lap. About two hours in the night, my sweet babe like a lamb departed this life on Feb. 18, 1675. It being about six years, and five months old. . . . In the morning, when they understood that my child was dead they sent for me home to my master's wigwam (by my master in this writing, must be understood Quinnapin, who was a Sagamore [subordinate chief], Webster's and married King Philip's wife's sister. . . . There were now besides myself nine English captives in this place (all of them children, except one woman). I got an opportunity to go and take my leave of them. They being to go one way, and I another. . . . And now I must part with that little company I had. Here I parted from my daughter Mary (whom I never saw again till I saw her in Dorchester, returned from captivity), and from four little cousins and neighbors, some of which I never saw afterward.

* * *

The Fifth Remove

. . . The first week of my being among them I hardly ate any thing; the second week I found my stomach grow very faint for want of something; and yet it was very hard to get down their filthy trash; but the third week, though I could think how formerly my stomach would turn against this or that, and I could starve and die before I could eat such things, yet they were sweet and savory to my taste. I was at this time knitting a pair of white cotton stockings for my mistress; and had not yet wrought upon a Sabbath day. When the Sabbath came they bade me go to work. I told them it was the Sabbath day, and desired them to let me rest, and told them I would do as much more tomorrow; to which they answered me they would break my face. And here I cannot but take notice of the strange providence of God in preserving the heathen. They were many hundreds, old and young, some sick, and some lame; many had papooses at their backs. The greatest number at this time with us were squaws, and they traveled with all they had, bag and baggage, and yet they got over this river aforesaid; and on Monday they set their wigwams on fire, and away they went. On that very day came the English army after them to this river, and saw the smoke of their wigwams, and yet this river put a stop to them. God did not give them courage or activity to go over after us. We were not ready for so great a mercy as victory and deliverance. If we had been God would have found out a way for the English to have passed this river, as well as for the Indians with their squaws and children, and all their luggage . . .

The Eighth Remove

. . . When I was in the canoe I could not but be amazed at the numerous crew of pagans that were on the bank on the other side. When I came ashore, they gathered all about me, I sitting alone in the midst. I observed they asked one another questions, and laughed, and rejoiced over their gains and victories. Then my heart began to fail: and I fell aweeping, which was the first time to my remembrance, that I wept before them. Although I had met with so much affliction, and my heart was many times ready to break, yet could I not shed one tear in their sight; but rather had been all this while in a maze, and like one astonished. But now I may say as Psalm 137.1, "By the Rivers of Babylon, there we sate down: yea, we wept when we remembered Zion." There one of them asked me why I wept. I could

hardly tell what to say: Yet I answered, they would kill me. "No," said he, "none will hurt you." Then came one of them and gave me two spoonfuls of meal to comfort me, and another gave me half a pint of peas; which was more worth than many bushels at another time. Then I went to see King Philip. He bade me come in and sit down, and asked me whether I would smoke it (a usual compliment nowadays amongst saints and sinners) but this no way suited me. For though I had formerly used tobacco, yet I had left it ever since I was first taken. It seems to be a bait the devil lays to make men lose their precious time. I remember with shame how formerly, when I had taken two or three pipes, I was presently ready for another, such a bewitching thing it is. But I thank God, He has now given me power over it; surely there are many who may be better employed than to lie sucking a stinking tobacco-pipe.

* * *

The Eighteenth Remove

. . . In this town there were four English children, captives; and one of them my own sister's. I went to see how she did, and she was well, considering her captive condition. I would have tarried that night with her, but they that owned her would not suffer it. Then I went into another wigwam, where they were boiling corn and beans, which was a lovely sight to see, but I could not get a taste thereof. Then I went to another wigwam, where there were two of the English children; the squaw was boiling horses feet; then she cut me off a little piece, and gave one of the English children a piece also. Being very hungry I had quickly eat up mine, but the child could not bite it, it was so tough and sinewy, but lay sucking, gnawing, chewing and slabbering of it in the mouth and hand. Then I took it of the child, and eat it myself, and savory it was to my taste. Then I may say as Job 6.7, "The things that my soul refused to touch are as my sorrowful meat." Thus the Lord made that pleasant refreshing, which another time would have been an abomination. Then I went home to my mistress's wigwam; and they told me I disgraced my master with begging, and if I did so any more, they would knock me in the head. I told them, they had as good knock me in head as starve me to death.

The Nineteenth Remove

. . . Then came Tom and Peter, with the second letter from the council, about the captives. . . . When the letter was come, the Sagamores met to consult about the captives, and called me to them to inquire how much my husband would give to redeem me. When I came I sat down among them, as I was wont to do, as their manner is. Then they bade me stand up, and said they were the General Court. They bid me speak what I thought he would give. Now knowing that all we had was destroyed by the Indians, I was in a great strait. I thought if I should speak of but a little it would be slighted, and hinder the matter; if of a great sum, I knew not where it would be procured. Yet at a venture I said "Twenty pounds," yet desired them to take less. But they would not hear of that, but sent that message to Boston, that for twenty pounds I should be redeemed. It was a Praying Indian that wrote their letter for them. . . . When my master came home, he came to me and bid me make a shirt for his papoose, of a holland-laced pillowbere. About that time there came an Indian to me and bid me come to his wigwam at night, and he would give me some pork and ground nuts. Which I did, and as I was eating, another Indian said to me, he seems to be your good friend, but he killed two Englishmen at Sudbury, and there lie their clothes behind you: I looked behind me, and there I saw bloody clothes, with bullet-holes in them. Yet the Lord suffered not this wretch to do me any hurt. Yea, instead of that, he many times refreshed me; five or six times did he and his squaw refresh my feeble carcass. If I went to their wigwam at any time, they would always give me something, and yet they were strangers that I never saw before. Another squaw gave me a piece of fresh pork, and a little salt with it, and lent me her pan to fry it in; and I cannot but remember what a sweet, pleasant and delightful relish that bit had to me, to this day. So little do we prize common mercies when we have them to the full.

The Twentieth Remove

[The Native Americans hold a general court (using the Massachusetts term for an assembly) to decide if Mary should be "redeemed." She digresses to query why God appeared to favor the Indians.]

. . . It was thought [by the English], if their [Indians'] corn were cut down, they would starve and die with hunger, and all their corn that could be found, was destroyed, and they driven from that little they had in store, into the woods in the midst of winter; and yet how to admiration did the Lord preserve them for His holy ends, and the destruction of many still amongst the English! strangely did the Lord provide for them; that I did not see (all the time I was among them) one man, woman, or child, die with hunger. Though many times they would eat that, that a hog or a dog would hardly touch; yet by that God strengthened them to be a scourge to His people. The chief and commonest food was ground nuts. They eat also nuts and acorns, artichokes, lilly roots, ground beans, and several other weeds and roots, that I know not. They would pick up old bones, and cut them to pieces at the joints, and if they were full of worms and maggots, they would scald them over the fire to make the vermine come out, and then boil them, and drink up the liquor, and then beat the great ends of them in a mortar, and so eat them. . . .

But to return again to my going home, where we may see a remarkable change of providence. At first they were all against it, except my husband would come for me, but afterwards they assented to it, and seemed much to rejoice in it; some asked me to send them some bread, others some tobacco, others shaking me by the hand, offering me a hood and scarfe to ride in; not one moving hand or tongue against it. Thus hath the Lord answered my poor desire, and the many earnest requests of others put up unto God for me. In my travels an Indian came to me and told me, if I were willing, he and his squaw would run away, and go home along with me. I told him no: I was not willing to run away, but desired to wait God's time, that I might go home quietly, and without fear. And now God hath granted me my desire. . . . Let the redeemed of the Lord say so, whom He hath redeemed from the hand of the enemy, especially that I should come away in the midst of so many hundreds of enemies quietly and peaceably, and not a dog moving his tongue. So I took my leave of them. . . .

. . . I see, when God calls a person to anything, and through never so many difficulties, yet He is fully able to carry them through and make them see, and say they have been gainers thereby. And I hope I can say in some measure, as David did, "It is good for me that I have been afflicted."

Source:

Department of History. The College of Staten Island/CUNY. "The Narrative . . . of Mary Rowlandson." Available on-line. URL: www.library.csi.cuny.edu/dept/history/lavender/ rownarr. html. Downloaded October 2003.

The Examination of Bridget Byshop, Salem Witchcraft Trials, 1692

The witchcraft trials, which occurred in Salem, Massachusetts, in 1692, have occupied historians, novelists, and playwrights, including Arthur Miller (*The Crucible*). The only completely accepted facts are that several teenaged girls ("the afflicted") started the process by accusing a West Indian slave in the household of the Reverend Samuel Parris of bewitching them. She confessed, as did more than 50 others, who in turn accused still others. By the time the authorities called a halt to the trials (because the accusations were reaching prominent people outside of Salem), 19 people, 14 of them women, were hanged, and one man, Giles Corey, was pressed to death. Explanations for the witchcraft hysteria run from foiled romance (Miller) to economic rivalries to hallucinations from tainted wheat. The excerpt below is representative. Bridget Byshop was executed June 10, 1692.

The Examination of Bridget Byshop at Salem Village 19. Apr. 1692
By John Hauthorn & Jonath: Corwin Esq'rs

As soon as she came near all [the afflicted girls] fell into fits Bridget Byshop, You are now brought before Authority to Give acco. of what witchcrafts you are conversant in.

I take all this people (turning her head & eyes about) to witness that I am clear.

Hath this woman hurt you speaking to the afflicted.

Eliz: Hubbard Ann Putman, Abigail Williams & Mercy Lewes affirmed she had hurt them. You are here accused by 4. or. 5. for hurting them, what do you say to it[?]

I never saw these persons before, nor I never was in this place before.

Mary Walcot said that her brother Jonathan stroke her appearance & she saw that he had tore her coat in striking, & she heard it tare.

Upon some search in the Court, a rent that seems to answere what was alledged was found.

They say you bewitch your first husband to death.

If it please your worship I know nothing of it.

She shake her head & the afflicted were tortured.

The like again upon the motion of her head. Sam: Braybrook affirmed that she told him to day that she had been accounted a Witch these 10 years, but she was no Witch, the Devil cannot hurt her.

* * *

I am no witch[.]

Why if you have not wrote in the book, yet tell me how far you have gone? Have you not to do with familiar Spirits?

I have no familiarity with the devil.

How is it then, that your appearance doth hurt these? I am innocent.

Why you seem to act witchcraft before us, by the motion of your body, which seems to have influence upon the afflicted.

I know nothing of it. I am innocent to a Witch. I know not what a Witch is[.]

How do you know then that you are not a witch[?]

I do not know what you say.

* * *

What do you say of those murders you are charged with?

I hope, I am not guilty of Murder

Then she turned up her eyes, the eyes of the afflicted were turned up[.]

It may be you do not know, that any have confessed to day, who have been examined before you, that they are Witches.

No. I know nothing of it. John Hutchinson & John Lewis in open Court affirmed that they had told her.

* * *

Salem Village Aprill the.19'th 1692 Mr Sam'l Parris being desired to take into wrighting the Examination of Bridget Byshop, hath delivered it as aforesaid. And upon hearing the same, and seeing what wee did then see, togather with the Charge of the afflicted persons then present: Wee Committed said Bridget Olliver.

John Hathorne.

Source:

Boyer, Paul, and Stephen Nissenbaum, eds. *The Salem Witchcraft Papers.* Vol. 1. Verbatim Transcripts of the Legal Documents of the Salem Witchcraft Outbreak of 1692, p. 34. Electronic Text Center. University of Virginia Library. Available on-line. URL: http://etext.lib.virginia.edu/salem/witchcraft/texts/BoySal1.html. Accessed October 2003.

Ebenezer Cook, "The Sotweed Factor or a Voyage to Maryland," 1707

Ebenezer Cook and his poem about Maryland may be best known as the subject of the John Barth novel *The Sotweed Factor.* *Sotweed* was another word for tobacco, and the word *factor* was the middleman between the tobacco growers and the English merchants who brought the dried leaves to England where they were sold for smoking and snuff. Perhaps surprisingly, many of the characters in the Barth novel, including the prostitute Joan Toast and Cook himself were actual people, and many of the tales Barth relates come straight out of the *Archives of Maryland.* Cook was probably born in London around 1670. Like the Barth character, he was Maryland's first poet laureate, and went to Maryland to handle an inherited estate on the Choptank River on the eastern shore of the Chesapeake Bay.

The excerpts below describe Cook's "seasoning," (thought to be malaria, a common affliction among new arrivals to the Chesapeake area), and his being swindled first out of his tobacco, then by his attorney. They also satirize the courts. Court days provided entertainment for settlers and were well-attended. An illiterate and drunken judge was certainly not unknown in this frontier colony, and many "attorneys" were self-taught, like the former apothecary Cook hires. Seventeenth-century Maryland, as a "tolerant" colony, was home to religious fugitives of all kinds. They included a significant number of Quakers, who were considered shrewd businesspeople. By the time Cook arrived, however, the Anglican Church was established there. Annapolis, on the western shore of the Chesapeake, was Maryland's capital.

The Sotweed Factor or
A Voyage to Maryland

A SATYR

Condemn'd by Fate to way-ward Curse,
Of Friends unkind, and empty Purse:
Plagues worse than fill'd *Pandora's* Box,
I took my leave of *Albion's* Rocks:
With heavy heart, concern'd that I
Was forc'd my Native soil to fly.
And the *Old World* must bid good-buy.
But Heav'n ordain'd it should be so.
And to repine is vain we know:
Freighted with Fools, from *Plymouth* sound,
To *Mary-Land* our ship was bound.
Where we arriv'd in dreadful Pain,
Shock'd by the Terrours of the Main

* * *

Waking next day, with aking Head,
And Thirst that made me quit my Bed;
I rigg'd myself, and soon got up,
to cool my Liver with a Cup
Of *Succahana* fresh and clear,
Not half so good as *English* Beer;
Which ready stood in Kitchin Pail,
And was in fact but *Adam's* Ale [water];

* * *

The soathing drought scarce down my throat,
Enough to put a ship a float,
With Cockerouse as I was sitting,
I felt a Feaver Intermitting:
A fiery Pulse beat in my Veins,
From Cold I felt resembling Pains:
This cursed seasoning I remember
Lasted from *March* to cold *December*:

* * *

But thanks to fortune and a Nurse
Whose Care depended on my Purse,
I saw myself in good Condition,
Without the help of a Physitian:
At length the shivering ill relieved,
Which long my Head and Heart had grieved;
I then began to think with Care,
How I might sell my British Ware,

* * *

While riding near a Sandy Bay,
I met a *Quaker, Yea* and *Nay*:
A Pious conscientious rogue,
As e'er woar Bonnet or a Brogue,
Who neither Swore nor kept his Word.

* * *

With this sly Zealot soon I struck
A Bargain for my *English* Truck,
Agreeing for ten thousand weight,
Of *Sot-weed* good and fit for freight,
Broad *Oronooko* bright and sound.
The growth and product of his ground;
In Cask that should contain compleat,
Five hundred of Tobacco neat
The contract thus betwixt us made,
Not well acquainted with the Trade,
My goods I trusted to the Cheat,
Whose crop was then aboard the Fleet;
And going to receive my own,
I found the Bird was newly flown:
Cursing this execrable Slave,
This damn'd pretended Godly Knave;
On due Revenge and Justice ent,
I instantly to Counsel went,
Unto an ambodexter *Quack*
learnedly had got the knack
Of giving Glisters, making Pills,
Of filling bonds, and forging Wills;
And with a stock of Impudence,
Supply'd his want of Wit and Sense;

* * *

Resolv'd to plauge the holy Brother,
I set one Rogue to catch another;
To try the Cause then fully bent,
Up to Annapolis I went,

* * *

The Judges left their Punch and Rum,
When Pettifogger Docter draws,
His Paper forth, and opens Cause:
And least I shou'd the better get,
Brib'd *Quack* supprest his Knavish Wit.
So Maid upon the downy Field,
Pretends a Force, and Fights to yeild:
The Byast Court without delay,
Adjudg'd my Debt in Country Pay:
In Pipe staves, Corn, or Flesh of Boar,
Rare Cargo for the *English* Shoar:
Raging with Grief, full speed I ran,
To join the Fleet at *Kicketan*;
Embarqu'd and waiting for a Wind,

I left this dreadful Curse behind.
May Canniballs transported o'er the Sea
Prey on these Slaves, as they have done on me:
May never Merchant's, trading Sails explore
This Cruel, this Inhospitable Shoar;
But left abandon'd by the World to starve,
May they sustain the Fate they well deserve:
May they turn Savage, or as *Indians* Wild,
From Trade, Converse, and Happiness exil'd:
Recreant to Heaven, may they adore the Sun,
And into pagan Superstitions run
For Vengeance ripe . . .
May Wrath Divine then lay those Regions wast
Where no Man's Faithful°, nor a Woman Chast.

15 January 1707

° The Author does not intend by this, any of the English Gentlemen resident here.

Source:

University of Oregon. Renascense Editions. "The Sotweed Factor.: Available on-line. URL: www.uoregon.edu/˜rbear.sotweed. htm. Accessed October 2003.

Smallpox in New England, 1721–1722

In the spring of 1621, a maritime fleet from Barbados arrived in Boston, Massachusetts, and brought with it the beginnings of a smallpox epidemic. By autumn the disease had spread throughout the city and reached the neighboring towns of Cambridge, Charlestown, and Roxbury. The epidemic was especially hard on the young and elderly populations, with mortality rates ranging from 15 percent to 50 percent. The clergyman Cotton Mather (1663–1728) sought the help of Dr. Zabdiel Boylston to innoculate New Englanders against the disease. According to some accounts, Mather learned about smallpox inoculations from a slave named Onesimus. Others say he had read of a method employed in Turkey. The idea was to produce a mild form of smallpox from which the patient would recover and, as a result, be protected against a more severe attack. After Boylston administered the smallpox vaccine to 250 slaves and his own son, the death rate dropped from one in 12 to about one in 40. According to the article below, it was even more successful. Mather's interest in science and particularly in various American phenomena—published in his *Curiosa Americana* (1712–24)—won him membership in the Royal Society of London. His account of the innoculation episode was published in the society's transactions.

While our brethren to the South struggle with the feared Malaria, New England continues to be the victim of repeated Smallpox epidemics. Common in England, it arrives cloaked by the scores of newcomers who then visit it upon the colony. Governor Bradford describes its effects upon the Plymouth Indians in horrific detail and concludes, "they fall into a lamentable condition . . . and die like rotten sheep." Fatal to the Indians, sometimes exceeding a 90 percent mortality rate, the dread "distemper" is only somewhat less kind to citizens as it sweeps through the colonies at unpredictable intervals devastating entire families, communities and commerce. Smallpox has claimed victims across all class boundaries including Deacon Samuel Fuller in 1633.

The disease was first documented in China in 1122, by the name variola.

The smallpox virus is described as a "mostly fatal" disease that runs its course fairly quickly. After initially inhaling the virus from an infected person, his clothes or bedding, the classic smallpox symptoms appear quickly. A few days after exposure, sever headaches, backaches, chills and a fever up to 105 degrees develop. Three to four days later, these symptoms may decline, but are replaced by a rash of hard red lumps. These lumps begin developing on the bodies extremities and then spread to the rest of the body. This rash continues to develop into small blisters that itch and are extremely painful. On the twelfth day, if the patient survives, the blisters scab over and leave permanent pitted scars.

One physician describes his patient who did not survive: "The smallpox came out by the thousands on his face which soon became one entire blister, and in two of three days after the body and limbs were beset with such numbers of them that the load bore down his strength before it in spite of every measure taken for his assistance."

So reviled is the disease that the infected have been known to be abandoned, sent to "pest" houses, and fearfully buried in common graves.

Among "cures" suggested are those of "A Brief Rule to Guide the Common-People of New-England How to Order Themselves and Theirs in the Small Pocks, or Measels," by Reverend Thomas Thacher, Old South Church, Boston. Rev. Thacher suggests that as soon as the disease appears, "Let the sick abstein from Flesh and Wine, and open Air, let him use small Bear warmed with a Tost for his ordinary drink, and moderately when he desires it." Suggested foodstuffs are water-gruel, water-potage, boild Apples, and milk, none of which should "manifest a hot quality."

A more radical and hotly debated cure of European origin proposed by Rev. Cotton Mather, is that of "innoculation," or the purposeful introduction of the disease so as to bring on a mild case of the disease and leave the patient henceforth immune. Mather's concept was at first heatedly debated and scorned by many of the medical community who scoffed at his lack of medical credentials.

In the recent 1721–22 epidemic, however, Mather and his clericals surreptitiously performed numerous inoculations. Victoriously, Mather proclaimed the procedure's veracity. Nearly 900 died who had no inoculation. Of about 300 persons who had inoculations, only five or six died, those possibly already infected with the disease before inoculation.

Source:

G.L. Kittredge. "Cotton Mather's Scientific Communications to the Royal Society." *Proceedings, American Antiquarian Society*, n.s., 26, 1916, pp. 18–57.

James Barbot, Jr., "Premeditated a Revolt," before 1732

These recollections of James Barbot, Jr., a sailor aboard the English slaver *Don Carlos,* were included in a 1732 collection. Barbot apparently held a certain degree of sympathy for slaves, as he concluded, ". . . Officers should consider these unfortunate creatures . . . men as well as themselves, tho' of a different colour, and pagans; and that they ought to do to others as they would be done by in like circumstances." In this episode, Barbot first recounts a slave revolt aboard his ship that involved deaths among both slaves and the crew. He goes on to describe the layout of the ship and how the slaves are treated. According to Barbot, they received better treatment on the *Don Carlos* than on most slave ships.

About one in the afternoon, after dinner, we, according to custom caused them, one by one, to go down between decks, to have each his pint of water; most of them were yet above deck, many of them provided with knives, which we had indiscreetly given them two or three days before, as not suspecting the least attempt of this nature from them; others had pieces of iron they had torn off our forecastle door, as having premeditated a revolt, and seeing all the ship's company, at best but weak and many quite sick, they had also broken off the shackles from several of their companions feet, which served them, as well as billets they had provided themselves with, and all other things they could lay hands on, which they imagin'd might be of use for this enterprize. Thus arm'd, they fell in crouds and parcels on our men, upon the deck unawares, and stabb'd one of the stoutest of us all, who receiv'd fourteen or fifteen wounds of their knives, and so expir'd. Next they assaulted our boatswain, and cut one of his legs so round the bone, that he could not move, the nerves being cut through; others cut our cook's throat to the pipe, and others wounded three of the sailors, and threw one of them over-board in that condition, from the fore-castle into the sea; who, however, by good providence, got hold of the bowline of the fore-sail, and sav'd himself . . . we stood in arms, firing on the revolted slaves, of whom we kill'd some, and wounded many: which so terrif'd the rest, that they gave way, dispersing themselves some one way and some another between decks, and under the fore-castle; and many of the most mutinous, leapt over board, and drown'd themselves in the ocean with much resolution, shewing no manner of concern for life. Thus we lost twenty seven or twenty eight slaves, either kill'd by us, or drown'd; and having master'd them, caused all to go betwixt decks, giving them good words. The next day we had them all again upon deck, where they unanimously declar'd, the Menbombe slaves had been the contrivers of the mutiny, and for an example we caused about thirty of the ringleaders to be very severely whipt by all our men that were capable of doing that office. . . .

I have observ'd, that the great mortality, which so often happens in slave-ships, proceeds as well from taking in too many, as from want of knowing how to manage them aboard. . . .

As to the management of our slaves aboard, we lodge the two sexes apart, by means of a strong partition at the main mast; the forepart is for men, the other behind the mast for the women. If it be in large ships carrying five or six hundred slaves, the deck in such ships ought to be at least five and a half or six foot high, which is very requisite for driving a continual trade of slaves: for the greater height it has, the more airy and convenient it is for such a considerable number of human creatures; and consequently far the more healthy for them, and fitter to look after them. We build a sort of half- decks along the sides with deals and spars provided for that purpose in Europe, that half-deck extending no father than the sides of our scuttles and so the slaves lie in two rows, one above the other, and as close together as they can be crouded. . . .

The planks, or deals, contract some dampness more or less, either from the deck being so often wash'd to keep it clean and sweet, or from the rain that gets in now and then through the scuttles or other openings, and even from the very sweat of the slaves; which being so crouded in a low place, is perpetual, and occasions many distempers, or at best great inconveniences dangerous to their health. . . .

It has been observ'd before, that some slaves fancy they are carry'd to be eaten, which make them desperate; and others are so on account of their captivity: so that if care be not taken, they will mutiny and destroy the ship's crue in hopes to get away.

To prevent such misfortunes, we use to visit them daily, narrowly searching every corner between decks, to see whether they have not found means, to gather any pieces of iron, or wood, or knives, about the ship, notwithstanding the great care we take not to leave any tools or nails, or other things in the way: which, however, cannot be always so exactly observ'd, where so many people are in the narrow compass of a ship.

We cause as many of our men as is convenient to lie in the quarter-deck and gun-room, and our principal officers in the great cabin, where we keep all our small arms in a readiness, with sentinels constantly at the doors and avenues to it; being thus ready to disappoint any attempts our slave might make on a sudden.

These precautions contribute very much to keep them in awe; and if all those who carry slaves duly observ'd them, we should not hear of so many revolts as have happen'd. Where I was concern'd, we always kept our slaves in such order, that we did not perceive the least inclination in any of them to revolt, or mutiny, and lost very few of our number in the voyage.

It is true, we allow'd them much more liberty, and us'd them with more tenderness than most other Europeans would think prudent to do; as, to have them all upon deck every day in good weather; to take their meals twice a- day, at fix'd hours, that is, at ten in the morning, and at five at night; which being ended, we made the men go down again between the decks; for the women were almost entirely at their own discretion, to be upon deck as long as they pleas'd, nay even many of the males had the same liberty by turns, successively; few or none being fetter'd or kept in shackles, and that only on account of some disturbances, or injuries, offer'd to their fellow captives, as will unavoidably happen among a numerous croud of such savage people. Besides, we allow'd each of them betwixt their meals a handful of Indian wheat and Mandioca, and now and then short pipes and tobacco to smoak upon deck by turns, and some coconuts; and to the women a piece of coarse cloth to cover them, and the same to many of the men, which we took care they did wash from time to time, to prevent vermin, which they are very subject to; and because it look'd sweeter and more agreeable. Toward the evening they diverted themselves on the deck, as they thought fit, some conversing together, others dancing, singing, and sporting after their manner, which pleased them highly, and often made us pastime; especially the female sex, who being apart from the males, on the quar-

terdeck, and many of them young sprightly maidens, full of jollity and good-humour, afforded us abundance of recreation; as did several little fine boys, which we mostly kept to attend on us about the ship.

We mess'd the slaves twice a day, as I have observed; the first meal was of our large beans boil'd, with a certain quantity of Muscovy lard. . . . The other meal was of pease, or of Indian wheat, and sometimes meal of Mandioca . . . boiled with either lard, or suet, or grease by turns: and sometimes with palm-oil and malaguette or Guinea pepper I found they had much better stomachs for beans, and it is a proper fattening food for captives. . . .

At each meal we allow'd every slave a full coconut shell of water, and from time to time a dram of brandy, to strengthen their stomachs. . . .

Much more might be said relating to the preservation and maintenance of slaves in such voyages, which I leave to the prudence of the officers that govern aboard, if they value their own reputation and their owners advantage; and shall only add these few particulars, that tho' we ought to be circumspect in watching the slaves narrowly, to prevent or disappoint their ill designs for our own conservation, yet must we not be too severe and haughty with them, but on the contrary, caress and humor them in every reasonable thing. Some commanders, of a morose peevish temper are perpetually beating and curbing them, even without the least offence, and will not suffer any upon deck but when unavoidable to ease themselves does require; under pretence it hinders the work of the ship and sailors and that they are troublesome by their nasty nauseous stench, or their noise; which makes those poor wretches desperate, and besides their falling into distempers thro' melancholy, often is the occasion of their destroying themselves.

Such officers should consider, those unfortunate creatures are men as well as themselves, tho' of a different colour, and pagans; and that they ought to do to others as they would be done by in like circumstances. . . .

Source:
Awnsham Churchill and John Churchill, eds. *Collection of Voyages and Travels.* London, 1732.

Jonathan Edwards, "Sinners in the Hands of an Angry God," 1741

Sermon written by the New England minister Jonathan Edwards in 1741 in order to convince his congregants to confess and be saved. Edwards was just one of the many preachers of his time trying to revive religious ardor to the colonies in what is known as the First Great Awakening. This sermon from which these excerpts come was written in order to scare his audience into converting.

———————— ⌗⌗⌗ ————————

Deuteronomy 32:35.—Their foot shall slide in due time.

In this verse is threatened the vengeance of God on the wicked unbelieving Israelites, that were God's visible people, and lived under means of grace; and that notwithstanding all God's wonderful works that he had wrought towards that people, yet remained, as is expressed verse 28, void of counsel, having no understanding in them; and that, under all the cultivations of heaven, brought forth bitter and poisonous fruit. . . .

The expression that I have chosen for my text, *their foot shall slide in due time,* seems to imply the following things relating to the punishment and destruction that these wicked Israelites were exposed to:

❋   ❋   ❋

3. Another thing implied is, that they are liable to fall of themselves, without being thrown down by the hand of another; as he that stands or walks on slippery ground needs nothing but his own weight to throw him down.

4. That the reason why they are not fallen already, and do not fall now, is only that God's appointed time is not come. For it is said that when that due time, or appointed time comes, *their feet shall slide.* Then they shall be left to fall, as they are inclined by their own weight. God will not hold them up in these slippery places any longer, but will let them go; and then, at that very instant, they shall fall into destruction; as he that stands in such slippery declining ground on the edge of a pit that he cannot stand alone, when he is let go he immediately falls and is lost.

The observation from the words that I would now insist upon is this.

[H]ere is nothing that keeps wicked men at any one moment out of hell, but the mere pleasure of God.

The truth of this observation may appear by the following considerations:

1. There is no want of power in God to cast wicked men into hell at any moment. Men's hands cannot be strong when God rises up: the strongest have no power to resist him, nor can any deliver out of his hands.

❋   ❋   ❋

They deserve to be cast into hell; so that divine justice never stands in the way, it makes no objection against God's using his power at any moment to destroy them. Yea, on the contrary, justice calls aloud for an infinite punishment of their sins. Divine justice says of the tree that brings forth such grapes of Sodom, "Cut it down, why cumbereth it the ground?" Luke 13:7. The sword of divine justice is every moment brandished over their heads and it is nothing but the hand of arbitrary mercy, and God's mere will, that holds it back.

❋   ❋   ❋

4. They are now the objects of that very same anger and wrath of God, that is expressed in the torments of hell: and the reason why they do not go down to hell at each moment, is not because of God, in whose power they are, is not then very angry with them; as angry, as he is with many of those miserable creatures that he is now tormenting in hell, and do there feel and bear the fierceness of his wrath. Yea, God is a great deal more angry with great numbers that are now on earth; yea, doubtless, with many that are now in this congregation, that, it may be, are at ease and quiet, than he is with many of those that are now in the flames of hell.

So that it is not because God is unmindful of their wickedness, and does not resent it, that he does not let loose his hand and cut them off. God is not altogether such a one as themselves, though they may imagine him to be so. The wrath of God burns against them; their damnation does not slumber; the pit is prepared; the fire is made ready; the furnace is now hot; ready to receive them; the flames do now rage and glow. The glittering sword is whet, and held over them, and the pit hath opened her mouth under them.

5. The devil stands ready to fall upon them, and seize them as his own, at what moment God shall permit him. They belong to him; and he has their soul in his possession, and under his dominion. The Scripture represents them as his goods, Luke 11:21. The devils watch them, like greedy hungry lions that see their prey, and except to have it, but are for the present kept back; if God should withdraw his hand by which they are restrained, they would in one moment fly upon their poor souls. The old serpent is gaping for them; hell opens its mouth wide to receive them; and if God should permit it, they would be hastily swallowed up and lost.

❋   ❋   ❋

7. It is no security to wicked men for one moment, that there are no visible means of death at hand. It is no security to a natural man, that he is now in health, and that he does not see which way he should now immediately go out of the world by any accident, and that there is no visible danger in any respect in his circumstances. The manifold and continual experience of the world in all ages, shows that this is no evidence that a man is not on the very brink of eternity, and that the next step will not be into another world. The unseen, unthought of ways and means of persons going suddenly out of the world are innumerable and

inconceivable. Unconverted men walk over the pit of hell on rotten covering, and there are innumerable places in this covering so weak that they will not bear their weight, and these places are not seen. The arrows of death fly unseen at noonday; the sharpest sight cannot discern them. God has so many different, unsearchable ways of taking wicked men out of the world and sending them to hell, that the is nothing to make it appear, that God had need to be at the expense of a miracle, or go out of the ordinary course of his providence, to destroy any wicked man, at any moment. All the means that there are of sinners going out of the world, are so in God's hands, and so absolutely subject to his power and determination, that it does not depend at all less on the mere will of God, whether sinners shall at any moment go to hell, than if means were never made use of, or at all concerned in the case.

8. Natural men's prudence and care to preserve their own lives, or the care of others to preserve them, do not secure them a moment. . . .

* * *

10. God has laid himself under no obligation, by any promise, to keep any natural man out of hell one moment: God certainly has made no promises either of eternal life, or of any deliverance or preservation from eternal death, but what are contained in the covenant of grace, the promises that are given in Christ, in whom all the promises are yea and amen. But surely they have no interest in the promises of the covenant of grace that are not the children of the covenant, and that do not believe in any of the promises of the covenant, and have no interest in the Mediator of the covenant.

So that, whatever some have imagined and pretended about promises made to natural men's earnest seeking and knocking, it is plain and manifest, that whatever pains a natural man takes in religion, whatever prayers he makes, that he believes in Christ, God is under no manner of obligation to keep him a moment from eternal destruction.

So that thus it is, that natural men are held in the hand of God over the pit of hell; they have deserved the fiery pit, and are already sentenced to it; and God is dreadfully provoked, his anger is as great towards them as to those that are actually suffering the executions of the fierceness of his wrath in hell, and they have done nothing in the least, to appease or abate that anger, neither is God in the least bound by any promise to hold them up one moment; the devil is waiting for them, hell is gaping for them, the flames gather and flash about them, and would fain lay hold on them and swallow them up; the fire pent up in their own hearts is struggling to break out; and they have no interest in any Mediator, there are no means within

reach that can be any security to them. In short, they have no refuge, nothing to take hold of; all that preserves them every moment is the mere arbitrary will, and uncovenanted, unobliged forbearance of an incensed God.

Application

[H]e use may be of awakening to unconverted persons in this congregation. This that you have heard is the case of every one of you that are out of Christ. That world of misery, that lake of burning brimstone, is extended abroad under you. There is the dreadful pit of the glowing flames of the wrath of God; there is hell's wide gaping mouth open; and you have nothing to stand upon, nor any thing to take hold of. There is nothing between you and hell but the air; it is only the power and mere pleasure of God that holds you up.

* * *

Your wickedness makes you as it were heavy as lead, and to tend downwards with great weight and pressure towards hell; and if God should let you go, you would immediately sink and swiftly descend and plunge into the bottomless gulf, and your healthy constitution, and your own care and prudence, and best contrivance, and all your righteousness, would have no more influence to uphold you and keep you out of hell, than a spider's web would have to stop a falling rock. Were it not that so is the sovereign pleasure of God, the earth would not bear you one moment; for you are a burden to it; the creation groans with you; the creature is made subject to the bondage of your corruption, not willingly; the sun does not willingly shine upon you to give you light to serve sin and Satan; the earth does not willingly yield her increase to satisfy your lusts; nor is it willingly a stage for your wickedness to be acted upon; the air does not willingly serve you for breath to maintain the flame of life in your vitals, while you spend your life in the service of God's enemies. God's creatures are good, and were made for men to serve God with, and do not willingly subserve to any other purpose, and groan when they are abused to purposes so directly contrary to their nature and end. And the world would spew you out, were it not for the sovereign hand of him who hath subjected it in hope. There are the black clouds of God's wrath now hanging directly over your heads, full of the dreadful storm, and big with thunder; and were it not for the restraining hand of God, it would immediately burst forth upon you. The sovereign pleasure of God, for the present, stays his rough wind; otherwise it would come with fury, and your destruction would come like a whirlwind, and you would be like the chaff of the summer threshing floor.

* * *

. . . God that holds you over the pit of hell, much as one holds a spider, or some loathsome insect, over the fire, abhors you, and is dreadfully provoked; his wrath towards you burns like fire; he looks upon you as worthy of nothing else, but to be cast into the fire; he is of purer eyes than to bear to have you in his sight; you are ten thousand times so abominable in his eyes, as the most hateful and venomous serpent is in ours. You have offended him infinitely more than ever a stubborn rebel did his prince: and yet it is nothing but his hand that holds you from falling into the fire every moment: it is ascribed to nothing else, that you did not go to hell the last night; that you were suffered to awake again in this world, after you closed your eyes to sleep; and there is no other reason to be given, why you have not dropped into hell since you arose in the morning, but that God's hand has held you up: there is no other reason to be given why you have not gone to hell, since you have sat here in the house of God, provoking his pure eyes by your sinful wicked manner of attending his solemn worship: yea, there is nothing else that is to be given as a reason why you do not this very moment drop down into hell.

O sinner! consider the fearful danger you are in: it is a great furnace of wrath, a wide and bottomless pit, full of the fire of wrath, that you are held over in the hand of that God, whose wrath is provoked and incensed as much against you, as against many of the damned in hell: you hang by a slender thread, with the flames of divine wrath flashing about it, and ready every moment to single it, and burn it asunder; and you have no interest in any Mediator, and nothing to lay hold of to save yourself, nothing to keep off the flames of wrath, nothing of your own, nothing that you ever have done, nothing that you can do, to induce God to spare you one moment.

And consider here more particularly several things concerning that wrath that you are in such danger of.

※　※　※

It is the fierceness of his wrath that you are exposed to. We often read of the fury of God; as in Isaiah 59:18: "According to their deeds, accordingly he will repay fury to his adversaries." So Isaiah 66:15, "For behold, the Lord will come with fire and with his chariots like a whirlwind, to render his anger with fury, and his rebuke with flames of fire." And so in many other places. So we read of God's fierceness, Rev. 19:15. There we read of "the wine-press of the fierceness and wrath of Almighty God." The words are exceedingly terrible: if it had only been said, "the wrath of God," the words would have implied that which is infinitely dreadful: but it is not only said so, but "the fierceness and wrath of God": the fury of God! the fierceness of Jehovah! Oh how dreadful must that be! Who can utter or

conceive what such expressions carry in them! But it is not only said so, but "the fierceness and wrath of Almighty God." As though there would be a very great manifestation of his almighty power in what the fierceness of his wrath should inflict, as though omnipotence should be as it were enraged, and exerted, as men are wont to exert their strength in the fierceness of their wrath. Oh! then, what will be the consequence! What will become of the poor worm that shall suffer it! Whose hands can be strong! And whose heart endure! To what a dreadful, inexpressible, inconceivable depth of misery must the poor creature be sunk who shall be the subject of this!

. . . Thus it will be with you that are in an unconverted state, if you continue in it; the infinite might, and majesty, and terribleness, of the omnipotent God shall be magnified upon you in the ineffable strength of your torments: you shall be tormented in the presence of the holy angels, and in the presence of the Lamb; and when you shall be in this state of suffering, the glorious inhabitants of heaven shall go forth and look on the awful spectacle, that they may see what the wrath and fierceness of the Almighty is; and when they have seen it, they will fall down and adore that great power and majesty. Isa. 66:23, 24, "And it shall come to pass, that from one moon to another, and from one Sabbath to another, shall all flesh come to worship before me, saith the Lord. And they shall go forth and look upon the carcasses of the men that have transgressed against me; for their worm shall not die, neither shall their fire be quenched, and they shall be abhorring unto all flesh."

4. It is everlasting wrath. It would be dreadful to suffer this fierceness and wrath of Almighty God one moment; but you must suffer it to all eternity: there will be no end to this exquisite, horrible misery: when you look forward, you shall see a long forever, a boundless duration before you, which will swallow up your thoughts, and amaze your soul; and you will absolutely despair of ever having any deliverance, any end, any mitigation, any rest at all; you will know certainly that you must wear out long ages, millions of millions of ages, in wrestling and conflicting with this Almighty merciless vengeance; and then when you have so done, when so many ages have actually been spent by you in this manner, you will know that all is but a point to what remains. So that your punishment will indeed be infinite. Oh, who can express what the state of a soul in such circumstances is! All that we can possibly say about it, gives but a very feeble, faint representation of it; it is inexpressible and inconceivable: for "who knows the power of God's anger?"

How dreadful is the state of those that are daily and hourly in danger of this great wrath and infinite misery! But this is the dismal case of every soul in this congregation that has not been born again, however moral and strict, sober and religious, they may otherwise be. Oh that you would consider it, whether you be young or old! There is reason to think, that there are many in this congregation now hearing this discourse, that will actually be the subjects of this very misery to all eternity. We know not who they are, or in what seats they sit, or what thoughts they now have. It may be they are now at ease, and hear all these things without much disturbance, and are now flattering themselves that they are not the persons; promising themselves that they shall escape. If we knew that there was one person, and but one, in the whole congregation, that was to be the subject of this misery, what an awful thing it would be to think of! If we knew who it was, what an awful sight would it be to see such a person! How might all the rest of the congregation lift up a lamentable and bitter cry over him! But alas! Instead of one, how many is it likely will remember this discourse in hell! And it would be a wonder, if some that are now present should not be in hell in a very short time, before this year is out. And it would be no wonder if some persons, that now sit here in some seats of this meeting-house in health, and quiet and secure, should be there before tomorrow morning.

Source:
John Scott, ed. *Living Documents in American History.* New York: Washington Square Press, 1964–68.

The Development of Political, Religious, and Social Institutions in the Colonies

Virginia Blue Laws, 1623–1624

A set of colonial laws that regulated conduct, including making church attendance on Sunday mandatory. The penalty for absence was one pound of tobacco. The laws also required that each plantation have a house or a room for worship. The Anglicans (members of the Church of England) in Virginia advocated the measures, which are often considered the first blue laws in colonial America (although later the term was used more frequently to refer to the certain statutes passed by the Puritans in New England in the 1600s).

Laws and Orders
Concluded on by the General Assembly, March the 5th, 1623–4.
No. of the Acts.

1. That there shall be in every plantation, where the people use to meete for the worship of God, a house or roome sequestred for that purpose, and not to be for any temporal use whatsoever, and a place empaled in, sequestred only to the buryal of the dead.

2. That whosoever shall absent himselfe from divine service any Sunday without an allowable excuse shall forfeite a pound of tobacco, and he that absenteth himselfe a month shall forfeit 50lb. of tobacco.

3. That there be an uniformity in our church as neere as may be to the canons in England; both in substance and circumstance, and that all persons yeild readie obedience unto them under paine of censure.

4. That the 22d of March by yeerly solemnized as holliday, and all other hollidays (except when they fall two together) betwixt the feast of the annuntiation of the blessed virgin and St. Michael the archangell, then only the first to be observed by reason of our necessities.

5. That no minister be absent from his church above two months in all the yeare upon penalty of forfeiting halfe his means, and whosoever shall absent above fowre months in the year shall forfeit his whole means and cure.

6. That whosoever shall disparage a minister without bringing sufficient proofe to justify his reports whereby the mindes of his parishioners may be alienated from him, and his ministry prove the less effectual by their prejudication, shall not only pay 500lb. waight of tobacco but also aske the minister so wronged forgiveness publickly in the congregation.

7. That no man dispose of any of his tobacco before the minister be satisfied, upon pain of forfeiture double his

part of the minister's means, and one man of every plantation to collect his means out of the first and best tobacco and corn.

8. That the Governor shall not lay any taxes or ympositions upon the colony their lands or comodities other way than by the authority of the General Assembly, to be levyed and ymployed as the said Assembly shall appoynt.

9. The governor shall not withdraw the inhabitants from their private labors to any service of his own upon any colour whatsoever and in case the publick service require ymployments of many hands before the holding a General Assemblie to give order for the same, in that case the levying of men shall be done by order of the governor and whole body of the counsell and that in such sorte as to be least burthensome to the people and most free from partiali . . .

10. That all the old planters that were here before or came in at the last coming of sir Thomas Gates they and their posterity shall be exempted from their personal service to the warrs and any publick charge (church duties excepted) that belong particularly to their persons (not exempting their families) except such as shall be ymployed to command in chief.

11. That no burgesses of the General Assembly shall be arrested during the time of the assembly, a week before and a week after upon pain of the creditors forfeiture of his debt and such punishment upon the officer as the court shall award.

12. That there shall be courts kept once a month in the corporations of Charles City and Elizabeth Citty for the decyding of suits and controversies not exceeding the value of one hundred pounds of tobacco and for punishing of petty offences, that the commanders of the places and such others as the governor and council shall appoint by commission shall be the judges, with reservation of apeal after sentence to the governor and counsell and whosoever shall appeal yf he be there cast in suit shall pay duble damages, The commanders to be of the quorum and sentence to be given by the major parties.

13. That every privatt planters devident shall be surveyed and laid out in several and the bounds recorded by the survey; yf there be any pettie differences betwixt neighbours about their devidents to be divided by the surveyor if of much importance to be referred to the governor and counsell: the surveyor to have 10 lbs. of tobacco upon every hundred acres.

14. For the encouragement of men to plant store of corne, the prise shall not be stinted, but it shall be free for every man to sell it as deere as he can.

15. That there shall be in every parish a publick garnary unto which there shall be contributed for every planter exceeding the adge of 18 years alive at the crop after he hath been heere a year a bushell of corne, the

which shall be disposed for the publique uses of every parish by the major part of the freemen, the remainder yearly to be taken out by the owners at St. Tho's his day and the new bushell to be putt in the roome.

16. That three sufficient men of every parish shall be sworne to see that every man shall plant and tende sufficient of corne for his family. Those men that have neglected so to do are to be by the said three men presented to be censured by the governor and counsell.

17. That all trade for corne with the salvages as well publick as private after June next shall be prohibited.

18. That every freeman shall fence in a quarter of an acre of ground before Whitsuntide next to make a garden for planting of vines, herbs, roots, &c. subpoena ten pounds of tobacco a man, but that no man for his own family shall be tyed to fence above an acre of land and that whosoever hath fenced a garden and of the land shall be paid for it by the owner of the soyle; they shall also plant Mulberry trees.

19. The proclamations for swearing and drunkenness sett out by the governor and counsel are confirmed by this Assembly; and it is further ordered that the churchwardens shall be sworne to present them to the commanders of every plantation and that the forfeitures shall be collected by them to be for publique uses.

20. That a proclamation be read aboard every ship and afterwards fixed to the maste of such in, prohibiting them to break boulke or make privatt sales of any commodity until James City, without special order from the governor and counsell.

21. That the proclamation of the rates of commodities be still in force and that there be some men in every plantation to censure the tobacco.

22. That there be no weights nor measures used but such as shall be sealed by officers appointed for that purpose.

23. That every dwelling house shall be pallizaded in for defence against the Indians.

24. That no man go or send abroad without a sufficient partie will armed.

25. That men go not to worke in the ground without their arms (and a centinell upon them.)

26. That the inhabitants go not abroad ships or upon any other occasions in such numbers, as thereby to weaken and endanger the plantations.

27. That the commander of every plantation take care that there be sufficient of powder and amunition within the plantation under his command and their pieces fixt and their arms compleate.

28. That there be dew watch kept by night.

29. That no commander of any plantation do either himselfe or suffer others to spend powder unneccessarily in drinking or entertainments, &c.

30. That such persons of quality as shall be founde delinquent in their duties being not fitt to undergoe corporal punishment may notwithstanding be ymprisoned at the discretione of the commander & for greater offenses to be subject to a ffine inflicted by the monthlie court, so, that it exceed not the value aforesaid.

31. That every man that hath not contributed to the finding a man at the castell shall pay for himself and servants five pounds of tobacco a head, towards the discharge of such as had their servants there.

32. That at the beginning of July next the inhabitants of every corporation shall fall upon their adjoyning salvages as we did the last yeare, those that shall be hurte upon service to be cured at the publique charge; in case any be lamed to be maintained by the country according to his person and quality.

33. That for defraying of such publique debts our troubles have brought upon us. There shall be levied 10 pounds of tobacco upon every male head above sixteen years of adge now living (not including such as arrived since the beginning of July last.)

34. That no person within this colony upon the rumur of supposed change and alteration, presume to be disobedient to the present government, nor servants to their private officers, masters or overseers at their uttermost perills.

35. That Mr. John Pountis, counsellor of state, goin to England, (being willing by our intreatie to accept of that imployment,) to solicite the general cause of the country to his majesty and the counsell, towards the charges of which voyage, the country consente to pay for every male head above sixteen years of adge then living, which have been here a yeare ffour pounds of the best merchantable tobacco, in leafe, at or before the last of October next.

Subscript.
Sir Francis Wyatt, Knt. Governor, &c.
Capt Fran's West, Sir George Yeardley,
George Sandys Trear, William Tucker,
Jabez Whitakers, William Peeine,
Rauleigh Croshaw, Richard Kingsmell,
Edward Blany, Luke Boyse, John Pollington,
Nath'l. Causey, Robert Addams,
Thomas Harris, Richard Stephens,
John Pountis, John Pott, Capt. Roger Smith,
Capt. Raphe Hamer, Nathaniel Bass,
John Willcox, Nicho: Marten,
Clement, Dilke, Isaeck Chaplin,
John Cew, John Utie, John Southerne,
Richard Bigge, Henry Watkins,
Gabriel Holland, Thomas Morlatt,
Copia Test,
R. Hickman, Cl. Sec. off.

Source:
Samuel Shepherd. *The Statutes at Large of Virginia.* Vol 1. New York: AMS Press, 1970, pp. 121–129.

Fundamental Orders of Connecticut, 1639

Document that fused three riverside settlements into the "Public State or Commonwealth" of Connecticut in January 1639. The orders formalized a representative style of government that had been in use in three towns—Windsor, Hartford, and Wethersfield—since 1636. Led by the Reverend Thomas Hooker, John Haynes, and Roger Ludlow, delegates from each town gathered in Hartford to establish a process for choosing government officials and passing laws. Ludlow, a lawyer, is often credited with the strength of the document's final version. The Fundamental Orders do not mention any king or sovereign. Instead, all ruling power is invested in freely chosen representatives. The document also contains methods for overriding the power of these representatives should they cease to act in the people's best interests. The orders served as the basic law of Connecticut until 1662, when a new charter, which incorporated many of their basic tenets, was granted by King Charles II.

For as much as it hath pleased Almighty God by the wise disposition of his divine providence so to order and dispose of things that we the Inhabitants and Residents of Windsor, Hartford and Wethersfield are now cohabiting and dwelling in and upon the River of Connectecotte and the lands thereunto adjoining; and well knowing where a people are gathered together the word of God requires that to maintain the peace and union of such a people there should be an orderly and decent Government established according to God, to order and dispose of the affairs of the people at all seasons as occasion shall require; do therefore associate and conjoin ourselves to be as one Public State or Commonwealth; and do for ourselves and our successors and such as shall be adjoined to us at any time hereafter, enter into Combination and Confederation together, to maintain and preserve the liberty and purity of the Gospel of our Lord Jesus which we now profess, as also, the discipline of the Churches, which according to the truth of the said Gospel is now practiced amongst us; as also in our civil affairs to be guided and governed according to such Laws, Rules, Orders and Decrees as shall be made, ordered, and decreed as followeth:

1

It is Ordered, sentenced, and decreed, that there shall be yearly two General Assemblies or Courts, the one the second Thursday in April, the other the second Thursday in September following; the first shall be called the Court of Election, wherein shall be yearly chosen from time to time, so many Magistrates and other public Officers as shall be found requisite: Whereof one to be chosen Governor for the year ensuing and until another be chosen, and no other Magistrate to be chosen for more than one year: provided always there be six chosen besides the Governor, which being chosen and sworn according to an Oath recorded for that purpose, shall have the power to administer justice according to the Laws here established, and for want thereof, according to the Rule of the Word of God; which choice shall be made by all that are admitted freemen and have taken the Oath of Fidelity, and do cohabit within this Jurisdiction having been admitted Inhabitants by the major part of the Town wherein they live or the major part of such as shall be then present.

2

It is Ordered, sentenced, and decreed, that the election of the aforesaid Magistrates shall be in this manner: every person present and qualified for choice shall bring in (to the person deputed to receive them) one single paper with the name of him written in it whom he desires to have Governor, and that he that hath the greatest number of papers shall be Governor for that year. And the rest of the Magistrates or public officers to be chosen in this manner: the Secretary for the time being shall first read the names of all that are to be put to choice and then shall severally nominate them distinctly, and every one that would have the person nominated to be chosen shall bring in one single paper written upon, and he that would not have him chosen shall bring in a blank; and every one that hath more written papers than blanks shall be a Magistrate for that year; which papers shall be received and told by one or more that shall be then chosen by the court and sworn to be faithful therein; but in case there should not be six chosen as aforesaid, besides the Governor, out of those which are nominated, than he or they which have the most writen papers shall be a Magistrate or Magistrates for the ensuing year, to make up the aforesaid number.

3

It is Ordered, sentenced, and decreed, that the Secretary shall not nominate any person, nor shall any person be chosen newly into the Magistracy which was not propounded in some General Court before, to be nominated the next election; and to that end it shall be lawful for each of the Towns aforesaid by their deputies to nominate any two whom they conceive fit to be put to election; and the Court may add so many more as they judge requisite.

4

It is Ordered, sentenced, and decreed, that no person be chosen Governor above once in two years, and that the Governor be always a member of some approved Congregation, and formerly of the Magistracy within this Jurisdiction; and that all the Magistrates, Freemen of this Commonwealth; and that no Magistrate or other public officer shall execute any part of his or their office before they are severally sworn, which shall be done in the face of the court if they be present, and in case of absence by some deputed for that purpose.

5

It is Ordered, sentenced, and decreed, that to the aforesaid Court of Election the several Towns shall send their deputies, and when the Elections are ended they may proceed in any public service as at other Courts. Also the other General Court in September shall be for making of laws, and any other public occasion, which concerns the good of the Commonwealth.

6

It is Ordered, sentenced, and decreed, that the Governor shall, either by himself or by the Secretary, send out summons to the Constables of every Town for the calling of these two standing Courts one month at least before their several times: And also if the Governor and the greatest part of the Magistrates see cause upon any special occasion to call a General Court, they may give order to the Secretary so to do within fourteen days' warning: And if urgent necessity so required, upon a shorter notice, giving sufficient grounds for it to the deputies when they meet, or else be questioned for the same; And if the Governor and major part of Magistrates shall either neglect or refuse to call the two General standing Courts or either of them, as also at other times when the occasions of the Commonwealth require, the Freemen thereof, or the major part of them, shall petition to them so to do; if then it be either denied or neglected, the said Freemen, or the major part of them, shall have the power to give order to the Constables of the several Towns to do the same, and so may meet together, and choose to themselves a Moderator, and may proceed to do any act of power which any other General Courts may.

7

It is Ordered, sentenced, and decreed, that after there are warrants given out for any of the said General Courts, the Constable or Constables of each Town, shall forthwith give notice distinctly to the inhabitants of the same, in some public assembly or by going or sending from house to house, that at a place and time by him or them limited and set, they meet and assemble themselves together to elect and choose certain deputies to be at the General Court then following to agitate the affairs of the Commonwealth; which said deputies shall be chosen by all that are admitted Inhabitants in the several Towns and have taken the oath of fidelity; provided that none be chosen a Deputy for any General Court which is not a Freeman of this Commonwealth.

The aforesaid deputies shall be chosen in manner following: every person that is present and qualified as before expressed, shall bring the names of such, written in several papers, as they desire to have chosen for that employment, and these three or four, more or less, being the number agreed on to be chosen for that time, that have the greatest number of papers written for them shall be deputies for that Court; whose names shall be endorsed on the back side of the warrant and returned into the Court, with the Constable or Constables' hand unto the same.

8

It is Ordered, sentenced, and decreed, that Windsor, Hartford, and Wethersfield shall have power, each Town, to send four of their Freemen as their deputies to every General Court; and Whatsoever other Town shall be hereafter added to this Jurisdiction, they shall send so many deputies as the Court shall judge meet, a reasonable proportion to the number of Freemen that are in the said Towns being to be attended therein; which deputies shall have the power of the whole Town to give their votes and allowance to all such laws and orders as may be for the public good, and unto which the said Towns are to be bound.

9

It is Ordered, sentenced, and decreed, that the deputies thus chosen shall have power and liberty to appoint atime and a place of meeting together before any General Court, to advise and consult of all such things as may concern the good of the public, as also to examine their own Elections, whether according to the order, and if they or the greatest part of them find any election to be illegal they may seclude such for present from their meeting, and return the same and their reasons to the Court; and if it be proved true, the Court may fine the party or parties so intruding, and the Town, if they see cause, and give out a warrant to go to a new election in a legal way, either in part or in whole. Also the said deputies shall have power to fine any that shall be disorderly at their meetings, or for not coming in due time or place according to appointment; and they may return the said fines into the Court if it be refused to be paid, and the Treasurer to take notice of it, and to escheat or levy the same as he does other fines.

10

It is Ordered, sentenced, and decreed, that every General Court, except such as through neglect of the Governor and the greatest part of the Magistrates the Freemen themselves do call, shall consist of the Governor, or some one chosen to moderate the Court, and four other Magistrates at least, with the major part of the deputies of the several Towns legally chosen; and in case the Freemen, or major part of them, through neglect or refusal of the Governor and major part of the Magistrates, shall call a Court, it shall consist of the major part of Freemen that are present or their deputiues, with a Moderator chosen by them: In which said General Courts shall consist the supreme power of the Commonwealth, and they only shall have power to make laws or repeal them, to grant levies, to admit of Freemen, dispose of lands undisposed of, to several Towns or persons, and also shall have power to call either Court or Magistrate or any other person whatsoever into question for any misdemeanor, and may for just causes displace or deal otherwise according to the nature of the offense; and also may deal in any other matter that concerns the good of this Commonwealth, except election of Magistrates, which shall be done by the whole body of Freemen.

In which Court the Governor or Moderator shall have power to order the Court, to give liberty of speech, and silence unseasonable and disorderly speakings, to put all things to vote, and in case the vote be equal to have the casting voice. But none of these Courts shall be adjourned or dissolved without the consent of the major part of the Court.

11

It is Ordered, sentenced, and decreed, that when any General Court upon the occasions of the Commonwealth have agreed upon any sum, or sums of money to be levied upon the several Towns within this Jurisdiction, that a committee be chosen to set out and appoint what shall be the proportion of every Town to pay of the said levy, provided the committee be made up of an equal number out of each Town.

14th January 1639 the 11 Orders above said are voted.

Source:

Francis Newton Thorpe, ed. *The Federal and State Constitutions, Colonial Charters, and Other Organic Laws of the States, Territories, and Colonies Now or Heretofore Forming the United States of America.* Washington, D.C.: Government Printing Office, 1909.

Plantation Agreement at Providence, 1640

Agreement written by the inhabitants of Providence, later to become the capital of Rhode Island, on August 27, 1640, based on the consent of the settlers. The Plantation Agreement set up laws for local home rule and distribution of land, a flexible constitution, and frequent elections. Leading a small band of settlers from Massachusetts Bay Colony, Roger Williams founded Providence in 1636 on land bought from two Narragansett chiefs and based it on a policy of religious and political freedom. Other settlements were set up in 1638 and 1639, but these were not united until 1644, when Williams obtained a charter from the English Parliamentary Commission.

Wee, Robert Coles, Chad Browne, William Harris, and John Warner, being freely chosen by the consent of our loveing freinds and neighbours the Inhabitants of this Towne of Providence, having many differences amongst us, they being freely willing and also bound themselves to stand to our Arbitration in all differences amongst us to rest contented in our determination, being so betrusted we have seriously and carefully indeavoured to weigh and consider all those differences, being desirous to bringe to vnity and peace, although our abilities are farr short in the due examination of such weighty things, yet so farre as we conceive in laying all things together we have gone the fairest and the equallest way to produce our peace.

I. Agreed, We have with one consent agreed that in the parting those particler proprieties which some of our friends and neighbours have in Patuxit, from the general Common of our towne of Providence, to run vppon a streight line from a fresh spring being in the Gulley, at at the head of that cove running by that point of land called Saxafras vnto the towne of Mashipawog, to an oake tree standing neere vnto the corne field, being at this time the neerest corne field vnto Patuxit, the oake tree having four marks with an axe, till some other land marke be set for a certaine bound. Also, we agree that if any meadow ground lyeing and joineing to that Meadow, that borders upon the River of Patuxit come within the aforesaid line, which will not come within a streight line from long Cove to the marked tree, then for that meadow to belong to Pawtuxit, and so beyond the towne of Mashipawog from the oake tree between the two fresh Rivers Pawtuxit and Wanasquatucket of an even Distance.

II. Agreed, We have with one consent agreed that for the disposeing, of those lands that shall be disposed belonging to this towne of Providence to be in the whole Inhabitants by the choise of five men for generall disposeall, to be betrusted with disposeall of lands and also of the townes Stocke, and all Generall things and not to receive in any six dayes as townesmen, but first to give the Inhabitants notice to consider if any have just cause to shew against the receiving of him as you can apprehend, and to receive none but such as subscribe to this our determination. Also, we agree that if any of our neighbours doe apprehend himselfe wronged by these or any of these 5 disposers, that at the Generall towne meeting he may have a tryall.

Alsoe wee agree for the towne to choose beside the other five men one or more to keepe Record of all things belonging to the towne and lying in Common.

Wee agree, as formerly hath bin the liberties of the town, so still, to hould forth liberty of Conscience.

III. Agreed, that after many Considerations and Consultations of our owne State and alsoe of States abroad in way of government, we apprehend, no way so suitable to our Condition as government by way of arbitration. But if men agree themselves by arbitration, no State we know of disallows that, neither doe we: But if men refuse that which is but common humanity betweene man and man, then to compel such vnreasonable persons to a reasonable way, we agree that the 5 disposers shall have power to compell him either to choose two men himselfe, or if he refuse, for them to choose two men to arbitrate his cause, and if these foure men chosen by every partie do end the cause, then to see theire determination performed and the faultive to pay the Arbitrators for theire time spent in it: But if those foure men doe not end it, then for the 5 disposers to choose three men to put an end to it, and for the certainty hereof, wee agree the major part of the 5 disposers to choose the 3 men, and the major part of the 3 men to end the cause haueing power from the 5 disposers by a note under theire hand to performe it, and the faultive not agreeing in the first to pay the charge of the last, and for the Arbitrators to follow no imployment till the cause be ended without consent of the whole that have to doe with the cause.

Instance. In the first Arbitration to offendor may offer reasonable terms of peace, and the offended may exact upon him and refuse and trouble men beyond reasonable satisfaction; so for the last arbitrators to judge where the fault was, in not agreeing in the first, to pay the charge of the last.

IV. Agreed, that if any person damnify any man, either in goods or good name, and the person offended follow not the cause vppon the offendor, that if any person giue notice to the 5 Disposers, they shall call the party delinquent to answer by Arbitration.

Instance. Thus, if any person abuse an other in person or goods, may be for peace sake, a man will at present put it vp, and it may so be resolue to revenge: therefore, for the peace of the state, the disposers are to look to it in the first place.

V. Agreed, for all the whole Inhabitants to combine ourselves to assist any man in the pursuit of any party delinquent, with all our best endeavours to attack him: but if any man raise a hubbub, and there be no just cause, then for the party that raised the hubbub to satisfy men for their time lost in it.

VI. Agreed, that if any man have a difference with any of the 5 Disposers which cannot be deferred till general meeting of the towne, then he may have the Clerk call the towne together at his [discretion] for a tryall.

Instance. It may be, a man may be to depart the land, or to a farr parte of the land; or his estate may lye vppon a speedy tryall or the like case may fall out.

VII. Agreed, that the towne, by the five men shall give every man a deed of all his lands lying within the bounds of the Plantation, to hould it by for after ages.

VIII. Agreed, that the 5 disposers shall from the date hereof, meete every month-day vppon General things and at the quarter-day to yeeld a new choice and give vp theire old Accounts.

IX. Agreed, that the Clerke shall call the 5 Disposers together at the month-day, and the generall towne together every quarter, to meete vppon general occasions from the date hereof.

X. Agreed, that the Clerke is to receive for every cause that comes to the towne for a tryall 4 *d.* for making each deed 12 *d.* and to give vp the booke to the towne at the yeeres end, and yeeld to a new choice.

XI. Agreed, that all acts of disposall on both sides to stand since the difference.

XII. Agreed, that every man that hath not paid in his purchase money for his Plantation shall make vp his 10 *s.* to be 30 *s* eqval with the first purchasers: and for all that are received townsmen hereafter, to pay the like summe of money to the towne stocke.

These being those things wee have generally concluded on, for our peace, we desireing our loveing friends to receive as our absolute determination, laying ourselves downe as subjects to it.

Source:

John Russell Bartlett, ed. *Records of the Colony of Rhode Island and Providence Plantations in New England.* Vol. 1. Providence, R.I.: A. C. Greene and Brothers, 1856. pp. 27–31.

Surrender of the Patent of Plymouth Colony, 1640

In 1629 William Bradford, a founding member of Plymouth Colony and its longtime governor, received a charter granting him and his associates (the "Old Planters") full rights to the land on which the colony was situated. In 1640 he relinquished that control to the freemen, or voters, of Plymouth Colony, keeping two tracts of land for himself and a third one for "the chief habitation of the Indians and reserved for them to dwell upon."

Whereas divers and sundry Treaties have beene in the Publicke generall courts of New Plymouth his majestie our dread Sovereigne Charles by the grace of God King of England Scotland France and Ireland &c. concerning the proper Right and title of the Lands within the bounds and

limitts of his said majestie's Letters Patents graunted by the Right Honorable his majestic's counsell for New England ratified by theire Comon Seale and signed by the hand of the Right Honorable Earle of Warwicke then Presidente of the said counsell to William Bradford his heirs associates and assignee beareing date &c And whereas the said William Bradford and divers others the first Instruments of God in the beginninge of this Create work of Plantacon together with such as the Alorderinge God in his Providence scone added unto them have beene at very grease charges to procure the said lands priviledges and freedomes from all entanglements as may appeare by divers and sondry deeds enlargements of graunts purchases payments of debts &c by reason whereof the title to the day of this present remayneth in the said William his heirs associate and assignee now for the better settling of the state of the said land aforesaid the said William Bradford and those their Instruments termed and called in sondry orders upon publick Record the Purchasers or Old Comers witnes two in especiall the one beareing date the third of March 1639 the other in December the first 1640 whereunto these presents have speciall relacon and agreement and whereby they are distinguished from other freemen and Inhabitants of the said Corporation. Be is Knowne unto all men therefore by these presents That the said William Bradford for himself his heires together with the said purchasers do onely reserve unto themselves their heires and assignee those three tracts of land menconed in the said resolucon order and agreement beareing date the first day of December 1640 viz. first from the bounds of Yarmouth three miles to the Eastward of Naemskeckett and from Sea to Sea crosse the said neck of land. The second of a place called Acconguesse (alias) Acockus which lyeth in the bottome of the Bay adjoyneing to the west side of Poynt Perrill and two miles to the westerne side of the said River to another place called Acqussent River which entereth at the western end of Nickatay and two miles to the Eastward therof and to extend eight miles up into the countrey. The third place of Sowawsett River to Patuckquett River with Consumpsit Neck which is the chief habitation of the Indians and reserved for them to dwell upon extending into the land eight miles through the whole breadth thereof, together with such other smale percells of lands as they or any of them are personally possessed of or interessed in by vertue of any former titles or graunts whatsoever and the said William Bradford doth by the free and full consent approbacon and agreement of the said Old Planters or Purchasers together with the likeing approbacon and acceptacon of the other part of the said Corporacon surrender into the hands of the whole court consisting of the Freemen of this Corporacon of New Plymouth all that ther right and title power authorytie priviledges immunities and freedomes graunted in the said

Letters Patents by the said Right Honorable Councell for New England reserveing his and their personall Right of Freemen together with the said Old Planters aforesaid except the said Lands before excepted, declaring the Freemen of this Corporacon together with all such as shall be legally admitted into the same his associates And the said William Bradford for him his heires and assignee doe further hereby promise and graunt to doe and performe whatsoever further thinge or thinges act or acts which in him lieth which shalbe needfull and expedient for the better confirmeing and establishinge the said premisses as by Counsell learned in the Laws shalbe reasonably advised and devised when he shalbe thereunto required In witnes whereof the said William Bradford hath in Publicke Court surrendered the said Letters Patents actually into the hands and power of the said Court bynding himselfe his heires executors administrators and assignee to deliver up whatsoever specialties are in his hands that do or may concerne the same.

Source:

Francis Newton Thorpe, ed. *The Federal and State Constitutions, Colonial Charters, and Other Organic Laws of the States, Territories, and Colonies Now or Heretofore Forming the United States of America.* Washington, D.C.: Government Printing Office, 1909.

Massachusetts Body of Liberties, 1641

Code of law put forth by the Massachusetts General Court in December 1641 and sent to towns for recommendations. It was based largely on English common law, leaving much authority to the magistrates, yet it indicated an incipient spirit of colonial independence. The general court, responding to criticism of the Body of Liberties in 1646, stated that "our allegiance binds us not to the laws of England any longer than while we live in England." At the end of a probation period, the Body of Liberties was replaced with *The Book of General Lawes and Libertyes* (1648).

The Liberties of the Massachusetts Colony in New England

The free fruition of such liberties immunities and privileges as humanity, and Christianity call for as due to every man in his place and proportion without impeachment and infringement, hath ever been and ever will be the tranquillity and stability of churches and commonwealths. And the denial or deprival thereof, the disturbance if not the ruin of both.

We hold it therefore our duty and safety, whilst we are about the further establishing of this government, to col-

lect and express all such freedoms as for present we foresee may concern us, and our posterity after us, and to ratify them with our solemn consent.

We do therefore this day religiously and unanimously decree and confirm these following rights, liberties, and privileges concerning our churches and civil state, to be respectively impartially inviolably enjoyed and observed throughout our jurisdiction for ever.

1. No man's life shall be taken away, no man's honor or good name shall be stained, no man's person shall be arrested, restrained, banished, dismembered, nor any ways punished, no man shall be deprived of his wife and children, no man's goods or estate shall be taken away from him, nor any way endamaged under color of law or countenance of authority, unless it be by virtue or equity of some express law of the country warranting the same, established by a General Court and sufficiently published, or in case of the defect of a law in any particular case, by the word of God. And in capital cases, or in cases concerning dismembering banishment, according to that word to be judged by the General Court.

2. Every person within this jurisdiction, whether inhabitant verdict so much as they can. If the bench and jurors shall so suffer at any time about their verdict that either of them cannot proceed with peace of conscience, the case shall be referred to the General Court, who shall take the question from both and determine it.

3. No man shall be urged to take any oath or subscribe any articles, covenants, or remonstrance, of a public and civil nature, but such as the General Court hath considered, allowed and required.

4. No man shall be punished for not appearing at or before any civil assembly, court, council, magistrate, or officer, nor for the omission of any office or service, if he shall be necessarily hindered by any apparent act or providence of God, which he could neither foresee nor avoid. Provided that this law shall not prejudice any person of his just cost and damage, in any civil action.

5. No man shall be compelled to any public work or service unless the press be grounded upon some act of the General Court, and have reasonable allowance therefor.

6. No man shall be pressed in person to any office, work, wars or other public service, that is necessarily and sufficiently exempted by any natural or personal impediment, as by want of years, greatness of age, defect of mind, failing of senses, or impotency of limbs.

7. No man shall be compelled to go out of the limits of this plantation upon any offensive wars which this Commonwealth or any of our friends or confederates shall voluntarily undertake. But only upon such vindictive and defensive wars in our own behalf or the behalf of our friends and confederates as shall be enterprized by the

counsel and consent of a Court General, or by authority derived from the same.

8. No man's cattle or goods of what kind soever shall be pressed or taken for any public use or service, unless it be by warrant grounded upon some act of the General Court, nor without such reasonable prices and hire as the ordinary rates of the country do afford. And if his cattle and goods shall perish or suffer damage in such service, the owners shall be sufficiently recompensed.

9. No monopolies shall be granted or allowed amongst us, but of such new inventions that are profitable to the country, and that for a short time.

10. All our lands and heritages shall be free from all fines and license upon alienations, and from all hariots, wardships, liveries, primer-seizins, year day and waste, escheats, and forfeitures, upon the deaths of parents or ancestors, be they natural, casual, or judicial.

11. All persons which are of the age of 21 years, and of right understanding and memories, whether excommunicate or condemned, shall have full power and liberty to make their wills and testaments, and other lawful alienations of their lands and estates.

12. Every man whether inhabitant or foreigner, free or not free, shall have liberty to come to any public court, council, or town meeting, and either by speech or writing to move any lawful, seasonable, and material question, or to present any necessary motion, complaint, petition, bill or information, whereof that meeting hath proper cognizance, so it be done in convenient time, due order, and respective manner.

13. No man shall be rated here for any estate or revenue he hath in England, or in any foreign parts til it be transported hither.

14. Any conveyance or alienation of land or other estate whatsoever, made by any woman that is married, any child under age, idiot or distracted person, shall be good if it be passed and ratified by the consent of a General Court.

15. All covetous or fraudulent alienations or conveyances of lands, tenements, or any hereditaments, shall be of no validity to defeat any man from due debts or legacies, or from any just title, claim or possession, of that which is so fraudulently conveyed.

16. Every inhabitant that is a householder shall have free fishing and fowling in any great ponds and bays, coves and rivers, so far as the sea ebbs and flows within the precincts of the town where they dwell, unless the free men of the same town or the General Court have otherwise appropriated them, provided that this shall not be extended to give leave to any man to come upon others property without their leave.

17. Every man of or with this jurisdiction shall have free liberty, notwithstanding any civil power, to remove both himself, and his family at their pleasure out of the

same, provided there be no legal impediment to the contrary.

Rights, Rules and Liberties concerning Judicial Proceedings

18. No man's person shall be restrained or imprisoned by any authority whatsoever, before the law hath sentenced him thereto, if he can put in sufficient security, bail or mainprise for his appearance and good behavior in the meantime, unless it be in crimes capital, and contempts in open Court, and in such cases where some express act of Court doth allow it.

19. If in a General Court any miscarriage shall be amongst the assistants when they are by themselves that may deserve an admonition or fine under 20/-, it shall be examined and sentenced by themselves. If amongst the deputies when they are by themselves, it shall be examined and sentenced amongst themselves. If it be when the whole Court is together, it shall be judged by the whole Court, and not severally as before.

20. If any which are to sit as judges in any other Court shall demean themselves offensively in the Court, the rest of the judges present shall have power to censure him for it; if the cause be of a high nature it shall be presented to and censured at the next superior Court.

21. In all cases where the first summons are not served six days before the Court, and the cause briefly specified in the warrant, where appearance is to be made by the party summoned, it shall be at his liberty whether he will appear or no, except all cases that are to be handled in courts suddenly called, upon extraordinary occasions. In all cases where there appears present and urgent cause any assistant or officer appointed shall have power to make out attachments for the first summons.

22. No man in any suit or action against another shall falsely pretend great debts or damages to vex his adversary, if it shall appear he doth so, the Court shall have power to set a reasonable fine on his head.

23. No man shall be adjudged to pay for detaining any debt from any creditor above eight pounds in the hundred for one year, and not above that rate proportionable for all sums whatsoever, neither shall this be a color or countenance to allow any usury amongst us contrary to the law of God.

24. In all trespasses or damages done to any man or men, if it can be proved to be done by the mere default of him or them to whom the trespass is done, it shall be judged no trespass, nor any damage given for it.

25. No summons pleading judgment, or any kind of proceeding in Court or course of justice shall be abated, arrested or reversed upon any kind of circumstantial errors or mistakes, if the person and cause be rightly understood and intended by the Court.

26. Every man that findeth himself unfit to plead his own cause in any Court shall have liberty to employ any man against whom the Court doth not except, to help him, provided he give him no fee or reward for his pains. This shall not exempt the party himself from answering such questions in person as the Court shall think meet to demand of him.

27. If any plaintiff shall give into any Court a declaration of his cause in writing, the defendant shall also have liberty and time to give in his answer in writing, and so in all further proceedings between party and party, so it does not further hinder the dispatch of justice than the Court shall be willing unto.

28. The plaintiff in all actions brought in any Court shall have liberty to withdraw his action, or to be nonsuited before the jury hath given in their verdict, in which case he shall always pay full cost and charges to the defendant, and may afterwards renew his suit at another Court if he please.

29. In all actions at law it shall be the liberty of the plaintiff and defendant by mutual consent to choose whether they will be tried by the bench or by a jury, unless it be where the law upon just reason hath otherwise determined. The like liberty shall be granted to all persons in criminal cases.

30. It shall be in the liberty of plaintiff and defendant, and likewise every delinquent (to be judged by a jury) to challenge any of the jurors. And if his challenge be found just and reasonable by the bench, or the rest of the jury, as the challenger shall choose it shall be allowed him, and *tales de circumstantibus* impanelled in their room.

31. In all cases where evidence is so obscure or defective that the jury cannot clearly and safely give a positive verdict, whether it be a grand or petit jury, it shall have liberty to give a *non liquit,* or a special verdict, in which last— that is, in a special verdict—the judgment of the case shall be left to the Court. And all jurors shall have liberty in matters of fact, if they cannot find the main issue, yet to find and present in their public laws and orders of the country. And if any inhabitant shall neglect or refuse to observe them, they shall have power to levy the appointed penalties by distress.

32. Every man shall have liberty to replevy his cattle or goods impounded, distrained, seized, or extended, unless it be upon execution after judgment, and in payment of fines. Provided he puts in good security to prosecute his replevin, and to satisfy such demands as his adversary shall recover against him in law.

33. No man's person shall be arrested, or imprisoned upon execution of judgment for any debt or fine, if the law can find competent means of satisfaction otherwise from his estate, and if not, his person may be arrested and imprisoned where he shall be kept at his own charge, not

the plaintiff's, till satisfaction be made, unless the Court shall otherwise provide.

34. If any man shall be proved and judged a common barrator vexing others with unjust, frequent, and endless suit, it shall be in the power of courts both to deny him the benefit of the law, and to punish him for his barratry.

35. No man's corn nor hay that is in the field or upon the cart, nor his garden stuff, nor anything subject to present decay, shall be taken in any distress, unless he that takes it doth presently bestow it where it may not be embezzled nor suffer spoil or decay, or give security to satisfy the worth whereof if it comes to any harm.

36. It shall be in the liberty of every man cast, condemned or sentenced in any cause in any inferior Court, to make their appeal to the Court of Assistants, provided they tender their appeal and put in security to prosecute it before the Court be ended wherein they were condemned, and within six days next ensuing put in good security before some assistant to satisfy what his adversary shall recover against him; and if the cause be of a criminal nature, for his good behavior and appearance. And every man shall have liberty to complain to the General Court of any injustice done him in any Court of Assistants or other.

37. In all cases where it appears to the Court that the plaintiff hath willingly and wittingly done wrong to the defendant in commencing and prosecuting an action or complaint against him, they shall have power to impose upon him a proportionable fine to the use of the defendant or accused person, for his false complaint or clamor.

38. Every man shall have liberty to record in the public rolls of any Court any testimony given upon oath in the same Court, or before two assistants, or any deed or evidence legally confirmed, there to remain *in perpetuam rei memoriam,* that is, for perpetual memorial or evidence upon occasion.

39. In all actions both real and personal between party and party, the Court shall have power to respite execution for a convenient time, when in their prudence they see just cause so to do.

40. No conveyance, deed, or promise whatsoever shall be of validity, if it be gotten by illegal violence, imprisonment, threatening, or any kind of forcible compulsion called duress.

41. Every man that is to answer for any criminal cause, whether he be in prison or under bail, his cause shall be heard and determined at the next Court that hath proper cognizance thereof; and may be done without prejudice of justice.

42. No man shall be twice sentenced by civil justice for one and the same crime, offense, or trespass.

43. No man shall be beaten with above 40 stripes, nor shall any true gentleman, nor any man equal to a gentleman,

be punished with whipping , unless his crime be very shameful and his course of life vicious and profligate.

44. No man condemned to die shall be put to death within four days next after his condemnation, unless the Court see special cause to the contrary, or in case of martial law; nor shall the body of any man so put to death be unburied 12 hours unless it be in case of anatomy.

45. No man shall be forced by torture to confess any crime against himself nor any other unless it be in some capital case, where he is first fully convicted by clear and sufficient evidence to be guilty, after which, if the cause be of that nature, that it is very apparent there be other conspirators or confederates with him, then he may be tortured, yet not with such tortures as be barbarous and inhumane.

46. For bodily punishments we allow amongst us none that are inhumane, barbarous, or cruel.

47. No man shall be put to death without the testimony of two or three witnesses or that which is equivalent thereunto.

48. Every inhabitant of the country shall have free liberty to search and view any rules, records, or registers of any Court or office except the Council; and to have a transcript of exemplification thereof, written, examined, and signed by the hand of the officer of the office, paying the appointed fees therefor.

49. No free man shall be compelled to serve upon juries above two courts a year, except grand jurymen, who shall hold two courts together at the least.

50. All jurors shall be chosen continually by the freemen of the town where they dwell.

51. All associates selected at any time to assist the assistants in inferior courts, shall be nominated by the towns belonging to that court, by orderly agreement among themselves.

52. Children, idiots, distracted persons, and all that are strangers, or newcomers to our plantation, shall have such allowances and dispensations in any cause whether criminal or other as religion and reason require.

53. The age of discretion for passing away of lands or such kind of hereditaments, or for giving of votes, verdicts, or sentence in any civil courts or causes, shall be one and twenty years.

54. Whensoever anything is to be put to vote, any sentence to be pronounced, or any other matter to be proposed, or read in any court or assembly, if the president or moderator thereof shall refuse to perform it, the major part of the members of that court or assembly shall have power to appoint any other meet man of them to do it. And if there be just cause, to punish him that should and would not.

55. In all suits or actions, in any court, the plaintiff shall have liberty to make all the titles, and claims to that he sues for, he can. And the defendant shall have liberty to plead all the pleas he can in answer to them, and the court shall judge according to the entire evidence of all.

56. If any man shall behave himself offensively at any town meeting, the rest of the freemen then present shall have power to sentence him for his offence. So be it the fine or penalty exceed not twenty shillings.

57. Whensoever any person shall come to any very sudden, untimely, and unnatural death, some assistant, or the constables of that town, shall forthwith summon a jury of twelve freemen to inquire of the cause and manner of their death, and shall present a true verdict thereof to some near assistant, or the next court to be held for that town upon their oath.

Liberties More Peculiarly Concerning the Freemen

58. Civil authority hath power and liberty to see the peace, ordinances and rules of Christ observed in every church according to his word, so it be done in a civil and not an ecclesiastical way.

59. Civil authority hath power and liberty to deal with any church member in a way of civil justice, notwithstanding any church relation, office, or interest.

60. No church censure shall degrade or depose any man from any civil dignity, office, or authority he shall have in the Commonwealth.

61. No magistrate, juror, officer, or other man shall be bound to inform present or reveal any private crime or offense, wherein there is no peril or danger to this plantation or any member thereof, when any necessary tie of conscience binds him to secrecy grounded upon the word of God, unless it be in case of testimony lawfully required.

62. Any shire or town shall have liberty to choose their deputies whom and where they please for the General Court. So be it they be freemen, and have taken their oath of fealty, and inhabiting in this jurisdiction.

63. No governor, deputy governor, assistant, associate, or grand juryman at any court, nor any deputy for the General Court, shall at any time bear his own charges at any court, but their necessary expenses shall be defrayed either by the town or shire in whose service they are, or by the country in general.

64. Every action between party and party, and proceedings against delinquents in criminal causes, shall be briefly and distinctly entered on the rolls of every court by the recorder thereof. That such actions be not afterwards brought again to the vexation of any man.

65. No custom or prescription shall ever prevail amongst us in any moral cause; our meaning is to maintain anything that can be proved to be morally sinful by the word of God.

66. The freemen of every township shall have power to make such by-laws and constitutions as may concern the welfare of their town, provided they be not of a criminal, but only of a prudential nature, and that their penalties exceed not 20/sh. for one offence, and that they be not repugnant to the or foreigner, shall enjoy the same justice and law, that is general for the plantation, which we constitute and execute one toward another without partiality or delay.

67. It is the constant liberty of the freemen of this plantation to choose yearly at the court of election out of the freemen all the general officers of this jurisdiction. If they please to discharge them at the day of election by way of vote, they may do it without showing cause; but if at any other General Court, we hold it due justice, that the reasons thereof be alleged and proved. By general officers we mean, our governor, deputy governor, assistants, treasurer, general of our wars, and our admiral at sea, and such as are or hereafter may be of the like general nature.

68. It is the liberty of the freemen to choose such deputies for the General Court out of themselves, either in their own towns or elsewhere, as they judge fittest. And because we cannot foresee what variety and weight of occasions may fall into future consideration, and what counsels we may stand in need of, we decree: that the deputies (to attend the General Court in the behalf of the country) shall not at any time be stated or enacted, but from Court to Court, or at the most but for one year, that the country may have an annual liberty to do in that case what is most behooveful for the best welfare thereof.

69. No General Court shall be dissolved or adjourned without the consent of the major part thereof.

70. All freemen called to give any advice, vote, verdict, or sentence in any court, council, or civil assembly, shall have full freedom to do it according to their true judgments and consciences, so it be done orderly and inoffensively for the manner.

71. The governor shall have a casting voice whensoever an equivote shall fall out in the Court of Assistants or general assembly. So shall the president or moderator have in all civil courts or assemblies.

72. The governor and deputy governor jointly consenting, or any three assistants concurring in consent, shall have power out of court to reprieve a condemned malefactor til the next quarter or General Court. The General Court only shall have power to pardon a condemned malefactor.

73. The General Court hath liberty and authority to send out any member of this Commonwealth of what quality, condition, or office whatsoever into foreign parts about any public message or negotiation. Provided the party sent be acquainted with the affair he goeth about, and be willing to undertake the service.

74. The freemen of every town or township shall have full power to choose yearly or for less time out of themselves a convenient number of fit men to order the planting or prudential occasions of that town, according to instructions given them in writing; provided nothing be done by them contrary to the public laws and orders of the country, provided also the number of such select persons be not above nine.

75. It is and shall be the liberty of any member or members of any court, council, or civil assembly in cases of making or executing any order or law, the properly concern religion, or any cause capital, or wars, or subscription to any public articles or remonstrance, in case they cannot in judgment and conscience consent to that way the major vote or suffrage goes, to make their contra-remonstrance or protestation in speech or writing, and upon request to have their dissent recorded in the rolls of that court. So it be done christianly and respectfully for the manner. And their dissent only be entered without the reasons thereof, for the avoiding of tediousness.

76. Whensoever any jury of trials or jurors are not clear in their judgments or consciences concerning any cause wherein they are to give their verdict, they shall have liberty in open court to advise with any man they think fit to resolve or direct them, before they give in their verdict.

77. In all cases wherein any freeman is to give his vote, be it in point of election, making constitutions and orders, or passing sentence in any case of judicature or the like, if he cannot see reason to give it positively one way or another, he shall have liberty to be silent, and not pressed to a determined vote.

78. The general or public treasure or any part thereof shall never be expended but by the appointment of a General Court, nor any shire treasure, but by the appointment of the freemen thereof, nor any town treasure but by the freemen of that township.

Liberties of Women

79. If any man at his death shall not leave his wife a competent portion of his estate, upon just complaint made to the General Court she shall be relieved.

80. Every married woman shall be free from bodily correction or stripes by her husband, unless it be in his own defence upon her assault. If there be any just cause of correction, complaint shall be made to authority assembled in some court, from which only she shall receive it.

Liberties of Children

81. When parents die intestate, the elder son shall have a double portion of his whole estate real and personal, unless the General Court upon just cause alleged shall judge otherwise.

82. When parents die intestate having no [male] heir of their bodies, their daughters shall inherit as co-partners, unless the General Court upon just reason shall judge otherwise.

83. If any parents shall willfully and unreasonably deny any child timely or convenient marriage, or shall exercise any unnatural severity towards them, such children shall have free liberty to complain to authority for redress.

84. No orphan during their minority which was not committed to tuition or service by the parents in their lifetime, shall afterwards be absolutely disposed of by any kindred, friend, executor, township, or church, nor by themselves, without the consent of some court wherein two assistants at least shall be present.

Liberties of Servants

85. If any servants shall flee from the tyranny and cruelty of their masters to the house of any freeman of the same town, they shall be there protected and sustained till due order be taken for their relief. Provided due notice thereof be speedily given to their masters from whom they fled, and [to] the next assistant or constable where the party flying is harbored.

86. No servant shall be put off for above a year to any other neither in the lifetime of their master nor after their death by their executors of administrators, unless it be by consent of authority assembled in some court or two assistants.

87. If any man smite out the eye or tooth of his manservant, or maid-servant, or otherwise maim or much disfigure him, unless it be by mere casualty, he shall let them go free from his service. And shall have such further recompense as the court shall allow him.

88. Servants that have served diligently and faithfully to the benefit of their masters seven years, shall not be sent away empty. And if any have been unfaithful, negligent, or unprofitable in their service, notwithstanding the good usage of their masters, they shall not be dismissed till they have made satisfaction according to the judgment of authority.

Liberties of Foreigners and Strangers

89. If any people of other nations professing the true Christian religion shall flee to us from the tyranny or oppression of their persecutors, or from famine, wars, or the like necessary and compulsory cause, they shall be entertained and succored amongst us, according to that power and prudence God shall give us.

90. If any ships or other vessels, be it friend or enemy, shall suffer shipwreck upon our coast, there shall be no violence or wrong offered to their persons or goods. But their persons shall be harbored, and relieved, and their goods preserved in safety till authority may be certified thereof, and shall take further order therein.

91. There shall never be any bond slavery, villeinage or captivity amongst us unless it be lawful captives taken in just wars, and such strangers as willingly sell themselves or are sold to us. And these shall have all the liberties and Christian usages which the law of God established in Israel concerning such persons doth morally require. This exempts none from servitude who shall be judged thereto by authority.

Of the Brute Creature

92. No man shall exercise any tyranny or cruelty towards any brute creature which are usually kept for man's use.

93. If any man shall have occasion to lead or drive cattle from place to place that is far off, so that they be weary, or hungry, or all sick, or lame, it shall be lawful to rest or refresh them, for competent time, in any open place that is not corn, meadow, or enclosed for some peculiar use.

94. Capital Laws

I

If any man after legal conviction shall have or worship any other God, but the lord God, he shall be put to death (Deut. 13:6, 10; Deut. 17:2, 6; Ex. 22:20).

II

If any man or woman be a witch (that is, hath or consulteth with a familiar spirit), they shall be put to death (Ex. 22:18; Lev. 20:27; Deut. 18:10).

III

If any person shall blaspheme the name of God, the Father, Son, or Holy Ghost, with direct, express, presumptuous or high-handed blasphemy, or shall curse God in the like manner, he shall be put to death (Lev. 24:15, 16).

IV

If any person commit any wilful murder, which is manslaughter, committed upon premeditated malice, hatred, or cruelty, not in a man's necessary and just defence, nor by mere casualty against his will, he shall be put to death (Ex. 21:12; Numb. 35:13, 14, 30, 31).

V

If any person slayeth another suddenly in his anger or cruelty of passion, he shall be put to death (Numb. 25:20, 21; Lev. 24:17).

VI

If any person shall slay another through guile, either by poisoning or other such devilish practice, he shall be put to death (Ex. 21:14).

VII

If any man or woman shall lie with any beast or brute creature by carnal copulation, they shall surely be put to death. And the beast shall be slain, and buried and not eaten (Lev. 20:15, 16).

VIII

If any man lieth with mankind as he lieth with a woman, both of them have committed abomination, they both shall surely be put to death (Lev. 20:13).

IX

If any person committeth adultery with a married or espoused wife, the adulterer and adulteress shall surely be put to death (Lev: 20:19 and 18:20; Deut. 22:23, 24).

X

If any man stealeth a man or mankind, he shall surely be put to death (Ex. 21:16).

XI

If any man rise up by false witness, wittingly and of purpose to take away any man's life, he shall be put to death (Deut. 19:16, 18, 19).

XII

If any man shall conspire and attempt any invasion, insurrection, or public rebellion against our commonwealth, or shall endeavor to surprise any town or towns, fort or forts therein, or shall treacherously and perfidiously attempt the alteration and subversion of our frame of polity or government fundamentally, he shall be put to death.

95. A Declaration of the Liberties the Lord Jesus Hath Given to the Churches

I

All the people of God within this jurisdiction who are not in a church way, and be orthodox in judgment, and not scandalous in life, shall have full liberty to gather themselves into a church estate; provided they do it in a Christian way, with due observation of the rules of Christ revealed in his word.

II

Every church hath full liberty to exercise all the ordinances of God, according to the rules of scripture.

III

Every church hath free liberty of election and ordination of all their officers from time to time, provided they be able, pious and orthodox.

IV

Every church hath free liberty of admission, recommendation, dismission, and expulsion or deposal of their officers and members, upon due cause, with free exercise of the discipline and censures of Christ according to the rules of his word.

V

No injunctions are to be put upon any church, church officers or member in point of doctrine, worship or discipline, whether for substance or circumstance besides the institutions of the Lord.

VI

Every church of Christ hath freedom to celebrate days of fasting and prayer, and of thanksgiving according to the word of God.

VII

The elders of churches have free liberty to meet monthly, quarterly, or otherwise, in convenient numbers and places, for conferences and consultations about Christians and church questions and occasions.

VIII

All churches have liberty to deal with any of their members in a church way that are in the hand of justice. So it be not to retard or hinder the course thereof.

IX

Every church hath liberty to deal with any magistrate, deputy of court, or other officer whatsoever that is a member in a church way in case of apparent and just offence given in their places, so it be done with due observance and respect.

X

We allow private meetings for edification in religion amongst Christians of all sorts of people. So it be without just offence for number, time, place, and other circumstances.

XI

For the preventing and removing of error and offence that may grow and spread in any of the churches in this jurisdiction, and for the preserving of truth and peace in the several churches within themselves, and for the maintenance and exercise of brotherly communion amongst all the churches in the country, it is allowed and ratified, by the authority of this General Court as a lawful liberty of the churches of Christ: that once in every month of the year (when the season will bear it) it shall be lawful for the ministers and elders of the churches near adjoining together, with any other of the brethren, with the consent of the churches, to assemble by course in each several church one after another. To the intent, after the preaching of the word by such a minister as shall be requested thereto by the elders of the church where the assembly is held, the rest of the day may be spent in public Christian conference about the discussing and resolving of any such doubts and cases of conscience concerning matter of doctrine or worship or government of the church as shall be propounded by any of the brethren of that church, will leave also to any other brother to propound his objections or answers for further satisfaction according to the word of God. Provided that the whole action be guided and moderated by the elders of the church where the assembly is held, or by such others as they shall appoint. And that nothing be concluded and imposed by way of authority from one or more churches upon another, but only by way of brotherly conference and consultations. That the truth may be searched out to the satisfying of every man's conscience in the sight of God according to his word. And because such an assembly and the work thereof cannot be duly attended to if other lectures be held in the same week, it is therefore agreed with the consent of the churches, that in that week when such an assembly is held, all the lectures in all the neighboring churches for that week shall be forborne. That so the public service of Christ in this more solemn assembly may be transacted with greater diligence and attention.

96. Howsoever these above specified rites, freedoms, immunities, authorities and privileges, both civil and ecclesiastical, are expressed only under the name and title of liberties, and not in the exact form of laws or statutes, yet we do with one consent fully authorize, and earnestly entreat all that are and shall be in authority, to consider them as laws, and not to fail to inflict condign and proportionable punishments upon every man impartially, that shall infringe or violate any of them.

97. We likewise give full power and liberty to any person that shall at any time be denied or deprived of any of them, to commence and prosecute their suit, complaint or action against any man that shall so do in any court that hath proper cognizance or judicature thereof.

98. Lastly, because our duty and desire is to do nothing suddenly which fundamentally concerns us, we decree that these rights and liberties shall be audibly read and deliberately weighed at every General Court that shall be held within three years next ensuing. And such of them as shall not be altered or repealed, they shall stand so ratified, that no man shall infringe them without due punishment.

And if any General Court within these next three years shall fail or forget to read and consider them as above said,

the governor and deputy governor for the time being, and every assistant present at such courts, shall forfeit 20/sh. a man, and every deputy 10/sh a man for each neglect, which shall be paid out of their proper estate, and not by the country or the towns which choose them; and whensoever there shall arise any question in any court among the assistants and associates thereof about the explanation of these rights and liberties, the General Court only shall have power to interpret them.

Source:

John Scott, ed. *Living Documents in American History.* New York: Washington Square Press, 1964–68.

New England Articles of Confederation, 1643

The first attempt at a unified federal government among the English colonies in North America. In 1643, in response to increasing Indian attacks and the expansion of Dutch settlement, the four Puritan colonies—Massachusetts Bay, Plymouth, Connecticut, and New Haven—formed the United Colonies of New England to ensure their "mutual safety and welfare." Each colony retained its individual sovereignty but pledged its allegiance to the confederation as a whole. A commission was established that consisted of two representatives from each colony. All defensive or offensive wars were to be justified and approved by the commission. Commissioners also had the power to legislate Indian affairs, settle interstate quarrels, and extradite fugitive servants or criminals. While the commission was an important step toward intercolonial cooperation, in practice it was little more than an advisory board. Petty rivalries, a narrow religious outlook that refused membership to the Maine and Rhode Island settlements, and the tendency of Massachusetts, the largest colony, to ignore the commission's decisions all led to the confederacy's demise. Despite briefly regaining its significance during King Philip's War (1675–76), the confederacy returned to its mostly inactive state shortly afterward. When the Massachusetts charter was revoked in 1684, the commission was dissolved, and the confederacy came to an end.

William Penn's Plan of Union (1697) appears to be the first such prescription for a union of all the northern American colonies. It, too, called for a congress made up of two representatives from each colony, who would meet at least once a year and twice during wartime. This congress would have held legal jurisdiction over such intercolonial activities as the prevention of frauds and the regulation of abuses in the plantation trade. It appointed the colony of New York as the meeting place for the congress and appointed the governor of New York to act as the king's high commissioner for each session. However, it was never implemented

The Articles of Confederation between the Plantations under the Government of the Massachusetts, the Plantations under the Government of New Plymouth, the Plantations under the Government of Connecticut, and the Government of New Haven with the Plantations in Combination therewith:

1

Whereas we all came into these parts of America with one and the same end and aim, namely, to advance the Kingdom of our Lord Jesus Christ and to enjoy the liberties of the Gospel in purity with peace; and whereas in our settling (by a wise providence of God) we are further dispersed upon the sea coasts and rivers than was at first intended, so that we can not according to our desire with convenience communicate in one government and jurisdiction; and whereas we live encompassed with people of several nations and strange languages which hereafter may prove injurious to us or our posterity. And forasmuch as the natives have formerly committed sundry insolence and outrages upon several Plantations of the English and have of late of late combined themselves against us: and seeing by reason of those sad distractions in England which they have heard of, and by which they know we are hindered from that humble way of seeking advice, or reaping those comfortable fruits of protection, which at other times we might well expect. We therefore do conceive it our bounden duty, without delay to enter into a present Consociation amongst ourselves, for mutual help and strength in all our future concernments: That, as in nation and religion, so in other respects, we be and continue one according to the tenor and true meaning of the ensuing articles: Wherefore it is fully agreed and concluded by and between the parties or Jurisdictions above named, and they jointly and severally do by these presents agree and conclude that they all be and henceforth be called by the name of the United Colonies of New England.

2

The said United Colonies for themselves and their posterities do jointly and severally hereby enter into a firm and perpetual league of friendship and amity for offence and defence, mutual advice and succor upon all just occasions both for preserving and propagating the truth and liberties of the Gospel and for their own mutual safety and welfare.

3

It is further agreed that the Plantations which at present are or hereafter shall be settled within the limits of the Massachusetts shall be forever under the Massachusetts and shall have peculiar jurisdiction among themselves in all cases as an entire body, and that Plymouth, Connecticut, and New Haven shall each of them have like peculiar jurisdiction and government within their limits; and in reference to the Plantations which already are settled or shall hereafter be erected, or shall settle within their limits respectively; provided no other Jurisdiction shall hereafter be taken in as a distinct head or member of this Confederation, nor shall any other Plantation or Jurisdiction in present being, and not already in combination or under the jurisdiction of any of these Confederates, be received by any of them; nor shall any two of the Confederates join in one Jurisdiction without the consent of the rest, which consent to be interpreted as is expressed in the sixth article ensuing.

4

It is by these Confederates agreed that the charge of all just wars, whether offensive or defensive, upon what part or member of this Confederation soever they fall, shall both in men, provisions, and all other disbursements be borne by all the parts of this Confederation in different proportions according to their different ability in manner following, namely, that the Commissioners for each Jurisdiction from time to time, as there shall be occasion, bring a true account and number of all their males males in every Plantation, or any way belonging to or under their several Jurisdictions, of what quality or condition soever they be, from sixteen to threescore, being inhabitants there. And that according to the different numbers from which from time to time shall be found in each Jurisdiction upon a true and just account, the service of men and all charges of the war be borne by the poll: each Jurisdiction or Plantation being left to their own just course and custom of rating themselves and people according to their different estates with due respects to their qualities and exemptions amongst themselves though the Confederation take no notice of any such privilege: and that according to their different charge of each Jurisdiction and Plantation the whole advantage of the war (if it please God so to bless their endeavors) whether it be in lands, goods, or persons, shall be proportionately divided among the said Confederates.

5

It is further agreed, that if any of these Jurisdictions or any Plantation under or in combination with them, be invaded by any enemy whomsoever, upon notice and request of any three magistrates of that Jurisdiction so invaded, the rest of the Confederates without any further meeting or expostulation shall forthwith send aid to the Confederate in danger but in different proportions; namely, the

Massachusetts an hundred men sufficiently armed and provided for such a service and journey, and each of the rest, forty five so armed and provided, or any less number, if less be required according to this proportion. But if such Confederate in danger may be supplied by their next Confederates, not exceeding the number hereby agreed, they may crave help there, and seek no further for the present: the charge to be borne as in this article is expressed: and at the return to be victualled and supplied with the powder and shot for their journey (if there be need) by that Jurisdiction which employed or sent for them; But none of the Jurisdictions to exceed these numbers until by a meeting of the Commissioners for this Confederation a greater aid appear necessary. And this proportion to continue till upon knowledge of greater numbers in each Jurisdiction which shall be brought to the next meeting, some other proportion be ordered. But in any such case of sending men for present aid, whether before or after such order or alteration, it is agreed that at the meeting of the Commissioners for this Confederation, the cause of such war or invasion be duly considered: and if it appear that the fault lay in the parties so invaded then that Jurisdiction or Plantation make just satisfaction, both to the invaders whom they have injured, and bear all the charges of the war themselves, without requiring any allowance from the rest of the Confederates towards the same. And further that if any Jurisdiction see any danger of invasion approaching, and there be time for a meeting, that in such a case three magistrates of the Jurisdiction may summon a meeting at such convenient place as themselves shall think meet, to consider and provide against the threatened danger; provided when they are met they may remove to what place they please; only whilst any of these four Confederates have but three magistrates in their Jurisdiction, their requests, or summons, from any of them shalm be accounted of equal force with the three mentioned in both the clauses of this article, till there be an increase of magistrates there.

6

It is also agreed, that for the managing and concluding of all affairs proper, and concerning the whole Confederation two Commissioners shall be chosen by and out of each of these four Jurisdictions: namely, two for the Massachusetts, two for Plymouth, two for Connecticut, and two for New Haven, being all in Church fellowship with us which shall bring full power from their several General Courts respectively to hear, examine, weigh and determine all affairs of our war, or peace, leagues, aids, charges, and numbers of men for war, division of spoils and whatsoever is gotten by conquest, receiving of more Confederates for Planatations into combination with any of the Confederates, and all things of like nature, which are the proper concomitants or consequents of such a Confederation for

amity, offence, and defence: not intermeddling with the government of any of the Jurisdictions, which by the third article is preserved entirely, to themselves. But if these eight Commissioners when they meet shall not all agree yet it [is] concluded that any six of the eight agreeing shall have power to settle and determine the business in question. But if six do not agree, that then such propositions with their reasons so far as they have been debated, be sent and referred to the four General Courts; namely, the Massachusetts, Plymouth, Connecticut, and New Haven; and if at all the said General Courts the business so referred be concluded, then to be prosecuted by the Confederates and all their members. It is further agreed that these eight Commissioners shall meet once every year besides extraordinary meetings (according to the fifth article) to consider, treat, and conclude of all affairs belonging to this Confederation, which meeting shall ever be the first Thursday in September. And that the next meeting after the date of these presents, which shall be accounted the second meeting, shall be at Boston in the Massachusetts, the third at Hartford, the fourth at New Haven, the fifth at Plvmouth, the sixth and seventh at Boston; and then Hartford, New Haven, and Plymouth, and so in course successively, if in the meantime some middle place be not found out and agreed on, which may be commodious for all the Jurisdictions.

7

It is further agreed that at each meeting of these eight Commissioners, whether ordinary or extraordinary they or six of them agreeing as before, may choose their President out of themselves whose office and work shall be to take care and direct for order and a comely carrying on of all proceedings in the present meeting but he shall be invested with no such power or respect, which he shall hinder the propounding or progress of any business or any way cast the scales otherwise than in the precedent article is agreed.

8

It is also agreed that the. Commissioners for this Confederation hereafter a their meetings, whether ordinary or extraordinary as they may have commission or opportunity, do endeavor to frame and establish agreements and orders in general cases of a civil nature, wherein all the Plantations are interested, for preventing as much as may be all occasion of war or differences with others, as about the free and speedy pasage of justice in every Jurisdiction, to all the Confederates equally as to their own, receiving those that remove from one Plantation to another without due certificate, how all the Jurisdictions, may carry it towards the Indians, that they neither grow insolent nor be injured without due satisfaction, lest war break in upon the Confederates through such miscarriages. It is also agreed that if any servant run away from his master into any other of these confederated Jurisdictions, that in such case, upon the certificate of one magistrate in the Jurisdiction out of which the said servant fled or upon other due proof; the said servant shall be delivered, either to his master or any other that pursues and brings such certificate or proof. And that upon the escape of any prisoner whatsoever, or fugitive for any criminal cause, whether breaking prison, or getting from the officer, or otherwise escaping,, upon the certificate of two magistrates of the Jurisdiction out of which the escape is made, that he was a prisoner, or such an offender at the time of the escape, the magistrates, or some of them of that Jurisdiction where for the present the said prisoner or fugitive abideth, shall forthwith grant such a warrant as the case will bear, for the apprehending of any such person, and the delivery of him into the hands of the officer or person who pursues him. And if there be help required for safe returning of any such offender, then it shall be granted to him that craves the same, paying the charges thereof.

9

And for that the justest wars may be of dangerous consequence, especially to the smaller Plantations in the United Colonies, it is agreed that neither the Massachusetts, Plymouth, Connecticut, nor New Haven, nor any of the members of them, shall at any time hereafter begin, undertake, or engage themselves, or this Confederation,or any part thereof in any war whatsoever (sudden exigencies, with the necessary consequents thereof excepted), which are also to be moderated as much as the case will permit, without the consent and agreement of the formentioned eight Commissioners, or at least six of them. as in the sixth article is provided: and that no charge be required of any of the Confederates, in case of a defensive war, till the Commissioners have met, and approved the justice of the war, and have agreed upon the sum of money to be levid, which sum is then to be paid by the several Confederates in proportion according to the fourth article.

Source:

Francis Newton Thorpe, ed. *The Federal and State Constitutions Colonial Charters, and Other Organic Laws of the States, Territories, and Colonies Now or Heretofore Forming the United States of America.* Washington, D.C.: Government Printing Office, 1909.

John Winthrop, "On Liberty," 1645

Document written by John Winthrop in 1645 for the purpose of addressing the assembly of the Massachusetts Bay Colony. after he was impeached and acquitted before the Massachusetts General Court. Never one to bow to popular demand, Winthrop made an unpopular decision concerning the issue of who should be chosen captain of the Higham mili-

tia, which led to his trial. The Massachusetts Bay Colony was based entirely on religious ideals, and Winthrop would not tolerate civil liberty in its government. He governed with these motivations in mind and, in this document, called for blithe and peaceful submission to authority from his subjects. He was reelected to governor until his death in 1649, though many independent citizens of Massachusetts did not go along with his strictly religious views.

I suppose something may be expected from me upon this charge that has befallen me, which moves me to speak now to you; yet I intend not to intermeddle in the proceedings of the court or with any of the persons concerned therein. Only I bless God that I see an issue of this troublesome business. I also acknowledge the justice of the court, and for mine own part I am well satisfied. I was publicly charged, and I am publicly and legally acquitted, which is all I did expect or desire. And thought this be sufficient for my justification before men, yet not so before the God who hath seen so much amiss in my dispensations (and even in this affair) as calls me to be humble.

For to be publicly and criminally charged in this court is matter of humiliation (and I desire to make a right use of it), notwithstanding I be thus acquitted. If her father had spit in her face (saith the Lord concerning Miriam), should she not have been ashamed seven days? Shame had lien upon her, whatever the occasion had been. I am unwilling to stay you from your urgent affairs, yet give me leave (upon this special occasion) to speak a little more to this assembly. It may be of some good use to inform and rectify the judgments of some of the people, and may prevent such distempers as have arisen amongst us. The great questions that have troubled the country are about the authority of the magistrates and the liberty of the people. It is yourselves who have called us to this office, and, being called by you, we have our authority from God, in way of an ordinance, such as hath the image of God eminently stamped upon it, the contempt and violation whereof hath been vindicated with examples of divine vengeance.

I entreat you to consider that, when you choose magistrates, you take them from among yourselves, men subject to like passions as you are. Therefore, when you see infirmities in us, you should reflect upon your own, and that would make you bear the more with us, and not be severe censurers of the failings of your magistrates, when you have continual experience of the like infirmities in yourselves and others.

We account him a good servant who breaks not his covenant. The covenant between you and us is the oath you have taken of us, which is to this purpose, that we shall govern you and judge your causes by the rules of God's laws and our own, according to our best skill. When you agree with a workman to build you a ship or house, etc., he undertakes as well for his skill as for faithfulness; for it is his profession, and you pay him for both. But when you call one to be a magistrate he doth not profess or undertake to have sufficient skill for that office, nor can you furnish him with gifts, etc., therefore you must run the hazard of his skill and ability. But if he fail in faithfulness, which by his oath he is bound unto, that he must answer for. If it fall out that the case be clear to common apprehension, and the rule clear also, if he transgress here, the error is not in the skill, but in the evil of the will: it must be required of him. But if the case be doubtful, or the rule doubtful, to men of such understanding and parts as your magistrates are, if your magistrates should err here, yourselves must bear it.

For the other point concerning liberty, I observe a great mistake in the country about that. There is a twofold liberty, natural (I mean as our nature is now corrupt) and civil or federal. The first is common to man with beasts and other creatures. By this man, as he stands in relation to man simply, hath liberty to do what he lists: it is a liberty to evil as well as to good. This liberty is incompatible and inconsistent with authority, and cannot endure the least restraint of the most just authority. The exercise and maintaining of this liberty makes men grow more evil, and in time to be worse than brute beasts: *omnes sumus licentia deteriores*. This is that great enemy of truth and peace, that wild beast, which all the ordinances of God are bent against, to restrain and subdue it.

The other kind of liberty I call civil or federal; it may also be termed moral, in reference to the covenant between God and man in the moral law, and the politic covenants and constitutions amongst men themselves. This liberty is the proper end and object of authority, and cannot subsist without it; and it is a liberty to that only which is good, just, and honest. This liberty you are to stand for, with the hazard (not only of your goods, but) of your lives, if need be. Whatsoever crosseth this is not authority, but a distemper thereof. This liberty is maintained and exercised in a way of subjection to authority; it is of the same kind of liberty wherewith Christ hath made us free. The woman's own choice makes such a man her husband; yet, being so chosen, he is her lord, and she is to be subject to him, yet in a way of liberty, not of bondage; and a true wife accounts her subjection her honor and freedom, and would not think her condition safe and free but in her subjection to her husband's authority. Such is the liberty of the church under the authority of Christ, her king and husband; his yoke is so easy and sweet to her as a bride's ornaments; and if, through forwardness or wantonness, etc., she shake it off at any time, she is at no rest in her spirit until she take it up again; and whether her lord smiles upon her, and embraceth her in his arms, or whether her frowns, or rebukes, or smites her, she appre-

hends the sweetness of his love in all, and is refreshed, supported, and instructed by every such dispensation of his authority over her. On the other side, ye know who they are that complain of this yoke and say, let us break their bands, etc., we will not have this man to rule over us.

Even so, brethren, it will be between you and your magistrates. If you stand for your natural corrupt liberties, and will do what is good in your own eyes, you will not endure the least weight of authority, but will murmur, and oppose, and be always striving to shake off that yoke; but if you will be satisfied to enjoy such civil and lawful liberties, such as Christ allows you, then will you quietly and cheerfully submit unto that authority which is set over you, in all the administrations of it, for your good. Wherein, if we fail at any time, we hope we shall be willing (by God's assistance) to hearken to good advice from any of you, or in any other way to God; so shall your liberties be preserved, in upholding the honor and power of authority amongst you.

Source:

James Andrews and David Zarefsky, eds. *American Voices: Significant Speeches in American History, 1640–1945*. New York: Longman, 1989.

Roger Williams, "Plea for Religious Liberty," 1645

Small part of the longer document, *The Bloudy Tenent of Persecution,* written by Roger Williams in 1645, based on views and principles he expressed at different times in his life. This small vignette of the man who founded the colony of Rhode Island and fought for the freedom of religion gives 12 reasons as to why civil and religious liberty should be separated. The document also advocates complete religious freedom as a distinct right of the people, rather than a right the government simply tolerates. Williams was banished from the colony of Massachusetts in 1636 and fled to the surrounding wilderness, where he became friendly with the Native Americans, learning their customs and language. Finally securing land from the Native Americans in 1636, he settled Providence, declaring it "a place where no man should be molested for his conscience."

First, that the blood of so many hundred thousand souls of Protestant and Papists, split in the wars of present and former ages, for their respective consciences, is not required nor accepted by Jesus Christ the Prince of Peace.

Secondly, pregnant scriptures and arguments are throughout the work proposed against the doctrine of persecution for cause of conscience.

Thirdly, satisfactory answers are given to scriptures, and objections produced by Mr. Calvin, Beza, Mr. Cotton, and the ministers of the New England churches and others former and later, tending to prove the doctrine of persecution for cause of conscience.

Fourthly, the doctrine of persecution for cause of conscience is proved guilty of all the blood of the souls crying for vengeance under the altar.

Fifthly, all civil states with their officers of justice in their respective constitutions and administrations are proved essentially civil, and therefore not judges, governors, or defenders of the spiritual or Christians state and worship.

Sixthly, it is the will and command of God that (since the coming of his Son the Lord Jesus) a permission of the most paganish, Jewish, Turkish, or antichristian conscience and worships, be granted to all men in all nations and countries; and they are only to be fought against with that sword which is only (in soul matters) able to conquer, to wit, the sword of God's Spirit, the Word of God.

Seventhly, the state of the Land of Israel, the kings and people thereof in peace and war, is proved figurative and ceremonial, and no pattern nor precedent for any kingdom or civil state in the world to follow.

Eighthly, God requireth not a uniformity of religion to be enacted and enforced in any civil state; which enforced uniformity (sooner or later) is the greatest occasion of civil war, ravishing of conscience, persecution of Christ Jesus in his servants, and of the hypocrisy and destruction of millions of souls.

Ninthly, in holding an enforced uniformity of religion in a civil state, we must necessarily disclaim our desires and hopes of the Jew's conversion to Christ.

Tenthly, an enforced uniformity of religion throughout a nation or civil state, confounds the civil and religious, denies the principles of Christianity and civility, and that Jesus Christ is come in the flesh.

Eleventhly, the permission of other consciences and worships than a state professeth only can (according to God) procure a firm and lasting peace (good assurance being taken according to the wisdom of the civil state for uniformity of civil obedience from all forts).

Twelfthly, lastly, true civility and Christianity may both flourish in a state or kingdom, notwithstanding the permission of divers and contrary consciences, either of Jew or Gentile. . . .

Truth: I acknowledge that to molest any person, Jew or Gentile, for either professing doctrine, or practicing worship merely religious or spiritual, it is to persecute him, and such a person (whatever his doctrine or practice be, true or false) suffereth persecution for conscience.

But withal I desire it may be well observed that this distinction is not full and complete: for beside this that a man may be persecuted because he holds or practices what he believes in conscience to be a truth (as Daniel did, for which he was cast into the lions' den. Dan. 6), and many thousands of Christians, because they durst not cease to preach and practice what they believed was by God commanded, as the Apostles answered (Acts 4 & 5), I say besides this a man may also be persecuted, because he dares not be constrained to yield obedience to such doctrines and worships as are by men invented and appointed. . . .

*   *   *

Dear Truth, I have two sad complaints:

First, the most sober of the witnesses, that dare to plead thy cause, how are they charged to be mine enemies, contentious, turbulent, seditious?

Secondly, thine enemies, though they speak and rail against thee, though they outrageously pursue, imprision, banish, kill thy faithful witnesses, yet how is all vermilion'd o'er for justice against the heretics? Yea, if they kindle coals, and blow the flames of devouring wars, that leave neither spiritual nor civil state, but burn up branch and root, yet how do all pretend an holy war? He that kills, and heaven, if he bring any other faith or doctrine. . . .

Peace: I add that a civil sword (as woeful experience in all ages has proved) is so far from bringing or helping forward an opposite in religion to repentance that magistrates sin grievously against the work of God and blood of souls by such proceedings. Because as (commonly) the sufferings of false and antichristian teachers harden their followers, who being blind, by this means are occasioned to tumble into the ditch of hell after their blind leaders, with more inflamed zeal of lying confidence. So, secondly, violence and a sword of steel begets such an impression in the sufferers that certainly they conclude (as indeed that religion cannot be true which needs such instruments of violence to uphold it so) that persecutors are far from soft and gentle commiseration of the blindness of others. . . .

For (to keep to the similitude which the Spirit useth, for instance) to batter down a stronghold, high wall, fort, tower, or castle, men bring not a first and second admonition, and after obstinacy, excommunication, which are spiritual weapons concerning them that be in the church: nor exhortation to repent and be baptized, to believe in the Lord Jesus, etc., which are proper weapons to them that be without, etc. But to take a stronghold, men bring cannons, culverins, saker, bullets, powder, muskets, swords, pikes, etc., and these to this end are weapons effectual and proportionable.

On the other side, to batter down idolatry, false worship, heresy, schism, blindness, hardness, out of the soul and spirit, it is vain, improper, and unsuitable to bring those weapons which are used by persecutors, stocks, whips, prisons, swords, gibbets, stakes, etc. (where these seem to prevail with some cities or kingdoms, a stronger force sets up again, what a weaker pull'd down), but against these spiritual strongholds in the souls of men, spiritual artillery and weapons are proper, which are mighty through God to subdue and bring under the very thought to obedience, or else to bind fast the soul with chains of darkness, and lock it up in the prison of unbelief and hardness to eternity. . . .

Peace: I pray descend now to the second evil which you observe in the answerer's position, viz., that it would be evil to tolerate notorious evildoers, seducing teachers, etc.

Truth: I say the evil is that he most improperly and confusedly joins and couples seducing teachers with scandalous livers.

Peace: But is it not true that the world is full of seducing teachers, and is it not true that seducing teachers are notorious evildoers?

Truth: I answer, far be it from me to deny either, and yet in two things I shall discover the great evil of this joining and coupling seducing teachers, and scandalous livers as one adequate or proper object of the magistrate's care and work to suppress and punish.

First, it is not an homogeneal (as we speak) but an hetergeneal commixture or joining together of things most different in kinds and natures, as if they were both of one consideration. . . .

Truth: I answer, in granting with Brentius that man hath not power to make laws to bind conscience, he overthrows such his tenent and practice as restrain men from their worship, according to their conscience and belief, and constrain them to such worships (though it be out of a pretense that they are convinced) which their own souls tell them they have no satisfaction nor faith in.

Secondly, whereas he affirms that men may make laws to see the law of God observed.

I answer, as God needeth not the help of a material sword of steel to assist the sword of the Spirit in the affairs of conscience, to those men, those magistrates, yea that commonwealth which makes such magistrates, must needs have power and authority from Christ Jesus to fit judge and to determine in all the great controversies concerning doctrine, discipline, government, etc.

And then I ask whether upon this ground it must not evidently follow that:

Either there is no lawful commonwealth nor civil state of men in the world, which is not qualified with this spiritual discerning (and then also that the very commonwealth hath more light concerning the church of Christ than the church itself).

Or, that the commonwealth and magistrates thereof must judge and punish as they are persuaded in their own belief and conscience (be their conscience paganish, Turkish, or antichristian) what is this but to confound heaven and earth together, and not only to take away the being of Christianity out of the world, but to take away all civility, and the world out of the world, and to lay all upon heaps of confusion? . . . peace: The fourth head is the proper means of both these powers to attain their ends.

First, the proper means whereby the civil power may and should attain its end are only political, and principally these five.

First, the erecting and establishing what form of civil government may seem in wisdom most meet, according to general rules of the world, and state of the people.

Secondly, the making, publishing, and establishing of wholesome civil laws, not only such as concern civil justice, but also the free passage of true religion; for outward civil peace ariseth and is maintained from them both, from the latter as well as from the former.

Civil peace cannot stand entire, where religion is corrupted (2 Chron. 15. 3. 5. 6; and Judges 8). And yet such laws, though conversant about religion, may still be counted civil laws, as, on the contrary, an oath doth still remain religious though conversant about civil matters.

Thirdly, election and appointment of civil officers to see execution to those laws.

Fourthly, civil punishments and rewards of transgressors and observers of these laws.

Fifthly, taking up arms against the enemies of civil peace.

Secondly, the means whereby the church may and should attain her ends are only ecclesiastical, which are chiefly five.

First, setting up that form of church government only of which Christ hath given them a pattern in his Word.

Secondly, acknowledging and admitting of no lawgiver in the church but Christ and the publishing of His laws.

Thirdly, electing and ordaining of such officers only, as Christ hath appointed in his Word.

Fourthly, to receive into their fellowship them that are approved and inflicting spiritual censures against them that offend.

Fifthly, prayer and patience in suffering any evil from them that be without, who disturb their peace.

So that magistrates, as magistrates, have no power of setting up the form of church government, electing church officers, punishing with church censures, but to see that the church does her duty herein. And on the other side, the churches as churches, have no power (though as members of the commonweal they may have power) or erecting or altering forms of civil government, electing of civil officers, inflicting civil punishments (no not on persons excommunicate) as by deposing magistrates from their civil authority, or withdrawing the hearts of the people against them, to their laws, no more than to discharge wives, or children, or servants, from due obedience to their husbands, parents, or masters; or by taking up arms against their magistrates, though he persecute them for conscience: for though members of churches who are public officers also of the civil state may suppress by force the violence of usurpers, as Ieholada did Athaliah, yet this they do not as members of the church but as officers of the civil state.

Truth: Here are divers considerable passages which I shall briefly examine, so far as concerns our controversy.

First, whereas they say that the civil power may erect and establish what form of civil government may seem in wisdom most meet, I acknowledge the proposition to be most true, both in itself and also considered with the end of it, that a civil government is an ordinance of God, to conserve the civil peace of people, so far as concerns their bodies and goods, as formerly hath been said.

But from this grant I infer (as before hath been touched) that the sovereign, original, and foundation of civil power lies in the people (whom they must needs mean by the civil power distinct from the government set up). And, if so, that a people may erect and establish what form of government seems to them most meet for their civil condition; it is evident that such governments as are by them erected and established have no more power, nor for no longer time, than the civil power or people consenting and agreeing shall betrust them with. This is clear not only in reason but in the experience of all commonweals, where the people are not deprived of their natural freedom by the power of tyrants.

And, if so, that the magistrates receive their power of governing the church from the people, undeniably it follows that a people, as a people, naturally considered (of what nature of nation soever in Europe, Asia, Africa, or America), have fundamentally and originally, as men, a power to govern the church, to see her do her duty, to correct her, to redress, reform, establish, etc. And if this be not to pull God and Christ and Spirit out of heaven, and subject them unto natural, sinful, inconstant men, and so consequently to Satan himself, by whom all peoples naturally are guided, let heaven and earth judge. . . .

Peace: Some will here ask: Why may the magistrate then lawfully do with his civil horn or power in matters of religion?

Truth: His horn not being the horn of that unicorn or rhinoceros, the power of the Lord Jesus in spiritual cases, his sword not the two-edged sword of the spirit, the word of God (hanging not about the loins or side, but at the lips, and proceeding out of the mouth of his ministers) but of an humane and civil nature and constitution, it must consequently be of a humane and civil operation, for who knows not that operation follows constitution? And therefore I shall end this passage with this consideration:

The civil magistrate either respecteth that religion and worship which his conscience is persuaded is true, and upon which he ventures his soul; or else that and those which he is persuaded are false.

Concerning the first, if that which the magistrate believeth to be true, be true, I say he owes a threefold duty unto it:

First, approbation and countenance, a reverent esteem and honorable testimony, according to Isa. 49, and Revel. 21, with a tender respect of truth, and the professors of it.

Secondly, personal submission of his own soul to the power of the Lord Jesus in that spiritual government and kingdom, according to Matt. 18 and 1 Cor. 5.

Thirdly, protection of such true professors of Christ, whether apart, or met together, as also of their estates from violence and injury, according to Rom. 13.

Now, secondly, if it be a false religion (unto which the civil magistrate dare not adjoin, yet) he owes:

First, permission (for approbation he owes not what is evil) and this according to Matthew 13.30 for public peace ad quiet's sake.

Secondly, he owes protection to the persons of his subjects (though of a false worship), that no injury be offered either to the persons or goods of any. . . .

. . . The God of Peace, the God of Truth will shortly seal this truth, and confirm this witness, and make it evident to the whole world, that the doctrine of persecution for cause of conscience, is most evidently and lamentably contrary to the doctrine of Christ Jesus the Prince of Peace.

Amen.

Source:

James Andrews and David Zarefsky, eds. *American Voices: Significant Speeches in American History, 1640–1945.* New York: Longman, 1970.

Margaret Brent, Requests for a Seat in the Maryland Assembly; Helps Quell a Rebellion, 1646, 1647

Margaret Brent, born in England around 1601, was an influential property owner in Maryland. She arrived in the colony in 1638 to take over an estate granted to her by the absent proprietor, Cecilius Calvert, Second Lord Baltimore, on the same grounds as any of the first settlers, which in effect made her a feudal lord, presumably with equal privileges over her tenants. Neither she nor her sister Mary, another landowner, married, which would have compromised their authority. She appears a number of times in the records as an attorney representing herself or others. (A number of women appeared as attorneys prior to the establishment of a more formal bar.) She also was appointed executor for the provincial governor, Leonard Calvert. In his absence she exercised his power of attorney for Lord Baltimore. The first document records her request for a seat and two votes in one of Maryland's general assemblies, which all freemen were entitled to attend. She claimed one vote for herself, and one as the proprietor's attorney (proxies were permitted in Maryland's early assemblies). She was not allowed to participate, most likely because of her gender, since she was otherwise qualified to have at least one vote.

Prior to this event, she exercised the governor's responsibilities during a two-year rebellion instigated by Protestants against the Catholic proprietorship. Because the rebels did not form a government, the province remained in a state of virtual anarchy called the "Plundering Time." Governor Calvert fled to Virginia, leaving Margaret Brent in charge of his estate, which he pledged to pay the soldiers who eventually put down the rebellion. When the proprietor criticized how she handled matters, the assembly defended her in the second document. There is no way to tell for certain whether an early feminism motivated Brent. However, her apparent refusal to marry and her tenacity in exercising every privilege to which she felt entitled earn her a place in feminist history.

General Assembly, January 21, 1648

Came Mrs Margarett Brent and requested to have vote in the howse for her selfe and voyce allso for that att the last Court[.]

3d Jan: [I]t was ordered that the said Mrs Brent was to be lookd uppon and received as his LPS [Lordship's] Attorney. The Gout [Government] denyed that the sd. Mrs Brent should have any uote in the howse. And the sd. Mrs Brent protested agst all proceedings in this pnt [present] Assembly, unlesse shee may be pnt. [present] and have vote as aforesd.

Assembly Proceedings, April 21, 1649

A Letter sent to his Lordship from the Assembly held at Saint Marys in April Anno Dni 1649

Right honble Great and many have been the miseries calamities and other Sufferings which your Poor distressed People Inhabitants of this Province have sustained and undergone here since the beginning of that Heinous Rebellion . . . almost for two years continued . . . in which time most of your Lordships Loyal friends here were spoiled of their whole Estate and sent away as banished persons out of the Province those few that remained were plundered and deprived in a manner of all Livelyhood and subsistance only Breathing under that intoilerable Yoke which they were forced to bear under those Rebells which

then assumed the Govt of your Lordships Province unto themselves ever endeavouring by Oaths and what other inventions and Practices they might to withdraw the Ears and Affections of the Inhabitants here from their wonted Obedience to your Lordship and to assure themselves of the Province so wrongfully taken and unjustly Possessed by them which our sufferings we hope your honr apprehends and is sensible and which tho they were ever Violent even like a Tempest for the time yet now (thanks be to God all is past and Calm and the whole Province in perfect Subjection again under your lawful Government amid Authority during all which time your Honour cannot be ignorant what pains and travell your Friends under went in aiding your dear Brother for the subduing of those Rebells and after again in conserving the Prove for your Lordship never sparing labour cost or Estate which they were or Could be Possessed of until they had accomplished their intended Purpose and desires in regaining it again and setled it under your Lordships Protection and dominion as for Mrs Brents undertaking and medling with your Lordships Estate here (whether she procured it with her own and others importtunity or no) we do Verily Believe and in Conscience report that it was better for the Collonys safety at that time in her hands then in any mans else in the whole Province after your Brothers death for the Soldiers would never have treated any other with that Civility and respect and though they were even ready at several times to run into mutiny yet she still pacified them till at the last things were brought to that strait that she must be admitted and declared your Lordships Attorney by an order of Court (the Copy whereof is herewith inclosed) or else all must go to ruin Again and then the second mischief had been doubtless far greater than the former so that if there hath not been any sinister use made of your Lordships Estate by her from what it was intended and ingaged for by Mr Calvert before his death as we verily Believe she hath not then we conceive from that time she rather deserved favour and thanks from your Honour for her so much Concurring to the publick safety then to be justly liable to all those bitter invectives you have been pleased to Express against her.

Source:
Proceedings and Acts of the General Assembly, January 1637/38–September 1664. Archives of Maryland Online. Vol 1, p. 215. Available on-line. URL: www.mdarchives.state.md.us. Accessed October 2003.

Maryland Toleration Act of 1649

Both George and Cecilius Calvert (the first and second lords Baltimore) advocated freedom of religious expression. As long as the Catholic proprietary government ruled in the colony's earliest years, religion was not a barrier to residency or participation in government. (Several anti-Catholic rebellions, during which Catholics were discriminated against, occurred in England in the 1640s.) During the tumultuous years under Oliver Cromwell in England, dissenters, including members of Unitarian Christian sects, emigrated to the colony. Catholic scholars of early Maryland like to claim that a Jew, former indentured servant Mathias da Sousa, participated in a general assembly of freemen; however, except for his swarthy complexion and name, which was shared by both Christians and Sephardic Jews, there is no reason to believe that da Sousa was Jewish. (Interestingly, da Sousa is described on entering Maryland as "mulatto"; at the time the term referred to skin color rather than race. As a result, Maryland claims that he is the first black to have voted in North America.) The Toleration Act passed an assembly, which may have had a Protestant majority, upon pressure from Lord Baltimore (Cecilius Calvert) to absolve Maryland from the charge of intolerance toward Protestantism. The act stated that no person within the province "professing to believe in Jesus Christ shall be troubled, molested or discountenanced for or in respect of his or her religion, or in the free exercise thereof." It also stated that no one shall be forced to the belief or exercise of any other religion against his or her conscience. By applying only to orthodox Christians who accepted the doctrine of the Trinity, the Act theoretically narrowed the toleration practices under the Catholic-dominated government. The only person prosecuted under it was a Jew, who was later pardoned.

An Act Concerning Religion

Forasmuch as in a well governed and Christian Common Wealth matters concerning Religion and the honor of God ought in the first place to bee taken, into serious consideracion and endeavoured to bee settled, Be it therefore ordered and enacted by the Right Honourable Cecilius Lord Baron of Baltemore absolute Lord and Proprietary of this Province with the advise and consent of this Generall Assembly:

That whatsoever person or persons within this Province and the Islands thereunto belonging shall from henceforth blaspheme God, that is Curse him, or deny our Saviour Jesus Christ to bee the sonne of God, or shall deny the holy Trinity the father sonne and holy Ghost, or the Godhead of any of the said Three persons of the Trinity or the Unity of the Godhead, or shall use or utter any reproachfull Speeches, words or language concerning the said Holy Trinity, or any of the said three persons thereof, shalbe punished with death and confiscation or forfeiture of all his or her lands and goods to the Lord Proprietary and his heires.

And bee it also Enacted by the Authority and with the advise and assent aforesaid, That whatsoever person or persons shall from henceforth use or utter any reproachfull words or Speeches concerning the blessed Virgin Mary the Mother of our Saviour or the holy Apostles or Evangelists or any of them shall in such case for the first offence forfeit to the said Lord Proprietary and his heirs Lords and Proprietaries of this Province the summe of five pound Sterling or the value thereof to be Levyed on the goods and chattells of every such person soe offending, but in case such Offender or Offenders, shall not then have goods and chattells sufficient for the satisfyeing of such forfeiture, or that the same bee not otherwise speedily satisfyed that then such Offender or Offenders shalbe publiquely whipt and bee imprisoned during the pleasure of the Lord Proprietary or the Lieutenant or cheife Governor of this Province for the time being. And that every such Offender or Offenders for every second offence shall forfeit tenne pound sterling or the value thereof to bee levyed as aforesaid, or in case such offender or Offenders shall not then have goods and chattells within this Province sufficient for that purpose then to bee publiquely and severely whipt and imprisoned as before is expressed. And that every person or persons before mentioned offending herein the third time, shall for such third Offence forfeit all his lands and Goods and bee for ever banished and expelled out of this Province.

And be it also further Enacted by the same authority advise and assent that whatsoever person or persons shall from henceforth uppon any occasion of Offence or otherwise in a reproachful manner or Way declare call or denominate any person or persons whatsoever inhabiting, residing, traffiqueing, trading or comerceing within this Province or within any the Ports, Harbors, Creeks or Havens to the same belonging an heritick, Scismatick, Idolator, puritan, Independant, Prespiterian popish prest, Jesuite, Jesuited papist, Lutheran, Calvenist, Anabaptist, Brownist, Antinomian, Barrowist, Roundhead, Separatist, or any other name or terme in a reproachfull manner relating to matter of Religion shall for every such Offence forfeit and loose the somme of tenne shillings sterling or the value thereof to bee levyed on the goods and chattells of every such Offender and Offenders, the one half thereof to be forfeited and paid unto the person and persons of whom such reproachfull words are or shalbe spoken or uttered, and the other half thereof to the Lord Proprietary and his heires Lords and Proprietaries of this Province. But if such person or persons who shall at any time utter or speake any such reproachfull words or Language shall not have Goods or Chattells sufficient and overt within this Province to bee taken to satisfie the penalty aforesaid or that the same bee not otherwise speedily satisfyed, that then the person or persons soe offending shalbe publickly whipt, and shall suffer imprisonment without baile or maineprise [bail] untill hee, shee or they respectively shall satisfy the party soe offended or greived by such reproachfull Language by asking him or her respectively forgivenes publiquely for such his Offence before the Magistrate of cheife Officer or Officers of the Towne or place where such Offence shalbe given.

And be it further likewise Enacted by the Authority and consent aforesaid That every person and persons within this Province that shall at any time hereafter prophane the Sabbath or Lords day called Sunday by frequent swearing, drunkennes or by any uncivill or disorderly recreacion, or by working on that day when absolute necessity doth not require it shall for every such first offence forfeit 2s 6d sterling or the value thereof, and for the second offence 5s sterling or the value thereof, and for the third offence and soe for every time he shall offend in like manner afterwards 10s sterling or the value thereof. And in case such offender and offenders shall not have sufficient goods or chattells within this Province to satisfy any of the said Penalties respectively hereby imposed for prophaning the Sabbath or Lords day called Sunday as aforesaid, That in Every such case the partie soe offending shall for the first and second offence in that kinde be imprisoned till hee or shee shall publickly in open Court before the cheife Commander Judge or Magistrate, of that County Towne or precinct where such offence shalbe committed acknowledg the Scandall and offence he hath in that respect given against God and the good and civill Governement of this Province, And for the third offence and for every time after shall also bee publickly whipt.

And whereas the inforceing of the conscience in matters of Religion hath frequently fallen out to be of dangerous Consequence in those commonwealthes where it hath been practised, And for the more quiett and peaceable governement of this Province, and the better to preserve mutuall Love and amity amongst the Inhabitants thereof, Be it Therefore also by the Lord Proprietary with the advise and consent of this Assembly Ordeyned and enacted (except as in this present Act is before Declared and sett forth) that noe person or persons whatsoever within this Province, or the Islands, Ports, Harbors, Creekes, or havens thereunto belonging professing to believe in Jesus Christ, shall from henceforth bee any waies troubled, Molested or discountenanced for or in respect of his or her religion nor in the free exercise thereof within this Province or the Islands thereunto belonging nor any way compelled to the beleife or exercise of any other Religion against his or her consent, soe as they be not unfaithfull to the Lord Proprietary, or molest or conspire against the civill Governement established or to bee established in this Province under him or his heires. And that all and every person and persons that shall presume Contrary to this Act and the true intent and meaning thereof directly or indirectly either in person or estate willfully to wrong disturbe trouble or molest any person whatsoever within this Province professing to beleive in Jesus Christ for or in respect of his or her religion or the free exercise thereof within this Province other than is provided for in this Act that such person or persons soe offending, shalbe compelled to pay trebble damages to the party soe wronged or molested, and for every such offence shall also forfeit 20s sterling in money or the value thereof, half thereof for the use of the Lord Proprietary, and his heires Lords and Proprietaries of this Province, and the other half for the use of the party soe wronged or molested as aforesaid, Or if the partie soe offending as aforesaid shall refuse or bee unable to recompense the party soe wronged, or to satisfy such fyne or forfeiture, then such Offender shalbe severely punished by publick whipping and imprisonment during the pleasure of the Lord Proprietary, or his Lieutenant or cheife Governor of this Province for the tyme being without baile or maineprise.

And bee it further alsoe Enacted by the authority and consent aforesaid That the Sheriff or other Officer or Officers from time to time to bee appointed and authorized for that purpose, of the County Towne or precinct where every particular offence in this present Act conteyned shall happen at any time to bee committed and whereupon there is hereby a forfeiture fyne or penalty imposed shall from time to time distraine and seise the goods and estate of every such person soe offending as aforesaid against this present Act or any part thereof, and sell the same or any part thereof for the full satisfaccion of such forfeiture, fine, or penalty as aforesaid, Restoring unto the partie soe offending the Remainder or overplus of the said goods or estate after such satisfaccion soe made as aforesaid.

The freemen have assented.

Source:
Proceedings and Acts of the General Assembly, January 1637/8– September 1664. Archives of Maryland Online. Vol 1, p. 224. Available on-line. URL: www.mdarchives.state.md.us. Accessed October 2003.

Flushing Remonstrance, 1657

Statement against the persecution of Quakers, written by English settlers at Flushing, Long Island, and addressed to Governor Peter Stuyvesant of New Amsterdam (New York) on December 27, 1657. Stuyvesant had ordered that Flushing "not receive any of those people called Quakers because they are supposed to be, by some, seducers of the people." The settlers remonstrated: "We desire in this case not to judged lest we be condemned, but rather to let every man stand and fall to his own Master." They probably made the first declaration of religious toleration in America. Nonetheless, five Quakers recently arrived at New Amsterdam were deported to Rhode Island.

Remonstrance of the Inhabitants of the Town of Flushing to Governor Stuyvesant

Right Honorable,

You have been pleased to send up unto us a certain prohibition or command that we should not receive or entertain any of those people called Quakers because they are supposed to be by some, seducers, of the people. For our part we cannot condemn them in this case, neither can we stretch out our hands against them, to punish, banish or persecute them, for out of Christ God is a consuming fire, and it is a fearful thing to fall into the hands of the living God.

We desire therefore in this case not to judge least we be judged, neither to condemn least we be condemned, but rather let every man stand and fall to his own Master. Wee are bounde by the Law to doe good unto all men, especially to those of the household of faith. And though for the present we seem to be unsensible of the law and the Law giver, yet when death and the Law assault us, if wee have our advocate to seeke, who shall plead for us in this case of conscience betwixt God and our own souls; the powers of this world can neither attack us, neither excuse us, for if God justifye who can condemn and if God condemn there is none can justifye.

And for those jealousies and suspicious which some have of them, that they are destructive unto Magistracy and Minstereye, that can not bee, for the magistrate hath the sword in his hand and the minister hath the sword in his hand, as witnesse those two great examples which all magistrates and ministers are to follow, Moses and Christ, whom God raised up maintained and defended against all the enemies both of flesh and spirit; and therefore that which is of God will stand, and that which is of man will come to nothing. And as the Lord hath taught Moses or the civil power to give an outward liberty in the state by the law written in his heart designed for the good of all, and can truly judge who is good, who is civil, who is true and who is false, and can pass definitive sentence of life or death against that man which rises up against the fundamental law of the States General; soe he hath made his ministers a savor of life unto life, and a savor of death unto death.

The law of love, peace and liberty in the states extending to Jews, Turks, and Egyptians, as they are considered the sonnes of Adam, which is the glory of the outward state of Holland, soe love, peace and liberty, extending to all in

Christ Jesus, condemns hatred, war and bondage. And because our Savior saith it is impossible but that offenses will come, but woe unto him by whom they cometh, our desire is not to offend one of his little ones, in whatsoever form, name or title hee appears in, whether Presbyterian, Independent, Baptist or Quaker, but shall be glad to see anything of God in any of them, desiring to doe unto all men as wee desire all men should doe unto us, which is the true law both of Church and State; for our Saviour saith this is the law and the prophets.

Therefore if any of these said persons come in love unto us, we cannot in conscience lay violent hands upon them, but give them free egresse and regresse unto our Town, and houses, as God shall persuade our consciences. And in this we are true subjects both of Church and State, for we are bounde by the law of God and man to doe good unto all men and evil to noe man. And this is according to the patent and charter of our Towne, given unto us in the name of the States General, which we are not willing to infringe, and violate, but shall houlde to our patent and shall remaine, your humble subjects, the inhabitants of Vlishing.

Written this 27th day of December, in the year 1657, by mee

Edward Hart, *Clericus*
Tobias Feake, The Marke of *William Noble, William Thorne, seignior,* The Marke of *William Thorne, junior, Edward Tarne, John Store, Nathaniel Hefferd, Benjamin Hubbard,* The Marke of *William Pidgion,* The Marke of *George Clere, Elias Doughtie, Antonie Feild, Richard Stocton, Edward Griffine, Nathaniell Tue, Nicolas Blackford,* The Marke of *Micah Tue,* The Marke of *Philipp Ud, Robert Field, senior, Robert Field, junior, Nicolas Parsell, Michael Milner, Henry Townsend, George Wright, John Foard, Henry Semtell, Edward Hart, John Mastine, John Townesend, Edward Farrington*

Source:
Edwin Tanjore Corwin, ed. *Ecclesiastical Records of the State of New York.* Albany, N.Y.: James B. Lyon, State Printer, 1901. pp. 412–413.

Fundamental Laws of West New Jersey, 1675

In 1674 one of the English proprietary owners of New Jersey, Lord John Berkeley, sold his interests in the western area of the colony to two Quakers, John Fenwick and George Billing. Like William Penn in Pennsylvania, Fenwick and Billing aspired to create a refuge for the Quakers. They were successful in this aim, and West Jersey became a Quaker stronghold. This charter, drafted two years after the settlement was established, was probably influenced by the group's experience with religious persecution in England. The charter guarantees religious freedom for all and the right to a fair trial by a jury of "twelve good and lawful men of his [the accused's] neighborhood." Other provisions include the requirement of a summons that clearly states the facts of the crime, the appointment of "justices" to instruct the jury in matters of the law throughout the trial, the establishment of standards of evidence, the prohibition of perjury, the right of plaintiffs to halt the proceedings if they wish, and the defendant's right of self-defense. The laws also state that all trials must be publicly and openly conducted. This last stipulation was cited as late as 1980 by the U.S. Supreme Court in *Richmond Newspapers v. Virginia*, a case that centered on the right of the public and press to attend criminal trials.

Chapter XIII
That These Following Concessions are the Common Law, or Fundamental Rights of the Province of West New Jersey

That the common law or fundamental rights and priviledges of West New Jersey, are individually agreed upon by the Proprietors and freeholders thereof, to be the foundation of the government, which is not to be altered by the Legislative authority, or free Assembly hereafter mentioned and constituted, but that the said Legislative authority is constituted according to these fundamentals, to make such laws as agree with, and maintain the said fundamentals, and to make no laws that in the least contradict, differ or vary from the said fundamentals, under what presence or alligation soever.

Chapter XIV
But if it so happen that any person or persons of the said General Assembly, shall therein designedly, willfully, and maliciously, move or excite any to move, any matter or thing whatsoever, that contradicts or any ways subverts, any fundamentals of the said laws in the Constitution of the government of this Province, it being proved by seven honest and reputable persons, he or they shall be proceeded against as traitors to the said government.

Chapter XV
That these Concessions, law or great charter of fundamentals, be recorded in a fair table in the Assembly House, and that they be read at the beginning and dissolving of every general free Assembly: And it is further agreed and ordained, that the said Concessions, common law, or great charter of fundamentals, be writ in fair tables in every common hall of justice within this Province, and that they

be read in solemn manner four times every year, in the presence of the people, by the chief magistrates of those places.

Chapter XVI
That no men, nor number of men upon earth, hath power or authority to rule over men's consciences in religious matters, therefore it is consented, agreed and ordained, that no person or persons whatsoever within the said Province, at any time or times hereafter, shall be any ways upon any presence whatsoever, called in question, or in the least punished or hurt, either in person, estate, or priviledge, for the sake of his opinion, judgment, faith or worship towards God in matters of religion. But that all and every such person, and persons may from time to time, and at all times, freely and fully have, and enjoy his and their judgments, and the exercises of their consciences in matters of religious worship throughout all the said Province.

Chapter XVII
That no Proprietor, freeholder or inhabitant of the said Province of West New Jersey, shall be deprived or condemned of life, limb, liberty, estate, property or any ways hurt in his or their privileges, freedoms or franchises, upon any account whatsoever, without a due tryal, and Judgment passed by twelve good and lawful men of his neighborhood first had: And that in all causes to be tryed, and in all tryals, the person or persons, arraigned may except against any of the said neghborhood, without any reason rendered, (not exceeding thirty five) and in case of any valid reason alleged, against every person nominated for that service.

Chapter XVIII
And that no Proprietor, freeholder, freedenison, or inhabitant in the said Province, shall be attached, arrested, or imprisoned for or by reason of any debt, duty, or thing whatsoever (cases felonious criminal and treasonable Excepted) before he or she have personal summon or summons, left at his or her last dwelling place, if in the said Province, by some legal authorized officer, constituted and appointed for that purpose, to appear in some court of judicature for the said Province, with a full and plain account of the cause or thing in demand, as also the name or names of the person or persons at whose suit, and the court where he is to appear, and that he hath at least fourteen days time to appear and answer the said suit, if he or she live or inhabit within forty miles English of the said court, and if at a further distance, to have for every twenty miles, two days time more, for his and their appearance, and so proportionately for a larger distance of place.

That upon the recording of the summons, and nonappearance of such person and persons, a writ or attachment shall or may be issued out to arrest, or attach the person or persons of such defaulters, to cause his or their appearance in such court, returnable at a day certain to answer the penalty or penalties, in such suit or suits; and if he or they shall be condemned by legal tryal and judgment, the penalty or penalties shall be paid and satisfied out of his or their real or personal estate so condemned, or cause the person or persons so condemned, to lie in execution till satisfaction of the debt and damages be made. *Provided always*, if such person or persons so condemned, shall pay and deliver such estate, goods, and chattles which he or any other person hath for his or their use, and shall solemnly declare and aver, that he or they have not any further estate, goods or chattles wheresoever to satisfy the person or persons, (at whose suit, he or they are condemned) their respective judgments, and shall also bring and produce three other persons as compurgators, who are well known and of honest reputation, and approved of by the commissioners of that division, where they dwell or inhabit, which shall in such open court, likewise solemnly declare and aver, that they believe in their consciences, such person and persons so condemned, have not werewith further to pay the said condemnation or condemnations, he or they shall be thence forthwith discharged from their said imprisonment, any law or custom to the contrary thereof, heretofore in the said Province, notwithstanding. And upon such summons and default of appearance, recorded as aforesaid, and such person and persons not appearing within forty days after, it shall and may be lawful for such court of judicature to proceed to tryal, of twelve lawful men to judgment, against such defaulters, and issue forth execution against his or their estate, real and personal, to satisfy such penalty or penalties, to such debt and damages so recorded, as far as it shall or may extend.

Chapter XIX

That there shall be in every court, three justices or commissioners, who shall sit with the twelve men of the neighborhood, with them to hear all causes, and to assist the said twelve men of the neighborhood in case of law; and that they the said justices shall pronounce such judgment as they shall receive from, and be directed by the said twelve men in whom only the judgment resides, and not otherwise.

And in case of their neglect and refusal, that then one of the twelve, by consent of the rest, pronounce their own judgment as the justices should have done.

And if any judgment shall be past, in any case civil or criminal, by any other person or persons, or ally other way, then according to this agreement and appointment, it shall be held null and void, and such person or persons so presuming to give judgment, shall be severely fin'd, and upon complaint made to the General Assembly, by them be declared incapable of any office or trust within this Province.

Chapter XX

That in all matters and causes, civil and criminal, proof is to be made by the solemn and plain averment, of at least two honest and reputable persons; arid in case that any person or persons shall bear false witness, and bring in his or their evidence, contrary to the truth of the matter as shall be made plainly to appear, that then every such person or persons, shall in civil causes, suffer the penalty which would be due to the person or persons he or they bear witness against. And in case any witness or witnesses, on the behalf of any person or persons, indicted in a criminal cause, shall be found to have borne false witness for fear, gain, malice or favour, and thereby hinder the due execution of the law, and deprive the suffering person or persons of their due satisfaction, that then and in all other cases of false evidence, such person or persons, shall be first severely fined, and next that he or they shall forever be disabled from being admitted in evidence, or into any public office, employment, or service within this Province.

Chapter XXI

That all and every person and persons whatsoever, who shall prosecute or prefer any indictment or information against others for any personal injuries, or matter criminal, or shall prosecute for any other criminal cause, (treason, murther, and felony, only excepted) shall and may be master of his own process, and llave full power to forgive and remit the person or persons offending against him or herself only, as well before as after judgment, and condemnation, and pardon and remit the sentence, fine and punishment of the person or persons offending, be it personal or other whatsoever.

Chapter XXII

That the tryals of all causes, civil and criminal, shall be heard and decided by the virdict or judgment of twelve honest men of the neighborhood, only to be summoned and presented by the sheriff of that division, or propriety where the fact or trespass is committed; and that no person or persons shall he compelled to fee any attorney or councillor to plead his cause, but that all persons have free liberty to plead his own cause, if he please: And that no person nor persons imprisoned upon any account whatsoever within this Province, shall be obliged to pay any fees to the officer or officers of the said prison, either when committed or discharged.

Chapter XXIII

That in all publick courts of justice for tryals of causes, civil or criminal, any person or persons, inhabitants of the said Province may freely come into, and attend the said courts, and hear and be present, at all or any such tryals as shall be there had or passed, that justice may not be done in a corner nor in any covert manner, being intended and resolved, by the help of the Lord, and by these our Concessions and Fundamentals, that all and every person and persons inhabiting the said Province, shall, as far as in us lies, be free from oppression and slavery.

Source:

Francis Newton Thorpe, ed. *The Federal and State Constitutions Colonial Charters, and Other Organic Laws of the States, Territories, and Colonies Now or Heretofore Forming the United States of America.* Washington, D.C.: Government Printing Office, 1909.

Nathaniel Bacon, "Declaration of the People," 1676

The migration of the Susquehannah Indians from Pennsylvania to the Virginia backcountry in the 1660s stiffened the resistance of Virginia's Native Americans to the further expansion of European agriculture. Western settlers demanded a policy of armed expansion, but coastal planters advised restraint. Led by the wealthy western planter Nathaniel Bacon—and in defiance of orders from William Berkeley, the governor of Virginia—westerners marched up the Potomac into Maryland in 1675, indiscriminately murdering Native Americans and precipitating a frontier war. With Bacon as leader, the westerners pushed a set of political reforms through the House of Burgesses, but, impatient with the pace of change, Bacon and his followers seized control of the colony, declaring the leader "General of Virginia" and, in a "Manifesto and Declaration of the People," demanded the death or removal of all Native Americans and an end to the rule of wealthy "parasites." Berkeley fled to the eastern shore of the Chesapeake. The civil war that followed shifted in Berkeley's favor only after Bacon's sudden death from dysentery. A short-lived rebellion with its own "Statement of Grievances" based on similar causes, but without a charismatic figure like Bacon, occurred in Maryland at the same time. Its leaders were hanged.

If virtue be a sin, if piety be guilt, all the principles of morality, goodness and justice be perverted, we must confess that those who are now called rebels may be in danger of those high imputations. Those loud and several bulls would affright innocents and render the defence of our

brethren and the inquiry into our sad and heavy oppressions, treason. But if there be, as sure there is, a just God to appeal to; if religion and justice be a sanctuary here; if to plead the cause of the oppressed; if sincerely to aim at his Majesty's honour and the public good without any reservation or by interest; if to stand in the gap after so much blood of our dear brethren bought and sold; if after the loss of a great part of his Majesty's colony deserted and dispeopled, freely with our lives and estates to endeavour to save the remainders be treason; God Almighty judge and let guilty die. But since we cannot in our hearts find one single spot of rebellion or treason, or that we have in any manner aimed at the subverting the settled government or attempting of the person of any either magistrate or private man, notwithstanding the several reproaches and threats of some who for sinister ends were disaffected to us and censured our innocent and honest designs, and since all people in all places where we have yet been can attest our civil, quiet, peaceable behaviour far different from that of rebellion and tumultuous persons, let truth be bold and all the world know the real foundations of pretended guilt. We appeal to the country itself what and of what nature their oppressions have been, or by what cabal and mystery the designs of many of those whom we call great men have been transacted and carried on; but let us trace these men in authority and favour to whose hands the dispensation of the country's wealth has been committed. Let us observe the sudden rise of their estates composed with the quality in which they first entered this country, or the reputation they have held here amongst wise and discerning men. And let us see whether their extractions and education have not been vile, and by what pretence of learning and virtue they could so soon [come] into employments of so great trust and consequence. Let us consider their sudden advancement and let us also consider whether any public work for our safety and defense or for the advancement and propagation of trade, liberal arts, or sciences is here extant in any way adequate to our vast charge. Now let us compare these things together and see what sponges have sucked up the public treasure, and whether it has not been privately contrived away by unworthy favourites and juggling parasites whose tottering fortunes have been repaired and supported at the public charge. Now if it be so, judge what greater guilt can be than to offer to pry into these and no unriddle the mysterious wiles of a powerful cabal; let all people judge what can be of more dangerous import than to suspect the so long safe proceedings of some of our grandees, and whether people may with safety open their eyes in so nice a concern.

Another main article of our guilt is our open and manifest aversion of all, not only the foreign but the protected and darling Indians. This, we are informed, is rebellion of a deep dye for that both the governor and council are by Colonel Cole's assertion bound to defend the queen and the Appamatocks with their blood. Now, whereas we do declare and can prove that they have been for these many years enemies to the king and country, robbers and thieves and invaders of his Majesty's right and our interest and estates, but yet have by persons in authority been defended and protected even against his Majesty's loyal subjects, and that in so high a nature that even the complaints and oaths of his Majesty's most loyal subjects in a lawful manner proffered by them against those barbarous outlaws, have been by the right honourable governor rejected and the delinquents from his presence dismissed, not only with pardon and indemnity, but with all encouragement and favour; their firearms so destructful to us and by our laws prohibited, commanded to be restored them, and open declaration before witness made that they must have ammunition, although directly contrary to our law. Now what greater guilt can be than to oppose and endeavour the destruction of these honest, quiet neighbours of ours?

Another main article of our guilt is our design not only to ruin and extirpate all Indians in general, but all manner of trade and commerce with them. Judge who can be innocent that strike at this tender eye of interest: since the right honourable the governor hath been pleased by his commission to warrant this trade, who dare oppose it, or opposing it can be innocent? Although plantations be deserted, the blood of our dear brethren spilled; on all sides our complaints; on all sides our complaints; continually murder upon murder renewed upon us; who may or dare think of the general subversion of all manner of trade and commerce with our enemies who can or dare impeach any of . . . traders at the heads of the rivers, if contrary to the wholesome provision made by laws for the country's safety; they dare continue their illegal practises and dare asperse the right honourable governor's wisdom and justice so highly to pretend to have his warrant to break that law which himself made; who dare say that these men at the heads of the rivers buy and sell our blood, and do still, notwithstanding the late act made to the contrary, admit Indians painted and continue to commerce; although these things can be proved, yet who dare be so guilty as to do it?

Another article of our guilt is to assert all those neighbour Indians as well as others, to be outlawed, wholly unqualified for the benefit and protection of the law, for that the law does reciprocally protect and punish, and that all people offending must either in person or estate make equivalent satisfaction or restitution, according to the manner and merit of the offences, debts, or trespasses. Now since the Indians cannot, according to the tenure and form of any law to us known, be prosecuted, seized, or complained against, their persons being difficultly distinguished or known; their many nations' languages, and their subterfuges such as makes them incapable to make us restitution or satisfaction, would it not be very guilty to say they have been unjustly defended and protected these many years?

If it should be said that the very foundation of all these disasters, the grant of the beaver trade to the right honourable governor was illegal, and not grantable by any power here present as being a monopoly, were not this to deserve the name of rebel and traitor?

Judge, therefore, all wise and unprejudiced men who may or can faithfully or truly with an honest heart, attempt the country's good, their vindication, and liberty without the aspersion of traitor and rebel, since as so doing they must of necessity gall such tender and dear concerns. But to manifest sincerity and loyalty to the world, and how much we abhor those bitter names; may all the world known that we do unanimously desire to represent our sad and heavy grievances to his most sacred Majesty as our refuge and sanctuary, where we do well know that all our causes will be impartially heard and equal justice administered to all men.

The Declaration of the People

For having upon specious pretences of the public works, raised unjust taxes upon the commonalty for the advancement of private favourites and other sinister ends, but no visible effects in any measure adequate.

For not having during the long time of his government in any measure advanced this hopeful colony, either by fortification, towns or trade.

For having abused and rendered contemptible the majesty of justice, of advancing to places of judicature scandalous and ignorant favourites.

For having wronged his Majesty's prerogative and interest by assuming the monopoly of the beaver trade.

By having in that unjust gain bartered and sold his Majesty's country and the lives of his loyal subjects to the barbarous heathen.

For having protected, favoured and emboldened the Indians against his Majesty's most loyal subjects, never contriving, requiring, or appointing any due or proper means of satisfaction for their many invasions, murders, and robberies committed upon us.

For having, when the army of the English was just upon the track of the Indians, which now in all places burn, spoil, and murder, and when we might with ease have destroyed them who then were in open hostility, for having expressly countermanded and sent back our army by passing his word for the peaceable demeanour of the said Indians, who immediately prosecuted their evil intentions, committing horrid murders and robberies in all places, being protected by the said engagement and word passed of him, the said Sir William Berkeley, having ruined and made desolate a great part of his Majesty's country, have now drawn themselves into such obscure and remote places and are by their successes so emboldened and confirmed, and by their confederacy so strengthened that the cries of blood are in all places, and the terror and consternation of the people so great, that they are now become not only a difficult, but a very formidable enemy who might ease have been destroyed, etc. When upon the loud outcries of blood, the Assembly had with all care raised and framed an army for the prevention of future mischiefs and safeguard of his Majesty's colony.

For having with only the privacy of some few favourites, without acquainting the people, only by the alteration of a figure, forged a commission by we know not what hand, not only without but against the consent of the people, for raising and effecting of civil wars and distractions, which being happily and without bloodshed prevented.

For having the second time attempted the same thereby calling down our forces from the defence of the frontiers, and most weak exposed places, for the prevention of civil mischief and ruin amongst ourselves, whilst the barbarous enemy in all places did invade, murder, and spoil us, his Majesty's most faithful subjects.

Of these, the aforesaid articles, we accuse Sir William Berkeley, as guilty of each and every one of the same, and as one who has traitorously attempted, violated and injured his Majesty's interest here, by the loss of a great part of his colony, and many of his faithful and loyal subjects by him betrayed, and in a barbarous and shameful manner exposed to the incursions and murders of the heathen.

And we further declare these, the ensuing persons in this list, to have been his wicked, and pernicious counsellors, aiders and assisters against the commonalty in these our cruel commotions:

Sir Henry Chicherly, Knt. Col. Charles Wormley, Phil. Dalowell, Robert Beverly, Robert Lee, Thos. Ballard, William Cole, Richard Whitacre, Nicholas Spencer, Mathew Kemp, Jos. Bridger, Wm. Clabourne, Thos. Hawkins, Jr., William Sherwood, Jos. Page, Clerk Jo. Cliffe, Hubberd Farrell, John West, Thos. Reade

And we do further demand, that the said Sir William Berkeley, with all the persons in this list, be forthwith delivered up, or surrender themselves, within four days after the notice hereof, or otherwise we declare as followeth: that in whatsoever house, place, or ship any of the said persons shall reside, be hid, or protected, we do declare that the owners, masters, or inhabitants of the said places, to be confederates and traitors to the people, and the estates of them, as also of all the aforesaid persons, to be confiscated. This we, the commons of Virginia, do

declare desiring a prime union amongst ourselves, that we may jointly, and with one accord defend ourselves against the common enemy. And let not the faults of the guilty be the reproach of the innocent, or the faults or crimes of the oppressors divide and separate us, who have suffered by their oppressions.

These are therefore in his Majesty's name, to command you forthwith to seize the persons above mentioned as traitors to the king and country, and them to bring to Middle Plantation, and there to secure them, till further order, and in case of opposition, if you want any other assistance, you are forthwith to demand it in the name of the people of all the counties of Virginia.

[Signed] Nath Bacon,
Gen'l. By the Consent of the People

Source:
Merrill Jensen, ed. *American Colonial Documents to 1776*, vol. 9 of *English Historical Documents*, ed. David C. Douglas. London: Eyre & Spottiswoode, 1955.

Habeas Corpus Act of 1679

Statute passed by Parliament in England (May 1679) making it compulsory for judges to issue a prisoner (at his request) the habeas corpus writ, which stated that no one could be imprisoned indefinitely without being charged in a court of law. The statute declared that prisoners were to be tried during the first term of their imprisonment and no later than the second. Once the court freed a prisoner, he could not be imprisoned again for the same crime. Judges were ordered to issue writs even when the courts were not in session, and any judge who failed to do so faced stiff penalties. The act applied initially only to criminal charges but was amended by the Habeas Corpus Act of 1816 to cover other charges. It is memorialized in Article I, Section 9 of the U.S. Constitution, which also permits its suspension in times of "rebellion or invasion."

An Act

For the better securing the liberty of the subject, and for prevention of imprisonments beyond the seas.

Whereas *great delays have been used by sheriffs, gaolers and other officers, to whose custody any of the King's subjects have been committed for criminal or supposed criminal matters, in making returns of writs of* habeas corpus *to them directed, by standing out an* alias *and* pluries habeas corpus, *and sometimes more, and by other shifts to avoid their yielding obedience of such writs, contrary to their duty and the known laws of the land, whereby many of the King's subjects have been and hereafter may be long detained in prison, in such cases where by law they are bailable, to their great charges and vexation:*

II. For the prevention whereof, and the more speedy relief of all persons imprisoned for any such criminal or supposed criminal matters; (2) be it enacted by the King's most excellent majesty, by and with the advice and consent of the lords spiritual and temporal, and commons, in this present parliament assembled, and by the authority thereof, That whensoever any person or persons shall bring any *habeas corpus* directed unto any sheriff or sheriffs, goaler, minister or other person whatsoever, for any person in his or their custody, and the said with shall be served upon the said officer, or left at the gaol or prison with any of the under-officers, under-keepers or deputy of the said officers or keepers, that the said officer or officers, his or their under-officers, under-keepers or deputies, shall within three days after the service thereof as aforesaid (unless the commitment aforesaid were for treason or felony, plainly and specially expressed in the warrant of commitment) upon payment or tender of the charges of bringing the said prisoner, to be ascertained by the judge or court that awarded the same, and endorsed upon the said writ, not exceeding twelve pence *per* mile, and upon security given by his own bond to pay the charges of carrying back the prisoner, if he shall be remanded by the court or judge to which he shall be brought according to the true intent of this present act, and that he will not make any escape by the way, make return of such writ; (3) and bring or cause to be brought the body of the party so committed or restrained, unto or before the lord chancellor, or lord keeper of the great seal of *England,* for the time being, or the judges or barons of the said court from whence the said writ shall issue, or unto and before such other person or persons before whom the said writ is made returnable, according to the command thereof; (4) and shall then likewise certify the true causes of his detainer or imprisonment, unless the commitment of the said party be in any place beyond the distance of twenty miles from the place or places where such court or person is or shall be residing; and if beyond the distance of twenty miles, and not above one hundred miles, then within the space of ten days, and if beyond the distance of one hundred miles, then within the space of twenty days, after such delivery aforesaid, and not longer.

III. And to the intent that no sheriff, gaoler or other officer may pretend ignorance of the import of any such writ; (2) be it enacted by the authority aforesaid, That all such writs shall be marked in this matter, *Per statutum tricesimo primo Caroli secundi Regis,* and shall be signed by the person that awards the same; (3) and if any person or persons shall be or stand committed or detained as aforesaid, for any crime, unless for felony or treason plainly

expressed in the warrant of commitment, in the vacation-time, and out of term, it shall and may be lawful to and for the person or persons so committed or detained (other than persons convict or in execution by legal process) or any one on his or their behalf, to appeal or complain to the lord chancellor or lord keeper, or any one of his Majesty's justices, either of the one bench or of the other, or the barons of the exchequer of the degree of the coif; (4) and the said lord chancellor, lord keeper, justices or barons or any of them, upon view of the copy or copies of the warrant or warrants of commitment and detainer, or otherwise upon oath made that such copy or copies were denied to be given by such person or persons in whole custody the prisoner or prisoners is or are detained, are hereby authorized and required, upon request made in writing by such person or persons, or any on his, her or their behalf, attested and subscribed by two witnesses who were present at the delivery of the same, to award and grant an *habeas corpus* under the seal of such court whereof he shall then be one of the judges, (5) to be directed to the officer or officers in whole custody the party so committed or detained shall be, returnable *immediate* before the said lord chancellor or lord keeper, or such justice, baron or any other justice or baron of the degree of the coif of any of the said courts; (6) and upon service thereof as aforesaid, the officer or officers, his or their under-officer or under-officers, under- keeper or under-keepers, or their deputy, in whose custody the party is so committed or detained, shall within the times respectively before limited, bring such prisoner or prisoners before the said lord chancellor or lord keeper, or such justices, barons or one of them, before whom the said writ is made returnable, and in case of his absence before any other of them, with the return of such writ, and the true causes of the commitment and detainer; (7) and thereupon within two days after the party shall be brought before them, the said lord chancellor or lord keeper, or such justice or baron before whom the prisoner shall be brought as aforesaid, shall discharge the said prisoner from his imprisonment, taking his or their recognizance, with one or more surety or sureties, in any sum according to their discretions, having regard to the quality of the prisoner and nature of the offence, for his or their appearance in the court of King's bench the term following, or at the next assizes, sessions or general gaol-delivery of and for such county, city or place where the commitment was, or where the offence was committed, or in such other court where the said offence is properly cognizable, as the case shall require, and then shall certify the said writ with the return thereof, and the said recognizance or recognizances into the said court where such appearance is to be made; (8) unless it shall appear unto the said lord chancellor or lord keeper, or justice or justices, or baron or barons, that the party so committed is detained upon a legal process, order or warrant, out of some court that hath jurisdiction of criminal matters, or by some warrant signed and sealed with the hand and seal of any of the said justices or barons, or some justice or justices of the peace, for such matters or offences for the which by the law the prisoner is not bailable.

IV. Provided always, and be it enacted, That if any person shall have wilfully neglected by the space of two whole terms after his imprisonment, to pray a *habeas corpus* for his enlargement, such person so wilfully neglecting shall not have any *habeas corpus* to be granted in vacation-time, in pursuance of this act.

V. And be it further enacted by the authority aforesaid, That if any officer or officers, his or their under-officer or under-officers, under-keeper or under-keepers, or deputy, shall neglect or refuse to make the returns aforesaid, or to bring the body or bodies of the prisoner or prisoners according to the command of the said writ, within the respective times aforesaid, or upon demand made by the prisoner or person in his behalf, shall refuse to deliver, or within the space of six hours after demand shall not deliver, to the person so demanding, a true copy of the warrant or warrants of commitment and detainer of such prisoner, which he and they are hereby required to deliver accordingly; all and every the head gaolers and keepers of such prisons, and such other person in whose custody the prisoner shall be detained, shall for the first offence forfeit to the prisoner or party grieved the sum of one hundred pounds; (2) and for the second offence the sum of two hundred pounds, and shall and is hereby made incapable to hold or execute his said office; (3) the said penalties to be recovered by the prisoner or party grieved, his executors or administrators, against such offender, his executors or administrators, by any action of debt, suit, bill, plaint or information, in any of the King's courts at *Westminster,* wherein no essoin, protection, privilege, injunction, wager of law, or stay of prosecution by *Non vult ulterius prosequi,* or otherwise, shall be admitted or allowed, or any more than one imparlance; (4) and any recovery or judgment at the suit of any party grieved, shall be a sufficient conviction for the first offence; and any after recovery or judgment at the suit of a party grieved for any offence after the first judgment, shall be a sufficient conviction to bring the officers or person within the said penalty for the second offence.

VI. And for the prevention of unjust vexation by reiterated commitments for the same offence; (2) be it enacted by the authority aforesaid, That no person or persons which shall be delivered or set at large upon any *habeas corpus,* shall at any time hereafter be again imprisoned or committed for the same offence by any person or persons whatsoever, other than by the legal order and process of such court wherein he or they shall be bound by

recognizance to appear, or other court having jurisdiction of the cause; (3) and if any other person or persons shall knowingly contrary to this act recommit or imprison, or knowingly procure or cause to be recommitted or imprisoned, for the same offence or pretended offence, any person or persons delivered or set at large as aforesaid, or be knowingly aiding or assisting therein, then he or they shall forfeit to the prisoner or party grieved the sum of five hundred pounds; any colourable pretence or variation in the warrant or warrants of commitment notwithstanding, to be recovered as aforesaid.

VII. Provided always, and be it further enacted, That if any person or persons shall be committed for high treason or felony, plainly and specially expressed in the warrant of commitment, upon his prayer or petition in open court the first week of the term, or first day of the sessions of *oyer* and *terminer* or general gaol-delivery, to be brought to his trial, shall not be indicted some time in the next term, sessions of *oyer* and *terminer* or general gaol-delivery, after such commitment; it shall and may be lawful to and for the judges of the court of King's bench and justices of *oyer* and *terminer* or general gaol-delivery, and they are hereby required, upon motion to them made in open court the last day of the term, sessions or gaol-delivery, either by the prisoner or any one in his behalf, to set at liberty the prisoner upon bail, unless it appear to the judges and justices upon oath made, that the witnesses for the King could not be produced the fame term, sessions or general gaol-delivery; (2) and if any person or persons committed as aforesaid, upon his prayer or petition in open court the first week of the term or first day of the sessions of *oyer* and *terminer* and general gaol-delivery, to be brought to his trial, shall not be indicted and tried the second term, sessions, of *oyer* and *terminer* or general gaol-delivery, after his commitment, or upon his trial shall be acquitted, he shall be discharged from his imprisonment.

VIII. Provided always, That nothing in this act shall extend to discharge out of prison any person charged in debt, or other action, or with process in any civil cause, but that after he shall be discharged of his imprisonment for such his criminal offence, he shall be kept in custody according to the law, for such other suit.

IX. Provided always, and be it enacted by the authority aforesaid, That if any person or persons, subjects of this realm, shall be committed to any prison or in custody of any officer or officers whatsoever, for any criminal or supposed criminal matter, that the laid person shall not be removed from the said prison and custody into the custody of any other officer or officers; (2) unless it be by *habeas corpus* or some other legal writ; or where the prisoner is delivered to the constable or other inferior officer to carry such prisoner to some common gaol; (3) or where any person is sent by order of any judge of assize or justice of the peace, to any common work-house or house of correction; (4) or where the prisoner is removed from one prison or place to another within the same county, in order to his or her trial or discharge in due course of law; (5) or in case of sudden fire or infection, or other necessity; (6) and if any person or persons shall after such commitment aforesaid make out and sign, our countersign any warrant or warrants for such removal aforesaid, contrary to this act; as well he that makes or signs, or countersigns such warrant or warrants, as the officer or officers that obey or execute the same, shall suffer and incur the pains and forfeitures in this act before mentioned, both for the first and second offence respectively, to be recovered in manner aforesaid by the party grieved.

X. Provided also, and be it further enacted by the authority aforesaid, That it shall and may be lawful to and for any prisoner and prisoners as aforesaid, to move and obtain his or their *habeas corpus* as well out of the high court of chancery or court of exchequer, as out of the courts of King's bench or common pleas, or either of them; (2) and if the said lord chancellor or lord keeper, or any judge or judges, baron or barons for the time being, of the degree of the coif, or any of the courts aforesaid, in the vacation time, upon view of the copy or copies of the warrant or warrants of commitment or detainer, or upon oath made that such copy or copies were denied as aforesaid, shall deny any writ of *habeas corpus* by this act required to be granted, being moved for as aforesaid, they shall severally forfeit to the prisoner or party grieved the sum of five hundred pounds, to be recovered in manner aforesaid.

XI. And be it declared and enacted by the authority aforesaid, That an *habeas corpus* according to the true intent and meaning of this act, may be directed and run into any county palatine, the cinque-ports, or other privileged places within the kingdom of *England*, dominion of *Wales*, or town of *Berwick* upon *Tweed*, and the islands of *Jersey* or *Guernsey*; any law or usage to the contrary notwithstanding.

XII. And for preventing illegal imprisonments in prisons beyond the seas; (2) be it further enacted by the authority aforesaid, That no subject of this realm than now is, or hereafter shall be an inhabitant or resiant of this kingdom of *England*, Dominion of *Wales*, or town of *Berwick* upon *Tweed*, shall or may be sent prisoner into *Scotland, Ireland, Jersey, Guernsey, Tangier*, or into parts, garrisons, islands or places beyond the seas, which are or at any time hereafter shall be within or without the dominions of his Majesty, his heirs or successors; (3) and that every such imprisonment is hereby enacted and adjudged to be illegal; (4) and that if any of the said subjects now is or hereafter shall be so imprisoned, every such person and persons so imprisoned, shall and may for every such imprisonment maintain by virtue of this act an action or

actions of false imprisonment, in any of his Majesty's courts of record, against the person or persons by whom he or she shall be so committed, detained, imprisoned, sent prisoner or transported, contrary to the true meaning of this act, and against all or any person or persons that shall frame, contrive, write, seal or countersign any warrant or writing for such commitment, detainer, imprisonment or transportation, or shall be advising, aiding, or assisting in the same, or any of them; (5) and the plaintiff in every such action, shall have judgment to recover his treble costs, besides damages, which damages so to be given, shall not be less than five hundred pounds; (6) in which action no delay stay or stop of proceeding by rule, order or command, nor no injunction, protection or privilege whatsoever, nor any more than one imparlance shall be allowed, excepting such rule of the court wherein the action shall depend, made in open court, as shall be thought in justice necessary, for special cause to be expressed in the said rule; (7) and the person or persons who shall knowingly frame, contrive, write, seal or countersign any warrant for such commitment, detainer, or transportation, or shall so commit, detain, imprison or transport any person or persons contrary to this act, or be any ways advising, aiding or assisting therein, being lawfully convicted thereof, shall be disabled from thenceforth to bear any office of trust or profit within the said realm of *England*, dominion of *Wales*, or town of *Berwick* upon *Tweed*, or any of the islands, territories or dominions thereunto belonging; (8) and shall incur and sustain the pains, penalties and forfeitures limited, ordained and provided in and by the statute of provision and *praemunire* made in the sixteenth year of King *Richard* the Second; (9) and be incapable of any pardon from the King, his heirs or successors, of the said forfeitures, losses or disabilities, or any of them.

XIII. Provided always, That nothing in this act shall extend to give benefit to any person who shall by contract in writing agree with any merchant or owner of any plantation, or other person whatsoever, to be transported to any parts beyond the seas, and receive earnest upon such agreement, although that afterwards such person shall renounce such contract.

XIV. Provided always, and be it enacted, That if any person or persons lawfully convicted of any felony, shall in open court pray to be transported beyond the seas, and the court shall think fit to leave him or them in prison for that purpose, such person or persons may be transported into any parts beyond the seas; this act or any thing therein contained to the contrary notwithstanding.

XV. Provided also, and be it enacted, That nothing herein contained shall be deemed, construed or taken, to extend to the imprisonment of any person before the first day of *June* one thousand six hundred seventy and nine, or to any thing advised, procured, or otherwise done, relating to such imprisonment; any thing herein contained to the contrary notwithstanding.

XVI. Provided also, That if any person or persons at any time resiant in this realm, shall have committed any capital offence in *Scotland* or *Ireland,* or any of the islands, or foreign plantations of the King, his heirs or successors, where he or the ought to be tried for such offence, such person or persons may be sent to such place, there to receive such trial, in such manner as the same might have been used before the making of this act; any thing herein contained to the contrary notwithstanding.

XVII. Provided also, and be it enacted, That no person or persons shall be sued, impleaded, molested, or troubled for any offence against this act, unless the party offending be sued or impleaded for the same within two years at the most after such time wherein the offence shall be committed, in case the party grieved shall not then in prison; and if he shall be in prison, then within the space of two years after the decease of the person imprisoned, or his or her delivery out of prison, which shall first happen.

XVIII. And to the intent no person may void his trial at the assizes or general gaol-delivery, by procuring his removal before the assizes, at such time as he cannot be brought back to receive his trial there; (2) be it enacted, That after the assizes proclaimed for that county where the prisoner is detained, no person shall be removed from the common gaol upon any *habeas corpus* granted in pursuance of this act, but upon any such *habeas corpus* shall be brought before the judge of assize in open court, who is thereupon to do what to justice shall appertain.

XIX. Provided nevertheless, That after the assizes are ended, any person or persons detained, may have his or her *habeas corpus* according to the direction and intention of this act.

XX. And be it also enacted by the authority aforesaid, That if any information, suit or action shall be brought or exhibited against any person or persons for any offence committed or to be committed against the form of this law, it shall be lawful for such defendants to plead the general issue, that they are not guilty, or that they owe nothing, and to give such special matter in evidence to the jury that shall try the same, which matter being pleaded had been good and sufficient matter in law to have discharged the said defendant or defendants against the said information, suit or action, and the said matter shall be then as available to him or them, to all intents and purposes, as if he or they had sufficiently pleaded, set forth or alledged the same matter in bar or discharge of such information suit or action.

XXI. And because many times persons charged with petty treason or felony, or as accessaries thereunto, are committed upon suspicion only, whereupon they are bailable, or not, according as the circumstances making out that suspicion are more or less weighty, which are best known to the justices of peace that committed the persons, and have the examination before them, or to other justices of the peace in the county; (2) be it therefore enacted, That where any person shall appear to be committed be any judge or justice of the peace and charged as accessary before the fact, to any petty treason or felony, or upon suspicion thereof, or with suspicion of petty treason or felony, which petty treason or felony shall be plainly and specially expressed in the warrant of commitment, that such person shall not be removed or bailed by virtue of this act, or in any other manner than they might have been before the making of this act.

Source:
Statutes of the Realm, 22 Charles II.

William Penn, Frame of Government, 1682

Liberal governmental structure drawn up and issued (April 25, 1682) by William Penn, an English Quaker and founder of the proprietary colony of Pennsylvania. It provided for a governor (the proprietor or his deputy), a council (where the governor served as presiding officer and had three votes), and an assembly. The council had 72 members, of whom a third were to be elected by the colony's freemen each year, while the assembly had 200 to 500 members, elected annually by the freemen. The governor and council held broad governing powers, including the ability to initiate legislation, and the assembly's vote was to ratify or reject legislation. Penn's plan also provided for friendly relations with the Native Americans and religious freedom.

The Preface
When the great and wise God had made the world of all His creatures, it pleased him to choose man His deputy to rule it; and to fit him for so great a charge and trust, He did not only qualify him with skill and power but with integrity to use them justly. This native goodness was equally his honor and his happiness; and while he stood here, all went well. There was no need of coercive or compulsive means; the precept of divine love and truth, in his bosom, was the guide and keeper of his innocency. But lust prevailing against duty made a lamentable breach upon it; and the law, that before had no power over him, took place upon him, and his disobedient posterity, that such as would not live conformable to the holy law within should fall under the reproof and correction of the just law without in a judicial administration.

This the apostle teaches in diverse of his epistles: "The law (says he) was added because of transgression."

In another place, "Knowing that the law was not made for the righteous man but for the disobedient and ungodly, for sinners, for unholy and profane, for murderers, for whoremongers, for them that defile themselves with mankind, and for man-stealers, for liars, for perjured persons," etc., But this is not all; he opens and carries the matter of government a little further: "Let every soul be subject to the higher powers; for there is no power but of God. The powers that be are ordained of God; whosoever therefore resisteth the power, resisteth the ordinance of God. For rulers are not a terror to good works but to evil; wilt thou then not be afraid of the power? Do that which is good, and thou shalt have praise of the same." "He is the minister of God to thee for good." "Wherefore ye must needs be subject, not only for wrath but for conscience sake."

This settles the divine right of government beyond exception, and that for two ends: first, to terrify evildoers; second, to cherish those that do well, which gives government a life beyond corruption and makes it as durable in the world, as good men shall be; so that government seems to me a part of religion itself, a thing sacred in its institution and end. For, if it does not directly remove the cause, it crushes the effects of evil, and is as such (though a lower, yet) an emanation of the same Divine Power that is both author and object of pure religion; the difference lying here, that the one is more free and mental, the other more corporal and compulsive in its operations. But that is only to evildoers; government itself being otherwise as capable of kindness, goodness, and charity as a more private society.

They weakly err that think there is no other use of government than correction, which is the coarsest part of it. Daily experience tells us that the care and regulation of many other affairs, more soft and daily necessary, make up much of the greatest part of government; and which must have followed the peopling of the world, had Adam never fell, and will continue among men on earth under the highest attainments they may arrive at, by the coming of the blessed Second Adam, the Lord from heaven. Thus much of government in general, as to its rise and end.

For particular frames and models, it will become me to say little; and comparatively I will say nothing. My reasons are:

First, that the age is too nice and difficult for it, there being nothing the wits of men are more busy and divided upon. It is true, they seem to agree to the end, to wit, happiness; but, in the means, they differ as to divine, so to this human felicity; and the cause is much the same, not always want of light and knowledge, but want of using them rightly. Men side with their passions against their reason, and their sinister interests have so strong a bias upon their minds that they lean to them against the good of the things they know.

Second, I do not find a model in the world that time, place, and some singular emergencies have not necessarily altered; nor is it easy to frame a civil government, that shall serve all places alike.

Third, I know what is said by the several admirers of monarchy, aristocracy, and democracy, which are the rule of one, a few, and many, and are the three common ideas of government, when men discourse on the subject. But I choose to solve the controversy with this small distinction, and it belongs to all three: Any government is free to the people under it (whatever be the frame) where the laws rule, and the people are at party to those laws, and more than this is tyranny, oligarchy, or confusion.

But, lastly, when all is said, there is hardly one frame of government in the world so ill designed by its first founders that, in good hands, would not do well enough; and story tells us the best, in ill ones, can do nothing that is great or good—witness the Jewish and Roman states. Governments, like clocks, go from the motion men give them; and as governments are made and moved by men, so by them they are ruined too. Wherefore, governments rather depend upon men than men upon governments. Let men be good, and the government cannot be bad; if it be ill, they will cure it. But, if men be bad, let the government be never so good, they will endeavor to warp and spoil it to their turn.

I know some say let us have good laws, and no matter for the men that execute them; but let them consider that though good laws do well, good men do better; for good laws may want good men, and be abolished or evaded by ill men; but good men will never want good laws, nor suffer ill ones. It is true, good laws have some awe upon ill ministers, but that is where they have not power to escape or abolish them, and the people are generally wise and good; but a loose and depraved people (which is the question) love laws and an administration like themselves. That, therefore, which makes a good constitution must keep it, viz.: men of wisdom and virtue, qualities, that because they descend not with worldly inheritances must be carefully propagated by a virtuous education of youth; for which after ages will owe more to the care and prudence of founders, and the successive magistracy, than to their parents, for their private patrimonies. These considerations of the weight of government, and the nice and various opinions about it, made it uneasy to me to think of publishing the ensuing frame and conditional laws, foreseeing both the censures they will meet with, from men of differing humors and engagements, and the occasion they may give of discourse beyond my design.

But, next to the power of necessity (which is a solicitor that will take no denial) this induced me to a compliance that we have (with reverence to God, and good conscience to men) to the best of our skill, contrived and composed the frame and laws of this government, to the great end of all government, viz.: To support power in reverence with the people, and to secure the people from the abuse of power; that they may be free by their just obedience, and the magistrates honorable, for their just administration; for liberty without obedience is confusion, and obedience without liberty is slavery. To carry this evenness is partly owing to the constitution, and partly to the magistracy; where either of these fail, government will be subject to convulsions; but where both are wanting, it must be totally subverted; then where both meet, the government is like to endure. Which I humbly pray and hope God will please to make the lot of this of Pennsylvania. Amen.

The Frame

To all persons to whom these presents may come.

Whereas, King Charles II, by his letters patents, under the great seal of England, bearing date the 4th day of March in the thirty-and-third year of the King, for diverse considerations therein mentioned, hath been graciously pleased to give and grant unto me, William Penn, by the name of William Penn, Esquire, son and heir of Sir William Penn, deceased, and to my heirs and assigns forever, all that tract of land, or province, called Pennsylvania, in America, with diverse great powers, preeminences, royalties, jurisdictions, and authorities necessary for the well-being and government thereof: Now know ye, that for the well-being and government of the said province, and for the encouragement of all the freemen and planters that may be therein concerned, in pursuance of the powers aforementioned, I, the said William Penn, have declared, granted, and confirmed, and by these presents, for me, my heirs, and assigns, do declare, grant, and confirm unto all the freemen, planters, and adventurers of, in, and to the said province, these liberties, franchises, and properties, to be held, enjoyed and kept by the freemen, planters, and inhabitants . . . forever.

Imprimis, that the government of this province shall, according to the powers of the patent, consist of the governor and freemen of the said province, in form of a provincial Council and General Assembly, by whom all laws shall be made, officers chosen, and public affairs transacted, as is hereafter respectively declared, that is to say—

II. That the freemen of the said province shall, on the 20th day of the twelfth month, which shall be in this present year 1682, meet and assemble in some fit place, of which timely notice shall be beforehand given by the governor or his deputy; and then and there shall choose out of themselves seventy- two persons of most note for their wisdom, virtue, and ability, who shall meet, on the 10th day of the first month next ensuing, and always be called, and act as, the provincial Council of the said province.

III. That, as the first choice of such provincial Council, one-third part of the said provincial Council shall be chosen to serve for three years, then next ensuing; one-third part, for two years then next ensuing; and one-third part, for one year then next ensuing such election, and no longer; and that the said third part shall go out accordingly. And on the 20th day of the twelfth month, as aforesaid, yearly forever afterward, the freemen of the said province shall, in like manner, meet and assemble together, and then choose twenty-four persons, being one-third of the said number, to serve in provincial Council for three years; it being intended that one-third part of the whole provincial Council (always consisting, and to consist, of seventy-two persons, as aforesaid) falling off yearly, it shall be yearly supplied by such new yearly elections, as aforesaid; and that no one person shall continue therein longer than three years. And, in case any member shall decease before the last election during his time, that then at the next election ensuing his decease, another shall be chosen to supply his place for the remaining time he was to have served and no longer.

IV. That after the first seven years, every one of the said third parts, that goeth yearly off, shall be incapable of being chosen again for one whole year following; that so all may be fitted for government, and have experience of the care and burden of it.

V. That the provincial Council, in all cases and matters of moment, as their arguing upon bills to be passed into laws, erecting courts of justice, giving judgment upon criminals impeached, and choice of officers, in such manner as is hereinafter mentioned, not less than two-thirds of the whole provincial Council shall make a quorum, and that the consent and approbation of two-thirds of such quorum shall be had in all such cases and matters of moment. And moreover that, in all cases and matters of lesser moment, twenty-four members of the said provincial Council shall make a quorum, the majority of which twenty-four shall, and may, always determine in such cases and causes of lesser moment.

VI. That in this provincial Council, the governor or his deputy shall or may always preside, and have a treble voice; and the said provincial Council shall always continue and sit upon its own adjournments and committees.

VII. That the governor and provincial Council shall prepare and propose to the General Assembly, hereafter mentioned, all bills which they shall, at any time, think fit to be passed into laws, within the said province; which bills shall be published and affixed to the most noted places, in the inhabited parts thereof, thirty days before the meeting of the General Assembly, in order to the passing them into laws or rejecting of them, as the General Assembly shall see meet.

VIII. That the governor and provincial Council shall take care that all laws, statutes, and ordinances, which shall at any time be made within the said province, be duly and diligently executed.

IX. That the governor and provincial Council shall, at all times, have the care of the peace and safety of the province, and that nothing be by any person attempted to the subversion of this frame of government.

X. That the governor and provincial Council shall, at all times, settle and order the situation of all cities, ports, and market towns in every country, modeling therein all public buildings, streets, and market places, and shall appoint all necessary roads and highways in the province.

XI. That the governor and provincial Council shall, at all times, have power to inspect the management of the public treasury, and punish those who shall convert any part thereof to any other use than what hath been agreed upon by the governor, provincial Council, and General Assembly.

XII. That the governor and provincial Council shall erect and order all public schools, and encourage and reward the authors of useful sciences and laudable inventions in the said province.

XIII. That, for the better management of the powers and trust aforesaid, the provincial Council shall, from time to time, divide itself into four distinct and proper committees for the more easy administration of the affairs of the province, which divides the seventy-two into four eighteens, every one of which eighteens shall consist of six out of each of the three orders, or yearly elections, each of which shall have a distinct portion of business, as followeth: First, a committee of plantations, to situate and settle cities, ports, and market towns, and highways, and to hear and decide all suits and controversies relating to plantations. Second, a committee of justice and safety, to secure the peace of the province, and punish the maladministration of those who subvert justice to the prejudice of the public, or private, interest. Third, a committee of trade and treasury, who shall regulate all trade and commerce according to law, encourage manufacture and country growth, and defray the public charge of the province. And, fourth, a committee of manners, education, and arts, that all wicked and scandalous living may be prevented, and that youth may be successively trained up in virtue and useful knowledge and arts. The quorum of each of which committees being six, that is, two out of each of the three orders, or yearly elections, as aforesaid, make a constant and standing Council of twenty-four, which will have the power of the provincial Council, being the quorum of it, in all cases not excepted in the 5th Article; and in the said committees, and standing Council of the province, the governor, or his deputy, shall or may preside, as aforesaid; and in the absence of the governor, or his deputy, if no one

is by either of them appointed, the said committees or Council shall appoint a president for that time, and not otherwise; and what shall be resolved at such committees shall be reported to the said Council of the province, and shall be by them resolved and confirmed before the same shall be put in execution; and that these respective committees shall not sit at one and the same time, except in cases of necessity.

XIV. And to the end that all laws prepared by the governor and provincial Council aforesaid may yet have the more full concurrence of the freemen of the province, it is declared, granted, and confirmed that, at the time and place or places for the choice of a provincial Council, as aforesaid, the said freemen shall yearly choose members to serve in a General Assembly, as their representatives, not exceeding 200 persons, who shall yearly meet on the 20th day of the second month, which shall be in the year 1683 following, in the capital town or city of the said province, where, during eight days, the several members may freely confer with one another; and, if any of them see meet, with a committee of the provincial Council (consisting of three out of each of the four committees aforesaid, being twelve in all) which shall be, at that time, purposely appointed to receive from any of them proposals for the alterations or amendment of any of the said proposed and promulgated bills. And on the ninth day from their so meeting, the said General Assembly, after reading over the proposed bills by the clerk of the provincial Council, and the occasions and motives for them being opened by the governor or his deputy, shall give their affirmative or negative, which to them seemeth best, in such manner as hereinafter is expressed. But not less than two-thirds shall make a quorum in the passing of laws, and choice of such officers as are by them to be chosen.

XV. That the laws so prepared and proposed, as aforesaid, that are assented to by the General Assembly, shall be enrolled as laws of the province, with this style: By the governor, with the assent and approbation of the freemen in provincial Council and General Assembly.

XVI. That, for the establishment of the government and laws of this province, and to the end there may be a universal satisfaction in the laying of the fundamentals thereof: the General Assembly shall, or may, for the first year, consist of all the freemen of and in the said province; and ever after it shall be yearly chosen, as aforesaid; which number of 200 shall be enlarged as the country shall increase in people, so as it do not exceed 500 at any time. The appointment and proportioning of which, is also the laying and methodizing of the choice of the provincial Council and General Assembly, in future times, most equally to the divisions of the hundreds and counties, which the country shall hereafter be divided into, shall be in the power of the provincial Council to propose, and the General Assembly to resolve.

XVII. That the governor and the provincial Council shall erect, from time to time, standing courts of justice, in such places and number as they shall judge convenient for the good government of the said province. And that the provincial Council shall, on the 13th day of the first month, yearly elect and present to the governor, or his deputy, a double number of persons, to serve for judges, treasurers, masters of rolls within the said province for the next year ensuing. And the freemen of the said province, in the country courts, when they shall be erected, and till then in the General Assembly, shall, on the 23rd of the second month, yearly, elect and present to the governor, or his deputy, a double number of persons to serve for sheriffs, justices of the peace, and coroners, for the year next ensuing; out of which respective elections and presentments, the governor or his deputy shall nominate and commissionate the proper number for each office, the third day after the said presentments, or else the first named in such presentment for each office shall stand and serve for that office the year ensuing.

XVIII. But forasmuch as the present condition of the province requires some immediate settlement, and admits not of so quick a revolution of officers; and to the end the said province may, with all convenient speed, be well ordered and settled. I, William Penn, do therefore think fit to nominate and appoint such persons for judges, treasurers, masters of the rolls, sheriffs, justices of the peace, and coroners as are most fitly qualified for those employments, to whom I shall make and grant commission for the said offices, respectively, to hold to them, to whom the same shall be granted for so long time as every such person shall well behave himself in the office, or place to him respectively granted, and no longer. And upon the decease or displacing of any of the said officers, the succeeding officer or officers, shall be chosen, as aforesaid.

XIX. That the General Assembly shall continue so long as may be needful to impeach criminals, fit to be there impeached, to pass bills into laws that they shall think fit to pass into laws, and till such time as the governor and provincial Council shall declare that they have nothing further to propose unto them for their assent and approbation; and that declaration shall be a dismiss to the General Assembly for that time; which General Assembly shall be, notwithstanding, capable of assembling together upon the summons of the provincial Council at any time during that year, if the said provincial Council shall see occasion for their so assembling.

XX. That all the elections of members, or representatives of the people, to serve in provincial Council and General Assembly, and all questions to be determined by both, or either of them, that relate to passing of bills into laws, to the choice of officers, to impeachments by the General Assembly, and judgment of criminals upon such impeachments by the provincial Council, and to all other cases by them respectively judged of importance, shall be resolved and determined by the ballot; and unless on sudden and indispensable occasions, no business in provincial Council, or its respective committees, shall be finally determined the same day that it is moved.

XXI. That at all times when, and so often as it shall happen that the governor shall or may be an infant, under the age of one-and-twenty years, and no guardians or commissioners are appointed in writing by the father of the said infant, or that such guardians or commissioners shall be deceased; that during such minority, the provincial Council shall, from time to time, as they shall see meet, constitute and appoint guardians or commissioners, not exceeding three; one of which three shall preside as deputy and chief guardian during such minority, and shall have and execute, with the consent of the other two, all the power of a governor, in all the public affairs and concerns of the said province.

XXII. That, as often as any day of the month, mentioned in any article of this charter, shall fall upon the first day of the week, commonly called the Lord's Day, the business appointed for that day shall be deferred till the next day, unless in case of emergency.

XXIII. That no act, law, or ordinance whatsoever shall, at any time hereafter, be made or done by the governor of this province, his heirs, or assigns, or by the freemen in the provincial Council, or the General Assembly to alter, change, or diminish the form, or effect, of this charter, or any part or clause thereof, without the consent of the governor, his heirs, or assigns, and six parts of seven of the said freemen in provincial Council and General Assembly.

XXIV. And lastly, that I, the said William Penn, for myself, my heirs, and assigns, have solemnly declared, granted and confirmed, and do hereby solemnly declare, grant, and confirm, that neither I, my heirs, nor assigns shall procure or do anything or things, whereby the liberties in this charter contained and expressed shall be infringed or broken; and if anything be procured by any person or persons contrary to these premises, it shall be held of no force or effect.

In witness whereof, I, the said William Penn, have unto this present charter of liberties set my hand and broad seal, this 25th day of the second month, vulgarly called April, in the year of Our Lord 1682.

Source:

James Otis. *The Annals of America.* Chicago: Encyclopaedia Britannica, 1926–87.

Charter of Liberties of 1683

Document enacted in 1683 by the New York Colony's first general (representative) assembly under English rule (under Thomas Dongan). The charter placed legislative power in the assembly, a council, and the governor. Written chiefly by the assembly speaker, Matthias Nicolls, it stipulated that the consent of the assembly, which was to meet no less than once every three years, was required for the imposition of taxes. The right to vote was given to all freeman; freedom of worship and trial by jury were guaranteed; and bases of landowning, inheritance, and court law were stated in the charter. Never fully confirmed, the charter became inoperative when King James II disapproved of it upon ascending to the English throne in 1685.

Colonel Thomas Dongan, English colonial governor of New York, granted and signed a charter of government to the people of the city of New York in 1686. It supplanted the 1683 Charter of Liberties and established a municipal government consisting of six aldermen and various other officials—all to be elected by freemen (citizens) of the town; the governor, however, was to appoint the mayor, recorder, clerk, and sheriff. The merchant class won a larger measure of home rule through the Dongan charter, which was rather liberal at times in furthering civil rights. Dongan granted similar charters to some Long Island towns, Schenectady, and Albany (whose similarly named Dongan charter confirmed upon it a monopoly of the fur trade). New York City's Dongan charter was in force until 1731.

That year, Governor John Montgomerie granted a colonial charter of government to the city of New York. It expanded the city's governing powers. The early municipal government empowered by this charter was similar to that of many boroughs (self-governing, incorporated towns) in Britain at the time. New York City's mayor remained an appointed and unsalaried official; the city, however, in addition to gaining some judicial powers, was given control over the establishment of ferries and docks and the construction of public buildings. The charter was in force until 1830.

FFOR The better Establishing the Government of this province of New Yorke and that Justice and Right may be Equally done to all persons within the same

BEE It Enacted by the Governour Councell and Representatives now in General Assembly mett and assembled and by the authority of the same.

1. —THAT The Supreme Legislative Authority under his Majesty and Royall Highnesse James Duke of Yorke Albany &c Lord proprietor of the said province shall forever be and reside in a Governour, Councell, and the people mett in Generall Assembly.

2. —THAT The Exercise of the Cheife Magistracy and Administracon of the Government over the said province shall bee in the said Governour assisted by a Councell with whose advice and Consent or with at least four of them he is to rule and Governe the same according to the Lawes thereof.

3. —THAT In Case the Governour shall dye or be absent out of the province and that there be noe person within the said province Comissionated by his Royall Highnesse his heires or Successours to be Governour or Comander in Cheife there That then the Councell for the time being or Soe many of them as are in the Said province doe take upon them the Administracon of the Governour and the Execucon of the Lawes thereof and powers and authorityes belonging to the Governour and Councell the first in nominacon in which Councell is to preside untill the said Governour shall returne and arrive in the said province againe, or the pleasure of his Royall Highnesse his heires or Successours Shall be further knowne.

4. —THAT According to the usage Custome and practice of the Realme of England a sessions of a Generall Assembly be held in this province once in three yeares at least.

5. —THAT Every ffreeholder within this province and ffreeman in any Corporacon Shall have his free Choise and Vote in the Electing of the Representatives without any manner of constraint or Imposicon. And that in all Eleccons the Majority of Voices shall carry itt and by freeholders is understood every one who is Soe understood according to the Lawes of England.

6. —THAT The persons to be Elected to sitt as representatives in the Generall Assembly from time to time for the severall Cittyes townes Countyes Shires or Divisions of this province and all places within the same shall be according to the proporcon and number hereafter Expressed that is to say for the Citty and County of New Yorke four, for the County of Suffolke two, for Queens County two, for Kings County two, for the County of Richmond two for the County of West Chester two, for the County of Ulster two for the County of Albany two and for Schenectade within the said County one for Dukes County two, for the County of Cornwall two and as many more as his Royall Highnesse shall think fitt to Establish.

7. —THAT All persons Chosen and Assembled in manner aforesaid or the Major part of them shall be deemed and accounted the Representatives of this province which said Representatives together with the Governour and his Councell Shall forever be the Supreame and only Legislative power under his Royall Highnesse of the said province.

8. —THAT The said Representatives may appoint their owne Times of meeting dureing their sessions and

may adjourne their house from time to time to such time as to them shall seeme meet and convenient.

9. —THAT THE said Representatives are the sole Judges of the Qualificacons of their owne members, and likewise of all undue Eleccons and may from time to time purge their house as they shall see occasion dureing the said sessions.

10. —THAT Noe mernber of the general Assembly or their servants dureing the time of their Sessions and whilest they shall be goeing to and returning from the said Assembly shall be arrested sued imprisoned or any wayes molested or troubled nor be compelled to make answere to any suite, Bill, plaint, Declaracon or otherwise, (Cases of High Treason and felony only excepted) provided the number of the said servants shall not Exceed three.

11. —THAT All bills agreed upon by the said Representatives or the Major part of them shall be presented unto the Governour and his Councell for their Approbacon and Consent All and Every which Said Bills soe approved of Consented to by the Governour and his Councell shall be Esteemed and accounted the Lawes of the province, Which said Lawes shall continue and remaine of force untill they shall be repealed by the authority aforesaid that is to say the Governour Councell and Representatives in General Assembly by and with the Approbacon of his Royal Highnesse or Expire by their owne Limittacons.

12. —THAT In all cases of death or removall of any of the said Representatives The Governour shall issue out Summons by Writt to the Respective Townes Cittyes Shires Countryes or Divisions for which he or they soe removed or deceased were Chosen willing and requireing the ffreholders of the Same to Elect others in their place and stead.

13. —THAT Noe freeman shall be taken and imprisoned or be disseized of his ffrehold or Libertye or ffree Customes or be outlawed or Exiled or any other wayes destroyed nor shall be passed upon adjudged or condemned But by the Law-full Judgment of his peers and by the Law of this province. Justice nor Right shall be neither sold denyed or deferred to any man within this province.

14. —THAT Noe aid, Tax, Tallage, Assessment, Custome, Loane, Benevolence or Imposicon whatsoever shall be layed assessed imposed or levyed on any of his Majestyes Subjects within this province or their Estates upon any manner of colour or pretence but by the act and Consent of the Governour Councell and Representatives of the people in Generall Assembly mett and Assembled.

15. —THAT Noe man of what Estate or Condicon soever shall be putt out of his Lands or Tenements, nor taken, nor imprisoned, nor disherited, nor banished nor any wayes distroyed without being brought to Answere by due Course of Law.

16. —THAT A ffreeman Shall not be amerced for a small fault, but after the manner of his fault and for a great fault after the Greatnesse thereof Saveing to him his freehold, And a husbandman saveing to him his Wainage and a merchant likewise saveing to him his merchandize And none of the said Amerciaments shall be assessed but by the oath of twelve honest and Lawfull men of the Vicinage provided the faults and misdemeanours be not in Contempt of Courts of Judicature.

17. —ALL Tryalls shall be by the verdict of twelve men, and as neer as may be peers or Equalls And of the neighbourhood and in the County Shire or Division where the fact Shall arise or grow Whether the Same be by Indictment Infermacon Declaracon or otherwise against the person Offender or Defendant.

18. —THAT In all Cases Capitall or Criminall there shall be a grand Inquest who shall first present the offence and then twelve men of the neighbourhood to try the Offender who after his plea to the Indictment shall be allowed his reasonable Challenges.

19. —THAT In all Cases whatsoever Bayle by sufficient Suretyes Shall be allowed and taken unlesse for treason or felony plainly and specially Expressed and menconed in the Warrant of Committment provided Always that nothing herein contained shall Extend to discharge out of prison upon bayle any person taken in Execucon for debts or otherwise legally sentenced by the Judgment of any of the Courts of Record within the province.

20. —THAT Noe Comissions for proceeding by Marshall Law against any of his Majestyes Subjects within this province shall issue forth to any person or persons whatsoever Least by Colour of them any of his Majestyes Subjects bee destroyed or putt to death Except all such officers persons and Soldiers in pay throughout the Government.

21. —THAT From hence forward Noe Lands Within this province shall be Esteemed or accounted a Chattle or personall Estate but an Estate of Inheritance according to the Custome and practice of his Majestyes Realme of England.

22. —THAT Noe Court or Courts within this province have or at any time hereafter Shall have any Jurisdiccon power or authority to grant out any Execucon or other writt whereby any mans Land may be sold or any other way disposed off without the owners Consent provided Always That the issues or meane proffitts of any mans Lands shall or may be Extended by Execucon or otherwise to satisfye just debts Any thing to the Contrary hereof in any wise Notwithstanding.

23. —THAT Noe Estate of a feme Covert shall be sold or conveyed But by Deed acknowledged by her in Some Court of Record the Woman being secretly Examined if She doth it freely without threats or Compulsion of her husband.

24. —THAT All Wills in writeing attested by two Credible Witnesses shall be of the same force to convey Lands as other Conveyances being registered in the Secretaryes Office within forty dayes after the testators death.

25. —THAT A Widow after the death of her husband shall have her Dower And shall and may tarry in the Cheife house of her husband forty dayes after the death of her husband within which forty dayes her Dower shall be assigned her And for her Dower shall be assigned unto her the third part of all the Lands of husband dureing Coverture, Except shee were Endowed of Lesse before Marriage.

26. —THAT All Lands and Heritages within this province and Dependencyes shall be free from all fines and Lycences upon Alienacons, and from all Herriotts Ward Shipps Liveryes primer Seizins yeare day and Wast Escheats and forfeitures upon the death of parents and Ancestors naturall unaturall casuall or Judiciall, and that forever; Cases of High treason only Excepted.

27. —THAT Noe person or persons which professe ffaith in God by Jesus Christ Shall at any time be any wayes molested punished disquieted or called in Question for any Difference in opinion or Matter of Religious Concernment, who doe not actually disturb the Civill peace of the province, But that all and Every such person or persons may from time to time and at all times freely have and fully enjoy his or their Judgments or Consciencyes in matters of Religion throughout all the province, they behaveing themselves peaceably and quietly and not useing this Liberty to Lycentiousnesse nor to the Civill Injury or outward disturbance of others provided Always that this liberty or any thing contained therein to the Contrary shall never be Construed or improved to make void the Settlement of any publique Minister on Long Island Whether Such Settlement be by two thirds of the voices in any Towne thereon which shall alwayes include the Minor part Or by Subscripcons of perticuler Inhabitants in Said Townes provided they are the two thirds thereon Butt that all such agreements Covenants and Subscripcons that are there already made and had Or that hereafter shall bee in this Manner Consented to agreed and Subscribed shall at all time and times hereafter be firme and Stable And in Confirmacon hereof It is Enacted by the Governour Councell and Representatives; That all Such Sumes of money soe agreed and Consented to or Subscribed as aforesaid for maintenance of said Publick Ministers by the two thirds of any Towne on Long Island Shall alwayes include the Minor part who shall be regulated thereby And also Such Subscripcons and agreements as are before menconed are and Shall be always ratified performed and paid, And if any Towne on said Island in their publick Capacity of agreement with any Such minister or any perticuler persons by their private Subscripcons as aforesaid Shall make default deny or withdraw from Such payment Soe Covenanted to

agreed upon and Subscribed That in Such Case upon Complaint of any Collector appointed and Chosen by two thirds of Such Towne upon Long Island unto any Justice of that County Upon his hearing the Same he is hereby authorized impowered and required to issue out his warrant unto the Constable or his Deputy or any other person appointed for the Collection of said Rates or agreement to Levy upon the goods and Chattles of the Said Delinquent or Defaulter all such Sumes of money Soe covenanted and agreed to be paid by distresse with Costs and Charges without any further Suite in Law Any Lawe Custome or usage to the Contrary in any wise Notwithstanding.

PROVIDED Always the said sume or sumes be under forty shillings otherwise to be recovered as the Law directs.

AND WHEREAS All the Respective Christian Churches now in practice within the City of New Yorke and the other places of this province doe appeare to be priviledged Churches and have beene Soe Established and Confirmed by the former authority of this Government BEE it hereby Enacted by this Generall Assembly and by the authority thereof That all the Said Respective Christian Churches be hereby Confirmed therein And that they and Every of them Shall from henceforth forever be held and reputed as priviledged Churches and Enjoy all their former freedomes of their Religion in Divine Worshipp and Church Discipline And that all former Contracts made and agreed upon for the maintenances of the severall ministers of the Said Churches shall stand and continue in full force and virtue And that all Contracts for the future to be made Shall be of the same power And all persons that are unwilling to performe their part of the said Contract Shall be Constrained thereunto by a warrant from any Justice of the peace provided it be under forty Shillings Or otherwise as this Law directs provided allsoe that all Christian Churches that Shall hereafter come and settle with in this province shall have the Same priviledges.

Source:
The Historical Society of the Courts of the State of New York. Available on-line. URL: http://www.courts.state.ny.us/history/Sitemap.htm. Accessed December 2003.

Jacob Leisler, Form of Association Proposed to the Inhabitants, 1689

When James II became king of England in 1685, he moved to consolidate royal government in the colonies. The Glorious Revolution in England in 1688, in which Catholic king James was overthrown and replaced by Protestants William and

Mary, inspired rebellions in America against Maryland's Catholic Proprietors, the rule of Governor Edmund Andros in the Dominion of New England, and the newly appointed royal government in New York. After the rebellions, which lasted until 1691, royal governments regained ascendency, although Maryland's proprietor took back his colony after 1815, when he converted to Anglicanism. Jacob Leisler headed a faction of Dutch traders in New York who resented the English and feared Indian insurrections. He even dismissed the representative assembly when he didn't like its actions. After the royal government regained control of New York, Leisler was hanged as a traitor.

Wee the Committee &ca and other members of this Province of new yorke finding to our great grief after so wonderfull a deliverance from Popery and Arbitrary power, wrought by the goodnesse of God, and the Armes of the Prince of Orange (now our gracious King and Soveraigne) that notwithstanding there hath beene Such Certaine notice therof, and Evidence undeniable to the Conviction of all this Province (Except Papists and Such who affected them who will not believe the Marvellous transactions in Europe to their disadvantage) in So much that most have for Shame or feare taken the Oath of Allegiance to their Majesties King William & Queen Mary: Yet it hath not that due Efficacy upon many of the Same, but they abett, allow, uphold & Support the illegall and Arbitrary Commissions of the late King James granted to his late governors and their unlawfull actings, nay to that degree that they justifie them as good and warrantable untill Order from England, & that those who were in office both Civill and Military Ought So long to Remaine in Excercise of the Same. All which being pernicious and Eminently Dangerous unto the Interest of King William his Crowne and dignity in this Province and the welfare of his good Subjects therein, have thought fitt to propose to all true Protestants within this Province an Union amongst themselves by Solemne and Sacred Promise of mutuall defense and Assistance in the preservation of the true Protestant Religion his Majesties Person and Royall State and our Laws Liberties & Properties and wee hold it our bounden duty to joyn our Selves for the Same intent in a Declaration of our united affections & Resolutions in the Forme ensuing I doe in the Presence of God Solemnly promise, Vow & protest to maintaine and defend to the utmost of my power with my person and Estate the true Protestant Religion against Popery and all Papist Superstition, Idolatry, or Innovation, and all those who do or Shall endeavour to Spread or advance it within this Province; I will also as far as in mee lyes maintaine and defend their Majesties King William & Queen Marys Royall Persons & Estates as also the lawfull Rights and Liberties of the Sub-

jects against all encroachments and usurpation of arbitrary power whatsoever, and endeavour entirely Suppresse all such who Shall oppose the Same.

Moreover what Colonel Thomas Dongan & Sir Edmond Andros themselves in or with Councell have illegall acted or done by Virtue of their Commissions from the late King James, I do declare to be null and off no Effect as if Such had not been and Esteeme them no otherwise than betrayers of the lawfull Rights, and libertyes of the Subject, To this end Wee and every one of us whose hands are here underwritten do most willingly bind our Selves & every one of us unto the other jointly and Severally in the bond of one firm and Loyall Society, or Association & do promise and vow before God, That with our joynt and particular forces we will oppose and pursue unto destruction all Such as upon any title whatsoever Shall oppose the just and Righteous ends of this Association & maintaine, protect & defend all such as shall enter into it in the just performance of the true intent and meaning of itt and least this just and Pious work should be any wayes obstructed or hindred for want of discipline or Conduct or any evill persons under pretence of raising forces for the Service of this Association should attempt or Committ disorders Wee will follow Such Orders as wee Shall from time to time Receive from the Present Committee or the Major part of them and obey whom they Shall appoint or Set over us in this Severall Counties and Townes of this Province untill Orders from his Majestie King William doth arrive; Neither will wee for any Respect of Persons or Causes or for fear or reward Separate our Selves from this Association or fail in the prosecution thereof during our lives, upon paine of being by the rest of us prosecuted and Suppressed as Perjured persons, and publicq Enemies to God, the king and this Province; To which Pains and Punishments wee do Volentarily Submitt our Selves and Every one of us without benefit of any Colour or pretence to Excuse us, In witnesse of all which promises to be inviolably kept wee do to this present writing put our hands and Sealles & Shall be most Ready to accept & admit any others hereafter into this Society & Association.

Source:
New York University. The Jacob Leisler Papers Homepage. Available on-line. URL: www.nyu.edu/leisler./. Accessed October 2003.

Charter of Massachusetts Bay, 1691

This charter, issued in 1691, merged the Plymouth Colony and Maine into the Massachusetts Bay Colony and revoked the colony's independent rule. By the late 17th century, the Massachusetts Bay Colony was the most successful of England's settlements in the New World. Boston was the third busiest seaport in the British Empire, and it led all other colonial ports in trade with England. Massachusetts Bay, however, operated in a predominantly independent manner. When the Massachusetts Bay Company received a charter to begin a colony in 1629, the usual clause requiring the primary investors to meet in England was omitted. This allowed the dominant Puritan colonists to buy out the London stockholders and carry the charter with them to America. There the colonists, led by John Winthrop, instituted a home rule that resulted in a virtual theocracy. Under Winthrop's government, church and state operated as one, and only church members were allowed to vote. Anyone who openly disagreed with the Puritans' Congregationalist Church was exiled. Over the years, relations between England and the strong government of its prosperous colony grew tense. In 1684 the colony's original charter was revoked, and a royal government was installed. This government was annulled after King James II was deposed in the Glorious Revolution of 1688. The new rulers, William and Mary, issued the 1691 charter to restore royal control in Massachusetts. The new charter government lasted until 1774, when a provisional revolutionary government was established in the wake of the Boston Tea Party. The excerpts here concern the reasons why the former charter is abrogated, the general court and assembly, and some of the rights reserved to the king, including the right to use trees for masts, which becomes one of the reasons why Massachusetts decided to resist English rule. Note that freedom of worship was granted only to Protestants. Signers of this document Sir John Trevor, Sir William Rawlinson, and Sir George Hutchins were appointed lords commissioners of the great seal May 15, 1690, and were succeeded by Lord Somers as chancellor May 3, 1693.

WILLIAM & MARY by the grace of God King and Queene of England Scotland France and Ireland Defenders of the Faith &c To all to whome these presents shall come Greeting Whereas his late Majesty King James the First Our Royall Predecessor by his Letters Patents vnder the Greate Seale of England . . . established at Plymouth in the County of Devon for the Planting Ruleing Ordering and Governing of New England in America. . . . Our said Royall Grandfather King Charles the First did by his said Letters Patents Create and make the said. . .Company and Society therein after menconed one Body Politique and Corporate in fact and name by the Name of the Governour and Company of the Massachusetts Bay in New England and did grant onto them and their Successors divers powers Liberties and priviledges as in and by the said Letters Patents may more fully and at large appears *And whereas* the said Governour and Company of the Massachusetts Bay in New England by vertue of the said Letters Patents did settle a Collony of the English in

the said parts of America and divers good Subjects of this Kingdome incouraged and invited by the said Letters Patents did Transport themselves and their Edects into the same whereby the said Plantacon did become very populous and divers Counties Townes and Places were created erected made setforth or designed within the said parts of America by the said Governour and Company for the time being *And Whereas* in the Terme of the holy Trinity in the Thirty Sixth yeare of the Reigne of Our dearest Vncle King Charles the Second a Judgment was given in Our Court of Chancery then sitting at Westminster . . . brought and prosecuted in the said Court against the Governour and Company of the Massachusetts Bay in New England that the said Letters Patents of Our said Royall Grandfather King Charles the First . . . made and granted to the said Governour and Company of the Massachusetts Bay in New F,ngland and the Enrollment of the same should be cancelled vacated and annihilated . . . *And whereas* severall persons employed as Agents in behalfe of Our said Collony of the Massachusetts Bay in New England have made their humble application vnto Vs that Wee would be graciously pleased by Our Royall Charter to Incorporate Our Subjects in Our said Collony and to grant and confirms Into them such powers priviledges and Franchises as [in] Our Royall Wisdome should be thought most conduceing to Our Interest and Service and to the Welfare and happy State of Our Subjects in New England and Wee being graciously pleased to gratifie Our said Subjects And alsoe to the end.Our good Subjects within Our Collony of New Plymouth in New England aforesaid may be brought under such a forme of Government as may put them in a better Condicon of defence and considering aswell the granting vnto them as onto Our Subejcts in the said Collony of the Massachusetts Bay Our Royall Charter with reasonable Powers and Priviledges will much tend not only to the safety but to the Flourishing estate of Our Subjects in the said parts of New England and alsoe to the advanceing of the ends for which the said Plantancons were at first encouraged of Our especiall Grace certaine knowledge and meer Mocon have willed and ordeyned and Wee doe by these presents for Vs Our Heires and Successors Will and Ordeyne That the Territories and Collnyes camonly called or known by the Names of the Collony of the Massachusetts Bay and Collony of New Plymouth the Province of Main the Territorie called Accadia or Nova Scotia and all that Tract of Land lying betweene the said Territoritories of Nova Scotia and the said Province of Main be Erected ignited and Incorporated And Wee doe by these presents Vnite Erect and Incorporate the same into one reall Province by the Name of Our Province of the Massachusetts Bay in New England. . . . Wee doe for Vs Our Heires and Successors Grant and ordeyne that all and every such Lands Tenements and Hereditaments and all other estates which any person or persons or Bodyes-Politique or Corporate Townes Villages Colledges or Schooles doe hold and enjoy or ought to hold and enjoy within the bounds aforesaid by or vnder any Grant or estate duely made or granted by any Generall Court formerly held or by vertue of the Letters Patents herein before recited or by any other lawfull Right or Title whatsoever shall be by such person and persons Bodyes Politique and Corporate Townes Villages Colledges or Schoolss their respective Heires Successors and Assignes for ever hereafter held and enjoyed according to the purport and Intent of such respective Grant vnder and Subject neverthelesse to the Rents and Services thereby reserved or made payable any matter or thing whatsoever to the contrary notwithstanding. . . . Wee doe further for Vs Our Heires and Successors Will Establish and ordeyne that from henceforth for ever there shall be one Goverour One Leivtent or Deputy Governour and One Secretary of Our said Province or Territory to be from time to time appointed and Commissionated by Vs Our Heires and Successors and Eight and Twenty Assistants or Councillors to be advising and assisting to the Governour of Our said Province or Territory for the time being as by these presents is hereafter directed and appointed which said Councillors or Assistants are to be Constituted Elected and Chosen in such forme and manner as hereafter in these presents is expressed And for the better Execucon of Our Royall Pleasure and Grant in this behalfe Wee doe by these presents for Vs Our Heires and Successors Nominate Ordeyne make and Constitute Our Trusty and Welbeloved Simon Broadstreet John Richards Nathaniel Saltenstall Wait Winthrop John Phillipps James Russell Samuell Sewall Samuel Appleton Barthilomew Gedney John Hawthorn Elisha Hutchinson Robert Pike Jonathan Curwin John Jolliffe Adam Winthrop Richard Middlecot John Foster Peter Serjeant Joseph Lynd Samuell Hayman Stephen Mason Thomas Hinckley William Bradford John Walley Barnabas Lothrop Job Alcott Samuell Daniell and Silvanus Davis Esquires the first and present Councillors or Assistants of Our said Province to continue in their said respective Offices or Trusts of Councillors or Assistants vntill the last Wednesday in May which shall be in the yeare of Our Lord One Thousand Six Hundred Ninety and Three and vntill other Councillors or Assistants shall be chosen and appointed in their stead in such manner as in these presents is expressed And Wee doe further by these presents Constitute and appoint Our Trusty and welbeloved Isaac Addington Esquier to be Our first and present Secretary of Our said Province during Our Pleasure And Our Will and Pleasure is that the Governour of Our said Province from the time being shall have Authority from time to time at his discretion to assemble and call together the Councillors or Assistants of Our said Province for the time being and that the said Governour with the said Assistants or Councillors or Seaven of them at the least shall and may from time to time hold and keep a Councill for the ordering and directing the Affaires of Our said Province *And further* Wee Will and by these presents for Vs Our Heires and Successors doe ordeyne and Grant that there shall and may be convened held and kept by the Governour for the time being vpon every last Wednesday in the Moneth of May every yeare for ever and at all such other times as the Governour of Our said Province shall think fitt and appoint a great and Generall Court of Assembly Which said Great and Generall Court of Assembly shall consist of the Governour and Councill or Assistants for the time being and of such-Freeholders of Our said Province or Territory as shall be from time to time elected or deputed by the Major parse of the Freeholders and other Inhabitants of the respective Townes or Places who shall be present at such Eleccons Each of the said Townes and Places being hereby impowered to Elect and Depute Two Persons and noe more to serve for and represent them respectively in the said Great and Generall Court or Assembly To which Great and Generall Court or Assembly to be held as aforesaid Wee doe hereby for Vs Our Heires and Successors give and grant full power and authority from time to time to direct appoint and declare what Number each County Towne and Place shall Elect and Depute to serve for and represent them respectively in the said Great and Generall Court or Assembly *Provided* always that noe Freeholder or other Person shall have a Vote in the Eleccon of Members to serve in any Greate and Generall Court or Assembly to be held as aforesaid who at the time of such Eleccon shall not have an estate of Freehold in Land within Our said Province or Territory to the value of Forty Shillings per Annu at the least or other estate to the value of Forty pounds Sterl' And that every Person who shall be soe elected shall before he silt or Act in the said Great and Generall Court or Assembly take the Oaths menconed in an Act of Parliament made in the first yeare of Our Reigne Entituled an Act for abrogateing of the Oaths of Allegiance and Supremacy and appointing other Oaths and thereby appointed to be taken instead of the Oaths of Allegiance and Supremacy and shall make Repeat and Subscribe the Declaracon menconed in the said Act before the Governour and Lievtent or Deputy Governour or any two of the Assistants for the time being who shall be therevnto authorized and Appointed by Our said Governour and that the Governour for the time being shall have full power and Authority from time to time as he shall Judge necessary to adjourns Prorogue and dissolve all Great and

Generall Courts or Assemblyes met and convened as aforesaid And Our Will and Pleasure is and Wee doe hereby for Vs Our Heires and Successors Grant Establish and Ordeyne that yearly once in every yeare for ever hereafter the aforesaid Number of Eight and Twenty Councillors or Assistants shall be by the Generall Court or Assembly newly chosen that is to say Eighteen at least of the Inhabitants of or Proprietors of Lands within the Territory formerly called the Collony of the Massachusetts Bay and four at the least of the Inhabitants of or Proprietors of Lands within the Territory formerly called New Plymouth and three at the least of the Inhabitants of or Proprietors of Land within the Territory formerly called the Province of Main and one at the least of the Inhabitants of or Proprietors of Land within the Territory lying between the River of Sagadahoc and Nova Scotia And that the said Councillors or Assistants or any of them shall or may at any time hereafter be removed or displaced from their respective Places or Trust of Councillors or Assistants by any Great or Generall Court or Assembly And that if any of the said Councillors or Assistants shall happen to dye or be removed as aforesaid before the Generall day of Eleccon That then and in every such Case the Great and Generall Court or Assembly at their first sitting may proceed to a New Eleccon of one or more Councillors or Assistants in the roome or place of such Councillors or Assistants soe dying or removed And Thee doe further Grant and Ordeyne that it shall and may be lawfull for the said Governour with the advice and consent of the Councill or Assistants from time to time to nominate and appoint Judges Commissioners of Oyer and Terminer Sheriffs Provosts Marshalls Justices of the Peace and other Officers to Our Councill and Courts of Justice belonging *Provided* always that noe such Nominacon or Appointment of Officers be made without notice first given or sumons Issued out seaven dayes before such Nominacon or Appointment onto such of the said Councillors or Assistants as shall be at that time resideing within Our said Province *And Our* Will and Pleasure is that the Governour and Leivtent or Deputy Governour and Councillors or Assistants for the time being and all other Officers to be appointed or Chosen as aforesaid shall before the Vndertaking the Execucon of their Offices and Places respectively take their severall and respective Oaths for the due and faithfull performance of their duties in their severall and respective Offices and Places and alsoe the Oaths appointed by the said Act of Parliament made in the first yeare of Our Reigne to be taken instead of the Oaths of Allegiance and Supremacy and shall make repeate and subscribe the Declaracon menconed in the said Act before such Person or Persons as are by these presents herein after appointed (that is to

say) The Governour of Our said Province or Territory for the time being shall take the said Oaths and make repeate and subscribe the said Decleracon before the Leivtent or Deputy Governour or in his absence before any two or more of the said Persons hereby Nominated and appointed the present Councillors or Assistants of Our said Province or Territory to whom Wee doe by these presents give full power and Authority to give and administer the same to Our said Governour accordingly and after Our said Governour shall be sworn and shall have subscribed the said Declaracon that then Our Leivtent or Deputy Governour for the time being and the Councillors or Assistants before by these presents Nominated and appointed shall take the said Oaths and make repeat and subscribe the said Declaracon before Our said Governour and that every such person or persons as shall (at any time of the Annuall Eleccons or otherwise vpon death or removeall) be appointed to be the New Councillors or Assistants and all other Officers to bee hereafter chosen from time to time shall take the Oaths to their respective Offices and places belonging and alsoe the said Oaths appointed by the said Act of Parliament to be taken instead of the Oaths of Allegiance and Supremacy and shall make repeate and subscribe the declaracon menconed in the said Act before the Governour or Leivtent or Deputy Governour or any two or more Councillors or Assistants or such other Person or Persons as shall be appointed thereunto by the Governour for the time being to whom Wee doe therefore by these presents give full power and authority from time to time to give and administer the same respectively according to Our true meaning herein before declared without any Comission or further Warrant to bee had and obteyned from vs Our Heires and Successors in that behalfe And Our Will and Pleasure is and Wee doe hereby require and Comand that all and every person and persons hereafter by Vs Our Heires and Successors nominated and appointed to the respective Offices of Governour or I,eivt or Deputy Governour and Secretary of Our said Province or Territory (which said Governour or Leivt or Deputy Governour and Secretary of Our said Province or Territory for the time being Wee doe hereby reserve full power and Authority to Vs Our Heires and Successors to Nominate and appoint accordingly, shall before he or they be admitted to the Execucon of their respective Offices take as well the Oath for the due and faithfull performance of the said Offices respectively as alsoe the Oaths appointed by the said Act of Parliament made in the said First yeare of Our Reigne to be taken instead of the said Oaths of Allegiance and Supremacy and shall alsoe make repeate and subscribe the Declaracon appointed by the said Act in such manner and before such persons as aforesaid *And further* Our Will and Pleasure is and Wee doe hereby for Vs Our Heires and Successors Grant Establish and Ordaine That all and every of the Subjects of Vs Our Heires and Successors which shall goe to and Inhabit within Our said Province and Territory and every of their Children which shall happen to be born there or on the Seas in goeing thither or returning from thence shall have and enjoy all Libertyes and Immunities of Free and naturall Subjects within any of the Dominions of Vs Our Heires and Successors to all Intents Construccons and purposes whatsoever as if they and every of them were borne within this *Our Realme* of England and for the greater Ease and Encouragement of Our Loveing Subjects Inhabiting our said Province or Territory of the Massachusetts Bay and of such as shall come to Inhabit there Wee doe by these presents for vs Our heires and Successors Grant Establish and Ordaine that for ever hereafter there shall be a liberty of Conscience allowed in the Worshipp of God to all Christians (Except Papists) Inhabiting or which shall Inhabit or be Resident within our said Province or Territory And Wee doe hereby Grant and Ordaine that the Governor or leivtent or Deputy Gouernor of our said Province or Territory for the time being or either of them or any two or more of the Councill or Assistants for the time being as shall be "hereunto appointed by the said Gouernor shall and may at all times and from time to time hereafter have full Power and Authority to Administer and give the Oathes appointed by the said Act of Parliament made in the first yeare of Our Reigne to be taken instead of the Oathes of Allegiance and Supremacy to all and every person and persons which are now Inhabiting or resideing within our said Province or Territory or which shall at any time or times hereafter goe or passe thither And wee doe of our further Grace certaine knowledge and meer mocon Grant Establish and Ordaine for Vs our heires and Successors that the great and Generall Court or Assembly of our said Province or Territory for the time being Convened as aforesaid shall for ever have full Power and Authority to Erect and, Constitute Judicatories and Courts of Record or other Courts to be held in the name of Vs Our heires and successors for the Hearing Trying and Determining of all manner of Crimes Odences Pleas Processes Plaints Accons Matters Causes and things whatsoever ariseing or happening within Our said Province or Territory or between persons Inhabiting or resideing there whether the same be Criminall or Civill and whether the said Crimes be Capitall or not Capitall and whether the said Pleas be Reall personall or mixt and for the awarding and makeing out of Execution thereupon To which Courts and Judicatories wee doe hereby for vs our heirs and Successors Give and Grant full power and Authority from time to time to Administer oathes for the better Discovery of Truth in any matter in Controversy or depending before

them *And* wee doe for vs Our Heires and Successors Grant Establish and Ordaine that the Gouernor of our said Province or Territory for the time being with the Councill or Assistants may doe execute or performe all that is necessary for the Probate of Wills and Granting of Administracons for touching or concerning any Interest or Estate which any person or persons shall have within our said Province or Territory *And whereas* Wee judge it necessary that all our Subjects should have liberty to Appeale to vs our heires and Successors in Cases that may deserve the same Wee doe by these presents Ordaine that incase either party shall not rest satisfied with the Judgement or Sentence of any Judicatories or Courts within our said Province or Territory in any Personall Accon wherein the matter in difference doth exceed the value of three hundred Pounds Sterling that then he or they may appeale to vs Our heires and Successors in our or their Privy Councill Provided such Appeale be made within Fourteen dayes after ye Sentence or Judgement given and that before such Appeale be allowed Security be given by the party or parties appealing . . . we doe further for vs our Heires and Successors Give and Grant to the said Governor and the great and Generall Court or Assembly of our said Province or Territory for the time being full power and Authority from time to time to make ordaine and establish all manner of wholsome and reasonable Orders Laws Statutes and Ordinances Directions and Instructions either with penalties or without (soe as the same be not repugnant or contrary to the Lawes of this our Realme of England) as they shall Judge to be for the-good and welfare of our said Province or Territory And for the Gouernment and Ordering thereof and of the People Inhabiting or who shall Inhabit the same and for the necessary support and Defence of the Government thereof *And* wee doe for vs our Heires and Successors Giue and grant that the said Generall Court or Assembly shall have full power and Authority to name and settle annually all Civill Officers within the said Province such Officers Excepted the Election and Constitution of whome wee have by these presents reserved to vs Our Heires and Successors or to the Governor of our said Province for the time being and to Sett forth the severall Duties Powers and Lymitts of every such Officer to be appointed by the said Generall Court or Assembly and the formes of such Oathes not repugnant to the Lawes and Statutes of this, our Realme of England as shall be respectiuely Administered vnto them for the Execution of their severall Offices and places And alsoe to impose Fines mulcts Imprisonments and other Punishments And to impose and leavy proportionable and reasonable Assessments Rates and Taxes vpon the Estates and Persons of all and every the Proprietors and Inhabitants of our said Province or Territory to be Issued and disposed of by Warrant vnder the hand of the Governor of our said Province for the time being with the advice and Consent of the Councill for Our service in the necessary defence and support of our Government of our said Province or Territory and the Protection and Preservation of the Inhabitants there according to such Acts as are or shall be in force within our said Province and to dispose of matters and things whereby our Subjects inhabitants of our said Province may be Religiously peaceably and Civilly Governed Protected and Defended soe as their good life and orderly Conversation may win the Indians Natives of the Country to the knowledge and obedience of the onely true God and Saviour of Mankinde and the Christian Faith which his Royall Majestie our Royall Grandfather king Charles the first in his said Letters Patents declared was his Royall Intentions . . . . any time being and resideing within our said Province or Territory as aforesaid *Willing* Comanding and Requireing and by these presents for vs Our heires and Successors Ordaining and appointing that all such Orders Lawes Statutes and Ordinances Instructions and Directions as shall be soe made and published vnder our Seale of our said Province or Territory shall be Carefully and duely observed kept and performed and put in Execution according to the true intent and meaning of these presents *Provided* alwaies and Wee doe by these presents for vs Our Heires and Successors Establish and Ordaine that in the frameing and passing of all such Orders Laws Statutes and Ordinances and in all Elections and Acts of Government whatsoever to be passed made or done by the said Generall Court or Assembly or in Councill the Governor of our said Province or Territory of the Massachusetts Bay in New England for the time being shall have the Negative voice and that without his consent or Approbation signified and declared in Writing no such Orders Laws Statutes Ordinances Elections or other Acts of Government whatsoever soe to be made passed or done by the said Generall Assembly or in Councill shall be of any Force effect or validity anything herein contained to the contrary in anywise notwithstanding *And* wee doe for vs Our Heires and Successors Establish and Ordaine that the said Orders Laws Statutes and Ordinances be by the first opportunity after the makeing thereof sent or Transmitted vnto vs Our Heires and Successors under the Publique Seale to be appointed by vs for Our or their approbation or Disallowance And that incase all or any of them shall at any time within the space of three years next after the same shall have presented to vs our Heires and Successors in Our or their Privy Councill be disallowed and rejected . . . any time being and resideing within our said Province or Territory as aforesaid *Willing* Comanding and Requireing and by these presents for vs Our heires and Successors Ordaining and appointing that all such Orders Lawes Statutes and Ordinances Instructions and

Directions as shall be soe made and published vnder our Seale of our said Province or Territory shall be Carefully and duely observed kept and performed and put in Execution according to the true intent and meaning of these presents *Provided* alwaies and Wee doe by these presents for vs Our Heires and Successors Establish and Ordaine that in the frameing and passing of all such Orders Laws Statutes and Ordinances and in all Elections and Acts of Government whatsoever to be passed made or done by the said Generall Court or Assembly or in Councill the Governor of our said Province or Territory of the Massachusetts Bay in New England for the time being shall have the Negative voice and that without his consent or Approbation signified and declared in Writing no such Orders Laws Statutes Ordinances Elections or other Acts of Government whatsoever soe to be made passed or done by the said Generall Assembly or in Councill shall be of any Force effect or validity anything herein contained to the contrary in anywise notwithstanding *And* wee doe for vs Our Heires and Successors Establish and Ordaine that the said Orders Laws Statutes and Ordinances be by the first opportunity after the makeing thereof sent or Transmitted vnto vs Our Heires and Successors under the Publique Seale to be appointed by vs for Our or their approbation or Disallowance And that incase all or any of them shall at any time within the space of three years next after the same shall have presented to vs our Heires and Successors in Our or their Privy Councill be disallowed and rejected. . . . Wee doe by these presents for vs Our Heires and Successors Grant Establish and Ordaine that the Governor of our said Province or Territory for the time being shall have full Power by himselfe or by any Cheif Comander or other Officer or Officers to be appointed by him from time to time to traine instruct Exercise and Governe the Militia there and for the speciall Denfence and Safety of Our said Province or Territory to assemble in Martiall Array and put in Warlike posture the Inhabitants of Our said Province or Territory and to lead and Conduct them and with them to Encounter Expulse Repell Resist and pursue by force of Armes aswell by Sea as by Land within or without the limitts of Our said Province or Territory and alsoe to kill slay destroy and Conquer by all fitting wayes Enterprises and meanes whatsoever all and every such Person and Persons as shall at any time hereafter Attempt or Enterprize the destruccon Invasion Detriment or Annoyance of Our said Province or Territory and to vse and exercise the Law Martiall in time of actuall Warr Invasion or Rebellion as occasion shall necessarily require and alsoe from time to time to Erect Forts and to fortifie any place or Places within Our said Province or Territory and the same to furnish with all necessary Amunicon Provisions and Stores of Warr for Odence or Defence and to comitt from time to time the Custody and Government of the same to such Person or Persons as to him shall seem meet And the said Forts and Fortificacons to demolish at his Pleasure and to take and surprise by all waies and meanes whatsoever all and every such Person or Persons with their Shipps Arms Ammuncon and other goods as shall in a hostile manner Invade or attempt the Invading Conquering or Annoying of Our said Province or Territory *Provided* always and Wee doe by these presents for Vs Our Heires and Successors Grant Establish and Ordeyne That the said Governour shall not at any time hereafter by vertue of any power hereby granted or hereafter to be granted to him Transport any of the Inhabitants of Our said Province or Territory or oblige them to march out of the Limitts of the same without their Free and voluntary consent or the Consent of the Great and Generall Court or Assembly or Our said Province or Territory nor grant Comissions for exerciseing the Law Martiall vpon any the Inhabitants of Our said Province or Territory without the Advice and Consent of the Councill or Assistants of the same *Provided* in like manner and Wee doe by these presents for Vs Our Heires and Successors Constitute and Ordeyne that when and as often as the Governour of Our said Province for the time being shall happen to dye or be displaced by Vs Our Heires or Successors or be absent from his Government That then and in any of the said Cases the Leivtenant or Deputy Governour of Our said Province for the time being shall have full power and authority to doe and excoute all and every such Acts Matters and things which Our Governour of Our said Province for the time being might or could by vertue of these Our Letter Patents lawfully doe or execute if he were personally present vntill the returne of the Governour soe absent or Arrivall or Constitucon of such other Governour as shall or may be appointed by Vs Our Heires or Successors in his stead and that when and as often as the Governour and Leivtenant or Deputy Governour of Our said Province or Territory for the time being shall happen to dye or be displaced by Vs Our Heires or Successors or be absent from Our said Province and that there shall be no person within the said Province Comissionated by Vs Our Heires or Successors to be Governour within the same Then and in every of the said cases the Councill or Assistants of Our said Province shall have full power and Authority and Wee doe hereby give and grant vnto the said Councill or Assistants of Our said Province for the time being or the Major parse of them full power and Authority to doe and execute all and every such Acts matters and things which the said Governour or Leivtenant of Deputy Governour of Our said Province or Territory for the time being might or could lawfully doe or exercise if they or either of them were personally present. . . . *Provided* alwaies and it is hereby declared that nothing herein shall extend or be

taken to Erect or grant or allow the Exercise of any Admirall Court Jurisdicon Power or Authority but that the same shall be and is hereby reserved to Vs and Our Successors and shall from time to time be Erected Granted and exercised by vertue of Commissions to be yssued vnder the Great Seale of England or vnder the Seale of the High Admirall or the Comissioners for executing the Office of High Admirall of England *And further* Our expresse Will and Pleasure is And Wee doe by these present for Vs Our Heires and Successors Ordaine and appoint that these Our Letters Patents shall not in any manner Enure or be taken to abridge bar or hinder any of Our loveing Subjects whatsoever to vse and exercise the Trade of Fishing vpon the Coasts of New England. . . . *And lastly* for the better provideing and furnishing of Masts for Our Royall Navy Wee doe hereby reserve to Vs Our Heires and Successors all Trees of the Diameter of Twenty Four Inches and upwards of Twelve Inches from the ground growing vpon any soyle or Tract of Land within Our said Province or Territory not heretofore granted to any private persons And Wee doe restrains and forbid all persons whatsoever from felling cutting or destroying any such Trees without the Royall Lycence of Vs Our Heires and Successors first had and obteyned vpon penalty of Forfeiting One Hundred Pounds sterling. . . . Notwithstanding *In Witnesse* whereof Wee-have caused these our Letters to be made Patents *Witnesse* Ourselves att Westminster the Seaventh Day of October in the Third yeare of Our Reigne

By Writt of Privy Seale
Pigott
Pro Fine in Hanaperio quadragint Marcas
J. Trevor C. S.
K. W. Rawlinson C. S.
L. G. Hutchins C. S.

Source:

Francis Newton Thorpe, ed. *The Federal and State Constitutions, Colonial Charters, and Other Organic Laws of the States, Territories, and Colonies Now or Heretofore Forming the United States of America.* Washington, D.C.: Government Printing Office, 1909.

Albany Plan of Union, 1754

Proposal for a federation or union of the British colonies in America, drafted principally by Benjamin Franklin and approved by the Albany Congress in June 1754. Delegates from the colonial assemblies of New Hampshire, Massachusetts, Connecticut, Rhode Island, New York, Pennsylvania, and Maryland were summoned to Albany, New York, to work out a common plan of defense against the French and hostile Iroquois tribes. Threatened, they sought a treaty with the Native Americans and a permanent union of the colonies. Franklin's plan provided for a union with a representative council elected by the colonial assemblies triennially, which would have the power to impose taxes, nominate civil officials, regulate Native American affairs, and control the military. A president-general, appointed by the British Crown, would preside over the council and would hold veto power. The individual colonies, unwilling to give up so much power, rejected the Albany Plan, as did the British, thinking it would decrease the power of Parliament and the king.

It is proposed that humble application be made for an act of Parliament of Great Britain, by virtue of which one general government may be formed in America, including all the said colonies, within and under which government each colony may retain its present constitution, except in the particulars wherein a change may be directed by the said act, as hereafter follows.

1. That the said general government be administered by a President-General, to be appointed and supported by the crown; and a Grand Council, to be chosen by the representatives of the people of the several Colonies met in their respective assemblies.

2. That within—months after the passing such act, the House of Representatives that happen to be sitting within that time, or that shall be especially for that purpose convened, may and shall choose members for the Grand Council, in the following proportion, that is to say,

Massachusetts Bay 7 New Hampshire 2 Connecticut 5 Rhode Island 2 New York 4 New Jersey 3 Pennsylvania 6 Maryland 4 Virginia 7 North Carolina 4 South Carolina 4—48

3.—who shall meet for the first time at the city of Philadelphia, being called by the President-General as soon as conveniently may be after his appointment.

4. That there shall be a new election of the members of the Grand Council every three years; and, on the death or resignation of any member, his place should be supplied by a new choice at the next sitting of the Assembly of the Colony he represented.

5. That after the first three years, when the proportion of money arising out of each Colony to the general treasury can be known, the number of members to be chosen for each Colony shall, from time to time, in all ensuing elections, be regulated by that proportion, yet so as that the number to be chosen by any one Province be not more than seven, nor less than two.

6. That the Grand Council shall meet once in every year, and oftener if occasion require, at such time and place as they shall adjourn to at the last preceding meeting, or as they shall be called to meet at by the President-General on any emergency; he having first obtained in writing the consent of seven of the members to such call, and sent duly and timely notice to the whole.

7. That the Grand Council have power to choose their speaker; and shall neither be dissolved, prorogued, nor continued sitting longer than six weeks at one time, without their own consent or the special command of the crown.

8. That the members of the Grand Council shall be allowed for their service ten shillings sterling per diem, during their session and journey to and from the place of meeting; twenty miles to be reckoned a day's journey.

9. That the assent of the President-General be requisite to all acts of the Grand Council, and that it be his office and duty to cause them to be carried into execution.

10. That the President-General, with the advice of the Grand Council, hold or direct all Indian treaties, in which the general interest of the Colonies may be concerned; and make peace or declare war with Indian nations.

11. That they make such laws as they judge necessary for regulating all Indian trade.

12. That they make all purchases from Indians, for the crown, of lands not now within the bounds of particular Colonies, or that shall not be within their bounds when some of them are reduced to more convenient dimensions.

13. That they make new settlements on such purchases, by granting lands in the King's name, reserving a quitrent to the crown for the use of the general treasury.

14. That they make laws for regulating and governing such new settlements, till the crown shall think fit to form them into particular governments.

15. That they raise and pay soldiers and build forts for the defence of any of the Colonies, and equip vessels of force to guard the coasts and protect the trade on the ocean, lakes, or great rivers; but they shall not impress men in any Colony, without the consent of the Legislature.

16. That for these purposes they have power to make laws, and lay and levy such general duties, imposts, or taxes, as to them shall appear most equal and just (considering the ability and other circumstances of the inhabitants in the several Colonies), and such as may be collected with the least inconvenience to the people; rather discouraging luxury, than loading industry with unnecessary burdens.

17. That they may appoint a General Treasurer and Particular Treasurer in each government when necessary; and, from time to time, may order the sums in the treasuries of each government into the general treasury; or draw on them for special payments, as they find most convenient.

18. Yet no money to issue but by joint orders of the President-General and Grand Council; except where sums have been appropriated to particular purposes, and the President-General is previously empowered by an act to draw such sums.

19. That the general accounts shall be yearly settled and reported to the several Assemblies.

20. That a quorum of the Grand Council, empowered to act with the President-General, do consist of twenty-five members; among whom there shall be one or more from a majority of the Colonies.

21. That the laws made by them for the purposes aforesaid shall not be repugnant, but, as near as may be, agreeable to the laws of England, and shall be transmitted to the King in Council for approbation, as soon as may be after their passing; and if not disapproved within three years after presentation, to remain in force.

22. That, in case of the death of the President-General, the Speaker of the Grand Council for the time being shall succeed, and be vested with the same powers and authorities, to continue till the King's pleasure be known.

23. That all military commission officers, whether for land or sea service, to act under this general constitution, shall be nominated by the President-General; but the approbation of the Grand Council is to be obtained, before they receive their commissions. And all civil officers are to be nominated by the Grand Council, and to receive the President-General's approbation before they officiate.

24. But, in case of vacancy by death or removal of any officer, civil or military, under this constitution, the Governor of the Province in which such vacancy happens may appoint, till the pleasure of the President-General and Grand Council can be known.

25. That the particular military as well as civil establishments in each Colony remain in their present state, the general constitution notwithstanding; and that on sudden emergencies any Colony may defend itself, and lay the accounts of expense thence arising before the President-General and General Council, who may allow and order payment of the same, as far as they judge such accounts just and reasonable.

Source:
Henry Steele Commager, ed. *Documents of American History.* New York: F.S. Crofts & Co., 1934.

James Otis, Speech Opposing Writs of Assistance, 1761

Legal argument by Boston attorney James Otis, dated February 24, 1761, against the issuance by the British court of exchequer of writs of assistance (general search warrants that gave British customs officers the power to search any house for smuggled items without showing cause). Though no formal record of the speech exists, it is known from notes taken by John Adams. Representing a group of Boston merchants, Otis argued (before the Superior Court of Massachusetts) that such writs were unconstitutional and void because they violated

natural law; he argued that a man is "as secure in his house as a prince in his castle." Otis's speech is often, perhaps erroneously, credited as the source of the slogan, "Taxation without representation is tyranny." He lost the case in court but became an influential pamphleteer.

I was desired by one of the Court to look into the books and consider the question now before them concerning "Writs of Assistance." I have accordingly considered it, and now appear not only in obedience to your order but likewise in behalf of the inhabitants of this town who have presented another petition, and out of regard to the liberties of the subject. And I take this opportunity to declare that whether under a fee or not (for in such a cause as this I despise a fee), I will to my dying day oppose with all the powers and faculties God has given me all such instruments of slavery on the one hand and villainy on the other as this Writ of Assistance is.

It appears to me the worst instrument of arbitrary power, the most destructive of English liberty and the fundamental principles of law, that ever was found in an English lawbook. I must therefore beg Your Honors' patience and attention to the whole range of an argument that may perhaps appear uncommon in many things, as well as to points of learning that are more remote and unusual, that the whole tendency of my design may the more easily be perceived, the conclusions better descend, and the force of them be better felt. I shall not think much of my pains in this cause, as I engaged in it from principle.

I was solicited to argue this cause as advocate general, and because I would not, I have been charged with desertion from my office. To this charge I can give a very sufficient answer. I renounced that office, and I argue this cause from the same principle; and I argue it with the greater pleasure, as it is in favor of British liberty, at a time when we hear the greatest monarch upon earth declaring from his throne that he glories in the name of Britain, and that the privileges of his people are dearer to him than the most valuable prerogatives of his Crown, and as it is in opposition to a kind of power, the exercise of which, in former periods of history, cost one king of England his head and another his throne. I have taken more pains in this cause than I ever will take again, although my engaging in this and another popular cause has raised much resentment. But I think I can sincerely declare that I cheerfully submit myself to every odious name for conscience's sake, and from my soul I despise all those whose guilt, malice, or folly has made them my foes. Let the consequences be what they will, I am determined to proceed. The only principles of public conduct that are worthy of a gentleman or a man are to sacrifice estate, ease, health, and applause, and even life, to the sacred calls of his country.

These manly sentiments in private life make the good citizen; in public life, the patriot and the hero. I do not say that when brought to the test I shall be invincible. I pray God I may never be brought to the melancholy trial, but if ever I should, it will be then known how far I can reduce to practice principles which I know to be founded in truth. In the meantime I will proceed to the subject of this writ.

Your Honors will find in the old books concerning the office of a justice of the peace precedents of general warrants to search suspected houses. But in more modern books you will find only special warrants to search such and such houses, specially named, in which the complainant has before sworn that he suspects his goods are concealed, and will find it adjudged that special warrants only are legal. In the same manner, I rely on it that the writ prayed for in this petition, being general, is illegal. It is a power that places the liberty of every man in the hands of every petty officer. I say I admit that special writs of assistance, to search special places, may be granted to certain persons on oath; but I deny that the writ now prayed for can be granted, for I beg leave to make some observations on the writ itself before I proceed to other acts of Parliament.

In the first place, the writ in universal, being directed "to all and singular justices, sheriffs, constables, and all other officers and subjects"; so that, in short, it is directed to every subject in the King's dominions. Everyone, with this writ, may be a tyrant; if this commission be legal, a tyrant in a legal manner, also, may control, imprison, or murder anyone within the Realm. In the next place, it is perpetual, there is no return. A man is accountable to no person for his doings. Every man may reign secure in his petty tyranny and spread terror and desolation around him, until the trump of the archangel shall excite different emotions in his soul. In the third place, a person with this writ, in the daytime, may enter all houses or shops, at will, and command all to assist him. Fourth, by this writ, not only deputies but even their menial servants are allowed to lord it over us. What is this but to have the curse of Canaan with a witness on us; to be the servant of servants, the most despicable of God's creation?

Now, one of the most essential branches of English liberty is the freedom of one's house. A man's house is his castle; and while he is quiet, he is as well guarded as a prince in his castle. This writ, if it should be declared legal, would totally annihilate this privilege. Customhouse officers may enter our houses when they please; we are commanded to permit their entry. Their menial servants may enter, may break locks, bars, and everything in their way; and whether they break through malice or revenge, no man, no court can inquire. Bare suspicion without oath is sufficient.

This wanton exercise of this power is not chimerical suggestion of a heated brain. I will mention some facts. Mr.

Pew had one of these writs, and when Mr. Ware succeeded him, he endorsed this writ over to Mr. Ware, so that these writs are negotiable from one officer to another; and so Your Honors have no opportunity of judging the persons to whom this vast power is delegated. Another instance is this: Mr. Justice Walley had called this same Mr. Ware before him, by a constable, to answer for a breach of the Sabbath-Day acts, or that of profane swearing. As soon as he had finished, Mr. Ware asked him if he had done. He replied, "Yes." "Well, then," said Mr. Ware, "I will show you a little of my power. I command you to permit me to search your house for uncustomed goods"; and went on to search the house from the garret to the cellar; and then served the constable in the same manner!

But to show another absurdity in this writ, if it should be established, I insist upon it every person—by the 14th Charles II—has this power as well as the customhouse officers. The words are, "It shall be lawful for any person or persons authorized. . . ." What a scene does this open! Every man prompted by revenge, ill humor, or wantonness to inspect the inside of his neighbor's house, may get a writ of assistance. Others will ask it from self-defense; one arbitrary exertion will provoke another, until society be involved in tumult and in blood. [The rest of the speech exists only in a summary by John Adams.]

A dissertation on the rights of man in a state of nature. He asserted that every man, merely natural, was an independent sovereign, subject to no law but the law written on his heart and revealed to him by his Maker, in the constitution of his nature and the inspiration of his understanding and his conscience. His right to his life, his liberty, no created being could rightfully contest. Nor was his right to his property less incontestable. The club that he had snapped from a tree, for a staff or for defense, was his own. His bow and arrow were his own; if by a pebble he had killed a partridge or a squirrel, it was his own. No creature, man or beast, had a right to take it from him. If he had taken an eel or a smelt or a sculpin, it was his property. In short, he sported upon this topic with so much wit and humor, and at the same time with so much indisputable truth and reason, that he was not less entertaining than instructive.

He asserted that these rights were inherent and inalienable. That they never could be surrendered or alienated but by idiots or madmen and all the acts of idiots and lunatics were void and not obligatory, by all the laws of God and man. Nor were the poor Negroes forgotten. Not a Quaker in Philadelphia or Mr. Jefferson in Virginia ever asserted the rights of Negroes in stronger terms. Young as I was and ignorant as I was, I shuddered at the doctrine he taught; and I have all my life shuddered, and still shudder, at the consequences that may be drawn from such premises. Shall we say that the rights of masters and servants clash and can be decided only by force? I adore the idea of gradual abolitions! but who shall decide how fast or how slowly these abolitions shall be made?

From individual independence he proceeded to association. If it was inconsistent with the dignity of human nature to say that men were gregarious animals, like wild geese, it surely could offend no delicacy to say they were social animals by nature, that there were natural sympathies, and, above all, the sweet attraction of the sexes, which must soon draw them together in little groups, and by degrees in larger congregations, for mutual assistance and defense And this must have happened before any formal covenant, by express words or signs, was concluded.

When general councils and deliberations commenced, the objects could be no other than the mutual defense and security of every individual for his life, his liberty, and his property. To suppose them to have surrendered these in any other way than by equal rules and general consent was to suppose them idiots or madmen whose acts were never binding. To suppose them surprised by fraud or compelled by force into any other compact, such fraud and such force could confer no obligation. Every man had a right to trample it underfoot whenever he pleased. In short, he asserted these rights to be derived only from nature and the Author of nature; that they were inherent, inalienable, and indefeasible by any laws, pacts, contracts, covenants, or stipulations which man could devise. These principles and these rights were wrought into the English constitution as fundamental laws. And under this head he went back to the old Saxon laws and to Magna Carta and the fifty confirmations of it in Parliament and the executions ordained against the violators of it and the national vengeance which had been taken on them from time to time, down to the Jameses and Charleses, and to the position of rights and the Bill of Rights and the revolution.

He asserted that the security of these rights to life, liberty, and property had been the object of all those struggles against arbitrary power, temporal and spiritual, civil and political, military and ecclesiastical, in every age. He asserted that our ancestors, as British subjects, and we their descendants, as British subjects, were entitled to all those rights by the British constitution as well as by the law of nature and our provincial character as much as any inhabitant of London or Bristol or any part of England, and were not to be cheated out of them by any phantom of "virtual representation" or any other fiction of law or politics or any monkish trick of deceit and hypocrisy.

He then examined the Acts of Trade, one by one, and demonstrated that, if they were considered as revenue laws, they destroyed all our security of property, liberty, and life every right of nature and the English constitution and the charter of the province. Here he considered the distinction between "external and internal taxes," at that time a popular and commonplace distinction. But he asserted that there was no such distinction in theory or upon any principle but "necessity." The necessity that the commerce of the Empire should be under one direction was obvious. The Americans had been so sensible of this necessity that they had connived at the distinction between external and internal taxes, and had submitted to the Acts of Trade as regulations of commerce but never as taxations or revenue laws. Nor had the British government till now ever dared to attempt to enforce them as taxations or revenue laws.

The Navigation Act he allowed to be binding upon us because we had consented to it by our own legislature. Here he gave a history of the Navigation Act of the first of Charles II, a plagiarism from Oliver Cromwell. In 1675, after repeated letters and orders from the King, Governor Leverett very candidly informs His Majesty that the law had not been executed because it was thought unconstitutional, Parliament not having authority over us.

Source:
James Otis, *The Annals of America*. Chicago: Encyclopaedia Britannica, 1926–87.

SUGGESTED READING

The Establishment of Colonies and Settlements; Settlers and Native Americans in the Colonies
Bernard Bailyn, *The Peopling of British North America*. New York: Knopf, 1986.
Ira Berlin, *Many Thousands Gone: The First Two Centuries of Slavery in America*. Cambridge, Mass.: Belknap Press of Harvard University, 2000.
Timothy H. Breen, *Puritans and Adventurers: Change and Persistence in Early America*. New York: Oxford University Press, 1980.

Colin G. Calloway, *New Worlds for All: Indians, Europeans, and the Remaking of America*. Baltimore, Md.: Johns Hopkins University Press, 1997.
Lois Green Carr et al., eds., *Colonial Chesapeake Society*. Chapel Hill, N.C.: University of North Carolina Press, 1988.
John Demos, *A Little Commonwealth: Family Life in Plymouth Colony*. New York: Oxford University Press, 1970.
———, *The Unredeemed Captive: A Family Story from Early America*. New York: Knopf, 1994.

David W. Galenson, *White Servitude in Colonial America.* New York: Cambridge University Press, 1981.

Gerald W. Mullen, *Flight and Rebellion: Slave Resistance in Eighteenth-Century Virginia.* New York: Oxford University Press, 1972.

Gary Nash, *Red, White, and Black: The Peoples of Early America.* Englewood Cliffs, N.J.: Prentice-Hall, 1974.

Marcus Rediker, *Between the Devil and the Deep Blue Sea: Merchant Seamen, Pirates, an the Anglo-American Maritime World, 1700–1750.* New York: Cambridge University Press, 1987.

Laurel T. Ulrich, *Good Wives: Image and Reality in the Lives of Women in Northern New England, 1650–1750.* New York: Knopf, 1982.

The Development of Political, Religious, and Social Institutions in the Colonies

Philip D. Curtin, *The Atlantic Slave Trade: A Census.* Madison, Wis.: University of Wisconsin Press, 1969.

Gregory Evans Dowd, *A Spirited Resistance: The North American Indian Struggle for Unity, 1745–1815.* Baltimore, Md.: Johns Hopkins University Press, 1992.

Jack P. Greene, *Pursuits of Happiness: The Social Development of Early Modern British Colonies and the Formation of American Culture.* Chapel Hill, N.C.: University of North Carolina Press, 1988.

Peter Charles Hoffer, *The Devil's Disciples: Makers of the Salem Witchcraft Trials.* Baltimore, Md.: Johns Hopkins University Press, 1996.

Ronald Hoffman and Peter J. Albert, eds., *Religion in a Revolutionary Age.* Charlottesville, Va.: University Press of Virginia, 1994.

David S. Lovejoy, *The Glorious Revolution in America.* New York: Harper & Row, 1972.

Edmund S. Morgan, *American Slavery, American Freedom.* New York: W.W. Norton, 1975.

Margaret Ellen Newell, *From Dependency to Independence: Economic Revolution in Colonial New England.* Ithaca, N.Y.: Cornell University Press, 1998.

Mary Beth Norton, *In the Devil's Snare: The Salem Witchcraft Crisis of 1692.* New York: Knopf, 2002.

Carl Ubbelohde, *The American Colonies and the British Empire, 1607–1763.* New York: Crowell, 1968.

ERA 3
Revolution and New Nation (1763–1820s)

This era holds major significance primarily as the time in which the United States was founded and its seminal documents created. We continually refer to our founders and their thoughts to determine how those documents should be interpreted today. Therefore, understanding this era is crucial both in its own right and for evaluating American law, politics, and society as they have evolved over the next centuries.

The first section features the documents that highlight the road to revolution: the British efforts to tax and otherwise rein in their unruly colonists and the colonists' response. In reviewing this section, we should remember that the colonial assemblies and groups like Sam Adams's Sons of Liberty were located on the more settled eastern seaboard. Frontier people did not always agree with them, and colonial assemblies often ignored their problems. Some frontier people, though, took to arms, such as the North Carolina Regulators.

More than a year before the 13 colonies declared their independence from Great Britain, the fighting began. It is at that point that the second section, on the American Revolution, begins. Among the documents are those expressing an initial reluctance to become independent and Thomas Paine's "Common Sense," which asserted that no alternative to independence is realistic. Once the Conti-

nental Congress declared independence, the documents feature issues related to war, including the alliance with France. The famous "Remember the Ladies" letter of Abigail Adams to her husband, John Adams, represents those who were left behind.

The final two sections, on the formation of the new government and the establishment of political parties begin, with the failed attempt to build the new nation from semiautonomous sovereign states held together by a weak executive and central government. The Articles of Confederation embodied that vision. Its greatest success may well have been the Northwest Ordinance, which provided the means for governing territories and eventually bringing them in as equal states. When problems of taxation and interstate commerce threatened the viability of the articles, the Constitutional Convention was held. It produced the U.S. Constitution, what may be the most successful governmental compact in world history, one copied by other new nations. Although a Bill of Rights had to be added in order to insure its passage and a civil war had to be fought in order to preserve it as the foundation of American government, the Constitution has endured with few amendments. The discussion of its provisions, represented here by the Federalist papers, resonates today as Americans relate modern problems and current values to the ideas of the founders. This section and the next also show attempts by the founders and early government to deal with issues such as slavery and the situation of Native Americans. The needs and potential rights of both blacks and Indians were sacrificed to the creation of a nation embracing all 13 colonies and the desires of its leaders. Nevertheless, the vision of "all men . . . created equal" has endured, despite the persistence of prejudice against men of color and all women.

The first congress and the first presidential administration fleshed out the Constitution in ways that also provide guidance for solving modern problems. Most significant for the executive are the policies that produced a strong central government, such as the cabinet, and the absorption of state debts. Under Chief Justice John Marshall, the Supreme Court also upheld a strong federal system, and this section features some of its most significant early decisions. The last section also recounts the development of political parties, something not anticipated in the Constitution.

Events Leading Up to the American Revolution

The Proclamation of 1763

Royal order issued by Britain's King George III on October 7, 1763, in an effort to placate the Native Americans in the American colonies after the French and Indian War (1756–63). It organized Britain's American holdings (those lands acquired in the peace with France and not administered by the 13 colonies) into four governments—for East and West Florida, Grenada, and Quebec—and established the lands west of the Appalachian Mountains as a vast Native American reservation barred to colonial white settlers (those already there were ordered to leave). Land titles secured from western Native Americans were revoked, and the profitable Native American fur trade was placed under royal license. The proclamation was strongly denounced by many colonists, who disregarded the newly established native borders. As a result, Britain failed to enforce its authority in the western areas, and Native-settler tensions continued into the American Revolution. It was overturned by the Treaty of Fort Stanwix between the British and the Iroquois in 1768, which opened Indian hunting grounds to white settlement. In 1784, also at Fort Stanwix, the United States and the New York Iroquois signed a new treaty confirming American rights to settle on this land. However, the Ohio Indians refused to endorse it. The following year, the Cherokee peoples and the commissioners of the United States signed a treaty at Hopewell, South Carolina, confirming Cherokee rights to most lands held in 1777. The treaty gave the United States sovereignty over the tribe and control of its trade. It was the first general treaty signed by the United States and established definite boundaries for Native American lands. Similar treaties with the Choctaw and Chickasaw peoples were signed at Hopewell the following year.

Whereas we have taken into our royal consideration the extensive and valuable acquisitions in America, secured to our Crown by the late definitive treaty of peace concluded at Paris the 10th day of February last; and being desirous that all our loving subjects, as well of our Kingdom as of our colonies in America, may avail themselves, with all convenient speed, of the great benefits and advantages which must accrue therefrom to their commerce, manufactures, and navigation; we have thought fit, with the advice of our Privy Council, to issue this our Royal Proclamation, hereby to publish and declare to all our loving subjects that we have, with the advice of our said Privy Council, granted our letters patent under our great seal of Great Britain, to erect within the countries and islands ceded and confirmed to us by the said treaty, four distinct and separate governments, styled and called by the names of Quebec, East Florida, West Florida, and Grenada. . . .

And to the end that the open and free fishery of our subjects may be extended to and carried on upon the coast of Labrador and the adjacent islands, we have thought fit . . . to put all that coast, from the river St. John's to Hudson's Straits, together with the islands of Anticosti and Madelaine, and all other smaller islands lying upon the said coast, under the care and inspection of our governor of Newfoundland.

We have also . . . thought fit to annex the islands of St. John and Cape Breton, or Isle Royale, with the lesser islands adjacent thereto, to our government of Nova Scotia.

We have also . . . annexed to our province of Georgia all the lands lying between the rivers Altamaha and St. Mary's. And . . . so soon as the state and circumstances of the said colonies will admit thereof, they shall, with the advice and consent of the members of our Council, summon and call general assemblies within the said governments respectively, in such manner and form as is used and directed in those colonies and provinces in America, which are under our immediate government. And we have also given power to the said governors, with the consent of our said councils and the representatives of the people, so to be summoned as aforesaid, to make, constitute, and ordain laws, statutes, and ordinances for the public peace, welfare, and good government of our said colonies, and of the people and inhabitants thereof, as near as may be agreeable to the laws of England, and under such regulations and restrictions as are used in other colonies.

And, in the meantime and until such assemblies can be called as aforesaid, all persons inhabiting in, or resorting to, our said colonies may confide in our royal protection for the enjoyment of the benefit of the laws of our Realm of England. . . .

We have also thought fit . . . to give unto the governors and councils of our said three new colonies upon the continent full power and authority to settle and agree with the inhabitants of our said new colonies, or to any other person who shall resort thereto, for such lands, tenements, and hereditaments as are now, or hereafter shall be, in our power to dispose of; and . . . to grant to any such person or persons upon such terms and under such moderate quitrents, services, and acknowledgments as have been appointed and settled in other colonies, and under such other conditions as shall appear to us to be necessary and expedient for the advantage of the grantees and the improvement and settlement of our said colonies.

And whereas we are desirous, upon all occasions, to testify our . . . approbation of the conduct and bravery of the officers and soldiers of our armies, and to reward the same, we do hereby command and empower our governors of our said three new colonies and other our governors of our several provinces on the continent of North America to grant, without fee or reward, to such reduced officers as have served in North America during the late war, and are actually residing there, and shall personally apply for the same . . . quantities of land subject, at the expiration of ten years, to the same quitrents as other lands are subject to in the province within which they are granted, as also subject to the same conditions of cultivation and improvement. . . .

And whereas it is just and reasonable and essential to our interest and the security of our colonies that the sev-

eral nations or tribes of Indians with whom we are connected, and who live under our protection, should not be molested or disturbed in the possession of such parts of our dominions and territories as, not having been ceded to or purchased by us, are reserved to them, or any of them, as their hunting grounds; we do therefore, with the advice of our Privy Council, declare it to be our royal will and pleasure that no governor or commander in chief, in any of our colonies of Quebec, East Florida, or West Florida, do presume, upon any pretense whatever, to grant warrants of survey or pass any patents for lands beyond the bounds of their respective governments, as described in their commissions; as also that no governor or commander in chief of our other colonies or plantations in America do presume for the present, and until our further pleasure be known, to grant warrants of survey or pass patents for any lands beyond the heads or sources of any of the rivers which fall into the Atlantic Ocean from the west or northwest; or upon any lands whatever which, not having been ceded to or purchased by us, as aforesaid, are reserved to the said Indians or any of them.

And we do further declare it to be our royal will and pleasure, for the present as aforesaid, to reserve under our sovereignty, protection, and dominion, for the use of the said Indians, all the land and territories not included within the limits of our said three new governments, or within the limits of the territory granted to the Hudson's Bay Company; as also all the land and territories lying to the westward of the sources of the rivers which fall into the seas from the west northwest as aforesaid. And we do hereby strictly forbid, on pain of our displeasure, all our loving subjects from making any purchases or settlements whatever, or taking possession of any of the lands above reserved, without our special leave and license for that purpose first obtained.

And we do further strictly enjoin and require all persons whatever who have either willfully or inadvertently seated themselves upon any lands within the countries above described, or upon any other lands which, not having been ceded to or purchased by us, are still reserved to the said Indians as aforesaid, forthwith to remove themselves from such settlements.

And whereas great frauds and abuses have been committed in the purchasing lands of the Indians, to the great prejudice of our interests and to the great dissatisfaction of the said Indians; in order, therefore, to prevent such irregularities for the future, and to the end that the Indians may be convinced of our justice and determined resolution to remove all reasonable cause of discontent, we do, with the advice of our Privy Council, strictly enjoin and require that no private person do presume to make any purchase from the said Indians of any lands reserved to the said Indians within those parts of our colonies where we have thought proper to allow settlement; but that if at any time any of the said Indians should be inclined to dispose of the said lands, the same shall be purchased only for us, in our name, at some public meeting or assembly of the said Indians, to be held for that purpose by the governor or commander in chief of our colony, respectively, within which they shall lie. And in case they shall lie within the limits of any proprietary government, they shall be purchased only for the use and in the name of such proprietaries, conformable to such directions and instructions as we or they shall think proper to give for that purpose.

And we do, by the advice of our Privy Council, declare and enjoin that the trade with the said Indians shall be free and open to all out subjects whatever, provided that every person who may incline to trade with the said Indians do take out a license for carrying on such trade, from the governor or commander in chief of any of our colonies, respectively, where such person shall reside, and also give security to observe such regulations as we shall at any time think fit, by ourselves or commissaries to be appointed for this purpose, to direct and appoint for the benefit of the said trade. And we do hereby authorize, enjoin, and require the governors and commanders in chief of all our colonies, respectively, as well those under our immediate government as those under the government and direction of proprietaries, to grant such licenses without fee or reward, taking special care to insert therein a condition that such license shall be void and the security forfeited in case the person to whom the same is granted shall refuse or neglect to observe such regulations as we shall think proper to prescribe as aforesaid.

Source:
James Otis. *The Annuals of America,* vol. 2, 1755–83. Chicago: Encyclopaedia Britannica, 1926–87, pp. 84–86.

Stamp Act, 1765

Act passed by the British Parliament to go into effect on November 1, 1765, in order to raise revenue to pay the costs of governing and protecting the American colonies. A number of other acts passed by Parliament after the French and Indian War (1756–1763) had angered the colonists but were not considered abrogations of the rights of Englishmen. These include the Proclamation of 1763 and the British Currency Act of 1764. The latter prohibited the American colonies from issuing paper money. At the time, British traders (especially in Virginia) complained about being paid in depreciated American paper currency. The act also banned the use of colonial currency for payment of imported British goods. It resulted in a severe money shortage.

The Stamp Act, passed strictly to raise revenue, however, highlighted the British belief in their power to tax the colonies without providing them with governmental representation. Supported by George Grenville, Britain's chancellor of the exchequer (treasury department), it required stamps to be placed on all legal and commercial documents (licenses, liquor permits, newspapers, pamphlets, almanacs, advertisements, and so on) and various articles (such as dice, and playing cards). In October 1765 delegates from nine colonies met in New York City for the Stamp Act Congress, declaring in the Declaration of Rights and Grievances that the British Parliament did not have the power to impose taxes on the Americans without approval from the colonial legislatures. When the Stamp Act went into effect, not only did the colonists refuse to buy and use the stamps, but, in several colonies, they burned the ships that carried them, harassed the stamp distributors, and rioted.

An Act
For granting and applying certain Stamp Duties, and other Duties, in the British Colonies and Plantations in America, towards further defraying the Expenses of defending, protecting and securing the same; and for amending such Parts of the several Acts of Parliament relating to the Trade and Revenues of the said Colonies and Plantations, as direct the Manner of determining and recovering the Penalties and Forfeitures therein mentioned.

Whereas by an Act made in the last Session of Parliament, several Duties were granted, continued, and appropriated, towards defraying the Expenses of defending protecting, and securing, the *British* Colonies and Plantations in *America:* And whereas it is just and necessary, that Provision be made for raising a further Revenue within Your Majesty's Dominions in *America,* towards defraying the said Expenses: We, Your Majesty's most dutiful and loyal Subjects, the Commons of *Great Britain* in Parliament assembled, have therefore resolved to give and grant unto Your Majesty the several Rates and Duties herein after mentioned; and do most humbly beseech Your Majesty that it may be enacted, and be it enacted by the King's most Excellent Majesty, by and with the Advice and Consent of the Lords Spiritual and Temporal, and Commons, in this Parliament assembled, and by the Authority of the same, That from and after the First Day of *November,* one thousand seven hundred and sixty-five, there shall be raised, levied, collected, and paid unto his Majesty, his Heirs, and Successors, throughout the Colonies and Plantations in *America* which now are, or hereafter may be, under the Dominion of his Majesty, his Heirs, and Successors.

For every Skin or Piece of Vellum or Parchment, or Sheet or Piece of Paper, on which shall be ingrossed, written, or printed, any Declaration, Plea, Replication, Rejoinder, Demurrer, or other Pleading, or any Copy thereof, in any Court of Law within the *British* Colonies and Plantations in *America,* a Stamp Duty of three Pence.

For every Skin or Piece of Vellum or Parchment, or Sheet or Piece of Paper, on which shall be ingrossed, written, or printed, any Special Bail and Appearance upon such Bail in any such Court, a Stamp Duty of two Shillings.

For every Skin or Piece of Vellum or Parchment, or Sheet or Piece of Paper, on which shall be ingrossed, written, or printed, any Petition, Bill, Answer, Claim, Plea, Replication, Rejoinder, Demurrer, or other Pleading in any Court of Chancery or Equity within the said Colonies and Plantations, a Stamp Duty of one Shilling and Six Pence.

For every Skin or Piece of Vellum or Parchment, or Sheet or Piece of Paper, on which shall be ingrossed, written, or printed, any Copy of any Petition, Bill, Answer, Claim, Plea, Replication, Rejoinder, Demurrer, or other Pleading in any such Court, a Stamp Duty of three Pence.

For every Skin or Piece of Vellum or Parchment, or Sheet or Piece of Paper, on which shall be ingrossed, written, or printed, any Monition, Libel, Answer, Allegation, Inventory, or Renunciation in Ecclesiastical Matters in any Court of Probate, Court of the Ordinary, or other Court exercising Ecclesiastical Jurisdiction within the said Colonies and Plantations, a Stamp Duty of one Shilling.

For every Skin or Piece of Vellum or Parchment, or Sheet or Piece of Paper, on which shall be ingrossed, written, or printed, any Copy of any Will (other than the Probate thereof) Monition, Libel, Answer, Allegation, Inventory, or Renunciation in Ecclesiastical Matters, in any such Court, a Stamp Duty of six Pence.

For every Skin or Piece of Vellum or Parchment, or Sheet or Piece of Paper, on which shall be ingrossed, written, or printed, any Donation, Presentation, Collation, or Institution of or to any Benefice, or any Writ or Instrument for the like Purpose, or any Register, Entry, Testimonial, or Certificate of any Degree taken in any University, Academy, College, or Seminary of Learning, within the said Colonies and Plantations, a Stamp Duty of two Pounds.

For every Skin or Piece of Vellum or Parchment, or Sheet or Piece of Paper, on which shall be ingrossed, written, or printed, any Monition, Libel, Claim, Answer, Allegation, Information, Letter of Request, Execution, Renunciation, Inventory, or other Pleading in any Admiralty Court within the said Colonies and Plantations, a Stamp Duty of one Shilling.

For every Skin or Piece of Vellum or Parchment, or Sheet or Piece of Paper, on which any Copy of any such Monition, Libel, Claim, Answer, Allegation, Information, Letter of Request, Execution, Renunciation, Inventory, or

other Pleading, shall be ingrossed, written, or printed, a Stamp Duty of six Pence.

For every Skin or Piece of Vellum or Parchment, or Sheet or Piece of Paper, on which shall be ingrossed, written, or printed, any Appeal, Writ of Error, Writ of Dower, *Ad quod damnum, Certiorari,* Statute Merchant, Statute Staple, Attestation, or Certificate, by any Officer, or Exemplification of any Record or Proceeding in any Court whatsoever within the Colonies and Plantations (except Appeals, Writs of Error, *Certiorari,* Attestations, Certificates, and Exemplification's, for or relating to the Removal of any Proceedings from before a single Justice of the Peace) a Stamp Duty of ten Shillings.

For every Skin or Piece of Vellum or Parchment, or Sheet or Piece of Paper, on which shall be ingrossed, written, or printed, any Writ of Covenant for levying of Fines, Writ of Entry for suffering a Common Recovery, or Attachment issuing out of, or returnable into, any Court within the said Colonies and Plantations, a Stamp Duty of five Shillings.

For every Skin or Piece of Vellum or Parchment, or Sheet or Piece of Paper, on which shall be ingrossed, written, or printed, any Judgment, Decree, Sentence, or Dismission, or any Record of *Nisi Prius* or *Postea,* in any Court within the said Colonies and Plantations, a Stamp Duty of four Shillings.

For every Skin or Piece of Vellum or Parchment, or Sheet or Piece of Paper, on which shall be ingrossed, written, or printed, any Affidavit, Common Bail or Appearance, Interrogatory Deposition, Rule, Order, or Warrant of any Court, or any *Dedimus Potestatem, Capias, Subpoena,* Summons, Compulsory Citation, Commission, Recognizance, or any other Writ, Process, or Mandate, issuing out of, or returnable into, any Court, or any Office belonging thereto, or any other Proceeding therein whatsoever, or any Copy thereof, or of any Record not herein before charged, within the said Colonies and Plantations (except Warrants relating to Criminal Matters, and Proceedings thereon or relating thereto) a Stamp Duty of one Shilling.

For every Skin or Piece of Vellum or Parchment, or Sheet or Piece of Paper, on which shall be ingrossed, written, or printed, any License, Appointment, or Admission of any Counselor, Solicitor, Attorney, Advocate, or Proctor, to practice in any Court, or of any Notary within the said Colonies and Plantations, a Stamp Duty of ten Pounds.

For every Skin or Piece of Vellum or Parchment, or Sheet or Piece of Paper, on which shall be ingrossed, written, or printed, any Note or Bill, which shall be signed for any Kind of Goods, Wares, or Merchandise, to be exported from, or any Cocket of Clearance granted within the said Colonies and Plantations, a Stamp Duty of four Pence.

For every Skin or Piece of Vellum or Parchment, or Sheet or Piece of Paper, on which shall be ingrossed, written, or printed, Letters of Mart, or Commissions for Private Ships of War, within the said Colonies and Plantations, a Stamp Duty of twenty Shillings.

For every Skin or Piece of Vellum or Parchment, or Sheet or Piece of Paper, on which shall be ingrossed, written, or printed, any Grant, Appointment, or Admission of or to any public beneficial Office or Employment, for the Space of one Year, or any lesser Time, of or above the Value of twenty Pounds *per Annum* Sterling Money, in Salary, Fees, and Perquisites, within the said Colonies and Plantations (except Commissions and Appointments of Officers of the Army, Navy, Ordinance, or Militia, of Judges, and of Justices of the Peace) a Stamp Duty of ten Shillings.

For every Skin or Piece of Vellum or Parchment, or Sheet or Piece of Paper, on which any Grant of any Liberty, Privilege, or Franchise, under the Seal of any of the said colonies or Plantations, or under the Seal or Sign Manual of any Governor, Proprietor, or public Officer alone, or in Conjunction with any other Person or Persons, or with any Council, or any Council and Assembly, or any Exemplification of the same, shall be ingrossed, written, or printed, within the said Colonies and Plantations, a Stamp Duty of six Pounds.

For every Skin or Piece of Vellum or Parchment, or Sheet or Piece of Paper, on which shall be ingrossed, written, or printed, any License for Retailing of Spirituous Liquors, to be granted to any Person who shall take out the same, within the said Colonies and Plantations, a Stamp Duty of twenty Shillings.

For every Skin or Piece of Vellum or Parchment, or Sheet or Piece of Paper, on which shall be ingrossed, written, or printed, any License for Retailing of Wine, to be granted to any Person who shall not take out a License for Retailing of Spirituous Liquors, within the said Colonies and Plantations, a Stamp Duty of four Pounds.

For every Skin or Piece of Vellum or Parchment, or Sheet or Piece of Paper, on which shall be ingrossed, written, or printed, any License for Retailing of Wine, to be granted to any Person who shall take out a License for Retailing of Spirituous Liquors, within the said Colonies and Plantations, a Stamp Duty of three Pounds.

For every Skin or Piece of Vellum or Parchment, or Sheet or Piece of Paper, on which shall be ingrossed, written, or printed, any Probate of a Will, Letters of Administration, or of Guardianship for any Estate above the Value of Twenty Pounds Sterling Money, within the *British* Colonies and Plantations upon the Continent of *America,* the Islands belonging thereto, and the *Bermuda* and *Bahama* Islands, a Stamp Duty of five Shillings.

For every Skin or Piece of Vellum or Parchment, or Sheet or Piece of Paper, on which shall be ingrossed, written, or printed, any such Probate, Letters of Administration, or of Guardianship, within all other Parts of the *British* Dominions in *America,* a Stamp Duty of ten Shillings.

For every Skin or Piece of Vellum or Parchment, or Sheet or Piece of Paper, on which shall be ingrossed, written, or printed, any Bond for securing the Payment of any Sum of Money, not exceeding the Sum of ten Pounds Sterling Money, within the *British* Colonies and Plantations upon the Continent of *America,* the Islands belonging thereto, and the *Bermuda* and *Bahama* Islands, a Stamp Duty of six Pence.

For every Skin or Piece of Vellum or Parchment, or Sheet or Piece of Paper, on which shall be ingrossed, written, or printed, any Bond for securing the Payment of any Sum of Money above ten Pounds, and not exceeding the Sum of twenty Pounds Sterling Money, within such Colonies, Plantations, and Islands, a Stamp Duty of one Shilling.

For every Skin or Piece of Vellum or Parchment, or Sheet or Piece of Paper, on which shall be ingrossed, written, or printed, any Bond for securing the Payment of any Sum of Money above twenty Pounds, and not exceeding forty Pounds Sterling Money, within such Colonies, Plantations, and Islands, a Stamp Duty of one Shilling and six Pence.

For every Skin or Piece of Vellum or Parchment, or Sheet of Piece of Paper, on which shall be ingrossed, written, or printed, any Order or Warrant for surveying or setting out any Quantity of Land, not exceeding one hundred Acres, issued by any Governor, Proprietor, or any Public officer alone, or in Conjunction with any other Person or Persons, or with any Council, or any Council and Assembly, within the *British* Colonies and Plantations in *America,* a Stamp Duty of six Pence.

For every Skin or Piece of Vellum or Parchment, or Sheet or Piece of Paper, on which shall be ingrossed, written, or printed, any such Order or Warrant for surveying or setting out any Quantity of Land above one hundred, and not exceeding two hundred Acres, within the said Colonies and Plantations, a Stamp Duty of one Shilling.

For every Skin or Piece of Vellum or Parchment, or Sheet or Piece of Paper, on which shall be ingrossed, written, or printed, any such Order or Warrant for surveying or setting out any Quantity of Land above two hundred, and not exceeding three hundred and twenty Acres, and in proportion for every such Order or Warrant for surveying or setting out every other three hundred and twenty Acres, within the said Colonies and Plantations, a Stamp Duty of one Shilling and six Pence.

For every Skin or Piece of Vellum or Parchment, or Sheet or Piece of Paper, on which shall be ingrossed, written, or printed, any Original Grant, or any Deed, Mesne Conveyance, or other Instrument whatsoever, by which any Quantity of Land not exceeding one hundred Acres shall be granted, conveyed, or assigned, within the *British* Colonies and Plantations upon the Continent of *America* , the Island belonging thereto, and the *Bermuda* and *Bahama* Islands (except Leases for any Term not exceeding the Term of twenty-one Years) a Stamp Duty of one Shilling and six Pence.

For every Skin or Piece of Vellum or Parchment, or Sheet or Piece of Paper, on which shall be ingrossed, written, or printed any such Original Grant, or any such, Deed, Mesne Conveyance, or other Instrument whatsoever by which Quantity of Land above one hundred, and not exceeding two hundred Acres, shall be granted, conveyed, or assigned, within such Colonies, Plantations, and Islands, a Stamp Duty of two Shillings.

For every Skin or Piece of Vellum or Parchment, or sheet or Piece of Paper, on which shall be ingrossed, written, or printed, any such Original Grant, or any such Deed, Mesne Conveyance, or other Instrument whatsoever, by which any Quantity of Land above two hundred, and not exceeding three hundred and twenty Acres, shall be granted, conveyed, or assigned, and in proportion for every such Grant, Deed, Mesne Conveyance, or other Instrument, granting, conveying, or assigning, every other three hundred and twenty Acres, within such Colonies, Plantations, and Islands, a Stamp Duty of two Shillings and six Pence.

For every Skin or Piece of Vellum or Parchment, or Sheet or Piece of Paper, on which shall be ingrossed, written, or printed, any such Original Grant, or any such Deed, Mesne Conveyance, or other Instrument whatsoever, by which Quantity of Land not exceeding one hundred Acres shall be granted, conveyed, or assigned, within all other Parts of the *British* Dominions in *America*, a Stamp Duty of three Shillings.

For every Skin or Piece of Vellum or Parchment, or Sheet or Piece of Paper, on which shall be ingrossed, written, or printed, any such Original Grant, or any such Deed, Mesne Conveyance, or other Instrument whatsoever, by which any Quantity of Land above one hundred, and not exceeding two hundred Acres, shall be granted, conveyed, or assigned, within the same Parts of the said Dominions, a Stamp Duty of four Shillings.

For every Skin or Piece of Vellum or Parchment, or Sheet or Piece of Paper, on which shall be ingrossed, written, or printed, any such Original Grant, or any such Deed, Mesne Conveyance, or other Instrument whatsoever, whereby any Quantity of Land above two hundred, and not exceeding three hundred and twenty Acres, shall be granted, conveyed, or assigned, and in proportion for every such Grant, Deed, Mesne Conveyance, or other Instru-

ment, granting, conveying, or assigning, every other three hundred and twenty Acres, within the same Parts of the said Dominions, a Stamp Duty of five Shillings.

For every Skin or Piece of Vellum or Parchment, or Sheet or Piece of Paper, on which shall be ingrossed, written, or printed, any Grant, Appointment, or Admission, of or to any public beneficial Office or Employment, not herein before charged, above the Value of twenty Pounds *per Annum* Sterling Money in Salary, Fees, and Perquisites, or any Exemplification of the same, within the *British* Colonies and Plantations upon the Continent of *America*, the Islands belonging thereto, and the *Bermuda* and *Bahama* Islands (except Commissions of Officers of the Army, Navy, Ordnance, or Militia, and of Justices of the Peace) a Stamp Duty of four Pounds.

For every Skin or Piece of Vellum or Parchment, or Sheet or a Piece of Paper, on which shall be ingrossed, written, or printed, any such Grant, Appointment, or Admission, of or to any such public beneficial Office or Employment, or any Exemplification of the same, within all other Parts of the *British* Dominions in *America,* a Stamp Duty of six Pounds.

For every Skin or Piece of Vellum or Parchment, or sheet or Piece of Paper, on which shall be ingrossed, written, or printed, any Indenture, Leafe, Conveyance, Contract, Stipulation, Bill of Sale, Charter Party, Protest, Articles of Apprenticeship, or Covenant (except for the Hire of Servant not Apprentices, and also except such other Matters as are herein charged) within the *British* Colonies and Plantations in *America,* a Stamp Duty of two Shillings and six Pence.

For every Skin or Piece of Vellum or Parchment, or Sheet or Piece of Paper, on which any Warrant or Order for auditing any Public Accounts, beneficial Warrant, Order, Grant, or Certificate, under any Public Seal, or under the Seal or Sign Manual of any Governor, Proprietor, or public Officer alone, or in Conjunction with any other Person or Persons, or with any Council, or any Council and Assembly, not herein before charged, or any Passport or Let-pass, Surrender of Office, or Policy of Assurance, shall be ingrossed, written, or printed, within the said Colonies and Plantations (except Warrants or Orders for the Service of the Navy, Army, Ordnance, or Militia, and Grants of Offices under Twenty Pounds *per Annum* in Salary, Fees, and Perquisites) a Stamp Duty of five Shillings.

For every Skin or Piece of Vellum or Parchment, or Sheet or Piece of Paper, on which shall be ingrossed, written, or printed, any Notarial Act, Bond, Deed, Letter of Attorney, Procuration, Mortgage, Releafe, or other Obligatory Instrument, not herein before charged, within the said Colonies and Plantations, a Stamp Duty of two Shillings and three Pence.

For every Skin or Piece of Vellum or Parchment, or Sheet or Piece, on which shall be ingrossed, written, or printed, any Register, Entry, or Enrollment of any Grant, Deed, or other Instrument whatsoever herein before charged, within the said Colonies and Plantations, a Stamp Duty of three Pence.

For every Skin or Piece of Vellum or Parchment, or Sheet or Piece of Paper, on which shall be ingrossed, written, or printed, any Register, Entry, or Enrollment of any Grant, Deed, or other Instrument whatsoever not herein before charged, within the said Colonies and Plantations, a Stamp Duty of two Shillings.

And for and upon any Pack of Playing Cards, and all Dice, which shall be fold or used within the said Colonies and Plantations, the several Stamp Duties following (that is to say)

For every Pack of such Cards, the Sum of one Shilling.

And for every Pair of such Dice, the Sum of ten Shillings.

And for and upon every Paper commonly called 2 *Pamphlet,* and upon every News Paper, containing public News, Intelligence, or Occurrences, which shall be printed, dispersed, and made public, within any of the said Colonies and Plantations, and for and upon such Advertisements as are herein after mentioned, the respective Duties following (that is to say)

For every such Pamphlet and Paper contained in half a Sheet, or any lesser Piece of Paper, which shall be so printed, a Stamp Duty of one Halfpenny, for every printed Copy thereof.

For every such Pamphlet and Paper (being larger than Half a Sheet, and not exceeding one whole Sheet) which shall be so printed, a Stamp Duty of one Penny, for every printed Copy thereof.

For every Pamphlet and Paper being larger than one whole Sheet, and not exceeding six Sheets in Octavo, or in a lesser Page, or not exceeding twelve Sheets in Quarto, or twenty Sheets in Folio, which shall be so printed, a Duty after the Rate of one Shilling for every Sheet of any Kind of Paper which shall be contained in one printed Copy thereof.

For every Advertisement to be contained in any Gazette, News Paper, or other Paper, or any Pamphlet which shall be so printed, a Duty of two Shillings.

For every Almanac or Calendar for any one Particular Year, or for any Time less than a Year, which shall be written or printed on one Side only of any one Sheet, Skin, or Piece of Paper, Parchment, or Vellum, within the said Colonies or Plantations, a Stamp Duty of two Pence.

For every other Almanac or Calendar for any one particular Year, which shall be written or printed within the said Colonies and Plantations, a Stamp Duty of four Pence.

And for every Almanac or Calendar written or printed within the said Colonies and Plantations, to serve for several Years, Duties to the same Amount respectively shall be paid for every such Year.

For every Skin or Piece of Vellum or Parchment, or Sheet or Piece of Paper, on which any Instrument, Proceeding, or other Matter or Thing aforesaid, shall be ingrossed, written, or printed, within the said Colonies and Plantations, in any other than the *English* Language, a Stamp Duty of Double the Amount of the respective Duties before charged thereon.

And there shall be also paid in the said Colonies and Plantations, a Duty of six Pence for every twenty Shillings, in any Sum not exceeding fifty Pounds Sterling Money, which shall be given, paid, contracted, or agreed for, with, or in relation to any Clerk or Apprentice, which shall be put or placed to or with any Master or Mistress to learn any Profession, Trade, or Employment.

And also a Duty of one Shilling for every twenty Shillings, in any Sum exceeding fifty Pounds, which shall be given, paid, contracted, or agreed, for, with, or in relation to any such Clerk or Apprentice.

II. And be it further enacted by the Authority aforesaid, That every Deed, Instrument, Note, Memorandum, Letter, or other Minument or Writing, for or relating to the Payment of any Sum of Money, or for making any valuable Consideration for or upon the Loss of any Ship, Vessel, Goods, Wages, Money, Effects, or upon any Loss by Fire, or for any other Loss whatsoever, or for or upon any Life of Lives, shall be construed, deemed, and adjudged to be Policies of Assurance, within the Meaning of this Act: And if any such Deed, Instrument, Note, Memorandum, Letter, or other Minument or Writing, for insuring, or tending to insure, any more than one Ship or Vessel for more than any one Voyage, or any Goods, Wages, Money, Effects, or other Matter or Thing whatsoever, for more than one Voyage, or in more than one Ship or Vessel, or being the Property of, or belonging to, any more than one Person, or any particular Number of Persons in General Partnership, or any more than one Body Politic or Corporate, or for more than one Riscue; then, in every such Case, the Money insured thereon, or the valuable Consideration thereby agreed to be made, shall become the absolute Property of the Insured, and the Insurer shall also forfeit the Premium given for such Insurance, together with the Sum of one hundred Pounds.

III. And be it further enacted by the Authority aforesaid, That every Deed, Instrument, Note, Memorandum, Letter, or other Minument or Writing, between the Captain or Master or Owner of any Ship or Vessel, and any Merchant, Trader, or other Person, in respect to the Freight or Conveyance of any Money, Goods, Wares, Merchandises, or Effects, laden or to be laden on board of any such Ship or Vessel, shall be deemed and adjudged to be a Charter Party within the Meaning of this Act.

IV. And be it further enacted by the Authority aforesaid, That all Books and Pamphlets serving chiefly for the Purpose of an Almanac, by whatsoever Name or Names intituled or described, are and shall be charged with the Duty imposed by this Act on Almanacs, but not with any of the Duties charged by this Act on Pamphlets, or other printed Papers; any thing herein contained to the contrary notwithstanding.

V. Provided always, That this Act shall not extend to charge any Bills of Exchange, Accounts, Bills of Parcels, Bills of Fees, or any Bills or Notes not sealed for Payment of Money at Sight, or upon Demand, or at the End of certain Days of Payment.

VI. Provided, That nothing in this Act contained shall extend to charge the Probate of any Will, or Letters of Administration to the Effects of any Common Seaman or Soldier, who shall die in his Majesty's Service; a Certificate being produced from the Commanding Officer of the Ship or Vessel, or Troop or Company, in which such Seaman or Soldier served at the Time of his Death, and Oath, or if by a Quaker a Solemn Affirmation, made of the Truth thereof before the proper Judge or Officer by whom such Probate or Administration ought to be granted; which Oath or Affirmation such Judge or Officer is hereby authorized and required to administer, and for which no Fee or Reward shall be taken.

VII. Provided always, and be it enacted, That until after the Expiration of five Years from the Commencement of the said Duties, no Skin or Piece of Vellum or Parchment, or Sheet or Piece of Paper, on which any Instrument, Proceeding, or other Matter or Thing shall be ingrossed, written, or printed, within the Colonies of *Quebec* or *Granada*, in any other than the *English* Language, shall be liable to be charged with any higher Stamp Duty than if the same had been ingrossed, written, or printed in the *English* Language.

VIII. Provided always, That nothing in this Act contained shall extend to charge with any Duty, any Deed or other Instrument, which shall be made between any *Indian* Nation and the Governor, Proprietor of any Colony, Lieutenant Governor, or Commander in Chief, alone, or in Conjunction with any other Person or Persons, or with any Council, or any Council and Assembly of any of the said Colonies or Plantations, for or relating to the granting, surrendering, or conveying, any Lands belonging to such Nation, to, for, or on Behalf of his Majesty, or any such Proprietor, or to any Colony or Plantation.

IX. Provided always, That this Act shall not extend to charge any Proclamation, Forms of Prayer and Thanksgiving, or any printed Votes of any House of Assembly in any of the said Colonies and Plantations, with any of the said Duties on Pamphlets or News Papers; or to charge any Books commonly used in any of the Schools within the said Colonies and Plantations, or any Books containing only Matters of Devotion or Piety; or to charge any single Advertisement printed by itself, or the daily Accounts or Bill of Goods imported and exported, so as such Accounts or Bills do contain no other Matters than what have been usually comprised therein; any thing herein contained to the contrary notwithstanding.

X. Provided always, That nothing in this Act contained shall extend to charge with any of the said Duties, any Vellum, Parchment, or Paper, on which shall only be engrossed, written, or printed, any Certificate that shall be necessary to entitle any Person to receive a Bounty granted by Act of Parliament.

XI. And be it further enacted by the Authority aforesaid, That the said several Duties shall be under the Management of the Commissioners, for the time being, of the Duties charged on Stamped Vellum, Parchment, and Paper, in *Great Britain*: And the said Commissioners are hereby empowered and required to employ such Officers under them, for that Purpose, as they shall think proper; and to use such Stamps and Marks, to denote the Stamp Duties hereby charged, as they shall think fit; and to repair, renew, or alter the same, from time to time, as there shall be Occasion; and to do all other Acts, Matters, and Things, necessary to be done, for putting this Act in Execution with relation to the Duties hereby charged.

XII. And be it further enacted by the Authority aforesaid, That the Commissioners for managing the said Duties, for time being, shall and may appoint a fit Person for Persons to attend in every Court of Public Office within the said Colonies and Plantations, to take notice of the Vellum, Parchment, or Paper, upon which any of the Matters or Things hereby charged with a Duty shall be ingrossed, written, or printed, and of the Stamps or Marks thereupon, and of all other Matters and Things tending to secure the said Duties; and that the Judges in the several Courts, and all other Persons to whom it may appertain, shall, at the Request of any such Officer, make such Orders, and do such other Matters and Things, for the better securing of the said Duties, as shall be lawfully or reasonably desired in that Behalf: And every Commissioner and other Officer, before he proceeds to the Execution of any Part of this Act, shall take an Oath in the Words, or to the Effect following (that is to say)

I *A. B.* do swear, That I will faithfully execute the Trust reposed in me, pursuant to an Act of Parliament made in the Fifth Year of the Reign of his Majesty King *George* the Third, for granting certain Stamp Duties, and other Duties, in the *British* Colonies and Plantations in *America*, without Fraud or Concealment; and will from time to time true Account make of my Doing therein, and deliver the same to such Person or Persons as his Majesty, his Heirs, or Successors, shall appoint to receive such Account; and will take no Free, Reward, or Profit, for the Execution or Performance of the said Trust, or the Business relating thereto, from any Person or Persons, other than such as shall be allowed by his Majesty, his Heirs, and Successors, or by some other Person or Persons under him or them to that Purpose authorized.

Or if any such Officer shall be of the People commonly called *Quakers*, he shall take a Solemn Affirmation to the Effect of the said Oath; which Oath or Affirmation shall and may be administered to any such Commissioner or Commissioners by any two or more of the same Commissioners, whether they have or have not previously taken the same: and any of the said commissioners, or any Justice of the Peace, within the Kingdom of *Great Britain*, or any Governor, Lieutenant Governor, Judge, or other Magistrate, within he said Colonies or Plantations, shall and may administer such Oath or Affirmation to any subordinate Officer.

XIII. And be it further enacted by the Authority aforesaid, That the said Commissioners, and all Officers to be employed or entrusted by or under them as aforesaid, shall, from time to time, in and for the better Execution of their several Places and Trusts, observe such Rules, Methods, and Orders, as they respectively shall, from time to time, receive from the High Treasurer of *Great Britain*, or the Commissioners of the Treasury or any three or more such Commissioners of the Treasury, or any three or more of such Commissioners for the Time being; and that the said Commissioners for managing the Stamp Duties shall take especial Care, that the several Parts of the said Colonies and Plantations shall, from time to time, be sufficiently furnished with Vellum, Parchment, and Paper, stamped or marked with the said respective Duties.

XIV. And be it further enacted by the Authority aforesaid, That if any Person or Persons shall sign, engross, write, print, or sell, or expose to Sale, or cause to be signed, engrossed, written, printed, or sold, or exposed to Sale, in any of the said Colonies or Plantations, or in any other Part of his Majesty's Dominions, any Matter or Thing, for which the Vellum, Parchment, or Papers, is hereby charged to pay any Duty, before the same shall be marked or stamped with the Mark resembling the same; or shall sign, engross, write, print, or sell, or expose to Sale, or cause to be signed, ingrossed, written, printed, or sold, or exposed to Sale, any Matter or Thing upon any Vellum, Parchment, or Paper, that shall be marked or stamped for any lower Duty than the Duty by this Act made payable in respect thereof; every such Person so offending shall, for every such Offense, forfeit the Sum of ten Pounds.

XV. And be it further enacted by the Authority aforesaid, That no Matter or Thing whatsoever, by this Act charged with the Payment of a Duty, shall be pleaded or given in Evidence, or admitted in any Court within the said Colonies and Plantations, to be good, useful, or available, in Law or Equity, unless the same shall be marked or stamped, in pursuance of this Act, with the respective Duty hereby charged thereon, or with an higher Duty.

XVI. Provided nevertheless, and be it further enacted by the Authority aforesaid, That if any Vellum, Parchment, or Paper, containing any Deed, Instrument, or other Matter or Thing, shall not be duly stamped in pursuance of this Act, at the Time of the Signing, Sealing, or other Execution, or the Entry or Enrollment thereof, any Person interested therein, or any Person on his or her Behalf, upon producing the same to any one of the Chief Distributors of stamp Vellum, Parchment, and Paper, and paying to him the Sum of ten Pounds for every such Deed, Instrument, Matter, or Thing, and also Double the Amount of the Duties payable in respect thereof, shall be intitled to receive from such Distributor, Vellum, Parchment, or Paper, stamped pursuant to this Act, to the Amount of the Money so paid; a Certificate being first written upon every such Piece of Vellum, Parchment, or Paper, expressing the Name and Place of Abode of the Person by or on whose Behalf such Payment is made, the general Purport of such Deed, Instrument, Matter, or Thing, the Names of the Parties therein, and of the Witnesses (if any) thereto, and the Date thereof, which Certificate shall be signed by the said Distributor; and the Vellum, Parchment, or Paper, shall be then annexed to such Deed, Instrument, Matter, or Thing, by or in the Presence of such Distributor, who shall impress a Seal upon Wax, to be affixed on the Part where such Annexation shall be made, in the Presence of a Magistrate, who shall attest such Signature and Sealing; and the Deed, Instrument, or other Matter of Thing, from thenceforth shall and may, with the Vellum, Parchment, or Paper, so annexed, be admitted and allowed in Evidence in any Court whatsoever, and shall be as valid and effectual as if the proper Stamps had been impressed thereon at the Time of the Signing, Sealing, or other Execution, or Entry or Enrollment thereof: And the said Distributor shall, once in every six Months, or oftener if required by the Commissioners for managing the Stamp Duties, send to such Commissioners true Copies of all such Certificates, and an Account of the Number of Pieces of Vellum, Parchment, and Paper, so annexed, and of the respective Duties impressed upon every such Piece.

XVII. And be it further enacted by the Authority aforesaid, That if any Person shall forge, counterfeit, erase, or alter, any such Certificate, every such Person so offending shall be guilty of Felony, and shall suffer Death as in Cases of Felony, without the Benefit of Clergy.

XVIII. And be it further enacted by the Authority aforesaid, That if any Person or Persons shall, in the said Colonies or Plantations, or in any other Part of his Majesty's Dominions, counterfeit or forge any Seal, Stamp,

Mark, Type, Device, or Label, to resemble any Seal, Stamp, Mark, Type, Device, or Label, which shall be provided or made in pursuance of this Act; or shall counterfeit or resemble the Impression of the same upon any Vellum, Parchment, Paper, Cards, Dice, or other Matter or Thing, thereby to evade the Payment of any Duty hereby granted; or shall make, sign, print, utter, vend, or fell, any Vellum, Parchment, or Paper, or other Matter or Thing, with such counterfeit Mark or Impression thereon, knowing such Mark or Impression to be counterfeited; then every Person so offending shall be adjudged a Felon, and shall suffer Death as in Cases of Felony, without the Benefit of Clergy.

XIX. And it is hereby declared, That upon any Prosecution or Prosecutions for such Felony, the Dye, Tool, or other Instrument made use of in counterfeiting or forging any such Seal, Stamp, Mark, Type, Device, or Label, together with the Vellum, Parchment, Paper, Cards, Dice, or other Matter or Thing having such counterfeit Impression, shall, immediately after the Trial or Conviction of the Party or Parties accused, be broke, defaced, or destroyed, in open Court.

XX. And be it further enacted by the Authority aforesaid, That if any Register, Public Officer, Clerk, or other Person in any Court, Registry, or Office within any of the said Colonies or Plantations, shall, at any Time after the said First Day of *November*, one thousand seven hundred and sixty-five, enter, register, or enroll, any Matter or Thing hereby charged with a Stamp Duty, unless the same shall appear to be duly stamped; in every such Case such Register, Public Officer, Clerk, or other Person, shall, for every such Offense, forfeit the Sum of twenty Pounds.

XXI. And be it further enacted by the Authority aforesaid, That from and after the said First Day of *November*, one thousand seven hundred and sixty-five, if any Counselor, Clerk, Officer, Attorney, or other Person, to whom it shall appertain, or who shall be employed or entrusted, in the said Colonies or Plantations, to enter or file any Matter or Thing in respect whereof any Duty shall be payable by virtue of this Act, shall neglect to enter, file, or record the same, as by Law the same ought to be entered, filed, or recorded, within the Space of four Months after he shall have received any Money for or in respect of the same, or shall have promised or undertaken so to do; or shall neglect to enter, file, or record, any such Matter or Thing, before any subsequent, further, or other Proceeding, Matter, or Thing, in the same Suit, shall be had, entered, filed, or recorded; that then every such Counselor, Clerk, Officer, Attorney, or other Person so neglecting or offending, in each of the Cases aforesaid, shall forfeit the Sum of fifty Pounds for every such Offense.

XXII. And be it further enacted by the Authority aforesaid, That if any Person or Persons, at any Time after the said first Day of *November*, one thousand seven hundred and sixty-five, shall write, engross, or print, or cause to be written, ingrossed, or printed, in the said Colonies or Plantations, or any other Part of his said Majesty's Dominions, either the Whole or any Part of any Matter or Thing whatsoever in respect whereof any Duty is payable by this Act, upon any Part of any Piece of Vellum, Parchment, or Paper, whereon there shall have been before written any other Matter or Thing in respect whereof any Duty was payable by this Act; or shall fraudulently erase, or cause to be erased, the Name or Names of any Person or Persons, or any Sum, Date, or other Thing, ingrossed, written, or printed, in such Matter or Thing as aforesaid; or fraudulently cut, tear, or get off, any Mark or Stamp from any Piece of Vellum, Parchment, or Paper, or any Part thereof, with Intent to use such Stamp or Mark for any other Matter or Thing in respect whereof any Duty shall be payable by virtue of this Act; that then, and so often, and in every such Case, every Person so offending shall, for every such Offense, forfeit the Sum of fifty Pounds.

XXIII. And be it further enacted by the Authority aforesaid, That every Matter and Thing, in respect whereof any Duty shall be payable in pursuance of this Act, shall be ingrossed, written, or printed, in such Manner, that some Part thereof shall be either upon, or as near as conveniently may be to, the Stamps or Marks denoting the Duty; upon Pain that the Person who shall engross, write, or print, or cause to be ingrossed, written, or printed, any such Matter or Thing in any other Manner, shall, for every such Offense, forfeit the Sum of five Pounds.

XXIV. And be it further enacted by the Authority aforesaid, That every Officer of each Court, and every Justice of the Peace or other Person within the said Colonies and Plantations, who shall issue any Writ or Process upon which a Duty is by this Act payable, shall, at the Issuing thereof, set down upon such Writ or Process the Day and Year of his issuing the same, which shall be entered upon a Remembrance, or in a Book to be kept for that Purpose, setting forth the Abstract of such Writ or Process; upon Pain or forfeit the Sum of ten Pounds for every such Offense.

XXV. And, for the better collecting and securing the Duties hereby charged on Pamphlets containing more than one Sheet of Paper as aforesaid, be it further enacted by the Authority aforesaid, That from and after the said first Day of *November*, one thousand seven hundred and sixty-five, one printed Copy of every Pamphlet which shall be printed or published within any of the said Colonies or Plantations, shall, within the Space of fourteen Days after the printing thereof, be brought to the Chief Distributor in the Colony or Plantation where such Pamphlet shall be printed, and the Title thereof, with the Number of the

Sheets contained therein, and the Duty hereby charged thereon, shall be registered or entered in a Book to be there kept for that Purpose; which Duty shall be thereupon paid to the proper Officer or Officers appointed to receive the same, or his or their Deputy or Clerk, who shall thereupon forthwith give a Receipt for the same on such printed Copy, to denote the Payment of the Duty hereby charged on such Pamphlet; and if any such Pamphlet shall be printed or published, and the Duty hereby charged thereon shall not be duly paid, and the Title and Number of Sheets shall not be registered, and a Receipt for such Duty given on one Copy, where required so to be, within the Time herein before for that Purpose limited; that then the Author, Printer, and Publisher, and all other Persons concerned in or about the printing or publishing of such Pamphlet, shall, for every such Offense, forfeit the Sum of ten Pounds, and shall lose all Property therein, and in every other Copy thereof, so as any Person may freely print and publish the same, paying the Duty payable in respect thereof by virtue of this Act, without being liable to any Action, Prosecution, or Penalty for so doing.

XXVI. And it is hereby further enacted by the Authority aforesaid, That no Person whatsoever shall fell or expose to Sale any such Pamphlet, or any News Paper, without the true respective Name or Names, and Place or Places of Abode, of some known Person or Persons by or for whom the same was really and truly printed or published, shall be written or printed thereon; upon Pain that every Person offending therein shall, for every such Offense, forfeit the Sum of twenty Pounds.

XXVII. And be it further enacted by the Authority aforesaid, That no Officer appointed for distributing stamp Vellum, Parchment, or Paper, in the said Colonies or Plantations, shall sell or deliver any stamped Paper for printing any Pamphlet, or any public News, Intelligence, or Occurrences, to be contained in one Sheet, or any letter Piece of Paper, unless such Person shall give Security to the said Officer, for the Payment of the Duties for the Advertisements which shall be printed therein or thereupon.

XXVIII. And whereas it may be uncertain how many printed Copies of the said printed News Papers or Pamphlets, to be contained in one Sheet or in a letter Piece of Paper, may be sold; and to the Intent the Duties hereby granted thereupon may not be lessened by printing a less Number than may be sold, out of a Fear of a Loss thereby in printing more such Copies than will be sold; it is hereby provided, and be it further enacted by the Authority aforesaid, That the proper Officer or Officers appointed for managing the said Stamp Duties, shall and may cancel, or cause to be canceled, all the Stamps upon the Copies of any Impression of any News Paper or Pamphlet contained in one Sheet, or any lesser Piece of Paper, which shall

really and truly remain unsold, and of which no Profit or Advantage has been made; and upon Oath, or if by a Quaker, upon Solemn Affirmation, made before a Justice of the Peace, or other proper Magistrate, that all such Copies, containing the Stamps so tendered to be canceled, are really and truly remaining unsold, and that none of the said Copies have been fraudulently returned or rebought, or any Profit or Advantage made thereof; which Oath or Affirmation such Magistrate is hereby authorized to administer, and to examine upon Oath of Affirmation into all Circumstances relating to the selling of disposing of such printed Copies; shall and may deliver, or cause to be delivered, the like Number of other Sheets, Half Sheets, or less Pieces of Paper, properly stamped with the same respective Stamps, upon Payment made for such Paper, but no Duty shall be taken for the Stamps thereon; any thing herein contained to the contrary notwithstanding: And the said Commissioners for managing the Stamp Duties for the time being are hereby empowered, from time to time, to make such Rules and Orders for regulating the Methods, and limiting the Times, for such Canceling and Allowance as aforesaid, with respect to such News Papers and Pamphlets, as they shall, upon Experience and Consideration of the several Circumstances, find necessary or convenient, for the effectual securing the Duties thereon, and doing Justice to the Persons concerned in the printing and publishing thereof.

XXIX. Provided always, and be it further enacted by the Authority aforesaid, That any Officer or Officers employed by the said Commissioners for managing the Stamp Duties, shall and may deliver to any Person, by or for whom any Almanac or Almanacs shall have been printed, Paper marked or stamped according to the true Intent and Meaning hereof, for the Printing such Almanac or Almanacs, upon his or her giving sufficient Security to pay the Amount of the Duty hereby charged thereon within the Space of three Months after such Delivery; and that the said Officer or Officers, upon bringing to him or them any Number of the Copies of such Almanacs, within the Space of three Months from the said Delivery and Request to him or them in that Behalf made, shall cancel all the Stamps upon such Copies, and abate to every such Person so much of the Money due upon such Security as such canceled Stamps shall amount to.

XXX. Provided always, That where any Almanac shall contain more than one Sheet of Paper, it shall be sufficient to stamp only one of the Sheets or Pieces of Paper upon which such Almanac shall be printed, and to pay the Duty accordingly.

XXXI. And it is hereby further enacted by the Authority aforesaid, That from and after the said first Day of *November*, one thousand seven hundred and sixty-five, in case any Person or Persons, within any of the said Colonies or Plantations, shall fell, hawk, carry about, utter, or expose to Sale, any Almanac, or Calendar, or any News Paper, or any Book, Pamphlet, or Paper, deemed or construed to be, or serving the Purpose of, an Almanac or News Paper, within the Intention and Meaning of this Act, not being stamped or marked as by this Act is directed; every such Person shall, for every such Offense, forfeit the Sum of forty Shillings.

XXXII. And be it further enacted by the Authority aforesaid, That from and after the said first Day of *November*, one thousand seven hundred and sixty-five, the full Sum or Sums of Money, or other valuable Consideration received, or in any wife directly or indirectly given, paid, agreed, or contracted, for, with, or in relation to any Clerk or Apprentice, within any of the said Colonies or Plantations, shall be truly inserted, or written in Words at Length, in some Indenture or other Writing which shall contain the Covenants, Articles, Contracts, or Agreements, relating to the Service of such Clerk or Apprentice; and shall bear Date upon the Day of the signing, sealing, or other Execution of the same, upon Pain that every Master or Mistress to or with whom, or to whose Use, any Sum of Money, or other valuable Consideration whatsoever, shall be given, paid, secured, or contracted, for or in respect of any such Clerk or Apprentice, which shall not be truly and fully so inserted and specified in some such Indenture, or other Writing, shall, for every such Offense, forfeit double the Sum, or double the Amount of any other valuable Consideration so given, paid, agreed, secured, or contracted for; to be sued for and recovered at any Time, during the Term specified in the Indenture or Writing for the Service of such Clerk or Apprentice, or within one Year after the Determination thereof; and that all such Indentures, or other Writings, shall be brought, within the Space of three Months, to the proper Officer or Officers, appointed by the said Commissioners for collecting the said Duties within the respective Colony or Plantation; and the Duty hereby charged for the Sums, or other valuable Consideration inserted therein, shall be paid by the Master or Mistress of such Clerk or Apprentice to the said Officer or Officers, who shall give Receipts for such Duty on the Back of such Indentures or other Writings; and in case the Duty shall not be paid within the Time before limited, such Master or Mistress shall forfeit Double the Amount of such Duty.

XXXIII. And be it further enacted by the Authority aforesaid, That all Indentures or Writings within the said Colonies and Plantations, relating to the Service of Clerks or Apprentices, wherein shall not be truly or written the full Sum or Sums of Money, or other valuable Consideration, received, or in any wise directly or indirectly given, paid, agreed, secured, or contracted, for, with, or in relation to any such Clerk or Apprentice, and a Receipt given

for the same by the Officer or Officers aforesaid, or whereupon the Duties payable by this Act shall not be duly paid or lawfully tendered, according to the Tenor and true Meaning of this Act, within the Time herein for that Purpose limited, shall be void and not available in any Court or Place, or to any Purpose whatsoever.

XXXIV. And be it further enacted by the Authority aforesaid, That if any Master or Mistress of any Clerk or Apprentice shall neglect to pay the said Duty, within the Time herein before limited, and any such Clerk or Apprentice shall in that Case pay, or cause to be paid, to the Amount of Double the said Duty, either during the Term of such Clerkship or Apprenticeship, or within one Year after the Determination thereof, such Master or Mistress not having then paid the said Double Duty, although required by such Clerk or Apprentice so to do; then, and in such Case, it shall and may be lawful to and for any such Clerk or Apprentice, within three Months after such Payment of the said Double Duty, to demand of such Master or Mistress, or his or her Executors or Administrators, such Sum or Sums of Money, or valuable Consideration, as was or were paid to such Master or Mistress, for or in respect of such Clerkship or Apprenticeship; and in case such Sum or Sums of Money, or valuable Consideration, shall not be paid within three Months after such Demand thereof made, it shall and may be lawful to and for any such Clerk or Apprentice, or any other Person or Persons on his or her Behalf, to sue for and recover the same, in such Manner as any Penalty hereby inflicted may be sued for and recovered; and such Clerks or Apprentices shall, immediately after Payment of such Double Duty, be and are hereby discharged from their Clerkships or Apprenticeships, and from all Actions, Penalties, Forfeitures, and Damages, for not serving the Time for which they were respectively bound, contracted for, or agreed to serve, and shall have such and the same Benefit and Advantage of the Time they shall respectively have continued with and served such Master or Mistress, as they would have been entitled to in, case such Duty had been paid by such Master or Mistress within the Time herein before limited for that Purpose.

XXXV. And be it further enacted by the Authority aforesaid, That all printed Indentures, or Contracts for binding Clerks or Apprentices, after the said first Day of *November*, one thousand seven hundred and sixty-five, within the said Colonies and Plantations, shall have the following Notice or Memorandum printed under the same, or added thereto, *videlicet*,

The Indenture must bear Date the Day it is executed; and the Money, or other Thing, given or contracted for with the Clerk or Apprentice, must be inserted in Words at Length; and the Duty paid, and a Receipt given on the Back of the Indenture, by the Distributor of Stamps, or his

Substitute, within three Months after the Execution of such Indenture, under the Penalties inflicted by Law.

And if any Printer, Stationer, or other Person or Persons, within any of the said Colonies or Plantations, or any other Part of his Majesty's Dominions, shall sell, or cause to be sold, any such Indenture or Contract, without such Notice or Memorandum being printed under the same, or added thereto; then, and in every such Case, such Printer, Stationer, or other Person or Persons, shall, for every such Offense, forfeit the Sum of ten Pounds.

XXXVI. And, for the better securing the said Duty on Playing Cards and Dice, be it further enacted by the Authority aforesaid, That from and after the said first Day of *November,* one thousand seven hundred and sixty-five, no Playing Cards or Dice shall be sold, exposed to Sale, or used in Play, within the said Colonies or Plantations, unless the Paper and Thread enclosing, or which shall have enclosed, the same, shall be or shall have been respectively sealed and stamped, or marked, and unless one of the Cards of each Pack or Parcel of Cards, so sold, shall be also marked or stamped on the spotted or painted Side thereof with such Mark or Marks as shall have been provided in pursuance of this Act, upon Pain that every Person who shall sell, or expose to Sale, any such Cards or Dice which shall not have been so respectively sealed, marked, or stamped, as hereby is respectively required, shall forfeit for every Pack or Parcel of Cards, and every one of such Dice so sold or exposed to Sale, the Sum of ten Pounds.

XXXVII. And it is hereby enacted by the Authority aforesaid, That if any Person within the said Colonies or Plantations, or any other Part of his Majesty's Dominions, shall sell or buy any Cover or Label which has before been made use of for denoting the said Duty upon Cards, in order to be made use of for the enclosing any Pack or Parcel of Cards; every Person so offending shall, for every such Offense, forfeit twenty Pounds.

XXXVIII. Provided always, and be it enacted by the Authority aforesaid, That if either the Buyer of Seller of any such Cover or Label shall inform against the other Party concerned in buying of selling such Cover or Label, the Party so informing shall be admitted to give Evidence against the Party informed against, and shall be indemnified against the said Penalties.

XXXIX. And be it further enacted by the Authority aforesaid, That if any Person and Persons shall fraudulently enclose any Parcel or Pack of Playing Cards in any Outside Paper so sealed and stamped as aforesaid, the same having been made use of for the Purpose aforesaid; then, so often, and in every such Case, every Person so offending in any of the Particulars before-mentioned, shall, for every such Offense, forfeit the Sum of twenty Pounds.

XL. And be it further enacted by the Authority aforesaid, That from and after the said first Day of *November,*

one thousand seven hundred and sixty-five, every Clerk, Officer, and other Person employed or concerned in granting, making out, or delivering Licenses for retailing Spirituous Liquors or Wine within any of the said Colonies or Plantations, shall, and he is hereby required and directed, within two Months after delivering any such Licenses, to transmit to the Chief Distributor of stamped Vellum, Parchment, and Paper, a true and exact List or Account of the Number of Licenses so delivered, in which shall be inserted the Names of the Persons licensed, and the Places where they respectively reside; and if any such Clerk, Officer, or other Person, shall refuse or neglect to transmit any such List or Account to such Distributor, or shall transmit a false or untrue one, then, and in every such Case, such Clerk, Officer, or other Person, shall, for every such Offense, forfeit fifty Pounds.

XLI. And be it further enacted by the Authority aforesaid, That Licenses for selling or uttering by Retail Spirituous Liquors or Wine within any of the said Colonies and Plantations, shall be in Force and serve for no longer than One Year from the Date of each License respectively.

XLII. Provided nevertheless, and be it enacted by the Authority aforesaid, That if any Person licensed to sell Spirituous Liquors or Wine, shall die or remove from the House or Place wherein such Spirituous Liquors or Wine shall, by virtue of such License, be sold, it shall and may be lawful for the Executors, Administrators, or Assigns, of such Person so dying or removing, who shall be possessed of such House or Place, or for any Occupier of such House or Place, to sell Spirituous Liquors or Wine therein during the Residue of the Term for which such License shall have been granted, without any new License to be had or obtained in that Behalf; any thing to the contrary thereof in any wife notwithstanding.

XLIII. And it is hereby enacted by the Authority aforesaid, That if any Person or Persons shall fell or utter by Retail, that is so say, in any less Quantity than one Gallon at any one Time, any Kind of Wine, or any Liquor called or reputed Wine, or any Kind of Spirituous Liquors, in the said Colonies or Plantations, without taking out such License yearly and every Year, he, she, or they, so offending, shall, for every such Offense, forfeit the Sum of twenty Pounds.

XLIV. And be it further enacted by the Authority aforesaid, That every Person who shall retail Spirituous Liquors or Wine in any Prison or House of Correction, or any Workhouse appointed or to be appointed for the Reception of Poor Persons within any of the said Colonies or Plantations, shall be deemed a Retailer of Spirituous Liquors or Wine within this Act.

XLV. Provided always, and be it further enacted by the Authority aforesaid, That if at any Time after the said the first Day of *November,* one thousand seven hundred and sixty-five, there shall not be any Provision made for licensing the Retailers of Wine or Spirituous Liquors, within any of the said Colonies or Plantations; then, and in every such Cafe, and during such Time as no Provision shall be made, such Licenses shall and may be granted for the Space of one Year, and renewed from time to time by the Governor or Commander in Chief of every such respective Colony or Plantation.

XLVI. And it is hereby further enacted by the Authority aforesaid, That every Person who shall at any Time buy of any Chief Distributor within any of the said Colonies or Plantation, Vellum, Parchment, or Paper, the Duties whereof shall amount to five Pounds Sterling Money of *Great Britain,* or upward, shall be allowed after the Rate of four Pounds *per Centum,* upon the prompt Payment of the said Duties of such Chief Distributor.

XLVII. And be it further enacted by the Authority aforesaid, That all public Clerks or Officers within the said Colonies or Plantations, who shall from time to time have in their Custody any Public Books, or other Matters or Things hereby charged with a Stamp Duty, shall, at any seasonable Time or Times, permit any Officer or Officers thereunto authorized by the said Commissioners for managing the Stamp Duties, to inspect and view all such Public Books, Matters, and Things, and to take thereout such Notes and Memorandums as shall be necessary for the Purpose of ascertaining or securing the said Duties, without Free or Reward; upon Pain that every such Clerk or other Officer who shall refuse or neglect so to do, upon reasonable Request in that Behalf made, shall, for every such Refusal or Neglect, forfeit Sum of twenty Pounds.

XLVIII. And be it further enacted by the Authority aforesaid, That the high Treasurer or *Great Britain,* or the Commissioners of his Majesty's Treasury, or any three or more of such Commissioners, for the time being, shall, once in every Year at least, set the Prices at which all Sorts stamped Vellum, Parchment, and Paper, shall be sold by the said Commissioners for managing the Stamp Duties, and their Officers: and that the said Commissioners for the said Duties shall cause such Prices to be marked upon every such Skin and Piece of Vellum and Parchment, and Sheet and Piece of Paper: And if any Officer or Distributor to be appointed by virtue of this Act, shall sell, or cause to be sold, any Vellum, Parchment, or Paper, for a greater or a higher Price or Sum than the Price or Sum so set or affixed thereon, every such Officer or Distribution shall, for every such Offense, forfeit the Sum to twenty Pounds.

XLIX. And be it also enacted by the Authority aforesaid, That the several Officers who shall be respectively employed in the raising, receiving, collecting, or paying, the several Duties hereby charged, within the said Colonies and Plantations, shall every twelve Months, or oftener, if thereunto required by the said Commissioners for managing the said Duties, exhibit his and their respective Account and Accounts of the said several Duties upon Oath, or if a Quaker upon Affirmation, in the Presence of the Governor, or Commander in Chief, or principal Judge of the Colony or Plantation where such Officers shall be respectively resident, in such Manner as the High Treasurer, or the Commissioners of the Treasury, or any three or more of such Commissioners of the time being, shall, from time to time, direct and appoint, in order that the same may be immediately afterwards transmitted by the said Officer of Officers to the Commissioners for managing the said Duties, to be comptrolled and audited according to the usual Course and Form of comptrolling and auditing the Accounts of the Stamp Duties arising within this Kingdom: And if any of the said Officers shall neglect or refuse to exhibit any such Account, or to verify the same upon Oath or Affirmation, or to transmit any such Account to verified to the Commissioners for managing the said Duties, in such Manner, and within such Time, as shall be so appointed or directed; or shall neglect or refuse to pay, or cause to be paid, into the Hands of the Receiver General of the Stamp Duties in *Great Britain,* or to such other Person or Persons as the High Treasurer, or Commissioners of the Treasury, or any three or more of such Commissioners for the time being, shall, from time to time, nominate or appoint, the Moneys Respectively raised, levied, and received, by such Officers under the Authority of this Act, at such Times, and in such Manner, as they shall be respectively required by the said High Treasurer, or Commissioners of the Treasury; or if any such Officers shall divert, detain, or misapply, all or any Part of the said Moneys so by them respectively raised, levied, and received, or shall knowingly return any Person or Persons *insuper* for any Moneys or other Things duly answered, paid, or accounted for, by such Person or Persons, whereby he or they shall sustain any Damage or Prejudice; in every such Case, every such Officer shall be liable to pay Treble the Value of all and every Sum and Sums of Money so diverted or misapplied; and shall also be liable to pay Treble Damages to the Party grieved, by returning him *insuper.*

L. And be it further enacted by the Authority aforesaid, That the Commissioners, Receiver or Receivers General, or other Person or Persons, who shall be respectively employed in *Great Britain,* in the directing, receiving, or paying, the Moneys arising by the Duties hereby granted, shall, and are hereby required, between the tenth Day of *October* and the fifth Day of *January* following, and so from Year to Year, yearly, at those Times, to exhibit their respective Accounts thereof to his Majesty's Auditors of the Imprest in *England* for the time being, or one of them, to be declared before the High Treasurer, or Commissioners of the Treasury and Chancellor of the Exchequer for the time being, according to the Course of the Exchequer.

LI. And be it further enacted by the Authority aforesaid, That if the said Commissioners for managing the said Duties, or the said Receiver or Receivers General, shall neglect or refuse to pay into the Exchequer all or any of the said Moneys, in such Manner as they are required by this Act to pay the same, or shall divert or misapply any Part thereof; then they, and every of them so offending, shall be liable to pay double the Value of all and every Sum and Sums of Money so diverted or misapplied.

LII. And be it further enacted by the Authority aforesaid, That the Comptroller or Comptrollers for the time being of the Duties hereby imposed, shall keep perfect and distinct Accounts, in Books fairly written, of all the Moneys arising by the said Duties; and if any such Comptroller or Comptrollers shall neglect his or their Duty therein, then he or they, for every such Offense, shall forfeit the Sum of one hundred Pounds.

LIII. And be it further enacted by the Authority aforesaid. That all the Moneys which shall arise by the several Rates and Duties hereby granted (except the necessary Charges of raising, collecting, recovering, answering, paying, and accounting for the same, and the necessary Charges from time to time incurred in relation to this Act, and the Execution thereof shall be paid into the Receipt of his Majesty's Exchequer, and shall be entered separate and apart from all other Moneys, and shall be there reserved to be from time to time disposed of by Parliament, towards further defraying the necessary Expenses of defending, protecting, and securing, the said Colonies and Plantations.

LIV. And whereas it is proper that some Provision should be made for Payment of the necessary Expenses which have been, and shall be incurred in relation to this Act, and the Execution thereof, and of the Orders and Rules to be established under the Authority of the same, before the said Duties shall take effect, or the Moneys arising thereby shall be sufficient to discharge such Expenses; Be it therefore enacted by the Authority aforesaid, That his Majesty may, and he is hereby empowered by any Warrant or Warrants under his Royal Sign Manual, at any Time or Times before the Twentieth Day of *April,* one thousand seven hundred and sixty-six, to cause to be issued and paid out of any of the Surpluses, Excesses, Overplus Moneys, and other Revenues composing the Fund commonly called *The Sinking Fund,* (except such Moneys of the said Sinking Fund as are appropriated to any particular Use or Uses by any former Act or Acts of Parliament in that Behalf) such Sum and Sums of Money as shall be necessary to defray the said Expenses; and the Moneys so issued shall be reimbursed, by Payment into the Exchequer of the like Sum or Sums out of the first Moneys which shall arise by virtue of this Act; which Moneys, upon the Payment thereof into the Exchequer, shall be carried to the Account, and made Part of the said Fund.

LV. And it is hereby further enacted and declared, That all the Powers and Authorities by this Act granted to the Commissioners for managing the Duties upon stamped Vellum, Parchment, and Paper, shall and may be fully and effectually carried into Execution by any three, or more of the said Commissioners; any thing herein before contained to the contrary notwithstanding.

LVI. And be it further enacted by the Authority aforesaid, That all Forfeitures and Penalties incurred after the twenty-ninth Day of *September,* one thousand seven hundred and sixty-five, for Offenses committed against an Act passed in the Fourth Year of the Reign of his present Majesty, intituled, 'An Act for granting certain Duties in the *British* Colonies and Plantations in *America,* for continuing amending, and making perpetual, an Act passed in the Sixth Year of the Reign of his late Majesty King *George* the Second, intituled, *An Act for the better securing and encouraging the Trade of his Majesty's Sugar Colonies in* America; for applying the Produce of such Duties, and of the Duties to arise by virtue of the said Act, towards defraying the Expences of defending, protecting, and securing, the said Colonies and Plantations; for explaining an Act made in the twenty-fifth Year of the Reign of King *Charles* the Second, intituled, *An Act for the Encouragement of the* Greenland *and* Eastland *Trades, and for the better securing the Plantation Trade;* and for altering and disallowing several Drawbacks on Exports from this Kingdom, and more effectually preventing the clandestine Conveyance of Goods to and from the said Colonies and Plantations, and improving and securing the Trade between the same and *Great Britain,'* and for Offenses committed against any other Act or Acts of Parliament relating to the Trade or Revenues of the said Colonies or Plantations; shall and may be prosecuted, sued for, and recovered, in any Court of Record, or in any Court of Admiralty, in the respective Colony or Plantation where the Offense shall be committed, or in any Court of Vice Admiralty appointed or to be appointed, and which shall have Jurisdiction within such Colony, Plantation, or Place, (which Courts of Admiralty or Vice Admiralty are hereby respectively authorized and required to proceed, hear, and determine the same (at the Election of the Informer or Prosecutor.

LVII. And it is hereby further enacted and declared by the Authority aforesaid, That all Sums of Money granted and imposed by this Act as Rates or Duties, and also all Sums of Money imposed as Forfeitures or Penalties, and all Sums of Money required to be paid, and all other Moneys herein mentioned, shall be deemed and taken to be Sterling Money of *Great Britain,* and shall be collected, recovered, and paid, to the Amount of the Value which such nominal Sums bear in *Great Britain;* and that such Moneys shall and may be received and taken, according to the Proportion and Value of five Shillings and six Pence the Ounce in Silver; and that all the Forfeitures and Penalties hereby inflicted, and which shall be incurred in the said Colonies and Plantations, shall and may be prosecuted, sued for, and recovered, in any Court of Record, or in any Court of Admiralty, in the respective Colony or Plantation where the Offense shall be committed, or in any Court of Vice Admiralty appointed or to be appointed, and which shall have Jurisdiction within such Colony, Plantation, or Place, (which Courts of Admiralty or Vice Admiralty are hereby respectively authorized and required to proceed, hear, and determine the same) at the Election of the Informer or Prosecutor; and that from and after the Twenty-ninth Day of *September*, one thousand seven hundred and sixty-five, in all Cases, where any Suit or Prosecution shall be commenced and determined for any Penalty or Forfeiture inflicted by this Act, or by the said Act made in the fourth Year of his present Majesty's Reign, or by any other Act of Parliament relating to the Trade or Revenues of the said Colonies or Plantations, in any Court of Admiralty in the respective Colony or Plantation where the Offense shall be committed, either Party, who shall think himself aggrieved by such Determination, may appeal from such Determination, to any Court of Vice Admiralty, appointed or to be appointed, and which shall have Jurisdiction within such Colony, Plantation, or Place, (which Court of Vice Admiralty is hereby authorized and required to proceed, hear, and determine such Appeal) any Law, Custom, or Usage, to the contrary notwithstanding; and the Forfeitures and Penalties hereby inflicted, which shall be incurred in any other Part of his Majesty's Dominions, shall and may be prosecuted, sued for, and recovered, with full Costs of Suit, in any Court of Record within the Kingdom, Territory, or Place, where the Offense shall be committed, in such and the same Manner as any Debt or Damage, to the Amount of such Forfeiture or Penalty, can or may be sued for and recovered.

LVIII. And it is hereby further enacted, That all the Forfeitures and Penalties hereby inflicted shall be divided, paid, and applied, as follows; (that is to say) one third Part of all such Forfeitures and Penalties recovered in the said Colonies and Plantations, shall be paid into the Hands of one of the Chief Distributors of stamped Vellum, Parchment, and Paper, residing in the Colony or Plantation wherein the Offender shall be convicted, for the Use of his Majesty, his Heirs, and Successors; one third Part of the Penalties and Forfeitures, so recovered, to the Governor or Commander in Chief of such Colony or Plantation; and the other third Part thereof, to the Person who shall inform or sue for the same; and that one moiety of all such Penalties and Forfeitures recovered in any other Part of his Majesty's Dominions, shall be to the Use of his Majesty,

his Heirs, and Successors, and the other Moiety thereof, to the Person who shall inform or sue for the same.

LIX. And be it further enacted by the Authority aforesaid, That all the Offenses which are by this Act made Felony, and shall be committed within any Part of his Majesty's Dominions, shall and may be heard, tried, and determined, before any Court of Law within the respective Kingdom, Territory, Colony, or Plantation, where the Offense shall be committed, in such and the same Manner as all other Felonies can or may be heard, tried, and determined, in such Court.

LX. And be it further enacted by the Authority aforesaid, That all the present Governors or Commanders in Chief of any *British* Colony or Plantation, shall, before the said first Day of *November*, one thousand seven hundred and sixty-five, and all who hereafter shall be made Governors or Commanders in Chief of the said Colonies or Plantations, or any of them, before their Entrance into their Government, shall take a solemn Oath to do their utmost, that all and every the Clauses contained in this present Act, be punctually and *bona fide* observed, according to the true Intent and Meaning thereof, so far as appertains unto the said Governors or Commanders in Chief respectively, under the like Penalties, Forfeitures, and Disabilities, either for neglecting to take the said Oath, or for wittingly neglecting to do their Duty accordingly, as are mentioned and expressed in an Act made in the seventh and eighth Year of the Reign of King *William* the Third, intituled, *An Act for preventing Frauds, and regulating Abuses, in the Plantation Trade;* and the said Oath hereby required to be taken, shall be administered by such Person or Persons as hath or have been, or shall be, appointed to administer the Oath required to be taken by the said Act made in the seventh and eighth Year of the Reign of King *William* the Third.

LXI. And be it further enacted by the Authority aforesaid, That all Records, Writs, Pleadings, and other Proceedings in all Courts whatsoever, and all Deeds, Instruments, and Writings whatsoever, hereby charged, shall be ingrossed and written in such Manner as they have been usually accustomed to be ingrossed and written, or are now ingrossed and written within the said Colonies and Plantations.

LXII. And it is hereby further enacted, That if any Person or Persons shall be sued or prosecuted, either in *Great Britain or America,* for any thing done in pursuance of this Act, such Person and Persons shall and may plead the General Issue, and give this Act and the Special Matter in Evidence; and if it shall appear so to have been done, the Jury shall find for the Defendant or Defendants: And if the Plaintiff or Plaintiffs shall become nonsuited, or discontinue his or their Action after the Defendant or Defendants shall have appeared, or if Judgment shall be given upon any Verdict or Demurrer against the Plaintiff or Plaintiffs, the Defendant or Defendants shall recover Treble Costs, and have the like Remedy for the same, as Defendants have in other Cases by Law.

Source:

Danby Pickering, ed. *Statutes at Large.* Vol. 10. Cambridge, Mass. J. Bentham, 1762–1807. pp. 18–31.

Declarations of Rights and Grievances (Resolutions of the Stamp Act Congress), 1765

Petition issued on October 19, 1765, by the Stamp Act Congress in New York City, condemning the Stamp Act of 1765 and assuring the American colonies that "no taxes ever have been or can be constitutionally imposed on them, except by their respective legislatures." Twenty-eight delegates from nine colonies congregated at the meeting, which had been initiated by the Massachusetts legislature and influenced by Patrick Henry's Virginia Stamp Act Resolutions. The petition, which contained 14 resolutions and which was probably drafted by John Dickinson (a Pennsylvania delegate), protested that the colonists' individual rights and liberties as recognized subjects of the British Crown were being violated. It also denounced the increased powers of the nonjury vice admiralty courts, which were trying violators of recent British trade regulations. Probably more effective than even the declaration and the failure to pay the tax was a boycott of British goods conducted in many of the colonies. At that time, the American colonies purchased approximately one-quarter of British exports, and half of British shipping was engaged in American colonial commerce. The British government repealed the act on March 18, 1766, replacing it that same day with the Declaratory Act of 1766, which asserted Parliament's authority to legislate for the colonies.

The members of this Congress, sincerely devoted with the warmest sentiments of affection and duty to His Majesty's person and Government, inviolably attached to the present happy establishment of the Protestant succession, and with minds deeply impressed by a sense of the present and impending misfortunes of the British colonies on this continent; having considered as maturely as time will permit the circumstances of the said colonies, esteem it our indispensable duty to make the following declarations of our humble opinion respecting the most essential rights and liberties of the colonists, and of the grievances under which they labour, by reason of several late Acts of Parliament.

I. That His Majesty's subjects in these colonies owe the same allegiance to the Crown of Great Britain that is owing from his subjects born within the realm, and all due subordination to that august body the Parliament of Great Britain.

II. That His Majesty's liege subjects in these colonies are intitled to all the inherent rights and liberties of his natural born subjects within the kingdom of Great Britain.

III. That it is inseparably essential to the freedom of a people, and the undoubted right of Englishmen, that no taxes be imposed on them but with their own consent, given personally or by their representatives.

IV. That the people of these colonies are not, and from their local circumstances cannot be, represented in the House of Commons in Great Britain.

V. That the only representatives of the people of these colonies are persons chosen therein by themselves, and that no taxes ever have been, or can be constitutionally imposed on them, but by their respective legislatures.

VI. That all supplies to the Crown being free gifts of the people, it is unreasonable and inconsistent with the principles and spirit of the British Constitution, for the people of Great Britain to grant to His Majesty the property of the colonists.

VII. That trial by jury is the inherent and invaluable right of every British subject in these colonies.

VIII. That the late Act of Parliament, entitled *An Act for granting and applying certain stamp duties, and other duties, in the British colonies and plantations in America, etc.,* by imposing taxes on the inhabitants of these colonies; and the said Act, and several other Acts, by extending the jurisdiction of the courts of Admiralty beyond its ancient limits, have a manifest tendency to subvert the rights and liberties of the colonists.

IX. That the duties imposed by several late Acts of Parliament, from the peculiar circumstances of these colonies, will be extremely burthensome and grievous; and from the scarcity of specie, the payment of them absolutely impracticable.

X. That as the profits of the trade of these colonies ultimately center in Great Britain, to pay for the manufactures which they are obliged to take from thence, they eventually contribute very largely to all supplies granted there to the Crown.

XI. That the restrictions imposed by several late Acts of Parliament on the trade of these colonies will render them unable to purchase the manufactures of Great Britain.

XII. That the increase, prosperity, and happiness of these colonies depend on the full and free enjoyments of their rights and liberties, and an intercourse with Great Britain mutually affectionate and advantageous.

XIII. That it is the right of the British subjects in these colonies to petition the King or either House of Parliament.

Lastly, That it is the indispensable duty of these colonies to the best of sovereigns, to the mother country, and to themselves, to endeavour by a loyal and dutiful address to His Majesty, and humble applications to both Houses of Parliament, to procure the repeal of the Act for granting and applying certain stamp duties, of all clauses of any other Acts of Parliament, whereby the jurisdiction of the Admiralty is extended as aforesaid, and of the other late Acts for the restriction of American commerce.

Source:

Henry Steele Commager, ed. *Documents of American History.* New York: F.S. Crofts & Co., 1934.

Townshend Acts, 1767

Several acts sponsored by Britain's Chancellor of the Exchequer (or treasury department) Charles Townshend and passed by the British Parliament in an effort to exercise greater royal authority over the American colonies and to levy new taxes. The acts, sometimes called the American Import Duties Acts, levied import taxes on glass, lead, paint, tea, and paper sent into the colonies. The Townshend Acts were viewed as undue interference in colonial affairs and caused deep resentment and widespread resistance. The colonists, influenced by the writings of John Dickinson, Samuel Adams, and others, protested against the taxes. Boston merchants once again boycotted British goods. In 1768 the Massachusetts Assembly was dissolved for sending a circular letter to other colonies about their common plight. British troops were then sent in to enforce laws and to try to keep the peace. Conflicts resulted, leading to the Boston Massacre. The boycott affected trade, and in 1770 most of the acts were repealed, temporarily averting a major British-American colonial crisis, but retention of the tea tax culminated in the Boston Tea Party.

An act for granting certain duties in the British *colonies and plantations in* America; *for allowing a drawback of the duties of customs upon the exportation, from this kingdom, of coffee and cocoa nuts of the produce of the said colonies or plantations; for discontinuing the drawbacks payable on china earthen ware exported to* America; *and for more effectually preventing the clandestine running of goods in the said colonies and plantations.*

Whereas *it is expedient that a revenue should be raised, in your Majesty's dominions in* America, *for making a more certain and adequate provision for defraying the*

charge of the administration of justice, and the support of civil government, in such provinces where it shall be found necessary; and towards further defraying the expenses of defending, protecting, and securing, the said dominions; we, your Majesty's most dutiful and loyal subjects, the commons of Great Britain, *in parliament assembled, have therefore resolved to give and grant unto your Majesty the several rates and duties herein after mentioned;* and do most humbly beseech your Majesty that it may be enacted, and be it enacted by the King's most excellent majesty, by and with the advice and consent of the lords spiritual and temporal, and commons, in this present parliament assembled, and by the authority of the same, That from and after the twentieth day of *November,* one thousand seven hundred and sixty seven, there shall be raised, levied, collected, and paid, unto his Majesty, his heirs, and successors, for and upon the respective goods herein after mentioned, which shall be imported from *Great Britain* into any colony or plantation in *America* which now is, or hereafter may be, under the dominion of his Majesty, his heirs, or successors, the several rates and duties following; that is to say,

For every hundred weight avoirdupois of crown, plate, flint, and white glass, four shillings and eight pence.

For every hundred weight avoirdupois of green glass, one shilling and two peace.

For every hundred weight avoirdupois of red lead, two shillings.

For every hundred weight avoirdupois of white lead, two shillings.

For every hundred weight avoirdupois of painters colors, two shillings.

For every pound weight avoirdupois of tea, three pence.

For every ream of paper, usually called or known by the name of *Atlas Fine,* twelve shillings.

For every ream of paper called *Atlas Ordinary,* six shillings.

For every ream of paper called *Bastard,* or *Double Copy,* one shilling and six pence.

For every single ream of blue paper for sugar bakers, ten pence halfpenny.

For every ream of paper called *Blue Royal,* one shilling and six pence.

For every bundle of brown paper containing forty quires, not made in *Great Britain,* six pence.

For every ream of paper called *Brown Cap,* not made in *Great Britain,* nine pence.

For every ream of paper called *Brown Large Cap,* made in *Great Britain,* four pence halfpenny.

For every ream of paper called *Small Ordinary Brown,* made in *Great Britain,* three pence.

For every bundle, containing forty quires, of paper called *Whited Brown*, made in *Great Britain*, four pence halfpenny.

For every ream of cartridge paper, one shilling and one penny halfpenny.

For every ream of paper called *Chancery Double*, one shilling and six pence.

For every ream of paper called *Genoa Crown Fine*, one shilling and one penny halfpenny.

For every ream of paper called *Genoa Crown Second*, nine pence.

For every ream of paper called *German Crown*, nine pence.

For every ream of paper called *Fine Printing Crown*, nine pence.

For every ream of paper called *Second Ordinary Printing Crown*, six pence three farthings.

For every ream of paper called *Crown Fine*, made in *Great Britain*, nine pence.

For every ream of paper called *Crown Second*, made in *Great Britain*, six pence three farthings.

For every ream of paper called *Demy Fine*, not made in *Great Britain*, three shillings.

For every ream of paper called *Demy Second*, not made in *Great Britain*, one shilling and four pence halfpenny.

For every ream of paper called *Demy Fine*, made in *Great Britain*, one shilling and one penny halfpenny.

For every ream of paper called *Demy Second*, made in *Great Britain*, nine pence.

For every ream of paper called *Demy Printing*, one shilling the three pence.

For every ream of paper called *Genoa Demy Fine*, one shilling and six pence.

For every ream of paper called *Genoa Demy Second*, one shilling and one penny halfpenny.

For every ream of paper called *German Demy*, one shilling and one penny halfpenny.

For every ream of paper called *Elephant Fine*, six shillings.

For every ream of paper called *Elephant Ordinary*, two shillings and five pence farthing.

For every ream of paper called *Genoa Fools Cap Fine*, one shilling and one penny halfpenny.

For every ream of paper called *Genoa Fools Cap Second*, nine pence.

For every ream of paper called *German Fools Cap*, nine pence.

For every ream of paper called *Fine Printing Fools Cap*, nine pence.

For every ream of paper called *Second Ordinary Printing Fools Cap*, six pence three farthings.

For every ream of any other paper called *Fools Cap Fine*, not made in *Great Britain*, one shilling and ten pence halfpenny.

For every ream of any other paper called *Fools Cap Fine Second*, not made in *Great Britain*, one shilling and six pence.

For every ream of paper called *Fools Cap Fine*, made in *Great Britain*, nine pence.

For every ream of paper called *Fools Cap Second*, made in *Great Britain*, six pence three farthings.

For every ream of paper called *Imperial Fine*, twelve shillings.

For every ream of paper called *Second Writing Imperial*, eight shillings and three pence.

For every ream of paper called *German Lombard*, nine pence.

For every ream of paper called *Medium Fine*, four shillings and six pence.

For every ream of paper called *Genoa Medium*, one shilling and ten pence halfpenny.

For every ream of paper called *Second Writing Medium*, three shillings.

For every ream of painted paper, not made in *Great Britain*, six shillings.

For every ream of paper called *Fine Large Post*, one shilling and ten pence halfpenny.

For every ream of paper called *Small Post*, one shilling and one penny halfpenny.

For every ream of paper called *Fine Genoa Pot*, six pence three farthings.

For every ream of paper called *Second Genoa Pot*, six pence three farthings.

For every ream of paper called *Superfine Pot*, not made in *Great Britain*, one shilling and six pence.

For every ream of other paper called *Second Fine Pot*, not made in *Great Britain*, one shilling and one penny halfpenny.

For every ream of paper called *Ordinary Pot*, not made in *Great Britain*, six pence three farthings.

For every ream of paper called *Fine Pot*, made in *Great Britain*, nine pence.

For every ream of paper called *Second Pot*, made in *Great Britain*, four pence halfpenny.

For every ream of paper called *Super Royal Fine*, nine shillings.

For every ream of paper called *Royal Fine*, six shillings.

For every ream of paper called *Fine Holland Royal*, two shillings and five pence farthing.

For every ream of paper called *Fine Holland Second*, one shilling and six pence.

For every ream of paper called *Second Fine Holland Royal*, one shilling and six pence.

For every ream of paper called *Ordinary Royal,* nine pence.

For every ream of paper called *Genoa Royal,* two shillings and five pence farthing.

For every ream of paper called *Second Writing Royal,* four shillings and one penny halfpenny.

For every ream of paper called *Second Writing Super Royal,* six shillings.

For every hundred weight avoirdupois of pasteboards, mill-boards, and scale-boards, not made in *Great Britain,* three shillings and nine pence.

For every hundred weight avoirdupois of pasteboards, mill-boards, and scale-boards, made in *Great Britain,* two shillings and three pence.

And for and upon all paper which shall be printed, painted, or stained, in *Great Britain,* to serve for hangings or other uses, three farthings for every yard square, over and above the duties payable for such paper by this act, if the same had not been printed, painted, or stained; and after those rates respectively for any greater or less quantity.

II. And it is hereby further enacted by the authority aforesaid, That all other paper (not being particularly rated and charged in this act) shall pay the several and respective duties that are charged, by this act, upon such paper as is nearest above in size and goodness to such unrated paper.

III. And be it declared and enacted by the authority aforesaid, That a ream of paper, chargeable by this act, shall be understood to conflict of twenty quires, and each quire of twenty four sheets.

IV. And it is hereby further enacted by the authority aforesaid, That the said rates and duties, charged by this act upon goods imported into any *British American* colony or plantation, shall be deemed, and are hereby declared to be, sterling money of *Great Britain;* and shall be collected, recovered, and paid, to the amount of the value which such nominal sums bear in *Great Britain;* and that such moneys may be received and taken, according to the proportion and value of five shillings and six pence the ounce in silver; and shall be raised, levied, collected, paid, and recovered, in the same manner and form, and by such rules, ways, and means, and under such penalties and forfeitures, as any other duties, now payable to his Majesty upon goods imported into the said colonies or plantations, may be raised, levied, collected, paid, and recovered, by any act or acts or parliament now in force, as fully and effectually, to all intents and purposes, as if the several clauses, powers, directions, penalties, and forfeitures, relating thereto, were particularly repeated, and again enacted, in the body of this present act: and that all the moneys that shall arise by the said duties (except the necessary charges of raising, collecting, levying, recovering, answering, paying, and accounting for the same) shall be applied, in the first place, in such manner as is herein after mentioned, in making a more certain and adequate provision for the charge of the administration of justice, and the support of civil government, in such of the said colonies and plantations where it shall be found necessary; and that the residue of such duties shall be paid into the receipt of his Majesty's exchequer, and shall be entered separate and apart from all other moneys paid or payable to his Majesty, his heirs, or successors; and shall be there reserved, to be from time to time disposed of by parliament towards defraying the necessary expenses of defending, protecting, and securing, the *British* colonies and plantations in *America.*

V. And be it further enacted by the authority aforesaid, That his Majesty and his successors shall be, and are hereby, empowered, from time to time, by any warrant or warrants under his or their royal sign manual or sign manuals, countersigned by the high treasurer, or any three or more of the commissioners of the treasury for the time being, to cause such moneys to be applied, out of the produce of the duties granted by this act, as his Majesty, or his successors, shall think proper or necessary, for defraying the charges of the administration of justice, and the support of the civil government, within all or any of the said colonies or plantations.

VI. *And whereas the allowing a drawback of all the duties of customs upon exportation, from this kingdom, of coffee and cocoa nuts, the growth of the* British *dominions in* America, *may be a means of encouraging the growth of coffee and cocoa in the said dominions;* be it therefore enacted by the authority aforesaid, That from and after the said twentieth day of *November,* one thousand seven hundred and sixty seven, upon the exportation of any coffee or cocoa nuts, of the growth or produce of any *British* colony or plantation in *America,* from this kingdom as merchandise, the whole duties of customs, payable upon the importation of such coffee or cocoa nuts, shall be drawn back and repaid; in such manner, and under such rules, regulations, penalties, and forfeitures, as any drawback or allowance, payable out of the duties of customs upon the exportation of such coffee or cocoa nuts, was, could, or might be paid, before the passing of this act; any law, custom, or usage, to the contrary notwithstanding.

VII. And it is hereby further enacted by the authority aforesaid, That no drawback shall be allowed for any china earthen ware fold, after the paffing of this act, at the sale of the united company of merchants of *England* trading to the *East Indies,* which shall be entered for exportation from *Great Britain* to any part of *America;* any law, custom, or usage, to the contrary notwithstanding.

VIII. And it is hereby further enacted by the Authority aforesaid, That if any china earthen ware- fold, after the paffing of this act, at the sale of the said united company, shall be entered for exportation to any part of *America* as china earthen ware that had been fold at the sale of the said company before that time; or, if any china earthen ware shall be entered for exportation to any parts beyond the seas, other than to some part of *America,* in order to obtain any drawback thereon, and the said china earthen ware shall nevertheless be carried to any part of *America,* and landed there, contrary to the true intent and meaning of this act; that then, in each and every such case, the drawback shall be forfeited; and the merchant or other person making such entry, and the master or person taking the charge of the ship or vessel on board which the said goods shall be loaden for exportation, shall forfeit double the amount of the drawback paid, or to be paid, for the same, and also treble the value of the said goods; one moiety to and for the use of his Majesty, his heirs, and successors; and the other moiety to such officer of the customs as shall sue for the same; to be prosecuted, sued for, and recovered, in such manner and form, and by the same rules and regulations, as other penalties inflicted for offenses against the laws relating to the customs may be prosecuted, sued for, and recovered, by any act or acts of parliament now in force.

IX. *And, for the more effectual preventing the clandestine running of goods in the* British *dominions in* America, be it further enacted by the authority aforesaid, That form and after the said twentieth day of *November,* one thousand seven hundred and fifty seven, the master or other person having or taking the charge or command of every ship or vessel arriving in any *British* colony or plantation in *America* shall, before he proceeds with his vessel to the place of unloading, come directly to the custom house for the port or district where he arrives, and make a just and true entry, upon oath, before the collector and comptroller, or other principal officer of the customs there, of the burthen, contents, and lading, of such ship or vessel, with the particular marks, numbers, qualities, and contents, of every parcel of goods therein laden, to the best of his knowledge; also where and in what port she took in her lading; of what country built; how manned; who was master during the voyage, and who are owners thereof; and whether any, and what goods, during the course of such voyage, had or had not been discharged out of such ship or vessel, and where: and the master or other person having or taking the charge or command of every ship or vessel, going out from any *British* colony or plantation in *America,* before he shall take in, or suffer to be taken into or laden on board any such ship or vessel, any goods, wares, or merchandises, to be exported, shall, in like manner, enter and report outwards such ship or vessel, with her name and burthen, of what country built, and how manned, with the names of the master and owners thereof, and to what port or place he intends to pass or fail: and before he shall

depart with such ship or vessel out of any such colony or plantation, he shall also bring and deliver unto the collector and comptroller, or other principal officer of the customs at the port or place where he shall lade, a content in writing, under his hand, of the name of every merchant, or other person who shall have laden, or put on board any such ship or vessel, any goods or merchandise, together with the marks and numbers of such goods or merchandise: and such master or person having or taking the charge or command of every such ship or vessel, either coming into, or going out of, any *British* colony or plantation as aforesaid, whether such ship or vessel shall be laden or in ballast, or otherwise, shall likewise publicly, in the open custom house, to the best of his knowledge, answer upon oath to such questions as shall be demanded of him by the collector and comptroller, or other principal officer of the customs for such port or place, concerning such ship or vessel, and the destination of her voyage, or concerning any goods or merchandise that shall or may be laden on board her, upon forfeiture of one hundred pounds sterling money of *Great Britain.* for each and every default or neglect; to be sued for, prosecuted, recovered, and divided, in the same manner and form, by the same rules and regulations in all respects, as other pecuniary penalties, for offenses against the laws relating to the customs or trade of his Majesty's colonies in *America,* may, by any act or acts of parliament now in force, be prosecuted, sued for, recovered, and divided.

X. *And whereas by an act of parliament made in the fourteenth year of the reign of King* Charles *the Second, intituled,* An act for preventing frauds, and regulating abuses, in his Majesty's customs, *and several other acts now in force, it is lawful for any officer of his Majesty's customs, authorized by writ of assistance under the seal of his Majesty's court of exchequer, to take a constable, headborough, or other public officer inhabiting near unto the place, and in the day-time to enter and go into any house, shop, cellar, warehouse, or room or other place, and, in case of resistance, to break open doors, thefts, trunks, and other package there, to seize, and from thence to bring, any kind of goods or merchandize whatsoever prohibited or uncustomed, and to put and secure the same in his Majesty's shore-house next to the place where such seizure shall be made: and whereas by an act made in the seventh and eighth years of the reign of King* William *the Third, intituled,* An act for preventing frauds, and regulating abuses, in the plantation trade, *it is, amongst other things, enacted, that the officers for collecting and managing his Majesty's revenue, and inspecting the plantation trade, in* America, *shall have the same powers and authorities to enter houses or warehouses, to search for and seize goods prohibited to be imported or exported into or out of any of the said plantations, or for which any duties are payable, or ought to have been paid; and that the like assistance shall be given to the said officers in the execution of their office, as, by the said recited act of the fourteenth year of King* Charles *the Second, is provided for the officers in* England: *but, no authority being expressly given by the said act, made in the seventh and eighth years of the reign of King* William *the Third, to any particular court to grant such writs of assistance for the officers of the customs in the said plantation, it is doubted whether such officers can legally enter houses and other places on land, to search for and seize goods, in the manner directed by the said recited acts:* To obviate which doubts for the future, and in order to carry the intention of the said recited acts into effectual execution, be it enacted , and it is hereby enacted by the authority aforesaid, That from and after the said twentieth day of *November,* one thousand seven hundred and sixty seven, such writs of assistance, to authorize and impower the officers of his Majesty's customs to enter and go into any house, warehouse, shop, cellar, or other place, in the *British* colonies or plantations in *America* , to search for and seize prohibited or uncustomed goods, in the manner directed by the said recited acts, shall and may be granted by the said superior or supreme court of justice having jurisdiction within such colony or plantation respectively.

XI. And be it further enacted by the authority aforesaid, That if any action or suit shall be commenced, either in *Great Britain* or *America,* against any person or persons for any thing done in pursuance of this act, the defendant or defendants in such action or suit may plead the general issue, and give this act, and the special matter, in evidence at any trial to be had thereupon; and that the same was done in pursuance and by the authority of this act: and if it shall appear so to have been done, the jury shall find for the defendant or defendants: and if the plaintiff shall be nonsuited, or discontinue his action after the defendant or defendants shall have appeared, or if judgment shall be given upon any verdict or demurrer against the plaintiff; the defendant or defendants shall recover treble costs, and have the like remedy for the same as defendants have in other cases by law.

Source:
Danby. Pickering, ed. *The Statutes at Large.* Cambridge, Mass. J. Bentham, 1762–1807, pp. 505–512.

Boston Non-Importation Agreement, 1768

Agreement entered into by the city of Boston on August 1, 1768, to completely withhold any imports from Great Britain and to stop the purchasing of products, such as tea, paper, or glass imported from Britain by any American colony. Because of the heavy taxes and restrictions laid on trade by the Town-

shend Revenue Act, Boston merchants agreed in March 1768 to refuse to import any merchandise from Britain if merchants from Philadelphia and New York would do the same. This nonimportation league did not come into being, however, leaving Boston to put forth its own agreement independently. A few weeks after this decision was made, merchants of New York and other New England towns soon followed suit. These agreements, as well as several others similar to this one, cut down imports from Britain by more than 50 percent.

Agreement Entered into by the Inhabitants of Boston

The merchants and traders in the town of Boston having taken into consideration the deplorable situation of the trade, and the many difficulties it at present labours under on account of the scarcity of money, which is daily increasing for want of the other remittances to discharge our debts in Great Britain, and the large sums collected by the officers of the customs for duties on goods imported; the heavy taxes levied to discharge the debts contracted by the government in the late war; the embarrassments and restrictions laid on trade by several late acts of parliament; together with the bad success of our cod fishery, by which our principal sources of remittance are like to be greatly diminished, and we thereby rendered unable to pay the debts we owe the merchants in Great Britain, and to continue the importation of goods from thence;

We, the subscribers, in order to relieve the trade under those discouragements, to promote industry, frugality, and economy, and to discourage luxury, and every kind of extravagance, do promise and engage to and with each other as follows:

First, That we will not send for or import from Great Britain, either upon our own account, or upon commission, this fall, any other goods than what are already ordered for the fall supply.

Secondly, That we will not send for or import any kind of goods or merchandize from Great Britain, either on our own account, or on commissions, or any otherwise, from the 1st of January 1769, to the 1st of January 1770, except salt, coals, fish-hooks and lines, hemp, and duck bar lead and shot, wool-cards and card-wire.

Thirdly, That we will not purchase of any factor, or others, any kind of goods imported from Great Britain, from January 1769, to January 1770.

Fourthly, That we will not import, on our own account, or on commissions or purchase of any who shall import from any other colony in America, from January 1769, to January 1770, any tea, glass, paper, or other goods commonly imported from Great Britain.

Fifthly, That we will not, from and after the 1st of January 1769, import into this province any tea, paper, glass, or painters colours, until the act imposing duties on those articles shall be repealed.

In witness whereof, we have hereunto set our hands, this first day of August, 1768.

Source:

Henry Steele Commager, ed. *Documents of American History.* New York: F.S. Crofts & Co., 1934.

Massachusetts Circular Letter, 1768

Document written by American patriot Samuel Adams and approved by the Massachusetts House of Representatives in 1768 in response to the Townshend Acts, passed by the British Parliament in the previous year, which imposed duties on selected colonial imports. The letter informed the assemblies of the other 12 colonies that the Massachusetts General Court (assembly) was denouncing the Townshend Acts on the grounds that they represented taxation without representation and urged a united colonial protest. The British government used the threat of dissolution in an attempt to prevent other legislatures from endorsing the letter and did eventually dissolve the assemblies of Massachusetts, Virginia, and other supporting colonies, thus heightening the tension between the colonies and the British Crown. This letter presaged Adams's role in establishing the Massachusetts Committees of Correspondence in 1772 to communicate their resistence to British encroachments on what they considered their rights as English. By the end of 1773, Massachusetts had some 80 towns with committees, and Virginia had opened the way for intercolonial committees of correspondence by setting one up in the House of Burgesses.

The House of Representatives of this province have taken into their serious consideration the great difficulties that must accrue to themselves and their constituents by the operation of several Acts of Parliament, imposing duties and taxes on the American colonies.

As it is a subject in which every colony is deeply interested, they have no reason to doubt but your house is deeply impressed with its importance, and that such constitutional measures will be come into as are proper. It seems to be necessary that all possible care should be taken that the representatives of the several assemblies, upon so delicate a point, should harmonize with each other. The House, therefore, hope that this letter will be candidly considered in no other light than as expressing a disposition freely to communicate their mind to a sister colony, upon a common concern, in the same manner as they would be glad to receive the sentiments of your or any other house of assembly on the continent.

The House have humbly represented to the ministry their own sentiments, that his Majesty's high court of Parliament is the supreme legislative power over the whole empire; that in all free states the constitution is fixed, and as the supreme legislative derives its power and authority from the constitution, it cannot overleap the bounds of it without destroying its own foundation; that the constitution ascertains and limits both sovereignty and allegiance, and, therefore, his Majesty's American subjects, who acknowledge themselves bound by the ties of allegiance, have an equitable claim to the full enjoyment of the fundamental rules of the British constitution; that it is an essential, unalterable right in nature, engrafted into the British constitution, as a fundamental law, and ever held sacred and irrevocable by the subjects within the realm, that what a man has honestly acquired is absolutely his own, which he may freely give, but cannot be taken from him without his consent; that the American subjects may, therefore, exclusive of any consideration of charter rights, with a decent firmness, adapted to the character of free men and subjects, assert this natural and constitutional right.

It is, moreover, their humble opinion, which they express with the greatest deference to the wisdom of the Parliament, that the Acts made there, imposing duties on the people of this province, with the sole and express purpose of raising a revenue, are infringements of their natural and constitutional rights; because, as they are not represented in the British Parliament, his Majesty's commons in Britain, by those Acts, grant their property without their consent.

This House further are of opinion that their constituents, considering their local circumstances, cannot, by any possibility, be represented in the Parliament; and that it will forever be impracticable, that they should be equally represented there, and consequently, not at all; being separated by an ocean of a thousand leagues. That his Majesty's royal predecessors, for this reason, were graciously pleased to form a subordinate legislature here, that their subjects might enjoy the unalienable right of a representation; also, that considering the utter impracticability of their ever being fully and equally represented in Parliament, and the great expense that must unavoidably attend even a partial representation there, this House think that a taxation of their constituents, even without their consent, grievous as it is, would be preferable to any representation that could be admitted for them there.

Upon these principles, and also considering that were the right in Parliament ever so clear, yet, for obvious reasons, it would be beyond the rules of equity that their constituents should be taxed on the manufactures of Great Britain here, in addition to the duties they pay for them in England, and other advantages arising to Great Britain, from the Acts of trade, this House have preferred a humble, dutiful, and loyal petition, to our most gracious sovereign, and made such representations to his Majesty's ministers, as they apprehended would tend to obtain redress.

They have also submitted to consideration, whether any people can be said to enjoy any degree of freedom if the Crown, in addition to its undoubted authority of constituting a governor, should appoint him such a stipend as it may judge proper, without the consent of the people, and at their expense; and whether, while the judges of the land, and other civil officers, hold not their commissions during good behaviour, their having salaries appointed for them by the Crown, independent of the people, hath not a tendency to subvert the principles of equity, and endanger the happiness and security of the subject. In addition to these measures, the House have written a letter to their agent which he is directed to lay before the ministry; wherein they take notice of the hardships of the Act for preventing mutiny and desertion, which requires the governor and council to provide enumerated articles for the king's marching troops, and the people to pay the expenses; and also, the commission of the gentlemen appointed commissioners of the customs, to reside in America, which authorizes them to make as many appointments as they think fit, and to pay the appointees what sum they please, for whose malconduct they are not accountable; from whence it may happen that officers of the Crown may be multiplied to such a degree as to become dangerous to the liberty of the people, by virtue of a commission, which does not appear to this House to derive any such advantages to trade as many have supposed.

These are the sentiments and proceedings of this House; and as they have too much reason to believe that the enemies of the colonies have represented them to his Majesty's ministers, and to the Parliament, as factious, disloyal, and having a disposition to make themselves independent of the mother country, they have taken occasion, in the most humble terms, to assure his Majesty, and his ministers, that, with regard to the people of this province, and, as they doubt not, of all the colonies, the charge is unjust. The House is fully satisfied that your assembly is too generous and liberal in sentiment to believe that this letter proceeds from an ambition of taking the lead, or dictating to the other assemblies. They freely submit their opinions to the judgment of others; and shall take it kind in your house to point out to them anything further that may be thought necessary.

This House cannot conclude, without expressing their firm confidence in the king, our common head and father, that the united and dutiful supplications of his distressed American subjects will meet with his royal and favourable acceptance.

Source:

Merrill Jensen, ed. *American Colonial Documents to 1776,* vol. 9 of *English Historical Documents,* ed. David C. Douglas. London: Eyre & Spottiswoode, 1955.

The Regulators of North Carolina, Petition, 1769

While the eastern seaboard and tidewater communities of the colonies became more settled and peaceful, frontier problems such as relations with Indians and land policies persisted. Colonial assemblies were weighted toward the east as well, leaving frontier communities feeling unrepresented. Especially in the South, backcountry farmers differed from their tidewater leaders, most of whom held slaves and belonged to dissenting religious sects. The opposition in North and South Carolina organized into "regulators," who disrupted the courts and refused to pay rents and taxes. An army of North Carolina Regulators was defeated in May 1771 as they attempted to storm the governor's home. Six of 15 captured Regulators were hanged. After independence, a number of Regulators either left the state or became Loyalists, rather than support tidewater patriots.

This petition, sent to the North Carolina assembly, October 9, 1769, covers the grievances of the "inhabitants of Anson County" in the western part of the colony.

Petition dated 9 October 1769.

"Mr. Speaker and Gen't of the Assembly.
Humbly Showeth:
That the Province in General labour under general grievances, and the western part thereof under particular ones; which we not only see, but very sensibly feel, being crouch'd beneath our sufferings and not withstanding our sacred privileges, have too long yielded ourselves slaves to remorseless oppression.

Permit us to conceive it to be our inviolable right to make known our grievances, and to petition for redress as appears in the Bill of Rights pass'd in the reign of King Charles the first, as well as the Act of Settlement of the Crown of the Revolution. We therefore beg leave at the Act of the Settlement of the Crown of the Revolution. We therefore beg leave to lay before you a specimen thereof that your compassionate endeavors may tend to the relief of your injured Constituents, whose distressed condition call aloud for aid. The alarming cries of the oppressed possibly may reach your ears; but without your zeal how they shall ascend the throne—how relentless is the breast without sympathy, the heart that cannot bleed on a view of our calamity; to see tenderness removed, cruelty stepping in; and all our liberties and privileges invaded and abridg'd (by as it were) domestickes; who are conscious of their guilt and void of remorse. O how darling! how relentless whilst impending Judgements loudly threaten and gaze upon them, with every emblem of merited destruction. A few of the many grievances are as follows, (viz't)

1. That the poor inhabitants in general are much oppress'd by reason of the disproportionate Taxes, and those of the western Counties in particular; as they are geneally in mean circumstances.

2. That no method is prescribed by law for the payment of the taxes of the Western Counties in produce (in lieu of a currency) as in other Counties within this Province to the Peoples great oppression.

3. That Lawyers, Clerks, and other petitioners; in place of being obsequious Servants for the Country's use, are become a nuisance, as the business of the people is often transacted without the least degree of fairness, the intention of the law evaded, exorbitant fees extorted, and the sufferers left to mourn under their oppressions.

4. That an Attorney should have it in his power, either for the sake of ease or interest, or to gratify their malevolence and spite, or commence suits to what courts he pleases, however inconvenient it may be to the Defendants; is a very great oppression.

5. That all unlawful fees taken in Indictment, where the Defendant is acquited by his Country (however customary it may be) is an oppression.

6. That Lawyers, Clerks, and others, extorting more fees than is intended by law, is also an oppression.

7. That the violation of the King's Instructions to his Delegates, their artfulness in concealing the same from him; and the great injury the People thereby sustains: is a manifest oppression.

And for remedy whereof, we take the freedom to recommend the following mode of redress, not doubting audience and acceptance which will not only tend to our relief, but command prayers at a duty from your humble Petitioners.

1. That at all elections each suffrage be given by Ticket & Ballot.

2. That the mode of Taxation be altered, and each person pay in proportion to the proffits arising from his Estate.

3. That no future tax be laid in Money, until a currency is made.

4. That there may be established a Western as well as a Northern and Southern District, and a Treasurer for the same.

5. That when a currency is made it may be let out by a loan office (on land security) and not be called in by a tax.

6. That all debts above 60s (shillings) and under 10 pounds be tried and determined without lawyers, by a jury of six freeholders, impaneled by a Justice, and that their verdict be enter'd by the said Justice, and be a final judgement.

7. That the Chief Justice have no perquisites, but a Salary only.

8. That Clerks be restricted in respect to fees, costs, and other things within the course of their office.

9. That Lawyers be effectively Barr'd from exacting and extorting fees.

10. That all doubts may be removed in respect to the payment of fees and costs on Indictments whereas the Defendant is not found guilty by the jury, and therefore acquited.

11. That the Assembly make known the Remonstrance to the King, the conduct of the cruel and oppressive Receiver of the Quit Rents, for omitting the customary easie and effectual method of collecting by distress, and pursuing the expensive mode of commencing suits in the most distant Courts.

12. That the Assembly in like manner make known that the Governor and Council do frequently grant lands to as many as they think proper without regard to Head Rights, notwithstanding the contrariety of his Majesties instructions, by which means immence sums has been collected, and numerous Patents granted, for much of the most fertile lands in this Province, that is yet uninhabited and cultivated, environed by great numbers of poor people who are necessitated to toil in the cultivation of bad Lands whereon they hardly can subsist, who are thereby deprived of His Majesties liberality and Bounty nor is there the least regard paid to the cultivation clause in said Patent mentioned, as many of the said Council as well as their friends and favorites enjoy large quantities of Lands under the above-mentioned circumstances.

13. That the Assembly communicates in like manner the Violation of His Majesties Instructions respecting the Land Office by the Governor and Council, and of their own rules, customs and orders. If it be sufficiently proved, that after they had granted Warrants for some Tracts of Land, and that the same was in due time suvey'd and returned and the Patent fees timely paid into the said office; and that if a private Council was called to avoid spectators, and peremptory orders made that Patents should not be granted; and Warrants by their orders arbitrarily to have been issued in the names of other Persons for the same Lands, and if when intreated by a solicitor they refus'd to render so much as a reason for their so doing, or to refund any part of the money paid by them extorted.

14. That some method may be pointed out that every Improvement on Lands in any of the Proprietors part

be proved when begun, by whom, and every sale made, that the eldest may have the preference of at least 300 acres. 15. That all taxes in the following Counties be paid as in other Counties in the Province (i.e.) in the produce of the County and that warehouses be erected as follows (viz), In Anson County at Isom Haleys Ferry Landing on PeeDee River, Rowan and Orange at Cambleton in Cumberland County, Mecklenburg at __?___ on the Catawba River, and in Tryon County at __?__ on __?__ River. 16. That every denomination of People may marry according to their respective mode Ceremony and customs after due publication or License.

17. That Doc't Benjamin Franklin or some other known patriot be appointed agent, to represent the unhappy state of this Province to his Majesty, and to solicit the several Boards in England.

Source:
Henry Steele Commager, ed. *Documents of American History*. New York: F.S. Croft & Co., 1938.

Tea Act, 1773

Legislation enacted by the British Parliament on April 27, 1773, that gave the British East India Company, which possessed a huge surplus of tea, a monopoly on all tea exported to America. The company was allowed duty-free export of tea (though the import tax was retained) and could sell directly through its own agents. Thus, the company could undercut the prices of both legitimate colonial merchants and smugglers. In Massachusetts, protests against the company's monopoly culminated in the Boston Tea Party (December 16, 1773), in which a patriotic gang, the Sons of Liberty, dressed as Indians and led by Sam Adams, dumped 45 tons of tea from the British ship *Dartmouth* into Boston Harbor. Their actions led to punitive measures by Britain, labeled the Coercive or Intolerable Acts by the colonists. These increased colonial hostility toward the mother country.

An Act
For explaining and amending an act made in the seventh year of his present Majesty, intituled, An act for taking off the inland duty of one shilling *per* pound weight upon all black and singlo teas consumed in *Great Britain;* and for granting a drawback upon the exportation of teas to *Ireland,* and the *British* dominions in *America,* for a limited time, upon such indemnification to be made in respect thereof by the *East India Company* as is therein mentioned, for permitting the exportation of teas in smaller

quantities than one lot to *Ireland,* or the said dominions in *America; and for preventing teas seized and condemned from being consumed in Great Britain; and for settling certain doubts and disputes which have arisen upon the said act of parliament.*

Whereas *by an act of parliament made in the seventh year of his present Majesty, intituled,* An act for taking off the inland duty of one shilling *per* pound weight upon all black and singlo teas consumed in *Great Britain;* and for granting a drawback upon the exportation of teas to *Ireland* and the *British* dominions in *America,* for a limited time, upon such indemnification to be made in respect thereof by the *East India Company,* as is therein mentioned, for permitting the exportation of teas in smaller quantities than one lot to *Ireland,* or the said dominions in *America;* and for preventing teas seized and condemned from being consumed in *Great Britain; amongst other things reciting, That the taking off the inland duty of one shilling* per *pound weight, then payable as therein is mentioned, upon black and singlo teas, and the allowing, upon the exportation of all teas which shall be exported to* Ireland *and his Majesty's plantations in* America, *the whole of the duty paid upon the importation thereof into this kingdom, appear to be the most probable and expedient means of extending the consumption of teas legally imported within this kingdom, and of increasing the exportation of teas to* Ireland, *and to his Majesty's plantations in* America, *which are now chiefly furnished by foreigners in a course of illicit trade; and further reciting, that the united company of merchants of* England *trading to the* East Indies, *are willing and desirous to indemnify the publick in such manner as is therein after provided, with respect to any diminution of the revenue which should or might happen from this experiment, it is amongst other things enacted, That for and during the space of five years, to be computed from the fifth day of* July, *one thousand seven hundred and sixty-seven, the said inland duty of one shilling* per *pound weight upon teas shall not be paid for or in respect of any bohea, congo, souchong, or pekoe teas, commonly called* Black Teas, *or any teas known by the denomination of* Singlo Teas, *which shall be cleared for consumption within* Great Britain *out of the warehouses of the said united company, but that all such teas so to be cleared, whether the same have been already or shall be hereafter sold by the said company, or their successors, shall be, and are thereby free and discharged, during the said term, from the said inland duty; and it is thereby, amongst other things, further enacted, That for and during the like space of five years, to be computed from the fifty day of* July, *one thousand seven hundred and sixty- seven, there shall be drawn back and allowed for all teas exported from this kingdom, as mer-*

chandise to Ireland, *or any of the* British *colonies or plantations in* America, *the whole duties of customs, payable upon the importation of such teas, and for making good any diminution which might happen in the revenues of customs and excise, by the discontinuance of the said duty, and the allowance of the said drawback, during the term aforesaid; it was further enacted, That on or before the fifth day of* September, *one thousand seven hundred and sixty-eight, and on or before the first day of* September, *in each of the four succeeding years, a true and exact account shall be taken, stated, and made up, by the proper officers of the customs and excise respectively, of the net produce of all the duties of customs, for and in respect of teas sold by the said company, and also of the net produce of the duties of excise, upon teas cleared out of the warehouses, belonging to the said company within the year, ending the fifth day of* July *immediately preceding the taking, stating, and making up such accounts, and that a sum which shall be equal to the annual net produce of the duties of customs, paid upon the importation of teas which were exported to* Ireland, *and the* British *colonies and plantations in* America, *upon an average for five years, preceding the fifth day of* July, *one thousand seven hundred and sixty-seven, shall be deducted from the total of the net produce, so stated of the said duties of customs and excise in the said account for the year ending the said day of* July, *one thousand seven hundred and sixty-eight, and for each of the said four succeeding years respectively; and if after such deduction shall have been made, the remaining sum shall not amount to the sum as shall be equal to the annual net produce of all the duties of customs, for and in respect of teas sold by the said company, and also to the annual net produce of the duties of excise, upon teas cleared out of the warehouses of the said company, on an average for five years, preceding the said fifth day of* July, *one thousand seven hundred and sixty-seven, then, and in every such case, from time to time, as often as such case shall so happen, the said company or their successors, within forty days after a copy of such yearly account respectively, shall have been delivered to their chairman, deputy chairman, secretary, cashier, or accomptant general, shall advance and pay for every such year respectively, into the receipt of his Majesty's exchequer, for his Majesty's use, such sum of money as shall, with the monies remaining in such respective annual account, after the deduction aforesaid shall have been made, amount to such a sum, as shall be equal to the annual net produce of all the said duties of customs and excise upon teas, on the said average of five years, preceding the said fifth day of* July, *one thousand seven hundred and sixty-seven, so as the money to be paid by the said company, or their successors, in pursuance of the said act, shall not in any one of the said five years,* exceed *such a sum, as shall be equal to the annual net amount of the said inland duty of one shilling* per *pound weight, upon teas cleared from the warehouses of the said company for consumption within* Great Britain, *and also to the annual net amount of the duties of customs, paid on the importation of teas, which were exported to* Ireland, *and the* British *colonies and plantations in* America, *upon an average for five years, preceding the fifth day of* July, *one thousand seven hundred and sixty-seven: and whereas the annual net produce of the duties of customs, paid upon the importation of teas, which were exported to* Ireland, *and the* British *colonies an plantations in* America, *upon an average for five years, preceding the fifth day of* July, *one thousand seven hundred and sixty-seven, is found, to amount to the sum of thirty-two thousand three hundred and two pounds, four shillings, and sixpence, and the annual net produce of all the duties of customs, for or in respect of teas sold by the said company, together with the annual net produce of the duties of excise upon teas, cleared out from the warehouses of the said company, on an average of five years, preceding the fifth day of* July, *one thousand seven hundred and sixty-seven, is found to amount to the sum of seven hundred and eighteen thousand, nine hundred and sixty-six pounds, one shilling, and two-fifth parts of a penny: and whereas if the said sum of thirty-two thousand three hundred and two pounds, four shillings and sixpence, should be deducted from the total of the net produce of the customs of excise, upon teas sold by the said united company, and cleared out of their warehouses, after paying such drawbacks as are allowed by the said in part-recited act, in the year ending on the said fifth day of* July, *one thousand seven hundred and sixty-eight, and in each of the said four succeeding years; and, if the said united company should be bound to pay such sum, as will make the sum which shall remain after such deduction equal to the said sum of seven hundred and eighteen thousand nine hundred and sixty-six pounds, one shilling, and two-fifth parts of a penny, your Majesty would probably in every of the said years, receive from the said united company a greater sum of money, in the name of indemnity, than the actual deficiency of your Majesty's revenue, computed upon the average in the said recited act mentioned, would amount to; and, on the other hand, if the said deduction should be made from the said total of the produce of the customs and excise, upon teas sold by and cleared out of the warehouses of the said united company for the year, ending on the said fifth day of* July, *one thousand seven hundred and sixty-eight, and for each of the said four succeeding years, before paying or deducting such drawbacks as are allowed by the said recited act; and if the said company should only pay such sum, as would make the sum, in such case, remaining equal to the* said sum of seven hundred and eighteen thousand nine hundred and sixty-six pounds, one shilling, and two-fifth parts of a penny, your Majesty would probably in every of the said years, receive less than the actual deficiency of your Majesty's revenue, computed upon the average in the said act mentioned, would amount to; so that the rule prescribed by the said act, for estimating the indemnity therein provided, is inadequate and ineffectual, whereupon doubts and disputes have arisen between the officers of your Majesty's revenue, and the said united company concerning the manner of ascertaining the same: and whereas it appears to have been the true intent and meaning of the said act, That the said united company should fully indemnity your Majesty, for any diminution of your Majesty's revenue, which might happen from the experiment in the said act mentioned, by paying to your Majesty such sum of money as should be sufficient to make the net produce of the duties of customs and excise, upon teas sold by the cleared out of the warehouses of the said company in the said year, to be computed from the fifth day of July, one thousand seven hundred and sixty-seven, after paying the said drawbacks allowed by the said act, and in each of the said four succeeding years, after the like payment of the said drawbacks, equal to the said sum of seven hundred and eighteen thousand nine hundred and sixty-six pounds, one shilling, and two-fifth parts of a penny, and the said united company are willing, and have agreed, to indemnify your Majesty accordingly, provided the several sums so to be computed, may be accepted in satisfaction and discharge of their agreement, and of the act herein-before recited; May it therefore please your most excellent Majesty, that it may be declared and enacted; and be it declared and enacted by the King's most excellent majesty, by and with the advice and consent of the lords spiritual and temporal, and commons, in this present parliament assembled, and by the authority of the same, That instead of the rate of indemnity provided by the said act, and to be computed as therein is mentioned, the said united company shall be liable to pay and make good to his Majesty for the year ending on the fifth day of July, one thousand seven hundred and sixty-eight, and for each of the said four succeeding years, such sum of money as, together with the net produce of customs, upon teas so by the said company and the net produce of excise upon teas cleared out from the warehouses of the said company, shall, in and for each of the said years, amount to the sum of seven hundred and eighteen thousand nine hundred and sixty-six pounds, one shilling, and two-fifth parts of a penny, and no more.

II. *And whereas by an account stated and made up in conformity to the rate of indemnity herein before last mentioned, for the first four of the said five years, the said four years ending on the fifth day of* July, *one thousand seven hundred and seventy-one, the said united company of merchants of* England *trading to the* East Indies, *stand indebted to his Majesty in the sum of one hundred and seventeen thousand three hundred and fourteen pounds, one shilling, and three- pence, and seven-twentieth parts of a penny;* be it further enacted by the authority aforesaid, That the said company shall, on or before the fifth day of July, which will be in the year of our Lord one thousand seven hundred and seventy-two, advance and pay into the receipt of his Majesty's exchequer the said sum of one hundred and seventeen thousand three hundred and fourteen pounds, one shilling, and three-pence, and seven-twentieth parts of a penny, without any abatement or defalcation whatsoever.

III. And be it further enacted by the authority aforesaid, That all the monies that shall be paid into the receipt of his Majesty's exchequer, in pursuance of this act, shall be applied to and for the uses and purposes directed by the aforemention act of the seventh year of the reign of his present Majesty.

IV. And be it further enacted by the authority aforesaid, That on or before the first day of *September*, which shall be the year of our Lord one thousand seven hundred and seventy-two, a true and exact account shall be taken, stated, and made up by the proper officers of the customs and excise respectively of the net produce of all the duties of customs for and in respect of teas fold by the said united company, and also the net produce of all the duties of excise upon teas cleared out from the warehouses belonging to the said united company, within the year ending the fifth day of *July*, one thousand seven hundred and seventy-two: and if the net sum total of both the said revenues, after paying the said drawback allowed by the said recite act, shall not amount to the sum of seven hundred and eighteen thousand nine hundred and sixty-six pounds, one shilling, and two fifth parts of a penny, the said united company shall, within forty days after such account shall have been delivered to the chairman, deputy chairman, secretary, cashier, or accountant general, advance and pay into the receipt of his Majesty's exchequer, for his Majesty's use, such sum of money as shall, together with the said sum total of customs and excise, computed as aforesaid, make up the said sum of seven hundred and eighteen thousand nine hundred and sixty-six pounds, one shilling, and two fifth parts of a penny.

V. And be it further enacted, That the said sum of one hundred and seventeen thousand three hundred and fourteen pounds, one shilling, and three-pence, and seventh-twentieth parts of a penny, and also such sum of money as shall be payable by the said united company, in respect of the account herein before directed to be made up for the year ending on the fifth day of *July,* one thousand seven hundred and seventy-two, shall, in default of payment as aforesaid, be sued for and recovered in such manner and form as the several sums required to be paid-in and by the said recited act are therein directed to be sued for and recovered.

VI. And be it further declared and enacted by the authority aforesaid, That the said recited act is and shall be confirmed and established, except so far as the same is hereby explained, altered or repealed.

Source:
Statutes at Large, Vol. 29, pp. 4–8 .

Coercive or Intolerable Acts, 1774

Starting with the Boston Port Act, passed by the British Parliament on March 31, 1774, and effective June 1, 1774, these acts were meant as punishment for the Boston Tea Party (December 16, 1773), in which colonists threw tea from ships of the British East India Company into Boston Harbor.

Boston Port Act, 1774

This act closed the customhouse and port of Boston, Massachusetts, until the company was paid for the destroyed tea and until Britain's King George III was assured of the Boston colonists' loyalty. In the interim, Marblehead became the port of entry.

An Act
To discontinue, in such manner, and for such time as are therein mentioned, the landing and discharging, lading or shipping, of goods, wares, and merchandise, at the town, and within the harbour, of Boston, in the province of Massachuset's Bay, in North America.

Whereas *dangerous commotions and insurrections have been fomented and railed in the town of* Boston, *in the province of* Massachuset's Bay, *in New England, by divers ill-affected persons, to the subversion of his Majesty's government, and to the utter destruction of the publick peace, and good order of the said town; in which commotions and insurrections certain valuable cargoes of teas, being the property of the* East India Company, *and on board certain vessels lying within the bay or harbour of* Boston, *were seized and destroyed: And whereas, in the present condition of the said town and harbour, the commerce of his Majesty's subjects cannot be safely carried on there, nor the customs payable to his Majesty duly collected; and it is therefore expedient that the officers of his Majesty's customs should be forthwith removed from the*

said town: May it please your Majesty that it may be enacted; and be it enacted by the King's most excellent majesty, by and with the advice and consent of the lords spiritual and temporal, and commons, in this present parliament assembled, and by the authority of the fame, That from and after the first day *of June,* one thousand seven hundred and seventy-four, it shall not be lawful for any person or persons whatsoever to lade put, or cause or procure to be laden or put, off or from any quay, wharf, or other place, within the said town of *Boston,* or in or upon any part of the shore of the bay, commonly called *The Harbour of Boston,* between a certain headland or point called *Nabant Point,* on the eastern side of the entrance into the said bay, and a certain other headland or point called *Alderton Point,* on the western side of the entrance into the said bay, or in or upon any island, creek, landing place, bank, or other place, within the said bay or headlands, into any ship, vessel, lighter, boat, or bottom, any goods, wares, or merchandise whatsoever, to be transported or carried into any other country, province, or place whatsoever, or into any other part of the said province of the *Massachuset's Bay,* in *New England;* or to take up, discharge, or lay on land, or cause or procure to be taken up, discharged, or laid on land, within the said town, or in or upon any of the places aforesaid, out of any boat, lighter, ship, vessel, or bottom, any goods, wares, or merchandise whatsoever, to be brought from any other country, province, or place, or any other part of the said province of the *Massachuset's Bay* in *New England,* upon pain of the forfeiture of the said goods, wares, and merchandise, and of the said boat, lighter, ship, vessel, or other bottom into which the fame shall be put, or out of which the fame shall be taken, and of the guns, ammunition, tackle, furniture, and stores, in or belonging to the fame: And if any such goods, wares, or merchandise, shall, within the said town, or in any the places aforesaid, be laden or taken in from the shore into any barge, hoy, lighter, wherry, or boat, to be carried on board any ship or vessel outward-bound to any other country or province, or other part of the said province of the *Massachuset's Bay* in *New England,* or be laden or taken into such barge, hoy, lighter, wherry, or boat, from or out of any ship or vessel coming in and arriving from any other country or province, or other part of the said province of the *Massachuset's Bay* in *New England,* such barge, hoy, lighter, wherry, or boat, shall be forfeited and lost.

II. And be it further enacted by the authority aforesaid, That if any warfinger, or keeper of any wharf, crane, or quay, or their servants, or any of them, shall take up or land, or knowingly suffer to be taken up or landed, or shall ship off, or suffer to be waterborne, at or from any of their said wharfs, cranes, or quays, any such goods, wares, or merchandise; in every such case, all and every such wharfinger, and keeper of such wharf, crane, or quay, and every person whatever who shall be assisting, or otherwise concerned in the shipping or in the loading or putting on board any boat, or other vessel, for that purpose, or in the unshipping such goods, wares, and merchandise, or to whose hands the same shall knowingly come after the loading, shipping, or unshipping thereof, shall forfeit and lose treble the value thereof, to be computed at the highest price which such sort of goods, wares, and merchandise, shall bear at the place where such offence shall be committed, at the time when the same shall be so committed, together with the vessels and boats, and all the horses, cattle, and carriages, whatsoever made use of in the shipping, unshipping, landing, removing, carriage, or conveyance of any of the aforesaid goods, wares, and merchandise.

III. And be it further enacted by the authority aforesaid, That if any ship or vessel shall be moored or lie at anchor, or be seen hovering within the said bay, described and bounded as aforesaid, or within one league from the said bay so described, or the said headlands, or any of the islands lying between or within the same, it shall and may be lawful for any admiral, chief commander, or commissioned officer, of his Majesty's fleet or ships of war, or for any officer of his Majesty's customs, to compel such ship or vessel to depart to some other port or harbour, or to such station as the said officer shall appoint, and to use such force for that purpose as shall be found necessary: And if such ship or vessel shall not depart accordingly, within six hours after notice for that purpose given by such person as aforesaid, such ship or vessel, together with all the goods laden on board thereon, and all the guns, ammunition, tackle, and furniture, shall be forfeited and lost, whether bulk shall have been broken or not.

IV. Provided always, That nothing in this act contained shall extend, or be construed to extend, to any military or other shores for his Majesty's use, or to the ships or vessels whereon the same shall be laden, which shall be commissioned by, and in the immediate pay of, his Majesty, his heirs or successors; nor to any fuel or victual brought coastwise from any part of the continent of *America,* for the necessary use and sustenance of the inhabitants of the said town of *Boston,* provided the vessels wherein the same are to be carried shall be duly furnished with a cocket and let-pass, after having been duly searched by the proper officers of his Majesty's customs at *Marblehead,* in the port of *Salem,* in the said province of *Massachuset's Bay;* and that some officer of his majesty's customs be also there put on board the said vessel, who is hereby authorised to go on board, and proceed with the said vessel, together with a sufficient number of persons, properly armed, for his defence, to the said town or harbour of *Boston;* nor to any ships or vessels which may happen to be within the said

harbour of *Boston* on or before the first day of *June,* one thousand seven hundred and seventy four, and may have either laden or taken on board, or be there with intent to load or take on board, or to land or discharge any goods, wares, and merchandise, provided the said ships and vessels do depart the said harbour within fourteen days after the said first day of *June,* one thousand seven hundred and seventy-four.

V. And be it further enacted by the authority aforesaid, That all seizures, penalties, and forfeitures, inflicted by this act, shall be made and prosecuted by any admiral, chief commander, or commissioned officer, of his Majesty's fleet, or ships of war, or by the officers of his Majesty's customs, or some of them, or by some other person deputed or authorised, by warrant from the lord high treasurer, or the commissioners of his Majesty's treasury for the time being, and by no other person whatsoever: And if any such officer, or other person authorised as aforesaid, shall, directly or indirectly, take or receive any bribe or reward, to connive at such lading or unlading, or shall make or commence any collusive seizure, information, or agreement for that purpose, or shall do any other act whatsoever, whereby the goods, wares, or merchandise, prohibited as aforesaid, shall be suffered to pass, either inwards or outwards, or whereby the forfeitures and penalties inflicted by this act may be evaded, every such offender shall forfeit the sum of five hundred pounds for every such offence, and shall become incapable of any office or employment, civil or military; and every person who shall give, offer, or promise, any such bribe or reward, or shall contract, agree, or treat with any person, so authorised as aforesaid, to commit any such offence, shall forfeit the sum of fifty pounds.

VI. And be it further enacted by the authority aforesaid, That the forfeitures and penalties inflicted by this act shall and may be prosecuted, sued for, and recovered, and be divided, paid, and applied, in like manner as other penalties and forfeitures inflicted by any act or acts of parliament, relating to the trade or revenues of the *British* colonies or plantations in *America,* are directed to be prosecuted, sued for, or recovered, divided, paid, and applied, by two several acts of parliament, the one passed in the fourth year of his present Majesty, (intituled, *An act for granting certain duties in the* British *colonies and plantations in* America; *for continuing, amending, and making perpetual, an act passed in the sixth year of the reign of his late majesty King* George *the Second, intituled,* An act for the better securing and encouraging the trade of his Majesty's sugar colonies in *America: for applying the produce of such duties, and of the duties to arise by virtue of the said act, towards defraying the expences of defending, protecting, and securing, the said colonies and plantations; for explaining an act made in the twenty-fifth year of the reign of King* Charles *the Second, intituled,* An act for the encouragement of the *Greenland* and *Eastland* trades, and for the better securing the plantation trade; *and for altering and disallowing several drawback's on exports from this kingdom, and more effectually preventing the clandestine conveyance of goods to and from the said colonies and plantations, and improving and securing the trade between the same and* Great Britain;) the other passed in the eighth year of his present Majesty's reign, (intituled, *An act for the more easy and effectual recovery of the penalties and forfeitures inflicted by the acts of parliament relating to the trade or revenues of the* British *colonies and plantations in* America.)

VII. And be it further enacted by the authority aforesaid, That every charter party bill of loading, and other contract for consigning shipping, or carrying any goods, wares, and merchandize whatsoever, to or from the said town of *Boston,* or any part of the bay or harbour thereof, described as aforesaid, which have been made or entered into, or which shall be made or entered into, so long as this act shall remain in full force, relating to any ship which shall arrive at the said town or harbour, after the first day of *June,* one thousand seven hundred and seventy-four, shall be, and the same are hereby declared to be, utterly void, to all intents and purposes whatsoever.

VIII. And be it further enacted by the authority aforesaid, That whenever it shall be made to appear to his Majesty, in his privy council, that peace and obedience to the laws shall be so far restored in the said town of *Boston,* that the trade of *Great Britain* may safety be carried on there, and his Majesty's customs duly collected, and his Majesty, in his privy council, shall adjudge the same to be true, it shall and may be lawful for his Majesty, by proclamation, or order of council, to assign and appoint the extent, bounds, and limits, of the port or harbour of *Boston,* and of every creek or haven within the same, or in the islands within the precincts thereof, and also to assign and appoint such and so many open places, quays, and wharfs, within the said harbour, creeks, havens, and islands, for the landing, discharging, lading, and shipping of goods, as his Majesty, his heirs or successors, shall judge necessary and expedient; and also to appoint such and so many officers of the customs therein as his Majesty shall think fit; after which it shall be lawful for any person or persons to lade or put off from, or to discharge and land upon, such wharfs, quays, and places, so appointed within the said harbour, and none other, any goods, wares, and merchandise whatever.

IX. Provided always, That if any goods, wares, or merchandize, shall be laden or put off from, or discharged or landed upon, any other place than the quays, wharfs, or places, so to be appointed, the same, together with the ships, boats, and other vessels employed therein, and the

horses, or other cattle and carriages used to convey the same, and the person or persons concerned or assisting therein, or to whole hands the same shall knowingly come, shall suffer all the forfeitures and penalties imposed by this or any other act on the illegal shipping or landing of goods.

X. Provided also, and it is hereby declared and enacted, That nothing herein contained shall extend , or be construed, to enable his Majesty to appoint such port, harbour, creeks, quays, wharfs, places, or officers, in the said town of *Boston,* or in the said bay or islands, until it shall sufficiently appear to his Majesty that full satisfaction hath been made by or on behalf of the inhabitants of the said town of *Boston* to the united company of merchants of *England* trading to the *East Indies,* for the damage sustained by the said company by the destruction of their goods sent to the said town of *Boston,* on board certain ships or vessels as aforesaid; and until it shall be certified to his Majesty, in council, by the governor, or lieutenant governor, of the said province, that reasonable satisfaction hath been made to the officers of his Majesty's revenue, and others, who suffered by the riots and insurrections above mentioned, in the months of *November* and *December,* in the year one thousand seven hundred and seventy-three, and in the month of *January,* in the year one thousand seven hundred and seventy-four.

XI. And be it further enacted by the authority aforesaid, That if any action or suit shall be commenced, either in *Great Britain* or *America,* against any person or persons, for any thing done in pursuance of this act of parliament, the defendant or defendants, in such action or suit, may plead the general issue, and give the said act, and the special matter, in evidence, at any trial to be had thereupon, and that the same was done in pursuance and by the authority of this act; and if it shall appear so to have been done, the jury shall find for the defendant or defendants; and if the plaintiff shall be nonsuited, or discontinue his action, after the defendant or defendants shall have appeared; or if judgment shall be given upon any verdict or demurrer, against the plaintiff, the defendant or defendants shall recover treble costs, and have the like remedy for the same, as defendants have in other cases by law.

Massachusetts Government Act, 1774

Enacted by the British Parliament with royal assent May 20, 1774, this statute enlarged the British governor's powers in the colony of Massachusetts. It nullified the colony's charter, depriving the colonists of their rights and reducing Massachusetts to the status of a crown colony. Appointment or election of various officials passed out of the hands of citizens and their representatives and came under the control of the governor and the king of England. The act also abolished town meetings, except for the strict purpose of electing municipal officers.

An Act

For the better regulating the government of the province of the Massachuset's Bay, in New England.

Whereas, *by letters patent under the great seal of* England, *made in the third year of the reign of their late majesties King* William *and Queen* Mary, *for uniting, erecting, and incorporating, the several colonies, territories, and tracts of land therein mentioned, into one real province, by the name of* Their Majesties Province of the Massachuset's Bay, *in* New England; *whereby it was, amongst other things, ordained and established, That the governor of the said province should, from thenceforth, be appointed and commissionated by their Majesties, their heirs and successors: It was, however, granted and ordained, That, from the expiration of the term for and during which the eight and twenty persons named in the said letters patent were appointed to be the first counsellors or assistants to the governor of the said province for the time being, the aforesaid number of eight and twenty counsellors or assistants should yearly, once in every year, for ever thereafter, be, by the general court or assembly, newly chosen: And whereas the said method of electing such counsellors or assistants, to be vested with the several powers, authorities, and privileges, therein mentioned, although conformable to the practice theretofore used in such of the colonies thereby united, in which the appointment of the respective governors had been vested in the general courts or assemblies of the said colonies, hath, by repeated experience, been found to be extremely ill adapted to the plan of government established in the province of the* Massachuset's Bay, *by the said letters patent herein- before mentioned, and hath been so far from contributing to the attainment of the good ends and purposes thereby intended, and to the promoting of the internal welfare, peace, and good government, of the said province, or to the maintenance of the just subordination to, and conformity with, the laws of Great Britain, that the manner of exercising the powers, authorities, and privileges aforesaid, by the persons so annually elected, hath, for some time past, been such as had the most manifest tendency to obstruct, and, in great measure, defeat, the execution of the laws; to weaken the attachment of his Majesty's well-disposed subjects in the said province to his Majesty's government, and to encourage the ill- disposed among them to proceed even to acts of direct resistance to, and defiance of, his Majesty's authority: And it hath accordingly happened, that an open resistance to the execution of the laws hath actually taken place in the town of* Boston, *and the neighbourhood thereof, within the said province: And whereas it is, under these circumstances, become absolutely necessary, in order to the preservation of the peace and good order of the said province, the protection of his Majesty's well-disposed subjects therein resident, the continuance of the mutual benefits arising from the commerce and correspondence between this kingdom and the said province, and the maintaining of the just dependance of the said province upon the crown and parliament of* Great Britain, *that the said method of annually electing the counsellors or assistants of the said province should no longer be suffered to continue, but that the appointment of the said counsellors or assistants should henceforth be put upon the like footing as is established in such other of his Majesty's colonies or plantations in* America, *the governors whereof are appointed by his Majesty's commission, under the great seal of* Great Britain: Be it therefore enacted by the King's most excellent Majesty, by and with the advice and consent of the lords spiritual and temporal, and commons, in this present parliament assembled, and by the authority of the fame, That from and after the first day of *August,* one thousand seven hundred and seventy-four, so much of the charter, granted by their majesties King *William* and Queen *Mary* to the inhabitants of the said province of the *Massachuset's Bay,* in *New England,* and all and every clause, matter, and thing, therein contained, which relates to the time and manner of electing the assistants or counsellors for the said province, be revoked, and is hereby revoked and made void and of none effect; and that the offices of all counsellors and assistants, elected and appointed in pursuance thereof, shall from thenceforth cease and determine: And that, from and after the said first day of *August,* one thousand seven hundred and seventy-four, the council, or court of assistants of the said province for the time being, shall be composed of such of the inhabitants or proprietors of lands within the same as shall be thereunto nominated and appointed by his Majesty, his heirs and successors, from time to time, by warrant under his or their signer or sign manual, and with the advice of the privy council, agreeable to the practice now used in respect to the appointment of counsellors in such of his Majesty's other colonies in *America,* the governors whereof are appointed by commission under the great seal of *Great Britain:* provided, that the number of the said assistants or counsellors shall not, at any one time, exceed thirty-six, nor be less than twelve.

II. And it is hereby further enacted, That the said assistants or counsellors, so to be appointed as aforesaid, shall hold their offices respectively, for and during the pleasure of his Majesty, his heirs or successors; and shall have and enjoy all the powers, privileges, and immunities, at present held, exercised, and enjoyed, by the assistants or counsellors of the said province, constituted and elected, from time to time, under the said charter, (except as herein-after excepted); and shall also, upon their admission into the said council, and before they enter upon the execution of their offices respectively, take the oaths, and make, repeat, and subscribe, the declarations required, as well by the said charter as by any law or laws of the said province now in force, to be taken by the assistants or counsellors who have been so elected and constituted as aforesaid.

III. And be it further enacted by the authority aforesaid, That from and after the first day of *July,* one thousand seven hundred and seventy-four, it shall and may be lawful for his Majesty's governor for the time being of the said province, or, in his absence, for the lieutenant- governor, to nominate and appoint, under the seal of the province, from time to time, and also to remove, without the consent of the council, all judges of the inferior courts of common pleas, commissioners of *Oyer* and *Terminer,* the attorney general, provosts, marshals, justices of the peace, and other officers to the council or courts of justice belonging; and that all judges of the inferior courts of common pleas, commissioners of *Oyer* and *Terminer,* the attorney general, provosts, marshals, justices, and other officers so appointed by the governor, or, in his absence, by the lieutenant- governor alone, shall and may have, hold, and exercise, their said offices, powers, and authorities, as fully and completely, to all intents and purposes, as any judges of the inferior courts of common pleas, commissioners of *Oyer* and *Terminer,* attorney general, provosts, marshals, or other officers, have or might have done heretofore under the said letters patent, in the third year of the reign of their late majesties King *William* and Queen *Mary;* any law, statute, or usage, to the contrary notwithstanding.

IV. Provided always, and be it enacted, That nothing herein contained shall extend, or be construed to extend, to annual or make void the commission granted before the said first day of *July,* one thousand seven hundred and seventy-four, to any judges of the inferior courts of common pleas, commissioners of *Oyer* and *Terminer,* the attorney general, provosts, marshals, justices of the peace, or other officers; but that they may hold and exercise the same, as if this act had never been made, until the same shall be determined by death, removal by the governor, or other avoidance, as the cafe may happen.

V. And be it further enacted by the authority aforesaid, That, from and after the said first day of *July,* one thousand seven hundred and seventy-four, it shall and may be lawful for his Majesty's governor, or, in his absence, for the lieutenant-governor for the time being of the said province, from time to time, to nominate and appoint the sheriffs without the consent of the council, and to remove such sheriffs with such consent, and not otherwise.

VI. And be it further enacted by the authority aforesaid, That, upon every vacancy of the officers of chief justice and judges of the superior court of the SAID province, from and after the said first day of *July,* one thousand seven hundred and seventy-four, the governor for the time being, or, in his absence, the lieutenant-governor, without the consent of the council, shall have full power and authority to nominate and appoint the persons to succeed to the said offices, who shall hold their commissions during the pleasure of his Majesty, his heirs and successors; and that neither the chief justice or judges appointed before the said first day of *July,* one thousand seven hundred and seventy-four, nor those who shall hereafter be appointed pursuant to this act, shall be removed, unless by the order of his Majesty, his heirs or successors, under his or their sign manual.

VII. *And whereas, by several acts of the general court, which have been from time to time enacted and passed within the said province, the freeholders and inhabitants of the several townships, districts, and precincts, qualified, as is therein expressed, are authorised to assemble together, annually, or occasionally, upon notice given, in such manner as the said acts direct, for the choice of select men, constables, and other officers, and for the making and agreeing upon such necessary rules, orders, and bye- laws, for the directing, managing, and ordering, the prudential affairs of such townships, districts, and precincts, and for other purposes; and whereas a great abuse has been made of the power of calling such meetings, and the inhabitants have, contrary to the design of their institution, been misled to treat upon matters of the most general concern, and to pass many dangerous and unwarrantable resolves:* for remedy whereof, be it enacted, That from and after the said first day of *August,* one thousand seven hundred and seventy-four, no meeting shall be called by the select men, or at the request of any number of freeholders of any township, district, or precinct, without the leave of the governor, or, in his absence, of the lieutenant-governor, in writing, expressing the special business of the said meeting, first had and obtained, except the annual meeting in the months of *March* or *May,* for the choice of select men, constables, and other officers, or except for the choice of persons to fill up the offices aforesaid, on the death or removal of any of the persons first elected to such offices, and also, except any meeting for the election of a representative or representatives in the general court; and that no other matter shall be treated of at such meetings, except the election of their aforesaid officers or representatives, nor at any other meeting, except the business expressed in the leave given by the governor, or, in his absence, by the lieutenant-governor.

VIII. *And whereas the method at present used in the province of* Massachuset's Bay, *in* America *of electing per-*

sons to serve on grand juries, and other juries, by the free-holders and inhabitants of the several towns, affords occasion for many evil practices, and tends to pervert the free and impartial administration of justice: for remedy whereof, be it further enacted by the authority aforesaid, That, from and after the respective times appointed for the holding of the general sessions of the peace in the several counties within the said province, next after the month of *September,* one thousand seven hundred and seventy-four, the jurors to serve at the superior courts of judicature, courts of assize, general gaol delivery, general sessions of the peace, and inferior court of common pleas, in the several counties within the said province, shall not be elected, nominated, or appointed, by the freeholders and inhabitants of the several towns within the said respective counties, nor summoned or returned by the constables of the said towns, but that, from thenceforth, the jurors, to serve at the superior courts of judicature, courts of assize, general gaol delivery, general sessions of the peace, and inferior court of common pleas within the said province, shall be summoned and returned by the sheriffs of the respective counties within the said province; and all writs of *Venire Facias,* or other process or warrants to be issued for the return of jurors to serve at the said courts, shall be directed to the sheriffs of the said counties respectively, any law, custom, or usage, to the contrary notwithstanding.

IX. Provided always, and be it further enacted by the authority aforesaid, That wherever the sheriff of any county shall happen to be a party, or interested or related to any party or person interested in any prosecution or suit depending in any of the said courts; that then, in such case, the writ of *Venire Facias,* or other process or warrant for the summoning and return of a jury, for the trial of such prosecution or suit, shall be directed to, and executed by, the coroner of such county; and in case such coroner shall be also a party, or interested in, or related to, any party or person interested in such prosecution or suit, then the *Venire Facias,* or other process or warrant, for the summoning and return of a jury for the trial of such prosecution or suit shall be directed to, and executed by, a proper and indifferent person, to be appointed for that purpose by the court wherein such prosecution or suit shall be depending.

X. *And that all sheriffs may be the better informed of persons qualified to serve on juries at the superior courts of judicature, courts of assize, general gaol delivery, general sessions of the peace, and inferior court of common pleas, within the said province,* be it further enacted by the authority aforesaid, That the constables of the respective towns, within the several counties of the said province shall, at the general sessions of the peace to be holden for each county, next after the month of *September* in every

year, upon the first day of the said sessions, return and deliver to the justices of the peace, in open court, a true lift, in writing, of the names and places of abode of all persons within the respective towns for which they serve, or the districts thereof, qualified to serve upon juries, with their titles and additions, between the age of one and twenty years and the age of seventy years; which said justices, or any two of them, at the said sessions in the respective counties, shall cause to be delivered a duplicate of the aforesaid lifts, by the clerk of the peace of every county, to the sheriffs, or their deputies, within ten days after such sessions; and cause each of the said lifts to be fairly entered into a book, by the clerk of the peace, to be by him provided, and kept for that purpose amongst the records of the said court; and no sheriff shall impanel or return any person or persons to serve upon any grand jury, or petit jury, whatsoever, in any of the said courts that shall not be named or mentioned to such lift: and, to prevent a failure of justice, through the neglect of constables to make such returns of persons qualified to serve on juries, as in and by this act is directed, the clerks of the peace of the said several counties are hereby required and commanded, twenty days at least next before the month of *September,* years, and every year, to issue forth precepts or warrants, under their respective hands and seals, to the respective constables of the several towns within the said respective counties, requiring them and every of them, to make such return of persons qualified to serve upon juries as hereby respectively directed; and every constable failing at any time to make and deliver such return to the justices in open court, as aforesaid, shall forfeit and incur the penalty of five pounds sterling to his Majesty, and his successors: to be recovered by bill, plaint, or information, to be prosecuted in any of the courts aforesaid; and, in order that the constables may be the better enabled to make complete lists of all persons qualified to serve on juries, the constables of the several towns shall have free liberty, at all seasonable times, upon request by them made to any officer or officers, who shall have in his or their custody any book or account of rates of taxes on the freeholders or inhabitants within such respective towns, to inspect the fame, and take from thence the names of such persons qualified to serve on juries, dwelling within the respective towns for which such lists are to be given in and returned pursuant to this act; and shall, in the month of *September,* yearly, and every year, upon two or more *Sundays,* fix upon the door of the church, chapel, and every other publick place of religious worship within their respective precincts, a true and exact list of all such persons intended to be returned to the said general sessions of the peace, as qualified to serve on juries, pursuant to the directions of this act; and leave at the same time a duplicate of such list with the town clerk of the said place, to be perused by the freeholders and inhabitants thereof, to the end that notice may be given of persons duly qualified who are omitted, or of persons inserted by mistake who ought to be omitted out of such lists; and it shall and may be lawful to and for the justices, at the general sessions of the peace to which the said lists shall be so returned, upon due proof made before them of any person or persons duly qualified to serve on juries being omitted in such lists, or of any person or persons being inserted therein who ought to have been omitted, to order his or their name or names to be inserted or struck out, as the case may require: and in case any constable shall wilfully omit, out of such list, any person or persons, whose name or names ought to be inserted, or shall wilfully insert any person or persons who ought to be omitted, every constable so offending, shall, for every person so omitted or inserted in such list, contrary to the true intent and meaning of this act, be fined by the said justices, in the said general sessions of the peace, in the sum of forty shillings sterling.

XI. Provided always, and be it enacted by the authority aforesaid, That in case default shall at any time hereafter be made, by any constable or constables, to return lists of persons qualified to serve on juries within any of the said towns to the said court of general sessions of the peace; then, and in such case, it shall and may be lawful for the sheriff of the country, in which such default shall be made, to summon and return to the several courts aforesaid, or any of them, such and so many persons dwelling in such towns, or the districts thereof, qualified to serve on juries, as he shall think fit to serve on juries at such respective courts; any thing herein contained to the contrary thereof in any-wife notwithstanding.

XII. And be it further enacted by the authority aforesaid, That every summons of any person, to serve upon any of the juries at the said courts, or any of them, shall be made by the sheriff, or other person, ten days at the least before the holding of every such court; and in case any jurors, so to be summoned, be absent from the usual place of his habitation at the time of such summons, notice of such summons shall be given, by leaving a note, in writing, under the hand of such sheriff, or person, containing the contents thereof, at the dwelling-house of such juror, with some person inhabiting in the same.

XIII. Provided always, and be it further enacted by the authority aforesaid, That in case a sufficient number of persons qualified to serve on juries shall not appear at the said courts, or any of them, to perform the service of grand or petit jurors; that then, and in such case, it shall be lawful for the said court to issue a writ or precept to the sheriff, requiring him to summon a sufficient number of other persons qualified to serve on juries, immediately to appear at such court, to fill up and compleat the number of jurors to serve at such court; and such persons are hereby required to appear and serve as jurors at the said courts accordingly.

XIV. And be it further enacted by the authority aforesaid, That no person who shall as a juror, at any of the said courts, shall be liable to serve again as a juror at the same court, or any other of the courts aforesaid, for the space of three years the next following, except upon special juries.

XV. *And, in order that sheriffs, may be informed of the persons who have served as jurors,* it is hereby further enacted by the authority aforesaid, That every sheriff shall prepare and keep a book, or register, wherein the names of all such persons who have served as jurors, with their additions and places of abode, and the times when, and the courts in which they served, shall be alphabetically entered and registered; which books or registers shall, from time to time, be delivered over to the succeeding sheriff of the said county, within ten days after he shall enter upon his office; and every juror, who shall attend and serve at any of the courts aforesaid, may, at the expiration of the time of holding every such court, upon application to the sheriff, or his deputy, have a certificate immediately, *gratis,* from the sheriff, or his deputy, testifying such his attendance and service; which said certificate the said sheriff, or his deputy, is required to give to every such juror.

XVI. And be it further enacted by the authority aforesaid, That if, by reason of challenges, or otherwise, there shall not be a sufficient number of jurors for the trial of any prosecution for any misdemeanour, or any action depending in any of the said courts; then, and in such case, the jury shall be filled up *de Talibus Circumstantibus,* to be returned by the sheriff, unless he be a party, or interested or related to any party or person interested in such prosecution or action; and, in any of which cases, to be returned by the coroner, unless he be a party, or interested or related to any party or person interested in such prosecution or action; and, in any of these cases, to be returned by a proper and indifferent person, to be appointed by the court for that purpose.

XVII. And be it further enacted by the authority aforesaid, That in case any person summoned to serve upon the grand or petit jury, at any of the courts aforesaid, or upon the jury in any prosecution, action, or suit, depending in any of the said courts, shall not appear and serve at the said courts, according to the said summons, (not having any reasonable excuse to be allowed by the judges or justices of such court,) he shall be fined by the judges or justices of such court in any sum not exceeding the sum of ten pounds, nor less than twenty shillings sterling.

XVIII. And be it further enacted by the authority aforesaid, That every sheriff, or other officer, to whom the *Venire Facias,* or other process or warrant, for the trial of causes, or summoning of juries, shall be directed, shall, upon his return of every such writ, or other process or warrant, (unless in cases where a special jury shall be struck by order or rule of courts, pursuant to this act,) annex a pannel to the said writ, or process, or warrant, containing the christian and surnames, additions, and places of abode, of a competent number of jurors, named in such lists, which number of jurors shall not be less than twenty- four, nor more than forty-eight, without direction of the judges or justices of such court or session, or one of them, who are hereby respectively impowered and required, if he or they fee cause, by order, under his or their respective hand or hands, to direct a greater number; and then such number as shall be so directed shall be the number to be returned to serve on such jury.

XIX. And be it further enacted by the authority aforesaid, That for the trials of all actions or fruits depending in any of the said courts, the name of each and every person who shall be summoned and returned as aforesaid, with his addition, and the place of his abode, shall be written in several and distinct pieces of parchment, or paper, being all as near as may be of equal size and bigness, and shall be delivered unto the officer to be appointed by the court for that purpose, by the sheriff, under sheriff, or some agent of his; and shall, by direction and care of such officer, be rolled up all as near as may be, in the same manner, and put together in a box or glass, to be provided for that purpose; and when any cause shall be brought on to be tried, some indifferent person, by direction of the court, may and shall, in open court, draw out twelve of the said parchments or papers, one after another; and if any of the persons, whose names shall be so drawn, shall not appear, or shall be challenged, and such challenge allowed, then such person shall proceed to draw other parchments or papers from the said box, till twelve indifferent persons shall be drawn; which twelve indifferent persons being sworn shall be the jury to try the said cause: and the names of the persons so drawn and sworn shall be kept apart by themselves in some other box or glass, to be kept for that purpose, till such jury shall have given in their verdict, and the same is recorded, or until such jury shall, by consent of the parties, or leave of the court, be discharged; and then the same names shall be rolled up again, and returned to the former box or glass, there to be kept, with the other names remaining at that time undrawn, and so *toties quoties,* as long as any cause remains then to be tried.

XX. And be it further enacted by the authority aforesaid, That it shall and may be lawful to and for the superior court of assize, and court of common pleas, upon motion made on behalf of his Majesty, his heirs or successors, or on the motion of any prosecutor or defendant, in any indictment or information for any misdemeanor depending, or to be brought or prosecuted in the said court, or on the motion of any plaintiff or plaintiffs, defendant or defen-

dants, in any action, cause, or suit whatsoever, depending, or to be brought and carried on in the said court, and the said court is hereby authorised and required, upon motion as aforesaid, in any of the cases before mentioned, to order the appoint a jury to be struck for the trial of any issue joined in any of the said cases, and triable by a jury of twelve men, by such officer of the said court as the court shall appoint; and for that purpose the sheriff, or his deputy, shall attend such officer with the duplicate of the lists of persons qualified to serve on juries; and such officer shall thereupon take down, in writing, from the said duplicate, the names of forty-eight persons qualified to serve on juries, with their additions, and places of abode, a copy whereof shall forthwith be delivered to the prosecutors or plaintiffs, their attornies or agents, and another copy thereof to the defendants, their attornies or agents, in such prosecutions and causes; and the said officer of the court aforesaid shall, at a time to be fixed by him for that purpose, strike out the names of twelve of the said persons, at the nomination of the prosecutors or plaintiffs, their attornies or agents, and also the names of twelve others of the said persons, at the nomination of the said defendants in such prosecutions and suits, and the twenty-four remaining persons shall be struck and summoned, and returned to the said court as jurors, for the trial of such issues.

XXI. Provided always, that in case the prosecutors or plaintiffs, or defendants, their attornies or agents, shall neglect or refuse to attend the officer at the time fixed for striking the names of twenty-four persons as aforesaid, or nominate the persons to be struck out; then, and in such case, the said officer shall, and he is hereby required to strike out the names of such number of said persons as such prosecutors or plaintiffs, or defendants, might have nominated to be struck out.

XXII. And be it further enacted, That the person or party who shall apply for such special jury is aforesaid, shall not only bear and pay the fees for striking such jury, but shall also pay and discharge all the expenses occasioned by the trial of the cause by such special jury, and shall not have any further or other allowance for the same, upon taxation of costs, than such person or party would be intitled unto in case the cause had been tried by a common jury, unless the judge, before whom the cause is tried, shall, immediately after the trial, certify, in open court, under his hand, upon the back of the record, that the same was a cause proper to be tried by a special jury.

XXIII. And be it further enacted by the authority aforesaid, That, in all actions brought in any of the said courts, where it shall appear to the court in which such actions are depending, that it will be proper and necessary that the jurors who are to try the issues in any such actions, should have the view of the messuages, lands, or place in question, in order to their better understanding the evidence that will be given upon the trial of such issues; in every such case the respective courts in which such actions shall be depending may order the jury to the place in question, who then and there shall have the matters in question shewn them by two persons to be appointed by the court; and the special costs of all such views as allowed by the court, shall, before the trial, be paid by the party who moved for the view, (the adverse party not consenting thereto;) and shall, at the taxation of the bill of costs, have the same allowed him, upon his recovering judgement in such trial; and upon all views with the consent of parties, ordered by the court, the costs thereof, as allowed by the court, shall, before trial, be equally paid by the said parties; and in the taxation of the bill of costs, the party recovering judgement shall have the sum by him paid allowed to him; any law, usage, or custom, to the contrary notwithstanding.

XXIV. And be it further enacted by the authority aforesaid, That if any action shall be brought against any sheriff, for what he shall do in execution, or by virtue of this act, he may plead the general issue, and give the special matter in evidence; and if a verdict shall be found for him, he shall recover treble costs.

Administration of Justice Act, 1774

Passed by the British Parliament May 21, 1774, its purpose was to quell the fears of royal officials in Massachusetts by providing that judges, soldiers, and revenue officers indicted for murder or other serious crimes committed in the execution of their official duties could be tried in Great Britain or another colony, thus avoiding hostile juries in Massachusetts. The act was viewed by the colonists as an attempt by Britain to impose a military despotism on Massachusetts.

An Act

For the impartial administration of justice in the cases of persons questioned for any acts done by them in the execution of the law, or for the suppression of riots and tumults, in the province of the Massachuset's Bay, in New England.

Whereas *in his Majesty's province of* Massachuset's Bay, *in* New England, *an attempt hath lately ben made to throw off the authority of the parliament of* Great Britain *over the said province, and an actual and avowed resistance, by open force, to the execution of certain acts of parliament, hath been suffered to take place, uncontrouled and unpunished, in defiance of his Majesty's authority, and to the utter subversion of all lawful government: and whereas, in the present disordered state of the said province, it is of the utmost importance to the general welfare thereof, and to the re-establishment of lawful authority throughout the same, that neither the magistrates*

acting in support of the laws, nor any of his Majesty's subjects aiding and assisting them therein, or in the suppression of riots and tumults, raised in opposition to the execution of the laws and statutes of this realm, should be discouraged from the proper discharge of their duty, by an apprehension, that in case of their being questioned for any acts done therein, they may be liable to be brought to trial for the same before persons who do not acknowledge the validity of the laws, in the execution thereof, or the authority of the magistrate in the support of whom, such acts had been done: in order therefore to remove every such discouragement from the minds of his Majesty's subjects, and to induce them, upon all proper occasions, to exert themselves in support of the public peace of the province, and of the authority of the King and parliament of Great Britain *over the same;* be it enacted by the King's most excellent majesty, by and with the advice and consent of the lords spiritual and temporal, and commons, in this present parliament assembled, and by the authority of the same, That any inquisition or indictment shall be found, or if any appeal shall be sued or preferred against any person, for murther, or other capital offence, in the province of the *Massachuset's Bay,* and it shall appear, by information given upon oath to the governor, or, in his absence, to the lieutenant-governor of the said province, that the fact was committed by the person against whom such inquisition or indictment shall be found, or against whom such appeal shall be sued or perferred, as aforesaid, either in the execution of his duty as a magistrate, for the suppression of riots, or in the support of the laws of revenue, or in acting in his duty as an officer of revenue, or in acting under the direction and order of any magistrate, for the suppression of riots, or for the carrying into effect the laws of revenue, or in aiding and assisting in any of the cases aforesaid; and if it shall also appear, to the satisfaction of the said governor, or lieutenant-governor respectively, that an indifferent trial cannot be had within the said province, in that case, it shall and may be lawful for the governor, or lieutenant-governor, to direct, with the advice and consent of the council, that the inquisition, indictment, or appeal, shall be tried in some other of his Majesty's colonies, or in *Great Britain;* and for that purpose, to order the person against whom such inquisition or indictment shall be found, or against whom such appeal shall be sued of preferred, as aforesaid, to be sent, under sufficient custody, to the place appointed for his trial, or to admit such person to bail, taking a recognizance, (which the said governor, or, in his absence, the lieutenant-governor, is hereby authorized to take), from such person, with sufficient sureties, to be approved of by the said governor, or, in his absence, the lieutenant-governor, in such sums of money as the said governor, or, in his absence, the lieutenant-governor, shall deem reasonable, for the personal appearance of such person, if the trial shall be appointed to be had in any other colony, before the governor, or lieutenant-governor, or commander in chief of such colony, and if the trial shall be appointed to be had in *Great Britain,* then before his Majesty's court of *King's Bench,* at a time to be mentioned in such recognizances; and the governor, or lieutenant governor, or commander in chief of the colony where such trial shall be appointed to be had, or court of *King's Bench,* where the trial is appointed to be had in *Great Britain,* upon the appearance of such person, according to such recognizance, or in custody, shall either commit such person, or admit him to bail, until such trial; and which the said governor, or lieutenant-governor, or commander in chief, and court of *King's Bench,* are hereby authorised and impowered to do.

II. *And, to prevent a failure of justice, from the want of evidence on the trial of any such inquisition, indictment or appeal,* be it further enacted, That the governor, or, in his absence, the lieutenant-governor, shall, and he is hereby authorised and required, to bind in recognizances to his Majesty all such witnesses as the prosecutor or person against whom such inquisition or indictment shall be found, or appeal sued or preferred, shall desire to attend the trial of the said inquisition, indictment, or appeal, for their personal appearance, at the time and place of such trial, to give evidence: and the said governor, or in his absence, the lieutenant-governor, shall thereupon appoint a reasonable sum to be allowed for the expences of every such witness, and shall thereupon give to each witness a certificate, in writing, under his hand and seal, that such witness has entered into a recognizance to give evidence, and specifying the sum allowed for his expences; and the collector and collectors of the customs, or one of them, within the said province, upon the delivery of such certificate, are, and is hereby authorised and required, forthwith to pay to such witness the sum specified therein for his expences.

III. And be it further enacted by the authority aforesaid, That all prosecutors and witnesses, who shall be under recognizances to appear in any of his Majesty's colonies in *America,* or in *Great Britain,* in pursuance of this act, shall be free from all arrests and restraints, in any action or suit to be commenced against them during their going to such colony, or coming to *Great Britain,* and their necessary stay and abiding there, on occasion of such prosecution, and returning again to the said province of the *Massachusset's Bay.*

IV. And be it further enacted by the authority aforesaid, That all and every his Majesty's justices of the peace, and other justices and coroners, before whom any person shall be brought, charged with murther, or other capital crime, where it shall appear by proof, on oath, to such jus-

tice or coroners, that the fact was committed by such person, either in the execution of his duty as a magistrate, for the suppression of riots, or in the support of the laws of revenue, or in acting in his duty as an officer of revenue, or in acting under the direction and order of any magistrate, for the suppression of riots, or for the carrying into effect the laws of revenue, or in aiding and assisting in any of the cases aforesaid, are hereby authorised and required to admit every such person so brought before him or them, as aforesaid, to bail, any law, custom, or usage, to the contrary thereof in any-wife notwithstanding.

V. And be it further enacted by the authority aforesaid, That where it shall be made appear to the judges or justices of any court, within the said province of *Massachuset's Bay,* by any person, against whom any inquisition or indictment, shall be found or appeal sued or preferred for murther, or other capital crime that the fact was committed by such person, either in the execution of his duty as a magistrate, for the suppression of riots, or in the support of the laws of revenue, or in acting in his duty as an officer of revenue, or in acting under the direction and order of any magistrate, for the suppression of riots, or for the carrying into effect the laws of revenue, or in aiding and assisting in any of the cases aforesaid, and that he intends to make application to the governor, or lieutenant-governor of the said province that such inquisition, indictment, or appeal, may be tried in some other of his Majesty's colonies, or in *Great Britain,* the said judges or justices are hereby authorised and required to adjourn or postpone the trial of such inquisition, indictment, or appeal, for a reasonable time, and admit the person to bail, in order that he may make application to the governor, or lieutenant-governor, for the purpose aforesaid.

VI. And be it further enacted, That the governor, or, in his absence, the lieutenant-governor, if he shall direct the trial to be had in any other of his Majesty's colonies, shall transmit the inquisition, indictment, or appeal, together with recognizances of the witnesses, and other recognizances, under the seal of the province, to the governor, or lieutenant-governor, or commander in chief of such other colony, who shall immediately issue a commission of *Oyer* and *Terminer,* and deliver, or cause to be delivered, the said inquisition, indictment, or appeal, with the said recognizances to the chief justice, and such other persons as have usually been commissioners of *Oyer* and *Terminer,* justices of assize, or general goal delivery there; who shall have power to proceed upon the said inquisition, indictment, or appeal, as if the same had been returned, found, or preferred before them, and the trial shall thereupon proceed in like manner, to all intents and purposes, as if the offence had been committed in such place: and in case the governor, or, in his absence, the lieutenant-governor, shall direct the trial to be had in *Great Britain*, he shall then transmit the inquisition, indictment, or appeal, together with the recognizances, of the witnesses, and other recognizances, under the seal of the province, to one of Majesty's principal secretaries of slate, who shall deliver, or cause to be delivered, the same, to the master of the crown office, to be filed of record in the court of *King's Bench*, and the inquisition, indictment, or appeal, shall be tried and proceeded upon, in the next term, or at such other time as the court shall appoint, at the bar of the court of *King's Bench*, in like manner, to all intents and purposes, as if the offence had been committed in the county of *Middlesex*, or in any other county of that part of *Great Britain* called *England*, where the court of *King's Bench* shall sit, or else before such commissioners, and in such county, in that part of *Great Britain* called *England*, as shall be assigned by the King's majesty's commission, in like manner and form, to all intents and purposes, as if such offence had been committed in the same country where such inquisition, indictment, or appeal, shall be so tried.

VII. And be it enacted by the authority aforesaid, That in case, on account of any error or defect in any indictment, which, in virtue or under the authority of this act, shall be transmitted to any other colony, or to *Great Britain*, the same shall be qualified, or judgment thereon arrested, or such indictment adjudged bad upon demurrer, it shall and may be lawful to prefer a new indictment or indictments against the person or persons accused in the said colony, to which such indictment, so qualified or adjudged bad, shall have been transmitted, or before the grand jury of any country in *Great Britain*, in safe such former indictment shall have been transmitted to *Great Britain*, in the same manner as could be done in safe the party accused should return to the place where the offence was committed; and the grant jury and petty jury of such other colony or county in *Great Britain* shall have power to find and proceed upon such indictment or indictments, in the same manner as if the offence, by such indictment or indictments charged, had been committed within the limits of the colony or county for which such juries shall respectively be impanelled to serve.

VIII. And be it further enacted by the authority aforesaid, That this act, and every clause, provision, regulation, matter, and thing, herein contained, shall commence and take effect upon the first day of *June*, one thousand seven hundred and seventy-four; and be, and continue in force, for and during the term of three years.

Source:

Danby Pickering, ed. *Statutes at Large*. Vols. 25 and 30. Cambridge, Mass. J. Bentham, 1762–1867, pp. 336–341, 366–371; 381–390.

Quebec Act, 1774

Act passed by the British Parliament June 22, 1774, that provided Quebec with an appointed council and governor, preserved the authority of French civil law, permitted the practice of Roman Catholicism, and extended the boundaries of the province southward to the Ohio River and westward to the Mississippi River. The law was ostensibly passed to create a practical governmental framework for the former French colony, which had been without an official government since it became a British colony under the Proclamation of 1763. But to the American colonists, the act was another punishment for the Boston Tea Party of December 1773. Extending Quebec's boundaries so far south and north cut off colonial prospects for western expansion, and the recognition of Roman Catholicism was especially odious to many Protestants in the colonies. The colonists included the Quebec Act in their list of Coercive or Intolerable Acts, a series of laws adopted by Parliament in 1774 and deemed coercive and intolerable by the colonists, which served as one of the immediate causes of the Revolutionary War.

An Act for making more effectual Provision for the Government of the Province of Quebec in North America.

WHEREAS his Majesty, by his Royal Proclamation bearing Date the seventh Day of October, in the third Year of his Reign, thought fit to declare the Provisions which had been made in respect to certain Countries, Territories, and Islands in America, ceded to his Majesty by the definitive Treaty of Peace, concluded at Paris on the tenth day of February, one thousand seven hundred and sixty-three: And whereas, by the Arrangements made by the said Royal Proclamation a very large Extent of Country, within which there were several Colonies and Settlements of the Subjects of France,.who claimed to remain therein under the Faith of the said Treaty, was left, without any Provision being made for the Administration of Civil Government therein; and certain Parts of the Territory of Canada, where sedentary Fisheries had been established and carried on by the Subjects of France, Inhabitants of the said Province of Canada under Grants and Concessions from the Government thereof, were annexed to the Government of Newfoundland, and thereby subjected to Regulations inconsistent with the Nature of such Fisheries:

I. May it therefore please your most Excellent Majesty that it may be enacted; and be it enacted by the King's most Excellent Majesty, by and with the Advice and Consent of the Lords Spiritual and Temporal, and Commons, in this present Parliament assembled, and by the Authority of the same: That all the Territories, Islands,.and Countries in North America, belonging to the Crown of Great

Britain, bounded on the South by a Line from the Bay of Chaleurs, along the High Lands which divide the Rivers that empty themselves into the River Saint Lawrence from those which fall into the Sea,.to a Point in forty-five Degrees of Northern Latitude, on the Eastern Bank of the River Connecticut, keeping the same Latitude directly West, through the Lake Champlain, until, in the same Latitude, it meets the River Saint Lawrence: from thence up the Eastern Bank of the said River to the Lake Ontario; thence through the Lake Ontario, and the River commonly call Niagara and thence along by the Eastern and South-eastern Bank of Lake Erie, following the said Bank, until the same shall be intersected by the Northern Boundary, granted by the Charter of the Province of Pennsylvania, in case the same shall be so intersected: and from thence along the said Northern and Western Boundaries of the said Province, until the said Western Boundary strike the Ohio: But in case the said Bank of the said Lake shall not be found to be so intersected, then following the said Bank until it shall arrive at that Point of the said Bank which shall be nearest to the North-western Angle of the said Province of Pensylvania, and thence by a right Line, to the said North-western Angle of the said Province; and thence along the Western Boundary of the said Province, until it strike the River Ohio; and along the Bank of the said River, Westward, to the Banks of the Mississippi, and Northward to the Southern Boundary of the Territory granted to the Merchants Adventurers of England, trading to Hudson's Bay; and also all such Territories, Islands, and Countries, which have, since the tenth of February, one thousand seven hundred and sixty-three, been made Part of the Government of Newfoundland, be, and they are hereby, during his Majesty's Pleasure, annexed to, and made Part and Parcel of, the Province of Quebec, as created and established by the said Royal Proclamation of the seventh of October, one thousand seven hundred and sixty-three.

II. Provided always:.That nothing herein contained, relative to the Boundary of the Province of Quebec, shall in anywise affect the Boundaries of any other Colony.

III. Provided always, and be it enacted: That nothing in this Act contained shall extend, or be construed to extend, to make void, or to vary or alter any Right, Title, or Possession, derived under any Grant, Conveyance, or otherwise nowsoever, of or to any Lands within the said Province, or the Provinces thereto adjoining; but that the same shall remain and be in Force, and have Effect, as if this Act had never been made.

IV. And whereas the Provisions, made by the said Proclamation, in respect to the Civil Government of the said Province of Quebec, and the Powers and Authorities given to the Governor and other Civil Officers of the said Province, by the Grants and Commissions issued in consequence thereof, have been found, upon Experience, to be inapplicable to the State and Circumstances of the said Province, the Inhabitants whereof amounted, at the Conquest, to above sixty-five thousand Persons professing the Religion of the Church of Rome, and enjoying an established Form of Constitution and System of Laws, by which their Persons and Property had been protected, governed, and ordered, for a long Series of Years, from the first Establishment of the said Province of Canada; be it therefore further enacted by the Authority aforesaid: That the said Proclamation, so far as the same relates to the said Province of Quebec, and the Commission under the Authority whereof the Government of the said Province is at present administered, and all and every the Ordinance and Ordinances made by the Governor and Council of Quebec for the Time being, relative to the Civil Government and Administration of Justice in the said Province, and all Commissions to Judges and other Officers thereof, be, and the same are hereby revoked, annulled, and made void, from and after the first Day of May, one thousand seven hundred and seventy-five.

V. And, for the more perfect Security and Ease of the Minds of the Inhabitants of the said Province, it is hereby declared: That his Majesty's Subjects, professing the Religion of the Church of Rome of and in the said Province of Quebec, may have, hold, and enjoy, the free Exercise of the Religion of the Church of Rome, subject to the King's Supremacy, declared and established by an Act, made in the first Year of the Reign of Queen Elizabeth, over all the Dominions and Countries which then did, or thereafter should belong, to the Imperial Crown of this Realm; and that the Clergy of the said Church may hold, receive, and enjoy, their accustomed Dues and Rights, with respect to such Persons only as shall profess the said Religion.

VI. Provided nevertheless: That it shall be lawful for his Majesty, his Heirs or Successors, to make such Provision out of the rest of the said accustomed Dues and Rights, for the Encouragement of the Protestant Religion, and for the Maintenance and Support of a Protestant Clergy within the said Province, as he or they shall, from Time to Time think necessary and expedient.

VII. Provided always, and be it enacted: That no Person professing the Religion of the Church of Rome, and residing in the said Province, shall be obliged to take the Oath required by the said Statute passed in the first Year of the Reign of Queen Elizabeth, or any other Oaths substituted by any other Act in the Place thereof; but that every such Person who, by the said Statute, is required to take the Oath therein mentioned, shall be obliged, and is hereby required, to take and subscribe the following Oath before the Governor, or such other Person in such Court of Record as his Majesty shall appoint, who are hereby authorized to administer the same; videlicet, I A.B., do sincerely promise and swear: That I will be faithful, and bear true Allegiance to his Majesty King George, and him will defend to the utmost of my Power, against all traitorous Conspiracies, and Attempts whatsoever, which shall be made against his Person, Crown, and Dignity; and I will do my utmost Endeavor to disclose and make known to his Majesty, his Heirs and Successors, all Treasons, and traitorous Conspiracies, and Attempts, which I shall know to be against him, or any of them; and all this I do swear without any Equivocation, mental Evasion, or secret Reservation, and renouncing all Pardons and Dispensations from any Power or Person whomsoever to the contrary. So help me GOD. And every such Person, who shall neglect or refuse to take the said Oath before mentioned, shall incur and be liable to the same Penalties, Forfeitures, Disabilities, and Incapacities, as he would have incurred and been liable to for neglecting or refusing to take the Oath required by the said Statute passed in the first Year of the Reign of Queen Elizabeth.

VIII. And be it further enacted by the Authority aforesaid: That all his Majesty's Canadian Subjects within the Province of Quebec, the religious orders and Communities only excepted, may also hold and enjoy their Property and Possessions, together with all Customs and Usages relative thereto, and all other their Civil Rights, in as large, ample, and beneficial Manner, as if the said Proclamation, Commissions, Ordinances, and other Acts and Instruments had not been made, and as may consist with their Allegiance to his Majesty, and Subjection to the Crown and Parliament of Great Britain; and that in all .Matters of Controversy, relative to Property and Civil Rights, Resort shall be had to the Laws of Canada, as the Rule for the Decision of the same; and all Causes that shall hereafter be instituted in any of the Courts of Justice, to be appointed within and for the said Province by his Majesty, his Heirs and Successors, shall, with respect to such Property and Rights, be determined agreeably to the said Laws and Customs of Canada, until they shall be varied or altered by any Ordinances that shall, from Time to Time, be passed in the said Province by the Governor, Lieutenant Governor, or Commander in Chief, for the Time being, by and with the Advice and Consent of the Legislative Council of the same, to be appointed in Manner herein-after mentioned.

IX. Provided always: That nothing in this Act contained shall extend, or be construed to extend, to any Lands that have been granted by his Majesty, or shall hereafter be granted by his Majesty, his Heirs and Successors, to be holden in free and common Soccage.

X. Provided also: That it shall and may be lawful to and for every Person that is Owner of any Lands, Goods, or Credits, in the said Province, and that has a Right to alienate the said Lands, Goods, or Credits, in his or her Lifetime, by Deed of Sale, Gift, or otherwise, to devise or bequeath the same at his or her Death, by his or her last Will and Testament; any Law, Usage, or Custom, heretofore or now prevailing in the Province, to the contrary hereof in any-wise notwithstanding; such Will being executed either according to the Laws of Canada, or according to the Forms prescribed by the Laws of England.

XI. And whereas the Certainty and Lenity of the Criminal Law of England, and the Benefits and Advantages resulting from the Use of it, have been sensibly felt by the Inhabitants, from an Experience of more than nine Years, during which it has been uniformly administered: be it therefore further enacted by the Authority aforesaid: That the same shall continue to be administered, and shall be observed as Law in the Province of Quebec, as well in the Description and Quality of the Offence as in the Method of Prosecution and Trial; and the Punishments and Forfeitures thereby inflicted to the Exclusion of every other Rule of Criminal Law, or Mode of Proceeding thereon, which did or might prevail in the said Province before the Year of our Lord one thousand seven hundred and seventy-four; any Thing in this Act to the contrary thereof in any respect notwithstanding; subject nevertheless to such Alterations and Amendments as the Governor, Lieutenant-governor, or Commander in Chief for the Time being, by and with the Advice and Consent of the legislative Council of the said Province, hereafter to be appointed, shall, from Time to Time, cause to be made therein, in Manner hereinafter directed.

XII. And whereas it may be necessary to ordain many Regulations for the future Welfare and good Government of the Province of Quebec, the Occasions of which cannot now be foreseen, nor, without much Delay and Inconvenience, be provided for, without intrusting that Authority, for a certain Time, and under proper Restrictions, to Persons resident there, and whereas it is at present inexpedient to call an Assembly; be it therefore enacted b~ the Authority aforesaid: That it shall and may be lawful for his Majesty, his Heirs and Successors, by Warrant under his or their Signet or Sign Manual, and with the Advice of the Privy Council, to constitute and appoint a Council for the Affairs of the Province of Quebec, to consist of such Persons resident there, not exceeding twenty-three, nor less than seventeen, as his Majesty, his Heirs and Successors, shall be pleased to appoint, and, upon the Death, Removal, or Absence of any of the Members of the said Council, in like Manner to constitute and appoint such and so many other Person or Persons as shall be necessary to supply the Vacancy or Vacancies; which Council, so appointed and nominated, or the major Part thereof; shall have Power and Authority to make Ordinances for the Peace, Welfare, and good Government, of the said Province, with the Consent of his Majesty's Governor, or, in his Absence, of the Lieutenant-governor, or Commander in Chief for the Time being.

XIII. Provided always: That nothing in this Act contained shall extend to authorize or impower the said legislative Council to lay any Taxes or Duties within the said Province, such Rates and Taxes only excepted as the Inhabitants of any Town or District within the said Province may be authorized by the said Council to assess, levy, and apply, within the said Town or District, for the Purpose of making Roads, erecting and repairing publick Buildings, or for any other Purpose respecting the local Convenience and Oeconomy of such Town or District.

XIV. Provided also, and be it enacted by the Authority aforesaid: That every Ordinance so to be made, shall, within six Months, be transmitted by the Governor, or, in his Absence, by the Lieutenant-governor, or Commander in Chief for the Time being, and laid before his Majesty for his Royal Approbation; and if his Majesty shall think fit to disallow thereof, the same shall cease and be void from the Time that his Majesty's Order in Council thereupon shall be promulgated at Quebec.

XV. Provided also: That no Ordinance touching Religion, or by which any Punishment may be inflicted greater than Fine or Imprisonment for three Months, shall be of any Force or Effect, until the same shall have received his Majesty's Approbation.

XVI. Provided also: That no Ordinance shall be passed at any Meeting of the Council where less than a Majority of the whole Council is present, or at any Time except between the first Day of January and the first Day of May, unless upon some urgent Occasion, in which Case every Member thereof resident at Quebec, or within fifty Miles thereof, shall be personally summoned by the Governor, or, in his absence, by the Lieutenant-governor, or Commander in Chief for the Time being, to attend the same.

XVII. And be it further enacted by the Authority aforesaid: That nothing herein contained shall extend, or be construed to extend, to prevent or hinder his Majesty, his Heirs and Successors, by his or their Letters Patent under the Great Seal of Great Britain, from erecting, constituting, and appointing, such Courts of Criminal, Civil, and Ecclesiastical Jurisdiction within and for the said Province of Quebec, and appointing, from Time to Time, the Judges and Officers thereof, as his Majesty, his Heirs and Successors, shall think necessary and proper for the Circumstances of the said Province.

XVIII. Provided always, and it is hereby enacted: That nothing in this Act contained shall extend, or be construed to extend, to repeal or make void, within the said Province of Quebec, any Act or Acts of the Parliament of Great Britain heretofore made, for prohibiting, restraining, or regulating, the Trade or Commerce of his Majesty's Colonies and Plantations in America; but that all and every the said Acts, and also all Acts of Parliament heretofore made concerning or respecting the said Colonies and Plantations, shall be, and are hereby declared to be, in Force, within the said Province of Quebec, and every Part thereof.

Source:

America's Homepage. Available on-line. URL: http://ahp.gatech.edu/quebec_act_1774.html

Suffolk Resolves, 1774

Set of resolutions written by Dr. Joseph Warren and presented at a convention in Suffolk County, Massachusetts, on September 9, 1774. The meeting was one of many convened in Massachusetts to protest the Coercive (or Intolerable) Acts. The Suffolk Resolves declared the Coercive Acts unconstitutional and refused obedience to them; urged withholding taxes from the royal government until the Coercive Acts were repealed and recommended that, in the interim, the people of Massachusetts form a government with the power to collect taxes; advised the formation of an armed militia; and recommended the imposition of economic sanctions against Britain. Adopted unanimously by the convention, the resolutions were immediately carried by Paul Revere to the First Continental Congress, which was meeting in Philadelphia. They were endorsed by that body on September 17, 1774.

While Virginia was preparing to elect its delegates to the First Continental Congress, in July 1774, Thomas Jefferson (absent due to illness) drafted instructions for them. Printed as a pamphlet, it outlined his republicanism and enhanced his reputation as a revolutionary. Another 1774 pamphlet, by future signer of the U.S. Constitution James Wilson of Pennsylvania, argued that the British Parliament had no power over the colonies, and that allegiance was only owed to the Crown.

The Congress met according to adjournment.

Richard Caswell, Esqr. one of the deputies from North-Carolina, appeared, and took his seat in Congress.

The Resolutions entered into by the delegates from the several towns and districts in the county of Suffolk, in the province of the Massachusetts-bay, on Tuesday the 6th instant, and their address to his excellency Govr. Gage, dated the 9th instant, were laid before the congress, and are as follows:

At a meeting of the delegates of every town & district in the county of Suffolk, on Tuesday the 6th of Septr., at the house of Mr. Richard Woodward, of Deadham, & by adjournment, at the house of Mr. [Daniel] Vose, of Milton, on Friday the 9th instant, Joseph Palmer, esq. being chosen moderator, and William Thompson, esq. clerk, a committee was chosen to bring in a report to the convention, and the following being several times read, and put paragraph by paragraph, was unanimously voted, viz. Whereas the power but not the justice, the vengeance but not the wisdom of Great-Britain, which of old persecuted, scourged, and exiled our fugitive parents from their native shores, now pursues us, their guiltless children, with unrelenting severity: And whereas, this, then savage and uncultivated desart, was purchased by the toil and treasure, or acquired by the blood and valor of those our venerable progenitors; to us they bequeathed the dearbought inheritance, to our care and protection they consigned it, and the most sacred obligations are upon us to transmit the glorious purchase, unfettered by power, unclogged with shackles, to our innocent and beloved offspring. On the fortitude, on the wisdom and on the exertions of this important day, is suspended the fate of this new world, and of unborn millions. If a boundless extent of continent, swarming with millions, will tamely submit to live, move and have their being at the arbitrary will of a licentious minister, they basely yield to voluntary slavery, and future generations shall load they memories with incessant execrations.—On the other hand, if we arrest the hand which would ransack our pockets, if we disarm the parricide which points the dagger to our bosoms, if we nobly defeat that fatal edict which proclaims a power to frame laws for us in all cases whatsoever, thereby entailing the endless and numberless curses of slavery upon us, our heirs and their heirs forever; if we successfully resist that unparalleled usurpation of unconstitutional power, whereby our capital is robbed of the means of life; whereby the streets of Boston are thronged with military executioners; whereby our coasts are lined and harbours crouded with ships of war; whereby the charter of the colony, that sacred barrier against the encroachments of tyranny, is mutilated and, in effect, annihilated; whereby a murderous law is framed to shelter villains from the hands of justice; whereby the unalienable and inestimable inheritance, which we derived from nature, the constitution of Britain, and the privileges warranted to us in the charter of the province, is totally wrecked, annulled, and vacated, posterity will acknowledge that virtue which preserved them free and happy; and while we enjoy the rewards and blessings of the faithful, the torrent of panegyrists will roll our reputations to that latest period, when the streams of time shall be absorbed in the abyss of eternity.—Therefore, we have resolved, and do *resolve,*

1. That whereas his majesty, George the Third, is the rightful successor to the throne of Great-Britain, and justly entitled to the allegiance of the British realm, and agreeable to compact, of the English colonies in America— therefore, we, the heirs and successors of the first planters of this colony, do cheerfully acknowledge the said George the Third to be our rightful sovereign, and that said

covenant is the tenure and claim on which are founded our allegiance and submission.

2. That it is an indispensable duty which we owe to God, our country, ourselves and posterity, by all lawful ways and means in our power to maintain, defend and preserve those civil and religious rights and liberties, for which many of our fathers fought, bled and died, and to hand them down entire to future generations.

3. That the late acts of the British parliament for blocking up the harbour of Boston, for altering the established form of government in this colony, and for screening the most flagitious violators of the laws of the province from a legal trial, are gross infractions of those rights to which we are justly entitled by the laws of nature, the British constitution, and the charter of the province.

4. That no obedience is due from this province to either or any part of the acts above-mentioned, but that they be rejected as the attempts of a wicked administration to enslave America.

5. That so long as the justices of our superior court of judicature, court of assize, &c. and inferior court of common pleas in this county are appointed, or hold their places, by any other tenure than that which the charter and the laws of the province direct, they must be considered as under undue influence, and are therefore unconstitutional officers, and, as such, no regard ought to be paid to them by the people of this county.

6. That if the justices of the superior court of judicature, assize, &c. justices of the court of common pleas, or of the general sessions of the peace, shall sit and act during their present disqualified state, this county will support, and bear harmless, all sheriffs and their deputies, constables, jurors and other officers who shall refuse to carry into execution the orders of said courts; and, as far as possible, to prevent the many inconveniencies which must be occasioned by a suspension of the courts of justice, we do most earnestly recommend it to all creditors, that they shew all reasonable and even generous forbearance to their debtors; and to all debtors, to pay their just debts with all possible speed, and if any disputes relative to debts or trespasses shall arise, which cannot be settled by the parties, we recommend it to them to submit all such causes to arbitration; and it is our opinion that the contending parties or either of them, who shall refuse so to do, ought to be considered as co-operating with the enemies of this country.

7. That it be recommended to the collectors of taxes, constables and all other officers, who have public monies in their hands, to retain the same, and not to make any payment thereof to the provincial county treasurer until the civil government of the province is placed upon a constitutional foundation, or until it shall otherwise be ordered by the proposed provincial Congress.

8. That the persons who have accepted seats at the council board, by virtue of a mandamus from the King, in conformity to the late act of the British parliament, entitled, an act for the regulating the government of the Massachusetts-Bay, have acted in direct violation of the duty they owe to their country, and have thereby given great and just offence to this people; therefore, resolved, that this county do recommend it to all persons, who have so highly offended by accepting said departments, and have not already publicly resigned their seats at the council board, to make public resignations of their places at said board, on or before the 20th day of this instant, September; and that all persons refusing so to do, shall, from and after said day, be considered by this county as obstinate and incorrigible enemies to this country.

9. That the fortifications begun and now carrying on upon Boston Neck, are justly alarming to this county, and gives us reason to apprehend some hostile intention against that town, more especially as the commander in chief has, in a very extraordinary manner, removed the powder from the magazine at Charlestown, and has also forbidden the keeper of the magazine at Boston, to deliver out to the owners, the powder, which they had lodged in said magazine.

10. That the late act of parliament for establishing the Roman Catholic religion and the French laws in that extensive country, now called Canada, is dangerous in an extreme degree to the Protestant religion and to the civil rights and liberties of all America; and, therefore, as men and Protestant Christians, we are indispensably obliged to take all proper measures for our security.

11. That whereas our enemies have flattered themselves that they shall make an easy prey of this numerous, brave and hardy people, from an apprehension that they are unacquainted with military discipline; we, therefore, for the honour, defence and security of this county and province, advise, as it has been recommended to take away all commissions from the officers of the militia, that those who now hold commissions, or such other persons, be elected in each town as officers in the militia, as shall be judged of sufficient capacity for that purpose, and who have evidenced themselves the inflexible friends to the rights of the people; and that the inhabitants of those towns and districts, who are qualified, do use their utmost diligence to acquaint themselves with the art of war as soon as possible, and do, for that purpose, appear under arms at least once every week.

12. That during the present hostile appearances on the part of Great-Britain, notwithstanding the many insults and oppressions which we most sensibly resent, yet, nevertheless, from our affection to his majesty, which we have at all times evidenced, we are determined to act merely upon the defensive, so long as such conduct may be vindi-

cated by reason and the principles of self-preservation, but no longer.

13. That, as we understand it has been in contemplation to apprehend sundry persons of this county, who have rendered themselves conspicuous in contending for the violated rights and liberties of their countrymen; we do recommend, should such an audacious measure be put in practice, to seize and keep in safe custody, every servant of the present tyrannical and unconstitutional government throughout the county and province, until the persons so apprehended be liberated from the hands of our adversaries, and restored safe and uninjured to their respective friends and families.

14. That until our rights are fully restored to us, we will, to the utmost of our power, and we recommend the same to the other counties, to withhold all commercial intercourse with Great-Britain, Ireland, and the West-Indies, and abstain from the consumption of British merchandise and manufactures, and especially of East-India teas and piece goods, with such additions, alterations, and exceptions only, as the General Congress of the colonies may agree to.

15. That under our present circumstances, it is incumbent on us to encourage arts and manufactures amongst us, by all means in our power, and that be and are hereby appointed a committee, to consider of the best ways and means to promote and establish the same, and to report to this convention as soon as may be.

16. That the exigencies of our public affairs, demand that a provincial Congress be called to consult such measures as may be adopted, and vigorously executed by the whole people; and we do recommend it to the several towns in this county, to chuse members for such a provincial Congress, to be holden at Concord, on the second Tuesday of October, next ensuing.

17. That this county, confiding in the wisdom and integrity of the continental Congress, now sitting at Philadelphia, pay all due respect and submission to such measures as may be recommended by them to the colonies, for the restoration and establishment of our just rights, civil and religious, and for renewing that harmony and union between Great-Britain and the colonies, so earnestly wished for by all good men.

18. That whereas the universal uneasiness which prevails among all orders of men, arising from the wicked and oppressive measures of the present administration, may influence some unthinking persons to commit outrage upon private property; we would heartily recommend to all persons of this community, not to engage in any routs, riots, or licentious attacks upon the properties of any person whatsoever, as being subversive of all order and government; but, by a steady, manly, uniform, and persevering opposition, to convince our enemies, that in a contest so

important, in a cause so solemn, our conduct shall be such as to merit the approbation of the wise, and the admiration of the brave and free of every age and of every country.

19. That should our enemies, by any sudden manoeuvres, render it necessary to ask the aid and assistance of our brethren in the country, some one of the committee of correspondence, or a select man of such town, or the town adjoining, where such hostilities shall commence, or shall be expected to commence, shall despatch couriers with written messages to the select men, or committees of correspondence, of the several towns in the vicinity, with a written account of such matter, who shall despatch others to committees more remote, until proper and sufficient assistance be obtained, and that the expense of said couriers be defrayed by the county, until it shall be otherwise ordered by the provincial Congress.

At a meeting of delegates from the several towns and districts in the county of Suffolk, held at Milton, on Friday, the 9th day of September, 1774—*Voted,*

That Dr. Joseph Warren, of Boston, &c. be a committee to wait on his excellency the governor, to inform him, that this county are alarmed at the fortifications making on Boston Neck, and to remonstrate against the same, and the repeated insults offered by the soldiery, to persons passing and repassing into that town, and to confer with him upon those subjects.

Attest,
William Thompson, *Clerk.*

"To his excellency Thomas Gage, Esq. captain-general, and commander in chief of his majesty's province of Massachusetts-Bay.

"May it please your excellency,

"The county of Suffolk, being greatly, and, in their opinion, justly alarmed at the formidable appearances of hostility, now threatening his majesty's good subjects of this county, and more particularly of the town of Boston, the loyal and faithful capital of this province, beg leave to address your excellency, and represent, that the apprehensions of the people are more particularly encreased by the dangerous design, now carrying into execution, of repairing and manning the fortifications at the south entrance of the town of Boston, which, when completed, may, at any time, be improved to aggravate the miseries of that already impoverished and distressed city, by intercepting the wonted and necessary intercourse between the town and country, and compel the wretched inhabitants to the most ignominious state of humiliation and vassalage, by depriving them of the necessary supplies of provision, for which they are chiefly dependant on that communication. We have been informed, that your excellency, in consequence of the application of the select men

of Boston, has, indeed, disavowed any intention to injure the town in your present manoeuvres, and expressed your purpose to be for the security of the troops and his majesty's subjects in the town, we are therefore at a loss to guess, may it please your excellency, from whence your want of confidence in the loyal and orderly people of this vicinity could originate; a measure, so formidable, carried into execution from a pre-conceived though causeless jealousy of the insecurity of this majesty's troops and subjects in the town, deeply wounds the loyalty, and is an additional injury to the faithful subjects of this county, and affords hem a strong motive for this application. We therefore intreat your excellency to desist from your design, assuring your excellency, that the people of this county, are by no means disposed to injure his majesty's troops; they think themselves aggrieved and oppressed by the late acts of parliament, and are resolved, by Divine assistance, never to submit to them, but have no inclination to commence a war with his majesty's troops, and beg leave to observe to your excellency, that the ferment now excited in the minds of the people, is occasioned by some late transactions, by seizing the powder in the arsenal at Charlestown; by withholding the powder lodged in the magazine of the town of Boston, from the legal proprietors; insulting, beating, and abusing passengers to and from the town by the soldiery, in which they have been encouraged by some of their officers; putting the people in fear, and menacing them in their nightly patrole into the neighbouring towns, and more particularly by the fortifying the sole avenue by land to the town of Boston.

"In duty therefore to his majesty and to your excellency, and for the restoration of order and security to this county, we the delegates from the several towns in this county, being commissioned for this purpose, beg your excellency's attention to this our humble and faithful address, assuring you, that nothing less than an immediate removal of the ordnance, and restoring the entrance into the town to its former state, and an effectual stop of all insults and abuses in future, can place the inhabitants of this county in that state of peace and tranquillity, in which every free subject ought to be."

His excellency was waited on to know if he would receive the committee with the above written address, but desiring he might have a copy of it in a private way, that so when he received it from the committee, he might have an answer prepared for them, he was accordingly furnished with a copy. His excellency than declared, that he would receive the committee on Monday, at 12 o'clock.

Saturday, September 18, 1774
The Congress, taking the foregoing into consideration,

Resolved unan, That this assembly deeply feels the suffering of their countrymen in the Massachusetts-Bay, under the operation of the late unjust, cruel, and oppressive acts of the British Parliament—that they most thoroughly approve the wisdom and fortitude, with which opposition to these wicked ministerial measures has hitherto been conducted, and they earnestly recommend to their brethren, a perseverance in the same firm and temperate conduct as expressed in the resolutions determined upon, at a [late] meeting of the delegates for the county of Suffolk, on Tuesday, the 6th instant, trusting that the effect [s] of the united efforts of North America in their behalf, will carry such conviction to the British nation, on the unwise, unjust, and ruinous policy of the present administration, as quickly to introduce better men and wiser measures.

Resolved unan, That contributions from all the colonies for supplying the necessities, and alleviating the distresses of our brethren at Boston, ought to be continued, in such manner, and so long as their occasions may require.

Ordered, That a copy of the above resolutions be transmitted to Boston by the president.

Ordered, That these resolutions, together with the resolutions of the County of Suffolk, be published in the newspapers.

The committee appointed to examine & report the several statutes, which affect the trade and manufacturers of the colonies, brought in their report, which was ordered to lie on the table.

Source:

Worthington Chauncey Ford. *Journals of the Continental Congress, 1774–1789.* New York: Johnson Reprint, 1968.

Plan of Union, 1774

Proposal submitted to the First Continental Congress, meeting in Philadelphia on September 28, 1774, by Joseph Galloway of Pennsylvania. Favored by moderates at the Congress as a means of resolving the conflict between Britain and the colonies, the plan recommended the establishment of an American legislature equal to Parliament that would deal with general American affairs. The proposed governmental structure would include a Grand Council, whose members would be chosen by the colonial assemblies to serve three-year terms, and a president-general, who would be appointed by the king and would have veto power over the council. The colonial legislature would be considered a branch of the British Parliament, and the consent of both bodies would be required to pass legislation. Galloway's plan was defeated by only one vote.

Resolution submitted by Joseph Galloway:

Resolved, That the Congress will apply to his Majesty for a redress of grievances under which his faithful subjects in America labour; and assure him, that the Colonies hold in obhorrence the idea of being considered independent communities on the British government, and most ardently desire the establishment of a Political Union, not only among themselves, but with the Mother State, upon those principles of safety and freedom which are essential in the constitution of all free governments, and particularly that of the British Legislature; and as the Colonies from their local circumstances, cannot be represented in the Parliament of Great-Britain, they will humbly propose to his Majesty and his two Houses of Parliament, the following plan, under which the strength of the whole Empire may be drawn together on any emergency, the interest of both countries advanced, and the rights and liberties of America secured.

Plan of a Proposed Union Between Great Britain and the Colonies

That a British and American legislature, for regulating the administration of the general affairs of America, be proposed and established in America, including all the said colonies; within, and under which government, each colony shall retain its present constitution, and powers of regulating and governing its own internal police, in all cases what[so]ever.

That the said government be administered by a President General, to be appointed by the King, and a grand Council, to be chosen by the Representatives of the people of the several colonies, in their respective assemblies, once in every three years.

That the several assemblies shall choose members for the grand council in the following proportions, viz.

New Hampshire. Massachusetts-Bay. Rhode Island. Connecticut. New-York. New-Jersey. Pennsylvania. Delaware Counties. Maryland. Virginia. North Carolina. South-Carolina. Georgia.

Who shall meet at the city of   for the first time, being called by the President-General, as soon as conveniently may be after his appointment.

That there shall be a new election of members for the Grand Council every three years; and on the death, removal or resignation of any member, his place shall be supplied by a new choice, at the next sitting of Assembly of the Colony he represented.

That the Grand Council shall meet once in every year, if they shall think it necessary, and oftener, if occasions shall require, at such time and place as they shall adjourn to, at the last preceding meeting, or as they shall be called to meet at, by the President-General, on any emergency.

That the Grand Council shall have power to choose their Speaker, and shall hold and exercise all the like rights, liberties and privileges, as are held and exercised by and in the House of Commons of Great-Britain.

That the President-General shall hold his office during the pleasure of the King, and his assent shall be requisite to all acts of the Grand Council, and it shall be his office and duty to cause them to be carried into execution.

That the President-General, by and with the advice and consent of the Grand-Council, hold and exercise all the legislative rights, powers, and authorities, necessary for regulating and administering all the general police and affairs of the colonies, in which Great-Britain and the colonies, or any of them, the colonies in general, or more than one colony, are in any manner concerned, as well civil and criminal as commercial.

That the said President-General and the Grand Council, be an inferior and distinct branch of the British legislature, united and incorporated with it, for the aforesaid general purposes; and that any of the said general regulations may originate and be formed and digested, either in the Parliament of Great Britain, or in the said Grand Council, and being prepared, transmitted to the other for their approbation or dissent; and that the assent of both shall be requisite to the validity of all such general acts or statutes.

That in time of war, all bills for granting aid to the crown, prepared by the Grand Council, and approved by the President General, shall be valid and passed into a law, without the assent of the British Parliament.

Source:

Worthington Chauncey Ford. *Journals of the Continental Congress,1774–1789.* New York: Johnson Reprint, 1968.

Declaration of Resolves of the First Continental Congress, 1774

Opinions and complaints of the First Continental Congress and adopted by the congress on October 14, 1774. The document argued that the American colonists were being deprived of their rights as Englishmen and included 10 resolutions describing those rights (such as "life, liberty, and property," the benefits of English common law, and peaceable assembly and petition) and protesting the colonists' lack of representation in the British Parliament. It declared that their rights were violated specifically by 13 acts passed by Parliament since 1763, including the Stamp Act of 1765, the Townshend Revenue Act of 1767, the Coercive Acts, and the

Quebec Act. In reaction to these violations of rights, it pledged economic sanctions against Britain until the protested laws were repealed. As a result of this declaration, the Continental Congress adopted the Continental Association on October 20, 1774, in an attempt to use economic coercion to force Britain to redress American colonial grievances. The colonies would cease importing goods from Britain as of December 1; the slave trade in the colonies would also be discontinued on December 1; consumption of British goods would stop by March 1, 1775; and exports to Britain, Ireland, and the West Indies would end by September 1, 1775. The Association was to be enforced by committees elected in each county, town, and city, and the principal means of enforcement would be publicity and the boycotting of goods from any province that failed to follow its provisions. The Association was widely adopted and was operating in 12 colonies by April 1775. The grievances also prompted such independent resolutions as one drafted by the women of Edenton, North Carolina, to protest punitive taxes enforced by the king of England. The women asserted their patriotism by resolving to abstain from tea, cloth, and other luxuries imported from England (Edenton was a seat of unrest both prior to and following the American Revolution.)

Friday, October 14, 1774

The Congress met according to adjournment, & resuming the consideration of the subject under debate—came into the following Resolutions:

Sullivan's Draught.

Whereas since the accession of the present King, Parliament has claimed a power of right to bind the people of the Colonies in North America by statutes in all cases whatsoever; and for carrying the said power into execution, has, by some statutes, expressly taxed the people of the said Colonies, and by divers other statutes under various pretences, but in fact for the purpose of raising a revenue, has imposed 'rates and duties.' payable in the said Colonies, established a Board of Commissioner, and extended the jurisdiction of Courts of Admiralty therein, for the collection of such 'rates and duties.'

And whereas some of the said statutes are also intended to render all Judges in the said Colonies dependent upon the Crown only.

And whereas since the said accession, statutes have been made for quartering and supplying troops to be kept in the said Colonies.

And whereas since the conclusion of the last war, orders have been issued by the King, that the authority of the commander-in-chief, and under him, of the Brigadier-General in the Northern and Southern departments, in all military affairs shall be supreme, and must be obeyed by the troops as such, in all the civil governments in America.

And whereas a statute was made in the seventh year of this reign 'for suspending the proceedings of the assembly of New York, &c.,' and assemblies in these Colonies have of late years very frequently dissolved.

And whereas, during the present reign, dutiful and reasonable petitions to the Crown, from the representatives of the people in these Colonies, have been repeatedly with contempt.

And whereas, it has been lately resolved in Parliament, that, by force of a statute made in the thirty-fifth year of Henry VIII, Colonists may be carried to England, and tried there, on accusations for offences committed in these Colonies. And by a statute made in the twelfth year of this reign such trials are directed in the cases therein mentioned.

And whereas in the last session of Parliament three statutes were made and declared to have force within the Province of Massachusetts Bay, one of them 'for discontinuing, &c. the landing, &c. goods, wares, and merchandises, at the town and within the harbor of Boston,' &c.; and another, 'for the better regulating the government, &c.;' and the third, 'for the impartial administration of justice,' &c.

And whereas, in the same session, another statute was made, 'for making more effectual provision for the government of the Province of Quebec,' &c.

And whereas the good people of these, And whereas justly alarmed by the proceedings of Parliament and Administration, have duly appointed and directed delegates to meet and sit in General Congress at Philadelphia, in this month of September, 1774, in order to such establishment as that their religion, laws, and liberties, may not be subverted; upon which appointment and direction, the said delegates being now assembled in a full and free representation of these, Colonies taking into their most serious consideration the best means for attaining the ends aforesaid, do, in the first place, (as their ancestors in like cases have usually done,) for vindicating and asserting their rights and liberties, declare—

1. That the power of making laws for ordering or regulating the internal polity of these Colonies, is, within the limits of each Colony, respectively and exclusively vested in the Provincial Legislature of such Colony; and that all statutes for ordering or regulating the internal polity of the said Colonies, or any of them, in any manner or in any case whatsoever, are illegal and void.

2. That all statutes, for taxing the people of the said colonies, are illegal and void.

3. That all the statutes before mentioned, for the purpose of raising a revenue, by imposing 'rates and duties' payable in these Colonies, establishing a Board of Commissioner, and extending the jurisdiction of Courts of Admiralty, for the collection of such 'rates and duties' are illegal and void.

4. That Judges, within these Colonies, ought not to be dependent on the Crown only; and that their commissions ought to be during good behavior.

5. That the raising or keeping a standing army within these Colonies in time of peace, unless it be with the consent of the Provincial Legislatures, is illegal, pernicious, and dangerous; and that every statute for quartering or supplying troops within the said Colonies is illegal and void.

6. That the orders aforesaid for rendering the authority of the Commander-in-chief, and under him, of the Brigadiers-General, supreme, and illegal and void.

7. That for redress of all grievances, and for the amending, strengthening, and preserving of the laws, assemblies ought to be held in each of these Colonies frequently, and at least once in every year; that such Assemblies ought not to be prorogued or dissolved, before they have had sufficient time to deliberate, determine, and bring to conclusion their counsels on public affairs; that any statute for suspending the proceedings of any such assembly, is illegal and void; and that every dissolution of an assembly within these Colonies, during the present reign, on pretence of misbehavior in the representatives of the people, has been arbitrary and oppressive.

8. That it is the right of the subjects to petition the King; and that a contemptuous treatment of such petitions has a most pernicious tendency.

9. That the resolution in Parliament on the statute made in the thirty-fifth year of Henry VIII, was arbitrary and erroneous; and that any statute directing the trials of Colonists to be had in England or elsewhere, on accusation for offences committed in the Colonies, is illegal and void.

10. That the three statutes made in the last session of Parliament, and declared to have force within the Province of Massachusetts Bay, are oppressive to the people of that Province, dangerous to the liberties of these colonies, illegal and void.

11. That the statute made in the same session, 'for making more effectual provision for the government of the Province of Quebec,' &c. is not only unjust to the people in that Province, but dangerous to the interests of the Protestant religion and of these Colonies, and ought to be repealed.

12. And they do claim, demand, and insist, on all and singular the rights and liberties before mentioned as indubitably belonging to them; and no declarations, judgments, doings, proceedings or statutes, to the prejudice of the people in any of the premises, ought in any wise to be drawn hereafter into consequence or example; and these, their undoubted rights and liberties, with the blessings of

Divine Providence, which they humbly and ardently implore in favor of their just exertions to preserve the freedom of rendering to their Creator the worship they judge most acceptable to him, and of promoting the happiness of his creatures, they are resolved, to the utmost of their power, to maintain and defend.

Whereas, since the close of the last war, the British parliament, claiming a power of right to bind the people of America, by statute in all cases whatsoever, hath in some acts expressly imposed taxes on them, and in others, under various pretences, but in fact for the purpose of raising a revenue, hath imposed rates and duties payable in these colonies, established a board of commissioners, with unconstitutional powers, and extended the jurisdiction of courts of Admiralty, not only for collecting the said duties, but for the trial of causes merely arising within the body of a county.

And whereas, in consequence of other statutes, judges, who before held only estates at will in their offices, have been made dependant on the Crown alone for their salaries, and standing armies kept in times of peace:

And it has lately been resolved in Parliament, that by force of a statute, made in the thirty-fifth year of the reign of King Henry the eighth, colonists may be transported to England, and tried there upon accusations for treasons, and misprisions, or concealments of treasons committed in the colonies; and by a late statute, such trials have been directed in cases therein mentioned.

And whereas, in the last session of parliament, three statutes were made; one, intituled "An act to discontinue, in such manner and for such time as are therein mentioned, the landing and discharging, lading, or shipping of goods, wares & merchandise, at the town, and within the harbour of Boston, in the province of Massachusetts-bay, in North-America;" another, intituled "An act for the better regulating the government of the province of the Massachusetts-bay in New-England;" and another, intituled "An act for the impartial administration of justice, in the cases of persons questioned for any act done by them in the execution of the law, or for the suppression of riots and tumults, in the province of the Massachusetts-bay, in New-England." And another statute was then made, "for making more effectual provision for the government of the province of Quebec, &c." All which statutes are impolitic, unjust, and cruel, as well as unconstitutional, and most dangerous and destructive of American rights.

And whereas, Assemblies have been frequently dissolved, contrary to the rights of the people, when they attempted to deliberate on grievances; and their dutiful, humble, loyal, & reasonable petitions to the crown for redress, have been repeatedly treated with contempt, by his majesty's ministers of state:

The good people of the several Colonies of New-hampshire, Massachusetts-Bay, Rhode-Island and Providence plantations, Connecticut, New-York, New-Jersey, Pennsylvania, Newcastle, Kent and Sussex on Delaware, Maryland, Virginia, North Carolina, and South Carolina, justly alarmed at these arbitrary proceedings of parliament and administration, have severally elected, constituted, and appointed deputies to meet and sit in general congress, in the city of Philadelphia, in order to obtain such establishment, as that their religion, laws, and liberties may not be subverted:

Whereupon the deputies so appointed being now assembled, in a full and free representation of these Colonies, taking into their most serious consideration, the best means of attaining the ends aforesaid, do, in the first place, as Englishmen, their ancestors in like cases have usually done, for asserting and vindicating their rights and liberties, declare,

That the inhabitants of the English Colonies in North America, by the immutable laws of nature, the principles of the English constitution, and the several charters or compacts, have the following Rights:

Resolved, N.C.D. 1. That they are entitled to life, liberty, & property, and they have never ceded to any sovereign power whatever, a right to dispose of either without their consent.

Resolved, N.C.D. 2. That our ancestors, who first settled these colonies, were at the time of their emigration from the mother country, entitled to all the rights, liberties, and immunities of free and natural-born subjects, within the realm of England.

Resolved, N.C.D. 3. That by such emigration they by no means forfeited, surrendered, or lost any of those rights, but that they were, and their descendants now are, entitled to the exercise and enjoyment of all such of them, as their local and other circumstances enable them to exercise and enjoy.

Resolved, N.C.D. 4. That the foundation of English liberty, and of all free government, is a right in the people to participate in their legislative council: and as the English colonists are not represented, and from their local and other circumstances, cannot properly be represented in the British parliament, they are entitled to a free and exclusive power of legislation in their several provincial legislatures, where their right of representation can alone be preserved, in all cases of taxation and internal polity, subject only to the negative of their sovereign, in such manner as has been heretofore used and accustomed. But, from the necessity of the case, and a regard to the mutual interest of both countries, we cheerfully consent to the operation of such acts of the British parliament, as are bona fide, restrained to the regulation of our external commerce, for the purpose of securing the commercial advantages of the whole empire to the mother country, and the commercial benefits of its respective members; excluding every idea of taxation, internal or external, for raising a revenue on the subjects in America, without their consent.

Resolved, N.C.D. 5. That the respective colonies are entitled to the common law of England, and more especially to the great and inestimable privilege of being tried by their peers of the vicinage, according to the course of that law.

Resolved, N.C.D. 6. That the are entitled to the benefit of such of the English statutes as existed at the time of their colonization; and which they have, by experience, respectively found to be applicable to their several local and other circumstances.

Resolved, N.C.D. 7. That these, his majesty's colonies, are likewise entitled to all the immunities and privileges granted & confirmed to them by royal charters, or secured by their several codes of provincial laws.

Resolved, N.C.D. 8. That they have a right peaceably to assemble, consider of their grievances, and petition the King; and that all prosecutions, prohibitory proclamations, and commitments for the same, are illegal.

Resolved, N.C.D. 9. That they keeping a Standing army in these colonies, in times of peace, without the consent of the legislature of that colony, in which such army is kept, is against law.

Resolved, N.C.D. 10. It is indispensably necessary to good government, and rendered essential by the English constitution, that the constituent branches of the legislature be independent of each other; that, therefore, the exercise of legislative power in several colonies, by a council appointed, during pleasure, by the crown, is unconstitutional, dangerous, and destructive to the freedom of America legislation.

All and each of which the aforesaid deputies, in behalf of themselves and their constituents, do claim, demand, and insist on, as their indubitable rights and liberties; which cannot be legally taken from them, altered or abridged by any power whatever, without their own consent, by their representatives in their several provincial legislatures.

In the course of our inquiry, we find many infringements and violations of the foregoing rights, which, from an ardent desire, that harmony and mutual intercourse of affection and interest may be restored, we pass over for the present, and proceed to state such acts and measures as have been adopted since the last war, which demonstrate a system formed to enslave America.

Resolved, N.C.D. That the following acts of Parliament are infringements and violations of the rights of the colonists; and that the repeal of them is essentially necessary in order to restore harmony between Great-Britain and the American colonies, viz:

The several acts of 4 Geo. 3. ch. 15, & ch. 34.—5 Geo. 3. ch. 25.—6 Geo 3. ch. 52.—7 Geo. 3. ch. 41, & ch. 46.—8 Geo. 3. ch. 22, which impose duties for the purpose of raising a revenue in America, extend the powers of the admiralty courts beyond their ancient limits, deprive the American subject of trial by jury, authorize the judges' certificate to indemnity the prosecutor from damages, that he might otherwise be liable to, requiring oppressive security from a claimant of ships and goods seized, before he shall be allowed to defend his property, and are subversive of American rights.

Also the 12 Geo. 3. ch. 24, entitled "An act for the better securing his Majesty's dock-yards, magazines, ships, ammunition, and stores," which declares a new offence in America, and deprives the American subject of a constitutional trial by a jury of the vicinage, by authorizing the trial of any person, charged with the committing any offense described in the said act, out of the realm, to be indicted and tried for the same in any shire or county within the realm.

Also the three acts passed in the last session of parliament, for stopping the port and blocking up the harbour of Boston, for altering the charter & government of the Massachusetts-bay, and that which is entitled "An act for the better administration of Justice," &c.

Also the act passed in the same session for establishing the Roman Catholick Religion in the province of Quebec, abolishing the equitable system of English laws, and erecting a tyranny there, to the great danger, from so total a dissimilarity of Religion, law, and government of the neighbouring British colonies, by the assistance of whose blood and treasure the said country was conquered from France.

Also the act passed in the same session for the better providing suitable quarterly for officers and soldiers in his Majesty's services in North-America.

Also, that the keeping a standing army in several of these colonies, in time of peace, without the consent of the legislature of that colony in which such army is kept, is against law.

To these grievous acts and measures, Americans cannot submit, but in hopes that their fellow subjects in Great-Britain will, on a revision of them, restore us to that state in which both countries found happiness and prosperity, we have for the present only resolved to pursue the following peaceable measures:

Resolved, unanimously, That from and after the first day of December next, there be no importation into British America, from Great Britain or Ireland of any goods, wares or merchandize whatsoever, or from any other place of any such goods, wares or merchandize.

1st. To enter into a non-importation, non-consumption, and non-exportation agreement or association.

2. To prepare an address to the people of Great-Britain, and a memorial to the inhabitants of British America, &

3. To prepare a loyal address to his Majesty; agreeable to Resolutions already entered into.

Source:

Worthington Chauncey Ford. *Journals of the Continental Congress,1774–1789.* New York: Johnson Reprint, 1968.

Patrick Henry, "Give Me Liberty" Speech, 1775

Address delivered by American colonial leader Patrick Henry to the Second Virginia Convention on March 23, 1775, in St. John's Church in Richmond. Henry addressed the reluctance of many in the colonies to confront the likelihood of armed conflict with Britain. He argued that hope for the peaceful resolution of differences with Britain was futile, pointed to Britain's preparations for war, and urged that the colonists arm and organize themselves without delay. The speech ended with these memorable words: "Is life so dear, or peace so sweet, as to be purchased at the price of chains and slavery? Forbid it, Almighty God! I know not what course others may take; but as for me, give me liberty or give me death!"

Henry's was one of a number of speeches that aroused colonists. While his eloquence made this speech a staple of American education, others, such as John Hancock's 1774 memorial of the so-called Boston Massacre, were published and widely circulated. The event occurred March 5, 1770, when several Bostonians including a black man, Crispus Attucks, were killed and others injured by British soldiers. The shooting responded to an attack on the soldiers after a weekend of provocation by the colonists. However, radicals like Samuel Adams (and later Hancock) used the massacre as propaganda against the British occupation of Boston. An engraving of the event by Paul Revere was widely distributed and added to the propaganda value of the incident. John Adams helped defend the soldiers, who were acquitted of murder.

Delivered
In the Convention of Delegates of Virginia.

Mr. President,

No man thinks more highly than I do of the patriotism, as well as abilities, of the very worthy gentlemen who have just addressed the House. But different men often see the same subject in different lights; and, therefore, I hope it will not be thought disrespectful to those gentlemen, if, entertaining as I do, opinions of a character very opposite to theirs, I shall speak forth my sentiments freely and without reserve. This is no time for ceremony. The question, before the House, is one of awful moment to this country. For my own part, I consider it as nothing less than a question of freedom or slavery: and in proportion to the magnitude of the subject ought to be freedom of the debate. It is only in this way that we can hope to arrive at truth, and fulfil the great responsibility which we hold to God and our country. Should I keep back my opinions at such a time, through fear of giving offence, I should consider myself as guilty of treason towards my country, and of an act of disloyalty toward the majesty of heaven, which I revere above all earthly kings.

Mr. President, it is natural to man to indulge in the illusions of hope. We are apt to shut our eyes against a painful truth, and listen to the song of that syren, till she transforms us into beasts. Is this the part of wise men, engaged in a great and arduous struggle for liberty? Are we disposed to be of the number of those, who having eyes, see not, and having ears, hear not, the things which so nearly concern their temporal salvation? For my part, whatever anguish of spirit it may cost, I am willing to know the whole truth; to know the worst, and to provide for it.

I have but one lamp by which my feet are guided; and that is the lamp of experience. I know of no way of judging of the future but by the past. And judging by the past, I wish to know what there has been in the conduct of the British ministry for the last ten years, to justify those hopes with which gentlemen have been pleased to solace themselves and the House? Is it that insidious smile with which our petition has been lately received? Trust it not, sir; it will prove a snare to your feet. Suffer not yourselves to be betrayed with a kiss. Ask yourselves how this gracious reception of our petition comports with those warlike preparations which cover our waters and darken our land. Are fleets and armies necessary to a work of love and reconciliation? Have we shown ourselves so unwilling to be reconciled, that force must be called in to win back our love? Let us not deceive ourselves, sir. These are the implements of war and subjugation; the last arguments to which kings resort. I ask gentlemen, sir, what means this martial array, if its purpose be not to force us to submission? Can gentlemen assign any other possible motive for it? Has Great Britain any enemy, in this quarter of the world, to call for all this accumulation of navies and armies? No, sir, she has none. They are meant for us: they can be meant for no other. They are sent over to bind and rivet upon us those chains, which the British ministry have been so long forging. And what have we to oppose to them? Shall we try argument? Sir, we have been trying that for the last ten years. Have we any thing new to offer upon the subject? Nothing. We have held the subject up in every light of which it is capable; but it has been all in vain. Shall we resort to entreaty and humble supplication? What terms shall we find, which have not been already exhausted? Let us not, I beseech you, sir, deceive ourselves longer. Sir, we have done every thing that could be done, to avert the storm which is now coming on. We have petitioned; we have remonstrated; we have supplicated; we have prostrated ourselves before the throne, and have implored its interposition to arrest the tyrannical hands of the ministry and parliament. Our petitions have been slighted; our remonstrances have produced additional violence and insult; our supplications have been disregarded; and we have been spurned, with contempt, from the foot of the throne! In vain, after these things, may we indulge the fond hope of peace and reconciliation. There is no longer any room for hope. If we wish to be free—if we mean to preserve, inviolate those inestimable privileges for which we have been so long contending—if we mean not basely to abandon the noble struggle in which we have been so long engaged, and which we have pledged ourselves never to abandon, until the glorious object of our contest shall be obtained—we must fight! I repeat it, sir, we must fight! An appeal to arms and to the God of Hosts is all that is left us!

They tell us, sir, that we are weak; unable to cope with so formidable an adversary. But when shall we be stronger? Will it be the next week, or the next year? Will it be when we are totally disarmed, and when a British guard shall be stationed in every house? Shall we gather strength by irresolution and inaction? Shall we acquire the means of effectual resistance, by lying supinely on our backs, and hugging the delusive phantom of hope, until our enemies

shall have bound us hand and foot? Sir, we are not weak, if we make a proper use of those means which the God of nature hath placed in our power. Three millions of people, armed in the holy cause of liberty, and in such a country as that which we possess, are invincible by any force which our enemy can send against us. Besides, sir, we shall not fight our battles alone. There is a just God who presides over the destinies of nations; and who will raise up friends to fight our battles for us. The battle, sir, is not to the strong alone; it is to the vigilant, the active, the brave. Besides, sir, we have no election. If we were base enough to desire it, it is now too late to retire from the contest. There is no retreat, but in submission and slavery! Our chains are forged! Their clanking may be heard on the plains of Boston! The war is inevitable—and let it come! I repeat it, sir, let it come!

It is in vain, sir, to extenuate the matter. Gentlemen may cry, peace, peace—but there is no peace. The war is actually begun! The next gale, that sweeps from the north, will bring to our ears the clash of resounding arms! Our brethren are already in the field! Why stand we here idle? What is it that gentlemen wish? What would they have? Is life so dear, or peace so sweet, as to be purchased at the price of chains and slavery? Forbid it, Almighty God! I know not what course others may take; but as for me, give me liberty, or give me death!

Source:

Williston, Ebenezer Bancroft. *Eloquence of the United States.* Middletown, Conn.: E. & H. Clark, 1827.

The American Revolution

Declaration of the Causes and Necessity of Taking Up Arms, 1775

Document drafted by Thomas Jefferson and John Dickinson on July 6, 1775, declaring the right to and just causes for taking up arms against the British. The Revolutionary War officially began on April 19, 1775, when a group of colonists fought British soldiers in Lexington, Massachusetts. The war was instigated by the many acts passed by Parliament—such as the Navigation Acts, the Quartering Act of 1774 (which replaced the Quartering Act of 1765), the Stamp Acts, and the Tea

Acts—that taxed the American colonists unfairly. These acts were passed by Great Britain to maintain a standing army in North America and to slow down the westward expansion of the colonies. The Second Continental Congress ordered the Declaration of Causes and Necessity of Taking Up Arms to be written to proclaim the causes of and the events leading up to the war against Britain and to defend the honor of the colonists involved in the fighting.

Shortly before passing the declaration, the Continental Congress appointed George Washington "General and Commander in Chief" of all colonial forces. Although Washington, a proven military leader, had impressed the delegates with his poise, dedication, and skill, his commission was partly the result of a political compromise. Most of the soldiers in the colonial army were from New England, but Washington, as a Virginian, tied the different regions of the fledgling country closer together and shored up support from the southern colonies. He refused a salary for his new position, requesting only that his expenses be covered while he remained in command. Washington's energy and decisive character helped him manage the ragtag colonial army and win the support he needed from Congress to keep them fed, quartered, and focused on defeating the more seasoned and experienced British troops.

If it was possible for men who exercise their reason to believe that the Divine Author of our existence intended a part of the human race to hold an absolute property in and an unbounded power over others, marked out by his infinite goodness and wisdom, as the objects of a legal domination never rightfully resistible, however severe and oppressive, the inhabitants of these colonies might at least require from the Parliament of Great Britain some evidence that this dreadful authority has been granted to that body. But a reverence for our great Creator, principles of humanity, and the dictates of common sense, must convince all those who reflect upon the subject that government was instituted to promote the welfare of mankind and ought to be administered for the attainment of that end. The legislature of Great Britain, however, stimulated by an inordinate passion for a power not only unjustifiable, but which they know to be peculiarly reprobated by the very constitution of that kingdom, and desperate of success in any mode of contest where regard should be had to truth, law, or right, have at length, deserting those, attempted to effect their cruel and impolitic purpose of enslaving these colonies by violence, and have thereby rendered it necessary for us to close with their last appeal from reason to arms. Yet, however blinded that assembly may be, by their intemperate rage for unlimited domination, so to slight justice and the opinion of mankind, we esteem ourselves bound by obligations of respect to the rest of the world to make known the justice of our cause.

Our forefathers, inhabitants of the island of Great Britain, left their native land to seek on these shores a residence for civil and religious freedom. At the expense of their blood; at the hazard of their fortunes; without the least charge to the country from which they removed; by unceasing labor and an unconquerable spirit, they effected settlements in the distant and inhospitable wilds of America, then filled with numerous and warlike nations of barbarians. Societies or governments, vested with perfect legislatures, were formed under charters from the crown, and an harmonious intercourse was established between the colonies and the kingdom from which they derived their origin.

The mutual benefits of this union became in a short time so extraordinary as to excite astonishment. It is universally confessed that the amazing increase of the wealth, strength, and navigation of the realm arose from this source; and the minister who so wisely and successfully directed the measures of Great Britain in the late war publicly declared that these colonies enabled her to triumph over her enemies. Toward the conclusion of that war it pleased our sovereign to make a change in his counsels. From that fatal moment the affairs of the British empire began to fall into confusion, and gradually sliding from the summit of glorious prosperity to which they had been advanced by the virtues and abilities of one man are at length distracted by the convulsions that now shake its deepest foundations. The new ministry, finding the brave foes of Britain, though frequently defeated, yet still contending, took up the unfortunate idea of granting them a hasty peace and of then subduing her faithful friends.

These devoted colonies were judged to be in such a state as to present victories without bloodshed and all the easy emoluments of statutable plunder. The uninterrupted tenor of their peaceable and respectful behavior from the beginning of colonization; their dutiful, zealous, and useful services during the war, though so recently and amply acknowledged in the most honorable manner by his Majesty, by the late King and by Parliament, could not save them from the meditated innovations. Parliament was influenced to adopt the pernicious project, and assuming a new power over them have in the course of eleven years given such decisive specimens of the spirit and consequences attending this power as to leave no doubt concerning the effects of acquiescence under it.

They have undertaken to give and grant our money without our consent, though we have ever exercised an exclusive right to dispose of our own property; statutes have been passed for extending the jurisdiction of courts of admiralty and vice-admiralty beyond their ancient limits; for depriving us of the accustomed and inestimable privilege of trial by jury in cases affecting both life and property; for suspending the legislature of one of the colonies; for interdicting all commerce to the capital of another, and for altering, fundamentally, the form of government established by charter and secured by acts of its own legislature, solemnly confirmed by the crown; for exempting the "murderers" of colonists from legal trial, and in effect from punishment; for erecting in a neighboring province, acquired by the joint arms of Great Britain and America, a despotism dangerous to our very existence; and for quartering soldiers upon the colonists in time of profound peace. It has also been resolved in Parliament that colonists charged with committing certain offences shall be transported to England to be tried.

But why should we enumerate our injuries in detail? By one statute it is declared that Parliament can "of right make laws to bind us in all cases whatsoever." What is to defend us against so enormous, so unlimited a power? Not a single man of those who assume it is chosen by us or is subject to our control or influence; but on the contrary they are all of them exempt from the operation of such laws, and an American revenue, if not diverted from the ostensible purposes for which it is raised, would actually lighten their own burden in proportion as they increase ours. We saw the misery to which such despotism would reduce us. We, for ten years, incessantly and ineffectually besieged the throne as supplicants; we reasoned, we remonstrated with Parliament in the most mild and decent language.

Administration, sensible that we should regard these oppressive measures as freemen ought to do, sent over fleets and armies to enforce them. The indignation of the Americans was roused, it is true, but it was the indignation of a virtuous, loyal, and affectionate people. A congress of delegates from the united colonies was assembled at Philadelphia on the 5th day of last September. We resolved again to offer an humble and dutiful petition to the King, and also addressed our fellow subjects of Great Britain. We have pursued every temperate, every respectful measure; we have even proceeded to break off our commercial intercourse with our fellow subjects, as the last peaceable admonition that our attachment to no nation upon earth should supplant our attachment to liberty. This, we flattered ourselves, was the ultimate step of the controversy, but subsequent events have shown how vain was this hope of finding moderation in our enemies.

Several threatening expressions against the colonies were inserted in his Majesty's speech; our petition, though we were told it was a decent one, and that his Majesty had been pleased to receive it graciously, and to promise laying it before his Parliament, was huddled into both Houses among a bundle of American papers and there neglected. The Lords and Commons in their address in the month of February said that "a rebellion at that time actually existed within the province of Massachusetts Bay, and that those concerned in it had been countenanced and encouraged by unlawful combinations and engagements entered into by his Majesty's subjects in several of the other colonies; and therefore they besought his Majesty that he would take the most effectual measures to enforce due obedience to the laws and authority of the supreme legislature." Soon after, the commercial intercourse of whole colonies with foreign countries and with each other was cut off by an act of Parliament; by another, several of them were entirely prohibited from the fisheries in the seas near their coasts,

on which they always depended for their subsistence, and large reinforcements of ships and troops were immediately sent over to General Gage.

Fruitless were all the entreaties, arguments, and eloquence of an illustrious band of the most distinguished peers and commoners, who nobly and strenuously asserted the justice of our cause to stay or even to mitigate the heedless fury with which these accumulated and unexampled outrages were hurried on. Equally fruitless was the interference of the city of London, of Bristol, and many other respectable towns, in our favor. Parliament adopted an insidious manoeuvre, calculated to divide us, to establish a perpetual auction of taxations, where colony should bid against colony, all of them uninformed what ransom would redeem their lives; and thus to extort from us, at the point of the bayonet, the unknown sums that should be sufficient to gratify, if possible to gratify, ministerial rapacity, with the miserable indulgence left to us of raising in our own mode the prescribed tribute. What terms more rigid and humiliating could have been dictated by remorseless victors to conquered enemies? In our circumstances to accept them would be to deserve them.

Soon after the intelligence of these proceedings arrived on this continent, General Gage, who in the course of the last year had taken possession of the town of Boston, in the province of Massachusetts Bay, and still occupied it as a garrison, on the 19th day of April sent out from that place a large detachment of his army, who made an unprovoked assault on the inhabitants of the said province at the town of Lexington, as appears by the affidavits of a great number of persons, some of whom were officers and soldiers of that detachment, murdered, eight of the inhabitants and wounded many others. From thence the troops proceeded in warlike array to the town of Concord, where they set upon another party of the inhabitants of the same province, killing several and wounding more, until compelled to retreat by the country people suddenly assembled to repel this cruel aggression.

Hostilities thus commenced by the British troops have been since prosecuted by them without regard to faith or reputation. The inhabitants of Boston being confined within that town by the general, their governor, and having, in order to procure their dismission, entered into a treaty with him, it was stipulated that the said inhabitants, having deposited their arms with their own magistrates, should have liberty to depart, taking with them their other effects. They accordingly delivered up their arms, but in open violation of honor, in defiance of the obligation of treaties which even savage nations esteem sacred, the governor ordered the arms deposited as aforesaid that they might be preserved for their owners, to be seized by a body of soliders, detained the greatest part of the inhabitants in the town, and compelled the few who were permitted to retire to leave their most valuable effects behind.

By this perfidy wives are separated from their husbands, children from their parents, the aged and the sick from their relations and friends who wish to attend and comfort them, and those who have been used to live in plenty and even elegance are reduced to deplorable distress.

The general, further emulating his ministerial masters, by a proclamation bearing date on the 12th day of June, after venting the grossest falsehoods and calumnies against the good people of these colonies, proceeds to "declare them all, either by name or description, to be rebels and traitors to supesede the course of common law, and instead thereof to publish and order the use and exercise of the law martial." His troops have butchered our countrymen, have wantonly burnt Charlestown, besides a considerable number of houses in other places; our ships and vessels are seized; the necessary supplies of provisions are intercepted, and he is exerting his utmost power to spread destruction and devastation around him.

We have received certain intelligence that General Carleton, the Governor of Canada, is instigating the people of that province and the Indians to fall upon us; and we have but too much reason to apprehend that schemes have been formed to excite domestic enemies against us. In brief, a part of these colonies now feel, and all of them are sure of feeling, as far as the vengeance of administration can inflict them, the complicated calamities of fire, sword, and famine. We are reduced to the alternative of choosing an unconditional submission to the tyranny of irritated ministers or resistance by force. The latter is our choice. We have counted the cost of this contest and find nothing so dreadful as voluntary slavery! Honor, justice, and humanity forbid us tamely to surrender that freedom which we received from our gallant ancestors, and which our innocent posterity have a right to receive from us. We cannot endure the infamy and guilt of resigning succeeding generations to that wretchedness which inevitably awaits them if we basely entail hereditary bondage upon them.

Our cause is just. Our union is perfect. Our internal resources are great, and, if necessary, foreign assistance is undoubtedly attainable. We gratefully acknowledge, as signal instances of Divine favor toward us, that his providence would not permit us to be called into his severe controversy until we were grown up to our present strength, had been previously exercised in warlike operations, and possessed the means of defending ourselves. With hearts fortified by these animating reflections we most solemnly, before God and the world, declare, that, exerting the utmost energy of those powers which our beneficent Creator has graciously bestowed upon us, the arms we have been compelled by our enemies to assume, we will, in defi-

nance of every hazard, with unabating firmness and perseverance, employ for the preservation of our liberties; being with one mind resolved to die freemen rather than to live slaves.

Lest this declaration should disquiet the minds of our friends and fellow subjects in any part of the Empire, we assure them that we mean not to dissolve that union which has so long and so happily subsisted between us, and which we sincerely wish to see restored. Necessity has not yet driven us into that desperate measure or induced us to excite any other nation to war against them. We have not raised armies with ambitious designs of separating from Great Britain and establishing independent states. We fight not for glory or for conquest. We exhibit to mankind the remarkable spectacle of a people attacked by unprovoked enemies, without any imputation or even suspicion of offense. They boast of their privileges and civilization, and yet proffer no milder conditions than servitude or death.

In our own native land, in defense of the freedom that is our birthright, and which we ever enjoyed till the late violation of it—for the protection of our property, acquired solely by the honest industry of our forefathers and ourselves, against violence actually offered, we have taken up arms. We shall lay them down when hostilities shall cease on the part of the aggressors and all danger of their being renewed shall be removed, and not before.

With an humble confidence in the mercies of the Supreme and impartial Judge and Ruler of the universe, we most devoutly implore his divine goodness to protect us happily through this great conflict, to dispose our adversaries to reconciliation on reasonable terms, and thereby to relieve the Empire from the calamities of civil war.

See also COERCIVE OR INTOLERABLE ACTS, 1774; STAMP ACT, 1765; TEA ACT, 1773; SECOND CONTINENTAL CONGRESS, ADDRESS OF THE CONTINENTAL CONGRESS TO THE AMERICAN PEOPLE, 1778.

Source:

James Andrews and David Zarefsky, eds. *American Voices: Significant Speeches in American History, 1640–1945*. New York: Longman, 1989.

Proclamation for Suppressing Rebellion and Sedition, 1775

Proclamation by King George III declaring the colonies to be in open rebellion against the king and government of England. The first shots of the Revolution were fired at the Battles of Lexington and Concord on April 19, 1775. When the Second

Continental Congress met in Philadelphia the next month, they raised an army, set up committees to handle domestic and foreign issues, and drafted the *Declaration of the Causes and Necessity of Taking Up Arms*. England viewed these measures as acts of war. In his proclamation, King George denounced the rebels as traitors and reminded all "obedient and loyal subjects" of their duty to resist this rebellion and "to disclose and make known all traitorous conspiracies." Parliament added a Restraining Act, December 22, 1775, which prohibited "all manner of trade and commerce" with the American colonies. It further stated that American ships found trading at any port would be captured, and their cargoes would be distributed among British crew members. However, instead of suppressing the rebellion, the act only strengthened the colonies' resolve to free themselves from British rule, leading ultimately to the Declaration of Independence in 1776. The document below followed the British Restraining Act for New England enacted by the British Parliament on March 30, 1775. That act was a retaliation against the colonial boycott of British goods that the First Continental Congress initiated in 1774 as a protest against British taxes and repression. This law restricted the trade of the New England colonies to England, Ireland, and the British West Indies and prohibited New England fishermen from fishing in North Atlantic waters.

Whereas many of our subjects in divers parts of our Colonies and Plantations in North America, misled by dangerous and ill designing men, and forgetting the allegiance which they owe to the power that has protected and supported them; after various disorderly acts committed in disturbance of the publick peace, to the obstruction of lawful commerce, and to the oppression of our loyal subjects carrying on the same; have at length proceeded to open and avowed rebellion, by arraying themselves in a hostile manner, to withstand the execution of the law, and traitorously preparing, ordering and levying war against us: And whereas, there is reason to apprehend that such rebellion hath been much promoted and encouraged by the traitorous correspondence, counsels and comfort of divers wicked and desperate persons within this Realm: To the end therefore, that none of our subjects may neglect or violate their duty through ignorance thereof, or through any doubt of the protection which the law will afford to their loyalty and zeal, we have thought fit, by and with the advice of our Privy Council, to issue our Royal Proclamation, hereby declaring, that not only all our Officers, civil and military, are obliged to exert their utmost endeavours to suppress such rebellion, and to bring the traitors to justice, but that all our subjects of this Realm, and the dominions thereunto belonging, are bound by law to be aiding and assisting in the suppression of such rebellion, and to disclose and make known all traitorous conspiracies and

attempts against us, our crown and dignity; and we do accordingly strictly charge and command all our Officers, as well civil as military, and all others our obedient and loyal subjects, to use their utmost endeavours to withstand and suppress such rebellion, and to disclose and make known all treasons and traitorous conspiracies which they shall know to be against us, our crown and dignity; and for that purpose, that they transmit to one of our principal Secretaries of State, or other proper officer, due and full information of all persons who shall be found carrying on correspondence with, or in any manner or degree aiding or abetting the persons now in open arms and rebellion against our Government, within any of our Colonies and Plantations in North America, in order to bring to condign punishment the authors, perpetrators, and abetters of such traitorous designs.

Given at our Court at St. James's the twenty-third day of August, one thousand seven hundred and seventy-five, in the fifteenth year of our reign.

GOD save the KING.

See also DECLARATION OF THE CAUSES AND NECESSITY OF TAKING UP ARMS.

Source:
America's Homepage. Available on-line. URL: http://ahp.gatech. edu/proclamation_bp_1775. html. Accessed November 2003.

Thomas Paine, *Common Sense*, 1776

Pamphlet written by Thomas Paine and published in Philadelphia in January 1776. It strongly urged Americans to claim independence from Britain. Paine argued that reconciliation was impossible and described some of the disadvantages suffered by the American colonies through their connection with Britain. He asserted that the colonies tended to get entangled in foreign wars because they acquired Britain's enemies and had also recently become the target of Britain's hostilities. He argued that it was impossible for Britain to govern effectively from such a distance and that the colonies were capable of governing themselves. He described a possible plan of representative government and urged formation of a constitutional convention. *Common Sense*, with 120,000 copies circulated in its first three months, was highly influential in advancing the idea of American independence.

In a number of his comments reproduced here, he is quite prescient concerning such ideas as checks and balances and population diversity. The pamphlet opens with a section on the necessity of government: "a mode rendered necessary by the inability of moral virtue to govern the world; here too is the design and end of government, viz. Freedom and security." He goes on to criticize the English constitution which, unlike the

American version, consists of unwritten precepts drawn from historic documents such as the Magna Carta (1215) and the Declaration of Rights (1689). The next section excerpted here contains some of Paine's specific responses to opponents of independence.

On the Origin and Design of Government in General, with Concise Remarks on the English Constitution

I draw my idea of the form of government from a principle in nature which no art can overturn, viz. that the more simple any thing is, the less liable it is to be disordered, and the easier repaired when disordered; and with this maxim in view I offer a few remarks on the so much boasted constitution of England. That it was noble for the dark and slavish times in which it was erected, is granted. When the world was overrun with tyranny the least remove therefrom was a glorious rescue. But that it is imperfect, subject to convulsions, and incapable of producing what it seems to promise, is easily demonstrated.

Absolute governments, (tho' the disgrace of human nature) have this advantage with them, they are simple: if the people suffer, they know the head from which their suffering springs; know likewise the remedy; and are not bewildered by a variety of causes and cures. But the constitution of England is so exceedingly complex, that the nation may suffer for years together without being able to discover in which part the fault lies; some will say in one and some in another, and every political physician will advise a different medicine.

I know it is difficult to get over local or long standing prejudices, yet if we will suffer ourselves to examine the component parts of the English constitution, we shall find them to be the base remains of two ancient tyrannies, compounded with some new Republican materials.

❧   ❧   ❧

[Monarchy and peers or lords], by being hereditary, are independent of the People; wherefore in a *constitutional sense* they contribute nothing towards the freedom of the State. To say that the constitution of England is an *union* of three powers [The third power is the House of Commons.], reciprocally *checking* each other, is farcical; either the words have no meaning, or they are flat contradictions.

❧   ❧   ❧

That the crown is this overbearing part in the English constitution needs not be mentioned, and that it derives its whole consequence merely from being the giver of places and pensions is self-evident; wherefore, though we have been wise enough to shut and lock a door against absolute Monarchy, we at the same time have been foolish enough to put the Crown in possession of the key.

The prejudice of Englishmen, in favour of their own government, by King, Lords and Commons, arises as much or more from national pride than reason. Individuals are undoubtedly safer in England than in some other countries: but the will of the King is as much the law of the land in Britain as in France, with this difference, that instead of proceeding directly from his mouth, it is handed to the people under the formidable shape of an act of parliament.

❧   ❧   ❧

Thoughts on the Present State of American Affairs

Volumes have been written on the subject of the struggle between England and America. Men of all ranks have embarked in the controversy, from different motives, and with various designs; but all have been ineffectual, and the period of debate is closed. Arms as the last resource decide the contest; the appeal was the choice of the King, and the Continent has accepted the challenge.

❧   ❧   ❧

The Sun never shined on a cause of greater worth. 'Tis not the affair of a City, a County, a Province, or a Kingdom; but of a Continent—of at least one eighth part of the habitable Globe. 'Tis not the concern of a day, a year, or an age; posterity are virtually involved in the contest, and will be more or less affected even to the end of time, by the proceedings now. Now is the seed-time of Continental union, faith and honour. The least fracture now will be like a name engraved with the point of a pin on the tender rind of a young oak; the wound would enlarge with the tree, and posterity read it in full grown characters.

By referring the matter from argument to arms, a new aera for politics is struck—a new method of thinking hath arisen. All plans, proposals, &c. prior to the nineteenth of April, *i.e.* to the commencement of hostilities, are like the almanacks of the last year; which tho' proper then, are superseded and useless now. Whatever was advanced by the advocates on either side of the question then, terminated in one and the same point, viz. a union with Great-Britain; the only difference between the parties was the method of effecting it; the one proposing force, the other friendship; but it hath so far happened that the first hath failed, and the second hath withdrawn her influence.

As much hath been said of the advantages of reconciliation, which, like an agreeable dream, hath passed away and left us as we were, it is but right that we should examine the contrary side of the argument, and enquire into some of the many material injuries which these Colonies sustain, and always will sustain, by being connected with and dependant on Great-Britain. To examine that connection and dependance, on the principles of nature and common sense, to see what we have to trust to, if separated, and what we are to expect, if dependant.

I have heard it asserted by some, that as America has flourished under her former connection with Great-Britain, the same connection is necessary towards her future happiness, and will always have the same effect. Nothing can be more fallacious than this kind of argument. . . . America would have flourished as much, and probably much more, had no European power taken any notice of her. The commerce by which she hath enriched herself are the necessaries of life, and will always have a market while eating is the custom of Europe.

But she has protected us say some . . . [but] she would have defended Turkey from the same motive, viz. for the sake of trade and dominion.

❖   ❖   ❖

But Britain is the parent country, say some. Then the more shame upon her conduct.

❖   ❖   ❖

Europe, and not England, is the parent country of America. This new World hath been the asylum for the persecuted lovers of civil and religious liberty from *every part* of Europe. Hither have they fled, not from the tender embraces of the mother, but from the cruelty of the monster; and it is so far true of England, that the same tyranny which drove the first emigrants from home, pursues their descendants still. . . . We claim brotherhood with every European Christian, and triumph in the generosity of the sentiment. . . . It is pleasant to observe by what regular gradations we surmount the force of local prejudices, as we enlarge our acquaintance with the World. . . .

❖   ❖   ❖

. . . Our plan is commerce, and that, well attended to, will secure us the peace and friendship of all Europe; because it is the interest of all Europe to have America a free port. Her trade will always be a protection, and her barrenness of gold and silver secure her from invaders.

I challenge the warmest advocate for reconciliation to show a single advantage that this continent can reap by being connected with Great Britain. I repeat the challenge; not a single advantage is derived. Our corn will fetch its price in any market in Europe, and our imported goods must be paid for, buy them where we will.

But the injuries and disadvantages which we sustain by that connection, are without number; and our duty to mankind at large, as well as to ourselves, instruct us to renounce the alliance: because, any submission to, or dependance on, Great Britain, tends directly to involve this Continent in European wars and quarrels, and set us at variance with nations who would otherwise seek our

friendship, and against whom we have neither anger nor complaint. As Europe is our market for trade, we ought to form no partial connection with any part of it. It is the true interest of America to steer clear of European contentions, which she never can do, while, by her dependance on Britain, she is made the make-weight in the scale of British politics.

❖   ❖   ❖

Though I would carefully avoid giving unnecessary offence, yet I am inclined to believe, that all those who espouse the doctrine of reconciliation, may be included within the following descriptions.

Interested men, who are not to be trusted, weak men who *cannot* see, prejudiced men who will not see, and a certain set of moderate men who think better of the European world than it deserves; and this last class, by an ill-judged deliberation, will be the cause of more calamities to this Continent than all the other three.

It is the good fortune of many to live distant from the scene of present sorrow; the evil is not sufficiently brought to their doors to make them feel the precariousness with which all American property is possessed. But let our imaginations transport us a few moments to Boston; that seat of wretchedness will teach us wisdom, and instruct us for ever to renounce a power in whom we can have no trust. The inhabitants of that unfortunate city who but a few months ago were in ease and affluence, have now no other alternative than to stay and starve, or turn out to beg. Endangered by the fire of their friends if they continue within the city, and plundered by the soldiery if they leave it, in their present situation they are prisoners without the hope of redemption, and in a general attack for their relief they would be exposed to the fury of both armies.

❖   ❖   ❖

Europe is too thickly planted with Kingdoms to be long at peace, and whenever a war breaks out between England and any foreign power, the trade of America goes to ruin, because of her connection with Britain. . . Every thing that is right or reasonable pleads for separation. The blood of the slain, the weeping voice of nature cries, 'Tis time to part. . . .

Every quiet method for peace hath been ineffectual. Our prayers have been rejected with disdain; and hath tended to convince us that nothing flatters vanity or confirms obstinacy in Kings more than repeated petitioning—and nothing hath contributed more than that very measure to make the Kings of Europe absolute. Witness Denmark and Sweden. Wherefore, since nothing but blows will do, for God's sake let us come to a final separation, and not leave the next generation to be cutting throats under the violated unmeaning names of parent and child.

To say they will never attempt it again is idle and visionary; we thought so at the repeal of the stamp act, yet a year or two undeceived us; as well may we suppose that nations which have been once defeated will never renew the quarrel . . .

Small islands not capable of protecting themselves are the proper objects for government to take under their care; but there is something absurd, in supposing a Continent to be perpetually governed by an island. . . .

❋   ❋   ❋

I am not induced by motives of pride, party, or resentment to espouse the doctrine of separation and independence; I am clearly, positively, and conscientiously persuaded that it is the true interest of this Continent to be so; that every thing short of *that* is mere patchwork, that it can afford no lasting felicity,—that it is leaving the sword to our children, and shrinking back at a time when a little more, a little further, would have rendered this Continent the glory of the earth.

As Britain hath not manifested the least inclination towards a compromise, we may be assured that no terms can be obtained worthy the acceptance of the Continent, or any ways equal to the expence of blood and treasure we have been already put to.

❋   ❋   ❋

. . . No man was a warmer wisher for a reconciliation than myself, before the fatal nineteenth of April, 1775, but the moment the event of that day was made known, I rejected the hardened, sullen-tempered Pharaoh of England for ever; and disdain the wretch, that with the pretended title of Father of his people can unfeelingly hear of their slaughter, and composedly sleep with their blood upon his soul.

❋   ❋   ❋

But the most powerful of all arguments is, that nothing but independence, *i.e.* a Continental from of government, can keep the peace of the Continent and preserve it inviolate from civil wars. I dread the event of a reconciliation with Britain now, as it is more than probable that it will be followed by a revolt some where or other, the consequences of which may be far more fatal than all the malice of Britain.

Thousands are already ruined by British barbarity; (thousands more will probably suffer the same fate.) Those men have other feelings than us who have nothing suffered. All they now possess is liberty; what they before enjoyed is sacrificed to its service, and having nothing more to lose they disdain submission. Besides, the general temper of the Colonies, towards a British government will be like that of a youth who is nearly out of his time; they

will care very little about her: And a government which cannot preserve the peace is no government at all, and in that case we pay our money for nothing; and pray what is it that Britain can do, whose power will be wholly on paper, should a civil tumult break out the very day after reconciliation? I have heard some men say, many of whom I believe spoke without thinking, that they dreaded an independance, fearing that it would produce civil wars . . . I make the sufferer's case my own, and I protest, that were I driven from house and home, my property destroyed, and my circumstances ruined, that as a man, sensible of injuries, I could never relish the doctrine of reconciliation, or consider myself bound thereby.

❋   ❋   ❋

If there is any true cause of fear respecting independance, it is because no plan is yet laid down. Men do not see their way out. Wherefore, as an opening into that business I offer the following hints; at the same time modestly affirming, that I have no other opinion of them myself, than that they may be the means of giving rise to something better. . . .

Let the assemblies be annual, with a president only. The representation more equal, their business wholly domestic, and subject to the authority of a Continental Congress.

Let each Colony be divided into . . . convenient districts, each district to send a proper number of Delegates to Congress. . . . Each congress to sit and to choose a President by the following method. When the Delegates are met, let a Colony be taken from the whole thirteen Colonies by lot, after which let the Congress choose (by ballot) a president from out of the Delegates of that Province. In the next Congress, let a Colony be taken by lot from twelve only, omitting that Colony from which the president was taken in the former Congress, and so proceeding on till the whole thirteen shall have had their proper rotation. And in order that nothing may pass into a law but what is satisfactorily just, not less than three-fifths of the Congress to be called a majority. He that will promote discord, under a government so equally formed as this, would have joined Lucifer in his revolt.

❋   ❋   ❋

But as there is a peculiar delicacy from whom, or in what manner, this business must first arise, and as it seems most agreeable and consistent that it should come from some intermediate body between the governed and the governors, that is, between the Congress and the People, let a Continental Conference be held in the following manner, and for the following purpose, A Committee of twenty-six members of congress [selected in various ways "in behalf of the whole province" to] be united the two grand principles of business, *knowledge* and *power*. The Members of Congress, Assemblies, or Conventions, by having had experience in national concerns, will be able and useful counsellors, and the whole, being empowered by the people, will have a truly legal authority.

The conferring members being met, let their business be to frame a Continental Charter, or Charter of the United Colonies; (answering to what is called the Magna Charta of England) fixing the number and manner of choosing Members of Congress, Members of Assembly, with their date of sitting; and drawing the line of business and jurisdiction between them: Always remembering, that our strength is Continental, not Provincial. Securing freedom and property to all men, and above all things, the free exercise of religion, according to the dictates of conscience; with such other matter as it is necessary for a charter to contain. Immediately after which, the said conference to dissolve, and the bodies which shall be chosen conformable to the said charter, to be the Legislators and Governors of this Continent for the time being: Whose peace and happiness, may God preserve. Amen.

❋ ❋ ❋

A government of our own is our natural right: and when a man seriously reflects on the precariousness of human affairs, he will become convinced, that it is infinitely wiser and safer, to form a constitution of our own in a cool deliberate manner, while we have it in our power, than to trust such an interesting event to time and chance. . . .

❋ ❋ ❋

Ye that tell us of harmony and reconciliation, can ye restore to us the time that is past? Can ye give to prostitution its former innocence? Neither can ye reconcile Britain and America. The last cord now is broken, the people of England are presenting addresses against us. There are injuries which nature cannot forgive; she would cease to be nature if she did. As well can the lover forgive the ravisher of his mistress, as the Continent forgive the murders of Britain. The Almighty hath implanted in us these unextinguishable feelings for good and wise purposes. They are the Guardians of his Image in our hearts. They distinguish us from the herd of common animals. The social compact would dissolve, and justice be extirpated from the earth, or have only a casual existence were we callous to the touches of affection. The robber and the murderer would often escape unpunished, did not the injuries which our tempers sustain, provoke us into justice.

O! ye that love mankind! Ye that dare oppose not only the tyranny but the tyrant, stand forth! Every spot of the old world is overrun with oppression. Freedom hath been hunted round the Globe. Asia and Africa hath long expelled her. Europe regards her like a stranger, and En-

gland hath given her warning to depart. O! receive the fugitive, and prepare in time an asylum for mankind.

Source:

Selections from the Writings of Thomas Paine, New York: Boni and Liveright, 1922, pp. 1–40.

Abigail and John Adams, "Remember the Ladies," 1776

These are excerpts from correspondence between Massachusetts delegate to the Continental Congress and future U.S. vice president and president John Adams and his wife, Abigail. The first letter was written shortly after the British evacuated Boston on March 17, 1776, and excerpts not reproduced here describe the condition in which the fleeing troops left the city. Abigail also expressed fear of smallpox. Left in charge of the family's farm, she wrote of planting crops. In addition to the passages below, asking her husband to "remember the ladies," she also questioned whether "the passion for Liberty cannot be Eaquelly Strong in the Breasts of those who have been accustomed to deprive their fellow Creatures of theirs." In his reply, John made light of Abigail's "remember the Ladies" request, and she answered in kind.

[Abigail Adams to John Adams, March 31, April 5, 1776:] . . . I long to hear that you have declared an independancy—and by the way in the new Code of Laws which I suppose it will be necessary for you to make I desire you would Remember the Ladies, and be more generous and favourable to them than your ancestors. Do not put such unlimited power into the hands of the Husbands. Remember all Men would be tyrants if they could. If perticuliar care and attention is not paid to the Laidies we are determined to foment a Rebellion, and will not hold ourselves bound by any Laws in which we have no voice, or Representation. That your Sex are Naturally Tyrannical is a Truth so thoroughly established as to admit of no dispute, but such of you as wish to be happy willingly give up the harsh title of Master for the more tender and endearing one of Friend. Why then, not put it out of the power of the vicious and the Lawless to use us with cruelty and indignity with impunity. Men of Sense in all Ages abhor those customs which treat us only as the vassals of your Sex. Regard us then as Beings placed by providence under your protection and in immitation of the Supreem Being make use of that power only for our happiness.

[John to Abigail, April 14, 1776:] As to Declarations of Independency, be patient. . . . As to your extraordinary

Code of Laws, I cannot but laugh. We have been told that our Struggle has loosened the bands of Government every where. That Children and Apprentices were disobedient—that schools and Colledges were grown turbulent—that Indians slighted their Guardians and Negroes grew insolent to their Masters. But your Letter was the first Intimation that another Tribe more numerous and powerfull than all the rest were grown discontented.—This is rather too coarse a Compliment but you are so saucy, I wont blot it out.

Depend upon it, We know better than to repeal our Masculine systems. Altho they are in full Force, you know they are little more than Theory. We dare not exert our Power in its full Latitude. We are obliged to go fair, and softly, and in Practice you know We are the subjects. We have only the Name of Masters, and rather than give up this, which would compleatly subject Us to the Despotism of the Peticoat, I hope General Washington, and all our brave Heroes would fight. . . . After stirring up Tories, Landjobbers, Trimmers, Bigots, Canadians, Indians, Negroes, Hanoverians, Hessians, Russians, Irish Roman Catholicks, Scotch Renegadoes, at last they have stimulated the [women] to demand new Priviledges and threaten to rebell.

[Abigail to John, May 7, 1776:] I can not say that I think you very generous to the Ladies, for whilst you are proclaiming peace and good will to Men, Emancipating all Nations, you insist upon retaining an absolute power over Wives. But you must remember that Arbitrary power is like most other things which are very hard, very liable to be broken—and notwithstanding all your wise Laws and Maxims we have it in our power not only to free our selves but to subdue our Masters, and without violence throw both your natural and legal authority at our feet—

> "Charm by accepting, by submitting sway
> Yet have our Humour most when we obey."

Source:
[electronic edition]. *Adams Family Papers: An Electronic Archive.* Boston, Mass.: Massachusetts Historical Society, 2002. http.www.masshist.org/digital_adams/

Declaration of Independence, 1776

Whatever Thomas Jefferson and the Continental Congress meant by the specific words in the Declaration of Independence, this document has inspired men and women of all colors, national origins, and economic conditions to believe that they "are created equal and endowed . . . with [the] unalienable rights of life, liberty, and the pursuit of happiness." It pre-

sents the vision of America that still beckons people from all over the world and has influenced incipient democracies abroad.

The document penned by Thomas Jefferson and made public on July 4, 1776, responded to resolutions proposed on June 7, 1776, by Virginia delegate Richard Henry Lee. Jefferson was a member of the committee appointed to draft the declaration. The other members were Benjamin Franklin, John Adams, Robert R. Livingston, and Roger Sherman. Final adoption of Lee's resolutions by the Congress took place on July 2 by a vote of 12 to 0, with New York abstaining.

The declaration opened with the theoretical explanation for America's separation from Great Britain, justifying the split with an appeal to the doctrine of natural rights. Arguing that governments derive "their just powers from the consent of the governed," Jefferson went on to assert the right to revolt against an unjust government. The abuses of King George III against the colonists were then listed in order to legitimize the renunciation of all ties with Great Britain.

Though edited by members of the Second Continental Congress (notably Benjamin Franklin and John Adams), Jefferson's ideas remained basically intact. Revisions were completed on July 4 and sent immediately to a printer in Philadelphia, who published it under that date. The official signing of the document by all the delegates to the Congress took place on August 2, 1776; most of the 56 names on the document were signed before August 6, but at least six signatures were attached later.

Declaration of Independence

When in the course of human events it becomes necessary for one people to dissolve the political bonds which have connected them with another, and to assume among the powers of earth the separate and equal station to which the laws of nature and of nature's god entitle them, a decent respect to the opinions of mankind requires that they should declare the causes which impel them to the separation.

We hold these truths to be self-evident; that all men are created equal; that they are endowed by their Creator with inherent and inalienable rights; that among these are life, liberty, and the pursuit of happiness; that to secure these rights, governments are instituted among men, deriving their just powers from the consent of the governed; that whenever any form of government becomes destructive of these ends, it is the right of the people to alter or to abolish it, and to institute new government, laying its foundation on such principles, and organizing its powers in such form as to them shall seem most likely to effect their safety and happiness. Prudence indeed will dictate that governments long established should not be changed for light and transient causes. And accordingly all experience hath shown that mankind are more disposed to suffer, while evils are sufferable, than to right themselves by abolishing the forms to which they are accustomed. But when a long train of abuses and usurpations, begun at a distinguished period and pursuing invariably the same object, evinces a design to reduce them under absolute despotism, it is their right, it is their duty, to throw off such government, and to provide new guards for their future security. Such has been the patient sufferance of these colonies, and such is now the necessity which constrains them to expunge their former systems of government. The history of the present king of Great Britain is a history of unremitting injuries and usurpations, among which appears no solitary fact to contradict the uniform tenor of the rest, but all have in direct object the establishment of an absolute tyranny over these states. To prove this let facts be submitted to a candid world, for the truth of which we pledge a faith yet unsullied by falsehood.

He has refused his assent to laws the most wholesome and necessary for the public good.

He has forbidden his governors to pass laws of immediate and pressing importance, unless suspended in their operation till his assent should be obtained; and when so suspended, he has neglected utterly to attend to them.

He has refused to pass other laws for the accommodation of large districts of people, unless those people would relinquish the right of representation in the legislature; a right in-estimable to them, and formidable to tyrants only.

He has called together legislative bodies at places unusual, uncomfortable, and distant from the depository of their public records, for the sole purpose of fatiguing them into compliance with his measures.

He has dissolved Representative houses repeatedly and continually, for opposing with manly firmness his invasions on the rights of the people.

He has refused for a long time after such dissolutions to cause others to be elected whereby the legislative powers, incapable of annihilation, have returned to the people at large for their exercise, the state remaining in the meantime exposed to all the dangers of invasion from without, and convulsions within.

He has endeavored to prevent the population of these states; for that purpose obstructing the laws for naturalization of foreigners; refusing to pass others to encourage their migrations hither; and raising the conditions of new appropriations of lands.

He has suffered the administration of justice totally to cease in some of these states, refusing his assent to laws for establishing judiciary powers.

He has made our judges dependent on his will alone, for the tenure of their offices, and the amount and payment of their salaries.

He has erected a multitude of new offices by a self-assumed power, and sent hither swarms of officers to harass our people, and eat out their substance.

He has kept among us, in times of peace, standing armies and ships of war, without the consent of our legislatures.

He has affected to render the military independent of, and superior to, the civil power.

He has combined with others to subject us to a jurisdiction foreign to our constitutions and unacknowledged by our laws; giving his assent to their acts of pretended legislation for quartering large bodies of armed troops among us;

For protecting them by a mock-trial from punishment for any murders which they should commit on the inhabitants of these states;

For cutting off our trade with all parts of the world;

For imposing taxes on us without our consent;

For depriving us of the benefits of trial by jury;

For transporting us beyond seas to be tried for pretended offenses;

For abolishing the free system of English laws in a neighboring province, establishing therein in arbitrary government, and enlarging its boundaries so as to render it at once an example and fit instrument for introducing the same absolute rule into these states;

For taking away our charters, abolishing our most valuable laws, and altering fundamentally the forms of our governments;

For suspending our own legislatures, and declaring themselves to be invested with power to legislate for us in all cases whatsoever.

He has abdicated government here, withdrawing his governors, and declaring us out of his allegiance and protection.

He has plundered our seas, ravaged our coasts, burnt our towns, and destroyed the lives of our people.

He is at this time transporting large armies of foreign mercenaries, to complete the works of death, desolation, and tyranny, already begun with circumstances of cruelty and perfidy unworthy the head of a civilized nation.

He has endeavored to bring on the inhabitants of our frontiers the merciless Indian savages, whose known rule of warfare is an undistinguished destruction of all ages, sexes, and conditions of existence.

He has incited treasonable insurrections of our fellow citizens, with the allurements of forfeiture and confiscation of property.

He has constrained others, taken captives on the high seas, to bear arms against their country, to become the executioners of their friends and brethren, or to fall themselves by their hands.

He has waged cruel war against human nature itself, violating its most sacred rights of life and liberty in the persons of a distant people, who never offended him, captivating and carrying them into slavery in another hemisphere, or to incur miserable death in their transportation thither. This piratical warfare, the opprobrium of *infidel* powers, is the warfare of the *Christian* king of Great Britain. Determined to keep open a market where MEN should be bought and sold, he has prostituted his negative for suppressing every legislative attempt to prohibit or restrain this execrable commerce; and that this assemblage of horrors might want no fact of distinguished die, he is now exciting those very people to rise in arms among us, and to purchase that liberty of which *he* has deprived them, by murdering the people upon whom *he* also obtruded them: thus paying off former crimes committed against the liberties of one people, with crimes which he urges them to commit against the *lives* of another.

In every stage of these oppressions we have petitioned for redness in the most humble terms; our repeated petitions have been answered only by repeated injury. A prince whose character is thus marked by every act which may define a tyrant, is unfit to be the ruler of a people who mean to be free. Future ages will scarce believe that the hardiness of one man adventured, within the short compass of twelve years only, to lay a foundation, so broad and undisguised, for tyranny over a people fostered and fixed in principles of freedom.

Nor have we been wanting in attentions to our British brethren. We have warned them from time to time of attempts by their legislature to extend a jurisdiction over these our states. We have reminded them of the circumstances of our emigration and settlement here, no one of which could warrant so strange a pretension: that these were affected at the expence of our own blood and treasure, unassisted by the wealth or the strength of Great Britain: that in constituting indeed our several forms of government, we had adopted one common king, thereby laying a foundation for perpetual league and amity with them: but that submission to their parliament was no part of our constitution, nor ever in idea, if history may be credited: and we appealed to their native justice and magnanimity, as well as to the ties of our common kindred, to disavow these usurpations, which were likely to interrupt our condition and correspondence. They too have been deaf to the voice of justice and of consanguinity; and when occasions have been given them, by the regular course of their laws, of removing from their councils the disturbers of our harmony, they have by their free election re-established them in power. At this very time, too, they are permitting their chief magistrate to send over not only soldiers of our common blood, but Scotch and foreign mercenaries

to invade and destroy us. These facts have given the last stab to agonizing affection; and manly spirit bids us to renounce forever these unfeeling brethren. We must therefore endeavor to forget our former love for them, and to hold them as we hold the rest of mankind, enemies in war, in peace friends. We might have been a great and free people together; but a communication of grandeur and of freedom, it seems, is below their dignity. Be it so, since they will have it. The road to happiness and to glory is open to us too; we will climb it apart from them, and acquiesce in the necessity which denounces our eternal separation!

We therefore the Representatives of the United States of America in General Congress assembled, do, in the name and by the authority of the good people of these states, reject and renounce all allegiance and subjection to the kings of Great Britain, and all others who may hereafter claim by, through, or under them; we utterly dissolve all political connection which may heretofore have subsisted between us and the people or parliament of Great Britain; and finally we do assert and declare these colonies to be free and independent states, and that as free and independent states, they have full power to levy war, conclude peace, contract alliances, establish commerce, and to do all other acts and things which independent states may of right do. And for the support of this declaration, we mutually pledge to each other our lives, our fortunes, and our sacred honor.

See also THOMAS PAINE, *COMMON SENSE*, 1776; MASSACHUSETTS BILL OF RIGHTS, 1780.

Source:
John Scott, ed. *Living Documents in American History*. New York: Washington Square Press, 1964–68.

First Treaty of Paris, 1778

French foreign minister Charles Gravier, count de Vergennes, and American commissioners Silas Deane and Benjamin Franklin signed two Franco-American treaties, February 6, 1778, in Paris. The first established a formal alliance, directed toward continuing the war against the common enemy (Britain) until American independence was "formally or tacitly assured" and vowing not to make separate peace. France granted America the rights to Bermuda and all British colonies on the mainland, reserving for itself the rights to Britain's territories in the West Indies. By the second, a treaty of amity and commerce, both countries received most-favored-nation status in each other's ports (that is they had the same rights as "the most favored nation"). Capping several years of French aid to America, the treaties ensured its continuation during the

American Revolution (1775–83), when France provided both manpower and financial resources. The treaties were ratified by the American Congress on May 4, 1778. The Franco-American alliance of 1778 ended formally with a new Franco-American treaty, known as the Treaty of Mortefontaine, signed September 30, 1800. That treaty also ended an undeclared naval war over French raids on U.S. shipping, which began in 1798 following publication of the XYZ report.

Between the United States of America and His Most Christian Majesty.

Treaty of Alliance

The Most Christian King and the United States of North America; to wit: New-Hampshire, Massachusetts-bay, Rhode-Island, Connecticut, New-York, New-Jersey, Pennsylvania, Delaware, Maryland, Virginia, North-Carolina, South-Carolina, and Georgia, having this day concluded a treaty of Amity and Commerce, for the reciprocal advantage of their subjects and citizens, have thought it necessary to take into consideration the means of strengthening those engagements, and of rendring them useful to the safety and tranquility of the two parties; particularly in case Great Britain, in resentment of that connection and of the good correspondence which is the object of the said treaty, should break the peace with France, either by direct hostilities, or by hindring her commerce and navigation in a manner contrary to the rights of nations, and the peace subsisting between the two crowns: And his Majesty and the said United States, having resolved in that case to join their councels and efforts against the enterprises of their common enemy, the respective plenipotentiaries empowered to concert the clauses and conditions proper to fulfil the said intentions, have, after the most mature deliberation, concluded and determined on the following articles:

Art. I

If war should break out between France and Great Britain during the continuance of the present war between the United States and England, his Majesty and the said United States shall make it a common cause and aid each other mutually with their good offices, their counsels and their forces, according to the exigence of conjunctures, as becomes good and faithful allies.

Art. II

The essential and direct end of the present defensive alliance is to maintain effectually the liberty, sovereignty and independence absolute and unlimited, of the said United States, as well in matters of gouvernement as of commerce.

Art. III

The two contracting parties shall each on its own part, and in the manner it may judge most proper, make all the efforts in its power against their common enemy, in order to attain the end proposed.

Art. IV

The contracting parties agree that in case either of them should form any particular enterprise in which the concurrence of the other may be desired, the party whose concurrence is desired, shall readily and with good faith, join to act in concert for that purpose, as far as circumstances and its own particular situation will permit; and in that case, they shall regulate, by a particular convention, the quantity and kind of succour to be furnished, and the time and manner of its being brought into action, as well as the advantages which are to be its compensation.

Art. V

If the United States should think fit to attempt the reduction of the British power, remaining in the northern parts of America, or the islands of Bermudas, those countries or islands in case of success, shall be confederated with, or dependent upon the said United States.

Art. VI

The Most Christian King renounces for ever the possession of the islands of Bermudas, as well as of any part of the continent of North America, which before the treaty of Paris in 1763, or in virtue of that treaty, were acknowledged to belong to the crown of Great Britain, or to the United States, heretofore called British colonies, or which are at this time, or have lately been under the power of the king and crown of Great Britain.

Art. VII

If his Most Christian Majesty shall think proper to attack any of the islands situated in the Gulph of Mexico, or near that Gulph, which are at present under the power of Great Britain, all the said isles, in case of success, shall appertain to the crown of France.

Art. VIII

Neither of the two parties shall conclude either truce or peace, with Great Britain, without the formal consent of the other first obtained; and they mutually engage not to lay down their arms until the independence of the United States shall have been formally or tacitly assured, by the treaty or treaties that shall terminate the war.

Art. IX

The contracting parties declare, that being resolved to fulfil each on its own part, the clauses and conditions of the present treaty of alliance, according to its own power and circumstances, there shall be no after claim of compensation on one side or the other, whatever may be the event of the war.

Art. X

The Most Christian King and the United States agree, to invite or admit other powers who may have received injuries from England, to make common cause with them, and to accede to the present alliance, under such conditions as shall be freely agreed to, and settled between all the parties.

Art. XI

The two parties guarantee mutually from the present time, and forever against all other powers, to wit: The United States to his Most Christian Majesty, the present possessions of the crown of France in America, as well as those which it may acquire by the future treaty of peace: And his Most Christian Majesty guarantees on his part to the United States, their liberty, sovereignty and independence, absolute and unlimited, as well in matters of government as commerce, and also their possessions, and the additions or conquests, that their confederation may obtain during the war, from any of the dominions now, or heretofore possessed by Great Britain in North America, conformable to the 5th and 6th articles above written, the whole as their possessions shall be fixed and assured to the said states, at the moment of the cessation of their present war with England.

Art. XII

In order to fix more precisely the sense and application of the preceding article, the contracting parties declare, that in case of a rupture between France and England, the reciprocal guarantee declared in the said article, shall have its full force and effect the moment such war shall break out; and if such rupture shall not take place, the mutual obligations of the said guarantee shall not commence until the moment of the cessation of the present war, between the United States and England, shall have ascertained their possessions.

Art. XIII

The present treaty shall be ratified on both sides, and the ratifications shall be exchanged in the space of six months, or sooner if possible.

In faith whereof the respective plenipotentiaries, to wit: On the part of the Most Christian king, Conrad Alexander Gerard, Royal Syndic of the city of Strasbourgh, and Secretary of his Majesty's Council of State; and on the part of the United States, Benjamin Franklin, Deputy to the General Congress from the state of Pennsylvania and

President of the Convention of the same state; Silas Deane, heretofore Deputy from the state of Connecticut, and Arthur Lee, Councellor at Law, have signed the above articles both in the French and English languages, declaring nevertheless, that the present treaty was originally composed and concluded in the French language, and they have hereunto affixed their seals.

Done at Paris, this sixth day of February, one thousand seven hundred and seventy-eight.

See also TREATY OF PARIS OF 1783.

Source:
Charles I. Bevans, comp. *Treaties and Other Agreements of the United States of America, 1776–1949.* Washington, D.C.: Government Printing Office, 1968–76.

Second Continental Congress, Address of the Continental Congress to the American People, 1778

In this address of May 9, 1778, Congress hoped to renew the American dedication to the war effort by citing past and present British abuses and promising a life of freedom and prosperity after American independence was achieved. It responded to peace concessions offered by England, which feared the consequences of the recent American alliance with France. The British offered to repeal the Tea Act (1773) and the Coercive Acts (1774) and vowed not to impose any new taxes if the Americans renounced independence. British "peace commissioners" were dispatched to persuade key citizens and members of Congress to lobby for a reunion with Great Britain. Direct appeals in the form of printed broadsides were issued by both British and American forces.

This address from the Continental Congress was directed to be read in churches all over America. Given the inflammatory language of the address, Congress must have feared that many Americans, tired of the violence of war, still harbored loyalist feelings toward England and could be easily persuaded to return to the security of the British Empire. In any case, the British peace offers were rejected, and the defeated commissioners returned to England.

Friends and Countrymen, three years have now passed away since the commencement of the present war, a war without parallel in the annals of mankind. It hath displayed a spectacle the most solemn that can possibly be exhibited. On one side, we behold fraud and violence labouring in the service of despotism, on the other, virtue and fortitude supporting and establishing the rights of human nature.

You cannot but remember how reluctantly we were dragged into this arduous contest, and how repeatedly, with the earnestness of humble entreaty, we supplicated a redress of our grievances from him who ought to have been the father of his people. In vain did we implore his protection, in vain appeal to the justice, the generosity, of Englishmen—of men who had been the guardians, the asserters and vindicators of liberty, through a succession of ages; men who, with their swords, had established a firm barrier of freedom, and cemented it with the blood of heroes. Every effort was vain; for, even whilst we were prostrated at the foot of the throne that fatal blow was struck which hath separated us for ever. Thus spurned, contemned, insulted, thus driven by our enemies into measures which our souls abhorred, we made a solemn appeal to the tribunal of unerring wisdom and justice, to that Almighty Ruler of Princes, whose kingdom is over all.

We were then quite defenceless—without arms, without ammunition, without clothing, without ships, without money, without officers skilled in war, with no other reliance but the bravery of our people, and the justice of our cause. We had to contend with a nation great in arts and in arms, whose fleets covered the ocean, whose banners had waved in triumph through every quarter of the globe. However unequal this contest, our weakness was still farther increased by the enemies which America had nourished in her bosom. Thus exposed on the one hand, to external force and internal divisions, on the other, to be compelled to drink of the bitter cup of slavery, and to go sorrowing all our lives long in this sad alternative, we chose the former. To this alternative we were reduced by men who, had they been animated by one spark of generosity, would have disdained to take such mean advantage of our situation, or, had they paid the least regard to the rules of justice, would have considered with abhorrence a proposition to injure those who had faithfully fought their battles, and industriously contributed to rear the edifice of their glory.

But however great the injustice of our foes in commening this war, it is by no means equal to the cruelty with which they have conducted it. The course of their armies is marked by rapine and devastation. Thousands, without distinction of age or sex, have been driven from their peaceful abodes, to encounter the rigours of inclement seasons; and the face of heaven hath been insulted by the wanton conflagration of defenceless towns. Their victories have been followed by the cool murder of men, no longer able to resist; and those who escaped from the first act of carnage have been exposed, by cold, hunger, and nakedness, to wear out a miserable existence in the tedious hours of confinement, or to become the destroyers of their countrymen, of their friends, perhaps, dreadful idea! of their parents or children. Nor was this the outrageous barbarity of an individual, but a system of deliberate malice, stamped with the concurrence of the British legislature, and sanctioned with all the formalities of law. Nay, determined to dissolve the closest bonds of society, they have stimulated servants to slay their masters in the peaceful hour of domestick security. And, as if all this were insufficient to stake their thirst of blood, the blood of brothers of unoffending brothers, they have excited the indians against us; and a General, who calls himself a Christian, a follower of the merciful Jesus, hath dared to proclaim to all the world his intention of letting loose against us whole hosts of savages, whose rule of warfare is promiscuous carnage, who rejoice to murder the infant smiling in its mother's arms, to inflict on their prisoners the most excruciating torments, and exhibit scenes of horrour from which nature recoils.

Were it possible, they would have added to this terrible system, for they have offered the inhabitants of these states to be exported by their merchants to the sickly, baneful climes of India, there to perish. An offer not accepted of, merely from the impracticability of carrying it into execution.

Notwithstanding these great provocations, we have treated such of them as fell into our hands with tenderness, and studiously endeavoured to alleviate the afflictions of their captivity. This conduct we have pursued so far as to be by them stigmatised with cowardice, and by our friends with folly. But our dependence was not upon man, it was upon him who hath commanded us to love our enemies, and to render good for evil. And what can be more wonderful than the manner of our deliverances? How often have we been reduced to distress, and yet been raised up? When the means to prosecute the war have been wanting to us, have not our foes themselves been rendered instrumental in producing them? This hath been done in such a variety of instances, so peculiarly marked almost by the direct interposition of Providence, that not to feel and acknowledge his protection would be the height of impious ingratitude.

At length that God of Battles, in whom was our trust, hath conducted us through the paths of danger and distress to the thresholds of security. It hath now become morally certain that, if we have courage to persevere, we shall establish our liberties and independence. The haughty Prince who spurned us from his feet with contumely and disdain, and the parliament which proscribed us, how descend to offer terms of accommodation. Whilst in the full career of victory, they pulled off the mask, and avowed their intended despotism; but, having lavished in vain the blood and treasure of their subjects in pursuit of this execrable purpose, they now endeavour to ensnare us with the insidious offers of peace. They would seduce you into a dependence, which necessarily, inevitably leads to the most humiliating slavery. And, do they believe that you will accept these fatal terms? Because you have suffered the distresses of war, do they suppose that you will basely lick the dust before the feet of your destroyer? Can there be an American so lost to the feelings which adorn human nature? To the generous price, the elevation, the dignity of freedom! Is there a man who would not abhor a dependence upon those who have deluged his country in the blood of its inhabitants? We cannot suppose this, neither is it possible that they themselves can expect to make many converts. What then is their intention? Is is not to lull you with the fallacious hopes of peace, until they can assemble new armies to prosecute their nesarious designs? If this is not the case, why do they strain every nerve to levy men throughout their islands? Why do they meanly court each little tyrant of Europe to sell them his unhappy slaves? Why do they continue to imbitter the minds of the savages against you? Surely this is not the way to conciliate the affections of America. Be not therefore deceived. You have still to expect one severe conflict. Your foreign alliances, though they secure your independence, cannot secure your country from desolation, your habitations from plunder, your wives from insult or violation, nor your children from butchery. Foiled in their principal design, you must expect to feel the rage of disappointed ambition. Arise then! to your tents! and gird you for the battle. It is time to turn the headlong current of vengeance upon the head of the destroyer. They have filled up the measure of their abominations; and, like ripe fruit, must soon drop from the tree. Although much is done, yet much remains to do. Expect not peace whilst any corner of America is in possession of your foes. You must drive them away from this land of promise, a land flowing indeed with milk and honey. Your brethren at the extremities of the continent already implore your friendship and protection. It is your duty to grant their request. They hunger and thirst after liberty. Be it yours to dispense to them the heavenly gift. And what is there now to prevent it?

After the unremitted efforts of our enemies, we are stronger than before; nor can the wicked emissaries who so assiduously labour to promote their cause point out any one reason to suppose that we shall not receive daily accessions of strength. They tell you, it is true, that your money is of no value, and your debts so enormous they can never be paid. But we tell you, that if Britain prosecutes the war another campaign, that single campaign will cost her more than we have hitherto expended. And yet these men would prevail upon you to take up that immense load, and for it to sacrifice your dearest rights; for, surely, there is no man so absurd as to suppose, that the least shadow of liberty can be preserved in a dependent connexion with Great Britain. From the nature of the thing, it is evident that the only security you could obtain would be the justice and moder-

ation of a Parliament who have sold the rights of their own constituents; and this slender security is still farther weakened, by the consideration that it was pledged to rebels (as they unjustly call the good people of their State) with whom they think they are not bound to keep faith by any law whatsoever. Thus would you be cast bound among men, whose minds (by your virtuous resistance) have been sharpened to the keenest edge of revenge. Thus would your children, and your childrens children, be by you forced to a participation in all their debts, their wars, their luxuries, and their crimes. And this mad, this impious system, they would lead you to adopt, because of the derangement of your finances.

It becomes you deeply to reflect on this subject. Is there a country on earth which hath such resources for the payment of her debts as America? Such an extensive territory? So fertile, so blessed in its climate and productions? Surely there is none. Neither is there any to which the wife Europeans will sooner confide their property. What then are the reasons that your money hath depreciated? Because no taxes have been imposed to carry on the war. Because your commerce hath been interrupted by your enemies fleets. Because their armies have ravages and desolated a part of your country. Because their agents have villainously conterfeited your bills. Because extortioners among you, inflamed with the lust of gain, have added to the price of every article of life. And because weak men have been artfully led to believe that it is of no value. How is this dangerous disease to be remedied? Let those among you, who have leisure and opportunity, collect the monies which individuals in their neighbourhood are desirous of placing in the publick funds. Let the several legislatures sink their respective emissions, that so, there being but one kind of bills, there may be less danger of counterfeits. Refrain a little while from purchasing those things which are not absolutely necessary, that so those who have engrossed commodities may suffer (as they deservedly will) the loss of their ill-gotten hoards, by reason of the commerce with foreign nations, which their fleets will protect. Above all, bring forward your armies into the field. Trust not to appearance of peace or safety. Be assured, that, unless you persevere, you will be exposed to every species of barbarity. But if you exert the means of defence which God and nature have given you, the time will soon arrive when every man shall sit under his own vine, and under his own fig tree, and there shall be none to make him afraid.

The sweets of a free commerce with every part of the earth will soon reimburse you for all the losses you have sustained, The full tide of wealth will flow in upon your shores, free from the arbitrary impositions of those whose interest, and whose declared policy, it was to check your growth. Your interests will be fostered and nourished by governments that derive their power from your grant, and will therefore be obliged, by the influence of cogent necessity, to exert it in your favour.

It is to obtain these things that we call for your strenuous, unremitted exertions. Yet do not believe that you have been, or can be saved, merely by your own strength. No! it is by the assistance of Heaven, and this you must assiduously cultivate, by acts which Heaven approves. Thus shall the power and the happiness of these sovereign, free, and independent states, founded on the virtue of their citizens, increase, extend, and endure, until the Almighty shall blot out all the empires of the earth.

Source:
Library of Congress, Rare Book and Special Collections Division, Continental Congress Broadside Collection.

Letters from an American Farmer, Letter II, 1782

Book written by Michel-Guillaume Saint-Jean de Crèvecoeur using the pen name J. Hector St. John de Crevecoeur. This French-American writer had settled in New York following his service in the French and Indian War (1756–63). *Letters from An American Farmer* is a series of essays that he wrote describing American life and the coming revolution. The purpose, as explained in Letter I, is to "[remark] throughout these provinces the causes which render so many people happy[by] delineating the unnoticed means by which we daily increase the extent of our settlements [and to show h]ow we convert huge forests into pleasing fields, and exhibit through these thirteen provinces so singular a display of easy subsistence and political felicity."

First published in 1782, the book is considered a classic of its type because of its outstanding descriptions of American rural life during this period. Letter II describes what it means to be an American and includes descriptions of inhabitants, including individuals of many different nationalities, as well as the local Indians, but leaving out blacks. In Letter I, however, Crevecoeur writes, "My negroes are tolerably faithful and healthy."

Letter II
On the Situations, Feelings, and Pleasures of an American Farmer

As you are the first enlightened European I have ever had the pleasure of being acquainted with, you will not be surprised that I should, according to your earnest desire and my promise, appear anxious of preserving your friendship and correspondence. By your accounts, I observe a material difference subsists between your husbandry, modes, and customs, and ours; everything is local; could we enjoy the advantages of the English farmer, we should be much happier, indeed, but this wish, like many others, implies a contradiction; and could the English farmer have some of those privileges we possess, they would be the first of their class in the world. Good and evil I see is to be found in all societies, and it is in vain to seek for any spot where those ingredients are not mixed. I therefore rest satisfied, and thank God that my lot is to be an American farmer, instead of a Russian boor, or an Hungarian peasant. I thank you kindly for the idea, however dreadful, which you have given me of their lot and condition; your observations have confirmed me in the justness of my ideas, and I am happier now than I thought myself before. It is strange that misery, when viewed in others, should become to us a sort of real good, though I am far from rejoicing to hear that there are in the world men so thoroughly wretched; they are no doubt as harmless, industrious, and willing to work as we are. Hard is their fate to be thus condemned to a slavery worse than that of our negroes. Yet when young I entertained some thoughts of selling my farm. I thought it afforded but a dull repetition of the same labours and pleasures. I thought the former tedious and heavy, the latter few and insipid; but when I came to consider myself as divested of my farm, I then found the world so wide, and every place so full, that I began to fear lest there would be no room for me. My farm, my house, my barn, presented to my imagination objects from which I adduced quite new ideas; they were more forcible than before. Why should not I find myself happy, said I, where my father was before? He left me no good books it is true, he gave me no other education than the art of reading and writing; but he left me a good farm, and his experience; he left me free from debts, and no kind of difficulties to struggle with.—I married, and this perfectly reconciled me to my situation; my wife rendered my house all at once cheerful and pleasing; it no longer appeared gloomy and solitary as before; when I went to work in my fields I worked with more alacrity and sprightliness; I felt that I did not work for myself alone, and this encouraged me much. My wife would often come with her knitting in her hand, and sit under the shady trees, praising the straightness of my furrows, and, the docility of my horses; this swelled my heart and made everything light and pleasant, and I regretted that I had not married before.

I felt myself happy in my new situation, and where is that station which can confer a more substantial system of felicity than that of an American farmer, possessing freedom of action, freedom of thoughts, ruled by a mode of government which requires but little from us? I owe nothing, but a pepper corn to my country, a small tribute to my king, with loyalty and due respect; I know no other landlord than the lord of all land, to whom I owe the most sincere gratitude. My father left me three hundred and seventy-one acres of land, forty-seven of which are good timothy meadow, an excellent orchard, a good house, and a substantial barn. It is my duty to think how happy I am that he lived to build and to pay for all these improvements; what are the labours which I have to undergo, what are my fatigues when compared to his, who had everything to do, from the first tree he felled to the finishing of his house? Every year I kill from 1500 to 2000 weight of pork, 1200 of beef, half a dozen of good wethers in harvest: of fowls my wife has always a great stock: what can I wish more? My negroes are tolerably faithful and healthy; by a long series of industry and honest dealings, my father left behind him the name of a good man; I have but to tread his paths to be happy and a good man like him. I know enough of the law to regulate my little concerns with propriety, nor do I dread its power; these are the grand outlines of my situation, but as I can feel much more than I am able to express, I hardly know how to proceed.

When my first son was born, the whole train of my ideas were suddenly altered; never was there a charm that acted so quickly and powerfully; I ceased to ramble in imagination through the wide world; my excursions since have not exceeded the bounds of my farm, and all my principal pleasures are now centred within its scanty limits: but at the same time there is not an operation belonging to it in which I do not find some food for useful reflections. This is the reason, I suppose, that when you were here, you used, in your refined style, to denominate me the farmer of feelings; how rude must those feelings be in him who daily holds the axe or the plough, how much more refined on the contrary those of the European, whose mind is improved by education, example, books, and by every acquired advantage! Those feelings, however, I will delineate as well as I can, agreeably to your earnest request. . . .

Source:
Crevecoeur, J. Hector St. John. *Letters from an American Farmer.* New York: E.P. Dutton & Co. Inc., 1926.

Treaty of Paris of 1783 (Treaty of Versailles of 1783)

Peace agreement concluded at Versailles, near Paris, France, on September 3, 1783, between Great Britain and the United States (the former 13 colonies), officially ending the American Revolution (1775–83). Britain also signed separate treaties with France and Spain. Britain recognized American independence and agreed to withdraw its troops. The boundaries of the United States were established: the Mississippi River as the western boundary (navigation on the river was open), Canada

as the northern, and Florida as the southern (Spain reacquired Florida and the island of Majorca in its treaty with Britain, which retained Gibraltar). The United States and Britain agreed that creditors of either side could collect just debts. The former promised also to press several states to return property confiscated from American Tories (supporters of Britain) during the Revolution. The Americans were given fishing rights off Newfoundland too. In separate treaties with Spain and France, Britain exchanged territory and guaranteed fishing and other rights. A formal declaration ending hostilities between Great Britain and the new United States of America was still necessary to end various military actions and return confiscated properties after the war. Cessation of Hostilities (1783) bound all parties to abide by the agreements forged in France.

Definitive Treaty of Peace
Between the United States of America and his Britannic Majesty
In the name of the Most Holy and Undivided Trinity.

It having pleased the Divine Providence to dispose the hearts of the most serene and most potent Prince George the Third, by the Grace of God King of Great-Britain, France and Ireland, Defender of the Faith, Duke of Brunswick and Lunebourg, Arch-Treasurer and Prince Elector of the Holy Roman Empire, &c. and of the United States of America, to forget all past misunderstandings and differences that have unhappily interrupted the good correspondence and friendship which they mutually wish to restore; and to establish such a beneficial and satisfactory intercourse between the two countries, upon the ground of reciprocal advantages and mutual convenience, as may promote and secure to both perpetual peace and harmony: And having for this desirable end, already laid the foundation of peace and reconciliation, by the provisional articles, signed at Paris, on the thirtieth of November, one thousand seven hundred and eighty-two, by the commissioners empowered on each part, which articles were agreed to be inserted in, and to constitute the treaty of peace proposed to be concluded between the crown of Great-Britain and the said United States, but which treaty was not to be concluded until terms of peace should be agreed upon between Great-Britain and France, and his Britannic Majesty should be ready to conclude such treaty accordingly; and the treaty between Great-Britain and France, having since been concluded, his Britannic Majesty and the United States of America, in order to carry into full effect the provisional articles abovementioned, according to the tenor thereof, have constituted and appointed, that is to say, His Britannic Majesty on his part, David Hartley, Esquire, Member of the Parliament of Great-Britain; and the said United States on their part, John Adams, Esquire, late a Commissioner of the United States of America at the

Court of Versailles, late Delegate in Congress from the state of Massachusetts, and Chief Justice of the said state, and Minister Plenipotentiary of the said United States to their High Mightinesses the States General of the United Netherlands; Benjamin Franklin, Esquire, late Delegate in Congress from the state of Pennsylvania, President of the Convention of the said state, and Minister Plenipotentiary from the United States of America at the Court of Versailles; John Jay, Esquire, late President of Congress, and Chief Justice of the state of New-York, and Minister Plenipotentiary from the said United States at the Court of Madrid, to be the Plenipotentiaries for the concluding and signing the present definitive treaty; who after having reciprocally communicated their respective full powers, have agreed upon and confirmed the following articles.

Article I

His Britannic Majesty acknowledges the said United States, viz. New-Hampshire, Massachusetts-Bay, Rhode-Island and Providence Plantations, Connecticut, New-York, New-Jersey, Pennsylvania, Delaware, Maryland, Virginia, North-Carolina, South-Carolina, and Georgia, to be free, sovereign and independent States; that he treats with them as such; and for himself, his heirs and successors, relinquishes all claims to the government, propriety and territorial rights of the same, and every part thereof.

Article II

And that all disputes which might arise in future, on the subject of the boundaries of the said United States, may be prevented, it is hereby agreed and declared, that the following are, and shall be their boundaries, viz. From the north-west angle of Nova-Scotia, viz. that angle which is formed by a line, drawn due north from the source of St. Croix river to the Highlands; along the said Highlands which divide those rivers, that empty themselves into the river St. Lawrence, from those which fall into the Atlantic ocean, to the northwesternmost head of Connecticut river, thence down along the middle of that river, to the forty-fifth degree of north latitude; from thence, by a line due west on said latitude, until it strikes the river Iroquois or Cataraquy; thence along the middle of said river into lake Ontario, through the middle of said lake until it strikes the communication by water between that lake and lake Erie; thence along the middle of said communication into lake Erie, through the middle of said lake until it arrives at the water-communication between that lake and lake Huron; thence along the middle of said water-communication into the lake Huron; thence through the middle of said lake to the water-communication between that lake and lake

Superior; thence through lake Superior northward of the isles Royal and Phelipeaux, to the Long Lake; thence through the middle of said Long Lake, and the water-communication between it and the Lake of the Woods, to the said Lake of the Woods; thence through the said lake to the most north-western point thereof, and from thence on a due west course to the river Mississippi; thence by a line to be drawn along the middle of the said river Mississippi until it shall intersect the northernmost part of the thirty-first degree of north latitude. South by a line to be drawn due east from the determination of the line last mentioned, in the latitude of thirty-one degrees north of the Equator, to the middle of the river Apalachicola or Catahouche; thence along the middle thereof to its junction with the Flint river; thence strait to the head of St. Mary's river; and thence down along the middle of St. Mary's river to the Atlantic ocean. East by a line to be drawn along the middle of the river St. Croix, from its mouth in the Bay of Fundy to its source, and from its source directly north to the aforesaid Highlands which divide the rivers that fall into the Atlantic ocean, from those which fall into the river St. Lawrence; comprehending all islands within twenty leagues of any part of the shores of the United States, and lying between lines to be drawn due east from the points where the aforesaid boundaries between Nova-Scotia on the one part, and East-Florida on the other, shall respectively touch the Bay of Fundy and the Atlantic ocean; excepting such islands as now are, or heretofore have been within the limits of the said province of Nova-Scotia.

Article III

It is agreed that the people of the United States shall continue to enjoy unmolested the right to take fish of every kind on the Grand Bank, and on all the other banks of Newfoundland; also in the gulph of St. Lawrence, and at all other places in the sea, where the inhabitants of both countries used at any time heretofore to fish; and also that the inhabitants of the United States shall have liberty to take fish of every kind on such part of the coast of Newfoundland as British fishermen shall use (but not to dry or cure the same on that island); and also on the coasts, bays and creeks of all other of his Britannic Majesty's dominions in America; and that the American fishermen shall have liberty to dry and cure fish in any of the unsettled bays, harbours and creeks of Nova-Scotia, Magdalen islands, and Labrador, so long as the same shall remain unsettled; but so soon as the same or either of them shall be settled, it shall not be lawful for the said fishermen to dry or cure fish at such settlement, without a previous agreement for that purpose with the inhabitants, proprietors or possessors of the ground.

Article IV

It is agreed that creditors on either side, shall meet with no lawful impediment to the recovery of the full value in sterling money, of all bona fide debts heretofore contracted.

Article V

It is agreed that the Congress shall earnestly recommend it to the legislatures of the respective states, to provide for the restitution of all estates, rights and properties, which have been confiscated, belonging to real British subjects, and also of the estates, rights and properties of persons resident in districts in the possession of his Majesty's arms, and who have not borne arms against the said United States. And that persons of any other description shall have free liberty to go to any part or parts of any of the thirteen United States, and therein to remain twelve months, unmolested in their endeavours to obtain the restitution of such of their estates, rights and properties, as may have been confiscated; and that Congress shall also earnestly recommend to the several states a reconsideration and revision of all acts or laws regarding the premises, so as to render the said laws or acts perfectly consistent, not only with justice and equity, but with that spirit of conciliation, which on the return of the blessings of peace should universally prevail. And that Congress shall also earnestly recommend to the several states, that the estates, rights and properties of such last mentioned persons, shall be restored to them, they refunding to any persons who may be now in possession, the bona fide price (where any has been given) which such persons may have paid on purchasing any of the said lands, rights or properties, since the confiscation. And it is agreed, that all persons who have any interest in confiscated lands, either by debts, marriage settlements, or otherwise, shall meet with no lawful impediment in the prosecution of their just rights.

Article VI

That there shall be no future confiscations made, nor any prosecutions commenced against any person or persons for, or by reason of the part which he or they may have taken in the present war; and that no person shall, on that account, suffer any future loss or damage, either in his person, liberty or property; and that those who may be in confinement on such charges, at the time of the ratification of the treaty in America, shall be immediately set at liberty, and the prosecutions so commenced be discontinued.

Article VII

There shall be a firm and perpetual peace between his Britannic Majesty and the said States, and between the subjects of the one and the citizens of the other, wherefore all hostilities, both by sea and land, shall from henceforth cease: all prisoners on both sides shall be set at liberty, and his Britannic Majesty shall, with all convenient speed, and without causing any destruction, or carrying away any negroes or other property of the American inhabitants, withdraw all his armies, garrisons and fleets from the said United States, and from every post, place and harbour within the same; leaving in all fortifications the American artillery that may be therein; and shall also order and cause all archives, records, deeds and papers, belonging to any of the said states, or their citizens, which in the course of the war may have fallen into the hands of his officers, to be forthwith restored and delivered to the proper states and persons to whom they belong.

Article VIII

The navigation of the river Mississippi, from its source to the ocean, shall for ever remain free and open to the subjects of Great-Britain, and the citizens of the United States.

Article IX

In case it should so happen that any place or territory belonging to Great-Britain or to the United States, should have been conquered by the arms of either from the other, before the arrival of the said provisional articles in America, it is agreed, that the same shall be restored without difficulty, and without requiring any compensation.

Article X

The solemn ratifications of the present treaty, expedited in good and due form, shall be exchanged between the contracting parties, in the space of six months, or sooner if possible, to be computed from the day of the signature of the present treaty. In witness whereof, we the undersigned, their Ministers Plenipotentiary, have in their name and in virtue of our full powers, signed with our hands the present definitive treaty, and caused the seals of our arms to be affixed thereto.

Done at Paris, this third day of September, in the year of our Lord one thousand seven hundred and eighty-three.

Source:

Charles I. Bevans. *Treaties and Other Agreements of the United States of America, 1776–1949*. Washington, D.C.: Government Printing Office, 1968–76.

Formation of the New Government

Articles of Confederation, 1776

Plan of union for the newly independent United States, framed by a committee appointed by the Second Continental Congress and presented on July 12, 1776. A draft, approved on November 15, 1777, was sent to the 13 states (former colonies) for ratification, which had to be unanimous. Although 12 states had signed by 1779, the articles did not become law until March 1, 1781, when Maryland finally ratified them. The government established a congress made up of two to seven delegates from each state, possessing one vote each. A committee of representatives from each state ran national matters between sessions. Congress would have the power to manage Native American and foreign affairs, establish a postal system, regulate coinage, borrow money, and settle disputes between states. All rights not specifically granted to the federal government were retained by the states. Each state was obliged to contribute to a common treasury in proportion to the value of surveyed lands and improvements and to supply its quota of troops, based on the number of white inhabitants. However, no enforcement mechanism for tax collection or filling military quotas was established. Moreover, except for admiralty questions, the articles did not contain a method to resolve interstate commercial or territorial disputes. The system came to be widely viewed as deficient, and in 1787 the Constitutional Convention was called to overhaul it; the result was an entirely new system of federal government.

The Articles of Confederation

To all to whom these presents shall come, we the undersigned delegates of the states affixed to our names send greeting. Whereas the delegates of the United States of America in Congress assembled did on the fifteenth day of November in the year of our Lord one thousand seven hundred and seventy-seven, and in the second year of the independence of America agree to certain Articles of Confederation and Perpetual Union between the states of New Hampshire, Massachusetts Bay, Rhode Island and Providence plantations, Connecticut, New York, New Jersey, Pennsylvania, Delaware, Maryland, Virginia, North Carolina, South Carolina and Georgia in the words following, viz.: Articles of Confederation and Perpetual Union between the states [as aforesaid].

Article I

The stile of this confederacy shall be "The United States of America."

Article II

Each state retains its sovereignty, freedom and independence, and every power, jurisdiction and right, which is not by this confederation expressly delegated to the United States, in Congress assembled.

Article III

The said states hereby severally enter into a firm league of friendship with each other, for their common defence, the security of their liberties, and their mutual and general welfare, binding themselves to assist each other, against all force offered to, or attacks made upon them, or any of them, on account of religion, sovereignty, trade, or any other pretence whatever.

Article IV

The better to secure and perpetuate mutual friendship and intercourse among the people of the different states in this Union, the free inhabitants of each of these states, paupers, vagabonds and fugitives from justice excepted, shall be entitled to all privileges and immunities of free citizens in the several states; and the people of each state shall have free ingress and regress to and from any other state, and shall enjoy therein all the privileges of trade and commerce, subject to the same duties, impositions and restrictions as the inhabitants thereof respectively, provided that such restrictions shall not extend so far as to prevent the removal of property imported into any state, to any other state of which the owner is an inhabitant; provided also that no imposition, duties or restriction shall be laid by any state, on the property of the United States, or either of them.

If any person guilty of, or charged with treason, felony, or other high misdemeanor in any state, shall flee from justice, and be found in any of the United States, he shall upon demand of the governor of executive power, of the state from which he fled, be delivered to the state having jurisdiction of his offence.

Full faith and credit shall be given in each of these states to the records, acts and judicial proceedings of the courts and magistrates of every other state.

Article V

For the more convenient management of the general interests of the United States, delegates shall be annually appointed in such manner as the legislature of each state shall direct, to meet in Congress on the first Monday in November, in every year, with a power reserved to each state, to recall its delegates, or any of them, at any time within the year, and to send others in their stead, for the remainder of the year. No state shall be represented in Congress by less than two, nor by more than seven members; and no person shall be capable of being a delegate for more than three years in any term of six years; nor shall any person, being a delegate, be capable of holding any office under the United States, for which he, or another for his benefit receives any salary, fees, or emolument of any kind.

Each state shall maintain its own delegates in a meeting of the states, and while they act as members of the committee of the states.

In determining questions in the United States, in Congress assembled, each state shall have one vote. Freedom of speech and debate in Congress shall not be impeached or questioned in any court, or place out of Congress, and the members of Congress shall be protected in their persons from arrests and imprisonments, during the time of their going to and from, and attendance on Congress, except for treason, felony, or breach of the peace.

Article VI

No state without the consent of the United States in Congress assembled, shall send any embassy to, or receive any embassy from, or enter into any conference, agreement, alliance or treaty with any king, prince or state; nor shall any person holding any office or profit or trust under the United States, or any of them, accept of any present, emolument, office or title of any kind whatever from any king, prince or foreign state; nor shall the United States in Congress assembled, or any of them, grant any title of nobility. No two or more states shall enter into any treaty, confederation or alliance whatever between them, without the consent of the United States in Congress assembled, specifying accurately the purposes for which the same is to be entered into, and how long it shall continue.

No state shall lay any imposts or duties, which may interfere with any stipulations in treaties, entered into by the United States in Congress assembled, with any king, prince or state, in pursuance of any treaties already proposed by Congress, to the courts of France and Spain.

No vessels of war shall be kept up in time of peace by any state, except such number only, as shall be deemed necessary by the United States in Congress assembled, for the defence of such state, or its trade; nor shall any body of forces be kept up by any state, in time of peace, except such number only, as in the judgment of the United States, in Congress assembled, shall be deemed requisite to garrison the forts necessary for the defence of such state; but every state shall always keep up a well regulated and disciplined militia, sufficiently armed and accoutred, and shall provide and constantly have ready for use, in public stores,

a due number of field pieces and tents, and a proper quantity of arms, ammunition and camp equipage.

No state shall engage in any war without the consent of the United States in Congress assembled, unless such state be actually invaded by enemies, or shall have received certain advice of a resolution being formed by some nation of Indians to invade such state, and the danger is so imminent as not to admit of a delay, till the United States in Congress assembled can be consulted: nor shall any state grant commissions to any ships or vessels of war, nor letters of marque or reprisal, except it be after a declaration of war by the United States in Congress assembled, and then only against the kingdom or state and the subjects thereof, against which war has been so declared, and under such regulations as shall be established by the United States in Congress assembled, unless such state be infested by pirates, in which case vessels of war may be fitted out for that occasion, and kept so long as the danger shall continue, or until the United States in Congress assembled shall determine otherwise.

Article VII

When land-forces are raised by any state for the common defence, all officers of or under the rank of colonel, shall be appointed by the legislature of each state respectively by whom such forces shall be raised, or in such manner as such state shall direct, and all vacancies shall be filled up by the state which first made the appointment.

Article VIII

All charges of war, and all other expenses that shall be incurred for the common defence or general welfare, and allowed by the United States in Congress assembled, shall be defrayed out of a common treasury, which shall be supplied by the several states, in proportion to the value of all land within each state, granted to or surveyed for any person, as such land and the buildings and improvements thereon shall be estimated according to such mode as the United States in Congress assembled, shall from time to time direct and appoint.

The taxes for paying that proportion shall be laid and levied by the authority and direction of the legislatures of the several states within the time agreed upon by the United States in Congress assembled.

Article IX

The United States in Congress assembled, shall have the sole and exclusive right and power of determining on peace and war, except in the cases mentioned in the sixth article—of sending and receiving ambassadors—entering into treaties and alliances, provided that no treaty of commerce shall be made whereby the legislative power of the respective states shall be restrained from imposing such imposts and duties on foreigners, as their own people are subjected to, or from prohibiting the exportation or importation of any species of good or commodities whatsoever—of establishing rules for deciding in all cases, what captures on land or water shall be legal, and in what manner prizes taken by land or naval forces in the service of the United States shall be divided or appropriated—of granting letters of marque and reprisal in times of peace—appointing courts for the trial of piracies and felonies committed on the high seas and establishing courts for receiving and determining finally appeals in all cases of captures, provided that no member of Congress shall be appointed a judge of any of the said courts.

The United States in Congress assembled shall also be the last resort on appeal in all disputes and differences now subsisting or that hereafter may arise between two or more states concerning boundary, jurisdiction or any other cause whatever; which authority shall always be exercised in the manner following. Whenever the legislative or executive authority or lawful agent of any state in controversy with another shall present a petition to Congress, stating the matter in question and praying for a hearing, notice thereof shall be given by order of Congress to the legislative or executive authority of the other state in controversy, and a day assigned for the appearance of the parties by their lawful agents, who shall then be directed to appoint by joint consent, commissioners or judges to constitute a court for hearing and determining the matter in question: but if they cannot agree, Congress shall name three persons out of each of the United States, and from the list of such persons each party shall alternately strike out one, the petitioners beginning, until the number shall be reduced to thirteen; and from that number not less than seven, nor more than nine names as Congress shall direct, shall in the presence of Congress be drawn out by lot, and the persons whose names shall be so drawn or any five of them, shall be commissioners or judges, to hear and finally determine the controversy, so always as a major part of the judges who shall hear the cause shall agree in the determination: and if either party shall neglect to attend at the day appointed, without showing reasons, which Congress shall judge sufficient, or being present shall refuse to strike, the Congress shall proceed to nominate three persons out of each state, and the Secretary of Congress shall strike in behalf of such party absent or refusing; and the judgment and sentence of the court to be appointed, in the manner before prescribed, shall be final and conclusive; and if any of the parties shall refuse to submit to the authority of such court, or to appear or defend their claim or cause, the court shall nevertheless proceed to pronounce sentence, or judgment, which shall in like manner be final and decisive, the judgment or sentence and other proceedings being in either case transmitted to Congress, and lodged among the acts

of Congress for the security of the parties concerned: provided that every commissioner, before he sits in judgment, shall take an oath to be administered by one of the judges of the supreme or superior court of the state where the cause shall be tried, "well and truly to hear and determine the matter in question, according to the best of his judgment, without favour, affection or hope of reward": provided also that no state shall be deprived of territory for the benefit of the United States.

All controversies concerning the private right of soil, claimed under different grants of two or more states, whose jurisdictions as they may respect such lands, and the states which passed such grants, are adjusted, the said grants or either of them being at the same time claimed to have originated antecedent to such settlement of jurisdiction, shall on the petition of either party to the Congress of the United States, be finally determined as near as may be in the same manner as is before prescribed for deciding disputes respecting territorial jurisdiction between different states.

The United States in Congress assembled shall also have the sole and exclusive right and power of regulating the alloy and value of coin struck by their own authority, or by that of the respective states—fixing the standard of weights and measures throughout the United States—regulating the trade and managing all affairs with the Indians, not members of any of the states, provided that the legislative right of any state within its own limits be not infringed or violated—establishing and regulating post-offices from one state to another, throughout all the United States, and exacting such postage on the papers passing thro' the same as may be requisite to defray the expenses of the said office—appointing all officers of the land forces in the service of the United States, excepting regimental officers—appointing all the officers of the naval forces, and commissioning all officers whatever in the service of the United States—making rules for the government and regulation of the said land and naval forces, and directing their operations.

The United States in Congress assembled shall have authority to appoint a committee, to sit in the recess of Congress, to be denominated "a committee of the states," and to consist of one delegate from each state; and to appoint such other committees and civil officers as may be necessary for managing the general affairs of the United States under their direction—to appoint one of their number to preside, provided that no person be allowed to serve in the office of President more than one year in any term of three years; to ascertain the necessary sums of money to be raised for the service of the United States, and to appropriate and apply the same for defraying the public expenses—to borrow money, or emit bills on the credit of the United States, transmitting every half year to the respective states an account of the sums of money so borrowed or emitted—to build and equip a navy—to agree upon the number of land forces, and to make requisitions from each state for its quota, in proportion to the number of white inhabitants in such state; which requisitions shall be binding, and thereupon the legislature of each state shall appoint the regimental officers, raise the men and clothe, arm and equip them in a soldier-like manner, at the expense of the United States; and the officers and men so clothed, armed and equipped shall march to the place appointed, and within the time agreed on by the United States in Congress assembled: but if the United States in Congress assembled shall, on consideration of circumstances, judge proper that any state should not raise men, or should raise a smaller number of men than its quota, and that any other state should raise a greater number of men than the quota thereof, such extra number shall be raised, officered, clothed, armed and equipped in the same manner as the quota of such state, unless the legislature of such state shall judge that such extra number cannot be safely spared out of the same, in which case they shall raise, officer, clothe, arm and equip as many of such extra number as they judge can be safely spared. And the officers and men so clothed, armed and equipped, shall march to the place appointed, and within the time agreed on by the United States in Congress assembled.

The United States in Congress assembled shall never engage in a war, nor grant letters of marque and reprisal in time of peace, nor enter into any treaties or alliances, nor coin money, nor regulate the value thereof, nor ascertain the sums and expenses necessary for the defence and welfare of the United States, or any of them, nor emit bills, nor borrow money on the credit of the United States, nor appropriate money, nor agree upon the number of vessels of war to be built or purchased, or the number of land or sea forces to be raised, nor appoint a commander in chief of the army or navy, unless nine states assent to the same: nor shall a question on any other point, except for adjourning from day to day be determined, unless by the votes of a majority of the United States in Congress assembled.

The Congress of the United States shall have power to adjourn to any time within the year, and to any place within the United States, so that no period of adjournment be for a longer duration than the space of six months, and shall publish the journal of their proceedings monthly, except such parts thereof relating to treaties, alliances or military operations, as in their judgment require secrecy; and the yeas and nays of the delegates of each state on any question shall be entered on the journal, when it is desired by any delegate; and the delegates of a state, or any of them, at his or their request shall be furnished with a transcript of the said journal, except such parts as are above excepted, to lay before the legislatures of the several states.

Article X
The committee of the states, or any nine of them, shall be authorized to execute, in the recess of Congress, such of the powers of Congress as the United States in Congress assembled, by the consent of nine states, shall from time to time think expedient to vest them with; provided that no power be delegated to the said committee, for the exercise of which, by the Articles of Confederation, the voice of nine states in the Congress of the United States assembled is requisite.

Article XI
Canada acceding to this confederation, and joining in the measures of the United States, shall be admitted into, and entitled to all the advantages of this Union: but no other colony shall be admitted into the same, unless such admission be agreed to by nine states.

Article XII
All bills of credit emitted, monies borrowed and debts contracted by, or under the authority of Congress, before the assembling of the United States, in pursuance of the present confederation, shall be deemed and considered as a charge against the United States, for payment and satisfaction whereof the said United States, and the public faith are hereby solemnly pledged.

Article XIII
Every state shall abide by the determinations of the United States in Congress assembled, on all questions which by this confederation are submitted to them. And the articles of this confederation shall be inviolably observed by every state, and the Union shall be perpetual; nor shall any alteration at any time hereafter be made in any of them; unless such alteration be agreed to in a Congress of the United States, and be afterwards confirmed by the legislatures of every state.

And whereas it has pleased the Great Governor of the world to incline the hearts of the legislatures we respectively represent in Congress, to approve of, and to authorize us to ratify the said Articles of Confederation and Perpetual Union. Know ye that we the undersigned delegates, by virtue of the power and authority to us given for that purpose, do by these presents, in the name and in behalf of our respective constituents, fully and entirely ratify and confirm each and every of the said Articles of Confederation and Perpetual Union, and all and singular the matters and things therein contained: and we do further solemnly plight and engage the faith of our respective constituents, that they shall abide by the determinations of the United States in Congress assembled, on all questions, which by the said Confederation are submitted to them. And that the articles thereof shall be inviolably observed by the states we respectively represent, and that the Union shall be perpetual.

Source:

John Scott, ed. *Living Documents in American History.* New York: Washington Square Press, 1964–68.

Massachusetts Bill of Rights, 1780

Just prior to and after independence, the former colonies established constitutions, several of which included bills of rights. The Virginia Declaration of Rights, for example, influenced Thomas Jefferson's version of the Declaration of Independence. The Massachusetts bill consisted of 30 articles, which were incorporated into the commonwealth's constitution and adopted in 1780. Drafted largely by John Adams, the document declared that "all men are born free and equal, and have certain natural, essential, and unalienable rights." It specified the right of the people to bear arms; to assemble; to be free of unreasonable searches; to participate in free elections; to be protected in life, liberty, and property; to obtain justice freely; and to have a free press. Declaring that "it is the right as well as the duty of all men . . . to worship the Supreme Being," it granted religious freedom to all Christian denominations.

Art. I. All men are born free and equal, and have certain, natural, essential, and unalienable rights, among which may be reckoned the right of enjoying and defending their lives and liberties; that of acquiring, possessing, and protecting property; in fine, that of seeking and obtaining their safety and happiness.

II. It is the right as well as the duty of all men in society, publicly, and at stated seasons, to worship the Supreme Being, the great creator and preserver of the universe. And no subject shall be hurt, molested, or restrained, in his person, liberty, or estate, for worshiping God in the manner and season most agreeable to the dictates of his own conscience; or for his religious profession or sentiments; provided he doth not disturb the public peace, or obstruct others in their religious worship.

III. As the happiness of a people, and the good order and preservation of civil government, essentially depend upon piety, religion and morality; and as these cannot be generally diffused through a community, but by the institution of the public worship of God, and of public instructions

in piety, religion and morality: Therefore, to promote their happiness, and to secure the good order and preservation of their government, the people of this Commonwealth have a right to invest their legislature with power to authorize and require, and the legislature shall, from time to time, authorize and require, the several towns, parishes, precincts, and other bodies politic, or religious societies, to make suitable provision, at their own expence, for the institution of the public worship of God, and for the support and maintenance of public protestant teachers of piety, religion and morality, in all cases where such provision shall not be made voluntarily. And the people of this Commonwealth have also a right to, and do, invest their legislature with authority to enjoin upon all the subjects an attendance upon the instructions of the public teachers aforesaid, at stated times and seasons, if there be any on whose instructions they can conscienciously and conveniently attend.

Provided notwithstanding that the several towns, parishes, precincts, and other bodies politic, or religious societies, shall, at all times, have the exclusive right of electing their public teachers, and of contracting with them for their support and maintenance.

And all monies paid by the subject to the support of public worship, and of the public teachers aforesaid, shall, if he require it, be uniformly applied to the support of the public teacher or teachers of his own religious sect or denomination, provided there be any on whose instructions he attends; otherwise it may be paid towards the support of the teacher or teachers of the parish or precinct in which the said monies are raised.

And every denomination of christians, demeaning themselves peaceably, and as good subjects of the Commonwealth, shall be equally under the protection of the law: and no subordination of any one sect or denomination to another shall ever be established by law.

IV. The people of this Commonwealth have the sole and exclusive right of governing themselves as a free, sovereign, and independent state, and do, and forever he easter shall, exercise and enjoy every power, jurisdiction, and right, which is not, or may not hereafter, be by them expresly delegated to the United States of America in Congress assembled.

V. All power residing originally in the people, and being derived from them, the several magistrates and officers of government, vested with authority, whether legislative, executive, or judicial, are their substitutes and agents, and are at all times accountable to them.

VI. No man, nor corporation, or association of men, have any other title to obtain advantages, or particular and exclusive privileges distinct from those of the community, than what arises from the consideration of services rendered to the public, and this title being in nature neither hereditary, nor transmissible to children, or decendents, or relations by blood, the idea of a man born a magistrate, lawgiver, or judge, is absurd and unnatural.

VII. Government is instituted for the common good; for the protection, safety, prosperity, and happiness of the people; and not for the profit, honor, or private interest of any one man, family or class of men: therefore the people alone have an incontestible, unalienable, and indefeasible right to institute government; and to reform, alter, or totally change the same, when their protection, safety, prosperity and happiness require it.

VIII. In order to prevent those, who are vested with authority, from becoming oppressors, the people have a right, at such periods and in such manner as they shall establish by their frame of government, to cause their public officers to return to private life; and to fill up vacant places by certain and regular elections and appointments.

IX. All elections ought to be free; and all the inhabitants of this Commonwealth, having such qualifications as they shall establish by their frame of government, have an equal right to elect officers, and to be elected, for public employments.

X. Each individual of the society has a right to be protected by it in the enjoyment of his life, liberty and property, according to standing laws. He is obliged, consequently, to contribute his share to the expence of this protection; to give his personal service, or an equivalent, when necessary: but no part of the property of any individual, can, with justice, be taken from him, or applied to public uses, without his own consent, or that of the representative body of the people: In fine, the people of this Commonwealth are not controulable by any other laws, than those to which their constitutional representative body have given their consent. And whenever the public exigencies require, that the property of any individual should be appropriated to public uses, he shall receive a reasonable compensation therefor.

XI. Every subject to the Commonwealth ought to find a certain remedy, by having recourse to the laws for all injuries or wrongs which he may receive in his person, property, or character. He ought to obtain right and justice freely, and without being obliged to purchase it; compleatly, and without any denial; promptly, and without delay; conformably to the laws.

XII. No subject shall be held to answer for any crime or offence, until the same is fully and plainly, substantially and formally, described to him; or be compelled to accuse, or furnish evidence against himself. And every subject shall have a right to produce all proofs that may be favorable to him; to meet the witnesses against him face to face; and to be fully heard in his defence by himself, or his council, at his election. And no subject shall be arrested, imprisoned, despoiled, or deprived of his property, immunities, or privileges, put out of the protection of the law, exiled, or deprived of his life, liberty, or estate, but by the judgment of his peers, or the law of the land.

And the legislature shall not make any law that shall subject any person to a capital or infamous punishment, excepting for the government of the army and navy, without trial by jury.

XIII. In criminal prosecutions, the verification of facts, in the vicinity where they happen, is one of the greatest securities of the life, liberty, and property of the citizen.

XIV. Every subject has a right to be secure from all unreasonable searches and seizures of his person, his houses, his papers, and all his possessions. All warrants, therefore, are contrary to this right, if the cause or foundation of them be not previously supported by oath or affirmation; and if the order in the warrant to a civil officer, to make search in suspected places, or to arrest one or more suspected persons, or to seize their property, be not accompanied with a special designation of the persons or objects of search, arrest, or seizure: and no warrant ought to be issued but in cases, and with the formalities prescribed by the laws.

XV. In all controversies concerning property, and in all suits between two or more persons, except in cases in which it has heretofore been otherways used and practiced, the parties have a right to a trial by a jury; and this method of procedure shall be held sacred, unless, in causes arising on the high feas, and such as relate to mariners wages, the legislature shall hereafter find it necessary to alter it.

XVI. The liberty of the press is essential to the security of freedom in a state; it ought not, therefore, to be restrained in this Commonwealth.

XVII. The people have a right to keep and to bear arms for the common defence. And as in time of peace armies are dangerous to liberty, they ought not to be maintained without the consent of the legislature; and the military power shall always be held in an exact subordination to the civil authority and be governed by it.

XVIII. A frequent recurrence to the fundamental principles of the constitution, and a constant adherence to those of piety, justice, moderation, temperature, industry, and frugality, are absolutely necessary to preserve the advantages of liberty, and to maintain a free government: the people ought, consequently, to have a particular attention to all those principles, in the choice of their officers and representatives: and they have a right to require of their law givers and magistrates, an exact and constant observance of them, in the formation and execution of the laws necessary for the good administration of the Commonwealth.

XIX. The people have a right, in an orderly and peaceable manner, to assemble to consult upon the common good: give instructions to their representatives; and to request of the legislative body, by the way of addresses, petitions, or remonstrances, redress of the wrongs done them, and of the grievances they suffer.

XX. The power of suspending the laws, or the execution of the laws, ought never to be exercised but by the legislature, or by authority derived from it, to be exercised in such particular cases only as the legislature shall expressly provide for.

XXI. The freedom of deliberation, speech and debate in either house of the legislature, is so essential to the rights of the people, that it cannot be the foundation of any accusation or prosecution, action or complaint, in any other court or place whatsoever.

XXII. The legislature ought frequently to assemble for the redress of grievances, for correcting, strengthening, and confirming the laws and for making new laws, as the common good may, require.

XXIII. No subsidy, charge, tax, impost, or duties, ought to be established, fixed, laid, or levied, under any pretext whatsoever, without the consent of the people, or their representatives in the legislature.

XXIV. Laws made to punish for actions done before the existence of such laws, and which have not been declared crimes by preceding laws, are unjust, oppressive, and inconsistent with the fundamental principles of a free government.

XXV. No subject ought, in any case, or in any time to be declared guilty of treason or felony by the legislature.

XXVI. No magistrate or court of law, shall demand excessive bail or sureties, impose excessive fines, or inflict cruel or unusual punishments.

XXVII. In time of peace no soldier ought to be quartered in any house without the consent of the owner; and in time of war such quarters ought not to be made but by the civil magistrate, in a manner ordained by the legislature.

XXVIII. No person can in any case be subjected to law-martial, or to any penalties or pains, by virtue of that law, except those employed in the army or navy, and except the militia in actual service, but by authority of the legislature.

XXIX. It is essential to the preservation of the rights of every individual, his life, liberty, property and character, that there be an impartial interpretation of the laws, and administration of justice. It is the right of every citizen to be tried by judges are free, impartial and independents as the lot of humanity will admit. It is therefore not only the best policy, but for the security of the rights of the people, and of every citizen, that the judges of the supreme judicial court should hold their offices as long as they behave themselves well; and that they should have honorable salaries ascertained and established by standing laws.

XXX. In the government of this Commonwealth, the legislative department shall never exercise the executive and judicial powers, or either of them; the executive shall never exercise the legislative and judicial powers, or either of them; the judicial shall never exercise the legislative and executive powers, or either of them: to the end it may be a government of laws and not of men.

See also VIRGINIA STATUTE OF RELIGIOUS LIBERTY, 1786.

Source:
A Constitution or Frame of Government Agreed Upon by the Delegates of the People of the State of Massachusetts Bay, 3rd ed. Boston: Benjamin Edes & Sons, 1780. pp. 7–13.

Land Ordinance of 1785

Plan enacted by Congress on May 20, 1785, that outlined a systematic survey and subdivision of land in the western territories and provided for clear-cut boundaries and titles. The land was to be divided into townships, each six miles square, which would be further subdivided into 36 lots of 640 acres each. Boundaries were based on meridians of longitude and parallels of latitude with lines running, wherever possible, due north and south by due east and west. Land was sold in 640-acre parcels for one dollar an acre. A proportion of the land was reserved for the United States government, and one lot in every township was set aside for public schools. This system of land disposal remained in effect, with a few changes, until the passage of the Homestead Act of 1862.

On May 18, 1796, Congress passed its first significant act to administer public lands in the western territories of the United States. It established the office of surveyor general and provided for a rectangular survey system, as in the Land Ordinance of 1785. Lands were to be divided into townships of six miles square. Half of the townships were to be divided into sections of 640 acres, the smallest unit available for sale; the other half of the townships were offered in 5,120-acre blocks. Lands were to be sold at public auction to the highest bidder, with a minimum price of two dollars per acre. The buyer was required to pay in full within a year of purchase. The law was unsuccessful because the minimum price was high, and the minimum parcel for sale was large.

Congress assembled. Present as yesterday.

Congress proceeded in the third reading of the Ordinance for ascertaining the mode of disposing of lands in the western territory, and the same being gone through, was passed as follows:

An Ordinance for ascertaining the mode of disposing of Lands in the Western Territory.

Be it ordained by the United States in Congress assembled, that the territory ceded by individual States to the United States, which has been purchased of the Indian inhabitants, shall be disposed of in the following manner:

A surveyor from each state shall be appointed by Congress, or a committee of the States, who shall take an Oath for the faithful discharge of his duty, before the Geographer of the United States, who is hereby empowered and directed to administer the same; and the like oath shall be administered to each chain carrier, by the surveyor under whom he acts.

The Geographer, under whose direction the surveyors shall act, shall occasionally form such regulations for their conduct, as he shall deem necessary; and shall have authority to suspend them for misconduct in Office, and shall make report of the same to Congress, or to the Committee of the States; and he shall make report in case of sickness, death, or resignation of any surveyor.

The Surveyors, as they are respectively qualified, shall proceed to divide the said territory into townships of six miles square, by lines running due north and south, and others crossing these at right angles, as near as may be, unless where the boundaries of the late Indian purchase may render the same impracticable, and then they shall depart from this rule no farther than such particular circumstances may require; and each surveyor shall be allowed and paid at the rate of two dollars for every mile, in length, he shall run, including the wages of chain carriers, markers, and every other expense attending the same. The first line, running north and south as aforesaid, shall begin on the river Ohio, at a point that shall be found to be due north from the western termination of a line, which has been run as the southern boundary of the state of Pennsylvania; and the first line, running east and west, shall begin at the same point, and shall extend throughout the whole territory. Provided, that nothing herein shall be construed, as fixing the western boundary of the state of Pennsylvania. The geographer hall designate the townships, or fractional parts of townships, by numbers progressively from south to north; always beginning each range with number one; and the ranges shall be distinguished by their progressive numbers of the westward. The first range, extending from the Ohio to the lake Erie, being marked number one. The Geographer shall personally attend to the running of the first east and west line; and shall take the latitude of the extremes of the first north and south line, and of the mouths of the principal rivers.

The lines shall be measured with a chain; shall be plainly marked by chaps on the trees, and exactly described on a plat; whereon shall be noted by the surveyor, at their proper distances, all mines, salt springs, salt licks and mill seats, that shall come to his knowledge, and all water courses, mountains and other remarkable and permanent things, over and near which such lines shall pass, and also the quality of the lands.

The plots of the townships respectively, shall be marked by subdivisions into lots of one mile square, or 640 acres, in the same direction as the external lines, and numbered from 1 to 36; always beginning the succeeding range of the lots with the number next to that with which the preceding one concluded. And where, from the causes before mentioned, only a fractional part of a township shall be surveyed, the lots, protracted thereon, shall bear the same numbers as if the township had been entire. And the surveyors, in running the external lines of the townships, shall, at the interval of every mile, mark corners for the lots which are adjacent, always designating the same in a different manner from those of the townships.

The geographer and surveyors shall pay the utmost attention to the variation of the magnetic needle; and shall run and note all lines by the true meridian, certifying, with every plat, what was the variation at the times of running the lines thereon noted.

As soon as seven ranges of townships, and fractional part of townships, in the direction from south to north, shall have been surveyed, the geographer shall transmit plats thereof to the board of treasury, who shall record the same, with the report, in well bound books to be kept for that purpose. And the geographer shall make similar returns, from time to time, of every seven ranges as they may be surveyed. The Secretary at War shall have recourse thereto, and shall take by lot therefrom, a number of townships, and fractional parts of townships, as well from those to be sold entire as from those to be sold in lots, as will be equal to one seventh part of the whole of such seven ranges, as nearly as may be, for the use of the late continental army; and he shall make a similar draught, from time to time, until a sufficient quantity is drawn to satisfy the same, to be applied in manner hereinafter directed. The board of treasury shall, from time to time, cause the remaining numbers, as well those to be sold entire, as those to be sold in lots, to be drawn for, in the name of the thirteen states respectively, according to the quotas in the last preceding requisition on all the states; provided, that in case more land than its proportion is allotted for sale, in any state, at any distribution, a deduction be made therefor at the next.

The board of treasury shall transmit a copy of the original plats, previously noting thereon, the townships, and fractional parts of townships, which shall have fallen to the several states, by the distribution aforesaid, to the Commissioners of the loan office of the several states, who, after giving notice of not less than two nor more than six months, by causing advertisements to be posted up at the court houses, or other noted places in every county, and to be inserted in one newspaper, published in the state of their residence respectively, shall proceed to sell the townships, or fractional parts of townships, at public vendue, in the following manner, viz: The township, or fractional part of a township, N 1, in the first range, shall be sold entire; and N 2, in the same range, by lots; and thus in alternate order through the whole of the first range. The township, or fractional part of a township, N 1, in the second range, shall be sold by lots; and N 2, in the same range, entire; and so in alternate order through the whole of the second range; and the third range shall be sold in the same manner as the first, and the fourth in the same manner as the second, and thus alternately throughout all the ranges; provided, that none of the lands, within the said territory, be sold under the price of one dollar the acre, to be paid in specie, or loan office certificates, reduced to specie value, by the scale of depreciation, or certificates of liquidated debts of the United States, including interest, besides the expense of the survey and other charges thereon, which are hereby rated at thirty six dollars the township, in specie, or certificates as aforesaid, and so in the same proportion for a fractional part of a township, or of a lot, to be paid at the time of sales; on failure of which payment, the said lands shall again be offered for sale.

There shall be reserved for the United States out of every township, the four lots, being numbered 8, 11, 26, 29, and out of every fractional part of a township, so many lots of the same numbers as shall be found thereon, for future sale. There shall be reserved the lot N 16, of every township, for the maintenance of public schools, within the said township; also one third part of all gold, silver, lead and copper mines, to be sold, or otherwise disposed of as Congress shall hereafter direct.

When any township, or fractional part of a township, shall have been sold as aforesaid, and the money or certificates received therefor, the loan officer shall deliver a deed in the following terms:

The United States of America, to all to whom these presents shall come, Greeting:

Know ye, That for the consideration of dollars, we have granted, and hereby do grant and confirm unto the township, (or fractional part of a township, as the case may be) numbered in the range excepting therefrom, and reserving one third part of all gold, silver, lead and copper mines within the same; and the lots Ns 8, 11, 26 and 29, for future sale or disposition, and the lot N 16, for the maintenance of public schools. To have to the said his heirs and assigns for ever; (or if more than one purchaser, to the said their heirs and assigns forever as tenants in Common.) In witness whereof, (A.B.) Commissioner of the loan office, in the State of hath, in conformity to the Ordinance passed by the United States in Congress assembled, the twentieth day of May, in the year of our Lord one thousand seven hundred and eighty five, hereunto set his hand, and affixed his seal, this day of in the year of our Lord and of the independence of the United States of America.

And when any township, or fractional part of a township, shall be sold by lots as aforesaid, the Commissioner of the loan office shall deliver a deed therefor in the following form:

The United States of America, to all to whom these presents shall come, Greeting:

Know ye, That for the consideration of dollars, we have granted, and hereby do grant and confirm unto the lot (or lots, as the case may be, in the township or fractional part of the township, as the case may be) numbered in the range excepting and reserving one third part of all gold, silver, lead and copper mines within the same, for future sale or disposition. To have to the said his heirs and assigns for ever; (or if more than one purchaser, to the said their heirs and assigns for ever as tenants in common.) In witness whereof, (A. B.) Commissioner of the continental loan office in the state of hath, in conformity to the Ordinance passed by the United States in Congress assembled, the twentieth day of May, in the year of our Lord 1785, hereunto set his hand, and affixed his seal, this day of in the year of our Lord and of the independence of the United States of America.

Which deeds shall be recorded in proper books, by the commissioner of the loan office, and shall be certified to have been recorded, previous to their being delivered to the purchaser, and shall be good and valid to convey the lands in the same described.

The commissioners of the loan offices respectively, shall transmit to the board of treasury every three months, an account of the townships, fractional parts of townships, and lots committed to their charge; specifying therein the names of the persons to whom sold, and the sums of money or certificates received for the same; and shall cause all certificates by them received, to be struck through with a circular punch; and they shall be duly charged in the books of the treasury, with the amount of the moneys or certificates, distinguishing the same, by them received as aforesaid.

If any township, or fractional part of a township or lot, remains unsold for eighteen months after the plat shall have been received, by the commissioners of the loan office, the same shall be returned to the board of treasury, and shall be sold in such manner as Congress may hereafter direct.

And whereas Congress, by their resolutions of September 16 and 18 in the year 1776, and the 12th of August, 1780, stipulated grants of land to certain officers and soldiers of the late continental army, and by the resolution of the 22d September, 1780, stipulated grants of land to certain officers in the hospital department of the late continental army; for complying therefore with such engagements, Be it ordained, That the secretary at war, from the returns in his office, or such other sufficient evidence as the nature of the case may admit, determine who are the objects of the above resolutions and engagements, and the quantity of land to which such persons or their representatives are respectively entitled, and cause the townships, or fractional parts of townships, hereinbefore reserved for the use of the late continental army, to be drawn for in such manner as he shall deem expedient, to answer the purpose of an impartial distribution. He shall, from time to time, transmit certificates to the commissioners of the loan offices of the different states, to the lines of which the military claimants have respectively belonged, specifying the name and rank of the party, the terms of his engagement and time of his service, and the division, brigade, regiment or company to which he belonged, the quantity of land he is entitled to, and the township, or fractional part of a township, and range out of which his portion is to be taken.

The commissioners of the loan offices shall execute deeds for such undivided proportions in manner and form herein before-mentioned, varying only in such a degree as to make the same conformable to the certificate from the Secretary at War.

Where any military claimants of bounty in lands shall not have belonged to the line of any particular state, similar certificates shall be sent to the board of treasury, who shall execute deeds to the parties for the same.

The Secretary at War, from the proper returns, shall transmit to the board of treasury, a certificate, specifying the name and rank of the several claimants of the hospital department of the late continental army, together with the quantity of land each claimant is entitled to, and the township, or fractional part of a township, and range out of which his portion is to be taken; and thereupon the board of treasury shall proceed to execute deeds to such claimants.

The board of treasury, and the commissioners of the loan offices in the states, shall, within 18 months, return receipts to the secretary at war, for all deeds which have been delivered, as also all the original deeds which remain in their hands for want of applicants, having been first recorded; which deeds so returned, shall be preserved in the office, until the parties or their representatives require the same.

And be it further Ordained, That three townships adjacent to lake Erie be reserved, to be hereafter disposed of by Congress, for the use of the officers, men, and others, refugees from Canada, and the refugees from Nova Scotia, who are or may be entitled to grants of land under resolutions of Congress now existing, or which may hereafter be made respecting them, and for such other purposes as Congress may hereafter direct.

And be it further Ordained, That the towns of Gnadenhutten, Schoenbrun and Salem, on the Muskingum, and so much of the lands adjoining to the said towns, with the buildings and improvements thereon, shall be reserved for the sole use of the Christian Indians, who were formerly settled there, or the remains of that society, as may, in the judgment of the Geographer, be sufficient for them to cultivate.

Saving and reserving always, to all officers and soldiers entitled to lands on the northwest side of the Ohio, by donation or bounty from the commonwealth of Virginia, and to all persons claiming under them, all rights to which they are so entitled, under the deed of cession executed by the delegates for the state of Virginia, on the first day of March, 1784, and the act of Congress accepting the same: and to the end, that the said rights may be fully and effectually secured, according to the true intent and meaning of the said deed of cession and act aforesaid, Be it Ordained, that no part of the land included between the rivers called little Miami and Sciota, on the northwest side of the river Ohio, be sold, or in any manner alienated, until there shall first have been laid off and appropriated for the said Officers and Soldiers, and persons claiming under them, the lands they are entitled to, agreeably to the said deed of cession and act of Congress accepting the same.

Done by the United States in Congress assembled, the 20th day of May, in the year of our Lord 1785, and of our sovereignty and independence the ninth.

Source:
Journals of the Continental Congress, 1774–1789. Vol. 28, pp. 375–381.

Virginia Statute of Religious Liberty, 1786

Thomas Jefferson considered the Virginia Statute for Religious Liberty one of his main achievements, ranking it second only to the Declaration of Independence. The statute is one of the earliest American statements of absolute religious liberty—a model for the First Amendment to the Constitution—and was adopted by the state of Virginia on January 16, 1786. It barred discrimination based on religious belief, outlawed compulsory church attendance, and ended a tax that was used to support Anglican Church operations. While Anglican ministers had largely remained on the British side during the American Revolution 10 years previously, Congregational and Baptist ministers had been very strong supporters of the revolutionaries. As a result, American sentiment turned against the Anglican

Church. The Virginia Declaration of Rights (1776) inspired a growing number of Virginia dissenters to demand the disestablishment of the Anglican Church as soon as the new legislature met. Although majority opinion favored Anglican disestablishment, no consensus emerged on the separation of church and state or on eliminating the distinctions between religions in the United States. Jefferson, returning from Congress to broaden Virginia's guarantees of freedom, opened the debate in the first assembly. Jefferson envisioned a future where "All men [shall] be free to profess, and by argument maintain, their opinion in matters of religion." Although he drafted the document earlier, he found no appropriate time to submit it until 1779. Fellow Virginian James Madison championed Jefferson's statute, writing that it "extinguished forever the ambitious hope of making laws for the human mind."

An Act for Establishing Religious Freedom

I. Whereas Almighty God hath created the mind free; that all attempts to influence it by temporal punishments or burthens, or by civil incapacitations, tend only to beget habits of hypocrisy and meanness, and are a departure from the plan of the Holy author of our religion, who being Lord both of body and mind, yet chose not to propagate it by coercions on either, as was in his Almighty power to do; that the impious presumption of legislators and rulers, civil as well as ecclesiastical, who being themselves but fallible and uninspired men, have assumed dominion over the faith of others, setting up their own opinions and modes of thinking as the only true and infallible, and as such endeavouring to impose them on others, hath established and maintained false religions over the greatest part of the world, and through all time; that to compel a man to furnish contributions of money for the propagation of opinions which he disbelieves, is sinful and tyrannical; that even the forcing him to support this or that teacher of his own religious persuasion, is depriving him of the comfortable liberty of giving his contributions to the particular pastor whose morals he would make his pattern, and whose powers he feels most persuasive to righteousness, and is withdrawing from the ministry those temporary rewards, which proceeding from an approbation of their personal conduct, are an additional incitement to earnest and unremitting labours for the instruction of mankind; that our civil rights have no dependence on our religious opinions, any more than our opinions in physics or geometry; that therefore the proscribing any citizen as unworthy the public confidence by laying upon him an incapacity of being called to offices of trust and emolument, unless he profess or renounce this or that religious opinion, is depriving him injuriously of those privileges and advantages to which in common with his fellow-citizens he has a natural right, that it tends only to corrupt the principles of that religion it is meant to encourage, by bribing with a monopoly of worldly honours and emoluments, those who will externally profess and conform to it; that though indeed these are criminal who do not withstand such temptation, yet neither are those innocent who lay the bait in their way; that to suffer the civil magistrate to intrude his powers into the field of opinion, and to restrain the profession or propagation of principles on supposition of their ill tendency, is a dangerous fallacy, which at once destroys all religious liberty, because he being of course judge of that tendency will make his opinions the rule of judgment, and approve or condemn the sentiments of others only as they shall square with or differ from his own; that it is time enough for the rightful purposes of civil government, for its officers to interfere when principles break out into overt acts against peace and good order; and finally, that truth is great and will prevail if left to herself, that she is the proper and sufficient antagonist to error, and has nothing to fear from the conflict, unless by human interposition disarmed of her natural weapons, free argument and debate, errors ceasing to be dangerous when it is permitted freely to contradict them.

II. *Be it enacted by the General Assembly,* that no man shall be compelled to frequent or support any religious worship, place or ministry whatsoever, nor shall be enforced, restrained, molested, or burthened in his body or goods, nor shall otherwise suffer on account of his religious opinions or belief; but that all men shall be free to profess, and by argument to maintain, their opinion in matters of religion, and that the same shall in no wise diminish, enlarge or affect their civil capacities.

III. And though we well know that this assembly, elected by the people for the ordinary purposes of legislation only, have no power to restrain the acts of succeeding assemblies, constituted with powers equal to our own, and that therefore to declare this act to be irrevocable would be of no effect in law; yet as we are free to declare, and do declare, that the rights hereby asserted are of the natural rights of mankind, and that if any act shall hereafter be passed to repeal the present, or to narrow its operation, such act will be an infringement of natural right.

See also MASSACHUSETTS BILL OF RIGHTS, 1780.

Source:
Henry Steele Commager, ed. *Documents of American History.* New York: F.S. Crofts & Co., 1934.

Annapolis Convention Address, 1786

Convention on interstate commerce held at Annapolis, Maryland in September 1786, and attended by 12 commissioners from New York, New Jersey, Pennsylvania, Delaware, and Virginia. Dissatisfaction with the Articles of Confederation and financial difficulties had led Virginia to call for the convention, but the scanty attendance precluded solutions to the problems. Instead, the convention report, drafted by Alexander Hamilton, called for a new convention to be held at Philadelphia in May 1787 to discuss not just problems of interstate commerce but all matters "necessary to render the Constitution of the Federal Government adequate to the exigencies of the Union."

Address of the Annapolis Convention

To the Honorable the Legislatures of Virginia, Delaware Pennsylvania, New Jersey, and New York.

The Commissioners from the said states, respectively assembled at Annapolis, humbly beg leave to report.

That, pursuant to their several appointments, they met, at Annapolis in the State of Maryland, on the eleventh day of September Instant, and having proceeded to a Communication of their powers; they found, that the States of New York, Pennsylvania and Virginia had, in substance, and nearly in the same terms, authorized their respective Commissioners "to meet such commissioners as were, or might be, appointed by the other States in the Union, at such time and place, as should be agreed upon by the said Commissioners to take into consideration the trade and Commerce of the United States, to consider how far an uniform system in their commercial intercourse and regulations might be necessary to their common interest and permanent harmony, and to report to the several States, such an Act, relative to this great object, as when unanimously ratified by them would enable the United States in Congress assembled effectually to provide for the same."

That the State of Delaware, had given similar powers to their Commissioners, with this difference only that the Act to be framed in virtue of those powers, is required to be reported "to the United States in Congress Assembled, to be agreed to by them, and confirmed by the Legislatures of every State."

That the State of New Jersey had enlarged the object of their Appointment, empowering their Commissioners, "to consider how far an uniform system in their commercial regulations and other important matters, might be necessary to the common interest and permanent harmony of the several States," and to report such an Act on the subject, as when ratified by them "would enable the United States in Congress Assembled, effectually to provide for the exigencies of the Union."

That appointments of Commissioners have also been made by the States of New Hampshire, Massachusetts, Rhode Island, and North Carolina, none of whom however have attended; but that no information has been received by your Commissioners of any appointments having been made by the States of Connecticut, Maryland, South Carolina, or Georgia.

That the express terms of the powers to your Commissioners supposing a deputation from all the States, and having for object the Trade and Commerce of the United States, Your Commissioners did not conceive it advisable to proceed on the business of their mission, under the Circumstance of so partial and defective a representation.

Deeply impressed however with the magnitude and importance of the object confided to them on this occasion, your Commissioners cannot forbear to indulge an expression of their earnest and unanimous wish, that speedy measures may be taken, to effect a general meeting, of the States, in a future Convention, for the same and such other purposes, as the situation of public affairs, may be found to require.

If in expressing this wish, or in intimating any other sentiment, your Commissioners should seem to exceed the strict bounds of their appointment, they entertain a full confidence, that a conduct, dictated by an anxiety for the welfare, of the United States, will not fail to receive an indulgent construction.

In this persuasion your Commissioners submit an opinion, that the Idea of extending the powers of their Deputies, to other objects, than those of Commerce, which has been adopted by the State of New Jersey, was an improvement on the original plan, and will deserve to be incorporated into that of a future Convention; they are the more naturally led to this conclusion, as in the course of their reflections on the subject, they have been induced to think, that the power of regulating trade is of such comprehensive extent, and will enter so far into the general System of the federal government, that to give it efficacy, and to obviate questions and doubts concerning its precise nature and limits, may require a correspondent adjustment of other parts of the Federal System.

That there are important defects in the system of the Federal Government is acknowledged by the Acts of all those States, which have concurred in the present Meeting; That the defects, upon a closer examination, may be found greater and more numerous, than even these acts imply, is at least so far probable, from the embarrassments which characterize the present State of our national affairs—foreign and domestic, as may reasonably be supposed to merit a deliberate and candid discussion, in some mode, which will unite the Sentiments and Councils of all the States. In the choice of the mode your Commissioners are of opinion, that a Convention of Deputies from the different States, for the special and sole purpose of entering into this investigation, and digesting a plan for supplying such defects as may be discovered to exist, will be entitled to a preference from consideration, which will occur, without being particularized.

Your Commissioners decline an enumeration of those national circumstances on which their opinion respecting the propriety of a future Convention with more enlarged powers, is founded; as it would be an useless intrusion of facts and observations, most of which have been frequently the subject of public discussion, and none of which can have escaped the penetration of those to whom they would in this instance be addressed. They are however of a nature so serious, as, in the view of your Commissioners to render the Situation of the United States delicate and critical, calling for an exertion of the united virtue and wisdom of all the members of the Confederacy.

Under this impression, Your Commissioners, with the most respectful deference, beg leave to suggest their unanimous conviction, that it may essentially tend to advance the interests of the union, if the States, by whom they have been respectively delegated, would themselves concur, and use their endeavors to procure the concurrence of the other States, in the appointment of Commissioners, to meet at Philadelphia on the second Monday in May next, to take into consideration the situation of the United States, to devise such further provisions as shall appear to them necessary to render the constitution of the Federal Government adequate to the exigencies of the Union; and to report such an Act for that purpose to the United States in Congress Assembled, as when agreed to, by them, and afterwards confirmed by the Legislatures of every State will effectually provide for the same.

Though your Commissioners could not with propriety address these observations and sentiments to any but the States they have the honor to Represent, they have nevertheless concluded from motives of respect, to transmit Copies of this report to the United States in Congress assembled, and to the executives of the other States.

Source:

Harold C. Syrett, ed. *The Papers of Alexander Hamilton.* New York: Columbia University Press, 1961-87.

Virginia Plan and New Jersey Plan, 1787

William Paterson submitted the New Jersey Plan to the Constitutional Convention on June 15, 1787. As a representative of a small state, Paterson aligned with the states' rights faction at the convention. In opposition to the Virginia Plan, Paterson's proposal called for a unicameral legislature similar to the Articles of Confederation Congress in which each state would have equal representation. The plan also included provisions that would strengthen the national government: Congress would have the power to tax and to regulate interstate and foreign commerce, a federal executive and judiciary branch

would be created, and the treaties and acts of Congress would be the supreme law in the states.

A committee of 11 set to resolve the differences between the two plans. Roger Sherman and Oliver Ellsworth, both from Connecticut, reported their compromise to the U.S. Federal Constitutional Convention on July 5, 1787. The new plan (sometimes called the Connecticut Compromise) was adopted by the convention on July 16. In its final form, it provided for a bicameral legislature with each state's representation in the lower house to be proportional to its population (based on the total white population and three-fifths of the black population), and each state having equal representation in the upper house.

The Great Compromise largely resolved the differences among the smaller states, which had favored the New Jersey Plan of representation by states, and the larger states, whose interests had been reflected in the Virginia Plan, which wanted representation by population.

Other participants in the excerpts below are Gunning Bedford, Delaware; Pierce Butler, South Carolina; Daniel Carroll, Maryland; William R. Davie, North Carolina; Benjamin Franklin, Pennsylvania; Elbridge Gerry, Massachusetts; Nathaniel Gorham, Massachusetts; Rufus King, Massachusetts; James Madison, Virginia; Luther Martin, Maryland; George Mason, Virginia; Gouveneur Morris, Pennsylvania; Charles Pinckney, South Carolina; Edmund Randolph, Virginia; John Rutledge, South Carolina; Hugh Williamson, North Carolina; and James Wilson, Pennsylvania.

Virginia Plan, 1787

1. Resolved that the Articles of Confederation ought to be so corrected and enlarged as to accomplish the objects proposed by their institution; namely "common defence, security of liberty and general welfare."

2. Resolved therefore that the rights of suffrage in the National Legislature ought to be proportioned to the Quotas of contribution, or to the number of free inhabitants, as the one or the other rule may seem best in different cases.

3. Resolved that the National Legislature ought to consist of two branches.

4. Resolved that the members of the first branch of the National Legislature ought to be elected by the people of the several States every for the terms of; to be of the age of years at least, to receive liberal stipends by which they may be compensated for the devotion of their time to public service, to be ineligible to any office established by a particular State, or under the authority of the United States, except those peculiarly belonging to the functions of the first branch, during the term of service, and for the space of after its expiration; to be incapable of reelection for the space of after the expiration of their term of service, and to be subject to recall.

5. Resolved that the members of the second branch of the National Legislature ought to be elected by those of the first, out of a proper number of persons nominated by the individual Legislatures, to be of the age of years at least; to hold their offices for a term sufficient to ensure their independency; to receive liberal stipends by which they may be compensated for the devotion of their time to public service; and to be ineligible to any office established by a particular State, or under the authority of the United States, except those peculiarly belonging to the functions of the second branch, during the term of service, and for the space of after the expiration thereof.

6. Resolved that each branch ought to possess the right of originating Acts; that the National Legislature ought to be impowered to enjoy the Legislative Rights vested in Congress by the Confederation and moreover to legislate in all cases to which the separate States are incompetent, or in which the harmony of the United States may be interrupted by the exercise of individual Legislation; to negative all laws passed by the several States, contravening in the opinion of the National Legislature the articles of Union; and to call forth the force of the Union against any member of the Union failing in its duty under the articles thereof.

7. Resolved that a National Executive be instituted; to be chosen by the National Legislature for the term of years; to receive punctually, at stated times, a fixed compensation for the services rendered, in which no increase or diminution shall be made so as to affect the Magistracy, existing at the time of the increase or diminution, and to be ineligible a second time; and that besides a general authority to execute the National laws, it ought to enjoy the Executive rights vested in Congress by the Confederation.

8. Resolved that the Executive and a convenient number of the National Judiciary, ought to compose a Council or revision with authority to examine every act of the National Legislature before it shall operate, and every act of a particular Legislature before a Negative thereon shall be final; and that the dissent of the said Council shall amount to a rejection, unless the Act of the National Legislature be passed again, or that of a particular Legislature be again negatived by of the members of each branch.

9. Resolved that a National Judiciary be established to consist of one or more supreme tribunals, and of inferior tribunals to be chosen by the National Legislature, to hold their offices during good behaviour; and to receive punctually at stated times fixed compensation for their services, in which no increase or diminution shall be made so as to affect the persons actually in office at the time of such increase or diminution. That the jurisdiction of the inferior tribunals shall be to hear and determine in the first instance, and of the supreme tribunal to hear and deter-

mine in the dernier resort, all piracies and felonies on the high seas, captures from an enemy; cases in which foreigners or citizens of other States applying to such jurisdictions may be interested, or which respect the collection of the National revenue; impeachments of any National officers, and questions which may involve the national peace and harmony.

10. Resolved that provision ought to be made for the admission of States lawfully arising within the limits of the United States, whether from a voluntary junction of Government and Territory or otherwise, with the consent of a number of voices in the National legislature less than the whole.

11. Resolved that a Republican Government and the territory of each State, except in the instance of a voluntary junction of Government and territory, ought to be guaranteed by the United States to each State.

12. Resolved that provision ought to be made for the continuance of Congress and their authorities and privileges, until a given day after the reform of the articles of Union shall be adopted, and for the completion of all their engagements.

13. Resolved that provision ought to be made for the amendment of the Articles of Union whensoever it shall seem necessary, and that the assent of the National Legislature ought not to be required thereto.

14. Resolved that the Legislative Executive and Judiciary powers within the several States ought to be bound by oath to support the articles of Union.

15. Resolved that the amendments which shall be offered to the Confederation, by the Convention ought at a proper time, or times, after the approbation of Congress to be submitted to an assembly or assemblies of Representatives, recommended by the several Legislatures to be expressly chosen by the people, to consider and decide thereon.

New Jersey Plan, 1787 (The Paterson Plan)

1. Resolved that the Articles of Confederation ought to be so revised, corrected, and enlarged as to render the federal Constitution adequate to the exigencies of Government, and the preservation of the Union.

2. Resolved that in addition to the powers vested in the United States in Congress, by the present existing articles of Confederation, they be authorized to pass acts for raising a revenue, by levying a duty or duties on all goods or merchandizes of foreign growth or manufacture, imported into any part of the United States, by Stamps on paper, velum or parchment, and by a postage on all letters or packages passing through the general post-office, to be applied to such federal purposes as they shall deem proper and expedient;

to make rules and regulations for the collection thereof; and the same from time to time, to alter and amend in such manner as they shall think proper: to pass Acts for the regulation of trade and commerce as well with foreign nations as with each other; provided that all punishments, fines, forfeitures and penalties to be incurred for contravening such acts rules and regulations shall be adjudged by the Common law Judiciaries of the State in which any offence contrary to the true intent and meaning of such Acts rules and regulations shall have been committed or perpetrated, with liberty of commencing in the first instance all suits and prosecutions for that purpose, in the superior common law Judiciary in such state, subject nevertheless, for the correction of errors, both in law and fact in rendering Judgement, to an appeal to the Judiciary of the United States.

3. Resolved that whenever requisitions shall be necessary, instead of the rule for making requisitions mentioned in the articles of Confederation, the United States in Congress be authorized to make such requisitions in proportion to the whole number of white and other free citizens and inhabitants of every age sex and condition including those bound to servitude for a term of years and three fifths of all other persons not comprehended in the foregoing description, except Indians not paying taxes; that if such requisitions be not complied with, in the time specified therein, to direct the collection thereof in the non-complying States and for that purpose to devise and pass acts directing and authorizing the same; provided that none of the powers hereby vested in the United States in Congress shall be exercised without the consent of at least States, and in that proportion if the number of Confederated States should hereafter be increased or diminished.

4. Resolved that the United States in Congress be authorized to elect a federal Executive to consist of persons, to continue in office for the term of years, to receive punctually at stated times a fixed compensation for their services, in which no increase or diminution shall be made so as to affect the persons composing the Executive at the time of such increase or diminution, to be paid out of the federal treasury; to be incapable of holding any other office or appointment during their time of service and for years thereafter; to be ineligible a second time, and removeable by Congress on application by a majority of the Executives of the several States; that the Executives besides their general authority to execute the federal acts ought to appoint all federal officers not otherwise provided for, and to direct all military operations; provided that none of the persons composing the federal Executive shall on any occasion take command of any troops so as personally to conduct any enterprise as General or in other capacity.

5. Resolved that a federal Judiciary be established to consist of a supreme tribunal the Judges of which to be appointed by the Executive, and to hold their offices during good behaviour, to receive punctually at stated times a fixed compensation for their services in which no increase or diminution shall be made so as to affect persons actually in office at the time of such increase or diminution; that the Judiciary so established shall have authority to hear and determine in the first instance on all impeachments of federal officers, and by way of appeal in the dernier resort in all cases touching the rights of Ambassadors, in all cases of captures from an enemy, in all cases of piracies and felonies on the high Seas, in all cases in which foreigners may be interested, in the construction of any treaty or treaties, or which may arise on any of the Acts for regulation of trade, or the collection of the federal Revenue: that none of the Judiciary shall during the time they remain in office be capable of receiving or holding any other office or appointment during the time of service, or for thereafter.

6. Resolved that all Acts of the United States in Congress made by virtue and in pursuance of the powers hereby and by the articles of Confederation vested in them, and all Treaties made and ratified under the authority of the United States, shall be the supreme law of the respective States so far forth as those Acts or Treaties shall relate to the said States or their Citizens, and that the Judiciary of the several States shall be bound thereby in their decisions, any thing in the respective laws of the Individual States to the contrary notwithstanding; and that if any State, or any body of men in any State shall oppose or prevent carrying into execution such acts or treaties, the federal Executive shall be authorized to call forth the power of the Confederated States, or so much thereof as may be necessary to enforce and compel an obedience to such Acts or an observance of such Treaties.

7. Resolved that provision be made for the admission of new States into the Union.

8. Resolved the rule for naturalization ought to be the same in every State.

9. Resolved that a Citizen of one State committing an offence in another State of the Union, shall be deemed guilty of the same offence as if it had been committed by a Citizen of the State in which the offence was committed.

Source:
Henry Steele Commager, ed. *Documents of American History*. New York: F.S. Crofts & Co., 1934.

Great Compromise of 1787
THURSDAY JULY 5TH. IN CONVENTION
Mr. Gerry delivered in from the Committee appointed on Monday last the following Report.

"The Committee to whom was referred the 8th. Resol. of the Report from the Committee of the whole House, and so much of the 7th. as has not been decided on, submit the following Report: That the subsequent propositions be recommended to the Convention on condition that both shall be generally adopted. I. that in the 1st. branch of the Legislature each of the States now in the Union shall be allowed 1 member for every 40,000 inhabitants of the description reported in the 7th. Resolution of the Come. of the whole House: that each State not containing that number shall be allowed 1 member: that all bills for raising or appropriating money, and for fixing the Salaries of the officers of the Governt. of the U. States shall originate in the 1st. branch of the Legislature, and shall not be altered or amended by the 2d. branch: and that no money shall be drawn from the public Treasury. but in pursuance of appropriations to be originated in the 1st. branch II. that in the 2d. branch each State shall have an equal vote."

Mr. Ghorum observed that as the report consisted of proportions mutually conditional he wished to hear some explanations touching the grounds on which the conditions were estimated.

Mr. Gerry. The Committee were of different opinions as well as the Deputations from which the Come. were taken, and agree to the Report merely in order that some ground of accommodation might be proposed. Those opposed to the equality of votes have only assented conditionally; and if the other side do not generally agree will not be under any obligation to support the Report.

Mr. Wilson thought the Committee had exceeded their powers.

Mr. Martin was for taking the question on the whole report.

Mr. Wilson was for a division of the question: otherwise it wd. be a leap in the dark.

Mr. Madison. could not regard the exclusive privilege of originating money bills as any concession on the side of the small States. Experience proved that it had no effect. If seven States in the upper branch wished a bill to be originated, they might surely find some member from some of the same States in the lower branch who would originate it. The restriction as to amendments was of as little consequence. Amendments could be handed privately by the Senate to members in the other house. Bills could be navigated that they might be sent up in the desired shape. If the Senate should yield to the obstinacy of the 1st. branch the use of that body as a check would be lost. If the 1st. branch should yield to that of the Senate, the privilege would be nugatory. Experience had also shewn both in G. B. and the States having a similar regulation that it was a source of frequent & obstinate altercations. These considerations had produced a rejection of a like motion on a former occasion when judged by its own merits. It could not therefore be deemed any concession on the present, and left in force all the objections which had prevailed

agst. allowing each State an equal voice. He conceived that the Convention was reduced to the alternative of either departing from justice in order to conciliate the smaller States, and the minority of the people of the U.S. or of displeasing these by justly gratifying the larger States and the majority of the people. He could not himself hesitate as to the option he ought to make. The Convention with justice & the majority of the people on their side, had nothing to fear. With injustice and the minority on their side they had every thing to fear. It was in vain to purchase concord in the Convention on terms which would perpetuate discord among their Constituents. The Convention ought to pursue a plan which would bear the test of examination, which would be espoused & supported by the enlightened and impartial part of America, & which they could themselves vindicate and urge. It should be considered that altho' at first many may judge of the system recommended, by their opinion of the Convention, yet finally all will judge of the Convention by the System. The merits of the System alone can finally & effectually obtain the public suffrage. He was not apprehensive that the people of the small States would obstinately refuse to accede to a Govt. founded on just principles, and promising them substantial protection. He could not suspect that Delaware would brave the consequences of seeking her fortunes apart from the other States, rather than submit to such a Govt. much less could he suspect that she would pursue the rash policy of courting foreign support, which the warmth of one of her representatives [Mr. Bedford] had suggested, or if she shd. that any foreign nation wd. be so rash as to hearken to the overture. As little could he suspect that the people of N. Jersey notwithstanding the decided tone of the gentlemen from that State, would choose rather to stand on their own legs, and bid defiance to events, than to acquiesce under an establishment founded on principles the justice of which they could not dispute, and absolutely necessary to redeem them from the exactions levied on them by the commerce of the neighbouring States. A review of other States would prove that there was as little reason to apprehend an inflexible opposition elsewhere. Harmony in the Convention was no doubt much to be desired. Satisfaction to all the States, in the first instance still more so. But if the principal States comprehending a majority of the people of the U.S. should concur in a just & judicious plan, he had the firmest hopes, that all the other States would by degrees accede to it.

Mr. Butler said he could not let down his idea of the people, of America so far as to believe they would from mere respect to the Convention adopt a plan evidently unjust. He did not consider the privilege concerning money bills as of any consequence. He urged that the 2d. branch ought to represent the States according to their property.

Mr. Govr. Morris. thought the form as well as the matter of the Report objectionable. It seemed in the first place to render amendments impracticable. In the next place, it seemed to involve a pledge to agree to the 2d. part if the 1st. shd. be agreed to. He conceived the whole aspect of it to be wrong. He came here as a Representative of America; he flattered himself he came here in some degree as a Representative of the whole human race; for the whole human race will be affected by the proceedings of this Convention. He wished gentlemen to extend their views beyond the present moment of time; beyond the narrow limits of place from which they derive their political origin. It he were to believe some things which he had heard, he should suppose that we were assembled to truck and bargain for our particular States. He can-not descend to think that any gentlemen are really actuated by these views. We must look forward to the effects of what we do. These alone ought to guide us. Much has been said of the sentiments of the people. They were unknown. They could not be known. All that we can infer is that if the plan we recommend be reasonable & right; all who have reasonable minds and sound intentions will embrace it, notwithstanding what had been said by some gentlemen. Let us suppose that the larger States shall agree; and that the smaller refuse: and let us trace the consequences. The opponents of the system in the smaller States will no doubt make a party, and a noise for a time, but the ties of interest, of kindred & of common habits which connect them with the other States will be too strong to be easily broken. In N. Jersey particularly he was sure a great many would follow the sentiments of Pena. & N. York. This Country must be united. If persuasion does not unite it, the sword will. He begged that this consideration might have its due weight. The scenes of horror attending civil commotion can not be described, and the conclusion of them will be worse than the term of their continuance. The stronger party will then make traytors of the weaker; and the Gallows & Halter will finish the work of the sword. How far foreign powers would be ready to take part in the confusions he would not say. Threats that they will be invited have it seems been thrown out. He drew the melancholy picture of foreign intrusions as exhibited in the History of Germany, & urged it as a standing lesson to other nations. He trusted that the Gentlemen who may have hazarded such expressions, did not entertain them till they reached their own lips. But returning to the Report he could not think it in any respect calculated for the public good. As the 2d. branch is now constituted, there will be constant disputes & appeals to the States which will undermine the Genl. Government & controul & annihilate the 1st. branch. Suppose that the delegates from Massts. & Rho I. in the Upper House disagree, and that the former are outvoted. What Results? they will immediately declare that their State will not abide by the decision, and make such representations as will produce that effect. The same may happen as to Virga. & other States. Of what avail then will be what is on paper. State attachments, and State importance have been the bane of this Country. We can not annihilate; but we may perhaps take out the teeth of the serpents. He wished our ideas to be enlarged to the true interest of man, instead of being circumscribed within the narrow compass of a particular Spot. And after all how little can be the motive yielded by selfishness for such a policy. Who can say whether he himself, much less whether his children, will the next year be an inhabitant of this or that State.

Mr. Bedford. He found that what he had said as to the small States being taken by the hand, had been misunderstood; and he rose to explain. He did not mean that the small States would court the aid & interposition of foreign powers. He meant that they would not consider the federal compact as dissolved untill it should be so by the Acts of the large States. In this case The consequence of the breach of faith on their part, and the readiness of the small States to fulfill their engagements, would be that foreign Nations having demands on this Country would find it their interest to take the small States by the hand, in order to do themselves justice. This was what he meant. But no man can foresee to what extremities the small States may be driven by oppression. He observed also in apology that some allowance ought to be made for the habits of his profession in which warmth was natural & sometimes necessary. But is there not an apology in what was said by [Mr. Govr. Morris] that the sword is to unite; by Mr. Ghorum that Delaware must be annexed to Penna. and N. Jersey divided between Pena. N. York. To hear such language without emotion, would be to renounce the feelings of a man and the duty of a Citizen—As to the propositions of the Committee, the lesser States have thought it necessary to have a security somewhere. This has been thought necessary for the Executive Magistrate of the proposed Govt. who has a sort of negative on the laws; and is it not of more importance that the State should be protected, than that the Executive branch of the Govt. shd. be protected. In order to obtain this, the smaller States have conceded as to the constitution of the first branch, and as to money bills. If they be not gratified by correspondent concessions as to the 2d. branch is it to be supposed they will ever accede to the plan; and what will be the consequence if nothing should be done! The condition of the U. States requires that something should be immediately done. It will be better that a defective plan should be adopted, than that none should be recommended. He saw no reason why defects might not be supplied by meetings 10, 15, or 20 years, hence.

Mr. Elseworth said he had not attended the proceedings of the Committee, but was ready to accede to the compromise they had reported. Some compromise was necessary; and he saw none more convenient or reasonable.

Mr. Williamson hoped that the expressions of individuals would not be taken for the sense of their colleagues, much less of their States which was not & could not be known. He hoped also that the meaning of those expressions would not be misconstrued or exaggerated. He did not conceive that [Mr. Govr. Morris] meant that the sword ought to be drawn agst. the smaller States. He only pointed out the probable consequences of anarchy in the U.S. A similar exposition ought to be given of the expressions [of Mr. Ghorum]. He was ready to hear the Report discussed; but thought the propositions contained in it, the most objectionable of any he had yet heard.

Mr. Patterson said that he had when the Report was agreed to in the Come. reserved to himself the right of freely discussing it. He acknowledged that the warmth complained of was improper; but he thought the Sword & the Gallows as little calculated to produce conviction. He complained of the manner in which Mr. M—& Mr. Govr. Morris had treated the small States.

Mr. Gerry. Tho' he had assented to the Report in the Committee, he had very material objections to it. We were however in a peculiar situation. We were neither the same Nation or different Nations. We ought not therefore to pursue the one or the other of these ideas too closely. If no compromise should take place what will be the consequence. A secession he foresaw would take place; for some gentlemen seem decided on it; two different plans will be proposed; and the result no man could foresee. If we do not come to some agreement among ourselves some foreign sword will probably do the work for us.

Mr. Mason. The Report was meant not as specific propositions to be adopted; but merely as a general ground of accommodation. There must be some accommodation on this point, or we shall make little further progress in the work. Accommodation was the object of the House in the appointment of the Committee; and of the Committee in the Report they had made. And however liable the Report might be to objections, he thought it preferable to an appeal to the world by the different sides, as had been talked of by some Gentlemen. It could not be more inconvenient to any gentlemen to remain absent from his private affairs, than it was for him: but he would bury his bones in this City rather than expose his Country to the Consequences of a dissolution of the Convention without any thing being done.

The 1st. proposition in the report for fixing the representation in the 1st. branch, one member for every 40,000 inhabitants, being taken up.

Mr. Govr. Morris objected to that scale of apportionment. He thought property ought to be taken into the estimate as well as the number of inhabitants. Life & liberty were generally said to be of more value, than property. An accurate view of the matter would nevertheless prove that property was the main object of Society. The savage State was more favorable to liberty than the Civilized; and sufficiently so to life. It was preferred by all men who had not acquired a taste for property; it was only renounced for the sake of property which could only be secured by the restraints of regular Government. These ideas might appear to some new, but they were nevertheless just. If property then was the main object of Govt. certainly it ought to be one measure of the influence due to those who were to be affected by the Governmt. He looked forward also to that range of New States which wd. soon be formed in the West. He thought the rule of representation ought to be so fixed as to secure to the Atlantic States a prevalence in the National Councils. The new States will know less of the public interest than these, will have an interest in many respects different, in particular will be little scrupulous of involving the Community in wars the burdens & operations of which would fall chiefly on the maritime States. Provision ought therefore to be made to prevent the maritime States from being hereafter outvoted by them. He thought this might be easily done by irrevocably fixing the number of representatives which the Atlantic States should respectively have, and the number which each new State will have. This wd. not be unjust, as the Western settlers wd. previously know the conditions on which they were to possess their lands. It would be politic as it would recommend the plan to the present as well as future interest of the States which must decide the face of it.

Mr. Rutlidge. The gentleman last up had spoken some of his sentiments precisely. Property was certainly the principal object of Society. If numbers should be made the rule of representation, the Atlantic States will be subjected to the Western. He moved that the first proposition in the report be postponed in order to take up the following viz "that the suffrages of the several States be regulated and proportioned according to the sums to be paid towards the general revenue by the inhabitants of each State respectively. that an apportionment of suffrages, according to the ratio aforesaid shall be made and regulated at the end of years from the 1st. meeting of the Legislature of the U.S. and at the end of every years but that for the present, and until the period above mentioned, the suffrages shall be for N. Hampshire Massachts. &c.—

Col. Mason said the case of new States was not unnoticed in the Committee; but it was thought and he was himself decidedly of opinion that if they made a part of the Union, they ought to be subject to no unfavorable discriminations. Obvious considerations required it.

Mr. Radolph concurred with Col. Mason.

On Question on Mr. Rutlidges motion.

Masts. no. Cost. no. N.Y. no. N.J. no. Pa. no. Del. no. Maryd. no. Va. no. N.C. no. S.C. ay. Geo. not on floor.
Adjd.

FRIDAY JULY 6TH. IN CONVENTION

Mr. Govr. Morris moved to commit so much of the Report as relates to "1 member for every 40,00 inhabitants" His view was that they might absolutely fix the number for each State in the first instance; leaving the Legislature at liberty to provide for changes in the relative importance of the States, and for the case of new States.

Mr. Wilson 2ded. the motion; but with a view of leaving the Committee under no implied shackles.

Mr. Ghorum apprehended great inconveniency from fixing directly the number of Representatives to be allowed to each State. He thought the number of Inhabitants the true guide; tho' perhaps some departure might be expedient from the full proportion. The State also would vary in their relative extent by separations of parts of the largest States. A part of Virga. is now on the point of a separation. In the province of Mayne a Convention is at this time deliberating on a separation from Masts. In such events the number of representatives ought certainly to be reduced. He hoped to see all the States made small by proper divisions, instead of their becoming formidable as was apprehended, to the Small States. He conceived that let the Genl. Government be modified as it might, there would be a constant tendency in the State Governments. to encroach upon it: it was of importance therefore that the extent of the States shd. be reduced as much & as fast as possible. The stronger the Govt. shall be made in the first instance the more easily will these divisions be effected; as it will be of less consequence in the opinion of the States whether they be of great or small extent.

Mr. Gerry did not think with his Colleague that the large States ought to be cut up. This policy has been inculcated by the middling and smaller States, ungenerously & contrary to the spirit of the Confederation. Ambitious men will be apt to solicit needless divisions, till the States be reduced to the size of Counties. If this policy should still actuate the small States, the large ones cou'd not confederate safely with them; but would be obliged to consult their safety by confederating only with one another. He favored the Commitment and thought that Representation ought to be in the Combined ratio of numbers of Inhabitants and of wealth, and not of either singly.

Mr. King wished the clause to be committed chiefly in order to detach it from the Report with which it had no connection. He thought also that the Ratio of Representation proposed could not be safely fixed, since in a century & a half our computed increase of population would carry the number of representatives to an enormous excess; that

ye. number of inhabitants was not the proper index of ability & wealth; that property was the primary object of Society; and that in fixing a ratio this ought not to be excluded from the estimate. With regard to new States, he observed that there was something peculiar in the business which had not been noticed. The U.S. were now admitted to be proprietors of the Country N. West of the Ohio. Congs. by one of their ordinances have impoliticly laid it out into ten States, and have made it a fundamental article of compact with those who may become settlers, that as soon as the number in any one State shall equal that of the smallest of the 13 original States, it may claim admission into the union. Delaware does not contain it is computed more than 35,000 souls, and for obvious reasons will not increase much for a considerable time. It is possible then that if this plan be persisted in by Congs. 10 new votes may be added, without a greater addition of inhabitants than are represented by the single vote of Pena. The plan as it respects one of the new States is already irrevocable, the sale of the lands having commenced, and the purchasers & settlers will immediately become entitled to all the privileges of the compact.

Mr. Butler agreed to the Commitment if the Committee were to be left at liberty. He was persuaded that the more the subject was examined, the less it would appear that the number of inhabitants would be a proper rule of proportion. If there were no other objection the changeableness of the standard would be sufficient. He concurred with those who thought some balance was necessary between the old & new States. He contended strenuously that property was the only just measure of representation. This was the great object of Governt: the great cause of war; the great means of carrying it on.

Mr. Pinkney saw no good reason for committing. The value of land had been found on full investigation to be an impracticable rule. The contributions of revenue including imports & exports, must be too changeable in their amount; too difficult to be adjusted; and too injurious to the non- commercial States. The number of inhabitants appeared to him the only just & practicable rule. He thought the blacks ought to stand on an equality with whites: But wd. agree to the ratio settled by Congs. He contended that Congs. had not right under the articles of Confederation to authorize the admission of new States; no such case having been provided for.

Mr. Davy, was for committing the clause in order to get at the merits of the question arising on the Report. He seemed to think that wealth or property ought to be represented in the 2d. branch; and numbers in the 1st. branch.

On the Motion for committing as made by Mr. Govr. Morris.

Masts. ay. Cont. ay. N.Y. no. N.J. no. Pa. ay. Del. no. Md. divd. Va. ay. N.C. ay. S.C. ay. Geo. ay.

The members appd. by Ballot were Mr. Govr. Morris, Mr. Gorham, Mr. Randolph, Mr. Rutlidge, Mr. King.

Mr. Wilson signified that his view in agreeing to the commitmt. was that the Come. might consider the propriety of adopting a scale similar to that established by the Constitution of Masts. which wd. give an advantage to ye. small States without substantially departing from a rule of proportion.

Mr. Wilson & Mr. Mason moved to postpone the clause relating to money bills in order to take up the clause relating to an equality of votes in the second branch.

On the question Masts. no. Cont. no. N.Y. ay. N.J. ay. Pa. ay. Del. ay. Md. ay. Va. ay. N.C. no. S.C. ay. Geo. ay.

The clause relating to equality of votes being under consideration,

Docr. Franklin observed that this question could not be properly put by itself, the Committee having reported several propositions as mutual conditions of each other. He could not vote for it if separately taken, but should vote for the whole together.

Col. Mason perceived the difficulty & suggested a reference of the rest of the Report to ye' Committee just appointed, that the whole might be brought into one view.

Mr. Randolph disliked ye. reference to that Committee, as it consisted of members from States opposed to the wishes of the smaller States, and could not therefore be acceptable to the latter.

Mr. Martin & Mr. Jennifer moved to postpone the clause till the Come. last appointed should report.

Mr. Madison observed that if the uncommitted part of the Report was connected with the part just committed, it ought also to be committed; if not connected, it need not be postponed till report should be made.

On the question for postponing moved by Mr. Martin & Mr. Jennifer

Cont. N.J. Del. Md. Va. Geo., ay

Pa. N.C.S.C. no

Mas. N.Y. divided

The 1st. clause relating to the originating of money bills was then resumed.

Mr. Governr. Morris was opposed to a restriction of this right in either branch, considered merely in itself and as unconnected with the point of representation in the 2d. branch. It will disable the 2d. branch from proposing its own money plans, and giving the people an opportunity of judging by comparison of the merits of those proposed by the 1st. branch.

Mr. Wilson could see nothing like a concession here on the part of the smaller States. If both branches were to say yes or no, it was of little consequence which should say yes or no first, which last. If either was indiscriminately to

have the right of originating, the reverse of the Report, would he thought be most proper; since it was a maxim that the least numerous body was the fittest for deliberation; the most numerous for decision. He observed that this discrimination had been transcribed from the British into several American constitutions. But he was persuaded that on examination of the American experiments it would be found to be a trifle light as air. Nor could he ever discover the advantage of it in the Parliamentary history of G. Britain. He hoped if there was any advantage in the privilege, that it would be pointed out.

Mr. Williamson thought that if the privilege were not common to both branches it ought rather to be confined to the 2d. as the bills in that case would be more narrowly watched, than if they originated with the branch having most of the popular confidence.

Mr. Mason. The consideration which weighed with the Committee was that the 1st. branch would be the immediate representatives of the people, the 2d. would not. Should the latter have the power of giving away the people's money, they might soon forget the source from whence they received it. We might soon have an aristocracy. He had been much concerned at the principles which had been advanced by some gentlemen, but had the satisfaction to find they did not generally prevail. He was a friend to proportional representation in both branches; but supposed that some points must be yielded for the sake of accommodation.

Mr. Wilson. If he had proposed that the 2d. branch should have an independent disposal of public money, the observations of [Col Mason] would have been a satisfactory answer. But nothing could be farther from what he had said. His question was how is the power of the 1st. branch increased or that of the 2d. diminished by giving the proposed privilege to the former? Where is the difference, in which branch it begins if both must concur, in the end?

Mr. Gerry would not say that the concession was a sufficient one on the part of the small States. But he could not but regard it in the light of a concession. It wd. make it a constitutional principle that the 2d branch were not possessed of the Confidence of the people in money matters, which 2d. lessen their weight & influence. In the next place if the 2d. branch were dispossessed of the privilege, they wd. be deprived of the opportunity which their continuance in office 3 times as long as the 1st. branch would give them of making three successive essays in favor of a particular point.

Mr. Pinkney thought it evident that the Concession was wholly on one side, that of the large States, the privilege of originating money bills being of no account.

Mr. Govr. Morris had waited to hear the good effects of the restriction. As to the alarm sounded, of an aristocracy, his creed was that there never was, nor ever will be a civilized Society without an aristocracy. His endeavor was to keep it as much as possible from doing mischief. The restriction if it has any real operation will deprive us of the services of the 2d. branch in digesting & proposing money bills of which it will be more capable than the 1st. branch. It will take away the responsibility of the 2d. branch, the great security for good behavior. It will always leave a plea, as to an obnoxious money bill that it was disliked, but could not be constitutionally amended; nor safely rejected. It will be a dangerous source of disputes between the two Houses. We should either take the British Constitution altogether or make one for ourselves. The Executive there has dissolved two Houses as the only cure for such disputes. Will our Executive be able to apply such a remedy? Every law directly or indirectly take money out of the pockets of the people. Again What use may be made of such a privilege in case of great emergency? Suppose an Enemy at the door, and money instantly & absolutely necessary for repelling him, may not the popular branch avail itself of this duress, to extort concessions from the Senate destructive of the Constitution itself. He illustrated this danger by the example of the Long Parliament's expedts. for subverting the H. of Lords; concluding on the whole that the restriction would be either useless or pernicious.

Docr. Franklin did not mean to go into a justification of the Report; but as it had been asked what would be the use of restraining the 2d. branch from medling with money bills, he could not but remark that it was always of importance that the people should know who had disposed of their money, & how it had been disposed of. It was a maxim that those who feel, can best judge. This end would, he thought, be best attained, if money affairs were to be confined to the immediate representatives of the people. This was his inducement to concur in the report. As to the danger or difficulty that might arise from a negative in the 2d. where the people wd. not be proportionally represented, it might easily be got over by declaring that there should be no such Negative: or if that will not do, by declaring that there shall be no such branch at all.

Mr. Martin said that it was understood in the Committee that the difficulties and disputes which had been apprehended, should be guarded agst. in the detailing of the plan.

Mr. Wilson. The difficulties & disputes will increase with the attempts to define & obviate them. Queen Anne was obliged to dissolve her Parliamt. in order to terminate one of these obstinate disputes between the two Houses. Had it not been for the mediation of the Crown, no one can say what the result would have been. The point is still *sub judice* in England. He approved of the principles laid down by the Hon'ble President [Docr. Franklin] his Colleague, as to the expediency of keeping the people informed of their money affairs. But thought they would know as much, and be as well satisfied, in one way as in the other.

Genl. Pinkney was astonished that this point should have been considered as a concession. He remarked that the restriction to money bills had been rejected on the merits singly considered, by 8 States agst. 3. and that the very States which now called it a concession, were then agst. it as nugatory or improper in itself.

On the Question whether the clause relating to money bills in the Report of the Come. consisting of a member from each State, shd. stand as part of the Report—

Massts. dividd. Cont. ay. N.Y. divd. N.J. ay. Pa. no. Del. ay. Md. ay. Va. no. N.C. ay. S.C. no. Geo. divd.

A Question was then raised whether the question was carried in the affirmative: there being but 5 ays out of II States present. The words of the rule are (see May 28).

On the question: Mas. Cont. N.J. Pa. Del. Md. N.C. S.C.

Geo. ay

N.Y.Va. no

[In several preceding instances like votes had *sub silentio* been entered as decided in the affirmative.]

Adjourned

SATURDAY, JULY 7TH. IN CONVENTION

"Shall the clause allowing each State one vote in the 2d. branch, stand as part of the Report"? being taken up—

Mr. Gerry. This is the critical question. He had rather agree to it than have no accommodation. A Governt. short of a proper national plan, if generally acceptable, would be preferable to a proper one which if it could be carried at all, would operate on discontented States. He thought it would be best to suspend the question till the Comme. yesterday appointed, should make report.

Mr. Sherman Supposed that it was the wish of every one that some Genl. Govt. should be established. An equal vote in the 2d. branch would, he thought, be most likely to give it the necessary vigor. The small States have more vigor in their Govts. than the large ones, the more influence therefore the large ones have, the weaker will be the Govt. In the large States it will be most difficult to collect the real & fair sense of the people. Fallacy & undue influence will be practiced with most success: and improper men will most easily get into office. If they vote by States in the 2d. branch, and each State has an equal vote, there must be always a majority of States as well as a majority of the people on the side of public measures, & the Govt. will have decision and efficacy. If this be not the case in the 2d. branch there may be a majority of the States agst. public measures, and the difficulty of compelling them to abide by the public determination, will render the Government feebler than it has ever yet been.

Mr. Wilson was not deficient in a conciliating temper, but firmness was sometimes a duty of higher obligation. Conciliation was also misapplied in this instance. It was pursued here rather among the Representatives, than among the Constituents; and it wd. be of little consequence, if not established among the latter; and there could be little hope of its being established among them if the foundation should not be laid in justice and right.

On Question shall the words stand as part of the Report?

Massts. divd. Cont. ay. N.Y. ay. N.J. ay. Pa. no. Del. ay. Md. ay. Va. no. N.C. ay. S.C. no. Geo. divd.

[Note: Several votes were given here in the affirmative or were divd. because another final question was to be taken on the whole report.]

Mr. Gerry thought it would be proper to proceed to enumerate & define the powers to be vested in the Genl. Govt. before a question on the report should be taken, as to the rule of representation in the 2d. branch.

Mr. Madison, observed that it wd. be impossible to say what powers could be safely & properly vested in the Govt. before it was known, in what manner the States were to be represented in it. He was apprehensive that if a just representation were not the basis of the Govt. it would happen, as it did when the Articles of Confederation were depending, that every effectual prerogative would be withdrawn or withheld, and the New Govt. wd. be rendered as impotent and as shortlived as the old.

Mr. Patterson would not decide whether the privilege concerning money bills were a valuable consideration or not: But he considered the mode & rule of representation in the 1st. branch as fully so. and that after the establishment of that point, the small States would never be able to defend themselves without an equality of votes in the 2d. branch. There was no other ground of accommodation. His resolution was fixt. He would meet the large States on that Ground and no other. For himself he should vote agst. the Report, because it yielded too much.

Mr. Govr. Morris. He had no resolution unalterably fixed except to do what should finally appear to him right. He was agst. the Report because it maintained the improper Constitution of the 2d. branch. It made it another Congress, a mere whisp of straw. It had been sd. (by Mr. Gerry] that the new Governt. would be partly national, partly federal; that it ought in the first quality to protect individuals; in the second, the States. But in what quality was it to protect the aggregate interest of the whole. Among the many provisions which has been urged, he had seen none for supporting the dignity and splendor of the American Empire. It had been one of our greatest misfortunes that the great objects of the nation had been sacrificed constantly to local views; in like manner as the general interests of States had been sacrificed to those of the Counties. What is to be the check in the Senate? none; unless it be to keep the majority of the people from injuring particular States. But particular States ought to be injured for the sake of a majority of the people, in case their conduct should deserve it. Suppose they should insist on claims evidently unjust, and pursue them in a manner detrimental to the whole body. Suppose they should give themselves up to foreign influence. Ought they to be protected in such cases. They were originally nothing more than colonial corporations. On the declaration of Independence, a Governmt. was to be formed. The small States aware of the necessity of preventing anarchy, and taking advantage of the moment, extorted from the large ones an equality of votes. Standing now on that ground, they demand under the new system greater rights as men, than their fellow Citizens of the large States. The proper answer to them is that the same necessity of which they formerly took advantage, does not now exist, and that the large States are at liberty now to consider what is right, rather than what may be expedient. We must have an efficient Govt. and if there be an efficiency in the local Govts. the former is impossible. Germany alone proves it. Notwithstanding their common diet, notwithstanding the great prerogatives of the Emperor as head of the Empire, and his vast resources, as sovereign of his particular dominions, no union is maintained: foreign influence disturbs every internal operation, & there is no energy whatever in the general Governmt. Whence does this proceed? From the energy of the local authorities; from its being considered of more consequence to support the Prince of Hesse, than the Happiness of the people of Germany. Do Gentlemen wish this to be ye case here. Good God, Sir, is it possible they can so delude themselves. What if all the Charters & Constitutions of the States were thrown into the fire, and all their demagogues into the ocean. What would it be to the happiness of America. And will not this be the case here if we pursue the train in wch. the business lies. We shall establish an Aulic Council without an Emperor to execute its decrees. The same circumstances which unite the people here, unite them in Germany. They have there a common language, a common law, common usages and manners, and a common interest in being united; yet their local jurisdictions destroy every tie. The case was the same in the Grecian States. The United Netherlands are at this time torn in factions. With these examples before our eyes shall we form establishments which must necessarily produce the same effects. It is of no consequence from what districts the 2d. branch shall be drawn, if it be so constituted as to yield an asylum agst. these evils. As it is now constituted he must be agst. its being drawn from the States in equal portions. But shall he was ready to join in devising such an amendment of the plan, as will be most likely to secure our liberty & happiness.

Mr. Sherman & Mr. Elseworth moved to postpone the Question on the Report from the Committee of a member from each State, in order to wait for the Report from the Come. of 5 last appointed.

Masts. ay. Cont. ay. N.Y. no. N.J. ay. Pa. ay. Del. ay. Maryland ay. Va. no. N.C. no. S.C. no. Geo. no.

Adjd.

MONDAY JULY 9TH. IN CONVENTION

Mr. Daniel Carroll from Maryland took his Seat.

Mr. Govr. Morris delivered a report from the Come. of 5 members to whom was committed the clause in the Report of the Come. consisting of a member from each State, stating the proper ratio of Representatives in the 1st. branch, to be as 1 to every 40,000 inhabitants, as follows viz

"The Committee to whom was referred the 1st. clause of the 1st. proposition reported from the grand Committee, beg leave to report

I. that in the 1st. meeting of the Legislature the 1st. branch thereof consist of 56. members of which Number, N. Hampshire shall have 2. Massts. 7. R.Id. 1. Cont 4. N.Y. 5. N.J. 3. Pa. 8. Del. 1. Md. 4. Va. 9. N.C. 5. S.C. 5. Geo. 2.—

II. But as the present situation of the States may probably alter as well in point of wealth as in the number of their inhabitants, that the Legislature be authorized from time to time to augment ye. number of Representatives. And in case any of the States shall hereafter be divided, or any two or more States united, or any new States created within the limits of the United States, the Legislature shall possess authority to regulate the number of Representatives in any of the foregoing cases, upon the principles of their wealth and number of inhabitants."

Mr. Sherman wished to know on what principles or calculations the Report was founded. It did not appear to correspond with any rule of numbers, or of any requisition hitherto adopted by Congs.

Mr. Gorham. Some provision of this sort was necessary in the outset. The number of blacks & whites with some regard to supposed wealth was the general guide Fractions could not be observed. The Legislre. is to make alterations from time to time as justice & propriety may require. Two objections prevailed agst. the rate of 1 member for every 40,000. inhts. The 1st. was that the Representation would soon be too numerous: the 2d. that the Westn. States who may have a different interest, might if admitted on that principle by degrees, outvote the Atlantic. Both these objections are removed. The number will be small in the first instance and may be continued so; and the Atlantic States having ye. Govt. in their own hands, may take care of their own interest, by dealing out the right

of Representation in safe proportions to the Western States. These were the views of the Committee.

See also THREE-FIFTHS COMPROMISE, 1787.

Source:

Notes of Debates in the Federal Convention of 1787 Reported by James Madison, Athens: Ohio University Press, 1966, pp. 237–257.

Three-fifths Compromise, 1787

Agreement reached at the Constitutional Convention of 1787 to resolve the dispute over apportioning direct taxes and representation in the House of Representatives, where representation is based on population. Northern states argued that slaves were property and should not be counted for apportionment purposes but should be counted for direct taxes. Southern states claimed that slaves should be counted for representation, but not for direct taxes. Under the terms of the compromise, spelled out in Article 1 of the U.S. Constitution, in addition to all free persons and "those bound to Service for a Term of Years, excluding Indians not taxed, three-fifths of all other Persons" would be counted for both representation and direct taxation. Noteworthy in the debate are the repeated assumptions that blacks were synonymous with slaves (although many free blacks lived in the United States) and were inferior to whites. Part of the lengthy discussion also centers around whether population is a legitimate basis for calculating wealth and the future role of western states (that is, those west of the original 13). Although use of direct taxes based on population passed the Constitutional Convention, they were never implemented, and other types of taxation were used to raise federal revenue. Also worth noting is the unchallenged comment by Pierce Butler of South Carolina that the government "was instituted principally for the protection of property, and was itself to be supported by property." Other participants in the excerpts below are William R. Davie, North Carolina; Oliver Ellsworth, Connecticut; Elbridge Gerry, Massacusetts; Nathaniel Gorham, Massachusetts; Samuel Johnson, Connecticut; Rufus King, Massachusetts; James Madison, Virginia; George Mason, Virginia; Gouveneur Morris, Pennsylvania; Charles Pinckney, South Carolina; General Charles Cotesworth Pinckney, South Carolina; Edmund Randolph, Virginia; John Rutledge, South Carolina; Roger Sherman, Connecticut; Hugh Williamson, North Carolina; and James Wilson, Pennsylvania. (Note: the spellings of names below are James Madison's; those in this introduction are correct.)

Although neither the debates nor the Constitution use the construction, this compromise is the origin of the charge that the New Nation declared a black to be "three-fifths of a man."

WEDNESDAY, JULY 11TH. IN CONVENTION

Mr. Butler & Gen. Pinkney, insisted that blacks be included in the rule of Representation, *equally*, with the Whites: and for that purpose moved that the words "three fifths" be struck out.

Mr. Gerry thought that 3/5 of them was to say the least the full proportion that could be admitted.

Mr. Ghorum. This ratio was fixed by Congs. as a rule of taxation. Then it was urged by the Delegates representing the States having slaves that the blacks were still more inferior to freemen. At present when the ratio of representation is to be established, we are assured that they are equal to freemen. The arguments on ye. former occasion had convinced him that 3/5 was pretty near the just proportion and he should vote according to the same opinion now.

Mr. Butler insisted that the labour of a slave in S. Carola. was as productive & valuable as that of a freeman in Massts., that as wealth was the great means of defence and utility to the Nation they were equally valuable to it with freemen; and that consequently an equal representation ought to be allowed for them in a Government which was instituted principally for the protection of property, and was itself to be supported by property.

Mr. Mason, could not agree to the motion, notwithstand it was favorable to Virga. because he though it unjust. It was certain that the slaves were valuable, as they raised the value of land, increased the exports & imports, and of course the revenue, would supply the means of feeding & supporting an army, and might in cases of emergency become themselves soldiers. As in these important respects they were useful to the community at large, they ought not to be excluded from the estimate of Representation. He could not however regard them as equal to freemen and could not vote for them as such. He added as worthy of remark, that the Southern States have this peculiar species of property, over & above the other species of property common to all the States.

Mr. Williamson reminded Mr. Ghorum that if the Southn. States contended for the inferiority of blacks to whites when taxation was in view, the Eastern States on the same occasion contended for their equality. He did not however either then or now, concur in either extreme, but approved of the ratio of 3/5.

On Mr. Butlers motion for considering blacks as equal to Whites in the apportionmt. of Representation.

Masts. no. Cont. no. [N.Y. not on floor.] N.J. no. Pa. no. Del. ay. Md. no. Va. no. N.C. no. S.C. ay. Geo. ay.

✻ ✻ ✻

Mr. Govr. Morris said he had several objections to the proposition of Mr. Williamson. 1. It fettered the Legislature too much. 2. it would exclude some States altogether who would not have a sufficient number to entitle them to a single Representative. 3. it will not consist with the Resolution passed on Saturday last authorising the Legislature to adjust the Representation from time to time on the principles of population & wealth or with the principles of equity. If slaves were to be considered as inhabitants, not as wealth, then the sd. Resolution would not be pursued: If as wealth, then why is no other wealth but slaves included? These objections may perhaps be removed by amendments. His great objection was that the number of inhabitants was not a proper standard of wealth. The amazing difference between the comparative numbers & wealth of different Countries, rendered all reasoning superfluous on the subject. Numbers might with greater propriety be deemed a measure of strength, than of wealth, yet the late defence made by G. Britain, ag.st her numerous enemies proved in the clearest manner, that it is entirely fallacious even in this respect.

Mr. King thought there was great force in the objections of Mr. Govr. Morris: he would however accede to the proposition for the sake of doing something.

Mr. Rutlidge contended for the admission of wealth in the estimate by which Representation should be regulated. The Western States will not be able to contribute in proportion to their numbers; they shd. not therefore be represented in that proportion. The Atlantic States will not concur in such a plan. He moved that "at the end of years after the 1st. meeting of the Legislature, and of every years thereafter, the Legislature shall proportion the Representation according to the principles of wealth & population."

✻ ✻ ✻

Mr. Govr. Morris. The argts. of others & his own reflections had led him to a very different conclusion. If we can't agree on a rule that will be just at this time, how can we expect to find one that will be just in all times to come. Surely those who come after us will judge better of things present, than we can of things future. He could not persuade himself that numbers would be a just rule at any time. The remarks of [Mr. Mason] relative to the Western Country had not changed his opinion on that head. Among other objections it must be apparent they would not be able to furnish men equally enlightened, to share in the administration of our common interests. The Busy haunts of men not the remote wilderness, was the proper school of political Talents. If the Western people get the power into their hands they will ruin the Atlantic interests. The Back members are always most averse to the best measures. He mentioned the case of Pena. formerly. The lower part of the State had ye. power in the first instance. They kept it in yr. own hands & the Country was ye. better for it. Another objection with him agst. admitting the blacks into the census, was that the people of Pena would revolt at the idea of being put on a footing with slaves. They would reject any plan that was to have such an effect. Two objections had been raised agst. leaving the adjustment of the Representation from time, to time, to the discretion of the Legislature. The 1. was they would be unwilling to revise it at all. The 2. that by referring to *wealth* they would be bound by a rule which if willing, they would be unable to execute. The 1st. objn. distrusts their fidelity. But if their duty, their honor & their oaths will not bind them, let us not put into their hands our liberty, and all our other great interests: let us have no Govt. at all. 2. If these ties will bind them, we need not distrust the practicability of the rule. It was followed in part by the Come. in the apportionment of Representatives yesterday reported to the House. The best course that could be taken would be to leave the interests of the people to the Representatives of the people.

✢   ✢   ✢

The next clause as to 3/5 of the negroes considered.

Mr. King. being much opposed to fixing numbers as the rule of representation, was particularly so on account of the blacks. He thought the admission of them along with Whites at all, would excite great discontents among the States having no slaves. He had never said as to any particular point that he would in no event acquiesce in & support it; but he wd. say that if in any case such a declaration was to be made by him, it would be in this. He remarked that in the temporary allotment of Representatives made by the Committee, the Southern States had received more than the number of their white & three fifths of their black inhabitants entitled them to.

Mr. Sherman. S. Carola. had not more beyond her proportion than N. York & N. Hampshire, nor either of them more than was necessary in order to avoid fractions or reducing them below their proportion. Georgia had more; but the rapid growth of that State seemed to justify it. In general the allotment might not be just, but considering all circumstances, he was satisfied with it.

Mr. Ghorum. supported the propriety of establishing numbers as the rule. He said that in Massts. estimates had been taken in the different towns, and that persons had been curious enough to compare these estimates with the respective numbers of people; and it had been found even including Boston, that the most exact proportion prevailed between numbers & property. He was aware that there might be some weight in what had fallen from his colleague, as to the umbrage which might be taken by the people of the Eastern States. But he recollected that when the proportion of Congs. for changing the 8th. art: of Con-

fedn. was before the Legislature of Massts. the only difficulty then was to satisfy them that the negroes ought not to have been counted equally with whites instead of being counted in the ratio of three fifths only.

Mr. Wilson did not well see on what principle the admission of blacks in the proportion of three fifths could be explained. Are they admitted as Citizens? then why are they not admitted on an equality with White Citizens? are they admitted as property? then why is not other property admitted into the computation? These were difficulties however which he thought must be overruled by the necessity of compromise. He had some apprehensions also from the tendency of the blending of the blacks with the whites, to give disgust to the people of Pena. as had been intimated by his Colleague [Mr. Govr. Morris]. But he differed from him in thinking numbers of inhabts. so incorrect a measure of wealth. He had seen the Western settlemts. of Pa. and on a comparison of them with the City of Philada. could discover little other difference, than that property was more unequally divided among individuals here than there. Taking the same number in the aggregate in the two situations he believed there would be little difference in their wealth and ability to contribute to the public wants.

Mr. Govr. Morris was compelled to declare himself reduced to the dilemma of doing injustice to the Southern States or to human nature, and he must therefore do it to the former. For he could never agree to give such encouragement to the slave trade as would be given by allowing them a representation for their negroes, and he did not believe those States would ever confederate on terms that would deprive them of that trade.

On Question for agreeing to include 3/5 of the blacks

Massts. no. Cont. ay. N.J. no. Pa. no. Del. no. Mard. no. Va. ay. N.C. ay. S.C. no. Geo. ay

Mr. Govr. Morris moved to add to the clause empowering the Legislature to vary the Representation according to the principles of wealth & number of inhabts. a "proviso that taxation shall be in proportion to Representation."

Mr. Butler contended again that Representation sd. be according to the full number of inhabts. including all the blacks; admitting the justice of Mr. Govr. Morris's motion.

Mr. Mason also admitted the justice of the principle, but was afraid embarrassments might be occasioned to the Legislature by it. It might drive the Legislature to the plan of Requisitions.

Mr. Govr. Morris, admitted that some objections lay agst. his motion, but supposed they would be removed by restraining the rule to *direct* taxation. With regard to indirect *exports* & imports & on consumption, the rule would be inapplicable. Notwithstanding what had been said to the contrary he was persuaded that the imports &

consumption were pretty nearly equal throughout the Union.

General Pinkney liked the idea. He thought it so just that it could not be objected to. But foresaw that if the revision of the census was left to the discretion of the Legislature, it would never be carried into execution. The rule must be fixed, and the execution of it enforced by the Constitution. He was alarmed at what was said yesterday, concerning the negroes. He was now again alarmed at what had been thrown out concerning the taxing of exports. S. Carola. has in one year exported to the amount of 600,000 pounds Sterling all which was the fruit of the labor of her blacks. Will she be represented in proportion to this amount? She will not. Neither ought she then to be subject to a tax on it. He hoped a clause would be inserted in the system, restraining, the Legislature from a taxing Exports.

Mr. Wilson approved the principle, but could not see how it could be carried into execution; unless restrained to direct taxation.

Mr. Govr. Morris having so varied his Motion by inserting the word "direct." It passd. nem. con. as follows—"provided the always that direct taxation ought to be proportioned to representation.

Mr. Davie, said it was high time now to speak out. He saw that it was meant by some gentlemen to deprive the Southern States of any share of Representation for their blacks. He was sure that No. Carola. would never confederate on any terms that did not rate them at least as 3/5. If the Eastern States meant therefore to exclude them altogether the business was at an end.

Dr. Johnson, thought that wealth and population were the true, equitable rule of representation; but he conceived that these two principles resolved themselves into one; population being the best measure of wealth. He concluded therefore that ye. number of people ought to be established as the rule, and that all descriptions including blacks *equally* with the whites, ought to fall within the computation. As various opinions had been expressed on the subject, he would move that a Committee might be appointed to take them into consideration and report thereon.

Mr. Govr. Morris. It has been said that it is high time to speak out, as one member, he would candidly do so. He came here to form a compact for the good America. He was ready to do so with all the States. He hoped & believed that all would enter into such a Compact. If they would not he was ready to join with any States that would. But as the Compact was to be voluntary, it is in vain for the Eastern States to insist on what the Southn. States will never agree to. It is equally vain for the latter to require what the other States can never admit; and he verily believed the people of Pena. will never agree to representation of Negroes. What can be desired by these States more than has been

already proposed; that the Legislature shall from time to time regulate Representation according to population & wealth.

Genl. Pinkney desired that the rule of wealth should be ascertained and not left to the pleasure of the Legislature; and that property in slaves should not be exposed to danger under a Govt. instituted for the protection of property. . . .

Mr. Elseworth. In order to carry into effect the principle established, moved to add to the last clause adopted by the House the words following "and that the rule of contribution by direct taxation for the support of the government of the U. States shall be the number of white inhabitants, and three fifths of every other description in the several States, until some other rule that shall more accurately ascertain the wealth of the several States can be devised and adopted by the Legislature."

Mr. Butler seconded the motion in order that it might be committed.

Mr. Randolph was not satisfied with the motion. The danger will be revived that the ingenuity of the Legislature may evade or pervert the rule so as to perpetuate the power where it shall be lodged in the first instance. He proposed in lieu of Mr. Elseworth's motion, "that in order to ascertain the alterations in Representation that may be required from time to time by changes in the relative circumstances of the States, a census shall be taken within two years from the 1st. meeting of the Genl. Legislature of the U.S., and once within the term of every year afterwards, of all the inhabitants in the manner & according to the ratio recommended by Congress in their resolution of the 18th day of Apl. 1783; [rating the blacks at 3/5 of their number] and, that the Legislature of the U.S. shall arrange the Representation accordingly."—He urged strenuously that express security ought to be provided for including slaves in the ratio of Representation. He lamented that such a species of property existed. But as it did exist the holders of it would require this security. It was perceived that the design was entertained by some of excluding slaves altogether; the Legislature therefore ought not to be left a liberty.

Mr. Elseworth withdraws his motion & seconds that of Mr. Randolph.

Mr. Wilson observed that less umbrage would perhaps be taken agst. an admission of the slaves into the Rule of representation, if it should be so expressed as to make them indirectly only an ingredient in the rule, by saying that they should enter into the rule of taxation: and as representation was to be according to taxation, the end would be equally attained. He accordingly moved & was 2ded. so to alter the last clause adopted by the House, that together with the amendment proposed the whole should read as follows—provided always that the representation ought to be proportioned according to direct taxation, and in order to ascertain the alterations in the direct taxation which may be required from time to time by the changes in the relative circumstances of the States. Resolved that a census be taken within two years from the first meeting of the Legislature of the U. States, and once within the term of every years afterwards of all the inhabitants of the U.S. in the manner and according to the ratio recommended by Congress in their Resolution of April 18. 1783; and that the legislature of the U.S. shall proportion the direct taxation accordingly.

Mr. King. Altho' this amendment varies the aspect somewhat, he had still two powerful objections agst. tying down the Legislature to the rule of numbers. 1. they were at this time an uncertain index of the relative wealth of the States. 2. if they were a just index at this time it can not be supposed always to continue so. He was far from wishing to retain any unjust advantage whatever in one part of the Republic. If justice was not the basis of the connection it could not be of long duration. He must be shortsighted indeed who does not foresee that whenever the Southern States shall be more numerous than the Northern, they can & will hold a language that will awe them into justice. If they threaten to separate now in case injury shall be done them, will their threats be less urgent or effectual, when force shall back their demands. Even in the intervening period, there will no point of time at which they will not be able to say, do us justice or we will separate. He urged the necessity of placing confidence to a certain degree in every Govt. and did not conceive that the proposed confidence as to a periodical readjustment, of the representation exceeded that degree.

Mr. Pinkney moved to amend Mr. Randolph's motion so as to make "blacks equal to the whites in the ratio of representation." This he urged was nothing more than justice. The blacks are the labourers, the peasants of the Southern States: they are as productive of pecuniary resources as those of the Northern States. They add equally to the wealth, and considering money as the sinew of war, to the strength of the nation. It will also be politic with regard to the Northern States, as taxation is to keep pace with Representation.

      ❋   ❋   ❋

Mr. Elseworth. In case of a poll tax there wd. be no difficulty. But there wd. probably be none. The sum allotted to a State may be levied without difficulty according to the plan used by the State in raising its own supplies. On the question on ye. whole proposition; as proportioning representation to direct taxation & both to the white & 3/5 of black inhabitants, & requiring a Census within six years— & within every ten years afterwards.

Mas. divd. Cont. ay. N.J. no. Pa. ay. Del. no. Md. ay. Va. ay. N.C. ay. S.C. divd. Geo. ay.

Source:
Notes of Debates in the Federal Convention of 1787 Reported by James Madison. Athens: Ohio University Press, 1966.

Northwest Ordinance of 1787

U.S. law, enacted by Congress on July 13, 1787, that provided for the organization and government of the Northwest Territory and laid out procedures for the admission of new states to the Union. It was based on and replaced the Land Ordinance of 1784 which established procedures for the survey and sale of the territories northwest of the Ohio River and for the admission of new states into the Union. The 1787 plan was written principally by Massachusetts jurist Nathan Dane. It stipulated that the Northwest Territory would initially be governed by a governor, secretary, and three judges, who would be appointed by Congress, and that a representative bicameral legislature was to be created when the colony included 5,000 adult free males. The territory could ultimately be divided into three to five states, and a population of 60,000 free inhabitants was necessary for statehood. Slavery was forbidden in the Northwest Territory (a provision that had failed to pass in 1784), and freedom of worship, trial by jury, and public support of education were guaranteed. The Northwest Ordinance is considered to be the most significant achievement of the Congress formed the Articles of Confederation.

An Ordinance for the government of the territory of the United States northwest of the river Ohio

Be it ordained by the United States in Congress assembled, that the said territory, for the purposes of temporary government, be one district, subject, however, to be divided into two districts, as future circumstances may, in the opinion of Congress, make it expedient.

Be it ordained by the authority aforesaid, that the estates, both of resident and non-resident proprietors in the said territory, dying intestate, shall descend to, and be distributed among their children, and the descendants of a deceased child, in equal parts; the descendants of a deceased child or grandchild to take the share of their deceased parent in equal parts among them: And where there shall be no children or descendants, then in equal parts to the next of kin in equal degree; and among collaterals, the children of a deceased brother or sister of the intestate shall have, in equal parts among them, their deceased parent's share; and there shall in no case be a distinction between kindred of the whole and half-blood;

saving, in all cases, to the widow of the intestate her third part of the real estate for life, and one-third part of the personal estate; and this law relative to descents and dower, shall remain in full force until altered by the legislature of the district. And until the governor and judges shall adopt laws as hereinafter mentioned, estates in the said territory may be devised or bequeathed by wills in writing, signed and sealed by him or her in whom the estate may be (being of full age), and attested by three witnesses; and real estates may be conveyed by lease and release, or bargain and sale, signed sealed and delivered by the person, being of full age, in whom the estate may be, and attested by two witnesses, provided such wills be duly proved, and such conveyances be acknowledged, or the execution thereof duly proved, and be recorded within one year after proper magistrates, courts, and registers shall be appointed for that purpose; and personal property may be transferred by delivery; saving, however to the French and Canadian inhabitants and other settlers of the Kaskaskies, St. Vincents and the neighboring villages, who have heretofore professed themselves citizens of Virginia, their laws and customs now in force among them relative to the descent and conveyance of property.

Be it ordained by the authority aforesaid, that there shall be appointed from time to time by Congress, a governor, whose commission shall continue in force for the term of three years, unless sooner revoked by Congress; he shall reside in the district, and have a freehold estate therein in 1,000 acres of land, while in the exercise of his office.

There shall be appointed from time to time by Congress, a secretary, whose commission shall continue in force for four years unless sooner revoked; he shall reside in the district, and have a freehold estate therein in 500 acres of land, while in the exercise of his office. It shall be his duty to keep and preserve the acts and laws passed by the legislature, and the public records of the district, and the proceedings of the governor in his executive department, and transmit authentic copies of such acts and proceedings, every six months, to the secretary of Congress: there shall also be appointed a court to consist of three judges, any two of whom to form a court, who shall have a common law jurisdiction, and reside in the district, and have each therein a freehold estate in 500 acres of land while in the exercise of their offices; and their commissions shall continue in force during good behavior.

The governor and judges, or a majority of them, shall adopt and publish in the district such laws of the original states, criminal and civil, as may be necessary and best suited to the circumstances of the district, and report them to Congress from time to time: which laws shall be in force in the district until the organization of the general assembly therein, unless disapproved of by Congress; but afterwards the legislature shall have authority to alter them as they shall think fit.

The governor, for the time being, shall be commander-in-chief of the militia, appoint and commission all officers in the same below the rank of general officers; all general officers shall be appointed and commissioned by Congress.

Previous to the organization of the general assembly, the governor shall appoint such magistrates and other civil officers in each county or township, as he shall find necessary for the preservation of the peace and good order in the same: after the general assembly shall be organized, the powers and duties of the magistrates and other civil officers shall be regulated and defined by the said assembly; but all magistrates and other civil officers not herein otherwise directed, shall, during the continuance of this temporary government, be appointed by the governor.

For the prevention of crimes and injuries, the laws to be adopted or made shall have force in all parts of the district, and for the execution of process, criminal and civil, the governor shall make divisions thereof; and he shall proceed from time to time as circumstances may require, to lay out the parts of the district in which the Indian titles shall have been extinguished, into counties and townships, subject however to such alterations as may thereafter be made by the legislature.

So soon as there shall be five thousand free male inhabitants of full age in the district, upon giving proof thereof to the governor, they shall receive authority, with time and place, to elect representatives from their counties or townships to represent them in the general assembly: provided, that, for every five hundred free male inhabitants, there shall be one representative, and so on progressively with the number of free male inhabitants shall the right of representation increase, until the number of representatives shall amount to twenty-five; after which, the number and proportion of representatives shall be regulated by legislature: provided, that no person be eligible or qualified to act as a representative unless he shall have been a citizen of one of the United States three years, and be a resident in the district, or unless he shall have resided in the district three years; and, in either case, shall likewise hold in his own right, in fee simple, two hundred acres of land within the same: provided, also, that a freehold in fifty acres of land in the district, having been a citizen of one of the states, and being resident in the district, or the like freehold and two years residence in the district, shall be necessary to qualify a man as an elector of a representative.

The representatives thus elected, shall serve for the term of two years; and, in case of death of a representative, or removal from office, the governor shall issue a writ to the county or township for which he was a member, to elect another in his stead, to serve for the residue of the term.

The general assembly or legislature shall consist of the governor, legislative council, and a house of representatives. The legislative council shall consist of five members, to continue in office five years, unless sooner removed by Congress; any three of whom to be a quorum: and the members of the council shall be nominated and appointed in the following manner, to wit: as soon as representatives shall be elected, the governor shall appoint a time and place for them to meet together; and, when met, they shall nominate ten persons, residents in the district, and each possessed of a freehold in five hundred acres of land, and return their names to Congress; five of whom Congress shall appoint and commission to serve as aforesaid; and, whenever a vacancy shall happen in the council, by death or removal from office, the house of representatives shall nominate two persons, qualified as aforesaid, for each vacancy, and return their names to Congress; one of whom Congress shall appoint and commission for the residue of the term. And every five years, four months at least before the expiration of the time of service of the members of the council, the said house shall nominate ten persons, qualified as aforesaid, and return their names to Congress; five of whom Congress shall appoint and commission to serve as members of the council five years, unless soon removed. And the governor, legislative council, and house of representatives, shall have authority to make laws in all cases, for the good government of the district, not repugnant to the principles and articles in this ordinance established and declared. And all bills, having passed by a majority in the house, and by a majority in the council, shall be referred to the governor for his assent; but no bill, or legislative act whatever, shall be of any force without his assent. The governor shall have power to convene, prorogue, and dissolve the general assembly, when, in his opinion, it shall be expedient.

The governor, judges, legislative council, secretary, and such other officers as Congress shall appoint in the district, shall take an oath or affirmation of fidelity and of office; the governor before the president of congress, and all other officers before the governor. As soon as a legislature shall be formed in the district, the council and house assembled in one room, shall have authority by joint ballot, to elect a delegate to Congress, who shall have a seat in Congress, with a right of debating but not of voting during this temporary government.

II

And, for extending the fundamental principles of civil and religious liberty, which form the basis whereon these republics, their laws and constitutions are erected; to fix and establish those principles as the basis of all laws, constitutions, and governments, which forever hereafter shall be formed in the said territory: to provide also for the establishment of states, and permanent government therein, and for their admission to a share in the federal councils on an equal footing with the original states, at as early periods as may be consistent with the general interest:

It is hereby ordained and declared by the authority aforesaid, that the following articles shall be considered as articles of compact between the original states and the people and states in the said territory and forever remain unalterable, unless by common consent, to wit:

Article 1

No person, demeaning himself in a peaceable and orderly manner, shall ever be molested on account of his mode of worship or religious sentiments, in the said territory.

Article 2

The inhabitants of the said territory shall always be entitled to the benefits of the writ of habeas corpus, and of the trial by jury; of a proportionate representation of the people in the legislature; and of judicial proceedings according to the course of the common law. All persons shall be bailable, unless for capital offences, where the proof shall be evident or the presumption great. All fines shall be moderate; and no cruel or unusual punishments shall be inflicted. No man shall be deprived of his liberty or property, but by the judgment of his peers or the law of the land; and, should the public exigencies make it necessary, for the common preservation, to take any person's property, or to demand his particular services, full compensation shall be made for the same. And, in the just preservation of rights and property, it is understood and declared, that no law ought ever to be made, or have force in the said territory, that shall, in any manner whatever, interfere with or affect private contracts or engagements, bona fide, and without fraud, previously formed.

Article 3

Religion, morality, and knowledge, being necessary to good government and the happiness of mankind, schools and the means of education shall forever be encouraged. The utmost good faith shall always be observed towards the Indians; their lands and property shall never be taken from them without their consent; and, in their property, rights, and liberty, they shall never be invaded or disturbed, unless in just and lawful wars authorized by Congress; but laws founded in justice and humanity, shall from time to time be made for preventing wrongs being done to them, and for preserving peace and friendship with them.

Article 4

The said territory, and the states which may be formed therein, shall forever remain a part of this Confederacy of the United States of America, subject to the Articles of Confederation, and to such alterations therein as shall be constitutionally made; and to all the acts and ordinances of the United States in Congress assembled, conformable thereto. The inhabitants and settlers in the said territory shall be subject to pay a part of the federal debts contracted or to be contracted, and a proportional part of the expenses of government, to be apportioned on them by Congress according to the same common rule and measure by which apportionments thereof shall be made on the other states; and the taxes for paying their proportion shall be laid and levied by the authority and direction of the legislatures of the district or districts, or new states, as in the original states, within the time agreed upon by the United States in Congress assembled. The legislatures of those districts or new states, shall never interfere with the primary disposal of the soil by the United States in Congress assembled, nor with any regulations Congress may find necessary for securing the title in such soil to the bona fide purchasers. No tax shall be imposed on lands the property of the United States; and, in no case, shall nonresident proprietors be taxed higher than residents. The navigable waters leading into the Mississippi and St. Lawrence, and the carrying places between the same, shall be common highways and forever free, as well to the inhabitants of the said territory as to the citizens of the United States, and those of any other states that may be admitted into the Confederacy, without any tax, impost, or duty therefor.

Article 5

There shall be formed in the said territory, not less than three nor more than five states; and the boundaries of the states, as soon as Virginia shall after her act of cession, and consent to the same, shall become fixed and established as follows, to wit: the western state in the said territory, shall be bounded by the Mississippi, the Ohio, and Wabash Rivers; a direct line drawn from the Wabash and Post Vincents, due north, to the territorial line between the United States and Canada; and, by the said territorial line, to the Lake of the Woods and Mississippi. The middle state shall be bounded by the said direct line, the Wabash from Post Vincents to the Ohio, by the Ohio, by a direct line, drawn due north from the mouth of the Great Miami, to the said territorial line, and by the said territorial line. The eastern state shall be bounded by the last mentioned direct line, the Ohio, Pennsylvania, and the said territorial line: provided, however, and it is further understood and declared, that the boundaries of these three states shall be subject so far to be altered, that, if Congress shall hereafter find it expedient, they shall have authority to form one or two states in that part of the said territory which lies north of an east and west line drawn through the southerly bend or extreme of Lake Michigan. And, whenever any of the said states shall have sixty thousand free inhabitants therein, such state shall be admitted, by its delegates, into the Congress of the United States, on an equal footing with the original states in all respects whatever, and shall be at liberty to form a permanent constitution and state government: provided, the constitution and government so to be formed, shall be republican, and in conformity to the principles contained in these articles; and, so far as it can be consistent with the general interest of the Confederacy, such admission shall be allowed at an earlier period, and when there may be a less number of free inhabitants in the state than sixty thousand.

Article 6

There shall be neither slavery nor involuntary servitude in the said territory, otherwise than in the punishment of crimes whereof the party shall have been duly convicted: provided, always, that any person escaping into the same, from whom labor or service is lawfully claimed in any one of the original states, such fugitive may be lawfully reclaimed and conveyed to the person claiming his or her labor or service as aforesaid.

Be it ordained by the authority aforesaid, that the resolutions of the 23rd of April 1784, relative to the subject of this ordinance, be, and the same are hereby repealed and declared null and void.

Source:

John Scott, ed. *Living Documents in American History.* Vol. 2 New York: Washington Square Press, 1964–68, pp. 615–621.

Constitution of the United States, 1787

Document embodying the fundamental laws and principles of the United States. Drafted by the Constitutional Convention in 1787 and ratified by the required nine states in 1788, the document replaced the Articles of Confederation and went into effect on March 4, 1789. Because the Articles of Confederation required unanimity for amendments, proponents of a new system decided to meet in secret and not disclose their deliberations. The new document called for ratification by only nine of the 13 states and changed the amendment procedure by requiring only two-thirds of the states.

The finished constitution was the result of a number of compromises. It consists of the preamble, seven articles, and 26 amendments (which were added later). The preamble itself was a compromise, originally saying, "We the People of," and listing all the states. The individual state names were eliminated, and ratification of the constitution was to be achieved through special ratifying conventions, rather than the state legislatures, signifying the preeminence the national government. The Tenth Amendment, however, ratified in 1791, protected state sovereignty: "The powers not delegated to the United States by the Constitution, nor prohibited by it to the States, are reserved to the States respectively, or to the people."

The first three articles of the Constitution define the three branches of government: the legislature, or Congress (consisting of the Senate and the House of Representatives); the executive, or president and vice president; and the judiciary, or Supreme Court, with provisions for Congress to establish lower federal courts. The fourth article outlines the relations between the various states and between the national government and the states. Article 5 sets the procedures for amending the Constitution. Article 6 defines the Constitution as the "supreme law of the land," binding on all federal and state officials. The final article provides for ratification of the Constitution.

Since John Marshall's time, the Supreme Court generally has been recognized as the final arbiter of constitutional interpretation. The Court's legitimacy, nevertheless, has been challenged on a number of occasions most notably after the Dred Scott decision (1857), a prelude to the Civil War.

While the Constitution was written by men of property, the most influential members of the Constitutional Convention set out not to protect their personal interests but to create "a more perfect union." A number of them actually died heavily in debt. The most unfortunate legacy of the convention were the compromises favoring slavery. Because many of the northern members were convinced that the Constitution would not be acceptable to southern convention delegates nor ratified by a sufficient number of states without those compromises, they put the interests of the Union ahead of the rights of African-Americans. However, it is legitimate to wonder if southern states in 1787 (before the invention of the cotton gin) might have capitulated if they otherwise would have been excluded from the Union. The Constitution does not guarantee equality of opportunity, and its most progressive possibilities are still challenged regularly. Women, for example, have not yet specifically achieved equality under it. Nevertheless, the United States Constitution produced the most enduring democratic government in world history, and with its post–Civil War amendments, it embodies the ideals of freedom and justice for all.

We the People of the United States, in order to form a more perfect Union, establish Justice, ensure domestic Tranquility, provide for the common defence, promote the general Welfare, and secure the Blessings of Liberty to ourselves and our Posterity, do ordain and establish this Constitution for the United States of America.

Article I

Section 1. All legislative powers herein granted shall be vested in a Congress of the United States, which shall consist of a Senate and House of Representatives.

Section 2. The House of Representatives shall be composed of members chosen every second year by the people of the several states, and the electors in each state shall have the qualifications requisite for electors of the most numerous branch of the state legislature.

No person shall be a representative who shall not have attained to the age of twenty-five years, and been seven years a citizen of the United States, and who shall not, when elected, be an inhabitant of that state in which he shall be chosen.

Representatives and direct taxes shall be apportioned among the several states which may be included within this union, according to their respective numbers, *[which shall be determined by adding to the whole number of free persons, including those bound to service for a term of years, and excluding Indians not taxed, three-fifths of all other persons.]* The actual enumeration shall be made within three years after the first meeting of the Congress of the United States, and within every subsequent term of ten years, in such manner as they shall by law direct. The number of representatives shall not exceed one for every 30,000, but each state shall have at least one representative; *[and until such enumeration shall be made, the state of New Hampshire shall be entitled to choose three, Massachusetts eight, Rhode Island and Providence Plantations one, Connecticut five, New York six, New Jersey four, Pennsylvania eight, Delaware one, Maryland six, Virginia ten, North Carolina five, South Carolina five, and Georgia three.]*

When vacancies happen in the representation from any state, the executive authority thereof shall issue writs of election to fill such vacancies.

The House of Representatives shall choose their speaker and other officers; and shall have the sole power of impeachment.

Section 3. The Senate of the United States shall be composed of two senators from each state, chosen *[by the legislature thereof,]* for six years, and each senator shall have one vote.

[Immediately after they shall be assembled in consequence of the first election, they shall be divided as equally as may be into three classes. The seats of the senators of the first class shall be vacated at the expiration of the second year, of the second class at the expiration of the fourth year, and of the third class at the expiration of the sixth year, so that one-third may be chosen every second

year; and if vacancies happen by resignation, or otherwise, during the recess of the legislature of any state, the executive thereof may make temporary appointments until the next meeting of the legislature, which shall then fill such vacancies.]

No person shall be a senator who shall not have attained to the age of 30 years, and been nine years a citizen of the United States, and who shall not, when elected, be an inhabitant of that state for which he shall be chosen.

The Vice-President of the United States shall be president of the Senate, but shall have no vote, unless they be equally divided.

The Senate shall choose their other officers, and also a president *pro tempore*, in the absence of the Vice-President, or when he shall exercise the office of President of the United States.

The Senate shall have the sole power to try all impeachments. When sitting for that purpose, they shall be on oath or affirmation. When the President of the United States is tried, the chief justice shall preside: And no person shall be convicted without the concurrence of two-thirds of the members present.

Judgment in cases of impeachment shall not extend further than to removal from office, and disqualification to hold and enjoy any office of honor, trust or profit under the United States; but the party convicted shall nevertheless be liable and subject to indictment, trial, judgment and punishment, according to law.

Section 4. The times, places and manner of holding elections for senators and representatives, shall be prescribed in each state by the legislature thereof: but the Congress may at any time by law make or alter such regulations, *[except as to the places of choosing senators.]*

The Congress shall assemble at least once in every year, *[and such meeting shall be on the first Monday in December, unless they shall by law appoint a different day.]*

Section 5. Each house shall be the judge of the elections, returns and qualifications of its own members, and a majority of each shall constitute a quorum to do business; but a small number may adjourn from day to day, and may be authorized to compel the attendance of absent members, in such manner, and under such penalties as each house may provide.

Each house may determine the rules of its proceedings, punish its members for disorderly behaviour, and, with the concurrence of two-thirds, expel a member.

Each house shall keep a journal of its proceedings, and from time to time publish the same, excepting such parts as may, in their judgment, require secrecy; and the yeas and nays of the members of either house on any question shall, at the desire of one-fifth of those present, be entered on the journal.

Neither house, during the session of Congress, shall, without the consent of the other, adjourn for more than three days, nor to any other place than that in which the two houses shall be sitting.

Section 6. The senators and representatives shall receive a compensation for their services, to be ascertained by law, and paid out of the Treasury of the United States. They shall in all cases, except treason felony and breach of the peace, be privileged from arrest during their attendance at the session of their respective houses, and in going to and returning from the same; and for any speech or debate in either house, they shall not be questioned in any other place.

No senator or representative shall, during the time for which he was elected, be appointed to any civil office under the authority of the United States, which shall have been created, or the emoluments whereof shall have been increased during such time; and no person holding any office under the United States, shall be a member of either house during his continuance in office.

Section 7. All bills for raising revenue shall originate in the House of Representatives; but the Senate may propose or concur with amendments as on other bills.

Every bill which shall have passed the House of Representatives and the Senate, shall before it become a law, be presented to the President of the United States; if he approve, he shall sign it, but if not, he shall return it, with his objections, to that house in which it shall have originated, who shall enter the objections at large on their journal, and proceed to reconsider it. If after such reconsideration, two-thirds of that house shall agree to pass the bill, it shall be sent, together with the objections, to the other house, by which it shall likewise be reconsidered, and if approved by two-thirds of that house, it shall become a law. But in all such cases the votes of both houses shall be determined by yeas and nays, and the names of the persons voting for and against the bill shall be entered on the journal of each house respectively. If any bill shall not be returned by the president within ten days (Sundays excepted), after it shall have been presented to him, the same shall be a law, in like manner as if he had signed it, unless the Congress by their adjournment prevent its return, in which case it shall not be a law.

Every order, resolution, or vote to which the concurrence of the Senate and House of Representatives may be necessary (except on a question of adjournment), shall be presented to the President of the United States; and before the same shall take effect, shall be approved by him, or, being disapproved by him, shall be re-passed by two-thirds of the Senate and House of Representatives, according to the rules and limitations prescribed in the case of a bill.

Section 8. The Congress shall have power:

To lay and collect taxes, duties, imposts and excises, to pay the debts and provide for the common defence and general welfare of the United States; but all duties, imposts and excises shall be uniform throughout the United States:

To borrow money on the credit of the United States:

To regulate commerce with foreign nations, and among the several states, and with the Indian tribes:

To establish an uniform rule of naturalization, and uniform laws on the subject of bankruptcies throughout the United States:

To coin money, regulate the value thereof, and of foreign coin, and fix the standard of weights and measures:

To provide for the punishment of counterfeiting the securities and current coin of the United States:

To establish post-offices and post-roads:

To promote the progress of science and useful arts, by securing for limited times to authors and inventors the exclusive right to their respective writings and discoveries:

To constitute tribunals inferior to the Supreme Court:

To define and punish piracies and felonies committed on the high seas, and offences against the law of nations:

To declare war, *[grant letters or marque and reprisal,]* and make rules concerning captures on land and water:

To raise and support armies, but no appropriation of money to that use shall be for a longer term than two years:

To provide and maintain a navy:

To make rules for the government and regulation of the land and naval forces:

To provide for calling forth the militia to execute the laws of the Union, suppress insurrections and repel invasions:

To provide for organizing, arming and disciplining the militia, and for governing such part of them as may be employed in the service of the United States, reserving to the states respectively, the appointment of the officers, and the authority of training the militia according to the discipline prescribed by Congress:

To exercise exclusive legislation in all cases whatsoever, over such district (not exceeding ten miles square) as may, by cession of particular states, and the acceptance of Congress, became the seat of the government of the United States, and to exercise like authority over all places purchased by the consent of the legislature of the state in which the same shall be, for the erection of forts, magazines, arsenals, dockyards, and other needful buildings: and,

To make all laws which shall be necessary and proper for carrying into execution the foregoing powers, and all other powers vested by this constitution in the government of the United States, or in any department or officer thereof.

Section 9. *[The migration or importation of such persons as any of the states now existing shall think proper to admit, shall not be prohibited by the Congress prior to the year 1808, but a tax or duty may be imposed on such importations, not exceeding ten dollars for each person.]*

The privilege of the writ of *habeas corpus* shall not be suspended, unless when in cases of rebellion or invasion the public safety may require it.

No bill of attainder or *ex post facto* law shall be passed.

No capitation, or other direct tax shall be laid unless in proportion to the *census* or enumeration herein before directed to be taken.

No tax or duty shall be laid on articles exported from any state.

No preference shall be given by any regulation of commerce or revenue to the ports of one state over those of another: nor shall vessels bound to, or from one state, be obliged to enter, clear, or pay duties in another.

No money shall be drawn from the Treasury but in consequence of appropriations made by law; and a regular statement and account of the receipts and expenditures of all public money shall be published from time to time.

No title of nobility shall be granted by the United States: and no person holding any office of profit or trust under them, shall, without the consent of the Congress, accept of any present, emolument, office, or title, of any kind whatever, from any king, prince or foreign state.

Section 10. No state shall enter into any treaty, alliance, or confederation; grant letters of marque and reprisal; coin money; emit bills of credit; make any thing but gold and silver coin a tender in payment of debts; pass any bill of attainder, *ex post facto* law, or law impairing the obligation of contracts, or grant any title of nobility.

No state shall, without the consent of the Congress, lay any imposts or duties on imports or exports, except what may be absolutely necessary for executing its inspection laws; and the net produce of all duties and imposts, laid by any state on imports and exports, shall be for the use of the Treasury of the United States; and all such laws shall be subject to the revision and control of the Congress.

No state shall, without the consent of Congress, lay any duty of tonnage, keep troops, or ships of war in time of peace, enter into any agreement or compact with another state, or with a foreign power, or engage in war, unless actually invaded, or in such imminent danger as will not admit of delay.

Article II
Section 1. The executive power shall be vested in a President of the United States of America. He shall hold his office during the term of four years, and, together with the

Vice-President, chosen for the same term, be elected as follows:

Each state shall appoint, in such manner as the legislature thereof may direct, a number of electors, equal to the whole number of senators and representatives to which the state may be entitled in the Congress; but no senator or representative, or person holding an office of trust or profit under the United States, shall be appointed an elector.

[The electors shall meet in their respective states, and vote by ballot for two persons, of whom one at least shall not be an inhabitant of the same state with themselves. And they shall make a list of all the persons voted for, and of the number of votes for each; which list they shall sign and certify, and transmit sealed to the seat of the government of the United States, directed to the president of the Senate. The president of the Senate shall, in the presence of the Senate and House of Representatives, open all the certificates and the votes shall then be counted. The person having the greatest number of votes shall be the President, if such number be a majority of the whole number of electors appointed; and if there be more than one who have such majority, and have an equal number of votes, then the House of Representatives shall immediately choose by ballot one of them for President; and if no person have a majority, then from the five highest on the list, the said House shall, in like manner, choose the President. But in choosing the President, the votes shall be taken by states, the representation from each state having one vote; a quorum for this purpose shall consist of a member or members from two-thirds of the states, and a majority of all the states shall be necessary to a choice. In every case, after the choice of the President, the person having the greatest number of votes of the electors shall be the Vice-President. But if there should remain two or more who have equal votes, the Senate shall choose from them by ballot the Vice-President.]

The Congress may determine the time of choosing the electors, and the day on which they shall give their votes; which day shall be the same throughout the United States.

No person except a natural born citizen, *[or a citizen of the United States, at the time of the adoption of this constitution]*, shall be eligible to the office of President; neither shall any person be eligible to that office, who shall not have attained to the age of thirty-five years, and been fourteen years a resident within the United States.

In case of the removal of the President from office, or of his death, resignation, or inability to discharge the powers and duties of the said office, the same shall devolve on the Vice-President, and the Congress may by law provide for the case of removal, death, resignation, or inability, both of the President and Vice-President, declaring what officer shall then act as President, and such officer shall act accordingly, until the disability be removed, or a President shall be elected.

The President shall, at stated times, receive for his services, a compensation, which shall neither be increased nor diminished during the period for which he shall have been elected, and he shall not receive within that period any other emolument from the United States, or any of them.

Before he enter on the execution of his office, he shall take the following oath or affirmation:

"I do solemnly swear (or affirm) that I will faithfully execute the office of President of the United States, and will to the best of my ability, preserve, protect and defend the Constitution of the United States."

Section 2. The President shall be commander-in-chief of the army and navy of the United States, and of the militia of the several states, when called into the actual service of the United States; he may require the opinion, in writing, of the principal officer in each of the executive departments, upon any subject relating to the duties of their respective offices, and he shall have power to grant reprieves and pardons for offences against the United States, except in cases of impeachment.

He shall have power, by and with the advice and consent of the Senate, to make treaties, provided two-thirds of the senators present concur; and he shall nominate, and by and with the advice and consent of the Senate, shall appoint ambassadors, other public ministers and consuls, judges of the Supreme Court, and all other officers of the United States, whose appointments are not herein otherwise provided for, and which shall be established by law. But the Congress may by law vest the appointment of such inferior officers, as they think proper in the President alone, in the courts of law, or in the heads of departments.

The President shall have power to fill up all vacancies that may happen during the recess of the Senate, by granting commissions, which shall expire at the end of their next session.

Section 3. He shall, from time to time, give to the Congress information of the state of the Union, and recommend to their consideration, such measures as he shall judge necessary and expedient; he may, on extraordinary occasions, convene both houses, or either of them, and in case of disagreement between them, with respect to the time of adjournment, he may adjourn them to such time as he shall think proper; he shall receive ambassadors and other public ministers; he shall take care that the laws be faithfully executed, and shall commission all the officers of the United States.

Section 4. The President, Vice-President, and all civil officers of the United States shall be removed from office on impeachment for, and conviction of, treason, bribery, or other high crimes and misdemeanors.

Article III

Section 1. The judicial power of the United States, shall be vested in one Supreme Court, and in such inferior courts as the Congress may, from time to time, ordain and establish. The judges, both of the Supreme and inferior courts, shall hold their offices during good behavior, and shall, at stated times, receive for their services a compensation, which shall not be diminished during their continuance in office.

Section 2. The judicial power shall extend to all cases, in law and equity, arising under this Constitution, the laws of the United States, and treaties made, or which shall be made under their authority; to all cases affecting ambassadors, other public ministers and consuls; to all cases of admiralty and maritime jurisdiction; to controversies to which the United States shall be a party: to controversies between two or more states, between a state and citizens of another state, between citizens of different states, between citizens of the same state, claiming lands under grants of different states, and between a state, or the citizens thereof, and foreign states, citizens or subjects.

In all cases affecting ambassadors, other public ministers and consuls, and those in which a state shall be party, the Supreme Court shall have original jurisdiction. In all the other cases before-mentioned, the Supreme Court shall have appellate jurisdiction, both as to law and fact, with such exceptions, and under such regulations as the Congress shall make.

The trial of all crimes, except in cases of impeachment, shall be by jury; and such trial shall be held in the state where the said crimes shall have been committed; but when not committed within any state, the trial shall be at such place or places as the Congress may by law have directed.

Section 3. Treason against the United States shall consist only in levying war against them, or in adhering to their enemies, giving them aid and comfort. No person shall be convicted of treason unless on the testimony of two witnesses to the same overt act, or on confession in open court.

The Congress shall have power to declare the punishment of treason, but no attainder of treason shall work corruption of blood, or forfeiture, except during the life of the person attainted.

Article IV

Section 1. Full faith and credit shall be given in each state to the public acts, records and judicial proceedings of every other state. And the Congress may by general laws prescribe the manner in which such acts, records and proceedings shall be proved, and the effect thereof.

Section 2. The citizens of each state shall be entitled to all privileges and immunities of citizens in the several states.

A person charged in any state with treason, felony, or other crime, who shall flee from justice, and be found in another state, shall, on demand of the executive authority of the state from which he fled, be delivered up, to be removed to the state having jurisdiction of the crime.

[No person held to service or labor in one state, under the laws thereof, escaping into another, shall, in consequence of any law or regulation therein, be discharged from such service or labour, but shall be delivered up on claim of the party to whom such service or labor may be due.] Section 3. New states may be admitted by the Congress into this Union; but no new state shall be formed or erected within the jurisdiction of any other state, nor any state be formed by the junction of two or more states, or parts of states, without the consent of the legislatures of the states concerned, as well as of the Congress.

The Congress shall have power to dispose of and make all needful rules and regulations respecting the territory or other property belonging to the United States; and nothing in this Constitution shall be so construed as to prejudice any claims of the United States, or of any particular state.

Section 4. The United States shall guarantee to every state in this Union, a republican form of government, and shall protect each of them against invasion; and on application of the legislature, or of the executive (when the legislature cannot be convened), against domestic violence.

Article V

The Congress, whenever two-thirds of both houses shall deem it necessary, shall propose amendments to this Constitution, or on the application of the legislatures of two-thirds of the several states, shall call a convention for proposing amendments, which, in either case, shall be valid to all intents and purposes, as part of this Constitution, when ratified by the legislatures of three-fourths of the several states, or by conventions in three-fourths thereof, as the one or the other mode of ratification may be proposed by the Congress: Provided, *[that no amendment which may be made prior to the year 1808, shall in any manner affect the first and fourth clauses in the ninth section of the first article; and]* that no state, without its consent, shall be deprived of its equal suffrage in the Senate.

Article VI

All debts contracted and engagements entered into, before the adoption of this Constitution, shall be as valid against the United States under this Constitution, as under the Confederation.

This Constitution, and the laws of the United States which shall be made in pursuance thereof; and all treaties made, or which shall be made, under the authority of the United States, shall be the supreme law of the land; and the judges in every state shall be bound thereby, any thing in the constitution or laws of any state to the contrary notwithstanding.

The senators and representatives before-mentioned, and the members of the several state legislatures, and all executive and judicial officers, both of the United States and of the several states, shall be bound by oath or affirmation, to support this Constitution; but no religious test shall ever be required as a qualification to any office or public trust under the United States.

Article VII

The ratification of the conventions of nine states, shall be sufficient for the establishment of this Constitution between the states so ratifying the same.

Done in convention, by the unanimous consent of the states present, the 17th day of September, in the year of our Lord 1787, and of the independence of the United States of America the 12th. In witness whereof we have hereunto subscribed our names.

> George Washington, President, And Deputy from Virginia.
> New Hampshire John Langdon, Nicholas Gilman.
> Massachusetts Nathaniel Gorham, Rufus King.
> Connecticut William Samuel Johnson, Roger Sherman.
> New York Alexander Hamilton
> William Livingston, New Jersey David Brearly, William Paterson, Jonathan Dayton.
> Benjamin Franklin, Thomas Mifflin, Robert Morris, Pennsylvania George Clymer, Thomas Fitzsimmons, Jared Ingersoll, James Wilson, Gouveneur Morris.
> George Read, Gunning Bedford, jun., Delaware John Dickinson, Richard Bassett, Jacob Broom.
> James McHenry, Maryland Daniel of St. Thomas Jenifer, Daniel Carroll.
> Virginia John Blair, James Madison, jun.

> William Blount, North Carolina Richard Dodds Spaight, Hugh Williamson.
> John Rutledge, South Carolina Charles Cotesworth Pinckney, Charles Pinckney, Pierce Butler.
> Georgia William Few, Abraham Baldwin.
> Attest: William Jackson, Secretary.

AMENDMENTS TO THE CONSTITUTION

Amendment I

Congress shall make no law respecting an establishment of religion, or prohibiting the free exercise thereof; or abridging the freedom of speech or of the press; or the right of the people peaceably to assembly, and to petition the government for a redress of grievances.

Amendment II

A well-regulated militia being necessary to the security of a free state, the right of the people to keep and bear arms shall not be infringed.

Amendment III

No soldier shall, in time of peace, be quartered in any house without the consent of the owner, nor in time of war but in a manner to be prescribed by law.

Amendment IV

The right of the people to be secure in their persons, houses, papers, and effects, against unreasonable searches and seizures, shall not be violated, and no warrants shall issue but upon probable cause, supported by oath or affirmation, and particularly describing the place to be searched, and the persons or things to be seized.

Amendment V

No person shall be held to answer for a capital or otherwise infamous crime unless on a presentment or indictment of a grand jury, except in cases arising in the land or naval forces, or in the militia, when in actual service, in time of war or public danger; nor shall any person be subject for the same offence to be twice put in jeopardy of life or limb; nor shall be compelled in any criminal case to be a witness against himself, nor be deprived of life, liberty, or property, without due process of law; nor shall private property be taken for public use without just compensation.

Amendment VI

In all criminal prosecutions, the accused shall enjoy the right to a speedy and public trial, by an impartial jury of the state and district wherein the crime shall have been committed, which district shall have been previously ascertained by law, and to be informed of the nature and cause of the accusation; to be confronted with the witnesses against him; to have compulsory process for obtaining witnesses in his favor, and to have the assistance of counsel for his defence.

Amendment VII

In suits at common law, where the value in controversy shall exceed twenty dollars, the right of trial by jury shall be preserved, and no fact tried by a jury shall be otherwise re-examined in any court of the United States than according to the rules of the common law.

Amendment VIII

Excessive bail shall not be required, nor excessive fines imposed, nor cruel and unusual punishments inflicted.

Amendment IX

The enumeration in the Constitution of certain rights shall not be construed to deny or disparage others retained by the people.

Amendment X

The powers not delegated to the United States by the Constitution, nor prohibited by it to the states, are reserved to the states respectively, or to the people.

[These 10 amendments, known as the Bill of Rights, were adopted at the first session of Congress and were declared to be in force on December 15, 1791.]

Source:
John Scott, ed., *Living Documents in American History.* New York: Washington Square Press, 1964–68.

Federalist Papers Numbers 10 and 78, 1787–1788

The *Federalist* Papers consist of 85 essays written to promote the ratification of the proposed constitution; they were published in New York papers in 1787 and 1788. Though all the essays were signed with the pseudonym *Publius,* the actual authors were Alexander Hamilton, who wrote most of the essays and emphasized economic issues; John Jay, who dealt with international relations; and James Madison, who discussed political theory. The essays consider the nature of republican government and promote the new federal system as an attempt to preserve state sovereignty and to protect individual liberty. Madison and Hamilton, the authors of the majority of these papers, played other major—even the most signifi-

cant—roles in establishing the Constitution and the framework of the federal government: Madison in the Constitutional Convention and first Congress, and Hamilton as President George Washington's most influential adviser. As a result, these documents are still used today to understand the government established by its founders. Moreover, the *Federalist* Papers are widely viewed as a classic work of political philosophy.

Federalist Number 10, written by Madison and published in the *New York Packet,* November 23, 1787, is probably the best known and most frequently cited of the Publius letters. It concerns the danger of "factions" (Madison did not anticipate the development of political parties) and outlines the advantages of a large republic—that is, a representative democracy—to check a faction from developing undue influence. *Federalist* Number 78 (which should be read in conjunction with *Federalist* Numbers 80 and Number 81) expands upon the role of the federal judiciary as expressed in Article 3 of the U.S. Constitution. Chief Justice John Marshall referred to it in his seminal *Marbury v. Madison* opinion. Hamilton wrote *Federalist* Number 78, and it was published in New York in 1788.

Federalist Number 10 (1787–1788)

Among the numerous advantages promised by a well-constructed Union, none deserves to be more accurately developed than its tendency to break and control the violence of faction. The friend of popular governments never finds himself so much alarmed for their character and fate as when he contemplates their propensity to this dangerous vice. He will not fail, therefore, to set a due value on any plan which, without violating the principles to which he is attached, provides a proper cure for it. The instability, injustice, and confusion introduced into the public councils, have, in truth, been the mortal diseases under which popular governments have everywhere perished; as they continue to be the favourite and fruitful topics from which the adversaries to liberty derive their most specious declamations. The valuable improvements made by the American constitutions on the popular models, both ancient and modern, cannot certainly be too much admired; but it would be an unwarrantable partiality, to contend that they have as effectually obviated the danger on this side, as was wished and expected. Complaints are everywhere heard from our most considerate and virtuous citizens, equally the friends of public and private faith, and of public and personal liberty, that our governments are too unstable, that the public good is disregarded in the conflicts of rival parties, and that measures are too often decided, not according to the rules of justice and the rights of the minor party, but by the superior force of an interested and overhearing majority. However anxiously we may wish that these complaints had no foundation, the evidence of known facts will not permit us to deny that they are in some degree true. It will be found, indeed, on a candid review of our situation, that some of the distresses under which we labour have been erroneously charged on the operation of our governments; but it will be found, at the same time, that other causes will not alone account for many of our heaviest misfortunes; and, particularly, for that prevailing and increasing distrust of public engagements, and alarm for private rights, which are echoed from one end of the continent to the other. These must be chiefly, if not wholly, effects of the unsteadiness and injustice with which a factious spirit has tainted our public administrations.

By a faction, I understand a number of citizens, whether amounting to a majority or minority of the whole, who are united and actuated by some common impulse of passion, or of interest, adverse to the rights of other citizens, or to the permanent and aggregate interests of the community.

There are two methods of curing the mischiefs of faction: the one, by removing its causes; the other, by controlling its effects.

There are again two methods of removing the causes of faction: the one, by destroying the liberty which is essential to its existence; the other, by giving to every citizen the same opinions, the same passions, and the same interests.

It could never be more truly said than of the first remedy, that it was worse than the disease. Liberty is to faction what air is to fire, an aliment without which it instantly expires. But it could not be less folly to abolish liberty, which is essential to political life, because it nourishes faction, than it would be to wish the annihilation of air, which is essential to animal life, because it imparts to fire its destructive agency. The second expedient is as impracticable as the first would be unwise. As long as the reason of man continues fallible, and he is at liberty to exercise it, different opinions will be formed. As long as the connection subsists between his reason and his self-love, his opinions and his passions will have a reciprocal influence on each other; and the former will be objects to which the latter will attach themselves. The diversity in the faculties of men, from which the rights of property originate, is not less an insuperable obstacle to a uniformity of interests. The protection of these faculties is the first object of government. From the protection of different and unequal faculties of acquiring property, the possession of different degrees and kinds of property immediately results; and from the influence of these on the sentiments and views of the respective proprietors, ensues a division of the society into different interests and parties.

The latent causes of faction are thus sown in the nature of man; and we see them everywhere brought into different degrees of activity, according to the different circumstances of civil society. A zeal for different opinions concerning religion, concerning government, and many other points, as well as speculation as of practice; an attachment of different leaders ambitiously contending for pre-eminence and power; or to persons of other descriptions whose fortunes have been interesting to the human passions, have, in turn, divided mankind into parties, inflamed them with mutual animosity, and rendered them much more disposed to vex and oppress each other than to cooperate for their common good. So strong is this propensity of mankind to fall into mutual animosities, that where no substantial occasion presents itself, the most frivolous and fanciful distinctions have been sufficient to kindle their unfriendly passions and excite their most violent conflicts. But the most common and durable source of factions has been the various and unequal distribution of property. Those who hold and those who are without property have ever formed distinct interests in society. Those who are creditors, and those who are debtors, fall under a like discrimination. A landed interest, a manufacturing interest, a mercantile interest, a moneyed interest, with many lesser interests, grow up of necessity in civilised nations, and divide them into different classes, actuated by different sentiments and views. The regulation of these various and interfering interests forms the principal task of modern legislation, and involves the spirit of party and faction in the necessary and ordinary operations of the government.

No man is allowed to be a judge in his own cause, because his interest would certainly bias his judgment, and, not improbably, corrupt his integrity. With equal, nay, with greater reason, a body of men are unfit to be both judges and parties at the same time; yet what are many of the most important acts of legislation but so many judicial determinations, not indeed concerning the rights of single persons, but concerning the rights of large bodies of citizens? And what are the different classes of legislators but advocates and parties to the causes which they determine? Is a law proposed concerning private debts? It is a question to which the creditors are parties on one side and the debtors on the other. Justice ought to hold the balance between them. Yet the parties are, and must be, themselves the judges; and the most numerous party, or, in other words, the most powerful faction must be expected to prevail. Shall domestic manufactures be encouraged, and in what degree, by restrictions on foreign manufacturers? are questions which would be differently decided by the landed and the manufacturing classes, and probably by neither with a sole regard to justice and the public good. The apportionment of taxes on the various descriptions of property is an act which seems to require the most exact impartiality; yet there is, perhaps, no legislative act in which greater opportunity and temptation are given to a predominant party to trample on the rules of justice. Every shilling with which they overburden the inferior number is a shilling saved to their own pockets.

It is in vain to say that enlightened statesmen will be able to adjust these clashing interests, and render them all subservient to the public good. Enlightened statesmen will not always be at the helm. Nor, in many cases, can such an adjustment be made at all without taking into view indirect and remote considerations, which will rarely prevail over the immediate interest which one party may find in disregarding the rights of another or the good of the whole.

The inference to which we are brought is, that the *causes* of faction cannot be removed, and that relief is only to be sought in the means of controlling its *effects*.

If a faction consists of less than a majority, relief is supplied by the republican principle, which enables the majority to defeat its sinister views by regular vote. It may clog the administration, it may convulse the society; but it will be unable to execute and mask its violence under the forms of the Constitution. When a majority is included in a faction, the form of popular government, on the other hand, enables it to sacrifice to its ruling passion or interest both the public good and the rights of other citizens. To secure the public good and private rights against the danger of such faction, and at the same time to preserve the spirit and the form of popular government, is then the great object to which our inquiries are directed. Let me add that it is the great desideratum by which this form of government can be rescued from the opprobrium under which it has so long laboured, and be recommended to the esteem and adoption of mankind. By that means is this object obtainable? Evidently by one of two only. Either the existence of the same passion or interest in a majority at the same time must be prevented, or the majority, having such co-existent passion or interest, must be rendered, by their number and local situation, unable to concert and carry into effect schemes of oppression. If the impulse and the opportunity be suffered to coincide, we well know that neither moral nor religious motives can be relied on as an adequate control. They are not found to be such on the injustice and violence of individuals, and lose their efficacy in proportion to the number combined together, that is, in proportion as their efficacy becomes needful.

From this view of the subject it may be concluded that a pure democracy, by which I mean a society consisting of a small number of citizens, who assemble and administer the government in person, can admit of no cure for the mischiefs of faction. A common passion or interest will, in almost every case, be felt by a majority of the whole; a communication and concert result from the form of government itself; and there is nothing to check the inducements to sacrifice the weaker party or an obnoxious individual. Hence it is that such democracies have ever been spectacles of turbulence and contention; have ever been found incompatible with personal security or the rights of property; and have in general been as short in their lives as they have been violent in their deaths. Theoretic politicians, who have patronised this species of government, have erroneously supposed that by reducing mankind to a perfect equality in their political rights, they would, at the same time, be perfectly equalised and assimilated in their possessions, their opinions, and their passions.

A republic, by which I mean a government in which the scheme of representation takes place, opens a different prospect, and promises the cure for which we are seeking. Let us examine the points in which it varies from pure democracy, and we shall comprehend both the nature of the cure and the efficacy which it must derive from the Union.

The two great points of difference between a democracy and a republic are: first, the delegation of the government, in the latter, to a small number of citizens elected by the rest secondly, the greater number of citizens, and greater sphere of country, over which the latter may be extended.

The effect of the first difference is, on the one hand, to refine and enlarge the public views, by passing them through the medium of a chosen body of citizens, whose wisdom may best discern the true interest of their country, and whose patriotism and love of justice will be least likely to sacrifice it to temporary or partial considerations. Under such a regulation, it may well happen that the public voice, pronounced by the representatives of the people, will be more consonant to the public good than if pronounced by the people themselves, convened for the purpose. On the other hand, the effect may be inverted. Men of factious tempers, of local prejudices, or of sinister designs, may, by intrigue, by corruption, or by other means, first obtain the suffrages, and then betray the interests, of the people. The question resulting is, whether small or extensive republics are more favourable to the election of proper guardians of the public weal; and it is clearly decided in favour of the latter by two obvious considerations:

In the first place, it is to be remarked that, however small the republic may be, the representatives must be raised to a certain number, in order to guard against the cabals of a few; and that, however large it may be, they must be limited to a certain number, in order to guard against the confusion of a multitude. Hence the number of representatives in the two cases not being in proportion to that of the two constituents, and being proportionally greater in the small republic, it follows that, if the proportion of fit characters be not less in the large than in the small republic, the former will present a greater option, and consequently a greater probability of a fit choice.

In the next place, as each representative will be chosen by a greater number of citizens in the large than in the small republic, it will be more difficult for unworthy candidates to practise with success the vicious arts by which elections are too often carried; and the suffrages of the people being more free, will be more likely to centre in men who possess the most attractive merit and the most diffusive and established character.

It must be confessed that in this, as in most other cases, there is a mean, on both sides of which inconveniences will be found to lie. By enlarging too much the number of electors, you render the representative too little acquainted with all their local circumstances and lesser interests; as by reducing it too much, you render him unduly attached to these, and too little fit to comprehend and pursue great and national objects. The federal Constitution forms a happy combination in this respect; the great and aggregate interests being referred to the national, the local and particular to the State legislatures. The other point of difference is, the greater number of citizens and extent of territory which may be brought within the compass of republican than of democratic government; and it is this circumstance principally which renders factious combinations less to be dreaded in the former than in the latter. The smaller the society, the fewer probably will be the distinct parties and interests composing it; the fewer the distinct parties and interests, the more frequently will a majority be found of the same party; and the smaller the number of individuals composing a majority, and the smaller the compass within which they are placed, the more easily will they concert and execute their plans of oppression. Extend the sphere, and you take in a greater variety of parties and interests; you make it less probable that a majority of the whole will have a common motive to invade the rights of other citizens; or if such a common motive exists, it will be more difficult for all who feel it to discover their own strength, and to act in unison with each other. Besides other impediments, it may be remarked that, where there is a consciousness of unjust or dishonourable purposes, communication is always checked by distrust in proportion to the number whose concurrence is necessary.

Hence, it clearly appears, that the same advantage which a republic has over a democracy, in controlling the effects of faction, is enjoyed by a large over a small republic—is enjoyed by the Union over the States composing it. Does the advantage consist in the substitution of representatives whose enlightened views and virtuous sentiments render them superior to local prejudices and to schemes of injustice? It will not be denied that the representation of the Union will be most likely to possess these requisite endowments. Does it consist in the greater security afforded by a greater variety of parties, against the event of any one party being able to outnumber and oppress the rest? In an equal degree does the increased variety of parties comprised within the Union increase this security? Does it, in fine, consist in the greater obstacles opposed to the concert and accomplishment of the secret wishes of an unjust and interested majority? Here, again, the extent of the Union gives it the most palpable advantage.

The influence of factious leaders may kindle a flame within their particular States, but will be unable to spread a general conflagration through the other States. A religious sect may degenerate into a political faction in a part of the Confederacy; but the variety of sects dispersed over the entire face of it must secure the national councils against any danger from that source. A rage for paper money, for an abolition of debts, for an equal division of property, or for any other improper or wicked project, will be less apt to pervade the whole body of the Union than a particular member of it; in the same proportion as such a malady is more likely to taint a particular county or district, than an entire State.

In the extent and proper structure of the Union, therefore, we behold a republican remedy for the diseases most incident to republican government. And accordingly to the degree of pleasure and pride we feel in being republicans, ought to be our zeal in cherishing the spirit and supporting the character of Federalists.

Federalist **Number 78 (1787–788)**

*We proceed now to an exami*nation of the judiciary department of the proposed government.

In unfolding the defects of the existing Confederation, the utility and necessity of a federal judicature have been clearly pointed out. It is the less necessary to recapitulate the considerations there urged, as the propriety of the institution in the abstract is not disputed; the only questions which have been raised being relative to the manner of constituting it, and to its extent. To these points, therefore, our observations shall be confirmed.

The manner of constituting it seems to embrace these several objects: 1st. The mode of appointing the judges. 2nd. The tenure by which they are to hold their places. 3rd. The partition of the judiciary authority between different courts, and their relations to each other.

First. As to the mode of appointing the judges; this is the same with that of appointing the officers of the Union in general, and has been so fully discussed in the two last numbers that nothing can be said here which would not be useless repetition.

Second. As to the tenure by which the judges are to hold their places: this chiefly concerns their duration in office; the provisions for their support; the precautions for their responsibility.

According to the plan of the convention, all judges who may be appointed by the United States are to hold their offices *during good behaviour;* which is conformable to the most approved of the Senate constitutions, and among the rest, to that of this State. Its propriety having been drawn into question by the adversaries of that plan is no light symptom of the rage for objection which disorders their imaginations and judgments. The standard of good behaviour for the continuance in office of the judicial magistracy is certainly one of the most valuable of the modern improvements in the practice of government. In a monarchy it is an excellent barrier to the despotism of the prince; in a republic it is a no less excellent barrier to the encroachments and oppressions of the representative body. And it is the best expedient which can be devised in any government to secure a steady, upright, and impartial administration of the laws.

Whoever attentively considers the different departments of power must perceive that, in a government in which they are separated from each other, the judiciary, from the nature of its functions, will always be the least dangerous to the political rights of the Constitution; because it will be least in a capacity to annoy or injure them. The Executive not only dispenses the honours, but holds the sword of the community. The legislature not only commands the purse, but prescribes the rules by which the duties and rights of every citizen are to be regulated. The judiciary, on the contrary, has no influence over either the sword or the purse; no direction either of the strength or of the wealth of the society; and can take no active resolution whatever. It may truly be said to have neither force nor will, but merely judgment; and must ultimately depend upon the aid of the executive arm even for the efficacy of its judgments.

This simple view of the matter suggests several important consequences. It proves incontestably that the judiciary is beyond comparison the weakest of the three departments of power; that it can never attack with success either of the other two; and that all possible care is requisite to enable it to defend itself against their attacks. It equally proves that though individual oppression may now and then proceed from the courts of justice, the general liberty of the people can never be endangered from that quarter; I mean so long as the judiciary remains truly distinct from both the legislature and the Executive. For I agree that "there is no liberty, if the power of judging be not separated from the legislative and executive powers." And it proves, in the last place, that as liberty can have nothing to fear from the judiciary alone, but would have everything to fear from its union with either of the other departments; that as all the effects of such a union must ensue from a dependence of the former on the latter, notwithstanding a nominal and apparent separation; that

as, from the natural feebleness of the judiciary, it is in continual jeopardy of being overpowered, awed, or influenced by its co-ordinate branches; and that as nothing can contribute so much to its firmness and independence as permanency in office, this quality may therefore be justly regarded as an indispensable ingredient in its constitution, and, in a great measure, as the citadel of the public justice and the public security.

The complete independence of the courts of justice is peculiarly essential in a limited Constitution. By a limited Constitution I understand one which contains certain specified exceptions to the legislative authority; such, for instance, as that it shall pass no bills of attainder, no *ex post facto* laws, and the like. Limitations of this kind can be preserved in practice no other way than through the medium of courts of justice, whose duty it must be to declare all acts contrary to the manifest tenor of the Constitution void. Without this, all the reservations of particular rights or privileges would amount to nothing.

Some perplexity respecting the rights of the courts to pronounce legislative acts void, because contrary to the Constitution, has arisen from an imagination that the doctrine would imply a superiority of the judiciary to the legislative power. It is urged that the authority which can declare the acts of another void must necessarily be superior to the one whose acts may be declared void. As this doctrine is of great importance in all the American constitutions, as a brief discussion of the ground on which it rests cannot be unacceptable.

There is no position which depends on clearer principles than that every act of a delegated authority, contrary to the tenor of the commission under which it is exercised, is void. No legislative act, therefore, contrary to the Constitution can be valid. To deny this would be to affirm that the deputy is greater than his principal; that the servant is above his master; that the representatives of the people are superior to the people themselves; that men acting by virtue of powers may do not only what their powers do not authorise, but what they forbid.

If it be said that the legislative body are themselves the constitutional judges of their own powers, and that the construction they put upon them is conclusive upon the other departments, it may be answered that this cannot be the natural presumption where it is not to be collected from any particular provisions in the Constitution. It is not otherwise to be supposed that the Constitution could intend to enable the representatives of the people to substitute their *will* to that of their constituents. It is far more rational to suppose that the courts were designed to be an intermediate body between the people and the legislature, in order, among other things, to keep the latter within the limits assigned to their authority. The interpretation of the laws is the proper and peculiar province of the courts. A constitution is, in fact, and must be regarded by the judges, as a fundamental law. It therefore belongs to them to ascertain its meaning, as well as the meaning of any particular act proceeding from the legislative body. If there should happen to be an irreconcilable variance between the two, that which has the superior obligation and validity ought, of course, to be preferred; or, in other words, the Constitution ought to be preferred to the statute, the intention of the people to the intention of their agents.

Nor does this conclusion by any means suppose a superiority of the judicial to the legislative power. It only supposes that the power of the people is superior to both; and that where the will of the legislature, declared in its statutes, stands in opposition to that of the people, declared in the Constitution, the judges ought to be governed by the latter rather than the former. They ought to regulate their decisions by the fundamental laws, rather than by those which are not fundamental.

This exercise of judicial discretion, in determining between two contradictory laws, is exemplified in a familiar instance. It not uncommonly happens that there are two statutes existing at one time, clashing in whole or in part with each other, and neither of them containing any repealing clause or expression. In such a case it is the province of the courts to liquidate and fix their meaning and operation. So far as they can, by any fair construction, be reconciled to each other, reason and law conspire to dictate that this should be done; where this is impracticable, it becomes a matter of necessity to give effect to one in exclusion of the other. The rule which has obtained in the courts for determining their relative validity is, that the last in order of time shall be preferred to the first. But this is a mere rule of constructions, not derived from any positive law, but from the nature and reason of the thing. It is a rule not enjoined upon the courts by legislative provision, but adopted by themselves, as consonant to truth and propriety, for the direction of their conduct as interpreters of the law. They thought it reasonable that between the interfering acts of an *equal* authority, that which was the last indication of its will should have the preference.

But in regard to the interfering acts of a superior and subordinate authority, of an original and derivative power, the nature and reason of the thing indicate the converse of that rule as proper to be followed. They teach us that the prior act of a superior ought to be preferred to the subsequent act of an inferior and subordinate authority; and that accordingly, whenever a particular statute contravenes the Constitution, it will be the duty of the judicial tribunals to adhere to the latter and disregard the former.

It can be of no weight to say that the courts, on the pretence of a repugnancy, may substitute their own pleasure to the constitutional intentions of the legislature. This might as well happen in the case of two contradictory statutes; or it might as well happen in every adjudication upon any single statute. The courts must declare the sense of the law; and if they should disposed to exercise will instead of Judgment, the consequence would equally be the substitution of their pleasure to that of the legislative body. The observation, if it prove anything, would prove that there ought to be no judges distinct from that body. If, then, the courts of justice are to be considered as the bulwarks of a limited Constitution against legislative encroachments, this consideration will afford a strong argument for the permanent tenure of judicial offices, since nothing will contribute so much as this to that independent spirit in the judges which must be essential to the faithful performance of so arduous a duty.

This independence of the judges is equally requisite to guard the Constitution and the rights of individuals from the effects of those ill humours, which the arts of designing men, or the influence of particular conjunctures, sometimes disseminate among the people themselves, and which, though they speedily give place to better information, and more deliberate reflection, have a tendency, in the meantime, to occasion dangerous innovations in the government, and serious oppressions of the minor party in the community. Though I trust the friends of the proposed Constitution will never concur with its enemies, in questioning that fundamental principle of republican government which admits the right of the people to alter or abolish the established Constitution, whenever they find it inconsistent with their happiness, yet it is not to be inferred from this principle that the representatives of the people, whenever a momentary inclination happens to lay hold of a majority of their constituents, incompatible with the provisions in the existing constitution, would, on that account, be justifiable in a violation of those provisions; or that the courts would be under a greater obligation to connive at infractions in this shape than when they had proceeded wholly from the cabals of the representative body. Until the people have, by some solemn and authoritative act, annulled or changed the established form, it is binding upon themselves collectively, as well as individually; and no presumption, or even knowledge, of their sentiments, can warrant their representatives in a departure from it, prior to such an act. But it is easy to see that it would require an uncommon portion of fortitude in the judges to do their duty as faithful guardians of the Constitution where legislative invasions of it had been instigated by the major voice of the community.

But it is not with a view to infractions of the Constitution only that the independence of the judges may be an essential safeguard against the effects of occasional ill humours in the society. These sometimes extend no farther than to the injury of the private rights of particular classes of citizens by unjust and partial laws. Here also the firmness of the judicial magistracy is of vast importance in mitigating the severity and confining the operation of such laws. It not only serves to moderate the immediate mischiefs of those which may have been passed, but it operates as a check upon the legislative body in passing them; who, perceiving that obstacles to the success of iniquitous intention are to be expected from the scruples of the courts, are in a manner compelled, by the very motives of the injustice they meditate to qualify their attempts. This is a circumstance calculated to have more influence upon the character of our governments than but few may be aware of. The benefits of the integrity and moderation of the judiciary have already been felt in more States than one; and though they may have displeased those whose sinister expectations they may have disappointed, they must have commanded the esteem and applause of all the virtuous and disinterested. Considerate men, of every description, ought to prize whatever will tend to beget or fortify that temper in the courts; as no man can be sure that he may not be to-morrow the victim of a spirit of injustice, by which he may be a gainer to-day. And every man must now feel that the inevitable tendency of such a spirit is to sap the foundations of public and private confidence, and to introduce in its stead universal distrust and distress.

That inflexible and uniform adherence to the rights of the Constitution, and of individuals, which we perceive to be indispensable in the courts of justice, can certainly not be expected from judges who hold their offices by a temporary commission. Periodical appointments, however regulated, or by whomsoever made, would, in some way or other, be fatal to their necessary independence. If the power of making them was committed either to the Executive or legislature, there would be danger of an improper complaisance to the branch which possessed it; if to both, there would be an unwillingness to hazard the displeasure of either; if to the people, or to persons chosen by them for the special purpose, there would be too great a disposition to consult popularity, to justify a reliance that nothing would be consulted but the Constitution and the laws.

There is yet a further and a weightier reason for the permanency of the judicial offices which is deducible from the nature of the qualifications they require. It has been frequently remarked, with great propriety, that a voluminous code of laws is one of the inconveniences necessarily connected with the advantages of a free government. To avoid an arbitrary discretion in the courts, it is indispensable that they should be bound down by strict rules and precedents, which serve to define and point out their duty in every particular case that comes before them; and it will readily be conceived from the variety of controversies which grow out of the folly and wickedness of mankind that the records of those precedents must unavoidably

swell to a very considerable bulk, and must demand long and laborious study to acquire a competent knowledge of them. Hence, it is, that there can be but few men in the society who will have sufficient skill in the laws to qualify them for the stations of judges. And making the proper deductions for the ordinary depravity of human nature, the number must be still smaller of those who unite the requisite integrity with the requisite knowledge. These considerations apprise us that the government can have no great option between fit character; and that a temporary duration in office, which would naturally discourage such characters from quitting a lucrative line of practice to accept a seat on the bench, would have a tendency to throw the administration of justice into hands less able, and less well qualified, to conduct it with utility and dignity. In the present circumstances of this country, and in those in which it is likely to be for a long time to come, the disadvantages on this score would be greater than they may at first sight appear; but it must be confessed that they are far inferior to those which present themselves under the other aspects of the subject.

Upon the whole, there can be no room to doubt that the convention acted wisely in copying from the models of those constitutions which have established *good behaviour* as the tenure of their judicial offices, in point of duration; and that so far from being blamable on this account, their plan would have been inexcusably defective, if it had wanted this important feature of good government. The experience of Great Britain affords an illustrious comment on the excellence of the institution.

Source:

Robert Maynard Hutchins, ed. *Great Books of the Western World*, Chicago: Encyclopaedia Britannica, 1952, pp. 49–53; 229–233.

Benjamin Franklin, "On the Constitution," 1787

Document written by Benjamin Franklin at the end of the congressional convention convened in 1787 to consider the revision of the Articles of Confederation. The convention was held in secret and attended by carefully chosen delegates to hammer out a constitution agreeable to everyone. Because of the diversity of the states, the constitution was conceived of as a great compromise, and it became clear that it must be released from the private convention with as much support from the delegates as possible. Franklin, being the oldest delegate there at 81 years of age, was known for his skills in politics and compromise. His document "On the Constitution" was written to launch the new charter as successfully as possible and unite the country in support of ". . . this Constitution, because I expect no better, and because I am not sure that it is not the best."

Mr. President:—I confess that I do not entirely approve of this Constitution at present; but, sir, I am not sure I shall never approve it; for, having lived long, I have experienced many instances of being obliged, by better information or fuller consideration, to change opinions even on important subjects, which I once thought right, but found to be otherwise. It is therefore that, the older I grow, the more apt I am to doubt my own judgment of others. Most men, indeed, as well as most sects in religion, think themselves in possession of all truth, and that wherever others differ from them, it is so far error. Steele, a Protestant, in a dedication, tells the Pope that the only difference between our two churches in their opinions of the certainty of their doctrine is, the Romish Church is *infallible,* and the Church of England is *never in the wrong.* But though many private persons think almost as highly of their own infallibility as that of their sect, few express it so naturally as a certain French lady, who, in a little dispute with her sister, said: "But I meet with nobody but myself that is *always* in the right." *"Je ne trouve que moi qui aie toujours raison."*

In these sentiments, sir, I agree to this Constitution, with all its faults—if they are such;—because I think a general government necessary for us, and there is no *form* of government but what may be a blessing to the people, if well administered; and I believe further, that this is likely to be well administered for a course of years, and can only end in despotism, as other forms have done before it, when the people shall become so corrupted as to need despotic government, being incapable of any other. I doubt, too, whether any other convention we can obtain, may be able to make a better Constitution; for, when you assemble a number of men, to have the advantage of their joint wisdom, you inevitably assemble with those men, all their prejudices, their passions, their errors of opinion, their local interests, and their selfish views. From such an assembly can a *perfect* production be expected? It therefore astonishes me, sir, to find this system approaching so near to perfection as it does; and I think it will astonish our enemies, who are waiting with confidence to hear that our counsels are confounded like those of the builders of Babel, and that our States are on the point of separation, only to meet hereafter for the purpose of cutting one another's throats. Thus I consent, sir, to this Constitution, because I expect no better, and because I am not sure that it is not the best. The opinions I have had of its *errors* I sacrifice to the public good. I have never whispered a syllable of them abroad. Within these walls they were born,

and here they shall die. If every one of us, in returning to our constituents, were to report the objections he has had to it, and endeavor to gain partisans in support of them, we might prevent its being generally received, and thereby lose all the salutary effects and great advantages resulting naturally in our favor among foreign nations, as well as among ourselves, from our real or apparent unanimity. Much of the strength and efficiency of any government in procuring and securing happiness to the people, depends on *opinion,* on the general opinion, of the goodness of that government, as well as of the wisdom and integrity of its governors. I hope, therefore, for our own sakes, as a part of the people, and for the sake of our posterity, that we shall act heartily and unanimously in recommending this Constitution, wherever our influence may extend, and turn our future thoughts and endeavors to the means of having it *well administered.*

On the whole, sir, I cannot help expressing a wish that every member of the convention who may still have objections to it would with me on this occasion doubt a little of his own infallibility, and, to make *manifest* our *unanimity,* put his name to this instrument.

Source:

James Andrews and David Zarefsky, eds. *American Voices: Significant Speeches in American History, 1640–1945.* New York: Longman, 1989, pp. 86–87.

Patrick Henry
"Against the Constitution," 1788

Speech given by Patrick Henry on June 5, 1788, opposing the new constitution produced by the Philadelphia convention of 1787. The proceedings of the constitutional convention were kept secret for many years. However, anticipating controversy, the delegates needed to defend the document in order to gain support in the ratifying conventions to be held in each state. Benjamin Franklin (Pennsylvania), being the oldest delegate there at 81 years of age, was known for his skills in politics and compromise. His document "On the Constitution" was written to launch the new charter as successfully as possible and to unite the country in support of "this Constitution, because I expect no better, and because I am not sure that it is not the best." Those supporting the Constitution called themselves Federalists.

The opposition then became known as Anti-Federalists. Patrick Henry of Virginia, the eloquent defender of the rights of the colonists, was one of the most influential Anti-Federalists. To ratify the document, nine states were needed to approve it. By the spring of 1788, as Virginia was beginning its debate, eight states had already agreed to ratify it. Henry's speech at the Virginia ratifying convention included his beliefs that the Constitution was dangerous to the states because it gave too much power to the central government and not enough to the individual states. He used the corruption of the British House of Commons as an example of his fears and argued that the constitution lacked a bill of rights. James Madison responded with a speech favoring the Constitution.

Mr. Chairman, I am much obliged to the very worthy gentleman for his encomium. I wish I was possessed with talents, or possessed of any thing that might enable me to elucidate this great subject. I am not free from suspicion: I am apt to entertain doubts. I rose yesterday to ask a question which arose in my own mind. When I asked that question, I thought the meaning of my interrogation was obvious. The fate of this question and of America may depend on this. Have they said, We, the states? Have they made a proposal of a compact between states? If they had, this would be a confederation. It is otherwise most clearly a consolidated government. The question turns, sir, on that poor little thing—the expression, We, the *people,* instead of the *states,* of America. I need not take much pains to show that the principles of this system are extremely pernicious, impolitic, and dangerous. Is this a monarchy, like England—a compact between prince and people, with checks on the former to secure the liberty of the latter? Is this a confederacy, like Holland—an association of a number of independent states, each of which retains its individual sovereignty? It is not a democracy, wherein the people retain all their rights securely. Had these principles been adhered to, we should not have been brought to this alarming transition, from a confederacy to a consolidated government. We have no detail of these great considerations, which, in my opinion, ought to have abounded before we should recur to a government of this kind. Here is a resolution as radical as that which separated us from Great Britain. It is radical in this transition; our rights and privileges are endangered, and the sovereignty of the states will be relinquished: and cannot we plainly see that this is actually the case? The rights of conscience, trial by jury, liberty of the press, all your immunities and franchises, all pretensions to human rights and privileges, are rendered insecure, if not lost, by this change, so loudly talked of by some, and inconsiderately by others. Is this tame relinquishment of rights worthy of freemen? Is it worthy of that manly fortitude that ought to characterize republicans? It is said eight states have adopted this plan. I declare that if twelve states and a half had adopted it, I would, with manly firmness, and in spite of an erring world, reject it. You are not to inquire how your trade may be increased, nor how you are to become a great and powerful people, but how your liber-

ties can be secured; for liberty ought to be the direct end of your government.

Having premised these things, I shall, with the aid of my judgment and information, which, I confess, are not extensive, go into the discussion of this system more minutely. Is it necessary for your liberty that you should abandon those great rights by the adoption of this system? Is the relinquishment of the trial by jury and the liberty of the press necessary for your liberty? Will the abandonment of your most sacred rights tend to the security of your liberty? Liberty, the greatest of all earthly blessings—give us that precious jewel, and you may take every thing else! But I am fearful I have lived long enough to become an old-fashioned fellow. Perhaps an invincible attachment to the dearest rights of man may, in these refined, enlightened days, be deemed old-fashioned; if so, I am contented to be so. I say, the time has been when every pulse of my heart beat for American liberty, and which, I believe, had a counterpart in the breast of every true American; but suspicions have gone forth—suspicions of my integrity—publicly reported that my professions are not real. Twenty-three years ago was I supposed a traitor to my country? I was then said to be the bane of sedition, because I supported the rights of my country. I may be thought suspicious when I say our privileges and rights are in danger. But, sir, a number of the people of this country are weak enough to think these things are too true. I am happy to find that the gentleman won the other side declares they are groundless. But, sir, suspicion is a virtue as long as its object is the preservation of the public good, and as long as it stays within proper bounds: should it fall on me, I am contented: conscious rectitude is a powerful consolation. I trust there are many who think my professions for the public good to be real. Let your suspicion look to both sides. There are many on the other side, who possibly may have been persuaded to the necessity of these measures, which I conceive to be dangerous to your liberty. Guard with jealous attention the public liberty. Suspect every one who approaches that jewel. Unfortunately, nothing will preserve it but downright force. Whenever you give up that force, you are inevitably ruined. I am answered by gentlemen, that, though I might speak of terrors, yet the fact was, that we were surrounded by none of the dangers I apprehended. I conceive this new government to be one of those dangers: it has produced those horrors which distress many of our best citizens. We are come hither to preserve the poor commonwealth of Virginia, if it can be possibly done: something must be done to preserve your liberty and mine. The Confederation, this same despised government, merits, in my opinion, the highest encomium: it carried us through a long and dangerous war; it rendered us victorious in that bloody conflict with a powerful nation; it has secured us a territory greater than any European monarch possesses: and shall a government which has been thus strong and vigorous, be accused of imbecility, and abandoned for want of energy? Consider what you are about to do before you part with the government. Take longer time in reckoning things; revolutions like this have happened in almost every country in Europe; similar examples are to be found in ancient Greece and ancient Rome—instances of the people losing their liberty by their carelessness and the ambition of a few. We are cautioned by the honorable gentleman, who presides, against faction and turbulence. I acknowledge that licentiousness is dangerous, and that it ought to be provided against; I acknowledge, also, the new form of government may effectually prevent it: yet there is another thing it will as effectually do—it will oppress and ruin the people.

There are sufficient guards placed against sedition and licentiousness; for, when power is given to this government to suppress these, or for any other purpose, the language it assumes is clear, express, and unequivocal; but when this Constitution speaks of privileges, there is an ambiguity, sir, a fatal ambiguity—an ambiguity which is very astonishing. In the clause under consideration, there is the strangest language that I can conceive. I mean, when it says that there shall not be more representatives than one for every thirty thousand. Now, sir, how easy is it to evade this privilege! "The number shall not exceed one for every thirty thousand." This may be satisfied by one representative from each state. Let our numbers be ever so great, this immense continent may, by this artful expression, be reduced to have but thirteen representatives. I confess this construction is not natural; but the ambiguity of the expression lays a good ground for a quarrel. Why was it not clearly and unequivocally expressed, that they should be entitled to have one for every thirty thousand? This would have obviated all disputes; and was this difficult to be done? What is the inference? When population increases, and a state shall send representative in this proportion, Congress *may* remand them, because the right of having one for every thirty thousand is not clearly expressed. This possibility of reducing the number to one for each state approximates to probability by that other expression—"but each state shall at least have one representative." Now, is it not clear that, from the first expression, the number might be reduced so much that some states should have no representatives at all, were it not for the insertion of this last expression? And as this is the only restriction upon them, we may fairly conclude that they *may* restrain the number of one from each state. Perhaps the same horrors may hang over my mind again. I shall be told I am continually afraid: but, sir, I have strong cause of apprehension. In some parts of the plan before you, the great rights of freemen are endangered; in other parts, absolutely taken away. How does your trial by jury stand? In civil cases gone—not sufficiently secured in criminal—this best privilege is gone. But we are told that we need not fear; because those in power, being our representatives, will not abuse the power we put in their hands. I am not well versed in history, but I will submit to your recollection, whether liberty has been destroyed most often by the licentiousness of the people, or by the tyranny of rulers. I imagine, sir, you will find the balance on the side of tyranny. Happy will you be if you miss the fate of those nations, who, omitting to resist their oppressors, or negligently suffering their liberty to be wrested from them, have groaned under intolerable despotism! Most of the human race are now in this deplorable condition; and those nations who have gone in search of grandeur, power, and splendor, have also fallen a sacrifice, and been the victims of their own folly. While they acquired those visionary blessings, they lost their freedom. My great objection to this government is, that it does not leave us the means of defending our rights, or of waging war against tyrants. It is urged by some gentlemen, that his new plan will brings us an acquisition of strength—an army, and the militia of the states. This is an idea extremely ridiculous: gentlemen cannot be earnest. This acquisition will trample on our fallen liberty. Let my beloved Americans guard against that fatal lethargy that has pervaded the universe. Have we the means of resisting disciplined armies, when our only defence, the militia, is put into the hands of Congress? The honorable gentleman said that great danger would ensue if the Convention rose without adopting this system. I ask, Where is that danger? I see none. Other gentlemen have told us, within these walls, that the union is gone, or that the union will be gone. Is not this trifling with the judgment of their fellow-citizens? Till they tell us the grounds of their fears, I will consider them as imaginary. I rose to make inquiry where those dangers were; they could make no answer: I believe I never shall have that answer. Is there a disposition in the people of this country to revolt against the dominion of laws? Has there been a single tumult in Virginia? Have not the people of Virginia, when laboring under the severest pressure of accumulated distresses, manifested the most cordial acquiescence in the execution of the laws? What could be more awful than their unanimous acquiescence under general distresses? Is there any revolution in Virginia? Whither is the spirit of America gone? Whither is the genius of America fled? It was but yesterday, when our enemies marched in triumph through our country. Yet the people of this country could not be appalled by their pompous armaments: they stopped their career, and victoriously captured them. Where is the peril, now, compared to that? Some minds are agitated by foreign alarms. Happily for us, there is no real danger from Europe; that country is engaged in more arduous business: from that quarter there is no cause of fear: you may sleep in safety forever for them.

Where is the danger? If, sir, there was any, I would recur to the Americans spirit to defend us; that spirit which has enabled us to surmount the greatest difficulties: to that illustrious spirit I address my most fervent prayer to prevent our adopting a system destructive to liberty. Let no gentlemen be told that it is not safe to reject this government. Wherefore is it not safe? We are told there are dangers, but those dangers are ideal; they cannot be demonstrated. To encourage us to adopt it, they tell us that there is a plain, easy way of getting amendments. When I come to contemplate this part, I suppose that I am mad, or that my countrymen are so. The way to amendment is, in my conception, shut. Let us consider this plain, easy way. "The Congress, whenever two thirds of both houses shall deem it necessary, shall propose amendments to this Constitution, or on the application of the legislatures of two thirds of the several states, shall call a Convention for proposing amendments, which, in either case, shall be valid to all intents and purposes, as part of this Constitution, when ratified by the legislatures of three fourths of the several states, or by the Conventions in three fourths thereof, as the one or the other mode of ratification may be proposed by the Congress. Provided, that no amendment which may be made prior to the year 1808, shall in any manner affect the 1st and 4th clauses in the 9th section of the 1st article; and that no state, without its consent, shall be deprived of its equal suffrage in the Senate."

Hence it appears that three fourths of the states must ultimately agree to any amendments that may be necessary. Let us consider the consequence of this. However uncharitable it may appear, yet I must tell my opinion—that the most unworthy character may get into power, and prevent the introduction of amendments. Let us suppose—for the case is supposable, possible, and probable—that you happen to deal those powers to unworthy hands; will they relinquish powers already in their possession, or agree to amendments? Two thirds of the Congress, or of the state legislatures, are necessary even to propose amendments. If one third of these be unworthy men, they may prevent the application for amendments; but what is destructive and mischievous, is, that three fourths of the state legislatures, or of the state conventions, must concur in the amendments when proposed! In such numerous bodies, there must necessarily be some designing, bad men. To suppose that so large a number as three fourths of the states will concur, is to suppose that they will possess genius, intelligence, and integrity, approaching to miraculous. It would indeed be miraculous that they should concur in the same amendments, or even in such as would bear some likeness to one another; for four of the smallest states, that do not collectively contain one tenth part of the population of the United States, may obstruct the most salutary and necessary amendments. Nay, in these four states, six tenths of the people may reject these amendments; and suppose that amendments shall be opposed to amendments, which is highly probable,—is it possible that three fourths can ever agree to the same amendments? A bare majority in these four small states may hinder the adoption of amendments; so that we may fairly and justly conclude that one twentieth part of the American people may prevent the removal of the most grievous inconveniences and oppression, by refusing to accede to amendments. A trifling minority may reject the most salutary amendments. Is this an easy mode of securing the public liberty? It is, sir, a most fearful situation, when the most contemptible minority can prevent the alteration of the most oppressive government; for it may, in many respects, prove to be such. Is this the spirit of republicanism?

What, sir, is the genius of democracy? Let me read that clause of the bill of rights of Virginia which relates to this: 3d clause:—that government is, or ought to be, instituted for the common benefit, protection, and security of the people, nation, or community. Of all the various modes and forms of government, that is best, which is capable of producing the greatest degree of happiness and safety, and is most effectually secured against the danger of maladministration; and that whenever any government shall be found inadequate, or contrary to those purposes, a majority of the community hath an indubitable, unalienable, and indefeasible right to reform, alter, or abolish it, in such manner as shall be judged most conducive to the public weal.

This, sir, is the language of democracy—that a majority of the community have a right to alter government when found to be oppressive. But how different is the genius of your new Constitution form this! How different from the sentiments of freemen, that a contemptible minority can prevent the good of the majority! If, then, gentlemen, standing on this ground, are come to that point, that they are willing to bind themselves and their posterity to be oppressed, I am amazed and inexpressibly astonished. If this be the opinion of the majority, I must submit; but to me, sir, it appears perilous and destructive. I cannot help thinking so. Perhaps it may be the result of my age. These may be feelings natural to a man of my years, when the American spirit has left him, and his mental powers, like the members of the body, are decayed. If, sir, amendments are left to the twentieth, or tenth part of the people of America, your liberty is gone forever. We bribery practised in the House of Commons, in England, and that many of the members raise themselves to preferments by selling the rights of the whole of the people. But, sir, the tenth part of that body cannot continue oppressions on the rest of the people. English liberty is, in this case, on a firmer foundation than American liberty. It will be easily contrived to procure the opposition of one tenth of the people to any alteration, however judicious. The honorable gentleman who presides told us that, to prevent abuses in our government, we will assemble in Convention, recall our delegated powers, and punish our servants for abusing the trust reposed in them. O sir, we should have fine times, indeed, if, to punish tyrants, it were only sufficient to assemble the people! Your arms, wherewith you could defend yourselves are gone; and you have no longer an aristocratical, no longer a democratical spirit. Did you ever read of any revolution in a nation, brought about by the punishment of those in power, inflicted by those who had no power at all? You read of a riot act in a country which is called one of the freest in the world, where a few neighbors cannot assemble without the risk of being shot by a hired soldiery, the engines of despotism. We may see such an act in America.

A standing army we shall have, also, to execute the execrable commands of tyranny; and how are you to punish them? Will you order them to be punished? Who shall obey these orders? Will your macebearer be a match for a disciplined regiment? In what situation are we to be? The clause before you gives a power to direct taxation, unbounded and unlimited, exclusive power of legislation, in all cases whatsoever, for ten miles square, and over all places purchased for the erection of forts, magazines, arsenals, dockyards, &c. What resistance could be made? The attempt would be madness. You will find all the strength of this country in the hands of your enemies; their garrisons will naturally be the strongest places in the country. Your militia is given up to Congress, also, in another part of this plan: they will therefore act as they think proper: all power will be in their own possession. You cannot force them to receive their punishment: of what service would militia be to you, when, most probably, you will not have a single musket in the state? for, as arms are to be provided by Congress, they may or may not furnish them.

Let me here call your attention to that part which gives the Congress power "to provide for organizing, arming, and disciplining the militia, and for governing such part of them as may be employed in the service of the United States—reserving to the states, respectively, the appointment of the officers, and the authority of training the militia according to the discipline prescribed by Congress." By this, sir, you see that their control over our last and best defence is unlimited. If they neglect or refuse to discipline or arm our militia, they will be useless: the states can do neither—this power being exclusively given to Congress. The power of appointing officers over men not disciplined or armed is ridiculous; so that this pretended little remains of power left to the states may, at the pleasure of Congress, be rendered nugatory. Our situ-

ation will be deplorable indeed: nor can we ever expect to get this government amended, since I have already shown that a very small minority may prevent it, and that small minority interested in the continuance of the oppression. Will the oppressor let go the oppressed? Was there even an instance? Can the annals of mankind exhibit one single example where rulers overcharged with power willingly let go the oppressed, though solicited and requested most earnestly? The application for amendments will therefore be fruitless. Sometimes, the oppressed have got loose by one of those bloody struggles that desolate a country; but a willing relinquishment of power is one of those things which human nature never was, nor ever will be, capable of.

The honorable gentleman's observations, respecting the people's right of being the agents in the information of this government, are not accurate, in my humble conception. The distinction between a national government and confederacy is not sufficiently discerned. Had the delegates, who were sent to Philadelphia, a power to propose a consolidated government instead of a confederacy? Were they not deputed by states, and not by the people? The assent of the people, in their collective capacity, is not necessary to the formation of a federal government. The people have no right to enter into leagues, alliances, or confederations; they are not the proper agents for this purpose. States and foreign powers are the only proper agents for this kind of government. Show me an instance where the people have exercised this business. Has it not always gone through the legislatures? I refer you to the treaties with France, Holland, and other nations. How were they made? Were they not made by the states? Are the people, therefore, in their aggregate capacity, the proper persons to form a confederacy? This, therefore, ought to depend on the consent of the legislatures, the people having never sent delegates to make any proposition for changing the government. Yet I must say, at the same time, that it was made on grounds the most pure; and perhaps I might have been brought to consent to it so far as to the change of government. But there is one thing in it which I never would acquiesce in. I mean, the changing it into a consolidated government, which is so abhorrent in my mind. *[The honorable gentleman then went on to the figure we make with foreign nations; the contemptible one we make in France and Holland; which according to the substance of the notes, he attributes to the present feeble government.]* An opinion has gone forth, we find, that we are contemptible people: the time has been when we were thought otherwise. Under the same despised government, we commanded the respect of all Europe: wherefore are we now reckoned otherwise? The American spirit has fled from hence: it has gone to regions where it has never been expected; it has gone to the people of France, in search of a splendid government—a strong, energetic government. Shall we imitate the example of those nations who have gone from a simple to a splendid government? Are those nations more worthy of our imitations? What can make an adequate satisfaction to them for the loss they have suffered in attaining such a government—for the loss of their liberty? If we admit this consolidated government, it will be because we like a great, splendid one. Some way or other we must be a great and mighty empire; we must have an army, and a navy, and a number of things. When the American spirit was in its youth, the language of America was different: liberty, sir, was then the primary object. We are descended from a people whose government was founded on liberty: our glorious forefathers of Great Britain made liberty the foundation of everything. That country is become a great, mighty, and splendid nation; not because their government is strong and energetic, but, sir, because liberty is its direct end and foundation. We drew the spirit of liberty from our British ancestors: by that spirit we have triumphed over every difficulty. But now, sir, the American spirit, assisted by the ropes and chains of consolidation, is about to convert this country into a powerful and mighty empire. If you make the citizens of this country agree to become the subjects of one great consolidated empire of America, your government will not have sufficient energy to keep them together. Such a government is incompatible with the genius of republicanism. There will be no checks, no real balances, in this government. What can avail your specious, imaginary balance, your rope-dancing, chain-rattling, ridiculous ideal checks and contrivances? But, sir, we are not feared by foreigners; we do not make nations tremble. Would this constitute happiness, or secure liberty? I trust, sir, our political hemisphere will ever direct their operations to the security of those objects.

Consider our situation, sir: go to the poor man, and ask him what he does. He will inform you that he enjoys the fruits of his labor, under his own fig-tree, with his wife and children around him, in peace and security. Go to every other member of society,—you will find the same tranquil ease and content; you will find no alarms or disturbances. Why, then, tell us of danger, to terrify us into an adoption of this new form of government? And yet who knows the dangers that this new system may produce? They are out of the sight of the common people: they cannot foresee latent consequences. I dread the operation of it on the middling and lower classes of people: it is for them I fear the adoption of this system. I fear I tire the patience of the committee; but I beg to be indulged with a few more observations. When I thus profess myself an advocate for the liberty of the people, I shall be told I am a designing man, that I am to be a great man, that I am to be a demagogue; and many similar illib-

eral insinuations will be thrown out: but, sir, conscious rectitude outweighs those things with me. I see great jeopardy in this new government. I see none from our present one. I hope some gentleman or other will bring forth, in full array, those dangers, if there by any, that we may see and touch them. I have said that I thought this is a consolidated government: I will now prove it. Will the greats rights of the people be secured by this government? Suppose it should prove oppressive, how can it be altered? Our bill of rights declares, "that a majority of the community hath an indubitable, unalienable, and indefeasible right to reform, alter, or abolish it, in such manner as shall be judged most conducive to the public weal."

I have just proved that one tenth, or less, of the people of America—a most despicable minority—may prevent this reform or alteration. Suppose the people of Virginia should wish to alter their government; can a majority of them do it? No; because they are connected with other men, or, in other words, consolidated with other states. When the people of Virginia, at a future day, shall wish to alter their government, though they should be unanimous in this desire, yet they may be prevented therefrom by a despicable minority at the extremity of the United States. The founders of your Constitution made your government changeable: but the power of changing it is gone from you. Whither is it gone? It is placed in the same hands that hold the rights of twelve other states; and those who hold those rights have right and power to keep them. It is not the particular government of Virginia: one of the leading features of that government is, that a majority can alter it, when necessary for the public good. This government is not a Virginian, but an American government. Is it not, therefore, a consolidated government? The sixth clause of your bill of rights tells you, "that elections of members to serve as representatives of the people in the Assembly ought to be free, and that all men having sufficient evidence of permanent common interest with, and attachment to, the community, have the right of suffrage, and cannot be *taxed,* or deprived of their property for public uses, without their own consent, or that of their representatives so elected, nor bound by any law to which they have not in like manner assented for the public good." But what does this Constitution say? The clause under consideration gives an unlimited and unbounded power of taxation. Suppose every delegate from Virginia opposes a law laying a tax; what will it avail? They are opposed by a majority; eleven members can destroy their efforts; those feeble ten cannot prevent the passing the most oppressive tax law; so that, in direct opposition to the spirit and express language of your declaration of rights, you are taxed, not by your own consent, but by people who have no connection with you.

The next clause of the bill of rights tells you, "that all power of suspending law, or the execution of laws, by any authority, without the consent of the representatives of the people, is injurious to their rights, and ought not to be exercised." This tells us that there can be no suspension of government or laws without our own consent; yet this Constitution can counteract and suspend any of our laws that contravene its oppressive operation; for they have the power of direct taxation, which suspends our bill of rights; and it is expressly provided that they can make all laws necessary for carrying their powers into execution; and it is declared paramount to the laws and constitutions of the states. Consider how the only remaining defence we have left is destroyed in this manner. Besides the expenses of maintaining the Senate and other house in as much splendor as they please, there is to be a great and mighty President, with very extensive powers—the powers of a king. He is to be supported in extravagant magnificence; so that the whole of our property may be taken by this American government, by laying what taxes they please, giving themselves what salaries they please, and suspending our laws at their pleasure. I might be thought too inquisitive, but I believe I should take up very little of your time in enumerating the little power that is left to the government of Virginia; for this power is reduced to little or nothing: their garrisons, magazines, arsenals, and forts, which will be situated in the strongest places within the states; their ten miles square, with all the fine ornaments of human life, added to their powers, and taken from the states, will reduce the power of the latter to nothing.

The voice of tradition, I trust, will inform posterity of our struggles for freedom. If our descendants be worthy the name of Americans, they will preserve, and hand down to their latest posterity, the transactions of the present times; and, though I confess my exclamations are not worthy the hearing, they will see that I have done my utmost to preserve their liberty; for I never will give up the power of direct taxation but for the scourge. I am willing to give it conditionally; that is, after non-compliance with requisitions. I will do more, sir, and what I hope will convince the most skeptical man that I am a lover of the American Union—that, in case Virginia shall not make punctual payment, the control of our custom-houses, and the whole regulation of trade, shall be given to Congress, and that Virginia, shall depend on Congress even for passports, till Virginia shall have paid the last farthing, and furnished the last soldier. Nay, sir, there is another alternative to which I would consent;—even that they should strike us out of the Union, and take away from us all federal privileges, till we comply with federal requisitions: but let it depend upon our own pleasure to pay our money in the most easy manner for our people. Were all the states, more terrible than the mother country, to join against us, I hope Virginia

could defend herself; but sir, the dissolution of the Union is most abhorrent to my mind. The first thing I have at heart is American liberty: the second thing is American union; and I hope the people of Virginia will endeavor to preserve that union. The increasing population of the Southern States is far greater than that of New England; consequently, in a short time, they will be far more numerous than the people of that country. Consider this, and you find this state more particularly interested to support American liberty, and not bind our posterity by an improvident relinquishment of our rights. I would give the best security for a punctual compliance with requisitions; but I beseech gentlemen, at all hazards, not to give up this unlimited power of taxation. The honorable gentleman has told us that these powers, given to Congress, are accompanied by a judiciary which will correct all. On examination, you will find this very judiciary oppressively constructed; your jury trial destroyed, and the judges dependent on Congress.

In this scheme of energetic government, the people will find two sets of taxgatherers—the state and the federal sheriffs. This, it seems to me, will produce such dreadful oppression as the people cannot possibly bear. The federal sheriff may commit what oppression, make what distresses, he pleases, and ruin you with impunity; for how are you to tie his hands? Have you any sufficiently decided means of preventing him from sucking your blood by speculations, commissions, and fees? Thus thousands of your people will be most shamefully robbed: our state sheriffs, those unfeeling blood-suckers, have, under the watchful eye of our legislature, committed the most horrid and barbarous ravages on our people. It has required the most constant vigilance of the legislature to keep them from totally ruining the people; a repeated succession of laws has been made to suppress their iniquitous speculations and cruel extortions; and as often has their nefarious ingenuity devised methods of evading the force of those laws: in the struggle they have generally triumphed over the legislature.

It is a fact that lands have been sold for five shillings, which were worth one hundred pounds: if sheriffs, thus immediately under the eye of our state legislature and judiciary, have dared to commit these outrages, what would they not have done if their masters had been at Philadelphia or New York? If they perpetrate the most unwarrantable outrage on your person or property, you cannot get redress on this side of Philadelphia or New York; and how can you get it there? If your domestic avocations could permit you to go thither, there you must appeal to judges sworn to support this Constitution, in opposition to that of any state, and who may also be inclined to favor their own officers. When these harpies are aided by excisemen, who may search, at any time, your houses, and most secret recesses, will the people bear it? If you think so, you differ from me. Where I thought there was a possibility of such mischiefs, I would grant power with a niggardly hand; and here there is a strong probability that these oppressions shall actually happen. I may be told that it is safe to err on that side, because such regulations may be made by Congress as shall restrain these officers, and because laws are made by our representatives, and judged by righteous judges: but sir, as these regulations may be made, so they may not; and many reasons there are to induce a belief that they will not. I shall therefore be an infidel on that point till the day of my death. This Constitution is said to have beautiful features; but when I come to examine these features, sir, they appear to me horribly frightful. Among other deformities, it has an awful squinting; it squints toward monarchy; and does not this raise indignation in the breast of every true American?

Your President may easily become king. Your Senate is so imperfectly constructed that your dearest rights may be sacrificed by what may be a small minority; and a very small minority may continue forever unchangeably this government, although horridly defective. Where are your checks in this government? Your strongholds will be in the hands of your enemies. It is on a supposition that your American governors shall be honest, that all the good qualities of this government are founded; but its defective and imperfect construction puts it in their power to perpetrate the worst of mischiefs, should they be bad men; and, sir, would not all the world, from the eastern to the western hemisphere, blame our distracted folly in resting our rights upon the contingency of our rulers being good or bad? Show me that age and country where the rights and liberties of the people were placed on the sole chance of their rulers being good men, without a consequent loss of liberty! I say that the loss of that dearest privilege has ever followed, with absolute certainty, every such mad attempt.

If your American chief be a man of ambition and abilities, how easy is it for him to render himself absolute! The army is in his hands, and if he be a man of address, it will be attached to him, and it will be the subject of long mediation with him to seize the first auspicious moment to accomplish his design; and, sir, will the American spirit solely relieve you when this happens? I would rather infinitely—and I am sure most of this Convention are of the same opinion—have a king, lords, and commons, than a government so replete with such insupportable evils. If we make a king, we may prescribe the rules by which he shall rule his people, and interpose such checks as shall prevent him from infringing them; but the President, in the field, at the head of his army, can prescribe the terms on which he shall reign master, so far that it will puzzle any American ever to get his neck from under the galling yoke.

I cannot with patience think of this idea. If ever he violates the laws, one of two things will happen: he will come at the head of his army, to carry every thing before him; or he will give bail, or do what Mr. Chief Justice will order him. If he be guilty, will not the recollection of his crimes teach him to make one bold push for the American throne? Will not the immense difference between being master of every thing, and being ignominiously tried and punished, powerfully excite him to make this bold push? But, sir, where is the existing force to punish him? Can he not, at the head of his army, beat down every opposition? Away with your President! we shall have a king: the army will salute him monarch: your militia will leave you, and assist in making him king, and fight against you: and what have you to oppose this force? What will then become of you and your rights? Will not absolute despotism ensue? [Here Mr. Henry strongly and pathetically expatiated on the probability of the president's enslaving America, and the horrid consequences that must result.]

What can be more defective than the clause concerning the elections? The control given to Congress over the time, place, and manner of holding elections, will totally destroy the end of suffrage. The elections may be held at one place, and the most inconvenient in the state; or they may be at remote distances from those who have a right of suffrage: hence nine out of ten must either not vote at all, or vote for strangers; for the most influential characters will be applied to, to know who are the most proper to be chosen. I repeat, the control of Congress over the *manner, &c.,* of electing, well warrants this idea. The natural consequence will be, that this democratic branch will possess none of the public confidence; the people will be prejudiced against representatives chosen in such an injudicious manner. The proceedings in the northern conclave will be hidden from the yeomanry of this country. We are told that the yeas and nays shall be taken, and entered on the journals. This, sir, will avail nothing: it may be locked up in their chests, and concealed forever from the people; for they are not to publish what parts they think require secrecy: they *may* think, and *will think,* the whole requires it. Another beautiful feature of this Constitution is, the publication from time to time of the receipts and expenditures of the public money.

This expression, *from time to time,* is very indefinite and indeterminate: it may extend to a century. Grant that any of them are wicked; they may squander the public money so as to ruin you, and yet this expression will give you no redress. I say they may ruin you; for where, sir, is the responsibility? The yeas and nays will show you nothing, unless they be fools as well as knaves; for, after having wickedly trampled on the rights of the people, they would act like fools indeed, were they to publish and divulge their iniquity, when they have it equally in their power to suppress and conceal it. Where is the responsibility—that leading principle in the British government? In that government, a punishment certain and inevitable is provided; but in this, there is no real, actual punishment for the grossest mal-administration. They may go without punishment, though they commit the most outrageous violation on our immunities. That paper may tell me they will be punished. I ask, By what law? They must make the law, for there is no existing law to do it. What! will they make a law to punish themselves?

This, sir, is my great objection to the Constitution, that there is no true responsibility—and that the preservation of our liberty depends on the single chance of men being virtuous enough to make laws to punish themselves.

In the country from which we are descended, they have real and not imaginary responsibility; for the mal-administration has cost their heads to some of the most saucy geniuses that ever were. The Senate, by making treaties, may destroy your liberty and laws for want of responsibility. Two thirds of those that shall happen to be present, can, with the President, make treaties that shall be the supreme law of the land; they may make the most ruinous treaties; and yet there is no punishment for them. Whoever shows me a punishment provided for them will oblige me. So, sir, notwithstanding there are eight pillars, they want another. Where will they make another? I trust, sir, the exclusion of the evils wherewith this system is replete in its present form, will be made a condition precedent to its adoption by this or any other state. The transition, from a general unqualified admission to offices, to a consolidation of government, seems easy; for, though the American states are dissimilar in their structure, this will assimilate them. This, sir, is itself a strong consolidating feature, and is not one of the least dangerous in that system. Nine states are sufficient to establish this government over those nine. Imagine that nine have come into it. Virginia has certain scruples. Suppose she will, consequently, refuse to join with those states; may not she still continue in friendship and union with them? If she sends her annual requisitions in dollars, do you think their stomachs will be so squeamish as to refuse her dollars? Will they not accept her regiments? They would intimidate you into an inconsiderate adoption, and frighten you with ideal evils, and that the Union shall be dissolved. 'Tis a bugbear, sir: the fact is, sir, that the eight adopting states can hardly stand on their own legs. Public fame tells us that the adopting states have already heart-burnings and animosity, and repent their precipitate hurry: this, sir, may occasion exceeding great mischief. When I reflect on these and many other circumstances, I must think those states will be found to be in confederacy with us. If we pay our quota of

money annually, and furnish our ratable number of men, when necessary, I can see no danger from a rejection.

The history of Switzerland clearly proves that we might be in amicable alliance with those states without adopting this Constitution. Switzerland is a confederacy, consisting of dissimilar governments. This is an example which proves that governments of dissimilar structures may be confederated. That confederate republic has stood upwards of four hundred years; and, although several of the individual republics are democratic, and the rest aristocratic, no evil has resulted from this dissimilarity; for they have braved all the power of France and Germany during that long period. The Swiss spirit, sir, has kept them together; they have encountered and overcome immense difficulties with patience and fortitude. In the vicinity of powerful and ambitious monarchs, they have retained their independence, republican simplicity, and valor. [Here he makes a comparison of the people of that country and those of France, and makes a quotation from Addison illustrating the subject.] Look at the peasants of that country and of France; and mark the difference. You will find the condition of the former far more desirable and comfortable. No matter whether the people be great, splendid, and powerful, if they enjoy freedom. The Turkish Grand Signior, alongside of our President, would put us to disgrace; but we should be as abundantly consoled for this disgrace, when our citizens have been put in contrast with the Turkish slave. The most valuable end of government is the liberty of the inhabitants. No possible advantages can compensate for the loss of this privilege. Show me the reason why the American Union is to be dissolved. Who are those eight adopting states? Are they averse to give us a little time to consider, before we conclude? Would such a disposition render a junction with them eligible; or is it the genius of that kind of government to precipitate people hastily into measures of the utmost importance, and grant no indulgence? If it be, sir, is it for us to accede to such a government? We have a right to have time to consider: we shall therefore insist upon it. Unless the government be amended, we can never accept it. The adopting states will doubtless accept our money and our regiments; and what is to be the consequence, if we are disunited? I believe it is yet doubtful, whether it is not proper to stand by a while, and see the effect of its adoption in other states. In forming a government, the utmost care should be taken to prevent its becoming oppressive; and this government is of such an intricate and complicated nature, that no man on this earth can know its real operation. The other states have no reason to think, from the antecedent conduct of Virginia, that she has any intention of seceding from the Union, or of being less active to support the general welfare. Would they not, therefore, acquiesce in our taking time to deliberate—deliberate whether the measure be not perilous, not only for us, but the adopting states?

Permit me, sir, to say, that a great majority of the people, even in the adopting states, are averse to this government. I believe I would be right to say, that they have been egregiously misled. Pennsylvania has, *perhaps*, been tricked into it. If the other states who have adopted it have not been tricked, still they were too much hurried into its adoption. There were very respectable minorities in several of them; and if reports be true, a clear majority of the people are averse to it. If we also accede, and it should prove grievous, the peace and prosperity of our country, which we all love, will be destroyed. This government has not the affection of the people at present. Should it be oppressive, their affections will be totally estranged from it; and, sir, you know that a government, without their affections, can neither be durable nor happy. I speak as one poor individual; but when I speak, I speak the language of thousands. But, sir, I mean not to breathe the spirit, nor utter the language, of secession.

I have trespassed so long on your patience, I am really concerned that I have something yet to say. The honorable member has said, we shall be properly represented. Remember, sir, that the number of our representatives is but ten, whereof six is a majority. Will those men be possessed of sufficient information? A particular knowledge of particular districts will not suffice. They must be well acquainted with agriculture, commerce, and a great variety of other matters throughout the continent; they must know not only the actual state of nations in Europe and America, the situations of their farmers, cottagers, and mechanics, but also the relative situations and intercourse of those nations. Virginia is as large as England. Our proportion of representatives is but ten men. In England they have five hundred and fifty-eight. The House of Commons, in England, numerous as they are, we are told, are bribed, and have bartered away the rights of their constituents: what, then, shall become of us? Will these few protect our rights? Will they be incorruptible? You say they will be better men than the English commoners. I say they will be infinitely worse men, because they are to be chosen blindfolded: their election (the term, as applied to their appointment, is inaccurate) will be an involuntary nomination, and not a choice.

I have, I fear, fatigued the committee; yet I have not said the one hundred thousandth part of what I have on my mind, and wish to impart. On this occasion, I conceived myself bound to attend strictly to the interest of the state, and I thought her dearest rights at stake. Having lived so long—been so much honored—my efforts, though small, are due to my country. I have found my mind hurried on, from subject to subject, on this very great occasion. We have been all out of order, from the gentleman who opened to-day to myself. I did not come prepared to speak, on so multifarious a subject, in so general a manner. I trust you will indulge me another time. Before you abandon the present system, I hope you will consider not only its defects, most maturely, but likewise those of that which you are to substitute for it. May you be fully apprized of the dangers of the latter, not by fatal experience, but by some abler advocate tha[n] I!

See also BENJAMIN FRANKLIN, "ON THE CONSTITUTION," 1787.

Source:

James Andrews and David Zarefsky, eds. *American Voices: Significant Speeches in American History, 1640–1945.* New York: Longman, 1989.

George Washington, First Inaugural Address, 1789

Speech delivered to both houses of Congress by George Washington on April 30, 1789, in New York City's Federal Hall, at his inauguration as first president of the United States. Washington opened his address with a modest disclaimer of his qualifications, stating that he had been summoned from his longed-for retreat at Mount Vernon by the voice of his country. He spoke hopefully about a government without local prejudices or party animosities, of honesty and magnanimity in conjunction with public prosperity, and of "the enlarged views, the temperate consultations, and the wise measures" on which he believed the success of the American government would depend. He noted that "the preservation of the sacred fire of liberty and the destiny of the republican model of government are . . . staked on the experiment entrusted to the hands of the American people." The delivery of this speech also set a precedent for presidents to deliver inaugural addresses.

Washington established a government that included a cabinet, although none was mentioned in the Constitution. Congress set up the cabinet in which its members were selected by the president with the advice and assent of the Senate. However, the president had the sole power of removal. Its members were the secretaries of state (Thomas Jefferson), treasury (Alexander Hamilton), and war (Henry Knox), and an attorney general (Edmund Randolph). In case of a vacancy in the presidency, the U.S. Constitution provided that the vice president should succeed. The rest of the succession was established in the Presidential Succession Law of 1792 (the president *pro tempore* of the Senate, followed by the Speaker of the House).

Fellow-Citizens of the Senate and of the House of Representatives:

Among the vicissitudes incident to life no event could have filled me with greater anxieties than that of which the notification was transmitted by your order, and received on the 14th day of the present month. On the one hand, I was summoned by my country, whose voice I can never hear but with veneration and love, from a retreat which I had chosen with the fondest predilection, and, in my flattering hopes, with an immutable decision, as the asylum of my declining years—a retreat which was rendered every day more necessary as well as more dear to me by the addition of habit to inclination, and of frequent interruptions in my health to the gradual waste committed on it by time. On the other hand, the magnitude and difficulty of the trust to which the voice of my country called me, being sufficient to awaken in the wisest and most experienced of her citizens a distrustful scrutiny into his qualifications, could not but overwhelm with despondence one who (inheriting inferior endowments from nature and unpracticed in the duties of civil administration) ought to be peculiarly conscious of his own deficiencies. In this conflict of emotions all I dare aver is that it has been my faithful study to collect my duty from a just appreciation of every circumstance by which it might be affected. All I dare hope is that if, in executing this task, I have been too much swayed by a grateful remembrance of former instances, or by an affectionate sensibility to this transcendent proof of the confidence of my fellow-citizens, and have thence too little consulted my incapacity as well as disinclination for the weighty and untried cares before me, my error will be palliated by the motives which mislead me, and its consequences be judged by my country with some share of the partiality in which they originated.

Such being the impressions under which I have, in obedience to the public summons, repaired to the present station, it would be peculiarly improper to omit in this first official act my fervent supplications to that Almighty Being who rules over the universe, who presides in the councils of nations, and whose providential aids can supply every human defect, that His benediction may consecrate to the liberties and happiness of the people of the United States a Government instituted by themselves for these essential purposes, and may enable every instrument employed in its administration to execute with success the functions allotted to his charge. In tendering this homage to the Great Author of every public and private good, I assure myself that it expresses your sentiments not less than my own, nor those of my fellow-citizens at large less than either. No people can be bound to acknowledge and adore the Invisible Hand which conducts the affairs of men more than those of the United States. Every step by which they have advanced to the character of an independent nation seems to have been distinguished by some token of providential agency; and in the important revolution just accomplished in the system of their united government the tranquil deliberations and voluntary consent of so many distinct communities from which the event has resulted can not be compared with the means by which most governments have been established without some return of pious gratitude, along with an humble anticipation of the future blessings which the past seem to presage. These reflections, arising out of the present crisis, have forced themselves too strongly on my mind to be suppressed. You will join with me, I trust, in thinking that there are none under the influence of which the proceedings of a new and free government can more auspiciously commence.

By the article establishing the executive department it is made the duty of the President "to recommend to your consideration such measures as he shall judge necessary and expedient." The circumstances under which I now meet you will acquit me from entering into that subject further than to refer to the great constitutional charter under which you are assembled, and which, in defining your powers, designates the objects to which your attention is to be given. It will be more consistent with those circumstances, and far more congenial with the feelings which actuate me, to substitute, in place of a recommendation of particular measures, the tribute that is due to the talents, the rectitude, and the patriotism which adorn the characters selected to devise and adopt them. In these honorable qualifications I behold the surest pledges that as on one side no local prejudices or attachments, no separate views nor party animosities, will misdirect the comprehensive and equal eye which ought to watch over this great assemblage of communities and interests, so, on another, that the foundation of our national policy will be laid in the pure and immutable principles of private morality, and the preeminence of free government be exemplified by all the attributes which can win the affections of its citizens and command the respect of the world. I dwell on this prospect with every satisfaction which an ardent love for my country can inspire, since there is no truth more thoroughly established than that there exists in the economy and course of nature an indissoluble union between virtue and happiness; between duty and advantage; between the genuine maxims of an honest and magnanimous policy and the solid rewards of public prosperity and felicity; since we ought to be no less persuaded that the propitious smiles of Heaven can never be expected on a nation that disregards the eternal rules of order and right which Heaven itself has ordained; and since the preservation of the sacred fire of liberty and the destiny of the republican model of government are justly considered, perhaps, as *deeply*, as *finally*, staked on the experiment intrusted to the hands of the American people.

Besides the ordinary objects submitted to your care, it will remain with your judgment to decide how far an exercise of the occasional power delegated by the fifth article of the Constitution is rendered expedient at the present juncture by the nature of objections which have been urged against the system, or by the degree of inquietude which has given birth to them. Instead of undertaking particular recommendations on this subject, in which I could be guided by no lights derived from official opportunities, I shall again give way to my entire confidence in your discernment and pursuit of the public good; for I assure myself that whilst you carefully avoid every alternation which might endanger the benefits of an united and effective government, or which ought to await the future lessons of experience, a reverence for the characteristics rights of freemen and a regard for the public harmony will sufficiently influence your deliberations on the question how far the former can be impregnably forfeited or the latter be safely and advantageously promoted.

To the foregoing observations I have one to add, which will be most properly addressed to the House of Representatives. It concerns myself, and will therefore be as brief as possible. When I was first honored with a call into the service of my country, then on the eve of an arduous struggle for its liberties, the light in which I contemplated my duty required that I should renounce every pecuniary compensation. From this resolution I have in no instance departed; and being still under the impressions which produced it, I must decline as inapplicable to myself any share in the personal emoluments which may be indispensably included in a permanent provision for the executive department, and must accordingly pray that the pecuniary estimates for the station in which I am placed may during my continuance in it be limited to such actual expenditures as the public good may be thought to require.

Having thus imparted to you my sentiments as they have been awakened by the occasion which brings us together, I shall take my present leave; but not without resorting once more to the benign Parent of the Human Race in humble supplication that, since He has been pleased of favor the American people with opportunities for deliberating in perfect tranquility, and dispositions for deciding with unparalleled unanimity on a form of government for the security of their union and the advancement of their happiness, so His divine blessing may be equally *conspicuous* in the enlarged views, the temperate consultations, and the wise measures on which the success of this Government must depend.

See also GEORGE WASHINGTON'S FAREWELL ADDRESS, 1796.

Source:
Inaugural Addresses of the Presidents of the United States, 1789–1965. Washington, D.C.: Government Printing Office, 1965.

Judiciary Act of 1789

Federal legislation enacted September 24, 1789, creating the federal court system. The U.S. Constitution had established a Supreme Court but had given Congress the power to organize it and the rest of the judiciary. The 1789 act provided for the Supreme Court to consist of a chief justice and five associates and established three intermediate circuit courts and 13 federal district courts. For each district court, a U.S. attorney and deputies were to serve as federal prosecutors, and U.S. marshals were to serve as federal police. The act established an attorney general for the United States to conduct all suits in the Supreme Court and to advise the executive branch. (The Department of Justice was not created, however, until 1870.) The act also gave the Supreme Court the right to hear and decide certain appeals from state courts. President George Washington appointed John Jay the first Chief Justice, and the Court sat for the first time February 2, 1790.

An Act
To establish the Judicial Courts of the United States.

Section 1. *Be it enacted by the Senate and House of Representatives of the United States of America in Congress assembled,* That the supreme court of the United States shall consist of a chief justice and five associate justices, any four of whom shall be a quorum, and shall hold annually at the seat of government two sessions, the one commencing the first Monday of February, and the other the first Monday of August. That the associate justices shall have precedence according to the date of their commissions, or when the commissions of two or more of them bear date on the same day, according to their respective ages.

Sec. 2. *And be it further enacted,* That the United States shall be, and they hereby are divided into thirteen districts, to be limited and called as follows, to wit: one to consist of that part of the State of Massachusetts which lies easterly of the State of New Hampshire, and to be called Maine District; one to consist of the State of New Hampshire, and to be called New Hampshire District; one to consist of the remaining part of the State of Massachusetts, and to be called Massachusetts district; one to consist of the State of Connecticut, and to be called Connecticut

District; one to consist of the State of New York, and to be called New York District; one to consist of the State of New Jersey, and to be called New Jersey District; one to consist of the State of Pennsylvania, and to be called Pennsylvania District; one to consist of the State of Delaware, and to be called Delaware District; one to consist of the State of Maryland, and to be called Maryland District; one to consist of the State of Virginia, except that part called the District of Kentucky, and to be called Virginia District; one to consist of the remaining part of the State of Virginia, and to be called Kentucky District; one to consist of the State of South Carolina, and to be called South Carolina District; and one to consist of the State of Georgia, and to be called Georgia District.

Sec. 3. *And be it further enacted,* That there be a court called a District Court, in each of the afore mentioned districts, to consist of one judge, who shall reside in the district for which he is appointed, and shall be called a District Judge, and shall hold annually four sessions, the first of which to commence as follows, to wit: in the districts of New York and of New Jersey on the first, in the district of Pennsylvania on the second, in the district of Connecticut on the third, and in the district of Delaware on the fourth, Tuesdays of November next; in the districts of Massachusetts, of Maine, and of Maryland, on the first, in the district of Georgia on the second, and in the districts of New Hampshire, of Virginia, and of Kentucky, on the third Tuesdays of December next; and the other three sessions progressively in the respective districts on the like Tuesdays of every third calendar month afterwards, and in the district of South Carolina, on the third Monday in March and September, the first Monday in July, and the second Monday in December of each and every year, commencing in December next; and that the District Judge shall have power to hold special courts at his discretion. That the stated District Court shall be held at the places following, to wit: in the district of Maine, at Portland and Pownalsborough alternately, beginning at the first; in the district of New Hampshire, at Exeter and Portsmouth alternately, beginning at the first; in the district of Massachusetts, at Boston and Salem alternately, beginning at the first; in the district of Connecticut, alternately at Hartford and New Haven, beginning at the first; in the district of New York, at New York; in the district of New Jersey, alternately at New Brunswick and Burlington, beginning at the first; in the district of Pennsylvania, at Philadelphia and York Town alternately, beginning at the first; in the district of Delaware, alternately at Newcastle and Dover, beginning at the first; in the district of Maryland, alternately at Baltimore and Easton, beginning at the first; in the district of Virginia, alternately at Richmond and Williamsburgh, beginning at the first; in the district of Kentucky, at Harrodsburgh; in the district of South Carolina, at Charleston;

and in the district of Georgia, alternately at Savannah and Augusta, beginning at the first; and that the special courts shall be held at the same place in each district as the stated courts, or in districts that have two, at either of them, in the discretion of the judge, or at such other place in the district, as the nature of the business and his discretion shall direct. And that in the districts that have but one place for holding the District Court, the records thereof shall be kept at that place; and in districts that have two, at that place in each district which the judge shall appoint.

Sec. 4. *And be it further enacted,* That the before mentioned districts, except those of Maine and Kentucky, shall be divided into three circuits, and be called the eastern, the middle, and the southern circuit. That the eastern circuit shall consist of the districts of New Hampshire, Massachusetts, Connecticut and New York; that the middle circuit shall consist of the districts of New Jersey, Pennsylvania, Delaware, Maryland and Virginia; and that the southern circuit shall consist of the districts of South Carolina and Georgia, and that there shall be held annually in each district of said circuits, two courts, which shall be called Circuit Courts, and shall consist of any two justices of the Supreme Court, and the district judge of such districts, any two of whom shall constitute a quorum: *Provided,* That no district judge shall give a vote in any case of appeal or error from his own decision; but may assign the reasons of such his decision.

Sec. 5. *And be it further enacted,* That the first session of the said circuit court in the several districts shall commence at the times following, to wit: in New Jersey on the second, in New York on the fourth, in Pennsylvania on the eleventh, in Connecticut on the twenty-second, and in Delaware on the twenty-seventh, days of April next; in Massachusetts on the third, in Maryland on the seventh, in South Carolina on the twelfth, in New Hampshire on the twentieth, in Virginia on the twenty-second, and in Georgia on the twenty-eight, days of May next, and the subsequent sessions in the respective districts on the like days of every sixth calendar month afterwards, except in South Carolina, where the session of the said court shall commence on the first, and in Georgia where it shall commence on the seventeenth day of October, and except when any of those days shall happen on a Sunday, and then the session shall commence on the next day following. And the sessions of the said circuit court shall be held in the district of New Hampshire, at Portsmouth and Exeter alternately, beginning at the first; in the district of Massachusetts, at Boston; in the district of Connecticut, alternately at Hartford and New Haven, beginning at the last; in the district of New York, alternately at New York and Albany, beginning at the first; in the district of New Jersey, at Trenton; in the district of Pennsylvania, alternately at Philadelphia and Yorktown, beginning at the first; in the district of Delaware, alternately at New Castle and Dover, beginning at the first; in the district of Maryland, alternately at Annapolis and Easton, beginning at the first; in the district of Virginia, alternately at Charlottesville and Williamsburgh, beginning at the first; in the district of South Carolina, alternately at Columbia and Charleston, beginning at the first; and in the district of Georgia, alternately at Savannah and Augusta, beginning at the first. And the circuit courts shall have power to hold special sessions for the trial of criminal causes at any other time at their discretion, or at the discretion of the Supreme Court.

Sec. 6. *And be it further enacted,* That the Supreme Court may, by any one or more of its justices being present, be adjourned from day to day until a quorum be convened; and that a circuit court may also be adjourned from day to day by any one of its judges, or if none are present, by the marshal of the district until a quorum be convened; and that a district court, in case of the inability of the judge to attend at the commencement of a session, may by virtue of a written order from the said judge, directed to the marshal of the district, be adjourned by the said marshal to such day, antecedent to the next stated session of the said court, as in the said order shall be appointed; and in case of the death of the said judge, and his vacancy not being supplied, all process, pleadings and proceedings of what nature soever, pending before the said court, shall be continued of course until the next stated session after the appointment and acceptance of the office by his successor.

Sec. 7. *And be it [further] enacted,* That the Supreme Court, and the district courts shall have power to appoint clerks for their respective courts, and that the clerk for each district court shall be clerk also of the circuit court in such district, and each of the said clerks shall, before he enters upon the execution of his office, take the following oath or affirmation, to wit: "I, A.B., being appointed clerk of , do solemnly swear, or affirm, that I will truly and faithfully enter and record all the orders, decrees, judgments and proceedings of the said court, and that I will faithfully and impartially discharge and perform all the duties of my said office, according to the best of my abilities and understanding. So help me God." Which words, so help me God, shall be omitted in all cases where an affirmation is admitted instead of an oath. And the said clerks shall also severally give bond, with sufficient sureties, (to be approved of by the Supreme and district courts respectively) to the United States, in the sum of two thousand dollars, faithfully to discharge the duties of his office, and seasonably to record the decrees, judgments and determinations of the court of which he is clerk.

Sec. 8. *And be it further enacted,* That the justices of the Supreme Court, and the district judges, before they proceed to execute the duties of their respective offices, shall take the following oath or affirmation, to wit: "I, A.B.,

do solemnly swear or affirm, that I will administer justice without respect to persons, and do equal right to the poor and to the rich, and that I will faithfully and impartially discharge and perform all the duties incumbent on me as , according to the best of my abilities and understanding, agreeably to the constitution and laws of the United States. So help me God."

Sec. 9. *And be it further enacted,* That the district courts shall have, exclusively of the courts of the several States, cognizance of all crimes and offences that shall be cognizable under the authority of the United States, committed within their respective districts, or upon the high seas; where no other punishment than whipping, not exceeding thirty stripes, a fine not exceeding one hundred dollars, or a term of imprisonment not exceeding six months, is to be inflicted; and shall also have exclusive original cognizance of all civil causes of admiralty and maritime jurisdiction, including all seizures under laws of impost, navigation or trade of the United States, where the seizures are made, on waters which are navigable from the sea by vessels of ten or more tons burthen, within their respective districts as well as upon the high seas; saving to suitors, in all cases, the right of a common law remedy, where the common law is competent to give it; and shall also have exclusive original cognizance of all seizures on land, or other waters than as aforesaid, made, and of all suits for penalties and forfeitures incurred, under the laws of the United States. And shall also have cognizance, concurrent with the courts of the several States, or the circuit courts, as the case may be, of all causes where an alien sues for a tort only in violation of the law of nations or a treaty of the United States. And shall also have cognizance, concurrent as last mentioned, of all suits at common law where the United States sue, and the matter in dispute amounts, exclusive of costs, to the sum or value of one hundred dollars. And shall also have jurisdiction exclusively of the courts of the several States, of all suits against consuls or vice-consuls, except for offences above the description aforesaid. And the trial of issues in fact, in the district courts, in all causes except civil causes of admiralty and maritime jurisdiction, shall be by jury.

Sec. 10. *And be it further enacted,* That the district court in Kentucky district shall, besides the jurisdiction aforesaid, have jurisdiction of all other causes, except of appeals and writs of error, hereinafter made cognizable in a circuit court, and shall proceed therein in the same manner as a circuit court, and writs of error and appeals shall lie from decisions therein to the Supreme Court in the same causes, as from a circuit court to the Supreme Court, and under the same regulations. And the district court in Maine district shall, besides the jurisdiction herein before granted, have jurisdiction of all causes, except of appeals and writs of error herein after made cognizable in a circuit court, and shall proceed therein in the same manner as a circuit court: And writs of error shall lie from decisions therein to the circuit court in the district of Massachusetts in the same manner as from other district courts to their respective circuit courts.

Sec. 11. *And be it further enacted,* That the circuit courts shall have original cognizance, concurrent with the courts of the several States, of all suits of a civil nature at common law or in equity, where the matter in dispute exceeds, exclusive of costs, the sum or value of five hundred dollars, and the United States are plaintiffs, or petitioners; or an alien is a party, or the suit is between a citizen of the State where the suit is brought, and a citizen of another State. And shall have exclusive cognizance of all crimes and offences cognizable under the authority of the United States, except where this act otherwise provides, or the laws of the United States shall otherwise direct, and concurrent jurisdiction with the district courts of the crimes and offences cognizable therein. But no person shall be arrested in one district for trial in another, in any civil action before a circuit or district court. And no civil suit shall be brought before either of said courts against an inhabitant of the United States, by any original process in any other district than that whereof he is an inhabitant, or in which he shall be found at the time of serving the writ, nor shall any district or circuit court have cognizance of any suit to recover the contents of any promissory note or other chose in action in favour of an assignee, unless a suit might have been prosecuted in such court to recover the said contents if no assignment had been made, except in cases of foreign bills of exchange. And the circuit courts shall also have appellate jurisdiction from the district courts under the regulations and restrictions herein after provided.

Sec. 12. *And be it further enacted,* That if a suit be commenced in any state court against an alien, or by a citizen of the state in which the suit is brought against a citizen of another state, and the matter in dispute exceeds the aforesaid sum or value of five hundred dollars, exclusive of costs, to be made to appear to the satisfaction of the court; and the defendant shall, at the time of entering his appearance in such state court, file a petition for the removal of the cause for trial into the next circuit court, to be held in the district where the suit is pending, or if in the district of Maine to the district court next to be holden therein, or if in Kentucky district to the district court next to be holden therein, and offer good and sufficient surety for his entering in such court, on the first day of its session, copies of said process against him, and also for his there appearing and entering special bail in the cause, if special bail was originally requisite therein, it shall then be the duty of the state court to accept the surety, and proceed no further in the cause, and any bail that may have been originally taken shall be discharged, and the said copies being entered as aforesaid, in such court of the United States, the cause shall there proceed in the same manner as if it had been brought there by original process. And any attachment of the goods or estate of the defendant by the original process, shall hold the goods or estate so attached, to answer the final judgment in the same manner as by the laws of such state they would have been holden to answer final judgment, had it been rendered by the court in which the suit commenced. And if in any action commenced in a state court, the title of land be concerned, and the parties are citizens of the same state, and the matter in dispute exceeds the sum or value of five hundred dollars, exclusive of costs, the sum or value being made to appear to the satisfaction of the court, either party, before the trial, shall state to the court and make affidavit if they require it, that he claims and shall rely upon a right or title to the land, under a grant from a state other than that in which the suit is pending, and produce the original grant or an exemplification of it, except where the loss of public records shall put it out of his power, and shall move that the adverse party inform the court, whether he claims a right or title to the land under a grant from the state in which the suit is pending; the said adverse [party] shall give such information, or otherwise not be allowed to plead such grant, or give it in evidence upon the trial, and if he informs that he does claim under such grant, the party claiming under the grant first mentioned may then, on motion, remove the cause for trial to the next circuit court to be holden in such district, or if in the district of Maine, to the court next to be holden therein; or if in Kentucky district, to the district court next to be holden therein; but if he is the defendant, shall do it under the same regulations as in the before-mentioned case of the removal of a cause into such court by an alien; and neither party removing the cause, shall be allowed to plead or give evidence of any other title than that by him stated as aforesaid, as the ground of his claim; and the trial of issues in fact in the circuit courts shall, in all suits, except those of equity, and of admiralty, and maritime jurisdiction, be by jury.

Sec. 13. *And be it further enacted,* That the Supreme Court shall have exclusive jurisdiction of all controversies of a civil nature, where a state is a party, except between a state and its citizens; and except also between a state and citizens of other states, or aliens, in which latter case it shall have original but not exclusive jurisdiction. And shall have exclusively all such jurisdiction of suits or proceedings against ambassadors, or other public ministers, or their domestics, or domestic servants, as a court of law can have or exercise consistently with the law of nations; and original, but not exclusive jurisdiction of all suits brought by ambassadors, or other public ministers, or in which a consul, or vice consul, shall be a party. And the trial of issues in fact in the Supreme Court, in all actions at law against citizens of the United States, shall be by jury. The Supreme Court shall also have appellate jurisdiction from the circuit courts and courts of the several states, in the cases herein after specially provided for; and shall have power to issue writs of prohibition to the district courts, when proceeding as courts of admiralty and maritime jurisdiction, and writs of *mandamus,* in cases warranted by the principles and usages of law, to any courts appointed, or persons holding office, under the authority of the United States.

Sec. 14. *And be it further enacted,* That all the before-mentioned courts of the United States, shall have power to issue writs of *scire facias, habeas corpus,* and all other writs not specially provided for by statute, which may be necessary for the exercise of their respective jurisdiction, and agreeable to the principles and usages of law. And that either of the justices of the supreme court, as well as judges of the district courts, shall have power to grant writs of *habeas corpus* for the purpose of an inquiry into the cause of commitment.—*Provided,* That writs of *habeas corpus* shall in no case extend to prisoners in gaol, unless where they are in custody, under or by colour of the authority of the United States, or are committed for trial before some court of the same, or are necessary to be brought into court to testify.

Sec. 15. *And be it further enacted,* That all the said courts of the United States, shall have power in the trial of actions at law, on motion and due notice thereof being given, to require the parties to produce books or writings in their possession or power, which contain evidence pertinent to the issue, in cases and under circumstances where they might be compelled to produce the same by the ordinary rules of proceeding in chancery; and if a plaintiff shall fail to comply with such order, to produce books or writings, it shall be lawful for the courts respectively, on motion, to give the like judgment for the defendant as in cases of nonsuit; and if a defendant shall fail to comply with such order, to produce books or writings, it shall be lawful for the courts respectively on motion as aforesaid, to give judgment against him or her by default.

Sec. 16. *And be it further enacted,* That suits in equity shall not be sustained in either of the courts of the United States, in any case where plain, adequate and complete remedy may be had at law.

Sec. 17. *And be it further enacted,* That all the said courts of the United States shall have power to grant new trials, in cases where there has been a trial by jury for reasons for which new trials have usually been granted in the courts of law; and shall have power to impose and administer all necessary oaths or affirmations, and to punish by fine or imprisonment, at the discretion of said courts, all contempts of authority in any cause or hearing before the

same; and to make and establish all necessary rules for the orderly conducting business in the said courts, provided such rules are not repugnant to the laws of the United States.

Sec. 18. *And be it further enacted,* That when a circuit court, judgment upon a verdict in a civil action shall be entered, execution may on motion of either party, at the discretion of the court, and on such conditions for the security of the adverse party as they may judge proper, be stayed forty-two days from the time of entering judgment, to give time to file in the clerk's office of said court, a petition for a new trial. And if such petition be there filed within said term of forty-two days, with a certificate thereon from either of the judges of such court, that he allows the same to be filed, which certificate he may make or refuse at his discretion, execution shall of course be further stayed to the next session of said court. And if a new trial be granted, the former judgment shall be thereby rendered void.

Sec. 19. *And be it further enacted,* That it shall be the duty of circuit courts, in causes in equity and of admiralty and maritime jurisdiction, to cause the facts on which they found their sentence or decree, fully to appear upon the record either from the pleadings and decree itself, or a state of the case agreed by the parties, or their counsel, or if they disagree by a stating of the case by the court.

Sec. 20. *And be it further enacted,* That where in a circuit court, a plaintiff in an action, originally brought there, or a petitioner in equity, other than the United States, recovers less than the sum or value of five hundred dollars, or a libellant, upon his own appeal, less than the sum or value of three hundred dollars, he shall not be allowed, but at the discretion of the court, may be adjudged to pay costs.

Sec. 21. *And be it further enacted,* That from final decrees in a district court in causes of admiralty and maritime jurisdiction, where the matter in dispute exceeds the sum or value of three hundred dollars, exclusive of costs, an appeal shall be allowed to the next circuit court, to be held in such district. *Provided nevertheless,* That all such appeals from final decrees as aforesaid, from the district court of Maine, shall be made to the circuit court, next to be holden after each appeal in the district of Massachusetts.

Sec. 22. *And be it further enacted,* That final decrees and judgments in civil actions in a district court, where the matter in dispute exceeds the sum or value of fifty dollars, exclusive of costs, may be re-examined, and reversed or affirmed in a circuit court, holden in the same district, upon a writ of error, whereto shall be annexed and returned therewith at the day and place therein mentioned, an authenticated transcript of the record, an assignment of errors, and prayer for reversal, with a citation to the adverse party, signed by the judge of such district court, or a justice of the Supreme Court, the adverse party having at least twenty days' notice. And upon a like process, may final judgments and decrees in civil actions, and suits in equity in a circuit court, brought there by original process, or removed there from courts of the several States, or removed there by appeal from a district court where the matter in dispute exceeds the sum or value of two thousand dollars, exclusive of costs, be re-examined and reversed or affirmed in the Supreme Court, the citation being in such case signed by a judge of such circuit court, or justice of the Supreme Court, and the adverse party having at least thirty days notice. But there shall be no reversal in either court on such writ of error for error in ruling any plea in abatement, other than a plea to the jurisdiction of the court, or such plea to a petition or bill in equity, as is in the nature of a demurrer, or for any error in fact. And writs of error shall not be brought but within five years after rendering or passing the judgment or decree complained of, or in case the person entitled to such writ of error be an infant, *feme covert, non compos mentis,* or imprisoned, then within five years as aforesaid, exclusive of the time of such disability. And every justice or judge signing a citation on any writ of error as aforesaid, shall take good and sufficient security, that the plaintiff in error shall prosecute his writ of effect, and answer all damages and costs if he fail to make his plea good.

Sec. 23. *And be it further enacted,* That a writ of error as aforesaid shall be a supersedeas and stay execution in cases only where the writ of error is served, by a copy thereof being lodged for the adverse party in the clerk's office where the record remains, within ten days, Sundays exclusive, after rendering the judgment or passing the decree complained of. Until the expiration of which term of ten days, executions shall not issue in any case where a writ of error may be a supersedeas; and whereupon such writ of error the Supreme or a circuit court shall affirm a judgment or decree, they shall adjudge or decree to the respondent in error just damages for his delay, and single or double costs at their discretion.

Sec. 24. *And be it further enacted,* That when a judgment or decree shall be reversed in circuit court, such court shall proceed to render such judgment or pass such decree as the district court should have rendered or passed; and the Supreme Court shall do the same on reversals therein, except where the reversal is in favour of the plaintiff, or petitioner in the original suit, and the damages to be assessed, or matter to be decreed, are uncertain, in which case they shall remand the cause for a final decision. And the Supreme Court shall not issue execution in causes that are removed before them by writs of error, but shall send a special mandate to the circuit court to award execution thereupon.

Sec. 25. *And be it further enacted,* That a final judgment or decree in any suit, in the highest court of law or equity of a State in which a decision in the suit could be had, where is drawn in question the validity of a treaty or statute of, or an authority exercised under the United States, and the decision is against their validity; or where is drawn in question the validity of a statute of, or an authority exercised under any State, on the ground of their being repugnant to the constitution, treaties or laws of the United States, and the decision is in favour of such their validity, or where is drawn in question the construction of any clause of the constitution, or of a treaty, or statute of, or commission held under the United States, and the decision is against the title, right, privilege or exemption specially set up or claimed by either party, under such clause of the said Constitution, treaty, statute or commission, may be re- examined and reversed or affirmed in the Supreme Court of the United States upon a writ of error, the citation being signed by the chief justice, or judge or chancellor of the court rendering or passing the judgment or decree complained of, or by a justice of the Supreme Court of the United States, in the same manner and under the same regulations, and the writ shall have the same effect, as if the judgment or decree complained of had been rendered or passed in a circuit court, and the proceeding upon the reversal shall also be the same, except that the Supreme Court, instead of remanding the cause for a final decision as before provided, may at their discretion, if the cause shall have been once remanded before, proceed to a final decision of the same, and award execution. But no other error shall be assigned or regarded as a ground of reversal in any such case as aforesaid, than such as appears on the face of the record, and immediately respects the before mentioned questions of validity or construction of the said constitution, treaties, statutes, commissions, or authorities in dispute.

Sec. 26. *And be it further enacted,* That in all causes brought before either of the courts of the United States to recover the forfeiture annexed to any articles of agreement, covenant, bond, or other speciality, where the forfeiture, breach or non-performance shall appear, by the default or confession of the defendant, or upon demurrer, the court before whom the action is, shall render judgment therein for the plaintiff to recover so much as is due according to equity. And when the sum for which judgment should be rendered is uncertain, the same shall, if either of the parties request it, be assessed by a jury.

Sec. 27. *And be it further enacted,* That a marshal shall be appointed in and for each district for the term of four years, but shall be removable from office at pleasure, whose duty it shall be to attend the district and circuit courts when sitting therein, and also the Supreme Court in the district in which that court shall sit. And to execute throughout the district, all lawful precepts directed to him, and issued under the authority of the United States, and he shall have power to command all necessary assistance in the execution of his duty, and to appoint as there shall be occasion, one or more deputies, who shall be removable from office by the judge of the district court, or the circuit court sitting within the district, at the pleasure of either; and before he enters on the duties of his office, he shall become bound for the faithful performance of the same, by himself and by his deputies before the judge of the district court to the United States, jointly and severally, with two good and sufficient sureties, inhabitants and freeholders of such district, to be approved by the district judge, in the sum of twenty thousand dollars, and shall take before said judge, as shall also his deputies, before they enter on the duties of their appointment, the following oath of office: "I, A. B., do solemnly swear or affirm, that I will faithfully execute all lawful precepts directed to the marshal of the district of under the authority of the United States, and true returns make, and in all things well and truly, and without malice or partiality, perform the duties of the office of marshal (or marshal's deputy, as the case may be) of the district of , during my continuance in said office, and take only my lawful fees. So help me God."

Sec. 28. *And be it further enacted,* That in all causes wherein the marshal or his deputy shall be a party, the writs and precepts therein shall be directed to such disinterested person as the court, or any justice or judge thereof may appoint, and the person so appointed, is hereby authorized to execute and return the same. And in case of the death of any marshal, his deputy or deputies shall continue in office, unless otherwise specially removed; and shall execute the same in the name of the deceased, until another marshall shall be appointed and sworn: And the defaults of misfeasances in office of such deputy or deputies in the mean time, as well as before, shall be adjudged a breach of the condition of the bond given, as before directed, by the marshal who appointed them; and the executor or administrator of the deceased marshal shall have like remedy for the defaults and misfeasances in office of such deputy or deputies during such interval, as they would be entitled to if the marshal had continued in life and in the exercise of his said office, until his successor was appointed, and sworn or affirmed: And every marshal or his deputy when removed from office, or when the term for which the marshal is appointed shall expire, shall have power notwithstanding to execute all such precepts as may be in their hands respectively at the time of such removal or expiration of office; and the marshal shall be held answerable for the delivery to his successor of all prisoners which may be in his custody at the time of his removal, or when the term for which he is appointed shall expire, and for that purpose may retain such prisoners in his custody

until his successor shall be appointed and qualified as the law directs.

Sec. 29. *And be it further enacted,* That in cases punishable with death, the trial shall be had in the county where the offence was committed, or where that cannot be done without great inconvenience, twelve petit jurors at least shall be summoned from thence. And jurors in all cases to serve in the courts of the United States shall be designated by lot or otherwise in each State respectively according to the mode of forming juries therein now practised, so far as the laws of the same shall render such designation practicable by the courts or marshals of the United States; and the jurors shall have the same qualifications as are requisite for jurors by the laws of the State of which they are citizens, to serve in the highest courts of law of such State, and shall be returned as there shall be occasion for them, from such parts of the district from time to time as the court shall direct, so as shall be most favourable to an impartial trial, and so as not to incur an unnecessary expense, or unduly to burthen the citizens of any part of the district with such services. And writs of *venire facias* when directed by the court shall issue from the clerk's office, and shall be served and returned by the marshal in his proper person, or by his deputy, or in case the marshal or his deputy is not an indifferent person, or is interested in the event of the cause, by such fit person as the court shall specially appoint for that purpose, to whom they shall administer on oath or affirmation that he will truly and impartially serve and return such writ. And when from challenges or otherwise there shall not be a jury to determine any civil or criminal cause, the marshal or his deputy shall, by order of the court where such defect of jurors shall happen, return jurymen *de talibus circumstantibus* sufficient to complete the pannel; and when the marshal or his deputy are disqualified as aforesaid, jurors may be returned by such disinterested person as the court shall appoint.

Sec. 30. *And be it further enacted,* That the mode of proof by oral testimony and examination of witnesses in open court shall be the same in all the courts of the United States, as well in the trial of causes in equity and of admiralty and maritime jurisdiction, as of actions at common law. And when the testimony of any person shall be necessary in any civil cause depending in any district in any court of the United States, who shall live at a greater distance from the place of trial than one hundred miles, or is bound on a voyage to sea, or is about to go out of the United States, or out of such district, and to a greater distance from the place of trial than as aforesaid, before the time of trial, or is ancient or very infirm, the deposition of such person may be taken *de bene esse* before any justice or judge of any of the courts of the United States, or before any chancellor, justice or judge of a supreme or superior court, major or chief magistrate of a city, or judge of a county court or court of common pleas of any of the United States, not being of counsel or attorney to either of the parties, or interested in the event of the cause, provided that a notification from the magistrate before whom the deposition is to be taken to the adverse party, to be present at the taking of the same, and to put interrogatories, if he think fit, be first made out and served on the adverse party or his attorney as either may be nearest, if either is within one hundred miles of the place of such caption, allowing time for their attendance after notified, not less than at the rate of one day, Sundays exclusive, for every twenty miles travel. And in causes of admiralty and maritime jurisdiction, or other cases of seizure when a libel shall be filed, in which an adverse party is not named, and depositions of persons circumstanced as aforesaid shall be taken before a claim be put in, the like notification as aforesaid shall be given to the person having the agency or possession of the property libelled at the time of the capture or seizure of the same, if known to the libellant. And every person deposing as aforesaid shall be carefully examined and cautioned, and sworn or affirmed to testify the whole truth, and shall subscribe the testimony by him or her given after the same shall be reduced to writing, which shall be done only by the magistrate taking the deposition, or by the deponent in his presence. And the depositions so taken shall be retained by such magistrate until he deliver the same with his own hand into the court for which they are taken, or shall, together with a certificate of the reasons as aforesaid of their being taken, and of the notice if any given to the adverse party, be by him the said magistrate sealed up and directed to such court, and remain under his seal until opened in court. And any person may be compelled to appear and depose as aforesaid in the same manner as to appear and testify in court. And in the trial of any cause of admiralty or maritime jurisdiction in a district court, the decree in which may be appealed from, if either party shall suggest to and satisfy the court that probably it will not be in his power to produce the witnesses there testifying before the circuit court should an appeal be had, and shall move that their testimony be taken down in writing, it shall be so done by the clerk of the court. And if an appeal be had, such testimony may be used on the trial of the same, if it shall appear to the satisfaction of the court which shall try the appeal, that the witnesses are then dead or gone out of the United States, or to a greater distance than as aforesaid from the place where the court is sitting, or that by reason of age, sickness, bodily infirmity or imprisonment, they are unable to travel and appear at court, but not otherwise. And unless the same shall be made to appear on the trial of any cause, with respect to witnesses whose depositions may have been taken therein, such depositions shall not be admitted or used in the

cause. *Provided,* That nothing herein shall be construed to prevent any court of the United States from granting a *dedimus potestatem* to take depositions according to common usage, when it may be necessary to prevent a failure or delay of justice, which power they shall severally possess, nor to extend to depositions taken in *perpetuam rei memoriam,* which if they relate to matters that may be cognizable in any court of the United States, a circuit court on application thereto made as a court of equity, may, according to the usages in chancery direct to be taken.

Sec. 31. *And be it [further] enacted,* That where any suit shall be depending in any court of the United States, and either of the parties shall die before final judgment, the executor or administrator of such deceased party who was plaintiff, petitioner, or defendant, in case the cause of action doth by law survive, shall have full power to prosecute or defend any such suit or action until final judgment; and the defendant or defendants are hereby obliged to answer thereto accordingly; and the court before whom such cause may be depending, is hereby empowered and directed to hear and determine the same, and to render judgment for or against the executor or administrator, as the case may require. And if such executor or administrator having been duly served with a *scire facias* from the office of the clerk of the court where such suit is depending, twenty days beforehand, shall neglect or refuse to become a party to the suit, the court may render judgment against the estate of the deceased party, in the same manner as if the executor or administrator had voluntarily made himself a party to the suit. And the executor or administrator who shall become a party as aforesaid, shall, upon motion to the court where the suit is depending, be entitled to a continuance of the same until the next term of the said court. And if there be two or more plaintiffs or defendants, and one or more of they shall die, if the cause of action shall survive to the surviving plaintiff or plaintiffs, or against the surviving defendant or defendants, the writ or action shall not be thereby abated; but such death being suggested upon the record, the action shall proceed at the suit of the surviving plaintiff or plaintiffs against the surviving defendant or defendants.

Sec. 32. *And be it further enacted,* That no summons, writ, declaration, return, process, judgment, or other proceedings in civil causes in any of the courts of the United States, shall be abated, arrested, quashed or reversed, for any defect or want of form, but the said courts respectively shall proceed and give judgment according as the right of the cause and matter in law shall appear unto them, without regarding any imperfections, defects, or want of form in such writ, declaration, or other pleading, return, process, judgment, or course of proceeding whatsoever, except those only in cases of demurrer, which the party demurring shall specially sit down and express together with his demurrer as the cause thereof. And the said courts respectively shall and may, by virtue of this act, from time to time, amend all and every such imperfections, defects and wants of form, other than those only which the party demurring shall express as aforesaid, and may at any time permit either of the parties to amend any defect in the process or pleadings, upon such conditions as the said courts respectively shall in their discretion, and by their rules prescribed.

Sec. 33. *And be it further enacted,* That for any crime or offence against the United States, the offender may, by any justice or judge of the United States, or by any justice of the peace, or other magistrate of any of the United States where he may be found agreeably to the usual mode of process against offenders in such state, and at the expense of the United States, be arrested, and imprisoned or bailed, as the case may be, for trial before such court of the United States as by this act has cognizance of the offence. And copies of the process shall be returned as speedily as may be into the clerk's office of such court, together with the recognizances of the witnesses for their appearance to testify in the case; which recognizances the magistrate before whom the examination shall be, may require on pain of imprisonment. And if such commitment of the offender, or the witnesses shall be in a district other than that in which the offence is to be tried, it shall be the duty of the judge of that district where the delinquent is imprisoned, seasonably to issue, and of the marshal of the same district to execute, a warrant for the removal of the offender, and the witnesses, or either of them, as the case may be, to the district in which the trial is to be had. And upon all arrests in criminal cases, bail shall be admitted, except where the punishment may be death, in which cases it shall not be admitted but by the supreme or a circuit court, or by a justice of the supreme court, or a judge of a district court, who shall exercise their discretion therein, regarding the nature and circumstances of the offence, and of the evidence, and the usages of law. And if a person committed by a justice of the supreme or a judge of a district court for an offence not punishable with death, shall afterwards procure bail, and there be no judge of the United States in the district to take the same, it may be taken by any judge of the supreme or superior court of law of such state.

Sec. 34. *And be it further enacted,* That the laws of the several states, except where the constitution, treaties or statutes of the United States shall otherwise require or provide, shall be regarded as rules of decision in trials at common law in the courts of the United States in cases where they apply.

Sec. 35. *And be it further enacted,* That in all the courts of the United States, the parties may plead and manage their own causes personally or by the assistance of such counsel or attorneys at law as by the rules of the said courts respectively shall be permitted to manage and conduct causes therein. And there shall be appointed in each district a meet person learned in the law to act as attorney for the United States in such district, who shall be sworn or affirmed to the faithful execution of his office, whose duty it shall be to prosecute in such district all delinquents for crimes and offences, cognizable under the authority of the United States, and all civil actions in which the United States shall be concerned, except before the supreme court in the district in which that court shall be holden. And he shall receive as a compensation for his services such fees as shall be taxed therefor in the respective courts before which the suits or prosecutions shall be. And there shall also be appointed a meet person, learned in the law, to act as attorney-general for the United States, who shall be sworn or affirmed to a faithful execution of his office; whose duty it shall be to prosecute and conduct all suits in the Supreme Court in which the United States shall be concerned, and to give his advice and opinion upon questions of law when required by the President of the United States, or when requested by the heads of any of the departments, touching any matters that may concern their departments, and shall receive such compensation for his services as shall by law be provided.

Source:
United States Statutes at Large, 1789, 1st Cong., Sess. I, pp. 73–93.

Alexander Hamilton, First Report on the Public Credit, 1790

Report submitted to the U.S. Congress by Secretary of the Treasury Alexander Hamilton on January 14, 1790, outlining his fiscal program. With the goals of establishing public credit domestically and abroad and of strengthening the central government at the expense of the states, Hamilton recommended that the United States fund the foreign and domestic debt at full value, allowing creditors to replace depreciated securities with new interest-bearing bonds at face value, and that the federal government assume the debts incurred by the states during the American Revolution (1775–83). The foreign debt was set at $11 million and the domestic debt at $40 million; the state debts were estimated at $25 million.

Despite opposition in states that had paid their debts, Congress enacted the Assumption Act on August 4, 1790, amended on March 3, 1791. The issue was settled by compromise. Most of the states that had paid their debts were in the South. Hamilton agreed to support a plan to locate the nation's capital along the Potomac in exchange for southern support of the Assumption Act. Congress authorized the president to borrow up to $12 million to discharge the overdue interest and payments on the foreign debt and to pay off the entire debt, if possible. It also authorized a loan of $21.5 million to pay off the state debts. Income from import duties was set aside to pay the interest and principal of the public debt, and proceeds from the sale of public lands in the West were designated to discharge the principal. The Funding Act helped to reestablish commerce in the United States.

The Secretary of the Treasury, in obedience to the resolution of the House of Representatives, of the twenty-first day of September last, has, during the recess of Congress, applied himself to the consideration of a proper plan for the support of the Public Credit, with all the attention which was due to the authority of the House, and to the magnitude of the object.

In the discharge of this duty, he has felt, in no small degree, the anxieties which naturally flow from a just estimate of the difficulty of the task, from a well-founded diffidence of his own qualifications for executing it with success, and from a deep and solemn conviction of the momentous nature of the truth contained in the resolution under which his investigations have been conducted, "That an *adequate* provision for the support of the Public Credit, is a matter of high importance to the honor and prosperity of the United States."

With an ardent desire that his well-meant endeavors may be conducive to the real advantage of the nation, and with the utmost deference to the superior judgment of the House, he now respectfully submits the result of his enquiries and reflections, to their indulgent construction.

In the opinion of the Secretary, the wisdom of the House, in giving their explicit sanction to the proposition which has been stated, cannot but be applauded by all, who will seriously consider, and trace through their obvious consequences, these plain and undeniable truths.

That exigencies are to be expected to occur, in the affairs of nations, in which there will be a necessity for borrowing.

That loans in times of public danger, especially from foreign war, are found an indispensable resource, even to the wealthiest of them.

And that in a country, which, like this, is possessed of little active wealth, or in other words, little monied capital, the necessity for that resource, must in such emergencies, be proportionably urgent.

And as on the one hand, the necessity for borrowing in particular emergencies cannot be doubted, so on the other, it is equally evident, that to be able to borrow upon *good terms*, it is essential that the credit of a nation should be well established.

For when the credit of a country is in any degree questionable, it never fails to give an extravagant premium, in one shape or another, upon all the loans it has occasion to make. Nor does the evil end here; the same disadvantage must be sustained upon whatever is to be bought on terms of future payment.

From this constant necessity of *borrowing* and *buying dear*, it is easy to conceive how immensely the expences of a nation, in a course of time, will be augmented by an unsound state of the public credit.

To attempt to enumerate the complicated variety of mischiefs in the whole system of the social economy, which proceed from a neglect of the maxims that uphold public credit, and justify the solicitude manifested by the House on this point, would be an improper intrusion on their time and patience.

In so strong a light nevertheless do they appear to the Secretary, that on their due observance at the present critical juncture, materially depends, in his judgment, the individual and aggregate prosperity of the citizens of the United States; their relief from the embarrassments they now experience; their character as a People; the cause of good government.

If the maintenance of public credit, then, be truly so important, the next enquiry which suggests itself is, by what means it is to be affected? The ready answer to which question is, by good faith, by a punctual performance of contracts. States, like individuals, who observe their engagements, are respected and trusted: while the reverse is the fate of those, who pursue an opposite conduct.

Every breach of the public engagements, whether from choice or necessity, is in different degrees hurtful to public credit. When such a necessity does truly exist, the evils of it are only to be palliated by a scrupulous attention, on the part of the government, to carry the violation no farther than the necessity absolutely requires, and to manifest, if the nature of the case admits of it, a sincere disposition to make reparation, whenever circumstances shall permit. But with every possible mitigation, credit must suffer, and numerous mischiefs ensue. It is therefore highly important, when an appearance of necessity seems to press upon the public councils, that they should examine well its reality, and be perfectly assured, that there is no method of escaping from it, before they yield to its suggestions. For though it cannot safely be affirmed, that occasions have never existed, or may not exist, in which violations of the public faith, in this respect, are inevitable; yet there is great reason to believe, that they exist far less frequently than precedents indicate; and are oftenest either pretended through levity, or want of firmness, or supposed through want of knowledge. Expedients might often have been devised to effect, consistently with good faith, what has been done in contravention of it. Those who are most commonly creditors of a nation, are, generally speaking, enlightened men; and there are signal examples to warrant a conclusion, that when a candid and fair appeal is made to them, they will understand their true interest too well to refuse their concurrence in such modifications of their claims, as any real necessity may demand.

While the observance of that good faith, which is the basis of public credit, is recommended by the strongest inducements of political expediency, it is enforced by considerations of still greater authority. There are arguments for it, which rest on the immutable principles of moral obligation. And in proportion as the mind is disposed to contemplate, in the order of Providence, as intimate connection between public virtue and public happiness, will be its repugnancy to a violation of those principles.

This reflection derives additional strength from the nature of the debt of the United States. It was the price of liberty. The faith of America has been repeatedly pledged for it, and with solemnities, that give peculiar force to the obligation. There is indeed reason to regret that it has not hitherto been kept; that the necessities of the war, conspiring with inexperience in the subjects of finance, produced direct infractions; and that the subsequent period has been a continued scene of negative violation, or noncompliance. But a diminution of this regret arises from the reflection, that the last seven years have exhibited an earnest and uniform effort, on the part of the government of the union, to retrieve the national credit, by doing justice to the creditors of the nation; and that the embarrassments of a defective constitution, which defeated this laudable effort, have ceased.

From this evidence of a favorable disposition, given by the former government, the institution of a new one, cloathed with powers competent to calling forth the resources of the community, has excited correspondent expectations. A general belief, accordingly, prevails, that the credit of the United States will quickly be established on the firm foundation of an effectual provision for the existing debt. The influence, which this has had at home, is witnessed by the rapid increase, that has taken place in the market value of the public securities. From January to November, they rose thirty-three and a third per cent, and from that period to this time, they have risen fifty per cent more. And the intelligence from abroad announces effects proportionably favourable to our national credit and consequence.

It cannot but merit particular attention, that among ourselves the most enlightened friends of good government are those, whose expectations are the highest.

To justify and preserve their confidence; to promote the encreasing respectability of the American name; to answer the calls of justice; to restore landed property to its due value; to furnish new resources both to agriculture and commerce; to cement more closely the union of the states; to add to their security against foreign attack; to establish public order on the basis of an upright and liberal policy. These are the great and invaluable ends to be secured, by a proper and adequate provision, at the present period, for the support of public credit.

To this provision we are invited, not only by the general considerations, which have been noticed, but by others of a more particular nature. It will procure to every class of the community some important advantages, and remove some no less important disadvantages.

The advantage to the public creditors from the increased value of that part of their property which constitutes the public debt, needs no explanation.

But there is a consequence of this, less obvious, though not less true, in countries in which every other citizen in interested. It is a well known fact, that in which the national debt is properly funded, and an object of established confidence, it answers most of the purposes of money. Transfers of stock or public debt are there equivalent to payments in specie; or in other words, stock, in the principal transactions of business, passes current as specie. The same thing would, in all probability happen here, under the like circumstances.

The benefits of this as various and obvious.

First. Trade is extended by it; because there is a larger capital to carry it on, and the merchant can at the same time, afford to trade for smaller profits; as his stock, which, when unemployed, brings him in an interest from the government, serves him also as money, when he has a call for it in his commercial operations.

Secondly. Agriculture and manufactures are also promoted by it: For the like reason, that more capital can be commanded to be employed in both; and because the merchant, whose enterprize in foreign trade, gives to them activity and extension, has greater means for enterprize.

Thirdly. The interest of money will be lowered by it; for this is always in a ratio, to the quantity of money, and to the quickness of circulation. This circumstance will enable both the public and individuals to borrow on easier and cheaper terms.

And from the combination of these effects, additional aids will be furnished to labour, to industry, and to arts of every kind.

But these good effects of a public debt are only to be looked for, when, by being well funded, it has acquired an *adequate* and *stable* value. Till then, it has rather a contrary tendency. The fluctuation and insecurity incident to it in an unfunded state, render it a mere commodity, and a precarious one. As such, being only an object of occasional and particular speculation, all the money applied to it is so much diverted from the more useful channels of circulation, for which the thing itself affords no substitute: So that, in fact, one serious inconvenience of an unfunded debt is, that it contributes to the scarcity of money.

This distinction which has been little if at all attended to, is of the greatest moment. It involves a question immediately interesting to every part of the community; which is no other than this—Whether the public debt, by a provision for it on true principles, shall be rendered a *substitute* for money; or whether, by being left as it is, or by being provided for in such a manner as will wound those principles, and destroy confidence, it shall be suffered to continue, as it is, a pernicious drain of our cash from the channels of productive industry.

The effect, which the funding of the public debt, on right principles, would have upon landed property, is one of the circumstances attending such an arrangement, which has been least adverted to, though it deserves the most particular attention. The present depreciated state of that species of property is a serious calamity. The value of cultivated lands, in most of the states, has fallen since the revolution from 25 to 50 per cent. In those farthest south, the decrease is still more considerable. Indeed, if the representations, continually received from that quarter, may be credited, lands there will command no price, which may not be deemed an almost total sacrifice.

This decrease, in the value of lands, ought, in a great measure, to be attributed to the scarcity of money. Consequently whatever produces an augmentation of the monied capital of the country, must have a proportional effect in raising that value. The beneficial tendency of a funded debt, in this respect, has been manifested by the most decisive experience in Great-Britain.

The proprietors of lands would not only feel the benefit of this increase in the value of their property, and of a more prompt and better sale, when they had occasion to sell; but the necessity of selling would be, itself, greatly diminished. As the same cause would contribute to the facility of loans, there is reason to believe, that such of them as are indebted, would be able through that resource, to satisfy their more urgent creditors.

It ought not however to be expected, that the advantages, described as likely to result from funding the public debt, would be instantaneous. It might require some time to bring the value of stock to its natural level, and to attach to it that fixed confidence, which is necessary to its quality as money. Yet the late rapid rise of the public securities encourages an expectation, that the progress of stock to the desireable point, will be such more expeditous than could have been foreseen. And as in the mean time it will be increasing in value, there is room to conclude, that it will, from the outset, answer many of the purposes in contemplation. Particularly it seems to the probable, that from

creditors, who are not themselves necessitous, it will early meet with a ready reception in payment of debts, at its current price.

Having now taken a concise view of the inducements to a proper provision for the public debt, the next enquiry which presents itself is, what ought to be the nature of such a provision? This requires some preliminary discussions.

It is agreed on all hands, that that part of the debt which has been contracted abroad, and is denominated the foreign debt, ought to be provided for, according to the precise terms of the contracts relating to it. The discussions, which can arise, therefore, will have reference essentially to the domestic part of it, or to that which has been contracted at home. It is to be regretted, that there is not the same unanimity of sentiment on this part, as on the other.

The Secretary has too much deference for the opinions of every part of the community, not to have observed one, which has, more than once, made its appearance in the public prints, and which is occasionally to be met with in conversation. It involves this question, whether a discrimination ought not to be made between original holders of the public securities, and present possessors, by purchase. Those who advocate a discrimination are for making a full provision for the securities of the former, at their nominal value; but contend, that the latter ought to receive no more than the cost to them, and the interest: And the idea is sometimes suggested of making good the difference to the primitive possessor.

In favor of this scheme, it is alledged, that it would be unreasonable to pay twenty shillings in the pound, to one who had not given more for it than three or four. And it is added, that it would be hard to aggravate the misfortune of the first owner, who, probably through necessity, parted with his property at so great a loss, by obliging him to contribute to the profit of the person, who had speculated on his distresses.

The Secretary, after the most mature reflection on the force of this argument, is induced to reject the doctrine it contains, as equally unjust and impolitic, as highly injurious, even to the original holders of public securities; as ruinous to public credit.

It is inconsistent with justice, because in the first place, it is a breach of contract; in violation of the rights of a fair purchaser.

The nature of the contract in its origin, is, that the public will pay the sum expressed in the security, to the first holder, or his *assignee*. The *intent*, in making the security assignable, is, that the proprietor may be able to make use of his property, by selling it for as much as it *may be worth in the market*, and that the buyer may be *safe* in the purchase.

Every buyer therefore stands exactly in the place of the seller, has the same right with him to the identical sum expressed in the security, and having acquired that right, by fair purchase, and in conformity to the original *agreement* and *intention* of the government, his claim cannot be disputed, without manifest injustice.

That he is to be considered as a fair purchaser, results from this: Whatever necessity the seller may have been under, was occasioned by the government, in not making a proper provision for its debts. The buyer had no agency in it, and therefore ought not to suffer. He is not even chargeable with having taken an undue advantage. He paid what the commodity was worth in the market, and took the risks of reimbursement upon himself. He of course gave a fair equivalent, and ought to reap the benefit of his hazard; a hazard which was far from inconsiderable, and which, perhaps, turned on little less than a revolution in government.

That the case of those, who parted with their securities from necessity, is a hard one, cannot be denied. But whatever complaint of injury, or claim of redress, they may have, respects the government solely. They have not only nothing to object to the persons who relieved their necessities, by giving them the current price of their property, but they are even under an implied condition to contribute to the reimbursement of those persons. They knew, that by the terms of the contract with themselves, the public were bound to pay to those, to whom they should convey their title, the sums stipulated to be paid to them; and, that as citizens of the United States, they were to bear their proportion of the contribution for that purpose. This, by the act of assignment, they tacitly engage to do; and if they had an option, they could not, with integrity or good faith, refuse to do it, without the consent of those to whom they sold.

But though many of the original holders sold from necessity, it does not follow, that this was the case with all of them. It may well be supposed, that some of them did it either through want of confidence in an eventual provision, or from the allurements of some profitable speculation. How shall these different classes be discriminated from each other? How shall it be ascertained, in any case, that the money, which the original holder obtained for his security, was not more beneficial to him, than if he had held it to the present time, to avail himself of the provision which shall be made? How shall it be known, whether if the purchaser had employed his money in some other way, he would not be in a better situation, than by having applied it in the purchase of securities, though he should now receive their full amount? And if neither of these things can be known, how shall it be determined whether a discrimination, independent of the breach of contract, would not do a real injury to purchasers; and if it included

a compensation to the primitive proprietors; would not give them an advantage, to which they had no equitable pretension. It may well be imagined, also, that there are not wanting instances, in which individuals, urged by a present necessity, parted with the securities received by them from the public, and shortly after replaced them with others, as an indemnity for their first loss. Shall they be deprived of the indemnity which they have endeavoured to secure by so provident an arrangement?

Questions of this sort, on a close inspection, multiply themselves without end, and demonstrate the injustice of a discrimination, even on the most subtle calculations of equity, abstracted from the obligation of contract.

The difficulties too of regulating the details of a plan for that purpose, which would have even the semblance of equity, would be found immense. It may well be doubted whether they would not be insurmountable, and replete with such absurd, as well as inequitable consequences, as to disgust even the proposers of the measure.

As a specimen of its capricious operation, it will be sufficient to notice the effect it would have upon two persons, who may be supposed two years ago to have purchased, each, securities at three shillings in the pound, and one of them to retain those bought by him, till the discrimination should take place; the other to have parted with those bought by him, within a month past, at nine shillings. The former, who had had most confidence in the government, would in this case only receive at the rate of three shillings and the interest; while the latter, who had had less confidence would receive *for what cost him the same money* at the rate of nine shillings, and his representative, *standing in his place,* would be entitled to a like rate.

The impolicy of a discrimination results from two considerations; one, that is proceeds upon a principle destructive of that *quality* of the public debt, or the stock or the nation, which is essential to its capacity for answering the purposes of money—that is the *security* of *transfer;* the other, that as well on this account, as because it includes a breach of faith, it renders property in the funds less valuable; consequently induces lenders to demand a higher premium for what they lend, and produces every other inconvenience of a bad state of public credit.

It will be perceived at first sight, that the transferable quality of stock is essential to its operation as money, and that this depends on the idea of complete security to the transferee, and a firm persuasion, that no distinction can in any circumstances be made between him and the original proprietor.

The precedent of an invasion of this fundamental principle, would of course tend to deprive the community of an advantage, with which no temporary saving could bear the least comparison.

And it will as readily be perceived, that the same cause would operate a diminution of the value of stock in the hands of the first, as well as of every other holder. The price, which any man, who should incline to purchase, would be willing to give for it, would be in a compound ratio to the immediate profit it afforded, and to the chance of the continuance of his profit. If there was supposed to be any hazard of the latter, the risk would be taken into the calculation, and either there would be no purchase at all, or it would be at a proportionably less price.

For this diminution of the value of stock, every person, who should be about to lend to the government, would demand a compensation; and would add to the actual difference, between the nominal and the market value, and equivalent for the chance of greater decrease; which, in a precarious state of public credit, is always to be taken into the account.

Every compensation of this sort, it is evident, would be an absolute loss to the government. In the preceding discussion of the impolicy of a discrimination, and injurious tendency of it to those, who continue to be the holders of the securities, they received from the government, has been explained. Nothing need be added, on this head, except that his is an additional and interesting light, in which the injustice of the measure may be seen. It would not only divest present proprietors by purchase, of the rights they had acquired under the sanction of public faith, but it would depreciate the property of the remaining original holders.

It is equally unnecessary to add any thing to what has been already said to demonstrate the fatal influence, which the principle of discrimination would have on the public credit.

But there is still a point in view in which it will appear perhaps even more exceptionable, than in either of the former. It would be repugnant to an express provision of the Constitution of the United States. This provision is, that "all debts contracted and engagements entered into before the adoption of that Constitution shall be as valid against the United States under it, as under the confederation." which amounts to a constitutional ratification of the contracts respecting the debt, in the state in which they existed under the confederation. And resorting to that standard, there can be no doubt, that the rights of assignees and original holders, must be considered as equal.

In exploding thus fully the principle of discrimination, the Secretary is happy in reflecting, the he is the only advocate of what has already been sanctioned by the formal and express authority of the government of the Union, in these emphatic terms—"The remaining class of creditors (say Congress in their circular address to the states, of the 26th of April 1783) is composed, partly of such of our fellow-citizens as originally lent to the public the use of their funds, or have since manifested *most confidence* in their country, by receiving transfers from the lenders; and partly of those, whose property has been either advanced or assumed for the public service. To *discriminate* the merits of these several descriptions of creditors, would be a task equally unnecessary and invidious. If the voice of humanity plead more loudly in favor of some than of others, the voice of policy, no less than of justice, pleads in favor of all. A wise nation will never permit those who relieve the wants of their country, or who *rely most* on its *faith,* its *firmness,* and its *resources* when either of them is distrusted, to suffer by the event."

The Secretary concluding, that a discrimination, between the different classes of creditors of the United States, cannot with propriety be *made,* proceeds to examine whether a difference ought to be permitted to *remain* between them, and another description of public creditors—Those of the states individually.

The Secretary, after mature reflection on this point, entertains a full conviction, that an assumption of the debts of the particular states by the union, and a like provision for them, as for those of the union, will be a measure of sound policy and substantial justice.

It would, in the opinion of the Secretary, contribute, in an eminent degree, to an orderly, stable and satisfactory arrangement of the national finances.

Admitting, as ought to be the case, that a provision must be made in some way or other, for the entire debt; it will follow, that no greater revenues will be required, whether that provision be made wholly by the United States, or partly by them, and partly by the states separately.

The principal question then must be, whether such a provision cannot be more conveniently and effectually made, by one general plan issuing from one authority, than by different plans originating in different authorities.

In the first case there can be no competition for resources; in the last, there must be such a competition. The consequences of this, without the greatest caution on both sides, might be interfering regulations, and thence collision and confusion. Particular branches of industry might also be oppressed by it. The most productive objects of revenue are not numerous. Either these must be wholly engrossed by one side, which might lessen the efficacy of the provisions by the other; or both must have recourse to the same objects in different modes, which might occasion an accumulation upon them beyond what they could properly bear. If this should not happen, the caution requisite to avoiding it, would prevent the revenue's deriving the full benefit of each object. The danger of interference and of excess would be apt to impose restraints very unfriendly to the complete command of those resources, which are the most convenient; and to compel the having recourse to others, less eligible in themselves, and less agreeable to the community.

The difficulty of an effectual command of the public resources, in case of separate provisions for the debt, may be seen in another, and perhaps more striking light. It would naturally happen that different states, from local considerations, would in some instances have recourse to different objects, in others, to the same objects, in different degrees, for procuring the funds of which they stood in need. It is easy to conceive how this diversity would affect the aggregate revenue of the country. By the supposition, articles which yielded a full supply in some states, would yield nothing, or an insufficient product, in others. And hence the public revenue would not deprive the full benefit of those articles, from state regulations. Neither could the deficiencies be made good by those of the union. It is a provision of the national constitution that "all duties, imposts and excises, shall be uniform throughout the United States." And as the general government would be under a necessity from motives of policy, of paying regard to the duty, which may have been previously imposed upon any article, though but in a single state it would be constrained, either to refrain wholly from any further imposition upon such article, where it had been already rated (sp) as high as was proper, or to confine itself to the difference between the existing rate, and what the article would reasonably bear. Thus the pre-occupancy of an article by a single state would tend to arrest or abridge the impositions of the union on the article. And as it is supposeable, that a great variety of articles might be placed in this situation, by dissimilar arrangements of the particular states, it is evident, that the aggregate revenue of the country would be likely to be very materially contracted by the plan of separate provisions.

If all the public creditors receive their dues from one source, distributed with an equal hand, their interest will be the same. And having the same interests, they will unite in the support of the fiscal arrangements of the government: As these, too, can be made with more convenience, where there is not competition: These circumstances combined will insure to the revenue laws a more ready and more satisfactory execution.

If on the contrary there are distinct provisions, there will be distinct interests, drawing different ways. That union and concert of views, among the creditors, which in every government is of great importance to their security, and to that of public credit, will not only not exist, but will be likely to give place to mutual jealousy and opposition. And from this cause, the operation of the systems which may be adopted, both by the particular states, and by the union with relation to their respective debts, will be in danger of being enumerated.

There are several reasons, which render it probable, that the situation of the state creditors would be worse, than that of the creditors of the union, if there be not a national assumption of the same debts. Of these it will be sufficient to mention two; one, that a principal branch of revenue is exclusively vested in the union; the other, that a state must always be checked in the imposition of taxes on articles of consumption, from the want of power to extend the same regulation to the other states, and from the tendency of partial duties to injure its industry and commerce. Should the state creditors stand upon a less eligible footing than the others, it is unnatural to expect they would see with pleasure a provision for them. The influence which their dissatisfaction might have, could not but operate injuriously, both for the creditors, and the credit, of the United States.

Hence it is even the interest of the creditors of the union, that those of the individual states should be comprehended in a general provision. Any attempt to secure to the former either exclusive or peculiar advantages, would materially hazard their interests.

Neither would it be just, that one class of the public creditors should be more favoured than the other. The objects for which both descriptions of the debt were contracted, are in the main the same. Indeed a great part of the particular debts of the States has arisen from assumptions by them on account of the union. And it is most equitable, that there should be the same measure of retribution for all.

There is an objection, however, to an assumption of the state debts, which deserves particular notice. It may be supposed, that it would increase the difficulty of an equitable settlement between them and the United States.

The principles of that settlement, whenever they shall be discussed, will require all the moderation and wisdom of the government. In the opinion of the Secretary, that discussion, till further lights are obtained, would be premature.

All therefore which he would now think adviseable on the point in question, would be, that the amount of the debts assumed and provided for, should be charged to the respective states, to abide an eventual arrangement. This, the United States, as assignees to the creditors, would have an indisputable right to do.

But as it might be a satisfaction to the House to have before them some plan for the liquidation of accounts between the union and its members, which, including the assumption of the state debts, would consist with equity: The Secretary will submit in this place such thoughts on the subject, as have occurred to his own mind, or been suggested to him, most compatible, in his judgment, with the end proposed.

Let each state be charged with all the money advanced to it our of the treasury of the United States, liquidated according to the specie value, at the time of each advance, with interest at six percent.

Let it also be charged with the amount, in specie value, of all its securities which shall be assumed, with the interest upon them to the time, when interest shall become payable by the United States.

Let it be credited for all monies paid and articles furnished to the United States, and for all other expenditures during the was, either towards general or particular defence, whether authorized or unauthorized by the United States; the whole liquidated to specie value, and bearing an interest of six per cent. from the several times at which the several payments, advances and expenditures accrued.

And let all sums of continental money now in the treasuries of the respective states, which shall be paid into the treasury of the United States, be a credited at specie value.

Upon a statement of the accounts according to these principles, there can be little doubt, that balances would appear in favor of all the states, against the United States.

To equalize the contributions of the states, let each be then charged with its proportion of the aggregate of those balances, according to some equitable ratio, to be devised for that purpose.

If the contributions should be found disproportionate, the result of this adjustment would be, that some states would be creditors, some debtors to the union.

Should this be the case, as it will be attended with less inconvenience for the United States, to have to pay balances to, than to receive them from the particular states, it may perhaps, be practicable to effect the former by a second process, in the nature of a transfer of the amount of the debts of debtor states, to the credit of creditor states, observing the ratio by which the first apportionment shall have been made. This, whilst it would destroy the balances due from the former, would increase those due to the latter. These to be provided for by the United States, at a reasonable interest, but not to be transferable.

The expediency of this second process must depend on a knowledge of the result of the first. If the inequalities should be too great, the arrangement may be impracticable, without unduly increasing the debt of the United States. But it is not likely, that this would be the case. It is also to be remarked, that thought this second process might not, upon the principle of apportionment, bring the thing to the point aimed at, yet it may approach so nearly to it, as to avoid essentially the embarrassment, having considerable balances to collect from any of the states.

The whole of this arrangement to be under the superintendence of commissioners, vested with equitable discretion, and final authority.

The operation of the plan is exemplified in the schedule A.

The general principle of it seems to be equitable, for it appears difficult to conceive a good reason, why the expences for the particular defence of a part in a common war, should not be a common charge, as well as those incurred professedly for the general defence. The defence of each part is that of the whole; and unless all the expenditures are brought into a common mass, the tendency must be, to add, to the calamities suffered, by being the most exposed to the ravages of war, an increase of burthens.

This plan seems to be susceptible of no objection, which does not belong to every other, that proceeds on the idea of a final adjustment of accounts. The difficulty of settling a ratio, is common to all. This must, probably, either be sought for in the proportions of the requisitions, during the war, or in the decision of commissioners appointed with plenary power. The rule prescribed in the Constitution, with regard to representation and direct taxes, would evidently not be applicable to the situation of parties, during the period in question.

The existing debt of the United States is excluded from the computation, as it ought to be, because it will be provided for out of a general fund.

The only discussion of a preliminary kind, which remains, relates to the distinctions of the debt into principal and interest. It is well known, that the arrears of the latter bear a large proportion to the amount of the former. The immediate payment of these arrears is evidently impracticable, and a question arises, what ought to be done with them?

There is good reason to conclude, that the impressions of many are more favorable to the claim of the principal than to that of the interest; at least so far, as to produce an opinion, that an inferior provision might suffice for the latter.

But to the Secretary, this opinion does not appear to be well founded. His investigations of the subject, have led him to a conclusion, that the arrears of interest have pretensions, at least equal to the principal. The liquidated debt, traced to its origin, falls under two principal discriminations. One, relating to loans; the other to services performed and articles supplied.

The part arising from loans, was at first made payable at fixed periods, which have long since elapsed, with an early option to lenders, either to receive back their money at the expiration of those periods, or to continue it at interest, till the whole amount of continental bills circulating should not exceed the sum in circulation at the time of each loan. This contingency, in the sense of the contract, never happened; and the presumption is, that the creditors preferred continuing their money indefinitely at interest, to receiving it in a depreciated and depreciating state.

The other parts of it were chiefly for objects, which ought to have been paid for at the time, that is, when the services were performed or the supplies furnished; and were not accompanied with any contract for interest.

But by different acts of government and administration, concurred in by the creditors, these parts of the debt have been converted into a capital, bearing an interest of six per cent. per annum, but without any definite period of redemption. A portion of the loan-office debt has been exchanged for new securities of that import. And the whole of it seems to have acquired that character, after the expiration of the periods prefixed for repayment.

If this view of the subject be a just one, the capital of the debt of the United States, may be considered in the light of an annuity at the rate of six per cent. per annum, redeemable at the pleasure of the government, by payment of the principal. For it seems to be a clear position, that when a public contracts a debt payable with interest, without any precise time being stipulated or understood for payment of the capital, that time is a matter of pure discretion with the government, which is at liberty to consult its own convenience respecting it, taking care to pay the interest with punctuality.

Wherefore, as long as the United States should pay the interest of their debt, as it accrued, their creditors would have no right to demand the principal.

But with regard to the arrears of interest, the case is different. These are now due, and those to whom they are due, have a right to claim immediate payment. To say, that it would be impracticable to comply, would not vary the nature of the right. Nor can this idea of impracticability be honorably carried further, than to justify the proposition of a new contract upon the basis of a commutation of that right for an equivalent. This equivalent too ought to be real and fair one. And what other fair equivalent can be imagined for the detention of money, but a reasonable interest? Or what can be the standard of that interest, but the market rate, or the rate which the government pays in ordinary cases?

From this view of the matter, which appears to be the accurate and true one, it will follow, that the arrears of interest are entitled to an equal provision with the principal of the debt.

The result of the foregoing discussions is this—That there ought to be no discrimination between the original holders of the debt, and present possessors by purchase— That it is expedient, there should be an assumption of the state debts by the Union, and that the arrears of interest should be provided for on an equal footing with the principal.

The next enquiry, in order, towards determining the nature of a proper provision, respects the quantum of the debt, and the present rates of interest.

The debt of the union is distinguishable into foreign and domestic. . . .

This includes all that has been paid in indents (except what has come into the treasury of the United States) which, in the opinion of the Secretary, can be considered in no other light, than as interest due. . . .

The unliquidated part of the domestic debt, which consists chiefly of the continental bills of credit, is not ascertained, but may be estimated at 2,000,000 dollars.

These several sums constitute the whole of the debt of the United States, amounting together to 54,124,464 dollars, and 56 cents.

That of the individual states is not equally well ascertained. The schedule E. shews the extent to which it has been ascertained by returns pursuant to the order of the House of the 21st September last; but this not comprehending all the states, the residue must be estimated from less authentic information. The Secretary, however, presumes, that the total amount may be safely stated at 25 millions of dollars, principal and interest. The present rate of interest of the state debts is in general, the same with that of the domestic debt of the union.

On the supposition, that the arrears of interest ought to be provided for, on the same terms with the principal, the annual amount of the interest, which, at the existing rates, would be payable on the entire mass of the public debt, would be—

On the foreign debt, computing the interest on the principal, as it stands, and allowing four per cent. on the arrears of interest, . . . $542,599.66

On the domestic debt, including that of the States 4,044,845.81

Making, together, . . . $4,587,444.81.

The interesting problem now occurs. Is it in the power of the United States, consistently with those prudential considerations, which ought not to be overlooked, to make a provision equal to the purpose of funding the whole debt, at the rates of interest which it now bears, in addition to the sum which will be necessary for the current service of the government?

The Secretary will not say that such provision would exceed the abilities of the country; but he is clearly of opinion, that to make it, would require the extension of taxation to a degree, and to objects, which the true interest of the public creditors forbids. It is therefore to be hoped, and even to be expected, that they will chearfully concur in such modifications of their claims, on fair and equitable principles, as will facilitate to the government an arrangement substantial, durable and satisfactory to the community. The importance of the last characteristic will strike every discerning mind. No plan, however flattering in appearance, to which it did not belong, could be truly entitled to confidence.

It will not be forgotten, that exigencies may, ere long, arise, which would call for resources greatly beyond what is now deemed sufficient for the current service; and that, should the faculties of the country be exhausted or even *strained* to provide for the public debt, there could be less reliance on the sacredness of the provision.

But while the Secretary yields to the force of these considerations, he does not lose sight of those fundamental principles of good faith, which dictate, that every practicable exertion ought to be made, scrupulously to fulfil the engagements of the government; than no change in the rights of its creditors ought to be attempted without their voluntary consent; and that this consent ought to be voluntary in fact, as well as in name. Consequently, that every proposal of a change ought to be in the shape of an appeal to their reason and to their interest; not to their necessities. To this end it is requisite, that a fair equivalent should be offered for what may be asked to be given up, and unquestionable security for the remainder. Without this, an alteration, consistently with the credit and honor of the nation, would be impracticable. It remains to see, what can be proposed in conformity to these views.

It has been remarked, that the capital of the debt of the union is to be viewed in the light of an annuity at the rate of six per cent. per annum, redeemable at the pleasure of the government, by payment of the principal. And it will not be required, that the arrears of interest should be considered in a more favourable light. The same character, in general, may be applied to the debts of the individual states.

This view of the subject admits, that the United States would have it in their power to avail themselves of any fall in the market rate of interest, for reducing that of the debt.

This property of the debt is favourable to the public; unfavourable to the creditor. And may facilitate an arrangement for the reduction of interest, upon the basis of a fair equivalent.

Probabilities are always a rational ground of contract. The Secretary conceives, that there is good reason to believe, if effectual measures are taken to establish public credit, that the government rate of interest in the United States, will, in a very short time, fall at least as low as five per cent. and that in a period not exceeding twenty years, it will sink still lower, probably to four.

There are two principal causes which will be likely to produce this effect; one, the low rate of interest in Europe; the other, the increase of the monied capital of the nation, by the funding of the public debt. From three to four per cent. is deemed good interest in several parts of Europe. Even less is deemed so, in some places. And it is on the

decline; the increasing plenty of money continually tending to lower it. It is presumable, that no country will be able to borrow of foreigners upon better terms, than the United States, because none can, perhaps, afford so good security. Our situation exposes us less, than that of any other nation, to those casualties, which are the chief causes of expence; our incumbrances, in proportion to our real means, are less, though these cannot immediately be brought so readily into action, and our progress in resources from the early state of the country, and the immense tracts of unsettled territory, must necessarily exceed that of any other. The advantages of this situation have already engaged the attention of the European money-lenders, particularly among the Dutch. And as they become better understood, they will have the greater influence. Hence as large a proportion of the cash of Europe as may be wanted, will be, in a certain sense, in our market, for the use of government. And this will naturally have the effect of a reduction of the rate of interest, not indeed to the level of the places, which send their money to market, but to something much nearer to it, than our present rate.

The influence which the funding of the debt is calculated to have, in lowering interest, has been already remarked and explained. It is hardly possible, that it should not be materially affected by such an increase of the monied capital of the nation, as would result from the proper funding of seventy millions of dollars. But the probability of a decrease in the rate of interest, acquires confirmation from facts, which existed prior to the revolution. It is well known, that in some of the states, money might with facility be borrowed, on good security, at five per cent. and, not unfrequently, even at less.

The most enlightened of the public creditors will be most sensible of the justness of this view of the subject, and of the propriety of the use which will be made of it.

The Secretary, in pursuance of it, will assume, as a probability, sufficiently great to be a ground of calculation, both on the part of the government and of its creditors— That the interest of money in the United States will, in five years, fall to five per cent. and, in twenty, to four. The probability, in the mind of the Secretary, is rather that the fall may be more rapid and more considerable; but he prefers a mean, as most likely to engage the assent of the creditors, and more equitable in itself; because it is predicated on probabilities, which may err on one side, as well as on the other.

Premising these things, the Secretary submits to the House, the expediency of proposing a loan to the full amount of the debt, as well of the particular states, as of the union, upon the following terms.

First—That for every hundred dollars subscribed, payable in the debt (as well interest as principal) the subscribed be entitled, at his option, either

To have two thirds funded at an annuity, or yearly interest of six per cent. redeemable at the pleasure of the government, by payment of the principal; and to receive the other third in lands in the Western Territory, at the rate of twenty cents per acre. Or,

To have the whole sum funded at an annuity or yearly interest of four per cent. irredeemable by any payment exceeding five dollars per annum on account both of principal and interest; and to receive; as a compensation for the reduction of interest, fifteen dollars and eighty cents, payable in lands, as in the preceding case. Or,

To have sixty-six dollars and two thirds of a dollar funded immediately at an annuity or yearly interest of six per cent. irredeemable by any payment exceeding four dollars and two thirds of a dollar per annum, on account both of principal and interest; and to have, at the end of ten years, twenty-six dollars and eighty-eight cents, funded at the like interest and rate of redemption. Or,

To have an annuity for the remainder of life, upon the contingency of living to a given age, not less distant than ten years, computing interest at four per cent. Or,

To have an annuity for the remainder of life, upon the contingency of the survivorship of the youngest of two persons, computing interest, in this case also, at four per cent.

In addition to the foregoing loan, payable wholly in the debt, the Secretary would propose, that one should be opened for ten millions of dollars, on the following plan.

That for every hundred dollars subscribed, payable one half in specie, and the other half in debt (as well principal as interest) the subscriber be entitled to an annuity or yearly interest of five per cent. irredeemable by any payment exceeding six dollars per annum, on account both of principal and interest.

The principles and operation of these different plans may now require explanation.

The first is simply a proposition for paying one third of the debt in land, and funding the other two thirds, at the existing rate of interest, and upon the same terms of redemption, to which it is at present subject.

Here is no conjecture, no calculation of probabilities. The creditor is offered the advantage of making his interest principal, and he is asked to facilitate to the government an effectual provision for his demands, by accepting a third part of them in land, at a fair valuation.

The general price, at which the western lands have been, heretofore, sold, has been a dollar per acre in public securities; but at the time the principal purchases were made, these securities were worth, in the market, less than three shillings in the pound. The nominal price, therefore, would not be the proper standard, under present circumstances, nor would the precise specie value then given, be a just rule. Because, as the payments were to be made by instalments, and the securities were, at the times of the

purchases, extremely low, the probability of a moderate rise must be presumed to have been taken into the account. Twenty cents, therefore, seem to bear an equitable proportion to the two considerations of value at the time, and likelihood of increase.

It will be understood, that upon this plan, the public retains the advantage of availing itself of any fall in the market rate of interest, for reducing that upon the debt, which is perfectly just, as no present sacrifice, either in the quantum of the principal, or in the rate of interest, is required from the creditor.

The inductment of the measure is, the payment of one third of the debt in land.

The second plan is grounded upon the supposition, that interest, in five years, will fall to five per cent. in fifteen more, to four. As the capital remains entire, but bearing an interest of four per cent. only, compensation is to be made to the creditor, for the interest of two per cent. per annum for five years, and of one per cent, per annum, for fifteen years, to commence at the distance of five years. The present value of these two sums or annuities, computed according to the terms of the supposition, is, by strict calculation, fifteen dollars and seven hundred and ninety-two thousandth parts of a dollar; a fraction less than the sum proposed.

The inducement to the measure here is, the reduction of interest to a rate, more within the compass of a convenient provision; and the payment of the compensation in lands.

The inducements to the individual are—the accommodation afforded to the public, the high probability of a complete equivalent—the chance even of gain, should the rate of interest fall, either more speedily or in a greater degree, than the calculation supposes. Should it fall to five percent, sooner than five years; should it fall lower than five before the additional fifteen were expired; or should it fall below four, previous to the payment of the debt, there would be, in each case, an absolute profit to the creditor. As his capital will remain entire, the value of it will increase, with every decrease of the rate of interest.

The third plan proceeds upon the like supposition of a successive fall in the rate of interest. And upon that supposition offers an equivalent to the creditor. One hundred dollars, bearing an interest of six per cent. for five years; of five per cent. for fifteen years, and thenceforth of four per cent. (these being the successive rates of interest in the market) is equal to a capital of 122 dollars, 510725 parts, bearing an interest of four per cent. which, converted into a capital, bearing a fixed rate of interest of six per cent, is equal to 81 dollars, 6738166 parts.

The difference between sixty-six dollars and two thirds of a dollar (the sum to be funded immediately) and this last sum is 15 dollars, 0172 parts, which at six per cent per annum, amounts at the end of ten years, to 26 dollars, 8755 parts, the sum to be funded at the expiration of that period.

It ought, however, to be acknowledged, that this calculation does not make allowance for the principle of redemption, which the plan itself includes; upon which principle the equivalent in a capital of six per cent. would be by strict calculation, 87 dollars, 50766 parts.

But there are two considerations which induce the Secretary to think, that the one proposed would operate more equitably than this: One is, that it may not be very early in the power of the United States to avail themselves of the right of redemption reserved in the plan: The other is, that with regard to the part to be funded at the end of ten years, the principal of redemption is suspended during that time, and the full interest at six per cent. goes on *improving* at the *same rate; which* for the *last five years* will exceed the market rate of interest, according to the supposition.

The equivalent is regulated in this plan, by the circumstance of fixing the rate of interest higher, than it is suppose it will continue to be in the market; permitting only a gradual discharge of the debt, in an established proportion, and consequently preventing advantage being taken of any decrease of interest below the stipulated rate.

Thus the true value of eighty-one dollars and sixty-seven cents, the capital proposed, considered as a perpetuity, and bearing six per cent. interest, when the market rate of interest was five per cent. would be a small fraction more than ninety-eight dollars, when it was four per cent. would be one hundred and twenty-two dollars and fifty-one cents. But the proposed capital being subject to gradual redemption, it is evident, that its value, in each case, would be somewhat less. Yet from this may be perceived, the manner in which a less capital at a fixed rate of interest, becomes an equivalent for a greater capital, at a rate liable to variation and diminution.

It is presumable, that those creditors, who do not entertain a favorable opinion of property in western lands, will give a preference to this last mode of modelling the debt. The Secretary is sincere in affirming, that, in his opinion, it will be likely to prove, *to the full* as beneficial to the creditors, as a provision for his debt upon its present terms.

It is not intended, in either case to oblige the government to redeem, in the proportion specified, but to secure to it, the right of doing so, to avoid the inconvenience of a perpetuity.

The fourth and fifth plans abandon the supposition which is the basis of the two preceding ones, and offer only four per cent. throughout.

The reason of this is, that the payment being deferred, there will be an accumulation of compound interest, in the intermediate period against the public, which, without a very provident administration, would turn to its detriment. And the suspension of the burthen would be too apt to beget a relaxation of efforts in the mean time. The measure therefore, its object being temporary accommodation, could only be adviseable upon a moderate rate of interest.

With regard to individuals, the inducement will be sufficient at four per cent. There is no disposition of money, in private loans, making allowance for the usual delays and casualties, which would be equally beneficial as a future provision.

A hundred dollars advanced upon the life of a person of eleven years old, would produce an annuity. The same sum advanced upon the chance of the survivorship of the youngest of two lives, one of the person being twenty-five, the other, thirty years old, would produce, if the youngest of the two, should survive, an annuity for the remainder of life of 23 dollars, 556 parts.

From these instances may readily be discerned, the advantages, which these deferred annuities afford, for securing a comfortable provision for the evening of life, or for wives, who survive their husbands.

The sixth plan also relinquishes the supposition, which is the foundation of the second, and third, and offers a higher rate of interest upon similar terms of redemption, for the consideration of the payment of one half of the loan is specie. This is a plan highly advantageous to the creditors, who may be able to make that payment; while the specie itself could be applied in purchases of the debt, upon terms, which would fully indemnify the public for the increased interest.

It is not improbable, that foreign holders of the domestic debt, may embrace this as a desireable arrangement.

As an auxiliary expedient, and by way of experiment, the Secretary would propose a loan upon the principles of a tontine.

To consist of six classes, composed respectively of persons of the following ages:

First class, of those 20 years and under.

Second class, of those above 20, and not exceeding 30.

Third class, of those above 30, and not exceeding 40.

Fourth class, of those above 40 and not exceeding 50.

Fifth class, of those above 50, and not exceeding 60.

Sixth class, of those above 60.

Each share to be two hundred dollars. The number of shares in each class, to be indefinite. Persons to be at liberty to subscribe on their own lives, or on those of others, nominated by them.

The annuities of those who die, to be equally divided among the survivors, until four-fifths shall be dead, when the principle of survivorship shall cease, and each annuitant thenceforth enjoy his dividend as a several annuity during the life, upon which it shall depend.

These annuities are calculated upon the best life in each class, and at a rate of interest of four per cent. with some deductions in favor of the public. To the advantages which these circumstances present, the cessation of the right of survivorship on the death of four-fifths of the annuitants, will be no considerable addition.

The inducements to individuals are, a competent interest for their money from the outset, secured for life, and the prospect of continual encrease, and even of large profit to those, whose fortune it is, to survive their associates.

It will have appeared, that in all the proposed loans, the Secretary has contemplated the putting the interest upon the same footing with the principal: *That* on the debt of the United States, he would have computed to the last of the present year: *That* on the debt of the particular states, to the last of the year 1791; the reason for which distinction will be seen hereafter.

In order to keep up a due circulation of money, it will be expedient, that the interest of the debt should be paid quarter-yearly. This regulation will, at the same time, conduce to the advantage of the public creditors, giving them, in fact, by the anticipation of payment, a higher rate of interest; which may, with propriety, be taken into the estimate of the compensation to be made to them. Six per cent. per annum, paid in this mode, will truly be worth six dollars, and one hundred and thirty-five thousandth parts of a dollar, computing the market interest at the same rate.

The Secretary thinks it advisable, to hold out various propositions, all of them compatible with the public interest, because it is, in his opinion, of the greatest consequence, that the debt should, with the consent of the creditors, be remoulded into such a shape, as will bring the expenditure of the nation to a level with its income. 'Till this shall be accomplished, the finances of the United States will never wear a proper countenance. Arrears of interest, continually accruing, will be as continual a monument, either of inability, or of ill faith; and will not cease to have an evil influence on public credit. In nothing are appearance of greater moment, than in whatever regards credit. Opinion is the soul of it, and this is affected by appearance, as well as realities. By offering an option to the creditors, between a number of plans, the change meditated will be more likely to be accomplished. Different tempers will be governed by different views of the subject.

But while the Secretary would endeavour to effect a change in the form of the debt, by new loans, in order to render it more susceptible of an adequate provision; he would not think it proper to aim at procuring the concurrence of the creditors by operating upon their necessities.

Hence whatever surplus of revenue might remain, after satisfying the interest of the new loans, and the demand for the current service, ought to be divided among those creditors, if any, who may not think fit to subscribe to them. But for this purpose, under the circumstance of depending propositions, a temporary appropriation will be most adviseable, and the sum must be limited to four per cent. as the revenues will only be calculated to produce, in that proportion, to the entire debt.

The Secretary confides for the success of the propositions, to be made, on the goodness of the reasons upon which they rest; on the fairness of the equivalent to be offered in each case; on the discernment of the creditors of their true interest; and on their disposition to facilitate the arrangements of the government, and to render them satisfactory to the community.

The remaining part of the task to be performed is, to take a view of the means of providing for the debt, according to the modification of it, which is proposed.

On this point the Secretary premises, that, in his opinion, the funds to be established, ought, for the present, to be confined to the existing debt of the United States; as well because a progressive augmentation of the revenue will be most convenient, as because the consent of the state creditors is necessary, to the assumption contemplated; and though the obtaining of that consent may be inferred with great assurance, from their obvious interest to give it; yet 'till it shall be obtained, an actual provision for the debt, would be premature. Texas could not, with propriety, be laid for an object, which depended on such a contingency.

All that ought now to be done, respecting it, is, to put the matter in an effectual train for a future provision. For which purpose, the Secretary will, in the course of this report, submit such propositions, as appear to him adviseable.

The Secretary now proceeds to a consideration of the necessary funds.

It has been stated that the debt of the United States consists of . . .

The interest on the domestic debt is computed to the end of this year, because the details of carrying any plan into execution, will exhaust the year.

Thus to pay the interest of the foreign debt, and to pay four per cent on the whole of the domestic debt, principal and interest, forming a new capital, will require a yearly income of 2,239,163 dollars, 9 cents.

The sum which, in the opinion of the Secretary, ought now to be provided in addition to what the current service will require.

For, though the rate of interest, proposed by the third plan, exceeds four per cent. on the whole debt, and the annuities on the tontine will also exceed four per cent. on the sums which may be subscribed; yet, as the actual provision for a part is, in the former case, suspended; as measures for reducing the debt, by purchases, may be advantageously pursued, and as the payment of the deferred annuities will of course be postponed, four per cent. on the whole, will be a sufficient provision.

With regard to the instalments of the foreign debt, these, in the opinion of the Secretary, ought to be paid by new loans abroad. Could funds be conveniently spared, from other exigencies, for paying them, the United States could ill bear the drain of cash, at the present juncture, which the measure would be likely to occasion.

But to the sum which has been stated for payment of the interest must be added a provision for the current service. This the Secretary estimates at six hundred thousand dollars; making, with the amount of the interest, two millions, eight hundred and thirty-nine thousand, one hundred and sixty-three dollars, and nine cents.

This sum may, in the opinion of the Secretary, be obtained from the present duties on imports and tonnage, with the additions, which, without any possible disadvantage either to trade, or agriculture, may be made on wines, spirits, including those distilled within the United States, teas and coffee.

The Secretary conceives, that it will be sound policy, to carry the duties upon articles of this kind, as high a will be consistent with the practicability of a safe collection. This will lessen the necessity, both of having recourse of direct taxation, and of accumulating duties where they would be more inconvenient to trade, and upon objects, which are more to be regarded as necessaries of life.

That the articles which have been enumerated, will, better than most others, bear high duties, can hardly be a question. They are all of them, in reality—luxuries—the greatest part of them foreign luxuries; some of them, in the excess in which they are used, pernicious luxuries. And there is, perhaps, none of them, which is not consumed in so great abundance, as may, justly, denominate it, a source of national extravagance and impoverishment. The consumption of ardent spirits particularly, no doubt very much on account of their cheapness, is carried to an extreme, which is truly to be regretted, as well in regard to the health and the morals, as to the oeconomy of the community.

Should the increase of duties tend to a decrease of the consumption of those articles, the effect would be, in every respect desirable. The saving which it would occasion, would leave individuals more as their ease, and promote a more favourable balance of trade. As far as this decrease might be applicable to distilled spirits, it would encourage the substitution of cyder and malt liquors, benefit agriculture, and open a new and productive source of revenue.

It is not however, probable, that this decrease would be in a degree, which would frustrate the expected benefit to the revenue from raising the duties. Experience has shewn, that luxuries of every kind, lay the strongest hold on the attachments of mankind, which, especially when confirmed by habit, are not easily alienated from them.

The same fact affords a security to the merchant, that he is not likely to be prejudiced by considerable duties on such articles. They will usually command a proportional price. The chief things in this view to be attended to, are, that the terms of payment be so regulated, as not to require inconvenient advances, and that the mode of collection be secure.

To other reasons, which plead for carrying the duties upon the articles which have been mentioned, to as great an extent as they will bear, may be added these; that they are of a nature, from their extensive consumption, to be very productive, and are amongst the most difficult objects of illicit introduction.

Invited by so many motives to make the best use of the resource, which these articles afford, the essential enquiry is—in what mode can the duties upon them be most effectually collected?

With regard to such of them, as will be brought from abroad, a duty on importation recommends itself by two leading considerations; one is, that meeting the object at its first entrance into the country, the collection is drawn to a point, and so far simplified; the other is, that it avoids the possibility of interference between the regulations of the United States, and those of the particular states.

But a duty, the precautions for the collection of which should terminate with the landing of the goods, as is essentially the case in the existing system, could not, with safety, be carried to the extent, which is contemplated.

In that system, the evasion of the duties, depends as it were, on a single risk. To land the goods in defiance of the vigilance of the officers of the customs, is almost, the sole difficulty. No future pursuit, is materially, to be apprehended. And where the inducement is equivalent to the risk, there will be found too many, who are willing to run it. Consequently there will be extensive frauds of the revenue, against which the utmost rigor of the penal laws, has proved, as often as it has been tried, an ineffectual guard.

The only expedient which has been discovered, for conciliating high duties with a safe collection, is, the establishment of a *second*, or interior scrutiny.

By pursuing the article, from its importation, into the hands of the dealers in it, the risk of detection is so greatly enhanced, that few, in comparison, will venture to incur it.

Indeed every dealer, who is not himself the fraudulent importer, then becomes, in some sort, a centinel upon him.

The introduction of a system, founded on this principle, in some shape or other, is, in the opinion of the Secretary, essential to the efficacy of every attempt, to render the revenues of the United States equal to their exigencies, their safety, their prosperity, their honor.

Nor is it less essential to the interest of the honest and fair trader. It might even be added, that every individual citizen, besides his share in the general weal, has a particular interest in it. The practice of smuggling never fails to have one of two effects, and sometimes unites them both. Either the smuggler undersells the fair trader, as, by saving the *duty* he can afford to do, and makes *it* a charge upon him; or he sells at the increased price occasioned by the duty, and defrauds every man, who buys of him, of his share of what the public ought to receive. For it is evident, that the loss falls ultimately upon the citizens, who must be charged with other taxes to make good the deficiency, and supply the wants of the state.

The Secretary will not presume, that the plan, which he shall submit to the consideration of the house, is the best that could be devised. But it is the one, which has appeared to him freest from objections of any, that has occurred of equal efficacy. He acknowledges too, that it is susceptible of improvement, by other precautions in favor of the revenue, which he did not think it expedient to add. The chief outlines of the plan are not original, but it is no ill recommendation of it, that it has been tried with success.

The Secretary accordingly proposes,

That the duties heretofore laid upon wines, distilled spirits, teas and coffee, should, after the last day of May next, cease, and that instead of them, the following duties be laid.

Upon every gallon of Madeira Wine, of the quality of London particular, thirty-five cents.

Upon every gallon of other Madeira Wine, thirty cent.

Upon every gallon of Sherry, twenty-five cents.

Upon every gallon of other Wine, twenty cents.

Upon every gallon of distilled Spirits, more than ten per cent. below proof, according to Dicas's hydrometer, twenty cents.

Upon every gallon of those Spirits under five, and not more than ten per cent. below proof, according to the same hydrometer, twenty-one cents.

Upon every gallon of those Spirits of proof, and not more than five per cent. below proof, according to the same hydrometer, twenty-two cents.

Upon every gallon of those Spirits above proof, but not exceeding twenty per cent. according to the same hydrometer, twenty-five cents.

Upon every gallon of those spirits more than twenty, and not more than forty per cent. above proof, according to the same hydrometer, thirty cents.

Upon every gallon of those spirits more than forty per cent, above proof, according to the same hydrometer, forty cents.

Upon every pound of Hyson Tea, forty cents.

Upon every pound of other Green Tea, twenty-four cents.

Upon every pound of Souchong and other black Teas, except Bohea, twenty cents.

Upon every pound of Bohea Tea, twelve cents.

Upon every pound of Coffee, five cents.

That upon Spirits distilled within the United States, from Molasses, Sugar, or other foreign materials, there be paid—

Upon every gallon of those Spirits, more than ten percent below proof, according to Dicas's hydrometer, eleven cents.

Upon every gallon of those spirits under five, and not more than ten per cent, below proof, according to the same hydrometer, twelve cents.

Upon every gallon of those Spirits of proof, and not more than five per cent. below proof, according to the same hydrometer, thirteen cents.

Upon every gallon of those Spirits, above proof, but not exceeding twenty per cent. according to the same hydrometer, fifteen cents.

Upon every gallon of those Spirits, more than twenty, and not more than forty per cent. above proof, according to the same hydrometer, twenty cents.

Upon every gallon of those Spirits more than forty per cent. above proof, according to the same hydrometer, thirty cents.

That upon Spirits distilled within the United States, in any city, town or village, from materials of the growth or production of the United States, there be paid—

Upon every gallon of those Spirits more than ten per cent. below proof, according to Dicas's hydrometer, nine cents.

Upon every gallon of those Spirits under five, and not more than ten per cent. below proof, according to the same hydrometer, ten cents.

Upon every gallon of those Spirits of proof, and not more than five per cent. below proof, according to the same hydrometer, eleven cents.

Upon every gallon of those Spirits above proof, but not exceeding twenty per cent. according to the same hydrometer, thirteen cents.

Upon every gallon of those Spirits more than twenty, and not more than forty per cent. above proof, according to the same hydrometer, seventeen cents.

Upon every gallon of those Spirits, more than forty per cent. above proof, according to the same hydrometer, twenty-five cents.

That upon all Stills employed in distilling Spirits from materials of the growth or production of the United States, in any other place, than a city, town or village, there be paid the yearly sum of sixty cents, for every gallon, English wine measure, of the capacity of each Still, including its head.

The Secretary does not distribute the duties on Teas into different classes, as has been done in the impost act of the last session; because this distribution depends on considerations of commercial policy, not of revenue. It is sufficient, therefore, for him to remark, that the rates, above specified, are proposed with reference to the lowest class.

The Secretary conceiving, that he could not convey an accurate idea of the plan contemplated by him, for the collection of these duties, in any mode so effectual as by the draft of a bill for the purpose, begs leave respectfully to refer the House to that, which will be found annexed to this report, relatively to the article of distilled spirits; and which, for the better explanation of some of its parts, is accompanied with marginal remarks.

It would be the intention of the Secretary, that the duty on wines should collected upon precisely the same plan with that on imported spirits.

But with regard to teas and coffee, the Secretary is inclined to think, that it will be expedient, till experience shall evince the propriety of going further, to exclude the *ordinary* right of the officers to visit and inspect the places in which those articles may be kept. The other precautions, without this, will afford, though not complete, considerable security.

It will not escape the observation of the House, that the Secretary, in the plan submitted, has taken the most scrupulous care, that those citizens upon whom it is immediately to operate, be secured from every species of injury by the misconduct of the officers to be employed. There are not only strong guards against their being guilty of abuses of authority; they are not only punishable, criminally, for any they may commit, and made answerable in damages, to individuals, for whatever prejudice these may sustain by their acts or neglects: But even where seizures are made with probable cause, if there be an acquittal of the article seized, a compensation to the proprietors for the injury their property may suffer, and even for its detention, is to be made out of the public treasury.

So solicitous indeed has the Secretary been, to obviate every appearance of hardship, that he has even included a compensation to the dealers, for their agency in aid of the revenue.

With all these precautions to manifest a spirit of moderation and justice on the part of government: And when it

is considered, that the object of the proposed system is the firm establishment of public credit; that on this depends the character, security and prosperity of the nation; that advantages in every light important, may be expected to result from it; that the immediate operation of it will be upon an enlightened class of citizens, zealously devoted to good government, and to a liberal and enlarged policy, and that it is peculiarly the interest of the virtuous part of them to co-operate in whatever will restrain the spirit of illicit traffic; there will be perceived to exist, the justest ground of confidence, that the plan, if eligible in itself, will experience the chearful and prompt acquiescence of the community.

The Secretary computes the nett product of the duties proposed in this report at about one million seven hundred and three thousand four hundred dollars, according to the estimate in schedule K, which if near the truth, will, together with the probable product of the duties on imports and tonnage, complete the sum required. But it will readily occur, that in so unexplored a field there must be a considerable degree of uncertainty in the data. And that, on this account, it will be prudent to have an auxiliary resource for the first year, in which the interest will become payable, that there may be no possibility of disappointment to the public creditors, ere there may be an opportunity of providing for any deficiency, which the experiment may discover. This will accordingly be attended to.

The proper appropriation of the funds provided, and to the provided, seems next to offer itself to consideration.

On this head, the Secretary would propose, that the duties on distilled spirits, should be applied in the first instance, to the payment of the interest of the foreign debt.

That reserving out of the residue of those duties an annual sum of six hundred thousand dollars, for the current service of the United States; the surplus, together with the product of the other duties, be applied to the payment of the interest on the new loan, by an appropriation, co-extensive with the duration of the debt.

And that if any part of the debt should remain unsubscribed, the excess of the revenue be divided among the creditors of the unsubscribed part, by a temporary disposition; with a limitation, however, to four per cent.

It will hardly have been unnoticed, that the Secretary had been thus far silent on the subject of the post-office. The reason is, that he has had in view the application of the revenue arising from that source, to the purposes of a sinking fund. The post-master-general gives it as his opinion, that the immediate product of it, upon a proper arrangement, would probably be, not less than one hundred thousand dollars. And from its nature, with good management, it must be a growing, and will be likely to become a considerable fund. The post-master-general is now engaged in preparing a plan, which will be the foundation of a proposition for a new arrangement of the establishment. This, and some other points relative to the subject referred to the Secretary, he begs leave to reserve for a future report.

Persuaded as the Secretary is, that the proper funding of the present debt, will render it a national blessing: Yet he is so far from acceding to the position, in the latitude in which it is sometimes laid down, that "public debts are public benefits," a position inviting to prodigality, and liable to dangerous abuse,—that he ardently wishes to see it incorporated, as a fundamental maxim, in the system of public credit of the United States, that the creation of debt should always be accompanied with the means of extinguishment. This he regards as the true secret for rendering pubic credit immortal. And he presumes, that it is difficult to conceive a situation, in which there may not be an adherence to the maxim. At least he feels an unfeigned solicitude, that this may be attempted by the United States, and that they may commence their measures for the establishment of credit, with the observance of it.

Under this impression, the Secretary proposes, that the next product of the post-office, to a sum not exceeding one million of dollars, be vested in commissioners, to consist of the Vice-President of the United States or President of the Senate, the Speaker of the House of Representatives, the Chief Justice, Secretary of the Treasury and Attorney-General of the United States, for the time being, in trust, to be applied, by them, or any three of them, to the discharge of the existing public debt, either by purchases of stock in the market, or by payments on account of the principal, as shall appear to them most adviseable, in conformity to the public engagements; to continue so vested, until the whole of the debt shall be discharged.

As an additional expedient for effecting a reduction of the debt, and for other purposes which will be mentioned, the Secretary would further propose that the same commissioners be authorised, with the approbation of the President of the United States, to borrow, on their credit, a sum, not exceeding twelve millions of dollars, to be applied,

First. To the payment of the interest and instalments of the foreign debt, to the end of the present year, which will require 3,491,923 dollars, and 46 cents.

Secondly. To the payment of any deficiency which may happen in the product of the funds provided for paying the interest of the domestic debt.

Thirdly. To the effecting a change in the form of such part of the foreign debt, as bears an interest of five per cent. It is conceived, that, for this purpose, a new loan, at a lower interest, may be combined with other expedients. The remainder of this part of the debt, after paying the instalments, which will accrue in the course of 1790, will be 3,888,888 dollars, and 81 cents.

Fourthly. To the purchase of the public debt at the price it shall bear in the market, while it continues below its true value. This measure, which would be, in the opinion of the Secretary, highly dishonorable to the government, if it were to precede a provision for funding the debt, would become altogether unexceptionable, after that had been made. Its effect would be in favor of the public creditors, as it would tend to raise the value of stock. And all the difference, between its true value, and the actual price, would be so much clear gain to the public. The payment of foreign interest on the capital to be borrowed for this purpose, should that be a necessary consequence, would not, in the judgment of the Secretary, be a good objection to the measure. The saving by the operation would be itself, a sufficient indemnity; and the employment of that capital, in a country situated like this, would much more than compensate for it. Besides, if the government does not undertake this operation, the same inconvenience, which the objection in question supposes, would happen in another way, with a circumstance of aggravation. As long, at least, as the debt shall continue below its proper value, it will be an object of speculation to foreigners, who will not only receive the interest, upon what they purchase, and remit it abroad, as in the case of the loan, but will reap the additional profit of the difference in value. By the government's entering into competition with them, it will not only reap a part of this profit itself, but will contract the extent, and lessen the extra profit of foreign purchases. That competition will accelerate the rise of stock; and whatever greater rate this obliges foreigners to pay, for what they purchase, is so much clear saving to the nation. In the opinion of the Secretary, and contrary to an idea which is not without patrons, it ought to be the policy of the government, to raise the value of stock to its true standard as fast as possible. When it arrives to that point, foreign speculations (which, till then, must be deemed pernicious, further than as they serve to bring it to that point) will become beneficial. Their money laid out in this country, upon our agriculture, commerce and manufactures, will produce much more to us, than the income they will receive from it.

The Secretary contemplates the application of this money, through the medium of a national bank, for which, with the permission of the House, he will submit a plan in the course of the session.

The Secretary now proceeds, in the last place, to offer to the consideration of the House, his ideas, of the steps, which ought at the present session, to be taken, towards the assumption of the state debts.

These are briefly, that concurrent resolutions of the two Houses, with the approbation of the President, be entered into, declaring in substance,

That the United States do assume, and will at the first session in the year 1791, provide, on the same terms with the present debt of the United States, for all such part of the debts of the respective states, or any of them, as shall, prior to the first day of January in the said year 1791, be subscribed towards a loan to the United States, upon the principles of either of the plans, which shall have been adopted by them, for obtaining a re-loan of their present debt.

Provided that the provision to be made as aforesaid, shall be suspended, with respect to the debt, of any state, which may have exchanged the securities of the United States for others issued by itself, until the whole of the said securities shall, either be re-exchanged, or surrendered to the United States.

And provided also, that the interest upon the debt assumed, be computed to the end of the year 1791; and that the interest to be paid by the United States, commence on the first day of January, 1792.

That the amount of the debt of each state so assumed and provided for, be charged to such state in account with the United States, upon the same principles, upon which it shall be lent to the United States.

That subscriptions be opened for receiving loans of the said debts at the same times and places, and under the like regulations, as shall have been prescribed in relation to the debt of the United States.

The Secretary has now completed the objects, which he proposed to himself, to comprise in the present report. He has, for the most part, omitted details, as well to avoid fatiguing the attention of the House, as because more time would have been desirable even to digest the general principles of the plan. If these should be found right, the particular modifications will readily suggest themselves in the progress of the work.

The Secretary, in the views which have directed his pursuit of the subject, has been influenced, in the first place, by the consideration, that his duty from the very terms of the resolution of the House, obliged him to propose what appeared to him an adequate provision for the support of the public credit, adapted at the same time to the real circumstances of the United States; and in the next, by the reflection, that measures which will not bear the test of future unbiassed examination, can neither be productive of individual reputation, nor (which is of much greater consequence) public honor, or advantage.

Deeply impressed, as the Secretary is, with a full and deliberate conviction, that the establishment of public credit, upon the basis of a satisfactory provision, for the public debt, is, under the present circumstances of this country, the true desideratum towards relief from individual and national embarrassments; that without it, these embarrassments will be likely to press still more severely upon the community—He cannot but indulge an anxious wish, that an effectual plan for that purpose may, during the present session, be the result of the united wisdom of the legislature.

He is fully convinced, that it is of the greatest importance, that no further delay should attend the making of the requisite provision; not only, because it will give a better impression of the good faith of the country, and will bring earlier relief to the creditors; both which circumstances are of great moment to public credit; but, because the advantages to the community, from raising stock, as speedily as possible, to its natural value, will be incomparably greater, than any that can result from its continuance below that standard. No profit, which could be derived from purchases in the market, on account of the government, to any practicable extent, would be an equivalent for the loss, which would be sustained by the purchases of foreigners, at a low value. Not to repeat, that governmental purchases, to be honorable, ought to be preceded by a provision. Delay, by disseminating doubt, would sink the price of stock; and as the temptation to foreign speculations, from the lowness of the price, would be too great to be neglected, millions would probably be lost to the United States.

Source:
Harold C. Syrett, ed. *The Papers of Alexander Hamilton.* New York: Columbia University Press, 1961–87.

Alexander Hamilton, On the Constitutionality of an Act to Establish a Bank, 1791

A written opinion concerning the constitutionality of the plan to establish a national bank presented by Secretary of the Treasury Alexander Hamilton to President George Washington at his request on February 23, 1791. Hamilton authored the plan to establish the bank, a modified version of which had passed Congress on February 8, 1791. In his opinion, Hamilton stated "that a bank has a natural relation to the power of collecting taxes, to that of regulating trade, to that of providing for the common defense." Washington signed the bill on February 25. Although he avoided constitutional questions in the report, on the House floor, he argued that establishing a bank came under the "necessary and proper clause" (sometimes termed the "elastic" clause) of Article I, Section 8. James Madison, at that time a member of Congress from Virginia, and Secretary of State Thomas Jefferson disagreed. Those agreeing with Hamilton's "loose construction" of the Constitution tended to become Federalists, whereas those following the "strict construction" of Jefferson and Madison became Democratic-Republicans.

On April 2, 1792, Congress provided for a new national currency, establishing both gold and silver as national monetary standards and creating a national mint. The act established a decimal system of coinage, with the dollar as the basic monetary unit. The value of gold was set at 15 times the value of silver; the gold dollar was valued at 24.75 grains of gold and the silver dollar at 371.25 grains of silver. The act followed the recommendations of Hamilton's report to Congress of 1791.

———————⚬⚭⚬———————

In entering upon the argument it ought to be premised, that the objections of the Secretary of State and Attorney General are founded on a general denial of the authority of the United States to erect corporations. The latter indeed expressly admits, that if there be any thing in the bill which is not warranted by the constitution, it is the clause of incorporation.

Now it appears to the Secretary of the Treasury, that this *general principle* is *inherent* in the very *definition* of *Government* and *essential* to every step of the progress to be made by that of the United States; namely—that every power vested in a Government is in its nature *sovereign,* and includes by *force* of the *term,* a right to employ all the *means* requisite, and fairly *applicable* to the attainment of the *ends* of such power; and which are not precluded by restrictions & exceptions specified in the constitution; or not immoral, or not contrary to the essential ends of political society.

This principle in its application to Government in general would be admitted as an axiom. And it will be incumbent upon those, who may incline to deny it, to *prove* a distinction; and to shew that a rule which in the general system of things is essential to the preservation of the social order is inapplicable to the United States.

⚬　⚬　⚬

If it would be necessary to bring proof to a proposition so clear as that which affirms that the powers of the federal government, *as to its objects,* are sovereign, there is a clause of its constitution which would be decisive. It is that which declares, that the constitution and the laws of the United States made in pursuance of it, and all treaties made or which shall be made under their authority shall be the supreme law of the land. The power which can create the *Supreme law* of the land, in any case, is doubtless sovereign *as to such case.*

This general & indisputable principle puts at once an end to the *abstract* question—Whether the United States have power to *erect a corporation?* that is to say, to give a *legal* or *artificial capacity* to one or more persons, distinct from the natural. For it is unquestionably incident to *sovereign power* to erect corporations, and consequently to *that* of the United States, in *relation to the objects* intrusted to the management of the government. The difference is this—where the authority of the government is general, it can create corporations in *all cases;* where it is confined to certain branches of legislation, it can create corporations only in those cases.

⚬　⚬　⚬

For a more complete elucidation of the point nevertheless, the arguments which they have used against the power of the government to erect corporations, however, foreign they are to the great & fundamental rule which has been stated, shall be particularly examined. And after shewing that they do not tend to impair its force, it shall also be shewn, that the power of incorporation incident to the government in certain cases, does fairly extend to the particular case which is the object of the bill.

The first of these arguments is, that the foundation of the constitution is laid on this ground "that all powers not delegated to the United States by the Constitution nor prohibited to it by the States are reserved to the States or to the people", whence it is meant to be inferred, that congress can in no case exercise any power not included in those enumerated in the constitution. And it is affirmed that the power of erecting a corporation is not included in any of the enumerated powers.

⚬　⚬　⚬

. . . It is conceded, that implied powers are to be considered as delegated equally with express ones.

Then it follows, that as a power of erecting a corporation may as well be *implied* as any other thing; it may as well be employed as an *instrument* or *mean* of carrying into execution any of the specified powers, as any other instrument or mean whatever. The only question must be, in this as in every other case, whether the mean to be employed, or in this instance the corporation to be erected, has a natural relation to any of the acknowledged objects or lawful ends of the government. Thus a corporation may not be erected by congress, for superintending the police of the city of Philadelphia because they are not authorised to *regulate* the *police* of that city; but one may be erected in relation to the collection of the taxes, or to the trade with foreign countries, or to the trade between the States, or with the Indian Tribes, because it is the province of the federal government to regulate those objects & because it is incident to a general *sovereign* or *legislative power* to *regulate* a thing, to employ all the means which relate to its regulation to the *best & greatest advantage.*

⚬　⚬　⚬

To this mode of reasoning respecting the right of employing all the means requisite to the execution of the specified powers of the Government, it is objected that none but *necessary* & proper means are to be employed, & the Secretary of State maintains, that no means are to be considered as *necessary,* but those without which the grant of the power would be *nugatory.* Nay so far does he go in his restrictive interpretation of the word, as even to make the case of *necessity* which shall warrant the constitutional exercise of the power to depend on *casual & temporary* circumstances, an idea which alone refutes the construction. The *expediency* of exercising a particular power, at a particular time, must indeed depend on *circumstances;* but the constitutional right of exercising it must be uniform & invariable—the same to day, as to morrow.

      ✿   ✿   ✿

It is essential to the being of the National government, that so erroneous a conception of the meaning of the word *necessary,* should be exploded.

   . . . *Necessary* often means no more than *needful, requisite, incidental, useful,* or *conducive to.* It is a common mode of expression to say, that it is *necessary* for a government or a person to do this or that thing, when nothing more is intended or understood, than that the interests of the government or person require, or will be promoted, by the doing of this or that thing. The imagination can be at no loss for exemplifications of the use of the word in this sense.

   And it is the true one in which it is to be understood as used in the constitution. The whole turn of the clause containing it, indicates, that it was the intent of the convention, by that clause to give a liberal latitude to the exercise of the specified powers. The expressions have peculiar comprehensiveness. They are—"to make *all laws,* necessary & proper for *carrying into execution* the foregoing powers & all *other powers* vested by the constitution in the *government* of the United States, or in any *department* or *officer* thereof." To understand the word as the Secretary of State does, would be to depart from its obvious & popular sense, and to give it a *restrictive* operation…It would be to give it the same force as if the word *absolutely* or *indispensibly* had been prefixed to it.

   . . . To insist upon it, would be to make the criterion of the exercise of any implied power a *case of extreme necessity;* which is rather a rule to justify the overleaping of the bounds of constitutional authority, than to govern the ordinary exercise of it.

      ✿   ✿   ✿

The *degree* in which a measure is necessary, can never be a test of the *legal* right to adopt it. That must ever be a matter of opinion; and can only be a test of expediency. The *relation* between the *measure* and the *end,* between the *nature* of *the mean* employed towards the execution of a

power and the object of that power, must be the criterion of constitutionally not the more or less of *necessity* or *utility.*

      ✿   ✿   ✿

This restrictive interpretation of the word *necessary* is also contrary to this sound maxim of construction namely, that the powers contained in a constitution of government, especially those which concern the general administration of the affairs of a country, its finances, trade, defence &c ought to be construed liberally, in advancement of the public good. This rule does not depend on the particular form of a government or on the particular demarcation of the boundaries of its powers, but on the nature and objects of government itself. The means by which national exigencies are to be provided for, national inconveniences obviated, national prosperity promoted, are of such infinite variety, extent and complexity, that there must, of necessity, be great latitude of discretion in the selection & application of those means. Hence consequently, the necessity & propriety of exercising the authorities intrusted to a government on principles of liberal construction.

      ✿   ✿   ✿

But while, on the one hand, the construction of the Secretary of State is deemed inadmissible, it will not be contended on the other, that the clause in question gives any *new* or *independent* power. But it gives an explicit sanction to the doctrine of *implied* powers, and is equivalent to an admission of the proposition, that the government, *as to its specified powers* and *objects,* has plenary & sovereign authority, in some cases paramount to that of the States, in others coordinate with it. For such is the plain import of the declaration, that it may pass *all laws* necessary & proper to carry into execution those powers.

      ✿   ✿   ✿

That truth is that difficulties on this point are inherent in the nature of the federal constitution. They result inevitably from a division of the legislative power. The consequence of this division is, that there will be cases clearly within the power of the National Government; others clearly without its power; and a third class, which will leave room for controversy & difference of opinion & concerning which a reasonable latitude of judgment must be allowed.

   But the doctrine which is contended for is not chargeable with the consequence imputed to it. It does not affirm that the National government is sovereign in all respects, but that it is sovereign to a certain extent: that is, to the extent of the objects of its specified powers.

   It leaves therefore a criterion of what is constitutional, and of what is not so. This criterion is the *end* to which the measure relates as a *mean.* If the end be clearly comprehended within any of the specified powers, & if the measure have an obvious relation to that end, and is not forbidden by any particular provision of the constitution—it may safely be deemed to come within the compass of the national authority. . . . Does the proposed measure abridge a preexisting right of any State, or of any individual? If it does not, there is a strong presumption in favour of its constitutionality; & slighter relations to any declared object of the constitution may be permitted to turn the scale.

*   *   *

But if it were even to be admitted that the erection of a corporation is a direct alteration of the State laws in the enumerated particulars; it would do nothing towards proving, that the measure was unconstitutional. If the government of the United States can do no act, which amounts to an alteration of a State law, all its powers are nugatory. For almost every new law is an alteration, in some way or other of an old *law,* either *common,* or *statute.*

*   *   *

. . . the bill neither prohibits any State from erecting as many banks as they please, nor any number of Individuals from associating to carry on the business: & consequently is free from the charge of establishing a monopoly: for monopoly implies a *legal impediment* to the carrying on of the trade by others than those whom it is granted.

And with regard to the second point, there is still less foundation. The bye-law of such an institution as a bank can operate only upon its own members; can only concern the disposition of its own property and must essentially resemble the rules of a private mercantile partnership. They are expressly not to be contrary to law; and law must here mean the law of a State as well as of the United States. There never can be a doubt, that a law of the corporation, if contrary to a law of a state, must be overruled as void; unless the law of the State is contrary to that of the United States; and then the question will not be between the law of State and that of the corporation, but between the law of the State and that of the United States.

*   *   *

. . . Whatever may have been the intention of the framers of a constitution, or of a law, that intention is to be sought for in the instrument itself, according to the usual & established rules of construction. Nothing is more common than for laws to *express* and *effect,* more or less than was intended. If then a power to erect a corporation, in any case, be deducible by fair inference from the whole or any part of the numerous provisions of the constitutions of the United States, arguments drawn from extrinsic circumstances, regarding the intention of the convention, must be rejected.

*   *   *

There is a sort of evidence on this point, arising from an aggregate view of the constitution, which is of no inconsiderable weight. The very general power of laying & collecting taxes & appropriating their proceeds—that of borrowing money indefinitely—that of coining money & regulating foreign coins—that of making all needful rules and regulations respecting the property of the United States—these powers combined, as well as the reason & nature of the thing speak strongly this language: That it is the manifest design and scope of the constitution to vest in congress all the powers requisite to the effectual administration of the finances of the United States. As far as concerns this object, there appears to be no parsimony of power.

To suppose then, that the government is precluded from the employment of so usual as well as so important an instrument for the administration of its finances as that of a bank, is to suppose, what does not coincide with the general tenor & complexion of the constitution, and what is not agreeable to impressions that any mere spectator would entertain concerning it. Little less than a prohibitory clause can destroy the strong presumptions which result from the general aspect of the government. Nothing but demonstration should exclude the idea, that the power exists.

In all questions of this nature the practice of mankind ought to have great weight against the theories of Individuals.

The fact, for instance, that all the principal commercial nations have made use of trading corporations or companies for the purposes of *external commerce,* is a satisfactory proof, that the Establishment of them is an incident to the regulation of that commerce.

This other fact, that banks are an usual engine in the administration of national finances, & an ordinary & the most effectual instrument of loans & one which in this country has been found essential, pleads strongly against the supposition, that a government clothed with most of the most important prerogatives of sovereignty in relation to the revenues, its debts, its credit, its defence, its trade, its intercourse with foreign nations—is forbidden to make use of that instrument as an appendage to its own authority.

It has been stated as an auxiliary test of constitutional authority, to try, whether it abridges any preexisting right of any state, or any Individual. The proposed incorporation will stand the most severe examination on this point. Each state may still erect as many banks as it pleases; every individual may still carry on the banking business to any extent he pleases.

Another criterion may be this, whether the institution or thing has a more direct relation as to its uses, to the objects of the reserved powers of the State Governments, than to those of the powers delegated by the United States. This rule indeed is less precise than the former, but it may still serve as some guide. Surely a bank has more reference to the objects entrusted to the national government, than to those, left to the care of the State Governments. The common defence is decisive in this comparison.

❖   ❖   ❖

One or two remarks only shall be made: one is that he has taken on notice of a very essential advantage to trade in general which is mentioned in the report, as peculiar to the existence of a bank circulation equal, in the public estimation to Gold & silver. It is this, that it renders it unnecessary to lock up the money of the country to accumulate for months successively in order to the periodical payment of interest. The other is this; that his arguments to shew that treasury orders & bills of exchange from the course of trade will prevent any considerable displacement of the metals, are founded on a partial view of the subject. A case will prove this: The sums collected in a state may be small in comparison with the debt due to it. The balance of its trade, direct & circuitous, with the seat of government may be even or nearly so. Here then without bank bills, which in that state answer the purpose of coin, there must be a displacement of the coin, in proportion to the difference between the sum collected in the State and that to be paid in it. With bank bills no such displacement would take place, or, as far as it did, it would be gradual & insensible. In many other ways also, would there be at least a temporary & inconvenient displacement of the coin, even where the course of trade would eventually return it to its proper channels.

The difference of the two situations in point of convenience to the Treasury can only be appreciated by one, who experiences the embarrassments of making provision for the payment of the interest on a stock continually changing place in thirteen different places.

❖   ❖   ❖

Philadelphia February 23d. 1791.

Source:
Harold C. Syrett, ed. *The Papers of Alexander Hamilton.* New York: Columbia University Press, 1961–87.

Alexander Hamilton, Report on the Subject of Manufactures, 1791

Report submitted by U.S. secretary of the treasury Alexander Hamilton to Congress on December 5, 1791, proposing federal aid to infant industries through protective tariffs. It responded to an argument put forth most notably by Thomas Jefferson that "Agriculture is the most beneficial and *productive* object of human industry." Hamilton argued that the national welfare required the federal government to encourage manufacturing in order to increase productivity as well as the national income and provide a dependable home market for agriculture. Hamilton's views were influenced by Adam Smith's *Wealth of Nations* (1776), but he rejected Smith's laissez-faire view that the state must not direct economic processes. Of note are Hamilton's reliance on his own previous arguments favoring a national bank and establishment of a public debt. Also of note, considering more recent values, are his favoring immigration and also the employment of women (as being less costly than men) and children, even "of tender age." Congress took no action on the report, the only time a report of his failed. However, it later fueled arguments on both sides of the protection question.

To the Speaker of the House of Representatives
The Secretary of the Treasury in obedience to the order of ye House of Representatives, of the 15th day of January 1790, has applied his attention, at as early a period as his other duties would permit, to the subject of Manufactures; and particularly to the means of promoting such as will tend to render the United States, independent on foreign nations, for military and other essential supplies. And he there [upon] respectfully submits the following Report.

The expediency of encouraging manufactures in the United States, which was not long since deemed very questionable, appears at this time to be pretty generally admitted. The embarrassments, which have obstructed the progress of our external trade, have led to serious reflections on the necessity of enlarging the sphere of our domestic commerce: the restrictive regulations, which in foreign markets abridge the vent of the increasing surplus of our Agriculture produce, serve to beget an earnest desire, that a more extensive demand for that surplus may be created at home: And the complete success, which has rewarded manufacturing enterprise, in some valuable branches, conspiring with the promising symptoms, which attend some less mature essays, in others, justify a hope, that the obstacles to the growth of this species of industry are less formidable than they were apprehended to be; and that it is not difficult to find, in its further extension; a full indemnification for any external disadvantages, which are or may be experienced, as well as an accession of resources, favourable to national independence and safety.

❖   ❖   ❖

It is now proper to proceed a step further, and to enumerate the principal circumstances, from which it may be inferred—That manufacturing establishments not only occasion a positive augmentation of the Produce and Revenue of the Society, but that they contribute essentially to rendering them greater than they could possibly be, without such establishments. These circumstances are—

1. The division of Labour

2. An extension of the use of Machinery.

3. Additional employment to classes of the community not ordinarily engaged in the business.

4. The promoting of emigration from foreign Countries.

5. The furnishing greater scope for the diversity of talents and dispositions which discriminate men from each other.

6. The affording a more ample and various field for enterprize.

7. The creating in some instances a new, and securing in all, a more certain and steady demand for the surplus produce of the soil.

Each of these circumstances has a considerable influence upon the total mass of industrious effort in a community. Together, they add to it a degree of energy and effect, which are not easily conceived. Some comments upon each of them, in the order in which they have been stated, may serve to explain their importance.

I. As to the Division of Labour

It has justly been observed, that there is scarcely any thing of greater moment in the oeconomy of a nation, than the proper division of labour. The separation of occupations causes each to be carried to a much greater perfection, than it could possible acquire, if they were blended. This arises principally from three circumstances.

1st—The greater skill and dexterity naturally resulting from a constant and undivided application to a single object. . . . 2nd. The oeconomy of time—by avoiding the loss of it, incident to a frequent transition from one operation to another of a different nature. . . . 3rd. An extension of the use of Machinery. A man occupied on a single object will have it more in his power, and will be more naturally led to exert his imagination in devising methods to facilitate and abridge labour, than if he were perplexed by a variety of independent and dissimilar operations. . . . And from these causes united, the mere separation of the occupation of the cultivator, from that of the Artificer, has the effect of augmenting the *productive powers* of labour, and with them, the total mass of the produce or revenue of a Country. In this single view of the subject, therefore, the utility of Artificers or Manufacturers, towards promoting an increase of productive industry, is apparent.

II. As to an extension of the use of Machinery a point which though partly anticipated requires to be placed in one or two additional lights.

The employment of Machinery forms an item of great importance in the general mass of national industry. 'Tis an artificial force brought in aid of the natural force of man; and, to all the purposes of labour, is an increase of hands; an accession of strength, *unincumbered too by the expence of maintaining the laborer.* May it not therefore be fairly inferred, that those occupations, which give greatest scope to the use of this auxiliary, contribute most to the general Stock of industrious effort, and, in consequence, to the general product of industry?

. . . The substitution of foreign for domestic manufactures is a transfer to foreign nations of the advantages accruing from the employment of Machinery, in the modes in which it is capable of being employed, with most utility and to the greatest extent.

The Cotton Mill invented in England, within the last twenty years, is a signal illustration of the general proposition, which has been just advanced. In consequence of it, all the different processes for spining Cotton are performed by means of Machines, which are put in motion by water. . . . And it is an advantage of great moment that the operations of this mill continue with convenience, during the night, as well as through the day. The prodigious affect of such a Machine is easily conceived. To this invention is to be attributed essentially the immense progress, which has been so suddenly made in Great Britain in the various fabrics of Cotton.

III. As to the additional employment of classes of the community, not ordinarily engaged in the particular business.

This is not among the least valuable of the means, by which manufacturing institutions contribute to augment the general stock of industry and production. In places where those institutions prevail, besides the persons regularly engaged in them, they afford occasional and extra employment to industrious individuals and families, who are willing to devote the leisure resulting from the intermissions of their ordinary pursuits to collateral labours, as a resource of multiplying their acquisitions of [their] enjoyments. The husbandman himself experiences a new source of profit and support from the encreased industry of his wife and daughters; invited and stimulated by the demands of the neighboring manufactories.

. . . There is another of a nature allied to it [and] of a similar tendency. This is—the employment of persons who would otherwise be idle (and in many cases a burthen on the community), . . . In general, women and Children are rendered more useful and the latter more early useful by manufacturing establishments, than they would otherwise be. Of the number of persons employed in the Cotton Manufactories of Great Britain, it is computed that 4/7 nearly are women and children; of whom the greatest proportion are children and many of them of a very tender age.

And thus it appears to be one of the attributes of manufactures, and one of no small consequence, to give occasion to the exertion of a greater quantity of Industry, even by the *same number* of persons, where they happen to prevail, than would exist, if there were no such establishment.

IV. As to the promoting of emigration from foreign Countries. . . . Manufacturers, who listening to the powerful invitations of a better price for their fabrics, or their labour, of greater cheapness of provisions and raw materials, of an exemption from the chief part of the taxes burthens and restraints, which they endure in the old world, of greater personal independence and consequence, under the operation of a more equal government, and of what is far more precious than mere religious toleration—a perfect equality of religious privileges; would probably flock from Europe to the United States to pursue their own trades or professions, if they were once made sensible of the advantages they would enjoy, and were inspired with an assurance of encouragement and employment, will, with difficulty, be induced to transplant themselves, with a view to becoming Cultivators of Land.

✿   ✿   ✿

V. As to the furnishing greater scope for the diversity of talents and dispositions, which discriminate men from each other.

. . . The results of human exertion may be immensely increased by diversifying its objects. When all the different kinds of industry obtain in a community, each individual can find his proper element, and can call into activity the whole vigour of his nature. And the community is benefitted by the services of its respective members, in the manner, in which each can serve it with most effect.

If there be anything in a remark often to be met with—namely that there is, in the genius of the people of this country, a peculiar aptitude for mechanic improvements, it would operate as a forcible reason for giving opportunities to the exercise of that species of talent, by the propagation of manufactures.

VI. As to the affording a more ample and various field for enterprise.

. . . To cherish and stimulate the activity of the human mind, by multiplying the objects of enterprise, is not among the least considerable of the expedients, by which the wealth of a nation may be promoted. Even things in themselves not positively advantageous, sometimes become so, by their tendency to provoke exertion. Every new scene, which is opened to the busy nature of man to rouse and exert itself, is the addition of a new energy to the general stock of effort.

The spirit of enterprise, useful and prolific as it is, must necessarily be contracted or expanded in proportion to the simplicity or variety of the occupations and productions, which are to be found in a Society. It must be less in a nation of mere cultivators, than in a nation of cultivators and merchants; less in a nation of cultivators, and merchants, than in a nation of cultivators, artificers and merchants.

VII. As to the creating, in some instances, a new, and securing in all a more certain and steady demand, for the surplus produce of the soil.

This is . . . a principal mean, by which the establishment of manufactures contributes to an augmentation of the produce or revenue of a country, and has an immediate and direct relation to the prosperity of Agriculture.

It is evident, that the exertions of the husbandman will be steady or fluctuating, vigorous or feeble, in proportion to the steadiness or fluctuation, adequateness, or inadequateness of the markets on which he must depend.... For the purpose of this vent, a domestic market is greatly to be preferred to a foreign one; because it is in the nature of things, far more to be relied upon.

It is a primary object of the policy of nations, to be able to supply themselves with subsistence from their own soils; and manufacturing nations, as far as circumstances permit, endeavor to procure, from the same source, the raw materials necessary for their own fabrics. . .

✿   ✿   ✿

But it is also a consequence of the policy, which has been noted, that the foreign demand for the products of Agricultural Countries, is, in a great degree, rather casual and occasional, than certain or constant . . . .

✿   ✿   ✿

It merits particular observation, that the multiplication of manufactories not only furnishes a Market for those articles, which have been accustomed to be produced in abundance, in a country; but it likewise creates a demand for such as were either unknown or produced in inconsiderable quantities. The bowels as well as the surface of the earth are ransacked for articles which were before neglected. Animals, Plants and Minerals acquire an utility and value, which were before unexplored.

The foregoing considerations seem sufficient to establish, as general propositions, That it is the interest of nations to diversify the industrious pursuits of the individuals, who compose them—That the establishment of manufactures is calculated not only to increase the general stock of useful and productive labour; but even to improve the state of Agriculture in particular; certainly to advance the interests of those who are engaged in it. There are other views, that will be hereafter taken of the subject, which, it is conceived, will serve to confirm these inferences.

* * *

. . . The United States are to a certain extent in the situation of a country precluded from foreign Commerce. They can indeed, without difficulty obtain from abroad the manufactured supplies, of which they are in want; but they experience numerous and very injurious impediments to the emission and vent of their own commodities. Nor is this the case in reference to a single foreign nation only. The regulations of several countries, with which we have the most extensive intercourse, throw serious obstructions in the way of the principal staples of the United States.

In such a position of things, the United States cannot exchange with Europe on equal terms; and the want of reciprocity would render them the victim of a system, which should induce them to confine their views to Agriculture and refrain from Manufactures. A constant and encreasing necessity, on their part, for the commodities of Europe, and only a partial and occasional demand for their own, in return, could not but expose them to a state of impoverishment, compared with the opulence to which their political and natural advantages authorise them to aspire.

. . . Tis for the United States to consider by what means they can render themselves least dependent, on the combinations, right or wrong of foreign policy.

It is no small consolation, that already the measures which have embarrassed our Trade, have accelerated internal improvements, which upon the whole have bettered our affairs. To diversify and extend these improvements is the surest and safest method of indemnifying ourselves for any inconveniences, which those or similar measures have a tendency to beget. If Europe will not take from us the products of our soil, upon terms consistent with our interest, the natural remedy is to contract as fast as possible our wants of her.

* * *

The supposed want of Capital for the prosecution of manufactures in the United States is the most indefinite of the objections which are usually opposed to it.

It is very difficult to pronounce any thing precise concerning the real extent of the monied capital of a Country, and still more concerning the proportion which it bears to the objects that invite the employment of Capital. It is not less difficult to pronounce how far the *effect* of any given quantity of money, as capital, or in other words, as a medium for circulating the industry and property of a nation, may be encreased by the very circumstance of the additional motion, which is given to it by new objects of employment. That effect, like the momentum of descending bodies, may not improperly be represented, as in a compound ratio to *mass* and *velocity*. It seems pretty certain, that a given sum of money, in a situation, in which the

quick impulses of commercial activity were little felt, would appear inadequate to the circulation of as great a quantity of industry and property, as in one, in which their full influence was experienced.

It is not obvious, why the same objection might not as well be made to external commerce as to manufactures; since it is manifest that our immense tracts of land occupied and unoccupied are capable of giving employment to more capital than is actually bestowed upon them. It is certain, that the United States offer a vast field for the advantageous employment of Capital; but it does not follow, that there will not be found, in one way or another, a sufficient fund for the successful prosecution of any species of industry which is likely to prove truly beneficial.

The following considerations are of a nature to remove all inquietude on the score of want of Capital.

The introduction of Banks, as has been shewn on another occasion has a powerful tendency to extend the active Capital of a Country. Experience of the Utility of these Institutions is multiplying them in the United States. It is probable that they will be established wherever they can exist with advantage; and wherever, they can be supported, if administered with prudence, they will add new energies to all pecuniary operations.

The aid of foreign Capital may safely, and, with considerable latitude be taken into calculation. Its instrumentality has been experienced in our external commerce; and it has begun to be felt in various other modes. Not only our funds, but our Agriculture and other internal improvements have been animated by it. It has already in a few instances extended even to our manufactures.

It is a well known fact, that there are parts of Europe, which have more Capital, than profitable domestic objects of employment. Hence, among other proofs, the large loans continually furnished, to foreign states. And it is equally certain that the capital of other parts may find more profitable employment in the United States, than at home. . . . Both these Causes operate to produce a transfer of foreign capital to the United States. 'Tis certain, that various objects in this country hold out advantages, which are with difficulty to be equalled elsewhere; and under the increasingly favorable impressions, which are entertained of our government, the attractions will become more and More strong. These impressions will prove a rich mine of prosperity to the Country, if they are confirmed and strengthened by the progress of our affairs. And to secure this advantage, little more is now necessary, than to foster industry, and cultivate order and tranquility, at home and abroad.

* * *

And whatever be the objects which originally attract foreign Capital, when once introduced, it may be directed towards any purpose of beneficial exertion, which is desired. And to detain it among us, there can be no expedient so effectual as to enlarge the sphere, within which it may be usefully employed: Though induced merely with views to speculations in the funds, it may afterwards be rendered subservient to the Interests of Agriculture, Commerce & Manufactures.

❖   ❖   ❖

But while there are Circumstances sufficiently strong to authorise a considerable degree of reliance on the aid of foreign Capital towards the attainment of the object in view, it is satisfactory to have good grounds of assurance, that there are domestic resources of themselves adequate to it. It happens, that there is a species of Capital actually existing within the United States, which relieves from all inquietude on the score of want of Capital—This is the funded Debt.

❖   ❖   ❖

To all the arguments which are brought to evince the impracticability of success in manufacturing establishments in the United States, it might have been a sufficient answer to have referred to the experience of what has been already done. It is certain that several important branches have grown up and flourished with a rapidity which surprises: affording an encouraging assurance of success in future attempts: of these it may not be improper to enumerate the most considerable.

I. of Skins. Tanned and tawed leather dressed skins, shoes, boots and Slippers, harness and sadlery of all kinds. Portmanteau's and trunks, leather breeches, gloves, muffs and tippets, parchment and Glue.

II. of Iron. Barr and Sheet Iron, Steel, Nail-rods & Nails, implements of husbandry, Stoves, pots and other household utensils, the steel and Iron work of carriages and for Shipbuilding, Anchors, scale beams and Weights & Various tools of Artificers, arms of different kinds; though the manufacture of these last has of late diminished for want of demand.

III. of Wood. Ships, Cabinet Wares and Turnery, Wool and Cotton cards and other Machinery for manufactures and husbandry, Mathematical instruments, Coopers wares of every kind.

IV. of flax & Hemp. Cables, sail-cloth, Cordage, twine and packthread.

V. Bricks and coarse tiles & Potters Wares.

VI. Ardent Spirits, and malt liquors.

VII. Writing and printing Paper, sheathing and wrapping Paper, pasteboards, fillers or press papers, paper hangings.

VIII. Hats of furr and Wool and of mixtures of both, Womens Stuff and Silk shoes.

IX. Refined Sugars.

X. Oils of Animals and seeds; Soap, Spermaceti and Tallow Candles

XI. Copper and brass wares, particularly utensils for distillers, Sugar refiners and brewers, And—Irons and other Articles for household Use, philosophical apparatus

XII. Tin Wares, for most purposes of Ordinary use.

XIII. Carriages of all kinds

XIV. Snuff, chewing & smoaking Tobacco.

XV. Starch and Hairpowder.

XVI. Lampblack and other painters colours,

XVII. Gunpowder

Besides manufactories of these articles which are carried on as regular Trades, and have attained to a considerable degree of maturity, there is a vast scene of household manufacturing, which contributes more largely to the supply of the Community, than could be imagined; without having made it an object of particular enquiry. This observation is the pleasing result of the investigation, to which the subject of the report has led, and is applicable as well to the Southern as to the middle and Northern States; great quantities of coarse cloths, coatings, serges, and flannels, linsey Woolseys, hosiery of Wool, cotton & thread, coarse fustians, jeans and Muslins, check(ed) and striped cotton and linen goods, bed ticks, Coverlets and Counterpanes, Tow linens, coarse shirtings, sheetings, toweling and table linen, and various mixtures of wool and cotton, and of Cotton & flax are made in the household way, and in many instances to an extent not only sufficient for the supply of the families in which they are made, but for sale, and (even in some cases) for exportation. It is computed in a number of districts that 2/3 3/4 and even 4/5 of all the clothing of the Inhabitants are made by themselves. The importance of so great a progress, as appears to have been made in family Manufactures, within a few years, both in a moral and political view, renders the fact highly interesting.

Neither does the above enumeration comprehend all the articles, that are manufactured as regular Trades. Many other occur, which are equally well established, but which not being of equal importance have been omitted. And there are many attempts stills in their Infancy, which though attended with very favorable appearances, could not have been properly comprized in an enumeration of manufactories, already established. There are other articles also of great importance, which tho' strictly speaking manufactures are omitted, as being immediately connected with husbandry: such are flour, pot & pearl ash, Pitch, tar, turpentine and the like.

There remains to be noticed an objection to the encouragement of manufactures, of a nature different from those which question the probability of success. This is derived from its supposed tendency to give a monopoly of a advantages to particular classes at the expence of the rest of the community, who, it is affirmed, would be able to procure the requisite supplies of manufactured articles on better terms from foreigners, than from our own Citizens, and who it is alledged, are reduced to a necessity of paying an enhanced price for whatever they want, by every measure, which obstructs the free competition of foreign commodities.

✻ ✻ ✻

It is not an unreasonable supposition, that measures, which serve to abridge the free competition of foreign But though it were true, that the immediate and certain effect of regulations controuling the competition of foreign with domestic fabrics was an increase of price, it is universally true, that the contrary is the ultimate effect with every successful manufacture. When a domestic manufacture has attained to perfection, and has engaged in the prosecution of it a competent number of Persons, it invariably becomes cheaper. Being free from the heavy charges, which attend the importation of foreign commodities, it can be afforded, and accordingly seldom or never fails to be sold Cheaper, in process of time, than was the foreign Article for which it is a substitute. The internal competition, which takes place, soon does away every thing like Monopoly, and by degrees reduces the price of the Article to the *minimum* of a reasonable profit on the Capital employed. This accords with the reason of the thing and with experience.

Whence it follows, that it is the interest of a community with a view to eventual and permanent oeconomy, to encourage the growth of manufactures. In a national view, a temporary enhancement of price must always be well compensated by a permanent reduction of it.

✻ ✻ ✻

There seems to be a moral certainty, that the trade of a country which is both manufacturing and Agricultural will be more lucrative and prosperous, than that of a Country, which is, merely Agricultural. . . .

Another circumstance which gives a superiority of commercial advantages to states, that manufacture as well as cultivate, consists in the more numerous attractions, which a more diversified market offers to foreign Customers, and greater scope, which it affords to mercantile enterprise. It is a position of indisputable truth in Commerce, depending too on very obvious reasons, that the greatest resort will ever be to those marts where commodities, while equally abundant, are most various. . . .

. . . Two important inferences are to be drawn, one, that there is always a higher probability of a favorable balance of Trade, in regard to countries in which manufactures founded on the basis of a thriving Agriculture flourish, than in regard to those, which are confined wholly or almost wholly to Agriculture; the other (which is also a

consequence of the first) that countries of the former description are likely to possess more pecuniary wealth, or money, than those of the latter.

✻ ✻ ✻

Not only the wealth; but the independence and security of a Country, appear to be materially connected with the prosperity of manufactures. Every nation, with a view to those great objects, ought to endeavour to possess within itself all the essentials of national supply. These comprise the means of *Subsistence habitation clothing* and *defence*.

The possession of these is necessary to the perfection of the body politic, to the safety as well as to the welfare of the society; the want of either, is the want of an important organ of political life and Motion; and in the various crises which await a state, it must severely feel the effects of any such deficiency. The extreme embarrassments of the United States during the late War, from an incapacity of supplying themselves, are still matter of keen recollection: A future war might be expected again to exemplify the mischiefs and dangers of a situation, to which that incapacity is still in too great a degree applicable, unless changed by timely and vigorous exertion. To effect this change as fast as shall be prudent, merits all the attention and all the Zeal of our Public Councils; 'tis the next great work to be accomplished.

✻ ✻ ✻

One more point of view only remains in which to Consider the expediency of encouraging manufacturers in the United states.

It is not uncommon to meet with an opinion that though the promoting of manufactures may be the interest of a part of the Union, it is contrary to that of another part. The Northern & southern regions are sometimes represented as having adverse interest in this respect. Those are called Manufacturing, these Agricultural states; and a species of opposition is imagined to subsist between the Manufacturing and Agricultural interests.

This idea of an opposition between those two interest is the common error of the early periods of every country. . . . But it is nevertheless a maxim well established by experience, and generally acknowledged, where there has been sufficient experience, that the *aggregate* prosperity of manufactures, and the *aggregate* prosperity of Agriculture are intimately connected. . . .

✻ ✻ ✻

. . . If the Northern and middle states should be the principal scenes of such establishments, they would immediately benefit the more southern, by creating a demand for productions; some of which they have in common with the other states, and others of which are either peculiar to them, or more abundant, or of better quality, than elsewhere. These productions, principally are Timber, flax, Hemp, Cotton, Wool, raw silk, Indigo, iron, lead, furs, hides, skins and coals. Of these articles Cotton & Indigo are peculiar to the southern states; as are hitherto *Lead & Coal*. Flax and Hemp are or may be raised in greater abundance there, than in the More Northern states; and the Wool of Virginia is said to be of better quality than that of any other state: a Circumstance rendered the more probable by the reflection that Virginia embraces the same latitudes with the finest Wool Countries of Europe. The Climate of the south is also better adapted to the production of silk.

The extensive cultivation of Cotton can perhaps hardly be expected, but from the previous establishment of domestic Manufactories of the Article; and the surest encouragement and vent, for the others, would result from similar establishments in respect to them.

✿   ✿   ✿

In order to a better judgment of the Means proper to be resorted to by the United states, it will be of use to Advert to those which have been employed with success in other Countries. The principal of these are.

I Protecting duties—or duties on those foreign articles which are the rivals of the domestic ones, intended to be encouraged. . . . They enable the National Manufacturers to undersell all their foreign Competitors. . . .

II Prohibitions of rival articles or duties equivalent to prohibitions. . . . In general it is only fit to be employed when a manufacture, has made such a progress and is in so many hands as to insure a due competition, and an adequate supply on reasonable terms. Of duties equivalent to prohibitions, there are examples in the Laws of the United States, and there are other Cases to which the principle may be advantageously extended, but they are not numerous.

✿   ✿   ✿

VIII The encouragement of new inventions and discoveries, at home, and of the introduction into the United States of such as may have been made in other countries; particularly those, which relate to machinery.

This is among the most useful and unexceptionable of the aids, which can be given to manufactures. The usual means of that encouragement are pecuniary rewards, and, for a time, exclusive privileges. The first must be employed, according to the occasion, and the utility of the invention, or discovery: For the last, so far as respects "authors and inventors" provision has been made by Law. But it is desirable in regard to improvements and secrets of extraordinary value, to be able to extend the same benefit to Introducers, as well as Authors and Inventors; a policy which has been practiced with advantage in other countries. Here, however, as in some other cases, there is cause to regret, that the competency of the authority of the National Government to the *good*, which might be done, is not without a question. Many aids might be given to industry; many internal improvements of primary magnitude might be promoted, by an authority operating throughout the Union, which cannot be effected, as well, if at all, by an authority confined within the limits of a single state.

✿   ✿   ✿

IX Judicious regulations for the inspection of manufactured commodities. This is not among the least important of the means, by which the prosperity of manufactures may be promoted. It is indeed in many cases one of the most essential. Contributing to prevent frauds upon consumers at home and exporters to foreign countries—to improve the quality & preserve the character of the national manufactures, it cannot fail to aid the expeditious and advantageous Sale of them, and to serve as a guard against successful competition from other quarters. . . .

X The facilitating of pecuniary remittances from place to place is a point of considerable moment to trade in general, and to manufactures in particular; by rendering more easy the purchase of raw materials and provisions and the payment for manufactured supplies. A general circulation of Bank paper, which is to be expected from the institution lately established will be a most valuable mean to this end. But much good would also accrue from some additional provisions respecting inland bills of exchange. If those drawn in one state payable in another were made negotiable, everywhere, and interest and damages allowed in case of protest, it would greatly promote negotiations between the Citizens of different states, by rendering them more secure; and, with it the convenience and advantage of the Merchants and manufacturers of each.

XI The facilitating of the transportation of commodities. Improvements favoring this object intimately concern all the domestic interests of a community; but they may without impropriety be mentioned as having an important relation to manufactures. . . .

There can certainly be no object, more worthy of the cares of the local administrations; and it were to be wished, that there was no doubt of the power of the national Government to lend its direct aid, on a comprehensive plan.... "Good roads, canals, and navigable rivers, by diminishing the expence of carriage, put the *remote parts of a country* more nearly upon a level with those in the neighborhood of the town. They are *upon that account* the greatest of all improvements. They encourage the cultivation of the remote, which must always be the most extensive circle of the country. . . .

＊　＊　＊

All the additional duties which shall be laid…will yield a considerable surplus.

This surplus will serve.

First. To constitute a fund for paying the bounties which shall have been decreed.

Secondly. To constitute a fund for the operations of a Board, to be established, for promoting Arts, Agriculture, Manufactures and Commerce …

＊　＊　＊

In countries where there is great private wealth much may be effected by the voluntary contributions of patriotic individuals, but in a community situated like that of the United States, the public purse must supply the deficiency of private resource. In what can it be so useful as in prompting and improving the efforts of industry?

All which is humbly submitted.

Source:

Harold C. Syrett, ed. *The Papers of Alexander Hamilton.* New York: Columbia University Press, 1961–87.

Jonathan Edwards, "Injustices and Impolicy of the Slave Trade and of the Slavery of Africans," 1791

Sermon delivered before a Connecticut antislavery society in 1791 by Congregationalist minister Jonathan Edwards (1745–1801), son of the famous American theologian of the same name. In the early days of the abolition movement, putting an end to the slave trade was seen as an essential step toward abolishing the practice of slavery altogether. In the sermon below, Edwards lists and explains a few of the principal arguments against slavery and the slave trade, then methodically presents and refutes each of the most common proslavery arguments. Citing that esteemed tenet of the Revolution, "all men are created equal," Edwards questions how a nation that refused to live under the "political slavery" of Great Britain can justify holding an entire race of people in physical bondage. He goes on at length about the cruelty and violence of the slave trade and how the enormous death toll it exacts does not merit the commercial profit it gains. Edwards uses his position as a noted theologian to disprove many of the biblical arguments for slavery used by southern Christians, such as the Apostles' instructions to servants of their day to obey their masters. One of the earliest examples of a well-developed and established antislavery ideology, this sermon shows how quickly the question of slavery had moved to the center of national debate.

Matthew VII. 12.

Therefore all things whatsoever you would, that men should do it to you. Do ye even so to them; for this is the law and the prophets.

This precept of our divine Lord hath always been admired as most excellent; and doubtless with the greatest reason. Yet it needs some explanation. It is not surely to be understood in the most unlimited sense, implying that because a prince expects and wishes for obedience from his subjects, he is obliged to obey them: that because parents wish their children to submit to their government, therefore they are to submit to the government of their children: or that because some men wish that others would concur and assist them to the gratification of their unlawful desires therefore they also are to gratify the unlawful desires of others. But whatever we are conscious, that we should, in an exchange of circumstances, wish, and are persuaded that we might reasonably wish, that others would do to us; that we are bound to do to them. This is the general rule given us in the text; and a very extensive rule it is, reaching to the whole of our conduct: and is particularly useful to direct our conduct toward inferiors, and those whom we have in our power. I have therefore thought it a proper foundation for the discourse, which by the Society for the promotion of Freedom, and for the Relief of Persons unlawfully holden in Bondage, I have the honour to be appointed to deliver, on the present occasion.

This divine maxim is most properly applicable to the slave-trade, and to the slavery of the Africans. Let us then make the application.

Should we be willing, that the Africans or any other nation should purchase us, our wives and children, transport us into Africa and there sell us into perpetual and absolute slavery? Should we be willing, that they by large bribes and offers of a gainful traffic should entice our neighbours to kidnap and sell us to them, and that they should hold in perpetual and cruel bondage, not only ourselves, but our posterity through all generations? Yet why is it not as right for them to treat us in this manner, as it is for us to treat them in the same manner? Their colour indeed is different from our's. But does this give us a right to enslave them? The nations from Germany to Guinea have complexions of every shade from the fairest white, to a jetty black: and if a black complexion subject a nation or an individual to slavery; where shall slavery begin? or where shall it end?

I propose to mention a few reasons against the right of the slave-trade—and then to consider the principal arguments, which I have ever heard urged in favour of it.— What will be said against the slave-trade will generally be equally applicable to slavery itself; and if conclusive against the former, will be equally conclusive against the latter.

As to the slave-trade, I conceive it to be unjust in itself-abominable on account of the cruel manner in which it is conducted-and totally wrong on account of the impolicy of it, or its destructive tendency to the moral and political interests of any country.

I. It is unjust in itself—. It is unjust in the same sense, and for the same reason, as it is, to steal, to rob, or to murder. It is a principle, the truth of which hath in this country been generally, if not universally acknowledged, ever since the commencement of the late war, that all men are born equally free. If this be true, the Africans are by nature equally entitled to freedom as we are; and therefore we have no more right to enslave, or to afford aid to enslave them, than they have to do the same to us. They have the same right to their freedom, which they have to their property or to their lives. Therefore to enslave them is as really and in the same sense wrong, as to steal from them, to rob or to murder them.

There are indeed cases in which men may justly be deprived of their liberty and reduced to slavery; as there are cases in which they may be justly deprived of their lives. But they can justly be deprived of neither, unless they have by their own voluntary conduct forfeited it. Therefore still the right to liberty stands on the same basis with the right to life. And that the Africans have done something whereby they have forfeited their liberty must appear, before we can justly deprive them of it; as it must appear, that they have done something whereby they have forfeited their lives, before we may justly deprive them of these.

II. The slave-trade is wicked and abominable on account of the cruel manner in which it is carried on. Beside the stealing or kidnapping of men, women and children, in the first instance, and the instigation of others to this abominable practice; the inhuman manner in which they are transported to America, and in which they are treated on their passage and in their subsequent slavery, in such as ought forever to deter every man from acting any part in this business, who has any regard to justice or humanity. They are crowed so closely into the holds and between the decks of vessels, that they have scarcely room to lie down, and sometimes not room to sit up in an erect posture; the men at the same time fastened together with irons by two and two; and all this in the most sultry climate. The consequence of the whole is, that the most dangerous and fatal diseases are soon bred among them, whereby vast numbers of those exported from Africa perish in the voyage: others in dread of that slavery which is before them and in distress and despair from the loss their parents, their children, their husbands, their wives, all their dear connections, and their dear native country itself, starve themselves to death or plunge themselves into the ocean. Those who attempt in the former of those ways to escape from their persecutors, are tortured by live coals applied to their mouths. Those who attempt an escape in the latter and fail, are equally tortured by the most cruel beating, or otherwise as their persecutors please. If any of them make an attempt, as they sometimes do, to recover their liberty, some, and as the circumstances may be, many, are put to immediate death. Others beaten, bruised, cut and mangled in a most inhuman and shocking manner, are in this situation exhibited to the rest, to terrify them from the like attempt in future: and some are delivered up to every species of torment, whether by the application of the whip, or of any other instrument, even of fire itself, as the ingenuity of the ship-master and of his crew is able to suggest or their situation will admit; and these torments are purposely continued for several days, before death is permitted to afford relief to these objects of vengeance.

By these means, according to the common computation, twenty-five thousand, which is a fourth part of those who are exported from Africa, and by the concession of all, twenty thousand, annually perish, before they arrived at the places of their destination in America.

But this is by means the end of the suffering of this unhappy people. Bred up in a country spontaneously yielding the necessaries and conveniences of savage life, they have never been accustomed to labour: of course they are but ill prepared to go through the fatigue and drudgery to which they are doomed in their state of slavery. Therefore partly by this cause, partly by the scantiness and badness of their food, and partly from dejection of spirits, mortification and despair, another twenty-five thousand die in the seasoning, as it is called, i.e. within two years after their arrival in America. This I say is the common computation. Or if we will in particular be as favourable to the trade as in the estimate of the number which perishes on the passage, we may reckon the number which dies in the seasoning to be twenty thousand. So that of the hundred thousand annually exported from Africa to America, fifty thousand, as it is commonly computed, or on the most favourable estimate, forty thousand, die before they are seasoned to the country.

Nor is this all. The cruel sufferings of these pitiable beings are not yet at an end. Thenceforward they have to drag out a miserable life in absolute slavery, entirely at the disposal of their masters, by whom not only every venial fault, every mere inadvertence or mistake, but even real virtues, are liable to be construed into the most atrocious crimes, and punished as such, according to their caprice or rage, while they are intoxicated sometimes with liquor, with passion.

By these masters they are supplied with barely enough to keep them from starving, as the whole expence laid out on a slave for food, clothing and medicine is commonly computed on an average at thirty shillings sterling annually. At the same time they are kept at hard labour from five o'clock in the morning, till nine at night excepting time to eat twice during the day. And they are constantly under the watchful eye of overseers and Negro-driver more tyrannical and cruel than ever their masters themselves. From these drivers, for every imagined, as well as real neglect or want of exertion, they receive the lash, the smack of which is all day long in the ears of those who are on the plantation or in the vicinity; and it is used with such dexterity and severity, as not only to lacerate the skin, but to tear out small portions of the flesh at almost every stroke.

This is the general treatment of the slaves. But many individuals suffer still more severely. Many, many are knocked down; some have their eyes beaten out; some have an arm or a leg broken, or chopt off; and many for a very small or for no crime at all, have been beaten to death merely to gratify the fury of an enraged master or overseer.

Nor ought we on this occasion to overlook the wars among the nations of Africa excited by the trade, or the destruction attendant on those wars. Not to mention the destruction of property, the burning of towns and villages, &c. it hath been determined by reasonable computation, that are annually exported from Africa to the various parts of America, one hundred thousand slaves, as was before observed; that of these, six thousand are captives of war; that in the wars in which these are taken, ten persons of victors and vanquished are killed, to one taken; that therefore the taking of the six thousand captives is attend with the slaughter of sixty thousand of their countrymen. Now does not justice? does not humanity shrink from the idea, that in order to procure slave to gratify our avarice, we should put to death ten human beings? Or that in order to increase our property, and that only in some small degree, we should carry on a trade, or even connive at it, to support which sixty thousand of our own species are slain in war?

These sixty thousand, added to the forty thousand who perish on the passage and in the seasoning, give us an hundred thousand who are annually destroyed by the trade; and the whole advantage gained by this amazing destruction of human lives is sixty thousand slaves. For you will recollect, that the whole number exported from Africa is an hundred thousand; that of these forty thousand die on the passage and in the seasoning, and sixty thousand are destroyed in the wars. Therefore while one hundred and sixty thousand are killed in the wars and are exported from Africa, but sixty thousand are added to the stock of slaves.

Now when we consider all this; when we consider the miseries which this unhappy people suffer in their wars, in their captivity, in their voyage to America, and during a wretched life of cruel slavery: and especially when we consider the annual destruction of an hundred thousand lives in the manner before mentioned; who can hesitate to declare this trade and the consequent slavery to be contrary to every principle of justice and humanity, of the law of nature and of the law of God?

III. This trade and this slavery are utterly wrong on the ground of their impolicy. In a variety of respects they are exceedingly hurtful to the state which tolerates them.

1. They are hurtful, as they deprave the morals of the people.—The incessant and inhuman cruelties practised in the trade and in the subsequent slavery, necessarily tend to harden human heart against the tender feelings of humanity in the masters of vessels, in the sailors, in the factors, in the proprietors of the slaves, in their children, in the overseers, in the slaves themselves, and in all who habitually see those cruelties. Now the eradication or even the diminution of compassion, tenderness and humanity, is certainly a great depravation of heart, and must be followed with correspondent depravity of manners. And measures which lead to such depravity of heart and manners, cannot be extremely hurtful to the state, and consequently are extremely impolitic.

2. The trade is impolitic as it is so destructive of the lives of seamen. The ingenious Mr. Clarkson hath in a very satisfactory manner made it appear, that in the slave-trade alone Great-Britain loses annually about nineteen hundred seamen; and that this loss is more than double to the loss annually sustained by Great-Britain in all her other trade taken together. And doubtless we lose as many as Great-Britain in proportion to the number of seamen whom we employ in this trade.—Now can it be politic to carry on a trade which is so destructive of that useful part of our citizens, our seamen?

3. African slavery is exceedingly impolitic, as it discourages industry. Nothing is more essential to the political prosperity of any state, than industry in the citizens. But in proportion as slaves are multiplied, every kind of labour becomes ignominious: and in fact, in those of the United States, in which slaves are the most numerous, gentlemen and ladies of any fashion disdain to employ themselves in business, which in other states is consistent with the dignity of the first families and first offices. In a country with Negro slaves, labour belongs to them only, and a white man is despised in proportion as he applies to it.— Now how destructive to industry in all the lowest and middle class of citizens, such a situation and the prevalence of such ideas will be, you can easily conceive. The consequence is, that some will nearly starve, others will betake themselves to the most dishonest practices, to obtain the means of living.

As slavery produces indolence in the white people, so it produces all those vices which are naturally connected with it; such as intemperance lewdness and prodigality. These vices enfeeble both the body and the mind, and unfit men for any vigorous exertions and employments either external or mental. And those who are unfit for such exertions, are already a very degenerate race; degenerate, not only in a moral, but a natural sense. They are contemptible too, and will soon be despised even by their Negroes themselves.

Slavery tends to lewdness not only as it produces indolence, but as it affords abundant opportunity for that wickedness without either the danger and difficulty of an attack on the virtue of a woman of chastity, or the danger of a connection with one of ill fame. And we learn the too frequent influence and effect of such a situation, not only from common fame, but from the multitude of mulattoes in countries where slaves are very numerous.

Slavery has a most direct tendency to haughtiness also, and domineering spirit and conduct in the control of them. A man who has been bred up in domineering over Negroes, can scarcely avoid contracting such a habit of haughtiness and domination, as will express itself in his general treatment of mankind, whether in his private capacity, or in any office civil or military with which he may be vested. Despotism in economics naturally leads to despotism in politics, and domestic slavery in a free government is a perfect solecism in human affairs.

How baneful all these tendencies and effects of slavery must be to the public good, and especially to the public good of such a free country as ours, I need not inform you.

4. In the same proportion as industry and labour are discouraged, is population discouraged and prevented. This is another respect in which slavery is exceedingly impolitic. That population is prevented in proportion as industry is discouraged, is, I conceive, so plain that nothing needs to be said to illustrate it. Mankind in general will enter into matrimony as soon as they possess the means of supporting a family. But the great body of any people have no other way of supporting themselves or a family, than by their own labour. Of course as labour is discouraged, matrimony is discouraged and population is prevented.—But the impolicy of whatever produeces these effects will be acknowledge by all. The wealth, strength and glory of a state depend on the number of its virtuous citizens: and a state without citizens is at least a great an absurdity, as a king without subjects.

5. The impolicy of slavery still further appears from this, that it weakens the state, and in proportion to the degree in which it exist, exposes it to become an easy conquest.—The increase of free citizens is an increase of the strength of the state. But not so with regard to the increase of slaves. They not only add nothing to the strength of the state, but actually diminish it in proportion to their number. Every slave is naturally an enemy to the state in which he is holden in slavery, and wants nothing but an opportunity to assist in its overthrow. And an enemy within a state, is much more dangerous than one without it.

These observations concerning the prevention of population and weakening the state, are supported by facts which have fallen within our own observation. That the southern states, in which slaves are so numerous are in no measure so populous, according to the extent of territory, as the northern, is a fact of universal notoriety: and that during the late war, the southern states found themselves greatly weakened by their slaves, and therefore were so easily overrun by the British army, is equally notorious.

From the view we have now taken of this subject, we scruple not to infer, that to carry on the slave-trade and to introduce slaves into our country, is not only to be guilty of injustice, robbery and cruelty toward our fellow-men; but it is to injure ourselves and our country; and therefore it is altogether unjustifiable, wicked and abominable.

Having thus considered the injustice and ruinous tendency of the slave-trade, I proceed to attend to the principal arguments urged in favour of it.

1. It is said, that the Africans are the posterity of Ham, the son of Noah; that Canaan one of Ham's sons, was cursed by Noah to be a servant of servants; that by Canaan we are to understand Ham's posterity in general; that as his posterity are devoted by God to slavery, we have a right to enslave them.—This is the argument: to which I answer:

It is indeed generally thought that Ham peopled Africa; but that the curse on Canaan extended to all the posterity of Ham is a mere imagination. The only reason given for it is, that Canaan was only one of Ham's sons; and that it seems reasonable, that the curse of Ham's conduct should fall on all his posterity, if on any. But this argument is insufficient. We might as clearly argue, that the judgments denounced on the house of David, on account of his sin in the matter of Uriah, must equally fall on all his posterity. Yet we know, that many of them lived and died in great posterity. So in every case in which judgments are predicted concerning any nation or family.

It is allowed in this argument, that the curse was to fall on the posterity of Ham, and not immediately on Ham himself; If otherwise, it is nothing to the purpose of the slave-trade, or of any slaves now in existence. It being allowed then, that this curse was to fall on Ham's posterity, he who had a right to curse the whole of that posterity, had the same right to curse a part of it only, and the posterity of Canaan equally as any other part; and a curse on Ham's posterity in the line of Canaan was as real a curse on Ham himself, as a curse on all his posterity would have been.

Therefore we have no ground to believe, that this curse respected any others, than the posterity of Canaan, who lived in the land of Canaan, which is well known to be remote from Africa. We have a particular account, that all the sons of Canaan settled in the land of Canaan; as may be seen in Gen. x. 15–20. "And Canaan begat Sidon his "first born, and Heth, and the Jebusite, and the "Emorite, and the Girgasite, and the Hivite, and "the Arkite, and the Sinite, and the Arvadite, and "the Zemorite, and the Hamathite; and afterward "were the families of the Canaanites spread abroad. "And the border of the Canaanites was from Sidon, "as thou goest to Gerar, unto Gaza; as thou goest "unto Sodom and Gomorrah, Admah, and Zeboim, "even unto Lashah."—Nor have we account that any of their posterity except the Carthaginians afterward removed to any part of Africa: and none will pretend that these peopled Africa in general; especially considering, that they were subdued, destroyed and so far extirpated by the Romans.

This curse then of the posterity of Canaan, had no reference to the inhabitants of Guinea, or of Africa in general; but was fulfilled partly in Joshua's time, in the reduction and servitude of the Canaanites, and especially of the Gibeonites; partly by what the Phenicians suffered from the Chaldeans, Persians and Greeks; and finally by what the Carthagenians suffered from the Romans.

Therefore this curse gives us no right to enslave the Africans, as we do by the slave-trade, because it has no respect to the Africans whom we enslave. Nor if it had respected them, would it have given any such right; because it was not an institution of slavery, but a mere prophecy of it. And from this prophecy we have no more ground to infer the right of slavery, than we have from the prophecy of the destruction of Jerusalem by Nebuchadnezzar, or by the Romans, to infer their right respectively to destroy it in the manner they did; or from other prophecies to infer the right of Judas to betray his master, or of the Jews to crucify him.

2. The right of slavery is inferred from the instance of Abraham, who had servants born in his house and bought with his money.—But it is by no means certain, that these were slaves, as our Negroes are. If they were, it is unaccountable, that he went out at the head of an army of them to fight his enemies. No West-India planter would easily be induced to venture himself in such a situation. It is far more probable, that similar to some of the vassals under the feudal constitution, the servants of Abraham were only in a good measure dependent on him, and protected by him. But if they were to all intents and purposes slaves, Abraham's holding of them will no more prove the right of slavery, than his going in to Hagar, will prove it right for any man to indulge in criminal intercourse with his domestic.

3. From the divine permission given the Israelites to buy servants of the nations round about them, it is argued, that we have a right to buy the Africans and hold them in slavery. See Lev. xxv. 44–47.

"Both thy bondmen and thy bondmaids, which thou shalt have, shall be of the heathen that are round about you; of them shall ye buy bondmen and bondmaids. Moreover, of the children of the strangers that do sojourn among you, of them shall ye buy, and of their families, that are with you, which they begat in your land; and they shall be your possession. And ye shall take them as an inheritance for your children after you, to inherit them for a possession; they shall be your bondmen for ever : but over your brethren the children of Israel ye shall not rule one over another with rigour." But if this be at all to the purpose, it is a permission to every nation under heaven to buy slaves of the nations round about them; to us, to buy of our Indian neighbours; to them, to buy of us; to the French, to buy of the English, and to the English to buy of the French; and so through the world. If then this argument be valid, every man has an entire right to engage in this trade, and to buy and sell any other man of another nation, and any other man of another nation has an entire right to buy and sell him. Thus according to this construction, we have in Lev. xxv. 43, &c. an institution of an universal slave-trade, by which every man may not only become a merchant, but may rightfully become the merchandise itself of this trade, and may be bought and sold like a beast.—Now this consequence will be given up as absurd, and therefore also the construction of scripture from which it follows, must be given up. Yet it is presumed, that there is no avoiding that construction or the absurdity flowing from it, but by admitting, that this permission to the Israelites to buy slaves has no respect to us, but was in the same manner peculiar to them, as the permission and command to subdue, destroy and extirpate the whole Canaanitish nation; and therefore no more gives countenance to African slavery, than the command to extirpate the Canaanites, gives countenance to the extirpation of any nation in these days, by an universal slaughter of men and women, young men and maidens, infants and sucklings.

4. It is further pleaded, that there were slaves in the time of the apostles; that they did not forbid the holding of those slaves, but gave directions to servants, doubtless referring to the servants of that day, to obey their masters, and count them worthy of all honour.

To this the answer is, that the apostles teach the genteral duties of servants who are righteously in the state of servitude, as many are or may be, by hire, by indenture, and by judgment of a civil court. But they do not say, whether the servants in general of that day were justly holden in slavery or not. In like manner they lay down the general rules of obedience to civil magistrates, without deciding concerning the characters of the magistrates of the Roman empire in the reign of Nero. And as the apostle Paul requires masters to give their servants that which is just and equal, (Col. iv. i.) so if any were enslaved unjustly, of course he in this text requires of the masters of such, to give them their freedom.—Thus the apostles treat the slavery of that day in the same manner that they treat the civil government; and say nothing more in favour of the former, than they say in favour of the latter.

Besides, this argument from the slavery prevailing in the days of the apostles, if it prove any thing, proves too much, and so confutes itself. It proves, that we may enslave all captives taken in war, of any nation, and in any the most unjust war, such as the wars of the Romans, which were generally undertaken from the motives of ambition or avarice. On the ground of this argument we had a right to enslave the prisoners, whom we, during the late war, took from the British army; and they had the same right to enslave those whom they took from us; and so with respect to all other nations.

5. It is strongly urged, that the Negroes brought from Africa are all captives of war, and therefore are justly bought and holden in slavery.—This is a principal argument always urged by the advocates for slavery; and in a solemn debate on this subject, it hath been strongly insisted on, very lately in the British parliament. Therefore it requires our particular attention.

Captives in a war just on their part, cannot be justly enslaved; nor is this pretended. Therefore the captives who may be justly enslaved, must be taken in a war unjust on their part. But even on the supposition, that captives in such a war may be justly enslaved, it will not follow, that we can justly carry on the slave trade, as it is commonly carried on from the African coast. In this trade any slaves are purchased, who are offered for sale, whether justly or unjustly enslaved. No enquiry is made whether they were captives in any war; much less, whether they were captivated in a war unjust on their part.

By the most authentic accounts, it appears, that the wars in general in Africa are excited by the prospect of gain from the sale of the captives of the war. Therefore those taken by the assailants in such wars, cannot be justly enslaved. Beside these, many are kidnapped by those of neighbouring nations; some by their own neighbours; and some by their kings or his agents; others for debt or some trifling crime are condemned to perpetual slavery-But none of these are justly enslaved. And the traders make no enquiry concerning the mode or occasion of their first enslavement. They buy all that are offerred, provided they like them and the price.—So that the plea, that the African slaves are captives in war, is entirely insufficient to justify the slave trade as now carried on.

But this is not all; if it were ever so true, that all the Negroes exported from Africa were captives in war, and that they were taken in a war unjust on their part; still they could not be justly enslaved.—We have no right to enslave a private foe in a state of nature, after he is conquered.

Suppose in a state of nature one man rises against another and endeavours to kill him; in this case the person assaulted has no right to kill the assailant, unless it be necessary to preserve his own life. But in wars between nations, one nation may no doubt secure itself against another, by other means than slavery of its captives. If a nation be victorious in the war, it may exact some towns or a district of country, by way of caution; or it may impose a fine to deter from future injuries. If the nation be not victorious, it will do no good to enslave the captives whom it has taken. It will provoke the victors, and foolishly excite vengeance which cannot be repelled.

Or if neither nation be decidedly victorious, to enslave the captives on either side can answer no good purpose, but must at least occasion the enslaving of the citizens of the other nation, who are now, or in future may be in a state of captivity. Such a practice therefore necessarily tends to evil and not good. Besides; captives in war are generally common soldiers or common citizens; and they are generally ignorant of the true cause or causes of the war, and are by their superiours made to believe, that the war is entirely just on their part. Or if this be not the case, they may by force be compelled to serve in a war which they know to be unjust. In either of these cases they do not deserve to be condemned to perpetual slavery. To inflict perpetual slavery on these private soldiers and citizens is manifestly not to do, as we would wish that men should do to us. If we were taken in a war unjust on our part, we should not think it right to be condemned to perpetual slavery. No more right is it for us to condemn and hold in perpetual slavery others, who are in the same situation.

6. It is argued, that as the Africans in their own country, previously to the purchase of them by the African traders, are captives in war; if they were not bought up by those traders, they would be put to death: that therefore to purchase them and to subject them to slavery instead of death, is an act of mercy not only lawful, but meritorious.

If the case were indeed so as is now represented, the purchase of the Negroes would be no more meritorious, than the act of a man, who, if we were taken by the Algerines, should purchase us out of that slavery. This would indeed be an act of benevolence, if the purchaser should set us at liberty. But it is no act of benevolence to buy a man out of one state into another no better. Nay, the act of ransoming a man from death gives no right to the ransomer to commit a crime or an act of injustice to the person ransomed. The person ransomed is doubtless obligated according to his ability to satisfy the ransomer for his expence and trouble. Yet the ransomer has no more right to enslave the other, than the man who saves the life of another who was about to be killed by a robber or an assassin, has a right to enslave him.—The liberty of a man for life is a far greater good, than the property paid for a

Negro on the African coast. And to deprive a man of an immensely greater good, in order to recover one immensely, is an immense injury and crime.

7. As to the pretence, that to prohibit or lay aside this trade, would be hurtful to our commerce; it is sufficient to ask, whether on the supposition, that it were advantageous to the commerce of Great-Britain to send her ships to these states, and transport us into that perpetual slavery in the West Indies, it would be right that she should go into trade.

8. That to prohibit the slave trade would infringe on the property of those, who have expended large sums to carry on that trade, or of those who wish to purchase the slaves for their plantations, hath also been urged as an argument in favour of the trade.—But the same argument would prove, that if the skins and teeth of the Negroes were as valuable articles of commerce as furs and elephant's teeth, and a merchant were to lay out his property in this commerce, he ought by no means to be obstructed therein.

9. But others will carry on the trade, if we do not.-So others will rob, steal and murder, if we do not.

10. It is said, that some men are intended by nature to be slaves.—If this mean, that the author of nature has given some men a licence, to enslave others; this is denied and proof is demanded. If it mean, that God hath made some of capacities inferior to others, and that the last have a right to enslave the first; this argument will prove, that some of the citizens of every country, have a right to enslave other citizens of the same country; nay, that some have a right to enslave their own brothers and sisters.— But if this argument mean, that God in his providence suffers some men to be enslaved, and that this proves, that from the beginning he intended they should be enslaved, and made them with this intention; the answer is, that in like manner he suffers some men to be murdered, and in this sense, he intended and made them to be murdered. Yet no man in his senses will hence argue the lawfulness of murder.

11. It is further pretended, that no other men, than Negroes, can endure labour in the hot climates of the West Indies and the southern states.—But does this appear to be fact? In all other climates, the labouring people are the most healthy. And I confess I have not yet seen evidence, but that those who have been accustomed to labour and are inured to those climates, can bear labour there also.— However, taking for granted the fact asserted in this objection, does it follow, that the inhabitants of those countries have a right to enslave the Africans to labour for them? No more surely than from the circumstance, that you are feeble and cannot labour, it follows, that you have a right to enslave your robust neighbour. As in all other cases, the feeble and those who choose not to labour, and yet wish to

have their lands cultivated, are necessitated to hire the robust to labour for them; so no reason can be given, why the inhabitants of hot climates should not either perform their own labour, or hire those who can perform it, whether Negroes or others.

If our traders went to the coast of Africa to murder the inhabitants, or to rob them of their property, all would own that such murderous or piratical practices are wicked and abominable. Now it is as really wicked to rob a man of his liberty, as to rob him of his life; and it is much more wicked, than to rob him of his property. All men agree to condemn highway robbery. And the slave-trade is as much a greater wickedness than highway robbery, as liberty is more valuable than property. How strange is it then, that in the same nation highway robbery should be punished with death, and the slave-trade be encourage by national authority.

We all dread political slavery, or subjection to the arbitrary power of a king or of any man or men not deriving their authority from the people. Yet such a state is inconceivably preferable to the slavery of the Negroes. Suppose that in the late war we had been subdued by Great-Britain; we should have been taxed without our consent. But these taxes would have amounted to but a small part of our property. Whereas the Negroes are deprived of all their property; no part of their earnings is their own; the whole is their masters.-In a conquered state we should have been at liberty to dispose of ourselves and of our property in most cases, as we should choose. We should have been free to live in this or that town or place; in any part of the country, or to remove out of the country; to apply to this or that business; to labour or not; and excepting a sufficiency for the taxes, to dispose of the fruit of our labour to our own benefit, or that of our children, or of any other person. But the unhappy Negroes in slavery can do none of these things. They must do what they are commanded and as much as they are commanded, on pain of the lash. They must live where they are placed, and must confine themselves to that spot, on pain of death.

So that Great-Britain in her late attempt to enslave America, committed a very small crime indeed in comparison with the crime of those who enslave the Africans.

The arguments which have been urged against the slave-trade, are with little variation applicable to the holding of slaves. He who holds a slave, continues to deprive him of that liberty, which was taken from him on the coast of Africa. And if it were wrong to deprive him of it in the first instance, why not in the second? If this be true, no man hath a better right to retain his Negro in slavery, than he had to take him from from his native African shores. And every man who cannot show, that his Negro hath by his voluntary conduct forfeited his liberty, is obligated immediately to manumit him. Undoubtedly we should think so, were we holden in the same slavery in which the Negroes are: And our text required us to do to others, as we would that they should do to us.

To hold a slave, who has a right to his liberty, is not only a real crime, but a very great one. Many good christians have wondered how Abraham, the father of the faithful, could take Hagar to his bed; and how Sarah, celebrated as an holy woman, could consent to this transaction: Also, how David and Solomon could have so many wives and concubines, and yet be real saints. Let such inquire how it is possible, that our fathers and men now alive, universally reputed pious, should hold Negro slaves, and yet be the subjects of real piety? And whether to reduce a man, who hath the same right to liberty as any other man, to a state of absolute slavery, or to hold him in that state, be not as great a crime as concubinage or fornication. I presume it will not be denied, that to commit theft or robbery every day of a man's life, is as great a sin as to commit fornication in one instance. But to steal a man or to rob him of his liberty is a greater sin, than to steal his property, or to take it by violence. And to hold a man in a state of slavery, who has a right to his liberty, is to be every day guilty of robbing him of his liberty, or of manstealing. The consequence is inevitable, that other things being the same, to hold a Negro slave, unless he have forfeited his liberty, is a greater sin in the sight of God, than concubinage or fornication.

Does this conclusion seem strange to any of you? Let me entreat you to weigh it candidly before you reject it. You will not deny, that liberty is more valuable than property; and that it is a greater sin to deprive a man of his whole liberty during life, than to deprive him of his whole property; or that manstealing is a greater crime than robbery. Nor will you deny, that to hold in slavery a man who was stolen, is substantially the same crime as to steal him.

These principles being undeniable, I leave it to yourselves to draw the plain and necessary consequence. And if your consciences shall, in spite of all opposition, tell you, that while you hold your Negroes in slavery, you do wrong, exceedingly wrong; that you do not, as you would that men should do to you; that you commit sin in the sight of God; that you daily violate the plain rights of mankind, and that in a higher degree, than if you committed theft or robbery; let me beseech you not to stifle this conviction, but attend to it and act accordingly; lest you add to your former guilt, that of sinning against the light of truth, and of your own consciences.

To convince yourselves, that your information being the same, to hold a Negro slave is a greater sin than fornication, theft or robbery, you need only bring the matter home to yourselves. I am willing to appeal to your own consciences, whether you would not judge it to be a greater sin for a man to hold you or your child during life

in such slavery, as that of the Negroes, than for him to indulge in one instance of licentious conduct or in one instance to steal or rob. Let conscience speak, and I will submit to its decision.

This question seems to be clearly decided by revelation. Exod. xxi. 16. "He that stealeth a man "and selleth him, or if he be found in his hand, "he shall surely be put to death." Thus death is, by the divine express declaration, the punishment due to the crime of man-stealing. But death is not the punishment declared by God to be due to fornication theft or robbery in common cases. Therefore we have the divine authority to assert, that manstealing is a greater crime than fornication, theft or robbery. Now to hold in slavery a man who has a right to liberty, is substantially the same crime as to deprive him of his liberty. And to deprive of liberty and reduce to slavery, a man who has a right to liberty, is man-stealing. For it is immaterial whether he be taken and reduced to slavery clandestinely or by open violence. Therefore if the Negroes have a right to liberty, to hold them in slavery is man-stealing, which we have seen is, by God himself, declared to be a greater crime than fornication, theft or robbery.

Perhaps, though this truth be clearly demonstrable both from reason and revelation, you scarcely dare receive it, because it seems to bear hardly on the characters of our pious fathers, who held slaves. But they did it ignorantly and in unbelief of the truth; as Abraham, Jacob, David and Solomon were ignorant, that polygamy or concubinage was wrong. As to domestic slavery our fathers lived in a time of ignorance which God winked at; but now he commandeth all men every where to repent of this wickedness, and to break off this sin by righteousness, and this iniquity by shewing mercy to the poor, if it may be a lengthening out of their tranquillity . You therefore to whom the present blaze of light as to this subject has reached, cannot sin at so cheap a rate as our fathers.

But methinks I hear some say, I have bought my Negro; I have paid a large sum for him; I cannot lose this sum, and therefore I cannot manumit him.—Alas! this is hitting the nail on the head . This brings into view the true cause which makes it so difficult to convince men of what is right in this case—You recollect the story of Amaziah's hiring an hundred thousand men of Israel, for an hundred talents, to assist him against the Edomites; and that when by the word of the Lord, he was forbidden to take those hired men with him to the war, he cried out, "But what shall we do for the hundred talents, "which I have given to the army of Israel?" In this case, the answer of God was, "The Lord is "able to give thee much more than this."—To apply this to the subject before us, God is able to give thee much more than thou shalt lose by manumitting thy slave.

You may plead, that you use your slave well; you are not cruel to him, but feed and clothe him comfortably, &c.

Still every day you rob him of a most valuable and important right. And a highway-man, who robs a man of his money in the most easy and complaisant manner, is still a robber; and murder may be effected in a manner the least cruel and tormenting; still it is murder.

Having now taken that view of our subject, which was proposed, we may in reflection see abundant reason to acquiesce in the institution of this society. If the slave-trade be unjust, and as gross a violation of the rights of mankind, as would be, if the Africans should transport us into perpetual slavery in Africa; to unite our influence against it, is a duty which we owe to mankind, to ourselves and to God too. It is but doing as we would that men should do to us.—Nor is it enough that we have formed the society; we must do the duties of it. The first of these is to put an end to the slave-trade. The second is to relieve those who, contrary to the laws of the country, are holden in bondage. Another is to defend those in their remaining legal and natural rights, who are by law holden in bondage. Another and not the least important object of this society, I conceive to be, to increase and disperse the light of truth with respect to the subject of African slavery, and so prepare the way for its total abolition. For until men in general are convinced of the injustice of the trade and of the slavery itself, comparatively little can be done to effect the most important purposes of the institution.

It is not to be doubted, that the trade is even now carried on from this state. Vessels are from time to time fitted out for the coast of Africa, to transport the Negroes to the West-Indies and other parts. Nor will an end be put to this trade, without vigilance and strenuous exertion on the part of this society, or other friends of humanity, nor without a patient enduring of the opposition and odium of all who are concerned in it, of their friends and of all who are of the opinion that it is justifiable. Among these we are doubtless to reckon some of large property and considerable influence. And if the laws and customs of the country equally allowed of it, many, and perhaps as many as now plead for the right of the African slave-trade, would plead for the right of kidnapping us, the citizens of the United States, and of selling us into perpetual slavery.—If then we dare not incur the displeasure of such men, we may as well dissolve the society, and leave the slave-trade to be carried on, and the Negroes to be kidnapped, and though free in this state, to be sold into perpetual slavery in distant parts, at the pleasure of any man, who wishes to make gain by such abominable practices.

Though we must expect opposition, yet if we be steady and persevering, we need not fear, that we shall fail of success. The advantages, which the cause has already gained, are many and great. Thirty years ago scarcely a man in this country thought either the slave-trade or the slavery of Negroes to be wrong. But now how many and able advocates in private life, in our legislatures, in Congress, have appeared and have openly and irrefragably pleaded the rights of humanity in this as well as other instances? Nay the great body of the people from New-Hampshire to Virginia inclusively, have obtained such light, that in all those states the further importation of slaves is prohibited by law. And in Massachusetts and New-Hampshire, slavery is totally abolished.

Nor is the light concerning this subject confined to America. It hath appeared with great clearness in France, and produced remarkable effects in the National Assembly. It hath also shone in bright beams in Great-Britain. It flashes with splendour in the writings of Clarkson and in the proceedings of several societies formed to abolish the slave-trade. Nor hath it been possible to shut it out of the British parliament. This light is still increasing, and in time will effect a total revolution. And if we judge of the future by the past, within fifty years from this time, it will be as shameful for a man to hold a Negro slave, as to be guilty of common robbery or theft. But it is our duty to remove the obstacles which intercept the rays of this light, that it may reach not only public bodies, but every individual. And when it shall have obtained a general spread, shall have dispelled all darkness, and slavery shall be no more; it will be an honour to be recorded in history, as a society which was formed, and which exerted itself with vigour and fidelity, to bring about an event so necessary and conducive to the interests of humanity and virtue, to the support of the rights and to the advancement of the happiness of mankind.

Source:
Library of Congress, Rare Book and Special Collections Division, Daniel A. P. Murray Pamphlets Collection.

Fugitive Slave Law of 1793

Federal legislation enacted on February 12, 1793, providing for the seizure and return, from one state to another, of escaped slaves in the United States. The act authorized the owner or the owner's agent to arrest a runaway in any state and gave federal and state judges the authority to determine whether the fugitive owed the service claimed, based on oral testimony or an affidavit. No jury trial was required to return a fugitive to the state or territory he or she had fled. Any person who harbored a fugitive or obstructed the arrest was liable for a fine of $500. The act was loosely enforced in the North, and it was countered by the Underground Railroad (a network to help escaping slaves). The controversial Fugitive Slave Act of 1850 put a heavier burden on free states to return slaves. Both acts were repealed in 1864.

An Act

Respecting fugitives from justice, and persons escaping from the service of their masters.

Section 1. *Be it enacted by the Senate and House of Representatives of the United States of America in Congress assembled,* That whenever the executive authority of any state in the Union, or either of the territories northwest or south of the river Ohio, shall demand any person as a fugitive from justice, of the executive authority of any such state or territory to which such person shall have fled, and shall moreover produce the copy of an indictment found, or an affidavit made before a magistrate of any state or territory as aforesaid, charging the person so demanded, with having committed treason, felony or other crime, certified as authentic by the governor or chief magistrate of the state or territory from whence the person so charged fled, it shall be the duty of the executive authority of the state or territory to which such person shall have fled, to cause him or her to be arrested and secured, and notice of the arrest to be given to the executive authority making such demand, or to the agent of such authority appointed to receive the fugitive, and to cause the fugitive to be delivered to such agent when he shall appear: But if no such agent shall appear within six months from the time of the arrest, the prisoner may be discharged. And all costs or expenses incurred in the apprehending, securing, and transmitting such fugitive to the state or territory making such demand, shall be paid by such state or territory.

Sec. 2. *And be it further enacted,* That any agent, appointed as aforesaid, who shall receive the fugitive into his custody, shall be empowered to transport him or her to the state or territory from which he or she shall have fled. And if any person or persons shall by force set at liberty, or rescue the fugitive from such agent while transporting, as aforesaid, the person or persons so offending shall, on conviction, be fined not exceeding five hundred dollars, and be imprisoned not exceeding one year.

Sec. 3. *And be it also enacted,* That when a person held to labour in any of the United States, or in either of the territories on the northwest or south of the river Ohio, under the laws thereof, shall escape into any other of the said states or territory, the person to whom such labour or service may be due, his agent or attorney, is hereby empowered to seize or arrest such fugitive from labour, and to take him or her before any judge of the circuit or district courts of the United States, residing or being within the state, or before any magistrate of a county, city or town corporate, wherein such seizure or arrest shall be made, and upon proof to the satisfaction of such judge or magistrate, either by oral testimony or affidavit taken before and certified by a magistrate of any such state or territory, that the person so seized or arrested, doth, under the laws of the state or territory from which he or she fled, owe service or labour to the person claiming him or her, it shall be the duty of such judge or magistrate to give a certificate thereof to such claimant, his agent or attorney, which shall be sufficient warrant for removing the said fugitive from labour, to the state or territory from which he or she fled.

Sec. 4. *And be it further enacted,* That any person who shall knowingly and willingly obstruct or hinder such claimant, his agent or attorney in so seizing or arresting such fugitive from labour, or shall rescue such fugitive from such claimant, his agent or attorney when so arrested pursuant to the authority herein given or declared; or shall harbor or conceal such person after notice that he or she was a fugitive from labour, as aforesaid, shall, for either of the said offences, forfeit and pay the sum of five hundred dollars. Which penalty may be recovered by and for the benefit of such claimant, by action of debt, in any court proper to try the same; saving moreover to the person claiming such labour or service, his right of action for or on account of the said injuries or either of them.

See also FUGITIVE SLAVE ACT OF 1850.

Source:
Statutes at Large of the United States of America, 1789–1873. 17 vols. Washington, D.C. 1850–73. Vol. 1, pp. 302–305.

Chisholm v. Georgia, 1793

U.S. Supreme Court decision of February 18, 1793, upholding the right of citizens of one state to sue another state in federal courts. Citizens of South Carolina who were the heirs of Alexander Chisholm, a Loyalist whose property had been confiscated by the state of Georgia during the American Revolution (1775–83), sued that state for compensation. Georgia denied the Supreme Court's jurisdiction and refused to appear. The Court ruled in favor of Chisholm. State protests against the decision led to passage of the Eleventh Amendment (ratified in 1798), denying federal jurisdiction in suits by a citizen of one state against another state.

Chisholm, Executor, v. Georgia
The Court held the case under advisement, from the 5th to the 18th of February, when they delivered their opinions *seriatim.*

Iredell, Justice.—This great cause comes before the court, on a motion made by the attorney-general, that an order be made by the court to the following effect: "That unless the state of Georgia shall, after reasonable notice of this motion, cause an appearance to be entered on behalf of the said state, on the fourth day of next term, or show cause to the contrary, judgment shall be entered for the plaintiff, and a writ of inquiry shall be awarded." Before such an order be made, it is proper that this court should be satisfied it hath cognisance of the suit; for, to be sure, we ought not to enter a conditional judgment (which this would be), in a case where we were not fully persuaded we had authority to do so.

This is the first instance wherein the important question involved in this cause has come regularly before the court. In the Maryland case, it did not because the attorney-general of the state voluntarily appeared. We could not, therefore, without the greatest impropriety, have taken up the question suddenly. That case has since been compromised; but had it proceeded to trial, and a verdict been given for the plaintiff, it would have been our duty, previous to our giving judgment, to have well considered whether we were warranted in giving it. I had then great doubts upon my mind, and should, on such a case, have proposed a discussion of the subject. Those doubts have increased since, and after the fullest consideration I have been able to bestow on the subject, and the most respectful attention to the able argument of the attorney-general, I am now decidedly of opinion, that no such action as this before the court can legally be maintained.

The action is an action of *assumpsit.* The particular question then before the court, is, will an action of *assumpsit* lie against a state? This particular question (abstracted from the general one, viz., whether, a state can in any instance be sued?) I took the liberty to propose to the consideration of the attorney-general, last term. I did so, because I have often found a great deal of confusion to arise from taking too large a view at once, and I had found myself embarrassed on this very subject, until I considered the abstract question itself. The attorney-general has spoken to it, in deference to my request, as he has been pleased to intimate, but he spoke to this particular question slightly, conceiving it to be involved in the general one; and after establishing, as he thought, that point, he seemed to consider the other followed of course. He expressed, indeed, some doubt how to prove what appeared so plain. It seemed to him (if I recollect right), to depend principally on the solution of this simple question; can a state assume? But the attorney-general must know, that in England, certain judicial proceedings, not inconsistent with the sovereignty, may take place against the crown, but that an action of *assumpsit* will not lie. Yet, surely, the King can assume as well as a state. So can the United States themselves, as well as any state in the Union: yet, the attorney-general himself has taken some pains to show, that no action whatever is maintainable against the United States. I shall, therefore, confine myself, as much

as possible, to the particular question before the court, though every thing I have to say upon it will effect every kind of suit, the object of which is to compel the payment of money by a state.

The question, as I before observed, is—will an action of *assumpsit* lie against a state? If it will, it must be in virtue of the constitution of the United States, and of some law of congress conformable thereto. The part of the constitution concerning the judicial power, is as follows, viz: Art. III., Section 2. The judicial power shall extend, (1) To all cases, in law and equity, arising under the constitution, the law of the United States, and treaties made, or which shall be made, under their authority: (2) To all cases affecting ambassadors, or other public ministers and consuls: (3) To all cases of admiralty and maritime jurisdiction: (4) To all controversies to which the United States shall be party: (5) To controversies between two or more states; between a state and citizens of another state; between citizens of different states; between citizens of the same state, claiming lands under grants of different states; and between a state or the citizens thereof, and foreign states, citizens or subjects. The constitution, therefore, provides for the jurisdiction wherein a state is a party, in the following instances: 1st. Controversies between two or more states: 2d. Controversies between a state and citizens of another state: 3d. Controversies between a state, and foreign states, citizens or subjects. And it also provides, that in all cases in which a state shall be a party, the supreme court shall have original jurisdiction.

The words of the general judicial act, conveying the authority of the supreme court, under the constitution, so far as they concern this question, are as follows: Section 13. "That the supreme court shall have exclusive jurisdiction of all controversies of a civil nature, where a state is a party, except between a state and its citizens; and except also, between a state and citizens of other states or aliens, in which latter case, it shall have original, but not exclusive jurisdiction. And shall have, exclusively, all jurisdiction of suits or proceedings against ambassadors or other public ministers, or their domestics or domestic servants, as a court of law can have or exercise consistently with the law of nations; and original, but not exclusive jurisdiction, of all suits brought by ambassadors or other public ministers, or in which a consul or vice-consul shall be a party."

The supreme court hath, therefore, *first,* exclusive jurisdiction in every controversy of a civil nature: 1st. Between two or more states: 2d. Between a state and a foreign state: 3d. Where a suit or proceeding is depending against ambassadors, other public ministers, or their domestics or domestic servants. *Second,* original, but not exclusive jurisdiction, 1st. Between a state and citizens of other states: 2d. Between a state and foreign citizens or subjects: 3d. Where a suit is brought by ambassadors or other public ministers: 4th. Where a consul or vice-consul is a party. The suit now before the court (if maintainable at all) comes within the latter description, it being a suit against a state by a citizen of another state.

The constitution is particular in expressing the parties who may be the objects of the jurisdiction in any of these cases, but in respect to the subject matter upon which such jurisdiction is to be exercised, used the word "controversies" only. The act of congress more particularly mentions civil controversies, a qualification of the general word in the constitution, which I do not doubt every reasonable man will think well warranted, for it cannot be presumed, that the general word "controversies" was intended to include any proceedings that relate to criminal cases, which in all instances that respect the same governor only, are uniformly considered of a local nature, and to be decided by its particular laws. The word "controversy" indeed, would not naturally justify any such construction, but nevertheless it was perhaps a proper instance of caution in congress to guard against the possibility of it.

A general question of great importance here occurs. What controversy of a civil nature can be maintained against a state by an individual? The framers of the constitution, I presume, must have meant one of two things— Either, 1. In the conveyance of that part of the judicial power which did not relate to the execution of the other authorities of the general government (which it must be admitted are full and discretionary, within the restrictions of the constitution itself), to refer to antecedent laws for the construction of the general words they use: or, 2. To enable congress in all such cases to pass all such laws as they might deem necessary and proper to carry the purposes of this constitution into full effect, either absolutely at their discretion, or, at least, in cases where prior laws were deficient for such purposes, if any such deficiency existed.

The attorney-general has indeed suggested another construction a construction, I confess, that I never heard of before, nor can I now consider it grounded on any solid foundation, though it appeared to me to be the basis of the attorney-general's argument. His construction I take to be this: "That the moment a supreme court is formed, it is to exercise all the judicial power vested in it by the constitution, by its own authority, whether the legislature has prescribed methods of doing so, or not." My conception of the constitution is entirely different. I conceive, that all the courts of the United States must receive, not merely their *organization* as to the number of judges of which they are to consist; but all their authority, as to the manner of their proceeding, from the legislature only. This appears to me to be one of those cases, with many others, in which an

article of the constitution cannot be effectuated, without the intervention of the legislative authority. There being many such, at the end of the special enumeration of the powers of congress in the constitution, is this general one: "To make all laws which, shall be necessary and proper for carrying into execution the foregoing powers, and all other powers vested by this constitution in the government of the United States, or in any department or officer thereof." None will deny, that an act of legislation is necessary to say, at least, of what number the judges are to consist; the President, with the consent of the senate, could not nominate a number at their discretion. The constitution intended this article so far, at least, to be the subject of a legislative act. Having a right thus to establish the court, and it being capable of being established in no other manner, I conceive it necessarily follows, that they are also direct the manner of its proceedings. Upon this authority, there is, that I know, but one limit; that is, "that they shall not exceed their authority." If they do, I have no hesitation to say, that any act to that effect would be utterly void, because it would be inconsistent with the constitution, which is a fundamental law, paramount to all others, which we are not only bound to consult, but sworn to observe; and therefore, where there is an interference, being superior in obligation to the other, we must unquestionably obey that in preference. Subject to this restriction, the whole business of organizing the courts, and directing the methods of their proceeding, where necessary, I conceive to be in the discretion of congress. If it shall be found, on this occasion, or on any other, that the remedies now in being are defective, for any purpose, it is their duty to provide for, they no doubt will provide others. It is their duty to *legislate*, so far as is necessary to carry the constitution into effect. It is *ours* only to *judge*. We have no reason, nor any more right to distrust their doing their duty, than they have to distrust that we all do ours. There is no part of the constitution that I know of, that authorizes this court to take up any business where they left it, and in order that the powers given in the constitution may be in full activity, supply their omission by making *new laws* for *new cases;* or, which I take to be the same thing, applying *old principles to new cases* materially different from those to which they were applied before.

With regard to the attorney-general's doctrine of incidents, that was founded entirely on the supposition of the other I have been considering. The authority contended for is certainly not one of those necessarily incident to all courts merely as such.

If therefore, this court is to be (as I consider it) the organ of the constitution and the law, not of the *constitution* only, in respect to the manner of its proceeding, we must receive our directions from the legislature in this particular, and have no right to constitute ourselves an *officina brevium,* or take any other short method of doing what the constitution has chosen (and, in my opinion, with the most perfect propriety) should be done, in another manner.

But the act of congress has not been altogether silent upon this subject. The 14th section of the judicial act, provides in the following words: "All the before-mentioned courts of the United States shall have power to issue writs of *scire facias, habeas corpus,* and all other writs not specially provided for by statute, which may be necessary for the exercise of their respective jurisdictions, and agreeable to the principles and usages of law." These words refer as well to the supreme court as to the other courts of the United States. Whatever writs we issue, that are necessary for the exercise of our jurisdiction, must be agreeable to the principles and usages of law. This is a direction, I apprehend, we cannot supersede, because it may appear to us not sufficiently extensive. If it be not, we must wait until other remedies are provided by the same authority. From this it is plain, that the legislature did not choose to leave to our own discretion the path to justice, but has prescribed one of its own. In doing so, it has, I think, wisely, referred us to principles and usages of law, already well known, and by their precision calculated to guard against that innovating spirit of courts of justice, which the attorney-general, in another case, reprobated with so much warmth, and with whose sentiments in that particular, I most cordially join. The principles of law to which reference is to be had, either upon the general ground I first alluded to, or upon the special words I have above cited, from the judicial act, I apprehend, can be, either, 1st. Those of the particular laws of the state, against which the suit is brought. Or 2d. Principles of law, common to all the states. I omit any consideration arising from the word "usages," though a still stronger expression. In regard to the principles of the particular laws of the state of Georgia, if they in any manner differed, so as to affect this question, from the principles of law, common to all the states, it might be material to inquire, whether, there would be any propriety or congruity in laying down a rule of decision which would induce this consequence, that an action would lie in the supreme court against some states, whose laws admitted of a compulsory remedy against their own governments, but not against others, wherein no such remedy was admitted, or which would require, perhaps, if the principle was received, fifteen different methods of proceeding against states, all standing in the same political relation to the general government, and none having any pretence to a distinction in its favor, or justly liable to any distinction to its prejudice. If any such difference existed in the laws of the different states, there would seem to be a propriety, in order to induce uniformity (if a constitutional power for that purpose exists), that congress should prescribe a rule, fitted to this new case, to which no equal,

uniform and impartial mode of proceeding could otherwise be applied.

But this point, I conceive, it is unnecessary to determine, because I believe there is no doubt, that neither in the state now in question, nor in any other in the Union, any particular legislative mode, authorizing a compulsory suit for the recovery of money against a state, was in being, either when the constitution was adopted, or at the time the judicial act was passed. Since that time, an act of assembly for such a purpose has been passed in Georgia. But that surely could have no influence in the construction of an act of the legislature of the United States, passed before.

The only principles of law, then, that can be regarded, are those common to all the states. I know of none such, which can affect this case, but those that are derived from what is properly termed "the common law," a law which I presume is the ground-work of the laws in every state in the Union, and which I consider, so far as it is applicable to the peculiar circumstances of the country, and where no special act of legislation controls it, to be in force in each state, as it existed in England (unaltered by any statute), at the time of the first settlement of the country. The statutes of England that are in force in America differ perhaps in all the states; and therefore, it is probable, the common law in each is in some respects different. But it is certain, that in regard to any common-law principle which can influence the question before us, no alteration has been made by any statute, which could occasion the least material difference, or have any partial effect. No other part of the common law of England, it appears to me, can have any reference to this subject, but that part of it which prescribes remedies against the crown. Every state in the Union, in every instance where its sovereignty has not been delegated to the United States, I consider to be as completely sovereign, as the United States are in respect to the powers surrendered. The United States are sovereign as to all the powers of government actually surrendered: each state in the Union is sovereign, as to all the powers reserved. It must necessarily be so, because the United States have no claim to any authority but such as the states have surrendered to them: of course, the part not surrendered must remain as it did before. The powers of the general government, either of a legislative or executive nature, or which particularly concerns treaties with foreign powers, do for the most part (if not wholly) affect individuals, and not states: they require no aid from any state authority. This is the great leading distinction between the old articles of confederation, and the present constitution. The judicial power is of a peculiar kind. It is indeed commensurate with the ordinary legislative and executive powers of the general government, and the power which concerns treaties. But it also goes further.

Where certain parties are concerned, although the subject in controversy does not relate to any of the special objects of authority of the general government, wherein the separate sovereignties of the states are blended in one common mass of supremacy, yet the general government has a judicial authority in regard to such subjects of controversy, and the legislature of the United States may pass all laws necessary to give such judicial authority its proper effect. So far as states, under the constitution, can be made legally liable to this authority, so far, to be sure, they are subordinate to the authority of the United States, and their individual sovereignty is in this respect limited. But it is limited no further than the necessary execution of such authority requires. The authority extends only to the decision of controversies in which a state is a party, and providing laws necessary for that purpose. That surely can refer only to such controversies in which a state *can* be a party; in respect to which, if any question arises, it can be determined, according to the principles have supported, in no other manner than by a reference either to pre-existent laws, or laws passed under the constitution and in conformity to it.

Whatever be the true construction of the constitution in this particular; whether it is to be construed as intending merely a transfer of jurisdiction from one tribunal to another, or as authorizing the legislature to provide laws for the decision of all possible controversies in which a state may be involved with an individual, without regard to any prior exemption; yet it is certain, that the legislature has in fact proceeded upon the former supposition, and upon the latter. For, besides what I noticed before, as to an express reference to principles and usages of law, as the guide of our proceeding, it is observable, that in instances like this before the court, this court hath a *concurrent jurisdiction* only; the present being one of those cases where, by the judicial act, this court hath *original* but not *exclusive* jurisdiction. This court therefore, under that act, can exercise no authority, in such instances, but such authority as, from the subject-matter of it, may be exercised in some other court. There are no courts with which such a concurrence can be suggested but the circuit courts, or courts of the different states. With the former, it cannot be, for admitting that the constitution is not to have a restrictive operation, so as to confine all cases in which a state is a party, exclusively to the supreme court (an opinion to which I am strongly inclined), yet, there are no words in the definition of the powers of the circuit court, which give a color at an opinion, that where a suit is brought against a state, by a citizen of another state, the circuit court could exercise any jurisdiction at all. If they could, however, such a jurisdiction, by the very terms of their authority, could be only concurrent with the courts of the several states. It follows, therefore, unquestionably, I

think, that looking at the act of congress, which I consider is on this occasion the limit of our authority (whatever further might be constitutionally enacted), we can exercise no authority, in the present instance, consistently with the clear intention of the act, but such as a proper state court would have been, at least, competent to exercise, at the time the act was passed.

If therefore, no new remedy be provided (as plainly is the case), and consequently, we have no other rule to govern us, but the principles of the pre-existent laws, which must remain in force until superseded by others, then it is incumbent upon us to inquire, whether, previous to the adoption of the constitution (which period, or the period of passing the law, in respect to the object of this inquiry, is perfectly equal), an action of the nature like this before the court could have been maintained against one of the states in the Union, upon the principles of the common law, which I have shown to be alone applicable. If it could, I think, it is now maintainable here: if it could not, I think, as the law stands at present, it is not maintainable; whatever opinion may be entertained, upon the construction of the constitution as to the power of congress to authorize such as one. Now, I presume, it will not be denied, that in every state in the Union, previous to the adoption of the constitution, the only common-law principles in regard to suits that were in any manner admissible in respect to claims against the state, were those which, in England, apply to claims against the crown; there being certainly no other principles of the common law which, previous to the adoption of this constitution, could, in any manner, or upon any color, apply to the case of a claim against a state, in its own courts, where it was solely and completely sovereign, in respect to such cases, at least. Whether that remedy was strictly applicable or not, still, I apprehend, there was no other. The only remedy, in a case like that before the court, by which, by any possibility, a suit can be maintained against the crown, in England, or, at any period from which the common law, as in force in America, could be derived, I believe, is that which is called a *Petition of right*. It is stated, indeed, in Com Dig. 105, that "until the time of Edward I, the King might have been sued in all actions, as a common person." And some authorities are cited for their position, though it is even there stated as a doubt. But the same authority adds—"but now, none can have an action against the King, but one shall be put to sue to him by petition." This appears to be a quotation or abstract from Theloall's Digest, which is also one of the authorities quoted in the former case. And this book appear (from the law catalogue) to have been printed so long ago as the year 1579. The same doctrine appears (according to a quotation in Blackstone's Commentaries, 1 vol. 243) to be stated in Finch's Law 253, the first edition of which, it seems, was published in 1579. This also more fully appears in the case of *The Bankers,* and particularly from the celebrated argument of Somers, in the time of Wm. III, for, though that case was ultimately decided against Lord Somers's opinion, yet, the ground on which the decision was given, no way invalidates the reasoning of that argument, so far as it respects the simple case of a sum of money demandable from the King, and not by him secured on any particular revenues. The case is reported in Freeman, vol. 1, p. 331; 5 Mod. 29; Skin. 601; and lately very elaborately in a small pamphlet published by Mr. Harrgave, which contains all the reports at length, except Skinner's, together with the argument at large of Lord Somers; besides some additional matter.

The substance of the case was as follows: King Charles II. having received large sums of money from bankers, on the credit of the growing produce of the revenue, for the payment of which, tallies and orders of the exchequer were given (afterwards made transferable by statute), and the payment of these having been afterwards postponed, the King at length, in order to relieve the bankers, in 1677, granted annuities to them out of the hereditary excise, equal to six per cent interest on their several debts, but redeemable on payment of the principal. This interest was paid until 1683, but it then became in arrear, and continued so at the revolution; and the suits which were commenced to enforce the payment of these arrears, were the subject of this case. The bankers presented a petition to the barons of the exchequer, for the payment of the arrears of the annuities granted; to which petition the attorney-general demurred. Two points were made: First, whether the grant out of the excise was good; second, whether a petition to the barons of the exchequer was a proper remedy. On the first point, the whole court agreed, that, in general, the King could alienate the revenues of the crown; but Mr. Baron Lechmere differed from the other barons, by thinking that this particular revenue of the excise, was an exception to the general rule. But all agreed, that the petition was a proper remedy. Judgment was, therefore, given for the petition, by directing payment to the complainants, at the receipt of the exchequer. A writ of error was brought on this judgment, by the attorney-general, in the exchequer-chamber. There, all the judges who argued held the grant out of the excise good. A majority of them, including Lord Chief Justice Holt, also approved of the remedy by petition to the barons. But Lord Chief Justice Treby was of opinion, that the barons of the exchequer were not authorized to make order for payments on the receipt of the exchequer, and therefore, that the remedy by petition to the barons was inapplicable. In this opinion, Lord Somers concurred. A doubt then arose, whether the Lord Chancellor and Lord High Treasurer were at liberty to give judgment, according to their own opinion, in opposition to that of a majority of the attendant judges; in other

words, whether the judges called by the Lord Chancellor and Lord High Treasurer were to considered as mere assistants to them, without voices. The opinion of the judges being taken on this point, seven against three, held, that the Lord Chancellor and Lord Treasurer were not concluded by the opinions of the judges, and therefore, that the Lord Keeper, in the case in question, there being then no Lord Treasurer, might give judgment according to his own opinion. Lord Somers concurring in this idea, reversed the judgment of the court of exchequer. But the case was afterwards carried by error into parliament, and there the Lords reversed the judgment of the exchequer-chamber, and affirmed that of the exchequer. However, notwithstanding this final decision in favor of the bankers and their creditors, it appears by a subsequent statute, that they were to receive only one-half of their debts; the 12 & 14 *Wm. III.,* after appropriating certain sums out of the hereditary excise for public uses, providing that in lieu of the annuities granted to the bankers and all arrears, the hereditary excise should, after the 26th of December 1601, be charged with annual sums equal to an interest of three per cent., until redeemed by payment of one moiety of the principal sums. *Hargrave's Case of the Bankers,* 1, 2, 3.

Upon perusing the whole of this case, these inferences naturally follow: 1st. That admitting the authority of that decision, in its fullest extent, yet, it is an authority only in respect to such cases, where letters-patent from the crown have been granted for the payment of certain sums out of a particular revenue. 2d. That such relief was grantable in the exchequer, upon no other principle than that the court had a right to direct the issues of the exchequer as well after the money was deposited there, as while (in the exchequer language) is was *in transitu.* 3d. That such an authority could not have been exercised by any other court in Westminster Hall, nor by any court, that, from its particular constitution, had no control over the revenues of the kingdom. Lord C. J. Holt, and Lord Somers (though they differed in the main point) both agreed in that case, that the court of King's bench could not send a writ to the treasury. Hargrave's case, 45, 89. Consequently, no such remedy could, under any circumstances, I apprehend, be allowed in any of the American states, in none of which it is presumed any court of justice hath any express authority over the revenues of the state such as has been attributed to the court of exchequer in England.

The observations of Lord Somers, concerning the general remedy by petition to the King, have been extracted and referred to by some of the ablest law characters since; particularly, by Lord C. Baron Comyns, in his digest. I shall, therefore, extract some of them, as he appears to have taken uncommon pains to collect all the material learning on the subject; and indeed is said to have expended several hundred pounds in the procuring of records relative to that case. Hargrave's Preface to the Case of the Bankers.

After citing many authorities, Lord Somers proceeds thus: "By all these authorities, and by many others, which I could cite, both ancient and modern, it is plain, that is the subject was to recover a rent or annuity, or other charge from the crown; whether it was a rent or annuity, originally granted by the King, or issuing out of lands, which by subsequent title came to be in the King's hands; in all cases, the remedy to come at it was, by petition to the person of the King; and no other method can be shown to have been practised at common law. Indeed, I take it to be generally true, that in all cases where the subject is in the nature of a plaintiff, to recover anything from the King, his only remedy, at common law, is to sue by petition to the person of the King. I say, where the subject comes as a plaintiff. For, as I said before, when upon a title found for the King of office, the subject comes in to traverse the King's title, or to show his own right, he comes in the nature of a defendant; and is admitted to interplead in the case, with the King, in defence of his title, which otherwise would be defeated by finding the office. And to show that this was so, I would take notice of several instances. That, in cases of debts owing by the crown, the subject's remedy was by petition, appears by *Aynesham's Case*, Ryley, 251, which is a petition for 19 *l* due for work done at Carnarvon castle. So, Ryley 251, the executors of John Estrateling petition for 132 *l* due to the testator, for wages. The answer is remarkable; for there is a latitude taken, which will very well agree with the notion that is taken up in this case; *habeant bre. de liberate in canc. thes. et camerar, de 321. in partem solutionis.* So, the case of *Yerward de Galeys, for 561.* Ryley 414. In like manner, in the same book, 253 (33 *Edw. I.*), several parties sue by *petition* for money and goods taken for the King's use; and also for wages due to them; and for debts owing to them by the king. The answer is, *rex ordinavit per concilium thesaurarii et baronum de scaccario, quod satisfiet iis quam citius fieri poterit; ita quod contertos se tenebunt.* And this is an answer given to a petition presented to the king in parliament; and therefore; we have reason to conclude it to be warranted by law. They must be content, and they shall be paid, *quam citius fieri poterit.* The parties, in these cases, first go to the King by petition: it is by him they are sent to the exchequer; and it is by writ under the great seal, that the exchequer is impowered to act. Nor can any such writ be found (unless in a very few instances, where it is mere matter of account), in which the treasurer is not joined with the barons. So for was it from being taken to be law at the time, that the barons had any original power of paying the King's debts; or of commanding annuities, granted by the King or his progenitors, to be paid, when the person applied to them for such payment. But, perhaps, it may be objected, that it is not to be inferred, because petitions were brought in these cases, that, therefore, it was of necessity, that the subject should pursue that course, and could take no other way. It might be reasonable to require from those who object thus, that they should produce some precedents, at least, of another remedy taken. But I think, there is a good answer to be given to this objection. All these petitions which I have mentioned, are after the Stat. 8 *Edw. I.* (Ryley 442), where notice is taken that the business of parliament is interrupted by a multitude of petitions, which might be redressed by the chancellor and justices. Wherefore, it is thereby enacted, that petitions which touch the seal shall come first to the chancellor; those which touch the exchequer, to the exchequer; and those which touch the justices, or the law of the land, should come to the justices; and if the business be so great, or *fi de grace,* that the chancellor, or others, cannot do them without the King, then the petitions shall be brought before the King, to know his pleasure; so that no petitions come before the King and his council, but by the hands of the chancellor, and other chief ministers; that the King and his council may attend the great affairs of the King's realm, and his sovereign dominions. This law being made; there is reason to conclude, that all petitions brought before the King or parliament, after this time, and answered there, were brought according to the method of this law; and were of the nature of such petitions as ought to be brought before the person of the King. And that petitions did lie for a chattel, as well as for a freehold, does appear, 37 Ass. pl. ii.; Bro. Pet. 17. If tenant by the statute-merchant be ousted, he may have petition, and shall be restored. *Vide 9 Hen. IV., 4; Bro.* Pet. 9; 9 *Hen. VI., 21; Bro.* Pet. 2. If the subject be ousted of his term, he shall have his petition. 7 *Hen. VII., 2.* Of a chattel real, a man shall have his petition of right, as of his freehold. 34 *Hen. VI., 51; Bro.* Pet. 3. A man shall have a petition of right, for goods and chattels, and the King indorses it in the usual form. It is said, indeed, 1 *Hen. VII., 3; Bro.* Pet. 19, that a petition will not lie on a chattel. And admitting there was any doubt as to that point, in the present suit, we are in the case of a freehold." Lord Somers's argument in Hargrave's Case of the Bankers, 103-105.

The solitary case, noticed at the conclusion of Lord Somers's argument, "that a petition will not lie of a chattel," certainly is deserving of no consideration, opposed to so many other instances mentioned, and unrecognized (as I believe it is) by any other authority, either ancient or modern, whereas, the contrary, it appears to me, has long been received and established law. In Comyn's Dig. 4 vol. 458, it is said, expressly, "suit shall be to the king by petition, for goods as well as for land." He cites Staundf. Praer. 75 *b*, 72 *b,* for his authority, and takes no notice of any authority to the contrary. The same doctrine is also laid down, with equal explicitness, and without noticing any distinction whatever, in Blackstone's Commentaries, 3 vol. 256, where he points out the petition of right as one of the common-law methods of obtaining possession or restitution from the crown, either of real or personal property; and says expressly, the petition of right "is of use, where the King is in full possession of any hereditaments or chattels, and the petitioner suggests such a right as controverts the title of the crown, grounded on facts disclosed in the petition itself."

I leave out of the argument, from which I have made so long a quotation, everything concerning the restriction on the exchequer, so far as it concerned the case then before the court, as Lord Somers (although more perhaps by weight of authority than reasoning) was overruled in that particular. As to all others, I consider the authorities on which he relied, and his deduction from them, to be unimpeached.

Blackstone, in the first volume of his Commentaries (p. 203), speaking of demands in point of property upon the King, state the general remedy thus: "If any person has, in point of property, a just demand upon the King, he must petition him in his court of chancery, where his chancellor will administer right, as a matter of grace, though not upon compulsion. (For which he cites Finch L. 255.) "And this is exactly consonant to what is laid down by the writers on natural law. A subject, says Puffendorf, so long as he continues a subject, hath no way to oblige his prince to give him his due when he refuses it; though no wise prince will ever refuse to stand to a lawful contract. And if the prince gives the subject leave to enter an action against him upon such contract, in his own courts, the action itself proceeds rather upon natural equity than upon the municipal laws. For the end of such action is not to compel the prince to observe the contract, but to persuade him."

It appears, that when a petition to the person of the King is properly presented, the usual way is, for the King to indorse or to underwrite *soit droit fait al partie* (let right be done to the party); upon which, unless attorney-general confesses the suggestion, a commission is issued to inquire into the truth of it; after the return of which, the King's attorney is at liberty to plead in bar, and the merits shall be determined upon issue or demurrer, as in suits between subject and subject. If the attorney-general confesses the suggestion, there is no occasion for a commission, his admission of the truth of the facts being equally conclusive, as if they had been found by a jury. See 3 Blackstone's Commentaries, 256; and 4 Com. Dig. 458, and the authorities there cited. Though the above-mentioned indorsement be the usual one Lord Somers, in the course of his voluminous search, discovered a variety of other answers to what he considered were unquestionable petitions of

right, in respect to which he observes: "The truth is, the manner of answering petitions to the person of the King was very various; which variety did sometimes arise from the conclusion of the party's petition; sometimes, from the nature of the thing; and sometimes, from favor to the person; and according as the indorsement was, the party was sent into chancery or the other courts. If the indorsement was general, *soit droit fait al partie*, it must be delivered to the chancellor of England, and then a commission was to go, to find the right of the party, and that being found, so that there was a record for him, thus warranted, he is let in to interplead with the King; but if the indorsement was special, then the proceeding was to be according to the indorsement in any other court. This is fully explained by Staundfort in his treatise of the Prerogative, c. 22. The case Mich. 10 *Hen. IV.*, No. 4, 8, is full as to this matter. The King recovers in a *quare impedit,* by default, against one who was never summoned; the party cannot have a writ of deceit, without a petition. If, then, says the book, he concludes his petition generally *"que le Roy lui face droit"* (that the King will cause right to be done), and the answer be general, it must go into the chancery, that the right may be inquired of by commission; and upon the inquest found, an original writ must be directed to the justices, to examine the deceit, otherwise, the justices before who the suit was, cannot meddle. But if he conclude his petition especially, that it may please his highness to command his justices to proceed to the examination, and the indorsement be accordingly, *that* had given the justices a jurisdiction. They might, in such case, have proceeded upon the petition, without any commission or any writ to be sued out, the petition and answer indorsed giving a sufficient jurisdiction to the court to which it was directed. And as the book I have mentioned proves this, so many other authorities may be cited." He, accordingly, mentions many other instances, immaterial to be recited here, particularly remarking a very extraordinary difference in the case belonging to the revenue, in regard to which he said, he thought there was not an instance, to be found, where petitions were answered, *soit droit fait aux parties* (let right be done to the parties). The usual reference appears to have been to the treasurer and barons, commanding them to do justice. Sometimes, a writ under the great seal was directed to be issued to them for that purpose: sometimes, a writ from the chancery directing payment of money immediately, without taking notice of the barons. An other varieties appear to have taken place. See Hargrave's Case of the Bankers, p. 73, *et seq.* But in all cases of petition of right, of whatever nature is the demand, I think it is clear, beyond all doubt, that there must be some indorsement or order of the King himself, to warrant any further proceedings. The remedy, in the language of Blackstone, being a matter of grace and not on compulsion.

In a very late case in England, this point was incidentally discussed. The case I refer to, is that of *Macbeath* v. *Haldimand*, reported 1 T. R. 172. The action was against the defendant, for goods furnished by the defendant's order, in Canada, when the defendant was a governor of Quebec. The defence was, that the plaintiff was employed by the defendant, in his official capacity, and not upon his personal credit, and that the goods being, therefore, furnished for the use of the government, and the defendant not having undertaken personally to pay, he was not liable. The defence was set up at the trial, on the plea of the general issue, and the jury, by Judge Buller's direction, found a verdict for the defendant. Upon a motion for a new trial, he reported particularly all the facts given in evidence, and said, his opinion had been at the trial, that the plaintiff should be nonsuited; "but the plaintiff's counsel appearing for their client, when he was called, he left the question to the jury, telling them that they were bound to find for the defendant in point of law. And upon their asking him whether, in the event of the defendant not being liable, any other person was, he told them, that was no part of their consideration, but being willing to give them any information, he added, that he was of opinion, that if the plaintiff's demands were just, his proper remedy was by a petition of right to the crown. On which, they found a verdict for the defendant. The rule for granting a new trial was moved for, on the misdirection of two points. 1st. That the defendant had, by his own conduct, made himself liable, which question should have been left to the jury. 2d. That the plaintiff had no remedy against the crown, by a petition of right, on the supposition of which the jury had been induced to give their verdict." "Lord Mansfield, Chief Justice, now declared, that the court did not feel it necessary from them to give any opinion on the second ground. His lordship said, that great difference had arisen, since the revolution, with respect to the expenditure of the public money. Before that period, all the public supplies were given to the King, who, in his individual capacity, contracted for all expenses. he alone had the disposition of the public money. But since that time, the supplies had been appropriated by parliament to particular purposes, and now, whoever advances money for the public service, trusts to the faith of parliament. That according to the tenor of Lord Somer's argument in the *Banker's case*, though a petition of right would lie, yet it would probably produce no effect. No benefit was ever derived from it in the *Banker's case;* and parliament was afterwards obliged to provide a particular fund for the payment of those debts. Whether, however, this alteration in the mode of distributing the supplies had made any difference in the law upon this subject, it was necessary to determine; at any rate, if there were a recovery against the crown, application must be made to parliament, and it would come under the head

of supplies for the year." The motion was afterwards argued on the other ground (with which I have at present nothing to do), and rejected.

In the old authorities, there does not appear any distinction between debts that might be contracted personally by the King, for his own private use, and such as he contracted in his political capacity, for the service of the kingdom. As he had, however, then, fixed and independent revenues, upon which depended the ordinary support of government, as well as the expenditure for his own private occasions, probably, no material distinction, at that time, existed, or could easily be made. A very important distinction may, however, perhaps, now subsist between the two cases, for the reasons intimated by Lord Mansfield; since the whole support of government depends now on parliamentary provisions, and except in the case of the civil list, those for the most part annual.

Thus, it appears, that in England, even in the case of a private debt con tracted by the King, in his own person, there is no remedy but by petition, which must receive his express sanction, otherwise there can be no proceeding upon it. If the debts contracted be avowedly for the public uses of government, it is at least doubtful, whether that remedy will lie, and if it will, it remain afterwards in the power of parliament to provide for it, or not, among the current supplies of the year.

Now, let us consider the case of a debt due from a state. None can, I apprehend, be directly claimed but in the following instances. 1st. In case of a contract with the legislature itself. 2d. In case of a contract with the executive, or any other person, in consequence of an express authority from the legislature. 3d. In case of a contract with the executive, without any special authority. In the first and second cases, the contract is evidently made on the public faith alone. Every man must know that no suit can lie against a legislative body. His only dependence, therefore, can be, that the legislature, on principles of public duty, will make a provision for the execution of their own contracts, and if that fails, whatever reproach the legislature may incur, the case is certainly without remedy in any of the courts of the state. It never was pretended, even in the case of the crown in England, that if any contract was made with parliament or with the crown, by virtue of an authority from parliament, that a petition to the crown would in such case lie. In the third case, a contract with the governor of a state, without any special authority. This case is entirely different from such a contract made with the crown in England. The crown there has very high prerogatives; in many instances, is a kind of trustee for the public interest; in all cases, represents the sovereignty of the kingdom, and is the only authority which can sue or be sued in any manner, on behalf of the kingdom, in any court of justice. A governor of a state is a mere executive officer;

his general authority very narrowly limited by the constitution of the state; with no undefined or disputable prerogatives; without power to effect one shilling of the public money, but as he is authorized under the constitution, or by a particular law; having no color to represent the sovereignty of the state, so as to bind it in any manner, to its prejudice, unless specially authorized thereto. And therefore, all who contract with him, do it at their own peril, and are bound to see (or take the consequence of their own indiscretion) that he has strict authority for any contract he makes. Of course, such contract, when so authorized, will come within the description I mentioned, of cases where public faith alone is the ground of relief, and the legislative body, the only one that can afford a remedy, which, from the very nature of it, must be the effect of its discretion, and not of any compulsory process. If, however, any such cases were similar to those which would entitle a party to relief, by petition to the King, in England, that petition being only presentable to him, as he is the sovereign of the kingdom, so far as analogy is to take place, such petition in a state could only be presented to the sovereign power, which surely the governor is not. The only constituted authority to which such an application could, with any propriety, be made, must undoubtedly be the legislature, whose express consent, upon the principle of analogy, would be necessary to any further proceeding. So that this brings us (though by a different route) to the same goal—the discretion and good faith of the legislative body.

There is no other part of the common law, besides that which I have considered, which can, by any person, be pretended, in any manner, to apply to this case, but that which concerns corporations. The applicability of this, the attorney-general, with great candor, has expressly waived. But as it may be urged on other occasions, and as I wish to give the fullest satisfaction, I will say a few words to that doctrine. Suppose, therefore, it should be objected, that the reasoning I have now used, is not conclusive, because, inasmuch as a state is made subject to the judicial power of congress, its sovereignty must not stand in the way of the proper exercise of that power, and therefore, in all such cases (though in no other), a state can only be considered as a subordinate corporation merely. I answer: 1st. That this construction can only be allowed, at the utmost, upon the supposition that the judicial authority of the United States, as it respects states, cannot be effectuated, without proceeding against them in that light: a position, I by no means admit. 2d. That according to the principles I have supported in this argument, admitting that states ought to be so considered for that purpose, an act of the legislature is necessary to give effect to such a construction, unless the old doctrine concerning corporations will naturally apply to this particular case. 3d. That as it is evident, the act of

congress has not made any special provision in this case, grounded on any such construction, so it is to my mind perfectly clear, that we have no authority, upon any supposed analogy between the two cases, to apply the common doctrine concerning corporations, to the important case now before the court. I take it for granted, that when any part of an ancient law is to be applied to a new case, the circumstances of the new case must agree in all essential points with the circumstances of the old cases to which that ancient law was formerly appropriated. Now, there are, in my opinion, the most essential differences between the old cases of corporations, to which the law intimated has reference, and the great and extraordinary case of states separately possessing, as to everything simply relating to themselves, the fullest powers of sovereignty, and yet, in some other defined particulars, subject to a superior power, composed out of themselves, for the common welfare of the whole. The only law concerning corporations, to which I conceive the least reference is to be had, is the common law of England on the subject. I need not repeat the observations I made in respect to the operation of that law in this country. The word "corporations," in its largest sense, has a more extensive meaning than people generally are aware of. Any body politic (sole or aggregate), whether its power be restricted or transcendent, is in this sense, "a corporation." The king, accordingly, in England, is called a corporation. 10 Co. 29 *b*. So also, by a very respectable author (Sheppard, in his Abridgement, 1 vol. 431), is the parliament itself. In this extensive sense, not only each state singly, but even the United States may, without impropriety, be termed "corporations." I have, therefore, in contradistinction to this large and indefinite term, used the term "subordinate corporations," meaning to refer to such only (as alone capable of the slightest application, for the purpose of the objection) whose creation and whose powers are limited by law.

The differences between such corporations, and the several states in the Union, as relative to the general government, are very obvious, in the following particulars. 1st. A corporation is a mere creature of the king, or of parliament; very rarely, of the latter; most usually, of the former only. It owes its existence, its name, and its laws (except such laws as are necessarily incident to all corporations merely as such), to the authority which create it. A state does not owe its origin to the government of the United States, in the highest or in any of its branches. It was in existence before it. It derives its authority from the same pure and sacred source as itself: the voluntary and deliberate choice of the people. 2d. A corporation can do no act but what is subject to the revision either of a court of justice, or of some other authority within the government. A state is altogether exempt from the jurisdiction of the courts of the United States, or from any other exterior authority, unless in the special instances where the general government has power derived from the constitution itself. 3d. A corporation is altogether dependent on that government to which it owes its existence. Its charter may be forfeited by abuse: its authority may be annihilated, without abuse, by an act of the legislative body. A state, though subject, in certain specified particulars, to the authority of the government of the United States, is, in every other respect, totally independent upon it. The people of the state created, the people of the state can only change, its constitution. Upon this power, there is no other limitation but that imposed by the constitution of the United States; that its must be of the republican form. I omit minuter distinctions. These are so palpable, that I never can admit that a system of law, calculated for one of these cases, is to be applied, as a matter of course, to the other, without admitting (as I conceive) that the distinct boundaries of law and legislation may be confounded, in a manner that would make courts arbitrary, and, in effect, makers of a new law, instead of being (as certainly they alone ought to be) expositors of an existing one. If still it should be insisted, that though a state cannot be considered upon the same footing as the municipal corporations I have been considering, yet, as relative to the powers of the general government, it must be deemed in some measure dependent; admitting that to be the case (which to be sure is, so far as the necessary execution of the powers of the general government extends), yet, in whatever character this may place a state, this can only afford a reason for a new law, calculated to effectuate the powers of the general government in this new case: but it affords no reason whatever for the court admitting a new action to fit a case, to which no old ones apply, when the *application* of law, not the *making* of it, is the sole province of the court.

I have now, I think, established the following particulars. 1st. That the constitution, so far as it respects the judicial authority, can only be carried into effect, by acts of the legislature, appointing courts, and prescribing their methods of proceeding. 2d. That congress has provided no new law in regard to this case, but expressly referred us to the old. 3d. That there are no principles of the old law, to which we must have recourse, that in any manner authorize the present suit, either by precedent or by analogy. The consequence of which, in my opinion, clearly is, that the suit in question cannot be maintained, nor, of course, the motion made upon it be complied with.

From the manner in which I have viewed this subject, so different from that in which it has been contemplated by the attorney-general, it is evident, that I have not had occasion to notice many arguments offered by the attorney-general, which certainly were very proper, as to his extended view of the case, but do not affect mine. No part of the law of nations can apply to this case, as I apprehend,

but that part which is termed, "The conventional Law of Nations;" nor can this any otherwise apply, than as furnishing rules of interpretation, since, unquestionably, the people of the United States had a right to form what kind of union, and upon what terms they pleased, without reference to any former examples. If, upon a fair construction of the constitution of the United States, the power contended for really exists, it undoubtedly may be exercised, though it be a power of the first impression. If is does not exist, upon that authority, ten thousand examples of similar powers would not warrant its assumption. So far as this great question affects the constitution itself, if the present afforded, consistently with the particular grounds of my opinion, a proper occasion for a decision upon it, I would not shrink from its discussion. But it is of extreme moment, that no judge should rashly commit himself upon important questions, which it is unnecessary for him to decide. My opinion being, that even if the constitution would admit of the exercise of such a power, a new law is necessary for the purpose, since no part of the existing law applies this alone is sufficient to justify my determination in the present case. So much, however, has been said on the constitution, that it may not be improper to intimate, that my present opinion is strongly against any construction of it, which will admit, under any circumstances, a compulsive suit against a state for the recovery of money. I think, every word in the constitution may have its full effect, without involving this consequence, and that nothing but express words, or an insurmountable implication (neither of which I consider, can be found in this case), would authorize the deduction of so high a power. This opinion, I hold, however, with all the reserve proper for one, which, according to my sentiments in this case, may be deemed in some measure extra-judicial. With regard to the policy of maintaining such suits, that is not for this court to consider, unless the point in all other respects was very doubtful. Policy might then be argued from, with a view to preponderate the judgment. Upon the question before us, I have no doubt. I have, therefore, nothing to do with the policy. But I confess, if I was at liberty to speak on that subject, my opinion on the policy of the case would also differ from that of the attorney-general. It is, however, a delicate topic. I pray to God, that if the attorney-general's doctrine, as to the law, be established by the judgment of this court, all the good he predicts from it may take place, and none of the evils with which, I have the concern to say, it appears to me to be pregnant.

Blair Justice.—In considering this important case, I have thought it best to pass over all the strictures which have been made on the various European confederations; because, as, on the one hand, their likeness to our own is not sufficiently close to justify any analogical application; so, on the other, they are utterly destitute of any binding authority here. The constitution of the United States is the only fountain from which I shall draw; the only authority to which I shall appeal. Whatever be the true language of that, it is obligatory upon every member of the Union; for no state could have become a member, but by an adoption of it by the people of that state. What then do we find there, requiring the submission of individual states to the judicial authority of the United States? This is expressly extended, among other things, to controversies between a state and citizens of another state. Is, then, the case before us one of that description? Undoubtedly, it is, unless it may be a sufficient denial to say, that it is a controversy between a citizen of one state and another state. Can this change of order be an essential change in the thing intended? And is this alone a sufficient ground from which to conclude, that the jurisdiction of this court reaches the case where a state is plaintiff, but not where it is defendant? In this latter case, should any man be asked, whether it was not a controversy between a state and citizen of another state, must not the answer be in the affirmative? A dispute between A. and B. is surely a dispute between B. and A. Both cases, I have no doubt, were intended; and probably, the state was first named, in respect to the dignity of a state. But that very dignity seems to have been thought a sufficient reason for confining the sense to the case where a state is plaintiff. It is, however, a sufficient answer to say, that our constitution most certainly contemplates, in another branch of the cases enumerated, the maintaining a jurisdiction against a state, as defendant; this is unequivocally asserted, when the judicial power of the United States is extended to controversies between two or more states; for there, a state must, of necessity, be a defendant. It is extended also to controversies between a state and foreign states; and if the argument taken from the order of designation were good, it would be meant here, that this court might have cognisance of a suit, where a state is plaintiff, and some foreign state a defendant, but not where a foreign state brings a suit against a state. This, however, not to mention that the instances may rarely occur, when a state may have an opportunity of suing, in the American courts, a foreign state, seems to lose sight of the policy which, no doubt, suggested this provision, viz., that no state in the Union should, by withholding justice, have it in its power to embroil the whole confederacy in disputes of another nature. But if a foreign state, though last named, may, nevertheless, be a plaintiff against an individual state, how can it be said, that a controversy between a state and a citizen of another state means, from the mere force of the order of the words, only such cases where a state is plaintiff? After describing, generally, the judicial powers of the United States, the constitution goes on to speak of it distributively, and gives to the supreme court original jurisdiction, among other instances, in the case where a state

shall be a *party;* a but is not a state a party as well in the condition of a defendant, as in that of a plaintiff? And is the whole force of that expression satisfied, by confining its meaning to the case of a plaintiff-state? It seems to me, that if this court should refuse to hold jurisdiction of a case where a state is defendant, it would renounce part of the authority conferred, and consequently, part of the duty imposed on it by the constitution; because, it would be a refusal to take cognisance of a case, where a state is a party.

Nor does the jurisdiction of this court, in relation to a state, seem to me to be questionable, on the ground, that congress has not provided any form of execution, or pointed out any mode of making the judgment against a state effectual; the argument *ab inutile* may weigh much, in cases depending upon the construction of doubtful legislative acts, but can have no force, I think, against the clear and positive directions of an act of congress and of the constitution. Let us go on so far as we can; and if, at the end of the business, notwithstanding the powers given us in the 14th section of the judicial law, we meet difficulties insurmountable to us, we must leave it to those departments of government which have higher powers; to which, however, there may be no necessity to have recourse. Is it altogether a vain expectation, that a state may have other motives than such as arise from the apprehension of coercion, to carry into execution a judgment of the supreme court of the United States, though not conformable to their own ideas of justice? Besides, this argument takes it for granted, that the judgment of the court will be against the state; it possibly may be in favor of the state: and the difficulty vanishes. Should judgment be given against the plaintiff, could it be said to be void, because extra-judicial? If the plaintiff, grounding himself upon that notion, should renew his suit against the state, in any mode in which she may permit herself to be sued in her own courts, would the attorney-general for the state be obliged to go again into the merits of the case, because the matter, when here, was *coram non judice?* Might be not rely upon the judgment given by this court, in bar of the new suit? To me, it seems clear, that he might. And if a state may be brought before this court, as a defendant, I see no reason for confining the plaintiff to proceed by way of petition; indeed, there would even seem to be an impropriety in proceeding in that mode. When sovereigns are sued in their own courts, such a method may have been established, as the most respectful form of demand; but we are not now in a state court; and if sovereignty be an exemption from suit, in any other than the sovereign's own courts, it follows, that when a state, by adopting the constitution, has agreed to be amenable to the judicial power of the United States, she has, in that respect, given up her right of sovereignty.

With respect to the service of the summons to appear, the manner in which it has been served, seems to be as proper as any which could be devised for the purpose of giving notice of the suit, which is the end proposed by it, the governor being the head of the executive department, and the attorney-general the law officer, who generally represents the state in legal proceedings: and this mode is the less liable to exception, when it is considered, that in the suit brought in this court, by the state of *Georgia* against *Brailsford* and others, it is conceived in the name of the governor in behalf of the state. If the opinion which I have delivered, respecting the liability of a state to be sued in this court, should be the opinion of the court, it will come, in course, to consider, what is the proper step to be taken for inducing appearance, none having been yet entered in behalf of the defendant. A judgment by default, in the present state of the business, and writ of inquiry for damages, would be too precipitate in any case, and too incompatible with the dignity of a state in this. Further opportunity of appearing to defend the suit ought to be given. The conditional order moved for the last term, the consideration of which was deferred to this, seems to me to be a very proper mode; it will warn the state of the meditated consequence of a refusal to appear, and give an opportunity for more deliberate consideration. The order, I think, should be thus: "Ordered, that unless the state of Georgia should, after due notice of this order, by a service thereof upon the governor and attorney-general of the said state, cause an appearance to be entered in behalf of the state, on the 5th day of the next term, or then show cause to the contrary, judgment be then entered up against the state, and a writ of inquiry of damages be awarded."

Wilson, Justice—This is a case of uncommon magnitude. One of the parties to it is a State, certainly respectable, claiming to the sovereign. The question to be determined is, whether this state, so respectable, and whose claim soars so high, is amenable to the jurisdiction of the supreme court of the United States? This question, important in itself, will depend on others, more important still; and may, perhaps, be ultimately resolved into one, no less *radical* than this—"do the People of the United States form a Nation?"

A cause so conspicuous and interesting, should be carefully and accurately viewed, from every possible point of sight. I shall examine it, 1st. By the principles of general jurisprudence. 2d. By the laws and practice of particular states and kingdoms. From the law of nations, little or no illustration of this subject can be expected. By that law, the several states and governments spread over our globe, are considered as forming a society, not a nation. It has only been by a very few comprehensive minds, such as those of Elizabeth and the Fourth Henry, that this last great idea has been even contemplated. 3d. And chiefly, I shall examine the important question before us, by the constitution

of the United States, and the legitimate result of that valuable instrument.

I. I am first to examine this question by the principles of general jurisprudence. What I shall say upon this head, I introduce, by the observation of an original and profound writer, who, on the philosophy of mind, and all the sciences attendant on this prime one, has formed an era not less remarkable, and far more illustrious, than that formed by the justly celebrated Bacon, in another science, not prosecuted with less ability, but less dignified as to its object; I mean the philosophy of nature. Dr. Reid, in his excellent inquiry into the human mind, on the principles of common sense, speaking of the sceptical and illiberal philosophy, which, under bold, but false, pretensions to liberality, prevailed in many parts of Europe before he wrote, makes the following judicious remark: "The language of philosophers, with regard to the original faculties of the mind, is so adapted to the prevailing system, that it cannot fit any other; like the coat that fits the man whom it was made, and shows him to advantage, which yet will fit very awkward upon one of a different make, although as handsome and well proportioned. It is hardly possible to make any innovation in our philosophy concerning the mind and its operations, without using new words and phrases, 'or giving a different meaning to those that are received." With equal propriety, may this solid remark be applied to the great subject, on the principles of which the decision of this court is to be founded. The perverted use of *genus* and *species* in logic, and of *impressions* and *ideas* in metaphysics, have never done mischief so extensive or so practically pernicious, as has been done by *states* and *sovereigns,* in politics and jurisprudence; in the politics and jurisprudence even of those who wished and meant to be free. In the place of those expressions, I intend not to substitute new ones; but the expressions themselves I shall certainly use for purposes different from those, for which hitherto they have been frequently used; and one of them I shall apply to an object still more different from that, to which it has been hitherto, most frequently, I may say, almost universally, applied. In these purposes, and in this application, I shall be justified by example the most splendid, and by authority the most binding; the example of the most refined as well as the most free nation known to antiquity; and the authority of one of the best constitutions known to modern times. With regard to one of the terms, "state," this authority is declared: with regard to the other, "sovereign," the authority is implied only; but it is equally strong: for, in an instrument well drawn, as in a poem well composed, silence is sometimes most expressive.

To the constitution of the United States the term *sovereign* is totally unknown. There is but one place where it could have been used with propriety. But even in that place, it would not, perhaps, have comported with the delicacy of those who ordained and established that constitution. They might have announced themselves *sovereign* people of the United States: but serenely conscious of the past, they avoided the ostentatious declaration.

Having thus avowed my disapprobation of the purposes for which the terms *state* and *sovereign*, are frequently used, and of the object to which the application of the last of them is almost universally made; it is now proper, that I should disclose the meaning which I assign to both, and the application which I make of the latter. In doing this, I shall have occasion incidentally to evince, how true it is, that states and governments were made for man; and at the same time, how true it is, that his creatures and servants have first deceived, next vilified, and at last, oppressed their master and maker.

Man, fearfully and wonderfully made, is the workmanship of his all-perfect Creator: a state, useful and valuable as the contrivance is, is the inferior contrivance of man; and from his native dignity, derives all its acquired importance. When I speak of a state, as an inferior contrivance, I mean that it is a contrivance inferior only to that which is divine: Of all human contrivances, it is certainly most transcendently excellent. If is concerning this contrivance, that Cicero says so sublimely, "Nothing which is exhibited upon our globe, is more acceptable to that divinity which governs the whole universe, than those communities and assemblages of men, which, lawfully associated, are denominated states."

Let a state be considered as subordinate to the People: but let everything else be subordinate to the state. The latter part of this position is equally necessary with the former. For in the practice, and even, at length, in the science of politics, there has very frequently been a strong current against the natural order of things, and an inconsiderate or an interested disposition to sacrifice the end to the means. As the state has claimed precedence of the people; so, in the same inverted course of things, the government has often claimed precedence of the state; and to this perversion in the second degree, many of the volumes of confusion concerning sovereignty owe their existence. The ministers, dignified very properly by the appellation of the magistrates, have wished, and have succeeded in their wish, to be considered as the sovereigns of the state. This second degree of perversion is confined to the old world, and begins to diminish even there: but the first degree is still too prevalent, even in the several states of which our Union is composed. By a state, I mean, a complete body of free persons united together for their common benefit, to enjoy peaceably what is their own, and to do justice to others. It is an artificial person. It has its affairs and its interests: it has its rules: it has its rights: and it has its obligations. It may acquire property, distinct from that of its members: it may incur debts, to be discharged, out of the public stock, not out of the private fortunes of individuals. It may be found by contracts; and for damages arising from the breach of those contracts. In all our contemplations, however, concerning this feigned and artificial person, we should never forget, that, in truth and nature, those who think and speak and act, are men.

Is the foregoing description of a state, a true description? It will not be questioned, but it is. Is there any part of this description, which intimates, in the remotest manner, that a state, any more than the men who compose it, ought not to do justice and fulfil engagements? It will not be pretended, that there is. If justice is not done; if engagements are not fulfilled; is it, upon general principles of right, less proper, in the case of a great number, than in the case of an individual, to secure, by compulsion, that which will not be voluntarily performed? Less proper, it surely cannot be. The only reason, I believe, why a free man is bound by human laws, is, that he binds himself. Upon the same principles, upon which he becomes bound by the laws, he becomes amenable to the courts of justice, which are formed and authorized by those laws. If one freeman, an original sovereign, may do all this, why may not an aggregate of free men, a collection of original sovereigns, do this likewise? If the dignity of each, singly, is undiminished; the dignity of all, jointly, must be unimpaired. A state, like a merchant, makes a contract. A dishonest state, like a dishonest merchant, wilfully refuses to discharge it: the latter is amenable to a court of justice: upon general principles of right, shall the former, when summoned to answer the fair demands of its creditor, be permitted Proteus-like, to assume a new appearance, and to insult him and justice, by declaring I am a *sovereign* state? Surely not. Before a claim, so contrary, in its first appearance, to the general principles of right and equality, be sustained by a just and impartial tribunal, the person, natural or artificial, entitled to make such claim, should certainly be well known and authenticated. Who, or what, is a sovereignty? What is his or its sovereignty? On this subject, the errors and the mazes are endless and inexplicable. To enumerate all, therefore, will not be expected: to take notice of some, will be necessary to the full illustration of the present important cause. In one sense, the term *sovereign* has for its correlative, *subject*. In this sense, the term can receive no application; for it has no object in the constitution of the United States. Under that constitution, there are *citizens*, but no *subjects*. "Citizens of the *United States*." "Citizens of another state." "Citizens of different states." "A state or citizen thereof." The term *subject* occurs, indeed, once in the instrument; but no mark the contrast strongly, the epithet "foreign" is prefixed. In this sense, I presume the state of Georgia has no claim upon her own citizens: in this sense, I am certain, she can have no claim upon the citizens of another state.

In another sense, according to some writers, every state, which governs itself, without any dependence on another power, is a sovereign state. Whether, with regard to her own citizens, this is the case of the state of Georgia; whether those citizens have done, as the individuals of England are said, by their late instructors, to have done, surrendered the supreme power to the state or government, and reserved nothing to themselves; or whether, like the people of other states and of the United States, the citizens of Georgia have reserved the supreme power in their own hands; and on that supreme power, have made the state dependent, instead of being sovereign; these are questions, to which, as a judge in this cause, I can neither know nor suggest the proper answers; though, as a citizen of the Union, I know, and am interested to know, that the most satisfactory answers can be given. As a citizen, I know, the government of that state to be republican; and my short definition of such a government is—one constructed on this principle, that the supreme power resides in the body of the people. As a judge of this court, I know, and can decide, upon the knowledge, that the citizens of Georgia, when they acted upon the large scale of the Union, as a part of the "People of the United States," did *not* surrender the supreme or sovereign power to that state; but, *as to the purposes of the Union,* retained it to themselves. *As to the purposes of the Union,* therefore, Georgia *is not a sovereign state.* If the judicial decision of this case forms one of those purposes; the allegation that Georgia is a sovereign state, is unsupported by the fact. Whether the judicial decision of this cause is, or is not, one of those purposes, is a question which will be examined particularly, in a subsequent part of my argument.

There is a third sense, in which the term sovereign is frequently used, and which it is very material to trace and explain, as it furnishes a basis for what, I presume, to be one of the principal objections against the jurisdiction of this court over the State of Georgia. In this sense, sovereignty is derived from a feudal source; and like many other parts of that systems, so degrading to man, still retains it influence over our sentiments and conduct, though the cause, by which that influence was produced, never extended to the American states. The accurate and well informed President Henault, in his excellent chronological abridgment of the History of France, tells us, that, about the end of the second race of Kings, a new kind of possession was acquired, under the name of fief. The governors of cities and provinces usurped equally the property of land, and the administration of justice; and established themselves as proprietary seigniors over those places in which they had been only civil magistrates or military officers. By this means, there was introduced into the state a new kind of authority, to which was assigned the appellation of sovereignty (*b*). In process of time, the feudal system was extended over France, and almost all the other nations of Europe; and every kingdom became, in fact, a large fief. Into England, this system was introduced by the conqueror; and to this era we may, probably, refer the English maxim, that the King or sovereign is the fountain of justice. But in the case of the King, the sovereignty had a double operation. While it vested him with jurisdiction over others, it excluded all others from jurisdiction over him. With regard to him, there was no superior power; and consequently, on feudal principles, no right of jurisdiction. "The law," says Sir William Blackstone, ascribes to the King, the attribute of sovereignty: he is sovereign and independent, within his own dominions; and owes no kind of subjection to any other potentate upon earth. Hence it is, that no suit or action can be brought against the King, even in civil matters; because no court can have jurisdiction over him: for all jurisdiction implies superiority of power." This last position is only a branch of a much more extensive principle, on which a plan of systematic despotism has been lately formed in England, and prosecuted with unwearied assiduity and care. Of this plan, the author of the Commentaries was, if not the introducer, at least, the great supporter. He has been followed in it, by writers later and less known; and his doctrines have, both on the other and this side of the Atlantic, been implicitly and generally received by those, who neither examined their principles nor their consequences. The principle is, that all human law must be prescribed by a superior: this principle I mean not now to examine: suffice it, at present, to say, that another principle, very different in its nature and operations, forms, in my judgement, the basis of sound and genuine jurisprudence; laws derived from the pure source of equality and justice must founded on the *consent* of those whose obedience they require. The sovereign, when traced to his source, must be found in the man.

I have now fixed, in the scale of things, the grade of a state; and have described its composure: I have considered the nature of sovereignty; and pointed its application to the proper object. I have examined the question before us, by the principles of general jurisprudence. In those principles, I find nothing, which tends to evince an exemption of the State of Georgia, from the jurisdiction of the court. I find everything to have a contrary tendency.

II. I am, in the second place, to examine this question by the laws and practice of different states and kingdoms. In ancient Greece, as we learn from Isocrates, whole nations defended their rights before crowded tribunals. Such occasions as these excited, we are told, all the powers of persuasion; and the vehemence and enthusiasm of the sentiment was gradually infused into the Grecian language, equally susceptible of strength and harmony. In those days, law, liberty and refining science made their benign progress in strict and graceful union; the rude and degrading league between the bar and feudal barbarism was not yet formed.

When the laws and practice of particular states have any application to the question before us, that application will furnish what is called an argument *a fortiori;* because all the instances produced will be instances of subjects instituting and supporting suits against those who were deemed their own sovereigns. These instances are stronger than the present one, because between the present plaintiff and defendant, no such unequal relation is alleged to exist.

Columbus achieved the discovery of that country which, perhaps, ought to bear his name. A contract made by Columbus furnished the first precedent for supporting, in his discovered country, the cause of injured merit against the claims and pretensions of haughty and ungrateful power. His son Don Diego wasted two years in incessant, but fruitless, solicitation at the Court of Spain, for the rights which descended to him, in consequence of his father's original capitulation. He endeavored, at length, to obtain, by a legal sentence, what he could not procure from the favour of an interested monarch. He commenced a suit against Ferdinand, before the Council which managed Indian affairs, and that court, with integrity which reflects honor on its proceedings, decided against the King, and sustained Don Diego's claim.

Other states have instituted officers to judge the proceedings of their Kings. Of this kind, were the Ephori of Sparta; of this kind also, was the mayor of the palace, and afterwards, the constable of France.

But of all the laws and institutions relating to the present question, none is so striking as that described by the famous Hottoman, in his book entitled Franco Gallia. When the Spaniards of Arragon elect a King, they represent a kind of play, and introduce a personage whom they dignify by the name of Law, *la Justiza,* of Arragon. This person they declare, by a public decree, to be greater and more powerful than their king, and then address him in the following remarkable expressions: "We, who are of as great worth as you, and can do more than you can do, elect you to be our King, upon the conditions stipulated. But between you and us, there is one of greater authority than you."

In England, according to Sir William Blackstone, no suit can be brought against the King, even in civil matters. So, in that kingdom, is the law at this time received. But it was not always so. Under the Saxon government, a very different doctrine was held to be orthodox. Under that government, as we are informed by the Mirror of Justice, a book said by Sir Edward Coke, to have been written, in part, at least, before the conquest; under that government, it was ordained, that the King's court should be open to all plaintiffs, by which, without delay, they should have remedial writs, as well against the King or against the Queen, as against any other of the people. The law continued to be the same, for some centuries after the conquest. Until the time of Edward I., the King might have been sued as a common person. The form of the process was even imperative. "*Proecipe Henrico Regi Anglioe,*" &c. "Command Henry, King of England," &c. Bracton, who wrote in the time of Henry III., uses these very remarkable expressions concerning the King: "*In justitia recipienda, minimo de regno suo comparetur*"—in receiving justice, he should be placed on a level with the meanest person in the kingdom. True it is, that now, in England, the King must be sued in his courts, by petition; but even now, the difference is only in the form, not in the thing. The judgments or decrees of those courts will substantially be the same upon a precatory as upon a mandatory process. In the courts of justice, says the very able author of the considerations on the laws of forfeiture, the King enjoys many privileges; yet not to deter the subject from contending with him freely. The judge of the high court of admiralty, in England, made, in a very late cause, the following manly and independent declaration: "In any case, where the crown is a party, it is to observed, that the crown can no more withhold evidence of documents in its possession that a private person. If the court thinks proper to order the production of any public instrument, that order must be obeyed. It wants no *insignia* of an authority derived from the crown."

"Judges ought to know, that the poorest peasant is a man, as well as the king himself: all men ought to obtain justice, since, in the estimation of justice, all men are equal, whether the prince complain of a peasant, or a peasant complain of the prince." These are the words of a king, of the late Frederic of Prussia. In his courts of justice, that great man stood upon his native greatness, and disdained to mount upon the artificial stilts of sovereignty.

Thus much concerning the laws and practice of other states and kingdoms. We see nothing against, but much in favor of, the jurisdiction of this court over the state of Georgia, a party to this cause.

III. I am, thirdly, and chiefly, to examine the important question now before us, by the constitution of the United States, and the legitimate result of that valuable instrument. Under this view, the question is naturally subdivided into two others. 1. Could the constitution of the United States vest a jurisdiction over the state of Georgia? 2. Has that constitution vested such jurisdiction in this court? I have already remarked, that in the practice, and even in the science of politics, there has been frequently a strong current against the natural order of things; and an inconsiderate or an interested disposition to sacrifice the end to the means. This remark deserves a more particular illustration. Even in almost every nation which has been denominated free, the state has assumed a supercilious pre-eminence above the people who have formed it: hence, the haughty notions of state independence, state sovereignty, and state supremacy. In despotic governments, the government has usurped, in a similar manner, both upon the state and the people: hence, all arbitrary doctrines and pretensions concerning the supreme, absolute, and uncontrollable power of government. In each, man is degraded from the prime rank, which he ought to hold in human affairs: in the latter, the state as well as the man is degraded. Of both degradations, striking instances occur in history, in politics, and in common life. One of them is drawn from an anecdote, which is recorded concerning Louis XIV., who has been styled the Grand Monarch of France. This prince, who diffused around him so much dazzling splendor, and so little vivifying heat, was vitiated by that inverted manner of teaching and of thinking, which forms kings to be tyrants, without knowing or even suspecting that they are so. The oppression under which he held his subjects, during the whole course of his long reign, proceeded chiefly from the principles and habits of his erroneous education. By these, he had been accustomed to consider his kingdom as his patrimony, and his power over his subjects as his rightful and undelegated inheritance. These sentiments were so deeply and strongly imprinted on his mind, that when one of his ministers represented to him the miserable condition, to which those subjects were reduced, and in the course of his representation, frequently used the word *L' Etat,* the state, the King, though he felt the truth and approved the substance of all that was said, yet was shocked at the frequent repetition of the expression *L' Etat;* and complained of it as an indecency offered to his person and character. And, indeed, that kings should imagine themselves the final causes, for which men were made, and societies were formed, and governments were instituted, will cease to be a matter of wonder or surprise, when we find, that lawyers and statesmen and philosophers have taught or favored principles which necessarily lead to the same conclusions. Another instance, equally strong, but still more astonishing, is drawn from the British government, as described by Sir William Blackstone and his followers. As described by him and them, the British is a despotic government. It is a government without a people. In that government, as so described, the sovereignty is possessed by the parliament: in the parliament, therefore, the supreme and absolute authority is vested: in the parliament resides that uncontrollable and despotic power, which, in all governments, must reside somewhere. The constituent parts of the parliament are the King's Majesty, the Lords spiritual, the Lords temporal, and the Commons. The King and these three estates together form the great corporation or body politic of the kingdom. All these sentiments are found; the last expressons are found *verbatim,* in the Commentaries

upon the Laws of England. The parliament form the great body politic of England! What, then, or where, are the people? Nothing! Nowhere! They are not so much as even the "baseless fabric of a vision!" From legal contemplation, they totally disappear! Am I not warranted in saying that, if this is a just description, a government, so and justly so described, is a despotic government? Whether this description is or is not a just one, is a question of very different import.

In the United States, and in the several states which compose the Union, we got not so far: but still, we go one step farther than we ought to go, in this unnatural and inverted order of things. The states, rather than the *people,* for whose sakes the states exist, are frequently the objects which attract and arrest our principal attention. This, I believe, has produced much of the confusion and perplexity, which have appeared in several proceedings and several publications on state-politics, and on the politics, too, of the United States. Sentiments and expressions of this inaccurate kind prevail in our common, even in our convivial, language. Is a toast asked? "The United States," instead of the "People of the United States," is the toast given. This is not politically correct. The toast is meant to present to view the first great object in the Union: it presents only the second: it presents only the artificial person, instead of the natural persons, who spoke it into existence. A *state,* I cheerfully admit, is the noblest work of man: but man himself, free and honest, is, I speak as to this world, the noblest work of God!

Concerning the prerogative of Kings, and concerning the sovereignty of states, much has been said and written; but little has been said and written, concerning a subject much more dignified and important, the majesty of the people. The mode of expression, which I would substitute in the place of that generally used, in not only politically, but also (for between true liberty and true taste there is a close alliance) classically, more correct. On the mention of Athens, a thousand refined and endearing associations rush at once into the memory of the scholar, the philosopher, and the patriot. When Homer, one of the most correct, as well as the oldest of human authorities, enumerates the other nations of Greece, whose forces acted at the siege of Troy, he arranges them under the names of their different Kings or Princes: but when he comes to the Athenians, he distinguishes them by the peculiar appellation of the People of Athens. The well-known address used by Demosthenes, when he harangued and animated his assembled countrymen, was "O! men of Athens." With the strictest propriety, therefore, classical and political, our national scene opens with the most magnificent object, which the nation could present: "The People of the United States" are the first personages introduced. Who were those people? They were the citizens of thirteen states, each of which had a separate constitution and government, and all of which were connected together by articles of confederation. To the purposes of public strength and felicity, that confederacy was totally inadequate. A requisition on the several states terminated its legislative authority: executive or judicial authority it had none. In order, therefore, to form a more perfect union, to establish justice, to insure domestic tranquility, to provide for common defence, and to secure the blessings of liberty, those people, among whom were the people of Georgia, ordained and established the present constitution. By that constitution, legislative power is vested, executive power is vested, judicial power is vested.

The question now opens fairly to our view, could the people of those states, among whom were those of Georgia, bind those states, and Georgia, among the others, by the legislative, executive, and judicial power so vested? If the principles on which I have founded myself, are just and true; this question must unavoidably receive an affirmative answer. If those states were the work of those people; those people, and, that I may apply the case closely, the people of Georgia, in particular, could alter, as they pleased, their former work: to any given degree, they could *diminish* as well as enlarge it: any or all of the former state-powers, they could extinguish or transfer. The inference, which necessarily results, is, that the constitution ordained and established by those people; and, still closely to apply the case, in particular, by the people of Georgia, could vest jurisdiction or judicial power over those states, and over the state of Georgia in particular.

The next question under this head is—has the constitution done so? Did those people mean to exercise this, their undoubted power? These questions may be resolved, either by fair and conclusive deductions, or by direct and explicit declarations. In order, ultimately, to discover, whether the people of the United States intended to bind those states by the judicial power vested by the national constitution, a previous inquiry will naturally be: Did those people intend to bind those states by the legislative power vested by that constitution? The articles of confederation, it is well known, did not operate upon individual citizens, but operated only upon states. This defect was remedied by the national constitution, which, as all allow, has an operation on individual citizens. But if an opinion, which some seem to entertain, be just; the defect remedied, on one side, was balanced by a defect introduced on the other: for they seem to think, that the present constitution operates only on individual citizens, and not on states. This opinion, however, appears to be altogether unfounded. When certain laws of the states are declared to be "subject to the revision and control of the congress;" it cannot, surely, be contended, that the legislative power of the national government was meant to have no operation on

the several states. The fact, uncontrovertibly established in one instance, proves the principle in all other instances, to which the facts will be found to apply. We may then infer, that the people of the United States intended to bind the several states, by the legislative power of the national government.

In order to make the discovery, at which we ultimately aim, a second previous inquiry will naturally be—Did the people of the United States intend to bind the several states, by the executive power of the national government? The affirmative answer to the former question directs, unavoidably, an affirmative answer to this. Ever since the time of Bracton, his maxim, I believe, has been deemed a good one— *Supervacuum esset, leges condere, nisi esset qui leges tueretur."* (It would be superfluous to make laws, unless those laws, when made, were to be enforced.) When the laws are plain, and the application of them is uncontroverted, they are enforced immediately by the executive authority of government. When the application of them is doubtful or intricate, the interposition of the judicial authority becomes necessary. The same principle, therefore, which directed us from the first to the second step, will direct us from the second to the third and last step of our deduction. Fair and conclusive deduction, then, evinces that the people of the United States did vest this court with jurisdiction over the state of Georgia. The same truth may be deducted from the declared objects, and the general texture of the constitution of the United States. One of its declared objects is, to form an union more perfect than, before that time, had been formed. Before that time, the Union possessed legislative, but unenforced legislative power over the state. Nothing could be more natural than to intend that this legislative power should be enforced by powers executive and judicial. Another declared object is, "to establish justice." This points, in a particular manner, to the judicial authority. And when we view this object, in conjunction with the declaration, "that no state shall pass a law impairing the obligation of contracts;" we shall probably think, that this object points, in a particular manner, to the jurisdiction of the court over the several states. What good purpose could this constitutional provision secure, if a state might pass a law, impairing the obligation of its own contracts; and be amenable, for such a violation of right, to no controlling judiciary power? We have seen, that on the principles of general jurisprudence, a state, for the breach of a contract, may be liable for damages. A third declared object is—"to insure domestic tranquillity." This tranquillity is most likely to be disturbed by controversies between states. These consequences will be most peaceably and effectually decided, by the establishment and by the exercise of a superintending judicial authority. By such exercise and establishment, the law of nations—the rule between contending states—will be enforced among the several states, in the same manner as municipal law.

Whoever considers, in a combined and comprehensive view, the general texture of the constitution, will be satisfied, that the people of the United States intended to form themselves into a nation, for national purposes. They instituted, for such purposes, a national government, complete in all its parts, with powers legislative, executive and judiciary; and in all those powers extending over the whole nation. Is it congruous, that, with regard to such purposes, any man or body of men, any person, natural or artificial, should be permitted to claim successfully, an entire exemption from the jurisdiction of the national government? Would not such claims, crowned with success, be repugnant to our very existence as a nation? When so many trains of deduction, coming from different quarters, converge and unite at last, in the same point, we may safely conclude, as the legitimate result of this constitution, that the state of Georgia is amenable to the jurisdiction of this court.

But in my opinion, this doctrine rests not upon the legitimate result of fair and conclusive deduction from the constitution: it is confirmed, beyond all doubt, by the direct and explicit declaration of the constitution itself. "The judicial power of the United States shall extend, to controversy between *two* state." Two states are supposed to have a controversy between them: this controversy is supposed to be brought before those vested with the judicial power of the United States: Can the most consummate degree of professional ingenuity devise a mode by which this "controversy between the states" can be brought before a court of law; and yet neither of those states be a defendant? "The judicial power of the United States shall extend to controversies, between a state and citizens of another state." Could the strictest legal language; could even that language, which is peculiarly appropriated to an art, deemed, by a great master, to be one of the most honorable, laudable and profitable things in our law; could this strict and appropriate language, describe, with more precise accuracy, the cause now depending before the tribunal? Causes, and not parties to causes, are weighed by justice, in her equal scales: on the former solely, her attention is fixed: to the latter, she is, as she is painted, blind.

I have now tried this question by all the touchstones, to which I proposed to apply it. I have examined it by the principle of general jurisprudence; by the laws and practice of states and kingdoms; and by the constitutions of the United States. From all, the combined inference is, that the action lies.

Cushing, Justice.—The grand and principal question in this case is, whether a state can, by the federal constitution, be sued by an individual citizen of another state?

The point turns not upon the law or practice of England, although, perhaps, it may be in some measure elucidated thereby, nor upon the law of any other country whatever; but upon the constitution established by the people of the United States; and particularly, upon the extent of powers given to the federal judiciary in the 2d section of the 3d article of the constitution. It is declared, that "the judicial power shall extend to all cases in law and equity arising under the constitution, the laws of the United States, or treaties made or which shall be made under their authority; to all cases affecting ambassadors or other public ministers and consuls; to all cases of admiralty and maritime jurisdiction; to controversies, to which the United States shall be a party; to controversies between two or more state and citizens of another state; between citizens of different states; between citizens of same state, claiming lands under grants of different states; and between a state and citizens thereof and foreign states, citizens or subjects." The judicial power, then, is expressly extended to "controversies between a state and citizens of another state." When a citizen makes a demand against a state, of which he is not a citizen, it is as really a controversy between a state and a citizen of another state, as if such state made a demand against such citizen. The case, then, seems clearly to fall within the letter of the constitution. It may be suggested, that it could not be intended to subject a state to be a defendant, because it would affect the sovereignty of states. If that be the case, what a shall we do with the immediate preceding clause—"controversies between two or more states," where a state must of necessity be defendant? If it was not the intent, in the very next clause also, that a state might be made defendant, why was it so expressed, as naturally to lead to and comprehend that idea? Why was not an exception made, if one was intended?

Again, what are we to do with the last clause of the section of judicial powers, viz., "controversies between a state, or the citizens thereof, and foreign states or citizens." Here again, state must be suable or liable to be made defendants by this clause, which has a similar mode of language with the two other clauses I have remarked upon. For if the judicial power extends to a controversy between one of the United States and a foreign state, as the clause expresses, one of the must be defendant. And then, what becomes of the sovereignty of states so far as suing affects it? But although the words appear reciprocally to affect the state here and a foreign state, and put them on the same footing so far as may be, yet ingenuity may say, that the state here may sue, but cannot be sued; but that the foreign state may be sued, but cannot sue. We may touch foreign sovereignties, but not our own. But I conceive, the reason of the thing, as well as the words of the constitution, tend to show that the federal judicial power extends to a suit brought by a foreign state against any one of the United States. One design of the general government was, for managing the great affairs of peace and war and the general defence, which were impossible to be conducted, with safety, by the states separately. Incident to these powers, and for preventing controversies between foreign powers or citizens from rising to extremities and to an appeal to the sword, a national tribunal was necessary, amicably to decide them, and thus ward off such fatal, public calamity. Thus, states at home and their citizens, and foreign states and their citizens, are put together without distinction, upon the same footing, so far as may be, as to controversies between them. So also, with respect to controversies between a state and citizens of another state (at home), comparing all the clauses together, the remedy is reciprocal; the claim to justice equal. As controversies between state and state, and between a state and citizens of another state, might tend gradually to involve states in war and bloodshed, a disinterested civil tribunal was intended to be instituted to decide such controversies, and preserve peace and friendship. Further, if a state is entitled to justice in the federal court, against a citizen of another state, why not such citizen against the state, when the same language equally comprehends both? The rights of individuals and the justice due to them, are as dear and precious as those of states. Indeed, the latter are founded upon the former; and the great end and object of them must be, to secure and support the rights of individuals, or else, vain is government.

But still it may be insisted, that this will reduce states to mere corporations, and take away all sovereignty. As to corporations, all states whatever are corporations or bodies politic. The only question is, what are their powers? As to individual states and the United States, the constitution marks the boundary of powers. Whatever power is deposited with the Union by the people, for their own necessary security, is so far a curtailing of the power and prerogatives of states. This is, as it were, a self-evident proposition; at least, it cannot be contested. Thus, the power of declaring war, making peace, raising and supporting armies for public defense, levying duties, excises and taxes, if necessary, with many other powers, are lodged in congress; and are a most essential abridgement of state sovereignty. Again, the restrictions upon states: "No state shall enter into any treaty, alliance or confederation, coin money, emit bills of credit, make anything but gold and silver a tender in payment of debts, pass any law impairing the obligations of contracts;" these, with a number of others, are important restrictions of the power of states, and were thought necessary to maintain the Union; and to establish some fundamental uniform principles of public justice, throughout the whole Union. So that, I think, no argument of force can be taken from the sovereignty of

states. Where it has been abridged, it was thought necessary for the greater indispensable good of the whole. If the constitution is found inconvenient in practice, in this or any other particular, it is well that a regular mode is pointed out for amendment. But while it remains, all officers, legislative, executive and judicial, both of the states and of the Union, are bound by oath to support it.

One other objection has been suggested, that if a state may be sued by a citizen of another state, then the United States may be sued by a citizen of any of the states, or, in other words, by any of their citizens. If this be a necessary consequence, it must be so. I doubt the consequence, from the different wording of the different clauses, connected with other reasons. When speaking of the United States, the constitution says, "controversies to which the United States shall be a party," not controversies between the United States and any of their citizens. When speaking of states, it says "controversies between two or more states; between a state and citizens of another state." As to reasons for citizens suing a different state, which do not hold equally good for suing the United States; one may be, that as controversies between a state and citizens of another state, might have a tendency to involve both states in contest, perhaps in war, a common umpire to decide such controversies, may have a tendency to prevent the mischief. That an object of this kind was had in view, by the framers of the constitution, I have no doubt, when I consider the clashing interfering laws which were made in the neighboring states, before the adoption of the constitution, and some affecting the property of citizens of another state, in a very different manner from that of their own citizens. But I do not think it necessary to enter fully into the question, whether the United States are liable to be sued by an individual citizen? in order to decide the point before us. Upon the whole, I am of opinion, that the constitution warrants a suit against a state, by an individual citizen of another state.

A second question made in the case was, whether the particular action of *assumpsit* could lie against a state? I think *assumpsit* will lie, if any suit; provided a state is capable of contracting.

The third question respects the competency of service, which I apprehend is good and proper; the service being by summons and notifying the suit to the governor and the attorney-general; the governor, who is the supreme executive magistrate and representative of the state, who is bound by oath to defend the state, and by the constitution to give information to the legislature of all important matters which concern the interest of the states; the attorney-general, who is bound to defend the interests of the state in courts of law.

Jay, Chief Justice.—The question we are now to decide has been accurately stated, viz.: Is a state suable by individual citizens of another state?

It is said, that Georgia refuses to appear and answer to the plaintiff in this action, because she is a sovereign state, and therefore, not liable to such actions. In order to ascertain the merits of this objection, let us inquire, 1st. In what sense, Georgia is a sovereign state. 2d. Whether suability is compatible with such sovereignty. 3d. Whether the constitution (to which Georgia is a party) authorizes such an action against her.

Suability and suable are words not in common use, but they concisely and correctly convey the idea annexed to them.

1st. In determining the sense in which Georgia is a sovereign state, it may be useful to turn our attention to the political situation we were in, prior to the revolution, and to the political rights which emerged from the revolution. All the country, now possessed by the United States, was then a part of the dominions appertaining to the crown of Great Britain. Every acre of land in this country was then held, mediately or immediately, by grants from that crown. All the people of this country were then subjects of the King of Great Britain, and owned allegiance to him; and all the civil authority then existing, or exercised here, flowed from the head of the British Empire. They were, in strict sense, fellow-subjects, and in a variety of respects, one people. When the revolution commenced, the patriots did not assert that only the same affinity and social connection subsisted between the people of the colonies, which subsisted between the people of Gaul, Britain and Spain, while Roman provinces, viz., only that affinity and social connection which result from the mere circumstance of being governed by the same prince; different ideas prevailed, and gave occasion to the Congress of 1774 and 1775.

The revolution, or rather the Declaration of Independence, found the people already united for general purposes, and at the same time, providing for their more domestic concerns, by state conventions, and other temporary arrangements. From the crown of Great Britain, the sovereignty of their country passed to the people of it; and it was then not an uncommon opinion, that the unappropriated lands, which belonged to that crown, passed, not to the people of the colony or states within whose limits they were situated, but to the whole people; on whatever principles this opinion rested, it did not give way to the other, and thirteen sovereignties were considered as emerged from the principles of the revolution, combined with local convenience and considerations; the people, nevertheless, continued to consider themselves, in a national point of view, an one people; and they continued, without interruption, to manage their national concerns accordingly; afterwards, in the hurry of the war, and in the warmth of mutual confidence, they made a confederation of the states, the basis of a general government. Experi-

ence disappointed the expectations they had formed from it; and then the people, in their collective and national capacity, established the present constitution.

It is remarkable, that in establishing it, the people exercised their own rights, and their own proper sovereignty, and conscious of the plenitude of it, they declared with becoming dignity, "We, the people of the United States, do ordain and establish this constitution." Here we see the people acting as sovereigns of the whole country; and in the language of sovereignty, establishing a constitution by which it was their will, that the state governments, should be bound, and to which the state constitutions should be made to conform. Every state constitution is a compact made by and between the citizens of a state, to govern themselves in a certain manner; and the constitution of the United States is likewise a compact made by the people of the United States, to govern themselves, as to general objects, in a certain manner. By this great compact, however, many prerogatives were transferred to the national government, such as those of making war and peace, contracting alliances, coining money, &c.

If, then, it be true, that the sovereignty of the nation is in the people of the nation, and the residuary sovereignty of each state in the people of each state, it may be useful to compare these sovereignties with those in Europe, that we may thence be enabled to judge, whether all the prerogatives which are allowed to the latter, are so essential to the former. There is reason to suspect, that some of the difficulties which embarrass the present questions, arise from inattention to differences which subsist between them.

It will be sufficient to observe briefly, that the sovereignties in Europe, and particularly in England, exist on feudal principles. That system considers the prince as the sovereign, and the people as his subjects; it regards his person as the object of allegiance, and excludes the idea of his being on an equal footing with a subject, either in a court of justice or elsewhere. That system contemplates him as being the fountain of honor and authority; and from his grace and grant, derives all franchises, immunities and privileges; it is easy to perceive, that such a sovereign could not be amendable to a court of justice, or subjected to judicial control and actual constraint. It was of necessity, therefore, that suability became incompatible with such sovereignty. Besides, the prince having all the executive powers, the judgment of the courts would, in fact, be only monitory, not mandatory to him, and a capacity to be advised, is a distinct thing from a capacity to be sued. The same feudal ideas run through all their jurisprudence, and constantly remind us of the distinction between the prince and the subject. No such ideas obtain here; at the revolution, the sovereignty devolved on the people; and they are truly the sovereigns of the country, but they are sovereigns without subjects (unless the African slaves among us may be so called) and have none to govern but themselves; the citizens of America are equal as fellow-citizens, and as joint-tenants in the sovereignty.

From the differences existing between feudal sovereignties and governments founded on compacts, it necessarily follows, that their respective prerogatives must differ. Sovereignty is the right to govern; a nation or state-sovereign is the person or persons in whom that resides. In Europe, the sovereignty is generally ascribed to the prince; here it rests with the people; there, the sovereign actually administers the government; here, never in a single instance; our governors are the agents of the people, and at most stand in the same relations to their sovereign, in which regents in Europe stand to their sovereigns. Their princes have personal powers, dignities and pre-eminences, our rulers have none but official; nor do they partake in the sovereignty otherwise, or in any other capacity, than as private citizens.

2d. The second object of inquiry now presents itself, viz., whether suability is compatible with state sovereignty.

Suability by whom? Not a subject, for in this country there are none; not an inferior, for all the citizens being, as to civil rights, perfectly equal, there is not, in that respect, one citizen inferior to another. It is agreed, that one free citizen may sue another; the obvious dictates of justice, and the purposes of society demanding it. It is agreed, that one free citizen may sue any number on whom process can be conveniently executed; nay, in certain cases, one citizen may sue forty thousand; for where a corporation is sued, all the members of it are actually sued, though not personally sued. In this city, there are forty odd thousand free citizens, all of whom may be collectively sued by any individual citizen. In the state of Delaware, there are fifty odd thousand free citizens, and what reason can be assigned why a free citizen who has demands against them, should not prosecute them? Can the difference between forty odd thousand, and fifty odd thousand make any distinction as to right? Is it not as easy, and as convenient to the public and parties, to serve a summons on the governor and attorney-general of Delaware, as on the mayor or other officers of the corporation of Philadelphia? Will it be said, that the fifty odd thousand citizens in Delaware, being associated under a state government, stand in a rank so superior to the forty odd thousand of Philadelphia, associated under their charter, that although it may become the latter to meet an individual on an equal footing in a court of justice, yet that such a procedure would not comport with the dignity of the former? In this land of equal liberty, shall forty odd thousand, in one place, be compellable to do justice, and yet fifty odd thousand, in another place, be privileged to do justice only as they may think proper? Such objec-

tions would not correspond with the equal rights we claim; with the equality we profess to admire and maintain; and with that popular sovereignty in which every citizen partakes. Grand that the governor of Delaware holds an office of superior rank to the mayor of Philadelphia, they are both nevertheless the officers of the people; and however more exalted the one may be than the other, yet in the opinion of those who dislike aristocracy, that circumstance cannot be a good reason for impeding the course of justice.

If there be any such incompatibility as is pretended, whence does it arise? In what does it consist? There is at least one strong undeniable fact against this incompatibility, and that is this, any one state in the Union may sue another state, in this court, that is, all the people of one state may sue all the people of another state. It is plain, then, that a state may be sued, and hence it plainly follows, that suability and state sovereignty are not incompatible. As one state may sue another state in this court, it is plain, that no degradation to a state is thought to accompany her appearance in this court. It is not, therefore, to an appearance in this court, that the objection points. To what does it point? It points to an appearance at the suit of one or more citizens. But why it should be more incompatible, that all the people of a state should be sued by one citizen, than by one hundred thousand, I cannot perceive, the process in both cases being alike; and the consequences of a judgment alike. Nor can I observe any greater inconveniences in the one case than in the other, except what may arise from the feelings of those who may regard a lesser number in an inferior light. But if any reliance be made on this inferiority as an objection, at least one-half of its force is done away, by this fact, viz., that it is conceded that a state may appear in this court, as plaintiff, against a single citizen, as defendant; and the truth is, that the state of Georgia is at this moment prosecuting an action in this court against two citizens of South Carolina.

The only remnant of objection, therefore, that remains is, that the state is not bound to appear and answer as a defendant, at the suit of an individual; but why it is unreasonable that she should be so bound, is hard to conjecture: that rule is said to be a bad one, which does not work both ways; the citizens of Georgia are content with a right of suing citizens of other states; but are not content that citizens of others states should have a right to sue them.

Let us now proceed to inquire, whether Georgia has not, by being a party to the national compact, consented to be suable by individual citizens of another state. This inquiry naturally leads our attention, 1st. To the design of the constitution. 2d. To the letter and express declaration in it.

Prior to the date of the constitution, the people had not any national tribunal to which they could resort for justice; the distribution of justice was then confined to state judicatories, in whose institution and organization the people of the other states had no participation, and over whom they had not the least control. There was then no general court of appellate jurisdiction, by whom the errors of state courts, affecting either the nation at large, or the citizens of any other state, could be revised and corrected. Each state was obliged to acquiesce in the measure of justice which another state might yield to her, or to her citizens; and that, even in cases where state considerations were not always favorable to the most exact measure. There was danger that from this source animosities would in time result; and as the transition from animosities to hostilities was frequent in the history of independent states, a common tribunal for the termination of controversies became desirable, from motives both of justice and of policy.

Prior also to that period, the United States had, by taking a place among the nations of the earth, become amenable to the law of nations; and it was their interest, as well as their duty, to provide, that those laws should be respected and obeyed; in their national character and capacity, the United States were responsible to foreign nations for the conduct of each state, relative to the laws of nations, and the performance of treaties; and there the inexpediency of referring all such questions to state courts, and particularly to the courts of delinquent states, became apparent. While all the states were bound to protect each, and the citizens of each, it was highly proper and reasonable, that they should be in a capacity, not only to cause justice to be done to each, and the citizens of each; but also to cause justice to be done by each, and the citizens of each; and that, not by violence and force, but in a stable, sedate and regular course of judicial procedure.

These were among the evils which it was proper for the nation, that is, the people of all the United States, to provide by a national judiciary, to be instituted by the whole nation, and to be responsible to the whole nation.

Let us not turn to the constitution. The people therein declare, that their design in establishing it, comprehended six objects. 1st. To form a more perfect union. 2d. To establish justice. 3d. To ensure domestic tranquility. 4th. To provide for the common defense. 5th. To promote the general welfare. 6th. To secure the blessings of liberty to themselves and their posterity. It would be pleasing and useful, to consider and trace the relations which each of these objects bears to the others; and to show that they collectively comprise everything requisite, with the blessing of Divine Providence, to render a people prosperous and happy: on the present occasion, such disquisitions would be unseasonable, because foreign to the subject immediately under consideration.

It may be asked, what is the precise sense and latitude in which the words "to establish justice," as here used, are to be understood? The answer to this question will result from the provisions made in the constitution on this head. They are specified in the 2d section of the 3d article, where it is ordained, that the judicial power of the United States shall extend to ten descriptions of cases, viz.: 1st. To all cases arising under this constitution; because the meaning, construction and operation of a compact ought always to be ascertained by all the parties, or by authority derived only from one of them. 2d. To all cases arising under the laws of the United States; because as such laws, constitutionally made, are obligatory on each state, the measure of obligation and obedience ought not to be decided and fixed by the party from whom they are due, but by a tribunal deriving authority from both the parties. 3d. To all cases arising under treaties made by their authority; because, as treaties are compacts made by, and obligatory on, the whole nation, their operation ought not to be affected or regulated by the local laws or courts of a part of the nation. 4th. To all cases affecting ambassadors, or other public ministers and consuls; because, as these are officers of foreign nations, whom this nation are bound to protect and treat according to the laws of nations, cases affecting them ought only to be cognisable by national authority. 5th. To all cases of admiralty and maritime jurisdiction; because, as the seas are the joint property of nations, whose right and privileges relative thereto, are regulated by the law of nations and treaties, such cases necessarily belong to national jurisdiction. 6th. To controversies to which the United States shall be a party; because in cases in which the whole people are interested, it would not be equal or wise to let any one state decide and measure out the justice due to others. 7th. To controversies between two or more states; because domestic tranquillity requires, that the contentions of states should be peaceably terminated by a common judicatory; and because, in a free country, justice ought not to depend on the will of either of the litigants. 8th. To controversies between a state and citizens of another state; because, in case a state (that is, all the citizens of it) has demands against some citizens of another state, it is better that she should prosecute their demands in a national court, than in a court of the state to which those citizens belong; the danger of irritation and criminations arising from apprehensions and suspicions of partiality, being thereby obviated. Because, in cases where some citizens of one state have demands against all the citizens of another state, the cause of liberty and the rights of men forbid, that the latter should be the sole judges of the justice due to the latter; and true republican government requires, that free and equal citizens should have free, fair and equal justice. 9th. To controversies between citizens of the same state, claiming lands under grants of different states; because, as the rights of the two states grant the land, are drawn into question, neither of the two states ought to decide the controversy. 10th. To controversies between a state, or the citizens thereof, and foreign states, citizens or subjects; because, as every nation is responsible for the conduct of its citizens towards other nations, all questions touching the justice due to foreign nations or people, ought to be ascertained by, and depend on national authority. Even this cursory view of the judicial powers of the United States, leaves the mind strongly impressed with the importance of them to the preservation of the tranquillity, the equal sovereignty and the equal right of the people.

The question now before us renders it necessary to pay particular attention to that part of the 2d section, which extends the judicial power "to controversies between a state and citizens of another state." It is contended, that this ought to be construed to reach none of these controversies, excepting those in which a state may be plaintiff. The ordinary rules for construction will early decide, whether those words are to be understood in that limited sense.

This extension of power is remedial, because it is to settle controversies. It is, therefore, to be construed liberally. It is politics, wise and good, that, not only the controversies in which a state is plaintiff, but also those in which a state is defendant, should be settled; both cases, therefore, are within the reason of the remedy; and ought to be so adjudged, unless the obvious, plain and literal sense of the words forbid it. If we attend to the words, we find them to be express, positive, free from ambiguity, and without room for such implied expressions: "The judicial power of the United States shall extend to controversies between a state and citizens of another state." If the constitution really meant to extend these powers only to those controversies in which a state might be plaintiff, to the exclusion of those in which citizens had demands against a state, it is inconceivable, that it should have attempted to convey that meaning in words, not only so incompetent, but also repugnant to it; if it meant to exclude a certain class of these controversies, why were they not expressly excepted; on the contrary, not even an intimation of such intention appears in any part of the constitution. It cannot be pretended, that where citizens urge and insist upon demands against a state, which the state refuses to admit and comply with, that there is no controversy between them. If it is a controversy between them, then it clearly falls not only within the spirit, but the very words of the constitution. What is it to the cause of justice, and how can it affect the definition of the word *controversy,* whether the demands which cause the dispute, are made by a state against citizens of another state, or by the latter against the former? When power is thus extended to a *controversy,* it necessarily, as to all judicial purposes, is also extended to those between whom it subsists.

The exception contended for, would contradict and do violence to the great and leading principles of a free and equal national government, one of the great objects of which is, to ensure justice to all: to the few against the many, as well as to the many against the few. It would be strange, indeed, that joint and equal sovereigns of this country, should, in the very constitution by which they professed to establish justice, so far deviate from the plain path of equality and impartiality, as to give to the collective citizens of one state, a right of suing individual citizens of another state, and yet deny to those citizens a right of suing them. We find the same general and comprehensive manner of expressing the same ideas, in a subsequent clause; in which the constitution ordains, that "in all cases affecting ambassadors, other public ministers and consuls, and those in which a state shall be a party, the supreme court shall have original jurisdiction." Did it mean here party-plaintiff? If that only was meant, it would have been easy to have found words to express it. Words are to be understood in their ordinary and common acceptation, and the word party being, in common usage, applicable both to plaintiff and defendant, we cannot limit it to one of them, in the present case. We find the legislature of the United States expressing themselves in the like general and comprehensive manner; they speak in the 13th section of the judicial act, of controversies where a state is a party, and as they do not, impliedly or expressly, apply that term to either of the litigants, in particular, we are to understand them as speaking of both. In the same section, they distinguish the cases where ambassadors are plaintiffs, from those in which ambassadors are defendants, and make different provisions respecting those cases; and it is not unnatural to suppose, that they would, in like manner, have distinguished between cases where a state was plaintiff, and where a state was defendant, if they had intended to make any difference between them; or if they had apprehended that the constitution had made any difference between them.

I perceive, and therefore candor urges me to mention, a circumstance, which seems to favor the opposite side of the question. It is this: the same section of the constitution which extends the judicial power to controversies "between a state and the citizens of another state," does also extend that power to controversies to which the United States are a party. Now, it may be said, if the word party comprehends both plaintiff and defendant, it follows, that the United States may be sued by any citizen, between whom and them there may be a controversy. This appears to me to be fair reasoning; but the same principles of candor which urge me to mention this objection, also urge me to suggest an important difference between the two cases. It is this, in all cases of actions against states or individual citizens, the national courts are supported in all their legal and constitutional proceedings and judgments, by the arm of the executive power of the United States; but in cases of actions against the United States, there is no power which the courts can call to their aid. From this distinction, important conclusion are deducible, and they place the case of a state, and the case of the United States, in very different points of view.

I wish the state of society was so far improved, and the science of government advanced to such a degree of perfection, as that the whole nation could, in the peaceable course of law, be compelled to do justice, and be sued by individual citizens. Whether that is, or is not, now the case, ought not to be thus collaterally and incidentally decided: I leave it a question.

As this opinion, though deliberately formed, has been hastily reduced to writing, between the intervals of the daily adjournments, and while my mind was occupied and wearied by the business of the day, I fear, it is less concise and connected than it might otherwise have been. I have been made no references to cases, because I know of none that are not distinguishable from this case; nor does it appear to me necessary to show that the sentiments of the best writers on government and the rights of men, harmonise with the principles which direct my judgment on the present question. The acts of the former congresses, and the acts of many of the state conventions, are replete with similar ideas; and to the honor of the United States, it may be observed, that in no other country are subjects of this kind better, if so well, understood. The attention and attachment of the constitution to the equal rights of the people are discernible in almost every sentence of it; and it is to be regretted that the provision in it which we have been considering, has not, in every instance, received the approbation and acquiescence which it merits. Georgia has, in strong language, advocated the cause of republican equality: and there is reason to hope, that the people of that state will yet perceive that it would not have been consistent with that equality, to have exempted the body of her citizens from that suability, which they are at this moment exercising against citizens of another state.

For my own part, I am convinced, that the sense in which I understand and have explained the words "controversies between states and citizens of another state," is the true sense. The extension of the judiciary power of the United States to such controversies appears to me to be wise, because it is honest, and because it is useful. It is honest, because it provides for doing justice, without respect of persons, and by securing individual citizens, as well as states, in their respective rights, performs the promise which every free government makes to every free citizen, of equal justice and protection. It is useful, because it is honest, because it leaves not even the most obscure and friendless citizen without means of obtaining justice from a neighboring state; because it obviates occasions of quarrels between states on account of the claims of their respective citizens; because it recognises and strongly rests on this great moral truth, that justice is the same whether due from one man or a million, or from a million to one man; because it teaches and greatly appreciates the value of our free republican national government, which places all our citizens on an equal footing, and enables each and every of them to obtain justice, without any danger of being overborne by the weight and number of their opponents; and because it brings into action and enforces this great and glorious principle, that the people are the sovereign of this country, and consequently, that fellow-citizens and joint-sovereigns cannot be degraded, by appearing with each other, in their own courts, to have their controversies determined. The people have reason to prize and rejoice in such valuable privileges; and they ought not to forget, that nothing but the free course of constitutional law and government can ensure the continuance and enjoyment of them.

For the reasons before given, I am clearly of opinion, that a state is suable by citizens of another state; but lest I should be understood in a latitude beyond by meaning, I think it necessary to subjoin this caution, viz.: That such suability may nevertheless not extend to all the demands, and to every kind of action; there may be exceptions. For instance, I am far from being prepared to say, that an individual may sue a state on bills of credit issued before the constitution was established, and which were issued and received on the faith of the state, and at a time when no ideas or expectations of judicial interposition were entertained or contemplated.

Source:
2 U.S. 419 (1793).

Proclamation of Neutrality, 1793

Proclamation issued by U.S. president George Washington on April 22, 1793, after France had declared war on Great Britain; it stated that the United States would "adopt and pursue a conduct friendly and impartial toward the belligerent powers" and warned U.S. citizens to avoid aiding any hostile nations, under threat of punishment. Washington's statement carefully avoided the word *neutrality* in hopes of securing British maritime concessions in exchange for a U.S. promise to remain neutral. The proclamation, which was strictly enforced and was codified in the Neutrality Act of June 5, 1794, set important precedents in international law and American policy toward foreign wars. It prohibited U.S. citizens from enlisting in the service of a foreign power and prohibited the fitting out of foreign armed ships in U.S. ports. The act only partially relieved tension between the United States and Great Britain.

Whereas it appears that a state of war exists between Austria, Prussia, Sardinia, Great Britain, and the United Netherlands, on the one part, and France on the other; and the duty and interest of the United States require, that they should with sincerity and good faith adopt and pursue a conduct friendly and impartial towards the belligerent powers:

I have therefore thought fit by these presents, to declare the disposition of the United States to observe the conduct aforesaid towards those powers respectively; and to exhort and warn the citizens of the United States carefully to avoid all acts and proceedings whatsoever, which may in any manner tend to contravene such disposition.

And I do hereby also make known, that whosoever of the citizens of the United States shall render himself liable to punishment or forfeiture under the law of nations, by committing, aiding or abetting hostilities against any of the said powers, or by carrying to any of them, those articles which are deemed contraband by the modern usage of nations, will not receive the protection of the United States against such punishment or forfeiture; and further that I have given instructions to those officers to whom it belongs, to cause prosecutions to be instituted against all persons, who shall, within the cognizance of the Courts of the United States, violate the law of nations, with respect to the powers at war, or any of them.

Source:
John C. Fitzpatrick, ed. *The Writings of George Washington.* Vol. 32. Westport: Conn.: Greenwood Press, 1970, pp. 430–431.

Whiskey Rebellion Proclamations, 1794

President George Washington announced the first Whiskey Rebellion Proclamation on August 7, 1794, in order to put a stop to the violence created by the excise tax placed upon distilled spirits and stills in 1791. There was much unrest over this law in the western parts of both Pennsylvania and Virginia, as these regions found it economically pleasing to turn their corn into whiskey and transport it to the coast. The Whiskey Rebellion Proclamation stated that Washington would order the militia out if the erupting vehemence and blatant disregard of the tax, which was part of Alexander Hamilton's financial policy, did not come to an end. Despite Washington's order, public protest continued. Rioting broke out, forcing the president to send troops to quell the violence. Although the resistance stopped, Hamilton sought to make an example of the rebellious settlers, and many were arrested. In a Second Whiskey

Rebellion Proclamation issued on September 25, 1794, President Washington eloquently expresses his firm belief in upholding the young country's laws and his disappointment at having to bring force upon the settlers.

First Whiskey Rebellion Proclamation
Whereas combinations to defeat the execution of the laws laying duties upon spirits distilled within the United States, and upon stills, have from the time of the commencement of those laws existed in some of the Western parts of Pennsylvania:

And whereas the said combinations, proceeding in a manner subversive equally of the just authority of Government and of the rights of individuals, have hitherto effected their dangerous and criminal purpose; by the influence of certain irregular meetings, whose proceedings have tended to encourage and uphold the spirit of opposition; by misrepresentations of the laws calculated to render them odious; by endeavors to deter those, who might be so disposed from accepting offices under them, through fear of public resentment and of injury to person and property, and to compel those who had accepted such offices, by actual violence to surrender or forbear the execution of them; by circulating vindictive menaces against all those who should otherwise directly or indirectly aid in the execution of the said laws, or who, yielding to the dictates of conscience, and to a sense of obligation, should themselves comply therewith; by actually injuring and destroying the property of persons who were understood to have so complied; by inciting cruel and humiliating punishments upon private citizens for no other cause, than that of appearing to be friends of the laws; by intercepting the public officers on the highways, abusing, assaulting, and otherwise ill-treating them; by going to their houses in the night, gaining admittance by force, taking away their papers, and committing other outrages, employing for these unwarrantable purposes the agency of armed banditti disguised in such manner as for the most part to escape discovery:

And whereas the endeavors of the Legislature to obviate objections to the said laws, by lowering the duties and by other alterations conducive to the convenience of those whom they immediately affect (though they have given satisfaction in other quarters,) and the endeavors of the executive officers to conciliate, a compliance with the laws, by explanations, by forbearance, and even by particular accommodations, founded on the suggestions of local considerations, have been disappointed of their effect by the machinations of persons whose industry to excite resistance has increased with every appearance of a disposition among the people to relax in their opposition and to acquiesce in the laws, insomuch that many persons in the said

Western parts of Pennsylvania have at length been hardy enough to perpetrate acts which I am advised amount to treason, being overt acts of levying war against the United States; the said persons having on the sixteenth and seventeenth of July last past proceeded in arms (on the second day, amounting to several hundreds) to the house of John Neville, inspector of the revenue for the fourth survey of the district of Pennsylvania, having repeatedly attacked the said house with the persons therein, wounding some of them; having seized David Lenox, marshal of the district of Pennsylvania, who, previous thereto, had been fired upon while in the execution of his duty, by a party of armed men, detaining him for some time prisoner, till, for the preservation of his life and the obtaining of his liberty, he found it necessary to enter into stipulations to forbear the execution of certain official duties touching processes issuing out of a Court of the United States; and having finally obliged the said inspector of the revenue, and the said marshal, from considerations of personal safety, to fly from that part of the country, in order, by a circuitous route, to proceed to the seat of Government; avowing as the motives of these outrageous proceedings an intention to prevent by force of arms the execution of the said laws, to oblige the said inspector of the revenue to renounce his said office, to withstand by open violence the lawful authority of the Government of the United States, and to compel thereby an alteration in the measures of the Legislature and a repeal of the laws aforesaid.

And whereas, by a law of the United States, entitled "An act to provide for calling forth the militia to execute the laws of the Union, suppress insurrections, and repel invasions," it is enacted, that whenever the laws of the United States shall be opposed or the execution of them obstructed in any State by combination too powerful to be suppressed by the ordinary course of judicial proceedings, or by the powers vested in the marshals by that act, the same being notified by an Associate Justice or the District Judge, it shall be lawful for the President of the United States to call forth the militia of such State to suppress such combinations, and to cause the laws to be duly executed. And if the militia of a State where such combinations may happen shall refuse, or be insufficient to suppress the same, it shall be lawful for the President, if the Legislature of the United States shall not be in session, to call forth and employ such numbers of the militia of any other State or States, most convenient thereto, as may be necessary; and the use of the militia so to be called forth may be continued, if necessary, until the expiration of thirty days after the commencement of the ensuing session: *Provided, always,* That whenever it may be necessary, in the judgment of the President, to use the military force hereby directed to be called forth, the President shall forthwith, and previous thereto, by proclamation, command such insurgents to disperse and retire peaceably to their respective abodes within a limited time.

And whereas James Wilson, an Associate Justice, on the fourth instant, by writing under his hand, did, from evidence which had been laid before him, notify to me that in the counties of Washington and Alleghany, in Pennsylvania, laws of the United States are opposed, and the execution thereof obstructed by combinations too powerful to be suppressed by the ordinary course of judicial proceedings, or by the powers vested in the marshal of the district.

And whereas it is, in my judgment, necessary, under the circumstances of the case, to take measures for calling forth the militia, in order to suppress the combinations aforesaid, and to cause the laws to be duly executed, and I have accordingly determined so to do, feeling the deepest regret for the occasion, but withal the most solemn conviction that the essential interests of the Union demand it; that the very existence of Government, and the fundamental principles of social order, are materially involved in the issue, and that the patriotism and firmness of all good citizens are seriously called upon, as occasion may require, to aid in the effectual suppression of so fatal a spirit.

Wherefore, and in pursuance of the proviso above recited, I, George Washington, President of the United States, do hereby command all persons, being insurgents as aforesaid, and all others whom it may concern, on or before the first day of September next, to disperse and retire peaceably to their respective abodes. And I do moreover warn all persons whomsoever against aiding, abetting, or comforting the perpetrators of the aforesaid treasonable acts; and do require all officers and other citizens, according to their respective duties and the laws of the land, to exert their utmost endeavors to prevent and suppress such dangerous proceedings.

Second Whiskey Rebellion Proclamation

Whereas, from a hope that the combinations against the Constitution and laws of the United States, in certain of the Western counties of Pennsylvania, would yield to time and reflection, I thought it sufficient, in the first instance, rather to take measures for calling forth the militia than immediately to embody them; but the moment is now come, when the overtures of forgiveness, with no other condition than a submission to law, have been only partially accepted; when every form of conciliation not inconsistent with the being of Government has been adopted, without effect; when the well-disposed in those counties are unable by their influence and example to reclaim the wicked from their fury, and are compelled to associate in their own defence; when the proffered lenity has been perversely misinterpreted into an apprehension that the citizens will march with reluctance; when the opportunity of examining the serious consequences of a treasonable opposition has been employed in propagating principles of anarchy, endeavoring through emissaries to alienate the friends of order from its support, and inviting enemies to perpetrate similar acts of insurrection; when it is manifest, that violence would continue to be exercised upon every attempt to enforce the laws; when, therefore, Government is set at defiance, the contest being whether a small proportion of the United States shall dictate to the whole Union, and, at the expense of those who desire peace, indulge a desperate ambition;

Now, therefore, I, George Washington, President of the United States, in obedience to that high and irresistible duty, consigned to me by the Constitution, "to take care that the laws be faithfully executed;" deploring that the American name should be sullied by the outrages of citizens on their own Government; commiserating such as remain obstinate from delusion; but resolved, in perfect reliance on that gracious Providence which so signally displays its goodness towards this country, to reduce the refractory to a due subordination to the laws; do hereby declare and make known, that, with a satisfaction which can be equaled only by the merits of the militia summoned into service from the States of New Jersey, Pennsylvania, Maryland, and Virginia, I have received intelligence of their patriotic alacrity, in obeying the call of the present, though painful, yet commanding necessity; that a force, which, according to every reasonable expectation, is adequate to the exigency, is already in motion to the scene of disaffection; that those who have confided or shall confide in the protection of Government, shall meet full succor under the standard and from the arms of the United States; that those who having offended against the laws have since entitled themselves to indemnity, will be treated with the most liberal good faith, if they shall not have forfeited their claim by any subsequent conduct, and that instructions are given accordingly.

And I do, moreover, exhort all individuals, officers, and bodies of men, to contemplate with abhorrence the measures leading directly or indirectly to those crimes, which produce this resort to military coercion; to check, in their respective spheres, the efforts of misguided or designing men to substitute their misrepresentation in the place of truth, and their discontents in the place of stable government; and to call to mind, that as the people of the United States have been permitted, under the Divine favor, in perfect freedom, after solemn deliberation, in an enlightened age, to elect their own Government, so will their gratitude for this inestimable blessing be best distinguished by firm exertions to maintain the Constitution and the laws.

And, lastly, I again warn all persons, whomsoever and wheresoever, not to abet, aid, or comfort the insurgents aforesaid, as they will answer the contrary at their peril;

and I do also require all officers and other citizens, according to their several duties, as far as may be in their power, to bring under the cognizance of the law offenders in the premises.

Source:

John C. Fitzpatrick, ed. *The Writings of George Washington,* 1745–99. Vol. 33. Westport: Conn.: Greenwood Press, pp. 457–461; 507–509.

Jay Treaty of 1794

Agreement signed in London, England, on November 19, 1794, by John Jay, U.S. chief justice and special envoy, and William Grenville, a British foreign secretary. The treaty settled outstanding grievances and disputes between the two men's countries. Britain agreed to evacuate its forts in the Northwest Territory by June 1, 1796, to make monetary amends for seizure of American ships and to give the United States trading concessions in England and the British East Indies. The Mississippi River was to be accessible to both countries, and commissions were to be established to fix boundaries between the United States and Canada in the northwest and northeast regions. American debts owed to British merchants prior to the American Revolution were to be paid. Although the treaty was unpopular in the United States (mainly because it did not deal with the important issue of British impressment of U.S. seamen), it was ratified by the U.S. Congress in 1795.

Treaty of Amity, Commerce and Navigation
Between His Britannic Majesty and the United States of America, by their President, with the Advice and Consent of their Senate.

His Britannic Majesty and the United States of America, being desirous, by a treaty of amity, commerce and navigation, to terminate their differences in such a manner, as, without reference to the merits of their respective complaints and pretensions, may be the best calculated to produce mutual satisfaction and good understanding; and also to regulate the commerce and navigation between their respective countries, territories and people, in such a manner as to render the same reciprocally beneficial and satisfactory; they have, respectively, named their plenipotentiaries, and given them full powers to treat of, and conclude the said treaty; that is to say: His Britannic Majesty has named for his Plenipotentiary, the Right Honorable William Wyndham Baron Grenville of Wotton, one of his Majesty's Privy Council, and his Majesty's Principal Secretary of State for Foreign Affairs; and the President of the said United States, by and with the advice and consent of the Senate thereof, hath appointed for their plenipotentiary, the honorable John Jay, Chief Justice of the said United States, and their envoy extraordinary to his Majesty: who have agreed on and concluded the following articles.

Article I

There shall be a firm, inviolable and universal peace, and a true and sincere friendship between his Britannic Majesty, his heirs and successors, and the United States of America; and between their respective countries, territories, cities, towns and people of every degree, without exception of persons or places.

Article II

His Majesty will withdraw all his troops and garrisons from all posts and places within the boundary lines assigned by the treaty of peace to the United States. This evacuation shall take place on or before the first day of June, one thousand seven hundred and ninety-six, and all the proper measures shall in the interval be taken by concert between the government of the United States, and his Majesty's Governor-General in America, for settling the previous arrangements which may be necessary respecting the delivery of the said posts: The United States in the mean time at their discretion, extending their settlements to any part within the said boundary line, except within the precincts or jurisdiction of any of the said posts. All settlers and traders, within the precincts or jurisdiction of the said posts, shall continue to enjoy, unmolested, all their property of every kind, and shall be protected therein. They shall be at full liberty to remain there, or to remove with all or any part of their effects; and it shall also be free to them to sell their lands, houses, or effects, or to retain the property thereof, at their discretion; such of them as shall continue to reside within the said boundary lines, shall not be compelled to become citizens of the United States, or to take any oath of allegiance to the government thereof; but they shall be at full liberty so to do if they think proper, and they shall make and declare their election within one year after the evacuation aforesaid. And all persons who shall continue there after the expiration of the said year, without having declared their intention of remaining subjects of his Britannic Majesty, shall be considered as having elected to become citizens of the United States.

Article III

It is agreed that it shall at all times be free to his Majesty's subjects, and to the citizens of the United States, and also to the Indians dwelling on either side of the said boundary line, freely to pass and repass by land or inland navigation, into the respective territories and countries of the two parties, on the continent of America (the country within the limits of the Hudson's bay Company only excepted) and to navigate all the lakes, rivers and waters thereof, and freely to carry on trade and commerce with each other. But it is understood, that this article does not extend to the admission of vessels of the United States into the sea-ports, harbours, bays, or creeks of his Majesty's said territories; nor into such parts of the rivers in his Majesty's said territories as are between the mouth thereof, and the highest port of entry from the sea, except in small vessels trading bona fide between Montreal and Quebec, under such regulations as shall be established to prevent the possibility of any frauds in this respect. Nor to the admission of British vessels from the sea into the rivers of the United States, beyond the highest ports of entry for foreign vessels from the sea. The river Mississippi shall, however, according to the treaty of peace, be entirely open to both parties; and it is further agreed, that all the ports and places on its eastern side, to whichsoever of the parties belonging, may freely be resorted to and used by both parties, in as ample a manner as any of the Atlantic ports or places of the United States, or any of the ports or places of his Majesty in Great-Britain.

All goods and merchandize whose importation into his Majesty's said territories in America, shall not be entirely prohibited, may freely, for the purposes of commerce, be carried into the same in the manner aforesaid, by the citizens of the United States, and such goods and merchandize shall be subject to no higher or other duties, than would be payable by his Majesty's subjects on the importation of the same from Europe into the said territories. And in like manner, all goods and merchandize whose importation into the United States shall not be wholly prohibited, may freely, for the purposes of commerce, be carried into the same, in the manner aforesaid, by his Majesty's subjects, and such goods and merchandize shall be subject to no higher or other duties, than would be payable by the citizens of the United States on the importation of the same in American vessels into the Atlantic ports of the said states. And all goods not prohibited to be exported from the said territories respectively, may in like manner be carried out of the same by the two parties respectively, paying duty as aforesaid.

No duty of entry shall ever be levied by either party on peltries brought by land, or inland navigation into the said territories respectively, nor shall the Indians passing or repassing with their own proper goods and effects of whatever nature, pay for the same any impost or duty whatever. But goods in bales, or other large packages, unusual among Indians, shall not be considered as goods belonging bona fide to Indians.

No higher or other tolls or rates of ferriage than what are or shall be payable by natives, shall be demanded on either side; and no duties shall be payable on any goods which shall merely be carried over any of the portages or carrying-places on either side, for the purpose of being immediately re-imbarked and carried to some other place or places. But as by this stipulation it is only meant to secure to each party a free passage across the portages on both sides: it is agreed, that this exemption from duty shall extend only to such goods as are carried in the usual and direct road across the portage, and are not attempted to be in any manner sold or exchanged during their passage across the same, and proper regulations may be established to prevent the possibility of any frauds in this respect.

As this article is intended to render in a great degree the local advantages of each party common to both, and thereby to promote a disposition favorable to friendship and good neighbourhood, it is agreed, that the respective governments will mutually promote this amicable intercourse, by causing speedy and impartial justice to be done, and necessary protection to be extended to all who may be concerned therein.

Article IV

Whereas it is uncertain whether the river Mississippi extends so far to the northward, as to be intersected by a line to be drawn due west from the Lake of the Woods, in the manner mentioned in the treaty of peace between his Majesty and the United States: it is agreed, that measures shall be taken in concert between his Majesty's government in America and the government of the United States, for making a joint survey of the said river from one degree of latitude below the falls of St. Anthony, to the principal source or sources of the said river, and also of the parts adjacent thereto; and that if on the result of such survey, it should appear that the said river, would not be intersected by such a line as is above mentioned, the two parties will thereupon proceed by amicable negociation, to regulate the boundary line in that quarter, as well as all other points to be adjusted between the said parties, according to justice and mutual convenience, and in conformity to the intent of the said treaty.

Article V

Whereas doubts have arisen what river was truly intended under the name of the river St. Croix, mentioned in the said treaty of peace, and forming a part of the boundary therein described; that question shall be referred to the final decision of commissioners to be appointed in the following manner, viz.

One commissioner shall be named by his Majesty, and one by the President of the United States, by and with the advice and consent of the Senate thereof, and the said two commissioners shall agree on the choice of a third; or if they cannot so agree, they shall each propose one person, and of the two name so proposed, one shall be drawn

by lot in the presence of the two original commissioners. And the three commissioners so appointed, shall be sworn, impartially to examine and decide the said question, according to such evidence as shall respectively be laid before them on the part of the British government and of the United States. The said commissioners shall meet at Halifax, and shall have power to adjourn to such other place or places as they shall think fit. They shall have power to appoint a secretary, and to employ such surveyors or other persons as they shall judge necessary. The said commissioners shall, by a declaration, under their hands and seals, decide what river is the river St. Croix, intended by the treaty. The said declaration shall contain a description of the said river, and shall particularize the latitude and longitude of its mouth and of its source. Duplicates of this declaration and of the statements of their accounts, and of the journal of their proceedings, shall be delivered by them to the agent of his Majesty, and to the agent of the United States, who may be respectively appointed and authorized to manage the business on behalf of the respective governments. And both parties agree to consider such decision as final, and conclusive, so as that the same shall never thereafter be called into question, or made the subject of dispute or difference between them.

Article VI

Whereas it is alledged by divers British merchants and others his Majesty's subjects, that debts, to a considerable amount, which were bona fide contracted before the peace, still remain owing to them by citizens or inhabitants of the United States, and that by the operation of various lawful impediments since the peace, not only the full recovery of the said debts has been delayed, but also the value and security thereof have been, in several instances, impaired and lessened, so that by the ordinary course of judicial proceedings, the British creditors cannot not obtain, and actually have and receive full and adequate compensation for the losses and damages which they have thereby sustained. It is agreed, that in all such cases, where full compensation for such losses and damages cannot, for whatever reason, be actually obtained, had and received by the said creditors in the ordinary course of justice, the United States will make full and complete compensation for the same to the said creditors: But it is distinctly understood, that this provision is to extend to such losses only as have been occasioned by the lawful impediments aforesaid, and is not to extend to losses occasioned by such insolvency of the debtors, or other causes as would equally have operated to produce such loss, if the said impediments had not existed; nor to such losses or damages as have been occasioned by the manifest delay or negligence, or wilful omission of the claimant.

For the purpose of ascertaining the amount of any such losses and damages, five commissioners shall be appointed, and authorized to meet and act in manner following, viz. Two of them shall be appointed by his Majesty, two of them by the President of the United States by and with the advice and consent of the Senate thereof, and the fifth by the unanimous voice of the other four; and if they should not agree in such choice, then the commissioners named by the two parties shall respectively propose one person, and of the two names so proposed, one shall be drawn by lot, in the presence of the four original commissioners. When the five commissioners thus appointed shall first meet, they shall, before they proceed to act, respectively take the following oath, or affirmation, in the presence of each other; which oath, or affirmation, being so taken and duly attested, shall be entered on the recorder of their proceedings, viz. *I, A.B.* one of the commissioners appointed in pursuance of the sixth article of the treaty of amity, commerce, and navigation, between his Britannic Majesty and the United States of America, do solemnly swear (or affirm) that I will honestly, diligently, impartially, and carefully examine, and to the best of my judgment, according to justice and equity, decide all such complaints, as under the said article shall be preferred to the said commissioners: and that I will forbear to act as a commissioner, in any case in which I may be personally interested.

Three of the said commissioners shall constitute a board, and shall have power to do any act appertaining to the said commission, provided that one of the commissioners named on each side, and the fifth commissioner shall be present, and all decisions shall be made by the majority of the voices of the commissioners then present. Eighteen months from the day on which the said commissioners shall form a board, and be ready to proceed to business, are assigned for receiving complaints and applications; but they are nevertheless authorized, in any particular cases in which it shall appear to them to be reasonable and just, to extend the said term of eighteen months, for any term not exceeding six months, after the expiration thereof. The said commissioners shall first meet at Philadelphia, but they shall have power to adjourn from place to place as they shall see cause.

The said commissioners in examining the complaints and applications so preferred to them, are empowered and required, in pursuance of the true intent and meaning of this article, to take into their consideration all claims, whether of principal or interest, or balances of principal and interest, and to determine the same respectively, according to the merits of the several cases, due regard being had to all the circumstances thereof, and as equity and justice shall appear to them to require. And the said commissioners shall have power to examine all such persons as shall come before them, on oath or affirmation,

touching the premises; and also to receive in evidence, according as they may think most consistent with equity and justice, all written depositions, or books, or papers, or copies, or extracts thereof; every such deposition, book, or paper, or copy, or extract, being duly authenticated, either according to the legal forms now respectively existing in the two countries, or in such other manner as the said commissioners shall see cause to require or allow.

The award of the said commissioners, or of any three of them as aforesaid, shall in all cases be final and conclusive, both as to the justice of the claim, and to the amount of the sum to be paid to the creditor or claimant: And the United States undertake to cause the sum so awarded to be paid in specie to such creditor or claimant without deduction; and at such time or times, and at such place or places, as shall be awarded by the said commissioners; and on condition of such releases or assignments to be given by the creditor or claimant, as by the said commissioners may be directed: Provided always, that no such payment shall be fixed by the said commissioner to take place sooner than twelve months from the day of the exchange of the ratifications of this treaty.

Article VII
Whereas complaints have been made by divers merchants and others, citizens of the United States, during the course of the war in which his Majesty is now engaged, they have sustained considerable losses and damage, by reason of irregular or illegal captures or condemnations of their vessels and other property, under colour of authority or commissioners from his Majesty, and that from various circumstances belonging to the said cases, adequate compensation for the losses and damages so sustained cannot now be actually obtained, had and received by the ordinary course of judicial proceedings; it is agreed, that in all such cases, where adequate compensation cannot, for whatever reason, be now actually obtained, had and received by the said merchants and others, in the ordinary course of justice, full and complete compensation for the same will be made by the British government to the said complainants. But it is distinctly understood, that this provision is not to extend to such losses or damages as have been occasioned by the manifest delay or negligence, or wilful omission of the claimant.

That for the purpose of ascertaining the amount of any such losses and damages, five commissioners shall be appointed and authorized to act in London, exactly in the manner directed with respect to those mentioned in the preceding article, and after having taken the same oath or affirmation (mutatis mutandis) the same term of eighteen months is also assigned for the reception of claims, and they are in like manner authorized to extend the same in particular cases. They shall receive testimony, books, papers and evidence in the same latitude, and exercise the like discretion and powers respecting that subject; and shall decide the claims in question according to the merits of the several cases, and to justice, equity, and the laws of nations. The award of the said commissioners, or any such three of them as aforesaid, shall in all cases be final and conclusive, both as to the justice of the claim, and the amount of the sum to be paid to the claimant; and his Britannic Majesty undertakes to cause the same to be paid to such claimant in specie, without any deduction, at such place or places, and at such time or times, as shall be awarded by the said commissioners, and on condition of such releases or assignments to be given by the claimant, as by the said commissioners may be directed.

And whereas certain merchants and others his Majesty's subjects, complain, that in the course of the war they have sustained loss and damage, by reason of the capture of their vessels and merchandize, taken within the limits and jurisdiction of the states, and brought into the ports of the same, or taken by vessels originally armed in ports of the said states.

It is agreed that in all such cases where restitution shall not have been made agreeably to the tenor of the letter from Mr. Jefferson to Mr. Hammond, dated at Philadelphia, Sept. 5, 1793, a copy of which is annexed to this treaty; the complaints of the parties shall be and hereby are referred to the commissioners to be appointed by virtue of this article, who are hereby authorized and required to proceed in the like manner relative to these as to the other cases committed to them; and the United States undertake to pay to the complainants or claimants in specie, without deduction, the amount of such sums as shall be awarded to them respectively by the said commissioners, and at the times and places which in such awards shall be specified; and on condition of such releases or assignments to be given by the claimants as in the said awards may be directed: And it is further agreed, that not only the now-existing cases of both descriptions, but also all such as shall exist at the time of exchanging the ratifications of this treaty, shall be considered as being within the provisions, intent, and meaning of this article.

Article VIII

It is further agreed, that the commissioners mentioned in this and in the two preceding articles shall be respectively paid in such manner as shall be agreed between the two parties, such agreement being to be settled at the time of the exchange of the ratifications of this treaty. And all other expences attending the said commissions shall be defrayed jointly by the two parties, the same being previously ascertained and allowed by the majority of the commissioners. And in the case of death, sickness or necessary absence, the place of every such commissioner respectively shall be supplied in the same manner as such commissioner was first appointed, and the new commissioners shall take the same oath or affirmation and do the same duties.

Article IX

It is agreed that British subjects who now hold lands in the territories of the United States, and American citizens who now hold lands in the dominions of his Majesty, shall continue to hold them according to the nature and tenure of their respective estates and titles therein; and may grant, sell, or devise the same to whom they please, in like manner as if they were natives; and that neither they nor their heirs or assigns shall, so far as may respect the said lands and the legal remedies incident thereto, be regarded as aliens.

Article X

Neither the debts due from individuals of the one nation to individuals of the other, nor shares, nor monies which they may have in the public funds, or in the public or private banks, shall ever in any event of war or national differences be sequestered or confiscated, it being unjust and impolitic that debts and engagements contracted and made by individuals, having confidence in each other and in their respective governments, should ever be destroyed or impaired by national authority on account of national differences and discontents.

Article XI

It is agreed between his Majesty and the United States of America, that there shall be a reciprocal and entirely perfect liberty of navigation and commerce between their respective people, in the manner, under the limitations and on the conditions specified in the following articles:

Article XII

His Majesty consents that it shall and may be lawful during the time herein-after limited, for the citizens of the United States to carry to any of his Majesty's islands and ports in the West-Indies from the United States, in their own vessels, not being above the burthen of seventy tons, any goods or merchandizes, being of the growth, manufacture or produce of the said states, which it is or may be lawful to carry to the said islands or ports from the said states in British vessels; and that the said American vessels shall be subject there to no other or higher tonnage-duties or charges, than shall be payable by British vessels in the ports of the United States; and that the cargoes of the said American vessels shall be subject there to no other or higher duties or charges, than shall be payable on the like articles if imported there from the said states in British vessels.

And his Majesty also consents, that it shall be lawful for the said American citizens to purchase, load, and carry away in their said vessels to the United States from the said islands and ports, all such articles, being of the growth, manufacture or produce of the said islands, as may now by law be carried from thence to the said states in British vessels, and subject only to the same duties and charges on exportation, to which British vessels and their cargoes are or shall be subject in similar circumstances.

Provided always, that the said American vessels do carry and land their cargoes in the United States only, it being expressly agreed and declared, that during the continuance of this article, the United States will prohibit and restrain the carrying any molasses, sugar, coffee, cocoa or cotton in American vessels, either from his Majesty's islands, or from the United States to any part of the world except the United States, reasonable sea-stores excepted. Provided also, that it shall and may be lawful, during the same period, for British vessels to import from the said islands into the United States, and to export from the United States to the said islands, all articles whatever, being of the growth, produce or manufacture of the said islands, or of the United States respectively, which now may, by the laws of the said states, be so imported and exported. And that the cargoes of the said British vessels shall be subject to no other or higher duties or charges, than shall be payable on the same articles if so imported or exported in American vessels.

It is agreed that this article and every matter and thing therein contained, shall continue to be in force during the continuance of the war in which his Majesty is now engaged; and also for two years from and after the day of the signature of the preliminary or other articles of peace, by which the same may be terminated.

And it is further agreed, that at the expiration of the said term, the two contracting parties will endeavour further to regulate their commerce in this respect, according to the situation in which his Majesty may then find himself with respect to the West-Indies, and with a view to such arrangements as may best conduce to the mutual advantage and extension of commerce. And the said parties will then also renew their discussions, and endeavour to agree, whether in any and what cases, neutral vessels shall protect enemy's property; and in what cases provisions and other articles, not generally contraband, may become such. But in the mean time, their conduct towards each other in these respects, shall be regulated by the articles hereinafter inserted on those subjects.

Article XIII

His Majesty consents that the vessels belonging to the citizens of the United States of America, shall be admitted and hospitably received, in all the sea-ports and harbours of the British territories in the East-Indies. And that the citizens of the said United States, may freely carry on a trade between the said territories and the said United States, in all articles of which the importation or exportation respectively, to or from the said territories, shall not be entirely prohibited. Provided only, that it shall not be lawful for them in any time of war between the British government and any other power or state whatever, to export from the said territories, without the special permission of the British government there, any military stores, or naval stores, or rice. The citizens of the United States shall pay for their vessels when admitted into the said ports no other or higher tonnage-duty than shall be payable on British vessels when admitted into the ports of the United States. And they shall pay no other or higher duties or charges, on the importation or exportation of the cargoes of the said vessels, than shall be payable on the same articles when imported or exported in British vessels. But it is expressly agreed, that the vessels of the United States shall not carry any of the articles exported by them from the said British territories, to any port or place, except to some port or place in America, where the same shall be unladen, and such regulations shall be adopted by both parties, as shall from time to time be found necessary to enforce the due and faithful observance of this stipulation. It is also understood that the permission granted by this article, is not to extend to allow the vessels of the United States to carry on any part of the coasting-trade of the said British territories; but vessels going with their original cargoes, or part thereof, from one port of discharge to another, are not to be considered as carrying on the coasting-trade. Neither is this article to be construed to allow the citizens of the said states to settle or reside within the said territories, or to go into the interior parts thereof, without the permission of the British government established there; and if any transgression should be attempted against the regulations of the British government in this respect, the observance of the same shall and may be enforced against the citizens of America in the same manner as against British subjects or others transgressing the same rule. And the citizens of the United States, whenever they arrive in any port or harbour in the said territories, or if they should be permitted in manner aforesaid, to go to any other place therein, shall always be subject to the laws, government, and jurisdiction of what nature established in such harbour, port or place, according as the same may be. The citizens of the United States may also touch for refreshment at the island of St. Helena, but subject in all respects to such regulations as the British government may from time to time establish there.

Article XIV

There shall be between all the dominions of his Majesty in Europe and the territories of the United States, a reciprocal and perfect liberty of commerce and navigation. The people and inhabitants of the two countries respectively, shall have liberty freely and securely, and without hindrance and molestation, to come with their ships and cargoes to the lands, countries, cities, ports, places and rivers, within the dominions and territories aforesaid, to enter into the same, to resort there, and to remain and reside there, without any limitation of time. Also to hire and possess houses and warehouses for the purposes of their commerce, and generally the merchants and traders on each side, shall enjoy the most complete protection and security for their commerce; but subjects always as to what respects this article to the laws and statutes of the two countries respectively.

Article XV

It is agreed that no other or higher duties shall be paid by the ships or merchandize of the one party in the ports of the other, than such as are paid by the like vessels or merchandize of all other nations. Nor shall any other or higher duty be imposed in one country on the importation of any articles the growth, produce or manufacture of the other, than are or shall be payable on the importation of the like articles being of the growth, produce, or manufacture of any other foreign country. Nor shall any prohibition be imposed on the exportation or importation of any articles to or from the territories of the two parties respectively, which shall not equally extend to all other nations.

But the British government reserves to itself the right of imposing on American vessels entering into the British ports in Europe, a tonnage duty equal to that which shall be payable by British vessels in the ports of America: And also such duty as may be adequate to countervail the difference of duty now payable on the importation of European and Asiatic goods, when imported into the United States in British or in American vessels.

The two parties agree to treat for the more exact equalization of the duties on the respective navigation of their subjects and people, in such manner as may be most beneficial to the two countries. The arrangements for this purpose shall be made at the same time, with those mentioned at the conclusion of the twelfth article of this treaty, and are to be considered as a part thereof. In the interval it is agreed, that the United States will not impose any new or additional tonnage duties on British vessels, nor increase the now-subsisting difference between the duties payable on the importation of any articles in British or in American vessels.

Article XVI

It shall be free for the two contracting parties, respectively to appoint consuls for the protection of trade, to reside in the dominions and territories aforesaid; and the said consuls shall enjoy those liberties and rights which belong to them by reason of their function. But before any consul shall act as such, he shall be in the usual forms approved and admitted by the party to whom he is sent; and it is hereby declared to be lawful and proper, that in case of illegal or improper conduct towards the laws or government, a consul may either be punished according to law, if the laws will reach the case, or be dismissed, or even sent back, the offended government assigning to the other their reasons for the same.

Either of the parties may except from the residence of consuls such particular places, as such party shall judge proper to be so excepted.

Article XVII

It is agreed, that in all cases where vessels shall be captured or detained on just suspicion of having on board enemy's property, or of carrying to the enemy any of the articles which are contraband for war; the said vessel shall be brought to the nearest or most convenient port; and if any property of an enemy should be found on board such vessel, that part only which belongs to the enemy shall be made prize, and the vessel shall be at liberty to proceed with the remainder without any impediment. And it is agreed, that all proper measures shall be taken to prevent delay, in deciding the cases of ships or cargoes so brought in for adjudication; and in the payment or recovery of any indemnification, adjudged or agreed to be paid to the masters or owners of such ships.

Article XVIII

In order to regulate what is in future to be esteemed contraband of war, it is agreed, that under the said denomination shall be comprised all arms and implements serving for the purposes of war, by land or sea, such a cannon, muskets, mortars, petards, bombs, grenades, carcasses, saucisses, carriages for cannon, musket rests, bandoliers, gunpowder, match, saltpetre, ball, pikes, swords, headpieces, cuirasses, halberts, lances, javelins, horse-furniture, holsters, belts, and generally all other implements of war; as also timber for ship-building, tar or rozin, copper in sheets, sails, hemp, and cordage, and generally whatever may serve directly to the equipment of vessels, unwrought iron and fir planks only excepted; and all the above articles are hereby declared to be just objects of confiscation, whenever they are attempted to be carried to an enemy.

And whereas the difficulty of agreeing on the precise cases in which alone provisions and other articles not generally contraband may be regarded as such, renders it expedient to provide against the inconveniences and misunderstandings which might thence arise: It is further agreed, that whenever any such articles so becoming contraband, according to the existing laws of nations, shall for that reason be seized, the same shall not be confiscated, but the owners thereof shall be speedily and completely indemnified; and the captors, or in their default, the government under whose authority they act, shall pay to the masters or owners of such vessels, the full value of all such articles, with a reasonable mercantile profit thereon, together with the freight, and also the demurrage incident to such detention.

And whereas it frequently happens that vessels sail for a port or place belonging to an enemy, without knowing that the same is either besieged, blockaded or invested; it is agreed, that every vessel so circumstanced, may be turned away from such port or place, but she shall not be detained, nor her cargo, if not contraband, be confiscated, unless after notice she shall again attempt to enter; but she shall be permitted to go to any other port or place she may think proper: Nor shall any vessel or goods of either party, that may have entered into such port or place, before the same was besieged, blockaded, or invested by the other, and be found therein after the reduction or surrender of such place, be liable to confiscation, but shall be restored to the owners or proprietors thereof.

Article XIX

And that more abundant care may be taken for the security of the respective subjects and citizens of the contracting parties, and to prevent their suffering injuries by the men of war, or privateers of either party, all commanders of ships of war and privateers, and all others the said subjects and citizens, shall forbear doing any damage to those of the other party, or committing any outrage against them, and if they act to the contrary, they shall be punished, and shall also be bound in their persons and estates to make satisfaction and reparation for all damages, and the interest thereof, of whatever nature the said damages may be.

For this cause, all commanders of privateers, before they receive their commissions, shall hereafter be obliged to give, before a competent judge, sufficient security by at least two responsible sureties, who have no interest in the said privateer, each of whom, together with the said commander, shall be jointly and severally bound in the sum of fifteen hundred pounds sterling, or if such ships be provided with above one hundred and fifty seamen or soldiers, in the sum of three thousand pounds sterling, to satisfy all damages and injuries, which the said privateer, or her officers or men, or any of them may do or commit during their cruise, contrary to the tenor of this treaty, or to the laws and instructions for regulating their conduct; and further, that in all cases of aggressions, the said commissions shall be revoked and annulled.

It is also agreed that whenever a judge of a court of admiralty of either of the parties, shall pronounce sentence against any vessel, or goods or property belonging to the subjects or citizens of the other party, a formal and duly authenticated copy of all the proceedings in the cause, and of the said sentence, shall, if required, be delivered to the commander of the said vessel, without the smallest delay, he paying all legal fees and demands for the same.

Article XX

It is further agreed that both the said contracting parties, shall not only refuse to receive any pirates into any of their ports, havens, or towns, or permit any of their inhabitants to receive, protect, harbor, conceal or assist them in any manner, but will bring to condign punishment all such inhabitants as shall be guilty of such acts or offenses.

And all their ships with the goods or merchandizes taken by them and brought into the port of either of the said parties, shall be seized as far as they can be discovered, and shall be restored to the owners, or their factors or agents, duly deputed and authorized in writing by them (proper evidence being first given in the court of admiralty for proving the property) even in case such effects should have passed into other hands by sale, if it be proved that the buyers knew or had good reason to believe, or suspect that they had been piratically taken.

Article XXI

It is likewise agreed, that the subjects and citizens of the two nations, shall not do any acts of hostility or violence against each other, nor accept commissions or instructions so to act from any foreign prince or state, enemies to the other party; nor shall be enemies of one of the parties be permitted to invite, or endeavor to enlist in their military service, any of the subjects or citizens of the other party; and the laws against all such offenses and aggressions shall be punctually executed. And if any subject or citizen of the said parties respectively, shall accept any foreign commission, or letters of marque, for arming any vessel to act as a privateer against the other party, and be taken by the other party, it is hereby declared to be lawful for the said party, to treat and punish the said subject or citizen, having such commission or letters of marque, as a pirate.

Article XXII

It is expressly stipulated, that neither of the said contracting parties will order or authorize any acts of reprisal against the other, on complaints of injuries or damages, until the said party shall first have presented to the other a statement thereof, verified by competent proof and evidence, and demanded justice and satisfaction, and the same shall either have been refused or unreasonably delayed.

Article XXIII

The ships of war of each of the contracting parties shall, at all times, be hospitality received in the ports of the other, their officers and crews paying due respect to the laws and government of the country. The officers shall be treated with that respect which is due to the commissions which they bear, and if any insult should be offered to them by any of the inhabitants, all offenders in this respect shall be punished as disturbers of the peace and amity between the two countries. And his Majesty consents, that in case an American vessel should, by stress of weather, danger from enemies or other misfortune, be reduced to the necessity of seeking shelter in any of his Majesty's ports, into which such vessel could not in ordinary cases claim to be admitted, she shall, on manifesting that necessity to the satisfaction of the government of the place, be hospitably received and be permitted to refit, and to purchase at the market price, such necessaries as she may stand in need of, conformably to such orders and regulations as the government of the place, having respect to the circumstances of each case, shall prescribe. She shall not be allowed to break bulk or unload her cargo, unless the same shall be bona fide necessary to her being refitted. Nor shall be permitted to sell any part of her cargo, unless so much only as may be necessary to defray her expences, and then not without the express permission of the government of the place. Nor shall she be obliged to pay any duties whatever, except only on such articles as she may be permitted to sell for the purpose aforesaid.

Article XXIV

It shall not be lawful for any foreign privateers (not being subjects or citizens of either of the said parties) who have commissions from any other prince or state in enmity with either nation, to arm their ships in the ports of either of the said parties, nor to sell what they have taken, nor in any other manner to exchange the same; nor shall they be allowed to purchase more provisions, than shall be necessary for their going to the nearest port of that prince or state from whom they obtained their commissions.

Article XXV

It shall be lawful for the ships of war and privateers belonging to the said parties respectively, to carry whithersoever they please, the ships and goods taken from their enemies, without being obliged to pay any fee to the officers of the admiralty, or to any judges whatever; nor shall the said prizes when they arrive at, and enter the ports of the said parties, be detained or seized, neither shall the searchers or other officers of those places visit such prizes, (except for the purpose of preventing the carrying of any part of the cargo thereof on shore in any manner contrary to the established laws of revenue, navigation or commerce) nor shall such officers take cognizance of the validity of such prizes; but they shall be at liberty to hoist sail, and depart as speedily as may be, and carry their said prizes to the place mentioned in their commissions or patents, which the commanders of the said ships of war or privateers shall be obliged to show. No shelter or refuge shall be given in their ports to such as have made a prize upon the subjects or citizens of either of the said parties; but if forced by stress of weather, or the dangers of the sea, to enter therein, particular care shall be taken to hasten their departure, and to cause them to retire as soon as possible. Nothing in this treaty contained shall, however, be construed or operate contrary to former and existing public treaties with other sovereigns or states. But the two parties agree, that while they continue in amity, neither of them will in future make any treaty shall be inconsistent with this or the preceding article.

Neither of the said parties shall permit the ships or goods belonging to the subjects or citizens of the other, to be taken within cannon-shot of the coast, nor in any of the bays, ports, or rivers of their territories, by ships of war, or others having commission from any prince, republic, or state whatever. But in case it should so happen, the party whose territorial rights shall thus have been violated, shall use his utmost endeavours to obtain from the offending party, full and ample satisfaction for the vessel or vessels so taken, whether the same be vessels of war or merchant vessels.

Article XXVI

If at any time a rupture should take place, (which God forbid) between his Majesty and the United States, the merchants and other of each of the two nations, residing in the dominions of the other, shall have the privilege of remaining and continuing their trade, so long as they behave peaceably, and commit no offence against the laws; and in case their conduct should render them suspected, and the respective governments should think proper to order them to remove, the term of twelve months from the publication of the order shall be allowed them for that purpose, to remove with their families, effects and property; but this favour shall not be extended to those who shall act contrary to the established laws; and for greater certainty, it is declared, that such rupture shall not be deemed to exist, while negociations for accommodating differences shall be depending, nor until the respective ambassadors or ministers, if such there shall be, shall be recalled, or sent home on account of such differences, and not on account of personal misconduct, according to the nature and degrees of which, both parties retain their rights, either to request the recall, or immediately to send home the ambassador or minister of the other; and that without prejudice to their mutual friendship and good understanding.

Article XXVII

It is further agreed, that his Majesty and the United States, on mutual requisitions, by them respectively, or by their respective ministers or officers authorized to make the same, will deliver up to justice all persons, who, being charged with murder or forgery, committed within the jurisdiction of either, shall seek an asylum within any of the countries of the other, provided that this shall only be done on such evidence of criminality, as, according to the laws of the place, where the fugitive or person so charged shall be found, would justify his apprehension and commitment for trial, if the offence had there been committed. The expence of such apprehension and delivery shall be borne and defrayed, by those who make the requisition and receive the fugitive.

Article XXVIII

It is agreed, that the first ten articles of this treaty shall be permanent, and that the subsequent articles, except the twelfth, shall be limited in their duration to twelve years, to be computed from the day on which the ratifications of this treaty shall be exchanged, but subject to this condition, That whereas the said twelfth article will expire by the limitation therein contained, at the end of two years from the signing of the preliminary or other articles of peace, which shall terminate the present war in which his Majesty is engaged, it is agreed, that proper measures shall by concern be taken, for bringing the subject of that article into amicable treaty and discussion, so early before the expiration of the said term, as the new arrangements on that head, may, by that time, be perfected, and ready to take place. But if it should unfortunately happen, that this Majesty and the United States should not be able to agree on such new arrangements, in that case, all the articles of this treaty, except the first ten, shall then cease and expire together.

Lastly. This treaty, when the same shall have been ratified by his Majesty, and by the President of the United States, by and with the advice and consent of their Senate, and the respective ratifications mutually exchanged, shall be binding and obligatory on his Majesty and on the said states, and shall be by them respectively executed, and observed, with punctuality and the most sincere regard to good faith; and whereas it will be expedient, in order the better to facilitate intercourse and obviate difficulties, that other articles be proposed and added to this treaty, which articles, from want of time and other circumstances, cannot now be perfected; it is agreed that the said parties will, from time to time, readily treat of and concerning such articles, and will sincerely endeavour so to form them, as that they may conduce to mutual convenience, and tend to promote mutual satisfaction and friendship; and that the said articles, after having been duly ratified, shall be added to, and make a part of this treaty. In faith whereof, we, the undersigned ministers plenipotentiary of his Majesty the King of Great-Britain, and the United States of America, have signed this present treaty, and have caused to be affixed thereto the seal of our arms.

Done at London, this nineteenth Day of November, one thousand seven hundred and ninety-four.

Source:

Charles I. Bevans, comp. *Treaties and Other Agreements of the United States of America, 1776–1949.* Washington, D.C.: Government Printing Office, 1968–76.

Greenville Treaty of 1795

Agreement signed on August 3, 1795, at Fort Greenville (now Greenville, Ohio) by U.S. general Anthony Wayne and the leaders of 12 Native American tribes; it opened part of the Northwest Territory to white settlement. Native American parties to the agreement included the Delaware, Shawnee, Wyandot, and Miami Confederacy. The treaty followed Wayne's decisive victory over the Native Americans at the Battle of Fallen Timbers the previous year. For a payment of $20,000 in trade goods and an annual sum of $9,500, the Native Americans ceded to the United States much of present-day Ohio and southeastern Indiana, as well as the regions that would become Chicago and Detroit. The Native Americans agreed to move westward and settlers poured into the area.

On July 22, 1790, the U.S. Congress had enacted the first law regulating trade between Indians and colonists, the Federal Trade and Intercourse Act. It required a license in order to carry on trade with Indians. The law was designed to be temporary and expired after two years.

A Treaty of Peace

Between the United States of America and the Tribes of Indians, called the Wyandots, Delawares, Shawanoes, Ottawas, Chipewas, Putawatimes, Miamis, Eel-river, Weea's Kickapoos, Piankashaws, and Kaskaskias.

To put an end to a destructive war, to settle all controversies, and to restore harmony and a friendly intercourse between the said United States, and Indian Tribes; Anthony Wayne, major-general, commanding the army of the United States, and sole commissioner for the good purposes abovementioned, and the said tribes of Indians, by their Sachems, chiefs, and warriors, met together at Greeneville, the head quarters of the said army, have agreed on the following articles, which, when ratified by the President, with the advice and consent of the Senate of the United States, shall be binding on them and the said Indian tribes.

Article I

Henceforth all hostilities shall cease; peace is hereby established, and shall be perpetual; and a friendly intercourse shall take place, between the said United States and Indian tribes.

Article II

All prisoners shall on both sides be restored. The Indians, prisoners to the United States, shall be immediately set a liberty. The people of the United States, still remaining prisoners among the Indians, shall be delivered up in ninety days from the date hereof, to the general or commanding officer at Greeneville, Fort Wayne or Fort Defiance; and ten chiefs of the said tribes shall remain at Greeneville as hostages, until the delivery of the prisoners shall be effected.

Article III

The general boundary line between the lands of the United States, and the lands of the said Indian tribes, shall begin at the mouth of Cayahoga river, and run thence up the same to the portage between that and the Tuscarawas branch of the Muskingum; thence down that branch to the crossing place above Fort Lawrence; thence westerly to a fork of that branch of that great Miami river running into the Ohio, at or near which fork stood Loromie's store, and where commences the portage between the Miami of the Ohio, and St. Mary's river, which is a branch of the Miami, which runs into Lake Erie; thence a westerly course to Fort Recovery, which stands on a branch of the Wabash; then south-westerly in a direct line to the Ohio, so as to intersect that river opposite the mouth of Kentucke or Cuttawa river. And in consideration of the peace now established; of the goods formerly received from the United States; of those now to be delivered, and of the yearly delivery of goods now stipulated to be made hereafter, and to indemnify the United States for the injuries and expences they have sustained during the war; the said Indian tribes do hereby cede and relinquish forever, all their claims to the lands lying eastwardly and southwardly of the general boundary line now described; and these lands, or any part of them, shall never hereafter be made a cause or pretence, on the part of the said tribes or any of them, of war or injury to the United States, or any of the people thereof.

And for the same considerations, and as an evidence of the returning friendship of the said Indian tribes, of their confidence in the United States, and desire to provide for their accommodation, and for that convenient intercourse which will be beneficial to both parties, the said Indian tribes do also cede to the United States the following pieces of land; to wit. (1.) One piece of land six miles square at or near Loromie's store before mentioned. (2.) One piece two miles square at the head of the navigable water or landing on the St. Mary's river, near Girty's town. (3.) One piece six miles square at the head of the navigable water of the Au-Glaize river. (4.) One piece six miles square at the confluence of the Au-Glaize and Miami rivers, where Fort Defiance now stands. (5.) One piece six

miles square at or near the confluence of the rivers St. Mary's and St. Joseph's, where Fort Wayne now stands, or near it. (6.) One piece two miles square on the Wabash river at the end of the portage from the Miami of the lake, and about eight miles westward from Fort Wayne. (7.) One piece six miles square at the Ouatanon or old Weea towns on the Wabash river. (8.) One piece twelve miles square at the British fort on the Miami of the lake at the foot of the rapids. (9.) One piece six miles square at the mouth of the said river where it empties into the Lake. (10.) One piece six miles square upon Sandusky lake, where a fort formerly stood. (11.) One piece two miles square at the lower rapids of Sandusky river. (12.) The post of Detroit and all the land to the north, the west and the south of it, of which the Indian title has been extinguished by gifts or grants to the French or English governments; and so much more land to be annexed to the district of Detroit as shall be comprehended between the river Rosine on the south, lake St. Clair on the north, and a line, the general course whereof shall be six miles distant from the west end of lake Erie, and Detroit river. (13.) The post of Michillimackinac, and all the land on the island, on which that post stands, and the main land adjacent, of which the Indian title has been extinguished by gifts or grants to the French or English governments; and a piece of land on the main to the north of the island, to measure six miles on lake Huron, or the streight between lakes Huron and Michigan, and to extend three miles back from the water of the lake or streight, and also the island De Bois Blanc, being an extra and voluntary gift of the Chipewa nation. (14.) One piece of land six miles square at the mouth of Chikago river emptying into the south-west end of Lake Michigan, where a forth formerly stood. (15.) One piece twelve miles square at or near the mouth of the Illinois river, emptying into the Mississippi. (16.) One piece six miles square at the old Piorias fort and village, near the south end of the Illinois lake on said Illinois river: And whenever the United States shall think proper to survey and mark the boundaries of the lands hereby ceded to them, they shall give timely notice thereof to the said tribes of Indians, that they may appoint some of their wise chiefs to attend and see that the lines are run according to the terms of this treaty.

And the said Indian tribes will allow to the people of the United States a free passage by land and by water, as one and the other shall be found convenient, through their country, along the chain of posts herein before mentioned; that is to say, from the commencement of the portage aforesaid at or near Loromie's store, thence along said portage to the St. Mary's, and down the same to Fort Wayne, and then down the Miami to lake Erie: again from the commencement of the portage at or near Loromie's store along the portage from thence to the river Au-Glaize, and down the same to its junction with the Miami at Fort

Defiance: again from the commencement of the portage aforesaid, to Sandusky river and down the same to Sandusky bay and lake Erie, and from Sandusky to the post which shall be taken at or near the foot of the rapids of the Miami of the lake: and from thence to Detroit. Again from the mouth of Chikago, to the commencement of the portage, between that river and the Illinois, and down the Illinois river to the Mississippi, also from Fort Wayne along the portage aforesaid which leads to the Wabash, and then down the Wabash to the Ohio. And the said Indian tribes will also allow to the people of the United States the free use of the harbours and mouths of rivers along the lakes adjoining the Indian lands, for sheltering vessells and boats, and liberty to land their cargoes where necessary for their safety.

Article IV

In consideration of the peace now established and of the cessions and relinquishments of lands made in the preceding article by the said tribes of Indians, and to manifest the liberality of the United States, as the great means of rendering this peace strong and perpetual; the United States relinquish their claims to all other Indian lands northward of the river Ohio, eastward of the Mississippi, and westward and southward of the Great Lakes and the waters uniting them, according to the boundary line agreed on by the United States and the king of Great-Britain, in the treaty of peace made between them in the year 1783. But from this relinquishment by the United States, the following tracts of land, are explicitly excepted. 1st. The tract of one hundred and fifty thousand acres near the rapids of the river Ohio, which has been assigned to General Clark, for the use of himself and his warriors. 2d. The post of St. Vincennes on the river Wabash, and the lands adjacent, of which the Indian title has been extinguished. 3d. The lands at all other places in possession of the French people and other white settlers among them, of which the Indian title has been extinguished as mentioned in the 3d article; and 4th. The post of fort Massac towards the mouth of the Ohio. To which several parcels of land so excepted, the said tribes relinquish all the title and claim which they or any of them may have.

And for the same considerations and with the same views as above mentioned, the United States now deliver to the said Indian tribes a quantity of goods to the value of twenty thousand dollars, the receipt whereof they do hereby acknowledge; and henceforward every year forever the United States will deliver at some convenient place northward of the river Ohio, like useful goods, suited to the circumstances of the Indians, of the value of nine thousand five hundred dollars; reckoning that value at the first cost of the goods in the city or place in the United States, where they shall be procured. The tribes to which those goods are to be annually delivered, and the proportions in which they are to be delivered, are the following.

1st. To the Wyandots, the amount of one thousand dollars. 2d. To the Delawares, the amount of one thousand dollars. 3d. To the Shawanese, the amount of one thousand dollars. 4th. To the Miamis, the amount of one thousand dollars. 5th. To the Ottawas, the amount of one thousand dollars. 6th. To the Chippewas, the amount of one thousand dollars. 7th. To the Putawatimes, the amount of one thousand dollars. 8th. And to the Kickapoo, Weea, Eel-river, Piankashaw and Kaskaskias tribes, the amount of five hundred dollars each.

Provided, That if either of the said tribes shall hereafter at an annual delivery of their share of the goods aforesaid, desire that a part of their annuity should be furnished in domestic animals, implements of husbandry, and other utensils convenient for them, and in compensation to useful artificers who may reside with or near them, and be employed for their benefit, the same shall at the subsequent annual deliveries be furnished accordingly.

Article V

To prevent any misunderstanding about the Indian lands relinquished by the United States in the fourth article, it is now explicitly declared, that the meaning of that relinquishment is this: The Indian tribes who have a right to those lands, are quietly to enjoy them, hunting, planting, and dwelling thereon so long as they please, without any molestation from the United States; but when those tribes, or any of them, shall be disposed to sell their lands, or any part of them, they are to be sold only to the United States; and until such sale, the United States will protect all the said Indian tribes in the quiet enjoyment of their lands against all citizens of the United States, and against all other white persons who intrude upon the same. And the said Indian tribes again acknowledge themselves to be under the protection of the said United States and no other power whatever.

Article VI

If any citizen of the United States, or any other white person or persons, shall presume to settle upon the lands now relinquished by the United States, such citizen or other person shall be out of the protection of the United States; and the Indian tribe, on whose land the settlement shall be made, may drive off the settler, or punish him in such manner as they shall think fit; and because such settlements made without the consent of the United States, will be injurious to them as well as to the Indians, the United States shall be at liberty to break them up, and remove and punish the settlers as they shall think proper, and so effect that protection of the Indian lands herein before stipulated.

Article VII

The said tribes of Indians, parties to this treaty, shall be at liberty to hunt within the territory and lands which they have now ceded to the United States, without hindrance or molestation, so long as they demean themselves peaceably, and offer no injury to the people of the United States.

Article VIII

Trade shall be opened with the said Indian tribes; and they do hereby respectively engage to afford protection to such persons, with their property, as shall be duly licensed to reside among them for the purpose of trade, and to their agents and servants; but no person shall be permitted to reside at any of their towns or hunting camps as a trader, who is not furnished with a license for that purpose, under the hand and seal of the superintendant of the department north-west of the Ohio, or such other person as the President of the United States shall authorise to grant such licenses; to the end, that the said Indians may not be imposed on in their trade. And if any licensed trader shall abuse his privilege by unfair dealing, upon complaint and proof thereof, his license shall be taken from him, and he shall be further punished according to the laws of the United States. And if any person shall intrude himself as a trader, without such license, the said Indians shall take and bring him before the superintendant or his deputy, to be dealt with according to law. And to prevent impositions by forged licenses, the said Indians shall at least once a year give information to the superintendant or his deputies, of the names of the traders residing among them.

Article IX

Lest the firm peace and friendship now established should be interrupted by the misconduct of individuals, the United States, and the said Indian tribes agree, that for injuries done by individuals on either side, no private revenge or retaliation shall take place; but instead thereof, complaint shall be made by the party injured, to the other: By the said Indian tribes, or any of them, to the President of the United States, or the superintendant by him appointed; and by the superintendant or other person appointed by the President, to the principal chiefs of the said Indian tribes, or of the tribe to which the offender belongs; and such prudent measures shall then be pursued as shall be necessary to preserve the said peace and friendship unbroken, until the Legislature (or Great Council) of the United States, shall make other equitable provision in the case, to the satisfaction of both parties. Should any Indian tribes meditate a war against the United States or either of them, and the same shall come to the knowledge of the before-mentioned tribes, or either of them, they do hereby engage to give immediate notice thereof to the general or officer commanding the troops of the United States, at the nearest post. And should any tribe, with hostile intentions against the United States, or either of them, attempt to pass through their country, they will endeavour to prevent the same, and in like manner give information of such attempt, to the general or officer commanding, as soon as possible, that all causes of mistrust and suspicion may be avoided between them and the United States. In like manner the United States shall give notice to the said Indian tribes of any harm that may be mediated against them, or either of them, that shall come to their knowledge; and do all in their power to hinder and prevent the same, that the friendship between them may be uninterrupted.

Article X

All other treaties heretofore made between the United States and the said Indian tribes, or any of them, since the treaty of 1783, between the United States and Great Britain, that come within the purview of this treaty, shall henceforth cease and become void.

In Testimony whereof, the said Anthony Wayne, and the Sachems and War-Chiefs of the before- mentioned Nations and Tribes of Indians, have hereunto set their Hands, and affixed their Seals. Done at Greeneville, in the Territory of the United States, northwest of the river Ohio, on the third Day of August, one thousand seven hundred and ninety-five.

Source:

Statutes at Large of the United States of America, 1789–1873. 17 vols. Washington, D.C., 1850–73. Vol. 3, pp. 49–54.

Pinckney Treaty of 1795 (Treaty of San Lorenzo)

Agreement signed at San Lorenzo, Spain, on October 27, 1795, to resolve long-standing disputes between the United States and Spain over the southern and western boundaries of the United States, over Spanish encouragement of Native American discontent, and over free navigation of the Mississippi River for Americans. The terms of the treaty, negotiated by Thomas Pinckney, special U.S. commissioner to Spain, were favorable to the United States: Spain recognized the Mississippi River and the thirty-first parallel as the U.S. boundaries, gave Americans free navigation of the Mississippi and the right to deposit goods for shipment at New Orleans, and promised more peaceful relations with the Native Americans.

Between the United States of America and the King of Spain.

His Catholic Majesty and the United States of America, desiring to consolidate, on a permanent basis, the friendship and good correspondence, which happily prevails between the two parties, have determined to establish, by a convention, several points, the settlement whereof will be productive of general advantage and reciprocal utility of both nations.

With this intention, his Catholic Majesty has appointed the most excellent Lord, don Manuel de Godoy, and Alvarez de Faria, Rios, Sanchez, Zarzosa, Prince de la Paz, duke de la Alcudia, lord of the Soto de Roma, and of the state of Albala, Grandee of Spain of the first class, perpetual regidor of the city of Santiago, knight of the illustrious order of the Golden Fleece, and Great Cross of the Royal and distinguished Spanish order of Charles the III. commander of Valencia, del Ventoso, Rivera, and Acenchal in that of Santiago; Knight and Great Gross of the religious order of St. John; Counsellor of state; first Secretary of state and despacho; Secretary to the Queen; Superintendant General of the posts and highways; Protector of the royal Academy of the noble arts, and of the royal societies of natural history, botany, chemistry, and astronomy; Gentleman of the King's chamber in employment; Captain General of his armies; Inspector and Major of the royal corps of body guards, &c. &c. &c. and the President of the United States, with the advice and consent of their Senate, has appointed Thomas Pinckney, a citizen of the United States, and their Envoy Extraordinary to his Catholic Majesty. And the said Plenipotentiaries have agreed upon and concluded the following articles:

Article I

There shall be a firm and inviolable peace and sincere friendship between his Catholic Majesty, his successors and subjects, and the United States, and their citizens, without exception of persons or places.

Article II

To prevent all disputes on the subject of the boundaries which separate the territories of the two high contracting parties, it is hereby declared and agreed as follows, to wit. The southern boundary of the United States, which divides their territory from the Spanish colonies of East and West Florida, shall be designated by a line beginning on the river Missisippi, at the northernmost part of the thirty-first degree of latitude north of the equator, which from thence shall be drawn due east to the middle of the river Apalachicola, or Catahouche, thence along the middle thereof to its junction with the Flint: thence straight to the head of St.Mary's river, and thence down the middle thereof to the Atlantic ocean. And it is agreed, that if there should be any troops, garrisons, or settlements of either party, in the territory of the other, according to the above-

mentioned boundaries, they shall be withdrawn from the said territory within the term of six months after the ratification of this treaty, or sooner if it be possible; and that they shall be permitted to take with them all the goods and effects which they possess.

Article III

In order to carry the preceding article into effect, one commissioner and one surveyor shall be appointed by each of the contracting parties, who shall meet at the Natchez, on the left side of the river Missisippi, before the expiration of six months from the ratification of this convention, and they shall proceed to run and mark this boundary according to the stipulations of the said article. They shall make plats and keep journals of their proceedings, which shall be considered as part of this convention, and shall have the same force as if they were inserted therein. And if on any account it should be found necessary that the said commissioners and surveyors should be accompanied by guards, they shall be furnished in equal proportions by the commanding officer of his Majesty's troops in the two Floridas, and the commanding officer of the troops of the United States in their southwestern territory, who shall act by common consent, and amicably, as well with respect to this point as to the furnishing of provisions and instruments, and making every other arrangement which may be necessary or useful for the execution of this article.

Article IV

It is likewise agreed that the western boundary of the United States which separates them from the Spanish colony of Louissiana, is in the middle of the channel or bed of the river Missisippi, from the northern boundary of the said states to the completion of the thirty-first degree of latitude north of the equator. And his Catholic Majesty has likewise agreed that the navigation of the said river, in its whole breadth from its source of the ocean, shall be free only to his subjects and the citizens of the United States, unless he should extend this privilege to the subjects of other powers by special convention.

Article V

The two high contracting parties shall, by all the means in their power, maintain peace and harmony among the several Indian nations who inhabit the country adjacent to the lines and rivers, which, by the preceding articles, form the boundaries of the two Floridas. And the better to obtain this effect, both parties oblige themselves expressly to restrain by force all hostilities on the part of the Indian nations living within their boundary: so that Spain will not suffer her Indians to attack the citizens of the United States, nor the Indians inhabiting their territory; nor will the United States permit these last-mentioned Indians to commence hostilities against the subjects of his Catholic Majesty or his Indians, in any manner whatever. And whereas several treaties of friendship exist between the two contracting parties and the said nations of Indians, it is hereby agreed that in future no treaty of alliance or other whatever (except treaties of peace) shall be made by either party with the Indians living within the boundary of the other, but both parties will endeavour to make the advantages of the Indian trade common and mutually beneficial to their respective subjects and citizens, observing in all things the most complete reciprocity, so that both parties may obtain the advantages arising from a good understanding with the said nations, without being subject to the expence which they have hitherto occasioned.

Article VI

Each party shall endeavour, by all means in their power, to protect and defend all vessels and other effects belonging to the citizens or subjects of the other, which shall be within the extent of their jurisdiction by sea or by land, and shall use all their efforts to recover and cause to be restored to the right owners, their vessels and effects which may have been taken from them within the extent of their said jurisdiction, whether they are at war or not with the power whose subjects have taken possession of the said effects.

Article VII

And it is agreed that the subjects or citizens of each of the contracting parties, their vessels or effects, shall not be liable to any embargo or detention on the part of the other, for any military expedition or other public or private purpose whatever: And in all cases of seizure, detention, or arrest for debts contracted, or offences committed by any citizen or subject of the one party within the jurisdiction of the other, the same shall be made and prosecuted by order and authority of law only, and according to the regular course of proceedings usual in such cases. The citizens and subjects of both parties shall be allowed to employ such advocates, solicitors, notaries, agents and factors, as they may judge proper, in all their affairs, and in all their trials at law, in which they may be concerned, before the tribunals of the other party; and such agents shall have free access to be present at the proceedings in such causes, and at the taking of all examinations and evidence which may be exhibited in the said trials.

Article VIII

In case the subjects and inhabitants of either party, with their shipping, whether public and of war, or private and of merchants, be forced, through stress of weather, pursuit of pirates or enemies, or any other urgent necessity, for seeking of shelter and harbour, to retreat and enter into any of the rivers, bays, roads or ports belonging to the other party, they shall be received and treated with all humanity, and enjoy all favor, protection and help, and they shall be permitted to refresh and provide themselves, at reasonable rates, with victuals and all things needful for the sustenance of their persons, or reparation of their ships and prosecution of their voyage; and they shall no ways be hindered from returning out of the said ports or roads, but may remove and depart when and whither they please, without any let or hindrance.

Article IX

All ships and merchandize, of what nature soever, which shall be rescued out of the hands of any pirates or robbers on the high seas, shall be brought into some port of either state, and shall be delivered to the custody of the officers of that port, in order to be taken care of, and restored entire to the true proprietor, as soon as due and sufficient proof shall be made concerning the property thereof.

Article X

When any vessel of either party shall be wrecked, foundered, or otherwise damaged, on the coasts or within the dominion of the other, their respective subjects or citizens shall receive, as well for themselves as for their vessels and effects, the same assistance which would be due to the inhabitants of the country where the damage happens, and shall pay the same charges and dues only as the said inhabitants would be subject to pay in a like case: And if the operations of repair would require that the whole or any part of the cargo be unladen, they shall pay no duties, charges or fees on the part which they shall relade and carry away.

Article XI

The citizens and subjects of each party shall have power to dispose of their personal goods, within the jurisdiction of the other, by testament, donation or otherwise, and their representatives being subjects or citizens of the other party, shall succeed to their said personal goods, whether by testament or ab intestato, and they may take possession thereof, either by themselves or others acting for them, and dispose of the same at their will, paying such dues only as the inhabitants of the country wherein the said goods are, shall be subject to pay in like cases.

And in case of the absence of the representative, such care shall be taken of the said goods, as would be taken of the goods of a native in like case, until the lawful owner may take measures for receiving them. And if questions shall arise among several claimants to which of them the said goods belong, the same shall be decided finally by the laws and judges of the land wherein the said goods are. And where, on the death of any person holding real estate within the territories of the one party, such real estate would by the laws of the land descend on a citizen or subject of the other, were he not disqualified by being an alien, such subject shall be allowed a reasonable time to sell the same, and to withdraw the proceeds without molestation, and exempt from all rights of detraction on the part of the government of the respective states.

Article XII

The merchant-ships of either of the parties which shall be making into a port belonging to the enemy of the other party, and concerning whose voyage, and the species of goods on board her, there shall be just grounds of suspicion, shall be obliged to exhibit as well upon the high seas as in the ports and havens, not only her passports but likewise certificates, expressly showing that her goods are not of the number of those which have been prohibited as contraband.

Article XIII

For the better promoting of commerce on both sides, it is agreed, that if a war shall break out between the said two nations, one year after the proclamation of war shall be allowed to the merchants, in the cities and towns where they shall live, for collecting and transporting their goods and merchandizes: And if any thing be taken from them or any injury be done them within that term, by either party, or the people or subjects of either, full satisfaction shall be made for the same by the government.

Article XIV

No subject of his Catholic Majesty shall apply for, or take any commission or letters of marque, for arming any ship or ships to act as privateers, against the said United States, or against the citizens, people or inhabitants of the said United States, or against the property of any of the inhabitants of any of them from any prince or state with which the said United States shall be at war.

Nor shall any citizen, subject or inhabitant of the said United States apply for or take any commission or letters of marque for arming any ship or ships to act as privates against the subjects of his Catholic Majesty, or the property of any of them, from any prince or state with which the said king shall be at war. And if any person of either nation shall take such commissions or letters of marque, he shall be punished as a pirate.

Article XV

It shall be lawful for all and singular the subjects of his Catholic Majesty, and the citizens, people and inhabitants of the said United States, to sail with their ships, with all manner of liberty and security, no distinction being made who are the proprietors of the merchandizes laden thereon, from any port to the places of those who now are, or hereafter shall be at enmity with his Catholic Majesty or the United States. It shall be likewise lawful for the subjects and inhabitants aforesaid, to sail with the ships and merchandizes aforementioned, and to trade with the same liberty and security from the places, ports and havens of those who are enemies of both or either party, without any opposition or disturbance whatsoever, not only directly from the places of the enemy aforementioned, to neutral places, but also from one place belonging to an enemy, to another place belonging to an enemy, whether they be under the jurisdiction of the same prince or under several; and it is hereby stipulated, that free ships shall also give freedom to goods, and that every thing shall be deemed free and exempt which shall be found on board the ships belonging to the subjects of either of the contracting parties, although the whole lading, or any part thereof, should appertain to the enemies of either: Contraband goods being always excepted. It is also agreed, that the same liberty be extended to persons who are on board a free ship, so that although they be enemies to either party, they shall not be made prisoners or taken out of that free ship, unless they are soldiers and in actual service of the enemies.

Article XVI

This liberty of navigation and commerce shall extend to all kinds of merchandizes, excepting those only, which are distinguished by the name of contraband: And under this name of contraband or prohibited goods, shall be comprehended arms, great guns, bombs, with the fusees, and other things belonging to them, cannon-ball, gunpowder, match, pikes, swords, lances, speards, halberds, mortars, petards, grenades, saltpetre, muskets, musket-ball, bucklers, helmets, breast-plates, coats of mail, and the like kind of arms, proper for arming soldiers, musket-rests, belts, horses with their furniture, and all other warlike instruments whatever. These merchandizes which follows, shall not be reckoned among contraband or prohibited goods: That is to say, all sorts of cloths, and all other manufactures woven of any wool, flax, silk, cotton, or any other materials whatever; all kinds of wearing aparel, together with all species whereof they are used to be made; gold and silver, as well coined as uncoined, tin, iron, latton, copper, brass, coals; as also wheat, barley, oats, and any other kind of corn and pulse; tobacco, and likewise all manner of spices, salted and smoked flesh, salted fish, cheese and butter, beer, oils, wines, sugars, and all sorts of salts: And in general, all provisions which serve for the sustenance of life: Furthermore, all kinds of cotton, hemp, flax, tar, pitch, ropes, cables, sails, sail-cloths, anchors, and any parts of anchors, also ships' masts, planks, wood of all kind, and all other things proper either for building or repairing ships, and all other goods whatever, which have not been worked into the form of any instrument prepared for war, by land or by sea, shall not be reputed contraband, much less, such as have been already wrought and made up for any other use; all which shall be wholly reckoned among free goods: As likewise all other merchandizes and things which are not comprehended and particularly mentioned in the foregoing enumeration of contraband goods: So that they may be transported and carried in the freest manner by the subjects of both parties, even to places belonging to an enemy, such towns or places being only excepted, as are at that time besieged, blocked up, or invested. And except the cases in which any ship of war, or squadron shall, in consequence of storms or other accidents at sea, be under the necessity of taking the cargo of any trading vessel or vessels, in which case they may stop the said vessel or vessels, and furnish themselves with necessaries, giving a receipt, in order that the power to whom the said ship of war belongs, may pay for the articles so taken, according to the price thereof, at the port to which they may appear to have been destined by the ship's papers: and the two contracting parties engage, that the vessels shall not be detained longer than may be absolutely necessary for their said ships to supply themselves with necessaries: That they will immediately pay the value of the receipts, and indemnify the proprietor for all losses which he may have sustained in consequence of such transaction.

Article XVII

To the end, that all manner of dissentions and quarrels may be avoided and prevented on one side and the other, it is agreed, that in case either of the parties hereto, should be engaged in a war, the ships and vessels belonging to the subjects or people of the other party must be furnished with sea-letters or passports, expressing the name, property, and bulk of the ship, as also the name and place of habitation of the master or commander of the said ship, that it may appear thereby, that the ship really and truly belongs to the subjects of one of the parties, which passport shall be made out and granted according to the form annexed to this treaty. They shall likewise be recalled every year, that is, if the ship happens to return home within the space of a year.

It is likewise agreed, that such ships being laden, are to be provided not only with passports as above mentioned, but also with certificates, containing the several particulars of the cargo, the place whence the ship sailed, that so it may be known whether any forbidden or contraband goods be on board the same: which certificates shall be made out by the officers of the place whence the ship sailed in the accustomed form: And if any one shall think it fit or advisable to express in the said certificates, the person to whom the goods on board belong, he may freely do so: Without which requisites they may be sent to one of the ports of the other contracting party, and adjudged by the competent tribunal, according to what is above set forth,

that all the circumstances of this omission having been well examined, they shall be adjudged to be legal prizes, unless they shall give legal satisfaction of their property by testimony entirely equivalent.

Article XVIII

If the ships of the said subjects, people, or inhabitants, of either of the parties, shall be met with, either sailing along the coasts or on the high seas, by any ship of war of the other, or by any privateer, the said ship of war or privateer for the avoiding of any disorder, shall remain out of cannon shot, and may send their boats a-board the merchant ship, which they shall so meet with, and may enter her to number of two or three men only, to whom the master or commander of such ship or vessel shall exhibit his passports, concerning the property of the ship, made out according to the form inserted in this present treaty, and the ship when she shall have shewed such passports, shall be free and at liberty to pursue her voyage, so as it shall not be lawful to molest or give her chace in any manner, or force her to quit her intended course.

Article XIX

Consuls shall be reciprocally established, with the privileges and powers which those of the most favoured nations enjoy, in the ports where their consuls reside or are permitted to be.

Article XX

It is also agreed that the inhabitants of the territories of each party shall respectively have free access to the courts of justice of the other, and they shall be permitted to prosecute suits for the recovery of their properties, the payment of their debts, and for obtaining satisfaction for the damages which they may have sustained, whether the persons whom they may sue be subjects or citizens of the country in which they may be found, or any other persons whatsoever, who may have taken refuge therein; and the proceedings and sentences of the said courts shall be the same as if the contending parties had been subjects or citizens of the said country.

Article XXI

In order to terminate all differences on account of the losses sustained by the citizens of the United States in consequence of their vessels and cargoes having been taken by the subjects of his Catholic Majesty, during the late war between Spain and France, it is agreed that all such cases shall be referred to the final decision of commissioners to be appointed in the following manner. His Catholic Majesty shall name one commissioner, and the President of the United States, by and with the advice and consent of their Senate, shall appoint another, and the said two commissioners shall agree on the choice of a third, or if they cannot agree so, they shall each propose one person, and of the two names so proposed, one shall be drawn by lot in the presence of the two original commissioners, and the person whose name shall be so drawn, shall be the third commissioner: and the three commissioners so appointed, shall be sworn impartially to examine and decide the claims in question, according to the merits of the several cases, and to justice, equity, and the laws of nations. The said commissioners shall meet and sit at Philadelphia: and in the case of the death, sickness, or necessary absence of any such commissioner, his place shall be supplied in the same manner as he was first appointed, and the new commissioner shall take the same oaths, and do the same duties. They shall receive all complaints and applications authorized by this article, during eighteen months from the day on which they shall assemble. They shall have power to examine all such persons as come before them on oath or affirmation, touching the complaints in question, and also to receive in evidence all written testimony, authenticated in such manner as they shall think proper to require or admit. The award of the said commissioners, or any two of them, shall be final and conclusive, both as to the justice of the claim and the amount of the sum to be paid to the claimants; and his Catholic Majesty undertakes to cause the same to be paid in specie, without deduction, at such times and places, and under such conditions as shall be awarded by the said commissioners.

Article XXII

The two high contracting parties, hopping that the good correspondence and friendship which happily reigns between them, will be further encreased by this treaty, and that it will contribute to augment their prosperity and opulence, will in future give to their mutual commerce all the extension and favour which the advantages of both countries may require.

And in consequence of the stipulations contained in the IV. article, his Catholic Majesty will permit the citizens of the United States, for the space of three years from this time, to deposit their merchandizes and effects in the port of New-Orleans, and to export them from thence without paying any other duty than a fair price for the hire of the stores, and his Majesty promises either to continue this permission, if he finds during that time that it is not prejudicial to the interests of Spain, or if he should not agree to continue it there, he will assign to them, on another part of the banks of the Mississippi, an equivalent establishment.

Source:

Charles I. Bevans, comp. *Treaties and Other Agreements of the United States of America, 1776-1949.* Washington, D.C.: Government Printing Office, 1968–76.

Mazzei Letter, 1796

Letter written by Thomas Jefferson to his Italian friend Philip Mazzei, dated April 24, 1796, and first published in translation in Florence, Italy, on January 1, 1797. It was republished in English in May of that year in the *New York Minerva*. In the letter, Jefferson, who was the leader of America's Democratic-Republican Party, attacked George Washington and other Federalists; the letter led to a permanent split between Washington and Jefferson. (Jefferson's party, known as Anti-Federalists, called themselves Republicans or Democratic-Republicans—the name *Democratic* as we know it was not affixed to it until 1828.) Jefferson described the Federalists as "an Anglican, monarchical, & aristocratic party" and their chief leaders as taken in by "heresies," with "their heads shorn by the harlot England."

To Phillip Mazzei
Monticello, Apr. 24, 1796.

My Dear Friend,—Your letter of Oct. 26, 1795, is just received and gives me the first information that the bills forwarded for you to V. S. & H. of Amsterdam on V. Anderson for 39–17–10 1/2 pounds & on George Barclay for 70–8–6 pounds both of London have been protested. I immediately write to the drawers to secure the money if still unpaid. I wonder I have never had a letter from our friends of Amsterdam on that subject as well as acknoleging the subsequent remittances. Of these I have apprised you by triplicates, but for fear of miscarriage will just mention that on Sep. 8. I forwarded them Hodgden's bill on Robinson Saunderson & Rumney of Whitehaven for 300 pounds. and Jan. 31. that of the same on the same for 137–16-6 pounds both received from mr. Blair for your stock sold out. I have now the pleasure to inform you that Dohrman has settled his account with you, has allowed the New York damage of 20. per cent for the protest, & the New York interest of 7. per cent. and after deducting the partial payments for which he held receipts the balance was three thousand & eighty-seven dollars which sum he has paid into mr. Madison's hands & as he (mr. Madison) is now in Philadelphia, I have desired him to invest the money in good bills on Amsterdam & remit them to the V. Staphorsts & H. whom I consider as possessing your confidence as they do mine beyond any house in London. The pyracies of that nation lately extended from the sea to the debts due from them to other nations renders theirs an unsafe medium to do business through. I hope these remittances will place you at your ease & I will endeavor to execute your wishes as to the settlement of the other small matters you mention: tho' from them I expect little. E. R. is bankrupt, or tantamount to it. Our friend M. P. is embarrassed, having lately sold the fine lands he lives on, & being superlatively just & honorable I expect we may get whatever may be in his hands. Lomax is under greater difficulties with less means, so that I apprehend you have little more to expect from this country except the balance which will remain for Colle after deducting the little matter due to me, & what will be recovered by Anthony. This will be decided this summer.

I have written to you by triplicates with every remittance I sent to the V. S. & H. & always recapitulated in each letter the objects of the preceding ones. I enclosed in two of them some seeds of the squash as you desired. Send me in return some seeds of the winter vetch, I mean that kind which is sewn in autumn & stands thro the cold of winter, furnishing a crop of green fodder in March. Put a few seeds in every letter you may write to me. In England only the spring vetch can be had. Pray fail not in this. I have it greatly at heart.

The aspect of our politics has wonderfully changed since you left us. In place of that noble love of liberty, & republican government which carried us triumphantly thro' the war, an Anglican monarchical, & aristocratical party has sprung up, whose avowed object is to draw over us the substance, as they have already done the forms, of the British government. The main body of our citizens, however, remain true to their republican principles; the whole landed interest is republican, and so is a great mass of talents. Against us are the Executive, the Judiciary, two out of three branches of the legislature, all the officers of the government, all who want to be officers, all timid men who prefer the calm of despotism to the boisterous sea of liberty, British merchants & Americans trading on British capitals, speculators & holders in the banks & public funds, a contrivance invented for the purposes of corruption, & for assimilating us in all things to the rotten as well as the sound parts of the British model. It would give you a fever were I to name to you the apostates who have gone over to these heresies, men who were Samsons in the field & Solomons in the council, but who have had their heads shorn by the harlot England. In short, we are likely to preserve the liberty we have obtained only by unremitting labors & perils. But we shall preserve them; and our mass of weight & wealth on the good side is so great, as to leave no danger that force will ever be attempted against us. We have only to awake and snap the Lilliputian cords with which they have been entangling us during the first sleep which succeeded our labors. I will forward the testimonial of the death of mrs. Mazzei, which I can do the more incontrovertibly as she is buried in my grave yard, and I pass her grave daily. The formalities of the proof you require, will occasion delay. John Page & his son Mann as well. The father remarried to a lady from N. York. Beverley Randolph *e la sua consorte* living & well. Their only

child married to the 2d of T. M. Randolph. The eldest son you know married my eldest daughter, is an able learned & worthy character, but kept down by ill health. They have two children & still live with me. My younger daughter well. Colo. Innis is well, & a true republican still as are all those before named. Colo. Monroe is our M. P. at Paris a most worthy patriot & honest man. These are the persons you inquire after. I begin to feel the effects of age. My health has suddenly broke down, with symptoms which give me to believe I shall not have much to encounter of the *tedium vitae*. While it remains, however, my heart will be warn in it's friendships, and among these, will always foster the affection with which I am, dear Sir, your friend and servant.

Source:
Paul Leicester Ford, ed. *The Works of Thomas Jefferson*. Vol 3. New York: G.P. Putnam's Sons. 1904–1905, pp. 235–241.

George Washington, "Farewell Address," 1796

Address to the American people, dated September 17, 1796, and published two days later in Philadelphia's *American Daily Advertiser*. In it George Washington explained his resolution not to run for a third presidential term and offered advice on national policy. The address, which was never publicly read, was prepared in part as early as 1792 and was written with the help of Alexander Hamilton. It warned against regional divisiveness and urged a strong union of the states, enumerated the dangers of a political party system, advised that the public credit be carefully preserved and wisely disbursed, and counseled for "temporary alliances for extraordinary emergencies," rather than permanent alliances with foreign nations. The document has had a great influence on American political culture.

Friends, and Fellow-Citizens: The period for a new election of a Citizen, to Administer the Executive government of the United States, being not far distant, and the time actually arrived, when your thoughts must be employed in designating the person, who is to be cloathed with that important trust, it appears to me proper, especially as it may conduce to a more distinct expression of the public voice, that I should now apprise you of the resolution I have formed, to decline being considered among the number of those, our of whom a choice is to be made.

I beg you, at the same time, to do me the justice to be assured, that this resolution has not been taken, without a strict regard to all the considerations appertaining to the relation, which binds a dutiful citizen to his country, and that, in with drawing the tender of service which silence in my situation might imply, I am influenced by no diminution of zeal for your future interest, no deficiency of grateful respect for your past kindness; but am supported by a full conviction that the step is compatible with both.

The acceptance of, and continuance hitherto in, the office to which your Suffrages have twice called me, have been a uniform sacrifice of inclination to the opinion of duty, and to a deference for what appeared to be your desire. I constantly hoped, that it would have been much earlier in my power, consistently with motives, which I was not at liberty to disregard, to return to that retirement, from which I had been reluctantly drawn. The strength of my inclination to do this, previous to the last Election, had even led to the preparation of an address to declare it to you; but mature reflection on the then perplexed and critical posture of our Affairs with foreign Nations, and the unanimous advice of persons entitled to my confidence, impelled me to abandon the idea.

I rejoice, that the state of your concerns, external as well as internal, no longer renders the pursuit of inclination incompatible with the sentiment of duty, or propriety; and am persuaded whatever partiality may be retained for my services, that in the present circumstances of our country, you will not disapprove my determination to retire.

The impressions, with which I first undertook the arduous trust, were explained on the proper occasion. In the discharge of this trust, I will only say, that I have, with good intentions, contributed towards the Organization and Administration of the government, the best exertions of which a very fallible judgment was capable. Not unconscious, in the outset, of the inferiority of my qualifications, experience in my own eyes, perhaps still more in the eyes of others, has strengthened the motives to diffidence of myself; and every day the encreasing weight of years admonishes me more and more, that the shade of retirement is as necessary to me as it will be welcome. Satisfied that if any circumstances have given peculiar value to my services, they were temporary, I have the consolation to believe, that while choice and prudence invite me to quit the political scene, patriotim does not forbid it.

In looking forward to the moment, which is intended to terminate the career of my public life, my feelings do not permit me to suspend the deep acknowledgment of that debt of gratitude wch. I owe to my beloved country, for the many honors it has conferred upon me; still more for the stedfast confidence with which it has supported me; and for the opportunities I have thence enjoyed of manifesting my inviolable attachment, by services faithful and persevering, though in usefulness unequal to my zeal. If benefits have resulted to our country from these services, let it always be remembered to your praise, and as an instructive example in our annals, that, under circum-

stances in which the Passions agitated in every direction were liable to mislead, amidst appearances sometimes dubious, viscissitudes of fortune often discouraging, in situations in which not unfrequently want of Success has countenanced the spirit of criticism, the constancy of your support was the essential prop of the efforts, and a guarantee of the plans by which they were effected. Profoundly penetrated with this idea, I shall carry it with me to my grave, as a strong incitement to unceasing vows that Heaven may continue to you the choicest tokens of its beneficence; that your Union and brotherly affection may be perpetual; that the free constitution, which is the work of your hands, may be sacredly maintained; that its Administration in every department may be stamped with wisdom and Virtue; that, in fine, the happiness of the people of these States, under the auspices of liberty, may be made complete, by so careful a preservation and so prudent a use of this blessing as will acquire to them the glory of recommending it to the applause, the affection, and adoption of every nation which is yet a stranger to it.

Here, perhaps, I ought to stop. But a solicitude for your welfare, which cannot end but with my life, and the apprehension of danger, natural to that solicitude, urge me on an occasion like the present, to offer to your solemn contemplation, and to recommend to your frequent review, some sentiments; which are the result of much reflection, of no inconsiderable observation, and which appear to me all important to the permanency of your felicity as a People. These will be offered to you with the more freedom, as you can only see in them the disinterested warnings of a parting friend, who can possibly have no personal motive to biass his counsel. Nor can I forget, as an encouragement to it, your endulgent reception of my sentiments on a former and not dissimilar occasion.

Interwoven as is the love of liberty with every ligament of your hearts, no recommendation of mine is necessary to fortify or confirm the attachment.

The Unity of Government which constitutes you one people is also now dear to you. It is justly so; for it is a main Pillar in the Edifice of your real independence, the support of your tranquility at home; your peace abroad; of your safety; of your prosperity; of that very Liberty which you so highly prize. But as it is easy to foresee, that from different causes and from different quarters, much pains will be taken, many artifices employed, to weaken in your minds the conviction of this truth; as this is the point in your political fortress against which the batteries of internal and external enemies will be most constantly and actively (though often covertly and insidiously) directed, it is of infinite moment, that you should properly estimate the immense value of your national Union to your collective and individual happiness; that you should cherish a cordial, habitual and immoveable attachment to it; accustoming yourselves to think and speak of it as of the Palladium of your political safety and prosperity; watching for its preservation with jealous anxiety; discountenancing whatever may suggest even a suspicion that it can in any event be abandoned, and indignantly frowning upon the first dawning of every attempt to alienate any portion of our Country from the rest, or to enfeeble the sacred ties which now link together the various parts.

For this you have every inducement of sympathy and interest. Citizens by birth or choice, of a common country, that country has a right to concentrate your affections. The name of American, which belongs to you, in your national capacity, must always exalt the just pride of Patriotism, more than any appellation derived from local discriminations. With slight shades of difference, you have the same Religeon, Manners, Habits and political Principles. You have in a common cause fought and triumphed together. The independence and liberty you possess are the work of joint councils, and joint efforts; of common dangers, sufferings and successes.

But these considerations, however powerfully they address themselves to your sensibility are greatly outweighed by those which apply more immediately to your Interest. Here every portion of our country finds the most commanding motives for carefully guarding and preserving the Union of the whole.

The *North,* in an unrestrained intercourse with the *South,* protected by the equal Laws of a common government, finds in the productions of the latter, great additional resources of Maratime and commercial enterprise and precious materials of manufacturing industry. The *South,* in the same Intercourse, benefitting by the Agency of the *North,* sees its agriculture grow and its commerce expand. Turning partly into its own channels the seamen of the *North,* it finds its particular navigation envigorated; and while it contributes, in different ways, to nourish and increase the general mass of the National navigation, it looks forward to the protection of a Maratime strength, to which itself is unequally adapted. The *East,* in a like intercourse with the *West,* already finds, and in the progressive improvement of interior communications, by land and water, will more and more find a valuable vent for the commodities which it brings from abroad, or manufactures at home. The *West* derives from the *East* supplies requisite to its growth and comfort, and what is perhaps of still greater consequence, it must of necessity owe the *secure* enjoyment of indispensable *outlets* for its own productions to the weight, influence, and the future Maratime strength of the Atlantic side of the Union, directed by an indissoluble community of Interest as *one Nation.* Any other tenure by which the *West* can hold this essential advantage, whether derived from its own separate strength, or from an apostate and unnatural

connection with any foreign Power, must be intrinsically precarious.

While then every part of our country thus feels an immediate and particular Interest in Union, all the parts combined cannot fail to find in the united mass of means and efforts greater strength, greater resource, proportionably greater security from external danger, a less frequent interruption of their Peace by foreign Nations; and, what is of inestimable value! they must derive from Union an exemption from those broils and Wars between themselves, which so frequently afflict neighbouring countries, not tied together by the same government; which their own rivalships alone would be sufficient to produce, but which opposite foreign alliances, attachments and intriegues would stimulate and imbitter. Hence likewise they will avoid the necessity of those overgrown Military establishments, which under any form of Government are inauspicious to liberty, and which are to be regarded as particularly hostile to Republican Liberty: In this sense it is, that your Union ought to be considered as a main prop of your liberty, and that the love of the one ought to endear to you the preservation of the other.

These considerations speak a persuasive language to every reflecting and virtuous mind, and exhibit the continuance of the Union as a primary object of Patriotic desire. Is there a doubt, whether a common government can embrace so large a sphere? Let experience solve it. To listen to mere speculation in such a case were criminal. We are authorized to hope that a proper organization of the whole, with the auxiliary agency of governments for the respective Sub divisions, will afford a happy issue to the experiment. 'Tis well worth a fair and full experiment With such powerful and obvious motives to Union, affecting all parts of our country, while experience shall not have demonstrated its impracticability, there will always be reason, to distrust the patriotism of those, who in any quarter may endeavor to weaken its bands.

In contemplating the causes wch. may disturb our Union, it occurs as matter of serious concern, that any ground should have been furnished for characterizing parties by *Geographical* discriminations: *Northern* and *Southern; Atlantic* and *Western;* whence designing men may endeavour to excite a belief that there is a real difference of local interests and views. One of the expedients of Party to acquire influence, within particular districts, is to misrepresent the opinions and aims of other Districts. You cannot shield yourselves too much against the jealousies and heart burnings which spring from these misrepresentations. They tend to render Alien to each other those who ought to be bound together by fraternal affection. The Inhabitants of our Western country have lately had a useful lesson on this head. They have seen, in the Negociation by the Executive, and in the unanimous ratification by the

Senate, of the Treaty with Spain, and in the universal satisfaction at that event, throughout the United States, a decisive proof how unfounded were the suspicions propagated among them of a policy in the General Government and in the Atlantic States unfriendly to their Interests in regard to the Mississippi. They have been witnesses to the formation of two Treaties, that with G: Britain and that with Spain, which secure to them every thing they could desire, in respect to our Foreign relations, towards confirming their prosperity. Will it not be their wisdom to rely for the preservation of [*sic*] these advantages on the Union by wch. they were procured? Will they not henceforth be deaf to those advisers, if such there are, who would sever them from their Brethren and connect them with Aliens?

To the efficacy and permanency of Your Union, a Government for the whole is indispensable. No Alliances however strict between the parts can be an adequate substitute. They must inevitably experience the infractions and interruptions which all Alliances in all times have experienced. Sensible of this momentous truth, you have improved upon your first essay, by the adoption of a Constitution of Government, better calculated than your former for an intimate Union, and for the efficacious management of your common concerns. This government, the offspring of our own choice uninfluenced and unawed, adopted upon full investigation and mature deliberation, completely free in its principles, in the distribution of its powers, uniting security with energy, and containing within itself a provision for its own amendment, has a just claim to your confidence and your support. Respect for its authority, compliance with its Laws, acquiescence in its measures, are duties enjoined by the fundamental maxims of true Liberty. The basis of our political systems is the right of the people to make and to alter their Constitutions of Government. But the Constitution which at any time exists, 'till changed by an explicit and authentic act of the whole People, is sacredly obligatory upon all. The very idea of the power and the right of the People to establish Government presupposes the duty of every Individual to obey the established Government.

All obstructions to the execution of the Laws, all combinations and Associations, under whatever plausible character, with the real design to direct, controul counteract, or awe the regular deliberation and action of the Constituted authorities are distructive of this fundamental principle and of fatal tendency. They serve to organize faction, to give it an artificial and extraordinary force; to put in the place of the delegated will of the Nation, the will of a party; often a small but artful and enterprizing minority of the Community; and, according to the alternate triumphs of different parties, to make the public administration the Mirror of the ill concerted and incongruous projects of faction, rather than the organ of consistent and wholesome

plans digested by common councils and modefied by mutual interests. However combinations or Associations of the above description may now and then answer popular ends, they are likely, in the course of time and things, to become potent engines, by which cunning, ambitious and unprincipled men will be enabled to subvert the Power of the People, and to usurp for themselves the reins of Government; destroying afterwards the very engines which have lifted them to unjust dominion.

Towards the preservation of your Government and the permanency of your present happy state, it is requisite, not only that you steadily discountenance irregular oppositions to its acknowledged authority, but also that you resist with care the spirit of innovation upon its principles however specious the pretexts, one method of assault may be to effect, in the forms of the Constitution, alterations which will impair the energy of the system, and thus to undermine what cannot be directly overthrown. In all the changes to which you may be invited, remember that time and habit are at least as necessary to fix the true character of Governments, as of other human institutions; that experience is the surest standard, by which to test the real tendency of the existing Constitution of a country; that facility in changes upon the credit of mere hypotheses and opinion express to perpetual change, from the endless variety of hypotheses and opinion: and remember, especially, that for the efficient management of your common interests, in a country so extensive as ours, a Government of as much vigour as is consistent with the perfect security of Liberty is indispensable. Liberty itself will find in such a Government, with powers properly distributed and adjusted, its surest Guardian. It is indeed little else than a name, where the Government is too feeble to withstand the enterprises of faction, to confine each member of the Society within the limits prescribed by the laws and to maintain all in the secure and tranquil enjoyment of the rights of person and property.

I have already intimated to you the danger of Parties in the State, with particular reference to the founding of them on Geographical discriminations. Let me now take a more comprehensive view, and warn you in the most solemn manner against the baneful effects of the spirit of Party, generally this spirit, unfortunately, is inseperable from our nature, having its root in the strongest passions of the human Mind. It exists under different shapes in all Governments, more or less stifled, controuled, or repressed; but, in those of the popular form it is seen in its greatest rankness and is truly their worst enemy.

The alternate domination of one faction over another, sharpened by the spirit of revenge natural to party dissention, which in different ages and countries has perpetrated the most horrid enormities, is itself a frightful despotism. But this leads at length to a more formal and permanent despotism. The disorders and miseries, which result, gradually incline the minds of men to seek security and repose in the absolute power of an Individual: and sooner or later the chief of some prevailing faction more able or more fortunate than his competitors, turns this disposition to the purposes of his own elevation, on the ruins of Public Liberty.

Without looking forward to an extremity of this kind (which nevertheless ought not to be entirely out of sight) the common and continual mischiefs of the spirit of Party are sufficient to make it the interest and the duty of a wise People to discourage and restrain it.

It serves always to distract the Public Councils and enfeeble the Public Administration. It agitates the Community with ill founded jealousies and false alarms, kindles the animosity of one part against another, foments occasionally riot and insurrection. It opens the door to foreign influence and corruption, which find a facilitated access to the government itself through the channels of party passions. Thus the policy and and the will of the country, are subjected to the policy and will of another.

There is an opinion that parties in free countries are useful checks upon the Administration of the Government and serve to keep alive the spirit of Liberty. This within certain limits is probably true, and in Governments of a Monarchial cast Patriotism may look with endulgence, if not with favour, upon the spirit of party. But in those of the popular character, in Governments purely elective, it is a spirit not to be encouraged. From their natural tendency, it is certain there will always be enough of that spirit for every salutary purpose. And there being constant danger of excess, the effort ought to be, by force of public opinion, to mitigate and assuage it. A fire not to be quenched; it demands a uniform vigilance to prevent its bursting into a flame, lest instead of warming it should consume.

It is important, likewise that the habits of thinking in a free Country should inspire caution in those entrusted with its administration, to confine themselves within their respective Constitutional spheres; avoiding in the exercise of the Powers of one department to encroach upon another. The spirit of encroachment tends to consolidate the powers of all the departments in one, and thus to create whatever the form of government, a real despotism. A just estimate of that love of power, and proneness to abuse it, which predominates in the human heart if sufficient to satisfy us of the truth of this position. The necessity of reciprocal checks in the exercise of political power; by dividing and distributing it into different depositaries, and constituting each the Guardian of the Public Weal against invasions by the others, has been evinced by experiments ancient and modern; some of them in our country and under our own eyes. To preserve them must be as necessary as to institute them. If in the opinion of the People, the distribution or modification of the Constitutional pow-

ers be in any particular wrong, let it be corrected by an amendment in the way which the Constitution designates. But let there be no change by usurpation; for though this, in one instance, may be the instrument of good, it is the customary weapon by which free governments are destroyed. The precedent must always greatly overbalance in permanent evil any partial or transient benefit which the use at any time yield.

Of all the dispositions and habits which lead to political prosperity, Religion and morality are indispensable supports. In vain would that man claim the tribute of Patriotism, who should labour to subvert these great Pillars of human happiness, these firmest props of the duties of Men and citizens. The mere Politician, equally with the pious man ought to respect and to cherish them. A volume could not trace all their connections with private and public felicity. Let it simply be asked where is the security for property, for reputation, for life, if the sense of religious obligation *desert* the oaths, which are the instruments of investigation in Courts of Justice? And let us with caution indulge the supposition, that morality can be maintained without religion. Whatever may be conceded to the influence of refined education on minds of peculiar structure, reason and experience both forbid us to expect that National morality can prevail in exclusion of religious principle.

'Tis substantially true, that virtue or morality is a necessary spring of popular government. The rule indeed extends with more or less force to every species of free Government. Who that is a sincere friend to it, can look with indifference upon attempts to shake the foundation of the fabric.

Promote then as an object of primary importance, Institutions for the general diffusion of knowledge. In proportion as the structure of a government gives force to public opinion, it is essential that public opinion should be enlightened.

As a very important source of strength and security, cherish public credit. One method of preserving it is to use it as sparingly as possible: avoiding occasions of expence by cultivating peace, but remembering also that timely disbursements to prepare for danger frequently prevent much greater disbursements to repel it; avoiding likewise the accumulation of debt, not only by shunning occasions of expence, but by vigorous exertions in time of Peace to discharge the Debts which unavoidable wars may have occasioned, not ungenerously throwing upon posterity the burthen which we ourselves ought to bear. The execution of these maxims belongs to your Representatives, but it is necessary that public opinion should cooperate. To facilitate to them the performance of their duty, it is essential that you should practically bear in mind, that towards the payment of debts there must be Revenue; that to have Revenue there must be taxes; that no taxes can be devised which are not more or less inconvenient and unpleasant; that the intrinsic embarrassment inseperable from the selection of the proper objects (which is always a choice of difficulties) ought to be a decisive motive for a candid construction of the Conduct of the Government in making it, and for a spirit of acquiescence in the measures for obtaining Revenue which the public exigencies may at any time dictate.

Observe good faith and justice towds. all Nations. Cultivate peace and harmony with all. Religion and morality enjoin this conduct; and can it be that good policy does not equally enjoin it? It will be worthy of a free, enlightened, and, at no distant period, a great Nation, to give to mankind the magnanimous and too novel example of a People always guided by an exalted justice and benevolence. Who can doubt that in the course of time and things the fruits of such a plan would richly repay and temporary advantages wch. might be lost by a steady adherence to it? Can it be, that Providence has not connected the permanent felicity of a Nation with its virtue? The experiment, at least, is recommended by every sentiment which ennobles human Nature. Alas! is it rendered impossible by its vices?

In the execution of such a plan nothing is more essential than that permanent, inveterate antipathies against particular Nations and passionate attachments for others should be excluded; and that in place of them just and amicable feelings towards all should be cultivated. The Nation, which indulges towards another an habitual hatred, or an habitual fondness, is in some degree a slave. It is a slave to its animosity or to its affection, either of which is sufficient to lead it astray from its duty and its interest. Antipathy in one Nation against another, disposes each more readily to offer insult and injury, to lay hold of slight causes of umbrage, and to be haughty and intractable, when accidental or trifling occasions of dispute occur. Hence frequent collisions, obstinate envenomed and bloody contests. The Nation, prompted by illwill and resentment sometimes impels to War the Government, contrary to the best calculations of policy. The Government sometimes participates in the national propensity, and adopts through passion what reason would reject; at other times, it makes the animosity of the Nation subservient to projects of hostility instigated by pride, ambition and other sinister and pernicious motives. The peace often, sometimes perhaps the Liberty, of Nations has been the victim.

So likewise, a passionate attachment of one Nation for another produces a variety of evils. Sympathy for the favourite nation, facilitating the illusion of an imaginary common interest, in cases where no real common interest exists, and infusing into one the enmities of the other, betrays the former into a participation in the quarrels and Wars of the latter, without adequate inducement or justification: It leads also to concessions to the favourite Nation

of priviledges denied to others, which is apt doubly to injure the Nation making the concessions; by unnecessarily parting with what ought to have been retained; and by exciting jealousy, ill will, and a disposition to retaliate, in the parties from whom eql. privileges are withheld: And it gives to ambitious, corrupted, or deluded citizens (who devote themselves to the favourite Nation) facility to betray, or sacrifice the interests of their own country, without odium, sometimes even with popularity; gilding with the appearances of a virtuous sense of obligation a commendable deference for public opinion, or a laudable zeal for public good, the base or foolish compliances of ambition corruption or infatuation.

As avenues to foreign influence in innumerable ways, such attachments are particularly alarming to the truly enlightened and independent Patriot. How many opportunities do they afford to tamper with domestic factions, to practice the arts of seduction, to mislead public opinion, to influence or awe the public Councils! Such an attachment of a small or weak, towards a great and powerful Nation, dooms the former to be the satellite of the latter.

Against the insidious wiles of foreign influence, (I conjure you to believe me fellow citizens) the jealousy of a free people ought to be *constantly* awake; since history and experience prove that foreign influence is one of the most baneful foes of Republican Government. But that jealousy to be useful must be impartial; else it becomes the instrument of the very influence to be avoided, instead of a defence against it. Excessive partiality for one foreign nation and excessive dislike of another, cause those whom they actuate to see danger only on one side, and serve to veil and even second the arts of influence on the other. Real Patriots, who may resist the intriegues of the favourite, are liable to become suspected and odious; while its tools and dupes usurp the applause and confidence of the people, to surrender their interests.

The Great rule of conduct for us, in regard to foreign Nations is in extending our commercial relations to have with them as little *political* connection as possible. So far as we have already formed engagements let them be fulfilled, with perfect good faith. Here let us stop.

Europe has a set of primary interests, which to us have none, or a very remote relation. Hence she must be engaged in frequent controversies, the causes of which are essentially foreign to our concerns. Hence therefore it must be unwise in us to implicate ourselves, by artificial ties, in the ordinary vicissitudes of her politics, or the ordinary combinations and collisions of her friendships, or enmities:

Our detached and distant situation invites and enables us to pursue a different course. If we remain one People, under an efficient government, the period is not far off, when we may defy material injury from external annoyance; when we may take such an attitude as will cause the neutrality we may at any time resolve upon to be scrupulously respected; when belligerent nations, under the impossibility of making acquisitions upon us, will not lightly hazard the giving us provocation; when we may choose peace or war, as our interest guided by our justice shall Counsel.

Why forego the advantages of so peculiar a situation? Why quit our own to stand upon foreign ground? Why, by interweaving our destiny with that of any part of Europe, entangle our peace and prosperity in the toils of European Ambition, Rivalship, Interest, Humour or Caprice?

'Tis our true policy to steer clear of permanent Alliances, with any portion of the foreign world. So far, I mean, as we are now at liberty to do it, for let me not be understood as capable of patronising infidility to existing engagements (I hold the maxim no less applicable to public than to private affairs, that honesty is always the best policy). I repeat it therefore, let those engagements be observed in their genuine sense. But in my opinion, it is unnecessary and would be unwise to extend them.

Taking care always to keep ourselves, by suitable establishments, on a respectably defensive posture, we may safely trust to temporary alliances for extraordinary emergencies.

Harmony, liberal intercourse with all Nations, are recommended by policy, humanity and interest. But even our Commercial policy should hold an equal and impartial hand: neither seeking nor granting exclusive favours or preferences; consulting the natural course of things; diffusing and deversifying by gentle means the streams of Commerce, but forcing nothing; establishing with Powers so disposed; in order to give to trade a stable course, to define the rights of our Merchants, and to enable the Government to support them; conventional rules of intercourse, the best that present circumstances and mutual opinion will permit, but temporary, and liable to be from time to time abandoned or varied, as experience and circumstances shall dictate; constantly keeping in view, that 'tis folly in one Nation to look for disinterested favors from another; that it must pay with a portion of its Independence for whatever it may accept under that character; that by such acceptance, it may place itself in the condition of having given equivalents for nominal favours and yet of being reproached with ingratitude for not giving more. There can be no greater error than to expect, or calculate upon real favours from Nation to Nation. 'Tis an illusion which experience must cure, which a just pride ought to discard.

In offering to you, my Countrymen these counsels of an old and affectionate friend, I dare not hope they will make the strong and lasting impression, I could wish; that they will controul the usual current of the passions, or pre-

vent our Nation from running the course which has hitherto marked the Destiny of Nations: But if I may even flatter myself, that they may be productive of some partial benefit, some occasional good; that they may now and then recur to moderate the fury of party spirit, to warn against the mischiefs of foreign Intriegue, to guard against the Impostures of pretended patriotism; this hope will be a full recompence for the solicitude for your welfare, by which they have been dictated.

How far in the discharge of my Official duties, I have been guided by the principles which have been delineated, the public Records and other evidences of my conduct must Witness to You and to the world. To myself, the assurance of my own conscience is, that I have at least believed myself to be guided by them.

In relation to the still subsisting War in Europe, my Proclamation of the 22d. of April 1793 is the index to my Plan. Sanctioned by your approving voice and by that of Your Representatives in both Houses of Congress, the spirit of that measure has continually governed me; uninfluenced by any attempts to deter or diver me from it.

After deliberate examination with the aid of the best lights I could obtain I was well satisfied that our Country, under all the circumstances of the case, had a right to take, and was bound in duty and interest, to take a Neutral position. Having taken it, I determined, as far as should depend upon me, to maintain it, with moderation, perseverence and firmness.

The considerations, which respect the right to hold this conduct, it is not necessary on this occasion to detail. I will only observe, that according to my understanding of the matter, that right, so far from being denied by any of the Belligerent Powers has been virtually admitted by all.

The duty of holding a Neutral conduct may be inferred, without any thing more, from the obligation which justice and humanity impose on every Nation, in cases in which it is free to act, to maintain inviolate the relations of Peace and amity towards other Nations.

The inducements of interests for observing that conduct will best be referred to your own reflections and experience. With me, a predominant motive has been to endeavour to gain time to our country to settle and mature its yet recent institutions, and to progress without interruption, to that degree of strength and consistency, which is necessary to give it, humanly speaking, the command of its own fortunes.

Though in reviewing the incidents of my Administration, I am unconscious of international error, I am nevertheless too sensible of my defects not to think it probable that I may have committed many errors. Whatever they may be I fervently beseech the Almighty to avert or mitigate the evils to which they may tend. I shall also carry with me the hope that my Country will never cease to view them with indulgence; and that after forty five years of my life dedicated to its Service, with an upright zeal, the faults of incompetent abilities will be consigned to oblivion, as myself must soon be to the Mansions of rest.

Relying on its kindness in this as in other things, and actuated by that fervent love towards it, which is so natural to a Man, who views in it the native soil of himself and his progenitors for several Generations; I anticipate with pleasing expectation that retreat, in which I promise myself to realize, without alloy, the sweet enjoyment of partaking, in the midst of my fellow Citizens, the benign influence of good Laws under a free Government, the ever favourite object of my heart, and the happy reward, as I trust, of our mutual cares, labours and dangers.

See also GEORGE WASHINGTON, FIRST INAUGURAL ADDRESS, 1789.

Source:
John C. Fitzpatrick, ed. *The Writings of George Washington.* Vol. 35. Westport, Conn.: Greenwood Press, 1970, pp. 214–238.

Petition of Emancipated Slaves to North Carolina Congress, 1797

Petition to Congress by four emancipated slaves requesting that they be allowed to live in North Carolina. In 1788 North Carolina instituted a law that required manumitted slaves—those freed by their owners—to leave the state or face re-enslavement. Four former slaves—Jacob Nicholson, Jupiter Nicholson, Job Albert, and Thomas Pritchet—all of whom had been manumitted, were forced to flee the state. In 1797 they submitted this petition to Congress requesting that they be allowed to return. In their appeal, they stated that armed men chased them from their North Carolina homes and forced their family members back into slavery. This is the first known petition by African Americans to Congress. It may have been written by Absalom Jones, founder of the Free African Society and the African Methodist Episcopal Church.

To the President, Senate, and House of Representatives.

The Petition and Representation of the under-named Freemen, respectfully showeth: —

That, being of African descent, late inhabitants and natives of North Carolina, to you only, under God, can we apply with any hope of effect, for redress of our grievances, having been compelled to leave the State wherein we had a right of residence, as freemen liberated under the hand and seal of humane and conscientious masters, the validity of which act of justice in restoring us to our native right of

freedom, was confirmed by judgment of the Superior Court of North Carolina, wherein it was brought to trial; yet, not long after this decision, a law of that State was enacted, under which men of cruel disposition, and void of just principle, received countenance and authority in violently seizing, imprisoning, and selling into slavery, such as had been so emancipated; whereby we were reduced to the necessity of separating from some of our nearest and most tender connexions, and of seeking refuge in such parts of the Union where more regard is paid to the public declaration in favor of liberty and the common right of man, several hundreds, under our circumstances, having, in consequence of the said law, been hunted day and night, like beasts of the forest, by armed men with dogs, and made a prey of as free and lawful plunder. Among others thus exposed, I, Jupiter Nicholson, of Perquimans county, North Carolina, after being set free by my master, Thomas Nicholson, and having been about two years employed as a seaman in the service of Zachary Nickson, on coming on shore, was pursued by men with dogs and arms; but was favored to escape by night to Virginia, with my wife, who was manumitted by Gabriel Cosan, where I resided about four years in the town of Portsmouth, chiefly employed in sawing boards and scantling; from thence I removed with my wife to Philadelphia, where I have been employed, at times, by water, working along shore, or sawing wood. I left behind me a father and mother, who were manumitted by Thomas Nicholson and Zachary Dickson; they have been since taken up, with a beloved brother, and sold into cruel bondage.

I, Jacob Nicholson, also of North Carolina, being set free by my master, Joseph Nicholson, but continuing to live with him till, being pursued day and night, I was obliged to leave my abode, sleep in the woods, and stacks in the fields, &c., to escape the hands of violent men who, induced by the profit afforded them by law, followed this course as a business; at length, by night, I made by escape, leaving a mother, one child, and two brothers, to see whom I dare not return.

I, Job Albert, manumitted by Benjamin Albertson, who was my careful guardian to protect me from being afterwards taken and sold, providing me with a house to accommodate me and my wife, who was liberated by William Robertson; but we were night and day hunted by men armed with guns, swords, and pistols, accompanied with mastiff dogs; from whose violence, being one night apprehensive of immediate danger, I left my dwelling, locked and barred, and fastened with a chain, being at some distance from it, while my wife was by my kind master locked up under his roof. I heard them break into my house, where, not finding their prey, they got but a small booty, a handkerchief of about a dollar value, and some provisions; but, not long after, I was discovered and seized by Alexander Stafford, William Stafford, and Thomas Creesy, who were armed with guns and clubs. After binding me with my hands behind me, and a rope round my arms and body, they took me about four miles to Hartford prison, where I lay four weeks, suffering much for want of provision; from thence, with the assistance of a fellow-prisoner, (a white man,) I made my escape, and for three dollars was conveyed, with my wife, by a humane person, in a covered wagon by night, to Virginia, where, in the neighborhood of Portsmouth, I continued unmolested about four years, being chiefly engaged in sawing boards and plank. On being advised to move Northward, I came with my wife to Philadelphia, where I have labored for a livelihood upwards of two years, in Summer mostly along shore in vessels and stores, and sawing wood in the Winter. My mother was set free by Phineas Nickson, my sister by John Trueblood, and both taken up and sold into slavery, myself deprived of the consolation of seeing them, without being exposed to the like grievous oppression.

I, Thomas Pritchet, was set free by my master Thomas Pritchet, who furnished me with land to raise provisions for my use, where I built myself a house, cleared a sufficient spot of woodland to produce ten bushels of corn; the second year about fifteen, and the third, had as much planted as I suppose would have produced thirty bushels; this I was obliged to leave about one month before it was fit for gathering, being threatened by Holland Lockwood, who married my said master's widow, that if I would not come and serve him, he would apprehend me, and send me to the West Indies; Enoch Ralph also threatening to send me to jail, and sell me for the good of the country: being thus in jeopardy, I left my little farm, with my small stock and utensils, and my corn standing, and escaped by night into Virginia, where shipping myself for Boston, I was, through stress of weather landed in New York, where I served as a waiter for seventeen months; but my mind being distressed on account of the situation of my wife and children, I returned to Norfolk in Virginia, with a hope of at least seeing them, if I could not obtain their freedom; but finding I was advertised in the newspaper, twenty dollars the reward for apprehending me, my dangerous situation obliged me to leave Virginia, disappointed of seeing my wife and children, coming to Philadelphia, where I resided in the employment of a waiter upward of two years.

In addition to the hardship of our own case, as above set forth, we believe ourselves warranted, on the present occasion, in offering to your consideration the singular case of a fellow-black now confined in the jail of this city, under sanction of the act of General Government, called the Fugitive Law, as it appears to us a flagrant proof how far human beings, merely on account of color and complexion, are, through prevailing prejudice, outlawed and excluded from common justice and common humanity, by the operation of such partial laws in support of habits and customs cruelly oppressive. This man, having been many years past manumitted by his master in North Carolina, was under the authority of the aforementioned law of that State, sold again into slavery, and, after having served his purchaser upwards of six years, made his escape to Philadelphia, where he has resided eleven years, having a wife and four children; and, by an agent of the Carolina claimer, has been lately apprehended and committed to prison, his said claimer, soon after the man's escaping from him, having advertised him, offering a reward of ten silver dollars to any person that would bring him back, or five times that sum to any person that would make due proof of his being killed, and no questions asked by whom.

We beseech your impartial attention to our hard condition, not only with respect to our personal sufferings, as freemen, but as a class of that people who, distinguished by color, are therefore with a degrading partiality, considered by many, even of those in eminent stations, as unentitled to that public justice and protection which is the great object of Government. We indulge not a hope, or presume to ask for the interposition of your honorable body, beyond the extent of your Constitutional power or influence, yet are willing to believe your serious, disinterested, and candid consideration of the premises, under the benign impressions of equity and mercy, producing upright exertion of what is in your power, may not be without some salutary effect, both for our relief as a people, and towards the removal of obstructions to public order and well-being.

If, notwithstanding all that has been publicly avowed as essential principles respecting the extent of human right to freedom; notwithstanding we have had that right restored to us, so far as was in the power of those by whom we were held as slaves, we cannot claim the privilege of representation in your councils, yet we trust we may address you as fellow-men, who, under God, the sovereign Ruler of the Universe, are intrusted with the distribution of justice, for the terror of evil-doers, the encouragement and protection of the innocent, not doubting that you are men of liberal minds, susceptible of benevolent feelings and clear conception of rectitude to a catholic extent, who can admit that black people (service as their condition generally is throughout this Continent) have natural affections, social and domestic attachments and sensibilities; and that, therefore, we may hope for a share in your sympathetic attention while we represent that the unconstitutional bondage in which multitudes of our fellows in complexion are held, is to us a subject sorrowfully affecting; for we cannot conceive their condition (more especially those who have been emancipated and tasted the sweets of liberty, and again reduced to slavery by kidnappers and man-stealers) to be less afflicting or deplorable than the situation of citizens of the United States, captured and enslaved through the unrighteous policy prevalent in Algiers. We are far from considering all those who retain slaves as wilful oppressors, being well assured that numbers in the State from whence we are exiles, hold their slaves in bondage, not of choice, but possessing them by inheritance, feel their minds burdened under the slavish restraint of legal impediments to doing that justice which they are convinced is due to fellow-rationals. May we not be allowed to consider this stretch of power, morally and politically, a Government defect, if not a direct violation of the declared fundamental principles of the Constitution; and finally, is not some remedy for an evil of such magnitude highly worthy of the deep inquiry and unfeigned zeal of the supreme Legislative body of a free and enlightened people? Submitting our cause to God, and humbly craving your best aid and influence, as you may be favored and directed by that wisdom which is from above, wherewith that you may be eminently dignified and rendered conspicuously, in the view of nations, a blessing to the people you represent, is the sincere prayer of your petitioners.

Source:

African-American History and Culture. CD-ROM. Facts On File, 1999.

Alien and Sedition Acts of 1798

These acts, seen today as early challenges to the Bill of Rights, constituted a Federalist response to Democratic-Republican (Jeffersonian) sympathies to France.

Alien Act of 1798

Federal legislation enacted on June 25, 1798, that authorized the president to order the deportation from the United States of all aliens deemed dangerous to the public peace and safety or reasonably suspected of "treasonable or secret machinations against the government." Failure to obey such an order was punishable by imprisonment and loss of the possibility of U.S. citizenship. The Alien Act frightened many foreigners into leaving the country, although it was not enforced. The law expired in 1800 and was not renewed. On July 6, 1798, Congress authorized the U.S. president, in the Alien Enemies Act of 1798, in times of declared war, to arrest, imprison, and remove all male citizens or subjects of the hostile nation aged 14 years or older.

The Naturalization Act of 1798, enacted on June 18, 1798, changed the required period of residence for admission to U.S. citizenship established in the Naturalization Act of 1795 (enacted January 29, 1795) from five to 14 years. Aliens also had to declare their intention five years before they applied for citizenship. As one of the Alien and Sedition Acts, this law postponed citizenship, and thus voting privileges, for European refugees who tended to support the Jeffersonian Republicans. The act was repealed by the Republicans in 1802, when the U.S. Naturalization Act of 1795 was reinstated. The 1795 act modified a 1790 naturalization law, which required only two years of residence, because increasing unrest in Europe led some Americans to fear an influx of aristocratic political refugees from France. This act allowed free white aliens who complied with the residency requirement to become citizens if they swore to uphold the U.S. Constitution, showed themselves to be of good character, and renounced all hereditary titles and foreign allegiance.

An Act *Concerning Aliens*

Section 1. *Be it enacted by the Senate and House of Representatives of the United States of America in Congress assembled,* That it shall be lawful for the President of the United States at any time during the continuance of this act, to *order* all such *aliens* as he shall judge dangerous to the peace and safety of the United States, or shall have reasonable grounds to suspect are concerned in any treasonable or secret machinations against the government thereof, to depart out of the territory of the United States, within such time as shall be expressed in such order, which order shall be served on such alien by delivering him a copy thereof, or leaving the same at his usual abode, and returned to the office of the Secretary of State, by the marshal or other person to whom the same shall be directed. And in case any alien, so ordered to depart, shall be found at large within the United States after the time limited in such order for his departure, and not having obtained a *license* from the President to reside therein, or having obtained such *license* shall not have conformed thereto, every such alien shall, on conviction thereof, be imprisoned for a term not exceeding three years, and shall never after be admitted to become a citizen of the United States. *Provided always, and be it further enacted,* that if any alien so ordered to depart shall prove to the satisfaction of the President, by evidence to be taken before such person or persons as the President shall direct, who are for that purpose hereby authorized to administer oaths, that no injury or danger to the United States will arise from suffering such alien to reside therein, the President may grant a *license* to such alien to remain within the United States for such time as he shall judge proper, and at such place as he may designate. And the President may also require of such alien to enter into a bond to the United States, in such penal sum as he may direct, with one or more sufficient sureties to the satisfaction of the person authorized by the President to take the same, conditioned for the good behavior of such alien during his residence in the United States, and not violating his license, which license the President may revoke, whenever he shall think proper.

Sec. 2. *And be it further enacted,* That it shall be lawful for the President of the United States, whenever he may deem it necessary for the public safety, to order to be removed out of the territory thereof, any alien who may or shall be in prison in pursuance of this act; and to cause to be arrested and sent out of the United States such of those aliens as shall have been ordered to depart therefrom and shall not have obtained a license as aforesaid, in all cases where, in the opinion of the President, the public safety requires a speedy removal. And if any alien so removed or sent out of the United States by the President shall voluntarily return thereto, unless by permission of the President of the United States, such alien on conviction thereof, shall be imprisoned so long as, in the opinion of the President, the public safety may require.

Sec. 3. *And be it further enacted,* That every master or commander of any ship or vessel which shall come into any port of the United States after the first day of July next, shall immediately on his arrival make report in writing to the collector or other chief officer of the customs of such report, of all aliens, if any, on board his vessel, specifying their names, age, the place of nativity, the country from which they shall have come, the nation to which they belong and owe allegiance, their occupation and a description of their persons, as far as he shall be informed thereof, and on failure, every such master and commander shall forfeit and pay three hundred dollars, for the payment whereof on default of such master or commander, such vessel shall also be holden, and may by such collector or other officer of the customs be detained. And it shall be the duty of such collector or other officer of the customs, forthwith to transmit to the office of the department of state true copies of all such returns.

Sec. 4. *And be it further enacted,* That the circuit and district courts of the United States, shall respectively have cognizance of all crimes and offences against this act. And all marshals and other officers of the United States are required to execute all precepts and orders of the President of the United States issued in pursuance or by virtue of this act.

Sec. 5. *And be it further enacted,* That it shall be lawful for any alien who may be ordered to be removed from the United States, by virtue of this act, to take with him such part of his goods, chattels, or other property, as he may find convenient; and all property left in the United States by any alien, who may be removed, as aforesaid, shall be, and remain subject to his order and disposal, in the same manner as if this act had not been passed.

Sec. 6. *And be it further enacted,* That this act shall continue and be in force for and during the term of two years from the passing thereof.

Source:

Statutes at Large of the United States of America, 1789–1873. 17 vols. Washington, D.C., 1850–73. Vol. 4, pp. 570–572.

Sedition Act of 1798

U.S. federal legislation enacted on July 14, 1798, that gave the U.S. government broad powers to repress treasonable activities. One of the U.S. Alien and Sedition Acts of 1798, it prohibited citizens or aliens from conspiring against the operation of federal laws; from preventing federal officials from executing their duties; and from aiding any insurrection, riot, or unlawful assembly. It outlawed the publication of any "false, scandalous and malicious writing" against the government and any effort to incite opposition to the government. Twenty-five Anti-Federalist editors or printers were arrested, and 10 were convicted under this law. Opposition to the act, expressed in the Virginia Resolutions and the Kentucky Resolutions, led to the decline of the Federalist Party. The act expired in 1801.

An Act

In addition to the act, entitled "An act for the punishment of certain crimes against the United States."

Section 1. *Be it enacted by the Senate and House of Representatives of the United States of America, in Congress assembled,* That if any persons shall unlawfully combine or conspire together, with intent to oppose any measure or measures of the government of the United States, which are or shall be directed by proper authority, or to impede the operation of any law of the United States, or to intimidate or prevent any person holding a place or office in or under the government of the United States, from undertaking, performing or executing his trust or duty; and if any person or persons, with intent as aforesaid, shall counsel, advise or attempt to procure any insurrection, riot, unlawful assembly, or combination, whether such conspiracy, threatening, counsel, advise, or attempt shall have the proposed effect or not, he or they shall be deemed guilty of a high misdemeanor, and on conviction, before any court of the United States having jurisdiction thereof, shall be punished by a fine not exceeding five thousand dollars, and by imprisonment during a term not less than six months nor exceeding five years; and further, at the discretion of the court may be holden to find sureties for his good behaviour in such sum, and for such time, as the said court may direct.

Sec. 2. *And be it further enacted,* That if any person shall write, print, utter or publish, or shall cause or procure to be written, printed, uttered or published, or shall knowingly and willingly assist or aid in writing, printing, uttering or publishing any false, scandalous and malicious writing or writings against the government of the United States, or either house of the Congress of the United States, or the President of the United States, with intent to defame the said government, or either house of the said Congress, or the said President, or to bring them, or either of them, into contempt or disrepute; or to excite against them, or either or any of them, the hatred of the good people of the United States, or to stir up sedition within the United States, or to excite any unlawful combinations therein, for opposing or resisting any law of the United States, or any of the President of the United States, done in pursuance of any such law, or of the powers in him vested by the constitution of the United States, or to resist, oppose, or defeat any such law or act, or to aid, encourage or abet any hostile designs of any foreign nation against the United States, their people or government, then such person, being thereof convicted before any court of the United States having jurisdiction thereof, shall be punished by a fine not exceeding two thousand dollars, and by imprisonment not exceeding two years.

Sec. 3. *And be it further enacted and declared,* That if any person shall be prosecuted under this act, for the writing or publishing any libel aforesaid, it shall be lawful for the defendant, upon the trial of the cause, to give in evidence in his defence, the truth of the matter contained in the publication charged as a libel. And the jury who shall try the cause, shall have a right to determine the law and the fact, under the direction of the court, as in other cases.

Sec. 4. *And be it further enacted,* That this act shall continue and be in force until the third day of March, one thousand eight hundred and one, and no longer: *Provided,* that the expiration of the act shall not prevent or defeat a prosecution and punishment of any offence against the law, during the time it shall be in force.

Source:
Statutes at Large of the United States of America, 1789–1873. 17 vols. Washington, D.C., 1850–73. Vol. 4, pp. 596–597.

Kentucky and Virginia Resolutions, 1798, 1799

Thomas Jefferson drafted the resolutions passed by the Kentucky legislature on November 16, 1798, that declared the U.S. Alien and Sedition Acts to be unconstitutional and that expressed a strict constructionist view of the U.S. Constitution,

limiting the power of the national government. They outlined the belief that the federal government represented a "compact between the states" and that when the national government exercised powers not specifically granted it by the Constitution, each state had "an equal right to judge for itself" and to determine the mode of redress.

James Madison drafted the resolutions against the U.S. Alien and Sedition Acts of 1798 adopted by the Virginia legislature on December 24, 1798; they declared these acts to be unconstitutional and appealed to the other states to make similar declarations. Like the 1798 Kentucky Resolutions, the Virginia document expressed loyalty to the Union and urged Congress to repeal the acts. It also claimed that the federal government represented a "compact" between the states and therefore held only those powers specifically delegated to it by the states; passage of the Alien and Sedition Acts exceeded those powers.

Jefferson amplified these resolutions in 1799. The Kentucky legislature passed them unanimously February 22, 1799. They reaffirmed the state's position in the 1798 Kentucky Resolutions, which concerned the Alien and Sedition Acts. However, the 1799 resolutions added that the states had the right to judge infractions of the U.S. Constitution and to nullify federal actions that they believed to be in violation of the Constitution. These resolutions were passed after several northern states opposed the principles expressed in the 1798 document and declared the federal judiciary, rather than the states, to be the judge of constitutionality. Though Congress took no action, the resolutions contributed to the defeat of the Federalist Party in the election of 1800.

Virginia Resolutions of 1798

Resolved, That the General Assembly of Virginia doth unequivocally express a firm resolution to maintain and defend the Constitution of the United States, and the Constitution of this state, against every aggression either foreign or domestic; and that they will support the Government of the United States in all measures warranted by the former.

That this Assembly most solemnly declares a warm attachment to the union of the states, to maintain which it pledges all its powers; and that, for this end, it is their duty to watch over and oppose every infraction of those principles which constitute the only basis of that Union, because a faithful observance of them can alone secure its existence and the public happiness.

That this Assembly doth explicitly and peremptorily declare that it views the powers of the Federal Government as resulting from the compact to which the states are parties, as limited by the plain sense and intention of the instrument constituting that compact; as no further valid than they are authorized by the grants enumerated in that compact; and that, in case of a deliberate, palpable, and dangerous exercise of other powers not granted by the said compact, the states, who are parties thereto, have the right and are in duty bound to interpose for arresting the progress of the evil, and for maintaining within their respective limits the authorities, rights, and liberties appertaining to them.

That the General Assembly doth also express its deep regret, that a spirit has in sundry instances been manifested by the Federal Government to enlarge its powers by forced constructions of the constitutional charter which defines them; and that indications have appeared of a design to expound certain general phrases (which, having been copied from the very limited grant of powers in the former Articles of Confederation, were the less liable to be misconstrued) so as to destroy the meaning and effect of the particular enumeration which necessarily explains and limits the general phrases; and so as to consolidate the states, by degrees, into one sovereignty, the obvious tendency and inevitable consequence of which would be to transform the present republican system of the United States into an absolute, or, at best, a mixed monarchy.

That the General Assembly doth particularly Protest against the palpable and alarming infractions of the Constitution in the two late cases of the "Alien and Sedition Acts," passed at the last session of Congress; the first of which exercises a power nowhere delegated to the Federal Government, and which, by uniting legislative and judicial powers to those of [the] executive, subverts the general principles of free government, as well as the particular organization and positive provisions of the Federal Constitution: and the other of which acts exercises, in like manner, a power not delegated by the Constitution, but, on the contrary, expressly and positively forbidden by one of the amendments thereto,—a power which, more than any other, ought to produce universal alarm, because it is levelled against the right of freely examining public characters and measures, and of free communication among the people thereon, which has ever been justly deemed the only effectual guardian of every other right.

That this state having, by its Convention which ratified the Federal Constitution, expressly declared that, among other essential rights, "the liberty of conscience and of the press cannot be cancelled, abridged, restrained or modified by any authority of the United States," and from its extreme anxiety to guard these rights from every possible attack of sophistry or ambition, having, with other states, recommended an amendment for that purpose, which amendment was in due time annexed to the Constitution,—it would mark a reproachful inconsistency and criminal degeneracy, if an indifference were now shown to the palpable violation of one of the rights thus declared

and secured, and to the establishment of a precedent which may be fatal to the order.

That the good people of this commonwealth, having ever felt and continuing to feel the most sincere affection for their brethren of the other states, the truest anxiety for establishing and perpetuating the union of all and the most scrupulous fidelity to that Constitution, which is the pledge of mutual friendship, and the instrument of mutual happiness, the General Assembly doth solemnly appeal to the like dispositions of the other states, in confidence that they will concur with this Commonwealth in declaring, as it does hereby declare, that the acts aforesaid are unconstitutional; and that the necessary and proper measures will be taken by each for co-operating with this state, in maintaining unimpaired the authorities, rights, and liberties reserved to the states respectively, or to the people. . . .

Kentucky Resolutions of 1798
I

Resolved, that the several States composing the United States of America, are not united on the principle of unlimited submission to their general government; but that by compact under the style and title of a Constitution for the United States and of amendments thereto, they constituted a general government for special purposes, delegated to that government certain definite powers, reserving each State to itself, the residuary mass of right to their own self-government; and that whensoever the general government assumes undelegated powers, its acts are unauthoritative, void, and of no force: That to this compact each State acceded as a State, and is an integral party, its co-States forming, as to itself, the other party: That the government created by this compact was not made the exclusive or final judge of the extent of the powers delegated to itself; since that would have made its discretion, and not the Constitution, the measure of its powers; but that as in all other cases of compact among parties having no common Judge, *each party has an equal right to judge for itself, as well of infractions as of the mode and measure of redress.*

II

Resolved, that the Constitution of the United States having delegated to Congress a power to punish treason, counterfeiting the securities and current coin of the United States, piracies and felonies committed on the high seas, and offenses against the laws of nations, and no other crimes whatever, and it being true as a general principle, and one of the amendments to the Constitution having also declared "that the powers not delegated to the United States by the Constitution, nor prohibited by it to the States, are reserved to the States respectively, or to the people," therefore also [the Sedition Act of July 14, 1798];

as also the act passed by them on the 27th day of June, 1798, entitled "An act to punish frauds committed on the Bank of the United States" (and all other their acts which assume to create, define, or punish crimes other than those enumerated in the Constitution), are altogether void and of no force, and that the power to create, define, and punish such other crimes is reserved, and of right appertains solely and exclusively to the respective States, each within its own Territory.

III

Resolved, that it is true as a general principle, and is also expressly declared by one of the amendments to the Constitution that "the powers not delegated to the United States by the Constitution, nor prohibited by it to the States, are reserved to the States respectively or to the people;" and that no power over the freedom of religion, freedom of speech, or freedom of the press being delegated to the United States by the Constitution, nor prohibited by it to the States, all lawful powers respecting the same did of right remain, and were reserved to the States, or to the people: That thus was manifested their determination to retain to themselves the right of judging how far the licentiousness of speech and of the press may be abridged without lessening their useful freedom, and how far those abuses which cannot be separated from their use should be tolerated rather than the use be destroyed; and thus also they guarded against all abridgment by the United States of the freedom of religious opinions and exercises, and retained to themselves the right of protecting the same, as this State, by a law passed on the general demand of its citizens, had already protected them from all human restraint or interference: And that in addition to this general principle and express declaration, another and more special provision has been made by one of the amendments to the Constitution which expressly declares, that "Congress shall make no law respecting an establishment of religion, or prohibiting the free exercise thereof, or abridging the freedom of speech, or of the press," thereby guarding in the same sentence, and under the same words, the freedom of religion, of speech, and of the press, insomuch, that whatever violates either, throws down the sanctuary which covers the others, and that libels, falsehoods, defamation equally with heresy and false religion, are withheld from the cognizance of Federal tribunals. That therefore [the Sedition Act], which does abridge the freedom of the press, is not law, but is altogether void and of no effect.

IV

Resolved, that alien friends are under the jurisdiction and protection of the laws of the State wherein they are; that no power over them has been delegated to the United

States, nor prohibited to the individual States distinct from their power over citizens; and it being true as a general principle, and one of the amendments to the Constitution having also declared that "the powers not delegated to the United States by the Constitution, nor prohibited by it to the States, are reserved to the States respectively, or to the people," the [Alien Act of June 22, 1798], which assumes power over alien friends not delegated by the Constitution, is not law, but is altogether void and of no force.

V

Resolved, that in addition to the general principle as well as the express declaration, that powers not delegated are reserved, another and more special provision inserted in the Constitution from abundant caution has declared, "that the migration or importation of such persons as any of the States now existing shall think proper to admit, shall not be prohibited by the Congress prior to the year 1808." That this Commonwealth does admit the migration of alien friends described as the subject of the said act concerning aliens; that a provision against prohibiting their migration is a provision against all acts equivalent thereto, or it would be nugatory; that to remove them when migrated is equivalent to a prohibition of their migration, and is therefore contrary to the said provision of the Constitution, and void.

VI

Resolved, that the imprisonment of a person under the protection of the laws of this Commonwealth on his failure to obey the simple order of the President to depart out of the United States, as is undertaken by the said act entitled "An act concerning aliens," is contrary to the Constitution, one amendment to which has provided, that "no person shall be deprived of liberty without due process of law," and that another having provided "that in all criminal prosecutions, the accused shall enjoy the right to a public trial by an impartial jury, to be informed of the nature and cause of the accusation, to be confronted with the witnesses against him, to have compulsory process for obtaining witnesses in his favour, and to have the assistance of counsel for his defense," the same act undertaking to authorize the President to remove a person out of the United States who is under the protection of the law, on his own suspicion, without accusation, without jury, without public trial, without confrontation of the witnesses against him, without having witnesses in his favour, without defense, without counsel, is contrary to these provisions also of the Constitution, is therefore not law, but utterly void and of no force. That transferring the power of judging any person who is under the protection of the laws, from the courts to the President of the United States, as is undertaken by the same act concerning aliens, is against the article of the Constitution which provides, that "the judicial power of the United States shall be vested in courts, the judges of which shall hold their offices during good behavior," and that the said act is void for that reason also; and it is further to be noted, that this transfer of judiciary power is to that magistrate of the general government who already possesses all the executive, and a qualified negative in all the legislative powers.

VII

Resolved, that the construction applied by the general government (as is evinced by sundry of their proceedings) to those parts of the Constitution of the United States which delegate to Congress a power to lay and collect taxes, duties, imposts, and excises; to pay the debts, and provide for the common defense, and general welfare of the United States, and to make all laws which shall be necessary and proper for carrying into execution the powers vested by the Constitution in the government of the United States, or any department thereof, goes to the destruction of all the limits prescribed to their power by the Constitution: That words meant by that instrument to be subsidiary only to the execution of the limited powers ought not to be so construed as themselves to give unlimited powers, nor a part so to be taken as to destroy the whole residue of the instrument: That the proceedings of the general government under color of these articles will be a fit and necessary subject for revisal and correction at a time of greater tranquillity, while those specified in the preceding resolutions call for immediate redress.

VIII

Resolved, that the preceding Resolutions be transmitted to the Senators and Representatives in Congress from this Commonwealth, who are hereby enjoined to present the same to their respective Houses, and to use their best endeavors to procure, at the next session of Congress, a repeal of the aforesaid unconstitutional and obnoxious acts.

IX

Resolved, lastly, that the Governor of this Commonwealth be, and is hereby authorized and requested to communicate the preceding Resolutions to the Legislatures of the several States, to assure them that this Commonwealth considers Union for specified National purposes, and particularly for those specified in their late Federal Compact, to be friendly to the peace, happiness, and prosperity of all the States: that faithful to that compact according to the plain intent and meaning in which it was understood and acceded to by the several parties, it is sincerely anxious for its preservation: that it does also believe, that to take from the States all the powers of self-government,

and transfer them to a general and consolidated government, without regard to the special delegations and reservations solemnly agreed to in that compact, is not for the peace, happiness, or prosperity of these States: And that, therefore, this Commonwealth is determined, as it doubts not its co-States are, tamely to submit to undelegated and consequently unlimited powers in no man or body of men on earth: that if the acts before specified should stand, these conclusions would flow from them; that the general government may place any act they think proper on the list of crimes and punish it themselves, whether enumerated or not enumerated by the Constitution as cognizable by them: that they may transfer its cognizance to the President or any other person, who may himself be the accuser, counsel, judge, and jury, whose suspicions may be the evidence, his order the sentence, his officer the executioner, and his breast the sole record of the transaction: that a very numerous and valuable description of the inhabitants of these States being by this precedent reduced as outlaws to the absolute dominion of one man, and the barrier of the Constitution thus swept away from us all, no rampart now remains against the passions and the powers of a majority of Congress, to protect from a like exportation or other more grievous punishment the minority of the same body, the legislatures, judges, governors, and counselors of the States, nor their other peaceable inhabitants who may venture to reclaim the constitutional rights and liberties of the State and people, or who for other causes, good or bad, may be obnoxious to the views or marked by the suspicions of the President, or be thought dangerous to his or their elections or other interests, public or personal: that the friendless alien has indeed been selected as the safest subject of a first experiment, but the citizen will soon follow, or rather has already followed: for, already has a sedition act marked him as its prey: that these and successive acts of the same character, unless arrested on the threshold, may tend to drive these States into revolution and blood, and will furnish new calumnies against Republican governments, and new pretexts for those who wish it to be believed, that man cannot be governed but by a rod of iron: that it would be a dangerous delusion were a confidence in the men or our choice to silence our fears for the safety of our rights: that confidence is everywhere the parent of despotism: free government is founded in jealousy and not in confidence; it is jealousy and not confidence which prescribes limited Constitutions to bind down those whom we are obliged to trust with power: that our Constitution has accordingly fixed the limits to which and no further our confidence may go; and let the honest advocate of confidence read the alien and sedition acts, and say if the Constitution has not been wise in fixing limits to the government it created, and whether we should be wise in destroying those limits; let him say what the government is if it be not a tyranny, which the men of our choice have conferred on the President, and the President of our choice has assented to and accepted over the friendly strangers, to whom the mild spirit of our country and its laws had pledged hospitality and protection: that the men of our choice have more respected the bare suspicions of the President than the solid rights of innocence, the claims of justification, the sacred force of truth, and the forms and substance of law and justice. In questions of power then let no more be heard of confidence in man, but bind him down from mischief by the claims of the Constitution. That this Commonwealth does therefore call on its co-States for an expression of their sentiments on the acts concerning aliens, and for the punishment of certain crimes herein before specified, plainly declaring whether these acts are or are not authorized by the Federal Compact. And it doubts not that their sense will be so announced as to prove their attachment unaltered to limited government, whether general or particular, and that the rights and liberties of their co-States will be exposed to no dangers by remaining embarked on a common bottom with their own: That they will concur with this Commonwealth in considering the said acts so palpably against the Constitution as to amount to an undisguised declaration, that the compact is not meant to be the measure of the powers of the general government, but that it will proceed in the exercise over these States of all powers whatsoever: That they will view this as seizing the rights of the States and consolidating them in the hands of the general government with a power assumed to bind the States (not merely in cases made Federal) but in all cases whatsoever, by laws made, not with their consent, but by others against their consent: That this would be to surrender the form of government we have chosen, and to live under one deriving its powers from its own will, and not from our authority; and that the co-States, recurring to their natural right in cases not made Federal, will concur in declaring these acts void and of no force, and will each unite with this Commonwealth in requesting their repeal at the next session of Congress.

Kentucky Resolutions of 1799

The representatives of the good people of this commonwealth, in General Assembly convened, having maturely considered the answers of sundry states in the Union, to their resolutions passed the last session, respecting certain unconstitutional laws of Congress, commonly called the Alien and Sedition Laws, would be faithless, indeed, to themselves and to those they represent, were they silently to acquiesce in the principles and doctrines attempted to be maintained in all those answers, that of Virginia only expected. To again enter the field of argument, and

attempt more fully or forcibly to expose the unconstitutionality of those obnoxious laws, would, it is apprehended, be as unnecessary as unavailing. We cannot, however, but lament, that, in the discussion of those interesting subjects, by sundry of the legislatures of our sister states, unfounded suggestions, and uncandid insinuations, derogatory to the true character and principles of this commonwealth have been substituted in place of fair reasoning and sound argument. Our opinions of these alarming measures of the general government, together with our reasons for those opinions, were detailed with decency, and with temper, and submitted to the discussion and judgment of our fellow-citizens throughout the Union. Whether the like decency and temper have been observed in the answers of most of those States, who have denied or attempted to obviate the great truths contained in those resolutions, we have now only to submit to a candid world. Faithful to the true principles of the federal Union, unconscious of any designs to disturb the harmony of that Union, and anxious only to escape the fangs of despotism, the good people of this commonwealth are regardless of censure or calumniation. Lest, however, the silence of this commonwealth should be construed into an acquiescence in the doctrines and principles advanced and attempted to be maintained by the said answers, or at least those of our fellow-citizens throughout the Union who so widely differ from us on those important subjects, should be deluded by the expectation, that we shall be deterred from what we conceive our duty, or shrink from the principles contained in those resolutions—therefore,

Resolved, That this commonwealth considers the federal Union, upon the terms and for the purposes specified in the late compact, conducive to the liberty and happiness of the several states: That it does now unequivocally declare its attachment to the Union, and to that compact, agreeably to its obvious and real intention, and will be among the last to seek its dissolution: That if those who administer the general government be permitted to transgress the limits fixed by that compact, by a total disregard to the special delegations of power therein contained, an annihilation of the state governments, and the creation upon their ruins of a general consolidated government, will be the inevitable consequence: That the principle and construction contended for by sundry of the state legislatures, that the general government is the exclusive judge of the extent of the powers delegated to it, stop not short of *despotism*—since the discretion of those who administer the government, and not the *Constitution*, would be the measure of their powers: That the several states who formed that instrument being sovereign and independent, have the unquestionable right to judge of the infraction; and, *That a nullification of those sovereignties, of all unauthorized acts done under color of that instrument is the rightful remedy:* That this common-wealth does, under the most deliberate reconsideration, declare, that the said Alien and Sedition Laws are, in their opinion, palpable violations of the said Constitution; and, however cheerfully it may be disposed to surrender its opinion to a majority of its sister states, in matters of ordinary or doubtful policy, yet, in momentous regulations like the present, which so vitally wound the best rights of the citizen, it would consider a silent acquiescence as highly criminal: That although this commonwealth, as a party to the federal compact, will bow to the laws of the Union, yet, it does, at the same time declare, that it will not now, or ever hereafter, cease to oppose in a constitutional manner, every attempt at what quarter soever offered, to violate that compact. And, finally, in order that no pretext or arguments may be drawn from a supposed acquiescence, on the part of this commonwealth in the constitutionality of those laws, and be thereby used as precedents for similar future violations of the federal compact—this commonwealth does now enter against them its solemn PROTEST.

Source:

Henry Steele Commager, ed. *Documents of American History.* New York: F.S. Crofts & Co., 1934.

Thomas Jefferson, First Inaugural Address, 1801

Speech delivered by Thomas Jefferson on March 4, 1801, in Washington, D.C., at his inauguration as the third president of the United States and the first to take place in the federal city established in the U.S. Constitution. Jefferson's election has been termed "the revolution of 1801." The new president, a Democratic-Republican, replaced Federalist John Adams. This change of the party running the government occurred through an election, rather than through a bloody war or nonviolent coup d'etat. As such, it was revolutionary in world politics and represented a political revolution—a change in government. Jefferson sought to placate his foes by proclaiming, "we are all Republicans, we are all Federalists." The address also expounds Jefferson's political philosophy, stressing the need for limiting government powers; strict construction of the U.S. Constitution; support for the rights of state governments; economy in national administration; majority rule tempered by the recognition of equal rights for minorities; the protection of civil liberties; freedom of trade; minimal public debt; and "peace, commerce, and honest friendship with all nations, entangling alliances with none."

Friends and Fellow-Citizens:

Called upon to undertake the duties of the first executive office of our country, I avail myself of the presence of that portion of my fellow-citizens which is here assembled to express my grateful thanks for the favor with which they have been pleased to look toward me, to declare a sincere consciousness that the task is above my talents, and that I approach it with those anxious and awful presentiments which the greatness of the charge and the weakness of my powers so justly inspire. A rising nation, spread over a wide and fruitful land, traversing all the seas with the rich productions of their industry, engaged in commerce with nations who feel power and forget right, advancing rapidly to destinies beyond the reach of mortal eye—when I contemplate these transcendent objects, and see the honor, the happiness, and the hopes of this beloved country committed to the issue, and the auspices of this day, I shrink from the contemplation, and humble myself before the magnitude of the undertaking. Utterly, indeed, should I despair did not the presence of many whom I here see remind me that in the other high authorities provided by our Constitution I shall find resources of wisdom, of virtue, and of zeal on which to rely under all difficulties. To you, then, gentlemen, who are charged with the sovereign functions of legislation, and to those associated with you, I look with encouragement for that guidance and support which may enable us to steer with safety the vessel in which we are all embarked amidst the conflicting elements of a troubled world.

During the contest of opinion through which we have passed the animation of discussions and of exertions has sometimes worn an aspect which might impose on strangers unused to think freely and to speak and to write what they think; but this being now decided by the voice of the nation, announced according to the rules of the Constitution, all will, of course, arrange themselves under the will of the law, and unite in common efforts for the common good. All, too, will bear in mind this sacred principle, that though the will of the majority is in all cases to prevail, that will to be rightful must be reasonable; that the minority possesses their equal rights, which equal law must protect, and to violate would be oppression. Let us, then, fellow-citizens, unite with one heart and one mind. Let us restore to social intercourse that harmony and affection without which liberty and even life itself are but dreary things. And let us reflect that, having banished from our land that religious intolerance under which mankind so long bled and suffered, we have yet gained little if we countenance a political intolerance as despotic, as wicked, and capable of as bitter and bloody persecutions. During the throes and convulsions of the ancient world, during the agonizing spasms of infuriated man, seeking through blood and slaughter his long-lost liberty, it was not wonderful that the agitation of the billows should reach even this distant and peaceful shore; that this should be more felt and feared by some and less by others, and should divide opinions as to measures of safety. But every difference of opinion is not a difference of principle. We have called by different names brethren of the same principle. We are all Republicans, we are all Federalists. If there be any among us who would wish to dissolve this Union or to change its republican form, let them stand undisturbed as monuments of the safety with which error of opinion may be tolerated where reason is left free to combat it. I know, indeed, that some honest men fear that a republican government can not be strong, that this Government is not strong enough; but would the honest patriot, in the full tide of successful experiment, abandon a government which has so far kept us free and firm on the theoretic and visionary fear that this Government, the world's best hope, may by possibility want energy to preserve itself? I trust not. I believe this, on the contrary, the strongest Government on earth. I believe it the only one where every man, at the call of the law, would fly to the standard of the law, and would meet invasions of the public order as his own personal concern. Sometimes it is said that man can not be trusted with the government of himself. Can he, then, be trusted with the government of others? Or have we found angels in the forms of kings to govern him? Let history answer this question.

Let us, then, with courage and confidence pursue our own Federal and Republican principles, our attachment to union and representative government. Kindly separated by nature and a wide ocean from the exterminating havoc of one quarter of the glove; too high-minded to endure the degradations of the others; possessing a chosen country, with room enough for our descendants to the thousandth and thousandth generation; entertaining a due sense of our equal right to the use of our own faculties, to the acquisitions of our own industry, to honor and confidence from our fellow-citizens, resulting not from birth, but from our actions and their sense of them; enlightened by a benign religion, professed, indeed, and practiced in various forms, yet all of them inculcating honesty, truth, temperance, gratitude, and the love of man; acknowledging and adoring an overruling Providence, which by all its dispensations proves that it delights in the happiness of man here and his greater happiness hereafter—with all these blessings, what more is necessary to make us a happy and a prosperous people? Still one thing more, fellow-citizens—a wise and frugal Government, which shall restrain men from injuring one another, shall leave them otherwise free to regulate their own pursuits of industry and improvement, and shall not take from the mouth of labor the bread it has earned. This is the sum of good government, and this is necessary to close the circle of our felicities.

About to enter, fellow-citizens, on the exercise of duties which comprehend everything dear and valuable to you, it is proper you should understand what I deem the essential principles of our Government, and consequently those which ought to shape its Administration. I will compress them within the narrowest compass they will bear, stating the general principle, but not all its limitations. Equal and exact justice to all men, of whatever state or persuasion, religious or political; peace, commerce, and honest friendship with all nations, entangling alliances with none; the support of the State governments in all their rights, as the most competent administrations for our domestic concerns and the surest bulwarks against antirepublican tendencies; the preservation of the General Government in its whole constitutional vigor, as the sheet anchor of our peace at home and safety abroad; a jealous care of the right of election by the people—a mild and safe corrective of abuses which are lopped by the sword of revolution where peaceable remedies are unprovided; absolute acquiescence in the decisions of the majority, the vital principle of republics, from which is no appeal but to force, the vital principle and immediate parent of despotism; a well-disciplined militia, our best reliance in peace and for the first moments of war, till regulars may relieve them; the supremacy of the civil over the military authority; economy in the public expense, that labor may be lightly burthened; the honest payment of our debts and sacred preservation of the public faith; encouragement of agriculture, and of commerce as its handmaid; the diffusion of information and arraignment of all abuses at the bar of the public reason; freedom of religion; freedom of the press, and freedom of person under the protection of the habeas corpus, and trial by juries impartially selected. These principles form the bright constellation which has gone before us and guided our steps through an age of revolution and reformation. The wisdom of our sages and blood of our heroes have been devoted to their attainment. They should be the creed of our political faith, the text of civic instruction, the touchstone by which to try the services of those we trust; and should we wander from them in moments of error or of alarm, let us hasten to retrace our steps and to regain the road which alone leads to peace, liberty, and safety.

I repair, then, fellow-citizens, to the post you have assigned me. With experience enough in subordinate offices to have seen the difficulties of this the greatest of all, I have learnt to expect that it will rarely fall to the lot of imperfect man to retire from this station with the reputation and the favor which bring him into it. Without pretentions to that high confidence you reposed in our first and greatest revolutionary character, whose preeminent services had entitled him to the first place in his country's love and destined for him the fairest page in the volume of faithful history, I ask so much confidence only as may give firmness and effect to the legal administration of your affairs. I shall often go wrong through defect of judgment. When right, I shall often be thought wrong by those whose positions will not command a view of the whole ground. I ask your indulgence for my own errors, which will never be intentional, and your support against the errors of others, who may condemn what they would not if seen in all its parts. The approbation implied by your suffrage is a great consolation to me for the past, and my future solicitude will be to retain the good opinion of those who have bestowed it in advance, to conciliate that of others by doing them all the good in my power, and to be instrumental to the happiness and freedom of all.

Relying, then, on the patronage of your good will, I advance with obedience to the work, ready to retire from it whenever you become sensible how must better choice it is in your power to make. And may that Infinite Power which rules the destinies of the universe lead our councils to what is best, and give them a favorable issue for your peace and prosperity.

Source:

Inaugural Addresses of the Presidents of the United States, 1789–1965. Washington, D.C.: Government Printing Office, 1965.

Marbury v. Madison, 1803

U.S. Supreme Court decision, issued on February 24, 1803, that established the principle of judicial review, whereby the Court could declare acts passed by the Congress unconstitutional and void. In 1801, at the end of his term of office, President John Adams appointed William Marbury to be justice of the peace, but the commission was not delivered promptly. When Adams's successor (and political opponent) Thomas Jefferson ordered that the commission be withheld, Marbury asked the Supreme Court to mandate delivery of the commission under the powers granted to the Court by the Judiciary Act of 1789. The Court, in a decision written by Federalist appointee John Marshall, ruled that although Marbury had a right to the commission, the section of the Judiciary Act authorizing the Court to issue such an order was in conflict with the U.S. Constitution and was therefore void. Although this case set the precedent for judicial review, no other congressional statute was declared unconstitutional until the Dred Scott decision in 1857.

William Marbury v. James Madison, secretary of state of the United States

February 24, 1803

On the 24th February, the following opinion of the court was delivered by the Chief Justice:

Opinion of the Court.—At the last term, on the affidavits then read and filed with the clerk, a rule was granted in this case, requiring the secretary of state to show cause why a *mandamus* should not issue, directing him to deliver to William Marbury his commission as a justice of the peace for the county of Washington, in the district of Columbia.

No cause has been shown, and the present motion is for a *mandamus.* The peculiar delicacy of this case, the novelty of some of its circumstances, and the real difficulty attending the points which occur in it, require a complete exposition of the principles on which the opinion to be given by the court is founded. These principles have been, on the side of the applicant, very ably argued at the bar. In rendering the opinion of the court, there will be some departure in form, though not in substances, from the points stated in that argument.

In the order in which the court has viewed this subject, the following questions have been considered and decided: 1st. Has the applicant a right to the commission he demands? 2d. If he has a right, and that right has been violated, do the laws his country afford him a remedy? 3d. If they do afford him a remedy, is it a *mandamus* issuing from this court?

The first object of inquiry is—Has the applicant a right to the commission he demands? His right originates in an act of congress passed in February 1801, concerning the district of Columbia. After dividing the district into two countries, the 11th section of this law enacts, "that there shall be appointed in and for each of the said countries, such number of discreet persons to be justices of the peace, as the president of the United States shall, from time to time, think expedient, to continue in office for five years.

It appears, from the affidavits, that, in compliance with this law, a commission for William Marbury, as a justice of peace for the country of Washington, was signed by John Adams, then President of the United States; after which, the seal of the United States was affixed to it; but the commission has never reached the person for whom it was made out. In order to determine whether he is entitled to this commission, it becomes necessary to inquire, whether he has been appointed to the office. For if the has been appointed, the law continues him in office for five years, and he is entitled to the possession of those evidences of office, which, being completed, became his property.

The 2d section of the 2d article of the constitution declares, that "the president shall nominate, and by and with the advice and consent of the senate, shall appoint ambassadors, other public ministers and consuls, and all other officers of the United States, whose appointments are not otherwise provided for." The 3d section declares, that "he shall commission all the officers of the United States."

An act of congress directs the secretary of state to keep the seal of the United States, "to make out and record, and affix the said seal to all civil commissions to officers of the United States, to be appointed by the president, by and with the consent of the senate, or by the president alone; provided, that the said seal shall not be affixed to any commission, before the same shall have been signed by the president of the United States.

These are the clauses of the constitution and laws of the United States, which affect this part of the case. They seem to contemplate three distinct operations: 1st. The nomination: this is the sole act of the president, and is completely voluntary. 2d. The appointment: this is also the act of the president, and is also a voluntary act, though it can only be performed by and with the advice and consent of the senate. 3d. The commission: to grant a commission to a person appointed, might, perhaps, be deemed a duty enjoined by the constitution. "He shall," says that instrument, "commission all the officers of the United States."

1. The acts of appointing to office, and commissioning the person appointed, can scarcely be considered as one and the same; since the power to perform them is given in two separate and distinct sections of the constitution. The distinction between the appointment and the commission, will be rendered more apparent, by adverting to that provision in the second section of the second article of the constitution, which authorizes congress "to vest, by law, the appointment of such inferior officers, as they think proper, in the president alone, in the courts of law, or in the heads of departments;" thus contemplating cases where the law may direct the president to commission an officer appointed by the courts, or by the heads of departments. In such a case, to issue a commission would be apparently a duty distinct from the appointment, the performance of which, perhaps, could not legally be refused.

Although that clause of the constitution which requires the president to commission all the officers of the United States, may never have been applied to officers appointed otherwise than by himself, yet it would be difficult to deny the legislature power to apply it to such cases. Of consequence, the constitutional distinction between the appointment to an office and the commission of an officer who has been appointed, remains the same, as if, in practice, the president had commissioned officers appointed by an authority other than his own. It follows, too, from the existence of this distinction, that if an appointment was to be evidenced by any public act,

other than the commission, the performance of such public act would create the officer; and if was not removable at the will of the president, would either give him a right to his commission, or enable him to perform the duties without it.

These observations are premised, solely for the purpose of rendering more intelligible those which apply more directly to the particular case under consideration.

This is an appointment made by the president, by and with the advice and consent of the senate, and is evidenced by no act but the commission itself. In such a case, therefore, the commission and the appointment seem inseparable; it being almost impossible to show an appointment, otherwise than by providing the existence of a commission; still the commission is not necessarily the appointment, though conclusive evidence of it.

But at what stage, does it amount to this conclusive evidence? The answer to this question seems an obvious one. The appointment being the sole act of the president, must be completely evidenced, when it is shown that he has done everything to be performed by him. Should the commission, instead of being evidence of an appointment, even be considered as constituting the appointment itself; still, it would be made, when the last act to be done by the president was performed, or, at farthest, when the commission was complete.

The last act to be done by the president is the signature of the commission: he has ten acted on the advice and consent of the senate to his own nomination. The time for deliberation has then passed: he has decided. His judgment, on the advice and consent of the senate, concurring with his nomination, has been made, and the officer is appointed. This appointment is evidenced by an open unequivocal act; and being the last act required from the person making it, necessarily excludes the idea of its being, so far as respects the appointment, an inchoate and incomplete transaction.

Some point of time must be taken, when the power of the executive over an officer, not removable at his will, must cease. That point of time must be, when the constitutional power of appointment has been exercised. And this power has been exercised, when the last act, required from the person possessing the power, has been performed: this last act is the signature of the commission. This idea seems to have prevailed with the legislature, when the act passed converting the department of foreign affairs into the department of state. By that act, it is enacted, that the secretary of state shall keep the seal of the United States, "and shall make out and record, and shall affix the said seal to all civil commissions to officers of the United States, to be appointed by the president;" "provided, that the said seal shall not be affixed to any commission, before the same shall have been signed by the President of the United States; nor to any other instrument or act, without the special warrant of the president therefor."

The signature is a warrant for affixing the great seal to the commission; and the great seal is only to be affixed to an instrument which is complete. It attests, by an act, supposed to be of public notoriety, the verity of the presidential signature. It is never to be affixed, until the commission is signed, because the signature, which gives force and effect to the commission, is conclusive evidence that the appointment is made.

The commission being signed, the subsequent duty of the secretary of state is prescribed by law, and not to be guided by the will of the president. He is to affix the seal of the United States to the commission, and is to record it. This is not a proceeding which may be varied, if the judgment of the executive shall suggest one more eligible; but is a precise course accurately marked out by law, and is to be strictly pursued. It is the duty of the secretary of state, to conform to the law, and in this he is an officer of the United States, bound to obey the laws. He acts, in this respect, as has been very properly stated at the bar, under the authority of law, and not by the instructions of the president. It is a ministerial act, which the law enjoins on a particular officer or a particular purpose.

If it should be supposed, that the solemnity of affixing the seal is necessary, not only to the validity of the commission, but even to the completion of an appointment, still, when the seal is affixed, the appointment is made, and the commission is valid. No other solemnity is required by law; no other act is to be performed on the part of government. All that the executive can do, to invest the person with his office, is done; and unless the appointment be then made, the executive cannot make one without the co-operation of others.

After searching anxiously for the principles on which a contrary opinion may be supported, none have been found, which appear of sufficient force to maintain the opposite doctrine. Such as the imagination of the court could suggest, have been very deliberately examined, and after allowing them all the weight which it appears possible to give them, they do not shake the opinion which has been formed. In considering this question, it has been conjectured, that the commission may have been assimilated to a deed, to the validity of which delivery is essential. This idea is founded on the supposition, that the commission is not merely evidence of an appointment, but is itself the actual appointment; a supposition by no means unquestionable. But for the purpose of examining this objection fairly, let it be conceded, that the principle claimed for its support is established.

The appointment being, under the constitution, to be made by the president, personally, the delivery of the deed of appointment, if necessary to its completion, must be made by the president also. It is not necessary, that the delivery should be made personally to the grantee of the office: it never is so made. The law would seem to contemplate, that it should be made to the secretary of state, since it directs the secretary to affix the seal to the commission, after it shall have been signed by the president. If, then, the act of delivery be necessary to give validity to the commission, it has been delivered, when executed and given to the secretary, for the purpose of being sealed, recorded and transmitted to the party.

But in all cases of letters-patent, certain solemnities are required by law, which solemnities are the evidences of the validity of the instrument: a formal delivery to the person is not among them. In cases of commissions, the sign manual of the president, and the seal of the United States are those solemnities. This objection, therefore, does not touch the case.

It has also occurred as possible, and barely possible, that the transmission of the commission, and the acceptance thereof, might be deemed necessary to complete the right of the plaintiff. The transmission of the commission is a practice, directed by convenience, but not by law. It cannot, therefore, be necessary to constitute the appointment, which must precede it, and which is the mere act of the president. If the executive required that every person appointed to an office should himself take means to procure his commission, the appointment would not be the less valid on that account. The appointment is the sole act of the president; the transmission of the commission is the sole act of the officer to whom that duty is assigned, and may be accelerated or retarded by circumstances which can have no influence on the appointment. A commission is transmitted to a person already appointed; not to a person to be appointed or not, as the letter enclosing the commission should happen to get into the post-office and reach him in safety, or to miscarry.

It may have some tendency to elucidate this point, to inquire, whether the possession of the original commission be indispensably necessary to authorize a person, appointed to any office, to perform the duties of that office. If it was necessary, then a loss of the commission would lose the office. Not only negligence, but accident or fraud, fire or theft, might deprive an individual of his office. In such a case, I presume, it could not be doubted, but that a copy from the record of the office of the secretary of state would be, to every intent and purpose, equal to the original: the act of congress has expressly made it so. To give that copy validity, it would not be necessary to prove that the original had been transmitted and afterwards lost. The copy would be complete evidence that the original had existed, and that the appointment had been made, but not that the original had been transmitted. If, indeed, it should appear, that the original had been mislaid in the office of state, that circumstance would not affect the operation of the copy. When all the requisites have been performed, which authorize a recording officer to record any instrument whatever, and the order for that purpose has been given, the instrument is, in law, considered as recorded, although the manual labor of inserting it in a book kept for that purpose may not have been performed. In the case of commissions, the law orders the secretary of state to record them. When, therefore, they are signed and sealed, the order for their being recorded is given; and whether inserted in the book or not, they are in law recorded.

A copy of this record is declared equal to the original, and the fees to be paid by a person requiring a copy are ascertained by law. Can a keeper of a public record erase therefrom a commission which has been recorded? Or can he refuse a copy thereof to a person demanding it on the terms prescribed by law? Such a copy would, equally with the original, authorize the justice of peace to proceed in the performance of this duty, because it would, equally with the original, attest his appointment.

If the transmission of a commission be not considered as necessary to give validity to an appointment, still less is its acceptance. The appointment is the sole act of the president; the acceptance is the sole act of the officer, and is, in plain common sense, posterior to the appointment. As he may resign, so may he refuse to accept: but neither the one nor the other is capable of rendering the appointment a nonentity.

That this is the understanding of the government, is apparent from the whole tenor of its conduct. A commission bears date, and the salary of the officer commences, from his appointment; not from the transmission or acceptance of his commission. When a person appointed to any office refuses to accept that office, the successor is nominated in the place of the person who has declined to accept, and not in the place of the person who had been previously in office, and had created the original vacancy.

It is, therefore, decidedly the opinion of the court, that when a commission has been signed by the president, the appointment is made; and that the commission is complete, when the seal of the United States has been affixed to it by the secretary of state.

Where an officer is removable at the will of the executive, the circumstance which completes his appointment is of no concern; because the act is at any time revocable; and the commission may be arrested, if still in the office. But when the officer is not removable at the will of the executive, the appointment is not revocable, and cannot be annulled: it has conferred legal rights which cannot be resumed. The discretion of the executive is to be exercised, until the appointment has been made. But having

once made the appointment, his power over the office is terminated, in all cases where, by law, the officer is not removable by him. The right to the office is then in the person appointed, and he has the absolute unconditional power of accepting or rejecting it.

Mr. Marbury, then, since his commission was signed by the president, and sealed by the secretary of state, was appointed; and as the law creating the office, gave the officer a right to hold for five years, independent of the executive, the appointment was not revocable, but vested in the officer legal rights, which are protected by the laws of his country. To withhold his commission, therefore, is an act deemed by the court not warranted by law, but violative of a vested legal right.

2. This brings us to the second inquiry; which is: If he has a right, and that right has been violated, do the laws of his country afford him a remedy?

The very essence of civil liberty certainly consists in the right of every individual to claim the protection of the laws, whenever he receives an injury. One of the first duties of government is to afford that protection. In Great Britain, the king himself is sued in the respectful form of a petition, and he never fails to comply with the judgment of his court.

In the 3d vol. of his Commentaries (p. 23), Blackstone states two cases in which a remedy is afforded by mere operation of law. "In all other cases," he says, "it is a general and indisputable rule, that where there is a legal right, there is also a legal remedy by suit, or action at law, whenever that right is invaded." And afterwards (p. 109, of the same vol.), he says, "I am text to consider such injuries as are cognisable by the courts of the common law. And herein I shall, for the present, only remark, that all possible injuries whatsoever, that did not fall within the exclusive cognisance of either the ecclesiastical, military or maritime tribunals, are, for that very, reason, within the cognisance of the common-law courts of justice; for it is a settled and invariable principle in the laws of England, that every right, when withheld, must have a remedy, and every injury its proper redress."

The government of the United States has been emphatically termed a government of laws, and not of men. It will certainly cease to deserve this high appellation, if the laws furnish no remedy for the violation of a vested legal right. If this obloquy is to be cast on the jurisprudence of our country, it must arise from the peculiar character of the case.

It behooves us, then, to inquire whether there be in its composition any ingredient which shall exempt it from legal investigation, or exclude the injured party from legal redress. In pursuing this inquiry, the first question which presents itself is, whether this can be arranged with that class of cases which come under the description of *damnum absque injuria;* a loss without an injury. This description of cases never has been considered, and it is believed, never can be considered, as comprehending offices of trust, of honor or of profit. The office of justice of peace in the district of Columbia is such an office; it is, therefore, worthy of the attention and guardianship of the laws. It has received that attention and guardianship: it has been created by special act of congress, and has been secured, so far as the laws can give security, to the person appointed to fill it, for five years. It is not, then, on account of the worthlessness of the thing pursued, that the injured party can be alleged to be without remedy.

Is it in the nature of the transaction? Is the act of delivering or withholding a commission to be considered as a mere political act, belonging to the executive department alone, for the performance of which entire confidence is placed by our constitution in the supreme executive; and for any misconduct respecting which, the injured individual has no remedy? That there may be such cases is not to be questioned; but that every act of duty, to be performed in any of the great departments of government, constitutes such a case, is not to be admitted.

By the act concerning invalids, passed in June 1794 (1 U.S. Stat. 392), the secretary at war is ordered to place on the pension list, all persons whose names are contained in a report previously made by him to congress. If he should refuse to do so, would the wounded veteran be without remedy? Is it to be contended, that where the law, in precise terms, directs the performance of an act, in which an individual is interested, the law is incapable of securing obedience to its mandate? Is it on account of the character of the person against whom the complaint is made? Is it to be contended that the heads of departments are not amenable to the laws of their country? Whatever the practice on particular occasions may be, the theory of this principle will certainly never be maintained. No act of the legislature confers so extraordinary a privilege, nor can it derive countenance from the doctrines of the common law. After stating that personal injury from the king to a subject is presumed to be impossible, Blackstone (vol. 3, p. 255), says, "but injuries to the rights of property can scarcely be committed by the crown, without the intervention of its officers; for whom the law, in matters of right, entertains no respect or delicacy; but furnishes various methods of detecting the errors and misconduct of those agents, by whom the king has been deceived and induced to do a temporary injustice."

By the act passed in 1796, authorizing the sale of the lands above the mouth of Kentucky river (1 U.S. Stat. 464), the purchaser, on paying his purchase-money, becomes completely entitled to the property purchased; and on producing to the secretary of state the receipt of the treasurer, upon a certificate required by the law, the president of the United States is authorized to grant him a patent. It is further enacted, that all patents shall be countersigned by the secretary of state, and recorded in his office. If the secretary of state should choose to withhold this patent; or, the patent being lost, should refuse a copy of it; can it be imagined, that the law furnishes to the injured person no remedy? It is not believed, that any person whatever would attempt to maintain such a proposition.

It follows, then, that the question, whether the legality of an act of the head of a department be examinable in a court of justice or not, must always depend on the nature of that act. If some acts be examinable, and others not, there must be some rule of law to guide that court in the exercise of its jurisdiction. In some instances, there may be difficulty in applying the rule to particular cases; but there cannot, it is believed, be much difficulty in laying down the rule.

By the constitution of the United States, the president is invested with certain important political powers, in the exercise of which he is to use his own discretion, and is accountable only to his country in his political character, and to his own conscience. To aid him in the performance of these duties, he is authorized to appoint certain officers, who act by his authority, and in conformity with his orders. In such cases, their acts are his acts; and whatever opinion may be entertained of the manner in which executive discretion may be used, still there exists, and can exist, no power to control that discretion. The subjects are political: they respect the nation, not individual rights, and being entrusted to the executive, the decision of the executive is conclusive. The application of this remark will be perceived, by adverting to the act of congress for establishing the department of foreign affairs. This officer, as his duties were prescribed by that act, is to conform precisely to the will of the president: he is the mere organ by whom that will is communicated. The acts of such an officer, as an officer, can never be examinable by the courts. But when the legislature proceeds to impose on that officer other duties; when he is directed peremptorily to perform certain acts; when the rights of individuals are dependent on the performance of those acts; he is so far the officer of the law; is amenable to the laws for his conduct; and cannot, at his discretion, sport away the vested rights of others.

The conclusion from this reasoning is, that where the heads of departments are the political or confidential agents of the executive, merely to execute the will of the president, or rather to act in cases in which the executive possesses a constitutional or legal discretion, nothing can be more perfectly clear, than that their acts are only politically examinable. But where a specific duty is assigned by law, and individual rights depend upon the performance of that duty, it seems equally clear, that the individual who considers himself injured, has a right to resort to the laws of his country for a remedy.

If this be the rule, let us inquire, how it applies to the case under the consideration of the court. The power of nominating to the senate, and the power of appointing the person nominated, are political powers, to be exercised by the president, according to his own discretion. When he has made an appointment, he has exercised his whole power, and his discretion has been completely applied to the case. If, by law, the officer be removable at the will of the president, then a new appointment may be immediately made, and the rights of the officer are terminated. But as a fact which has existed, cannot be made never to have existed, the appointment cannot be annihilated; and consequently, if the officer is by law not removable at the will of the president, the rights he has acquired are protected by the law, and are not resumable by the president. They cannot be extinguished by executive authority, and he has the privilege of asserting them in like manner, as if they had been derived from any other source.

The question whether a right has vested or not, is, in its nature, judicial, and must be tried by the judicial authority. If, for example, Mr. Marbury had taken the oaths of a magistrate, and proceeded to act as one; in consequence of which, a suit has been instituted against him, in which his defense had depended on his being a magistrate, the validity of his appointment must have been determined by judicial authority. So, if he conceives that, by virtue of his appointment, he has a legal right either to the commission which has been made out for him, or to a copy of that commission, it is equally a question examinable in a court, and the decision of the court upon it must depend on the opinion entertained of his appointment. That question has been discussed, and the opinion is, that the latest point of time which can be taken as that at which the appointment was complete, and evidenced, was when, after the signature of the president, the seal of the United States was affixed to the commission.

It is, then, the opinion of the Court: 1st. That by signing the commission of Mr. Marbury, the President of the United States appointed him a justice of peace for the county of Washington, in the district of Columbia; and that the seal of the United States, affixed thereto by the Secretary of state, is conclusive testimony of the verity of the signature, land of the completion of the appointment; and that the appointment conferred on him a legal right to the office for the space of five years. 2d. That, having this legal title to the office, he has a consequent right to the commission; a refusal to deliver which is a plain violation of that right, for which the laws of his country afford him a remedy.

3. It remains to be inquired whether he is entitled to the remedy for which he applies? This depends on—1st.

The nature of the writ applied for; and 2d. The power of this court.

1st. The nature of the writ. Blackstone, in the 3d volume of his Commentaries, page 110, defines a *mandamus* to be "a command issuing in the king's name, from the court of king's bench, and directed to any person, corporation or inferior court of judicature, within the king's dominions, requiring them to do some particular thing therein specified, which appertains to their office and duty, and which the court of king's bench has previously determined, or at least supposes, to be consonant to right and justice."

Lord Mansfield, in 3 Burr. 1267, in the case of *The King* v. *Baker et al.*, states, with much precision and explicitness, the cases in which this writ may be used. "Whenever," says that very able judge, "there is a right to execute an office, perform a service, or exercise a franchise (more especially if it be in a matter of public concern, or attended with profit), and a person is kept out of possession, or dispossessed of such right, and has no other specific legal remedy, this court ought to assist by *mandamus,* upon reasons of justice, as the writ expresses, and upon reasons of public policy, to preserve peace, order and good government." In the same case, he says, "this writ ought to be used upon all occasions where the law has established no specific remedy, and where in justice and good government there ought to be one." In addition to the authorities now particularly cited, many others were relied on at the bar, which show how far the practice has conformed to the general doctrines that have been just quoted.

This writ, if awarded, would be directed to an officer of government, and its mandate to him would be, to use the words of Blackstone, "to do a particular thing therein specified, which appertains to his office and duty, and which the court has previously determined, or at least supposes, to be consonant to right and justice." Or, in the words of Lord Mansfield, the applicant, in this case, has a right to execute an office of public concern, and is kept out of possession of that right. These circumstances certainly concur in this case.

Still, to render the *mandamus* a proper remedy, the officer to whom it is to be directed, must be one to whom, on legal principles, such writ may be directed; and the person applying for it must be without any other specific and legal remedy.

1. With respect to the officer to whom it would be directed. The intimate political relation subsisting between the president of the United States and the heads of departments, necessarily renders any legal investigation of the acts of one of those high officers peculiarly irksome, as well as delicate; and excites some hesitation with respect to the propriety of entering into such investigation. Impressions are often received, without much reflection or

examination, and it is not wonderful, that in such a case as this, the assertion, by an individual, of his legal claims in a court of justice, to which claims it is the duty of that court to attend, should at first view be considered by some, as an attempt to intrude into the cabinet, and to intermeddle with the prerogatives of the executive.

It is scarcely necessary for the court to disclaim all pretensions to such a jurisdiction. An extravagance, so absurd and excessive, could not have been entertained for a moment. The province of the court is, solely, to decide on the rights of individuals, not to inquire how the executive, or executive officers, perform duties in which they have a discretion. Questions in their nature political, or which are, by the constitution and laws, submitted to the executive, can never be made in this court.

But, if this be not such a question; if, so far from being an intrusion into the secrets of the cabinet, it respects a paper which, according to law, is upon record, and to a copy of which the law gives a right, on the payment of ten cents; if it be no intermeddling with a subject over which the executive can be considered as having exercised any control; what is there, in the exalted station of the officer, which shall bar a citizen from asserting, in a court of justice, his legal rights, or shall forbid a court to listen to the claim, or to issue a *mandamus,* directing the performance of a duty, not depending on executive discretion, but no particular acts of congress, and the general principles of law?

If one of the heads of departments commits any illegal act, under color of his office, by which an individual sustains an injury, it cannot be pretended, that his office alone exempts him from being sued in the ordinary mode of proceeding, and being compelled to obey the judgment of the law. How then, can his office exempt him from this particular mode of deciding on the legality of his conduct, if the case be such a case as would, were any other individual the party complained of, authorize the process?

It is not by the office of the person to whom the writ is directed, but the nature of the thing to be done, that the propriety or impropriety of issuing a *mandamus* is to be determined. Where the head of a department acts in a case, in which executive will; it is again repeated, that any application to a court to control, in any respect, his conduct would be rejected without hesitation. But where he is directed by law to do a certain act, affecting the absolute rights of individuals, in the performance of which he is not placed under the particular direction of the president, and the performance of which the president cannot lawfully forbid, and therefore, is never presumed to have forbidden; as, for example, to record a commission or a patent for land, which has received all the legal solemnities; or to give a copy of such record; in such cases, it is not perceived, on what ground the courts of the country are fur-

ther excused from the duty of giving judgment that right be done to an injured individual, than if the same services were to be performed by a person not the head of a department.

This opinion seems not now, for the first time, to be taken up in this country. It must be well recollected, that in 1792, an act passed, directing the secretary at war to place on the pension list such disabled officers and soldiers as should be reported to him, by the circuit courts, which act, so far as the duty was imposed on the courts, was deemed unconstitutional; but some of the judges, thinking that the law might be executed by them in the character of commissioners, proceeded to act, and to report in that character. This law being deemed unconstitutional, at the circuits, was repealed, and a different system was established; but the question whether those persons who had been reported by the judges, as commissioners, were entitled, in consequence of that report, to be placed on the pension list, was a legal question, properly determinable in the courts, although the act of placing such persons on the list was to be performed by the head of a department.

That this question might be properly settled, congress passed an act, in February 1793, making it the duty of the secretary of war, in conjunction with the attorney-general, to take such measures as might be necessary to obtain an adjudication of the supreme court of the United States on the validity of any such rights, claimed under the act aforesaid. After the passage of this act, a *mandamus* was moved for, to be directed to the secretary of war, commanding him to place on the pension list, a person stating himself to be on the report of the judges. There is, therefore, much reason to believe, that this mode of trying the legal right of the complainant was deemed, by the head of a department, and by the highest law- officer of the United States, the most proper which could be selected for the purpose. When the subject was brought before the court, the decision was, not that a *mandamus* would not lie to the head of a department, directing him to perform an act, enjoined by law, in the performance of which an individual had a vested interest; but that a *mandamus* ought not to issue in that case; the decision necessarily to be made, if the report of the commissioners did not confer on the applicant a legal right. The judgment, in that case, is understood to have decided the merits of all claims of that description; and the persons, on the report of the commissioners, found it necessary to pursue the mode prescribed by the law, subsequent to that which had been deemed unconstitutional, in order to place themselves on the pension list. The doctrine, therefore, now advanced, is by no means a novel one.

It is true, that the *mandamus,* now moved for, is not for the performance of an act expressly enjoined by statute. It is to deliver a commission; on which subject, the acts of congress are silent. This difference is not considered as affecting the case. It has already been stated, that the applicant has, to that commission, a vested legal right, of which the executive cannot deprive him. He has been appointed to an office, from which he is not removable at the will of the executive; and being so appointed, he has a right to the commission which the secretary has received from the president for his use. The act of congress does not indeed order the secretary of state to send it to him, but it is placed in his hands for the person entitled to it; and cannot be more lawfully withheld by him, than by any other person.

It was at first doubted, whether the action of *detinue* was not a specific legal remedy for the commission which has been withheld from Mr. Marbury; in which case, a *mandamus* would be improper. But this doubt has yielded to the consideration, that the judgment in *detinue* is for the thing itself, *or* its value. The value of a public office, not to be sold, is incapable of being ascertained; and the applicant has a right to the office itself, or to nothing. He will obtain the office by obtaining the commission, or a copy of it, from the record.

This, then, is a plain case for a *mandamus* , either to deliver the commission, or a copy of it from the record; and it only remains to be inquired, whether it can issue from this court?

The act to establish the judicial courts of the United States authorizes the supreme court, "to issue writs of *mandamus*, in cases warranted by the principles and usages of law, to any courts appointed or persons holding office, under the authority of the United States." The secretary of state, being a person holding an office under the authority of the United States, is precisely within the letter of this description; and if this court is not authorized to issue a writ of *mandamus* to such an officer, if must be because the law is unconstitutional, and therefore, absolutely incapable of conferring the authority, and assigning the duties which its words purport to confer and assign.

The constitution vests the whole judicial power of the United States in one supreme court, and such inferior courts as congress shall, from time to time, ordain and establish. This power is expressly extended to all cases arising under the laws of the United States; and consequently, in some form, may be exercised over the present case; because the right claimed is given by a law of the United States.

In the distribution of this power, it is declared, the "the supreme court shall have original jurisdiction, in all cases affecting ambassadors, other public ministers and consuls, and those in which a state shall be a party. In all other cases, the supreme court shall have appellate jurisdiction." It has been insisted, at the bar, that as the original grant of jurisdiction to the supreme and inferior courts,

is general, and the clause, assigning original jurisdiction to the supreme court, contains no negative or restrictive words, the power remains to the legislature, to assign original jurisdiction to that court, in other cases than those specified in the article which has been recited; provided those cases belong to the judicial power of the United States.

If it had been intended to leave it in the discretion of the legislature, to apportion the judicial power between the supreme and inferior courts, according to the will of that body, it would certainly have been useless to have proceeded further than to have defined the judicial power, and the tribunals in which it should be vested. The subsequent part of the section is mere surplusage—is entirely without meaning, if such is to be the construction. If congress remains at liberty to give this court appellate jurisdiction, where the constitution has declared their jurisdiction shall be original; and original jurisdiction where the constitution has declared it shall be appellate; the distribution of jurisdiction, made in the constitution, if form without substance. Affirmative words are often, in their operation, negative of other objects than those affirmed; and in this case, a negative or exclusive sense must be given to them, or they have no operation at all.

It cannot be presumed, that any clause in the constitution is intended to be without effect; and therefore, such a construction is inadmissible, unless the words require it. If the solicitude of the convention, respecting our peace with foreign powers, induced a provision that the supreme court should take original jurisdiction in cases which might be supposed to affect them; yet the clause would have proceeded no further than to provide for such cases, if no further restriction on the powers of congress had been intended. That they should have appellate jurisdiction in all other cases, with such exceptions as congress might make, is no restriction; unless the words be deemed exclusive of original jurisdiction.

When an instrument organizing, fundamentally, a judicial system, divides it into one supreme, and so many inferior courts as the legislature may ordain and establish; then enumerates its powers, and proceeds so far to distribute them, as to define the jurisdiction of the supreme court, by declaring the cases in which it shall take original jurisdiction, and that in others it shall take appellate jurisdiction, the plain import of the words seems to be, that in one class of cases, its jurisdiction is original, and not appellate; in the other, it is appellate, and not original. If any other construction would render the clause inoperative, that is an additional reason for rejecting such other construction, and for adhering to their obvious meaning. To enable this court, then, to issue a *mandamus*, it must be shown to be an exercise of appellate jurisdiction, or to be necessary to enable them to exercise appellate jurisdiction.

It has been stated at the bar, that the appellate jurisdiction may be exercised in a variety of forms, and that if it be the will of the legislature that a *mandamus* should be used for that purpose, that will must be obeyed. This is true, yet the jurisdiction must be appellate, not original. It is the essential criterion of appellate jurisdiction, that it revises and corrects the proceedings in a cause already instituted, and does not create that cause. Although, therefore, a *mandamus* may be directed to courts, yet to issue such a writ to an officer, for the delivery of a paper, is, in effect, the same as to sustain an original action for that paper, and therefore, seems not to belong to appellate, but to original jurisdiction. Neither is it necessary in such a case as this, to enable the court to exercise its appellate jurisdiction. The authority, therefore, given to the supreme court by the act establishing the judicial courts of the United States, to issue writs of *mandamus* to public officers, appears not to be warranted by the constitution; and it becomes necessary to inquire, whether a jurisdiction so conferred can be exercised.

The question, whether an act, repugnant to the constitution, can become the law of the land, is a question deeply interesting to the United States; but happily, not of an intricacy proportioned to its interest. It seems only necessary to recognise certain principles, supposed to have been long and well established, to decide it. That the people have an original right to establish, for their future government, such principles as, in their opinion, shall most conduce to their own happiness, is the basis on which the whole American fabric has been erected. The exercise of this original right is a very great exertion; nor can it, nor ought it, to be frequently repeated. The principles, therefore, so established, are deemed fundamental: and as the authority from which they proceed is supreme, and can seldom act, they are designed to be permanent.

This original and supreme will organizes the government, and assigns to different departments their respective powers. It may either stop here, or establish certain limits not to be transcended by those departments. The government of the United States is of the latter description. The powers of the legislature are defined and limited; and that those limits may not be mistaken or forgotten, the constitution is written. To what purpose are powers limited, and to what purpose is that limitation committed to writing, if these limits may, at any time, be passed by those intended to be restrained? The distinction between a government with limited and unlimited powers is abolished, if those limits do not confine the persons on whom they are imposed, and if acts prohibited and acts allowed, are of equal obligation. It is a proposition too plain to be contested, that the constitution controls any legislative act repugnant to it; or that the legislature may alter the constitution by an ordinary act.

Between these alternatives, there is no middle ground. The constitution is either a superior paramount law, unchangeable by ordinary means, or it is on a level with ordinary legislative acts, and, like other acts, is alterable when the legislature shall please to alter it. If the former part of the alternative be true, then a legislative act, contrary to the constitution, is not law: if the latter part be true, then written constitutions are absurd attempts, on the part of the people, to limit a power, in its own nature, illimitable.

Certainly, all those who have framed written constitutions contemplate them as forming the fundamental and paramount law of the nation, and consequently, the theory of every such government must be, that an act of the legislature, repugnant to the constitution, is void. This theory is essentially attached to a written constitution, and is, consequently, to be considered, by this court, as one of the fundamental principles of our society. It is not, therefore, to be lost sight of, in the further consideration of this subject.

If an act of the legislature, repugnant to the constitution, is void, does it, notwithstanding its invalidity, bind the courts, and oblige them to give it effect? Or, in other words, though it be not law, does it constitute a rule as operative as if it was a law? This would be to overthrow, in fact, what was established in theory; and would seem, at first view, an absurdity too gross to be insisted on. It shall, however, receive a more attentive consideration.

It is, emphatically, the province and duty of the judicial department, to say what the law is. Those who apply the rule to particular cases, must of necessity expound and interpret that rule. If two laws conflict with each other, the courts must decide on the operation of each. So, if a law be in opposition to the constitution; if both the law and the constitution apply to a particular case, so that the court must either decide that case, conformable to the law, disregarding the constitution; or conformable to the constitution, disregarding the law; the court must determine which of these conflicting rules governs the case: this is of the very essence of judicial duty. If then, the courts are to regard the constitution, and the constitution is superior to any ordinary act of the legislature, the constitution, and not such ordinary act, must govern the case to which they both apply.

Those, then, who controvert the principle, that the constitution is to be considered, in court, as a paramount law, are reduced to the necessity of maintaining that courts must close their eyes on the constitution, and see only the law. This doctrine would subvert the very foundation of all written constitutions. It would declare that an act which, according to the principles and theory of our government, is entirely void, is yet, in practice, completely obligatory. It would declare, that if the legislature shall do what is expressly forbidden, such act, notwithstanding the express prohibition, is in reality effectual. It would be giving to the legislature a practical and real omnipotence, with the same breath which professes to restrict their powers within narrow limits. It is prescribing limits, and declaring that those limits may be passed at pleasure. That it thus reduces to nothing, what we have deemed the greatest improvement on political institutions, a written constitution, would, of itself, be sufficient, in America, where written constitutions have been viewed with so much reverence, for rejecting the construction. But the peculiar expressions of the constitution of the United States furnish additional arguments in favor of its rejection. The judicial power of the United States is extended to all cases arising under the constitution. Could it be the intention of those who gave this power, to say, that in using it, the constitution should not be looked into? That a case arising under the constitution should be decided, without examining the instrument under which it arises? This is too extravagant to be maintained. In some cases, then, the constitution must be looked into by the judges. And if they can open it at all, what part of it are they forbidden to read or to obey?

There are many other parts of the constitution which serve to illustrate this subject. It is declared, that "no tax or duty shall be laid on articles exported from any state." Suppose, a duty on the export of cotton, of tobacco or of flour; and a suit instituted to recover it. Ought judgment to be rendered in such a case? ought the judges to close their eyes on the constitution, and only see the law?

The constitution declares "that no bill of attainder or *ex post facto* law shall be passed." If, however, such a bill should be passed, and a person should be prosecuted under it; must the court condemn to death those victims whom the constitution endeavors to preserve?

"No person," says the constitution, "shall be convicted of treason, unless on the testimony of two witnesses to the same *overt* act, or on confession in open court." Here, the language of the constitution is addressed especially to the courts. It prescribes, directly for them, a rule of evidence not to be departed from. If the legislature should change that rule, and declare one witness, or a confession out of court, sufficient for conviction, must the constitutional principle yield to the legislative act?

From these, and many other selections which might be made, it is apparent, that the framers of the constitution contemplated that instrument as a rule for the government of courts, as well as of the legislature. Why otherwise does it direct the judges to take an oath to support it? This oath certainly applies in an especial manner, to their conduct in their official character. How immoral to impose it on them, if they were to be used as the instruments, and the knowing instruments, for violating what they swear to support!

The oath of office, too, imposed by the legislature, is completely demonstrative of the legislative opinion on this subject. It is in these words: "I do solemnly swear, that I will administer justice, without respect to persons, and do equal right to the poor and to the rich; and that I will faithfully and impartially discharge all the duties incumbent on me as—,according to the best of my abilities and understanding, agreeably to the constitution and laws of the United States." Why does a judge swear to discharge his duties agreeably to the constitution of the United States, if that constitution forms no rule for his government? if it is closed upon him, and cannot be inspected by him? If such be the real state of things, this is worse than solemn mockery. To prescribe, or to take this oath, becomes equally a crime.

It is also not entirely unworthy of observation, that in declaring what shall be the supreme law of the land, the constitution itself is first mentioned; and not the laws of the United States, generally, but those only which shall be made in pursuance of the constitution, have that rank.

Thus, the particular phraseology of the constitution of the United States confirms and strengthens the principle, supposed to be essential to all written constitutions, that a law repugnant to the constitution is void; and that courts, as well as other departments, are bound by that instrument.

The rule must be discharged.

Source:
5 U.S. 137 (1803).

Fletcher v. Peck, 1810

U.S. Supreme Court decision issued on March 16, 1810, concerning a Georgia land fraud case; the ruling was the first to declare a state law void under the U.S. Constitution. In the Yazoo land fraud case, the Georgia legislature had been bribed, in 1795, into selling 35 million acres to four land companies for $500,000. The following year a new Georgia legislature rescinded the sale on the grounds of fraud and corruption, and a suit concerning the land title eventually reached the Supreme Court. The Court was faced with a dilemma: How could it uphold the sanctity of contract, essential to promoting industry and commerce in the new nation, without appearing to sanction fraud and corruption and in the process reward speculators of dubious reputation. In a unanimous opinion written by Chief Justice John Marshall, the Court upheld the 1795 grant by declaring the new state law unconstitutional for abrogating contracts. He therefore preserved property and contractual rights. At the same time, he noted that legislative fraud and corruption must be rooted out through the electoral process, not the courts.

Fletcher v. Peck
March 16, 1810

Marshall, Ch. J. delivered the opinion of the court upon the pleadings, as follows:

In this cause there are demurrers to three pleas filed in the circuit court, and a special verdict found on an issue joined on the 4th plea. The pleas were all sustained, and judgment was rendered for the defendant.

To support this judgment, this court must concur in overruling all the demurrers; for, if the plea to any one of the counts be bad, the plaintiff below is entitled to damages on that count.

The covenant, on which the breach in the first count is assigned, is in these words; "that the legislature of the said state, (Georgia,) at the time of the passing of the act of sale aforesaid, had good right to sell and dispose of the same, in manner pointed out by the said act."

The breach of this covenant is assigned in these words; "now the said Fletcher saith that, at the time when the said act of the legislature of Georgia, entitled an act, &c. was passed, the said legislature had no authority to sell and dispose of the tenements aforesaid, or of any part thereof, in the manner pointed out in the said act."

The plea sets forth the constitution of the state of Georgia, and avers that the lands lay within that state. It then sets forth the act of the legislature, and avers that the lands, described in the declaration, are included within those to be sold by the said act; and that the *governor* was legally empowered to sell and convey the premises.

To this plea the plaintiff demurred; and the defendant joined in the demurrer.

If it be admitted that sufficient matter is shown, in this plea, to have justified the defendant in denying the breach alleged in the count, it must also be admitted that he has not denied it. The breach alleged is, that the legislature had not authority to sell. The bar set up is, that the governor had authority to convey. Certainly an allegation, that the principal has no right to give a power, is not denied by alleging that he has given a proper power to the agent.

It is argued that the plea shows, although it does not, in terms, aver, that the legislature had authority to convey. The court does not mean to controvert this position, but its admission would not help the case. The matter set forth in the plea, as matter of inducement, may be argumentatively good, may warrant an averment which negatives the averment in the declaration, but does not itself constitute that negative.

Had the plaintiff tendered an issue in fact upon this plea, that the governor was legally empowered to sell and convey the premises, it would have been a departure from his declaration; for the count to which this plea is intended as a bar alleges no want of authority in the governor. He was therefore under the necessity of demurring.

But it is contended that although the plea be substantially bad, the judgment, overruling the demurrer, is correct, because the declaration is defective.

The defect alleged in the declaration is, that the breach is not assigned in the words of the covenant. The covenant is, that the legislature had a *right* to convey, and the breach is, that the legislature had no *authority* to convey.

It is not necessary that a breach should be assigned in the very words of the covenant. It is enough that the words of the assignment show, unequivocally, a substantial breach. The assignment under consideration does show such a breach. If the legislature had no *authority* to convey, it had no *right* to convey.

It is, therefore, the opinion of this court, that the circuit court erred in overruling the demurrer to the first plea by the defendant pleaded, and that their judgment ought therefore to be reversed, and that judgment on that plea be rendered for the plaintiff.

After the opinion of the court was delivered, the parties agreed to amend the pleadings, and the cause was continued for further consideration.

The cause having been again argued at this term,

March 16, 1810

Marshall, Ch. J. delivered the opinion of the court as follows:

The pleadings being now amended, this cause comes on again to be heard on sundry demurrers, and on a special verdict.

The suit was instituted on several covenants contained in a deed made by John Peck, the defendant in error, conveying to Robert Fletcher, the plaintiff in error, certain lands which were part of a large purchase made by James Gunn and others, in the year 1795, from the state of Georgia, the contract for which was made in the form of a bill passed by the legislature of that state.

The first count in the declaration set forth a breach in the second covenant contained in the deed. The covenant is, "that the legislature of the state of Georgia, at the time of passing the act of sale aforesaid, had good right to sell and dispose of the same in manner pointed out by the said act." The breach assigned is, that the legislature had no power to sell.

The plea in bar sets forth the constitution of the state of Georgia, and avers that the lands sold by the defendant to the plaintiff, were within that state. It then sets forth the granting act, and avers the power of the legislature to sell and dispose of the premises as pointed out by the act.

To this plea the plaintiff below demurred, and the defendant joined in demurrer.

That the legislature of Georgia, unless restrained by its own constitution, possesses the power of disposing of the unappropriated lands within its own limits, in such manner as its own judgment shall dictate, is a proposition not to be controverted. The only question, then, presented by this demurrer, for the consideration of the court, is this, did the then constitution of the state of Georgia prohibit the legislature to dispose of the lands, which were the subject of this contract, in the manner stipulated by the contract?

The question, whether a law be void for its repugnancy to the constitution, is, at all times, a question of much delicacy, which ought seldom, if ever, to be decided in the affirmative, in a doubtful case. The court, when impelled by duty to render such a judgment, would be unworthy of its station, could it be unmindful of the solemn obligations which that station imposes. But it is not on slight implication and vague conjecture that the legislature is to be pronounced to have transcended its powers, and its acts to be considered as void. The opposition between the constitution and the law should be such that the judge feels a clear and strong conviction of their incompatibility with each other.

In this case the court can perceive no such opposition. In the constitution of Georgia, adopted in the year 1789, the court can perceive no restriction on the legislative power, which inhibits the passage of the act of 1795. The court cannot say that, in passing that act, the legislature has transcended its powers, and violated the constitution.

In overruling the demurrer, therefore, to the first plea, the circuit court committed no error.

The 3d covenant is, that all the title which the state of Georgia ever had in the premises had been legally conveyed to John Peck, the grantor.

The 2d count assigns, in substance, as a breach of this covenant, that the original grantees from the state of Georgia promised and assured divers members of the legislature, then sitting in general assembly, that if the said members would assent to, and vote for, the passing of the act, and if the said bill should pass, such members should have a share of, and be interested in, all the lands purchased from the said state by virtue of such law. And that divers of the said members, to whom the said promises were made, were unduly influenced thereby, and, under such influence, did vote for the passing of the said bill; by reason whereof the said law was a nullity, &c. and so the title of the state of Georgia did not pass to the said Peck, &c.

The plea to this count, after protesting that the promises it alleges were not made, avers, that until after the purchase made from the original grantees by James Greenleaf, under whom the said Peck claims, neither the said James Greenleaf, nor the said Peck, nor any of the mesne vendors between the said Greenleaf and Peck, had any notice or knowledge that any such promises or assurances were made by the said original grantees, or either of them, to any of the members of the legislature of the state of Georgia.

To this plea the plaintiff demurred generally, and the defendant joined in the demurrer.

That corruption should find its way into the governments of our infant republics, and contaminate the very source of legislation, or that impure motives should contribute to the passage of a law, or the formation of a legislative contract, are circumstances most deeply to be deplored. How far a court of justice would, in any case, be competent, on proceedings instituted by the state itself, to vacate a contract thus formed, and to annul rights acquired, under that contract, by third persons having no notice of the improper means by which it was obtained, is a question which the court would approach with much circumspection. It may well be doubted how far the validity of a law depends upon the motives of its framers, and how far the particular inducements, operating on members of the supreme sovereign power of a state, to the formation of a contract by that power, are examinable in a court of justice. If the principle be conceded, that an act of the supreme sovereign power might be declared null by a court, in consequence of the means which procured it, still would there be much difficulty in saying to what extent those means must be applied to produce this effect. Must it be direct corruption, or would interest or undue influence of any kind be sufficient? Must the vitiating cause operate on a majority, or on what number of the members? Would the act be null, whatever might be the wish of the nation, or would its obligation or nullity depend upon the public sentiment?

If the majority of the legislature be corrupted, it may well be doubted, whether it be within the province of the judiciary to control their conduct, and, if less than a majority act from impure motives, the principle by which judicial interference would be regulated, is not clearly discerned.

Whatever difficulties this subject might present, when viewed under aspects of which it may be susceptible, this court can perceive none in the particular pleadings now under consideration.

This is not a bill brought by the state of Georgia, to annul the contract, nor does it appear to the court, by this count, that the state of Georgia is dissatisfied with the sale that has been made. The case, as made out in the pleadings, is simply this. One individual who holds lands in the state of Georgia, under a deed covenanting that the title of Georgia was in the grantor, brings an action of covenant upon this deed, and assigns, as a breach, that some of the members of the legislature were induced to vote in favour of the law, which constituted the contract, by being promised an interest in it, and that therefore the act is a mere nullity.

This solemn question cannot be brought thus collaterally and incidentally before the court. It would be indecent, in the extreme, upon a private contract, between two individuals, to enter into an inquiry respecting the corruption of the sovereign power of a state. If the title be plainly deduced from a legislative act, which the legislature might constitutionally pass, if the act be clothed with all the requisite forms of a law, a court, sitting as a court of law, cannot sustain a suit brought by one individual against another founded on the allegation that the act is a nullity, in consequence of the impure motives which influenced certain members of the legislature which passed the law.

The circuit court, therefore, did right in overruling this demurrer.

The 4th covenant in the deed is, that the title to the premises has been, in no way, constitutionally or legally impaired by virtue of any subsequent act of any subsequent legislature of the state of Georgia. The third count recites the undue means practised on certain members of the legislature, as stated in the second count, and then alleges that, in consequence of these parties, and of other causes, a subsequent legislature passed an act annulling and, rescinding the law under which the conveyance to the original grantees was made, declaring that conveyance void, and asserting the title of the state to the lands it contained. The count proceeds to recite at large, this rescinding act, and concludes with averring that, by reason of this act, the title of the said Peck in the premises was constitutionally and legally impaired, and rendered null and void.

After protesting, as before, that no such promises were made as stated in this count, the defendant again pleads that himself and the first purchaser under the original grantees, and all intermediate holders of the property, were purchasers without notice.

To this plea there is a demurrer and joinder.

The importance and the difficulty of the questions, presented by these pleadings, are deeply felt by the court.

The lands in controversy vested absolutely in James Gunn and others, the original grantees, by the conveyance of the governor, made in pursuance of an act of assembly to which the legislature was fully competent. Being thus in full possession of the legal estate, they, for a valuable consideration, conveyed portions of the land to those who were willing to purchase. If the original transaction was infected with fraud, these purchasers did not participate in it, and had no notice of it. They were innocent. Yet the leg-

islature of Georgia has involved them in the fate of the first parties to the transaction, and, if the act be valid, has annihilated their rights also.

The legislature of Georgia was a party to this transaction; and for a party to pronounce its own deed invalid, whatever cause may be assigned for its invalidity, must be considered as a mere act of power which must find its vindication in a train of reasoning not often heard in courts of justice.

But the real party, it is said, are the people, and when their agents are unfaithful, the acts of those agents cease to be obligatory.

It is, however, to be recollected that the people can act only by these agents, and that, while within the powers conferred on them, their acts must be considered as the acts of the people. If the agents be corrupt, others may be chosen, and, if their contracts be examinable, the common sentiment, as well as common usage of mankind, points out a mode by which this examination may be made, and their validity determined.

If the legislature of Georgia was not bound to submit its pretensions to those tribunals which are established for the security of property, and no decide on human rights, if it might claim to itself the power of judging in its own case, yet there are certain great principles of justice, whose authority is universally acknowledged, that ought not to be entirely disregarded.

If the legislature be its own judge in its own case, it would seem equitable that its decision should be regulated by those rules which would have regulated the decision of a judicial tribunal. The question was, in its nature, a question of title, and the tribunal which decided it was either acting in the character of a court of justice, and performing a duty usually assigned to a court, or it was exerting a mere act of power in which it was controlled only by its own will.

If a suit be brought to set aside a conveyance obtained by fraud, and the fraud be clearly proved, the conveyance will be set aside, as between the parties; but the rights of third persons, who are purchasers without notice, for a valuable consideration, cannot be disregarded. Titles, which, according to every legal test, are perfect, are acquired with that confidence which is inspired by the opinion that the purchaser is safe. If there be any concealed defect, arising from the conduct of those who had held the property long before he acquired it, of which he had no notice, that concealed defect cannot be set up against him. He has paid his money for a title good at law, he is innocent, whatever may be the guilt of others, and equity will not subject him to the penalties attached to that guilt. All titles would be insecure, and the intercourse between man and man would be very seriously obstructed, if this principle be overturned.

A court of chancery, therefore, had a bill been brought to set aside the conveyance made to James Gunn and others, as being obtained by improper practices with the legislature, whatever might have been its decision as respected the original grantees, would have been bound, by its own rules, and by the clearest principles of equity, to leave unmolested those who were purchasers, without notice, for a valuable consideration.

If the legislature felt itself absolved from those rules of property which are common to all the citizens of the United States, and from those principles of equity which are acknowledged in all our courts, its act is to be supported by its power alone, and the same power may devest any other individual of his lands, if it shall be the will of the legislature so to exert it.

It is not intended to speak with disrespect of the legislature of Georgia, or of its acts. Far from it. The question is a general question, and is treated as one. For although such powerful objections to a legislative grant, as are alleged against this, may not again exist, yet the principle, on which alone this rescinding act is to be supported, may be applied to every case to which it shall be the will of any legislature to apply it. The principle is this; that a legislature may, by its own act, devest the vested estate of any man whatever, for reasons which shall, by itself, be deemed sufficient.

In this case the legislature may have had ample proof that the original grant was obtained by practices which can never be too much reprobated, and which would have justified its abrogation so far as respected those to whom crime was imputable. But the grant, when issued, conveyed an estate in fee- simple to the grantee, clothed with all the solemnities which law can bestow. This estate was transferrable; and those who purchased parts of it were not stained by that guilt which infected the original transaction. Their case is not distinguishable from the ordinary case of purchasers of a legal estate without knowledge of any secret fraud which might have led to the emanation of the original grant. According to the well known, course of equity, their rights could not be affected by such fraud. Their situation was the same, their title was the same, with that of every other member of the community who holds land by regular conveyances from the original patentee.

Is the power of the legislature competent to the annihilation of such title, and to a resumption of the property thus held?

The principle asserted is, that one legislature is competent to repeal any act which a former legislature was competent to pass; and that one legislature cannot abridge the powers of a succeeding legislature.

The correctness of this principle, so far as respects general legislation, can never be controverted. But, if an act be done under a law, a succeeding legislature cannot undo it. The past cannot be recalled by the most absolute power. Conveyances have been made, those conveyances have vested legal estates, and, if those estates may be seized by the sovereign authority, still, that they originally vested is a fact, and cannot cease to be a fact.

When, then, a law is in its nature a contract, when absolute rights have vested under that contract, a repeal of the law cannot devest those rights; and the act of annulling them, if legitimate, is rendered so by a power applicable to the case of every individual in the community.

It may well be doubted whether the nature of society and of government does not prescribe some limits to the legislative power; and, if any be prescribed, where are they to be found, if the property of an individual, fairly and honestly acquired, may be seized without compensation.

To the legislature all legislative power is granted; but the question, whether the act of transferring the property of an individual to the public, be in the nature of the legislative power, is well worthy of serious reflection.

It is the peculiar province of the legislature to prescribe general rules for the government of society; the application of those rules of individuals in society would seem to be the duty of other departments. How far the power of giving the law may involve every other power, in cases where the constitution is silent, never has been, and perhaps never can be, definitely stated.

The validity of this rescinding act, then, might well be doubted, were Georgia a single sovereign power. But Georgia cannot be viewed as a single, unconnected, sovereign power, on whose legislature no other restrictions are imposed than may be found in its own constitution. She is a part of a large empire; she is a member of the American union; and that union has a constitution the supremacy of which all acknowledge, and which imposes limits to the legislatures of the several states, which none claim a right to pass. The constitution of the United States declares that no state shall pass any bill of attainder, *ex post facto* law, or law impairing the obligation of contracts.

Does the case now under consideration come within this prohibitory section of the constitution?

In considering this very interesting question, we immediately ask ourselves what is a contract? Is a grant a contract?

A contract is a compact between two or more parties, and is either executory or executed. An executory contract is one in which a party binds himself to do, or not to do, a particular thing; such was the law under which the conveyance was made by the governor. A contract executed is one in which the object of contract is performed; and this, says Blackstone, differs in nothing from a grant. The contract between Georgia and the purchasers was executed by the grant. A contract executed, as well as one which is executory, contains obligations binding on the parties. A grant, in its own nature, amounts to an extinguishment of the right of the grantor, and implies a contract not to reassert that right. A party is, therefore, always estopped by his own grant.

Since, then, in fact, a grant is a contract executed, the obligation of which still continues, and since the constitution uses the general term contract, without distinguishing between those which are executory and those which are executed, it must be construed to comprehend the latter as well as the former. A law annulling conveyances between individuals, and declaring that the grantors should stand seised of their former estates, notwithstanding those grants, would be as repugnant to the constitution as a law discharging the vendors of property from the obligation of executing their contracts by conveyances. It would be strange if a contract to convey was secured by the constitution, while an absolute conveyance remained unprotected.

If, under a fair construction the constitution, grants are comprehended under the term contracts, is a grant from the state excluded from the operation of the provision? Is the clause to be considered as inhibiting the state from impairing the obligation of contracts between two individuals, but as excluding from that inhibition contracts made with itself?

The words themselves contain no such distinction. They are general, and are applicable to contracts of every description. If contracts made with the state are to be exempted from their operation, the exception must arise from the character to the contracting party, not from the words which are employed.

Whatever respect might have been felt for the state sovereignties, it is not to be disguised that the framers of the constitution viewed, with some apprehension, the violent acts which might grow out of the feelings of the moment; and that the people of the United States, in adopting that instrument, have manifested a determination to shield themselves and their property from the effects of those sudden and strong passions to which men are exposed. The restrictions on the legislative power of the states are obviously founded in this sentiment; and the constitution of the United States contains what may be deemed a bill of rights for the people of each state.

No state shall pass any bill of attainder *ex post facto* law, or law impairing the obligation of contracts.

A bill of attainder may affect the life of an individual, or may confiscate his property, or may do both.

In this form the power of the legislature over the lives and fortunes of individuals is expressly restrained. What motive, then, for implying, in words which import a general prohibition to impair the obligation of contracts, an exception in favour of the right to impair the obligation of those contracts into which the state may enter?

The state legislatures can pass no *ex post facto* law. An *ex post facto* law is one which renders an act punishable in a manner in which it was not punishable when it was committed. Such a law may inflict penalties on the person, or may inflict pecuniary penalties which swell the public treasury. The legislature is then prohibited from passing a law by which a man's estate, or any part of it, shall be seized for a crime which was not declared, by some previous law, to render him liable to that punishment. Why, then, should violence be done to the natural meaning of words for the purpose of leaving to the legislature the power of seizing, for public use, the estate of an individual in the form of a law annulling the title by which he holds the estate? The court can perceive no sufficient grounds for making this distinction. This rescinding act would have the effect of an *ex post facto* law. It forfeits the estate of Fletcher for a crime not committed by himself, but by those from whom he purchased.

This cannot be effected in the form of an *ex post facto* law, or bill of attainder; why, then, is allowable in the form of a law annulling the original grant?

The argument in favour of presuming an intention to except a case, not expected by the words of the constitution, is susceptible of some illustration from a principle originally ingrafted in that instrument, though no longer a part of it. The constitution, as passed, gave the courts of the United States jurisdiction in suits brought against individual states. A state, then, which violated its own contract was suable in the courts of the United States for that violation. Would it have been a defence in such a suit to say that the state had passed a law absolving itself from the contract? It is scarcely to be conceived that such a defence could be set up. And yet, if a state is neither restrained by the general principles of our political institutions, nor by the words, of the constitution, from impairing the obligation of its own contracts, such a defence would be a valid one. This feature is no longer found in the constitution; but it aids in the construction of those clauses with which it was originally associated.

It is, then, the unanimous opinion of the court, that, in this case, the estate having passed into the hands of a purchaser for a valuable consideration, without notice, the state of Georgia was restrained, either by general principles which are common to our free institutions, or by the particular provisions of the constitution of the United States, from passing a law whereby the estate of the plaintiff in the premises so purchased could be constitutionally and legally impaired and rendered null and void.

In overruling the demurer to the 3d plea, therefore, there is no error.

The first covenant in the deed is, that the state of Georgia, at the time of the act of the legislature thereof, entitled as aforesaid, was legally seised in fee of the soil thereof subject only to the extinguishment of part of the Indian title thereon.

The 4th count assigns, as a breach of this covenant, that the right to the soil was in the United States, and not in Georgia.

To this count the defendant pleads, that the state of Georgia *was seised;* and tenders an issue on the fact in which the plaintiff joins. On this issue a special verdict is found.

The jury find the grant of Carolina by Charles second to the Earl of Clarendon and others, comprehending the whole country from 36 deg. 30 min. north lat. to 29 deg. north lat., and from the Atlantic to the South Sea.

They find that the northern part of this territory was afterwards erected into a separate colony, and that the most northern part of the 35 deg. of north lat. was the boundary line between North and South Carolina.

That seven of the eight proprietors of the Carolinas surrendered to George 2d in the year 1729, who appointed a Governor of South Carolina.

That, in 1732, George the 2d granted, to the Lord Viscount Percival and others, seven eights of the territory between the Savannah and the Alatamaha, and extending west to the South Sea, and that the remaining eighth part, which was still the property of the heir of Lord Carteret, one of the original grantees of Carolina, was afterwards conveyed to them. This territory was constituted a colony and called Georgia.

That the Governor of South Carolina continued to exercise jurisdiction south of Georgia.

That, in 1752, the grantees surrendered to the crown.

That, in 1754, a governor was appointed by the crown, with a commission describing the boundaries of the colony.

That a treaty of peace was concluded between Great Britain and Spain, in 1763, in which the latter ceded to the former Florida, with Fort St. Augustin and the bay of Pensacola.

That, in October, 1763, the King of Great Britain issued a proclamation, creating four new colonies, Quebec, East Florida, West Florida, and Grenada; and prescribing the bounds of each, and further declaring that all the lands between the Alatamaha, and St. Mary's should be annexed to Georgia. The same proclamation contained a clause reserving, under the dominion and protection of the crown, for the use of the Indians, all the lands on the western waters, and forbidding a settlement on them, or a purchase of them from the Indians. The lands conveyed to the plaintiff lie on the western waters.

That, in November, 1763, a commission was issued to the Governor of Georgia, in which the boundaries of that province are described, as extending westward to the Mississippi. A commission, describing boundaries of the same extent, was afterwards granted in 1764.

That a war broke out between Great Britain and her colonies, which terminated in a treaty of peace acknowledging them as sovereign and independent states.

That in April, 1787, a convention was entered into between the states of South Carolina and Georgia settling the boundary line between them.

The jury afterwards describe the situation of the lands mentioned in the plaintiff's declaration, in such manner that their lying within the limits of Georgia, as defined in the proclamation of 1763, in the treaty of peace, and in the convention between that state and South Carolina, has not been questioned.

The counsel for the plaintiff rest their argument on a single proposition. They contend that the reservation for the use of the Indians, continued in the proclamation of 1763, excepts the lands on the western waters from the colonies within whose bounds they would otherwise have been, and that they were acquired by the revolutionary war. All acquisitions during the war, it is contended, were made by the joint arms, for the joint benefit of the United States, and not for the benefit of any particular state.

The court does not understand the proclamation as it is understood by the counsel for the plaintiff. The reservation for the use of the Indians appears to be a temporary arrangement suspending, for a time, the settlement of the country reserved, and the powers of the royal governor within the territory reserved, but is not conceived to amount to an alteration of the boundaries of the colony. If the language of the proclamation be, in itself, doubtful, the commissions subsequent thereto, which were given to the governors of Georgia, entirely remove the doubt.

The question, whether the vacant lands within the United States became a joint property, or belonged to the separate states, was a momentous question which, at one time, threatened to shake the American confederacy to its foundation. This important and dangerous contest has been compromised, and the compromise is not now to be disturbed.

It is the opinion of the court, that the particular land stated in the declaration appears, from this special verdict, to lie within the state of Georgia, and that the state of Georgia had power to grant it.

Some difficulty was produced by the language of the covenant, and of the pleadings. It was doubted whether a state can be seised in fee of lands, subject to the Indian title, and whether a decision that they were seised in fee, might not be construed to amount to a decision that their grantee might maintain an ejectment for them, notwithstanding that title.

The majority of the court is of opinion that the nature of the Indian title, which is certainly to be respected by all courts, until it be legitimately extinguished, is not such as to be absolutely repugnant to seisin in fee on the part of the state.

Judgment affirmed with costs.

Johnson, J. In this case I entertain, on two points, an opinion different from that which has been delivered by the court.

I do not hesitate to declare that a state does not possess the power of revoking its own grants. But I do it on a general principle, on the reason and nature of things: a principle which will impose laws even on the deity.

A contrary opinion can only be maintained upon the ground that no existing legislature can abridge the powers of those which will succeed it. To a certain extent this is certainly correct; but the distinction lies between power and interest, the right of jurisdiction ad the right of soil.

The right of jurisdiction is essentially connected to, or rather identified with, the national sovereignty. To part with it is to commit a species of political suicide. In fact, a power to produce its own annihilation is an absurdity in terms. It is a power as utterly incommunicable to a political as to a natural person. But it is not so with the interests or property of a nation. Its possessions nationally are in nowise necessary to its political existence; they are entirely accidental, and may be parted with in every respect similarly to those of the individuals who compose the community. When the legislature have once conveyed their interest or property in any subject to the individual, they have lost all control over it; have nothing to act upon; it has passed from them; is vested in the individual; becomes intimately blended with his existence, as essentially so as the blood that circulates through his system. The government may indeed demand of him the one or the other, not because they are not his, but because whatever is his is his country's.

As to the idea, that the grants of a legislature may be void because the legislature are corrupt, it appears to me to be subject to insuperable difficulties. The acts of the supreme power of a country must be considered pure for the same reason that all sovereign acts must be considered just; because there is no power that can declare them otherwise. The absurdity in this case would have been strikingly perceived, could the party who passed the act of cession have got again into power, and declared themselves pure, and the intermediate legislature corrupt.

The security of a people against the misconduct of their rulers, must lie in the frequent recurrence to first principles, and the imposition of adequate constitutional restrictions. Nor would it be difficult, with the same view, for laws to be framed which would bring the conduct of individuals under the review of adequate tribunals, and make them suffer under the consequences of their own immoral conduct.

I have thrown out these ideas that I may have it distinctly understood that my opinion on this point is not founded on the provision in the constitution of the United States, relative to laws impairing the obligation of contracts. It is much to be regretted that words of less equivocal signification, had not been adopted in that article of the constitution. There is reason to believe, from the letters of Publius, which are well known to be entitled to the highest respect, that the object of the convention was to afford a general protection to individual rights against the acts of the state legislatures. Whether the words, "acts impairing the obligation of contracts," can be construed to have the same force as must have been given to the words "obligation and *effect* of contracts," is the difficulty in my mind.

There can be no solid objection to adopting the technical definition of the word "contract," given by Blackstone. The etymology, the classical signification, and the civil law idea of the word, will all support it. But the difficulty arises on the word "obligation," which certainly imports an existing moral or physical necessity. Now a grant or conveyance by no means necessarily implies the continuance of an obligation beyond the moment of executing it. It is most generally but the consummation of a contract is *functus officio* the moment it is executed, and continues afterwards to be nothing more than the evidence that a certain act was done.

I enter with great hesitation upon this question, because it involves a subject of the greatest delicacy and much difficulty. The states and the United States are continually legislating on the subject of contracts, prescribing the mode of authentication, the time within which suits shall be prosecuted for them, in many cases affecting existing contracts by the laws which they pass, and declaring them to cease or lose their effect for want of compliance, in the parties, with such statutory provisions. All these acts appear to be within the most correct limits of legislative powers, and most beneficially exercised, and certainly could not have been intended to be affected by this constitutional provision; yet where to draw the line, or how to define or limit the words, "obligation of contracts," will be found a subject of extreme difficulty.

To give it the general effect of a restriction of the state powers in favour of private rights, is certainly going very far beyond the obvious and necessary import of the words, and would operate to restrict the states in the exercise of that right which every community must exercise, of possessing itself of the property of the individual, when necessary for public uses; a right which a magnanimous and just government will never exercise without amply indemnifying the individual, and which perhaps amounts to nothing more than a power to oblige him to sell and convey, when the public necessities require it.

The other point on which I dissent from the opinion of the court, is relative to the judgment which ought to be given on the first count. Upon that count we are called upon substantially to decide, "that the state of Georgia, at the time of passing the act of cession, was legally seised in fee of the soil, (then ceded,) subject only to the extinguishment of part of the Indian title." That is, that the state of Georgia was seised of an estate in fee-simple in the lands in question, subject to another estate, we know not what, nor whether it may not swallow up the whole estate decided to exist in Georgia. It would seem that the mere vagueness and uncertainty of this covenant would be a sufficient objection to deciding in favour of it, but to me it appears that the facts in the case are sufficient to support the opinion that the state of Georgia had not a *fee-simple* in the land in question.

This is a question of much delicacy, and more fitted for a diplomatic or legislative than a judicial inquiry. But I am called upon to make a decision, and I must make it upon technical principles.

The question is, whether it can be correctly predicated of the interest or estate which the state of Georgia had in these lands, "that the state was seised thereof, in fee-simple."

To me it appears that the interest of Georgia in that land amounted to nothing more than a mere possibility, and that her conveyance thereof could operate legally only as a covenant to convey or to stand seised to a use.

The correctness of this opinion will depend upon a just view of the state of the Indian nations. This will be found to be very various. Some have totally extinguished their national fire, and submitted themselves to the laws of the states: others have, by treaty, acknowledged that they hold their national existence at the will of the state within which they reside: others retain a limited sovereignty, and the absolute proprietorship of their soil. The latter is the case of the tribes to the west of Georgia. We legislate upon the conduct of strangers or citizens within their limits, but innumerable treaties formed with them acknowledge them to be an independent people, and the uniform practice of acknowledging their right of soil, by purchasing from them, and restraining all persons from encroaching upon their territory, makes it unnecessary to insist upon their right of soil. Can, then, one nation be said to be seised of a fee-simple in lands, the right of soil of which is in another nation? It is awkward to apply the technical idea of a fee-simple to the interests of a nation, but I must consider an absolute right of soil as an estate to them and their heirs. A fee-simple estate may be held in reversion, but our law will not admit the idea of its being limited after a free-simple. In fact, if the Indian nations be the absolute proprietors of their soil, no other nation can be said to have the same

interest in it. What, then, practically, is the interest of the states in the soil of the Indians within their boundaries? Unaffected by particular treaties, it is nothing more than what was assumed at the first settlement of the country, to wit, a right of conquest or of purchase, exclusively of all competitors within certain defined limits. All the restrictions upon the right of soil in the Indians, amount only to an exclusion of all competitors from their markets; and the limitation upon their sovereignty amounts to the right of governing every person within their limits except themselves. If the interest in Georgia was nothing more than a pre-emptive right, how could that be called a fee-simple, which was nothing more than a power to acquire a fee-simple by purchase, when the proprietors should be pleased to sell? And if this ever was any thing more than a mere possibility, it certainly was reduced to that state when the state of Georgia ceded, to the United States, by the constitution, both the power of pre-emption and of conquest, retaining for itself only a resulting right dependent on a purchase or conquest to be made by the United States.

I have been very unwilling to proceed to the decision of this cause at all. It appears to me to bear strong evidence, upon the face of it, of being a mere feigned case. It is our duty to decide on the rights, but not on the speculations of parties. My confidence, however, in the respectable gentlemen who have been engaged for the parties, has induced me to abandon my scruples, in the belief that they would never consent to impose a mere feigned case upon this court.

Source:
10 U.S. 87 (1810).

Martin v. Hunter's Lessee, 1816

U.S. Supreme Court decision of March 20, 1816, that upheld the Court's right to review the decisions of state courts in all cases involving the laws, treaties, and Constitution of the United States. In *Ware* v. *Hilton* (1796), the U.S. Supreme Court had established previously that a national treaty superseded a state law. The *Martin* decision, written by Justice Joseph Story, reversed a ruling of the Virginia Court of Appeals affirming the state's right to confiscate British-owned land, a right contrary to the Jay Treaty between the British and U.S. governments, which protected such property from exploration. Virginia argued that the state and federal governments were equal, with neither having the power to overrule the other. Story, however, ruled that the Supreme Court had primacy and appellate jurisdiction over state courts in constitutional cases.

Martin, heir at law and devisee of Fairfax, v. Hunter's Lessee
March 20, 1816

Story, J., delivered the opinion of the court.

This is a writ of error from the court of appeals of Virginia, founded upon the refusal of that court to obey the mandate of this court, requiring the judgment rendered in this very cause, at February term, 1813, to be carried into due execution. The following is the judgment of the court of appeals rendered on the mandate: "The court is unanimously of opinion, that the appellate power of the supreme court of the United States does not extend to this court, under a sound construction of the constitution of the United States; that so much of the 25th section of the act of congress to establish the judicial courts of the United States, as extends the appellate jurisdiction of the supreme court to this court, is not in pursuance of the constitution of the United States; that the writ of error, in this cause, was improvidently allowed under the authority of that act; that the proceedings thereon in the supreme court were, *coram non judice*, in relation to this court, and that obedience to its mandate be declined by the court."

The questions involved in this judgment are of great importance and delicacy. Perhaps it is not too much to affirm, that, upon their right decision, rest some of the most solid principles which have hitherto been supposed to sustain and protect the constitution itself. The great respectability, too, of the court whose decisions we are called upon to review, and the entire deference which we entertain for the learning and ability of that court, add much to the difficulty of the task which has so unwelcomely fallen upon us. It is, however, a source of consolidation, that we have had the assistance of most able and learned arguments to aid our inquiries; and that the opinion which is now to be pronounced has been weighed with every solicitude to come to a correct result, and matured after solemn deliberation.

Before proceeding to the principle questions, it may not be unfit to dispose of some preliminary considerations which have grown out of the arguments at the bar.

The constitution of the United States was ordained and established, not by the states in their sovereign capacities, but emphatically, as the preamble of the constitution declares, by "the people of the United States." There can be no doubt that it was competent to the people to invest the general government with all the powers which they might deem proper and necessary; to extend or restrain these powers according to their own good pleasure, and to give them a paramount and supreme authority. As little doubt can there be, that the people had a right to prohibit to the states the exercise of any powers which were, in their judgment, incompatible with the objects of the general compact; to make the powers of the state governments, in given cases, subordinate to those of the nation, or to reserve to themselves those sovereign authorities which they might not choose to delegate to either. The constitution was not, therefore, necessarily carved out of existing state sovereignties, nor a surrender of powers already existing in state institutions, for the powers of the states depend upon their own constitutions; and the people of every state had the right to modify and restrain them, according to their own views of policy or principle. On the other hand, it is perfectly clear that the sovereign powers vested in the state governments, by their respective constitutions, remained unaltered and unimpaired, except so far as they were granted to the government of the United States.

These deductions do not rest upon general reasoning, plain and obvious as they seem to be. They have been positively recognised by one of the articles in amendment of the constitution, which declares, that "the powers not delegated to the United States by the constitution, nor prohibited by it to the states, are reserved to the *states* respectively, or *to the people.*"

The government, then, of the United States, can claim no power which are not granted to it by the constitution, and the powers actually granted, must be such as are expressly given, or given by necessary implication. On the other hand, this instrument, like every other grant, is to have a reasonable construction, according to the import of its terms; and where a power is expressly given in general terms, it is not to be restrained to particular cases, unless that construction grow out of the context expressly, or by necessary implication. The words to be taken in their natural and obvious sense, and not in a sense reasonably restricted or enlarged.

The constitution unavoidably deals in general language. It did not suit the purposes of the people, in framing this great charter of our liberties, to provide for minute specifications of its powers, or to declare the means by which those powers should be carried into execution. It was foreseen that this would be a perilous and difficult, if not an impracticable, task. The instrument was not intended to provide merely for the exigencies of a few years, but was to endure through a long lapse of ages, the events of which were locked up in the inscrutable purposes of Providence. It could not be foreseen what new changes and modifications of power might be indispensable to effectuate the general objects of the charter; and restrictions and specifications, which, at the present, might seem salutary, might, in the end, prove the overthrow of the system itself. Hence its powers are expressed in general terms, leaving to the legislature, from time to time, to adopt its own means to effectuate legitimate objects, and to mould and model the exercise of its powers, and its own wisdom, and the public interests, should require.

With these principles in view, principles in respect to which no difference of opinion ought to be indulged, let us now proceed to the interpretation of the constitution, so far as regards the great points in controversy.

The third article of the constitution is that which must principally attract our attention. The 1st. section declares, "the judicial power of the United States shall be vested in one supreme court, and in such other inferior courts as the congress may, from time to time, ordain and establish." The 2d section declares, that "the judicial power shall extend to all cases in law or equity, arising under this constitution, the laws of the United States, and the treaties made, or which shall be made, under their authority; to all cases affecting ambassadors, other public ministers and consuls; to all cases of admiralty and maritime jurisdiction; to controversies to which the United States shall be a party; to controversies between two or more states; between a state and citizens of another state; between citizens of different states; between citizens of the same state, claiming lands under the grants of different states; and between a state or the citizens thereof, and foreign states, citizens, or subject." It then proceeds to declare, that "in all cases affecting ambassadors, other, public ministers and consuls, and those in which a state shall be a party, the supreme court shall have *original jurisdiction.* In all the other cases before mentioned the supreme court shall have *appellate jurisdiction,* both as to law and fact, with such exceptions, and under such regulations, as the congress shall make."

Such is the language of the article creating and defining the judicial power of the United States. It is the voice of the whole American people solemnly declared, in establishing one great department of that government which was, in many respects, national, and in all, supreme. It is a part of the very same instrument which was to act not merely upon individuals, but upon states; and to deprive them altogether of the exercise of some powers of sovereignty, and to restrain and regulate them in the exercise of others. Let this article be carefully weighed and considered. The language of the article throughout is manifestly designed to be mandatory upon the legislature. Its obligatory force is so imperative, that congress could not, without a violation of its duty, have refused to carry it into operation. The judicial power of the United States *shall be vested* (not may be vested) in one supreme court, and in such inferior courts as congress may, from time to time, ordain and establish. Could congress have lawfully refused to create a supreme court, or to vest in it the constitutional jurisdiction? "The judges, both of the supreme and inferior courts, *shall hold* their offices during good behavior, and

shall, at stated times, receive, for their services, a compensation which shall not be diminished during their continuance in office." Could congress create or limit any other tenure of the judicial office? Could they refuse to pay, at stated times, the stipulated salary, or diminish it during the continuance in office? But one answer can be given to these questions: it must be in the negative. The object of the constitution was to establish three great departments of government; the legislative, the executive, and the judicial departments. The first was to pass laws, the second to approve and execute them, and the third to expound and enforce them. Without the latter, it would be impossible to carry into effect some of the express provisions of the constitution. How, otherwise, could crimes against the United States be tried and punished? How could causes between two states be heard and determined? The judicial power must, therefore, be vested in some court, by congress; and to suppose that it was not an obligation binding on them, but might, at their pleasure, be omited or declined, is to suppose that, under the sanction of the constitution, they might defeat the constitution itself; a construction which would lead to such a result cannot be sound.

The same expression, "shall be vested," occurs in other parts of the constitution, in defining the powers of the other co-ordinate branches of the government. The first article declares that "all legislative powers herein granted *shall be vested* in a congress of the United States." Will it be contended that the legislative power is not absolutely vested? that the words merely refer to some future act, and mean only that the legislative power may hereafter be vested? The second article declares that "the executive power *shall be vested* in a president of the United States of America." Could congress vest it in any other person; or, is it to await their good pleasure, whether it is to vest at all? It is apparent that such a construction, in either case, would be utterly inadmissible. Why, then, is it entitled to a better support in reference to the judicial department?

If, then, it is a duty of congress to vest the judicial power of the United States, it is a duty to vest the *whole judicial power.* The language, if imperative as to one part, is imperative as to all. If it were otherwise, this anomaly would exist, that congress might successively refuse to vest the jurisdiction in any one class of cases enumerated in the constitution, and thereby defeat the jurisdiction as to all; for the constitution has not singled out any class on which congress are bound to act in preference to others. The next consideration is as to the courts in which the judicial power shall be vested. It is manifest that a supreme court must be established; but whether it be equally obligatory to establish inferior courts, is a question of some difficulty. If congress may lawfully omit to establish inferior courts, it might follow, that in some of the enumerated cases the judicial power could nowhere exist. The supreme court can have original jurisdiction in two classes of cases only, viz. in cases affecting ambassadors, other public ministers and consuls, and in cases in which a state is a party. Congress cannot vest any portion of the judicial power of the United States, except in courts ordained and established by itself; and if in any of the cases enumerated in the constitution, the state courts did not then possess jurisdiction, the appellate jurisdiction of the supreme court (admitting that it could act on state courts) could not reach those cases, and, consequently, the injunction of the constitution, that the judicial power *"shall be vested,"* would be disobeyed. It would seem, therefore, to follow, that congress are bound to create some inferior courts, in which to vest all that jurisdiction which, under the constitution, is *exclusively* vested in the United States, and of which the supreme court cannot take original cognizance. They might establish one or more inferior courts; they might parcel out the jurisdiction among such courts, from time to time, at their own pleasure. But the whole judicial power of the United States should be, at all times, vested either in an original or appellate form, in some courts created under its authority.

This construction will be fortified by an attentive examination of the second section of the third article. The words are "the judicial power *shall extend,*" &c. Much minute and elaborate criticism has been employed upon these words. It has been argued that they are equivalent to the words "may extend," and that "extend" means to widen to new cases not before within the scope of the power. For the reasons which have been already stated, we are of opinion that the words are used in an imperative sense. They import an absolute grant of judicial power. They cannot have a relative signification applicable to powers already granted; for the American *people* had not made any previous grant. The constitution was for a new government, organized with new substantive powers, and not a mere supplementary charter to a government already existing. The confederation was a compact between states; and its structure and powers were wholly unlike those of the national government. The constitution was an act of the people of the United States to supercede the confederation, and not to be ingrafted on it, as a stock through which it was to receive life and nourishment.

If, indeed, the relative signification could be fixed upon the term "extend," it could not (as we shall hereafter see) subserve the purposes of the argument in support of which it has been adduced. This imperative sense of the words "shall extend," is strengthened by the context. It is declared that "in all cases affecting ambassadors, &c., that the supreme court *shall have* original jurisdiction." Could congress withhold original jurisdiction in these cases from the supreme court? The clause proceeds—"in all the other cases before mentioned the supreme court shall have

appellate jurisdiction, both as to law and fact, with such exceptions, and under such regulations, as the congress shall make." The very exception here shows that the framers of the constitution used the words in an imperative sense. What necessity could there exist for this exception if the preceding words were not used in that sense? Without such exception, congress would, by the preceding words, have possessed a complete power to regulate the appellate jurisdiction, if the language were only equivalent to the words "may have" appellate jurisdiction. It is apparent, then, that the exception was intended as a limitation upon the preceding words, to enable congress to regulate and restrain the appellate power, as the public interests might, from time to time, require.

Other clauses in the constitution might be brought in aid of this construction; but a minute examination of them cannot be necessary, and would occupy too much time. It will be found that whenever a particular object is to be effected, the language of the constitution is always imperative, and cannot be disregarded without violating the first principles of public duty. On the other hand, the legislative powers are given in language which implies discretion, as from the nature of legislative power such a discretion must ever be exercised.

It being, then, established that the language of this clause is imperative, the next question is as to the cases to which it shall apply. The answer is found in the constitution itself. The judicial power shall extend to all the cases enumerated in the constitution. As the mode is not limited, it may extend to all such cases, in any form, in which judicial power may be exercised. It may, therefore, extend to them in the shape of original or appellate jurisdiction, or both; for there is nothing in the nature of the cases which binds to the exercise of the one in preference to the other.

In what cases (if any) is this judicial power exclusive, or exclusive at the election of congress? It will be observed that there are two classes of cases enumerated in the constitution, between which a distinction seems to be drawn. The first class includes cases arising under the constitution, laws, and treaties of the United States; cases affecting ambassadors, other public ministers and consuls, and cases of admiralty and maritime jurisdiction. In this class the expression is, and that the judicial power shall extend to *all cases;* but in the subsequent part of the clause which embraces all the other cases of national cognizance, and forms the second class, the word *"all"* is dropped seemingly *ex industria.* Here the judicial authority is to extend to controversies (not to *all* controversies) to which the United States shall be a party, &c. From this difference of phraseology, perhaps, a difference of constitutional intention may, with proprietary, be inferred. It is hardly to be presumed that the variation in the language could have been accidental. It must have been the result of some determinate reason; and it is not very difficult to find a reason sufficient to support the apparent change of intention. In respect to the first class, it may well have been the intention of the framers of the constitution imperatively to extend the judicial power either in an original or appellate form to *all cases;* and in the latter class to leave it to congress to qualify the jurisdiction, original or appellate, in such manner as public policy might dictate.

The vital importance of all the cases enumerated in the first class to the national sovereignty, might warrant such a distinction. In the first place, as to cases arriving under the constitution, laws, and treaties of the United States. Here the state courts could not ordinarily possess a direct jurisdiction. The jurisdiction over such cases could not exist in the state courts previous to the adoption of the constitution, and it could not afterwards be directly conferred on them; for the constitution expressly requires the judicial power to be vested in courts ordained and established by the United States. This class of cases would embrace civil as well as criminal jurisdiction, and affect not only our internal policy, but our foreign relations. It would, therefore, be perilous to restrain it in any manner whatsoever, inasmuch as it might hazard the national safety. The same remarks may be urged as to cases affecting ambassadors, other public ministers, and consuls, who are emphatically placed under the guardianship of the law of nations; and as to cases of admiralty and maritime jurisdiction, the admiralty jurisdiction embraces all questions of prize and salvage, in the correct adjudication of which foreign nations are deeply interested; it embraces also maritime torts, contracts, and offences, in which the principles of the law and comity of nations often form an essential inquiry. All these cases, then, enter into the national policy, affect the national right, and may compromit the national sovereignty. The original or appellate jurisdiction ought not, therefore, to be restrained, but should be commensurate with the mischiefs intended to be remedied, and, of course, should extend to all cases whatsoever.

A different policy might well be adopted in reference to the second class of cases; for although it might be fit that the judicial power should extend to all controversies to which the United States should be a party, yet this power night not have been imperatively given, least it should imply a right to take cognizance of original suits brought against the United States as defendants in their own courts. It might not have been deemed proper to submit the sovereignty of the United States, against their own will, to judicial cognizance, either to enforce rights or to prevent wrongs; and as to the other cases of the second class, they might well be left to be exercised under the exceptions and regulations which congress might, in their wisdom, choose to apply. It is also worthy of remark, that congress seem, in a good degree, in the establishment of

the present judicial system, to have adopted this distinction. In the first class of cases, the jurisdiction is not limited except by the subject matter; in the second, it is made materially to depend upon the value in controversy.

We do not, however, profess to place any implicit reliance upon the distinction which has here been stated and endeavoured to be illustrated. It has the rather been brought into view in deference to the legislative opinion, which has so long acted upon, and enforced, this distinction. But there is, certainly, vast weight in the argument which has been urged, that the constitution is imperative upon congress to vest all the judicial power of the United States, in the shape of original jurisdiction, in the supreme and inferior courts created under its own authority. At all events, whether the one construction or the other prevail, it is manifest that the judicial power of the United States is unavoidably, in some cases, exclusive of all state authority, and in all others, may be made so at the election of congress. No part of the criminal jurisdiction of the United States can, consistently with the constitution, be delegated to state tribunals. The admiralty and maritime jurisdiction is of the same exclusive cognizance; and it can only be in those cases where, previous to the constitution, state tribunals possessed jurisdiction independent of national authority, that they can now constitutionally exercise a concurrent jurisdiction. Congress, throughout the judicial act, and particularly in the 9th, 11th, and 13th sections, have legislated upon the supposition that in all the cases to which the judicial powers of the United States extended, they might rightfully vest exclusive jurisdiction in their own courts.

But, even admitting that the language of the constitution is not mandatory, and that congress may constitutionally omit to vest the judicial power in courts of the United States, it cannot be denied that when it is vested, it may be exercised to the utmost constitutional extent.

This leads us to the consideration of the great question as to the nature and extent of the appellate jurisdiction of the United States. We have already seen that appellate jurisdiction is given by the constitution of the supreme court in all cases where it has not original jurisdiction; subject, however, to such exceptions and regulations as congress may prescribe. It is, therefore, capable of embracing every case enumerated in the constitution, which is not exclusively to be decided by way of original jurisdiction. But the exercise of appellate jurisdiction is far from being limited by the terms of the constitution to the supreme court. There can be no doubt that congress may create a succession of inferior tribunals, in each of which it may vest appellate as well as original jurisdiction. The judicial power is delegated by the constitution in the most general terms, and may, therefore, be exercised by congress under every variety of form, of appellate or original jurisdiction. And as there is nothing in the constitution which restrains or limits this power, it must, therefore, in all other cases, subsist in the utmost latitude of which, in its own nature, it is susceptible.

As, then, by the terms of the constitution, the appellate jurisdiction is not limited as to the supreme court, and as to this court it may be exercised in all other cases than those of which it has original cognizance, what is there to restrain its exercise over state tribunals in the enumerated cases? The appellate power is not limited by the terms of the third article to any particular courts. The words are, "the judicial power (which includes appellate power) shall extend *to all cases,*" &c., and "in all other cases before mentioned the supreme court shall have appellate jurisdiction." It is the *case,* then, and not *the court,* that gives the jurisdiction. If the judicial power extends to the case, it will be in vain to search in the letter of the constitution for any qualification as to the tribunal where it depends. It is incumbent, then, upon those who assert such a qualification to show its existence by necessary implication. If the text be clear and distinct, no restriction upon its plain and obvious import ought to be admitted, unless the inference be irresistible.

If the constitution meant to limit the appellate jurisdiction to cases pending in the courts of the United States, it would necessarily follow that the jurisdiction of these courts would, in all the cases enumerated in the constitution, be exclusive of state tribunals. How otherwise could the jurisdiction extend to *all* cases arising under the constitution, laws, and treaties of the United States, or *to all cases* of admiralty and maritime jurisdiction? If some of these cases might be entertained by state tribunals, and no appellate jurisdiction as to them should exist, then the appellate power would not extend to *all,* but to *some* cases. If state tribunals might exercise concurrent jurisdiction over all or some of the other classes of cases in the constitution without control, then the appellate jurisdiction of the United States might, as to such cases, have no real existence, contrary to the manifest intent of the constitution. Under such circumstances, to give effect to the judicial power, it must be construed to be exclusive; and this not only when the *casus foederis* should arise directly, but when it should arise, incidentally, in cases pending in state courts. This construction would abridge the jurisdiction of such court far more than has been ever contemplated in any act of congress.

On the other hand, if, as has been contended, a discretion be vested in congress to establish, or not to establish, inferior courts at their own pleasure, and congress should not establish such courts, the appellate jurisdiction of the supreme court would have nothing to act upon, unless it could act upon cases pending in the state courts. Under such circumstances it must be held that the appel-

late power would extend to state courts; for the constitution is peremptory that it shall extend to certain enumerated cases, which cases could exist in no other courts. Any other construction, upon this supposition, would involve this strange contradiction, that a discretionary power vested in congress, and which they might rightfully omit to exercise, would defeat the absolute injunctions of the constitutions in relation to the whole appellate power.

But it is plain that the framers of the constitution did contemplate that cases within the judicial cognizance of the United States not only might but would arise in the state courts, in the exercise of their ordinary jurisdiction. With this view of the sixth article declares, that "this constitution, and the laws of the United States which shall be made in pursuance thereof, and all treaties made, or which shall be made, under the authority of the United States, shall be the supreme law of the land, and the judges in every state shall be bound thereby, and thing in the constitution or laws of any stat to the contrary notwithstanding." It is obvious that this obligation is imperative upon the state judges in their official, and not merely in their private, capacities. From the very nature of their judicial duties they would be called upon to pronounce the law applicable to the case in judgment. They were not to decide merely according to the laws or constitution of the state, but according to the constitution, laws and treaties of the United States—"the supreme law of the land."

A moment's consideration will show us the necessity and propriety of this provision in cases where the jurisdiction of the state court is unquestionable. Suppose a contract for the payment of money is made between citizens of the same state, and performance thereof is sought in the courts of that state; no person can doubt that the jurisdiction completely and exclusively attaches, in the first instance, to such courts. Suppose at the trial the defendant sets up in his defence a tender under a state law, making paper money a good tender, or a state law, impairing the obligation of such contract, which law, if binding, would defeat the suit. The constitution of the United States has declared that not state shall make any thing but gold or silver coin a tender in payment of debts, or pass a law impairing the obligation of contracts. If congress shall not have passed a law providing for the removal of such suit to the courts of the United States, must not the state court proceed to hear and determine it? Can a mere plea in defence be of itself a bar to further proceedings, so as to prohibit in inquiry into its truth or legal propriety, when no other tribunal exists to whom judicial cognizance of such cases is confided? Suppose an indictment for a crime in a state court, and the defendant should allege in his defence that the crime was created by an *ex post facto* act of the state, must not the state court, in the exercise of a jurisdiction which has already rightfully attached, have a right to pronounce on the validity and sufficiency of the defence? It would be extremely difficult, upon any legal principles, to give a negative answer to these inquiries. Innumerable instances of the same sort might be stated, in illustration of the position; and unless the state courts could sustain jurisdiction in such cases, this clause of the sixth article would be without meaning or effect, and public mischiefs, of a most enormous magnitude, would inevitably ensue.

It must, therefore, be conceded that the constitution not only contemplated, but meant to provide for cases within the scope of the judicial power of the United States, which might yet depend before state tribunals. It was foreseen that in the exercise of their ordinary jurisdiction, state courts would incidentally take cognizance of cases arising under the constitution, the laws, and treaties of the United States. Yet to all these cases the judicial power, by the very terms of the constitution, is to extend. It cannot extend by original jurisdiction if that was already rightfully and exclusively attached in the state courts, which (as has been already shown) may occur; it must, therefore, extend by appellate jurisdiction, or not at all. It would seem to follow that the appellate power of the United States must, in such cases, extend to state tribunals; and if in such cases, there is no reason why it should not equally attach upon all others within the purview of the constitution.

It has been argued that such an appellate jurisdiction over state courts is inconsistent with the genius of our governments, and the spirit of the constitution. That the latter was never designed to act upon state sovereignties, but only upon the people, and that if the power exists, it will materially impair the sovereignty of the states, and the independence of their courts. We cannot yield to the force of this reasoning; it assumes principles which we cannot admit, and draws conclusions to which we do not yield our assent.

It is a mistake that the constitution was not designed to operate upon states, in their corporate capacities. It is crowded with provisions which restrain or annul the sovereignty of the states in some of the highest branches of their prerogatives. The tenth section of the first article contains a long list of disabilities and prohibitions imposed upon the states. Surely, when such essential portions of state sovereignty are taken away, prohibited to be exercised it cannot be correctly asserted that the constitution does not act upon the states. The language of the constitution is also imperative upon the states as to the performance of many duties. It is imperative upon the state legislatures to make laws prescribing the time, places, and manner of holding elections for senators and representatives, and for electors of president and vice-president. And in these, as well as some other cases, congress have a right to revise, amend, or supercede the laws which may be passed by state legislature. When, therefore, the states are

stripped of some of the highest attributes of sovereignty, and the same are given to the United States; when the legislatures of the states are, in some respects, under the control of congress, and in every case are, under the constitution, bound by the paramount authority of the United States; it is certainly difficult to support the argument that the appellate power over the decisions of state courts is contrary to the genius of our institutions. The courts of the United States can, without question revise the proceedings of the executive and legislative authorities of the states, and if they are found to be contrary to the constitution, may declare them to be of no legal validity. Surely the exercise of the same right over judicial tribunals is not a higher or more dangerous act of sovereign power.

Nor can such a right be deemed to impair the independence of state judges. It is assuming the very ground in controversy to assert that they possess an absolute independence of the United States. In respect to the powers granted to the United States, they are not independent; they are expressly bound to obedience by the letter of the constitution; and if they should unintentionally transcend their authority, or misconstrue the constitution, there is no more reason for giving their judgments an absolute and irresistible force, than for giving it to the acts of the other co-ordinate departments of state sovereignty. The argument urged from the possibility of the abuse of the revising power, is equally unsatisfactory. It is always a doubtful course, to argue against the use or existence of a power, from the possibility of its abuse. It is still more difficult, by such an argument, to ingraft upon a general power a restriction which is not to be found in the terms in which it is given. From the very nature of things, the absolute right of decision, in the last resort, must rest somewhere—wherever it may be vested it is susceptible of abuse. In all questions of jurisdiction the inferior, or appellate court, must pronounce the final judgment; and common sense, as well as legal reasoning, has conferred it upon the latter.

It has been further argued against the existence of this appellate power, that it would form a novelty in our judicial institutions. This is certainly a mistake. In the articles of confederation, an instrument framed with infinitely more deference to state rights and state jealousies, a power was given to congress to establish "courts for revising and determining, finally, *appeals* in all cases of captures." It is remarkable, that no power was given to entertain *original* jurisdiction in such cases; and, consequently, the appellate power (although not so expressed in terms) was altogether to be exercised in revising the decisions of state tribunals. This was, undoubtedly, so far a surrender of state sovereignty; but it never was supposed to be a power fraught with public danger, or destructive of the independence of state judges. On the contrary, it was supposed to be a power indispensable to the public safety, inasmuch as our national rights might otherwise be compromised, and our national peace been dangered. Under the present constitution the prize jurisdiction is confined to the courts of the United States; and a power to revise the decisions of state courts, if they should assert jurisdiction over prize causes, cannot be less important, or less useful, than it was under the confederation.

In this connexion we are led again to the construction of the words of the constitution, "the judicial power shall extend," &c. If, as has been contended at the bar, the term "extend" have a relative signification, and mean to widen an existing power, it will then follow, that, as the confederation gave an appellate power over state tribunals, the constitution enlarged or widened that appellate power to all the other cases in which jurisdiction is given to the courts of the United States. It is not presumed that the learned counsel would choose to adopt such a conclusion.

It is further argued, that no great public mischief can result from a construction which shall limit the appellate power of the United States to cases in their own courts: first, because state judges are bound by an oath to support the constitution of the United States, and must be presumed to be men of learning and integrity; and, secondly, because congress must have an unquestionable right to remove all cases within the scope of the judicial power from the state courts to the courts of the United States, at any time before final judgment, though not after final judgment. As to the first reason—admitting that the judges of the state courts are, and always will be, of as much learning, integrity, and wisdom, as those of the courts of the United States, (which we very cheerfully admit,) it does not aid the argument. It is manifest that the constitution has proceeded upon a theory of its own, and given or withheld powers according to the judgment of the American people, by whom it was adopted. We can only construe its powers, and cannot inquire into the policy or principles which induced the grant of them. The constitution has presumed (whether rightly or wrongly we do not inquire) that state attachments, state prejudices, state jealousies, and state interests, might sometimes obstruct, or control, or be supposed to obstruct or control, the regular administration of justice. Hence, in controversies between states; between citizens of different states; between citizens claiming grants under different states; between a state and its citizens, or foreigners, and between citizens and foreigners, it enables the parties, under the authority of congress, to have the controversies heard, tried, and determined before the national tribunals. No other reason than that which has been stated can be assigned, why some, at least, of those cases should not have been left to the cognizance of the state courts. In respect to the other enumerated cases—the cases arising under the constitution, laws, and treaties of the United States, cases affecting

ambassadors and other public ministers, and cases of admiralty and maritime jurisdiction—reasons of a higher and more extensive nature, touching the safety, peace, and sovereignty of the nation, might well justify a grant of exclusive jurisdiction.

This is not all. A motive of another kind, perfectly compatible with the most sincere respect for state tribunals, might induce the grant of appellate power over their decisions. That motive is the importance, and even necessity of *uniformly* of decisions throughout the whole United States, upon all subjects within the purview of the constitution. Judges of equal learning and integrity, in different states, might differently interpret a statute, or a treaty of the United States, or even the constitution itself: If there were no revising authority to control these jarring and discordant judgments, and harmonize them into uniformity, the laws, the treaties, and the constitution of the United States would be different in different states, and might, perhaps, never have precisely the same construction, obligation, or efficacy, in any two states. The public mischiefs that would attend such a state of things would be truly deplorable; and it cannot be believed that they could have escaped the enlightened convention which formed the constitutional. What, indeed, might then have been only prophecy, has now become fact; and the appellate jurisdiction must continue to be the only adequate remedy for such evils.

There is an additional consideration, which is entitled to great weight. The constitution of the United States was designed for the common and equal benefit of all the people of the United States. The judicial power was granted for the same benign and salutary purposes. It was not to be exercised exclusively for the benefit of parties who might be plaintiffs, and would elect the national forum, but also for the protection of defendants who might be entitled to try their rights, or assert their privileges, before the same forum. Yet, if the construction contended for be correct, it will follow, that as the plaintiff may always elect the state court, the defendant may be deprived of all the security which the constitution intended in aid of his rights. Such a state of things can, in no respect, be considered as giving equal rights. To obviate this difficulty, we are referred to the power which it is admitted congress possess to remove suits from state courts to the national courts; and this forms the second ground upon which the argument we are considering has been attempted to be sustained.

This power of removal is not to be found in express terms in any part of the constitution; if it be given, it is only given by implication, as a power necessary and proper to carry into effect some express power. The power of removal is certainly not, in strictness of language; it presupposes in exercise of original jurisdiction to have attached elsewhere. The existence of this power of removal is familiar in courts acting according to the course of the common law in criminal as well as civil cases and it is exercised before as well as after judgment. But this is always deemed in both cases an exercise of appellate, and not of original jurisdiction. If, then, the right of removal be included in the appellate jurisdiction, it is only because it is one mode of exercising that power, and as congress is not limited by the constitution to any particular mode, or time of exercising it, it may authorize a removal either before or after judgment. The time, the process, and the manner, must be subject to its absolute legislative control. A writ of error is, indeed, but a process which removes the record of one court to the possession of another court, and enables the latter to inspect the proceedings, and give such judgment as its own opinion of the law and justice of the case may warrant. There is nothing in the nature of the process which forbids if from being applied by the legislature to interlocutory as well as final judgments. And if the right of removal from state courts exist before judgment, because it is included in the appellate power, it must, for the same reason, exist after judgment. And if the appellate power by the constitution does not include cases pending in state courts, the right of removal, which is but a mode of exercising that power, cannot be applied to them. Precisely the same objections, therefore, exist as to the right of removal before judgment, as after, and both must stand or fall together. Nor, indeed, would the force of the arguments on either side materially vary, if the right of removal were an exercise of original jurisdiction. It would equally trench upon the jurisdiction and independence of state tribunals.

The remedy, too, of removal of suits would be utterly inadequate to the purposes of the constitution, if it could act only on the parties, and not upon the state courts. In respect to criminal prosecutions, the difficulty seems admitted to be insurmountable; and in respect to civil suits, there would, in many cases, be rights without corresponding remedies. If state courts should deny the constitutionally of the authority to remove suit from their cognizance, in what manner could they be compelled to relinquish the jurisdiction? In respect to criminal cases, there would at once be an end of all control, and the state decisions would be paramount to the constitution; and though in civil suits the courts of the United States might act upon the parties, yet the state courts might act in the same way; and this conflict of jurisdictions would not only jeopardise private rights, but bring into imminent peril the public interests. On the whole, the court are of opinion, that the appellate power of the United States does extend to cases pending in the state courts; and that the 25th section of the judiciary act, which authorizes the exercise of this jurisdiction in the specified cases, by a writ of error, is supported by the letter and spirit of the constitution. We find no clause in that instrument which limits this power;

and we dare not interpose a limitation where the people have not been disposed to create one.

Strong as this conclusion stands upon the general language of the constitution, it may still derive support from other sources. It is an historical fact, that this exposition of the constitution, extending its appellate power to state courts, was, previous to its adoption, uniformly and publicly avowed by its friends, and admitted by its enemies, as the basis of their respective reasonings, both in and out of the state conventions. It is an historical fact, that at the time when the judiciary act was submitted to the deliberations of the first congress, composed, as it was, not only of men of great learning and ability, but of men who had acted a principal part in framing, supporting, or opposing that constitution, the same exposition was explicitly declared and admitted by the friends and by the opponents of that system. If is an historical fact, that the supreme court of the United States have, from time to time, sustained this appellate jurisdiction in a great variety of cases, brought from the tribunals of many of the most important states in the union, and that no state tribunal has ever breathed a judicial doubt on the subject, or declined to obey the mandate of the supreme court, until the present occasion. This weight of contemporaneous exposition by all parties, this acquiescence of enlightened state courts, and these judicial decisions of the supreme court through so long a period, do, as we think, place the doctrine upon a foundation of authority which cannot be shaken, without delivering over the subject to perpetual and irremediable doubts.

The next question which has been argued, is, whether the case at bar be within the purview of the 25th section of the judiciary act, so that this court may rightfully sustain the present writ of error. This section, stripped of passages unimportant in this inquiry, enacts, in substance, that a final judgment or decree in any suit in the highest court of law or equity of a state, where is drawn in question the validity of a treaty or statute of, or an authority excised under, the United States, and the decision is against their validity; or where is drawn in question the validity of a statute of, or an authority exercised under, any state, on the ground of their being repugnant to the constitution, treaties, or laws, of the United States, and the decision is in favour of such their validity; or of the constitution, or of a treaty or statute of, or commission held under, the United States, and *the decision is against the title, right, privilege, or exemption, specially set up or claimed by either party under such* clause of the said constitution, treaty, statute, or commission, may be re-examined and reversed or affirmed in the supreme court of the United States, upon a writ of error, in the same manner, and under the same regulations, and the writ shall have the same effect, as if the judgment or decree complained of had been rendered or passed in a circuit court, and the proceeding upon the reversal shall also be the same, *except that the supreme court, instead of remanding the cause for a final decision, as before provided, may, at their discretion, if the cause shall have been once remanded before, proceed to a final decision of the same, and award execution.* But no other error shall be assigned or regarded as a ground of reversal in any such case as aforesaid, *than such as appears upon the face of the record, and immediately respects the before-mentioned question* of validity or construction of the said constitution, treaties, statutes, commissions, or authorities in dispute.

That the present writ of error is founded upon a judgment of the court below, which drew in question and denied the validity of a statute of the United States, is controvertible, for it is apparent upon the face of the record. That this judgment is final upon the rights of the parties is equally true; for if well founded, the former judgment of that court was of conclusive authority, and the former judgement of this court utterly void. The decision was, therefore, equivalent to a perpetual stay of proceedings upon the mandate, and a perpetual denial of all the rights acquired under it. The case, then, falls directly within the terms of the act. It is a final judgment in a suit in a state court, denying the validity of a statute of the United States; and unless a distinction can be made between proceedings under a mandate, and proceedings in an original suit, a writ of error is the proper remedy to revise that judgment. In our opinion no legal distinction exists between the cases.

In causes remanded to the circuit courts, if the mandate be not correctly executed, a writ of error or appeal has always been supposed to be a proper remedy, and has been recognized as such in the former decisions of this court. The statute gives the same effect to writs of error from the judgments of state courts as of the circuit courts; and in its terms provides for proceedings where the same cause may be a second time brought up on writ of error before the supreme court. There is no limitation or description of the cases to which the second writ of error may be applied; and it ought, therefore, to be coextensive with the cases which fall within the mischiefs of the statute. It will hardly be denied that this cause stands in that predicament; and if so, then the appellate jurisdiction of this court has rightfully attached.

But it is contended, that the former judgment of this court was rendered upon a case not within the purview of this section of the judicial act, and that as it was pronounced by an incompetent jurisdiction, it was utterly void, and cannot be a sufficient foundation to sustain any subsequent proceedings. To this argument several answers may be given. In the first place, it is not admitted that, upon this writ of error, the former record is before us. The error now assigned is not in the former proceedings, but in the judgment rendered upon the mandate issued after the former judgment. The question now litigated is not upon the construction of a treaty, but upon the constitutionality of a statute of the United States, which is clearly within our jurisdiction. In the next place, in ordinary cases a second writ of error has never been supposed to draw in question the propriety of the first judgment, and it is difficult to perceive how such a proceeding could be sustained upon principle. A final judgment of this court is supposed to be conclusive upon the rights which it decides, and no statute has provided any process by which this court can revise its own judgments. In several cases which have been formerly adjudged in this court, the same point was argued by counsel, and expressly overruled. It was solemnly held at a final judgment of this court was conclusive upon the parties, and could not be re-examined.

In this case, however, from motives of a public nature, we are entirely willing to wave all objections, and to go back and re-examine the question of jurisdiction as it stood upon the record formerly in judgment. We have great confidence that our jurisdiction will, on a careful examination, stand confirmed as well upon principle as authority. It will be recollected that the action was an ejectment for a parcel of land in the Northern Neck, formerly belonging to Lord Fairfax. The original plaintiff claimed the land under a patent granted to him by the state of Virginia, in 1789, under a title supposed to be vested in that state by escheat or forfeiture. The original defendant claimed the land as devisee under the will of Lord Fairfax. The parties agreed to a special statement of facts in the nature of a special verdict, upon which the district court of Winchester, in 1793, gave a general judgment for the defendant, which judgment was afterwards reversed in 1810, by the court of appeals, and a general judgment was rendered for the plaintiff; and from this last judgment a writ of error was brought to the supreme court. The statement of facts contained a regular deduction of the title of Lord Fairfax until his death, in 1781, and also the title of his devisee. It also contained a regular deduction of the title of the plaintiff, under the state of Virginia, and further referred to the treaty of peace of 1783, and to the acts of Virginia respecting the lands of Lord Fairfax, and the supposed escheat or forfeiture thereof, as component parts of the case. No facts disconnected with the titles thus set up by the parties were alleged on either side. It is apparent, from this summary explanation, that the title thus set up by the plaintiff might be open to other objections; but the title of the defendant was perfect and complete, if it was protected by the treaty of 1783. If, therefore, this court had authority to examine into the whole record, and to decide upon the legal validity of the title of the defendant, as well as its application to the treaty of peace, it would be a case within the express purview of the 25th section of the act; for there was nothing in the record upon which the court below could have decided but upon the title as connected with the treaty; and if the title was otherwise good, its sufficiency must have depended altogether upon its protection under the treaty. Under such circumstances it was strictly a suit where was drawn in question the construction of a treaty, and the decision was against the title specially set up or claimed by the defendant. It would fall, then, within the very terms of the act.

The objection urged at the bar is, that this court cannot inquire into the title, but simply into the correctness of the construction put upon the treaty by the court of appeals; and that their judgment is not re- examinable here, unless it appear on the face of the record that some construction was put upon the treaty. If, therefore, that court might have decided the case upon the invalidity of the title, (and, *non constant,* that they did not,) independent of the treaty, there is an end of the appellate jurisdiction of this court. In support of this objection much stress is laid upon the last clause of the section, which declares, that no other cause shall be regarded as a ground of reversal than such as appears *on the face* of the record and *immediately* respects the construction of the treaty, &c., in dispute.

If this be the true construction of the section, it will be wholly inadequate for the purposes which it professes to have in view, and may be evaded at pleasure. But we see no reason for adopting this narrow construction; and there are the strongest reasons against it, founded upon the words as well as the intent of the legislature. What is the case for which the body of the section provides a remedy by writ of error? The answer must be in the words of the section, a suit where is drawn in question the construction of a treaty, and the decision is against *the title set up by the party.* It is, therefore, the decision against the title set up with reference to the treaty, and not the mere abstract construction of the treaty itself, upon which the statute intends to found the appellate jurisdiction. How, indeed, can it be possible to decide whether a title be within the protection of a treaty, until it is ascertained what that title is, and whether it have a legal validity? From the very necessity of the case, there must be a preliminary inquiry into the existence and structure of the title, before the court can construe the treaty in reference to that title. If the court below should decide, that the title was bad, and, therefore, not protected by the treaty, must not this court have a power to decide the title to be good, and, therefore, protected by the treaty? Is not the treaty, in both instances, equally construed, and the title of the party, in reference to the treaty, equally ascertained and decided? Nor does the clause relied on in the objection, impugn this construction. It requires, that the error upon which the appellate court is to decide, shall appear on the face of the record, and *immediately respect* the questions before mentioned in the section. One of the questions is as to the construction of a treaty upon a title specially set up by a party, and every error that immediately respects that question must, of course, be within the cognizance of the court. The title set up in this case is apparent upon the face of the record, and immediately respects the decision of that question; and error, therefore, in respect to that title must be re-examinable, or the case could never be presented to the court.

The restraining clause was manifestly intended for a very different purpose. It was foreseen that the parties might claim under various titles, and might assert various defences, altogether independent of each other. The court might admit or reject evidence applicable to one particular title, and not to all, and in such cases it was the intention of congress to limit what would otherwise have unquestionably attached to the court, the right of revising all the points involved in the cause. It therefore restrains this right to such errors as respect the questions specified in the section; and in this view, it has an appropriate sense, consistent with the preceding clauses. We are, therefore, satisfied, that, upon principle, the case was rightfully before us, and if the point were perfectly new, we should not hesitate to assert the jurisdiction.

But the point has been already decided by this court upon solemn argument. In Smith v. The State of Maryland, (6 *Cranch,* 286.,) precisely the same objection was taken by counsel, and overruled by the unanimous opinion of the court. That case was, in some respects, stronger than the present; for the court below decided, expressly, that the party had no title, and, therefore, the treaty could not operate upon it. This court entered into an examination of that question, and being of the same opinion, affirmed the judgment. There cannot, then, be an authority which could more completely govern the present question.

It has been asserted at the bar that, in point of fact, the court of appeals did not decide either upon the treaty or the title apparent upon the record, but upon a compromise made under an act of the legislature of Virginia. If it be true (as we are informed) that this was a private act, to take effect only upon certain condition, viz. the execution of a deed of release of certain lands, which was matter *in pais,* it is somewhat difficult to understand how the court could take judicial cognizance of the act, or of the performance of the condition, unless spread upon the record. At all events, we are bound to consider that the court did decide upon the facts actually before them. The treaty of peace was not necessary to have been stated, for it was the supreme law of the land, of which all courts must take notice. And at the time of the decision in the court of appeals and in this court, another treaty had intervened, which attached itself to the title in controversy, and, of course, must have been the supreme law to govern the decision, if it should be found applicable to the case. It was in this view that this court did not deem it necessary to rest its former decision upon the treaty of peace, believing that the title of the defendant was, at all events, perfect under the treaty of 1794.

The remaining questions respect more the practice than the principles of this court. The forms of process, and the modes of proceeding in the exercise of jurisdiction are, with few exceptions, left by the legislature to be regulated and changed as this court may, in its discretion, deem expedient. By a rule of this court, the return of a copy of a record of the proper court, under the seal of that court, annexed to the writ of error, is declared to be "a sufficient compliance with the mandate of the writ." The record, in this case, is duly certified by the clerk of the court of appeals, and annexed to the writ of error. The objection, therefore, which has been urged to the sufficiency of the return, cannot prevail.

Another objections is, that it does not appear that the judge who granted the writ of error did, upon issuing the citation, take the bond required by the 22d section of the judiciary act.

We consider that provision as merely directory to the judge; and that an omission does not avoid the writ of error. If any party be prejudiced by the omission, this court can grant him summary relief, by imposing such terms on the other party as, under all the circumstances, may be legal and proper. But there is nothing in the record by which we can judicially know whether a bond has been taken or not; for the statute does not require the bond to be returned to this court, and it might, with equal propriety, be lodged in the court below, who would ordinarily execute the judgment to be rendered on the writ. And the presumption of law is, until the contrary appears, that every judge who signs a citation has obeyed the injunctions of the act.

We have thus gone over all the principal questions in the cause, and we deliver our judgment with entire confidence, that it is consistent with the constitution and laws of the land.

We have not thought it incumbent on us to give any opinion upon the question, whether this court have authority to issue a writ of mandamus to the court of appeals to enforce the former judgments, as we do not think it necessarily involved in the decision of this cause.

It is the opinion of the whole court, that the judgment of the court of appeals of Virginia, rendered on the mandate in this cause, be reversed, and the judgment of the district court, held at Winchester, be, and the same is hereby affirmed.

Johnson, J. It will be observed in this case, that the court disavows all intention to decide on the right to issue compulsory process to the state courts; thus leaving us, in my opinion, where the constitution and laws place us—supreme over persons and cases as far as our judicial powers extend, but not asserting any compulsory control over the state tribunals.

In this view I acquiesce in their opinion, but not altogether in the reasoning, or opinion, of my brother who delivered it. Few minds are accustomed to the same habit of thinking, and our conclusions are most satisfactory to ourselves when arrived at in our own way.

I have another reason for expressing my opinion on this occasion. I view this question as one of the most momentous importance; as one which may affect, in its consequences, the permanence of the American union. It presents an instance of collision between the judicial powers of the union, and one of the greatest states in the union, on a point the most delicate and difficult to be adjusted. On the one hand, the general government must cease to exist whenever it loses the power of protecting itself in the exercise of its constitutional powers. Force, which acts upon the physical powers of man, or judicial process, which addresses itself to his moral principles or his fears, are the only means to which governments can resort in the exercise of their authority. The former is happily unknown to the genius of our constitution, except as far as it shall be sanctioned by the latter; but let the latter be obstructed in its progress by an opposition which it cannot overcome or put by, and the resort must be to the former, or government is no more.

On the other hand, so firmly am I persuaded that the American people can no longer enjoy the blessings of a free government, whenever the state sovereignties shall be prostrated at the feet of the general government, nor the proud consciousness of equality and security, any longer than the independence of judicial power shall be maintained consecrated and intangible, that I could borrow the language of a celebrated orator, and exclaim, "I rejoice that Virginia has resisted."

Yet here I must claim the privilege of expressing my regret, that the opposition of the high and truly respected tribunal of that state had not been marked with a little more moderation. The only point necessary to be decided in the case then before them was, *whether they were bound to obey the mandate emanating from this court?* But in the judgment entered on their minutes, they have affirmed that the case was, in this court, *coram non judice,* or, in other words, that this court had not jurisdiction over it. This is assuming a truly alarming latitude of judicial power. Where is it to end? It is an acknowledged principle of, I believe, every court in the world, that not only the decisions, but every thing done under the judicial process of courts, not having jurisdiction, are, *ipso facto,* void. Are, then, the judgments of this court to be reviewed in every court of the union? and is every recovery of money, every change of property, that has taken place under our process, to be considered as null, void, and tortious?

We pretend not to more infallibility than other courts composed of the same frail materials which compose this. It would be the height of affectation to close our minds upon the recollection that we have been extracted from the same seminaries in which originated the learned men who preside over the state tribunals. But there is one claim which we can with confidence assert *in our own name* upon those tribunals—the profound, uniform, and unaffected respect which this court has always exhibited for state decisions, give us strong pretentions to judicial comity. And another claim I may assert, in *the name of the American people;* in this court, every state in the union is represented; we are constituted by the voice of the union, and when decisions take place, which nothing but a spirit to give ground and harmonize can reconcile, ours is the superor claim upon the comity of the state tribunals. It is the nature of the human mind to press a favourite hypothesis too far, but magnanimity will always be ready to sacrifice the pride of opinion to public welfare.

In the case before us, the collision has been, on our part, wholly unsolicited. The exercise of this appellate jurisdiction over the state decisions has long been acquiesced in, and when the writ of error, in this case, was allowed *by the president of the court of appeals of Virginia,* we were sanctioned in supposing that we were to meet with the same acquiescence there. Had that court refused to grant the writ in the first instance, or had the question of jurisdiction, or on the mode of exercising jurisdiction, been made here originally, we should have been put on our guard, and might have so modelled the process of the court as to strip it of the offensive form of a mandate. In this case it might have been brought down to what probably the 25th section of the judiciary act meant it should be, to wit, an alternative judgment, either that the state court may finally proceed, at its option, to carry into effect the judgment of this court, or, if it declined doing so, that then this court would proceed itself to execute it. The language, sense, and operation of the 25th section on this subject, merit particular attention. In the preceding section, which has relation to causes brought up by writ of error from the circuit courts of the United States, this court is instructed not to issue executions, but to send a special mandate to the circuit court to award execution thereupon. In case of the circuit court's refusal to obey such mandate, there could be no doubt as to the ulterior measures; compulsory process might, unquestionably, be resorted to. Nor, indeed, was there any reason to suppose that they ever would refuse; and, therefore, there is no provision made for authorizing this court to execute its own judgment in cases of that description. But not so, in cases brought up

from the state courts; the framers of that law plainly foresaw that the state courts might refuse; and not being willing to leave ground for the implication, that compulsory process must be resorted to, because no specific provision was made, they have provided the means, by authorizing this court, in case of reversal of the state decision, to execute its own judgment. In case of *reversal* only was this necessary; for, in case of affirmance, this collision could not arise. It is true, that the words of this section are, that this court may, *in their discretion,* proceed to execute its own judgment. But these words were very properly put in, that it might not be made imperative upon this court to proceed indiscriminately in this way; as it could only be necessary in case of the refusal of the state courts; and this idea is fully confirmed by the words of the 13th section, which restrict this court in issuing the writ of mandamus, so as to confine it expressly to those courts which are constituted by the United States.

In this point of view the legislature is completely vindicated from all intention to violate the independence of the state judiciaries. Nor can this court, with any more correctness, have imputed to it similar intentions. The form of the mandate issued in this case is that known to appellate tribunals, and used in the ordinary cases of writs of error from the courts of the United States. It will, perhaps, not be too much, in such cases, to expect of those who are conversant in the forms, fictions, and technicality of the law, not to give the process of courts too literal a construction. They should be considered with a view to the ends they are intended to answer, and the law and practice in which they originate. In this view, the mandate was no more than a mode of submitting to that court the option which the 25th section holds out to them.

Had the decision of the court of Virginia been confined to the point of their legal obligation to carry the judgment of this court into effect, I should have thought it unnecessary to make any further observations in this cause. But we are called upon to vindicate our general revising power, and its due exercise in this particular case.

Here, that I may not be charged with arguing upon a hypothetical case, it is necessary to ascertain what the real question is which this court is now called to decide on.

In doing this, it is necessary to do what, although, in the abstract, of very questionable propriety, appears to be generally acquiesced in, to wit, to review the case as it originally came up to this court on the former writ of error. The cause, then, came up upon a case stated between the parties, and under the practice of that state, having the effect of a special verdict. The case stated brings into view the treaty of peace with Great Britain, and then proceeds to present the various laws of Virginia, and the facts upon which the parties found their respective titles. It then presents no particular question, but refers generally to the law arising out of the case. The original decision was obtained prior to the treaty of 1794, but before the case was adjudicated in this court, the treaty of 1794 had been concluded.

The difficulties of the case arise under the construction of the 25th section above alluded to, which, as far as it relates to this case, is in these words: "A final judgment or decree in any suit, in the highest court of law or equity of a state in which a decision in the suit could be had," "where is drawn in question the construction of any clause of the constitution or of a treaty," "and the decision is against *the title* set up or claimed by either party under such clause, may be re-examined and reversed, or affirmed." "But no other error shall be assigned or regarded as a ground of reversal in any such case as aforesaid, than such as appears on the face of the record, and immediately respects the before-mentioned questions of validity or construction of the said treaties," &c.

The first point decided under this state of the case was, that the judgment being a part of the record, if that judgment was not such as, upon that case, it ought to have been, it was an error apparent on the face of the record. But it was contended that the case there stated presented a number of points upon which the decision below may have been founded, and that it did not, therefore, necessarily appear to have been an error immediately respecting a question on the construction of a treaty. But the court held, that as the reference was general to the law arising out of the case, if one question arose, which called for the construction of a treaty, and the decision negatived the right set up under it, this court will reverse that decision, and that it is the duty of the party who would avoid the inconvenience of this principle, so to mould the case as to obviate the ambiguity. And under this point arises the question whether this court can inquire into the title of the party, or whether they are so restricted in their judicial powers as to be confined to decide on the operation of a treaty upon a title previously ascertained to exist. If there is any one point in the case on which an opinion may be given with confidence, it is this, whether we consider the letter of the statute, or the spirit, intent, or meaning, of the constitution and of the legislature, as expressed in the 27th section, it is equally clear that the title is the primary object to which the attention of the court is called in every such case. The words are, "and the decision be against *the title*," so set up, not against *the construction of the treaty* contended for by the party setting up the title. And how could it be otherwise? The title may exist, notwithstanding the decision of the state courts to the contrary; and in that case the party is entitled to the benefits intended to be secured by the treaty. The decision to his prejudice may have been the result of those very errors, partialities, or defects, in state jurisprudence against which the constitution intended to protect the individual. And if the contrary doc-

trine be assumed, what is the consequence? This court may then be called upon to decide on a mere hypothetical case—to give a construction to a treaty without first deciding whether there was any interest on which that treaty, whatever be its proper construction, would operate. This difficulty was felt, and weighed in the case of Smith and the State of Maryland, and that decision was founded upon the idea that this court was not thus restricted.

But another difficulty presented itself: the treaty of 1794 had become the supreme law of the land since the judgment rendered in the court below. The defendant, who was at that time an alien, had now become confirmed in his rights under that treaty. This would have been no objection to the correctness of the original judgment. Were we, then, at liberty to notice that treaty in rendering the judgment of this court? Having dissented from the opinion of this court in the original case, on the question of title, this difficulty did not present itself in my way in the view I then took of the case. But the majority of this court determined that, as a public law, the treaty was a part of the law of every case depending in this court; that, as such, it was not necessary that it should be spread upon the record, and that it was obligatory upon this court, in rendering judgment upon this writ of error, notwithstanding the original judgment may have been otherwise unimpeachable. And to this opinion I yielded my hearty consent; for it cannot be maintained that this court is bound to give a judgment unlawful at the time of rendering it, in consideration that the same judgment would have been lawful at any prior time. What judgment can now be lawfully rendered between the parties is the question to which the attention of the court is called. And if the law which sanctioned the original judgment expire, pending an appeal, this court has repeatedly reversed the judgment below, although rendered whilst the law existed. So, too, if the plaintiff in error die, pending suit, and his land descend on an alien, it cannot be contended that this court will maintain the suit in right of the judgment, in favour of his ancestor, notwithstanding his present disability.

It must here be recollected, that this is an action of ejectment. If the term formally declared upon expires pending the action, the court will permit the plaintiff to amend, by extending the term—why? Because, although the right may have been in him at the commencement of the suit, it has ceased before judgment, and without this amendment he could not have judgment. But suppose the suit were really instituted to obtain possession of a leasehold, and the lease expire before judgment, would the court permit the party to amend in opposition to the right of the case? On the contrary, if the term formally declared on were more extensive than the lease in which the legal title was founded, could they give judgment for more than costs? It must be recollected that, under this judgment, a *writ of restitution* is the fruit of the law. This, in its very nature, has relation to, and must be founded upon, a present existing right at the time of judgment. And whatever be the cause which takes this right away, the remedy must, in the reason and nature of things, fall with it.

When all these incidental points are disposed of, we find the question finally reduced to this—does the judicial power of the United States extend to the revision of decisions of state courts, in cases arising under treaties? But, in order to generalize the question, and present it in the true form in which it presents itself in this case, we will inquire whether the constitution sanctions the exercise of a revising power over the decisions of state tribunals in those cases to which the judicial power of the United States extends?

And here it appears to me that the great difficulty is on the other side. That the real doubt is, whether the state tribunals can constitutionally exercise jurisdiction in any of the cases to which the judicial power of the United States extends.

Some cession of judicial power is contemplated by the third article of the constitution: that which is ceded can no longer be retained. In one of the circuit courts of the United States, it has been decided (with what correctness I will not say) that the cession of a power to pass an uniform act of bankruptcy, although not acted on by the United States, deprives the states of the power of passing laws to that effect. With regard to the admiralty and maritime jurisdiction, it would be difficult to prove that the states could resume it, if the United States should abolish the courts vested with that jurisdiction; yet, it is blended with the other cases of jurisdiction, in the second section of the third article, and ceded in the same words. But it is contented that the second section of the third article contains no express cession of jurisdiction; that it only vests a power in congress to assume jurisdiction to the extent therein expressed. And under this head arose the discussion on the construction proper to be given to that article.

On this part of the case I shall not pause long. The rules of construction, where the nature of the instrument is ascertained, are familiar to every one. To me the constitution appears, in every line of it, to be a contract, which, in legal language, may be denominated tripartite. The parties are the people, the states, and the United States. It is returning in a circle to contend, that it professes to be the exclusive act of the people, for what have the people done but to form this compact? That the states are recognised as parties to it is evident from various passages, and particularly that in which the United States guaranty to each state a republican form of government.

The security and happiness of the whole was the object, and, to prevent dissertion and collision, each surrendered those powers which might make them dangerous to each other. Well aware of the sensitive irritability of sovereign states, where their wills or interests clash, they placed themselves, with regard to each other, on the footing of sovereigns upon the ocean; where power is mutually conceded to act upon the individual, but the national vessel must remain unviolated. And to remove all ground for jealousy and complaint, they relinquish the privilege of being any longer the exclusive arbiters of their own justice, where the rights of others come in question, or the great interests of the whole may be affected by those feelings, partialities, or prejudices, which they meant to put down for ever.

Nor shall I enter into a minute discussion on the meaning of the language of this section. I have seldom found much good result from hypercritical severity, in examining the distinct force of words. Language *is* essentially defective in precision; more so than those are aware of who are not in the habit of subjecting it to philological analysis. In the case before us, for instance, a rigid construction might be made, which would annihilate the powers intended to be ceded. The words are, "shall extend to;" now that which *extends to*, does not necessarily *include in*, so that the circle may enlarge until it reaches the objects that limit it, and yet not take them in. But the plain and obvious sense and meaning of the word *shall*, in this sentence, is in the future sense, and has nothing imperative in it. The language of the framers of the constitution is, "We are about forming a general government—when that government is formed, its powers shall extend," &c. I therefore see nothing imperative in this clause, and certainly it would have been very unnecessary to use the word in that sense; for, as there was no controlling power constituted, it would only, if used in an imperative sense, have imposed a moral obligation to act. But the same result arises from using it in a future sense, and the constitution everywhere assumes, as a postulate, that whenever power is given it will be used or at least used, as far as the interests of the American people require it, if not from the natural proneness of man to the exercise of power, at least from a sense of duty, and the obligation of an oath.

Nor can I see any difference in the effect of the words used in this section, as to the scope of the jurisdiction of the United States' courts over the cases of the first and second description, comprised in that section. "Shall extend to controversies," appears to me as comprehensive in effect, as "shall extend to all cases." For, if the judicial power extend "to controversies between citizen and alien," &c., to what controversies of that description does it not extend? If no case can be pointed out which is excepted, it then extends to *all controversies.*

But I will assume the construction as a sound one, that the cession of power to the general government, means no more than that they may assume the exercise of it whenever they think it advisable. It is clear that congress have hitherto acted under that impression, and my own opinion is in favour of its correctness. But does it not then follow that the jurisdiction of the state court, within the range ceded to the general government, is permitted, and may be withdrawn whenever congress think proper to do so? As it is a principal that every one may renounce a right introduced for his benefit, we will admit that as congress have not assumed such jurisdiction, the state courts may, constitutionally, exercise jurisdiction in such cases. Yet, surely, the general power to withdraw the exercise of it, includes in it the right to modify, limit, and restrain that exercise. "This is my domain, put not your foot upon it, if you do, you are subject to my laws, I have a right to exclude you altogether; I have, then, a right to prescribe the terms of your admission to a participation. As long as you conform to my laws, participate in peace, but I reserve to myself the right of judging how far your acts are comfortable to my laws." Analogy, then, to the ordinary exercise of sovereign authority, would sustain the exercise of this controlling or revising power.

But it is argued that a power to assume jurisdiction to the constitutional extent, does not necessarily carry with it a right to exercise appellate power over the state tribunals.

This is a momentous question, and one on which I shall reserve myself uncommitted for each particular case as it shall occur. It is enough, at present, to have shown that congress has not asserted, and this court has not attempted, to exercise that kind of authority in *personam* over the state courts which would place them in the relation of an inferior responsible body *without their own acquiescence*. And I have too much confidence in the state tribunals to believe that a case ever will occur in which it will be necessary for the general government to assume a controlling power over these tribunals. But is it difficult to suppose a case which will call loudly for some remedy or restraint? Suppose a foreign minister, or an officer, acting regularly under authority from the United States, seized to-day, tried to-morrow, and hurried the next day to execution. Such cases may occur, and have occurred, in other countries. The angry vindictive passions of men have too often made their way into judicial tribunals, and we cannot hope for ever to escape their baleful influence. In the case supposed, there ought to be a power somewhere to restrain or punish, or the union must be dissolved. At present the uncontrollable exercise of criminal jurisdiction is most securely confided to the state tribunals. The courts of the United States are vested with no power to scrutinize into the proceedings of the state courts in criminal cases; on the contrary, the general government has, in more than one instance, exhibited their confidence, by a wish to vest them with the execution of their own penal law. And

extreme, indeed, I flatter myself, must be the case in which the general government could ever be induced to assert this right. If ever such a case should occur, it will be time enough to decide upon their constitutional power to do so.

But we know that by the 3d article of the constitution, judicial power, to a certain extent, is vested in the general government, and that by the same instrument, power is given to pass all laws necessary to carry into effect the provisions of the constitution. At present it is only necessary to vindicate the laws which they have passed affecting civil cases pending in state tribunals.

In legislating on this subject, congress, in the true spirit of the constitution, have proposed to secure to every one the full benefit of the constitution, without forcing any one necessarily into the courts of the United States. With this view, in one class of cases, they have not taken away absolutely from the state courts all the cases to which their judicial power extends, but left it to the plaintiff to bring his action there, originally, if he choose, or to the defendant to force the plaintiff into the courts of the United States where they have jurisdiction, and the former has instituted his suit in the state courts. In this case they have not made it legal for the defendant to plead to the jurisdiction; the effect of which would be to put an end to the plaintiff's suit, and oblige him, probably at great risk or expense, to institute a new action; but the act has given him a right to obtain an order for a removal, on a petition to the state court, upon which the cause, with all its existing advantages, is transferred to the circuit court of the United States. This, I presume, can be subject to no objection; as the legislature has an unquestionable right to make the ground of removal a ground of plea to the jurisdiction, and the court must then do no more than it is now called upon to do, to wit, give an order or a judgment, or call it what we will, in favour of that defendant. And so far from asserting the inferiority of the state tribunal, this act is rather that of a superior, inasmuch as the circuit court of the United States becomes bound, by that order, to take jurisdiction of the case. This method, so much more unlikely to affect official delicacy than that which is resorted to in the other class of cases, might, perhaps, have been more happily applied to all the cases which the legislature thought it advisable to remove from the state courts. But the other class of cases, in which the present is included, was proposed to be provided for in a different manner. And here, again, the legislature of the union evince their confidence in the state tribunals; for they do not attempt to give original cognizance to their own circuit courts of such cases, or to remove them by petition and order; but still believing that their decisions will be generally satisfactory, a writ of error is not given immediately as a question within the jurisdiction of the United States shall occur, but only in case the decision shall finally, in the court of the last resort, be against the title set up under the constitution, treaty, &c.

In this act I can see nothing which amounts to an assertion of the inferiority or dependence of the state tribunals. The presiding judge of the state court is himself authorized to issue the writ of error, if he will, and thus give jurisdiction to the supreme court: and if he thinks proper to decline it, no compulsory process is provided by law to oblige him. The party who imagines himself aggrieved is then at liberty to apply to a judge of the United States, who issues the writ of error, which (whatever the form) is, in substance, no more than a mode of compelling the opposite party to appear before this court, and maintain the legality of his judgment obtained before the state tribunal. An exemplification of a record is the common property of every one who chooses to apply and pay for it, and thus the case and the parties are brought before us; and so far is the court itself from being brought under the revising power of this court, that nothing but the case, as presented by the record and pleadings of the parties, is considered, and the opinions of the court are never resorted to unless for the purpose of assisting this court in forming their own opinions.

The absolute necessity that there was for congress to exercise something of a revising power over cases and parties in the state courts, will appear from this consideration.

Suppose the whole extent of the judicial power of the United States vested in their own courts, yet such a provision would not answer all the ends of the constitution, for two reasons:

1st. Although the plaintiff may, in such case, have the full benefit of the constitution extended to him, yet the defendant would not; as the plaintiff might force him into the court of the state at his election.

2dly. Supposing it possible so to legislate as to give the courts of the United States original jurisdiction in all cases arising under the constitution, laws, &c., in the words of the 2d section of the 3d article, (a point on which I have some doubt, and which in time might, perhaps, under some *quo minus* fiction, or a willing construction, greatly accumulate the jurisdiction of those courts,) yet a very large class of cases would remain unprovided for. Incidental questions would often arise, and as a court of competent jurisdiction in the principal case must decide all such questions, whatever laws they arise under, endless might be the diversity of decisions throughout the union upon the constitution, treaties, and laws, of the United States; a subject on which the tranquility of the union, internally and externally, may materially depend.

I should feel the more hesitation in adopting the opinions which I express in this case, were I not firmly con-

vinced that they are practical, and may be acted upon without compromitting the harmony of the union, or bringing humility upon the state tribunals. God forbid that the judicial power in these states should ever, for a moment, even in its humblest departments, feel a doubt of its own independence. Whilst adjudicating on a subject which the laws of the country assign finally to the revising power of another tribunal, it can feel no such doubt. An anxiety to do justice is ever relieved by the knowledge that what we do is not final between the parties. And no sense of dependence can be felt from the knowledge that the parties, not the court, may be summoned before another tribunal. With this view, by means of laws, avoiding judgments obtained in the state courts in cases over which congress has constitutionally assumed jurisdiction, and inflicting penalties on parties who shall contumaciously persist in infringing the constitutional rights of others—under a liberal extension of the writ of injunction and the *habeas corpus ad subjiciendum*, I flatter myself that the full extent of the constitutional revising power may be secured to the United States, and the benefits of it to the individual, without ever resorting to compulsory or restrictive process upon the state tribunals; a right which, I repeat again, congress has not asserted, nor has this court asserted, nor does there appear any necessity for asserting.

The remaining points in the case being mere questions of practice, I shall make no remarks upon them.

Judgment affirmed.

Source:
14 U.S. 304 (1816).

Cohens v. Virginia, 1821

U.S. Supreme Court decision issued on March 3, 1821, asserting the right of the Supreme Court to review decisions of state courts. The unanimous ruling, written by Chief Justice John Marshall, emerged from the Court's review of the conviction of P. J. and M. J. Cohen for selling federal lottery tickets in Virginia in violation of state law. When the Cohens appealed their conviction in federal court, Virginia claimed that the Supreme Court had no jurisdiction, under the Eleventh Amendment. By hearing the case, the Supreme Court, using the principle of national supremacy, firmly established the right of federal courts to review state court decisions concerning constitutional issues. The Cohens' conviction, however, was upheld.

By 1833 Marshall had diluted his nationalist stance in *Barron v. Baltimore*. It held that the first 10 amendments to the U.S. Constitution (the Bill of Rights) were binding upon the federal government but not upon the state governments.

Cohens v. Virginia
March 3d, 1821.

Marshall, Ch. J., delivered the opinion of the court.—This is a writ of error to a judgment rendered in the Court of Husting for the borough of Norfolk, on an information for selling lottery-tickets, contrary to an act of the legislature of Virginia. In the state court, the defendant claimed the protection of an act of congress. A case was agreed between the parties, which states the act of assembly on which the prosecution was founded, and the act of congress on which the defendant relied, and concludes in these words: "If upon this case, the court shall be of opinion, that the acts of congress before mentioned were valid, and on the true construction of those acts, the lottery-tickets sold by the defendants as aforesaid, might lawfully be sold within the state of Virginia, notwithstanding the act or statute of the general assembly of Virginia prohibiting such sale, then judgment to be entered for the defendants: And if the court should be of opinion, that the statute or act of the general assembly, of the state of Virginia, prohibiting such sale, is valid, notwithstanding the said acts of congress, then judgment to be entered that the defendants are guilty, and that the commonwealth recover against them one hundred dollars and costs." Judgment was rendered against the defendants; and the court in which it was rendered being the highest court of the state in which the cause was cognisable, the record has been brought into this court by writ of error.

The defendant in error moves to dismiss this writ, for want of jurisdiction. In support of this motion, three points have been made, and argued with the ability which the importance of the question merits. These points are—1st. That a state is a defendant. 2d. That no writ of error lies from this court to a state court. 3d. The third point has been presented in different froms by the gentlemen who have argued it. The counsel who opened the cause said, that the want of jurisdiction was shown by the subject-matter of the case. The counsel who followed him said, that jurisdiction was not given by the judiciary act. The court has bestowed all its attention on the arguments of both gentlemen, and supposes that their tendency is, to show that this court has no jurisdiction of the case, or, in other words, has no right to review the judgment of the state court, because neither the constitution nor any law of the United States has been violated by that judgment.

The questions presented to the court by the first two points made at the bar are of great magnitude, and may be truly said vitally to affect the Union. They exclude the inquiry whether the constitution and laws of the United States have been violated by the judgment which the plaintiffs in error seek to review; and maintain that, admitting such violation, it is not in the power of the government to apply a corrective. They maintain that the nation does not possess a department capable of restraining, peaceably, and by authority of law, any attempts which may be made, by a part, against the legitimate powers of the whole; and that the government is reduced to the alternative of submitting to such attempts, or of resisting them by Force. The maintain that the constitution of the United States has provided no tribunal for the final construction of itself, or of the laws or treaties of the nation; but that this power may be exercised in the last resort by the courts of every state in the Union. That the constitution, laws and treaties may receive as many constructions as there are states; and that this is not a mischief, or, if a mischief, is irremediable. These abstract propositions are to be determined; for he who demands decision, without permitting inquiry, affirms that the decision he asks does not depend on inquiry.

If such be the constitution, it is the duty of the court to bow with respectful submission to its provisions. If such be not the constitution, it is equally the duty of the court to say so; and to perform that task which the American people have assigned to the judicial department.

1. The first question to be considered is, whether the jurisdiction of this court is excluded by the character of the parties, one of them being a state, and the other a citizen of that state. The second section of the third article of the constitution defines the extent of the judicial power of the United States. Jurisdiction is given to the courts of the Union, in two classes of cases. In the first, their jurisdiction depends on the character of the cause, whoever may be the parties. This class comprehends "all cases in law and equity arising under this constitution, the laws of the United States, and treaties made, or which shall be made, under their authority." This clause extends the jurisdiction of the court to all the cases described, without making in its terms any exception whatever, and without any regard to the condition of the party. If there be any exception, it is to be implied, against the express words of the article. In the seconds class, the jurisdiction depends entirely on the character of the parties. In this are comprehended "controversies between two or more states, between a state and citizens of another state," and "between a state and foreign states, citizens or subjects." If these be the parties, it is entirely unimportant, what may be the subject of controversy. Be it what it may, these parties have a constitutional right to come into the courts of the Union.

The counsel for the defendant in error have stated, that the cases which arise under the constitution must grow out of those provisions which are capable of self-execution; examples of which are to be found in the 2d section of the 4th article, and in the 10th section of the 1st article.

A case which arises under a law of the United States must, we are likewise told, be a right given by some act which becomes necessary to execute the powers given in the constitution, of which the law of naturalization is mentioned as an example.

The use intended to be made of this exposition of the first part of the section, defining the extent of the judicial power, is not clearly understood. If the intention be merely to distinguish cases arising under the constitution, from those arising under a law, for the sake of precision in the application of this argument, these propositions will not be controverted. If it be, to maintain that a case arising under the constitution, or a law, must be one in which a party comes into court to demand something conferred on him by the constitution or a law, we think, the construction too narrow. A case in law or equity consists of the right of the one party, as well as of other, and may truly be said to arise under the constitution or a law of the United States, whenever its correct decision depends on the construction of either. Congress seems to have intended to give its own construction of this part of the constitution in the 25th section of the judiciary act; and we perceive no reason to depart from that construction.

The jurisdiction of the court, then, being extended by the letter of the constitution to all cases arising under it, or under the laws of the United States, it follows, that those who would withdraw any case of this description from that jurisdiction, must sustain the exemption they claim, on the spirit and true meaning of the constitution, which spirit an true meaning must be so apparent as to overrule the words which its framers have employed. The counsel for the defendant in error have undertaken to do this; and have laid down the general proposition, that a sovereign independent state is not suable, except by its own consent.

This general proposition will not be controverted. But its consent is not requisite in each particular case. It may be given in a general law. And if a state has surrendered any portion of its sovereignty, the question, whether a liability to suit be a part of this portion, depends on the instrument by which the surrender is made. If, upon a just construction of that instrument, it shall appear, that the state has submitted to be sued, then it has parted with this sovereign right of judging, in every case, on the justice of its own pretensions, and has intrusted that power to a tribunal in whose impartiality it confides.

The American states, as well as the American people, have believed a close and firm union to be essential to their liberty and to their happiness. They have been taught by experience, that this union cannot exist, without a government for the whole; and they have been taught by the same experience, that this government would be a mere shadow, that must disappoint all their hopes, unless invested with large portions of that sovereignty which

belongs to independent states. Under the influence of this opinion, and thus instructed by experience, the American people, in the conventions of their respective states, adopted the present constitution.

If it could be doubted, whether, from its nature, it were not supreme, in all cases were it is empowered to act, that doubt would be removed by the declaration, that "this constitution, and the laws of the United States which shall be made in pursuance thereof, and all treaties made, or which shall be made, under the authority of the United States, shall be the supreme law of the land; and the judges in every state shall be bound thereby; anything in the constitution or laws of any state to the contrary notwithstanding." This is the authoritative language of the American people; and, if gentlemen please, of the American states. It marks, with lines too strong to be mistaken, the characteristic distinction between the government of the Union, and those of the states. The general government, though limited as to its objects, is supreme with respect to those objects. This principle is a part of the constitution; and if there be any who deny its necessity, none can deny its authority.

To this supreme government, ample powers are confided; and if it were possible to doubt the great purposes for which they were so confided, the people of the United States have declared, that they are given "in order to form a more perfect union, establish justice, ensure domestic tranquillity, provide for the common defence, promote the general welfare, and secure the blessings of liberty to themselves and their posterity." With the ample powers confided to this supreme government, for these interesting purposes, are connected many express and important limitations on the sovereignty of the states, which are made for the same purposes. The powers of the Union, on the great subjects of war, peace and commerce, and on many others, are in themselves limitations of the sovereignty of the states; but in addition to these, the sovereignty of the states is surrendered, in many instances, where the surrender can only operate to the benefit of the people, and where, perhaps, no other power is conferred on congress than a conservative power to maintain the principles established in the constitution. The maintenance of these principles in their purity, is certainly among the great duties of the government. One of the instruments by which this duty may be peaceably performed, is the judicial department. It is authorized to decide all cases of every description, arising under the constitution or laws of the United States. From this general grant of jurisdiction, no exception is made of those cases in which a state may be a party. When we consider the situation of the government of the Union and of a state, in relation to each other; the nature of our constitution; the subordination of the state governments to that constitution; the great purpose for which jurisdiction over all cases arising under the constitution and laws of the United States, is confided to the judicial department; are we at liberty to insert in this general grant, an exception of those cases in which a state may be a party? Will the spirit of the constitution justify this attempt to control its words? We think it will not. We think a case arising under the constitution or laws of the United States, is cognisable in the courts of the Union, whoever may be the parties to that case.

Had any doubt existed with respect to the just construction of this part of the section, that doubt would have been removed, by the enumeration of those cases to which the jurisdiction of the federal courts is extended, in consequence of the character of the parties. In that enumeration, we find "controversies between two or more states, between a state and citizens of another state," "and between a state and foreign states, citizens or subjects." One of the express objects, then, for which the judicial department was established, is the decision of controversies between states, and between a state and individuals. The mere circumstance, that a state is a party, gives jurisdiction to the court. How, then, can it be contended, that the very same instrument, in the very same section, should be so construed, as that this same circumstance should withdraw a case from the jurisdiction of the court, where the constitution or laws of the United States are supposed to have been violated? The constitution gave to every person having a claim upon a state, a right to submit his case to the court of the nation. However unimportant his claim might be, however little the community might be interested in its decision, the framers of our constitution thought it necessary, for the purposes of justice, to provide a tribunal as superior to influence as possible, in which that claim might be decided. Can it be imagined, that the same persons considered a case involving the constitution of our country and the majesty of the laws, questions in which every American citizen must be deeply interested, as withdrawn from this tribunal, because a state is a party?

While weighing arguments drawn from the nature of government, and from the general spirit of an instrument, and urged for the purpose of narrowing the construction which the words of that instrument seem to require, it is proper to place in the opposite scale those principles, drawn from the same sources, which go to sustain the words in their full operation and natural import. One of these, which has been pressed with great force by the counsel for the plaintiffs in error, is, that the judicial power of every well- constituted government must be co-extensive with the legislative, and must be capable of deciding every judicial question which grows out of the constitution and laws. If any proposition may be considered as a political axiom, this, we think, may be so considered. In reasoning upon it, as an abstract question, there would, probably, exist no contrariety of opinion respecting it. Every argu-

ment, proving the necessity of the principle, proves also the propriety of giving this extent to it. We do not mean to say, that the jurisdiction of the courts of the Union should be construed to be co-extensive with the legislative, merely because it is fit that it should be so; but we mean to say, that this fitness furnishes an argument in construing the constitution, which ought never to be overlooked, and which is most especially entitled to consideration, when we are inquiring, whether the words of the instrument which purport to establish this principle, shall be contracted for the purpose of destroying it.

The mischievous consequences of the constitution contended for on the part of Virginia, are also entitled to great consideration. It would prostrate, it has been said, the government and its laws at the feet of every state in the Union. And would not this be its effect? What power of the government could be executed, by its own means, in any state disposed to resist its execution by a course of legislation? The laws must be executed by individuals acting within the several states. If these individuals may be exposed to penalties, and if the courts of the Union cannot correct the judgments by which these penalties may be enforced, the course of the government may be, at any time, arrested by the will of one of its members. Each member will possess a veto on the will of the whole. The answer which has been given to this argument, does not deny its truth, but insists, that confidence is reposed, and may be safely reposed, in the state institutions; and that, if they shall ever become so insane, or so wicked, as to seek the destruction of the government, they may accomplish their object, by refusing to perform the functions assigned to them.

We readily concur with the counsel for the defendant, in the declaration, that the cases which have been put, of direct legislative resistance, for the purpose of opposing the acknowledged powers of the government, are extreme cases, and in the hope, that they will never occur; but we cannot help believing, that a general conviction of the total incapacity of the government to protect itself and its laws, in such cases, would contribute in no inconsiderable degree to their occurrence. Let it be admitted, that the cases which have been put, are extreme and improbable, yet there are gradations of opposition to the laws, far short of those cases, which might have a baneful influence on the affairs of the nation. Different states may entertain different opinions on the true construction of the constitutional powers of congress. We know, that at one time, the assumption of the debts contracted by the several states, during the war of our revolution, was deemed unconstitutional, by some of them. We know, too, that at other times, certain taxes, imposed by congress, have been pronounced unconstitutional. Other laws have been questioned partially, while they were supported by the great majority of the American people. We have no assurance that we shall be less divided than we have been. States may legislate in conformity to their opinions, and may enforce those opinions by penalties. It would be hazarding too much, to assert, that the judicatures of the states will be exempt from the prejudices by which the legislatures and people are influenced, and will constitute perfectly impartial tribunals. In many states, the judges are dependent for office and for salary, on the will of the legislature. The constitution of the United States furnishes no security against the universal adoption of this principle. When we observe the importance which that constitution attaches to the independence of judges, we are the less inclined to suppose, that it can have intended to leave these constitutional questions to tribunals where this independence may not exist, in all cases where a state shall prosecute an individual who claims the protection of an act of congress. These prosecutions may take place, even without a legislative act. A person making a seizure under an act of congress, may be indicted as a trespasser, if force has been employed, and of this, a jury may judge. How extensive may be the mischief, if the first decisions in such cases should be final!

These collisions may take place, in times of no extraordinary commotion. But a constitution is framed for ages to come, and is designed to approach immortality, as nearly as human institutions can approach it. Its course cannot always be tranquil. It is exposed to storms and tempests, and its framers must be unwise statesmen indeed, if they have not provided it, so far as its nature will permit, with the means of self-preservation from the perils it may be destined to encounter. No government ought to be so defective in its organization, as not to contain within itself, the means of securing the execution of its own laws against other dangers than those which occur every day. Courts of justice are the means most usually employed; and it is reasonable to expect, that a government should repose on its own courts, rather than on others. There is certainly nothing in the circumstances under which our constitution was formed—nothing in the history of the times—which would justify the opinion, that the confidence reposed in the states was so implicit, as to leave in them and their tribunals the power of resisting or defeating, in the form of law, the legitimate measures of the Union. The requisitions of congress, under the confederation, were as constitutionally obligatory, as the laws enacted by the present congress. That they were habitually disregarded, is a fact of universal notoriety. With the knowledge of this fact, and under its full pressure, a convention was assembled to change the system. Is it so improbable, that they should confer on the judicial department the power of construing the constitution and laws of the Union in every case, in the last resort, and or preserving them from all violation, from every quarter, so far as judicial decision can preserve them,

that this improbability should essentially affect the construction of a new system? We are told, and we are truly told, that the great change which is to give efficacy to the present system, is its ability to act on individuals directly, instead of acting through the instrumentality of state governments. But ought not this ability, in reason and sound policy, to be applied directly to the protection of individuals employed in the execution of the laws, as well as to their coercion. Your laws reach the individual, without the aid of any other power; why may they not protect him from punishment, for performing his duty in executing them?

The counsel for Virginia endeavor to obviate the force of these arguments, by saying, that the dangers they suggest, if not imaginary, are inevitable; that the constitution can make no provision against them; and that, therefore, in construing that instrument, they ought to be excluded from our consideration. This state of things, they say, cannot arise, until there shall be a disposition so hostile to the present political system, as to produce a determination to destroy it; and when that determination shall be produced, its effects will not be restrained by parchment stipulations; the fate of the constitution will not then depend on judicial decisions. But should no appeal be made to force, the states can put an end to the government by refusing to act; they have only not to elect senators, and it expires without a struggle. It is very true, that, whenever hostility to the existing system shall become universal, it will be also irresistible. The people made the constitution, and the people can unmake it. It is the creature of their will, and lives only by their will. But this supreme and irresistible power to make or to unmake, resides only in the whole body of the people; not in any subdivision of them. The attempt of any of the parts to exercise it, is usurpation, and ought to be repelled by those to whom the people have delegated their power of repelling it.

The acknowledged inability of the government, then, to sustain itself against the public will, and by force or otherwise, to control the whole nation, is no sound argument in support of it constitutional inability to preserve itself against a section of the nation, acting opposition to the general will.

It is true, that if all the states, or a majority of them, refuse to elect senators, the legislative powers of the Union will be suspended. But if any one state shall refuse to elect them, the senate will not, on that account, be the less capable of performing all its functions. The argument founded on this fact would seem rather to prove the subordination of the parts to the whole, than the complete independence of any one of them. The framers of the constitution were, indeed, unable to make any provisions which should protect that instrument against a general combination of the states, or of the people, for its destruction; and conscious of this inability, they have not made the attempt. But they were able to provide against the operation of measures adopted in any one state, whose tendency might be to arrest the execution of the laws, and this it was the part of true wisdom to attempt. We think, they have attempted it.

It has been also urged, as an additional objection to the jurisdiction of the court, that cases between a state and one of its own citizens, do not come within the general scope of the constitution; and were obviously never intended to be made cognisable in the federal courts. The state tribunals might be suspected of partiality, in cases between itself or its citizens and aliens, or the citizens of another state, but not in proceedings by a state against its own citizens. That jealousy which might exist in the first case, could not exist in the last, and therefore, the judicial power is not extended to the last. This is very true, so far as jurisdiction depends on the character of the parties; and the argument would have great force, if urged to prove that this court could not establish the demand of a citizen upon his state, but is not entitled to the same force, when urged to prove that this court cannot inquire whether the constitution or laws of the United States protect a citizen from a prosecution instituted against him by a state. If jurisdiction depended entirely on the character of the parties, and was not given, where the parties have not an original right to come into court, that part of the 2d section of the 3d article, which extends the judicial power to all cases arising under the constitution and laws of the United States, would be mere surplusage. It is to give jurisdiction, where the character of the parties would not give it, that this very important part of the clause was inserted. It may be true, that the partiality of the state tribunals, in ordinary controversies between a state and its citizens, was not apprehended, and therefore, the judicial power of the Union was not extended to such cases; but this was not the sole nor the greatest object for which this department was created. A more important, a much more interesting, object was, the preservation of the constitution and laws of the United States, so far as they can be preserved by judicial authority; and therefore, the jurisdiction of the courts of the Union was expressly extended to all cases arising under that constitution and those laws. If the constitution or laws may be violated by proceedings instituted by a state against its own citizens, and if that violation may be such, as essentially to affect the constitution and the laws, such as to arrest the progress of government in its constitutional course, why should these cases be excepted from that provision which expressly extends the judicial power of the Union to *all* cases arising under the constitution and laws?

After bestowing on this subject the most attentive consideration, the court can perceive no reason, founded on the character of the parties, for introducing an exception which the constitution has not made; and we think, that the judicial power, as originally given, extends to all cases

arising under the constitution or a law of the United States, whoever may be the parties.

It has been also contended, that this jurisdiction, if given, is original, and cannot be exercised in the appellate form. The words of the constitution are, "in all cases affecting ambassadors, other public ministers and consuls, and those in which a state shall be a party, the supreme court shall have original jurisdiction. In all the other cases before mentioned, the supreme court shall have appellate jurisdiction." This distinction between original and appellate jurisdiction, excludes, we are told, in all cases, the exercise of the one where the other is given.

The constitution gives the supreme court original jurisdiction, in certain enumerated cases, and gives it appellate jurisdiction in all others. Among those in which jurisdiction must be exercised, in the appellate form, are cases arising under the constitution and laws of the United States. These provisions of the constitution are equally obligatory, and are to be equally respected. If a state be a party, the jurisdiction of this court is original; if the case under a constitution or a law, the jurisdiction is appellate. But a case to which a state is a party may arise under the constitution or a law of the United States. What rule is applicable to such a case? What then, becomes the duty of the court? Certainly, we think, so to construe the constitution, as to give effect to both provisions, so far as it is possible to reconcile them, and not to permit their seeming repugnancy to destroy each other. We must endeavor so to construe them, as to preserve the true intent and meaning of the instrument.

In one description of cases, the jurisdiction of the court is founded entirely on the character of the parties; and the nature of the controversy is not contemplated by the constitution—the character of the parties is everything, the nature of the case nothing. In the other description of cases, the jurisdiction is founded entirely on the character of the case, and the parties are not contemplated by the constitution—in these, the nature of the case is everything, the character of the parties nothing. When, then, the constitution declares the jurisdiction, in cases where a state shall be a party, to be original, and in all cases arising under the constitution or a law, to be appellate, the conclusion seems irresistible, that its framers designed to include in the first class, those cases in which jurisdiction is given, because a state is a party; and to include in the second, those in which jurisdiction is given, because the case arises under the constitution or a law.

This reasonable construction is rendered necessary by other considerations. That the constitution or a law of the United States is involved in a case, and makes a part of it, may appear in the progress of a cause, in which the courts of the Union, but for that circumstances, would have no jurisdiction, and which, of consequence, could not originate in the supreme court; in such a case, the jurisdiction can be exercised only in its appellate form. To deny its exercise in this form, is to deny its existence, and would be to construe a clause, dividing the power of the supreme court, in such a manner, as in a considerable degree to defeat the power itself. All must perceive, that this construction can be justified only where it is absolutely necessary. We do not think the article under consideration presents that necessity.

It is observable, that in this distributive clause, no negative words are introduced. This observation is not made, for the purpose of contending, that the legislature may "apportion the judicial power between the supreme and inferior courts, according to its will." That would be, as was said by this court in the case of *Marbury* v. *Madison,* to render the distributive clause "mere surplusage," to make it "form without substance." This cannot, therefore, be the true construction of the article. But although the absence of negative words will not authorize the legislature to disregard the distribution of the power previously granted, their absence will justify a sound construction of the whole article, so as to give every part its intended effect. It is admitted, that "affirmative words are often, in their operation, negative of other objects than those affirmed;" and that where "a negative or exclusive sense must be given to them, or they have no operation at all," they must receive that negative or exclusive sense. But where they have full operation without it; where it would destroy some of the most important objects for which the power was created; then, we think, affirmative words ought not to be construed negatively.

The constitution declares, that in cases where a state is a party, the supreme court shall have original jurisdiction; but does not say, that its appellate jurisdiction shall not be exercised in cases where, from their nature, appellate jurisdiction is given, whether a state be or be not a party. It may be conceded, that where the case is of such a nature, as to admit of its originating in the supreme court, it ought to originate there; but where, from its nature, it cannot originate in that court, these words ought not to be so construed as to require it. There are many cases in which it would be found extremely difficult, and subversive of the spirit of the constitution, to maintain the construction, that appellate jurisdiction cannot be exercised, where one of the parties might sue or be sued in this court.

The constitution defines the jurisdiction of the supreme court, but does not define that of the inferior courts. Can it be affirmed, that a state might not sue the citizen of another state in a circuit court? Should the circuit court decide for or against its jurisdiction, should it dismiss the suit, or give judgment against the state, might not its decision be revised in the supreme court? The argument is, that it could not; and the very clause which is urged to prove, that the circuit court could give no judgment in the case, is also urged to prove, that its judgment is irreversible. A supervising court, whose peculiar province it is to correct the errors of an inferior court, has no power to correct a judgment given without jurisdiction, because, in the same case, that supervising court has original jurisdiction. Had negative words been employed, it would be difficult to give them this construction, if they would admit of any other. But without negative words, this irrational construction can never be maintained.

So, too, in the same clause, the jurisdiction of the court is declared to be original, "in cases affecting ambassadors, other public ministers and consuls." There is, perhaps, no part of the article under consideration so much required by national policy as this; unless it be that part which extends the judicial power "to all cases arising under the constitution, laws and treaties of the United States." It has been generally held, that the state courts have a concurrent jurisdiction with the federal courts, in cases to which the judicial power is extended, unless the jurisdiction of the federal courts be rendered exclusive by the words of the third article. If the words, "to all cases," give exclusive jurisdiction in cases affecting foreign ministers, they may also give exclusive jurisdiction, if such be the will of congress, in cases arising under the constitution, laws and treaties of the United States. Now, suppose an individual were to sue a foreign minister in a state court, and that court were to maintain its jurisdiction, and render judgment against the minister, could it be contended, that this court would be incapable of revising such judgment, because the constitution had given it original jurisdiction in the case? If this could be maintained, then a clause inserted for the purpose of excluding the jurisdiction of all other courts than this, in a particular case, would have the effect of excluding the jurisdiction of this court, in that very case, if the suit were to be brought in another court, and that court were to assert jurisdiction. This tribunal, according to the argument which has been urged, could neither revise the judgment of such other court, nor suspend its proceedings: for a writ of prohibition, or any other similar writ, is in the nature of appellate process.

Foreign consuls frequently assert, in our prize courts, the claims of their fellow-subjects. These suits are maintained by them, as consuls. The appellate power of this court has been frequently exercised in such cases, and has never been questioned. It would be extremely mischievous, to withhold its exercise. Yet the consul is a party on the record. The truth is, that where the words confer only appellate jurisdiction, original jurisdiction is most clearly not given; but where the words admit of appellate jurisdiction, the power to take cognisance of the suit originally, does not necessarily negative the power to decide upon it on an appeal, if it may originate in a different court.

It is, we think, apparent, that to give this distribute clause the interpretation contended for, to give to its affirmative words a negative operation, in every possible case, would, in some instances, defeat the obvious intention of the article. Such an interpretation would not consist with those rules which, from time immemorial, have guided courts, in their construction of instruments brought under their consideration. It must, therefore, be discarded. Every part of the article must be taken into view, and that construction adopted, which will consist with its words, and promote its general intention. The court may imply a negative from affirmative words, where the implication promotes, not where it defeats the intention.

If we apply this principle, the correctness of which we believe will not be controverted, to the distributive clause under consideration, the result, we think, would be this: the original jurisdiction of the supreme court, in cases where a state is a party, refers to those cases in which, according to the grant of power made in the preceding clause, jurisdiction might be exercised, in consequence of the character of the party, and an original suit might be instituted in any of the federal courts; not to those cases, in which an original suit might not be instituted in a federal court. Of the last description, is every case between a state and its citizens, and, perhaps, every case in which a state is enforcing its penal laws. In such cases, therefore, the supreme court cannot take original jurisdiction. In every other case, that is, in every case to which the judicial power extends, and in which original jurisdiction is not expressly given, that judical power shall be exercised in the appellate, and only in the appellate form. The original jurisdiction of this court cannot be enlarged, but its appellate jurisdiction may be exercised in every case cognisable under the third article of the constitution, in the federal courts, in which original jurisdiction cannot be exercised; and the extent of this judicial power is to be measured, not by giving the affirmative words of the distributive clause a negative operation in every possible case, but by giving their true meaning to the words which define its extent.

The counsel for the defendant in error urge, in opposition to this rule of construction, some *dicta* of the court, in the case of *Marbury* v. *Madison*. It is a maxim, not to be disregarded, that general expressions, in every opinion, are to be taken in connection with the case in which those expressions are used. If they go beyond the case, they may be respected, but ought not to control the judgment in a subsequent suit, when the very point is presented for decision. The reason of this maxim is obvious. The question actually before the court is investigated with care, and considered in its full extent. Other principles which may serve to illustrate it, are considered in their relation to the case decided, but their possible bearing on all other cases is sel-

dom completely investigated. In the case of *Marbury* v. *Madison*, the single question before the court, so far as that case can be applied to this, was, whether the legislature could give this court original jurisdiction, in a case in which the constitution had clearly not given it, and in which no doubt respecting the construction of the article could possibly be raised. The court decided, and we think very properly, that the legislature could not give original jurisdiction in such a case. But in the reasoning of the court in support of this decision, some expressions are used which go far beyond it. The counsel for Marbury had insisted on the unlimited discretion of the legislature in the apportionment of the judicial power; and it is against this argument that the reasoning of the court is directed. They say that, if such had been the intention of the article, "it would certainly have been useless to proceed farther than to define the judicial power, and the tribunals in which it should be vested." The court says, that such a construction would render the clause, dividing the jurisdiction of the court into original and appellate, totally useless; that "affirmative words are often, in their operation, negative of other objects than those which are affirmed; and in this case (in the case of *Marbury* v. *Madison*), a negative or exclusive sense must be given to them, or they have no operation at all." "It cannot be presumed," adds the court, "that any clause in the constitution is intended to be without effect; and therefore, such a construction is inadmissible, unless the words require it." The whole reasoning of the court proceeds upon the idea, that the affirmative words of the clause giving one sort of jurisdiction, must imply a negative of any other sort of jurisdiction, because, otherwise, the words would be totally inoperative, and this reasoning is advanced in a case to which it was strictly applicable. If, in that case, original jurisdiction could have been exercised, the clause under consideration would have been entirely useless. Having such cases only in its view, the court lays down a principle which is generally correct, in terms must broader than the decision, and not only much broader than the reasoning with which that decision is supported, but in some instances, contradictory to its principle. The reasoning sustains the negative operation of the words in that case, because, otherwise, the clause would have no meaning whatever, and because such operation was necessary to give effect to the intention of the article. The effort now made is, to apply the conclusion to which the court was conducted by that reasoning, in the particular case, to one in which the words have their full operation, when understood affirmatively, and in which the negative or exclusive sense, is to be so used as to defeat some of the great objects of the article. To this construction, the court cannot give assent. The general expressions in the case of *Marbury* v. *Madison* must be understood, with the limitations which are given to them in this opinion; limitations which in no degree affect the decision in that case, or the tenor of its reasoning.

The counsel who closed the argument, put several cases, for the purpose of illustration, which he supposed to arise under the constitution, and yet to be, apparently, without the jurisdiction of the court. Were a state to lay a duty of exports, to collect the money and place it in her treasury, could the citizen who paid it, he asks, maintain a suit in this court against such state, to recover back the money? Perhaps not. Without, however, deciding such supposed case, we may say, that it is entirely unlike that under consideration. The citizen who has paid his money to his state, under a law that is void, is in the same situation with every other person who has paid money by mistake. The law raises a *assumpsit* to return the money, and it is upon that *assumpsit,* that the action is to be maintained. To refuse to comply with this *assumpsit* may be no more a violation of the constitution, than to refuse to comply with any other; and as the federal courts never had jurisdiction over contracts between a state and its citizens, they may have none over this. But let us so vary the supposed case, as to give it a real resemblance to that under consideration. Suppose, a citizen to refuse to pay this export duty, and a suit to be instituted for the purpose of compelling him to pay it. He pleads the constitution of the United States in bar of the action, notwithstanding which the court gives judgment against him. This would be a case arising under the constitution, and would be the very case now before the court.

We are also asked, if a state should confiscate property secured by a treaty, whether the individual could maintain an action for that property? If the property confiscated be debts, our own experience informs us, that the remedy of the creditor against his debtor remains. If it be hand, which is secured by a treaty, and afterwards confiscated by a state, the argument does not assume, that this title, thus secured, could be extinguished by an act of confiscation. The injured party, therefore, has his remedy against the occupant of the land, for that which the treaty secures to him, not against the state for money which is not secured to him.

The case of a state which pays off its own debts with paper money, no more resembles this, than do those to which we have already adverted. The courts have no jurisdiction over the contract; they cannot enforce it, nor judge of its violation. Let it be, that the act discharging the debt is a mere nullity, and that it is still due. Yet, the federal courts have no cognisance of the case. But suppose, a state to institute proceedings against an individual, which depended on the validity of an act emitting bills of credit: suppose, a state to prosecute one of its citizens for refusing paper money, who should plead the constitution in bar of such prosecution. If his plea should be overruled, and judgment rendered against him, his case would resemble

this; and unless the jurisdiction of this court might be exercised over it, the constitution would be violated, and the injured party be unable to bring his case before that tribunal to which the people of the United States have assigned all such cases.

It is most true, that this court will not take jurisdiction if it should not: but it is equally true, that it must take jurisdiction, if it should. The judiciary cannot, as the legislature may, avoid a measure, because it approaches the confines of the constitution. We cannot pass it by, because it is doubtful. With whatever doubts, with whatever difficulties, a case may be attended, we must decide it, if it be brought before us. We have no more right to decline the exercise of jurisdiction which is given, than to usurp that which is not given. The one or the other would be treason to the constitution. Questions may occur, which we would gladly avoid; but we cannot avoid them. All we can do is, to exercise our best judgment, and conscientiously to perform our duty. In doing this, on the present occasion, we find this tribunal invested with appellate jurisdiction in all cases arising under the constitution and laws of the United States. We find no exception to this grant, and we cannot insert one.

To escape the operation of these comprehensive words, the counsel for the defendant has mentioned instances in which the constitution might be violated, without giving jurisdiction to this court. These words, therefore, however universal in their expression, must, he contends, be limited and controlled in their construction by circumstances. One of these instances is, the grant by a state of a patent of nobility. The court, he says, cannot annul this grant. This may be very true; but by no means justifies the inference drawn from it. The article does not extend the judicial power to every violation of the constitution which may possibly take place, but to "a case in law or equity," in which a right, under such law, is asserted in a court of justice. If the question cannot be brought into a court, then there is no case in law or equity, and no jurisdiction is given by the words of the article. But if, in any controversy depending in a court, the cause should depend on the validity of such a law, that would be a case arising under the constitution, to which the judicial power of the United States would extend.

The same observation applies to the other instances with which the counsel who opened the cause has illustrated this argument. Although they show that there may be violation, of the constitution, of which the court can take no cognisance, they do not show that an interpretation more restrictive than the words themselves import, ought to be given to this article. They do not show that there can be "a case in law or equity," arising under the constitution, to which the judicial power does not extend. We think, then, that, as the constitution originally stood, the appellate jurisdiction of this court, in all cases arising under the constitution, laws or treaties of the United States, was not arrested by the circumstance that a state was a party.

This lead to a consideration of the 11th amendment. It is in these words: "The judicial power of the United States shall not be construed to extend to any suit in law or equity commenced or prosecuted against one of the United States, by citizens of another state, or by citizens or subjects of any foreign state." It is a part of our history, that, at the adoption of the constitution, all the states were greatly indebted; and the apprehension that these debts might be prosecuted in the federal courts, formed a very serious objection to that instrument. Suits were instituted; and the court maintained its jurisdiction. The alarm was general; and, to quiet the apprehensions that were so extensively entertained, this amendment was proposed in congress, and adopted by the state legislatures. That its motive was not to maintain the sovereignty of a state from the degradation supposed to attend a compulsory appearance before the tribunal of the nation, may be inferred from the terms of the amendment. It does not comprehend controversies between two or more states, or between a state and a foreign state. The jurisdiction of the court still extends to these cases: and in these, a state may still be sued. We must ascribe the amendment, then, to some other cause than the dignity of a state. There is no difficulty in finding this cause. Those who were inhibited from commencing a suit against a state, or from prosecuting one which might be commenced before the adoption of the amendment, were persons who might probably be its creditors. There was not much reason to fear that foreign or sister states would be creditors to any considerable amount, and there was reason to retain the jurisdiction of the court in those cases, because it might be essential to the preservation of peace. The amendment, therefore, extended to suits commenced or prosecuted by individuals, but not to those brought by states.

The first impression made on the mind by this amendment is, that it was intended for those cases, and for those only, in which some demand against a state is made by an individual, in the courts of the Union. If we consider the causes to which it is to be traced, we are conducted to the same conclusion. A general interest might well be felt in leaving to a state the full power of consulting its convenience in the adjustment of its debts, or of other claims upon it; but no interest could be felt in so changing the relations between the whole and its parts, and so strip the government of the means of protecting, by the instrumentality of its courts, the constitution and laws from active violation.

The words of the amendment appear to the court to justify and require this construction. The judicial power is not "to extend to any suit in law er equity commenced or

prosecuted against one of the United States by citizens of another state, &c." What is a suit? We understand it to be prosecution or pursuit of some claim, demand or request; in law language, it is the prosecution of some demand in a court of justice. The remedy for every species of wrong is, says Judge Blackstone, "the being put in possession of that right whereof the party injured is deprived." "The instruments whereby this remedy is obtained, are a diversity of suits and actions, which are defined by the Mirror, to be 'the lawful demand of one's right;' or, as Bracton and Fleta express it, in the words of Justinian, *'jus prosequendi in judicio quod alicui debetur,'*" Blackstone then proceeds to describe every species of remedy by suit; and they are all cases where the party suing claims to obtain something to which he has a right.

To commence a suit is to demand something by the institution of process in a court of justice; and to prosecute the suit, is, according to the common acceptation of language, to continue that demand. By a suit commenced by an individual against a state, we should understand process sued out by that individual against the state, for the purpose of establishing some claim against it by the judgment of a court; and the prosecution of that suit is its continuance. Whatever may be the stages of its progress, the actor is still the same. Suits had been commenced in the supreme court against some of the states, before this amendment was introduced into congress, and others might be commenced, before it should be adopted by the state legislature, and might be depending at the time of its adoption. The object of the amendment was, not only to prevent the commencement of future suits, but to arrest the prosecution of those which might be commenced, when this article should form a part of the constitution. It, therefore, embraces both objects; and its meaning is, that the judicial power shall not be construed to extend to any suit which may be commenced, or which, if already commenced, may be prosecuted against a state by the citizen of another state. If a suit, brought in one court, and carried by legal process to a supervising court, be a continuation of the same suit, then this suit is not commenced nor prosecuted against a state. It is, clearly, in its commencement, the suit of a state against an individual, which suit is transferred to this court, not for the purpose of asserting any claim against the state, but for the purpose of asserting a constitutional defence against a claim made by a state.

A writ of error is defined to be, a commission by which the judges of one court are authorized to examine a record upon which a judgment was given in another court, and on such examination, to affirm or reverse the same according to law. If, says my Lord Coke, by the writ of error, the plaintiff may recover, or be restored to anything, it may be released by the name of an action. In Bacon's Abridgment, tit. Error, L, it is laid down, that "where, by a writ of error, the plaintiff shall recover, or be restored to any personal thing, as debt, damage or the like, a release of all actions personal, is a good plea; and when land is to be recovered or restored in a writ of error, a release of actions real, is a good bar; but where, by a writ of error, the plaintiff shall not be restored to any personal or real thing, a release of all actions, real or personal, is no bar. And for this we have the authority of Lord Coke, both in his Commentary on Littleton and in his reports. A writ of error, then, is in the nature of a suit or action, when it is to restore the party who obtains it to the possession of anything which is withheld from him, not when its operation is entirely defensive.

This rule will apply to writs of error from the courts of the United States, as well as to those writs in England. Under the judiciary act, the effect of a writ of error is simply to bring the record into court, and submit the judgment of the inferior tribunal to re-examination. It does not in any manner act upon the parties; it acts only on the record. It removes the record into the supervising tribunal. Where, then, a state obtains a judgment against an individual, and the court, rendering such judgment, over-rules a defence set up under the constitution or laws of the United States, the transfer of this record into the supreme court, for the sole purpose of inquiring whether the judgment violates the constitution or laws of the United States, can, with no propriety, we think, be denominated as suit commenced or prosecuted against the state whose judgment is so far re-examined. Nothing is demanded from the state. No claim against it, of any description, is asserted or prosecuted. The party is not to be restored to the possession of anything. Essentially, it is an appeal on a single point; and the defendant who appeals from a judgment rendered against him, is never said to commence or prosecute a suit against the plaintiff who has obtained the judgment. The writ of error is given, rather than an appeal, because it is the more usual mode of removing suits at common law; and because, perhaps, it is more technically proper, where a single point of law, and not the whole case, is to be re-examined. But an appeal might be given, and might be so regulated as to effect every purpose of a writ of error. The mode of removal is form, and not substance. Whether it be by writ of error or appeal, no claim is asserted, no demand is made by the original defendant; he only asserts the constitutional right to have his defence examined by that tribunal whose province it is to construe the constitution and laws of the Union.

The only part of the proceeding which is in any manner personal, is the citation. And what is the citation? It is simply notice to the opposite party, that the record is transferred into another court, where he may appear, or decline to appear, as his judgment or inclination may determine. As the party who has obtained a judgment is out of court, and may, therefore, not know that his cause is removed,

common justice requires that notice of the fact should be given him. But this notice is not a suit, nor has it the effect of process. If the party does not choose to appear, he cannot be brought into court, nor is his failure to appear considered as a default. Judgment cannot be given against him for his non-appearance, but the judgment is to be re-examined, and reversed or affirmed, in like manner as if the party had appeared and argued his cause.

The point of view in which this writ of error, with its citation, has been considered uniformly in the courts of the Union, has been well illustrated by a reference to the course to this court, in suits instituted by the United States. The universally received opinion is, that no suit can be commenced or prosecuted against the United States; that the judiciary act does not authorize such suits. Yet, writs of error, accompanied with citations, have uniformly issued for the removal of judgments in favor of the United States into a superior court, where they have, like those in favor of an individual, been re-examined, and affirmed or reversed. It has never been suggested, that such writ of error was a suit against the United States, and therefore, not within the jurisdiction of the appellate court.

It is then, the opinion of the court, that the dependant who removes a judgement rendered against him by a state court into this court, for the purpose of re-examining the question, whether that judgment be in violation of the constitution or laws of the United States, does not commence or prosecute a suit against the state, whatever may be its opinion, where the effect of the writ may be to restore the party to possession of a thing which he demands.

But should we in this be mistaken, the error does not affect the case now before the court. If this writ of error be a suit, in the sense of the 11th amendment, it is not a suit commenced or prosecuted "by a citizen of another state, by a citizen or subject of any foreign state." It is not, then, within the amendment, but is governed entirely by the constitution as originally framed, and we have already seen, that in its origin, the judicial power was extended to all cases arising under the constitution or laws of the United States, without respect to parties.

2. The second objection to the jurisdiction of the court is, that its appellate power cannot be exercised, in any case, over the judgment of a state court. This objection is sustained chiefly by arguments drawn from the supposed total separation of the judiciary of a state from that of the Union, and their entire independence of each other. The argument considers the federal judiciary as completely foreign to that of a state; and as being no more connected with it, in any respect whatever, than the court of a foreign state. If this hypothesis be just, the argument founded on it, is equally so; but if the hypothesis be not supported by the constitution, the argument fails with it. This hypothe-

sis is not founded on any words in the constitution, which might seem to countenance it, but on the unreasonableness of giving a contrary construction to words which seem to require it; and on the incompatibility of the application of the appellate jurisdiction to the judgments of state courts, with that constitutional relation which subsists between the government of the Union and the governments of those states which compose it.

Let this unreasonableness, this total incompatibility, be examined. That the United States form, for many, and for most important purposes, a single nation, has not yet been denied. In war, we are one people. In making peace, we are one people. In all commercial regulations, we are one and the same people. In many other respects, the American people are one; and the government which is alone capable of controlling and managing their interest in all these respects, is the government of the Union. It is their government, and in that character, they have no other. America has chosen to be, in many respects, and to many purposes, a nation; and for all these purposes, her government is complete; to all these objects, it is competent. The people have declared, that in the exercise of all powers given for these objects, it is supreme. It can, then, in effecting these objects, legitimately control all individuals or governments within the American territory. The constitution and laws of a state, so far as they are repugnant to the constitution and laws of the United States, are absolutely void. These states are constituent parts of the United States; they are members of one great empire—for some purposes sovereign, for some purposes subordinate.

In a government so constituted, is it unreasonable, that the judicial power should be competent to give efficacy to the constitutional laws of the legislature? That department can decide on the validity of the constitution or law of a state, if it be repugnant to the constitution or to a law of the United States. Is it unreasonable, that it should also be empowered to decide on the judgment of a state tribunal enforcing such unconstitutional law? Is it so very unreasonable, as to furnish a justification for controlling the words of the constitution? We think it is not. We think, that in a government, acknowledgedly supreme, with respect to objects of vital interest to the nation, there is nothing inconsistent with sound reason, nothing incompatible with the nature of government, in making all its departments supreme, so far as respects those objects, and so far as is necessary to their attainment. The exercise of the appellate power over those judgments of the state tribunals which may contravene the constitution or laws of the United States, is, we believe, essential to the attainment of those objects.

The propriety of intrusting the construction of the constitution, and laws made in pursuance thereof, to the judiciary of the Union, has not, we believe, as yet, been drawn into question. It seems to be a corollary from this political axiom, that the federal courts should either possess exclusive jurisdiction in such cases, on a power to revise the judgment rendered in them, by the state tribunals. If the federal and state courts have concurrent jurisdiction in all cases arising under the constitution, laws and treaties of the United States; and if a case of this description brought in a state court cannot be removed before judgment, nor revised after judgment, then the construction of the constitution, laws and treaties of the United States, is not confided particularly to their judicial department, but is confided equally to that department and to the state courts, however they may be constituted. "Thirteen independent courts," says a very celebrated statesman (and we have now more than twenty such courts) "of final jurisdiction over the same causes, arising upon the same laws, is a hydra in government, from which nothing but contradiction and confusion can proceed."

Dismissing the unpleasant suggestion, that any motives which may not be fairly avowed, or which ought not to exist, can ever influence a state or its courts, the necessity of uniformity, as well as correctness in expounding the constitution and laws of the United States, would itself suggest the propriety of vesting in some single tribunal, the power of deciding, in the last resort, all cases in which they are involved.

We are not restrained, then, by the political relations between the general and state governments, from construing the words of the constitution, defending the judicial power, in their true sense. We are not bound to construe them more restrictively than they naturally import. They give to the supreme court appellate jurisdiction, in all cases arising under the constitution, laws and treaties of the United States. The words are broad enough to comprehend all cases of this description, in whatever court they may be decided. In expounding them, we may be permitted to take into view those consideration to which courts have always allowed great weight in the exposition of laws.

The framers of the constitution would naturally examine the state of things existing at the time; and their work sufficiently attests that they did so. All acknowledge, that they were convened for the purpose of strengthening the confederation, by enlarging the powers of the government, and by giving efficacy to those which it before possessed, but could not exercise. The inform us, themselves, in the instrument they presented to the American public, that one of its objects was to form a more perfect union. Under such circumstances, we certainly should not expect to find, in that instrument, a diminution of the powers of the actual government. Previous to the adoption of the confederation, congress established courts which received appeals in prize causes decided in the courts of the respective states. This power of the government, to establish tribunals for these appeals, was thought consistent with, and was founded on, its political relations with the states. These courts did exercise appellate jurisdiction over those cases decided in the state courts, to which the judicial power of the federal government extended. The confederation gave to congress the power "of establishing courts for receiving and determining finally appeals in all cases of captures." This power was uniformly construed to authorize those courts to receive appeals from the sentences of state courts, and to affirm or reverse them. State tribunals are not mentioned; but this clause in the confederation, necessarily comprises them. Yet the relation between the general and state governments was must weaker, much more lax, under the confederation, than under the present constitution; and the states being much more completely sovereign, their institutions were much more independent.

The convention which framed the constitution, on turning their attention to the judicial power, found it limited to a few objects, but exercised, with respect to some of those objects, in its appellate form, over the judgments of the state courts. They extend it, among other objects, to all cases arising under the constitution, laws and treaties of the United States; and in a subsequent clause declare, that in such cases, the supreme court shall exercise appellate jurisdiction. Nothing seems to be given which would justify the withdrawal of a judgment rendered in a state court, on the constitution, laws or treaties of the United States, from this appellate jurisdiction.

Great weight has always being attached, and very rightly attached, to contemporaneous exposition.

No question, it is believed, has arisen, to which this principle applies more unequivocally than to that now under consideration. The opinion of the Federalist has always being considered as of great authority. It is a complete commentary on our constitution; and is appealed to by all parties, in the questions to which that instrument has given birth. Its intrinsic merit entitles it to this high rank; and the part two of its authors performed in framing the constitution, put it very much in their power to explain the views with which it was framed. These essays having being published, while the constitution was before the nation for adoption or rejection, and having been written in answer to objections founded entirely on the extent of its powers, and on its diminution of state sovereignty, are entitled to the more consideration, where they frankly avow that the power objected to is given, and defend it. In discussing the extent of the judicial power, the Federalist says, "Here another question occurs: what relation would subsist between the national and state courts in these instances of concurrent jurisdiction? I answer, that an appeal would certainly lie from the latter, to the supreme court of the United States. The constitution in direct terms gives an appellate jurisdiction to the supreme court, in all the enumerated cases of federal cognisance in which it is not to have an original one, without a single expression to confine its operation to the inferior federal courts. The objects of appeal, not the tribunals from which it is to be made, are alone contemplated. From this circumstance, and from the reason of the thing, it ought to be construed to extend to the state tribunals. Either this must be the case, or the local courts must be excluded from a concurrent jurisdiction in matters of national concern, else the judicial authority of the Union may be eluded, at the pleasure of every plaintiff or prosecutor. Neither of these consequences ought, without evident necessity, to be involved; the latter would be entirely inadmissible, as it would defeat some of the most important and avowed purposes of the proposed government, and would essentially embarrass its measures. Nor do I perceive any foundation for such a supposition. Agreeable to the remark already made, the national and state systems are to be regarded *as* one whole. The courts of the latter will, of course, be natural auxiliaries to the execution of the laws of the Union, and an appeal from them will as naturally lie to that tribunal which is destined to unite and assimilate the principles of natural justice, and the rules of natural decision. The evident aim of the plan of the national convention is, that all the causes of the specified classes shall, for weighty public reasons, receive their original or final determination in the courts of the Union. To confine, therefore, the general expression which give appellate jurisdiction to the supreme court, to appeals from the subordinate federal courts, instead of allowing their extension to the state courts, would be to abridge the latitude of the terms, in subversion of the intent, contrary to every sound rule of interpretation.

A contemporaneous exposition of the constitution, certainly of not less authority than that which has been just cited, is the judiciary act itself. We know, that in the congress which passed that act were many eminent members of the convention which formed the constitution. Not a single individual, so far as is known, supposed that part of the act which gives the supreme court appellate jurisdiction over the judgments of the state courts, in the cases therein specified, to be unauthorized by the constitution.

While on this part of the argument, it may be also material to observe, that the uniform decisions of this court on the point now under consideration, have been assented to, with a single exception, by the courts of every state in the Union whose judgments have been revised. It has been the unwelcome duty of this tribunal to reverse the judgments of many state courts, in cases in which the strongest state feelings were engaged. Judges, whose talents and character would grace any bench, to whom a disposition to submit to jurisdiction that is usurped, or to surrender their legitimate powers, will certainly not be imputed, have yielded without hesitation to the authority by which their judgments were reversed, while they, perhaps, disapproved the judgment of reversal. This concurrence of statesmen, of legislators, and of judges, in the same construction of the constitution, may justly inspire some confidence in that construction.

In opposition to it, the counsel who made this point has presented, in a great variety of forms, the idea already noticed, that the federal and state courts must, of necessity, and from the nature of the constitution, be in all things totally distinct and independent of each other. If this court can correct the errors of the courts of Virginia, he says, it makes them courts of the United States, or becomes itself a part of the judiciary of Virginia. But it has been already shown, that neither of these consequences necessarily follows: The American people may certainly give to a national tribunal a supervising power over those judgments of the state courts, which may conflict with the constitution, laws or treaties of the United States, without converting them into federal courts, or converting the national into a state tribunal. The one court still derives its authority from the state, the other still derives its authority from the nation.

If it shall be established, he says, that this court has appellate jurisdiction over the state courts, in all cases enumerated in the 3d article of the constitution, a complete consolidation of the states, so far as respects judicial power is produced. But, certainly, the mind of the gentleman who argued this argument is too accurate not to perceive that he has carried it too far; that the premises by no means justify the conclusion. "A complete consolidation of the states, so far as respects the judicial power," would authorize the legislature to confer on the federal courts appellate jurisdiction from the state courts in all cases whatsoever. The distinction between such a power, and that of giving appellate jurisdiction in a few specified cases, in the decision of which the nation takes an interest, is too obvious not to be perceived by all.

This opinion has been already drawn out to too great a length to admit of entering into a particular consideration of the various forms in which the counsel who made this point has, with much ingenuity, presented his argument to the court. The argument, in all its forms, is essentially the same. It is founded, not on the words of the constitution, but on its spirit—a spirit extracted, not from the words of the instrument, but from his view of the nature of our Union, and of the great fundamental principles on which the fabric stands. To this argument, in all its forms, the same answer may be given. Let the nature and objects of our Union be considered; let the great fundamental principles, on which the fabric stands, be examined; and we think, the result must be, that there is nothing so extravagantly absurd, in giving to the court of the nation the power of revising the decisions of local tribunals, on questions which affect the nation, as to require that words which import this power should be restricted by

a forced construction. The question then must depend on the words themselves; and on their construction, we shall be the more readily excused for not adding to the observations already made, because the subject was fully discussed and exhausted in the case of *Martin* v. *Hunter*.

3. We come now to the third objection, which, though differently stated by the counsel, is substantially the same. One gentleman has said, that the judiciary act does not give jurisdiction in the case. The cause was argued in the state court, on a case agreed by the parties, which states the prosecution under a law for selling lottery-tickets, which is set forth, and further states the act of congress by which the city of Washington was authorized to establish the lottery. It then states, that the lottery was regularly established by virtue of the act, and concludes with referring to the court the questions, whether the act of congress be valid? whether, on its just construction, it constitutes a bar to the prosecution? and whether the act of assembly, on which the prosecution is founded, be not itself invalid? These questions were decided against the operation of the act of congress, and in favor of the operation of the act of the state. If the 25th section of the judiciary act be inspected, it will at once be perceived, that it comprehends expressly the case under consideration.

But it is not upon the letter of the act that the gentleman who stated this point in this form, founds his argument. Both gentlemen concur substantially in their views of this part of the case. They deny that the act of congress, on which the plaintiff in error relies, is a law of the United States; or, if a law of the United States, is within the second clause of the sixth article. In the enumeration of the powers of congress, which is made in the 8th section of the first article, we find that of exercising exclusive legislation over such district as shall become the seat of government. This power, like all others which are specified, is conferred on congress as the legislature of the Union: for, strip them of that character, and they would not possess it. In no other character, can it be exercised. In legislating for the district, they necessarily preserve the character of the legislature of the Union; for it is in that character alone, that the constitution confers on them this power of exclusive legislation. This proposition need not be enforced.

The 2d clause of the 6th article declares, that "this constitution, and the laws of the United States, which shall be made in pursuance thereof, shall be the supreme law of the land." The clause which gives exclusive jurisdiction is, unquestionably, a part of the constitution, and as such, binds all the United States. Those who contend that acts of congress, made in pursuance of this power, do not, like acts made in pursuance of other powers, bind the nation, ought to show some safe and clear rule which shall support this construction, and prove, that an act of congress, clothed in all the forms which attend other legislative acts, and passed in virtue of a power conferred on, and exercised by congress, as the legislature of the Union, is not a law of the United States, and does not bind them.

One of the gentlemen sought to illustrate his proposition that congress, when legislating for the district, assumed a distinct character, and was reduced to a mere local legislature, whose laws could possess no obligation out of the ten miles square, by a reference to the complex character of this court. It is, they say, a court of common law and a court of equity. Its character, when sitting as a court of common law, is as distinct from its character when sitting as a court of equity, as if the powers belonging to those departments were vested in different tribunals. Though united in the same tribunal, they are never confounded with each other. Without inquiring how far the union of different characters in one court may be applicable, in principle, to the union in congress of the power of exclusive legislation in some places, and of limited legislation in others, it may be observed, that the forms of proceedings in a court of law are so totally unlike the forms of proceedings in a court of equity, that a mere inspection of the record gives decisive information of the character in which the court sits, and consequently, of the extent of its powers. But if the forms of proceeding were precisely the same, and the court the same, the distinction would disappear.

Since congress legislates in the same forms, and in the same character, in virtue of powers of equal obligation, conferred in the same instrument, when exercising its exclusive powers of legislation, as well as when exercising those which are limited, we must inquire, whether there be anything in the nature of this exclusive legislation, which necessarily confines the operation of the laws made in virtue of this power, to the place with a view to which they are made. Connected with the power to legislate within this district, is a similar power in forts, arsenals, dock-yards, &c. Congress has a right to punish murder in a fort, or other place within its exclusive jurisdiction; but no general right to punish murder committed within any of the states. In the act for the punishment of crimes against the United States, murder committed within a fort, or any other place or district of country, under the sole and exclusive jurisdiction of the United States, is punished with death. Thus, congress legislates in the same act, under its exclusive and its limited powers. The act proceeds to direct, that the body of the criminal, after execution, may be delivered to a surgeon for dissection, and punishes any person who shall rescue such body, during its conveyance from the place of execution to the surgeon to whom it is to be delivered. Let these actual provisions of the law, or any other provisions which can be made on the subject, be considered with a view to the character in which congress acts when exercising its powers of exclusive legislation.

If congress is to be considered merely as a local legislature, invested, as to this object, with powers limited to the fort, or other place, in which the murder may be committed, if its general powers cannot come in aid of these local powers, how can the offence be tried in any other court than that of the place in which it has been committed? How can the offender be conveyed to, or tried in, any other place? How can he be executed elsewhere? How can his body be conveyed through a country under the jurisdiction of another sovereign, and the individual punished, who, within that jurisdiction, shall rescue the body? Were any one state of the Union to pass a law for trying a criminal in a court not created by itself, in a place not within its jurisdiction, and direct the sentence to be executed without its territory, we should all perceive and acknowledge its incompetency to such a course of legislation. If congress be not equally incompetent, it is because that body unites the powers of local legislation with those which are to operate through the Union, and may use the last in aid of the first; or because the power of exercising exclusive legislation draws after it, as an incident, the power of making that legislation effectual, and the incidental power may be exercised throughout the Union, because the principal power is given to that body as the legislature of the Union.

So, in the same act, a person who, having knowledge of the commission of murder, or other felony, on the high seas, or within any fort, arsenal dock-yard, magazine, or other place, or district of country within the sole and exclusive jurisdiction of the United States, shall conceal the same, &c., he shall be adjudged guilty of misprision of felony, and shall be adjudged to be imprisoned, &c. It is clear, that congress cannot punish felonies generally; and, of consequence, cannot punish misprison of felony. It is equally clear, that a state legislature, the state of Maryland, for example, cannot punish those who, in another state, conceal a felony committed in Maryland. How, then, is it that congress, legislating exclusively for a fort, punishes those who, out of that fort, conceal a felony committed within it?

The solution, and the only solution of the difficulty, is, that the power vested in congress, as the legislature of the United States, to legislate exclusively within any place ceded by a state, carries with it, as an incident, the right to make that power effectual. If a felon escape out of the state in which the act has been committed, the government cannot pursue him into another state, and apprehend him there, but must demand him from the executive power of that other state. If congress were to be considered merely as the local legislature for the fort or other place in which the offence might be committed, then this principle would apply to them as to other local legislatures, and the felon who should escape out of the fort, or other place, in which the felony may have been committed, could not be apprehended by the marshal, but must be demanded from the executive of the state. But we know that the principle does not apply; and the reason is that congress is not a local legislature, but exercises this particular power, like all its other powers, in its high character, as the legislature of the Union. The American people thought it a necessary power, and they conferred it for their own benefit. Being so conferred, it carriers with it all those incidental powers which are necessary to its complete and effectual execution.

Whether any particular law be designed to operate without the district or not, depends on the words of that law. If it be designed so to operate, then the question, whether the power to exercised be incidental to the power of exclusive legislation, and be warranted by the constitution, requires a consideration of that instrument. In such cases, the constitution and the law must be compared and construed. This is the exercise of jurisdiction. It is the only exercise of it which is allowed in such a case. For the act of congress directs, that "no other error shall be assigned or regarded as a ground of reversal, in any such case as aforesaid, than such as appears on the face of the record, and immediately respects the before-mentioned questions of validity or construction of the said constitution, treaties," &c. The whole merits of this case, then, consist in the construction of the constitution and the act of congress. The jurisdiction of the court, if acknowledged, goes no further. This we are required to do, without the exercise of jurisdiction.

The counsel for the state of Virginia have, in support of this motion, urged many arguments of great weight against the application of the act of congress to such a case as this; but those arguments go to the construction of the constitution, or of the law, or of both; and seem, therefore, rather calculated to sustain their cause upon its merits, than to prove a failure of jurisdiction in the court.

After having bestowed upon this question the most deliberate consideration of which we are capable, the court is unanimously of opinion, that the objections to its jurisdiction are not sustained, and that the motion ought to be overruled.

Motion denied.

March 5th, 1821.

The opinion of the court was delivered by Marshall, Ch. J.—This case was stated in the opinion given on the motion for dismissing the writ or error for want of jurisdiction in the court. It now comes on to be decided, on the question, whether the borough court of Norfolk, in overruling the defence set up under the act of congress, has misconstrued that act. It is in these words: "The said corporation shall have full power to authorize the drawing of lotteries, for effecting any important improvement in the city, which the ordinary funds or revenue thereof will not accomplish; provided, that the sum to be raised in each year shall not exceed the amount of $10,000; and provided

also, that the object for which the money is intended to be raised shall be first submitted to the president of the United States, and shall be approved of by him."

Two question arise on this act. 1st. Does it purport to authorize the corporation to force the sale of these lottery-tickets in states where such sales may be prohibited by law? If it does, 2d. Is the law constitutional? If the first question be answered in the affirmative, it will become necessary to consider the second. If it should be answered in the negative, it will be unnecessary, and consequently, improper, to pursue any inquiries, which would then be merely speculative, respecting the power of congress in the case.

In inquiring into the extent of the power granted to the corporation of Washington, we must first examine the words of the grant. We find in them no expression which looks beyond the limits of the city. The powers granted are all of them local in the nature, and all of them such as would, in the common course of things, if not necessarily, be exercised within the city. The subject on which congress was employed when framing this act, was a local subject; it was not the establishment of a lottery, but the formation of a separate body for the management of the internal affairs of the city, for its internal government, for its police. Congress must have considered itself as delegating to this corporate body powers for these objects, and for these objects solely. In delegating these powers, therefore, it seems reasonable to suppose, that the mind of the legislature was directed to the city alone, to the action of the being they were creating within the city, and not to any extra-territorial operations. In describing the powers of such a being, no words of limitation need be used. They are limited by the subject. But, if it be intended to give its acts a binding efficacy beyond the natural limits of its power, and within the jurisdiction of a distinct power, we should expect to find, in the language of the incorporating act, some words indicating such intention. Without such words, we cannot suppose that congress designed to give to the acts of the corporation any other effect, beyond its limits, than attends every act having the sanction of local law, when anything depends upon it which is to be transacted elsewhere.

If this would be the reasonable construction of corporate powers generally, it is more especially proper, in a case where an attempt is made so to exercise those powers as to control and limit the penal laws of a state. This is an operation which was not, we think, in the contemplation of the legislature, while incorporating the city of Washington. To interfere with the penal laws of a state, where they are not levelled against the legitimate powers of the Union, but have for their sole object the internal government of the country, is a very serious measure, which congress cannot be supposed to adopt lightly or inconsiderately. The motives for it must be serious and weighty. It would be taken deliberately, and the intention would be clearly and unequivocally expressed. An act, such as that under consideration, ought not, we think, to be so construed as to imply this intention, unless its provisions were such as to render the construction inevitable.

We do not think it essential to the corporate power in question, that it should be exercised out of the city. Could the lottery be drawn in any state of the Union? Does the corporate power to authorize the drawing of a lottery, imply a power to authorize its being drawn without the jurisdiction of a corporation, in a place where it may be prohibited by law? This, we think, would scarcely be asserted. And what clear legal distinction can be taken between a power to draw a lottery, in a place where it is prohibited by law, and a power to establish an office for the sale of tickets, in a place where it is prohibited by law? It may be urged, that the place where lottery is drawn, is of no importance to the corporation, and therefore, the act need not be so construed as to give power over the place, but that the right to sell tickets throughout the United States is of importance, and therefore ought to be implied. That the power to sell tickets in every part of the United States might facilitate their sale, is not to be denied; but it does not follow, that congress designed, for the purpose of giving this increased facility, to overrule the penal laws of the several states. In the city of Washington, the great metropolis of the nation, visited by individuals, from every part of the Union, tickets may be freely sold to all who are willing to purchase. Can it be affirmed, that this is so limited a market, that the incorporating act must be extended beyond its words, and made to conflict with the internal police of the states, unless it be construed to give a more extensive market?

It has been said, that the states cannot make it unlawful to buy that which congress has made it lawful to sell. This proposition is not denied; and therefore, the validity of a law punishing a citizen of Virginia for purchasing a ticket in the city of Washington, might well be drawn into question. Such a law would be a direct attempt to counteract and defeat a measure authorized by the United States. But a law to punish the sale of lottery-tickets in Virginia, is of a different character. Before we can impeach its validity, we must inquire whether congress intended to empower this corporation to do any act within a state, which the laws of that state might prohibit.

In addition to the very important circumstances, that the act contains no words indicating such intention, and that this extensive construction is not essential to the execution of the corporate power, the court cannot resist the conviction, that the intention ascribed to this act, had it existed, would have been executed by very different means from those which have been employed. Had congress intended to establish a lottery for those improvements in the city which are deemed national, the lottery itself would have become the subject of legislative consideration. It would be organized by law, and agents for its execution would be appointed by the president, or in such other manner as the law might direct. If such agents were to act out of the district, there would be, probably, some provision made for such a state of things, and in making such provisions, congress would examine its power to make them. The whole subject would be under the control of the government, or of persons appointed by the government.

But in this case, no lottery is established by law, no control is exercised by the government over any which may be established. The lottery emanates from a corporate power. The corporation may authorize, or not authorize it, and may select the purposes to which the proceeds are to be applied. This corporation is a being intended for local objects only. All its capacities are limited to the city. This, as well as every other law it is capable of making, is a by-law, and, from its nature, is only co-extensive with the city. It is not probable, that such an agent would be employed in the execution of a lottery established by congress; but when it acts, not as the agent for carrying into effect a lottery established by congress, but in its own corporate capacity, from its own corporate powers, it is reasonable to suppose, that its acts were intended to partake of the nature of that capacity and of those powers; and like all its other acts, be merely local in its nature.

The proceeds of these lotteries are to come in aid of the revenues of the city. These revenues are raised by laws whose operation is entirely local, and for objects which are also local; for no person will suppose, that the president's house, the capitol, the navy-yard, or other public institution, was to be benefited by these lotteries, or was to form a charge on the city revenue. Coming in aid of the city revenue, they are of the same character with it—the mere creature of a corporate power.

The circumstances, that the lottery cannot be drawn without the permission of the president, and that this resource is to be used only for important improvements, have been relied on as giving to this corporate power a more extensive operation than is given to those with which it is associated. We do not think so. The president has no agency in the lottery. It does not originate with him, nor is the improvement to which its profits are to be applied to be selected by him. Congress has not enlarged the corporate power by restricting its exercise to cases of which the president might approve.

We very readily admit, that the act establishing the seat of government, and the act appointing commissioners to superintendent the public buildings, are laws of universal obligation. We admit, too, that the laws of any state to defeat the loan authorized by congress, would have been void, as would have been any attempt to arrest the progress of the canal, or of any other measure which congress may adopt. These, and all other laws relative to the district, have the authority which may be claimed by other acts of the national legislature; but their extent is to be determined by those rules of construction which are applicable to all laws. The act incorporating the city of Washington is, unquestionably, of universal obligation; but the extent of the corporate powers conferred by that act, is to be determined by those considerations which belong to the case.

Whether we consider the general character of a law incorporating a city, the objects for which such law is usually made, or the words in which this particular power is conferred, we arrive at the same result. The corporation was merely empowered to authorize the drawing of lotteries; and the mind of the congress was not directed to any provision for the sale of the tickets beyond the limits of the corporation. That subject does not seem to have been taken into view. It is the unanimous opinion of the court, that the law cannot be construed to embrace it.

Source:

19 U.S. 264 (1821).

SUGGESTED READING

Events Leading Up to the American Revolution

Ian R. Christie and Benjamin W. Labaree, *Empire and Independence, 1760–1776: A British-American Dialogue on the Coming of the American Revolution.* Oxford: Phaidon Press, 1976.

Patrick Conley and John P. Kaminski, eds., *The Bill of Rights and the States: The Colonial and Revolutionary Origins of American Liberties.* Madison, Wis.: Madison House, 1992.

Pauline Maier, *From Resistance to Revolution: Colonial Radicals and the Development of American Opposition to Britain, 1765–1776.* New York: Knopf, 1972.

Gary Nash, *The Urban Crucible: Social Change, Political Consciousness and the Origins of the American Revolution.* Cambridge, Mass.: Harvard University Press, 1979.

The American Revolution

Robert M. Calhoon,ed. *Loyalists and Community in Revolutionary America.* Westport, Conn.: Greenwood Press, 1994.

Colin G. Calloway, *The American Revolution in Indian Country: Crisis and Diversity in Native American Communities.* New York: Cambridge University Press, 1995.

David Brion Davis, *The Problem of Slavery in the Age of Revolution: 1770–1823.* Ithaca, N.Y.: Cornell University Press, 1975.

Jonathan R. Dull, *A Diplomatic History of the American Revolution.* New Haven, Conn.: Yale University Press, 1985.

David Hackett Fischer, *Paul Revere's Ride.* New York: Oxford University Press, 1994.

Sylvia Frey, *Water from the Rock: Black Resistance in a Revolutionary Age.* Princeton, N.J.: Princeton University Press, 1991.

Robert A. Gross, *The Minutemen and Their World.* New York: Hill and Wang, 1976.

Pauline Maier, *American Scripture: Making the Declaration of Independence.* New York: Knopf, 1997.

Mary Beth Norton, *Liberty's Daughters: The Revolutionary Experience of American Women.* Boston, Mass.: Little, Brown, 1980.

John Shy, *A People Numerous and Armed: Reflections on the Military Struggle for American Independence.* New York: Oxford University Press, 1976.

Formation of the New Government

Joyce Appleby, *Capitalism and a New Social Order: The Republican Vision of the 1790s.* New York: New York University Press, 1984.

Lance Banning, ed., *After the Constitution: Party Conflict in the New Republic.* Belmont, Calif.: Wadsworth, 1989.

Stanley Elkins and Eric McKittrick, *The Age of Federalism: The Early American Republic.* New York: Oxford University Press, 1993.

John P. Kaminski, ed., *A Necessary Evil? Slavery and the Debate over the Constitution.* Madison, Wis.: 1995.

Daniel G. Lang, *Foreign Policy in the Early Republic: The Law of Nations and the Balance of Power.* Baton Rouge, La.: Louisiana State University Press, 1985.

Forrest McDonald, *The Presidency of George Washington.* Lawrence, Kans.: University Press of Kansas, 1974.

Edmund S. Morgan, *Inventing the People: The Rise of Popular Sovereignty in England and America.* New York: W.W. Norton, 1988.

R. Kent Newmyer, *John Marshall and the Heroic Age of the Supreme Court.* Baton Rouge, La.: Louisiana State University Press, 2001.

Peter S. Onuf, *Statehood and Union: A History of the Northwest Ordinance.* Bloomington, Ind.: Indiana University Press, 1987.

Jack N. Rakove, *The Beginnings of National Politics: An Interpretive History of the Continental Congress.* New York, Knopf, 1979.

————, Oscar Handlin, eds. *James Madison and the Creation of the American Republic.* New York, Knopf, 1996.

Jack N. Rakove, *Original Meanings: Politics and Ideas in the Making of the Constitution.* New York: Longman, 2002.

Herbert J. Storing, *What the Anti-Federalists Were For.* Chicago, Ill.: University of Chicago Press, 1981.

Gordon S. Wood, *The Radicalism of the American Revolution.* New York, Knopf, 1991.

Index

Boldface page numbers denote extensive treatment of a topic.

A

Ableman v. Booth (1859) **840–847**

abolition movement. *See also* slavery
and the Anti-Slavery Convention of American Women (1838) 697–701
South Carolina resolutions against propaganda from (1835) 693–694
and *United States v. Libellants and Claimants of the Schooner Amistad* (1841) 697–701

abortion
and the Mexico City Policy 1,716
and *Roe v. Wade* (1973) 1,646–1,647

Abrams v. United States (1919) 1,285
and the Espionage Act (1917) 1,270
and the Sedition Act (1918) 1,278

ACLU. *See* American Civil Liberties Union

"Acres of Diamonds" (Conwell; 1876–1925) **986–989**

Act Abolishing the Slave Trade in the District of Columbia **787**. *See also* Compromise of 1850

Act of Chapultepec (1945) **1,453–1,456**

Adair v. United States (1908) **1,197–1,206**

Adams, Abigail, "Remember the Ladies," (correspondence; 1776) **286–287**

Adams, John
and the Declaration of Independence (1776) 287
and the Massachusetts Bill of Rights (1780) 302
"Remember the Ladies," (correspondence; 1776) 286–287

Adams, John Quincy, first annual message to Congress by (1825) **595–604**

Adamson Act (1916) 1,188, **1,254–1,255**

Adams-Onís Treaty (1821) 518

Addams, Jane, "Problems of Poverty" (1910) **1,209–1,214**

Addyston Pipe and Steel Company v. United States 1,003

Adkins v. Children's Hospital (1923) 1,206

Adler v. Board of Education (1952) 1,547

Administration of Justice Act (1774) **263–265**

affirmative action 1,656, 1,735

AFL-CIO Constitution (1955) **1,471–1,473**

African Americans
and the Constitution of the United States (1787) 328
and Executive Order 8802 (1941) 1,417–1,418
following the Civil War 751
"Injustices and Impolicy of the Slave Trade and of the Slavery of Africans," (Edwards; 1791) 388–396

and the Medal of Honor Recipients 1,015–1,016
and a Petition of Emancipated Slaves to North Carolina Congress (1797) 449–451
and *Smith v. Allwright* (1944) 1,432
and *The Souls of Black Folk* (DuBois; 1903) 1,166–1,186
and the Three-fifths Compromise (1787) 320–324
and the Trial of Mrs. Douglass (1853) 705–707
and the Tuskegee Study 1,775
and the UNIA declaration of rights (1920) 1,303–1,307
and World War II 1,352

African heritage, people of xviii

"Against the Constitution" (Henry; 1788) **341–350**

Agency for International Development 1,716

Agostini et al. v. Felton et al. (1997) 1,728

Agreement to End the Vietnam War (1973) **1,532–1,533**

agriculture
and the Agriculture Adjustment Act (1933) 1,362–1,363
and the Buckhead-Jones Farm Tenant Act (1937) 1,393–1,394
and the Carey Desert Land Grant Act (1894) 1,026
during the Industrial Age 986
and *Munn v. Illinois* (1877) 989–991

I